HANDBOOK OF INCOME DISTRIBUTION
VOLUME 1

HANDBOOKS
IN
ECONOMICS

16

Series Editors

KENNETH J. ARROW
MICHAEL D. INTRILIGATOR

ELSEVIER

AMSTERDAM · LAUSANNE · NEW YORK · OXFORD · SHANNON · SINGAPORE · TOKYO

HANDBOOK OF INCOME DISTRIBUTION

VOLUME 1

Edited by

ANTHONY B. ATKINSON

Nuffield College, Oxford

and

FRANÇOIS BOURGUIGNON

Ecole des Hautes Etudes en Sciences Sociales, Delta, Paris

2000

ELSEVIER

AMSTERDAM · LAUSANNE · NEW YORK · OXFORD · SHANNON · SINGAPORE · TOKYO

ELSEVIER SCIENCE B.V.
Sara Burgerhartstraat 25
P.O. Box 211, 1000 AE Amsterdam, The Netherlands

First edition 2000

Library of Congress Cataloging in Publication Data
A catalog record from the Library of Congress has been applied for.

ISBN: 0-444-81631-3

∞ The paper used in this publication meets the requirements of ANSI/NISO Z39.48-1992 (Permanence of Paper).
Printed in The Netherlands.

INTRODUCTION TO THE SERIES

The aim of the *Handbooks in Economics* series is to produce Handbooks for various branches of economics, each of which is a definitive source, reference, and teaching supplement for use by professional researchers and advanced graduate students. Each Handbook provides self-contained surveys of the current state of a branch of economics in the form of chapters prepared by leading specialists on various aspects of this branch of economics. These surveys summarize not only received results but also newer developments, from recent journal articles and discussion papers. Some original material is also included, but the main goal is to provide comprehensive and accessible surveys. The Handbooks are intended to provide not only useful reference volumes for professional collections but also possible supplementary readings for advanced courses for graduate students in economics.

KENNETH J. ARROW and MICHAEL D. INTRILIGATOR

PUBLISHER'S NOTE

For a complete overview of the Handbooks in Economics Series, please refer to the listing on the last page of this volume.

CONTENTS OF THE HANDBOOK

CONTENTS OF VOLUME 1

Chapter 3

Three Centuries of Inequality in Britain and America   167

P. H. LINDERT

Chapter 4

Historical Perspectives on Income Distribution: The Case of Europe   217

C. MORRISSON

Chapter 5

Empirical Evidence on Income Inequality in Industrial Countries   261

P. GOTTSCHALK and T. M. SMEEDING

INTRODUCTION: INCOME DISTRIBUTION AND ECONOMICS

A. B. ATKINSON and F. BOURGUIGNON*

Nuffield College, Oxford; Ecole des Hautes Etudes en Sciences Sociales, Delta, Paris

Contents

* In writing this Introduction, we have drawn very heavily on the chapters of the Handbook. This will be evident from the extent of cross-references, although we have tried to stop short of the point at which such references become tedious to the reader. We are most grateful to the following for their comments on the first draft of the Introduction: Sam Bowles, Jim Davies, John Flemming, John Micklewright, Christian Morrisson, Sherwin Rosen, Tony Shorrocks and Gert Wagner. None of them should be held responsible for errors or for the opinions expressed.

Handbook of Income Distribution, Volume 1. Edited by A. B. Atkinson and F. Bourguignon

The produce of earth—all that is derived from its surface by the united application of labour, machinery and capital, is divided among three classes of the community, namely, the proprietor of the land, the owner of the stock or capital necessary for its cultivation, and the labourers by whose industry it is cultivated.

But in different stages of society, the proportions of the whole produce of the earth which will be allotted to each of these classes, under the names of rent, profit and wages, will be essentially different. . . .

To determine the laws which regulate this distribution is the principal problem in Political Economy.

David Ricardo, Preface to *Principles of Political Economy*, 1817 (1911 edition, p. 1).

At the risk of appearing to lack imagination, it is difficult not to begin with this quotation from Ricardo, which is now a commonplace. Indeed, many people feel that it gives a better definition of economics in general than the other commonplace which begins so many textbooks, according to which economics is "the science of allocating scarce resources to competing uses". But of course these are only two aspects of the same fundamental problem. Scarce resources are controlled or owned by personal interests and allocating them in one way or another modifies individual benefits. The allocation of scarce resources may thus reflect as much the way conflicts of interests are resolved as the pursuit of efficiency. It is difficult to think of economic issues without distributive consequences and it is equally difficult to imagine distributive problems without some allocational dimension.

But distributional issues have not always been regarded as important by the economics profession. There have been times in the postwar period when interest in the distribution of income has been at a low ebb: in the 1950s and early 1960s, and in the 1980s. There are several possible explanations for this lack of interest. In response to the critiques of welfare economics in the 1930s and 1940s, economists could understandably have decided to concentrate on efficiency questions. Indeed, it may have been the case that distributive outcomes were of little social concern, with the social welfare function being explicitly or implicitly indifferent with regard to the distribution of income. At a time of full employment and rapid growth, people may have justified such lack of concern by the argument that those at the bottom would gain more from employment policies and the promotion of economic growth than from redistribution. In many countries, there had been a significant reduction in income inequality between the 1930s and the 1950s. It may have seemed that differences in distributive outcomes were now of second order in comparison with changes in aggregates. Or, on the textbook efficiency/equality trade-off, the cost of redistribution may have been judged too great in terms of reduced efficiency.

Today, at the end of the 1990s, the position is different. During the last quarter of a century, economic growth proved to be unsteady and rather slow on average. Europe has seen prolonged unemployment. There has been widening wage disparity in a number of OECD countries. It is no longer true of income distribution statistics, as Aaron once said, that "following these data was like watching the grass grow" (1978, p. 17). Rising affluence in rich countries coexists, in a number of such countries, with the persistence of poverty. Policy choices about privatisation, about monetary union, about the future of the Welfare State, all impinge on the distribution of income. It is difficult to think of an issue ranking high in the public economic debate without some strong distributive implications. Monetary policy, fiscal policy, taxes, prices and competition regulation, are all issues which are now often perceived as conflictual because of their strong redistributive content.

Economists have responded quickly to the renewed policy interest in distribution, and the contents of this Handbook are very different from those which would have been included had it been written 10 years ago. A large proportion of the references in this Handbook are to research published in the 1990s. It has now become common to have income distribution variables playing a pivotal role in economic models. The recent interest in the relationship between growth and distribution is a good example of this. The surge of political economy in the contemporary literature is also a route by which distribution is coming to re-occupy the place it deserves. Within economics itself, the development of models of imperfect information and informational asymmetries (see, for example, Chapters 8 and 10) have not only provided a means of resolving the puzzle as to why identical workers get paid different amounts, but have also caused reconsideration of the efficiency of market outcomes. These models indicate that redistribution can increase aggregate income. There may not be an efficiency/equity trade-off; it may be possible to make progress on both fronts.

Despite this, income distribution still remains rather peripheral in economics. We lack research that integrates distribution centrally into the examination of how the economy works. To the extent that it does enter the analysis, distribution is more like an input than an output. Distribution is taken as a parameter which affects the outcome of economic mechanisms. This is significant and has certainly changed our way of looking at many issues. We now understand that asset redistribution may improve allocative efficiency. However, distribution must also be the object of the analysis, or still more fundamentally, distribution must be considered jointly with other economic phenomena. When we look at it from this point of view, we then realize how little is actually understood about the determinants of distribution. The same is true at the empirical level. The conceptual and practical problems in using data on income distribution are not widely understood in the profession. As with the World Tables on economic growth, the ready availability of a secondary data-set such as that assembled by Deininger and Squire (1996), does not guarantee that users are aware of its subtleties. People do not always stop to ask "inequality of what among whom?". So that, even though we have made much progress over the last decade, a great deal is still to be done.

The aim of this Handbook is to survey the state of the art with regard to the economics of income distribution, and to provide a basis for the next generation of research in this important topic. Why do we say that it is important? First, as already indicated, the distribution of economic resources is a social phenomenon which has engaged social commentators and policy-makers. We believe that economists should be able to provide an explanation. This view sees distribution as the leading character in the play. We are asking how far economic theory is helpful in explaining the distribution of income, its evolution over time, the way it interacts with other economic and noneconomic phenomena, and the way it is affected by policy. This theoretical inquiry has an empirical counterpart. Statistical institutes or researchers publish evidence on the distribution of income on the basis of various statistical concepts and indices: dispersion of earnings, inequality of households net income after taxes and transfers, inequality of wealth, etc. Newspaper headlines proclaim that "poverty in Europe has increased" or that "the earnings gap is stretching" or that "the North-South divide is widening". Are such empirical assertions complete and satisfactory? Do we always have the theoretical background to read these data, or is it necessary to generate other types of data to fit the theories we may have in mind?

Instead of having the distribution of income as the leading character of the play, we may have it as a supporting actor (the "input" view of its role). Income distribution assists our understanding of various fields of economics. In some cases, the relation is relatively obvious. It would be difficult to ignore the distribution of income when dealing with political economy mechanisms. In public finance, the design of optimal taxes depends critically on the role of distribution, since without distributional differences a uniform lump sum tax may well suffice. But there are also less visible ways through which income distribution enters the core of economic analysis. Aggregation is the methodological bridge between many distribution issues and more standard economic analysis, with consumer demand as the leading field. But there are other areas where distribution has played or is beginning to play a prominent role. It was clearly central to Marxian economics. It has always been prominent in development economics and it is now featuring in growth economics. Even if there were no ethical reason for studying distribution, it would still be required as a conditioning parameter in other economic phenomena.

This Introduction gives an account of the progress of the study of income distribution in economics and argues strongly in favour of a more systematic interconnection between economic analysis in general and distribution issues. This is done through reviewing the channels through which various fields communicate with each other, the notable achievements of recent years, and what we believe are the directions that research should take in the future. This has led us to consider income distribution issues from various, sometimes overlapping points of view. Intentionally, we have not tried to avoid these overlaps which are essentially the proof that income distribution issues cannot simply be handled independently of the rest of economic analysis.

Section 1 starts the process of identifying the elements from which we can begin to construct a comprehensive theory of income distribution. Quite substantial progress has been achieved in developing various building blocks but their integration remains extremely difficult. We need to consider the way they should articulate with each other to get the complete picture. To this end, we commence with a simple model, showing how it relates to factor shares, to the unskilled/skilled wage differential debate and to computable general equilibrium modelling. Sections 2 and 3 develop this framework to allow for the accumulation of factors (Section 2), and for a richer treatment of the labour market (Section 3).

Section 4 is concerned with empirical research, illustrated by income distribution data for France in 1994. Finally, we turn to a set of issues which logically could perhaps have come first, and in the Handbook are indeed the subject of Chapter 1. The main character of the play we are watching should really be inequality, but like the "Arlesienne" in Bizet's opera, one never sees it. Here, it is elusive because it has many economic and noneconomic dimensions. Income dispersion is strictly equivalent to economic inequality only in the most simple version of the standard economic paradigm. As soon as we deviate from this model, income dispersion becomes an approximation—sometimes a bad one—of true inequality. Identifying the sources of inequality, and the relation with theories of justice, are the subjects of Section 5.

The final part of the Introduction, Section 6, provides a guide to the contents of the Handbook.

1. Factor share theories of income distribution

No unified theory of income distribution actually exists. Even though several titles of books and articles announce quite ambitiously the statement of such a "theory of income distribution",[1] they typically refer to only one part of what should actually be covered by such a theory: the determination of wages in the labour market, factor shares, the accumulation of wealth, etc. Rather than an unified theory, the literature thus offers a series of building blocks with which distribution issues are to be studied. Because of the natural complexity of the subject, however, no serious attempt at integrating them has really been made. We review in this section, and the next two sections, the various blocks and the most obvious links between them.

---

[1] The bibliography to this introductory chapter contains references to some of the key books and articles in the field. Among the general books in this field are Dalton (1920a), Meade (1964 and 1976), Bronfenbrenner (1971), Pen (1971), Johnson (1973), Blinder (1974), Tinbergen (1975), Thurow (1976), Lydall (1979), Atkinson (1983), Osberg (1984), Lambert (1989), Cowell (1995), Morrisson (1996), Jorgenson (1997), and Piketty (1997b).

1.1. A simple static and competitive framework

We open this review of the various building blocks of a theory of income distribution with a model inspired by the standard static Walrasian framework. This model works back from the end by taking as given the distribution of all productive factors in the economy and focusing on the rate at which they are paid. It is a simple model, but it underlies much of both applied and theoretical literature on income distribution, from the rudimentary practice of considering that income distribution is essentially linked to factor shares in the National Income to more elaborate treatments like the Computable General Equilibrium models of income distribution.

In a static framework, consider an economy made up of I individual units. We do not specify for the moment whether they are persons or households. Each individual i is endowed with a vector of productive factors, with components a_{im}. The number of components, M, of this vector may be large, so that this representation of individual endowments permits us to take into account not only aggregate factors like capital and labour, but also different types of (observable) capital or labour skills or abilities. Let there be K firms, indexed by k, each with some fixed factors of production, f_k, and able to produce various goods with some given technology. To close the model, assume full private ownership of the firms by individual agents and let θ_{ik} be the share of individual i in firm k. Supposing that all these goods and factors may be exchanged on competitive markets, with the vector of factor prices being denoted by w, the primary income of individual i is given by:

$$y_i = \sum_m a_{im} w_m + \sum_k \theta_{ik} \pi_k, \tag{1.1}$$

where π_k is the profit of firm k. The distribution of income $Y = (y_1, y_2, \ldots, y_I)$ thus results from the combination of the multidimensional distribution of endowments, the matrix $A = (a_{11}, a_{12}, \ldots, a_{1M}; a_{21}, a_{22}, \ldots, a_{2M}; \ldots; a_{I1}, a_{I2}, \ldots, a_{IM})$, and the per unit returns to these endowments, w, and of the distribution of the ownership of firms within the population, that is the distribution of financial wealth, where the matrix is denoted by Θ. In such a framework, a theory of income distribution is essentially a theory of factor rewards, and this explains the location of the subject in many economic textbooks as part of the theory of pricing. Given the ownership distributions A and Θ, knowledge of factor rewards, that is the vector of prices and profits, determines the distribution of income.

Closing the model requires that we specify the way the factor rewards and profit are determined. The competitive equilibrium model is closed by determining the set of prices and factor rewards which equilibrate the demand and supply of the various goods and (variable) factors. This set of prices and factor returns is therefore a function of the distribution of endowments and wealth (ownership shares in firms) among individuals and of the distribution of fixed factors among firms. The reduced form of this competitive model thus expresses the distribution of income Y as a function of the distribution of endowments, A, of wealth, Θ, and of technological factors summarised by the distribution F of the fixed factors among firms (see Bourguignon and Morrisson, 1990).

$$Y = H(A, \Theta, F). \tag{1.2}$$

This general equilibrium formulation, or its partial counterpart (1.1) may be seen as the heart of the theory of income distribution and the basis for policy analysis in that field. It is generally used with a small number of dimensions to the key matrices. Consider first the case where there are two factors of production, raw labour supplied by workers who make up a fixed fraction, n_w, of the population and capital owned by capitalists, who do not work and make up $(1 - n_w)$ of the population. Then, according to Eq. (1.1) the relative distribution of incomes in the population depends only on the share of labour, denoted by α, and of capital $(1 - \alpha)$, in total income. This two-class economy (see Chapter 9, Section 2), reminiscent of Ricardo's statement recalled above, is probably the simplest justification for reducing the issue of income distribution to that of factor shares.

The effect of variation in factor shares is shown in Fig. 1, where we have drawn the Lorenz curve for this two-class economy. The Lorenz curve (see Section 3 of Chapter 2) cumulates people below a given income level and shows on the vertical axis the cumulative share in total income of the bottom $x\%$ of the population. Where incomes are unequal, this curve lies below the 45° line (the bottom $x\%$ have less than $x\%$ of total income until we reach $x = 100\%$). If the factor shares and relative population sizes are such that income per head of workers is less than that of capitalists, we have the situation shown in Fig. 1. The slope of the first segment is equal to α divided by n_w; the slope of the second segment is equal to $(1 - \alpha)$ divided by $(1 - n_w)$. A rise in the wage share moves the Lorenz curve upwards and closer to the line of equal incomes. The overall extent of inequality is often measured by a summary measure, of which one of the most popular is the Gini coefficient, which is the ratio of the area between the Lorenz curve and the 45° line to the maximum such area (see Chapter 2, Section 4). In the present simple case, it is equal to the difference between n_w and α: if the wage share is 75% and workers are 90% of the population, then the Gini is 15%.

At the time that Ricardo wrote, the factor distribution was seen as directly relevant to the personal distribution, in that the different sources were identified with particular classes of people. As Musgrave described it,

For classical economists, this scheme was doubly attractive. For one thing, it was an analytically convenient grouping, the pricing of various factors being subject to different principles. For another, it was a socially relevant grouping, as the division of society into capitalists, landlords and workers gave a fair picture of social stratification in the England of the early nineteenth century (1959, p. 223).

Today, however, this is scarcely adequate, for several reasons. We need to explain the distribution of factor incomes *within* classes, such as the size distribution of wages. Why do Chief Executive Officers receive many times more than teachers? Why do airline

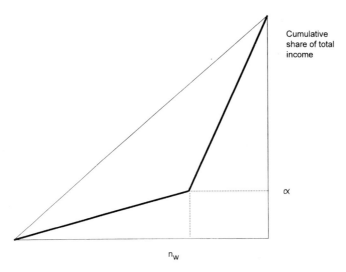

Fig. 1. Lorenz curve for a two-class economy.

pilots get paid more than train drivers? In terms of Fig. 1, the Lorenz curves for the two segments are not straight lines but are bowed outwards (the slope of the Lorenz curve at a particular point is equal to the income at that point divided by the mean, so a bow shape indicates that earnings are different). Second, there is human capital: the investment which people make in themselves in the form of education, training or other activities which raise their productivity represents a determinant of production which has analogous features to investment in physical capital, and needs to be incorporated into the production function.

Third, rather than people being identified with a single source of income, they now receive income from a range of sources, so that one individual may be in receipt of wages, interest income and rent (for example, through owning a house). A worker is not simply reliant on wages. This means that we cannot draw any direct implications for the personal distribution from observations of changes in factor prices. Fourthly, there are intervening institutions: the production model referred to above does not explicitly allow for the existence of institutions such as corporations, financial intermediaries or pension funds, which stand between the production side of the economy and the receipt of household incomes. Corporations receive profits, part of which are paid out in dividends, but part is retained for further investment. Pension funds act as intermediaries. They own shares, real property and other assets, receiving the income from these assets and paying it out, or accumulating it, on behalf of the members of the pension schemes. Perhaps the single most significant intervening institution is the state. The gross incomes generated by production are modified by taxation, used to finance public spending, including transfers which constitute a major source of personal incomes in industrialised countries.

These mechanisms modify the relation between factor returns and the personal distribution. Suppose that person i has a wage w_i and capital k_i:

$$y_i = w_i + rk_i. \tag{1.3}$$

Taking the coefficient of variation, V, as an alternative measure of inequality,[2] and defining ρ as the correlation between wages and capital, we find that the square of the coefficient of variation is given by

$$V^2 = \alpha^2 V_w^2 + (1 - \alpha)^2 V_k^2 + 2\rho\alpha(1 - \alpha)V_k V_w, \tag{1.4}$$

where V_w^2 and V_k^2 denote the squared coefficient of variation of wages and capital. The consequences of a rise in the profit share now depend on the relative dispersion of wages and capital and on the correlation between them. Already, the conclusions are becoming complex.

This treatment of distribution may be seen as the starting point of most competitive equilibrium theories of income distribution with a macro-economic focus. Other approaches, too, end up dealing with distributional issues in a similar way. Through the Stolper–Samuelson theorem which determines the way in which factor rewards change with the price of goods in international markets, the preceding formulation includes the analysis of the distributional consequences of international trade. (To introduce trade in the preceding framework, it is sufficient to assume that the prices of some goods are exogenously given and that the corresponding markets equilibrate through imports and exports.) It also includes the public finance approach to the distribution of incomes and the analysis of tax incidence which developed in the tradition of the Harberger model (see Harberger, 1962; Atkinson and Stiglitz, 1980: Lecture 6).

1.2. Skilled/unskilled wage differential

A second direct application of the preceding framework is the case where there are various types of labour, say, in the simplest case, skilled and unskilled labour. Thus, the endowment vector, a, in the preceding expressions has two components which take the value 0 or 1 depending on whether a person is skilled or not. A model of this kind

---

[2] The coefficient of variation is the standard deviation divided by the mean. Equation (1.4) is reached by using the formula for the variance of a sum, which is

$$\text{var}(X_1 + X_2) = \text{var}(X_1) + \text{var}(X_2) + 2\text{cov}(X_1, X_2)$$

(where cov denotes the covariance) and dividing by the mean squared. It should be noted that the coefficient of variation for wages is obtained by dividing by the mean *for wages*, which leads to the squared term in α, and the corresponding expression for capital income.

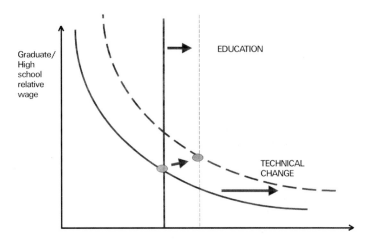

Fig. 2. Race between education and technical change.

was the basis for the "race" between technological development and education described by Tinbergen in his book *Income Distribution* (1975, Chapter 6). He referred to people being educated to graduate, or high-school, level. (The analysis refers to an advanced country, in that it assumes that everyone receives at least a high school education.) Total output is produced using graduate labour, high-school labour and capital. Tinbergen argued that the elasticity of substitution of the production function is sufficiently close to unity to warrant using a Cobb–Douglas form, with constant returns to scale and constant cost shares for graduate labour and for high-school labour. From this, we can obtain the profit-maximising choice of labour by competitive firms. Figure 2 shows the *relative* demands and relative wages of the two types of labour. If the relative supplies are fixed in the short-run, as shown by the vertical line, then we can solve for the market clearing wage ratio as indicated. The race is then between the growth in the relative numbers with graduate education and technological development increasing the importance of graduate labour in production. In the case shown, the demand shifts faster than the supply, so that the wage differential widens.

It is a model of this type which is invoked in the growing literature which tries to explain the recent increase in wage dispersion in several countries. This literature has sought to explain how, despite an increase in the relative supply of skilled workers, the wage differential could have increased over the last two decades, contributing to an increase in the dispersion of earnings. In terms of the preceding model, a natural explanation is that the evolution of technological factors produced a bias in favour of skilled labour, or in a multi-sectoral model, a bias in favour of sectors intensive in the use of skilled labour. An alternative explanation has to do with the effects of international trade and the drop in the relative price of goods which are relatively intensive in unskilled labour (Wood, 1994). At this point, we should point out that, to avoid overlapping with the forthcoming chapter by Katz in Volume III of the *Handbook of Labour Economics*, we have not covered the empirical literature on earnings in the present volume. The reader is also referred to Levy and Murnane (1992), Katz and Murphy (1992) and Burtless (1995). The theoretical explanation of the earnings distribution as a whole is the subject of Chapter 7.

We have noted the lack of integration of different parts of the income distribution story. The discussion of widening wage dispersion as a result of skill-biased technical change has been conducted largely independently of any consideration of the contemporaneous rise in the real rate of interest, or, in most G7 countries, the rise in the share of nonlabour income. Can the technical change explanation of the shift in demand for unskilled workers be reconciled with the rise in the rate of return and in the capital share? In the competitive equilibrium framework, this depends on the degree of complementarity between factors in the production function. It may also be questioned how far the technological developments to which reference is commonly made, such as the spread of information technology, are well represented by a standard constant returns to scale production function. Network externalities require us to provide a dynamic treatment of the diffusion of an innovation, such as e-mail, and its increasing value as the network becomes more extensive. The explicit modelling of such technical change, and its distributional impact, seems a fruitful area for future research.

1.3. CGE modelling

More elaborate specifications of the preceding model have been used for an empirical analysis of the determinants of the distribution of income and redistributional policies. This is the "computable general equilibrium" (CGE) tradition. In the fields of international trade and taxation, numerical models have been developed which extended the basic principles of factor reward determination beyond the Stolper–Samuelson theorem or the Harberger model to more complex economic structures with more than two factors and two sectors of production (for a survey, see Shoven and Whalley (1984)). These models have had much success in the field of economic development (for a survey of these models, see Robinson (1991)). By distinguishing urban and rural labour markets, skilled and unskilled labour, the land cultivated by peasants or used in large plantations, it is indeed possible to take into account many factors with a direct and strong influence on the overall distribution of income. The topic of income distribution and development is covered here in Chapter 13 and in the *Handbook of Development Economics* by Adelman and Robinson (1989).

1.4. Capitalism and socialism

A variation on the two factor model may be used to examine the difference in distribution between different economic systems. What reason is there to expect less inequality in the personal income distribution under socialism? The most evident contribution to the reduction in inequality is that resulting from the abolition of the private ownership of the means of production. In terms of factor incomes, that part of national income received as profit and rent (both referred to here as "capital income") in a pure market economy accrues under socialism to the state. Even if none of the spending by the state benefits individual citizens, this elimination of private capital income can in itself be expected to reduce substantially relative inequality.

Let us go back to the earlier class model, and assume, in an over-simplified way, that in a capitalist society a proportion $(1 - n_w)$ of the population receive income only from capital and they are all better off than the remainder who receive only income from work. The share of capital in total income is denoted by $(1 - \alpha)$, this being considerably greater than $(1 - n_w)$, and we have seen that this would lead to a Gini coefficient equal to $n_w - \alpha$. With n_w equal to 90% and α equal to 75%, the Gini is 15%. Suppose, more realistically, that we allow for differences among wage earners (in terms of Fig. 1, we allow the first section of the Lorenz curve to be bowed outwards rather than a straight line). Let the value of the Gini coefficient be G in a socialist society where there are only workers, with the same distribution of earnings as in the capitalist economy, and all capital income accrues to the state (and is not redistributed to the workers). In contrast, in the capitalist society the contribution of wage income to inequality will be proportionately smaller, by a factor $(1 - n_w)\alpha$, but the contribution of capital income will now add a term $(n_w - \alpha)$ to the Gini coefficient. With the figures used earlier, the Gini coefficient in the capitalist society is, as a percentage

$$G \times 0.9 \times 0.75 + 15.$$

If inequality in the socialist economy, G, were 20%, then the capitalist country would have a Gini coefficient of 28.5%. This comparison assumes that the profits accruing to the state provide no direct benefit to individual citizens. If profits accruing to the state were equally distributed to all workers, the difference between the two systems would be still wider. This would reduce the Gini coefficient among a society of pure workers by a factor of $(1 - \alpha)$, and, with the numbers used earlier, would mean a Gini coefficient for incomes of 15%. The combination of the abolition of private ownership, and the use of profits to finance social programmes (such as education, pensions, health care), has, on this basis, a substantial redistributive impact.

This simple model, taken from Atkinson and Micklewright (1992), is not meant to be a realistic description of any actual economy; it is intended only as an expositional device. It does not, for instance, allow for profit and other income being appropriated by the ruling elite (on this, see Morrisson, 1984 and Atkinson and Micklewright, 1992, pages

169–170). How far distribution of income was different under Communist regimes, and the impact of transition to market economies, is the subject of Chapter 14.

1.5. Limitations

The limitations of the simple static Walrasian approach to income distribution are obvious. It misses major sources of income inequality or considers them as exogenous. Practically, the capital–labour income dichotomy explains a limited proportion of observed differences among households. Decomposing the dispersion of individual earnings with respect to skill, or more generally education or other definitions of human capital, usually explains a larger share. However, a considerable heterogeneity is left unexplained. It cannot be satisfactory to consider this residual as exogenous or, equivalently, as the result of purely "natural", that is noneconomic, differences among individuals. This is especially so in view of the changes recently observed in this "unexplained" component of inequality in several countries and of the differences across societies.

To be more concrete, the distribution of income depends on that of personal endowments and assets, but nothing has been said so far about how the latter are determined. To do so, the theory must be made dynamic and must tackle the issue of the accumulation of productive factors. Moreover, the assumptions of competitive behaviour and market clearing may be questioned. In the macroeconomic theory of factor shares there has long been a strand of thinking that has emphasised the role of monopoly power (Kalecki, 1938). More within the mainstream, we may draw on recent work in labour economics, replacing the competitive assumption in the preceding framework by more realistic price, wage and employment determination mechanisms.

These two directions, of the dynamics of income generating factors and the microeconomics of the labour market, are the main aspects that we now consider.

2. Factor accumulation and income distribution

Making the preceding framework dynamic means that we have to model the way in which individuals accumulate the assets generating their current income and their shares in the various firms in the economy, as well as the way firms modify their fixed factors. The standard assumption is that these decisions are based on maximising behaviour, which means that the accumulation equations depend on the sequence of current and expected future factor rewards and prices. The accumulation equations have to be complemented, therefore, by equations giving the equilibrium prices of those factors, assets and firm shares which may be acquired on the market, as well as expectations of their future values. Together with Eqs (1.1)–(1.2), they would provide a full dynamic representation of the economy, the distribution of current income and that of all assets. It is a *dynamic general equilibrium* model of this type which should be invoked to explain the determinants of income distribution at a point of time, and the way it changes over time with the economy. Clearly, however, this model is much too complicated to be analyzed in general terms and the literature has focused on extremely simplified forms of it. Given the difficulties which economic theorists have found in explaining the dynamic behaviour of aggregates, this may perhaps be forgiven!

In what follows we briefly review the main directions which have been explored. The most elementary version of the accumulation equation—and practically the only one being used—refers to the case of a single asset being accumulated by individuals who are identical apart from their level of assetholding. The canonical model is written in its simplest discrete form as:

$$A_{i,t} = \rho A_{i,t-1} + a + \epsilon_{i,t}, \tag{2.1}$$

where $A_{i,t}$ is the level of assets owned by person i at time t, ρ and a are two positive constants, and $\epsilon_{i,t}$ a random term representing exogenous shocks to the accumulation process. The latter are supposed to have zero expected value and to be identically and independently distributed across periods and persons, with variance σ^2. In what follows, we shall refer to A as being the total "wealth" of a person, comprising both conventional financial wealth and human capital, except when otherwise specified.

As simple as it may be, model (2.1) can be invoked to represent various theories of income distribution.

2.1. Stochastic theories

Stochastic theories (see Chapters 7 and 11) emphasize the role of the term, ϵ. In the simplest model A stands for the logarithm of wealth, or income, and ρ is equal to unity (and a to zero). The logarithm of wealth thus follows a random walk. After some time, it is distributed lognormally among individuals whereas its variance increases linearly with time. This is simply another statement of the well-known Gibrat's law (Gibrat, 1931)—see Aitchison and Brown (1957). The model with $\rho < 1$ corresponds to the mean reversion process introduced by Galton (1879)—see also Kalecki (1945). Subtracting the mean of the (log) wealth from both sides of Eq. (2.1) shows that the expected value of the change in the deviation from the mean is negative for persons with wealth above the mean and positive below it. The distribution of wealth or income tends toward some limit which depends only on the characteristics of the distribution of ϵ and on ρ. Writing var$(A)_t$ for the variance of $A_{i,t}$, we have

$$\text{var}(A)_t = \rho^2 \text{var}(A)_{t-1} + \sigma^2, \tag{2.2}$$

so that the variance of the logarithm of wealth converges to $\sigma^2/(1 - \rho^2)$. There is continuing inequality, but it is generated by the stochastic term. The "economics" that enters via ρ determines the degree of magnification of the inequality due to the stochastic term, and the convergence or otherwise of the process. Where $\rho < 1$, the process converges more rapidly, the smaller is the value of ρ. If $\rho > 1$, then the process is explosive and leads in infinite time to a degenerate situation of maximum inequality, where the share of total income or wealth owned by the richest tends towards unity. Other models have been built along similar lines. They exhibit different dynamic patterns and limiting distributions. In the model of Champernowne (1953) the distribution tends toward a Pareto distribution rather than a lognormal distribution. This result is obtained by replacing the stochastic specification in Eq. (2.1) by a Markov stochastic process with a particular set of probabilities of transition across discrete wealth intervals of uniform proportionate extent.

These stochastic models have been repeatedly criticised as lacking economic content. According to Mincer,

From the economist's point of view, perhaps the most unsatisfactory feature of the stochastic models . . . is that they shed no light on the economics of the distribution process. (1958, p. 283)

By this he means that they do not incorporate individual optimising behaviour:

it is difficult to see how the factor of individual choice can be disregarded in analysing personal income distribution. (1958, p. 283)

From this point of view, the stochastic models are not fundamentally different from assuming that the distribution of productive assets in the economy is exogenous as was done in the preceding section. This criticism can be overstated, in that optimising models may simply push the explanation back one stage. But if we are to go beyond a description of the dynamics of income and wealth, then we need a fuller understanding of the determinants of the distribution of income. If we stick to the simple linear model (2.1), the economic analysis must bear on the mechanisms which determine ρ and whether $\rho \lessgtr 1$.

2.2. The dynastic consumption model as a benchmark and the ambiguity of bequest theories

The standard microeconomic model of intertemporal consumption allocation (see Chapter 11) should give some information on the value that may be expected for ρ. However, different assumptions in this model lead to different values. A benchmark is offered by the "dynastic" model where the altruism of a person extends to his/her descendants, their descendants, the descendants of their descendants, and so on for an infinite future. This is equivalent to assuming that the person lives forever and optimizes over an infinite horizon. Under the assumption of strict demographic replacement, the budget constraint is:

$$A_t = (1 + r)A_{t-1} - c_t + \epsilon_t, \qquad (2.3)$$

where c_t is the flow of consumption at period t, and, as before, A includes both conventional financial wealth and human capital, and ϵ is the stochastic term. If the utility of consumption is assumed to be additive and quadratic, and if the time discount rate is assumed to be equal to the rate of return, r, on wealth, then the maximization of the expected value of the discounted sum of utility leads to Eq. (2.1) above with $\rho = 1$ and $a = 0$—see Deaton (1992, p. 183). In other words, the optimal consumption at each point of time is simply the income flow from wealth. Wealth, income and consumption all follow a random walk. It follows that their variance in the population increases linearly with time.

There is evidence that the dispersion of consumption expenditures tends to increase continuously with age in a given cohort, see Deaton and Paxson (1994). So, the preceding model could be satisfactory for an intragenerational theory of income and wealth distribution. However, it does not seem to fit the most obvious stylized facts of the intergenerational transmission of inequality, and in particular the apparently nonincreasing variance of wealth. The reason why the preceding model may be less adapted for intergenerational issues is that it relies on a rather extreme form of altruism. If agents were selfish agents and indifferent to the fate of their descendants, then with a fixed and certain lifetime, wealth should decrease at the end of one's lifetime and be equal to zero at death. With such a theory, bequests should essentially be involuntary and mostly explained by the natural uncertainty of life duration, coupled with the absence of a good annuity market. But a host of intermediate cases may be envisaged where bequests enter personal utility and transfers to children are made at death or during one's lifetime under the form of human capital. Fertility behaviour must be taken into consideration since the number of descendants directly affects the intergenerational discount rate. Differences in family size are also important. Large families mean that, with equal division, wealth is divided more rapidly; where families die out, on the other hand, wealth passes into other hands.

There is a rich literature on the simultaneous determination of fertility and intergenerational transfers of wealth and/or human capital which has been largely influenced by Becker—see in particular Becker and Tomes (1979, 1986) and Becker and Murphy (1988). This explains why there seems to be regression to the mean in wealth and earnings across generations. However, this finding is consistent with many theories of intergenerational transmission of wealth and human capital and it does not seem to be possible to discriminate in any simple way between them. There remains considerable ambiguity about what motives actually drive bequests—see for instance the survey by Kessler and Masson (1989) and Chapter 11. Consideration has also to be given to the division of estates and the role of social and legal norms—see Meade (1964), Stiglitz (1969), Blinder (1973) and Atkinson (1980). In our view, the role of inheritance is an important area for future research.

2.3. Heterogeneity in the accumulation factor ρ and human capital theory

In the previous models, heterogeneity across individuals arises essentially because of the idiosyncratic shocks, ϵ, which are distributed independently across persons, and their accumulation over time through the factor ρ. The economic theory of distribution thus appears as a theory of the transformation, through wealth accumulation and inter-generational transmission behavior, of these idiosyncratic shocks into some permanent inequality of income and wealth. However, individuals are likely to differ not only in the income shocks that have hit them in the past but also in preferences and tastes. These may correspond to the degree of altruism of persons, their preferences for number of children, or their risk aversion. If there is independence of the idiosyncratic shocks, ϵ, and if ρ is the same and below unity for a group of persons, we know that the distribution of wealth within that group tends asymptotically toward a well-defined limit. With het-erogeneity of ρ within the population one can thus say that the overall limit distribution is a mixture of the preceding asymptotic distributions. But short-run dynamics may be much more complex.

Such heterogenity is behind the theory of human capital and income distribution initially introduced by Becker (1967), which is different from Mincer's (1958) original model where the accumulation of human capital in formal education is not essentially different from the accumulation of another financial asset. Becker's framework is in fact close to the static general model considered above. The total human capital asset owned over his/her lifetime by an individual is determined by the equalization of the (individual specific) marginal return and marginal cost. This essentially makes the total amount of the human capital asset operated by person i an individual specific function of the market prices which are behind the marginal cost and marginal return schedules, that is wage rates and the rate of interest.

An explicitly dynamic human capital accumulation framework with heterogeneity in ρ leads to the cross-over phenomenon of life-cycle earning paths noted by Mincer (1970). If human capital is accumulated continuously during one's lifetime according to a process of type (2.3) but if the return, r, on this investment is individual specific, then the corresponding accumulation speed, ρ, differs across persons. Two persons starting with the same initial human capital will end up with different levels after some time. Moreover the consumption of the more able person will be smaller at the beginning of his/her lifetime, since he/she invests more, and larger at the end since he/she has more capital. It follows—see Chapter 7—that the dispersion of earnings as a function of age is U-shaped, a conclusion different from that obtained above.

In such a model, and in Becker (1967), the cause of income differences, apart from the stochastic terms, is the difference in "abilities"; we have therefore simply pushed the explanation back one stage to the explanation of these ability differences. We return to this in Section 3.

2.4. Market imperfections and wealth dependent accumulation rates

A second source of nonstochastic heterogeneity lies in the initial endowments of wealth. In the shortrun, these are clearly important, and they may leave a long shadow on the dis-tribution. Differences in initial endowments acquire particular interest, however, when there are reasons to expect them to persist. This cannot happen with the simple linear

Eq. (2.1), but allowing ρ to depend on A in Eq. (2.1) makes the difference equation nonlinear and introduces new possibilities. This small change of assumption may allow us to account for what could be called "economic" as opposed to "natural" sources of inequality.

The simplest reason why the accumulation factor may depend on the level of wealth has to do with market imperfections. Because of asymmetries between lenders and borrowers leading to moral hazard and risk selection problems, people with a low level of wealth cannot borrow against future incomes or can do so at a rate of interest which depends negatively on their current wealth used as a collateral. This important aspect of the income distribution is treated in depth in Chapters 8 and 10. For people actually constrained by capital market imperfections, the optimal strategy in the standard life-cycle or dynastic consumption-saving model will be different from that described above, whether accumulation concerns conventional wealth or human capital. The significance of these factors is likely to vary from country to country depending on the institutional arrangements for the financing, in particular, of education.

In the field of human capital, and financing entrepreneurship, these imperfections can perpetuate inequalities. The argument which follows is inspired by Galor and Zeira (1993)—see also the synthetic presentation of this model in Atkinson (1997). Consider the case of human capital accumulation in children, and abstract for the present from stochastic factors. Poor parents are liquidity constrained. Even though accumulation increases with the initial level of capital, A, at rate ρ (assumed to be <1), it is taking place at a low rate (since human capital and hence earnings are low) and they know that their children will also be constrained. At the top of the distribution, rich parents are not liquidity constrained and do not expect their children to be. Therefore, accumulation proceeds at a higher level, although again it increases marginally with A at rate ρ. In the middle of the distribution, parents are in a situation such that if they accumulate enough, they will be able to borrow to pay for their children's education, or maybe to free their children from the liquidity constraint. Moreover, the more they accumulate the lower will be the rate of interest on their loan. The rate of return on their savings is thus marginally much higher than in the two preceding cases and they accumulate faster. Instead of being a linear locus in the (A_{t-1}, A_t) space, the wealth dynamic Eq. (2.1) now has the shape shown in Fig. 3. It is nonlinear, and—most importantly—it is nonconcave. There may be one or three intersections with the 45° line. In the case depicted in Fig. 3, there are two locally stable equilibria at points E_1 and E_3 to which individual wealth may converge. In the absence of random shocks, the limiting distribution is determined by the initial distribution: the proportion of people ending up at E_1 is the proportion of people initially on the left side of the unstable equilibrium point E_2. It is the nonconcavity introduced by the capital market imperfection which is important, as demonstrated by Bourguignon (1981) in a model with a nonconcave savings function which leads to a locally stable equilibrium with persistent inequality among otherwise identical people.

Unlike other models reviewed so far, where income and wealth inequality essentially result from "natural" differences across individual talents, preferences and chance,

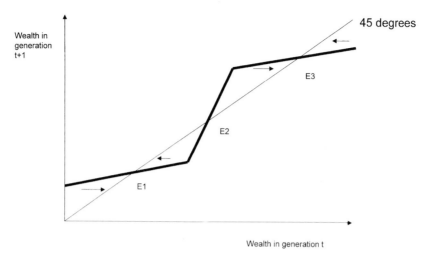

Fig. 3. Wealth accumulation process with imperfect capital market.

possibly compounded by economic phenomena, the nonconcave models just described generate inequality ex nihilo. Two persons, or dynasties, with very similar initial wealth, but on different sides of E_2, end up with different long-run wealth. Some people are "trapped" at a low wealth level. Of course, if we re-introduce stochastic terms into the Galor–Zeira model, then there is a positive probability that a family below E_2 will be taken above by the random shock. In this sense, the notion of a "trap" is a fragile one. One would expect that, taking into account the random shocks, ϵ, the asymptotic distribution of wealth would be a mixture of two distributions defined by the frequency of ϵ and, roughly speaking, centred around E_1 and E_3.

2.5. Accumulation rates with endogenous prices: distribution and growth

All the preceding dynamic theories of the distribution of productive assets assume that the price system, as summarized by the rate of return on wealth, is exogenous—even when depending on personal wealth as in the preceding model—and independent of this distribution itself. This is in contradiction with the dynamic general equilibrium frame-work outlined at the beginning of this section, where the personal distribution of assets, the distribution of fixed factor among firms and the price system all depend on each other and change simultaneously, except at a steady state. In this general framework, the rates of return of the various assets as well as their rates of accumulation should all be functions of the distribution of assets itself. A simpler case is when there is a single asset the return on which possibly depends on the total volume available of that asset. By allowing the accumulation rate, ρ to depend on the rate of return to the productive asset, the individual accumulation Eq. (2.1) then provides a link between growth theory, factor shares and the personal wealth or income distribution.

This relationship was first analyzed within the framework of Solow's aggregate neo-classical growth model by Stiglitz (1969). In the present framework, his argument may be summarized and generalized by rewriting the individual accumulation Eq. (2.1) as, taking A now to exclude human capital:

$$A_{i,t} = \rho[r(K_t)]A_{i,t-1} + \alpha_i(K_{t-1}) + \epsilon_{i,t}, \tag{2.4}$$

where K_t is wealth per capita in the economy, $r(\ )$ its rate of return which in the neoclassical model is a decreasing function of the mean wealth, $\rho(\ )$ is as before the rate of accumulation of wealth, but its positive dependence on the rate of return r is now explicit, and $\alpha_i(\ )$ stands for the effect of nonwealth income—essentially earnings—on accumulation.

The key new feature is the feedback from accumulation to the rate of return. Suppose we ignore the stochastic element. With an identical linear savings relationship, as in the main model analysed by Stiglitz, the behaviour of aggregate capital follows an aggregate version of Eq. (2.4):

$$K_t = \rho[r(K_t)]K_{t-1} + \alpha(K_{t-1}), \tag{2.5}$$

where $\alpha(K_{t-1})$ denotes the aggregate effect. If the aggregate economy converges to a steady-state level of capital, then this implies that $\rho(\ )$ is less than unity, and hence that ultimately the individual wealth-holdings also converge. Such steady-state convergence is guaranteed for example where savings are a constant proportion of total income. With no random component, the wealth distribution would tend toward an egalitarian distribution after some threshold of wealth per capita has been reached. Before then, however, $\rho(\ )$ is larger than unity so that inequality may initially increase. In summary, this modification of the original linear dynamic Eq. (2.1) consists of finding an economic reason for the accumulation rate ρ to vary over time and to end up at less than unity. The reason given here is the decline in the rate of return on wealth due to the aggregate accumulation.

In the preceding model, it is growth, or economic development, that determines the evolution of the distribution of wealth. Because of the linearity of the individual accumulation Eq. (2.4), the distribution of wealth or income has no impact on the ag-gregate evolution of the economy. Different results may be obtained by modifying the assumptions about the model of growth and factor shares behind the functions $r(\ )$ and $\alpha(\ )$. In the model of Bertola (1993), people are identical in all except their wealth and their labour endowment. There are no random disturbances. People are infinitely-lived and maximise identical iso-elastic and additive utility functions. They face the same interest rate, and choose the same rate of growth of consumption. The economy grows steadily at this rate. As Bertola shows (see Chapter 9), nonwealth income is optimally entirely consumed, so that the $a(\ )$ term itself disappears. People with no capital do not accumulate any. On the other hand, those with capital must save in order to keep up, and the initial heterogeneity is perpetuated. There is no feedback from growth to the distribution. On the other hand, Bertola goes on to posit a politico-economic mechanism for the determination by the median voter of taxation which affects the rate of growth. Different people have different interests depending on the ratio of capital to labour in their income. The growth rate is then potentially affected by changes in the location of the preferred choice of the median voter relative to that of a person with a factor bundle equal to the mean. In this way there is a link between distribution and growth.

To be complete, the imperfect capital market theory described earlier can be combined with the preceding endogenous determination of the rate of return on wealth. However, we can no longer simply assume that r and α are determined as previously by the aggregate wealth in the economy. Unlike the preceding models based on Eq. (2.6), there is no dichotomy any more between the (initial) distribution and the equilibrium price system, at least in a closed economy. Following the dynamic general equilibrium specification mentioned earlier, the price system at a point of time is that which equilibrates the demand for investment and the supply of savings. If this is the case, then the imperfection of the credit market implies that the current distribution of wealth and income in the economy affects its rate of growth, and that in turn the growth process modifies the distribution. Recent work on modelling this complex interaction includes Aghion and Bolton (1997) and Piketty (1997a)—see Chapter 8.

Here lies the frontier. Starting from a considerable simplification of the general dynamic specification of the distribution of assets, the literature is progressively integrating an increasing part of the complexity of this process. A better understanding of the basic mechanisms responsible for the evolution and the persistence of inequality has certainly been obtained. The research programme corresponding to the dynamic general equilibrium formulation is, however, far from realised, and further progress is to come. For instance, expectation formation and properties of expectational equilibria are being analysed as a possible cause of persistent inequalities—Piketty (1998) and Chapter 8.

3. Labour market and income distribution

The general static Walrasian theory of income distribution with which we began in Section 1 showed how income accrues to individuals as a remuneration of the various assets they own, which are supposed to be observable, homogeneous and therefore tradable on possibly perfectly competitive markets. Section 2 then reviewed how these assets were accumulated and how their distribution was determined. Such a framework seems adequate to handle income distribution issues where the underlying assets are readily identifiable factors like land or financial assets. For labour earnings, however, things are not that straightforward. Human capital theory allows us to represent that aspect of earnings which results from explicit accumulation behavior in formal education and further training, but it may be considered as too simple a view for earnings distribution issues. Presumably, there is more than the remuneration of a single factor in individual earnings and any theory of distribution should take explicitly into account such things as natural talents, abilities, or effort, which are commonly invoked to explain why one person earns more than another. In general, these determinants of earnings are not homogeneous within the population, they cannot be accumulated and they often are difficult to observe. There is no market for them and therefore no price, so that the basic income generation Eq. (2.1) above seems inappropriate to deal with such issues.

A possibility would be to simply ignore these factors altogether. Talents are unobserved determinants of earnings; and economic theory should concentrate on observable factors while allowing for some "residual" describing natural disparities among persons. Such a reasoning may be behind the numerous attempts since Pareto (1897) at finding a regularity in the distribution comparable to that of physical characteristics like size or weight. However, as with the stochastic term, ϵ, in the dynamic models above, the issue is whether the observed distribution of earnings is simply that of that random component—conditionally on observable earnings determinants like education or job experience as proxies for human capital—or whether economic mechanisms are responsible for the transformation of the natural distribution of talents and abilities into a distribution of earnings which is more or less skewed. We briefly review the various theories found in the literature, covering ground which is surveyed in detail in Chapter 7.

3.1. Selection theory as an economic explanation of skewness

One class of models explains the skewness of the distribution of earnings by the assumption that earnings result from the multiplication of many factors which are themselves independently and approximately normally distributed. This may be seen as largely ad hoc, and somewhat tautological. Although it was long ignored, a more economic explanation of the skewness of the distribution of earnings was offered in the 1950s by Roy (1951) and Tinbergen (1956). This model (see Chapter 7) contains the essence of what is nowadays referred to as "selection" mechanisms, which are at the heart of modern representations of the functioning of the labour market.

Suppose that individuals are endowed with quantities of various homogeneous talents which are distributed lognormally. Suppose also that there are two sectors in the economy which weight differently these talents. The earnings of an individual are y_1 in the first sector and y_2 in the second. If everyone works in the same sector, then the distribution of the logarithm of earnings is normal. But, with free entry and perfect competition in both sectors, each person selects the sector which pays him/her best. His/her actual earnings will thus be given by the self-explanatory "selection" rule:

$$y = \text{Max}(y_1, y_2). \tag{3.1}$$

It is easy to see that, if talents in the two sectors are not perfectly correlated, then the distribution of the logarithm of earnings is skewed to the right (see Heckman and Honoré, 1990, p. 1132). The nature of the sorting which takes place in this model is set out clearly by Neal and Rosen in Chapter 7.

This model may be made more complex by making different statistical assumptions about the primary distributions of earnings in the two (or more) sectors. From an economic point of view, in one sense this selection theory is not far from the basic competitive model (1.1): one could simply say that a person in the labour market is endowed with quantities of two assets which are themselves combinations of his/her innate talents. Each of these assets has a price which is set competitively. Indeed, if firms in sector 1 want to hire more people, they simply increase proportionally all the y_1, until the selection rule supplies them with as many people, or efficiency units of labour, as they require.[3] So each person is remunerated proportionally to the labour asset he/she owns. The difference is that he/she cannot sell both at the same time (being, in effect, rationed) and thus opts for the most remunerative. Choice therefore enters the explanation of the earnings distribution: it is not purely the result of a given distribution. To account for this choice, some form of supply function should be introduced in front of some of the assets in Eq. (1.1), as well as in the market equilibrium equations which determine the rates of return. Of course, things become much more complicated and the results which can be obtained from the standard Walrasian construct may not apply any more.

3.2. Involuntary selection, segmentation and discrimination

Interpreting the selection model as some kind of rationing makes it necessary to distinguish between voluntary and involuntary selection. In the preceding model, rationing occurs because a person cannot sell physically his/her labour twice. However, he/she remains free to choose in what sector or occupation he/she actually wants to work. On the contrary, involuntary selection imposes this choice.

This brings us to models of labour market segmentation. Wages are fixed in some firms or some sectors, at a level above the competitive rate for a given type of labour. Workers outside this privileged segment of the labour market would like to enter, but the number of openings is limited and rationing occurs according to some scheme which is arbitrary or partly dependent on the characteristics of the workers. Several mechanisms have been invoked to explain this segmentation of the labour market and the wage dispersion that it creates. Efficiency wages explain why competitive firms may prefer to pay a wage rate higher than that observed in the rest of the market. The existence or the uneven strength of labour unions, and more generally the distinction between insiders and outsiders in the internal labour market made up by large and medium firms, may

---

[3] For an illustration of these mechanisms and their implications for the distribution, as well as for an econometric estimation of the Roy model, see Heckman and Sedlacek (1985).

be another cause of segmentation. On these themes see respectively Akerlof and Yellen (1986) and Lindbeck and Snower (1988).

An extreme case of segmentation is labour market discrimination by which some individuals in the labour force are simply prevented from being hired in some jobs or at some wage levels on the basis of their ethnic origin or their gender. For references to different theories of the economics of racial discrimination, see—in addition to Chapter 8—Becker (1957), Arrow (1972), Phelps (1972), Marshall (1974) and Reich (1981). On gender, see among others, Amsden (1980), Fuchs (1988), Gunderson (1989), Folbre et al. (1992) and Polachek and Siebert (1993, Chapter 6).

3.3. *Imperfect information on workers' and jobs' characteristics: sorting and matching*

It was supposed until now that all players in the labour market had perfect information on the characteristics, ability and skill of employees or potential employees. This is not the case, however. Guessing the productivity in a specific firm of a person being hired is actually difficult not only for the employer but also for the employee. Productivity depends on imperfectly known characteristics of both the worker and the firm. It takes time to realize whether or not a marriage in the labour market is successful. From the point of view of the distribution of earnings, the uncertainty arising from this imperfect knowledge and the strategies to overcome its effects may explain why the shape of the observed distribution of earnings can differ from that of the distribution of abilities or productivities. More or less efficiency in learning about the quality of a match, or in sorting out employees or jobs with higher productivity, may mean more or less inequality in the distribution of earnings.

Matching and sorting models may be considered as dynamic extensions of the basic selection mechanism analyzed above and their distributive implications are similar. To understand the intuition of these models, suppose that the first match of any entrant on the labour market with an employer is random and yields some level of earnings, the logarithm of which is denoted by y_1. Suppose that another opportunity is given to all employees to change job at a subsequent period after some uncertainty on productivity or job characteristic has been resolved. This is more or less equivalent to assuming that the new matches are drawn randomly. Those finding a better match actually change jobs and others stay with their initial job. If y_2 is the second draw, earnings after round 2 are simply given by Eq. (3.1). If the "natural" distribution of abilities, that is of y_1 and y_2, is symmetric, then that of actual earnings after period 2 will be skewed. Assuming that new possible matches are drawn at regular time intervals, or equivalently that new information about a given match is revealed, then one should observe that: (a) individual earnings in a cohort increase with age, (b) the skewness of the distribution of earnings increases with age. Actual models are much more elaborate than this simple story, but they lead to the same kind of results (see Gibbons and Katz (1992) and Sattinger (1993)).

In addition to the selection mechanism that produces skewness starting from a symmetric distribution of personal abilities, random information acquisition and optimal dynamic job strategy give an interesting dynamic dimension to sorting and matching theories. They have something comparable to the dynamic models of asset accumulation briefly reviewed in the preceding section, the asset being here the information on the best jobs available. To the extent that this accumulation process is independent of the action of agents, it might enter the class of "stochastic" dynamic models defined above. However, it is possible to introduce in the basic framework described above some choice by employees among different sectors, search behavior and possibly some equilibrating wage setting mechanisms, all these extensions leading to more complex dynamics (see Jovanovic (1979) and Chapter 7).

3.4. Imperfect observability of effort and agency problems

The need to provide incentives to employees because of the unobservability of their effort gives another example of a situation where economic mechanisms introduce a wedge between the natural distribution of productivities and that of earnings. In the canonical model of agency theory of the determination of earnings, the observed productive performance of employees is equal to the sum of the effort they devote to their task and a zero mean stochastic term ("noise"). The latter prevents employers from observing and rewarding effort. To maintain effort incentives, the optimal labour contract consists then of remunerating workers whose performance is above some threshold, z, at a level, y_1, above the remuneration y_2 given to workers whose performance falls below z. The threshold, z, and therefore the number of workers paid the higher level of earnings, as well as the earnings differential $y_1 - y_2$, depend on the cost of effort for workers and the distribution of the noise term. (For references to contract theory, see Macho-Stadler and Pérez-Castrillo, 1997; Salanié, 1998.)

From a distributional point of view, this theory of earnings determination is interesting because it explains earnings differentials between persons who are strictly identical in the sense that they have strictly the same productivity and offer the same effort. Inequality arises here from the imperfect observability of these characteristics, and the impossibility for workers to insure against the risk of negative noise in the observation of their performance. It might be thought under these conditions that earnings would reflect actual productivities and would be distributed like the noise term in the observation of performances. The theory tells us, however, that this is not the case and that the ex-post distribution of earnings is biased in comparison with the distribution of actual performances, the extent of the bias depending on purely economic factors. Extensions of the preceding basic model to tournaments (Lazear and Rosen, 1981, Green and Stokey, 1983; Nalebuff and Stiglitz, 1983) allows us to understand the determinants of the hierarchichal structure of earnings within a company, whereas the extension to an intertemporal framework suggests determinants of individual earnings profiles over their career. Rewards and incentives within teams are discussed in Chapter 10.

3.5. *Conclusion of our theoretical tour d'horizon*

Our tour of various theories relevant to explaining the distribution of income has encompassed a number of theoretical developments in the micro- and macrotheory of factor
pricing and factor accumulation. This is not surprising. A theory of income distribution
must draw on the union of what is known about the pricing of the assets whose services
individuals can sell on the market, to which we should add the possible rents or quasi-
rents that may accrue to individuals for noncompetitive positions that they may hold and
the dynamics of the competitive structure of an economy. At the same time, it should be
clear why we initially referred to "building blocks" of a theory of income distribution
rather than to a unique theory. There is at present no unified economic theory of income
distribution. This should be seen as the reflection of the complexity of the world in which
we are living and not as the sign of some fundamental weakness of economics. As is
described in more detail in the following chapters of this Handbook, we have learned
a great deal about different pieces in the puzzle. These pieces all help us understand
why inequality of income is higher in one country than another, or in one sector than
another, or in one period than in another. There is little doubt that some countries are
more unequal than others in terms of the distribution of the ownership of land and capital
and that this has a direct impact on inequality comparisons. There is little doubt that
bequest behavior is important in explaining the persistence of such inequality. There is
little doubt that changes in factor shares have on occasions important effects on the distribution of income. There is little doubt that the functioning of the labour-market and its
regulation has a direct impact on the distribution of earnings. Taken independently, our
theoretical building blocks are thus useful analytical instruments, which have undergone
continuous progress over the last two or three decades and continue to do so. Thanks to
this progress there are certain things that we now understand much better. But this is not
a reason for not trying to integrate more closely all these components of the theory.

4. Working with income distribution data

The preceding section reviewed existing economic theories seeking to explain the distribution of income. The empirical counterpart of these theories consists of comparing
income distribution data across various societies or at different points of time for the
same society. The intellectual challenge is then to try to relate observed differences to
a set of exogenous characteristics of the societies being analyzed and to see whether
the relationship fits the predictions of the theory. Considerable work has been developed
along these lines since the pioneering comparisons undertaken by Pareto (see Chapter
4, and also Lydall, 1968; Creedy, 1977; Brandolini, 1998), but it must be recognized
that it does not permit us to identify in more than a rough way the determinants of the
distribution of income suggested by the theory. On one hand, this is because the number
of observations is limited and the numerous determinants of the distribution are likely

to change over time. On the other hand, switching from the theory to the data opens a large set of new questions—conceptual and practical. We review in this section the main issues arising in the comparison of income distribution data over time or space.

One of the conclusions which the reader will rightly draw from the Handbook is that there has been a very considerable improvement in the availability of data about the distribution of income. Advances have been made at the national level, where in many countries a significant investment has been made in carrying out new surveys, in linking administrative data, and in refining methods of analysis. Just to give one example, the conference volume edited by Gottschalk et al. (1997) contained studies of income distribution based on data for Australia, Canada, the Czech Republic, Finland, France, Germany, Greece, Hungary, Ireland, Israel, Japan, Netherlands, Sweden, the UK and the US. One major step has been the establishment of panel studies such as the Michigan Panel Study of Income Dynamics (see Brown et al., 1996) and the German Socio-Economic Panel (see Burkhauser and Wagner, 1994), which provide data on the same individuals or households over a span of years.

Of particular significance has been the assembly of datasets which can be compared across countries (although it should be stressed that comparability is a matter of degree). Here the way has been pioneered by the Luxembourg Income Study (LIS), which brings together microdata on households derived from sample surveys and other sources. The LIS database provided the basis, for example, for the comparative study of income inequality in OECD countries published by the OECD in 1995 (Atkinson et al., 1995). The PACO project, similarly based in Luxembourg, provides an assembly of panel data. In the European Union, the EUROMOD project to construct a tax benefit model for the European Union, brings together microdata for all member states which will allow analysis of the distributional impact of policy changes in the Union as a whole (see Sutherland, 1997b).

The particular data that we use to illustrate our discussion are drawn from the French household budget surveys, the "Enquête Budget de Famille", referred to as the EBF, for 1979 and 1994. The EBF is conducted periodically, and information is obtained by interview on expenditure, income and other variables. The initial sample of approximately 20,000 represents around 1 in 1000 households, although nonresponse reduced the effective sample size in 1994 to 11,344 cases. To adjust for differential nonresponse between different types of household in the EBF, a grossing-up procedure is applied to yield re-weighted results representative of the population. It should be emphasised that such re-weighting procedures cannot be relied upon to eliminate the problem. Response may vary not only by the characteristics employed in grossing-up, such as region, or age of head of household, but also by income.

There are other reasons why observed monetary disposable income may give a biased representation of the actual distribution of (monetary) income in a society. One potentially important source of nonsampling error is under-reporting. Comparisons of total household income reported in the surveys generally used to estimate the distribution of income with National Accounts data suggest an average rate of underestimation between

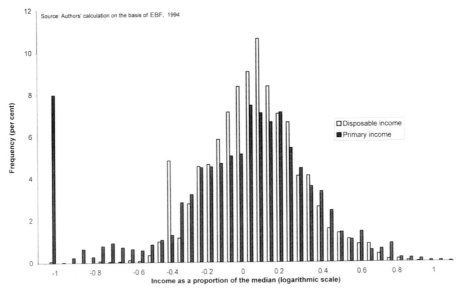

Fig. 4a. Histogram of the distribution of primary and disposable household income per adult equivalent in France (1994).

10 and 20% of total disposable income depending on the country,[4] and the type of statistical source. With such a gap, it is sufficient that some underreporting be proportionally more important at some levels of income than at others for potential biases in measuring inequality to become sizable. The correction of these biases is not easy, but it is possible to get some idea of the magnitude of the bias by matching various data sources. Note also that these biases are very troublesome when an absolute estimate of the distribution of income and its degree of inequality is needed, as for international comparisons at a given point of time. They may be less of a problem when examining changes in the distribution over time, if they can be assumed to be more or less constant over time, but even this is debatable, since the changes over time will themselves be smaller.

4.1. Representation of the distribution and inequality measurement

A first issue is that of the presentation of income distribution data. In Fig. 4 are shown four different representations which, up to normalisation by the mean, contain the same information: one representation is chosen over another essentially on grounds of practical convenience of comparison.

Traditionally, individual observations were arranged into a vector indicating the proportion of people falling in selected income bands. This is the frequency histogram

---

[4] See the estimates in Atkinson et al. (1995: 34). The underreporting is often larger in developing countries.

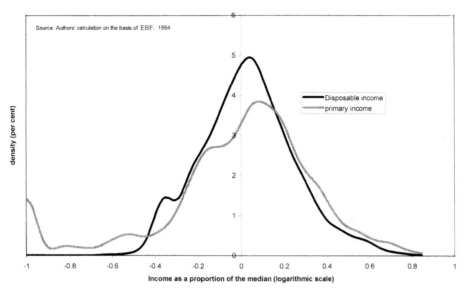

Fig. 4b. Kernel estimate of density of primary and disposable household income per adult equivalent in France (1994).

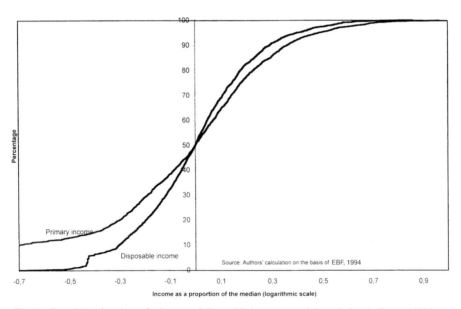

Fig. 4c. Cumulative functions of primary and disposable income per adult equivalent in France (1994).

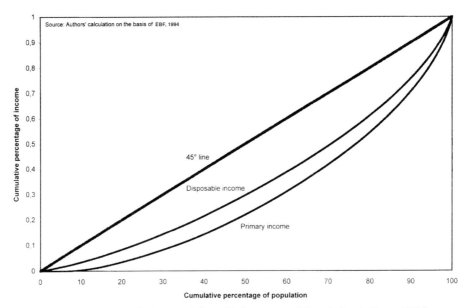

Fig. 4d. Lorenz curves of primary and disposable income per adult equivalent in France (1994).

shown in Fig. 4a for the distribution in France in 1994. The distributions are those of primary income, defined as income from labour and property plus replacement income (pensions and unemployment benefit), and of disposable income. Income is expressed as a proportion of the median on a logarithmic scale. A sizable proportion of the population had zero primary income, as indicated by the spike in the first range for that variable. Nowadays, modern computing possibilities permit us to work directly with the individual observations rather than grouping them and to obtain more flexible estimates of the income frequency function through Kernel techniques. Examples of such Kernel estimates of the "density function" are shown in Fig. 4b. In effect they smooth the histogram. (For a description and discussion of Kernel techniques, see Chapter 2 and Silverman (1986).)

Other representations of the distribution of income in a given sample include the "distribution curve" and the Lorenz curve. The former simply cumulates people below a given income level—see Fig. 4c. Looked at from the vertical axis and from bottom to top, this curve corresponds to the famous parade of Pen (1971) where all individuals in the population march in the order of their size, itself proportional to their income. Each distribution has been normalised to its median, so that the curves intersect at that point. The slope of the cumulative distribution gives the frequency at that point, so that we can work back to the frequency distribution. The small vertical segment at the bottom of the cumulative distribution of disposable income is due to some bunching of individuals around income minima guaranteed by the redistribution system. This bunching is also apparent on the discrete frequency histogram and the Kernel estimate of the density function.

The Lorenz curve, which we have used theoretically in Fig. 1, cumulating the population in increasing order of income, is depicted in Fig. 4d. Some of the data points for the Lorenz curve are shown in Table 1. For the distribution among persons of disposable income per equivalent adult in 1994 (line 14) the share of the bottom 10 per cent was 3.55%. The share of the bottom 50% was 30.1%. As pointed out earlier, the slope of the Lorenz curve is equal to the income at that point divided by the mean, so that a slope of 0.5 means that people to the left of this point have incomes less than half the mean.

Comparisons of curves like those appearing in Fig. 4 are often unclear or ambiguous because curves are close to each other or cross several times. This is one reason why so many authors prefer to rely on one or a few scalar "inequality measures" which summarize the departure of the distribution from equality and satisfy various basic properties. The Gini coefficient has for long been the most popular scalar inequality measure. The reasons for its popularity are not entirely clear, but may be due, as Cowell speculates in Chapter 2, to its graphical interpretation as the area between the Lorenz curve and the diagonal, relative to the whole triangle. In France in 1994, the Gini coefficient for the distribution of disposable income shown in Fig. 4 was 29.7%.

In considering the wide variety of other summary measures of inequality, one property of interest is the extent to which the measure allows for differing attitudes to inequality. The class of measures, I_ϵ, where the valuation of individual income, y_i, is given by y_i to the power of $(1 - \epsilon)$, as in Atkinson (1970), allows for such differences through the parameter ϵ.[5] A value of ϵ equal to zero means that society is indifferent about the distribution; the degree of aversion to inequality rises with ϵ; and as the parameter tends to infinity we reach a situation where society is only concerned with the lowest income group (a "Rawlsian" position). Where μ denotes the mean income, then $\mu(1 - I_\epsilon)$ may be interpreted as the "equally distributed equivalent income", or the amount of income which, if equally distributed, would be equally valued. This value depends both on the degree of dispersion, and on attitudes to inequality, as represented by ϵ.

A second property of interest is the degree to which the measure allows decomposition (see Chapter 2). Decomposability properties were initially studied by Bourguignon (1979) and Shorrocks (1980), who examined the conditions under which overall inequality could be decomposed in an additive way into inequality within subgroups and

---

[5] The formula for the index, I, where $\epsilon \neq 1$, is that

$$[1 - I]^{(1-\epsilon)} = \sum f_i (y_i/\mu)^{(1-\epsilon)},$$

where μ denotes the mean income and f_i is the proportion of the population with income Y_i.
Where $\epsilon = 1$, then

$$\log_e[1 - I] = \sum f_i \log_e (y_i/\mu).$$

Table 1
Various perspectives on income distribution data: France 1979 and 1994

Type of income	Recipient unit	Year	Income share of:							Gini Coef.	Theil Coef.	$I_{0.5}$	I_1	I_2
			Bottom 10%	Bottom 20%	Bottom 30%	Bottom 50%	Top 20%	Top 10%	Top 5%					
Wage (Monthly)	Salaried workers	1979	2.64	7.75	13.91	28.80	40.87	26.76	17.55	0.326	0.214	0.096	0.182	0.459
		1994	1.62	5.54	11.27	26.05	42.79	28.01	18.22	0.365	0.258	0.121	0.244	0.962
Gross per household	Household	1979	2.92	7.65	13.48	28.38	39.86	25.02	15.68	0.321	0.190	0.086	0.164	0.341
		1994	1.67	5.58	10.77	24.92	42.55	26.91	16.87	0.369	0.246	0.110	0.234	0.955
Gross per capita	Person	1979	2.14	5.92	10.89	24.42	43.65	27.76	17.66	0.377	0.257	0.115	0.220	0.430
		1994	1.55	5.01	9.79	23.16	45.06	29.17	18.65	0.399	0.296	0.129	0.260	0.956
Gross per adult equivalent	Person	1979	2.75	7.24	12.91	27.58	40.19	25.13	15.83	0.330	0.199	0.089	0.171	0.350
		1994	1.88	5.89	11.30	25.81	41.75	26.29	16.48	0.357	0.232	0.103	0.217	0.953
Disposable per household	Household	1979	3.19	8.34	14.65	30.20	37.95	23.60	14.81	0.295	0.165	0.076	0.145	0.308
		1994	2.77	7.22	12.93	27.74	40.14	25.18	15.68	0.328	0.192	0.090	0.173	0.363
Disposable per capita	Person	1979	3.17	7.86	13.50	27.82	40.74	25.69	16.22	0.328	0.201	0.091	0.168	0.319
		1994	3.11	7.68	13.25	27.35	41.71	26.76	16.96	0.338	0.213	0.095	0.175	0.326
Disposable per adult equivalent	Person	1979	3.76	9.23	15.60	31.09	37.32	23.12	14.58	0.281	0.152	0.069	0.129	0.263
		1994	3.55	8.79	14.97	30.10	38.65	24.26	15.11	0.297	0.162	0.074	0.139	0.280
Leisure adjusted disposable per adult equivalent	Person	1979	4.39	10.82	18.02	34.37	34.81	21.46	13.36	0.237	0.115	0.052	0.097	0.197
		1994	4.08	9.91	16.64	32.40	36.67	22.85	14.16	0.265	0.132	0.060	0.113	0.227

Source: Authors' calculation on the basis of EBF, 1979 and 1994.

inequality between groups. The ability to make such a breakdown, as with analysis of variance, is helpful when seeking to account for inequality differences, but its appropriateness as a judgment is open to question (see Chapter 1). In general, the Gini coefficient is not decomposable by population subgroups. If we insist on this property, and on certain other requirements (see Chapter 2), this means that attention has to be limited to the *generalised entropy* class of measures. This class includes two measures proposed by Theil (1967), as well as measures ordinally equivalent to I_ϵ.

Study of these summary measures has made explicit the underlying values. At the same time, it must be recognised that there may be considerations which they do not capture. We may, for instance, want to allow for social judgments which are concerned with notions of "distance". This may explain the continued popularity of measures such as the ratio of the top decile to the bottom decile (see Chapter 14). The same applies to measures of poverty (see Chapter 6), where people have sought to replace a simple headcount of poverty (those below the specified poverty line) by measures which reflect the intensity of poverty (see Sen, 1976a). The most straightforward such measure is the average poverty deficit, or the average amount by which the incomes of the poor would need to be increased to bring them to the poverty line. Other measures attach more weight to larger poverty deficits, as with the Sen measure which weights each person's poverty gap by the person's rank in the ordering of the poor. This gives a "smoother" measure of poverty, but, as noted in Chapter 6, the headcount continues to be widely used.

Using different scalar inequality and poverty measures to compare distributions may lead to contradictory conclusions, one distribution appearing more unequal than another with respect to one measure, but the opposite being true with another measure. A condition for such a contradiction not to occur, with distributions with the same mean and total population, is that the Lorenz curve for one distribution be everywhere above that of another, a condition referred to as "Lorenz dominance". Lorenz dominance ensures agreement for a wide class of inequality measures, and this is undoubtedly a central result of the literature on inequality measurement. Interestingly enough, this criterion is also linked to poverty measurement. Indeed, this condition is equivalent to saying (taking distributions with the same mean and total population) that there is *smaller poverty deficit* in the first than in the second distribution *for all possible poverty limits*, from zero to infinity. The same dominance result, with the poverty limit restricted to stay below its predetermined maximum, allows us to conclude that we would get the same ranking for all poverty measures such that the marginal valuation of income is nondecreasing, although it should be noted that this rules out the headcount.[6]

Where distributions differ in their mean incomes, as where comparing different countries, the Lorenz curve may be replaced by the *generalised Lorenz curve* (Shorrocks, 1983).[7] This replaces the relative percentage of total income on the vertical axis by

---

[6] The reformulation in terms of poverty dominance is given in Atkinson (1987) and Foster and Shorrocks (1988a, 1988b). A summary of the results is provided in Chapter 6 and Atkinson (1998).

[7] This idea, like many others in the field of inequality measurement, is contained in Kolm (1969).

the absolute total income per head, so that it is now denominated in currency. (For cross-country comparisons, this clearly raises issues of the appropriate conversion rate.) This amounts to multiplying by the mean the share in the standard Lorenz curve. The condition for one distribution to rank ahead of another is then that its generalised Lorenz curve be everywhere above. So that, comparing France and the US, we ask whether the absolute living standard of the bottom 10% (20%, ...) in the US is higher than that of the bottom 10% (20%, ...) in France. The country with the higher mean cannot be dominated, since the end point of the generalised Lorenz curve is the overall mean, but if its income is more unequally distributed then it may not itself dominate.

Even though the use of these instruments is spreading only slowly among empirical analysts of distribution issues, there is no doubt that considerable progress has been achieved over the last decades in the field of inequality measurement and the comparison of income distribution. (The reader is referred for fuller discussion to Chapter 2, Lambert (1989) and Sen and Foster (1997).) This is true to such an extent that one may wonder whether the problem may not be any more that of *how* to measure and to compare income distributions but that of *what* to measure and compare. This is the subject of the rest of this section.

4.2. *The recipient unit*

As a first element in answering the "what to compare" question, we consider the definition of the recipient unit. This was deliberately ignored in the preceding theoretical sections so as not to mix issues, but empirical analysts generally have to choose between a range of alternatives, depending on the data at hand and the issue to be addressed:
  − individuals, whether they have an income or not;
  − individual income recipients;
  − families, of related adults and dependent children;
  − spending units, that is individuals pooling their income together and sharing the same consumption budget; and
  − households, that is people living at the same address.
These definitions may lead to different evaluations of the degree of inequality of a distribution, and possibly to different representations of its evolution over time. Yet, they are often confused.

The main difference between distribution data defined with reference to these various recipient units has to do with the "matching" of individual earners into households and the size of these households. Clearly, if all households had the same size, if the number of earners were the same, and if individual earnings within a household were perfectly correlated—i.e., perfect "homogamy"—then there would be a straightforward relation between the definitions. On the other hand, random marriage, and independence between household size and the income of the adults in the household, would lead to a different relationship between the different definitions. Practically, the real world is at a changing position somewhere between these two extremes. The four first rows of Table

1 compare the distribution of individual earnings in France and that of the gross income of households in 1979 and 1994. Even though the Gini coefficient happens not to be very different for the two distributions, closer inspection reveals substantial differences. However, nothing general can be said of the direction these differences should take.

We must stress the gap between the empirical definition of the distribution of income and the theory reviewed in the preceding sections of this Introduction. In order to analyze and understand the evolution of the distribution of household income, a model of income generation at that level is required. Two factors make such a model substantially different from the basic model (1.1) above. On the one hand, it is necessary to correct the total income that a family gets from the assets and the talents of its members by its size or composition. We have to look at fertility, and, more generally, household formation and dissolution, and their correlation with the earnings potential and the assets of the household. On the other hand, labour supply becomes a key variable to explain differences in total monetary income across households since some members with given abilities choose not to work or to work part time, changing the relation between the individual and household distributions. These two dimensions are seldom considered explicitly, but it is increasingly realised that they are of considerable importance.[8] The last rows of Table 1 compare the distribution of income in France depending on whether differences in labour supply are or are not taken into account. Imputing some implicit income equal to the prediction of a conventional earning equation to nonparticipating household members contributes to a substantial equalization of the distribution.

The choice of recipient unit depends on the issue which is addressed. Individual earnings data are better adapted to positive studies focusing on the labour market, whereas household income may be more appropriate in normative studies addressing the issue of inequality in living standards, although this is influenced by the degree to which resources are shared within the household. What is appropriate for the Mr and Mrs Blanc and their children aged 2 and 5 may not be applicable to friends sharing an apartment but nothing else. In the former case we may want to aggregate the total household income; in the latter case we may want to look at their individual incomes. Even in the case of the Blanc family we may be interested in individual incomes if there is substantial inequality within the family (see, for example, Jenkins (1991) and Sutherland (1997a)). How far it is possible to calculate individual incomes depends in part on the nature of that income. Earnings are typically received on an individual basis, but income from investments may be in the joint names of a couple.

Whatever unit is chosen, an adjustment has to be made for the differing needs of units of different size and composition. The most meaningful concept from that point of view is the distribution of "equivalised incomes" where total income is expressed per adult

[8] See for instance the recurrent debate on the influence of wives' earnings on household income inequality. An early treatment is provided by Smith (1970) and Layard and Zabalza (1978). For an illustration of the role of the change in the correlation between spouses' earnings on the distribution of family income, see Karoly and Burtless (1995). A decomposition method permitting the isolation of these phenomena is proposed in Bourguignon et al. (1998).

equivalent. One such adjustment is to take per capita income. This is illustrated by rows
3–6 or 9–12 in Table 1. Here again there is no presumption on the consequences of this
change of income definition upon the appraisal of inequality. In the French case, moving
from household income to incomes per capita unambiguously increases inequality when
considering gross income whereas the change is somewhat ambiguous when disposable
income is considered. Per capita income makes no allowance for economies of scale,
and a commonly used alternative adjustment is to divide total household income by
the square root of the household size, so that the income of a family of 4 is divided
by 2. It must be kept in mind, however, that the definition of an equivalence scale is
problematic and that there is some ambiguity in the concept of adult equivalent. There
is a voluminous literature on equivalence scales: see, for example, Pollak and Wales
(1979), Deaton and Muellbauer (1980), Jorgenson and Slesnick (1984), Fisher (1987)
and Blundell and Lewbel (1991). See also the discussion in the next section.

There is a further choice to be made, which is the weighting to be given to each unit.
It is still quite common for income distribution statistics to treat each household as 1, so
that we are considering the distribution among households: i.e., the Blancs appear once
in the figures. But the welfare economic approach might lead more naturally to treat each
person as 1, so that we impute to every member in the household the per adult equivalent
income: i.e., the Blancs appear four times in the figures. This choice of weights should
not be confused with that for the equivalence scale, and there is no necessary reason
why total equivalent income for the household has to add to the household total. It may
be quite legitimate to look at the distribution among individuals of household income
divided by equivalent adults, so that the Blanc family is treated as 4 people each with
an income equal to the total divided by 2 (if the equivalence scale is the square root
of household size). Table 1 compares the distribution of income among individuals
when the income concept is household income per capita or household income per adult
equivalent. Because individuals living in numerous families tend to be poorer in terms
of income per capita, moving from the former to the latter definition of income generally
produces an unambiguous improvement of the distribution.

To sum up, in using income distribution data, one must ask—what unit, how is income adjusted for unit size and composition, and how are units weighted? The answers
to these three questions must be clearly signalled when reporting empirical findings: for
example, the distribution of wage income among individual wage-earners, or the distribution of total household income among households, or the distribution of household
income per equivalent adult among persons.

4.3. Definition of income

To a large extent, the definition of income in distribution data parallels that of the recipient unit. Earnings data generally refer to individuals whereas more comprehensive
definitions of income apply to households. There are, however, different definitions of

household income, leading in turn to different evaluation of income inequality and its evolution over time.

Total family income can come from various sources. Labour income and the issue of the labour supply of household members—to which we should logically add that of unemployment—have already been discussed above. The other source of primary income is capital and other property. It is much more difficult to measure. On one hand, capital income is generally paid on a less regular basis than earnings and therefore more difficult to observe in data sources other than income tax returns. On the other hand, it is often virtual rather than real. A person who has taken out a private pension for instance is receiving every year some income on the total accumulated savings, but by the very nature of the contract this income is automatically reinvested and will appear neither in income tax returns nor as a spontaneously reported income source. The same is true of nonrealized capital gains or losses on a portfolio of equities and bonds. For households who own their house, the same is true of the potential capital gain, or loss, and may be true of the implicit rent (although some surveys attempt to estimate such imputed rent).

For all these reasons, capital income is generally underestimated in distribution data, which probably means that the observed income distribution understates the dispersion of current incomes. The figures reported in Table 1 do not include any correction for this underestimation. A recent attempt has been made to correct capital incomes by type of assets so as to make them consistent with National Accounts data (INSEE, 1997, p. 37 and Appendix V). It suggests that the Gini coefficient of the distribution of household incomes in the original household budget survey could be underestimated by 2 percentage points. It must be noted, however, that the correction involved there is concerned only with taking into account the actual income of all financial assets owned by households and not all the virtual income like undistributed dividends or implicit rents. This imperfect observability of capital income may explain why the strong macroeconomic fluctuations in factor shares observed in most developed countries over the past 20 years have failed to produce the sizable change in income distribution that theory would predict.

There are situations where labour and property income are difficult to distinguish. Self-employment is the most obvious. In this respect, the case of farm households in developing countries is quite typical. Defining the income of these households often requires imputing values to flows of goods which do not go through the market and therefore have no explicit prices. The assumptions behind these imputations are debatable. Should income be estimated by imputing a value to the labour expended on the farm and a return to land and equipment? Or should it be estimated by imputing a price to all outputs produced in the household and subtracting the cost of market inputs? Considerable ambiguity may appear because of these imputations.

A different source of income is the transfers made by the public sector towards persons or households in specific situations. These transfers (discussed in Chapter 12) are often considered as part of the redistribution system and as such not directly comparable to "primary income" from labour or capital. Different cases must, however, be distinguished. The majority of transfers are the counterpart of contributions paid by beneficiaries at an earlier stage of their lifetime to insure themselves against unforeseen accidents like unemployment or invalidity, or simply for their old age. These schemes are generally administered by the State and the correspondence between contribution and payments is therefore less direct, but conceptually pension payments by the social security system should not be considered as different from capital income or annuities received by persons who would live partially or completely on their savings after retirement, even though not determined in the same way.

This being said, there often is some "redistributive" component in contributory transfer incomes which stems from the lack of direct correspondence between the contributions made by a person to an insurance scheme and the benefit to be obtained from it. This component is difficult to calculate, and it makes this replacement income not directly comparable to more obviously redistributive transfers like child benefits, income supplement or welfare support given to needy families on a noncontributory basis. In theory, this public transfer income should include the imputed value of publicly provided consumption goods like education or a national health service. The impact of noncash subsidies for health, education and housing is investigated by Smeeding et al. (1993). Although seldom observable, "private" transfers made directly between households should also be included under this heading, since they may be substitutes or complement to transfers made by the public sector. Several studies have shown how these transfers could modify our view of the distribution of income both in developing and in developed countries. See Cox and Jimenez (1986) and INSEE (1997).

Disposable income is typically defined as the sum of the preceding "primary" and transfer incomes minus the total amount of direct taxes paid, including income tax and social security contributions. Not only is this widely used definition incomplete in ways that we have already discussed, but it also fails to allow for indirect taxes which affect the purchasing power of households in a nonneutral way, or for spatial or other differences in the structure of prices, in the availability of public goods, or in the consumption of leisure. Several studies have done so. They generally have to rely on some extraneous tax or price incidence assumptions and to use additional information from other data sources, for instance household expenditure surveys. Because of this, they are not strictly comparable with other sources on income distribution and they tend to appear in the literature which specialises on redistribution. But, the fact that the concept of monetary disposable income does not rely on (possibly) debatable economic assumptions does not make it conceptually more appropriate than more sophisticated real income concepts. Given the diversity of rankings of distributions induced by the various concepts of income, this is certainly an issue about which practitioners should be more aware.

4.4. *The time dimension*

Income data generally refer to a well-defined observation period: the week, the month, or the year. There are good reasons to believe that the length of the unit-period is not without influence on the estimation of the distribution of income and its inequality. In the case of sample surveys, collecting earnings information for a current pay period, such as a month, may be less subject to inaccuracy than if the survey asks respondents to provide information for a longer period such as the previous calendar year. (This problem would not arise with administrative data, such as those from income tax records.) Working in the opposite direction is the fact that, the shorter the observation period, the more contaminated are the data by transitory income components—premium payments, sickness leave, delay in transfer payments, etc. In the case of investment incomes, payments may only be made annually.

Pushing the transitory argument further provides a rationale for using observed consumption expenditures rather than income to estimate income inequality. Indeed, according to the well-known permanent income hypothesis (Friedman, 1957), differences in consumption expenditures over time and between agents should reflect differences in permanent disposable household income rather than transitory shocks to income. As a matter of fact, it is typically true that the distribution of consumption expenditures is less unequal than that of current income, whatever the periodicity of observation.[9] Where people plan their consumption over the life-cycle (see, for example, Chapter 11), current income reflects the accumulation of assets with age. The resulting dispersion of current wealth is a compound of such age factors and the distribution of earnings: in the simple model of Flemming (1979), for example, the range of current wealth is at least twice that of earnings, even though the latter is the sole source of inequality. This being said, the use of consumption rather than income data raises problems of definition and observation. The main conceptual problem is the treatment of durables and the necessity of imputing a value for their services. The main observational problem is the infrequency of purchase. Other definitional problems for consumer expenditure are fully similar to those already stressed for income, and to this extent there is no clear advantage in using expenditure rather than income in studying distributional issues.

Another important issue related to the time dimension of income distribution data is whether it is justified to mix all age groups in the same analysis. The situation of a 60-year-old person is not comparable to that of a 25-year-old. Their income may well be unequal when observed in the same year, but this inequality is totally artificial if, 35 years from now, the 25 year old enjoys the same real income as the 60 year old today. In other words, it might be justified to restrict the analysis of income distribution to persons with the same age (or families whose head has the same age) and to distinguish between intragenerational and extragenerational inequality. It is important to stress that it is not necessary to rely on panel data for such an analysis. "Pseudo-panel" data provided by the repetition of cross-section surveys at various points of time allow us to follow the evolution of the mean income and the income inequality of various successive cohorts. Deaton and Paxson (1994) show that the dispersion of consumption expenditures tends

---

[9] For discussion of the differences found in using expenditure rather than income, see Cutler and Katz (1992), Goodman et al. (1995), and Johnson and Shipp (1997).

to increase with the age of a cohort, in conformity with standard life-cycle consumption theory. This dynamic dimension of repeated cross-sections should be increasingly exploited in the future as the number of available surveys increases.

Panel data do, however, ease, or at least transform, many of the preceding problems. Such data have been available for individual earnings for a rather long time in selected countries. Studies of the dynamics of individual earnings over a few years, along the lines of Eq. (2.1) above, confirm the presence of a sizable transitory component at all levels. Atkinson et al. (1992, p. 93) find that the share of the transitory component in the variance of the logarithm of earnings is quite similar across the samples and studies which they survey, ranging from 15–20% for homogeneous highly educated groups to around 35% for much more heterogeneous groups. Mobility means that the dispersion of earnings measured over a longer period is less than the average dispersion in individual years, with the extent of the reduction depending on the measure used and on the sample studied (see Atkinson et al., 1992, Table VIII).

For household incomes, panel studies such as those cited earlier (the Michigan Panel Study of Income Dynamics and the German Socio-Economic Panel) have been joined by others, which have proved a rich-yielding investment. Other nonlongitudinal surveys have increasingly made panel data available for short time intervals, say one to three years, thanks to rotating sampling techniques in essentially cross-sectional surveys. Administrative data also provide an important source of panel data. These confirm the presence of a sizable transitory component at all levels of income and a lower degree of income inequality when income is averaged over a longer period of time. However, the extent of mobility should not be exaggerated. In the UK, for example, Hills (1998) has pointed out that, while 35% of people in the bottom fifth leave from one year to the next, the occurrence of low income is far from random: 61% of observations of low income over a 4-year period were accounted for by people who were in the bottom fifth 3 or 4 times. Moreover, there are potential measurement problems. Use of panel data introduces the risk that there is a higher noise-to-signal ratio when considering differences in income. In the absence of a perfect capital market, the appropriate valuation of income streams is unclear, and different procedures may be appropriate at different points in the income scale. In the case of household incomes, the analysis is made difficult by the fact that the composition of households is changing over time, possibly in a way that is endogenous to the earnings dynamics of its members.

4.5. Conclusion

To conclude this brief review of empirical issues and problems in the analysis of income distribution, we should stress the multiplicity of perspectives offered by the available data and the way they are used and interpreted by statisticians and economists. Given the different perspectives offered by economic theory to explain the distribution of income, this may seem only natural. Empirical work is a matter of choosing the definition of data which fits the theory one wants to test or apply. Things are not that simple, however.

On one hand, empirical data may call for theories more complex and sophisticated than those so far developed. This seems to be the case, for instance, with household income data and the gaps in our understanding about household decision-making. On the other hand, the available data may not allow us to get close enough to the concepts put forward by the theory. The cure seems, simply, to lie in more work being undertaken to improve the adequacy of both theory and observation.

In the meantime, caution needs to be exercised in drawing conclusions about causal mechanisms and about even the extent of inequality. Definitional issues are too serious to be left to footnotes—or ignored altogether. Data on inequality are meaningless if they do not specify "of what among whom". Statements that one society is more unequal than another, or that it has become more unequal over time, cannot be based on data where definitions are different. Nor should we rely on a single definition. The picture may look different for one concept of income than for another; looking at households may conceal what is happening within the household unit. Lorenz dominance is seen as a better analytical tool than single income inequality measures because it encompasses most well-behaved inequality measures. Likewise, income distribution analysts should make use of alternative approaches to measurement, using a range of data and of definitions.

5. Income distribution, economic inequality and social justice

We have until now taken a largely positive view of income distribution, but there would be something paradoxical in not going beyond such a perspective, since income distribution may be considered the normative economic issue "par excellence". It is indeed rather difficult to study how the total produce of a society is shared among its members without having to consider whether it is "just" or "unjust", "fair" or "unfair". In our own case, even though we have tried in the preceding parts of this Introduction to avoid use of the word "inequality", because of its normative connotation, it proved unavoidable, and the discussion of measurement inevitably went beyond description to evaluation. In this section, we face this head on and review the main issues in the vast literature which bears upon the normative issues associated with income distribution.[10]

The elementary distributive issue is the "cake division problem", that is the allocation of a fixed resource among various individuals, under the key assumption that this allocation is without effect upon the total to be allocated. There is no equity/efficiency trade-off. This problem may be considered as the starting point of the theory of economic inequality and social justice. It provides the normative background for income inequality measurement, and we have learned a lot about these issues. There are, however, important aspects on which we have only touched so far, notably that a particular sized slice of the cake may mean different levels of well-being for different people. One standard slice may mean much more to Mr Noir, a single person, than to Mr and Mrs Blanc and

---

[10] Our coverage is very incomplete. The reader is referred to such recent works on economic theories of justice as those of Sen (1992), Kolm (1996a), and Roemer (1996).

their 2 children. This is one example of the problem of heterogeneity among individuals which is discussed later.

Division of a fixed cake provides a starting point but some of the key problems only become evident when the size of the cake is variable. This is apparent when there is a trade-off between the size of the cake and the fairness of its distribution. Much of the public finance literature has been concerned with the costs of redistribution in terms of reduced efficiency (see Atkinson and Stiglitz, 1980, Chapter 11). As, however, we have already stressed, and is developed in several chapters of this Handbook, redistribution may have a positive effect on the size of the cake. This causes us to have a different view of the problem.

The variable size of the cake introduces a second important set of issues, which is the relation between individual contributions and economic productivity. Individuals differ in their endowed productive abilities and in their effort. These two forms of heterogeneity are different, in that the former is not under the control of the individual, and we may want to distinguish between them in a normative evaluation. This is discussed later.

5.1. The cake division problem: utilitarianism, welfarism and the measurement of inequality

Consider first a fixed cake, that is a sum of money, and two allocations of that sum among individuals (the "Irene and Janet problem" of Chapter 2) who may be considered as identical in all respects except the share they receive. Assume that all individuals value the income they receive according to the same increasing and concave utility function. The standard maximisation of the corresponding utilitarian objective, that is the sum of individual utilities, leads to an optimal distribution which is perfectly egalitarian. Inequality may then be measured as the distance between the actual distribution and this egalitarian reference. Between two distributions with the same mean or total income, the socially preferred one is therefore the least unequal on this account. These are the ideas originally expressed in a utilitarian framework by Pigou (1912) and Dalton (1920b).

A broader welfarist perspective was developed at the end of the 1960s by Kolm (1969) and Atkinson (1970). In this framework, the utility function is to be interpreted as the way in which society, rather than individuals themselves, values individual incomes. More generally, the sum of society valued individual utilities can be replaced by a non-decreasing Schur-concave (s-concave) social welfare function with individual income as its arguments (Kolm, 1969; Dasgupta et al., 1973).[11] In that case too, maximum welfare under a fixed total income constraint is achieved with perfect equality. For a given total income, inequality can then be measured as some transformation of the gap between the level of social welfare corresponding to the observed distribution and this maximum.

---

[11] s-Concavity is weaker than quasi-concavity, as may readily be seen in the two person case: quasi-concavity requires that the social indifference curves be convex to the origin, whereas s-concavity requires only that a move towards the 45° line raise social welfare.

Social welfare itself may be expressed as a function of total or mean income and that inequality index.[12]

Given this one to one correspondence between social welfare functions and inequality measures, it is natural to expect that the same kind of dominance properties apply to social welfare functions as we considered in the case of inequality measures in the previous section. A distribution of income is said to dominate another if and only if social welfare is greater for the former for all possible social welfare functions in some given class. The main class of social welfare functions considered is that of nondecreasing, s-concave functions described in the previous paragraph (referred to as the class W_2). A central result of the literature is that, for constant total income and population, dominance of distribution A over distribution B for the class W_2 is equivalent to dominance of the Lorenz curve for A over that for B, the descriptive test described in Section 4. Moreover, this is equivalent to it being possible to reach distribution A from distribution B by making a series of mean preserving equalising transfers. (Where the means are different, the generalised Lorenz criterion applies: dominance of distribution A over distribution B for the class W_2 is equivalent to dominance of the generalised Lorenz curve for A over that for B.) We have therefore completed the triangle:

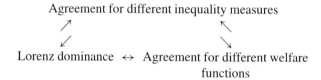

Agreement for different inequality measures

Lorenz dominance $\leftrightarrow$ Agreement for different welfare functions

Alternative normative measures of inequality rely on different classes of social welfare functions, such as those that, either explicitly or implicitly, allow the valuation of individual incomes to depend not only on the income of that individual but also on the income of others. For instance, the Gini coefficient may be interpreted as a transformation of an index of "envy" evaluated through the comparison of the income of an individual and that of all other individuals richer than him/her.[13] More formally, some authors have considered the case where the utility depends on both income and the rank on an individual in the distribution. A more general formulation leads to the introduction of the whole distribution as an argument of individual utility, as in Kolm (1969) and Thurow (1971).

---

[12] Dalton (1920b) used the gap between total utility and egalitarian utility. As explained earlier, Atkinson (1970) defines inequality, I_ϵ, as 1 minus the ratio to mean income of the equally distributed income giving the same social welfare as the actual distribution. In this framework, an income measure of social welfare is directly given by $\mu(1 - I_\epsilon)$. Sen (1976b) proposed the same combination of the Gini index and the mean income as a measure of social welfare. A general treatment of this point was provided by Blackorby and Donaldson (1978).

[13] A related concept is that of "relative deprivation", see Runciman (1966). See also the axiomatic justification of the Gini coefficient by Sen (1976b) which relies on this kind of externality between individuals.

5.2. Extending the concept of income to economic well-being and coping with heterogeneity

The issue of measuring income inequality and social welfare among otherwise identical individuals now seems satisfactorily understood. Widely accepted analytical tools, firmly linked to theories of justice, have been available for some time to make comparisons between distributions, even though they are still too rarely used. The situation is much less favourable when one wants to extend the definition of well being so as to take into account other dimensions of welfare than income or the natural heterogeneity among individuals.

In a perfectly competitive environment, and with identical individual preferences, there should be no difference between inequalities in income and inequalities in material well-being. If individuals have the same preferences among the goods and services they consume and if there is no restriction on buying and selling goods at posted prices, material well-being is a function of income and prices (the indirect utility function). If everybody faces the same prices, then differences in material well-being arise only from differences in income as was supposed in the preceding section. If prices differ across consumers, a correction of individual incomes becomes necessary to allow them to continue to express differences in well-being. As long as there is an unambiguous way to combine income and prices so as to express all differences across individuals in the single dimension of "real" income, it is possible to use the income inequality framework discussed before (although the concept of a fixed total income does not really make sense in that situation since changing the distribution of prices in the population changes total real income).

It would seem that the preceding argument might generalize to other situations where individuals do not face the same "market" conditions, as for instance with the rationing of some goods or the presence of public goods. Unfortunately, things are not that simple. Under the assumption of common preferences, it is in theory possible to define an indirect utility function of income, prices, rations and public goods available which represents well-being and makes individuals mutually comparable. The only issue is that of the form that this indirect utility function should take. Observed market behaviour may permit us in some cases to estimate an (ordinal) indirect utility function of income, prices and rations, and to agree on a particular cardinal representation. But this is much more debatable for nonmarket goods like most public goods. The original problem then becomes much more complicated.

Heterogeneity across individuals could be taken as a limit of the preceding case. Kolm (1972) noted that, conceptually, the assumption of identical preferences is not restrictive provided that preferences could be defined on a sufficiently rich vector of observed personal characteristics including taste for pleasure, handicaps, talents and the like. Since there is no market for variation in these characteristics, however, we cannot really envisage estimating an indirect utility function that would allow aggregation of these characteristics together with income and prices into some "super real income".

More assumptions are definitely needed; it is not clear, however, what these assumptions should be. The estimation of equivalence scales provides a case in point. Observed consumption behaviour allows us to recover an indirect utility function consistent with the conditional preferences over market consumption goods of households with different characteristics, but it gives no information whatsoever on cardinal utility. As in the case of otherwise identical households receiving different incomes, some normative assumption is necessary to compare the level of utility that is reached. In the present case, this assumption must also encompass the way different characteristics affect this cardinal utility. Normative judgments cannot be avoided. From that point of view, using an equivalence scale whereby a family of N persons needs $\sqrt{N}$ more than a single person is no more or less arbitrary than, say, counting a second adult for 0.7, and each child for 0.5 adult.

What can be done if different judgments about equivalence scales, or other adjustments for heterogeneity, lead to opposite conclusions when comparing two income distributions? A natural answer to this question seems to lie in a generalization of the social dominance criterion to other dimensions than income. Atkinson and Bourguignon (1987) provided such an extension in the case where an agreement may be obtained in ranking different households by increasing "needs"—this concept itself involves various dimensions like family size, age or health condition.[14] On the assumption that increasing needs are interpreted as meaning that the marginal social welfare of income, at the same income level, is higher and declines at a slower rate in more needy families, they showed that social dominance was equivalent to a sequential Lorenz dominance criterion whereby generalised Lorenz dominance should obtain for any subset of the original population that would comprise all the households with greater than a specified level of need. Suppose that this approach is applied to compare two distributions A and B with, say, three different groups, in increasing order of "need": single persons, couples and couples with children. We should first compare the generalised Lorenz curves for couples with children, then compare curves for couples and couples and children combined, and finally compare the curves for the whole population. Dominance requires that A be superior to B on all three tests (or vice versa). This is a strong requirement but it is weaker than requiring that dominance hold for each group separately.

The basic assumption leading to the criterion just described could be seen strictly as utilitarian, but it is important to stress that it is in fact consistent with the idea forcefully emphasised by Sen of the need for the distribution of income to *compensate* for differences in absolute levels of well-being across heterogeneous individuals (see the Weak Equity Axiom in Sen (1973, 1997)). Take for instance the simple case where the well-being of two individuals depends on their income plus a constant representing

---

[14] This extension derived from a previous attempt at comparing multidimensional distributions of various characteristics defining the well-being of an individual,see Atkinson and Bourguignon (1982). Other authors have pursued this direction of multidimensional inequality essentially by preimposing some aggregator function allowing the problem to be reduced to a single dimension. See in particular Maasoumi (1986) and Tsui (1995).

the effect of some noneconomic characteristics. If social welfare is then defined as a nondecreasing, s-concave function of individual levels of well-being, then assuming that the social marginal welfare associated with the income of the first person is always larger, at the same income level, than that with the second is equivalent to assuming that the noneconomic component of well-being is smaller, in some unknown amount, for the first person than for the second person. But of course, differences in marginal social welfare may also come from differences between the two persons in getting more well-being out of an increase in their income. The preceding dominance criterion thus includes both these aspects of inter-personal comparisons across persons with different characteristics.

Assuming that it is indeed possible to find some agreement on the ranking of persons according to needs, in the precise sense given to that concept above, a limitation of the sequential Lorenz dominance criterion is that it only allows for comparison of populations with the same distribution of needs. Indeed comparing distributions with distinct marginal distributions of needs requires making assumptions on the absolute level of well-being of households with different needs. Not being able to do so may not be too much of a problem if one is essentially interested in income redistribution issues within a given population. From an economic policy point of view, this is already of considerable interest. But comparing distributions where both the structure of income and that of personal characteristics or needs are different is sometimes necessary. Some generalisation of the sequential Lorenz dominance to cover such a situation has been proposed for some particular situations. Research in this domain is presently very active.[15]

5.3. *From the inequality of incomes to that of opportunities and social justice*

Recognizing that individuals or households differ by nonmarket characteristics and that this difference must be taken into account in comparing income distributions is conceptually clear when differences may be cast in terms of needs or innate abilities or handicaps: i.e., uncontrollable factors. Other sources of difference are less clear. Suppose that there are two low wage earners of whom one is handicapped and the other lazy. Compensating the former for his/her bad luck seems natural, but, for the majority of people, doing the same for the latter would seem to go against basic principles of justice. In other words, differences in innate abilities, needs or handicaps would seem to require some kind of income compensation, but not differences in effort, resulting from differences in tastes or preferences (see, for a discussion in terms of equality of opportunity, Roemer (1998)).

The distinction between heterogeneity in preferences and in innate abilities/handicaps is fundamental. Many authors in the literature on economic justice deem the former to be "irrelevant" and suggest that measures of economic inequality should be exclusively

---

[15] On the generalization of the sequential Lorenz dominance criterion to the case of different marginal distributions of needs, see Jenkins and Lambert (1993). On the general issue of comparing distributions when needs differ see Ebert (1995, 1997).

concerned with the latter. Loosely speaking, the basic idea is that preferences are under the full individual responsibility of individuals who should be given full liberty to exert them. Differences in economic outcomes attributable to differences in preferences must thus be considered essentially as the expression of individual liberty and diversity in a society rather than as a sign of inequality. An obvious example is that of a society where individuals would differ only by their preferences over leisure and consumption. In such a society income disparities should not be considered as economic inequalities. Suppose that, in an oil-rich country, oil revenues are divided equally, allowing some people not to work, while others choose to do so. We will then observe an unequal distribution of money income, but no equity significance need be attached. If all individuals have the possibility of earning the same income by working the same number of hours, this should be the only thing that matters. Individuals may decide to work more or to work less because they find more satisfaction in doing so, but this has nothing to do with social "equity".

"Equity" or "fairness", and "envy-freeness" in more recent literature, is the economic concept corresponding to the preceding ideas. The first statement was made by Tinbergen,[16] and developed in different forms by Foley (1967), Kolm (1972), Varian (1974) and others. It has now given rise to an abundant literature (see, among recent contributions, Baumol (1986), Arnsperger (1994), Young (1994) and Kolm (1996a and 1996b)). An allocation of goods is defined as *equitable* if there exists a common choice set such that every individual in that economy would have freely chosen in that set the bundle of goods actually allocated to him or her. The interest of this general nontechnical definition is to emphasise the direct relationship of equity with the concepts of liberty and equality (Kolm, 1972): all participants are *free* to choose their preferred bundle in a choice set which is *equal* for all. More technically, an equitable allocation of goods is "fair" if it is Pareto efficient. It is easily seen that the egalitarian allocation of existing supplies of goods is a fair allocation, as are all the allocations derived from it through competitive exchange. So, the notion of equity or fairness allows the introduction of the egalitarian allocation as a benchmark to evaluate other allocations without making use of cardinal utility functions defined on identical individuals as in the utilitarian or welfarist tradition. Even in a world of heterogeneous preferences and without invoking any interpersonal comparison rule, the egalitarian distribution of resources stands out.

The shift to considering commodity bundles as the primitive concepts with which we are concerned is an example of a move outside the welfarist approach based on personal utilities, but looked at in this way there is perhaps little difference from a social welfare function defined over individual incomes (not utilities), as previously discussed. More far-reaching is the move to considering the whole choice sets open to a person, and not just the actual outcome. One interpretation of the "capability" approach advocated by Sen (see below) is that we are concerned with the full set of options actually open to

---

[16] The "exchange principle" of Tinbergen is described in Pen (1971: pp. 303–305), who says that Tinbergen was influenced by his teacher, the physicist Paul Ehrenfest. See also Kolm (1996b: p. 202).

an individual to "function" in a given economic and social environment and not simply with the vector describing the functioning of the individual, however detailed might be that description. Other authors refer to the set of opportunities or resources offered to individuals to achieve their ends and to the *equality of opportunities or resources* (see Dworkin (1981a and 1981b), Arneson (1989)). Consider for example the leisure-consumption problem where some individuals in the population are unable to sell as much of their time as they wish because of rationing on the labour-market. In the standard indirect utility approach, no distinction would be made between the "unemployed" time of rationed individuals and voluntary consumption of leisure. Within an equity approach, on the contrary, the fact that individuals do not face the same choice set would be explicitly taken into account in evaluating that situation.

Accepting differences in preferences as irrelevant and considering differences in the choice sets on which these preferences must be applied as the true object of inequality measurement does not make measurement easier. In the simple case where innate productive abilities or handicaps determine the space where individuals must choose a particular consumption-leisure combination, standard income inequality measures provide a way of evaluating the inequality of opportunities offered to individuals. But what should be done if innate consumption abilities or handicaps make these consumption-leisure spaces noncomparable? Equivalently, how should noneconomic dimensions of choice sets be taken into account in economic analysis? Other things being equal, a disabled person cannot move as easily as another person and thus has a restricted set of opportunities. How much additional income capacity is necessary to compensate for being disabled, living in a polluted environment, or being responsible for a large family? There clearly cannot be a single and undisputed answer to such questions.

We are thus back to the problem we started from. Heterogeneity in preferences among individuals can be accommodated as long as they bear on goods and services which are freely exchanged. Heterogeneity in the capacity of individuals to generate income may then be considered as the unique source of inequality. But heterogeneity in the consumption ability of individuals or, equivalently, heterogeneity of preferences over goods or characteristics which are outside their control, reintroduces the initial ambiguity of income comparison. It is necessary to adopt a multidimensional framework where multiple trade-offs describing the frontier of the space of individual capabilities would have to be defined. For the moment, we lack the elements necessary to make these trade-offs explicit on a more or less consensual basis. This is probably the area in the measurement of inequality where progress is most needed.

The need to enrich the informational basis for welfare judgments is emphasised by Sen in Chapter 1 (see also Sen, 1992), which draws on his extensive contribution to the development of a nonwelfarist approach. In rejecting welfarism, Sen is not alone. The difference principle of Rawls (1971) is concerned with the position of the least advantaged defined not by personal welfare, but by "primary goods", or "things that every rational man is presumed to want". This takes us outside the traditional scope of welfare economics. The rejection of the welfarist approach is similarly to be found in

Marxist theories of exploitation, relating social judgements to the historical information that capital represents the product of past labour. Nozick's entitlement theory of justice (1974) is quite different but equally appeals to historical information. For him, it is not the distribution of income that matters but the *process* by which it is brought about, people being "entitled" to resources that were justly acquired or that were transferred to them according to a just process, even if this means they will be immensely rich, and that their riches may be of no benefit to the poor.

It is in his alternative to welfarism that Sen is distinctive. This is based on "capabilities", to which reference has already been made. He has made a forceful case that assessment of the standard of living should focus on

neither commodities, nor characteristics (in the sense of Gorman and Lancaster), nor utility, but something that may be called a person's capability. (Sen 1983, p. 160)

Capability refers to the freedom that a person has in terms of choice of functionings. Sen illustrates this by the example of a bicycle:

It is, of course, a commodity. It has several characteristics, and let us concentrate on one particular characteristic, viz., transportation. Having a bike gives a person the ability to move about in a certain way that he may not be able to do without the bike. So the transportation *characteristic* of the bike gives the person the *capability* of moving in a certain way. (Sen 1983, p. 160)

He recognises that the capability may generate utility, but argues that it is the capability to function that comes closest to the notion of standard of living. The challenge which this raises is to translate this concept into one which can be implemented in empirical analysis of distributional issues. There is scope for a great deal of future research.

We conclude this brief review of normative theories by some consideration of the issues of uncertainty and dynamics. Ever since Vickrey (1945), Harsanyi (1953 and 1955) and Rawls (1971), the theory of social justice has been intimately mixed with the theory of choice under uncertainty. Utilitarian social welfare is equivalent to expected income utility when the density associated with each income level is equal to the density of the population at that income level, and this can be seen as the criterion applied when a person has no knowledge of his/her position in society, other than the overall distribution. It follows that social welfare dominance is equivalent to stochastic dominance in the theory of choice under uncertainty. It also follows that it is possible to define social aversion toward inequality in line with the equivalent definition of individual aversion toward risk. A maxi-min principle of justice theory, maximising the welfare of the worst off in society, may be interpreted as infinite aversion towards risk, and therefore towards inequality.

Referring to uncertainty to justify theoretical principles for the comparison of distributions of certain incomes is one matter; comparing distributions of uncertain incomes is another, where we do not know much. Yet, this may be necessary. Measuring the inequality of "chances" among children born from different ethnic groups or in different social classes requires taking into account not only the inequality of their expected income but also that of the risk that they end up more or less far from the mean. A related domain is the measurement of income mobility over time or across generations. The existing theory of inequality measurement is static. However, the situation in which individuals are observed at a given point of time is most often temporary. Averaging over several periods may not be satisfactory, for reasons outlined in Section 4. It may be the case that situations of extreme poverty entail irreversible health or psychological costs which could not be compensated by better incomes at a later stage. Evidence of strong intergenerational associations of economic status mean that we have to address the normative issues surrounding inheritance. We cannot simply assume that all such equity issues were resolved at some primeval date. If one believes that preferences are transmitted by parents to their children, or the product of the social class to which one belongs, then they cannot be considered as irrelevant any more (on this see Arneson (1989) or Roemer (1985)). The social origin of individuals might have to be taken into account when comparing their present situation, thus leading to an intergenerational concept of inequality.

5.4. *Conclusion*

To conclude, the normative theory of income distribution and, more generally, of economic inequality, has been a very active domain of economic research over the last 30 years. Impressive progress has been made in the understanding of the issues at stake, and in some instances in developing the appropriate quantitative instruments. The difficulties which have been pointed out in the last sections of this Introduction are, however, equally impressive. They are true challenges to the economics profession.

6. Guide to the Handbook chapters

The first chapter, by Amartya Sen, covers in depth the issues which we have just been considering: the relation between ideas of social justice and the analysis of income distribution. One of the main conclusions is that we need to "liberate" the analysis of economic inequality from confinement to the space of incomes or commodity bundles. Income is only relevant, Sen argues, as an instrument to ends and the freedom to achieve ends. It is indeed true that much conventional analysis of inequality closes its eyes to the difficulties which Sen outlines so clearly. We therefore urge readers to study carefully his strictures on applied welfare economics. At the same time, we hope that this will not cause them to stop reading the rest of the volume. Sen himself has emphasized

the danger of falling prey to a kind of nihilism (which) takes the form of noting, quite legitimately, a difficulty of some sort, and then constructing from it a picture of total disaster. (Sen 1973: p. 78)

We need to be aware of the limitations of current measures, and to seek to refine them, not to throw in the towel.

In Chapter 2, Frank Cowell starts from the premise that we have a satisfactory measure of each individual's status and sets out the basis for comparing different distributions and measuring inequality. The chapter, whose content we have previewed in this Introduction, will be useful to those who wish to understand the formal relation to underlying axioms and welfare judgments; it will be useful to those who wish to apply the measures in practice. As we have noted, a number of the innovations have taken time to be adopted by practitioners, and this chapter should speed their diffusion.

The tendency for income distribution to go in and out of fashion means that a sense of history is especially important. Chapters 3 and 4 provide a historical perspective. In Chapter 3, Peter Lindert covers no less than three centuries, courageously starting with the 1688 estimates for England and Wales. From this rich account of inequality changes in Britain and the United States, he concludes that "the Kuznets curve flickers" and identifies the intriguing paradox that "Robin Hood's redistributive army is missing when and where it is most needed". In Chapter 4, Christian Morrisson presents evidence for mainland Europe, with particular reference to the explanation of developments over time within and between sectors. Going back as far as the early 1880s, he finds that the inverse U-curve hypothesis is verified in Finland, France, Germany and Sweden. He explains these changes by political factors as well as by economic ones (diffusion of education, accumulation of capital and dualistic development). The exploitation of historical evidence, especially through further use of fiscal data, is a potentially fruitful area for future research.

These OECD countries are among the twenty five studied in Chapter 5 by Peter Gottschalk and Tim Smeeding, who present evidence on the current level of inequality and on the changes since 1970. (The chapter illustrates the application of a number of the tools described in Chapter 2.) Such a comparability exercise is now possible as a result of the improvements in data availability noted earlier, notably the Luxembourg Income Study. The data indicate that the degree of income inequality varies considerably across countries, and that the changes over time are more similar, though not universally so. There is a lot to explain.

Chapter 6 by Sheldon Danziger and Markus Jäntti looks in detail at the bottom of the income distribution in advanced countries, drawing on the same kind of internationally comparable data source. Conceptual issues in the measurement of poverty, to which we have already alluded, are set out in greater depth, as are the practical problems in implementation which are faced by official and independent investigators. Among the interesting elements are the dynamics of poverty over time, the identification of poverty risks and the impact of public policy on poverty.

In Chapter 7, the volume turns to the theory of income distribution, starting with the distribution of earnings. Derek Neal and Sherwin Rosen provide a succinct account of different types of models which seek to explain the observed features of the earnings distribution. These models, which we have previewed in Sections 2 and 3, include stochastic theories, selection models, sorting models, human capital formation and agency models. Given the balkanisation of much of the journal literature, it is particularly valuable to have these approaches set side by side, helping the reader identify their relative strengths and weaknesses.

Earnings are brought together with wealth in Chapter 8 by Thomas Piketty, which deals with intergenerational mobility and the persistence of advantage or disadvantage from generation to generation. As he brings out clearly in the opening section, there are sharply conflicting claims about both theory and evidence regarding mobility in industrial societies. The chapter first considers models based on Pareto-efficient markets, and then goes on to theories based on market inefficiencies, this being—as we have signalled—one of the most important recent developments. The chapter is wide-ranging in that it not only covers both theory and evidence, but also covers sociological as well as economic research. Openness to other social science disciplines is a feature which we very much welcome in the current literature on distribution.

Chapter 9 relates the theory of distribution to other recent areas of economic research: growth theory and political economy. Giuseppe Bertola begins by noting that the macroeconomics of distribution is almost an oxymoron, but his chapter is highly successful in bringing together the two fields of macroeconomics and income distribution. The first part is concerned with the interaction of income and wealth distribution with aggregate accumulation and growth, which we have introduced earlier. The second part is concerned with the imperfections and/or incompleteness of capital markets, covering from a macroeconomic perspective elements which also appear in Chapter 8. The third part explores the political economy of taxation and redistribution; and the final section reviews empirical evidence about growth and inequality.

The role of distribution in a world where market outcomes are not Pareto efficient has already been evoked in Chapter 8. This subject is developed further by Pranab Bardhan, Samuel Bowles and Herbert Gintis in Chapter 10, where they examine the relation between redistribution of assets and productivity enhancement. They cover a variety of contexts including credit markets, farm tenancies, incentives in teams and local public goods. They show that where there is asymmetric, or nonverifiable, information, then an inequality-reducing redistribution of assets may be productivity-enhancing (in the sense defined). (See also Putterman et al., 1998). Again the chapter is welcome evidence of the willingness of economists to take on board the contributions of other disciplines, political scientists, sociologists and psychologists all being cited, but its implications are of central importance for economics.

Assets feature in all of the preceding theoretical chapters, but the distribution of personal wealth is the specific concern of Chapter 11 by Jim Davies and Tony Shorrocks. They summarise the evidence about the distribution for a number of countries, concluding that material wealth is more unequally distributed than labour income and that, while there has ben a general downward trend in inequality, there have been interruptions and reversals. They review a range of theories that can explain observed wealth-holding, covering both intra-generational accumulation and inter-generational transmission. As they point out, there are a number of areas where future research promises to be fruitful, including the intriguing suggestion that economists should make more use of the information on the wealth of named persons published by *Fortune* and other sources.

In Chapter 12, entitled "Redistribution", Robin Boadway and Michael Keen start from the motives for redistribution. The first of these—the pursuit of social justice—harks back to the issues considered in Chapter 1. In treating the second—achieving mutually advantageous efficiency gains—the authors develop a theme central to Chapter 10, with interesting applications to social insurance and other fiscal instruments. The third—the politics of redistribution—puts public choice considerations in centre stage, linking up with Chapter 9. As they point out, the distinctions between different motives become quickly blurred, but they provide a valuable organising framework.

The relationship between income distribution and economic development is clearly too important for the subject not to be covered even if we risk overlapping the territory of other Handbooks. In Chapter 13, Ravi Kanbur examines the distribution across countries and the distribution within developing countries. There are clear links with other chapters—with the long-run analyses in Chapters 3 and 4, with the measurement of poverty in Chapter 6, with growth theory in Chapter 9—but it is very valuable to view the material from a different perspective. Once again, our survey brings out the many challenges which remain.

Finally, in Chapter 14, John Flemming and John Micklewright survey the relation between economic systems and income distribution, with particular reference to the impact of transition from communism.[17] They first re-assess the starting point in socialist economies, drawing on material which was not available prior to 1990, emphasising the variety of experience. They then consider the distributional implications of transition and the role of policy intervention, followed by a review of the empirical evidence about earnings and incomes, underlining the problems of measurement and of interpretation. Earnings inequality appears to have increased during the 1990s, but the scale of the rise varied across countries, and the impact on household income was more modest (except in Russia). Transition may by definition be an impermant field of economics, but it highlights in an acute way some of the key questions of distribution and brings the reader back to a number of the fundamental issues raised in Chapter 1.

References

Aaron, H.J. (1978), Politics and the Professors (Brookings Institution, Washington, DC).

Adelman, I. and S. Robinson (1989), Income distribution and development, in H. Chenery and T.N. Srinivasan, eds., Handbook of Development Economics, Vol. 2 (North-Holland, Amsterdam), pp. 949–1003.

Aghion, P. and P. Bolton (1997), A theory of trickle-down growth and development, Review of Economic Studies 64: 151–172.

Akerlof, G.A. and J. Yellen, eds. (1986), Efficiency Wage Models of the Labour Market (Cambridge University Press, Cambridge).

Aitchison, J. and J.A.C. Brown (1957), The Lognormal Distribution (Cambridge University Press, Cambridge).

Amsden, A.H., ed. (1980), The Economics of Women and Work (Penguin Books, London).

---

[17] A special case of particular interest is the reunification of East and West Germany. See Hauser et al. (1994) and Hauser and Becker (1997) for analysis of the changes in income inequality.

Arneson, R. (1989), Equality and equal opportunity for welfare, Philosophical Studies 56: 77–93.

Arnsperger, C. (1994), Envy-freeness and distributive justice, Journal of Economic Surveys 8: 155–186.

Arrow, K.J. (1972), Models of job discrimination, and some mathematical models of race in the labor market, in A. Pascal, ed., Racial Discrimination in Economic Life (Lexington Books, Lexington), pp. 83–102 and pp. 187–203.

Atkinson, A.B. (1970), On the measurement of inequality, Journal of Economic Theory 2: 244–263.

Atkinson, A.B. (1980), Inheritance and the redistribution of wealth, in G.M. Heal and G.A. Hughes, eds., Public Policy and the Tax System (Allen and Unwin, London), pp. 36–66.

Atkinson, A.B. (1983), The Economics of Inequality, 2nd ed.(Oxford University Press, Oxford).

Atkinson, A.B. (1987), On the measurement of poverty, Econometrica 55: 749–764.

Atkinson, A.B. (1997), Bringing income distribution in from the cold, Economic Journal 107: 297–321.

Atkinson, A.B. (1998), Poverty in Europe (Basil Blackwell, Oxford).

Atkinson, A.B. and F. Bourguignon (1982), The comparison of multidimensioned distributions of economic status, Review of Economic Studies 49: 183–201.

Atkinson, A.B. and F. Bourguignon (1987), Income distribution and differences in needs, in G. Feiwel, ed., Arrow and the Foundations of the Theory of Economic Policy (Macmillan, London).

Atkinson, A.B., F. Bourguignon and C. Morrisson (1992), Empirical studies of earnings mobility, Fundamentals of Pure and Applied Economics, Vol. 52 (Harwood Academic, Chur).

Atkinson, A.B. and J. Micklewright (1992), Economic Transformation in Eastern Europe and the Distribution of Income (Cambridge University Press, Cambridge).

Atkinson, A.B., L. Rainwater and T.M. Smeeding (1995), Income Distribution in OECD Countries (OECD, Paris).

Atkinson, A.B. and J.E. Stiglitz (1980), Lectures on public economics (McGraw-Hill, New York).

Baumol, W.J. (1986), Superfairness (MIT Press, Cambridge).

Becker, G.S. (1957), The Economics of Discrimination (University of Chicago Press, Chicago).

Becker, G.S. (1967), Human capital and the personal distribution of income, W.S. Woytinsky Lecture No. 1 (University of Michigan, Ann Arbor).

Becker, G.S. and K. Murphy (1988), The family and the state, Journal of Law and Economics 31: 1–18.

Becker, G.S. and N. Tomes (1979), An equilibrium theory of the distribution of income and intergenerational mobility, Journal of Political Economy 87: 1153–1189.

Becker, G.S. and N. Tomes (1986), Human capital and the rise and fall of families, Journal of Labor Economics 4: S1–S39.

Bertola, G. (1993), Factor shares and savings in endogenous growth, American Economic Review 83: 1184–1198.

Blackorby, C. and D. Donaldson (1978), Measures of relative equality and their meaning in terms of social welfare, Journal of Economic Theory 18: 59–80.

Blinder, A.S. (1973), A model of inherited wealth, Quarterly Journal of Economics 87: 608–626.

Blinder, A.S. (1974), Toward an Economic Theory of Income Distribution (MIT Press, Cambridge).

Blundell, R. and A. Lewbel (1991), The Information Content of Equivalence Scales, Journal of Econometrics 50: 49–68.

Bourguignon, F. (1979), Decomposable Income Inequality Measures, Econometrica 47: 901–920.

Bourguignon, F. (1981), Pareto Superiority of Unegalitarian Equilibria in Stiglitz' Model of Wealth Distribution with Convex Saving Function, Econometrica 49: 1469–1475.

Bourguignon, F. and C. Morrisson (1990), Income distribution, development and foreign trade: a cross-sectional analysis, European Economic Review 34: 1113–1132.

Bourguignon, F., M. Fournier and M. Gurgand (1998), Distribution, development and education: Taiwan, 1979–1994, mimeo.

Brandolini, A. (1998), Pareto's Law and Kuznets' Curve: A Bird's-eye View of Long-run Changes in Income Inequality, Bank of Italy.

Bronfenbrenner, M. (1971), Income Distribution Theory (Macmillan, London).

Brown, C., G. Duncan and F. Stafford (1996), Data Watch: the Panel Study of Income Dynamics, Journal of Economic Perspectives 10(2): 155–168.

Burkhauser, R.V. and G. Wagner (1991), The socio-economic panel after ten years, in R.V. Burkhauser and G. Wagner, eds., Proceedings of the 1993 International Conference of German Socio-Economic Panel Study Users, Vierteljahrsheft zur Wirtschaftsforschung, 1/2: 7–9.

Burtless, G. (1995), International trade and the rise in earnings inequality, Journal of Economic Literature 33: 800–816.

Champernowne, D.G. (1953), A model of income distribution, Economic Journal 63: 318–351.

Cowell, F.A. (1995), Measuring Inequality, 2nd ed. (Harvester Wheatsheaf, Hemel Hempstead).

Cox, D. and E. Jimenez (1986), Social security and private transfers in developing countries: the case of Peru, World Bank Economic Review 6(1): 155–169.

Creedy, J. (1977), Pareto and the distribution of income, Review of Income and Wealth 23: 405–411.

Cutler, D. and L. Katz (1992), Rising inequality? Changes in the distribution of income and consumption in the 1980's, American Economic Review 82: 546–551.

Dalton, H. (1920a), The Inequality of Incomes (Routledge and Kegan Paul, London).

Dalton, H. (1920b), Measurement of the inequality of incomes, Economic Journal 30: 348–361.

Dasgupta, P., A. Sen and D. Starrett (1973), Notes on the measurement of inequality, Journal of Economic Theory 6: 180–187.

Deaton, A. (1992), Understanding Consumption (Clarendon Press, Oxford).

Deaton, A. and J. Muellbauer (1980), Economics and Consumer Behavior (Cambridge University Press, Cambridge).

Deaton, A. and C. Paxson (1994), Intertemporal choice and inequality, Journal of Political Economy 102: 437–467.

Deininger, K. and L. Squire (1996), A new data set measuring income inequality, World Bank Economic Review 10: 565–591.

Dworkin, R. (1981a), What is equality? Part 1: Equality of welfare, Philosophy and Public Affairs 10: 185–246.

Dworkin, R. (1981b), What is equality? Part 2: Equality of resources, Philosophy and Public Affairs 10: 283–345.

Ebert, U. (1995), Income inequality and differences in household size, Mathematical Social Science 30: 37–55.

Ebert, U. (1997), Social welfare when needs differ: an axiomatic approach, Economica 64: 233–244.

Fisher, F.M. (1987), Household equivalence scales and interpersonal comparisons, Review of Economic Studies 54: 519–524.

Flemming, J.S. (1979), The effects of earnings inequality, imperfect capital markets and dynastic altruism on the distribution of wealth in life cycle models, Economica 46: 363–380.

Folbre, N., B. Bergmann and B. Agarwal, eds. (1992), Women's Work in the World Economy (Macmillan, London).

Foley, D. (1967), Resource allocation in the public sector, Yale Economic Essays 7: 45–98.

Foster, J. and A. Shorrocks (1988a), Poverty orderings, Econometrica 56: 173–177.

Foster, J. and A. Shorrocks (1988b), Inequality and poverty orderings, European Economic Review 32: 654–661.

Friedman, M. (1957), A Theory of the Consumption Function (Princeton University Press, Princeton).

Fuchs, V. (1988), Women's Quest for Economic Equality (Harvard University Press, Cambridge).

Galor, O. and J. Zeira (1993), Income distribution and macroeconomics, Review of Economic Studies 60: 35–52.

Galton, F. (1879), The geometric mean in vital and social statistics, Proceedings of the Royal Society 29: 365–366.

Gibbons, R. and L. Katz (1992), Does unmeasured ability explain inter-industry wage differentials?, Review of Economic Studies 59: 515–535.

Gibrat, R. (1931), Les inégalités économiques (Sirey, Paris).

Goodman, A., P. Johnson and S. Webb (1995), The distribution of UK household expenditure, 1979–1992, Fiscal Studies 16: 55–80.

Gottschalk, P., B. Gustafsson and E. Palmer, eds. (1997), Changing Patterns in the Distribution of Economic Welfare (Cambridge University Press, Cambridge).

Green, J. and N. Stokey (1983), A comparison of tournaments and contracts, Journal of Political Economy 91: 349–364.

Gunderson, M. (1989), Male-female wage differentials and policy responses, Journal of Economic Literature 27: 46–72.

Harberger, A.C. (1962), The incidence of the corporation income tax, Journal of Political Economy 70: 215–240.

Harsanyi, J.C. (1953), Cardinal utility in welfare economics and in the theory of risk-taking, Journal of Political Economy 61: 434–435.

Harsanyi, J.C. (1955), Cardinal welfare, individualistic ethics and interpersonal comparisons of utility, Journal of Political Economy 63: 309–321.

Hauser, R. and I. Becker (1997), The development of income distribution in the Federal Republic of Germany during the 1970s and 1980s, in P. Gottschalk, B. Gustafsson and E. Palmer, eds., Changing Patterns in the Distribution of Economic Welfare (Cambridge University Press, Cambridge), 184–219.

Hauser, R., J. Frick, K. Mueller and G.G. Wagner (1994), Inequality in income: a comparison of East and West Germans before reunification and during transition, Journal of European Social Policy 4: 277–295.

Heckman, J.J. and B.E. Honoré (1990), The empirical content of the Roy model, Econometrica 58: 1121–1149.

Heckman, J.J. and G. Sedlacek (1985), Heterogeneity, aggregation, and market wage functions: an empirical model of self-selection in the labor market, Journal of Political Economy 93: 1077–1125.

Hills, J. (1998), Does income mobility mean that we do not need to worry about poverty?, in A.B. Atkinson and J. Hills, eds., Exclusion, Employment and Opportunity (Centre for Analysis of Social Exclusion, LSE).

INSEE (1997), Revenus et Patrimoines des Ménages, Synthèses No. 11 (Documentation Française, Paris).

Jenkins, S.P. (1991), Poverty measurement and the within-household distribution: agenda for action, Journal of Social Policy 20: 457–483.

Jenkins, S. and P. Lambert (1993), Ranking income distributions when needs differ, Review of Income and Wealth 39: 337–356.

Johnson, D. and S. Shipp (1997), Trends in inequality using consumption-expenditures: The US from 1960 to 1993, Review of Income and Wealth 43: 133–152.

Johnson, H.G. (1973), The Theory of Income Distribution (Gray-Mills, London).

Jorgenson, D.W. (1997), Welfare, Vol. 2, Measuring Social Welfare (MIT Press, Cambridge).

Jorgenson, D.W. and D. Slesnick (1984), Aggregate consumer behaviour and the measurement of inequality, Review of Economic Studies 51: 369–392.

Jovanovic, B. (1979), Firm-specific capital and turnover, Journal of Political Economy 87: 1246–1260.

Kalecki, M. (1938), The determinants of distribution of the national income, Econometrica 6: 97–112.

Kalecki, M. (1945), On the Gibrat distribution, Econometrica 13: 161–170.

Karoly, L. and G. Burtless (1995), Demographic change, rising earnings inequality, and the distribution of personal well-being, 1959–1989, Demography 32: 379–405.

Katz, L. and K. Murphy (1992), Changes in relative wages, 1963–1987: Supply and demand factors, Quarterly Journal of Economics 107: 35–78.

Kessler, D. and A. Masson (1989), Bequest and wealth accumulation: are some pieces of the puzzle missing?, Journal of Economic Perspectives 3(3): 141–152.

Kolm, S.-C. (1969), The optimal production of social justice, in J. Margolis and H. Guitton, eds., Public Economics (Macmillan, London), pp. 145–200.

Kolm, S.-C. (1972), Justice et Equité (Editions du CNRS, Paris).

Kolm, S.-C. (1996a), Modern Theories of Justice (MIT Press, Cambridge).

Kolm, S.-C. (1996b), Playing fair with fairness, Journal of Economic Surveys 10: 199–215.

Lambert, P. (1989), The Distribution and Redistribution of Income (Basil Blackwell, Oxford).

Layard, J. and A. Zabalza (1978), Family income distribution: explanation and policy evaluation, Journal of Political Economy 87: S133–S161.

Lazear, E.P. and S. Rosen (1981), Rank-order tournaments as optimum labor contracts, Journal of Political Economy 89: 841–864.

Levy, F. and R.J. Murnane (1992), U.S. earnings levels and earnings inequality: a review of recent trends and proposed explanations, Journal of Economic Literature 30: 1333–1381.

Lindbeck, A. and D. Snower (1988), The Insider-outsider Theory of Employment and Unemployment (MIT Press, Cambridge).

Lydall, H.F. (1968), The Structure of Earnings (Clarendon Press, Oxford).

Lydall, H.F. (1979), A Theory of Income Distribution (Clarendon Press, Oxford).

Maasoumi, E. (1986), The measurement and decomposition of multi-dimensional inequality, Econometrica 54: 991–997.

Macho-Stadler, I. and D. Pérez-Castrillo (1997), An Introduction to the Economics of Information (Oxford University Press, Oxford).

Marshall, R. (1974), The economics of racial discrimination: a survey, *Journal of Economic Literature* 12: 849–871.

Meade, J.E. (1964), Efficiency, Equality and the Ownership of Property (Allen and Unwin, London).

Meade, J.E. (1976), The Just Economy (Allen and Unwin, London).

Mincer, J. (1958), Investment in human capital and personal income distribution, Journal of Political Economy 66: 281–302.

Mincer, J. (1970), The distribution of labor incomes: a survey, Journal of Economic Literature 8: 1–26.

Morrisson, C. (1984), Income distribution in east European and western countries, Journal of Comparative Economics 8: 121–138.

Morrisson, C. (1996), La répartition des revenus (Presses Universitaires de France, Paris).

Musgrave, R.A. (1959), The Theory of Public Finance (McGraw-Hill, New York).

Nalebuff, B. and J.E. Stiglitz (1983), Prizes and incentives: towards a general theory of compensation and competition, Bell Journal of Economics 14: 21–43.

Nozick, R. (1974), Anarchy, State and Utopia (Basil Blackwell, Oxford).

Osberg, L. (1984), Economic Inequality in the United States (ME Sharpe, Armonk).

Pareto, V. (1897), Cours d'Economie Politique, tome 2 (Pichon, Paris).

Pen, J. (1971), Income Distribution (Allen Lane, London).

Phelps, E.S. (1972), The statistical theory of racism and sexism, American Economic Review 62: 659–661.

Pigou, A.C. (1912), Wealth and Welfare (Macmillan, London).

Piketty, T. (1997a), The dynamics of the wealth distribution and the interest rate with credit rationing, Review of Economic Studies 64: 173–189.

Piketty, T. (1997b), L'économie des inégalités (La Découverte, Paris).

Piketty, T. (1998), Self-fulfilling beliefs about social status, Journal of Public Economics 70: 115–132.

Polachek, S.W. and W.S. Siebert (1993), The Economics of Earnings (Cambridge University Press, Cambridge).

Pollak, R.A. and T.J.Wales (1979), Welfare comparisons and equivalence scales, American Economic Review 69: 216–221.

Putterman, L., J.E. Roemer and J. Silvestre (1998), Does Egalitarianism Have a Future?, Journal of Economic Literature 36: 861–902.

Rawls, J. (1971) A Theory of Justice (Harvard University Press, Cambridge).

Reich, M. (1981), Racial Inequality (Princeton University Press, Princeton).

Ricardo, D. (1911), Principles of Political Economy, first published 1817, 1911 edition (Dent, London).

Robinson, S. (1991), Macroeconomics, financial variables, and computable general equilibrium models, World Development 19: 1509–1525.

Roemer, J.E. (1985), Equality of talent, Economics and Philosophy 1: 151–187.

Roemer, J.E. (1996), Theories of Distributive Justice (Harvard University Press, Cambridge).

Roemer, J.E. (1998), Equality of Opportunity (Harvard University Press, Cambridge).

Roy, A.D. (1951), Some thoughts on the distribution of earnings, Oxford Economic Papers 3: 135–146.

Runciman, W.G. (1966), Relative Deprivation and Social Justice (Routledge, London).

Salanié, B. (1998), The Economics of Contracts (MIT Press, Cambridge).

Sattinger, M. (1993), Assignment models of the distribution of earnings, Journal of Economic Literature 31: 831–880.

Sen, A. (1973, 1997), On Economic Inequality, Expanded edition with a substantial annexe by James Foster and Amartya Sen (Clarendon Press, Oxford).

Sen, A. (1976a), Poverty: An ordinal approach to measurement, Econometrica 44: 219–231.

Sen, A. (1976b), Real national income, Review of Economic Studies 43: 19–39.

Sen, A.K. (1983), Poor, relatively speaking, Oxford Economic Papers 35: 153–169.

Sen, A. (1992), Inequality Reexamined (Harvard University Press, Cambridge).

Shorrocks, A. (1980), The class of additively decomposable inequality measures, Econometrica 48: 613–625.

Shorrocks, A. (1983), Ranking income distributions, Economica 50: 3–17.

Shoven, J.B. and J. Whalley (1984), Applied general-equilibrium models of taxation and international trade, Journal of Economic Literature 2: 1007–1051.

Silverman, B.W. (1986) Density Estimation for Statistics and Data Analysis (Chapman and Hall, London).

Smeeding, T., P. Saunders, J. Coder, S. Jenkins, J. Fritzell, A.J.M. Hagenaars, R. Hauser and M. Wolfson (1993), Poverty, inequality, and family living standards impacts across seven nations: the effects of noncash subsidies for health, education and housing, Review of Income and Wealth 39: 229–256.

Smith J. (1970), The Distribution of Family Earnings, Journal of Political Economy 87: 163-92.

Stiglitz, J.E. (1969), Distribution of income and wealth among individuals, Econometrica 37: 382–397.

Sutherland, H. (1997a), Women, men and the redistribution of income, Fiscal Studies 18: 1–22.

Sutherland, H. (1997b), The EUROMOD preparatory study: a summary report, Microsimulation Unit Working Paper 9705.

Theil, H. (1967), Economics and Information Theory (North Holland, Amsterdam).

Thurow, L. (1971), The income distribution as a pure public good, Quarterly Journal of Economics 85: 327–336.

Thurow, L. (1976), Generating Inequality (Macmillan, London).

Tinbergen, J, (1956), On the theory of income distribution, Weltwirtschaftliches Archiv 77: 155–175.

Tinbergen, J. (1975), Income Distribution (North Holland, Amsterdam).

Tsui, K-Y. (1995), Multidimensional generalisations of the relative and absolute inequality indices: The Atkinson–Kolm-Sen approach, Journal of Economic Theory 67: 251–265.

Varian, H. (1974), Equity, envy, and efficiency, Journal of Economic Theory 9: 63–91.

Vickrey, W.S. (1945), Measuring marginal utility by reactions to risk, Econometrica: 13: 215–236.

Wood, A. (1994), North-South Trade, Employment and Inequality (Clarendon Press, Oxford).

Young, H.P. (1994), Equity (Princeton University Press, Princeton).

Chapter 1

SOCIAL JUSTICE AND THE DISTRIBUTION OF INCOME

AMARTYA SEN

Trinity College, Cambridge, UK

Contents

Handbook of Income Distribution, Volume 1. Edited by A. B. Atkinson and F. Bourguignon

1. Motivation

This chapter deals with the bearing of theories of social justice on the analysis and evaluation of income distribution and related features of economic inequality. The assessment of income distribution involves both descriptive and prescriptive issues, and ideas of social justice influence both. The connection is immediate in the case of normative analysis, since concepts of social justice can be central to ethical norms for assessing the optimality or acceptability of distributions of income. But the connections with descriptive and predictive issues can be, ultimately, no less important.

People's attitudes towards, or reactions to, actual income distributions can be significantly influenced by the correspondence—or the lack thereof—between (1) their ideas of what is normatively tolerable, and (2) what they actually see in the society around them. Ideas of social justice can sway actual behaviour and actions. In assessing the likelihood of discontent or protest or disapproval, or the political feasibility of particular policies, which are primarily descriptive and predictive issues (rather than prescriptive ones), it can be useful—indeed crucial—to have some understanding of the ideas of justice that command respect in the society in question.

If notions of social justice belong to the ethical world of norms, actual *beliefs*—implicit or explicit—in notions of social justice are parts of the phenomenal world in which we live. Frequently, these beliefs may not have the analytical sophistication or the perceptive clarity that can be found in the professional writings of, say, Mill, or Sidgwick, or Rawls, or Nozick, or Dworkin, but they do involve far-reaching ideas of what is good and proper, and what is shameful, inexcusable or intolerable.[1] Also, political debates and social discussions about the appropriateness of particular ideas of justice can help in the formation and evolution of norms.

The ideas entertained or championed by us as citizens can, of course, clash with each other, but this heterogeneity need not be seen as a sign of our cognitive or perceptive failure. Indeed, substantial heterogeneity is similarly present in the substantive ethical theories presented by trained moral philosophers as well: for example, Rawls's (1971) theory of justice does clash powerfully with the utilitarian theories of Sidgwick (1874) or Pigou (1920). Plurality of conceptions of justice is part of the moral and social universe, and to this phenomenon, the ethical discussions of inequality and income distribution have to be alive. Indeed, given the social perspicuity and ethical legitimacy of several different perspectives in judging what is just and what is not, it is possible to entertain some scepticism as to whether some grand general "principles of justice" would be unanimously acceptable, even when vested interests have been somehow subdued and eliminated, through some device such as Rawls's (1958, 1971) "original position", or

---

[1] For interesting investigations of widely held values on distributional issues, see Rae (1981), Yaari and Bar-Hillel (1984), Temkin (1986, 1993), Fields (1990), Amiel and Cowell (1992) and Marshall and Swift (1995).

Harsanyi's (1955) model of equi-probability of being in the position of any person in the society.[2] Heterogeneity of ideas may well be just as "basic" as conflicts of interests.

People may agree that inequality has increased when the Lorenz curve has shifted outward, but reasonably disagree about the ranking of two situations where the Lorenz curves cross. Thus, intersecting Lorenz curves may occasion heterogeneity of ideas about inequality which cannot be easily resolved and this can leave social assessment with an irreducible incompleteness.

As will be argued later on in this essay, this is also part of the reason why the characterization of social justice in the assessment of economic inequality has to accommodate *assertive incompleteness*, as opposed to only *tentative* lack of completeness. Even though some pairs may be unambiguously ranked, others may remain unrankable, given the clash of commitments and concerns that a full-bodied theory of justice may yield, even after the ranking has been extended as far as possible. In such a case, the incompleteness that remains is not a "defect", but a part of the articulation that the theory of justice demands. A complete theory of justice need not insist on a complete ranking of all possible alternatives (and may, on the contrary, include such assertions as "*x* and *y cannot* be ranked in terms of justice"). The resilient presence of competing grounds of justice has strong implications on the discipline of inequality evaluation in general and of the assessment of income distribution in particular.

2. Informational basis of theories of justice

Given the relevance of theories of justice in economic evaluation (and also in social appraisal and political understanding), we must try to achieve some systematic understanding of different concepts of justice as a prelude to searching for an evaluative framework for assessing income distribution. The systematization can be usefully done through a strategy of classification that identities the respective informational basis of the different theories. Each substantive approach concentrates on some information on the states, achievements and opportunities of the people involved as being *central* to assessing justice and injustice in that society. Also, each theory *rules out*—typically implicitly—some other information as being directly important for the evaluation of justice. For example, the utilitarian theory of justice attaches intrinsic importance to—and only to—the utilities of the individuals involved, and has no direct interest in information on such subjects as the fulfilment or violation of rights or liberties, or for that matter, in the levels of incomes that people enjoy (even though there may be an *indirect* interest in incomes or rights or liberties because of their effects on individual utilities). Most forms of libertarianism, in contrast, concentrates on—and only on—the fulfilment or violation

---

[2] Scepticism about the possibility of reaching unanimity in the Rawlsian "original position" was outlined in Runciman and Sen (1965) and Sen (1970a: Chapter 9), without disputing the great value of the Rawlsian exercise as a device for moral reflection and political discussion.

of classes of rights and liberties, and attaches no direct importance to levels of utilities or of incomes.[3]

It is particularly relevant in this context to examine three different but interrelated aspects of the informational basis of these theories, which I will respectively call:

(1) basal space;
(2) focal combination; and
(3) reference group.

The basal space of a theory of justice—perhaps the most fundamental part of its claims—refers to the general class of variables to which the assessment of justice is sensitive under that theory, and no less importantly, excludes other variables, which are not part of the basal space, from having any direct impact on the assessment of justice (even though they can be indirectly important through their *causal* influences on basal variables, or as informational *proxies* for unobserved basal variables). For example, the basal space for utilitarian theories of justice consists of the combinations of utilities of different individuals. The concept of utility is not uniform in different utilitarian theories, but these theories all deny the direct relevance of any variable that does not count as being part of its particular interpretation of utility.

The second aspect relates to the way discriminating use is made of the basal information in the respective theory of justice. For example, in the utilitarian theory, the utilities of the different individuals are simply added together to arrive at the relevant overall assessment of the social state. This focal combination contrasts with, say, concentrating on the utility of the least well-off, or on some measure of dispersion in addition to the sum-total of the utilities of the different people.[4]

The third aspect of the informational basis raises a different type of issue from the first two. When we examine the achievements and predicaments of different people in a particular group, should that assessment be independent of the states of others outside this group? Can every group of people we consider for assessing inequality be seen as an isolated "island" for the purpose of this evaluation? If not, how should we bring in the interdependences? This question relates closely to the difficult issue of the relationship between injustice or inequality in different groups and the assessment of injustice or inequality in the *union* of these different groups. Or, to look at the same problem in another way (as it is more typically seen), what is at issue is the relationship between injustice or inequality of any group and the extents of injustice or inequality in the respective *subgroups* into which the first group can be partitioned.[5]

---

[3] I have tried elsewhere (in Sen 1977, 1979) to understand and assess substantive ethical doctrines and normative social choice theories through the analysis of their respective "informational basis".

[4] The contrasts between different theories of justice which James Meade (1976) has illuminatingly discussed really relate to what we are calling focal combination: the alternative theories he considers all share the same basal space, viz., the space of individual utilities. Meade argues convincingly why we may have good reason to resist the summation formula of utilitarian theory even if we confine our attention entirely to utilities (see also Sen, 1973a; Atkinson, 1983, 1989; Broome, 1991; Le Grand, 1991).

[5] On the principles underlying "decomposability" and "subgroup consistency", see Atkinson (1973, 1983), Cowell (1980, 1985), Shorrocks (1980, 1984, 1988), Anand (1983), Foster et al. (1984), Kanbur (1984),

On this subject, utilitarianism goes forcefully for the adequacy of separated information in the *basal space*. If the utilities of different people in any group are fully specified, then that information is entirely sufficient for judging the overall goodness of that state for this group. There is no "external reference" beyond the group (for example, to the comparative performance of members of this group vis-à-vis others outside it). This does not, of course, imply that the utilitarian assessment of inequality or injustice can be done on the basis of individual *incomes* of members of that group only. For utilitarian evaluation of the state of a group, the adequacy of utility information concerning all the members of the group can co-exist with the inadequacy of income information about them, since the utility of a member of a group can depend on variables other than his or her own income and incomes of others within this group (for example, it may be influenced by the incomes of others outside this group). In order to make *income distributions* separately assessable (in isolation) in the utilitarian perspective, further assumptions would have to be made, for example, that each person's utility depends only on that person's income. That assumption is frequently made, but it is not a necessary part of utilitarian welfare economics, or of utilitarian assessment of justice and injustice.[6]

These different aspects of the informational basis of evaluation have to be examined to gain insights into the nature and operation of distinct theories of justice. This framework will be used as we proceed to outline and examine some of the principal concepts and theories of justice in contemporary social thought and their relevance to the assessment of income distribution and economic inequality.

3. Utilitarianism and welfarist justice

For well over a century welfare economics has been dominated by one particular approach, viz., utilitarianism. It was initiated, in its modern form, by Jeremy Bentham (1789), and championed by such economists as Mill (1861), Sidgwick (1874), Edgeworth (1881), Marshall (1890) and Pigou (1920). Utilitarianism has been, in many ways, the "official" theory of traditional welfare economics, and its pervasive influence has already been indirectly acknowledged in this essay in our decision to *illustrate* the different aspects of the information basis of evaluation through the nature and characteristics of utilitarianism (as the most familiar normative approach). Indeed, in many respects utilitarianism serves as the "default program" in welfare-economic analysis: the theory that is implicitly summoned when no others are explicitly invoked.

Foster (1985), Foster and Shorrocks (1988, 1991), Ravallion (1994), Foster and Sen (1997), among other contributions. See also Chapter 2 (Frank Cowell).

[6] Furthermore, insofar as a utilitarian theory of justice looks not only at the utilities achieved, but also at the utilities that *could have* been achieved (to see in particular, whether, or not, the interests of some people in this group were unnecessarily sacrificed), the interdependences between the different groups (for example, through trade and other interrelations) may also be importantly relevant. But that issue (viz., interdependences in the generation of feasible alternatives) has to be distinguished from the issue of interdependence in the evaluation of each fully specified alternative outcome.

The *basal space* of utilitarian evaluation, as has been already discussed, consists of individual utilities. This is sometimes called "welfarism". This is a generic term, since the exact content of the space can differ depending on how "utility" is defined (for example, whether as pleasure, or as fulfilled desires, or as representation of choice). The *focal combination* takes the form of simple summation of individual utilities. This is sometimes called "sum-ranking". The *reference group* in assessing the social state of a group is that group itself, separately considered on its own (that is, the focus is on the utilities of the individuals only in that group, without any direct note being taken of the utilities of others not in the group). The normative maximand in assessing the state of a group is, as a result, just the sum-total of the utilities of the members of that group.

The "separability" already implicit in utilitarianism in the basal space can be extended to the income space as well through additional assumptions, such as the requirement that person i's utility depends only on her individual income. Such a separable form is indeed used in Atkinson's (1970) classic formulation of ethical measurement of income inequality. The social-welfare maximand W is given by the summation of components u_i related to the respective individuals i, taking each u_i to be given by the same concave function $u(y_i)$ for every i:

$$W = \sum_i^n u_i . \tag{3.1}$$

The extent of income inequality is judged by an index A, given by the percentage difference between the actual mean income (y), and the minimal value of mean income (y_e) that would permit the same social welfare to be achieved through an optimal (in this case, equal) distribution:

$$A = 1 - (y_e/y). \tag{3.2}$$

The formulation characterized by Eqs. (3.1) and (3.2) is, of course, quite general, and need not involve any separability in the income space. But the Atkinson formula does invoke this separability through making each individual u_i a function $u(y_i)$ of that person's income only.

Furthermore, these *separable components* u_i of the aggregate social welfare (associated with the respective individual i) need not be interpreted as the *utility* of the individual (and for this reason the principal limitations of the utilitarian approach need not apply to Atkinson's general formulation). Indeed, nonseparable and nonutilitarian uses of the Atkinson framework involves only a minor extension (see Sen, 1973a). However, the Atkinson framework is typically interpreted as being within the utilitarian tradition. This is not only because the formulae used are consistent with utilitarianism (and, furthermore, u_i sound very like utility), but also because—as noted earlier—utilitarianism tends to serve as a "default program" in standard welfare economics.

I postpone for the moment (indeed up to Section 8), the issue of the "reference group" and the operation of separability and decomposition, and concentrate instead on the choice of basal space and that of the focal combination. How adequate is utilitarianism in these respects?

To start with "welfarism", how acceptable is it as a general basis of judgments of justice? One of the major limitations of this approach lies in the fact that the same collection of individual welfares may go with very different social arrangements, opportunities, freedoms and consequences.[7] It may, in one case, involve significant violations of accepted individual rights, but not in another case. The utilitarian formula, in its Benthamite form, cannot discriminate between the pain of torture and the pain of being taxed, but that identification goes against widely held values as well as mainstream ethical reasoning (even though the contemporary political climate seems to encourage the view that taxation *is* torture). So long as the utilities generated end up being the same (no matter through what process), welfarism demands that the two alternatives are treated as equivalent (and no intrinsic importance be given to the differences between the scenarios in the ultimate assessment).

This informational neglect applies both to overall freedoms (sometimes called "positive" freedoms) which may entail claims on others or on the state (e.g., the right to free elementary education, unemployment insurance or basic health care), and to "negative" freedoms which demand noninterference by others (e.g., the requirements of personal liberty and autonomy). Welfarism's neglect of negative freedom (such as libertarian immunities) is obvious enough, but the overall (or positive) freedoms are also neglected since they are quite different from individual welfare achievements.

The informational limitation is made even stronger by the particular utilitarian interpretation of individual welfare, seeing it simply in terms of pleasures or desires, or as representations of choice. The last—utility as the real-valued representation of choice—does not, on its own, yield any obvious way of making interpersonal comparisons, since people do not get to choose between being one person or another. There have been fine attempts to close this gap through the consideration of *hypothetical* choices (as in Harsanyi's 1955 framework), but the resulting structure is neither interpretationally unambiguous, nor easy to apply in practice, even though it is illuminating and very useful as a conceptual device. In practice, the force of interpersonal comparison, which is necessary for using the utilitarian and other standard welfarist approaches, is sought—often implicitly—in the more classical understandings of utility as pleasure or as fulfilled desires (not as a numerical representation of choice).

Both these approaches rely ultimately on mental metrics—indicators of the extent of pleasure or of the strength of desire. The kind of scepticism that Lionel Robbins (1938) and others have expressed on this raises one type of problems. But one can argue that this may not be an insuperable objection, since there are many practical ways in

---

[7] I have tried to discuss some of the limitations of utilitarianism in Sen (1970a, 1973a, 1992).

which we do make these comparisons, which need not take an all or nothing form.[8] The difficulty that may be more basic in the context of a theory of justice and of inequality arises from the mental adaptation that makes the extent of pleasure or the strength of desire a very unreliable guide to real deprivation. Our desires and expectations adjust to circumstances, particularly to make life bearable in adverse situations. The hopeless underdog does not lead a life of constantly desiring what she thinks is unfeasible, nor one of seeking pleasures that are unobtainable. Rather, the focus is on cutting desires to size and on taking joy from smaller successes. In so far as they succeed in getting these more attainable pleasures and in fulfilling the restrained desires, their deprivation may look less intense in the mental metrics of pleasures and desires, even though their lack of real opportunities remains. Such adjustments in chronically deprived positions are easy to understand as a sensible strategy of coming to terms with deprivation, but they also have the incidental effect of distorting the scale of utilities with the effect that the deprivations are not adequately recognized in the basal space of utilities.

The utilitarian calculus can, thus, be insensitive and unfair to those who are persistently deprived: traditional outcasts, oppressed minorities, exploited labourers, subdued housewives, or the persistently poverty-stricken. Indeed, aside from its effect on the utilitarian calculus, this utility-based notion of interpersonal comparisons is itself deeply problematic for the informational basis of social justice and for the evaluative assessment of inequality.

Has this problem plagued applied welfare economics given its basically utilitarian character? The answer, oddly enough, is no. This is not because applied welfare economics has tried hard to avoid this bias (in fact, there has been little discussion of this issue); rather, it has avoided the problem because it has not tried hard enough to live up to its utilitarian foundations and justifications. Despite basing its underpinning on utilitarian theory, standard welfare economics makes no real effort at all to estimate utilities in line with utilitarian theory. There are few comparisons of mental states—whether of pleasure or of desire—and the choice interpretation of utility, which does not yield any interpersonal comparison, is simply combined—often implicitly—with the arbitrary assumption that if two persons have the same demand function, then they must get the same utility level from a given commodity basket. This is, of course, totally illegitimate; for example, if one person were to get exactly one quarter of the utility that another gets from each basket of commodities, they would still have exactly the same demand function.

The psychology behind this arbitrary practice rests on the continuing scepticism that most economists have about the scientific status of utility comparisons (Robbins remains the unsung hero who is followed without being praised), so that any assumption about interpersonal comparison looks as good—or as bad—as any other. The economic practitioner has not been able to work up enough enthusiasm to do any real "fact finding"

---

[8] These issues have been discussed in Little (1957), Sen (1970a, 1973a), Davidson (1986) and Gibbard (1986), among others.

about interpersonal correspondences of different persons' utilities.[9] And given the absence of any evidence on interpersonal comparison, the assumption that everyone gets the same utility from the same commodity basket (and by adaptation, from the same income level) has seemed good enough. This assumption is standardly made, and this is typically done even without the requirement of checking that people do have identical demand functions. One liberty taken is heaped on another.

This practice has the contingent merit of avoiding the mental-adaptation bias against the deprived (discussed above). But this it does by being totally insensitive to interpersonal differences. In particular, it judges adversity of circumstances only by the lowness of income, or of the commodity basket owned, over which a common utility function is defined. For example, a person with a disability or a handicap, or more prone to illness, is assumed to have the same utility so long as they have they same level of income or consumption, when the utility function is defined only on income or consumption. It is also in this form that the utilitarian framework and other welfarist approaches inspired by utilitarianism are typically used in the literature on the measurement and evaluation of economic inequality. The main problem with this is the neglect of relevant information in judging injustice and inequity. It avoids the perverse treatment of persistent deprivation in classical utilitarianism through lack of enterprise in living up to its utilitarian foundations, but that "laziness" has other penalties, in particular a lack of interest in causal factors that work—along with low income—to make people wretched and miserable, and confined to lives of great deprivation. Since some of these factors are matters of public policy (for example, health care, epidemiology, basic education, old-age security, support of the disabled), their neglect in basic welfare economics is a limitation of considerable practical moment. There is certainly a strong case for more integration of welfare-economic theory with the work that does go on in these fields—often without the benefit of much theory or foundational ethical reasoning.

In addition to these general difficulties that relate to various interpretations of "welfarism", there are other problems for the utilitarian theory that arise from the special limitations of "sum-ranking", i.e., the procedure of aggregating collections of utilities simply by *addition*. Utilitarianism cannot tell between two distributions of the same total utility. For example, it makes no difference in utilitarian evaluation whether one person has 10 units of utility and another has 2, or both have 6 units of utility each. This lack of concern with the distribution of welfares is a further limitation of utilitarianism.

To be sure, sum-ranking does not eliminate a preference for income equality when everyone is attributed the same concave utility function defined on the respective income level. But even within this framework, it can be argued that of the two reasons for censuring income inequality, only one is recognized here. Income inequality is *inefficient* in generating high utility sums given a shared and strictly concave utility function of this type. It is also *iniquitous* in the basal space of utilities in generating disparities in utilities.

---

[9] Among the few exceptions are the members of the "Leiden school", such as van Praag (1968, 1977) and van Praag and Kapteyn (1973).

The evaluation of inequality within the sum-ranking utilitarian framework, in this case, takes on board the "inefficiency" aspect of income inequality in the basal space, but not the "inequity" aspect of it in the same space. This problem can be compounded when there are people with handicaps and disadvantages, since their equitable treatment call for a very different framework which requires rejection, at once, of sum-ranking and welfarism (both constitutive features of utilitarianism).

4. Libertarian theories of justice

While various libertarian arguments against utilitarianism and egalitarianism have been presented for a long time (some of the finest arguments were presented by a great utilitarian himself, viz., John Stuart Mill, 1859), it is only recently that fully worked out libertarian theories have been offered in the professional literature, particularly by Robert Nozick (1973, 1974). They have drawn on earlier—more general—concerns (for example, those expressed by Hayek 1960), but they have gone on to make liberty and rights the constitutive components of an exclusive basal space (in a way that Hayek and others had not).

The *basal space* of rights in the formulation chosen by Nozick (1974) consists of the fulfilment or violation of different rights. Since these judgments are not of the "more-or-less" kind, but of the "zero-one" type (either a right is violated, or it is not), the metric of the space is quite compressed. The *focal combination* seeks the fulfilment of all the specified rights, and if there is any violation of any such rights, there is a failure of justice. No trade-offs are permitted. Furthermore, the *reference group* is the group directly involved, and nothing need be brought into the evaluation from outside the statistics regarding the group itself.

Once this basic system is honoured, libertarianism permits the introduction of other concerns, even those of utilities, at a lower level of decisional status, "if there are any choices left to make" (Nozick, 1973: pp. 60–61; Nozick, 1974: pp. 165–166). There can be, thus, a hierarchy of spaces, but the most powerful basal space is that of liberties and rights of various kinds. What is, thus, at issue in this theory of justice is the *priority of rights and liberties*. The idea of a priority of liberty has figured also in other theories of justice (for example, in John Rawls's 1971, immensely influential theory of "justice as fairness"), and there is an interesting comparison here which will be discussed in the next section.

In the purely libertarian theory, an extensive class of rights are treated as nonrelaxable constraints that must be fulfilled and which, accordingly, bind political action.[10] They cannot be overridden by other goals, including the social interest in better satisfying other goals, or for that matter, other rights.[11] People's entitlements related to their lib-

---

[10] On related issues see also Buchanan (1954), Buchanan and Tullock (1962) and Sugden (1981, 1986).

[11] These stark requirements are somewhat qualified by Nozick (1974) in the case of "catastrophic moral horrors", and more qualifications have been introduced since then in Nozick (1989).

ertarian rights cannot be outweighed by the nature of their results — even when those results are clearly rather nasty. This version of libertarianism is, thus, quite insensitive to the actual social consequences of these constraints and requirements. This insensitivity can be particularly problematic since the actual consequences of libertarian entitlements include the possibility of results that must be seen as quite terrible. For example, even famines can result without anyone's libertarian rights being violated: the destitutes such as the unemployed may starve precisely because their entitlements do not give them enough food to eat.[12]

It is hard to argue that a libertarian theory with its extremely narrow informational focus, and its neglect of human welfare and misery, can provide an adequate theory of justice in general, and in particular a sufficient theory for analyzing inequality and inequity. There is, of course, an "egalitarianism" implicit in Nozick's libertarianism, to wit, everyone's liberties count—and count the same. But this basic equality has a very special coverage, given the nature of its basal space, and the demand for equality does not go beyond everyone having the same right to liberty in the form of constraints on the actions of others. The theory builds on a reasoned intuition which many people have: that liberty is rather special and must not be substitutable by other kinds of individual advantages. When, for example, we hear of a person being killed by a religious bigot, or by an oppressive state, we have reason to be more upset than we might be when he hear of a death caused by natural events, even though the principal end-result, in a limited sense, is much the same (viz., a death). But the presence of this asymmetry is not ground enough to make liberty have irresistible force over all other concerns. Nor does it give us reason to demand the same priority for a whole class of other putative rights, which relate importantly to the functioning of economic instruments (like the role of property rights, including exchange and bequeathal, for the working of the market mechanism), but are not easily seen as immovable components of unrelaxable political requirements. It is the severe limitation of the basal space, combined with the absence of trade-offs in the focal combination, that makes this type of libertarianism an inadequate theory of justice, despite its useful pointer to an important asymmetry in the social importance of liberty.

5. Rawlsian theory of justice

John Rawls's concept of justice as fairness grounds the requirements of justice on the need for fairness. One form that fairness can take is to demand that the social arrangements should reflect decisions that would be arrived at in a hypothetical state of primordial equality, where the nature of the basic structure of the society can be agreed upon without each person knowing who s/he is in fact going to be in that society. In spelling out a just structure that would be arrived at, Rawls invokes two principles. The first principle demands the most extensive liberty for each consistent with similar liberty for

[12] See Sen (1981) and Drèze and Sen (1989).

others. This has priority over the second principle, which insists on keeping offices and opportunities open to all, and under the Difference Principle (a component of the second principle) also demands that inequalities be regarded as unjust except to the extent that they work out to be in the interest of the worst-off.

The basal space in this theory is rather complicated. Like in the libertarian theory, there is a hierarchy, but the space of liberties is quite narrow (it does not include property rights or rights of exchange or bequeathal), and is essentially concerned with basic personal and political liberties. Beyond this first round of concern, there is a basal space—lower down in hierarchy but forceful once the minimal liberties have been met—which includes the holding of "primary goods". These are general-purpose *resources* that are useful for the pursuit of different objectives that the individuals may have, and are "things that citizens need as free and equal persons, and claims to these goods are counted as appropriate claims" (Rawls, 1988: p. 257). Primary goods are "things that every rational man is presumed to want", and include "income and wealth", "the basic liberties", "freedom of movement and choice of occupation", "powers and prerogatives of offices and positions of responsibility", and "the social bases of self-respect" (see Rawls, 1971: pp. 60–65; Rawls, 1988: pp. 256–257). The coverage of "resources" can be extended to include other means, and Ronald Dworkin (1981) has taken his system of ethical accounting in that direction.

In the basal space of primary goods, Rawlsian Difference Principle demands that the least well-off groups are made as well-off as possible, in terms of an overall index of the holding of primary goods. A lexicographic form can be given to this priority (as proposed in Sen, 1970a, and accepted in Rawls, 1971), so that whenever the worst-off groups are equally well-off in a pairwise comparison, the attention is shifted to the next worst-off group, and so on. This focal combination has clearly egalitarian features, though the concentration is specifically on inequalities that cut into the lives of the least advantaged people.

The "priority of liberty" in the Rawlsian system is much less extensive and less restraining than in the libertarian arrangements. The rights that are given priority in this theory are far fewer and less demanding than those in the libertarian proposals (and in particular do not include property rights in general). However, these circumscribed rights (concerning personal and basic political liberties) have complete precedence over other social concerns, including the fulfilment of our most elementary needs and reasoned desires.

The case for this complete priority (even though applied to rather a limited class of rights) can be disputed by demonstrating the force of other considerations including that of needs, which occupy lower lexical priority, no matter how intense these needs may be. Herbert Hart (1973) raised this question forcefully in an early critique of Rawls (1971), and Rawls (1993) himself has clarified that this total nontrade-off need not be fully insisted on. It is, in fact, possible to distinguish between (1) Rawls's strict proposal that liberty should receive overwhelming *priority* in the case of a conflict, and (2) his general procedure of separating out personal liberty from other types of advantages for a *special* treatment. Acknowledging the pre-eminence of these rights need not take the sharp and extreme form that the claims of "priority of liberty" seems to demand—overriding every- thing with which it might conflict. The critical issue in the more general second claim is whether, or not, a person's liberty should get just the same kind of importance (no more) that other types of personal advantages—incomes, utilities, etc.—have. In particular, whether, or not, the significance of liberty for the society is adequately reflected by the weight that the person herself would tend to give to it in judging her *overall* advantage. The claim of pre-eminence of liberty and political rights can be seen as a denial of that symmetry.

The underlying issue, therefore, is that the social importance of liberty and basic political rights can far exceed the value that would be attached to them by individuals in judging their overall personal advantage. In order to prevent a misunderstanding, I should explain that the contrast is *not* with the value that citizens attach to liberty and rights in their *political* judgements. Quite the contrary, since the safeguarding of liberty rests ultimately on the general political acceptance of their importance. The contrast is, rather, with the extent to which having more liberty or rights increases an individual's own personal advantage. The citizens' judgement on the importance of liberty and other rights need not be based only on the extent to which they themselves expect to profit from these rights. So the claim is that the political significance of rights can far exceed the extent to which the personal advantage of the holders of these rights is enhanced by having these rights.[13] There is, thus, an asymmetry with other sources of individual advantage, for example incomes, which would be valued largely on the basis of how much they contribute to the respective personal advantages. The safeguarding of the basic political rights would have the policy priority that follows from this asymmetric prominence. While I will not further pursue this issue here, it is a distinction to which importance can be, I believe, sensibly attached.[14] One effect of this is to place the is- sue of income distribution—the subject matter of this collection of essays—in a wider context, and not to treat the distribution of incomes as the exclusive or even the most prominent area of social concern.

What about the Difference Principle? Much of the early criticism of the Rawlsian framework concerned his formula for aggregation, that is, the chosen focal combina- tion.[15] The maximin form (even when modified by its lexicographic extension) can be "extremist" in giving complete priority to the worst-off's gain (no matter how small) over the better-off's loss (no matter how great), and there is some indifference here to considerations of aggregative efficiency. But this is open to qualification and modifica-

---

[13] The discussion here is primarily within consequentialist frameworks, so that the relative importance of different types of objectives are judged vis-a-vis each other. In an alternative approach, rights can be seen as constraints that must be fulfilled, rather than being incorporated within the objectives of the society; on the distinction, see particularly Nozick (1974), Dworkin (1978) and Sugden (1981, 1986).

[14] This question is more fully discussed in my forthcoming *Freedom, Rationality and Social Choice: Arrow Lectures and Other Essays* (Clarendon Press).

[15] See particularly the collection of essays presented in Phelps (1973).

tion, without eliminating the concentration on the worst-off citizens—a focus in favour of which Rawls has provided strong arguments. Various compromises are possible, including using strictly concave transformations that take us, in an equity-conscious way, from individual fortunes to social assessment.[16]

A different type of criticism relates to the choice of basal space in Rawlsian theory. But before coming to that, it is important to see the merits of the space of primary goods. It does not suffer from the narrowness of focus of libertarianism, and while it includes liberties and rights among the primary goods (in addition to the role given to liberty under the first principle), it also includes other general-purpose means that give people the opportunity to pursue their respective objectives. Nor does the accounting of primary goods have the built-in bias against the persistently deprived that the mental metric of utilities have.

However, primary goods are *means*, not the *ends* that people seek. Nor do they reflect the *freedoms* that people have to pursue their ends. The concentration, rather, is on the means—and only *some* of the means—that are relevant in generating these freedoms. If we are interested in freedom, is it adequate to concentrate only on some of the means to freedom, rather than on the *extent* of the freedom that a person actually has? Since the conversion of these primary goods and resources into freedom of choice over alternative lives and achievements may vary from person to person, equality of holdings of primary goods or of resources can go hand in hand with serious inequalities in actual freedoms enjoyed by different persons. For example, a disabled person with a given basket of primary goods will enjoy less freedom in many significant respects than would an able-bodied person with an identical basket. An aged person with special difficulties would have a similar problem.[17] So would a person suffering from an adverse epidemiological environment at her native location, and similarly a person with a greater genetic proneness to some disease.[18]

Thus, despite the great advance that has been made in the theory of justice by Rawls's path-breaking work (most of the recent theories follow the routes explored by Rawls, even when they choose to vary their ultimate destination), there remain some difficulties

---

[16] This was the basic general idea behind Kolm's (1969) and Atkinson's (1970) departures in evaluative economics, even though the form of the concave functions were rather special ones.

[17] Sometimes the problems of old age are dismissed on the grounds that the Rawlsian calculus should be made to apply to expected lifetime stocks of primary goods. But this leaves open the distribution over the lifetime, which can be itself quite significant. Also lifetime accounting has to cope with the relevance of different life expectancies: the advantages of living longer as well as the greater needs experienced in the declining years.

[18] Although there are important differences between Rawls's and Dworkin's approaches, both focus on resources in making interpersonal comparisons, and both seek to answer the question "equality of what?" in terms of *means* rather than in terms of what people can obtain *from* the means. Dworkin (1981) has, however, proposed enriching the perspective of "resources" by including *as if* insurance mechanisms against certain types of personal handicaps. To the extent that these insurance mechanisms even out differences in different people's ability to convert resources into actual freedoms, the equality of insurance-adjusted values of resources would be an indirect way of *approaching* the equality of freedoms. Much would depend on the scope, coverage and versatility of the *as if* insurance mechanisms.

in seeing justice entirely in terms of the Rawlsian principles and their implications for the basal space and focal combination. In the context of assessing income distribution, the important lessons from Rawlsian analysis relate to the broadening of the context of the judgment. The relevance of liberty and rights has already been commented on, but there is also the need to see that income is only one of the means—one of the primary goods—that help people to pursue their objectives and to live in freedom. This broadening remains deeply insightful, even though we may want to go further (as the present writer certainly does).

6. Quality of life, functionings and capabilities

There is a different approach to justice that draws on some lines of analysis suggested by Aristotle, and to some extent Adam Smith, and which is concerned with the opportunities that people enjoy to achieve what Aristotle called "human flourishing". This approach can help to systematize the investigation of quality of life, in which a number of contributions have been made in recent years.[19] The widespread interest in an informationally rich evaluative framework especially in the literature on economic development provides excellent motivation for going in this direction. A theory of justice can use the ingredients of quality of living as the basal space.[20]

Concepts of quality of life are frequently used in an informal way, and often with an arbitrary choice of an indicator. This is to some extent inevitable in practice given the gaps in the relevant data and the vagueness of the underlying concepts. But it is important to be sure how in principle the formal analysis would proceed had the relevant data been available, and had there been an opportunity to separate out the inescapable ambiguities in the nature of the subject matter from unnecessary obscurities resulting from inadequate analysis. Informational lacuna or complexity of concepts need not serve as an excuse for tolerating avoidable conceptual murkiness. Difficulties in observing utilities have not prevented the development of utility theory at the conceptual level, and search for clarity is important here too, even when practical applicability may be contingently limited.

---

[19] See Pant et al. (1962), Adelman and Morris (1973), Sen (1973b, 1980, 1985b), Haq (1976), Herrera et al. (1976), ILO (1976), Ghai et al. (1977), Grant (1978), Griffin (1978), Streeten and Burki (1978), Morris (1979), Chichilnisky (1980), Streeten (1981, 1984), Streeten et al. (1981), Osmani (1982), Stewart (1985), Behrman and Deolalikar (1988), Drèze and Sen (1989), Anand and Kanbur (1990), Griffin and Knight (1990), Dasgupta (1993), Lipton and van der Gaag (1993), among other contributions.

[20] John Roemer (1996) has provided a rich analysis of competing theories of justice along with his evaluation of their respective merits and shortcomings, and has particularly explored the possibility of a structure more informed about the nature of human welfare and opportunities, and the role and limitations of the rewarding of talents (see also Roemer, 1985). Richard Arneson (1989, 1990) and G.A. Cohen (1989, 1990) have also enriched the theory of justice with another class of informational concerns. Their respective contributions can be examined and appreciated in terms of widening the informational basis of justice and the reasons they give for the direction in which they have chosen to proceed.

A fuller presentation can indeed be developed and conceptually defended in the lines already identified by Aristotle and Smith. A person's achieved living can be seen as a combination of "functionings" (i.e., doings and beings), and taken together, they can be broadly seen as constituting the quality of life.[21] The functionings on which human flourishing depend include such elementary things as being alive, being well nourished and in good health, moving about freely, and so on. It can also include more complex functionings such as having self-respect and respect of others, and taking part in the life of the community (including "appearing in public without shame"), on which Smith (1776) in particular placed much weight.[22]

Given **n** different types of functionings, an **n**-tuple of "functionings" represents the focal features of a person's living, with each of its "components" reflecting the extent of the achievement of a particular functioning. A person's "capability" is represented by the set of **n**-tuples of functionings from which the person can choose any one **n**-tuple. The "capability set", thus, stands for the actual freedom of choice a person has over the alternative lives that s/he can lead. There are many technical issues in the specification and analysis of functionings and capabilities, but the central idea is to see the basal space in terms of what people are able to be, or do (rather than in terms of the means they possess). In this view, individual claims are to be assessed not only by the incomes, resources or primary goods the persons respectively have, nor only with reference to the utilities they enjoy, but in terms of the freedoms they actually have to choose between different ways of living they can have reason to value.[23]

In the move from the basal space of primary goods to that of functionings and capabilities, there are two distinct steps. First, the basic shift is from the space of an individual's primary goods space (where each dimensions represents a primary good held by that individual) to the space where the dimensions stand for distinct functionings enjoyed by that person. In Rawlsian analysis, the primary goods bundles are converted into an index of primary goods (on the basis of agreed trade-off maps). A similar process would yield an index of functioning *n*-tuples. However, given the importance of recognizing possible incompleteness in valuation (and in implicit trade-offs), the indexing need not take quite the strong form that is demanded in the Rawlsian system; the representation of a partial ordering has some rather restrictive properties.[24] It is also possible to incorporate "fuzziness" in the specification as well as valuation of functionings in

---

[21] On different aspects of this identification, see the collection of essays in Nussbaum and Sen (1993).

[22] See also Townsend (1979).

[23] This has been the subject of a good deal theoretical and empirical work in recent years. On different ways of using functionings and capabilities, see Sen (1980, 1985a, b, 1992), Kakwani (1986), Hawthorn (1987), Kanbur (1987), Williams (1987), Muellbauer (1987), Dréze and Sen (1989, 1995), Bourguignon and Fields (1990), Griffin and Knight (1990), Hossain (1990), Schokkaert and Van Ootegem (1990), UNDP (1990), Crocker (1992, 1996), Anand and Ravallion (1993), Nussbaum and Sen (1993), Balestrino (1994, 1996), Chiappero Martinetti (1994, 1996), Cornia (1994), Desai (1994), Granaglia (1994), Lenti (1994), Arrow (1995), Atkinson (1995), Balestrino and Petretto (1995), Fleurbaey (1995a, b), Herrero (1995), Casini and Bernetti (1996) and Piacentino (1996), among other contributions.

[24] On the representation of a partial ordering, see Majumdar and Sen (1976).

well-structured ways, in line with inescapable ambiguities of concepts of this kind (as opposed to fogginess of analysis).[25]

When it comes to the evaluation of capability, the same structure can be extended, to assess the set of alternative functioning bundles. While judging a set by its chosen element is always a possibility (making the set evaluation problem "degenerate" into the evaluation of the chosen element), there is a good case for trying to go much beyond that. The indexing of such sets requires additional problems of set evaluation.[26]

The second step is to see the interpersonal basal space in terms of individual indices of primary goods in the case of the Rawlsian framework and the representations of achieved functionings or capabilities in the capability framework. While the nature of the respective approaches has been much discussed and developed at the conceptual level, they have not typically been much applied formally with empirical data. There is a gap here that is somewhat similar to the hiatus between utilitarian theory and the practice of utilitarian applied welfare economics (which was discussed earlier). The possibility of practical use is limited both by data availability and the ambiguities of parts of the subject matter (so that the practical uses have tended to be confined to a limited class of variables which are more precisely obtainable, such as life expectancy).[27] The practical value of these approaches lies in pointing to the relevance of some crucial information neglected in standard welfare economics as well as the main theories of justice, rather than in making great formal use of these spaces in exactly the same way the income space or the commodity space is used. The need to go beyond the income space does not immediately translate itself into an alternative space of the same degree of articulation.

Since the options that a person has is very often hard to ascertain, the main focus of the "capability approach" has been on functioning information, supplemented by considering, where possible, some of the more prominent options a person had, but did not choose to use. For example, a rich and healthy person who becomes ill-nourished through fasting can be distinguished from a person who is forced into undernutrition through a lack of means, or as a result of suffering from a parasitic disease. In doing studies of poverty, it is possible to distinguish between the meagreness of the actual functionings and the resentment of the lack of choice over other alternatives.[28] In practice such discrimination is often difficult to do when dealing with aggregate statistics (as

---

[25] See Chiappero Martinetti (1994, 1996), and also Basu (1987), Delbono (1989), Cerioli and Zani (1990), Balestrino (1994), Balestrino and Chiappero Martinetti (1994), Ok (1996) and Casini and Bernetti (1996).

[26] On these measurement issues and related problems, see Sen (1985b, 1993), Kanbur (1987), Muellbauer (1987), Bourguignon and Fields (1990), Balestrino (1994, 1996), Chiappero Martinetti (1994, 1996), Desai (1994), Granaglia (1994), Balestrino and Petretto (1995) and Herrero (1995), among other contributions.

[27] For interesting practical applications with a particular focus on life expectancy, see Kakwani (1986), UNDP (1990, 1997) and Anand and Ravallion (1993).

[28] For an insightful study on this distinction related to the Belgian unemployed, see Schokkaert and Van Ootegem (1990).

opposed to detailed microstudies of individuals), and the practical uses of the capability concept in poverty analysis has been mainly with simple functioning information.[29]

There is some methodological trade-off here in the analysis of justice and inequality. Information on incomes, consumption levels, and sometimes even primary goods may often be easier to obtain and use than the kind of data that the capability approch, in different forms, seeks. And yet to confine attention only to space of incomes or primary goods on this ground results in some real loss in the informational basis of judgments of justice and of socially relevant inequalities. Easier articulation can, to some extent, conflict with richer analysis, and the pragmatic case for combining the different approaches is undoubtedly strong.

7. Income inequality and non-income concerns

The heterogeneity of components in the basal space (such as different functionings) points inevitably to the need to weigh them against one another. This applies to all approaches that respect plurality in one form or another, including the Rawlsian focus on primary goods, or the Aristotelian focus on functionings and capabilities (and in other theories that take note of different aspects of quality of life).

This weighting requirement is often seen as a "difficulty" with these approaches. But the heterogeneity in our value system makes it necessary for us either to face this plurality, with its consequent problems, or to ignore it in some arbitrary way, which has problems of its own. While we can decide to close our eyes to this issue by simply *assuming* that there is something homogeneous called "the income" in terms of which everyone's overall advantage can be judged and interpersonally compared (and that variations of needs, personal circumstances, prices, etc. can be, correspondingly, assumed away), this does not resolve the problem—only evades it. Real income comparison involves aggregation over different commodities, and in judging comparative individual advantages, there is the further problem of interpersonal comparisons taking note of variations of individual conditions and circumstances. It is, of course, possible to reflect these variations in values of "adjusted income" that can be appropriately defined, but that is only another way of stating the same problem, requiring that attention be paid to the valuation of heterogeneous factors, though expressed in the "indirect" space of equivalent incomes.[30] Measurements in the direct space (e.g., quality of life, or capability indicators) and those in the indirect space (e.g., "equivalent incomes") would have a tight correspondence with each other, when the underlying values are the same. One way or another, the issue of valuation and weighting has to be, inescapably, faced.

---

[29] See, for example, Griffin and Knight (1990), Hossain (1990), UNDP (1990), Crocker (1992, 1996), Anand and Ravallion (1993), Balestrino (1994, 1996), Chiappero Martinetti (1994, 1996), Desai (1994), Granaglia (1994), Balestrino and Petretto (1995), Casini and Bernetti (1996) and Piacentino (1996), among others. See, however, Schokkaert and Van Ootegem (1990), Arrow (1995), Atkinson (1995) and Herrero (1995), who have been more concerned with the evaluation of freedom in this context.

[30] On the possibility of this, see particularly, Deaton and Muellbauer (1980) and Deaton (1995).

It is crucial to ask, in any evaluative exercise of this kind, how the weights are to be selected. This is a judgmental exercise, and it can be resolved only through reasoned evaluation. In making *personal* judgments, the selection of the weights will be done by a person in the way s/he thinks is reasonable. But in arriving at an "agreed" range for *social evaluation* (for example, in social studies of poverty), there has to be some kind of a reasoned "consensus" on weights (even if it is of an informal kind). While the possibility of arriving at a unique set of weights is rather unlikely, that uniqueness is not really necessary to make agreed judgments in many situations, and may not indeed be required even for arriving at a fully complete ordering.[31]

In the democratic context, values are given a foundation through their correspondence with informed judgements by the people involved. The discipline of social evaluation has been extensively explored in the contemporary literatures on social choice theory as well as public choice theory. There is, in fact, much complementarity between them, and a more complete characterization of basing social judgments on public acceptance can be obtained by combining the two disciplines. I have tried to argue elsewhere (Sen, 1995) why and how this combination is needed. Public choice theory has provided more exploration of the role of discussion and negotiation in arriving at a consensus, whereas social choice theory has made a more extensive contribution on acceptable compromises in areas in which disagreements remain. This type of exercise is needed not only for the informational basis and focal combination underlying theories of justice, but also in other areas of public policy and social action. Indeed, similar combinations (involving agreed norms and consensus, on the one hand, and acceptable compromises, on the other) are needed even for setting a "poverty line", or for the evaluation of an "environmentally adjusted national income", or for the use of an "inequality index" in national statistics (like Atkinson's 1970 measure for a chosen α).

The need to look for socially acceptable compromises also directs attention to the identification of issues for public discussion and scrutiny rather than to the immediate task of getting one grand general ordering and real-valued representation of such an ordering. The value of the capability perspective lies particularly in identifying problems that are central to the assessment of inequality and poverty which are nevertheless ignored in more immediate measures (such as incomes). Even if one were quite pessimistic about getting a general ranking of capability combinations (in the form of either a complete ordering, or in that of a practically adequate partial ranking), there would be uses for capability analysis in identifying neglected concerns in the more tranditional literature of inequality and poverty.[32]

The point has sometimes been made that it may be a mistake to move from the sure ground of real income statistics to the murky territory of other values and concerns. As Srinivasan (1994) has argued, quoting Sugden (1993), "the real-income framework

---

[31] On some methodological issues of ranking with "partial comparability", see Chapters 7 and 7* in Sen (1970a).

[32] See, for example, the analysis in Atkinson (1995) of capability differences brought about by the diversity of consumer opportunities and the associated marketing arrangments.

includes an operational metric for weighting commodities—the metric of exchange value".[33] Is this a good argument for sticking to the commodity space and market valuation in making comparative judgments on personal advantages, rather than using information on functionings and other features of quality of life?[34]

It is certainly true that market prices exist for commodities, and not for functionings. But how can evaluatively significant weights—whether of commodities or functionings—be simply "read off" from some *other* exercise (in this case, of commodity exchange), without addressing the issue of values in *this* exercise (the comparison of individual advantages)? There are two distinct issues here of practical importance. The first is the problem of externalities, inequalities and other concerns which suggest that market prices be "adjusted". We have to decide whether, or not, such adjustments *should* be made, and if so, *how* this should be done, and in the process an evaluative exercise cannot really be avoided.

The second—and the more fundamental—problem is that "the metric of exchange value", although operational in its own context, was not devised to give us—and indeed cannot give us—*interpersonal comparisons* of welfare or advantage. Some confounding has occurred on this subject because of misreading the tradition—sensible within its context—of taking utility to be simply the numerical representation of a person's choice. That is a useful way of defining utility for the analysis of consumption behaviour of each person taken separately, but it does not offer (as has been already discussed earlier on in this essay) any procedure whatever for substantive interpersonal comparison.[35] Samuelson's (1947) elementary point that "it was not necessary to make interpersonal comparisons of utility in describing exchange" (p. 205), is the other side of the same coin: nothing about interpersonal comparison of utility is learnt from observing exchange or "the metric of exchange value".

This is not just a theoretical difficulty of little practical interest; it can make a very big difference in practice as well. For example, *even if* a person who is disabled or ill or depressed happens to have the *same* demand function as another who is not disadvantaged in this way, it would be quite absurd to assume that she is having exactly the same utility or well-being from a given commodity bundle as the other can get from it. At the practical level, perhaps the biggest difficulty in basing interpersonal comparisons of advantage on real-income comparisons lies in the diversity of human beings. Differences in age, gender, special talents, disability, proneness to illness, etc., can make two different persons have quite divergent substantive opportunities *even when* they have the very same commodity bundle. When we have to go beyond simply observing market

---

[33] In fact, Sugden went on to say that it "remains to be seen whether, or not, analogous metrics can be developed for the capability approach", taking a position rather less "closed" than Srinivasan's.

[34] The discussion here follows the arguments considered in Foster and Sen (1997: pp. 203–209).

[35] Explanations on why interpersonal comparison do not follow from observing actual choices have been repeated persistently (see Samuelson, 1947; Graaff, 1957: pp. 157–158; Gintis, 1969; Fisher and Shell, 1972: p. 3). Evidently, this has not shaken the faith of the optimist.

choices, which tell us little about interpersonal comparisons, we have to use *additional* information, rather than simply the good old "metric of exchange value".

The market mechanism does not *preselect for evaluative use* some metric of social valuation; we have to do that ourselves. For informed scrutiny by the public, the implicit values have to be made more explicit, rather than being shielded from scrutiny on the false ground that they are part of an "already available" evaluative metric. There is a real need for openness to critical discussion of *evaluative* weights, and it is a need that applies to all procedures for devising such weights. It is not a special problem for assessing primary goods, or functionings, or the distinct components of quality of life, or the comparative evaluation of the demands of liberty and rights vis-à-vis the claims of needs and well-being. Collective decisions call for public discussion and social evaluation.

8. Is every subgroup a community?

So far, I have neglected the issue of "reference group" after the initial motivating presentation. There can be little doubt that the main informational focus in assessing the justice of a social arrangement, or the nature of economic inequality, has to be on the state of the people in the respective communities. Does this suggest the need for "separability" in social evaluation?

To some extent it does, particularly when we concentrate attention on the variables that ultimately matter, rather than those that are only contingently important, perhaps as instruments. For example, if it were to be agreed that welfarism is just right, then that would be ground enough to evaluate the state of each group by the levels of utilities of all the members of that group (and not members of other groups). Any relevant interdependence would be reflected through the determination of the utility levels. For example, a person's utility may depend not only on her own income but also on the income of others—not necessarily in the same group. That connection would have to be worked out in estimating utilities, but once that is done, the interdependences would have had their say.

It is still possible, in principle, that the criterion in judging social achievement or the extent of inequality may refer to what distributions of utilities obtain elsewhere, but this type of evaluative connection may often appear to be rather remote. More immediately, it must be noted that in the space of contingently valued variables (such as incomes), separability cannot be easily demanded. In judging how bad a particular pattern of income distribution is, we have to examine the consequences of that pattern on the distribution of what matters (say, utilities) for members of that group, and these effects may be conditional on the values of incomes of others not in the group.

This problem is sometimes ignored through the assumption that the interactions all work *within* each group, and not between members of different groups. For some partitions this assumption may be good enough, but in the general theory of inequality evaluation, the requirements are standardly applied to *all* partitions. The extensive and powerful results on "decomposability" and "subgroup consistency" draw on the possibility of applying the interconnection to *all* partitions.[36] However, if the interconnections all work within each component of some partition (e.g., when the British population is divided over the counties), then clearly some interconnections would go across different subgroups if some other principle of partitioning is used (e.g., by first names, no matter where the location). There is only one exception, to wit, when every individual is an "island" on her own. Indeed, this is precisely what the formal results draw on through the demands for decomposability or subgroup consistency over all partitions. The measures that survive, which belong to the generalized "entropy" class, all make the individuals' incomes respectively operate separately, on their own, without interdependence. These axiomatic requirements are, thus, particularly hostile to measures such as the Gini coefficient that permits interdependences of particular types.

It is tempting to think that decomposability or subgroup consistency can be demanded for some partition, and not for others. If this is done within the limits of income information only, this is certainly possible, and indeed some nondecomposable measures are contingently decomposable for specific income-based partitions (for example, the Gini coefficient is contingently decomposable for population subgroups belonging to nonintersecting income ranges, as Anand 1983 noted). But if we want to discriminate between different partitions on the basis of some information other than incomes, then the resulting exercise cannot evaluate inequality on the basis of income information alone, and the informational basis of the evaluation has to be correspondingly broadened.

Not all subgroups are communities. Some are, depending on location, social connections, and so on. To take note of interdependence *within* a community, and when sensible to ignore the relation between different communities, may well be a part of a useful social evaluational exercise. But this does call for a broadening of the informational basis of social evaluation.

9. Concluding remarks

One of the main conclusions to emerge from the different problems studied here is the general need for liberating the analysis of economic inequality from confinement to the space of incomes or commodity holdings. The main argument for this broadening lies in reasons discussed earlier, to wit, our basic concerns are not with incomes or commodities, which are only contingently important, mainly as instruments to ends and the freedom to achieve ends. This issue is particularly relevant in the context of the informational basis of social justice.

However, in addition to this basic reason, there are some other different, although not unrelated, grounds for broadening the informational inputs into the analysis of economic inequality. Even if we are primarily interested in measuring or evaluating *income distribution* as such, the axiomatic demands we impose on this measurement has to

---

[36] See Shorrocks (1980, 1984) and Foster and Shorrocks (1991).

distinguish between different types of partitions which call for information beyond the income space. The link between the two problems lies in the fact that income, like wealth, "is evidently not the good we are seeking", as Aristotle put it in *Nicomachean Ethics*, "for it is merely useful and for something else".

References

Adelman, I. and C.T. Morris (1973), Economic Growth and Social Equity in Developing Countries (Stanford University Press, Stanford).

Amiel, Y. and F.A. Cowell (1992), Measurement of income inequality, Journal of Public Economics 47: 3–26.

Anand, S (1983), Inequality and Poverty in Malaysia (Oxford University Press, London).

Anand, S. and M. Ravallion (1993), Human development in poor countries: on the role of private incomes and public services, Journal of Economic Perspectives 7: 133–150.

Anand, S. and R. Kanbur (1984), Inequality and development: a reconsideration, in H.P. Nissen, ed., Towards Income Distribution Policies (European Association of Development Research and Training, Tilburg).

Arneson, R. (1989), Equality and equality of opportunity for welfare, Philosophical Studies 56: 77–93.

Arneson, R. (1990), Liberalism, distributive subjectivism, and equal opportunity for welfare, Philosophy and Public Affairs 19: 159–194.

Arrow, K.J. (1995), A note on freedom and flexibility, in K. Basu, P. Pattanaik and K. Suzumura, eds., Choice, Welfare and Development (Oxford University Press, Oxford).

Atkinson, A.B. (1970), On the measurement of inequality, Journal of Economic Theory 2: 244–263.

Atkinson, A.B. (1973), More on measurement of inequality, unpublished notes, mimeographed.

Atkinson, A.B. (1983), Social Justice and Public Policy (MIT Press, Cambridge).

Atkinson, A.B. (1989), Poverty and Social Security (Wheatsheaf, New York).

Atkinson, A.B. (1995), Capabilities, exclusion, and the supply of goods, in K. Basu, P. Pattanaik and K. Suzumura, eds., Choice, Welfare and Development (Clarendon Press, Oxford): 17–31.

Balestrino, A. (1994), Poverty and functionings: issues in measurement and public action, Giornale degli Economisti e Annali di Economia 53: 389–406.

Balestrino, A. (1996), A note on functioning-poverty in affluent societies, Notizie de Politeia 12: 97–105.

Balestrino, A. and E. Chiappero Martinetti (1994), Poverty, differentiated needs, and information, mimeographed, University of Pisa and University of Pavia.

Balestrino, A. and A. Petretto (1995), Optimal taxation rules for 'functioning'-inputs, Economic Notes 23.

Basu, K. (1987), Axioms for fuzzy measures of inequality, Mathematical Social Sciences 14: 275–288.

Behrman, J.R. and A.B. Deolalikar (1988), Health and nutrition, in H.B. Chenery and T.N. Srinivasan, eds., Handbook of Development Economics, Vol. 1 (North-Holland, Amsterdam).

Bentham, J. (1789), An Introduction to the Principles of Morals and Legislation (Payne; also Clarendon Press, Oxford, 1907).

Broome, J. (1991), Utility, Economics and Philosophy 7.

Bourguignon, F. and G. Fields (1990), Poverty measures and anti-poverty policy, Recherches Economiques de Louvain 56.

Buchanan, J.M. (1954a), Social choice, democracy and free markets, Journal of Political Economy 62: 114—123.

Buchanan, J.M. (1954b), Individual choice in voting and the market, Journal of Political Economy 62: 334–343.

Buchanan, J.M. and G. Tullock (1962), The Calculus of Consent (University of Michigan Press, Ann Arbor, Michigan).

Casini, L. and I. Bernetti (1996), Environment, sustainability, and Sen's Theory, mimeographed, University of Naples and University of Florence, presented at the Politeia meeting on 'Environment and society in a changing world: a perspective from the functioning theory', 10 May 1996.

Cerioli, A. and S. Zani (1990), A fuzzy approach to the measurement of poverty, in C. Dagum and M. Zenga, eds., Income and Wealth Distribution, Inequality and Poverty (Springer-Verlag, Berlin).

Chiappero Martinetti, E. (1996), Standard of living evaluation based on Sen's approach: some methodological suggestions, Notizie di Politeia 12: 37–53..

Chichilnisky, G. (1980), Basic needs and global models, Alternatives 6.

Cohen, G.A. (1989), On the currency of egalitarian justice, Ethics 99: 906–944.

Cohen, G.A. (1990), Equality of what? On welfare, goods and capabilities, Recherches Économiques de Louvain 56.

Cornia, G.A. (1995), Poverty in Latin America in the 1980s: extent, causes and possible remedies, Giornale degli Economisti 54.

Cowell, F.A. (1980), On the structure of additive inequality measures, Review of Economic Studies 47: 521–531.

Cowell, F.A. (1985), Measures of distributional change: an axiomatic approach, Review of Economic Studies 52: 135–151.

Crocker, D. (1992), Functioning and capability: the foundations of Sen's and Nussbaum's development ethic, Political Theory 20.

Crocker, D. (1996), Consumption, well-being and capability, mimeographed, Institute of Philosophy and Public Policy, University of Maryland.

Dasgupta, P. (1993), An Inquiry into Well-Being and Destitution (Clarendon Press, Oxford).

Davidson, C. (1986), Judging interpersonal interests, in J. Elster and A. Hylland, eds., Foundation of Social Choice Theory (Cambridge University Press, Cambridge).

Deaton, A.S. (1995), Microeconometric Analysis for Development Policy: an Approach from Household Surveys (Johns Hopkins University Press for the World Bank, Baltimore).

Deaton, A.S. and J. Muellbauer (1980), Economics and Consumer Behaviour (Cambridge University Press, Cambridge).

Delbono, F. (1989), Poverta come incapacita: premesse teoriche, identificazion e misurazione, Rivista Internazionale di Scienze Sociali 97.

Desai, M. (1994), Poverty, Famine and Economic Development (Elgar, Aldershot).

Drèze, J. and A. Sen (1989), Hunger and Public Action (Clarendon Press, Oxford).

Drèze, J. and A. Sen (1995), India: Economic Development and Social Opportunity (Oxford University Press, Delhi and Oxford).

Dworkin, R. (1978) Taking Rights Seriously, 2nd edn (Duckworth, London).

Dworkin, R. (1981), What is equality? Part 1: Equality of welfare, and What is equality? Part 2: Equality of resources, Philosophy and Public Affairs 10: 185-246, 283–345.

Edgeworth, F.Y. (1881), Mathematical Psychics (Kegan Paul, London).

Fields, G.S. (1990), Do inequality measures measure inequality?, mimeographed, Cornell University.

Fisher, F.M. and K Shell (1972), The Economic Theory of Price Indices (Academic Press, New York).

Fleurbaey, M. (1995a), Three solutions for the compensation problem, Journal of Economic Theory 65: 505–521.

Fleurbaey, M. (1995b), Equality and responsibility, European Economic Review 39: 683–689.

Foster, J.E. (1985), Inequality measurement, in H.P. Young, ed., Fair Allocation (American Mathematical Society, Providence).

Foster, J.E. and A. Sen (1997), On Economic Inequality after a quarter century, Annexe, in A. Sen, On Economic Inequality, expanded edition (Clarendon Press, Oxford).

Foster, J.E. and A.F. Shorrocks (1988), Poverty orderings, Econometrica 56: 173–177.

Foster, J.E. and A.F. Shorrocks (1991), Subgroup consistent poverty indices, Econometrica 59.

Foster, J.E., J. Greer and E. Thorbecke (1984), A class of decomposable poverty measures, Econometrica 52: 761–766.

Ghai, D., A.R. Khan, E. Lee and T.A. Alfthan (1977), The Basic-needs Approach in Development (ILO, Geneva).

Gibbard, A. (1986), Interpersonal comparisons: preference, good, and the intrinsic reward of a life, in J. Elster and A. Hylland, eds., Foundation of Social Choice Theory (Cambridge University Press, Cambridge).

Gintis, H. (1969), Alienation and power: toward a radical welfare economics, Ph.D. dissertation, Harvard University.

Graaff, J. de V. (1957), Theoretical Welfare Economics (Cambridge University Press, Cambridge).

Granaglia, E. (1994), Più o meno eguaglianza di risorse? Un falso problema per le politiche sociali, Giornale degli Economisti e Annali de Economia 53 (Abstract in English: more or less equality? A misleading question for social policy).

Grant, J.P. (1978), Disparity Reduction Rates in Social Indicators (Overseas Development Council, Washington DC).

Griffin, K. (1978), International Inequality and National Poverty (Macmillan, London).

Griffin, K. and J. Knight, eds. (1990), Human Development and the International Development Strategies for the 1990s (Macmillan, London).

Haq, M. (1976), The Poverty Curtain Choices for the Third World (Columbia University Press, New York).

Harsanyi, J.C. (1955), Cardinal welfare, individualistic ethics and interpersonal comparisons of utility, Journal of Political Economy 63: 309–321.

Hart, H.L.A. (1973), Rawls on liberty and its priority, University of Chicago Law Review 40.

Hawthorn, G. (1987), Introduction, in A.K. Sen et al., The Standard of Living (Cambridge University Press, Cambridge).

Hayek, F.A. (1960), The Constitution of Liberty (Routledge and Kegan Paul, London).

Herrera, A.O. et al. (1976), Catastrophe or New Society? A Latin American World Model (IDRC, Ottawa).

Herrero, Carmen (1995), Capabilities and utilities, mimeographed, (University of Alicante and IVIE, Spain).

Hossain, I. (1990), Poverty as Capability Failure (Swedish School of Economics, Helsinki).

ILO (1976), Employment, Growth and Basic Needs: A One-world Problem (ILO, Geneva).

Kakwani, N.C. (1986), Analysing Redistribution Policies (Cambridge University Press, Cambridge).

Kanbur, R. (S.M.R.), The measurement and decomposition of inequality and poverty, in F. van der Ploeg, ed., Mathematical Methods in Economics (Wiley, New York).

Kanbur, R. (1987), The standard of living: uncertainty, inequality and opportunity, in A.K. Sen et al., The Standard of Living (Cambridge University Press, Cambridge).

Kolm, S.C. (1969), The optimal production of social justice, in J. Margolis and H. Guitton, eds., Public Economics (Macmillan, London).

Le Grand, J. (1991), Equity and Choice (Harper Collins, London).

Lenti, R.T. (1994), Sul contributo alla cultura dei grandi economisti: liberta, disenguaglianza e poverta di Amarta K. Sen, Rivista Milanese di Economica 53.

Lipton, M. and J. van der Gaag (1993), Including the Poor (Johns Hopkins, Baltimore).

Little, I.M.D. (1957), A Critique of Welfare Economics, 2nd edn (Clarendon Press, Oxford).

Majumdar, M. and A.K. Sen (1976), A note on representing partial orderings, Review of Economic Studies 43: 543–545.

Marshall, A. (1890), Principles of Economics (Macmillan, London).

Marshall, G. and A. Swift (1995), Distributional justice: does it matter what the people think? in J.R. Kluegel, ed., Social Justice and Political Change (Aldine, Chicago).

Meade, J.E. (1976), The Just Economy (Allen and Unwin, London).

Mill, J.S. (1859), On Liberty (republished, Penguin, Harmondsworth, 1974).

Mill, J.S. (1861), Utilitarianism (London).

Morris, M.D. (1979), Measuring the Conditions of the World's Poor: The Physical Quality of Life Index (Pergamon Press, Oxford).

Muellbauer, J. (1987), Professor Sen on the standard of living, in A.K. Sen et al., The Standard of Living (Cambridge University Press, Cambridge).

Nozick, R. (1973), Distributive justice, Philosophy and Public Affairs 3.

Nozick, R. (1974), Anarchy, State and Utopia (Basic Books, New York).

Nozick, R. (1989), The Examined Life (Simon & Schuster, New York).

Nussbaum, M.C. and A.K. Sen, eds. (1993), The Quality of Life (Clarendon Press, Oxford).

Ok, E. (1995), Fuzzy measurement of income inequality: a class of fuzzy inequality measures, Social Choice and Welfare 12: 111–136.

Osmani, S.R. (1982), Economic Inequality and Group Welfare (Clarendon Press, Oxford).

Pant, P. et al. (1962), Perspective of Development 1961–1976. Implications of Planning for a Minimum Level of Living (Planning Commission of India, New Delhi).

Phelps, E.S. (1973) (ed.), Economic Justice (Penguin, Harmondsworth).

Piacentino, D. (1996), Functioning and social equity, mimeographed, (University of Urbino); presented at the Politeia meeting on 'Environment and Society in a Changing World: A Perspective from the Functioning Theory', 10 May 1996.

Pigou, A.C. (1920), The Economics of Welfare (Macmillan, London).

Rae, D. (1981), Equalities (Harvard University Press, Cambridge).

Ravallion, M. (1994), Poverty Comparisons (Harwood Academic Publishers, Chur, Switzerland).

Rawls, J. (1958), Justice as fairness, Philosophical Review 67.

Rawls, J. (1971), A Theory of Justice (Harvard University Press, Cambridge).

Rawls, J. (1993), Political Liberalism (Columbia University Press, New York).

Rawls, J. (1988a), Priority of right and ideas of the good, Philosophy and Public Affairs 17.

Robbins, L (1938), Interpersonal comparisons of utility: a comment, Economic Journal 48.

Roemer, J.E. (1985), Equality of talent, Economics and Philosophy 1: 151–181.

Roemer, J.E. (1996), Theories of Distributive Justice (Harvard University Press, Cambridge).

Runciman, W.G. and A.K. Sen (1965), Games, justice and the general will, Mind 74.

Samuelson, P.A. (1947), Foundations of Economic Analysis (Harvard University Press, Cambridge).

Schokkaert, E. and L. Van Ootegem (1990), Sen's concept of the living standard applied to the Belgian unemployed, Recherches Économiques de Louvain 56: 429–450.

Sen, A.K. (1970a), Collective Choice and Social Welfare (Holden-Day, San Francisco; republished by North-Holland, Amsterdam, 1979).

Sen, A.K. (1973a) On Economic Inequality (Clarendon Press, Oxford).

Sen, A.K. (1973b), On the development of basic income indicators to supplement GNP measures, United Nations Economic Bulletin for Asia and the Far East 24.

Sen, A.K. (1977), On weights and measures: informational constraints in social welfare analysis, Econometrica 45: 1539–1572.

Sen, A.K. (1979), Informational analysis of moral principles, in R. Harrison, ed., Rational Action (Cambridge University Press, Cambridge).

Sen, A.K. (1980), Equality of what? in S. McMurrin, ed., Tanner Lectures on Human Values (Cambridge University Press, Cambridge).

Sen, A.K. (1981), Poverty and Famines: An Essay on Entitlement and Deprivation (Clarendon Press, Oxford).

Sen, A.K. (1985a), Commodities and Capabilities (North-Holland, Amsterdam).

Sen, A.K. (1985b), Well-being, agency and freedom: the Dewey Lectures 1984, Journal of Philosophy 82.

Sen, A.K. (1987), The standard of living: Tanner Lectures on human values, in A.K. Sen et al., The Standard of Living (Cambridge University Press, Cambridge).

Sen, A.K. (1992), Inequality Reexamined (Clarendon Press, Oxford and Harvard University Press, Cambridge, MA).

Sen, A.K. (1993), Internal consistency of choice, Econometrica 61: 495–521.

Sen, A.K. (1995), Rationality and social choice, American Economic Review 85:1–24.

Sen, A.K. (1997), On Economic Inequality, expanded edition, with an Annexe by James Foster and Amartya Sen (Clarendon Press, Oxford).

Shorrocks, A.F. (1980), The class of additively decomposable inequality measures, Econometrica 48: 613–625.

Shorrocks, A.F. (1984), Inequality decomposition by population subgroups, Econometrica 52: 1369–1385.

Shorrocks, A.F. (1988), Aggregation issues in inequality measurement, in W. Eichhorn, ed., Measurement in Economics (Physica Verlag, New York).

Sidgwick, H. (1874), The Methods of Ethics (Macmillan, London).

Smith, A. (1776), An Inquiry into the Nature and Causes of the Wealth of Nations (republished in R.H. Campbell and A.S. Skinner, eds., Clarendon Press, Oxford, 1976).

Srinivasan, T.N. (1994), Human development: a new paradigm or reinvention of the wheel?, American Economic Review 84: 238–243.

Stewart, F. (1985), Planning to Meet Basic Needs (Macmillan, London).

Streeten, P. (1981), Development Perspectives (Macmillan, London).

Streeten, P. (1984), Basic needs: some unsettled questions, World Development 12: 973–978.

Streeten, P. and S.J. Burki (1978), Basic needs: some issues, World Development 6.

Streeten, P., S.J. Burki, M. Haq, N. Hicks and F. Stewart (1981), First Things First: Meeting Basic Needs in Developing Countries (Oxford University Press, London).

Sugden, R. (1981), The Political Economy of Public Choice (Martin Robertson, Oxford).

Sugden, R. (1986), Review of 'Commodities and Capabilities', Economic Journal 96.

Sugden, R. (1993), Welfare, resources and capabilities: a review of inequality reexamined by Amartya Sen, Journal of Economic Literature 31: 1947–1962.

Temkin, L.S. (1993), Inequality (Oxford University Press, New York).

Temkin, L.S. (1986), Inequality, Philosophy and Public Affairs 15.

Townsend, P. (1979), Poverty in the United Kingdom (Penguin, London).

UNDP (1990), Human Development Report 1990 (Oxford University Press, New York).

UNDP (1997), Human Development Report 1997 (Oxford University Press, New York).

Van Praag, B.M.S. (1968), Individual Welfare Functions and Consumer Behaviour (North-Holland, Amsterdam).

Van Praag, B. (1977), The perception of welfare inequality, European Economic Review 10: 189–207.

Van Praag, B. and A. Kapteyn (1973), Further evidence on the individual welfare function of income, European Economic Review 4: 33–62.

Williams, B. (1987), The Standard of Living: Interests and Capabilities, in A.K. Sen et al., The Standard of Living (Cambridge University Press, Cambridge).

Yaari, M.E. and M. Bar-Hillel (1984), On dividing justly, Social Choice and Welfare 1: 1–24.

Chapter 2

MEASUREMENT OF INEQUALITY

F. A. COWELL*

STICERD, London School of Economics

Contents

* This work is partially supported by an ESRC Grant No. R000 23 5725. I am grateful to Tasneem Azad, Ceema Namazie, Lupin Rahman and Silva Ule for research assistance, and to Ramses Abul Naga, Yoram Amiel, Tony Atkinson, François Bourguignon, Russell Davidson, Udo Ebert, James Foster, Joanna Gomulka, Stephen Jenkins, Serge-Christophe Kolm, Teresa Kowalczyk, Peter Lambert, Patrick Moyes, Amartya Sen, Jacques Silber, Maria-Pia Victoria-Feser and Shlomo Yitzhaki for valuable comments on earlier versions.

Handbook of Income Distribution, Volume 1. Edited by A. B. Atkinson and F. Bourguignon

Abstract

The analysis of inequality is placed in the context of recent developments in economics and statistics.

Keywords: Inequality, social welfare, income distribution

JEL codes. C13, D63

1. Introduction

1.1. Inequality and income distribution

Inequality measurement is a subject where much energy can be spent arguing about the meaning of terms. This is not a matter of taxonomy for the sake of taxonomy. The problem is that "inequality" itself—as with many other economic concepts—is not self-defining and the definitions applied may derive from sometimes sharply contrasted intellectual positions. Inequality measurement is an attempt to give meaning to comparisons of income distributions in terms of criteria which may be derived from ethical principles, appealing mathematical constructs or simple intuition. In this respect, it is similar to other methods of characterising and comparing income distributions to which it is closely related. For this reason we shall take into account some of these other concepts—such as the general principles of distributional ranking—rather than just concentrating on the inequality measurement in the narrow sense.[1]

    Given that we are to focus on comparisons of "income distributions", we should acknowledge straight away that this is itself a flexible term and in the present context may

---

[1] For previous contributions that have surveyed the properties of inequality measures see Champernowne (1974), Cowell (1995), Foster (1995), Jenkins (1991), Lambert (1993), Sen (1973), Sen and Foster (1997). A good general introduction to the welfare-economic issues is also to be found in Atkinson (1983).

be interpreted broadly to apply to distributions of other economic entities that share some of the same analytical constructs or empirical characteristics. This remark refocuses our attention on another basic issue: What is an income distribution?

There is a variety of stylised answers to this question. For the present exposition we will concentrate on two useful paradigms.

1.1.1. The Irene and Janet approach

The essential idea can be presented in terms of a very simple two-person economy, as depicted in Fig. 1, but this can be easily generalised in a number of ways.[2] Specifically, if one assumes that "income" conveys all that one might want to know about an individual's economic status, then the income distribution can be represented as a list of persons and a list of corresponding incomes: in the n-person version, if x_i denotes the income of person i, $i = 1, \ldots, n$ then a common approach to the issue is just to provide a corresponding ordered list of the incomes. In the simplest case the distribution is simply represented as a finite-dimensioned vector:

$$\mathbf{x} = (x_1, x_2, \ldots, x_n). \tag{1}$$

In the two-person case, the set of all feasible income distributions out of a given total income is illustrated by the shaded area in Fig. 1 bounded by a 45° line.[3] Other features of income distributions which it may be desirable to model can be fitted within this general framework. For example if different income-receiving units consist of families of differing size we might want to represent this by introducing a corresponding set of population weights for the observations, so that the distribution becomes an ordered list of pairs:

$$((w_1, x_1), (w_2, x_2), \ldots, (w_n, x_n)) \tag{2}$$

Clearly, either the single variable case (1) or the multivariable case (2) can be applied to any situation that may be modelled as a known, finite set of individuals.

1.1.2. The Parade approach

Alternatively, we could depict an income distribution using some aspect of the general statistical concept of a probability distribution. This is brilliantly captured by the famous story of the "parade of dwarfs and a few giants" related by Jan Pen (1971). The simple and compelling imagery of the parade—according to which each person's income is represented by his physical height—provides more than just an appealing parable for inequality in terms that a lay person can appreciate. It also suggests that welfare in a

---

[2] This is the approach commonly adopted in the modern theoretical work on income inequality: see, for example, Dasgupta et al. (1973), Sen (1973).

[3] The shaded area (other than the 45° line) consists of distributions where some income is thrown away. The counterpart to this line in the case of an n-person economy this is an $(n - 1)$-dimensional simplex.

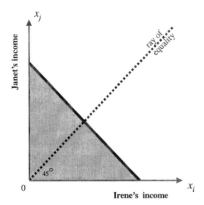

Fig. 1. The Irene and Janet approach to income distribution.

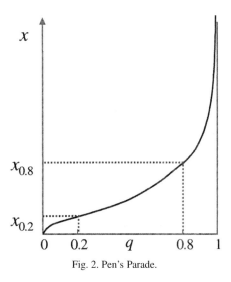

Fig. 2. Pen's Parade.

society can be expressed in the form of an "income profile" of members of the population. This idea is illustrated in Fig. 2: along the horizontal axis we measure proportions
of the population q, with income x along the vertical axis. The population is arranged
in ascending order of income ("height"), and the typical pattern shape of the resulting
profile is illustrated by the solid curve in Fig. 2: the points $x_{0.2}$ and $x_{0.8}$ give the income
("height") of the person who appears exactly 20 and 80% of the way along the Parade,
respectively.

   One reason that this is so useful is that we can immediately interpret ideas in inequality analysis in terms of analogous statistical concepts. By adopting the fiction that there
may be uncountably many income-receivers in the population, we obtain a device that

will permit a simple interpretation and implementation, and that is applicable to both discrete and continuous distributions. The Parade in Fig. 2 is a simple transformation of the statistical distribution function F (see Fig. 3). Trading on this important relationship we shall call this general approach the "F-form".

Which to use? Of course the two approaches are reconcilable. In effect, they are just alternative simplifying representations of an inherently complex subject. For reasons of both economic principle and statistical tractability, it is reasonable to apply each of the two approaches to different types of problems in distributional analysis. For example, the F-form approach can be especially useful in cases where it is appropriate to adopt a parametric model of income distribution and inequality; the Irene and Janet paradigm can be particularly convenient in approaches to the subject based primarily on individualistic welfare criteria, where a simplified, discrete representation of an income distribution is often appropriate. Because of the generality of the F-form[4] we will mainly use this in the discussion which follows.

These two analytical threads have been around for some time, as a brief glance at the history of the subject reveals. The line of argument pursued by Pigou (1912) and Dalton (1920)—who may be attributed to providing the basis for the welfare-theoretic approach to inequality—is based on the model-free Irene and Janet approach. In contrast, Pareto's (1896) insights on inequality comparisons were almost quintessentially those of a model-based approach to inequality; the seminal work of Gini (1912) and Lorenz (1905)—although originally formulated in F-form terminology—avoided the restrictions of the Paretian parametric approach and their insights are now commonly reinterpreted in terms of the Irene and Janet paradigm.

1.2. Overview

Perhaps it is appropriate to briefly mention what this chapter will not do. Because the primary focus is on inequality within a static framework, the broader issues of social welfare and poverty get a brief look-in, mobility and polarisation almost none. Furthermore, although we will consider issues of empirical implementation, there is no coverage of actual examples: one has to draw the line somewhere.

We will tackle the inequality-measurement problem within the general class of questions concerning distributional analysis. The order of attack will be as follows. Section 2 examines fundamental issues involved in representing the problem of inequality comparisons, and addresses questions of how we may represent an income distribution and the basis upon which distributional comparisons are to be made. The fundamental techniques of comparison in Section 3 lead to powerful and implementable criteria for ranking distributions. However, the general ranking criteria applied to income distributions—whether based on ad hoc methods or formal welfare economics—very

---

[4] Note that I do not claim it as more general than the Irene and Janet approach: it requires the use of a probability measure which will ensure that the anonymity axiom and population principle (see the discussion in Section 2.3) are automatically satisfied (see, for example Hoffmann-Jørgensen, 1994a, p. 100).

often result in indecisive comparisons. For some purposes it is desirable to have a unique inequality index, and we will consider the axiomatic and welfare-theoretic approaches to this in Sections 4 and 5. A number of ramifications and extensions of the basic analysis including the structure of inequality and multidimensional considerations and approaches are examined in Sections 6 and 7. Finally, Section 8 addresses the problems of empirical implementation.

2. Distributional judgements

A serious approach to inequality measurement should begin with a consideration of the entities to which the tools of distributional judgment are being applied: what is being distributed amongst whom? Many of these issues are well rehearsed in the literature and so we will only give a cursory treatment here touching on the points that bear directly upon inequality analysis.

2.1. Income and the individual

A coherent definition of "equality" in this context requires implementable definitions of income and of the income recipient. However, each of these concepts raises difficulties for the theoretician and practical analyst which should not just be brushed aside.

Even if we set aside the important theoretical difficulties associated with the definition of individual well-being, and the observation, measurement and valuation of assets,[5] there is an obvious gap in the meaning of "income": between an abstraction that represents "individual welfare", and a mundane practical concept such as "total family income" which may be dictated by accounting conventions. The standard approach to bridging this gap is to introduce an *equivalence scale* which defines a "rate of exchange" between conventionally-defined income y and an adjusted concept of income x—equivalised income—which acts as a money metric of utility. Imagine that a complete description of a family or household's circumstances other than money income can be given by some list of attributes $\mathbf{a}$ (age of each family member, health indicators, etc.), then we suppose that there is some functional relationship χ such that[6]

$$x = \chi(\mathbf{a}, y). \tag{3}$$

This relationship is usually expressed in the form

$$x = \frac{y}{\nu(\mathbf{a})}, \tag{4}$$

---

[5] For a discussion of the problems of valuing incomes see Fisher (1956), and on the issues raised by looking at the distribution of income rather than that of ability see Allingham (1972).

[6] The use of equivalised incomes can have major—and sometimes apparently bizarre—impacts on distributional comparisons (Glewwe, 1991).

where $\nu(.)$ is a function determining the number of *equivalent adults*. There is of course a range of difficulties associated with a specification such as Eq. (4). For example, it is not clear what the appropriate analytical basis for the function χ in Eq. (3) should be, nor even why there should be a proportional relationship between x and y.[7] An alternative approach to the modelling of needs is discussed in Section 7.

Again, the concept of "income recipient" is sometimes treated as though it was self-defining, when in practical application of inequality comparisons this is manifestly not the case. Given that the structure of conventional welfare economics is essentially based on the concept of the *individual person*, whereas data on income distribution is very often collected on a *family* or *household* basis, some transformation of income-recipient—logically separate from the equivalisation process (3)—is required for meaningful distributional comparisons to be made. In sum, if a dataset consists of household attribute-income pairs $(\mathbf{a}_i, y_i)$ then, in order to adduce the income distribution that is relevant according to individualistic welfare criteria, the standard approach requires that the incomes x_i in Eq. (2) should be the equivalised incomes found from a relationship such as Eq. (3), and the weights w_i in Eq. (2) should correspond to the number of persons in each household (Cowell, 1984; Danziger and Taussig, 1979), although alternative coherent views have been persuasively argued.[8]

2.2. Distributional concepts

We tackle the problem by introducing an abstract notation for the distribution that will encompass both the elementary Irene and Janet approach and also other important cases. It will also facilitate the development of the statistical approach to the analysis of income distributions.[9] Let $\mathfrak{F}$ be the space of all univariate probability distributions with support $\mathfrak{X} \subseteq \mathfrak{R}$, where $\mathfrak{R}$ denotes the set of real numbers and $\mathfrak{X}$ is a proper interval. We may use $\mathfrak{F}$ as the basis for modelling income distribution: $x \in \mathfrak{X}$ is then a particular value of income and $F \in \mathfrak{F}$ is one possible distribution of income in the population; so $F(x_0)$ captures the proportion of the population with income less than or equal to some value x_0 as shown in Fig. 3. The set $\mathfrak{X}$ is important, because it incorporates an implicit assumption about the logically possible values that x could adopt: in practice it will be determined by the precise economic definition of "income"—(see Section 8.1.1). In addition, we will write $\underline{x} := \inf(\mathfrak{X})$, and we use $\mathfrak{F}(\mu)$ for the subset of $\mathfrak{F}$ with given mean μ: we need this for the many cases in inequality measurement where we want to consider distributions

---

[7] On these issues see Coulter et al. (1992a) and Cowell and Mercader (1999). The ethical issues associated with equivalisation are considered in Sen (2000, Section 7), and the issues of estimation and implementation in Jäntti and Danziger (2000, Section 2.4) and Gottschalk and Smeeding, (2000).

[8] See, for example, Ebert (1995c, 1997d), Pyatt (1990); see also the discussion of this issue in Bruno and Habib (1976) and Ebert (1995a). The logic of using the family as a basic economic unit in this context is discussed in Bottiroli Civardi and Martinetti Chiappero (1995).

[9] See Section 8. Note that adoption of this analogy does not of course imply that an individual's income is stochastic. The analysis of inequality where incomes are stochastic—in particular the problems of reconciling *ex-ante* and *ex-post* concepts of inequality—is addressed in Ben-Porath et al. (1997).

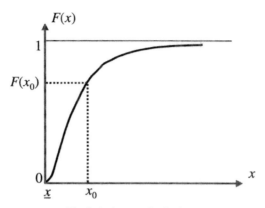

Fig. 3. An income distribution.

out of a fixed-size "cake". This basic framework can be extended to handle multivariate distributions (discussed further in Section 7 below), by introducing the corresponding space of r-dimensional probability distributions $\mathfrak{F}_r$ (so that $\mathfrak{F}_1 = \mathfrak{F}$).

The function F is our fundamental concept for economic and statistical approaches to the subject and represents a formalisation of the F-form concept of the income distribution introduced above (note that Fig. 3 is the inverse of—i.e., a simple rotation and reflection of—Fig. 2). The standard summary statistics of distributions can be easily expressed in terms of this concept. For example, the mean is a functional $\mu : \mathfrak{F} \mapsto \mathfrak{R}$ given by

$$\mu(F) := \int x \, dF(x). \tag{5}$$

Furthermore, using the concept of the F-function we can conveniently capture a very wide range of theoretical and empirical distributions, including some important special cases.

For example, if $F \in \mathfrak{F}$ is absolutely continuous over some interval $\mathcal{X}' \subseteq \mathcal{X}$ then we may also define the *density function* $f : \mathcal{X}' \mapsto \mathfrak{R}$ (see Fig. 4); if F is also differentiable[10] over $x \in \mathcal{X}'$ then f is given by

$$f(x) := \frac{dF(x)}{dx}. \tag{6}$$

In some cases, it is easier and more intuitive to work with f rather than with the corresponding F. On the other hand, the framework is sufficiently flexible to deal with cases

---

[10] Note that this is not a necessary requirement for f to exist. For example, the density could be positive everywhere, but discontinuous at some points.

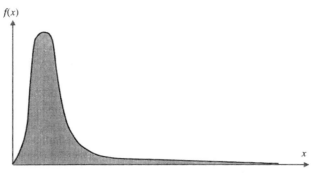

Fig. 4. The density function.

where F is not differentiable. For example, the elementary representation (1) can be expressed as:

$$F(x) = \frac{j}{n} \quad \text{if} \quad x \geq x_{[j]} \tag{7}$$

where $x_{[j]}$ represents the jth smallest component of Eq. (1).[11]

This basic framework for distributional analysis can be applied not only to inequality measurement, but also to other related issues such as social welfare and poverty comparisons. Each of these separate issues can be illuminated by considering the analytical linkages amongst them (Cowell, 1988b), (Foster and Shorrocks, 1998a, b).

2.3. Distributional and welfare axioms

Let us consider the key concepts that we use to compare distributions in the context of inequality measurement. First, let us use the term *inequality ordering* to mean a complete and transitive binary relation $\succcurlyeq_I$ on $\mathfrak{F}$;[12] if this ordering is continuous it can be represented as a functional $I : \mathfrak{F} \mapsto \mathfrak{R}$. Other distributional concepts to which inequality may be related can be similarly expressed. For example, a *social-welfare ordering* of

[11] If $x_1, x_2, \ldots, x_n$ are all distinct we can write Eq. (7) in a slightly more transparent form:

$$dF(x) = \begin{cases} \frac{1}{n} & \text{if} \quad x = x_1 \\ \cdots & \cdots \\ \frac{1}{n} & \text{if} \quad x = x_n \\ 0 & \text{otherwise} \end{cases}.$$

[12] This means $\forall F, G \in \mathfrak{F}$ either or both of the statements "$F \succcurlyeq_I G$", "$G \succcurlyeq_I F$" are true and, $\forall F, G, K \in \mathfrak{F}$, "$F \succcurlyeq_I G$" and "$G \succcurlyeq_I K$" together imply "$F \succcurlyeq_I K$". See, for example, the definition of strict order Fishburn (1970: p. 11) and ordering Suzumura (1983: p. 7) and, in the inequality context, the complete pre-ordering of Fields and Fei (1978). The representation of such an ordering by a continuous function follows from the classic work of Debreu (1954). However, representation results for some restricted types of orderings on subsets of the space of distributions can run into difficulties—see Wakker (1993).

distributions will be written $\succcurlyeq_W$; equivalently a *social-welfare function* (SWF) can be expressed in the form of a functional $W : \mathfrak{F} \mapsto \mathfrak{R}$. In each case the strict ordering part $\succ$ and the equivalence part $\sim$ will be defined in the usual way, and the properties of $\succcurlyeq_I$ and $\succcurlyeq_W$ will be determined by ethical principles or fundamental distributional axioms.[13] A brief overview of some of the standard axioms will be useful.

In our analytical framework, the first two basic assumptions that we need to make may be expressed in terms of an elementary vector-representation of a distribution (1). The first is very straightforward:

- *Anonymity.*[14]

$$(x_1, x_2, x_3, \ldots, x_n) \sim_I (x_2, x_1, x_3, \ldots, x_n) \sim_I (x_1, x_3, x_2, \ldots, x_n), \ldots.$$

This assumption—which is usually invoked for welfare orderings $\succcurlyeq_W$ also—states that all permutations of personal labels are regarded as distributionally equivalent. It requires that the ordering principle use only the information about the income variable and not about, for example, some other characteristic which might be discernible in a sample or an enumeration of the population. However, the axiom is neither trivial nor self-evident, and under certain circumstances for specific problems of distributional analysis it could make sense to relax it or modify its scope of application. For example, suppose one has information on a variety of income attributes of individuals: perhaps there is sufficient detail about personal circumstances to infer the bivariate income distribution $F(x_t, x_{t-1})$, where x_t is current income and x_{t-1} is income last period, then an analysis of the distribution of current income (only) that invokes the anonymity axiom is making the very strong assumption that $\succcurlyeq_I$ or $\succcurlyeq_W$ does not take account of the past (the marginal distribution of x_{t-1}), or of the links between the past and the present (for example, the correlation between x_t and x_{t-1}).

Similar considerations apply in situations where individual utility is presumed to depend both on income and on some other attribute which cannot be aggregated into the individual income concept.[15] In what follows we will assume that the distributional problem has been sufficiently well defined to make questioning of the anonymity principle unnecessary.

- *The population principle.* (Dalton, 1920)

$$(x_1, x_2, \ldots, x_n) \sim_I (x_1, x_1, x_2, x_2, \ldots, x_n, x_n) \sim_I \cdots$$
$$\sim_I (\underbrace{x_1, \ldots, x_1}_{m}, \underbrace{x_2, \ldots, x_2}_{m}, \ldots, \underbrace{x_n, \ldots, x_n}_{m}) \cdots$$

The population principle states that an income distribution is to be regarded as distributionally equivalent to a distribution formed by replications of it. Once again there

---

[13] See also Definition 1 below. The relationship between inequality and social welfare is discussed more fully in Section 5.

[14] Also known as symmetry.

[15] In this type of case, it may be appropriate to apply a more general version of the anonymity principle to the problem of multidimensional distributional comparisons. See, for example, Atkinson and Bourguignon (1982, 1987), Cowell (1985b) and Lambert and Yitzhaki (1995).

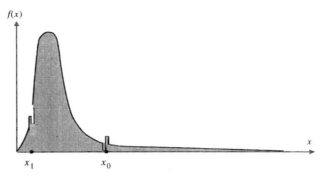

Fig. 5. A mean-preserving spread.

may be reasons for querying this principle under certain circumstances[16] but we shall not pursue them here.

These two axioms permit us to work with elementary distributions represented in the F-form. In particular they permit us to define an *equal* distribution, given that the concept of income and of income-receiver have been settled; this is the degenerate distribution $H^{(x*)}$ given by:

$$H^{(x*)}(x) = \begin{cases} 1 & \text{if } x \geq x^* \\ 0 & \text{otherwise} \end{cases} \tag{8}$$

which places a single point mass at x^*. But, of course, these two axioms do not get us very far by themselves. The following principle is usually taken to be indispensable in most of the inequality literature.[17]

- *Principle of transfers.* (Dalton, 1920; Pigou, 1912) $G \succ_I F$ if distribution G can be obtained from F by a *mean-preserving spread*.[18]

The idea of a mean-preserving spread is illustrated in Fig. 5 depicting two equal and opposite deformations of the income distribution at points x_0 and x_1. In the context of the Irene and Janet approach to distribution this principle can be represented thus: consider an arbitrary distribution $\mathbf{x}_A := (x_1, \ldots, x_i, \ldots, x_j, \ldots, x_n)$ and a number δ such that $0 <$

[16] See, for example, Cowell (1995: p. 56). This axiom is sometimes invoked also for welfare and poverty comparisons. The consistency of inequality comparisons across distributions with differing populations is discussed in Salas (1998).

[17] See, for example, Atkinson (1970, 1983), Cowell (1995) and Sen (1973).

[18] This is the way the axiom would be expressed if the ordering criterion were to be defined so as to correspond with an economic "bad" like inequality or poverty. For a "good", like social welfare, one simply reverses the sign: $F \succ_W G$ in the above definition. Note that Fig. 5 depicts a case where the two points of deformation are on opposite sides of the mean; of course the twin perturbations could occur on the same side of the mean. Note also that Dalton (1920) refined the concept of the transfer principle which was originally set out in Pigou (1912)—see Amiel and Cowell (1998); Castagnoli and Muliere (1990) give a broader interpretation of the transfer principle.

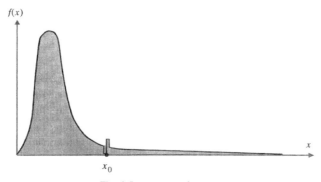

Fig. 6. Income growth at x_0.

$\delta < x_i \leq x_j$; from $\mathbf{x}_A$ we may form the distribution $\mathbf{x}_B := (x_1, \ldots, x_i - \delta, \ldots, x_j + \delta,$ $\ldots, x_n)$. The principle of transfers then ranks $\mathbf{x}_B$ as more unequal than $\mathbf{x}_A$.[19]

In addition to these principles, a large number of theoretical and empirical studies explicitly invoke additional axioms which may be motivated by principles of economic welfare or considerations of structure within the space of income distributions. The principal welfare axiom that bears upon distributional rankings may be expressed as:

- *Monotonicity.* $G \succ_W F$ if distribution G can be obtained from F by a rightward translation of some probability mass—see Fig. 6 in which this translation takes place at point x_0. In the Irene and Janet approach this can be represented thus: consider an arbitrary distribution $\mathbf{x}_A := (x_1, \ldots, x_i, \ldots, x_n)$ and a number $\delta > 0$; from $\mathbf{x}_A$ we form the distribution $\mathbf{x}_B := (x_1, \ldots, x_i + \delta, \ldots, x_n)$. The monotonicity principle then requires that welfare is higher in $\mathbf{x}_B$ than $\mathbf{x}_A$.[20]

To introduce the principal structure axioms, let $F^{(+k)}$ be the distribution derived from F by a shift or translation by an amount $k \in \mathfrak{R}$:

$$F^{(+k)}(x) = F(x - k). \tag{9}$$

Likewise, let $F^{(\times k)}$ be the distribution derived from F by transforming the income variable by a scalar multiple $k \in \mathfrak{R}_+$:

$$F^{(\times k)}(x) = F\left(\frac{x}{k}\right). \tag{10}$$

The following structural axioms are stated in terms of inequality, but could equally be applied also to welfare or poverty orderings.[21]

---

[19] Except for their ith and jth components the vectors $\mathbf{x}_A$ and $\mathbf{x}_B$ are identical.

[20] This axiom is commonly invoked also in the case of poverty orderings. Notice that it is similar, but not identical, to the Pareto criterion. The Pareto criterion is defined in terms of utilities rather than incomes, and will differ from monotonicity if individual utility functions are dependent on other people's incomes, as is reasonable in cases involving distributional judgments (Amiel and Cowell, 1994c).

[21] The terminology for the following concepts is not uniform throughout the literature. The terms "invariance" and "independence" are variously defined, and the particular interpretations of scale- and translation-

- *Scale invariance.* Given $F, G \in \mathfrak{F}(\mu)$ if $G \succcurlyeq_I F$ then $G^{(\times k)} \succcurlyeq_I F^{(\times k)}$.
- *Decomposability.* Given $F, G, K \in \mathfrak{F}(\mu)$ and $\delta \in [0, 1]$ then $G \succcurlyeq_I F$ implies $[1 - \delta] G + \delta K \succcurlyeq_I [1 - \delta] F + \delta K$.

This means that if the same distribution K is mixed with F and with G (where F, G, K all have the same mean) then ordering of the resulting mixture distribution is determined solely by the ordering of F and G—see also the discussion in Section 6.

The above list of axioms constitutes a brief summary of the standard approach to inequality measurement and associated welfare theory, and in Sections 3–5 we will see the role these play in making distributional comparisons and in determining an inequality index. However, it should be noted that in many cases reasonable alternative approaches are available. For example it could be argued that the monotonicity axiom is unacceptably strong; as an alternative we might require no more than the condition that welfare should increase if there were a uniform rightward translation of the whole distribution:[22]

- *Uniform income growth.* $k > 0 \Rightarrow F^{(+k)} \succ_W F$.

Again, in place of the scale-invariance concept it is sometimes argued that the following structural assumption is appropriate (Kolm 1976a, b):

- *Translation Invariance.* Given $F, G \in \mathfrak{F}(\mu)$ if $G \succcurlyeq_I F$ then $G^{(+k)} \succcurlyeq_I F^{(+k)}$.

In contrast to the standard axiom—where the inequality-contour map remains invariant under scalar transformations of income—this assumption ensures that the inequality-contour map remains invariant under uniform additions to income and under uniform subtractions from income; furthermore, "intermediate" versions of invariance can be specified (Bossert, 1988b; Bossert and Pfingsten, 1990; Kolm, 1969, 1976a, b).

Furthermore, other coherent approaches to inequality can be developed that do not assume the individualistic structure that is implied by acceptance of the transfer principle. For example, alternatives may be based on the concept of income differences—see Gastwirth (1974b), Kolm (1993) and Temkin (1986, 1993). These alternative approaches raise the question of what constitutes an "appropriate" axiom system for distributional comparisons. This issue has been investigated by questionnaire-experimental testing[23] which revealed that fundamental concepts such as the transfer principle do not correspond with the way in which people appear to make inequality comparisons in practice.

3. Ranking distributions

The basic concept in the comparison of income distributions is that of a *ranking* over the set of distributions $\mathfrak{F}$. This is more general than that of an ordering—as conventionally

---

invariance used here are often described as homotheticity and translatability and are to be distinguished from the corresponding concepts of independence introduced in Section 5.3.4.

[22] Note that monotonicity implies the uniform income growth principle but not *vice versa*.

[23] See, for example, Amiel (1999), Amiel and Cowell (1992, 1994b, 1998, 1999a, b), Ballano and Ruiz-Castillo (1992), Cowell (1985a), Harrison and Seidl (1994a, b) and Beckman et al. (1994); see also Kolm (1997c). Considerations of perceptions of income distribution also underlie recent interest in the topic of "polarisation" (Wolfson, 1994).

used in the analysis of individual preferences, for example—in that the idea encompasses "partial orderings" as well as orderings. Use the notation $\succeq_T$ to indicate the ranking that is induced by some comparison principle T. Then we need to distinguish three possibilities in any distributional comparison:[24]

DEFINITION 1. *For all* $F, G \in \mathfrak{F}$:
  (a) *(strict dominance)* $G \succ_T F \Leftrightarrow G \succeq_T F$ *and* $F \not\succeq_T G$.
  (b) *(equivalence)* $G \sim_T F \Leftrightarrow G \succeq_T F$ *and* $F \succeq_T G$.
  (c) *(non-comparability)* $G \perp_T F \Leftrightarrow G \not\succeq_T F$ *and* $F \not\succeq_T G$.

3.1. Formal and informal approaches

It is common practice in empirical studies to use informal easily computable ranking criteria; this typically takes the form of quantile rankings or distributional-shares rankings of income distributions. The use of these tools has a direct intuitive appeal: statements such as "the differential between the top decile and the bottom decile has narrowed" and "the share of the bottom 10% has risen", seem to be sensible ways of talking about inequality-reducing distributional changes. Furthermore, these basic ideas are related to other intuitive concepts in distributional analysis. For example, the *range*, $(x_{\max} - x_{\min})$, is sometimes used as an elementary—if extreme—inequality index, but the implementation of the range in practice may be as $(x_{0.99} - x_{0.01})$, for example.[25]

However, it is also possible to give rigorous theoretical support to these intuitive approaches. To do this we use the concept of the social-welfare function, introduced on page 96. In particular, we focus on a special class of SWF, those that can be expressed in *additively separable* form; these are given by[26]

$$W(F) = \int u(x)\, dF(x). \tag{11}$$

---

[24] Contrast this with the definition of an ordering given in note 12.

[25] For example, in Rawls' work on a theory of justice there is a discussion of how to implement his famous "difference principle" which focuses on the least advantaged. Rawls himself suggests that it might be interpreted relative to a particular quantile of the distribution (the median)—see Rawls (1972: p. 98). A number of useful pragmatic indices involving quantiles have been proposed such as the semidecile ratio (Wiles, 1974), (Wiles and Markowski, 1971) and the comparative function of Esberger and Malmquist (1972).

[26] Or a monotonic transformation of Eq. (11). The additively separable structure of W is quite a strong requirement. For example, if welfare and inequality are linked by a relation such as Eq. (32) below, then additively separability of W is stronger than the decomposability axiom of the inequality ordering (an additively separable W implies decomposability of $\succeq_I$ but not vice versa). Also note that Eq. (11) has the interpretation of "expected utility" where a representative person in the population regards it as equally likely that he should have any of the income-entitlements in the income distribution (Harsanyi, 1955). For a general discussion, see Broome (1991), Kolm (1996a, b), Roemer (1996) and Zajac (1996).

where $u : \mathfrak{X} \mapsto \mathfrak{R}$ is an *evaluation function* of individual incomes. Use the term $\mathfrak{W}_1$ for the subclass of SWFs of type (11) where u is increasing;[27] and use $\mathfrak{W}_2$ to denote the subclass of $\mathfrak{W}_1$ where u is also concave.

The SWF subclasses $\mathfrak{W}_1$ and $\mathfrak{W}_2$ will be found to play a crucial role in interpreting two fundamental ranking principles—first- and second-order distributional dominance[28]—and to have a close relationship with the intuitively appealing concepts of quantiles and shares.

3.2. First-order distributional dominance

First-order dominance criteria are based on the quantiles of the distribution that are yielded by the (generalised) inverse of the distribution function F. Let us make this more precise:

DEFINITION 2. *For all $F \in \mathfrak{F}$ and for all $0 \leq q \leq 1$, the* quantile functional *is defined by*[29]

$$Q(F; q) = \inf\{x | F(x) \geq q\} = x_q. \tag{12}$$

For example, $Q(F; 0.1)$ is the first decile of the distribution F, and $Q(F; 0.5)$ is the median of F. For any distribution of income F, the graph of Q describes, in formal terms, the concept of the Parade introduced in Section 1.1.2. This concept of the profile implies that if some persons "grow" (and nobody shrinks) social welfare also increases. In formal terms we may express these ideas by means of the following theorem (Quirk and Saposnik, 1962; Saposnik, 1981, 1983):

THEOREM 1. $G \succeq_Q F$ *if and only if,* $W(G) \geq W(F) \; \forall(W \in \mathfrak{W}_1).$[30]

---

[27] This specification is consistent with the assumption of the Pareto principle and the absence of externalities in the SWF—see Amiel and Cowell (1994c) for a discussion of the issues involved here.

[28] This terminology is inherited from the stochastic dominance literature (Bawa, 1975).

[29] See Gastwirth (1971). On the other hand the quantiles can be defined in the form of a correspondence. In this case, if the function F is not continuous the quantile may be a *set* of income values. Defining the collection of subsets of $\mathfrak{X}$:

$$\Xi := \{\{x : a \leq x \leq b\} : a, b \in \mathfrak{X}\}.$$

The quantile correspondence is

$$\tilde{Q} : \mathfrak{F} \times [0, 1] \mapsto \Xi,$$

such that

$$\tilde{Q}(F; q) = \{x : F(x) = q\}.$$

Cf. Kendall and Stuart (1977: pp. 39–41).

[30] See Definition 1.

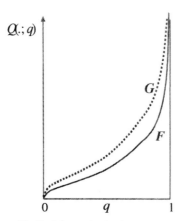

Fig. 7. *G* first-order dominates *F*.

This result means that the quantiles contain important information about economic welfare. If each quantile in distribution *G* is no less than the corresponding quantile in distribution *F*, and at least one quantile is strictly greater (as in Fig. 7), then distribution *G* will be assigned a higher welfare level by every SWF in class $\mathfrak{W}_1$.

3.3. Second-order distributional dominance

Unfortunately the first-order criterion—the ranking-principle $\succeq_Q$—has a couple of draw-backs. First, in practical applications, it is very often the case that neither distribution first-order dominates the other. Second, it does not employ all the standard principles of social welfare analysis: above all it does not incorporate the principle of transfers. For this reason it is useful to introduce the second-order dominance criterion.[31] The application of the second-order dominance criterion requires the following concept:

DEFINITION 3. *For all $F \in \mathfrak{F}$ and for all $0 \le q \le 1$, the* cumulative income functional *is defined by*

$$ C(F; q) := \int_{\underline{x}}^{Q(F;q)} x \, \mathrm{d}F(x). \tag{13} $$

Note that, by definition $C(F; 0) = 0$, $C(F; 1) = \mu(F)$, and that, for a given $F \in \mathfrak{F}$, the graph of $C(F, q)$ against q describes the *generalised Lorenz curve* (GLC) (see Fig. 8).[32]

---

[31] However, Bishop et al. (1991) argue that in international comparisons the second-order criterion $\succeq_C$ in Theorem 2 does not resolve many of the "incomparable cases" where $G \perp_Q F$.

[32] This terminology is not universal: Kolm (1969) refers to the graph of $C(F, q)$ as the "concentration curve" and Yitzhaki and Olkin (1991) uses the term "absolute Lorenz curve".

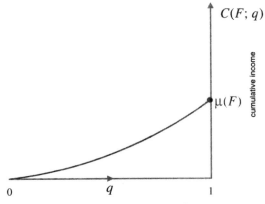

Fig. 8. The income-cumulation diagram.

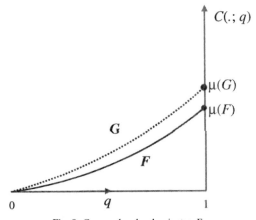

Fig. 9. G second-order dominates F.

The principal property of C can be summarised in the following theorem.[33]

THEOREM 2. $\forall F, G \in \mathfrak{F}$: $G \succeq_C F$ if, and only if, $W(G) \geq W(F) \ \forall(W \in \mathfrak{W}_2)$.

3.4. Tools for income distribution

The GLC is a fundamental tool for drawing conclusions about welfare from individual income data. Closely associated with it are other important tools of distributional analy-

[33] See Kakwani (1984), Kolm (1969), Marshall and Olkin (1979) and Shorrocks (1983). For more on GLC rankings and the relationship with first-order criteria, see Iritani and Kuga (1983), Thistle (1989a,b). For a discussion of the use of the GLC as a general criterion for ranking stochastic income streams, see Saposnik and Tutterow (1992).

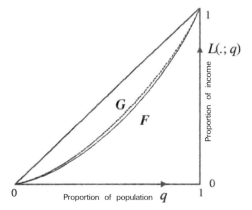

Fig. 10. G (relative) Lorenz-dominates F.

sis. Foremost among these is the conventional Lorenz curve (Lorenz, 1905)—or *relative Lorenz curve*—to distinguish it from other concepts with similar names.

3.4.1. The Lorenz ranking

To obtain the Lorenz ranking we normalise the cumulative income functional by the mean

$$L(F; q) := \frac{C(F; q)}{\mu(F)} \tag{14}$$

The Lorenz curve—the graph of $L(F; q)$ against q[34]—encapsulates the intuitive principle of the distributional-shares ranking referred to above: in Fig. 10 it is evident that the income share of the bottom $100q\%$ of the population must be higher in distribution G than in F, whatever the value of q.

The basic insights of Theorem 2 were originally obtained for distributions with a given mean $\mathfrak{F}(\mu)$:[35]

THEOREM 3. $\forall F, G \in \mathfrak{F}(\mu)$: $G \succeq_L F$ *if, and only if,* $W(G) \geq W(F)$ $\forall (W \in \mathfrak{W}_2)$.

---

[34] For a given F the first moment function $\Phi : \mathfrak{X} \mapsto [0, 1]$ is simply $\Phi(x) = L(F; F(x)) = \frac{1}{\mu(F)} \int_{\underline{x}}^{x} y \, dF(y)$ (Kendall and Stuart 1977). The general use of moment functions in measuring inequality is discussed in Butler and McDonald (1987).

[35] The principal reference is the seminal paper of Atkinson (1970) whose work was inspired by results in the stochastic dominance literature. However, based on the work of Hardy et al. (1934), Dasgupta et al. (1973) showed that the class of SWFs in Theorem 3 can be broadened to those that are S-concave but not necessarily additively separable. See also Arnold (1987), Fields and Fei (1978), Kolm (1966, 1968, 1969), Kurabayashi and Yatsuka (1977) and Rothschild and Stiglitz (1973).

3.4.2. Relative and absolute dominance

An alternative similar reinterpretation of Theorem 2 can be obtained by restricting the admissible SWFs to those in $\mathfrak{W}_2$ that have the additional property that proportional increases in all incomes yield welfare improvements:

$$\left\{ W \left| W \in \mathfrak{W}_2; \forall F \in \mathfrak{F}, k > 1 : W \left(F^{(\times k)} \right) > W(F) \right. \right\}. \tag{15}$$

Distribution G dominates F for SWFs in this restricted class if and only if G (relative) Lorenz-dominates F and $\mu(G) \geq \mu(F)$. Other special cases of Theorem 2 also yield useful insights. In particular, consider the welfare property analogous to Eq. (15) that uniform absolute increases in all incomes yield welfare improvements:[36]

$$\left\{ W \left| W \in \mathfrak{W}_2; \forall F \in \mathfrak{F}, k > 0 : W \left(F^{(+k)} \right) > W(F) \right. \right\}. \tag{16}$$

In this case, the counterpart to Eq. (14) is the *absolute Lorenz curve* (ALC) (Moyes, 1987):

$$A(F; q) := C(F; q) - q\mu(F). \tag{17}$$

Then, we find that $G \succeq_A F$ (see Fig. 11) and $\mu(G) \geq \mu(F)$ if, and only if, $W(G) \geq W(F)$ for all W that satisfy Eq. (16) (Shorrocks, 1983). The ALC is a particularly convenient tool for comparing distributions where a large proportion of the incomes are negative.[37]

3.4.3. Extensions

However, just as with the first-order criterion, one may often find in practice that second-order criteria are indecisive. In situations where Lorenz curves intersect there are essentially two routes forward.[38] The first is to supplement the restrictions on the class of SWFs (Eq. 11)—which means imposing a further restriction on the income-evaluation function; the second approach (discussed in Section 4) is to derive specific unambiguous indices of inequality. There is no shortage of additional restrictions that could reasonably be imposed upon the $\mathfrak{W}$-classes: one of the more useful is the so-called "principle of diminishing transfers" (Kolm, 1976a)—namely, that a small transfer from an individual with income x to one with income $x - \Delta$ (where Δ is some given absolute dollar amount)

---

[36] This is another way of stating the principle of uniform income growth (Champernowne and Cowell, 1998: p. 13) and is sometimes known as the incremental improvement condition (Chakravarty, 1990).

[37] If $\mu(F)$ is positive then the presence of negative incomes causes no problem for the relative Lorenz curve; but if there are so many negative incomes that $\mu(F) \leq 0$ then it is clear from Eq. (14) that there may be problems (Amiel et al., 1996).

[38] Basu (1987), following Sen (1973), argued that inequality comparisons are inhererently imprecise and that rather than seeking to make progress with incomplete partial orderings $\succeq$, one should approach the subject using the concept of a fuzzy binary relation. See also Ok (1995, 1996).

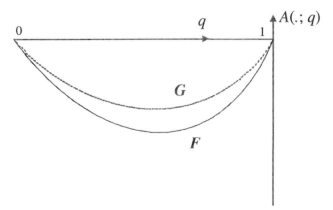

Fig. 11. G absolute Lornz-dominates F.

should have a greater impact on inequality the lower x is located in the distribution.[39] If this additional principle is invoked then a result is available for some cases where the Lorenz curves intersect.[40] This result is closely linked to a concept of "third-order" dominance (Shorrocks and Foster, 1987); an extension of the idea of dominance to an arbitrary order is discussed in Fishburn and Willig (1984) and Kolm (1974, 1976b), and Formby et al. (1996) discuss the topic of "normalised" dominance—essentially adapting nth-order dominance to $\mathfrak{F}(1)$, the subset of $\mathfrak{F}$ with mean unity.

4. An axiomatic approach to inequality measurement

As we have noted in Section 3.4, it is in the nature of general ranking principles that in many practical situations they yield an "indecisive" answer: "$F \perp G$". This is one reason why it is often considered desirable to go beyond the use of principles in order to derive practically implementable indices: specific examples of the inequality-measure concept introduced on page 96. The ways in which this step is to be done can be categorised roughly into three types of approaches:

---

[39] The principle is implied by the principle of "transfer sensitivity" (Shorrocks and Foster, 1987) which also goes by the name of "aversion to downside inequality" (Davies and Hoy, 1995), the latter based upon Menezes et al. (1980).

[40] Specifically $W(F) > W(G)$ for all SWFs in this restricted class if $F, G \in \mathfrak{F}$ have all three of the following properties: (i) $\mu(F) = \mu(G)$, (ii) var$(F) \leq$ var(G); and (iii) $\exists q^* \in (0, 1)$ such that $\forall q < q^*$: $L(F; q) > L(G; q)$ and $\forall q > q^* : L(F; q) < L(G; q)$—a single Lorenz intersection result (Atkinson, 1973; Davis and Hoy, 1994a, b; Dardanoni and Lambert, 1988; Muliere and Scarsini, 1989). Davies and Hoy (1995) extend the analysis to cases of multiple Lorenz intersections. Zoli (1998) discusses an extension of this to a "positionalist" interpretation of the principle of diminishing transfers (see Mehran, 1976 and Section 4.2, see also Subramanian, 1987).

- An ad hoc selection procedure for methods that may have a neat statistical or graphical interpretation.[41]
- The axiomatic approach which invites the "user" to specify what the basic principles are for comparing distributions; sufficiently tightly-specified principles may narrow down the range of tools to a small number of indices.
- The welfare-theoretic approach in which an explicit SWF is adopted as a basis for distributional judgment; an inequality measure may then be inferred from the specified SWF.

These three categories are by no means mutually exclusive. Rather they are complementary routes to a set of useful and implementable indices. It is appropriate to consider first the ad hoc and axiomatic approaches (there is little point in trying to separate them: it is nearly always possible to find some set of axioms to support the use of a particular ad hoc measure that happens to have intuitive appeal[42]) in order to see how properties of inequality indices can be linked to fundamental ideas about the meaning of inequality comparisons. The SWF route is considered in more detail in Section 5.

In all three types of approach we need the following basic concepts:

DEFINITION 4. *Two inequality indices* $I, \hat{I} : \mathfrak{F} \mapsto \mathfrak{R}$ *are* ordinally equivalent *if there is a function* $\psi : \mathfrak{R}^2 \mapsto \mathfrak{R}$, *increasing in its second argument, such that:*

$$\forall F \in \mathfrak{F} : \hat{I}(F) = \psi\left(\mu(F), I(F)\right). \tag{18}$$

DEFINITION 5. *An inequality index* $I : \mathfrak{F} \mapsto \mathfrak{R}$ *is* zero-normalised *if* $I(H^{(\mu)}) = 0$.[43]

DEFINITION 6. *Two zero-normalised ordinally equivalent inequality indices* $I, \hat{I} : \mathfrak{F} \mapsto \mathfrak{R}$ *are* cardinally equivalent *if the function* ψ *in Eq. (18) is linear in its second argument.*

Notice that the ordinal-equivalence relation embodied in the function ψ in Eq. (18) may depend on the mean of the distribution: this dependence will give rise to some problems of interpretation in Section 5.3.

---

[41] See, for example, the elegant and appealing interpretation of the Gini index described on page 112.

[42] For a discussion of these issues here, see Foster (1994).

[43] This normalisation—which means that inequality is zero for a distribution where everyone has the same income—can always be trivially ensured: for any measure I the zero-normalised index I^* is where $I^*(F) := I(F) - I\left(H^{(\mu(F))}\right)$. I and I^* will order all distributions in $\mathfrak{F}(\mu)$ in the same way. Sometimes great store is laid on normalisation such that maximum inequality is standardised at 1. Although this is of no great analytical significance it can always be arranged in the sense that, for a given I, an ordinally equivalent I^* can be found that is bounded in [0, 1]. Furthermore, if an inequality measure is bounded in [0, 1]. there are infinitely many ordinally-equivalent indices that are also bounded in [0, 1].

4.1. Insights from information theory

To obtain insights on the nature of income distribution comparisons one might reasonably look to the analysis of distributions in other fields of study. Using an analogy with the entropy concept in information theory Theil (1967) pioneered an approach to inequality measurement from which a number of lessons may be drawn for the axiomatic approach to inequality measurement.

4.1.1. The Theil approach

The information-theoretic idea incorporates the following main components (Kullback, 1959):

- A set of possible events each with a given probability of its occurrence.
- An information function ϕ for evaluating events according to their associated probabilities, similar in spirit to the income-evaluation function u in Eq. (11). The calibration of ϕ uses three key axioms: (1) if an event was considered to be a certainty ($p = 1$) the information that it had occurred would be valueless ($\phi(1) = 0$); (2) higher-probability events have a lower value ($p > p' \Rightarrow \phi(p) < \phi(p')$); and (3) the joint information of two independent events is the sum of the information of each event separately ($\phi(pp') = \phi(p) + \phi(p')$). These requirements ensure that the evaluation function is $\phi(p) = -\log(p)$.
- The entropy concept is the expected information in the distribution.

Theil's application of this to income distribution replaced the concept of event-probabilities by income shares, and introduced:

- A comparison distribution, usually taken to be perfect equality.

Given some appropriate normalisation this approach then found expression in the following inequality index (Theil, 1967):

$$I_{\text{Theil}}(F) := \int \frac{x}{\mu(F)} \log\left(\frac{x}{\mu(F)}\right) \, dF(x), \tag{19}$$

and also the following (which has since become more widely known as the *mean logarithmic deviation*):

$$I_{\text{MLD}}(F) := -\int \log\left(\frac{x}{\mu(F)}\right) \, dF(x). \tag{20}$$

4.1.2. A generalisation

However, in their original derivation, the Theil measures in Section 4.1.1 use an axiom (#3 in the abbreviated list above) which does not make much sense in the context of distributional shares. It has become common practice to see Eqs. (19) and (20) as two important special cases of a more flexible general class; in terms of the Theil analogy this is achieved by taking a more general evaluation function for income shares.

Then the *generalised entropy* (GE) family of measures (Cowell, 1977; Cowell and Kuga, 1981a, b; Toyoda, 1975) is given by

$$I_{GE}^{\alpha}(F) := \frac{1}{\alpha^2 - \alpha} \int \left[\left[\frac{x}{\mu(F)} \right]^{\alpha} - 1 \right] dF(x), \tag{21}$$

where $\alpha \in (-\infty, +\infty)$ is a parameter that captures the sensitivity of a specific GE index to particular parts of the distribution: for α large and positive the index is sensitive to changes in the distribution that affect the upper tail; for α negative the index is sensitive to changes in the distribution that affect the lower tail.[44] Measures ordinally equivalent to the GE class include a number of pragmatic indices such as the variance and the coefficient of variation

$$I_{CV}(F) := \sqrt{\int \left[\frac{x}{\mu(F)} - 1 \right]^2 dF(x)}, \tag{22}$$

standard statistical moments (Kendall and Stuart, 1977), and measures of industrial concentration (Gehrig, 1988; Hannah and Kay, 1977; Hart, 1971; Herfindahl, 1950).

However, the principal attraction of the GE class (Eq. 21) lies neither in the generalisation of Theil's insights, nor in the happy coincidence of its connection with well-known indices, but rather in the fact that the class embodies some of the key distributional assumptions discussed in Section 2.3.

THEOREM 4. *A continuous inequality measure* $I : \mathfrak{F} \mapsto \mathfrak{R}$ *satisfies the principle of transfers, scale invariance, and decomposability if and only if it is ordinally equivalent to Eq. (21) for some* α.[45]

4.1.3. The role of key axioms
The result of Theorem 4 might appear at first glance to have been produced like a conjuring trick. However, it is one of a number of similar results that can be generated by combinations of basic axioms listed in Section 2.3.[46] The decomposability assumption induces the additive structure, and the scale invariance (or homotheticity) property induces the power-function form of the income-evaluation function in Eq. (21). A simple

---

[44] Note that Eq. (21) is usually defined only on $[0, \infty)$ and is undefined for zero values of x if $\alpha < 0$; negative values of x can be handled in the very special case where α is an even positive integer. For the special cases $\alpha = 0, 1$ the general form Eq. (21) becomes Eqs. (20) and (19), respectively; see also Kuga (1973) and Foster (1983). Kuga (1979) examines the behaviour of these measures in a simulation study, and in a further contribution (Kuga, 1980) he shows that the experimental rankings of the Theil coefficient ($\alpha = 1$) are similar to those of the Gini coefficient—see Section 4.2. For recent reinterpretation of generalised entropy see, Chu et al. (1996) and Foster and Shneyerov (1997).

[45] See Bourguignon (1979), Cowell (1980b), Shorrocks (1980, 1984). Russell (1985) and Zagier (1982).

[46] These issues of structure are discussed in Blackorby and Donaldson (1978, 1980b, 1984), and Ebert (1988b). See also Sections 5 and 6.

generalisation of the approach illustrates how crucial to the determination of the general shape of the index is the invariance assumption. Apply the scale-invariance assumption to $F^{(+k)}$;[47] then Theorem 4 will yield the modified family of indices:

$$I_{\text{int}}^{\alpha,k}(F) := \frac{1}{\alpha^2 - \alpha} \int \left[\left[\frac{x+k}{\mu(F)+k} \right]^{\alpha} - 1 \right] dF(x) \tag{23}$$

We find that as $k \to \infty$ Eq. (23) adopts the form:

$$I_{\text{K}}^{\beta}(F) := \frac{1}{\beta} \left[\int e^{\beta[x-\mu(F)]} dF(x) - 1 \right], \tag{24}$$

where $\beta > 0$ is a sensitivity parameter.[48] The family of indices Eq. (24)—usually known as *Kolm indices* (Kolm, 1976a)—form the translation-invariant counterparts of the family Eq. (21) (Eichorn and Gehrig, 1982; Toyoda, 1980). The cases of Eq. (23) corresponding to $0 < k < \infty$ are usually known as *intermediate inequality* indices (Bossert and Pfingsten, 1990; Eichhorn, 1988).

4.2. Distance, rank and inequality

Of course the analysis outlined in Section 4.1 cannot be claimed as being the uniquely appropriate method of formulating an axiomatic approach to the analysis of inequality. It is also possible that considerable progress with alternative axiomatic approaches may be based on apparently pragmatic inequality-measurement tools: indices that have an appealing intuitive interpretation usually prove susceptible to the formulation of reasonably plausible systems of axioms.

We may illustrate this point with the *Gini index* which has long played a central role in the inequality literature. This index can be expressed in a number of equivalent forms:[49]

$$I_{\text{Gini}}(F) \quad : \quad = \frac{1}{2\mu(F)} \int \int |x - x'| \, dF(x) \, dF(x') \tag{25}$$

---

[47] This is equivalent to adopting the change of variable $z := x + k$ and assuming that the inequality rankings of distributions of z are scale-invariant; alternatively one shifts the origin from which one measures income from 0 to $-k$. The role of income transformations in defining inequality concepts and their relationship with social-welfare functions is discussed further in Ebert (1996, 1997b).

[48] See the discussion in Cowell (1998).

[49] Based on Gini's mean difference—see David (1968, 1981), Gini (1921), Glasser (1961), Helmert (1876) and Jasso (1979). There are other equivalent interpretations and formulae for the Gini coefficient and mean difference that are sometimes useful—see Berrebi and Silber (1984), de Finetti (1931), Dorfman (1979), Galvani (1931), Giaccardi (1950), Lerman and Yitzhaki (1984), Giorgi (1984, 1990, 1993), Stuart (1954) and Yitzhaki (1982b, 1998).

$$= 1 - 2 \int_0^1 L(F; q) \, dq \tag{26}$$

$$= \int x\kappa(x) \, dF(x), \tag{27}$$

where $x, x' \in \mathfrak{X}$ and $\forall F \in \mathfrak{F}, x \in \mathfrak{X} : \kappa(x) := \left[F(x^-) + F(x^+) - 1 \right] / \mu(F)$. The Gini coefficient has a number of practical advantages: for example it deals with negative incomes (Berrebi and Silber, 1985; Chen et al., 1982; Stich, 1996), and it satisfies both the scale-invariance and translation-invariance principles.[50] Furthermore, it suggests natural interpretations of income distribution and axiomatisation of inequality as may be illustrated by each of the above three forms:

- (Eq. 25) presents its standard interpretation as the normalised average absolute difference between all pairs of incomes in the population. It captures the idea of "average distance" between incomes in the population according to a particular definition of distance. Replacing this definition with an alternative concept of distance will yield other inequality measures: for example the Euclidean norm will yield a measure ordinally equivalent to the variance.[51]
- (Eq. 26) reveals its close link with the (relative-) Lorenz curve: the Gini is the normalised area between the curve and the 45° line in Fig. 10.[52]
- (Eq. 27) reveals a particularly important feature of the Gini coefficient: it is a weighted sum of all the incomes in the population where the weights $\kappa(x)$ depend on the *rank* of the income-receiving unit in the distribution $F(x)$.[53] This formulation has prompted a number of useful generalisations of the Gini coefficient—see Ben Porath and Gilboa (1994), Bossert (1988a), Donaldson and Weymark (1980, 1983), Weymark (1981), Yaari (1988), Yitzhaki (1983).[54]

[50] Such scale- and translation-invariant measures are sometimes known as *compromise indices* (Blackorby and Donaldson, 1980b). See Ebert (1988a) for a general characterisation based on the L^r metric in Hellwig (1982); see also Krtscha (1994), for a related index. Examples of the axiomatic approach in the context of Gini-type indices are: Bossert (1990), Milanovic (1994), Pyatt (1976), Ranadive (1965), Takayama (1979), Thon (1982), Tendulkar (1983) and Trannoy (1986).

[51] The distance concept in Eq. (25) can be seen as the counterpart of the ℓ^1 metric on $\mathfrak{R}^n$: $\sum_{j=1}^n |x_j - x'_j|$ for $\mathbf{x}, \mathbf{x}' \in \mathfrak{R}^n$. The Euclidean ℓ^2 metric is given by $\sqrt{\sum_{j=1}^n \left[x_j - x'_j \right]^2}$.

[52] Chakravarty (1988) and Shorrocks and Slottje (1995) suggested a simple generalisation of the Gini based on this formulation; see also Mehran (1976). For other measures based on intuitive interpretations of the Lorenz curve see Alker (1970), Alker and Russet (1964) and Basmann and Slottje (1987).

[53] In the case of continuous distributions $\kappa(x)$ simplifies to $(2F(x) - 1)/\mu(F)$. The intuitive interpretation is as follows. Imagine you have income x: then the number of persons below and above you are proportional to $F(x)$ and $1 - F(x)$, respectively. Let $\mathcal{E}$ be the expectations operator: given that $\mathcal{E}F(x) := \int F(x) \, dF(x) = \int_0^1 q \, dq = \frac{1}{2}$, we immediately see that the form (Eq. 27) is equivalent to $cov(x, F(x))/(\mathcal{E}x\mathcal{E}F(x))$. So the Gini coefficient is the normalised covariance of income and ranks in the population (Jenkins, 1988; Lerman and Yitzhaki, 1985; Stuart, 1954). It also happens that the Gini coefficient is the (normalised) Ordinary Least Squares slope of Pen's Parade.

[54] Other applications include the application of inequality to voting mechanisms treated as cooperative games: in this context Einy and Peleg (1991) argue a role for the generalised Gini of Weymark (1981).

5. Welfare functions

5.1. Insights from choice under uncertainty

As we noted in Section 4, the analysis of other economic problems involving probability distributions has served to inform the analysis of income distributions. So too with the topic of social welfare. The early modern literature on inequality measurement and the social evaluation of income distributions drew extensively on the parallel literature in the field of individual choice in the face of uncertainty, a cross-fertilisation which has continued.[55] The mapping from individual preferences over uncertain prospects into coherent utility functions, the formulation of riskiness and the concept of risk aversion, are all mirrored in the welfare analysis of distributional comparisons. Details of attitudes to risk are matched by "rightist", "centrist" and "leftist" interpretations (Kolm, 1976a, b) of attitudes to inequality associated with the structure of the contours of social-welfare functions. The resulting tools for distributional analysis are closely related to those already discussed in the context of the axiomatic approach.

5.2. Basic concepts

A social welfare function might not at first seem to be a very appealing basis for measuring income inequality. A welfare function—like utility functions in consumer theory—has an arbitrary cardinalisation; and even in the case of the special additive form (Eq. 11) the scale and origin of the evaluation function u are indeterminate. However, many may be persuaded by the idea that a more equitable income distribution would be a good thing, in which case one might reasonably expect to be able to construct a link between welfare theory and inequality measurement.[56]

However a simple transformation of the SWF yields a practical tool for distributional analysis: the *equally-distributed equivalent* can be defined as a money-metric of social welfare. Use the definition of an equal distribution $H^{(\cdot)}$—given by Eq. (8)—to provide an implicit definition of a number ξ such that

$$W(H^{(\xi)}) = W(F). \tag{28}$$

This can be used to yield the equally-distributed equivalent as a functional $\mathfrak{F} \mapsto \mathfrak{R}$; in other words, given a distribution F, $\xi(F)$ may be extracted from Eq. (28). The expression $\xi(F)$ is that income which, if it were imputed to every income-receiver in the population would yield the same level of social welfare as the actual income distribution

---

[55] See, for example, Atkinson (1970), Theil, (1967) and Yaari (1987, 1988).

[56] See, for example, Aigner and Heins (1967), Broome (1988), Dalton (1920) and Meade (1976); for a polemical case for equality as a social norm see Tawney (1964). Young (1994) sets income inequality in context with other notions of equity.

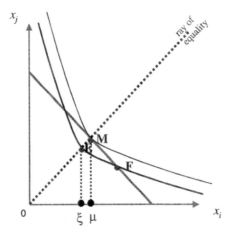

Fig. 12. The equally-distributed-equivalent is less than the mean.

F.[57] Figure 12 illustrates the idea. Let point F represent an income distribution in a two-person economy; then mean income μ can be found as the abscissa of the point M where the 45° line through F intersects the equality ray; the equally-distributed equivalent ξ is the abscissa of the point E where the W-contour through F intersects the equality ray. Clearly, the farther along the constant-total-income line is point F from perfect equality M, the lower is ξ; the normalised gap between ξ and μ then provides a natural basis for an inequality index:

$$I_A(F) := 1 - \frac{\xi(F)}{\mu(F)}. \tag{29}$$

The formulation (Eq. 29) permits a general approach to social-welfare values interpreted as aversion to inequality: for any given income-distribution the more sharply convex to the origin is the contour in Fig. 12, the greater is the gap between ξ and μ; in an extreme case, given that welfare is assumed additively separable (Eq. 11),[58] one would get situation such as Fig. 13 (Hammond, 1975).

However, in implementing this idea as a practical tool we need to address three specific issues:

- the derivation of an index;
- the nature of inequality aversion;
- the structure of the SWF.

[57] See Atkinson (1970) and Kolm (1969). The use of the equally-distributed-equivalent was anticipated by Champernowne (1952: p. 610).

[58] The restriction to the class (Eq. 11) is important. In the absence of this, other concepts of extreme inequality aversion could be introduced—see the discussion of "super-egalitarian" criterion in Meade (1976: p. 49), and the discussion of Fig. 14.

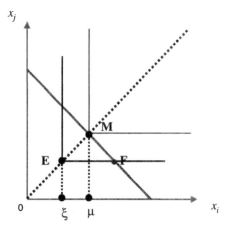

Fig. 13. Extreme inequality aversion?

5.2.1. The Atkinson index

To obtain a specific inequality measure we need to impose more structure on W. If we also require that the principle of scale invariance hold then ξ in Eq. (29) becomes a kind of generalised mean (Atkinson, 1970):[59]

$$I_A^\varepsilon(F) := 1 - \frac{1}{\mu(F)} \left[\int x^{1-\varepsilon} \, dF(x) \right]^{\frac{1}{1-\varepsilon}} \tag{30}$$

where $\varepsilon \geq 0$ is a parameter defining *(relative) inequality aversion*. A brief comparison of I_{GE}^α and I_A^ε (Eqs. 21 and 30) shows that they are ordinally equivalent—they will have the same shape of contours in $\mathfrak{F}(\mu)$—for cases where $\alpha = 1 - \varepsilon$.

Again it is clear that alternative sensible assumptions about structure and normalisation of W and ξ could be made which will induce alternative families of inequality measures: for example requiring that welfare comparisons satisfy translation invariance with a suitable normalisation will yield the "absolute" indices (Eq. 24) instead of the "relative" measures (Eqs. 21 and 30).

5.2.2. Inequality aversion

The inequality-aversion concept is clearly central to the Atkinson index (Eq. 30) and is implicit in the sensitivity parameters used in Eqs. (21) and (24). Two issues suggest themselves: How is the aversion to inequality to be interpreted? On what is it supposed to be based?

---

[59] Cf. the alternative approach by Chew (1983); see also Bossert (1988b) for the case where the strict scale-invariance assumption is replaced by a more general form of invariance. The limiting form of (30) as $\varepsilon \to 1$ is $I_A^1(F) := 1 - \exp\left(\int \log(x) \, dF(x)\right)$.

There are at least two ways of interpreting the idea of inequality aversion—or two types of inequality aversion—which may be summarised in the questions:

1. "How should transfers from the rich to the quite-well-off be ranked against transfers from the quite-well-off to the poor?"[60]

2. "At what rate should society be prepared to trade off equality against mean income?"

Question 1 is what is captured by the sensitivity parameter in Eq. (21); question 2 is the fundamental issue of political economy highlighted by Okun (1975) and others. The two questions are, in general, not identical (Cowell, 1985a) although sometimes the specification of the SWF obscures this point.

As far as the basis of inequality-aversion is concerned, we could consider it to be rooted in individual distributional judgments. These could take the form of the individual valuation of an externality involving other people's incomes or living standards (Hochman and Rodgers, 1969; Kolm, 1964, 1969; Thurow, 1971; Van Praag, 1977) or the form of risk perceptions (Amiel and Cowell, 1994a; Harsanyi, 1955). In the first case, inequality aversion is determined by the marginal utility of the externality, in the latter by risk aversion.[61] In both cases, social welfare can be taken as an embodiment of personal preferences, and it may be illuminating to investigate the strength of, and factors determining, inequality aversion.[62] An alternative approach is to suppose that social values, including inequality aversion, will be revealed by public policy decisions (Christiansen and Jansen, 1978; Stern, 1977), although this may run into the problems of falsely assuming coherence and rationality on the part of governments and their agents, as well as problems of specification of the SWF.[63]

5.2.3. The structure of the SWF

As we have seen, the derivation of the specific welfare-based index such as Eq. (30) required the introduction of some assumptions about the structure of W- or I-contours. However, there remains another important issue of structure of the SWF which will impact upon the interpretation of inequality aversion and the relationship between inequality and social welfare.

Consider a welfare function $\hat{W}$ derived from W in the following manner:

$$\hat{W}(F) = \Psi \left(\mu(F), W(F) \right),$$ (31)

---

[60] See the discussion of the related point for inequality measures in note 39.

[61] In this case, inequality measures can be interpreted as measures of riskiness of an income distribution (Dahlby, 1987).

[62] See Amiel et al. (1999), Gevers et al. (1979) and Glejser et al. (1977) for empirical studies on students; see also Van Praag (1977, 1978), Van Herwaarden et al. (1977) and Van Batenburg and Van Praag (1980) for an ambitious research programme focusing on welfare and inequality perceptions using a specific functional form for individual welfare functions.

[63] Guerrero (1987) suggests that, given the standard Atkinson-type evaluation function ("utility function") $u(x) = (x^{1-\epsilon} - 1)/(1 - \epsilon)$ in Eq. (30) one might determine use a Box-Cox (Box and Cox, 1964) method of estimating ϵ on the assumption that "utility" is normally distributed, but it is difficult to see why this data-driven statistical procedure should be appropriate to the selection of an essentially normative parameter.

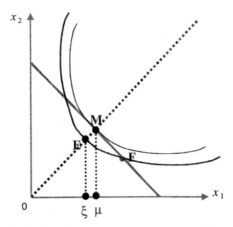

Fig. 14. Inequality aversion with a non-monotonic W.

where $\Psi : \mathfrak{R}^2 \mapsto \mathfrak{R}$ is increasing in its second argument. It is clear that $\hat{W}$ and W will have the same contours in $\mathfrak{F}(\mu)$, and therefore the same family of associated inequality measures, but also that they may have dramatically different responses to income growth:[64] the μ-dependent transformation Ψ will affect the implied trade-off between equality and mean income, and the choice of Ψ is not innocuous. To each distinct Ψ there will be a distinct value of type-2 inequality aversion, for any given type-1 inequality aversion.

What of the specific additive form of SWF (Eq. 11) that we used so extensively in the distributional ranking results of Section 3? It is clear that, despite its attractive simplicity of form and the fact that it can be supported by some a priori ethical arguments (see footnote 26 above), it is somewhat restrictive. First, there are some sensible systems of social values W for which there is no μ-dependent transformation Ψ such that $\hat{W}$ has an additive form.[65] Second, even where it is possible to find some Ψ that permits representation of a particular SWF in the form Eq. (11), insisting on additivity of the SWF may rule out some important aspects of social values.

For example if the SWF does not belong to the restrictive class given by Eq. (11) then it is possible that W may satisfy the principle of transfers, and the principle of uniform income growth, but violate the monotonicity principle. An example of this situation is given in Fig. 14. The distribution represented by point F is the same as in Fig. 12. By construction the equally-distributed-equivalent income—and hence inequality—is also the same as in Fig. 12; but it is evident that continually increasing one individual's income

[64] Consider for example the case where W is additive with scale-invariant contours and Ψ is simply the transformation by which one extracts $\xi(F)$ from $W(F)$ in Eq. (28), normalised by the mean: $\hat{W}(F) = \Psi(\mu(F), W(F)) = \xi(F)/\mu(F)$. W will increase with proportional increases in all incomes; $\hat{W}$ will not.

[65] See Newbery (1970). The additive separability assumption rules out "positionalist" welfare functions (Fine and Fine, 1974a, b; Gärdenfors, 1973).

has a dramatically different impact in the two cases: in Fig. 14 this raises social welfare if the individual has only a modest income, but may reduce welfare if the individual is already rich.

5.3. Social welfare and inequality

The SWF opens up an "indirect" approach to inequality. The mapping $W \to I$ presupposes that social values on distributional questions have already been settled,[66] and thus the "inequality map" is predetermined by the contours of the SWF. However the formal welfare-inequality link can be exploited in a number of other ways.

5.3.1. Reduced-form social welfare
Introduce the *reduced-form version* Ω of the SWF[67] implicitly defined by

$$W(F) = \Omega\left(\mu(F), I(F)\right), \tag{32}$$

where $\Omega : \mathfrak{X} \times \mathfrak{R} \mapsto \mathfrak{R}$ is increasing in its first argument and decreasing in its second argument; Ω encapsulates the concept of an equality-total-income trade-off (Dutta and Esteban, 1992). The form (Eq. 32) suggests some ways forward in examining the link between welfare and inequality, and some difficulties in the relationship.

For a start the relationship (Eq. 32) immediately opens the way for the discussion in welfare terms of ad hoc approaches to inequality measurement (Aigner and Heins, 1967; Bentzel, 1970; Champernowne, 1974; Kondor, 1975).[68] Even though a particular index may have been constructed for reasons of statistical convenience, mathematical elegance or seat-of-the-pants intuition, it may yet have interesting welfare properties that commend its use in a variety of applied welfare-economics problems.

Furthermore, from the relationship (Eq. 32) and the analysis in Section 4, it suggests that we might construct an approach to inequality in the "reverse direction". This $I \to W$ mapping is particularly useful when one has a clear idea on the basis for an inequality index and wants welfare rankings to be consistent with this inequality criterion, but otherwise is unable to specify a SWF completely—see Section 5.3.3.

Now for one of the principal difficulties. For a given Ω let $W^* := \Omega(\mu, I^*)$ denote the social-welfare functional corresponding to a given inequality functional I^*: the ordinal equivalence of I and I^* does not entail ordinal equivalence of W and W^* (Blackorby and Donaldson, 1984; Ebert, 1987).

[66] On the social-welfare basis for redistribution see, for example, Kolm (1995, 1997b), Roemer (1996) and Zajac (1996).

[67] This is the term used by Champernowne and Cowell (1998). See also the term "abbreviated social-welfare function" used in Lambert (1993: Chap. 5). See also Blackorby et al. (1981) who discuss the conditions under which W which is expressible in this form.

[68] For other approaches exploiting the connection between social welfare and inequality, see Dagum (1990, 1993).

5.3.2. The cardinalisation issue

It might seem that the ordinal properties of inequality measures alone contain the essentials of the problem. For example, given the ordinal equivalence of I_{GE}^{α} and $I_{\text{A}}^{\varepsilon}$, for $\alpha = 1 - \varepsilon$, we can mechanically transform one index into the other for any given distribution F using the formula

$$I_{\text{GE}}^{\alpha}(F) = \frac{\left[1 - I_{\text{A}}^{\varepsilon}(F)\right]^{\alpha} - 1}{\alpha\,[\alpha - 1]}. \qquad (33)$$

Need anything more be said? This over-simplification is misleading in two respects. First, cardinalisation has an important role to play in decomposition analysis (see Section 6). Second, as we have seen in Section 5.3.1, there are problems regarding the welfare interpretation of inequality measures.

Take the issue of interpreting inequality measures and consider the question: what constitutes an "important" change in inequality? The question is implicitly raised in, for example, comparative studies of the development of the income distribution over different time periods using an inequality index as a performance indicator. Here there appears to be a rôle for the social welfare function. For example, we could try using the welfare function to get an income-equivalent of a particular change in measured inequality using Eq. (29).[69] However, not only is a benchmark for numerical comparisons required ("is a 1% increase in the index 'big'?") but also a criterion for comparing the magnitude of one distributional change with another; the validity of a statement such as "inequality I increased more in period t_1 than it did in period t_2" is dependent on a particular cardinalisation of I;[70] but in order to interpret this in welfare-terms we need to make a non-trivial assumption about the structure of social welfare. To see this use the definition of ordinal equivalence for inequality measures (Eq. 18) and the reduced-form social welfare function (Eq. 32) to get the general relation:

$$W(F) = \Omega\left(\mu(F), \psi\left(\mu(F), I(F)\right)\right), \qquad (34)$$

from which we obtain:

$$\frac{\mathrm{d}\mu(F)}{\mathrm{d}I(F)} = -\frac{\psi_I}{\frac{\Omega_\mu}{\Omega_I} + \psi_\mu}, \qquad (35)$$

as the change in average income that exactly offsets a given inequality change. This income-equivalent depends on two factors:

---

[69] For a given change in I_{A} the method requires finding the offsetting change in μ that leaves $\xi(F) = \mu(F)\left[1 - I_{\text{A}}(F)\right]$ unchanged—see Cowell (1995, p. 132).

[70] To see this, consider I and $\hat{I}$ such that $\hat{I} = I^2$ and three distributions F_0, F_1, F_2 such that $I(F_0) = 0.8, I(F_1) = 1, I(F_2) = 1.19$: measure I indicates that $F_0 \rightarrow F_1$ is a greater change in inequality than $F_1 \rightarrow F_2$; measure $\hat{I}$ indicates the opposite. Note that, although it does not invoke the use of a SWF, the procedure suggested by Blackburn (1989) also depends on the cardinalisation of inequality.

- the inequality cardinalisation ψ;
- the shape of the reduced-form SWF Ω.

The first of these may be considered to be fairly arbitrary, and we will see some pragmatic arguments for particular "natural" inequality cardinalisations below; the second is not just arbitrary, but represents some basic social issues: the assumption of the additivity of W, or of the monotonicity of W, plays a fundamental role in the evaluation of inequality changes. Disentangling the two factors is inevitably problematic, and these issues impinge upon the topics considered next in Sections 5.3.3. and 5.3.4.

5.3.3. From inequality to welfare

The problem of building a full welfare function, or class of welfare functions, on the basis of a pre-specified inequality index requires additional information to fill an important gap. The principal point is that the conventionally defined ordinal inequality measure is defined on $\mathfrak{F}(\mu)$ and so, of itself, does not encode any information about what happens as one income increases. In particular we might wonder whether the resultant welfare function(s) satisfy monotonicity. In the *separable* case consisting of measures that are ordinally equivalent (in the sense of Eq. 18) to the form:

$$\int \phi(x)\, dF(x),\tag{36}$$

the issue is fairly transparent, if Ω and ϕ are differentiable. If the inequality measure I is cardinally equivalent to Eq. (36) then all we need to do is to ensure that a fairly mild condition on the slope of the reduced form welfare function is satisfied:

$$-\frac{\Omega_\mu}{\Omega_I} > \max\, \phi_x(x),\tag{37}$$

(where the subscripts denote partial derivatives); measures that are ordinally, but not cardinally, equivalent to Eq. (36) require a slightly modified form of Eq. (37). The nonseparable case is a little more difficult, since it includes indices such as the Gini coefficient which is non differentiable.[71] However, Amiel and Cowell (1997) demonstrate that a version of Eq. (37) applies as a bounding condition in this case too.

5.3.4. Inequality and growth

What happens to inequality as incomes grow? Apart from the practical question of whether the historical process of economic growth is typically accompanied by increasing income disparity (Kuznets, 1955) there is also an issue of interpretation: given a specific hypothetical change in one or more persons' income what would we "reasonably" expect to happen to inequality? (Fields, 1987; Glewwe, 1990; Kolm, 1976b).

---

[71] Examples of reduced-form Gini-SWFs in the literature include $n^2[1-I]\mu$ (Sheshinski, 1972), $\log\mu - I$ Katz (1972), and $\mu/(1+I)$ (Kakwani, 1986) all of which satisfy monotonicity, and $(1-I)\mu/(1+I)$ (Chipman, 1974; Dagum, 1990) which does not.

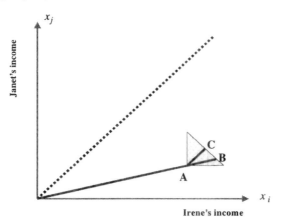

Fig. 15. Which direction leaves inequality unchanged?

The problem can be interpreted in standard individualistic welfare terms, as illustrated in Fig. 15: Suppose the income distribution currently is given by point A. In what direction from A should an increase in Irene's and Janet's incomes be made in order to keep inequality unchanged? Call this the *transformation direction*. Two obvious suggestions for the transformation direction would be $\overrightarrow{AB}$ (an equi-proportional increase in both persons' incomes) and $\overrightarrow{AC}$ (an equal absolute increase in both persons' incomes): but any direction in the shaded triangle would be valid. If there is a uniform transformation direction for all income distributions then this will induce a specific structure on the inequality measure: if inequality remains everywhere unchanged under scale transformations (like $\overrightarrow{AB}$ in the above example) this will force the inequality measure to be *scale-independent*, $I\left(F^{(\times k)}\right) = I(F)$; if inequality remains everywhere unchanged under translations (like $\overrightarrow{AC}$ in the above example) this produces a *translation-independent* inequality measure, $I\left(F^{(+k)}\right) = I(F)$.[72] More generally, we could imagine a general iso-inequality map where the transformation direction changed at different parts of the set of possible income distributions, such as the two examples in Fig. 16: case (a) depicts a situation where, at low incomes, equal absolute additions *increase* inequality, at moderate incomes there is (local) translation-independence, and at high incomes, equal proportional additions *reduce* inequality; case (b) depicts the situation suggested by Dalton, (1920) who argued that both absolute and proportionate additions to income would reduce inequality.[73]

Alternatively the relationship between inequality and income growth (or decline) may be taken as fundamental to the definition of the *meaning* of inequality: Temkin

---

[72] In general a uniform transformation direction will yield a form ordinally equivalent to Eq. (23) for $k \geq 0$. Note that the properties of scale- and translation-independence are stronger than those of scale- and translation-*invariance* introduced in Section 2.3.

[73] Questionnaire-experimental evidence suggests support for the Dalton view (Amiel and Cowell, 1999a).

(a)   (b)

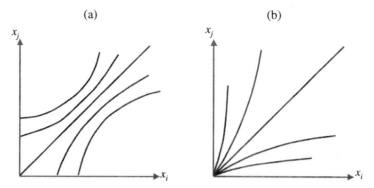

Fig. 16. Inequality maps: (a) a variety of transformation directions; (b) the Dalton conjecture.

(1986, 1993) has argued that inequality should be formulated in terms of "complaints", which Temkin further rationalises in terms of the changing pattern of income differences as individuals migrate between low- and high-income groups.[74]

5.3.5. Relative deprivation

Relative deprivation is a sociological concept whose social-welfare analytic counterpart may be seen as having grown out of the relationship between inequality measures and SWFs; it has some structural similarity to the formal work on poverty measurement (see Section 6.3.2).

In a sense, the economic insights on the topic of relative deprivation have made a virtue of the necessity of focusing on the Gini coefficient: the very features of the Gini that make it awkward for some branches of the modern literature on inequality (see, for example, Section 6) make it particularly attractive for embodying the relative depriva-tion concept of Runciman (1966).[75] Like the Temkin concept of complaint discussed in Section 5.3.4, relative deprivation seems to lend itself to a natural expression in terms of income differences: the rôle of rank in defining the Gini coefficient can surely be reinterpreted in terms of social disadvantage.

Suppose the relative deprivation experienced by a person with income x' is measured by

$$\int_{x'}^{\infty} \left[x - x' \right] \mathrm{d}F(x), \tag{38}$$

then the aggregated value of this over the distribution F is

$$\mu(F) - 2 \int_0^1 C(F; q) \,\mathrm{d}q, \tag{39}$$

[74] See also the "isolation" and "elitism" concepts in Fields (1993), Figini (1996) and the discussion in Fields (1998).

[75] However, for an alternative view, see Podder (1996).

which is simply $\mu(F)I_{\mathrm{Gini}}(F)$—the "absolute Gini".[76]

The form (Eq. 39) shows the close relationship between this interpretation of deprivation and GLC rankings (Hey and Lambert, 1980) and a number of straightforward generalisations of the concept have been proposed (see Berrebi and Silber, 1985, 1989; Chakravarty, 1998; Chakravarty and Chakraborty, 1984; Chakravarty and Mukherjee, 1997; Hey and Lambert, 1980; Stark and Yitzhaki, 1988; Yitzhaki, 1979, 1980, 1982a).

6. The structure of inequality

6.1. The basic problem

The discussion of the basic axioms of distributional analysis included decomposability as one of the fundamental properties that might be considered in the formal approach to income distribution. However, beyond its use in the specification of some convenient inequality tools and the discussion of the additivity of the SWFs, the issue of inequality decomposition raises a number of questions concerning the structure of distributional comparisons. These resolve into two major types of problem:

- *By population subgroup*. We assume that individuals may be distinguished by personal or group attributes which serve to partition the population into distinct subpopulations. This can be useful in the analysis of the relationship between inequality in a whole country and inequality within and between its regions, or between inequality in a heterogeneous group of persons and inequality within and between subgroups categorised by gender, ethnicity and the like. It is almost essential to attempts to "account for" the level of, or trend in, inequality by components of the population.
- *By income source*. For example, one might we wish to relate the inequality of total income to the inequality of income from work, inequality of income from property and so on.

In other words, the two types of decomposition involve looking at the structure of inequality by components of the population and by components of income. To implement either of these approaches one needs to recognise the multidimensional character

---

[76] Individual deprivation (38) may be written

$$\mu(F) - C(F; F(x)) - x + xF(x),$$

integrating this over the distribution F we get

$$= -\int_0^1 C(F; q)\,dq + \int_0^\infty x \int_0^x dF(y)\,dF(x);$$

a rearrangement of variables then gives Eq. (39).

of the underlying problem of distributional comparison, which will be discussed further in Section 7; in particular decomposition by income source is examined in Section 7.2.[77]

6.2. Approaches to decomposition by subgroup

Let a partition consist of a collection of a finite number J subgroups

$$\Pi = \{N_1, N_2, \ldots, N_J\}, \tag{40}$$

such that a proportion p_j of the population belong to subgroup j, $j = 1, 2, \ldots, J$; let $F^{(j)}$ be the income distribution in group j and $s_j := p_j \mu(F^{(j)})/\mu(F)$ be the income share of group j. Three issues need to be clarified:

- the exact requirements of decomposability;
- the type of partitions that are admissible;
- the nature of "between-group" inequality.

6.2.1. Types of decomposability
The definition of decomposability that we have used so far (see page 100) can be expressed in a number of equivalent forms. One of these is the *subgroup consistency* property which requires that inequality overall $I(F)$ can be rewritten in terms of any partition using the basic decomposition relation:

$$I(F) = \Phi\left(I\left(F^{(1)}\right), I\left(F^{(2)}\right), \ldots I\left(F^{(J)}\right); p_1, p_2, \ldots, p_J; s_1, s_2, \ldots, s_J\right), \tag{41}$$

where Φ is increasing in each of its first J arguments (Shorrocks, 1984, 1988). This can be seen as a minimal requirement for decomposability by subgroup: without this property one could have the remarkable situation in which inequality in every subgroup rises (while mean income and the population shares remain unchanged) and yet overall inequality *falls*. However, one might wish for a more demanding interpretation of decomposability, and so let us consider two ways of strengthening the subgroup consistency requirement.

Additive decomposability requires:

$$I(F) = \sum_{\substack{j=1 \\ \text{[within group]}}}^{J} \omega_j I(F^{(j)}) + \underbrace{I(F_\Pi)}_{\text{[between group]}}, \tag{42}$$

and

$$\omega_j = w(p_j, s_j) \geq 0, \tag{43}$$

---

[77] For a recent discussion and overview of the issues, see Deutsch and Silber (1999) and Morduch and Sicular (1996).

where the distribution F_Π will be discussed in Section 6.2.3.

One might perhaps require a yet more demanding interpretation of decomposability by adding to Eq. (42) the additional restriction

$$\sum_{j=1}^{J} \omega_j = 1 \tag{44}$$

which is perhaps an "accountant's approach" to decomposition: the weights in the within-group component sum exactly to 100%.

As we have seen in Section 4 if the basic consistency requirement is imposed for any arbitrary partition this will ensure that the measure must take a form that is ordinally equivalent (in the sense of Eq. 18) to the form (Eq. 36); so if one also requires the property of scale invariance one obtains the GE class (Eq. 21) and the weights in Eq. (42) take the form

$$\omega_j = \omega(p_j, s_j) = p_j^{1-\alpha} s_j^{\alpha}. \tag{45}$$

If one further requires the property (Eq. 44) then only two measures are available: the MLD index (Eq. 20) where the weights are population shares ($\alpha = 0$ in Eq. 45), and the Theil index (Eq. 19) where the weights are income shares ($\alpha = 1$) (Berry et al., 1981, 1983; Bourguignon, 1979; Cowell, 1980b; Shorrocks, 1980; Theil, 1979a, b; Yoshida, 1977).

6.2.2. Types of partition

In Section 6.2.1, we implicitly assumed that every sort of attribute partition Π of the population was valid. In some applications of decomposability it may be appropriate to consider a more restrictive subclass of partitions. In particular consider the concept of a *non-overlapping* partition in which all the constituent subgroups can be strictly ordered by their members' incomes; Fig. 17 illustrates this for the case $J = 2$: in case (a) every member of subgroup N_1 has an income less than any member of N_2; in case (b) N_1 "overlaps" N_2 in terms of income ranges (Ebert, 1988c).

In the light of this distinction, consider the problem of decomposing an inequality index excluded from the cases considered in Section 6.2.1: the case of the Gini index. It is well known that, in general, the Gini is not decomposable in the sense of sub-group consistency; if we attempt an exercise similar to that of Eq. (42); instead of a neat breakdown into two components we find three terms: a within-group component, a between-group component and an interaction term.[78] Whether the presence of this interaction term means that the Gini coefficient is "decomposable" in some more general sense is a moot point.

---

[78] See for example, Anand (1983, Appendix), Bhattacharya and Mahalanobis (1967), Fei et al. (1979), Mangahas (1975), Mehran (1975), Piesch (1975), Pyatt (1976), Rao (1969) and Silber (1989). For recent discussion on attempts to decompose the Gini coefficient, see Dagum (1997), and the discussion by Deutsch and Silber (1997) of Gini's concept of "trasvariazione" and the relationship to distance between income distributions.

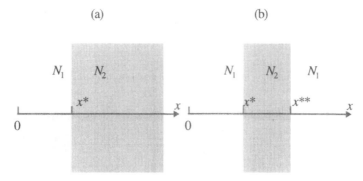

Fig. 17. (a) Non-overlapping partition; (b) overlapping partition.

What is particularly interesting to see is why, and under what circumstances, the Gini coefficient potentially gives rise to problems. Imagine that there is a small mean-preserving change in the distribution, let us say a transfer from a person with income x to someone with income x'. Inspection of the form (Eq. 27) of the Gini coefficient reveals that the effect of this depends on the expression

$$\kappa(x') - \kappa(x) = \frac{2}{\mu(F)} \left[F(x') - F(x) \right], \tag{46}$$

for continuous distributions. Contrast this to the corresponding impact of such a distributional change upon a measure that is ordinally equivalent to an additively separable index (Eqs. 18 and 36): it would be proportional to

$$\phi_x(x') - \phi_x(x). \tag{47}$$

Observe that Eq. (47) only needs minimal information about the specific affected income values x and x'; but for the Gini we find that Eq. (46) requires more detailed information about the distributions to which the affected persons belong: the effect of the transfer depends on the *rank* of the affected individuals in the relevant distributions. It is clear that the term $F(x') - F(x)$ will have the same value as $F^{(j)}(x') - F^{(j)}(x)$ if the relevant partition is non-overlapping (left-hand side of Fig. 17), but that the two values may differ if the partition is overlapping. For example consider x and x' in Fig. 17(b) so that $x < x^*$ and $x^{**} < x'$: clearly $F(x') - F(x) > F^{(1)}(x') - F^{(1)}(x)$. Now imagine a more complex mean-preserving change within $F^{(1)}$: the impact on the within-group Gini will depend on some aggregate of a collection of pairwise transfers like $F^{(1)}(x') - F^{(1)}(x)$, and the impact on the overall Gini will depend on the aggregate of the corresponding collection of pairwise transfers $F(x') - F(x)$. There is no guarantee that these two aggregates will have the same sign, so that the Gini of $F^{(1)}$ might decrease while the Gini of F increased. In sum, the Gini coefficient decomposes in the sense of Eqs. (41)

and (42) only if Π is non-overlapping, in which case the interaction term mentioned above will vanish.

6.2.3. Between-group inequality
What is the meaning of the between-group inequality component denoted by the distribution function F_Π in Eq. (42)? Perhaps the obvious answer is to suppose that the between-group distribution is a step function

$$F_\Pi(x) = \sum_{\ell=1}^{j} p_\ell \quad \text{if} \quad x \geq \mu\left(F^{(j)}\right), \tag{48}$$

where $\mu\left(F^{(1)}\right) \leq \mu\left(F^{(2)}\right) \ldots \leq \mu\left(F^{(J)}\right)$.[79] This is equivalent to assuming that all the probability mass in group N_j is concentrated at the mean $\mu\left(F^{(j)}\right)$. However, there are other possibilities. If the decomposable inequality index is explicitly based upon a social welfare function—such as Eq. (29)—then (Blackorby et al., 1981) suggest that the appropriate representative income for each subgroup is its equally-distributed-equivalent income $\xi\left(F^{(j)}\right)$ rather than the mean.[80] This decomposition scheme can be expressed by replacing the functional μ by ξ throughout Eq. (48); see also Foster and Shneyerov (1997).

6.2.4. The importance of decomposability
Decomposability of inequality might appear to be a luxury item, additional to other more basic criteria for selecting an inequality measurement tool. The issue of whether it is worth affording this luxury resolves into two questions:

- *Does decomposability matter?* Some commonly-used inequality measures do not satisfy even the minimal consistency properties such as the relative mean deviation[81]

$$I_{\mathrm{RMD}}(F) := \int \left| \frac{x}{\mu(F)} - 1 \right| \, dF(x), \tag{49}$$

  and the logarithmic variance

$$I_{\mathrm{logvar}}(F) := \int \left[\log\left(\frac{x}{\mu(F)} \right) \right]^2 \, dF(x). \tag{50}$$

  If these indices are used in empirical studies of inequality-decomposition it is difficult to avoid the conclusion that the wrong tool is being used for the job.

---

[79] Cf. Eq. (7).

[80] See also Ebert (1997a).

[81] See, for example, Cowell (1988a). The same difficulty affects other similar measures such as those suggested by Eltetö and Frigyes (1968) (see also Addo, 1976 and Schutz, 1951), and the variance of logarithms found by replacing the term $\mu(F)$ in Eq. (50) by the geometric mean. Moreover, the logarithmic variance and the variance of logarithms do not satisfy the principle of transfers everywhere (Cowell, 1995; Creedy, 1977; Ok and Foster, 1997).

- *Does a particular decomposition matter?* If one is concerned merely with the ordinal properties of inequality measures then the subgroup consistency requirement (Eq. 41) may be all that is required. However, Eq. (42) suggests a "natural" cardinalisation for decomposable measures, but the ordinal-equivalence function ψ in Eq. (18) can be used to derive to derive decomposition formulae for alternative cardinalisations (Das and Parikh, 1981, 1982). As we have seen, more than one logical way of defining the between-group components is available for a given partition, but it is important that the precise assignment of weights and the components in the decomposition are assigned in a fashion that is consistent under alternative partitions: for example, where one wants to carry out multilevel decompositions (say by age *and* gender *and* region ...), the within-group/between group definition in the finest partition should be consistent with that used in other, coarser partitions (age-and-region, or age alone perhaps) (Adelman and Levy, 1984; Cowell, 1985c). The type of decomposition that is appropriate—the cardinalisation, the partition, the definition of between-group inequality will ultimately depend on the economic question which one is trying to answer.

6.3. Applications

6.3.1. "Explaining" income inequality

Consider the problem of "accounting for" or "explaining" inequality alluded to on page 123. It seems intuitively reasonable that some specific partitions are more "important" than others in the analysis of a particular economy's income distribution. There are a number of ways of quantifying this (Cowell, 1984; Jenkins, 1995), and the framework of analysis in Section 6.2 should provide some help. For any distribution F and any partition Π consider the index

$$R(F, \Pi) := 1 - \frac{I_{\text{WITHIN}}(F, \Pi)}{I(F, \Pi)}, \tag{51}$$

where I_{WITHIN} is the within-group inequality component for a particular cardinalisation of inequality and a given definition of between-group inequality: in the case of a measure expressed in additively separable form this is the first term on the right-hand side of Eq. (42). Given two personal or social attributes a and b by which one might—separately or jointly—partition the population we obviously have

$$\left. \begin{array}{l} R(F, \Pi_{a\&b}) \geq R(F, \Pi_a) \\ R(F, \Pi_{a\&b}) \geq R(F, \Pi_b) \end{array} \right\}. \tag{52}$$

where, for example, $\Pi_{a\&b}$ refers to the fine partition by both attribute categories. Using the Atkinson-type inequality index (Eq. 30) for a variety of values of inequality aversion, Cowell and Jenkins (1995) show the impact on the R index of alternative assumptions about cardinalisation and between-group inequality, and that the amount of inequality "explained" by characteristics such as age, ethnicity and gender is relatively modest.

6.3.2. Poverty

As we have seen in the above discussion there are a number of connections between the modern theory of inequality measurement and poverty analysis (Cowell, 1988b; Le Breton, 1994; Osmani, 1982; Sen, 1976). One of the principal threads connecting the two is the structural analysis of the type considered in Section 6.

An operational approach to poverty requires the specification of a poverty line x^*: this may be an unique exogenously given value, some functional of the distribution F, or a set of possible values. Given x^* there is a fundamental partition of the population into poor and non-poor—a special case of the nonoverlapping partition discussed in Section 6.2.2. Now, in the case of the inequality applications that we have considered thus far, the anonymity axiom induces a symmetry of treatment of the component subgroups. However, in the case of the fundamental poor/non-poor partition this may be inappropriate: the nature of the poverty problem is such that one specifically wants to treat the members of the two groups differently. For this reason the *focus axiom* is introduced:[82] a perturbation of F that affects only the incomes of the non-poor should leave the poverty index unaltered.

Based on this the standard approach is to construct an ordering of distributions of poverty gaps $g := \max\{0, x^* - x\}$, a device which effectively filters out the (irrelevant) information about the non-poor (Jäntti and Danziger, 2000; Jenkins and Lambert, 1997; Shorrocks, 1998). The distribution of poverty gaps F^* is a simple transform of F, censored at the poverty line (Takayama, 1979), and many of the tools that are commonly applied to income distribution may be adapted to the problem of poverty measurement. Distributional dominance as discussed in Section 3 translate into criteria for poverty dominance (Atkinson, 1987; Foster and Shorrocks, 1988a, b) and standard families of non-overlapping-decomposable inequality indices translate into poverty indices (Foster, 1984; Blackorby and Donaldson, 1980a; Clark et al., 1981; Foster et al., 1984; Sen, 1976). As an example of the latter, consider the Foster et al. (1984) indices given by

$$\int \left[\frac{g}{x^*} \right]^a dF^*(g), \tag{53}$$

where $a \geq 1$ is a sensitivity parameter:[83] the family resemblance between Eq. (53) and the inequality indices (Eq. 21) and (Eq. 30) is evident.

---

[82] Notice that the anonymity axiom remains valid.

[83] The restriction $a \geq 1$ is required to ensure that Eq. (53) does not violate the principle of transfers: i.e., that a transfer from a poor person to someone less poor could not reduce measured poverty. However, the headcount ratio (which violates the principle) can be obtained as the special case of Eq. (53) where $a = 0$.

7. Multidimensional approaches

7.1. The general problem

As we have briefly noted in discussing the main body of analysis on inequality measurement, there is a good case for considering the problem of analysing income distributions as essentially one of multivariate rather than univariate analysis. That being the case we ought to consider as our fundamental tool a distribution function F—a typical member of $\mathfrak{F}_r$, the set of r-dimensional distributions; F is the joint distribution of variables $x_1, x_2, \ldots, x_r$. Let F_j be the marginal distribution of x_j and $\bar{F}$ the distribution of $\sum_{j=1}^{r} x_j$. Some aspects of the multivariate problem have already been developed in Sections 2.1 and 6.2 dealing with particular issues in the way households or families are to be distinguished by characteristics other than income; the remaining issues lie in three broadly defined areas:

1. The extension of ranking principles and measures (Bradburd and Ross, 1988; Flückiger and Silber, 1994; Maasoumi, 1986, 1989, 1999; Rietveld, 1990; Tsui, 1995).
2. Questions involved in multidimensional aggregation of income components (Maasoumi and Nickelsburg, 1988).
3. The applications of multidimensional analysis to general welfare criteria and to specific welfare-economic issues (Kolm, 1973, 1977; Foster et al., 1990).

The general problem (1 above) is inherently complex, principally because one has to take into account the interaction amongst variates, whether interpreted as the interrelations between income and non-income personal attributes, or as multiple components of income involved in a multidimensional generalisation of the Lorenz curve and related concepts (Atkinson and Bourguignon, 1982; Koshevoy, 1995). However, progress with interpretable results is possible in a number of interesting special cases. We will examine first the issue arising under item 2, and then two aspects of welfare economic issues (item 3).

7.2. Decomposition by income source

Assume that income x consists of two components; then, taking a bivariate distribution $F \in \mathfrak{F}_2$, we have by definition an elementary variance decomposition:

$$\text{var}(x_1 + x_2) = \text{var}(x_1) + \text{var}(x_2) + 2\text{cov}(x_1, x_2). \tag{54}$$

Using Eq. (54) we find that the standard inequality measure (Eq. 22) can be written as

$$I_{\text{CV}}(\bar{F})^2 = \lambda_1^2 I_{\text{CV}}(F_1)^2 + \lambda_2^2 I_{\text{CV}}(F_2)^2 + 2\lambda_1\lambda_2 I_{\text{CV}}(F_1) I_{\text{CV}}(F_2)\, \rho(F), \tag{55}$$

where $\lambda_j := \mu(F_j)/\mu(\bar{F})$ measures the "importance" in income terms of income type j, and $\rho(F)$ is the correlation coefficient for the bivariate distribution F. The technique can be extended with some elaboration to cases with $J > 2$ income components.

Of course it is not to be expected that other arbitrary inequality measures will have such a neat exact formula for decomposition by income source. However, it is interesting to see whether it is possible to assign a decomposition rule to determine the impact of the inequality of income component j upon the inequality of total income. There are two problems here. First, even in cases which appear to permit this sort of decomposition (typically those that can be written as a linear function of income) the result can be messy. For example there is considerable interest in applying the technique to the Gini coefficient (Podder, 1993, 1995; Sandström, 1983; Silber, 1989; Fei et al., 1978; Lerman and Yitzhaki, 1985; Pyatt et al., 1980; Stark et al., 1986, 1988); using Eq. (27) we get

$$I_{\text{Gini}}(F) = \int x\kappa(x)\, \mathrm{d}\bar{F}(x) = \sum_{j=1}^{J} \left[\int x_j \kappa(x)\, \mathrm{d}\bar{F}(x) \right]. \tag{56}$$

The term inside the brackets in Eq. (56) is typically used as the basis for specifying the "contribution" to inequality of income component j; but this term is not a true inequality index.[84] Second, without further restriction on the decomposition rule, the assignment of these inequality-contributions is non-unique (Shorrocks, 1982; Chakravarty, 1990).

7.3. Income and needs

Until now, we have assumed that the issue of differing needs could be handled by a transformation of the income variable. This is not entirely satisfactory because equivalence scales with different parameters or different methods of equivalisation could lead to dramatically different conclusions on welfare comparisons and because there is no generally accepted method of deriving a unique equivalence scale (Coulter et al., 1992b, 1994a, b; Jenkins and Cowell, 1993, 1994). An alternative approach would be to see how much can be said about distributional comparisons without precommitment to a particular equivalence scale.

Let us make use of the (attributes-income) method of describing individuals that we introduced in Section 2.1. Instead of assuming the existence of an equivalising function χ suppose instead that the population can be unambiguously partitioned into J different needs categories. Category j is a set N_j. Then a simple extension of the additive form of the SWF (Eq. 11) yields:

$$W(F) = \sum_{j} p_j \int_{\mathbf{a} \in N_j} u(y)\, \mathrm{d}F(\mathbf{a}, y), \tag{57}$$

where p_j is the proportion of the population that are of type j. This is no more than a relabelling. If we allow for the possibility that one has a "categorical" social evaluation

---

[84] This is usually known as a concentration coefficient (see Lambert, 1993: p. 50).

function—the income evaluation u also depends upon each person's needs category—we then would have:[85]

$$W(F) = \sum_j p_j \int_{\mathbf{a} \in N_j} u(j, y) \, dF(\mathbf{a}, y). \tag{58}$$

Assume that it is possible to label the needs categories j unambiguously and arrange them in descending order of need, independently of income. This requires that the marginal social-utility gap between needs levels become smaller at high levels of incomes; so for every category j, the expression

$$\frac{\partial u(j, y)}{\partial y} - \frac{\partial u(j + 1, y)}{\partial y}, \tag{59}$$

should be positive and decreasing in y.

Let us denote by $\mathfrak{W}_3$ the subclass of $\mathfrak{W}_2$ such that this condition on Eq. (59) holds. Then we can introduce the concept of *sequential generalised-Lorenz dominance*. Let $F^{(\leq j)}$ denote the distribution covering the subpopulation of the first j most needy groups. Notice the contrast here with subgroup-decomposition analysis: in Eq. (41) each observation in the income observation in the whole population appears in one and only one subgroup distribution; here if the attributes of a particular person i belong to N_j then his income will appear in the distribution $F^{(\leq j)}$ and also in $F^{(\leq j+1)}$, $F^{(\leq j+2)}$,.... .

Then we have:[86]

THEOREM 5. $W(G) \geq W(F) \; \forall (W \in \mathfrak{W}_3)$ *if, and only if*

$$G^{(\leq j)} \succeq_C F^{(\leq j)} \; \forall j = 1, 2, \ldots$$

Theorem 5 neatly extends the second-order-dominance criterion to the heterogeneous household case, although it is somewhat demanding since, apart from the stringent needs-ranking condition (Eq. 59), it also requires that the proportion of households in each of the needs categories is the same in the two distributions under comparison: this restriction has been relaxed in Jenkins and Lambert (1993).

---

[85] Cf. the "fundamental utility" in Kolm (1971, 1994, 1997a). If social welfare were expressed in Harsanyi-type terms (see footnote 14 above) then we can interpret Eq. (58) as:

$$W(F) = \sum_j \Pr\{\mathbf{a} \in N_j\} \, \mathcal{E} \left\{ u(j, y) | \mathbf{a} \in N_j \right\}.$$

The anonymity axiom applies within each needs category N_j but not between them (see the "partial symmetry" concept in Cowell, 1980b).

[86] See Atkinson and Bourguignon (1982, 1987) and also the general discussion in Bourguignon (1989) and Ebert (1997c).

7.4. Distributional change

The multidimensional approach to income distribution permits us to address a class of "from-to" questions that are a natural extension of the problem of inequality measurement. Perhaps the most obvious example of this class of question is the case highlighted on page 97: there may be substantial change in the distribution of income from period 1 to period 2, even though the two marginal distributions are identical; we may want to take into account *re-rankings* of individual income receivers in the distribution as well as changes in inequality at a point in time. This intertemporal aspect of the multivariate problem focuses attention on the concept of *mobility* (Fields and Ok, 1996, 1997), which may be useful in formalising important distributional concepts—such as the distinction between inequality of opportunity and inequality of outcome—that are logically separate from the issues on which we have focused in this chapter.

However, there are other important interpretations of the same idea. In the analysis of personal taxation systems one is also interested in rerankings of individuals induced by the operation of the tax schedule as well as any equalisation of the distribution of income that the tax system may produce (Berrebi and Silber, 1983; Ebert, 1995b; Jenkins and O'Higgins, 1989; Lambert and Ramos, 1997; Plotnick, 1981, 1982, 1985; Silber, 1995).

The way in which this class of problems may be addressed is to change the reference distribution from one of perfect equality to some given status quo distribution. So instead of the process

$$H^{(\bar{x})} \to F, \tag{60}$$

where $H^{(\bar{x})}$ is a notional state of primordial equality at $\bar{x}$ and F is the actual income distribution, one considers the process

$$F_1 \to F_2, \tag{61}$$

where F_1 and F_2 can be the "before" and "after" income distributions in a historical process, or the pre- and post-tax distributions. Cowell (1980a) shows how the ideas here are related to Theil (1967)'s insights on information theory, and a general axiomatisation of this class of problems is provided in Cowell (1985b).

8. Empirical implementation

8.1. Some general issues

The modern field of inequality measurement grew out of the intelligent application of quantitative methods to imperfect data in the hope of illuminating important social issues. The important social issues remain, and it is interesting to see the ways in which modern analytical techniques can throw some light on what it is possible to say about them.

A number of practical difficulties crop up throughout distributional analysis, some of which are common to applied statistics, and some which are associated with special problems that are characteristic of empirical income distributions (Sections 8.1.1 to 8.1.3 highlight some of the main issues).

8.1.1. Data problems

Apart from the routine problems associated with data collection and interpretation several issues arise from the nature of the problem of comparing income distributions. Empirical income distributions typically have long tails with sparse data, and are possibly highly aggregated in order to protect confidentiality—this issue is discussed further in Section 8.6. Difficulties with estimating what happens in the tails are further compounded by sensitivity of some estimation techniques and statistics to outliers and arbitrary truncation (Ben Horim, 1990; Nelson and Pope, 1990), and to the presence of negative or zero values.[87] Because of the way in which data are collected[88] estimates of the values of inequality indices and other distributional tools may be subject to the impact of data contamination (see Section 8.2.2).

8.1.2. The questions to be addressed

It is clear from the previous sections that there is a variety of tools that are of potential interest to a researcher working on income inequality. The appropriate way in which to address a specific question on income distribution may be to employ a single index, a family of indices, or a more general ranking principle. The standard approach is to use sample statistics as estimates of the "true" population values of the various numerical tools (see Section 8.2), and this strategy raises some basic questions about the type of test that will be appropriate when applying each of these types of tool. Clearly, the empirical implementation of a single index that induces a complete order on $\mathfrak{F}$ is likely to be relatively straightforward in comparison to the implementation of something like the Lorenz criterion, which induces a ranking but leaves open the possibility of non-comparability of distributions (see page 101).

8.1.3. Modelling strategy

Perhaps the simplest, and most appealing, approach to the implementation of the distributional concepts introduced above is to use microdata on incomes as though they represented a complete enumeration of a particular economy's income distribution. Using the raw data array in the form of Eqs. (1) or (2) appears to yield a straightforward

---

[87] This is basically a problem of the a priori specification of the support $\mathfrak{X}$: some interpretations of the "income" concept (expenditure, for example) explicitly rule out negative values, other interpretations (personal net worth, for example) allow them.

[88] It often happens that data providers will modify raw data so as to eliminate negatives or zeros (Jenkins, 1997) or to censor high incomes on the grounds of confidentiality (Fichtenbaum and Shahidi, 1988): this may amount to (well-meant) contamination of the data.

non-parametric approach to the analysis of income distribution. However, to do this is to sweep aside a number of statistical difficulties which we will consider in Section 8.2.[89]

An alternative approach to the problem is to develop an explicit model based on a parametric functional form. The functional form consists of two components:

- A general formula for a *class* of distribution functions $\mathfrak{F}'_1 \subset \mathfrak{F}$.
- A parameter vector $\boldsymbol{\theta}$ which distinguishes one element $F_\theta \in \mathfrak{F}'$ from another.

The empirical problem then consists of two parts: the specification of an appropriate functional form for the particular problem in hand, and then the estimation of the parameters of the selected functional forms according to appropriate statistical criteria. This is considered in Section 8.7.

8.2. Using sample data

The statistical approach to the subject exploits the analogy established between probability distributions and income distributions in Section 2.2. In this analogy, we take X to be a random variable which is distributed according to $F \in \mathfrak{F}$ where X is "income" and x is a particular realisation of X: the problem is to relate this abstract construct to the concrete objects in a real-world dataset. Of course it is only rarely that a microdataset represents a complete enumeration of an income distribution; typically we have to use a sample drawn from the distribution F; this is $F^{(n)}$, a distribution consisting of n-point masses, one at each observation in the sample. Fortunately several constructs that we have introduced in the abstract as appropriate tools for distributional analysis can be shown to be well-behaved when considering the relationship between the empirical representation and the underlying theoretical concept: for example, it can be shown that the empirical (sample) Lorenz curve converges to the population Lorenz curve (Goldie, 1977).[90]

8.2.1. Empirical measurement tools

The key concept that we require in empirical work is a *statistic*, which we have already met in other guises: in the case of univariate data a statistic is a functional T from $\mathfrak{F}$ to an appropriate range; for example, given the interpretation of the mean of a distribution in functional form (Eq. 5), the sample mean will simply be $\mu(F^{(n)})$. We may reinterpret other interesting entities used for distributional comparison—including inequality measures and ranking criteria—as statistics of a distribution. For a ranking or ordering $\succeq_T$ that embodies some given economic criterion T it is of particular interest to determine the properties of the corresponding statistic when applied to sample data.

---

[89] It is also an unsatisfactory approach to the modelling of income distribution in the form of a density function (Fig. 4); for discussion of the problems here see Cowell (1995: Chap. 5 and Appendix), and Silverman (1986).

[90] There are several useful results of this sort. For example, if we consider the inequality statistic $I(F^{(n)})$, introduced in Section 8.2.1, then, from the Glivenko-Cantelli theorem, as $n \to \infty$, $I(F^{(n)})$ converges to $I(F)$ (Hoffman-Jørgensen, 1994b, p. 105), (Victoria-Feser, 1999). On the convergence of the Lorenz curve, see also Csörgő and Zitikis (1995).

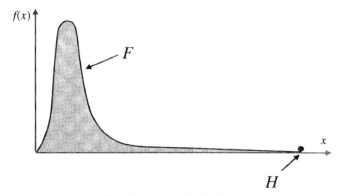

Fig. 18. A mixture distribution.

8.2.2. *Contamination and errors*

It would be idle to suppose that a carefully constructed sampling procedure will resolve the main practical problems of empirical implementation. One may reasonably suppose that, because of misunderstanding, misrecording or misreporting, some of the observations are just wrong, and this may have a serious impact upon estimates of inequality measures (Van Praag et al., 1983). There are two principal types of approach to this problem, which find counterparts in the theoretical work of Sections 6 and 7.

The first of these can be illustrated by the elementary case depicted in Fig. 18 where a mixture distribution has been constructed by combining the "true" distribution F with an elementary point mass at income z (see Eq. 8)

$$F_\delta^{(z)} = [1 - \delta] F + \delta H^{(z)} \tag{62}$$

as in the discussion of decomposability on page 100. The distribution $H^{(z)}$ represents a simple form of *data contamination* at point z, and δ indicates the importance of the contamination; $F_\delta^{(z)}$ is the observed distribution, and F remains unobservable.

Obviously if δ were large one would not expect to get sensible estimates of income-distribution statistics; but what if the contamination were very small? To address this question for any given statistic T one uses the *influence function* given by

$$IF(z; T, F) := \lim_{\delta \to 0} \left[\frac{T(F_\delta^{(z)}) - T(F)}{\delta} \right]. \tag{63}$$

Then, under the given model of data-contamination (Eq. 62) the statistic T is *robust* if IF in Eq. (63) is bounded for all $z \in \mathfrak{X}$. The simple rule of thumb is that first-order dominance criteria and most poverty indices are indeed robust, whereas most inequality measures and second- and higher-order dominance criteria are not; with such inherently non-robust tools it is important that consideration be given to the treatment of zeros and outliers by one's estimation method.[91]

The alternative approach is to consider that x is observed subject to measurement error. If this is so then presumably this will bias estimates of inequality (Chakravarty and Eichhorn, 1994). An informal argument based on the decomposition by income source in Section 7.2 illustrates this. What we actually observe is an income x which deviates from its "true" value $\tilde{x}$ thus:

$$x = \tilde{x} + v, \tag{64}$$

where v is the realisation of a random variable that captures the effect of errors in measurement. It is clear that the error-model (Eq. 64) has the same form as the source-decomposition problem in Section 7.2: the relationship between "true" and "apparent" inequality can be deduced from a formula such as Eq. (55).

8.3. A standard class of inequality measures

To make effective use of sample data on income-distribution one should have a full specification of the sampling distribution of inequality measures and other tools of distributional analysis. A general treatment of the problem requires a full book, but some of the main issues can be illustrated by restricting attention to a few important special cases of inequality measurement.[92] In order to make the analogies with the relevant statistical literature more transparent let us modify our notation by introducing the following family of weighted moments about zero

$$\mu_{j,\eta}(F) := \int w^j x^\eta \, dF(w, x), \tag{65}$$

where w is used to allow for the possibility of population weights, as in Eq. (2) above. The GE class of inequality measures (Eq. 21) can then be written[93]

$$I_{GE}^\alpha(F) = \frac{\mu_{1,0}(F)^{\alpha-1}\mu_{1,1}(F)^{-\alpha}\mu_{1,\alpha}(F) - 1}{\alpha^2 - \alpha}, \tag{66}$$

with appropriate limiting forms for the special cases $\alpha = 0, 1$.

[91] See the discussion in Section 8.7.3, and the results in Cowell and Victoria-Feser (1996a, b, c) and Monti (1991) whose approach is based on the work of Hampel (1968, 1974), Hampel et al. (1986) and Huber (1986). Notice that the problem may sometimes be generated by the procedures involved in collecting data (see footnote 87 in Section 8.1.1).

[92] For more details, see Cowell (1999).

[93] Note that in this notation moment $\mu_{1,0}$ can be interpreted as the "effective population size": if income-receivers are households and if the weight on each observation corresponds to the number of persons in each household, then $\mu_{1,0}(F)$ is exactly the number of persons in the population; if the weights are normalised by definition then $\mu_{1,0}(F) = 1$. Mean income is given by $\mu_{1,1}/\mu_{1,0}$.

8.3.1. Point estimates

To obtain the point estimates, assume that a simple random sample $F^{(n)}$ has been drawn consisting of n observations (w_i, x_i), $i = 1, \ldots, n$, where x_i is the income and w_i the weight of observation i. Cf. the specification in Eq. (7).[94] Then the sample-moment counterparts to Eq. (65) are

$$m_{j,\eta} := \mu_{j,\eta}\left(F^{(n)}\right) = \frac{1}{n}\sum_{i=1}^{n} w^j x^\eta, \qquad (67)$$

for any $j \in \{0, 1, 2\}$.

From Eqs. (65) and (67) a consistent estimator of Eq. (66) is then given by

$$\frac{1}{\alpha^2 - \alpha}\left[\frac{m_{1,\alpha}}{m_{1,1}^\alpha m_{1,0}^{1-\alpha}} - 1\right]. \qquad (68)$$

This approach can easily be extended to inequality measures that are ordinally equivalent to Eq. (66), to other fully decomposable inequality measures and to measures that are ordinally equivalent to the form:

$$\int \phi\left(\frac{x}{\mu(F)}\right) dF, \qquad (69)$$

which covers most of the specific indices introduced earlier. However, the Gini coefficient is a little more problematic; perhaps its most convenient form for computation is as a sample version of Eq. (27)—a weighted sum of the ordered incomes:[95]

$$\sum_{i=1}^{n} \kappa[i] x[i], \qquad (70)$$

where

$$\kappa[i] := \frac{w[i]}{m_{1,1} m_{1,0}}\left[2\sum_{j=1}^{i} w[j] - w[i] - 1\right], \qquad (71)$$

and $(w[i], x[i])$ is the observation with the ith smallest x-value in the sample.

---

[94] In the empirical distribution the weights usually play two roles: in addition to their use in reweighting the distribution by households to get the individual income distribution they may also incorporate sample weights: the weight for observation i is then $w_i = w_i' w_i''$ where w_i' is the ith observation's sampling weight and w_i'' is the household-to-individual weighting factor.

[95] Cf. Donaldson and Weymark (1980). On computational algorithms for the Gini, see Berrebi and Silber (1987), Lerman and Yitzhaki (1984, 1989) and Shalit (1985).

8.3.2. Inference

Now consider the problem of inference from microdata; for analytical convenience take first the class of scale-invariant, decomposable inequality measures. The basic result can be seen by examining the behaviour of $m_{1,\alpha}$, the sample estimate of $\mu_{1,\alpha}$, as an inequality measure which is essentially a non-normalised form of Eq. (66) with a sampling weight of unity for all observations.[96] We find:

$$\text{var}\left(m_{1,\alpha}\right) = \frac{1}{n}\left[\mu_{2,2\alpha} - \mu_{1,\alpha}^2\right], \tag{72}$$

$$\widehat{\text{var}}\left(m_{1,\alpha}\right) = \frac{1}{n-1}\left[m_{2,2\alpha} - m_{1,\alpha}^2\right], \tag{73}$$

$$\mathcal{E}\left(\widehat{\text{var}}\left(m_{1,\alpha}\right)\right) = \text{var}\left(m_{1,\alpha}\right). \tag{74}$$

From Eqs. (72)–(74) we can obtain a result for all measures ordinally equivalent to the GE class—see Eqs. (18) and (66). Define

$$\boldsymbol{\mu} := \left(\mu_{1,0},\ \mu_{1,1},\ \mu_{1,\alpha}\right) \tag{75}$$

and **m** as the sample counterpart of $\boldsymbol{\mu}$. Then the relevant class of inequality measures can be written as $\psi(\boldsymbol{\mu})$ and $\psi(\mathbf{m})$ in the population and the sample respectively (Cowell, 1989; Thistle, 1990). Given that:

$$\sqrt{n}[\mathbf{m} - \boldsymbol{\mu}]_{n\to\infty} \sim N(0, \boldsymbol{\Sigma}), \tag{76}$$

$$\boldsymbol{\Sigma} := \left[n\,\text{cov}(m_{1i}, m_{1j})\right]_{i,j=0,1,\alpha}$$

$$= \begin{bmatrix} \mu_{2,0} - \mu_{1,0}^2 & \mu_{2,1} - \mu_{1,0} & \mu_{2,\alpha} - \mu_{1,\alpha}\mu_{1,0} \\ \mu_{2,1} - \mu_{1,0} & \mu_{2,1} - \mu_{1,1}^2 & \mu_{2,\alpha+1} - \mu_{1,\alpha}\mu_{1,1} \\ \mu_{2,\alpha} - \mu_{1,\alpha}\mu_{1,0} & \mu_{2,\alpha+1} - \mu_{1,\alpha}\mu_{1,1} & \mu_{2,2\alpha} - \mu_{1,\alpha}^2 \end{bmatrix}, \tag{77}$$

where N denotes the normal distribution (Rao, 1973), we obtain as an asymptotic result:

$$\sqrt{n}[\psi(\mathbf{m}) - \psi(\boldsymbol{\mu})] \sim N(0, nV), \tag{78}$$

where

$$V := \frac{1}{n}\frac{\partial \psi^T}{\partial \boldsymbol{\mu}}\boldsymbol{\Sigma}\frac{\partial \psi}{\partial \boldsymbol{\mu}}, \tag{79}$$

$$\frac{\partial \psi}{\partial \boldsymbol{\mu}} := \left[\frac{\partial \psi(\boldsymbol{\mu})}{\partial \mu_{1,0}}, \frac{\partial \psi(\boldsymbol{\mu})}{\partial \mu_{1,1}}, \frac{\partial \psi(\boldsymbol{\mu})}{\partial \mu_{1,\alpha}}\right]^T. \tag{80}$$

---

[96] This is itself a valid non-normalised inequality measure for $\alpha > 1$ and $\alpha < -1$.

The quadratic form V in Eq. (79) is the asymptotic sampling variance of the inequality statistic, Σ is the variance-covariance matrix of the sample moments and ψ_μ encapsulates the role of the inequality-cardinalisation in the sampling variance. In applying this result to the case of the GE class (in its standard cardinalisation 21) we find:

$$\frac{\partial \psi}{\partial \mu} = \frac{1}{\mu_{1,1}^\alpha \mu_{1,0}^{1-\alpha}} \left[[\alpha - 1] \frac{\mu_{1,\alpha}}{\mu_{1,0}}, \alpha \frac{\mu_{1,\alpha}}{\mu_{1,1}}, 1 \right]. \tag{81}$$

The bottom right-hand term in Eq. (77) would be the only relevant term if the data were unweighted and one had independent information about the true mean of the distribution. The neighbouring off-diagonal terms show that, if the mean is to be estimated from the sample, then its covariance with the income-evaluation function must be accounted for; likewise the remaining off-diagonal terms in Eq. (77) illustrate the way individual weights are correlated with income (terms involving $\mu_{1,0}$) and with the income-evaluation function (bottom-left and top-right in the matrix): this correlation depends upon sample design and population heterogeneities which are inherent in inequality measurement. The variance of the inequality estimate in the case of weighted data could be larger or smaller than the corresponding variance in the unweighted case.

The normality of the sampling distribution (Eq. 78) means that it is straightforward to apply standard statistical tests to problems involving distributional comparisons. For example a straightforward difference-of-means test could be applied to test whether, or not, inequality in one year was higher than that in another.[97]

8.4. *Extensions*

The methodology of Section 8.3 can be extended to inequality indices that do not belong to the GE class such as the relative mean deviation (Gastwirth, 1974a) although the formulae for the standard errors are not so neat.

It can also be applied to order statistics which form the basis for empirical implementation of the Lorenz curve concept and so also to the Gini coefficient:[98] ordinates of Lorenz curves (regular, generalised or absolute) are basically the sum of order-statistics, or a simple function of such sums. Consider the estimation problem in this case. In drawing such a curve, one typically chooses a (finite) collection of population proportions $\Theta \subset [0, 1]$ and then for each $q \in \Theta$ computes

$$\hat{c}_q := C\left(F^{(n)}; q\right) = \frac{1}{n} \sum_{i=1}^{\text{int}(nq)} x_{[i]}, \tag{82}$$

---

[97] See Zheng and Cushing (1996) for a discussion of tests on marginal changes in inequality.

[98] The underlying theory of the sampling distribution of order statistics was developed by Hoeffding (1948)—see also Moore (1968), Shorack (1972) and Sillitto (1969). On the Gini coefficient, see also Gastwirth and Gail (1985), Glasser (1962), Nygård and Sandström (1981), Sandström (1982, 1983) and Sandström (1985, 1988).

using Eq. (13) where int(z) denotes the largest integer less than or equal to z. The set of pairs $\{(q, \hat{c}_q/q) : q \in \Theta\}$ gives points on the empirical generalised Lorenz curve, and $\hat{c}_1$ is the sample mean $\mu \left(F^{(n)} \right)$; the relative and absolute curves are found by a simple normalisation as in Eqs. (14) and (17). Under fairly mild conditions on the underlying distribution F the asymptotic distribution of the collection $\{\hat{c}_q\}$ is multivariate normal[99] (Beach and Davidson, 1983; Cowell and Victoria-Feser, 1998) and so standard tests are available for comparing distributions,[100] and it is possible to construct confidence bands for Lorenz curves and associated tools (Anderson, 1994; Beach and Richmond, 1985; Csörgő and Zitikis, 1996a, b). However, this procedure raises a further issue: given that one wants to *rank* distributions according to some criterion T (in the manner of Section 3—see Definition 1) rather than simply *ordering* distributions according to a unique index I then there are two logical ways of testing for T-dominance of distribution G over distribution F with a sample from each distribution using a set of population proportions Θ: (1) the null hypothesis is $T(G; q) \geq T(F; q)$ for some $q \in \Theta$ and the alternative hypothesis is $T(G; q) < T(F; q)$ for all $q \in \Theta$, (2) the null hypothesis is $T(G; q) \geq T(F; q)$ for all $q \in \Theta$ and the alternative hypothesis is $T(G; q) < T(F; q)$ for some $q \in \Theta$; which approach is preferable depends on the significance level and the power of the test (Howes, 1993).

8.5. Small sample problems

The asymptotic results in Section 8.3.2 may not be valid for some empirical applications for reasons that are readily apparent. First, it is often the case that the particular problem of economic interest requires a subsample that is of fairly modest size: the sample or subsample may be so small that the asymptotic results which are commonly invoked are invalid. The assumption is sometimes made that sample data on income distribution

---

[99] Beach and Davidson (1983) assume that F is twice differentiable. For any $q, q' \in \Theta$ such that $q \leq q'$ then the asymptotic covariance of $\sqrt{n}\hat{c}_q$ and $\sqrt{n}\hat{c}_{q'}$ is

$$n \left[q\sigma_q^2 + [qx_q - c_q] \left[x_{q'} - q'x_{q'} + c_{q'} - \frac{c_q}{q} \right] \right],$$

where x_q and c_q are the population quantiles and income cumulants

$$x_q := Q(F; q),$$
$$c_q := C(F; q),$$

(see Eqs. 12 and 13), and σ_q^2 is the conditional variance

$$\frac{1}{q} \int^{Q(F;q)} x^2 dF(x) - \left[\frac{c_q}{q} \right]^2.$$

[100] For applications of classical hypothesis testing to ranking criteria see, for example, Beach et al. (1994), Bishop et al. (1987, 1988, 1989a, b, 1991, 1994, 1997), Davidson and Duclos (1997), Stein et al. (1987) and Zheng (1996).

will, of their nature, have a large n so that in practice the issue of sampling error can be neglected as being of secondary importance. Second, some particularly sensitive indices (for example the coefficient of variation) have a standard error of estimate that it is very large even for apparently large samples. Under these circumstances it may be appropriate to use statistical methods which involve resampling with ("the bootstrap") or without ("the jackknife") replacement using the empirical distribution $F^{(n)}$ as raw materials.[101]

8.6. The problem of grouped data

Even though microdata are widely available today it is still necessary to work with grouped data on income distributions; if one wishes to examine historical data then the issue of grouping is almost unavoidable. Typically we have the following situation. The structure of the data imply that there is a partially specified income distribution of the form:

$$F(x) = \sum_{i=1}^{j} p_i, \ x = a_{j+1}, j = 1, 2, \ldots, J - 1.$$ (83)

However, detailed information on the distribution within each interval $[a_j, a_{j+1})$ is usually unavailable except that one sometimes has the information

$$\frac{1}{p_j} \int_{a_j}^{a_{j+1}} x \, dF(x) = \bar{x}_j \,,$$ (84)

the mean of the empirical distribution within interval j. The situation is as though one had a partition of the nonoverlapping form described in Section 6.2.2 with limited information about the within-group income distributions $F^{(j)}$. Furthermore, not only is information unavailable about the shape of the distribution in the top income interval $[a_J, a_{J+1})$, but the value of a_{J+1} is also usually left unspecified.

It is clear that this information structure will result in the loss of some important distributional information (Howes, 1996) and will complicate some standard statistical problems such as inference—see Gastwirth et al. (1986, 1989). However, there are a number of additional problems—special to this type of data—concerning the possibility of an appropriate assumed distribution $\tilde{F}^{(j)}$ in interval j:

- Is it possible to choose $\tilde{F}^{(j)}$ so as to put *bounds* on inequality estimates in the light of the partial information?

---

[101] Although bootstrap estimates have a smaller sampling variance than their jackknife counterparts, they are usually much more time-consuming computationally. For a discussion of the bootstrap and jackknife approaches see Bhattacharya and Qumsiyeh (1989), Csörgő and Mason (1989), Efron (1979, 1982), Efron and Tibshirani (1993), Hall (1982), Rubin (1981) and Shao and Tu (1995); see also Kish and Frankel (1970) for a discussion of cases where samples are complex. However, the bootstrap does not work in every case, especially when—as with relative Lorenz ordinates—the statistic to be bootstrapped is bounded; see Schenker (1985) and Andrews (1997). For an application of the bootstrap and jackknife to inequality statistics, see Efron and Stein (1981), Maasoumi et al. (1997), Mills and Zandvakili (1997) and Yitzhaki (1991).

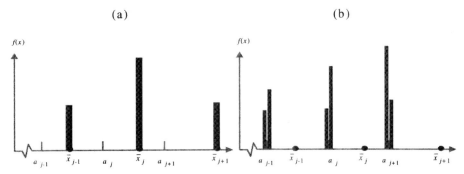

Fig. 19. Assumed distribution for (a) lower-bound inequality, (b) upper-bound inequality.

- Are there appropriate interpolation methods to fit *compromise* estimates $\tilde{F}^{(j)}$ of the underlying distribution?
- How is one to choose $\tilde{F}^{(J)}$ so as to handle the problem of the open-ended interval $[a_J, \infty)$?[102]

8.6.1. *The bounding problem*

Unsophisticated methods of choosing $\tilde{F}^{(j)}$ to obtain bounding values of inequality measures are easily obtained. Given the information (Eqs. 83, 84) the lower bound on inequality is found by assigning a point mass p_j at point $\bar{x}_j$ in each closed interval j, and the upper bound is found by assigning a point mass λp_j at the lower boundary a_j and a point mass $[1 - \lambda]p_j$ at the upper boundary a_{j+1} of each closed interval j where $\lambda := (a_{j+1} - \bar{x}_j)/(a_{j+1} - a_j)$—see Fig. 19.

If it is legitimate to make more specific assumptions about $F^{(j)}$, the unknown distribution within a particular interval $[a_j, a_{j+1})$, namely that there is decreasing frequency over that interval, then it is possible to obtain more refined bounds on the values of measures that have the additively separable form (Eq. 36). For the refined lower-bound value of inequality the assumed distribution $\tilde{F}^{(j)}$ within the interval is assumed to be rectangular over the subinterval $[a_j, 2\mu_j - a_j)$ and zero elsewhere; the refined upper-bound case is found by supposing $\tilde{F}^{(j)}$ to consist of a point mass $p_j[a_{j+1} + a_j - 2\bar{x}_j][a_{j+1} - a_j]^{-1}$ at a_j and a rectangular distribution $2p_j[\bar{x}_j - a_j][a_{j+1} - a_j]^{-2}$ over (a_j, a_{j+1})—see Fig. 20 (Gastwirth, 1975). Other bounding results are obtainable for alternative assumptions about the amount of information available about the grouped income data (Cowell, 1991; Gastwirth, 1972; McDonald and Ransom, 1981; Murray, 1978).

---

[102] In some cases a_1 is left unspecified so that a similar problem arises with $\tilde{F}^{(1)}$.

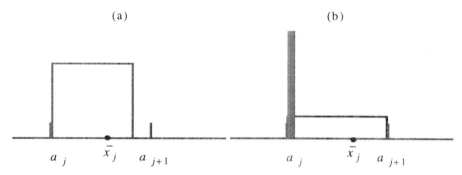

Fig. 20. Assumed distribution for refined bounds: (a) lower, (b) upper.

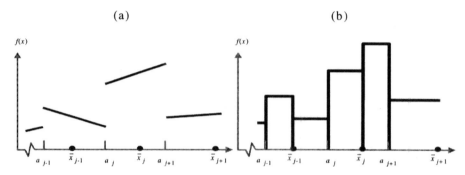

Fig. 21. (a) Linear and (b) Split-histogram interpolation.

8.6.2. *Interpolation methods*

If one were trying to choose $\tilde{F}^{(j)}$ to obtain a compromise estimate of inequality what type of restrictions on the distribution would it be reasonable to impose? It might be that essentially aesthetic properties—such as smoothness or flexibility of form of $\tilde{F}^{(j)}$, or continuity of the implied density across interval boundaries, or familiarity of the functional form used in interpolation—appear as particularly attractive. However, relatively simple interpolation schemes—such as those depicted[103]—actually perform as well as more elegant formulae (Cowell and Mehta, 1982; Gastwirth and Glauberman, 1976). What is far more important than the detail of the interpolation formula is the fineness of the information provided by the data source.[104]

---

[103] In Fig. 21(a) the interpolation formula is piecewise linear with discontinuities at the interval boundaries a_j; in Fig. 21(b) the interpolation formula is piecewise rectangular in the subintervals $[a_j, \bar{x}_j)$ and $[\bar{x}_j, a_{j+1})$– see Cowell and Mehta (1982) for details.

[104] The question of optimal grouping by data providers is discussed by Aghevli and Mehran (1981) and Davies and Shorrocks (1989).

8.6.3. The upper tail

Unbounded intervals are convenient for information providers but present a difficult problem for the distributional analyst. Although in some cases it is possible to use the data to impose an upper bound on inequality estimates (see the references in Section 8.6.1) the standard approach is to model the distribution in the top one or two intervals using an explicit functional form, usually a Pareto distribution (Needleman, 1978; Fuller, 1979) (see Section 8.7).

8.7. Modelling with functional forms

The use of the parametric approach to distributional analysis runs counter to the general trend towards the pursuit of non-parametric methods, although is extensively applied in the statistical literature. Perhaps it is because some versions of the parametric approach have had a bad press: Pareto's seminal works led to some fanciful interpretations of "laws" of income distribution (Davis, 1941, 1954); perhaps it is because the non-parametric method seems to be more general in its approach.[105]

Nevertheless a parametric approach can be particularly useful for estimation of inequality indices or other statistics in cases where information is sparse (Braulke, 1983, 1988; Chotikapanich et al., 1997). Furthermore, some standard functional forms claim attention, not only for their suitability in modelling some features of many empirical income distributions but also because of their role as equilibrium distributions in economic processes.

8.7.1. The choice of functional form

In the inequality literature there is a substantial number of formulae F_θ used to model various aspects of income distribution, most of which have natural intuitive interpretations of the parameters θ. Some of the most important include the following:

- the Pareto model (Arnold, 1983; Chipman, 1974),

$$F_{\underline{x},\alpha}(x) = 1 - \left[\frac{\underline{x}}{x}\right]^\alpha , \tag{85}$$

where $\underline{x} > 0$ is a location parameter and α is a parameter that is inversely related to dispersion.

- the lognormal model (Aitchison and Brown, 1954, 1957)

$$F_{m,\sigma^2}(x) = \int_0^x \frac{1}{y\sqrt{2\pi}\sigma} e^{-\frac{1}{2\sigma^2}[\log(y)-m]^2} \, \mathrm{d}y , \tag{86}$$

where m and σ^2 are parameters specifying the mean and variance of log-income.

---

[105] Although for some issues, such as kernel density estimation, specialised structural assumptions are required (Silverman, 1986).

• the gamma model (Salem and Mount, 1974)

$$F_{\alpha,\lambda}(x) = \int_0^x \frac{\lambda^\alpha}{\Gamma(\alpha)} y^{\alpha-1} e^{-\lambda y} \, \mathrm{d}y \tag{87}$$

where Γ is the standard gamma function.

The functional form that is appropriate for modelling distributions depends on the definition of income and the particular part of the distribution in which we happen to be interested. For example, the Pareto model is appropriate for analysing upper incomes; in general lognormal models are appropriate for individual earnings in a homogeneous population; the gamma model approximates the majority of data in the "middle" of the distribution (Harrison, 1981).

The families of two-parameter models (Eqs. 85–87) are evidently limited in the variety of shapes of income distributions that they can be expected to describe. One way forward is to consider extensions to the basic forms to make them more flexible—for example multiparameter generalisations of the Pareto and of the lognormal have been suggested.[106] Several other families of distributions have been shown to have merit in capturing some important features of the distribution; many of these functional forms are interrelated, in the sense that one is a special form of another, or one approximates another asymptotically.[107] But it should be borne in mind that, however attractive greater flexibility may seem to be, proliferation of parameters in the model specification may impose a considerably greater burden in terms of interpretation and computation. Four parameter models can be very unwieldy, and even three-parameter models may not give a huge advantage over their two-parameter counterparts. Complicated empirical distributions may not be much illuminated by complicated functional forms: it may be better to piecemeal focus on readily interpretable chunks of the distribution.

8.7.2. Inequality in parametric models

In most cases the use of a functional form induces a structure on $\mathfrak{F}'$ that makes the distributional ranking problem very easy—perhaps deceptively so. For example, the Lorenz curves of Pareto distributions never intersect; the same is true for lognormal distributions (the Lorenz curve lies further from the line of equality the lower is the parameter α and the higher is the parameter σ^2 in Eqs. (85) and (86), respectively); so adoption of either of these families as a paradigm for the admissible class of distributions means that first- and second-order dominance criteria are always very clear. Of course one has to be careful that one is not squeezing a foot into an ill-fitting standardised shoe: unambiguous dominance results are of little use if the adoption of the functional form is at the price of ignoring important information in some part of the distribution.

---

[106] See, for example, Rasche et al. (1980), Gupta (1984), Rao and Tam (1987) and Singh and Maddala (1976) on Pareto-type indices, Esteban (1986), Kloek and Van Dijk (1977, 1978) and Taille (1981) on the generalised gamma, Metcalf (1969) on the generalised lognormal, and also Cowell (1995, Appendix) for a discussion of these alternative forms.

[107] See McDonald (1984, p. 698) and Merkies (1994) for a useful diagram showing the principal family connections. See also Majumder and Chakravarty (1990).

If one does adopt a specific functional form, then inequality can be expressed in terms of its parameters:[108]

$$I(F_\theta) = \iota(\boldsymbol{\theta}).\tag{88}$$

For example, the Atkinson family of indices (Eq. 30) can be written

$$I_A^\varepsilon\left(F_{\underline{x},\alpha}\right) = 1 - \frac{\alpha - 1}{\alpha}\left[\frac{\alpha}{\alpha + \varepsilon - 1}\right]^{1/(1-\varepsilon)}\tag{89}$$

and

$$I_A^\varepsilon\left(F_{m,\sigma^2}\right) = 1 - e^{-(1/2)\varepsilon\sigma^2}\tag{90}$$

in the case of the Pareto and the lognormal, respectively. Again, note that inequality is monotonic decreasing in α (Eq. 89) and monotonic increasing in σ^2 (Eq. 90), respectively.

8.7.3. The estimation method

The general nature of the problem can be described as follows. First, it is necessary to choose a functional form or model that is appropriate in an economic sense—i.e., a general family form F_θ that captures the general shape of the distribution, or part of the distribution, that one wishes to model, as described in Section 8.7.1. Then the model parameters are estimated using an appropriate algorithm: this means an algorithm chosen according to criteria which implicitly define the term "appropriate" in the statistical sense.

For example, "appropriateness" is often interpreted in terms of efficiency of the estimator: given a model F_θ with density function f_θ, the *maximum likelihood estimators* (MLE) are then obtained as the solution in $\boldsymbol{\theta}$ of the m equations[109]

$$\sum_{i=1}^{n} \mathbf{S}(x_i; \boldsymbol{\theta}) = 0,\tag{91}$$

where $m := \dim(\boldsymbol{\theta})$ and $\mathbf{S}$ is the scores function defined by

$$\mathbf{S}(x; \boldsymbol{\theta}) = \frac{\partial}{\partial \boldsymbol{\theta}} \log f_\theta(x).\tag{92}$$

Of course it is clear that this efficiency criterion cannot take account of the problem of contamination mentioned in Section 8.2.2. It may be realistic to assume that the data

---

[108] See, for example, Cowell (1995, Chap. 4), Wilfling (1996) and Wilfling and Krämer (1993); also see Aitchison and Brown (1957) for the lognormal and Chipman (1974) for the Pareto.

[109] For the MLE in the case of the Pareto, see Baxter (1980); and for the MLE for a variety of functional forms, see McDonald and Ransom (1979).

come from a distribution in the neighbourhood of the true model of the distribution—that they are actually generated by the parametric model F_θ with probability $1 - \delta$, and by an alien distribution (the contamination) H with probability δ, where δ is small. The MLE procedures would be optimal given the assumption that the data are generated by F_θ (the case $\delta = 0$), but will be invalid for any variation around F_θ (the case $\delta > 0$)—see Hampel et al. (1986) and Victoria-Feser (1993). To handle this requires an alternative statistical criterion of appropriateness that takes into account the robustness considerations outlined in Section 8.2.2. In the robust approach to estimation, instead of applying Eqs. (91) and (92), one requires an algorithm to filter outlying observations systematically. The MLE belong to a general class of so-called *M-estimators* which are defined as the solution in $\boldsymbol{\theta}$ of

$$\sum_{i=1}^{n} \psi(x_i; \boldsymbol{\theta}) = 0, \tag{93}$$

where ψ belongs to a very general class of functions (Huber, 1964). The robust approach consists of a search for the minimum (asymptotic) variance M-estimator with a bounded IF: efficiency is sacrificed to some extent in favour of robustness. There is a number of optimal estimators, depending on the exact method of bounding the IF.[110]

Other criteria of appropriateness could be applied. For example the *method of moments* has the advantages of simplicity and relative transparency: by equating the theoretical values, conditional on $\boldsymbol{\theta}$, of some of the moments to their counterparts computed

---

[110] For example, consider the standardised *Optimal Bias-Robust Estimators (OBRE)* which also belong to Eq. (93); given a constant $c \in [\sqrt{m}, \infty)$ which plays the role of upper bound on the IF, the OBRE is defined as the solution in $\boldsymbol{\theta}$ to

$$\sum_{i=1}^{n} \psi_c^{\mathbf{A},\mathbf{a}}(x_i; \boldsymbol{\theta}) = 0,$$

where

$$\psi_c^{\mathbf{A},\mathbf{a}}(x; \boldsymbol{\theta}) = \mathbf{A}(\boldsymbol{\theta}) \left[\mathbf{S}(x; \boldsymbol{\theta}) - \mathbf{a}(\boldsymbol{\theta}) \right] w_c(x; \boldsymbol{\theta})$$

$$w_c(x; \boldsymbol{\theta}) = \min \left\{ 1; \frac{c}{\|\mathbf{A}(\boldsymbol{\theta}) \left[\mathbf{S}(x; \boldsymbol{\theta}) - \mathbf{a}(\boldsymbol{\theta}) \right] \|} \right\}$$

$\mathbf{A}$ is an $m \times m$-matrix, and $\mathbf{a}$ is an m-vector; $\mathbf{A}$ and $\mathbf{a}$ are determined by:

$$E \left[\psi_c^{\mathbf{A},\mathbf{a}}(x; \boldsymbol{\theta}) \psi_c^{\mathbf{A},\mathbf{a}}(x; \boldsymbol{\theta})^T \right] = \mathbf{I}$$

$$E \left[\psi_c^{\mathbf{A},\mathbf{a}}(x; \boldsymbol{\theta}) \right] = \mathbf{0}$$

$\mathbf{A}$ and $\mathbf{a}$ can be considered as Lagrange multipliers for these last two restrictions; ψ is a modified and standardised scores function, weighted using w_c. The constant c may be selected as a "regulator" between the two statistical criteria, efficiency and robustness. Lower values of c yield more robust, but less efficient, estimators: the maximum-robustness estimator corresponds to the lower bound of the constant $c = \sqrt{m}$; on the other hand $c = \infty$ yields the MLE (Prieto-Alaiz and Victoria-Feser, 1996; Victoria-Feser, 1995). On robust estimation for grouped data, see Victoria-Feser and Ronchetti (1997).

from the data one can obtain a set of simultaneous equations for the explicit computation of the parameter estimates. How many moments should be used, and which ones, will of course depend on the particular form of F_θ; but typically one sets up two equations in the mean and variance of income or log-income.

8.8. Re-using inequality measures

The computation of inequality in the case of parametric approaches to income distribution has suggested a number of alternative applications of measurement tools. Prominent among these are instances where the inequality measures are "turned on their heads" and used as the basis of goodness-of-fit tests (Gail and Gastwirth,1978a, b) or devices for quantifying the distance of one distribution from another (Atkinson et al., 1988). The inequality index is used to give meaning to the deviations between the sample data and a particular functional form proposed as a model of the underlying income distribution.

Applying inequality measures in this sort of way continues to be a promising idea. For some time distributional tools developed for the purpose of inequality analysis have been applied in contexts other than income distribution—such as in the study of industrial concentration, political science, for example. It seems appropriate that these measurement techniques which have been underpinned by careful analytical work on their axiomatic bases and their structural properties should be applied in contexts other than a narrow welfare-economic interpretation of inequality. An example of this is the development of the concept of the "Gini regression" technique (Olkin and Yitzhaki, 1992; Yitzhaki, 1996). Re-using inequality measures in this way can provide important insights in other fields of economics and gives the prominence to the analysis that it justly deserves.

9. A brief conclusion

A conclusion section provides an ideal opportunity to pass judgment on deadends and promising discoveries, and to make hopeful remarks about further work in the subject. I shall not try such grand things: instead, let us briefly consider the natural limitations of the subject as it is currently understood.

The formal approach to inequality measurement is a good discipline for training us in thinking about what we are doing when income distributions are to be compared. It does not matter much what the ethical or intellectual standpoint is from which one comes to the subject; the analysis can assist in providing systematic answers to a number of basic questions. Is inequality about individual incomes or about income differences? Is the shape of the income distribution relevant to inequality judgments? How can theoretical reasoning in the economics discipline illuminate practical questions of economic and social policy?

On the other hand some major issues are sidestepped or are deliberately left open for work by scholars in related fields: Why *should* social welfare be concerned with inequality? Does inequality "matter" in a social sense? How should inequality be related to broader concepts of "fairness" in economics?

Finally, an odd question. Why is something like the Gini coefficient so consistently popular? A trawl through the empirical literature (which I shamefully neglected in this survey) reveals an overwhelming propensity to use this index rather than other tools reviewed above. For many practical people doing important applied work it is *the* inequality index. Yet the index has many apparent drawbacks. It is not decomposable, at least not in the sense that it will satisfy consistency requirements for arbitrary partitions of the population. Its statistical properties are far less tractable than those of easily available alternatives. It does not emerge naturally from the welfare-economics of the subject (although it can be made to fit in). It is certainly not new. Here are two possible answers, both of which are offered tentatively:

(1) There is also considerable cultural inertia in the field of inequality analysis, as in other fields.

(2) Perhaps it is because people can "see" inequality immediately once the idea of the Lorenz curve is accepted.

Each of these reasons may be no bad thing. However, the question, and its possible answer, may illuminate some of the problems that academic researchers in this field could have in connecting theory with an understanding of the real world.

References

Addo, H. (1976), Trends in international value-inequality 1969–1970: an empirical study, Journal of Peace Research 13: 13–34.

Adelman, I. and A. Levy (1984), Decomposing Theil's index of income inequality into between and within components. The Review of Income and Wealth 30: 119–121. (Reply: 1986, Vol. 32: 107–108.)

Aghevli, B.B. and F. Mehran (1981), Optimal grouping of income distribution data, Journal of the American Statistical Association 76.

Aigner, D.J. and A.J. Heins (1967), A social welfare view of the measurement of income equality, Review of Income and Wealth 13(3): 12–25.

Aitchison, J. and J.A.C. Brown (1954), On the criteria for descriptions of income distribution, Metroeconomica 6.

Aitchison, J. and J.A.C. Brown (1957), The Lognormal Distribution. (Cambridge University Press, Cambridge).

Alker, H.R.J. (1970), Measuring inequality, in E.R. Tufte, ed., The Quantitative Analysis of Social Problems, (Addison-Wesley, Reading, MA).

Alker, H.R.J. and B. Russet (1964), On measuring inequality, Behavioral Science 9: 207–218.

Allingham, M.G. (1972), The measurement of inequality, Journal of Economic Theory 5: 163–169.

Amiel, Y. (1999), The subjective approach to the measurement of income inequality, in J. Silber, ed., Income Inequality Measurement: From Theory to Practice (Kluwer, Deventer).

Amiel, Y. and F.A. Cowell (1992), Measurement of income inequality: experimental test by questionnaire, Journal of Public Economics 47: 3–26.

Amiel, Y. and F.A. Cowell (1994a), Income inequality and social welfare, in J. Creedy, ed., Taxation, Poverty and Income Distribution, (Edward Elgar) pp. 193–219.

Amiel, Y. and F.A. Cowell (1994b), Inequality changes and income growth, In W. Eichhorn, ed., Models and measurement of welfare and inequality, (Springer-Verlag, Heidelberg) pp. 3–26.

Amiel, Y. and F.A. Cowell (1994c), Monotonicity, dominance and the Pareto principle, Economics Letters 45: 447–450.

Amiel, Y. and F.A. Cowell (1997), Inequality, welfare and monotonicity, Distributional Analysis Discussion Paper 29, (London School of Economics, STICERD: London).

Amiel, Y. and F.A. Cowell (1998), Distributional orderings and the transfer principle: a re-examination, Research on Economic Inequality 8.

Amiel, Y. and F.A. Cowell (1999a), Income transformations and income inequality, in D. Slottje, ed., Festschrift for Camilo Dagum (Springer Verlag, Heidelberg).

Amiel, Y. and F.A. Cowell (1999b), Thinking about Inequality, (Cambridge University Press, Cambridge).

Amiel, Y., F.A. Cowell, and A. Polovin (1996), Inequality amongst the kibbutzim, Economica 63: S63–S85.

Amiel, Y., J. Creedy, and D. Hurn (1999), Attitudes towards inequality, The Scandinavian Journal of Economics 101: 83–96.

Anand, S. (1983), Inequality and poverty in Malaysia, (Oxford University Press, London).

Anderson, G. (1994), Nonparametric tests of stochastic dominance in income distributions, Department of economics and institute for policy analysis discussion paper, University of Toronto.

Andrews, D.W.K. (1997), A simple counterpart to the bootstrap, Discussion Paper 1157, Cowles Foundation for Research in Economics at Yale University, New Haven, Connecticut.

Arnold, B.C. (1983), Pareto Distributions, Fairland, MD: International Cooperative Publishing House.

Arnold, B.C. (1987), Majorization and the Lorenz Order: A Brief Introduction, Heidelberg: Springer-Verlag.

Atkinson, A.B. (1970), On the measurement of inequality, Journal of Economic Theory 2: 244–263.

Atkinson, A.B. (1973), More on the measurement of inequality, mimeo, University of Essex.

Atkinson, A.B. (1983), The Economics of Inequality, 2nd edn., Oxford: Clarendon Press.

Atkinson, A.B. (1987), On the measurement of poverty, Econometrica 55: 749–764.

Atkinson, A.B. and F. Bourguignon (1982), The comparison of multi-dimensional distributions of economic status, Review of Economic Studies 49: 183–201.

Atkinson, A.B. and F. Bourguignon (1987), Income distribution and differences in needs, in G.R. Feiwel, ed., Arrow and the Foundations of the Theory of Economic Policy (Macmillan, New York).

Atkinson, A.B., J. Gomulka, and H. Sutherland (1988), Grossing-up FES data for tax-benefit models, in A.B. Atkinson and H. Sutherland, eds., Tax-Benefit Models (London School of Economics, STICERD: London).

Ballano, C. and J. Ruiz-Castillo (1992), Searching by questionnaire for the meaning of income inequality, Technical Report 43, Universidad Carlos III de Madrid, Departmento de Economia.

Basmann, R.L. and D.J. Slottje (1987), A new index of income inequality—the B measure, Economics Letters 24: 385–389.

Basu, K. (1987), Axioms for a fuzzy measure of inequality, Mathematical Social Sciences 14(12): 275–288.

Bawa, V. (1975), Optimal rules for ordering uncertain prospects, Journal of Financial Economics 2: 95–121.

Baxter, M.A. (1980), Minimum-variance unbiased estimation of the parameters of the Pareto distribution, Metrika 27.

Beach, C.M., K. Chow, J. Formby, and G. Slotsve (1994), Statistical inference for decile means, Economics Letters 45: 161–167.

Beach, C.M. and R. Davidson (1983), Distribution-free statistical inference with Lorenz curves and income shares, Review of Economic Studies 50: 723–725.

Beach, C.M. and J. Richmond (1985), Joint confidence intervals for income shares and Lorenz curves, International Economic Review 26(6): 439–450.

Beckman, S., D. Cheng, J.P. Formby, and W.J. Smith (1994), Preferences for income distributions and redistributions: evidence from experiments with real income at stake, Technical Report (University of Colorado, Denver, and University of Alabama).

Ben Horim, M. (1990), Stochastic dominance and truncated sample data. Journal of Financial Research 13: 105–116.

Ben-Porath, E. and I. Gilboa (1994), Linear measures, the Gini index, and the income-equality trade-off, Journal of Economic Theory 64: 443–467.

Ben-Porath, E., I. Gilboa, and D. Schmeidler (1997), On the measurement of inequality under uncertainty, Journal of Economic Theory 75: 194–204.

Bentzel, R. (1970), The social significance of income distribution statistics, Review of Income and Wealth, 253–264.

Berrebi, Z. M. and J. Silber (1983), On an absolute measure of distributional change, European Economic Review 22: 139–146.

Berrebi, Z.M. and J. Silber (1984), Interquantile differences, income inequality measurement and the Gini concentration index, Technical Report 2 (Bar Ilan University).

Berrebi, Z.M. and J. Silber (1985), Income inequality indices and deprivation: a generalization, Quarterly Journal of Economics 99: 807–810.

Berrebi, Z.M. and J. Silber (1987), Dispersion, asymmetry and the Gini index of inequality, International Economic Review 28(6): 331–338.

Berrebi, Z.M. and J. Silber (1989), Deprivation, the Gini index of inequality and the flatness of an income distribution, Mathematical Social Sciences 18(12): 229–237.

Berry, A., F. Bourguignon, and C. Morrisson (1981), The level of world inequality: how much can one say? Review of Income and Wealth 29: 217–243.

Berry, A., F. Bourguignon, and C. Morrisson (1983), Changes in the world distributions of income between 1950 and 1977, Economic Journal 93: 331–350.

Bhattacharya, N. and B. Mahalanobis (1967), Regional disparities in household consumption in India, Journal of the American Statistical Association 62: 143–161.

Bhattacharya, R.N. and M. Qumsiyeh (1989), Second order Lp-comparisons between the bootstrap and empirical Edgeworth expansion methodologies, The Annals of Statistics 17: 160–169.

Bishop, J.A., S. Chakraborti, and P.D. Thistle (1987), Distribution-free statistical inference for generalized Lorenz curves, Working Paper (University of Alabama).

Bishop, J.A., S. Chakraborti, and P.D. Thistle (1988), Large sample tests for absolute Lorenz dominance, Economics Letters 26: 291–294.

Bishop, J.A., S. Chakraborti, and P.D. Thistle (1989a), Asymptotically distribution-free statistical inference for generalized Lorenz curves, Review of Economics and Statistics 71(11): 725–727.

Bishop, J.A., S. Chakraborti, and P.D. Thistle (1994), Relative inequality, absolute inequality, and welfare: large sample tests for partial orders, Bulletin of Economic Research 46: 41–60.

Bishop, J.A., J.P. Formby, and W.P. Smith (1991), International comparisons of income inequality: Tests for Lorenz dominance across nine countries, Economica 58: 461–477.

Bishop, J.A., J.P. Formby, and P.D. Thistle (1989b), Statistical inference, income distributions, and social welfare, in D.J. Slottje, ed., Research on Economic Inequality I (JAI Press, Connecticut).

Bishop, J.A., J.P. Formby, and P.D. Thistle (1991), Rank dominance and international comparisons of income distributions, European Economic Review 35: 1399–1409.

Bishop, J.A., J.P. Formby, and P. Thistle (1997), Changing American earnings distributions: one-half century of experience, Empirical Economics 22(4): 501–514.

Blackburn, M.L. (1989), Interpreting the magnitude of changes in measures of income inequality, Journal of Econometrics 42: 21–25.

Blackorby, C. and D. Donaldson (1978), Measures of relative equality and their meaning in terms of social welfare, Journal of Economic Theory 18: 59–80.

Blackorby, C. and D. Donaldson (1980a), Ethical indices for the measurement of poverty, Econometrica 48: 1053–1860.

Blackorby, C. and D. Donaldson (1980b), A theoretical treatment of indices of absolute inequality, International Economic Review 21: 107–136.

Blackorby, C. and D. Donaldson (1984), Ethically significant ordinal indices of relative inequality, in R.L. Basmann and G.G. Rhodes, eds., Advances in Econometrics, Vol. 3 (JAI Press, Connecticut, pp. 83–86).

Blackorby, C., D. Donaldson, and M. Auersperg (1981), A new procedure for the measurement of inequality within and among population subgroup, Canadian Journal of Economics 14: 665–685.

Bossert, W. (1988a), Generalized Gini social evaluation functions and low income group aggregation, Discussion Paper 343 (Karlsruhe University).

Bossert, W. (1988b), A note on intermediate inequality indices which are quasilinear means, Discussion Paper 289 (Karlsruhe University).

Bossert, W. (1990), An axiomatization of the single series Ginis, Journal of Economic Theory 50: 89–92.

Bossert, W. and A. Pfingsten (1990), Intermediate inequality: concepts, indices and welfare implications, Mathematical Social Science 19: 117–134.

Bottiroli Civardi, M. and E. Martinetti Chiappero (1995), Family as economic unit in the analyses of income inequality and poverty, Research on Economic Inequality 6: 157–176.

Bourguignon, F. (1979), Decomposable income inequality measures, Econometrica 47: 901–920.

Bourguignon, F. (1989), Family size and social utility: Income distribution dominance criteria, Journal of Econometrics 42: 67–80.

Box, G.E.P. and D.R. Cox (1964), An analysis of transformations, Journal of the Royal Statistical Society, Series B 26: 211–252.

Bradburd, R.M. and D.R. Ross (1988), A general measure of multidimensional inequality, Oxford Bulletin of Economics and Statistics 50: 429–433.

Braulke, M. (1983), An approximation to the Gini coefficient for population based on sparse information for sub-groups, Journal of Development Economics 2(12): 75–81.

Braulke, M. (1988), How to retrieve the Lorenz curve from sparse data, in W. Eichhorn, ed., Measurement in Economics, (Physica-Verlag, Heidelberg).

Broome, J. (1988), What's the good of equality? in J. Hey, ed., Current Issues in Microeconomics (Macmillan, Basingstoke, Hampshire).

Broome, J. (1991), Weighing Goods (Basil Blackwell, Oxford).

Bruno, M. and J. Habib (1976), Taxes, family grants and redistribution, Journal of Public Economics 5: 57–79.

Butler, R.J. and J.B. McDonald (1987), Interdistributional income inequality, Journal of Business and Economic Statistics 5: 13–18.

Castagnoli, E. and P. Muliere (1990), A note on inequality measures and the Pigou-Dalton principle of transfer, in C. Dagum and M. Zenga, eds., Income and Wealth Distribution, Inequality and Poverty, (Springer-Verlag, Heidelberg, pp. 171–182).

Chakravarty, S.R. (1988), Extended Gini indices of inequality. International Economic Review 29(2): 147–156.

Chakravarty, S.R. (1990), Ethical Social Index Numbers (Springer-Verlag, Berlin).

Chakravarty, S.R. (1998), Relative deprivation and satisfaction orderings, Keio Economic Studies.

Chakravarty, S.R. and A.B. Chakraborty (1984), On indices of relative deprivation, Economics Letters 14: 283–287.

Chakravarty, S.R. and W. Eichhorn (1994), Measurement of income inequality: Observed versus true data, in W. Eichhorn, ed., Models and Measurement of Welfare and Inequality, (Springer-Verlag, Heidelberg, pp. 28–32).

Chakravarty, S.R. and D. Mukherjee (1997), Lorenz transformation, utilitarian deprivation rule and equal sacrifice principle, The Manchester School.

Champernowne, D.G. (1952), The graduation of income distribution, Econometrica 20: 591–615.

Champernowne, D.G. (1974), A comparison of measures of income distribution, The Economic Journal 84: 787–816.

Champernowne, D.G. and F.A. Cowell (1998), Inequality and Income Distribution (Cambridge University Press, Cambridge).

Chen, C.-N., T.-W. Tsaur, and T.-S. Rhai (1982), The Gini coefficient and negative income, Oxford Economic Papers 34(11): 473–476.

Chew, S.-H. (1983), A generalization of the quasi-linear mean with application to the measurement of income inequality, Econometrica 51: 1065–1092.

Chipman, J.S. (1974), The welfare ranking of Pareto distributions, Journal of Economic Theory 9: 275–282.

Chotikapanich, D., R. Valenzuela, and D. Prasada Rao (1997), Global and regional inequality in the distribution of income: estimation with limited and incomplete data.

Christiansen, V. and E.S. Jansen (1978), Implicit social preferences in the Norwegian system of social welfare, Journal of Public Economics 10: 217–245.

Chu, C.Y.C., D.-Y. Huang, and H.-W. Koo (1996), The preference foundation of the generalized entropy measures, Working paper, Department of Economics, National Taiwan University.

Clark, S., R. Hemming, and D. Ulph (1981), On indices for the measurement of poverty, Economic Journal 91: 515–526.

Coulter, F.A.E., F.A. Cowell, and S.P. Jenkins (1992a), Differences in needs and assessement of income distributions, Bulletin of Economic Research 44: 77–124.

Coulter, F.A.E., F.A. Cowell, and S.P. Jenkins (1992b), Equivalence scale relativities and the extent of inequality and poverty, Economic Journal 102: 1067–1082.

Coulter, F.A.E., F.A. Cowell, and S.P. Jenkins (1994b), Equivalence scale relativities and the extent of inequality and poverty, in J. Creedy, ed., Taxation, Poverty and Income Distribution, (Edward Elgar, pp. 87–103).

Coulter, F.A.E., F.A. Cowell, and S.P. Jenkins (1994a), Equivalence scales and assessment of income distribution, European Journal of Population.

Cowell, F.A. (1977), Measuring Inequality 1st edn., Oxford: Phillip Allan.

Cowell, F.A. (1980a), Generalized entropy and the measurement of distributional change, European Economic Review 13: 147–159.

Cowell, F.A. (1980b), On the structure of additive inequality measures, Review of Economic Studies 47: 521–531.

Cowell, F.A. (1984), The structure of American income inequality, Review of Income and Wealth 30: 351–375.

Cowell, F.A. (1985a), 'A fair suck of the sauce bottle'-or what do you mean by inequality? Economic Record 6: 567–579.

Cowell, F.A. (1985b), The measurement of distributional change: an axiomatic approach, Review of Economic Studies 52: 135–151.

Cowell, F.A. (1985c), Multilevel decomposition of Theil's index of inequality, Review of Income and Wealth 31: 201–205.

Cowell, F.A. (1988a), Inequality decomposition—three bad measures, Bulletin of Economic Research 40: 309–312.

Cowell, F.A. (1988b), Poverty measures, inequality and decomposability, in D. Bös, M. Rose, and C. Seidl, eds., Welfare and Efficiency in Public Economics (Springer-Verlag, Heidelberg, pp. 149–166).

Cowell, F.A. (1989), Sampling variance and decomposable inequality measures, Journal of Econometrics 42: 27–41.

Cowell, F.A. (1991), Grouping bounds for inequality measures under alternative informational assumptions, Journal of Econometrics 48: 1–14.

Cowell, F.A. (1995), Measuring Inequality 2nd edn., Hemel Hempstead: Harvester Wheatsheaf.

Cowell, F.A. (1998), Intermediate and other inequality measures, Distributional Analysis Discussion Paper 42, (London School of Economics, STICERD: London).

Cowell, F.A. (1999), Estimation of inequality indices, in J. Silber, ed., Income Inequality Measurement: From Theory to Practice (Kluwer, Deventer).

Cowell, F.A. and S.P. Jenkins (1995), How much inequality can we explain? A methodology and an application to the USA. Economic Journal 105.

Cowell, F.A. and K. Kuga (1981a), Additivity and the entropy concept: an axiomatic approach to inequality measurement, Journal of Economic Theory 25: 131–143.

Cowell, F.A. and K. Kuga (1981b), Inequality measurement: an axiomatic approach, European Economic Review 15: 287–305.

Cowell, F.A. and F. Mehta (1982), The estimation and interpolation of inequality measures, Review of Economic Studies 49: 273–290.

Cowell, F.A. and M. Mercader-Prats (1999), Equivalence scales and inequality, in J. Silber ed., Income Inequality Measurement: From Theory to Practice (Kluwer, Deventer).

Cowell, F.A. and M.-P. Victoria-Feser (1996a), Poverty measurement with contaminated data: A robust approach, European Economic Review 40: 1761–1771.

Cowell, F.A. and M.-P. Victoria-Feser (1996b), Robustness properties of inequality measures, Econometrica 64: 77–101.

Cowell, F.A. and M.-P. Victoria-Feser (1996c), Welfare judgements in the presence of contaminated data, Distributional Analysis Discussion Paper 13, (London School of Economics, STICERD: London).

Cowell, F.A. and M.-P. Victoria-Feser (1998), Statistical inference for Lorenz curves with censored data, Distributional Analysis Discussion Paper 35, (London School of Economics, STICERD: London).

Creedy, J. (1977), The principle of transfers and the variance of logarithms, Oxford Bulletin of Economics and Statistics 39: 153–158.

Csörgő, M. and D. Mason (1989), Bootstrapping empirical functions, Annals of Statistics 17: 1447–1471.

Csörgő, M. and R. Zitikis (1995), On the Vervaat, Lorenz and Goldie Processes I, II, III, Technical Report for Research in Statistics and Probability 279.

Csörgő, M. and R. Zitikis (1996a), On confidence bands for the Lorenz and Goldie curves, in A Volume in Honor of Samuel Kotz (Wiley, New York).

Csörgő, M. and R. Zitikis (1996b), Strassen's LIL for the Lorenz Curve, Journal of Multivariate Analysis.

Dagum, C. (1990), On the relationship between income inequality measures and social welfare functions, Journal of Econometrics 43: 91–102.

Dagum, C. (1993), The social welfare bases of Gini and other income inequality measures, Statistica 8: 3–30.

Dagum, C. (1997), A new approach to the decomposition of the Gini income inequality ratio, Empirical Economics 22(4): 515–531.

Dahlby, B. G. (1987), Interpreting inequality measures in a Harsanyi framework, Theory and Decision 22: 187–202.

Dalton, H. (1920), Measurement of the inequality of incomes, The Economic Journal 30(9): 348–361.

Danziger, S. and M.K. Taussig (1979), The income unit and the anatomy of income distribution, Review of Income and Wealth 25: 365–375.

Dardanoni, V. and P. Lambert (1988), Welfare ranking of income distribution: a role for the variance and some insights for tax reform, Social Choice and Welfare 5: 1–17.

Das, T. and A. Parikh (1981), Decompositions of Atkinson's measures of inequality, Australian Economic Papers 6: 171–178.

Das, T. and A. Parikh (1982), Decomposition of inequality measures and a comparative analysis, Empirical Economics 7: 23–48.

Dasgupta, P.S., A.K. Sen, and D.A. Starrett (1973), Notes on the measurement of inequality, Journal of Economic Theory 6: 180–187.

David, H.A. (1968), Gini's mean difference rediscovered, Biometrika 55: 573–575.

David, H.A. (1981), Order Statistics, 2nd ed., New York: Wiley.

Davidson, R. and J.-Y. Duclos (1997), Statistical inference for the measurement of the incidence of taxes and transfers. Econometrica 65: 1453–1466.

Davies, J.B. and M. Hoy (1994a), Comparing income distributions when Lorenz curves intersect, Department of Economics Research Report 9414, University of Western Ontario.

Davies, J.B. and M. Hoy (1994b), The normative significance of using third-degree stochastic dominance in comparing income distributions, Journal of Economic Theory 64: 520–530.

Davies, J.B. and M. Hoy (1995), Making inequality comparisons when Lorenz curves intersect, American Economic Review 85: 980–986.

Davies, J.B. and A.F. Shorrocks (1989), Optimal grouping of income and wealth data, Journal of Econometrics 42: 97–108.

Davis, H.T. (1941), The Analysis of Economic Time Series, (The Principia Press, Bloomington IA).

Davis, H.T. (1954), Political Statistics. (Principia Press, Evanston, IL).

de Finetti, B. (1931), Sui metodi proposti per il calcolo della differenza media, Metron 9: 47–52.

Debreu, G. (1954), Representation of a preference ordering by a numerical function, in R. Thrall, C. Coombs, and R. Davis, eds., Decision Processes (John Wiley, New York).

Deutsch, J. and J. Silber (1997), Gini's 'Transvariazione' and the measurement of distance between distributions, Empirical Economics 22(4): 547–554.

Deutsch, J. and J. Silber (1999), The decomposition of inequality by population subgroups and the analysis of interdistributional inequality, in J. Silber, ed., Income Inequality Measurement: From Theory to Practice: (Kluwer, Chap 13).

Donaldson, D. and J.A. Weymark (1980), A single parameter generalization of the Gini indices of inequality, Journal of Economic Theory 22: 67–68.

Donaldson, D. and J.A. Weymark (1983), Ethically flexible Gini indices for income distribution in the continuum, Journal of Economic Theory 29(4): 353–358.

Dorfman, P. (1979), A formula for the Gini coefficient, Review of Economics and Statistics 61: 146–149.

Dutta, B. and J. Esteban (1992), Social welfare and equality, Social Choice and Welfare 9: 267–276.

Ebert, U. (1987), Size and distribution of incomes as determinants of social welfare, Journal of Economic Theory 41: 25–33.

Ebert, U. (1988a), A family of aggregative compromise inequality measure, International Economic Review 29:(5), 363–376.

Ebert, U. (1988b), Measurement of inequality: an attempt at unification and generalization, Social Choice and Welfare 5: 147–169.

Ebert, U. (1988c), On the decomposition of inequality: Partitions into nonoverlapping sub-groups, in W. Eichhorn, eds., Measurement in Economics (Physica Verlag, Heidelberg).

Ebert, U. (1995a), Income inequality and differences in household size, Mathematical Social Sciences 30(V-83-92): 37–55.

Ebert, U. (1995b), Income inequality and redistribution in heterogenous populations, Discussion paper, Institut für Volkswirtschaftslehre, Carl von Ossietzky Universität Oldenburg, D-26111 Oldenburg.

Ebert, U. (1995c), Using equivalence scales to compare household types when needs are different, Discussion paper, Institut für Volkswirtschaftslehre, Carl von Ossietzky Universität Oldenburg, D-26111 Oldenburg.

Ebert, U. (1996), Inequality concepts and social welfare, Discussion paper, Institut für Volkswirtschaftslehre, Carl von Ossietzky Universität Oldenburg, D-26111 Oldenburg.

Ebert, U. (1997a), Dual decomposable inequality measures, Discussion paper, Institut für Volkswirtschaftslehre, Carl von Ossietzky Universität Oldenburg, D-26111 Oldenburg.

Ebert, U. (1997b), Linear inequality concepts and social welfare, Distributional Analysis Discussion Paper 33, (London School of Economics, STICERD: London).

Ebert, U. (1997c), Sequential generalised Lorenz dominance and transfer principles, Discussion paper, Institut für Volkswirtschaftslehre, Carl von Ossietzky Universität Oldenburg, D-26111 Oldenburg.

Ebert, U. (1997d), Social welfare when needs differ, Economica 64.

Efron, B. (1979), Bootstrap methods: Another look at the jackknife, The Annals of Statistics 7: 1–26.

Efron, B. (1982), The Jackknife, the Bootstrap and Other Resampling Plans. (Philadelphia: SIAM).

Efron, B. and C. Stein (1981), The jackknife estimate of variance, The Annals of Statistics 9.

Efron, B. and R. Tibshirani (1993), An Introduction to the Bootstrap. (Chapman and Hall, London).

Eichhorn, W. (1988), On a class of inequality measures, Social Choice and Welfare 5: 171–177.

Eichhorn, W. and W. Gehrig (1982), Measurement of inequality in economics, in B. Korte, ed., Modern Applied Mathematics—optimization and operations research (North Holland, Amsterdam, pp. 657–693).

Einy, E. and B. Peleg (1991), Linear measures of inequality for cooperative games, Journal of Economic Theory 53: 328–344.

Eltetö, O. and E. Frigyes (1968), New income inequality measures as efficient tools for causal analysis and planning, Econometrica 36: 383–396.

Esberger, S.E. and S. Malmquist (1972), En Statisk Studie av Inkomstutveklingen. Stockholm: Statisk Centralbyrån och Bostadssyrelsen.

Esteban, J. (1986), Income share elasticity and the size distirbution of income, International Economic Review 27: 439–444.

Fei, J.C.H., G. Ranis, and S.W.Y. Kuo (1978), Growth and family distribution of income by factor components, Quarterly Journal of Economics 92: 17–53.

Fei, J.C.H., G. Ranis, and S.W.Y. Kuo (1979), Growth with Equity: the Taiwan Case. (Oxford University Press, London).

Fichtenbaum, R. and H. Shahidi (1988), Truncation bias and the measurement of income inequality, Journal of Business and Economic Statistics 6: 335–337.

Fields, G.S. (1987), Measuring inequality change in an economy with income growth, Journal of Development Economics 26: 357–374.

Fields, G.S. (1993), Inequality in dual economy models, The Economic Journal 103: 1228–1235.

Fields, G.S. (1998), Do inequality measures measure inequality? in S.P. Jenkins, A. Kapteyn, and B.M.S. Van Praag, eds., The Distribution of Welfare and Household Production: International Perspectives Cambridge University Press, Chap. 10, pp. 233–249).

Fields, G.S. and J.C.H. Fei (1978), On inequality comparisons, Econometrica 46: 303–316.

Fields, G.S. and E.A. Ok (1996), The meaning and measurement of income mobility, Journal of Economic Theory 71(2): 349–377.

Fields, G.S. and E.A. Ok (1997), The measurement of income mobility: An introduction to the literature, Working paper, Cornell University.

Figini, P. (1996), On the Fields' index of income inequality: generalisation and properties, Working paper, Trinity College, Dublin.

Fine, B. and K. Fine (1974a), Social choice and individual ranking I, Review of Economic Studies 41: 303–322.

Fine, B. and K. Fine (1974b), Social choice and individual ranking II, Review of Economic Studies 41: 459–475.

Fishburn, P.C. (1970), Utility theory for decision making. (John Wiley, New York).

Fishburn, P.C. and R.D. Willig (1984), Transfer principles in income redistribution, Journal of Public Economics 25: 323–328.

Fisher, F.M. (1956), Income distribution, value judgement and welfare, Quarterly Journal of Economics 70: 380–424.

Flückiger, Y. and J. Silber (1994), The Gini index and the measurement of multidimensional inequality, Oxford Bulletin of Economics and Statistics 56(5): 225–228.

Formby, J.P., W.J. Smith, and B. Zheng (1996), Inequality orderings, normalized stochastic dominance and statistical inference, Working paper, (University of Alabama).

Foster, J.E. (1983), An axiomatic characterization of the Theil measure of income inequality, Journal of Economic Theory 31: 105–121.

Foster, J.E. (1984), On economic poverty: a survey of aggregate measures, Advances in Econometrics 3: 215–251.

Foster, J.E. (1985), Inequality measurement, in H.P. Young, ed., Fair Allocation (American Mathematical Society, Providence RI, pp. 38–61).

Foster, J.E. (1994), Normative measurement: is theory relevant? American Economic Review ,Papers and Proceedings 84(2): 365–370.

Foster, J.E., J. Greer, and E. Thorbecke (1984), A class of decomposable poverty measures, Econometrica 52: 761–776.

Foster, J.E., M.K. Majumdar, and T. Mitra (1990), Inequality and welfare in market economies, Journal of Public Economics 41(3): 351–367.

Foster, J.E. and A.A. Shneyerov (1997), Path independent inequality measures, Working paper, Department of Economics, Vanderbilt University.

Foster, J.E. and A.F. Shorrocks (1988a), Poverty ordering, Econometrica 56(1): 173–177.

Foster, J.E. and A.F. Shorrocks (1988b), Poverty orderings and welfare dominance, Social Choice and Welfare 5: 171–198.

Fuller, M. (1979), The estimation of Gini coefficients from grouped data, Economics Letters 3: 187–192.

Gail, M.H. and J.L. Gastwirth (1978a), A scale-free goodness-of-fit test for the exponential distribution based on the Gini statistic, Journal of the Royal Statistical Society, Series B. 40: 350–357.

Gail, M.H. and J.L. Gastwirth (1978b), A scale-free goodness-of-fit test for exponential distribution based on the Lorenz curve, Journal of the American Statistical Association 73: 787–793.

Galvani, L. (1931), Contributi alla determinazione degli indici di variabilità per alcuni tipi di distribuzione, Metron 9: 3–45.

Gärdenfors, P. (1973), Positionalist voting functions, Theory and Decision 4: 1–24.

Gastwirth, J.L. (1971), A general definition of the Lorenz curve, Econometrica 39: 1037–1039.

Gastwirth, J.L. (1972), The estimation of the Lorenz curve and Gini index, Review of Economics and Statistics 54: 306–316.

Gastwirth, J.L. (1974a), Large-sample theory of some measures of inequality, Econometrica 42: 191–196.

Gastwirth, J.L. (1974b), A new index of income inequality, International Statistical Institute Bulletin 45(1): 437–441.

Gastwirth, J.L. (1975), The estimation of a family of measures of economic inequality, Journal of Econometrics 3: 61–70.

Gastwirth, J.L. and M.H. Gail (1985), Simple asymptotically distribution-free methods for comparing Lorenz curves and Gini-indices obtained from complete data, Advances in Econometrics 4: 229–243.

Gastwirth, J.L. and M. Glauberman (1976), The interpolation of the Lorenz curve and Gini index from grouped data, Econometrica 44: 479–483.

Gastwirth, J.L., T. Nayak, and A. Krieger (1986), Large sample theory for the bounds on the Gini and related indices of inequality estimated from grouped data, Journal of Business and Economics Statistics 4: 269–274.

Gastwirth, J.L., T.K. Nayak, and J.L. Wang (1989), Statistical properties of between-group income differentials, Journal of Econometrics 42: 5–19.

Gehrig, W. (1988), On the Shannon-Theil concentration measure and its characterizations, in W. Eichhorn, ed., Measurement in Economics (Physica Verlag, Heidelberg).

Gehrig, W. and K. Hellwig (1982), Eine Charakterisierung der gewichteten Lr-distanz, OR Spektrum 3: 233–237.

Gevers, L., H. Glejser, and J. Rouyer (1979), Professed inequality aversion and its error component, Scandinavian Journal of Economics 81: 238–243.

Giaccardi, F. (1950), Un criterio per la costruzione di indici di concentrazione, Rivista Italiana di Economia, Demografia e Statistica 4: 527–538.

Gini, C. (1912), Variabilità e mutabilità, Studi Economico-Giuridici dell'Università di Cagliari 3: 1–158.

Gini, C. (1921), Measurement of inequality of incomes, The Economic Journal 31: 124–126.

Giorgi, G.M. (1984), A methodological survey of recent studies for the measurement of inequality of economic welfare carried out by some Italian statisticians, Economic Notes 1: 146–158.

Giorgi, G.M. (1990), Bibliographic portrait of the Gini concentration ratio, Metron 48(1–4): 183–221.

Giorgi, G.M. (1993), A fresh look at the topical interest of the Gini concentration ratio, Metron 51(1–2): 83–98.

Glasser, G.J. (1961), Relationship between the mean difference and other measures of variation, Metron 21.

Glasser, G.J. (1962), Variance formulas for the mean difference and coefficient of concentration, Journal of the American Statistical Association 57.

Glejser, H., L. Gevers, P. Lambot, and J.A. Morales (1977), An econometric study of the variables determining inequality aversion among students, European Economic Review 10: 173–188.

Glewwe, P. (1990), The measurement of income inequality under inflation, Journal of Development Economics 32: 43–67.

Glewwe, P. (1991), Household equivalence scales and the measurement of inequality: Transfers from the poor to the rich could decrease inequality, Journal of Public Economics 44: 211–216.

Goldie, C.M. (1977), Convergence theorems for empirical Lorenz curves and their inverses, Advances in Applied Probability 9: 765–791.

Gottschalk, P. and T.M. Smeeding (2000), Empirical evidence on income inequality in industrialized countries, in A.B. Atkinson and F. Bourguignon, eds., Handbook of Income Distribution (North Holland, Amsterdam, Chap. 3).

Guerrero, V.M. (1987), A note on the estimation of Atkinson's index of inequality, Economics Letters 25: 379–384.

Gupta, M.R. (1984), Functional forms for estimating the Lorenz curve, Econometrica 52: 1313–1314.

Hall, P. (1982), The Bootstrap and Edgeworth Expansion (Springer-Verlag, New York).

Hammond, P.J. (1975), A note on extreme inequality aversion, Journal of Economic Theory 11: 465–467.

Hampel, F.R. (1968), Contribution to the Theory of Robust Estimation. Ph. D. thesis, University of California, Berkeley.

Hampel, F.R. (1974), The influence curve and its role in robust estimation, Journal of the American Statistical Association 69: 383–393.

Hampel, F.R., E.M. Ronchetti, P.J. Rousseeuw, and W.A. Stahel (1986), Robust Statistics: The Approach Based on Influence Functions, (John Wiley, New York).

Hannah, L. and J.A. Kay (1977), Concentration in British Industry: Theory, Measurement and the UK Experience, (MacMillan, London).

Hardy, G., J. Littlewood, and G. Polya (1934), Inequalities, (Cambridge University Press, Cambridge).

Harrison, A. (1981), Earnings by size: A tale of two distributions, Review of Economic Studies 48: 621–631.

Harrison, E. and C. Seidl (1994a), Acceptance of distributional axioms: Experimental findings, in W. Eichhorn, ed., Models and Measurement of Welfare and Inequality (Springer-Verlag, Heidelberg, pp. 67–99).

Harrison, E. and C. Seidl (1994b), Perceptional inequality and preferential judgements: An empirical examination of distributional judgments, Public Choice 19: 61–81.

Harsanyi, J.C. (1955), Cardinal welfare, individualistic ethics and interpersonal comparisons of utility, Journal of Political Economy 63: 309–321.

Hart, P.E. (1971), Entropy and other measures of concentration, Journal of the Royal Statistical Society, Series A 134: 423–34.

Helmert, F.R. (1876), Die Berechnung des wahrscheinlichen Beobachtungsfehlers aus den ersten Potenzen der Differenzen gleichgenauer direkter Beobachtungen, Astronomische Nachrichten 88: 127–132.

Herfindahl, O.C. (1950), Concentration in the Steel Industry, Ph. D. thesis, Columbia University.

Hey, J.D. and P.J. Lambert (1980), Relative deprivation and the Gini coefficient: comment, Quarterly Journal of Economics 95: 569–573.

Hochman, H. and J.D. Rodgers (1969), Pareto-optimal redistribution, American Economic Review 59: 542–557.

Hoeffding, W. (1948), A class of statistics with asymptotically normal distribution, The Annals of Mathematical Statistics 19: 293–325.

Hoffman-Jørgensen, J. (1994a), Probability with a View Toward Statistics: Volume I (Chapman and Hall, London).

Hoffman-Jørgensen, J. (1994b), Probability with a View Toward Statistics: Volume II (Chapman and Hall, London).

Howes, S.R. (1993), Income Distribution: Measurement, Transition and Analysis of Urban China, 1981—1990, Ph.D. Thesis, (London School of Economics, UK).

Howes, S.R. (1996), The influence of aggregation on the ordering of distributions, Economica 63: 253–272.

Huber, P.J. (1964), Robust estimation of a location parameter, Annals of Mathematical Statistics 35: 73–101.

Huber, P.J. (1986), Robust Statistics (John Wiley, New York).

Iritani, J. and K. Kuga (1983), Duality between the Lorenz curves and the income distribution functions, Economic Studies Quarterly 34(4): 9–21.

Jäntti, M. and Danziger, S. (2000), Income poverty in advanced countries, in A.B. Atkinson and F. Bourguignon, eds., Handbook of Income Distribution (North Holland, Amsterdam, Chap. 10).

Jasso, G. (1979), On Gini's mean difference and Gini's index of concentration, American Sociological Review 44: 867–70.

Jenkins, S.P. (1988), Calculating income distribution indices from micro data, National Tax Journal 41: 139–142.

Jenkins, S.P. (1991), The measurement of economic inequality, in L. Osberg, ed., Readings on Economic Inequality (M.E. Sharpe, Armonk, NY).

Jenkins, S.P. (1995), Accounting for inequality trends: Decomposition analyses for the UK, Economica 62: 29–64.

Jenkins, S.P. (1997), Trends in real income in Britain: a microeconomic analysis, Empirical Economics 22(4): 483–500.

Jenkins, S.P. and F.A. Cowell (1993), Dwarfs and giants in the 1980s: The UK income distribution and how it changed, Department of Economics, Discussion Paper 93-3, University College of Swansea.

Jenkins, S.P. and F.A. Cowell (1994), Dwarfs and giants in the 1980s: The UK income distribution and how it changed, Fiscal Studies 15(1): 99–118.

Jenkins, S.P. and P.J. Lambert (1993), Ranking income distributions when needs differ, Review of Income and Wealth 39: 337–356.

Jenkins, S.P. and P.J. Lambert (1997), Three 'I's of Poverty Curves, with an analysis of UK Poverty Trends, Oxford Economic Papers 49: 317–327.

Jenkins, S.P. and M. O'Higgins (1989), Inequality measurement using norm incomes, The Review of Income and Wealth 35(9): 245–282.

Kakwani, N.C. (1984), Welfare ranking of income distributions, in R.L. Basmann and G.G. Rhodes, eds., Advances in Econometrics (JAI Press, Greenwich, Vol. 3, pp. 191–213).

Kakwani, N.C. (1986), Analyzing Redistribution Policies (Cambridge University Press, Cambridge).

Katz, A. (1972), On the social welfare function and the parameters of income distribution, Journal of Economic Theory 5: 377–382.

Kendall, M. and A. Stuart (1977), The Advanced Theory of Statistics, (Griffin, London).

Kish, L. and M. Frankel (1970), Balanced repeated replications for standard errors, Journal of the American Statistical Association 65: 1071–1093.

Kloek, T. and H.K. Van Dijk (1977), Further results on efficient estimation of income distribution parameters, Economie Appliquée 30(3), 439–459.

Kloek, T. and H.K. Van Dijk (1978), Efficient estimation of income distribution parameters, Journal of Econometrics 8: 61–74.

Kolm, S.-C. (1964), Les Fondements de l'Économie Publique: Introduction a la théorie du rôle économique de l'état (IFP, Paris).

Kolm, S.-C. (1966), Les Choix Financiers et Monétaires: Théorie et Technique Modernes) (Dunod, Paris).

Kolm, S.-C. (1968), The optimal production of social justice, in J. Margolis and H. Guitton, eds., Économie Publique (CNRS, Paris).

Kolm, S.-C. (1969), The optimal production of social justice, in J. Margolis and H. Guitton, eds., Public Economics (Macmillan, London, pp. 145–200).

Kolm, S.-C. (1971), Justice et equité (CEPREMAP, Paris).

Kolm, S.-C. (1973), More equal distributions of bundles of commodities, mimeo (CEPREMAP, Paris).

Kolm, S.-C. (1974), Rectifiances et dominances intégrales de tous dégrés, Technical report (CEPREMAP, Paris).

Kolm, S.-C. (1976a), Unequal inequalities I, Journal of Economic Theory 12: 416–442.

Kolm, S.-C. (1976b), Unequal inequalities II, Journal of Economic Theory 13: 82–111.

Kolm, S.-C. (1977), Multidimensional egalitarianisms, Quarterly Journal of Economics 91: 1–13.

Kolm, S.-C. (1993), Distributive justice, in R. Goodin and P. Pettit, eds., A Companion to Political Philosophy (Basil Blackwell, Oxford, pp. 30–66).

Kolm, S.-C. (1994), The meaning of fundamental preferences, Social Choice and Welfare 11: 193–198.

Kolm, S.-C. (1995), Economic justice: The central question, Euorpean Economic Review 39(3–4): 661–673.

Kolm, S.-C. (1996a), Chance and justice: Social policy and the Harsanyi-Vickery-Rawls problem, European Economic Review, (forthcoming).

Kolm, S.-C. (1996b), Modern Theories of Justice, (MIT Press, Cambridege MA).

Kolm, S.-C. (1997a), Justice and Equity, (MIT Press, Cambridege MA), English translation with new Foreword.

Kolm, S.-C. (1997b), Macrojustice, Avances théoriques en Economie Sociale.

Kolm, S.-C. (1997c), Rational measurement of income inequality, Working paper, CGPC, 4eme Section, Affaires Economiques, France.

Kondor, Y. (1975), Value judgement implied by the use of various measures of income inequality, The Review of Income and Wealth, 309–321.

Koshevoy, G. (1995), Multivariate Lorenz majorization, Social Choice and Welfare 12: 93–102.

Krtscha, M. (1994), A new compromise measure of inequality, in W. Eichhorn, ed., Models and Measurement of Welfare and Inequality (Springer-Verlag, Heidelberg, pp. 111–119).

Kuga, K. (1973), Measures of income inequality: An axiomatic approach, Discussion Paper 76, Institute of Social and Economic Research, Osaka University.

Kuga, K. (1979), Comparison of inequality measures: a Monte Carlo study, Economic Studies Quarterly 30: 219–235.

Kuga, K. (1980), The Gini index and the generalised entropy class: further results and a vindication, Economic Studies Quarterly 31: 217–228.

Kullback, S. (1959), Information Theory and Statistics (Wiley, New York).

Kurabayashi, Y. and A. Yatsuka (1977), Redistribution of income and measures of income inequality, in T. Fuji and R. Sato, eds., Resource Allocation and Division of Space (Springer-Verlag, New York).

Kuznets, S. (1955), Economic growth and income inequality, American Economic Review 45: 1–28.

Lambert, P. and X. Ramos (1997), Horizontal inequity and vertical redistribution, International Tax and Public Finance 4: 25–37.

Lambert, P.J. (1993), The Distribution and Redistribution of Income: 2nd edn., (Manchester University Press, Manchester UK).

Lambert, P.J. and S. Yitzhaki (1995), Equity, equality and welfare, European Economic Review 39: 674–682.

Le Breton, M. (1994), Inequality, poverty measurement and welfare dominance: At attempt at unification. in W. Eichhorn, ed., Models and Measurement of Welfare and Inequality (Springer-Verlag, Heidelberg, pp. 120–140).

Lerman, R. I. and S. Yitzhaki (1984), A note on the calculation and interpretation of the Gini index, Economics Letters 15: 363–368.

Lerman, R.I. and S. Yitzhaki (1985), Income inequality effects by income source: A new approach and applications to the US, Review of Economics and Statistics 67: 151–156.

Lerman, R.I. and S. Yitzhaki (1989), Improving the accuracy of estimates of the Gini coefficient, Journal of Econometrics 42: 43–47.

Lorenz, M.O. (1905), Methods for measuring concentration of wealth, Journal of the American Statistical Association 9: 209–219.

Maasoumi, E. (1986), The measurement and decomposition of multi- dimensional inequality, Econometrica 54:(7), 991–997.

Maasoumi, E. (1989), Continuously distributed attributes and measures of multivariate inequality, Journal of Econometrics 42: 131–144.

Maasoumi, E. (1999), Multidimensioned approaches to welfare analysis, in J. Silber, ed., Income Inequality Measurement: From Theory to Practice (Kluwer).

Maasoumi, E., J. Mills, and S. Zandvakili (1997), Consensus ranking of US income distributions: a boot-strap application of tests for stochastic dominance, Technical report, Department of Economics, SMU, Department of Economics, SMU, Dallas.

Maasoumi, E. and G. Nickelsburg (1988), Multivariate measures of well-being and an analysis of inequality in the Michigan data, Journal of Business and Economic Statistics 6: 327–334.

Majumder, A. and S.R. Chakravarty (1990), Distribution of personal income: Development of a new model and its application to US income data, Journal of Applied Econometrics 5: 189–196.

Mangahas, M. (1975), Income inequality in the Philippines: A decomposition analysis, Population and employment working paper, International Labor Organization, Geneva.

Marshall, A.W. and I. Olkin (1979), Inequalities: Theory and Majorization (Academic Press, New York).

McDonald, J.B. (1984), Some generalized functions for the size distribution of income, Econometrica 52: 647–664.

McDonald, J.B. and M.R. Ransom (1979), Functional forms, estimation techniques and the distribution of income, Econometrica 47: 1513–1525.

McDonald, J.B. and M.R. Ransom (1981), An analysis of the bounds for the Gini coefficient, Journal of Econometrics 17: 177–188.

Meade, J.E. (1976), The Just Economy- Ch. VII Measurement and patterns of inequality (Allen and Unwin).

Mehran, F. (1975), A statistical analysis on income inequality based on decomposition of the Gini index, Proceeding of the 40th Session of ISI.

Mehran, F. (1976), Linear measures of income inequality, Econometrica 44:(7), 805–809.

Menezes, C., C. Geiss, and J. Tressler (1980), Increasing downside risk, American Economic Review 70: 921–931.

Merkies, A.H.Q.M. (1994), The scope of inequality coefficients, in W. Eichhorn, ed., Models and Measurement of Welfare and Inequality (Springer-Verlag, Heidelberg, pp. 141–161).

Metcalf, C.E. (1969), The size distribution of income during the business cycle, American Economic Review 59: 657–668.

Milanovic, B. (1994), The Gini-type functions: an alternative derivation, Bulletin of Economic Research 46: 81–90.

Mills, J.A. and S. Zandvakili (1997), Statistical inference via bootstrapping for measures of inequality, Journal of Applied Econometrics 12: 133–150.

Monti, A.C. (1991), The study of the Gini concentration ratio by means of the influence function, Statistica 51: 561–577.

Moore, D.S. (1968), An elementary proof of asymptotic normality of linear functions of order statistics, Annals of Mathematical Statistics 39: 263–265.

Morduch, J. and T. Sicular (1996), Rethinking inequality decomposition, with evidence from China, Working paper, Harvard University.

Moyes, P. (1987), A new concept of Lorenz domination, Economics Letters 23: 203–207.

Muliere, P. and M. Scarsini (1989), A note on stochastic dominance and inequality measures, Journal of Economic Theory 49: 314–323.

Murray, D. (1978), Extreme values for Gini coefficients calculated from grouped data, Economics Letters 1: 389–393.

Needleman, L. (1978), On the approximation of the Gini coefficient of concentration, Manchester School, pp. 105–122.

Nelson, R.D. and R.D. Pope (1990), Imprecise tail estimation and the empirical failure of stochastic dominance, American Statistical Association Proceedings, Business and Economic Statistics Section, pp. 374–379.

Newbery, D.M.G. (1970), A theorem on the measurement of inequality, Journal of Economic Theory 2: 264–266.

Nygård, F. and A. Sandström (1981), Measuring Income Inequality, Stockholm, Sweden: Almqvist Wicksell International.

Ok, E.A. (1995), Fuzzy measurement of income inequality: a class of fuzzy inequality measures, Social Choice and Welfare 12(2): 111–136.

Ok, E.A. (1996), Fuzzy measurement of income inequality: some possibility results on the fuzzification of the Lorenz ordering, Economic Theory 7(3): 513–530.

Ok, E.A. and J. Foster (1997), Lorenz dominance and the variance of logarithms, Economic Research Reports 97-22, C.V. Starr Center for Applied Economics, New York University, Faculty of Arts and Science, Dept. of Economics, New York.

Okun, A.M. (1975), Equality and Efficiency: the Big Trade-off (Brookings Institute, Washington).

Olkin, I. and S. Yitzhaki (1992), Gini regression analysis, International Statistical Review 60: 185–196.

Osmani, S.R. (1982), Economic Inequality and Group Welfare (Clarendon Press, Oxford).

Pareto, V. (1896), Ecrits sur la courbe de la répartition de la richesse, in Oeuvres complètes de Vilfredo Pareto, Giovanni Busino, Librairie Droz, Genève, 1965.

Pen, J. (1971), Income Distribution, (Allen Lane, Harmondsworth).

Piesch, W. (1975), Statistische Konzentrationsmasse, (J.C.B. Mohr-Paul Siebeck, Tübingen).

Pigou, A.C. (1912), Wealth and Welfare, (Macmillan, London).

Plotnick, R. (1981), A measure of horizontal inequity, Review of Economics and Statistics 63: 282–288.

Plotnick, R. (1982), The concept and measurement of horizontal inequity, Journal of Public Economics 17: 373–391.

Plotnick, R. (1985), A comparison of measures of horizontal inequity, in D. Martin and T. Smeeding, eds., Horizontal Equity, Uncertainty and Economic Well-being: Number 50 in Studies in Income and Wealth. Chicago: NBER and the University of Chicago Press.

Podder, N. (1993), A new decomposition of the Gini coefficient among groups and its interpretations with applications to Australia, Sankhya , Ser. B 55: 262–271.

Podder, N. (1995), On the relationship of the Gini coefficient and income elasticity, Sankhya , Ser. B 57: 428–432.

Podder, N. (1996), Relative deprivation, envy and economic inequality, Kyklos 49: 353–376.

Prieto-Alaiz, M. and M.P. Victoria-Feser (1996), Income distribution in Spain: A robust parametric approach, Distributional Analysis Discussion Paper 20, (London School of Economics, STICERD: London).

Pyatt, G. (1976), On the interpretation and disaggregation of Gini coefficient, Economic Journal 86: 243–255.

Pyatt, G. (1990), Social evaluation criteria, in D.C. and M. Zenga, eds., Income and Wealth Distribution, Inequality and Poverty (Springer-Verlag, Heidelberg, pp. 243–253).

Pyatt, G., C.N. Chen, and J. Fei (1980), The distribution of income by factor components, Quarterly Journal of Economics 95: 451–473.

Quirk, J.D. and R. Saposnik (1962), Admissibility and measurable utility functions, Review of Economic Studies 29: 140–146.

Ranadive, K.R. (1965), The equality of incomes in India, Bulletin of the Oxford Institute of Statistics 27: 119–134.

Rao, C.R. (1973), Linear Statistical Inference and Its Applications (Wiley, New York).

Rao, U.L.P. and A.Y.P. Tam (1987), An empirical study of selection and estimation of alternative models of the Lorenz curve, Journal of Applied Statistics 14: 275–280.

Rao, V.M. (1969), Two decompositions of the concentration ratio, Journal of the Royal Statistical Society, Series A 132: 418–425.

Rasche, R.H., J. Gaffney, A.Y.C. Koo, and N. Obst (1980), Functional forms for estimating the Lorenz curve, Econometrica 48: 1061–1062.

Rawls, J. (1972), A Theory of Justice (Oxford University Press, Oxford).

Rietveld, P. (1990), Multidimensional inequality comparisons, Economics Letters 32: 187–192.

Roemer, J.E. (1996), Theories of Distributive Justice (Harvard University Press, Cambridge, MA).

Rothschild, M. and J.E. Stiglitz (1973), Some further results on the measurement of inequality, Journal of Economic Theory 6: 188–203.

Rubin, D.B. (1981), The Bayesian bootstrap, Annals of Statistics 9: 130–134.

Runciman, W.G. (1966), Relative Deprivation and Social Justice (Routledge, London).

Russell, R.R. (1985), A note on decomposable inequality measures, Review of Economic Studies 52:(4), 347–352.

Salas, R. (1998), Welfare-consistent inequality indices in changing populations: the marginal population replication axiom. a note, Journal of Public Economics 67(1): 145–150.

Salem, A.B.Z. and T.D. Mount (1974), A convenient descriptive model of income distribution: The Gamma density, Econometrica 42: 1115–1127.

Sandström, A. (1982), Estimating the Gini coefficient, Working Paper 1982:18, Department of Statistics, University of Stockholm.

Sandström, A. (1983), Estimating income inequality: Large sample inference in finite populations, Working Paper 1983:5, Department of Statistics, University of Stockholm.

Sandström, A., J.H. Wretman, and B. Walden (1985), Variance estimators of the Gini coefficient: simple random sampling, Metron 43: 41–70.

Sandström, A., J.H. Wretman, and B. Walden (1988), Variance estimators of the Gini coefficient: probability sampling, Journal of Business and Economic Statistics 6: 113–120.

Saposnik, R. (1981), Rank dominance in income distribution, Public Choice 36: 147–151.

Saposnik, R. (1983), On evaluating income distributions: rank dominance, Public Choice 40: 329–336.

Saposnik, R. and R. Tutterow (1992), On the rank, generalised Lorenz and overtaking criteria for evaluating stochastic income regimes, Southern Economic Journal 59.

Schenker, N. (1985), Qualms about bootstrap confidence intervals, Journal of the American Statistical Association 80: 360–361.

Schutz, R.R. (1951), On the measurement of income inequality, American Economic Review 41: 107–122.

Sen, A.K. (1973), On Economic Inequality (Clarendon Press, Oxford).

Sen, A.K. (1976), Poverty: An ordinal approach to measurement, Econometrica 44: 219–231.

Sen, A.K. (2000), Social justice and the distribution of income, in A.B. Atkinson and F. Bourguignon, eds., Handbook of Income Distribution (North Holland, Amsterdam, Chap. 1).

Sen, A.K. and J.E. Foster (1997), On Economic Inequality, 2nd edn., (Clarendon Press, Oxford).

Shalit, H. (1985), Calculating the Gini index of inequality for individual data, Oxford Bulletin of Economics and Statistics 47: 185–189.

Shao, J. and D. Tu (1995), The Jackknife and the Bootstrap (Springer-Verlag, New York).

Sheshinski, E. (1972), Relation between a social welfare function and the Gini index of inequality, Journal of Economic Theory 4: 98–100.

Shorack, G.R. (1972), Functions of order statistics, Annals of Mathematical Statistics 43: 412–427.

Shorrocks, A. (1998), Deprivation profiles and deprivation indices, in S.P. Jenkins, A. Kapteyn, and B.M. Van Praag, eds., The Distribution of Welfare and Household Production: International Perspectives (Cambridge University Press, Cambridge, Chap. 11, pp. 250–267).

Shorrocks, A. F. (1980), The class of additively decomposable inequality measures, Econometrica 48: 613–625.

Shorrocks, A.F. (1982), Inequality decomposition by factor components, Econometrica 50:(1), 193–211.

Shorrocks, A.F. (1983), Ranking income distribution, Economica 50(197), 3–17.

Shorrocks, A.F. (1984), Inequality decomposition by population subgroups, Econometrica 52: 1369–1385.

Shorrocks, A.F. (1988), Aggregation issues in inequality measurement, in W. Eichhorn, ed., Measurement in Economics, (Physica Verlag, Heidelberg).

Shorrocks, A.F. and J.E. Foster (1987), Transfer-sensitive inequality measures, Review of Economic Studies 54: 485–498.

Shorrocks, A.F. and D.J. Slottje (1995), Approximating unanimity orderings: an application to Lorenz dominance, Department of economics discussion paper, University of Essex.

Silber, J. (1989), Factor components, population subgroups and the computation of the Gini index of inequality, The Review of Economics and Statistics 71: 107–115.

Silber, J. (1995), Horizontal inequity, the Gini index, and the measurement of distributional change, Research on Inequality 6: 379–392.

Sillitto, G.P. (1969), Derivation of approximations to inverse distribution function of a continuous univariate population from the order statistics of a sample, Biometrika 56: 641–650.

Silverman, B.W. (1986), Density Estimation for Statistics and Data Analysis, Chapman and Hall.

Singh, S.K. and G.S. Maddala (1976), A function for the size distribution of income, Econometrica 44: 963–970.

Stark, O., J.E. Taylor, and S. Yitzhaki (1986), Remittances and inequality, Economic Journal 96: 722–740.

Stark, O., J.E. Taylor, and S. Yitzhaki (1988), Migration, remittances and inequality, Journal of Development Economics 28: 309–322.

Stark, O. and S. Yitzhaki (1988), The migration response to relative deprivation, Journal of Population Economics, 1.

Stein, W.E., R.C. Pfaffenberger, and D.W. French (1987), Sampling error in first-order stochastic dominance, Journal of Financial Research 10: 259–269.

Stern, N.H. (1977), Welfare weights and the elasticity of the marginal valuation of income, in M. Artis and A.R. Nobay, eds., Studies in Modern Economic Analysis (Basil Blackwell, Oxford).

Stich, A. (1996), Inequality and negative income, Discussion paper in Statistics and Econometrics 04/96, Universität zu Köln, Köln, Germany.

Stuart, A. (1954), The correlation between variate values and ranks in samples from a continuous dstribution, British Journal of Statistical Psychology 7: 37–44.

Subramanian, S. (1987), On a simple transfer-sensitive index of inequality, Economics Letters 23: 389–392.

Suzumura, K. (1983), Rational Choice, Collective Decisions and Social Welfare (Cambridge University Press, Cambridge).

Taille, C. (1981), Lorenz ordering within the generalized gamma family of income distributions, in P. Taille, G.P. Patil, and B. Baldessari, eds., Statistical Distributions in Scientific Work (Reidel, Boston).

Takayama, N. (1979), Poverty, income inequality and their measures: Professor Sen's axiomatic approach reconsidered, Econometrica 47: 747–759.

Tawney, H.R. (1964), Equality, (Allen and Unwin, London).

Temkin, L.S. (1986), Inequality, Philosophy and Public Affairs 15: 99–121.

Temkin, L.S. (1993), Inequality, (Oxford University Press, Oxford).

Tendulkar, S. (1983), Economic inequality in an Indian perspective, in A. Beteille, ed., Equality and Inequality (Oxford University Press, Delhi).

Theil, H. (1967), Economics and Information Theory (North Holland, Amsterdam).

Theil, H. (1979a), The measurement of inequality by components of income, Economics Letters 2: 197–9.

Theil, H. (1979b), World income inequality and its components, Economics Letters 2: 99–102.

Thistle, P.D. (1989a), Duality between generalized Lorenz curves and distribution functions, Economic Studies Quarterly. 404(6): 183–187.

Thistle, P.D. (1989b), Ranking distributions with generalized Lorenz curves, Southern Economic Journal 56: 1–12.

Thistle, P.D. (1990), Large sample properties of two inequality indices, Econometrica 58: 725–728.

Thon, D. (1982), An axiomatization of the Gini coefficient, Mathematical Social Science 2: 131–143.

Thurow, L. (1971), The income distribution as a pure public good, Quarterly Journal of Economics 85: 327–336.

Toyoda, T. (1975), Inequalities of income distributions: their comparisons and inequality measures, Kokumin Keizai 134: 15–41 (In Japanese).

Toyoda, T. (1980), Decomposability of inequality measures, Economic Studies Quarterly 31(12): 207–246.

Trannoy, A. (1986), On Thon's axiomatization of the Gini index, Mathematical Social Sciences 11: 191–194.

Tsui, K.-Y. (1995), Multidimensional generalizations of the relative and absolute inequality indices: the Atkinson-Kolm-Sen approach, Journal of Economic Theory 67: 251–265.

Van Batenburg, P.C. and B.M.S. Van Praag (1980), The perception of welfare inequality: a correction note, European Economic Review 13(3), 259–261.

Van Herwaarden, F.G., A. Kapteyn, and B.M.S. Van Praag (1977), 12,000 individual welfare functions of income: a comparison of six samples in Belgium and the Netherlands, European Economic Review, 9.

Van Praag, B.M.S. (1977), The perception of welfare inequality, European Economic Review 10(11): 189–207.

Van Praag, B.M.S. (1978), The perception of income inequality, in W. Krelle and A.F. Shorrocks, eds., Personal Income Distribution (North Holland, Amsterdam).

Van Praag, B.M.S., A.J.M. Hagenaars, and W. Van Eck (1983), The influence of classification and observation errors on the measurement of income inequality, Econometrica 51: 1093–1108.

Victoria-Feser, M.-P. (1993), Robust Methods for Personal Income Distribution Models, Ph. D. thesis, University of Geneva, Switzerland. Thesis no 384.

Victoria-Feser, M.-P. (1995), Robust methods for personal income distribution models with application to Dagum's model, in C. Dagum and A. Lemmi, eds., Income Distribution, Social Welfare, Inequality and Poverty (JAI Press, Connecticut).

Victoria-Feser, M.-P. (1999), The sampling properties of inequality indices: comment, in J. Silber ed., Income Ineeqquality Measurement: from Theory to Practice (Kluwer, Deventer).

Victoria-Feser, M.-P. and E. Ronchetti (1997), Robust estimation for grouped data, Journal of the American Statistical Association 92: 333–340.

Wakker, P. (1993), Additive representations on rank-ordered sets: Ii. the topological approach, Journal of Mathematical Economics 22(1): 1–26.

Weymark, J.A. (1981), Generalized Gini inequality indices, Mathematical Social Sciences 1: 409–430.

Wilfling, B. (1996), The Lorenz-ordering of generalized beta-ii income distributions, Journal of Econometrics 71: 381–388.

Wilfling, B. and W. Krämer (1993), The Lorenz-ordering of Singh-Maddala income distributions, Economics Letters 43: 53–57.

Wiles, P.J.D. (1974), Income Distribution, East and West, (North Holland, Amsterdam).

Wiles, P.J.D. and Markowski, S. (1971), Income distribution under communism and capitalism, Soviet Studies 22: 344–369, 485–511.

Wolfson, M. (1994), Conceptual issues in normative measurement—when inequalities diverge, American Economic Review 84(5): 353–358.

Yaari, M.E. (1987), The dual theory of choice under risk, Econometrica 55: 99–115.

Yaari, M.E. (1988), A controversial proposal concerning inequality measurement, Journal of Economic Theory 44(4): 381–397.

Yitzhaki, S. (1979), Relative deprivation and the Gini coefficient, Quarterly Journal of Economics 93: 321–324.

Yitzhaki, S. (1980), Relative deprivation and the Gini coefficient: reply, Quarterly Journal of Economics 95: 575–6.

Yitzhaki, S. (1982a), Relative deprivation and economic welfare, European Economic Review 17(1): 99–114.

Yitzhaki, S. (1982b), Stochastic dominance, mean variance and Gini's mean difference, American Economic Review, 178–185.

Yitzhaki, S. (1983), On an extension of the Gini inequality index, International Economic Review 24(10): 617–628.

Yitzhaki, S. (1991), Calculating jackknife variance estimators for parameters of the Gini method, Journal of Business and Economic Statistics 9: 235–238.

Yitzhaki, S. (1996), On using linear regressions in welfare economics, Journal of Business and Economic Statistics 14: 478–486.

Yitzhaki, S. (1998), More than a dozen alternative ways of spelling Gini, Research on Economic Inequality 8: 13–30.

Yitzhaki, S. and I. Olkin (1991), Concentration indices and concentration curves, in K. Mosler and M. Scarsini, eds., Stochastic Orders and Decisions under Risk Institute of Mathematical Statistics: Lecture-Notes Monograph Series, Vol. 19, pp. 380–392.

Yoshida, T. (1977), The necessary and sufficient condition for additive separability of income inequality measures. Economic Studies Quarterly 28: 160–163.

Young, H. P. (1994), Equity in Theory and in Practice, (Princeton University Press, Princeton).

Zagier, D. (1982), On the decomposability of the Gini coefficient and other indices of inequality, Discussion paper, Institut für Gesellschafts-und Wirtschaftswissenschaften, Universität Bonn.

Zajac, E.E. (1996), Political Economy of Fairness (MIT Press, Cambridge MA).

Zheng, B. (1996), Statistical inferences for testing marginal changes in Lorenz and Generalized Lorenz curves, Working paper, Department of Economics, University of Colorado at Denver.

Zheng, B. and B.J. Cushing (1996), Large sample statistical inferences for testing marginal changes in inequality indices. Working paper, University of Colorado at Denver.

Zoli, C. (1998), Intersecting generalized Lorenz curves and the Gini index, Social Choice and Welfare, forthcoming.

Chapter 3

THREE CENTURIES OF INEQUALITY IN BRITAIN AND AMERICA

PETER H. LINDERT

University of California, Davis

Contents

Keywords: Income inequality, wealth inequality, income distribution, wealth distribution, history

JEL codes. D31, D63, N31, N32, N33, N34

Handbook of Income Distribution, Volume 1. Edited by A. B. Atkinson and F. Bourguignon

Abstract

Income and wealth inequality rose over the first 150 years of US history. They rose in Britain before 1875, especially 1740–1810. The first half of the 20th century equalized pre-fisc incomes both in Britain and in America. From the 1970s to the 1990s inequality rose in both countries, reversing most or all of the previous equalization. Government redistribution explains part but not all of the reversals in inequality trends. Factor-market forces and economic growth would have produced a similar timing of rises and falls in income inequality even without shifts in the progressivity of redistribution through government.

Redistribution toward the poor tends to happen least in those times and polities where it would seem most justified by the usual goals of welfare policy.

Arthur Burns was delighted with what he read in Simon Kuznets's massive new book in 1953. Kuznets found that incomes were getting more equal. For Burns, this finding re-wrote all the rules for the perennial debate over inequality and redistribution through government:

Few Americans and fewer Europeans are aware of the transformation in the distribution of our national income that has occurred within the past twenty years—a transformation that has been carried out peacefully and gradually, but which may already be counted as one of the great social revolutions of history ....

Considerable income inequalities still exist in our midst, but they require careful interpretation .... the upper stratum is dominated by the most productive age, sex, and educational groups in the population ....

These conclusions of Kuznets' investigation have great significance for the American people. If we are to look forward constructively to a material reduction of income inequalities in the future, we must seek to attain it principally by raising the productivity of those at the bottom of the income scale rather than by transferring income from the rich to the poor .... Substantial further government redistribution of income may .... affect adversely the size of the national income, while it cannot improve appreciably the living conditions of the great masses. (Burns, 1954: p. 137)

Burns was neither the first nor the last to base a sermon about inequality on some historical data. His enthusiasm stands out in retrospect, however, because it came at a time when an epochal equalization of incomes seemed tangible to many. Seeing him in that dawn of discovery, and marveling at his breath-taking leaps of logic, we naturally wonder about the longer and deeper history. Was he right? How long had that egalitarian trend been going on before the 1950s? Was the non-meritocratic part of inequality really stripped away in those past twenty years? Would the change be permanent? And what would Burns have written about inequality movements "within the past twenty years" if he were writing at the end of the twentieth century?

We can now take stock of past inequality movements in Britain and the United States with the help of recent progress on three fronts: (1) New experiences since the 1970s; (2) archeological progress, yielding better retrospective data on the more distant past; and (3) a highly-developed algebra that decomposes inequality movements into their proximate causes, in order to trace more fingerprints of the underlying causal forces than simple inequality aggregates can reveal.

A number of *conclusions* about inequality movements stand out, despite all the data flaws and the nuances we have learned to expect from movements in the distribution of incomes among fluctuating human populations:

1. Income and wealth inequality definitely rose over the first 150 years of US history. Britain may also have had an early period of rising inequality, but the most likely period of rising inequality (1740–1810) was earlier than most writers have imagined.
2. Britain and America, and indeed most high-income countries, did indeed experience a shift toward more equal pre-fisc incomes in the first half of the twentieth century, as Kuznets believed. The leveling was brief and sharp for America, but proceeded more gradually for Britain. Most or all of the leveling took the form of a narrowing of the gaps between the top and middle ranks.
3. From the 1970s to the 1990s income inequality clearly rose in these two countries. This widening reversed most or all of the previous equalization of pre-fisc incomes. There was probably still a net equalization of post-fisc (disposable) incomes over the whole three centuries, however.

   Exploring these movements has deepened our knowledge of their underlying causes:
4. Even "pre-fisc" income inequality moves partly in response to redistribution through government. The rise of tax-transfer progressivity equalized the ownership of human and non-human capital, and its later stasis played a permissive role in the recent return of rising inequality.
5. Government redistribution cannot explain all of the epochal reversals in inequality trends, however. Factor-market forces and economic growth would have produced a similar chronology of rises and falls in income inequality even without shifts in the progressivity of redistribution through government. The dominant causal forces here are demographic change, unbalanced technological advance, and income effects.
6. These underlying forces change overall inequality both through movements in relative factor prices and through compositional shifts in group weights.
7. The key to future improvements in our understanding of the forces driving income inequality lies in simultaneously explaining the pre-fisc inequality, the inequality of political voice, and government redistribution between rich and poor. Only with such a three-sided simultaneous system will we have a satisfactory explanation of the Robin Hood paradox, which notes that redistribution toward the poor tends to happen least in those times and polities where it would seem most justified by the usual goals of welfare policy.

1. Choosing issues, measures, and methods

Our conventions for addressing, measuring, and explaining inequality movements have governed what we are prepared to see, for better and for worse. Before turning to the long history that can now be mapped, and surveying the usual approaches, we should note where the literature has placed its lamp-posts, illuminating some aspects of inequality but leaving others in the dark.

1.1. Redistributable income or living standards?

Much follows from one's choice of a social issue for research and policy debate. Our whole view of inequality hinges on whether we care more about (1) the inequality of economic resources that economic policies might redistribute or (2) the overall inequality of living standards. The division is sharp here. Pursuing redistributable incomes, as in the rest of this chapter and this book, reveals a history of episodic swings in this kind of inequality. Pursuing the inequality of living standards among individual lifetimes reveals more of an equalizing trend.

Economists' exploration of inequality movements has seldom strayed far from the issue that dominates most of economics: What is the proper role of government in our lives? Income inequality is of interest primarily as an exhibit in the debate over how, or whether, government should redistribute income and wealth. The (valid) pre-occupation with this perennial debate shapes all choices of inequality measurement. In the choice of independent variables (influences on inequality trends), considerable attention is spent on allocating the credit or blame for inequality trends between government redistribution, market movements, and the distribution of human capital. It matters to most writers whether the credit for a reduction in inequality should be given to government and labor unions, or to the normal workings of the marketplace, or to equalization of individuals' human capital.

Similarly, the dependent variable of interest is typically one directly responsive to government manipulation and to market forces, such as taxable market income or full-time annual earnings. When the subject turns to the health and longevity side of inequality, our usual instinct is to view health and death as things experienced by families at different positions in the income ranks, or by families headed by persons in different socio-occupational classes. Thus infant mortality is something suffered differentially by poor and rich parents, and we measure its impact at the household level (e.g., Titmuss, 1943). The implicit policy question is how much mortality could be reduced and equalized by redistributing economic resources (income, health care, etc.) across households.

Yet one might care primarily about that other inequality concept, the inequality of overall living standards themselves, not just the income part of them most manipulable by changing government policy or other economic institutions. Such a broader concern for inequality of human living standards would give far more attention to inequalities in individuals' health and length of life in particular.[1] Even if we valued whole life-times only according to people's total lifetime consumption, the literature on economic inequality would look much different from the literature to be surveyed below. Robert Summers (1956) noted this, and Lee Lillard (1977) offered indirect measures of the inequality of lifetime income and consumption. Such measures, however, stay close to the annual income idea by positing a fixed economic lifetime. A bigger second step is to follow the inequality of lifetime consumption among birth cohorts of individuals, taking account of the inequality in the length of life. The inequality of living standards, as proxied by lifetime consumption, is governed more by movements in infant mortality than by movements in the inequality of annual income. Improved infant survival, even if evenly spread across economic classes, has probably converted an upward drift in income inequality into a clear trend toward *more equal* lifetime consumption across individuals (Lindert, 1991: pp. 213–214; Jackson, 1994).

The usual economic treatment of inequality resists giving such heavy weight to newborns as citizens, preferring to concentrate on infant death as something experienced differentially by parents in different social classes. The literature says much about mortality gaps by income or social class, little about how the greatest reduction in individual-lifetime inequality may have been achieved by advances in medicine and health care that did not favor any class. Since this chapter's task is to share the literature's preoccupation with the debate over income inequality, differentials in life expectancy will be noted only *en passant*, as extra twists on inequalities between income ranks.[2]

1.2. The pre-fisc focus

Much of the literature on income inequality movements chooses to follow measures of the inequality of pre-fisc, or original, incomes, rather than the post-fisc disposable incomes people actually receive. This frequent choice has a rationale and a major implication.

The rationale is to concentrate on the larger intellectual challenge. The directly redistributive component of post-fisc inequality is transparently attributable to government, at least in the accounting sense. The task of explaining movements in pre-fisc or original income is more challenging. Many economic forces compete for explanatory roles.

---

[1] For a review of alternative concepts of the standard of living, with some discussion of inequality movements, see Steckel (1994). There is a large literature on the economic valuation of gains in life expectancy (e.g., Usher, 1973; Williamson, 1984), but without quantification of its impact on the inequality of living standards, a task left to Jackson (1994).

[2] To emphasize that either view to the inequality of life expectancy seems valid, depending on the question being pursued, I should note that I have viewed it both ways. In Lindert (1991: p. 214) I suggested a focus on individual lifetime consumption patterns, so that, for example, infant deaths in any social class would raise the inequality of living standards among individuals. This view is developed and quantified in Jackson (1994). In a comment on Britain on the same page, and in Lindert (1994), I reverted to the implicit convention of viewing infant mortality as a subtraction from the well-being of households in the affected ranks of the income distribution.

Indeed pre-fisc is not even pre-fisc, inasmuch as prior fiscal interventions, such as estate tax, affect the inequality of this year's original incomes.

The implication to bear in mind is that the literature focusing on movements in pre-fisc inequality, even when it recognizes feedbacks from past taxes and transfers to current original income, hides much of the role of government in shaping the inequality of current disposable income.

1.3. Causal methods

Different analytical techniques compete for our energies and attention, so that using one more fully can crowd out other insights. The treatment of income inequality has passed from simple factor-price and factor-share tales, to a more sophisticated decompositional accounting based on identities, to the use of regressions and large-model simulations to weigh exogenous causal forces. Time spent at each step is time not spent at the next.

Before the mid-twentieth century the usual instinct was to imagine fixed shares of the population for different economic classes, each rewarded by a different factor price, and to assume that movements in rents and profit rates and wage rates summarized the movements in inequality. While this simple equation of factors and quantile ranks had some validity back when the classical economists wrote (Lindert, 1986), it was obsolete long before it was abandoned.

Simon Kuznets (1955) ushered in the current era of decompositional inequality accounting with his often-cited example of how shifting group weights could generate inequality trends without any movement at all in factor prices. The algebra has grown in sophistication, as evidenced by other chapters in this volume. Identifying the behavior of the different components makes it possible to test numerous side-implications of each hypothesis about the sources of inequality.

While decomposing inequality into its parts sharpens our sense of how inequality changes, it leaves open the question of why. Each of the classes into which decompositions divide an inequality change can be affected by several underlying forces in unknown proportions, and each of those forces typically shapes inequality though more than one component. Decompositional analysis must share the stage with statistical and simulation- model (e.g., computable general equilibrium) techniques for weighing the contributions of underlying forces.

1.4. The Kuznets conjecture

Finally, one other lamp-post has illuminated a corner of the subject rather well, a corner from which it is time to move. This is the literature testing whether or not inequality follows an inverted-U curve, a Kuznets curve, as per capita income rises.

Despite its name, Kuznets never drew such a curve. He was content to offer a verbal conjecture about how income inequality might move, and to use a tale of compositional shifts and some common sense to suggest explanations. He was rightly modest about the international data base he had at his disposal, and described his conjectures about trends as "...perhaps 5% empirical information and 95% speculation, some of it possibly tainted by wishful thinking" (Kuznets, 1955: p. 26).

Kuznets did not feel the same about the rise as he did about the fall of inequality. That inequality tended to decline at some advanced stage of development, he seemed quite confident. He barely asserted—rather, wondered about—the possibility of an earlier rise. His confidence in his explanations for it all were similarly mixed: He emphasized the role of sectoral shifts as an engine of inequality, and mused more vaguely about the possible importance of the demographic transition (Kuznets, 1955).

The Kuznets curve has to some extent tyrannized the literature on inequality trends. Energies that could have moved earlier into exploring the underlying causes of inequality were diverted into a debate over whether there was or was not an inverted U curve, either in history or in postwar international cross-sections. Like other writings, the rest of this chapter will show both theoretical and empirical reasons to doubt that countries must follow such a rise and fall in inequality. It is time to move onto explorations that proceed directly to the task of explaining any episodic movement, without bothering to relate it to the Kuznets curve.

2. Was there a rise in inequality sometime before 1914?

[As a] conjectural conclusion .... I would place the early phase in which income inequality might have been widening, from about 1780 to 1850 in England; from about 1840 to 1890, and particularly from 1870 on in the United States; and, from the 1840's to the 1890's in Germany. (Kuznets, 1955: p. 19)

The top candidates for rising inequality, in Kuznets's view, were those epochs that the debates of the 1960s would call "industrialization" or "take-off", including the classic dating of Britain's Industrial Revolution.

Was it true? Our interest has remained strong since 1955, and our views have changed. Pioneering work by Lee Soltow has amassed an impressive array of primary data. Soltow doubts that there was any period of sustained and serious widening of inequalities in either Britain or America. Rather, he emphasizes that inequalities were traditionally stark before they narrowed dramatically across the twentieth century. Jeffrey Williamson and I, by contrast, see early widening and later narrowing of inequality in both countries, though not with the timing conjectured by Kuznets. Jan Luiten van Zanden has posited an early rise in inequality by arguing that most economies of Western Europe ascended a "super-Kuznets curve" *before* industrialization, sometime between the sixteenth century and the late eighteenth century. The evidence, and the additional patterns of interest, need to be viewed for Britain and America separately.[3]

---

[3] See, in particular, Soltow (1968, 1969, 1971, 1975, 1984, 1989, 1990, 1992); Williamson and Lindert (1980); Lindert and Williamson (1983, 1985); Williamson (1985, 1991); Lindert (1986, 1991, 1994); criticisms of Williamson (1985) by Jackson (1987) and Feinstein (1988); criticisms of Lindert (1991) by Jackson (1994); Phelps Brown (1988); and van Zanden (1994).

2.1. Britain, 1688–1914

For Britain before 1914, our best guesses are necessarily eclectic. There is little choice but to weave an archival quilt of indirect clues on income inequality. The main pieces of primary material are: (1) the social tables used by the "political arithmeticians" from Gregory King through A.L. Bowley; (2) measures of personal wealth based on probate records and occasional tax assessments; (3) the paths followed by a few dozen wage series; (4) land-rent series, and (5) early partial tax returns.

Britain's early income distributions start from educated works of fiction, those social tables drawn up by Gregory King, Joseph Massie, Patrick Colquhoun, R. Dudley Baxter, A.L. Bowley and others. Each of these experts had access to the best miscellany of data available in London at the time. The first three of them, at least, had axes to grind. King seemed intent on warning that the nation had only a limited capacity to raise tax revenues for wars against France. Massie railed against the sugar monopoly. Colquhoun highlighted the nation's achievements and its ability to afford more poor relief. Such dangerous estimates need to be cross-checked and revised with the help of all the records unearthed by subsequent scholarship. Weighing them carefully has yielded useful tentative revised estimates of the whole distribution of class-average incomes per household (Lindert and Williamson 1982, 1983).[4]

Table 1 and Fig. 1 summarize the income distribution estimates for England-Wales and the UK since 1688. We focus on top-rank income shares because the underlying data aggregated the poorest ranks of society into a few large classes, blurring our view of inequalities below the median household before 1914. The estimates imply that Britain's inequality was higher between 1688 and 1911 than anytime since, though the gaps in the 1990s approach those of 1911. There is no clear early widening of the income gaps, though the period 1759–1802 (or, probably, from the 1740s to the 1810s) gives signals of a rise in the share received by the richest. There is also the suggestion that income inequality declined gently in the last five decades before World War I, though the 1911 figures are based on highly aggregated distributions.

The suggestion of overall stability in the income gaps, with a slight rise in 1759–1802 and a possible slight decline in 1867–1911, should not be accepted on the basis of the revised social tables alone. We need to see what other evidence says about the suggested long-run stability, the apparent net rise of 1759–1802 (or similar dates), and the possible decline between 1867 and 1911.

We have three main kinds of additional clues available: (1) Movements in factor-price ratios; (2) estimates of movements in the inequality of wealth or property income, and (3) estimates of movements in the inequality of human earnings.

---

[4] The choice of population units is driven by data availability. In this case it is expedient to compare estimates for households. The early social tables sometimes called them "families" but apparently included servants in wealthy households and unrelated adult individuals at the bottom of the distribution. The rest of this chapter alternates between households, earners, and adults, depending on which units are offered in the available series.

Table 1

Income inequality trends in the UK, 1688–1995

A. Rough estimates for early benchmark years[a]

	Shares of pre-tax nominal personal income received by			Real-income shares (1911 base)	
	Top 5% of households	Top 20% of households	Nominal Gini × 100	Top 5%	Top 20%
England and Wales					
1688 (King, revised)	35.6	58.1	55.6	n.a.	n.a.
1759 (Massie, revised)	35.4	57.5	52.2	21.1	46.4
1801/03 (Colquhoun, revised)	39.2	63.2	59.3	27.9	55.9
1867 (Baxter, revised)	41.2	57.3	49.0	37.4	55.6
United Kingdom					
1867 (Baxter, revised)	41.1	57.7	50.6	37.3	56.0
1911 (Bowley revised)	38.7	55.2	48.3	38.7	55.2

[a] The main sources for the 1688–1867 rough estimates are Lindert and Williamson (1982, 1983) and Williamson (1985), using the full class detail, not just the 13-class comparisons in Table 3 of Lindet and Williamson (1993). I have since revised the estimates for 1867, however, to adjust them for a distribution among Baxter's income-recipients to a distribution among households. I have done the same for the Bowley estimates of 1911, removing earnings of minors and atttributing them to adult-head households. The 1911 estimates may miss some paupers (who comprise about 3% of the total population), causing some understatement of inequality. The detailed re-calculations are available upon request.

The "real" top-group shares are based on separate deflators for the incomes of the top 5%, top 20%, and all households, 1759–1911, as explained in (Lindert, 1998). The deflators differ mainly because of pronounced movements in the relative prices of food and rent versus all commodities. Since the data on nominal incomes excluded income from owner-occupied housing, this housing should also be excluded from the cost-of-living bundle for the upper classes. The variant shown here assumes that the occupant-owned share of all housing was 100% for the top 5% of households, 67% for the next 15%, and 0% for the bottom 80% of households.

The first set of clues uses a crude factor-price ratio, the ratio of land rents to wage rates. For an early era in which land still commanded a significant share of national product, land rents alone can represent much of what was happening to the average reward for the use of property. And for England and Wales as late as 1867, land was almost exclusively an upper-class asset. Land rents accruing to the top decile of households were 13% of their income versus only 1% of the income of the other 90% of households. Stated differently, about 89% of land rents were earned by that top decile (Lindert, 1986: p. 1155). In such a society, any rise in the ratio of land rents to the wages of common labor would imply a rise in the top decile's income share, other things being equal. As it happens, the only period between 1688 and 1914 in which the rent/wage

Table 1

Income inequality trends in the UK, 1688–1995, continued

B. Inland Revenue, Survey of Personal Incomes (SPI)[a]

Financial year beginning	Shares of pre-tax income received by			
	Top 1% of tax units	Top 5% of tax units	Top 20% of tax units	Gini × 100
1938	17.1	31.5	52.4	42.3
1949	10.6	23.1	45.3	36.4
1954	8.8	19.7	42.1	34.2
1959	7.9	18.7	41.2	33.4
1964	7.7	18.3	40.9	33.0
1965	7.8	18.5	41.1	33.5
1966	7.2	17.6	40.3	32.8
1967	7.0	17.4	40.2	32.8
1968	6.9	17.3	40.4	33.1
1969	6.7	17.1	40.0	32.6
1970	6.2	16.6	39.9	32.2
1971	6.1	16.4	39.8	32.5
1972	6.0	15.9	38.9	30.5
1973	6.2	16.1	39.0	31.2
1974	5.9	15.8	39.4	32.0

[a] Royal Commission (1977: pp. 240–243).

ratio clearly rose was circa 1750–1810, roughly the period in which the social tables show their only rise in the top-decile and top-quintile income shares.[5]

By contrast, the separate estimates of wealthholding inequality and of earnings inequality do not follow the same chronology. The next set of clues consists of wealth distributions worked up from large samples of probate inventories.[6] Wealth is not in-

[5] This view of rent/wage trends rests on a miscellany of sources. The wage series are the Phelps Brown–Hopkins wage for building laborers and John's (1989) farm wage rates. The rents are those reported in John (1989), in my gleanings of several rent series in (Lindert, 1983, working paper), and in an updated version of Gregory Clark's (1991) rack-rent series. Clark's current estimates of the rental/wage ratio in English agriculture show a large sustained rise from 1740 all the way to 1840.

Another crude hint also points to the era ending in the French Wars as the top candidate for rising inequality in Britain. Between 1780 and 1801 the current-consensus estimates of national product per employed person grew substantially, whereas the real wages received by broad groups of workers stagnated or even declined (Feinstein, 1996b, and the sources cited there). Growth rates between the 1801 and 1831 benchmarks again suggest faster growth in average national product than in real wages, though the hint looks stronger for 1780–1801 than for 1801–1831.

[6] The wealth distributions for England and Wales 1670–1875 are detailed and interpreted in Lindert (1985, 1986, 1987). The financial and social position of the very top wealth-holders was described at length by Rubinstein (1981, 1986). See also Soltow (1990) on Scottish landed wealth in the eighteenth century.

Table 1

Income inequality trends in the UK, 1688–1995, continued

C. CSO hybrid estimates (Blue Books)[a]

Financial year beginning	Shares of pre-tax income received by			
	Top 1% of tax units	Top 5% of tax units	Top 20% of tax units	Gini × 100
1949	11.2	23.8	47.3	41.1
1954	9.3	20.8	45.2	40.3
1959	8.4	19.9	44.5	39.8
1962	8.3	19.5	44.4	39.7
1963	8.0	19.2	44.3	39.5
1964	8.2	19.5	44.6	39.9
1965	8.1	19.6	44.2	39.0
1966	7.7	18.8	43.7	38.6
1967	7.4	18.4	43.2	38.2
1968	7.1	17.8	42.5	37.4
1969	7.0	17.8	42.8	38.0
1970	6.6	17.7	43.4	38.5
1971	6.5	17.5	43.2	38.3
1972	6.4	17.2	42.7	37.0
1973	6.5	17.1	42.4	37.0
1974	6.2	16.8	42.4	37.1
1975 old	5.6	16.0	41.9	36.6
1975 new	5.7	16.4	42.3	37.3
1978	5.3	16.0	42.6	37.5
1981	6.0	17.6	45.0	40.0
1984	6.4	18.5	46.3	41.0

[a] The CSO hybrid estimates combine date from the SPI and the Family Expenditure Survey (FES), as reported in the May 1978, July 1984, and November 1987 issues of *Economic Trends*.

In this series CSO defines households as "individual tax-units, i.e., married couples or single people over school-leaving age not at school" (*Economic Trends*, November 1987: p. 94).

come, of course, but it sheds indirect light in two ways: by showing the assets on which current property income is based, and by reflecting the wealth accumulated from earlier total incomes.

When one follows the average levels of estimated net worth by social classes— landed gentry, merchants, yeomen, craftsmen, and so forth—one finds a striking widening of the wealth gaps between 1810 and 1875. The top landed groups and mer-

Future research could narrow the wide confidence intervals on wealth inequality for the mid-nineteenth century reported in Lindert (1986), by using the death duty returns in the Public Record Office, which were unavailable at the time of my research. These returns attach real estate to personal estate more closely than I could do by collating materials from separate sources.

Table 1

Income inequality trends in the UK, 1688–1995, continued

D. CSO-UNS equivalised-income series[a]

Financial year beginning	Original income of households:		Disposable income of households:	
	Top 20% share	Gini × 100	Top 20%	Gini × 100
1977	43	43	36	27
1978	43	43	35	27
1979	43	44	36	27
1980	44	44	37	28
1981	46	46	38	28
1982	46	47	37	28
1983	47	48	38	28
1984	47	49	37	28
1985	47	49	38	29
1986	49	50	40	31
1987	50	51	41	33
1988	50	51	42	35
1989	49	50	41	34
1990	51	52	43	36
1991	50	51	42	35
1992	50	52	42	35
1993/4	52	54	42	35
1994/5	51	53	41	33
1995	50	52	40	33

[a] The source is the set of articles in *Economic Trends* entitled "The Effects of Taxes and Benefits on Household Income", here cited from the December 1994, December 1995, and March 1997 issues.

The estimates distribute equivalised original income among households ranked by equivalised disposable (not original) income, except for the Gini coefficients on original income, which seem to be (correctly) ranked by original income. "Equivalised" here means that income has been divided by "equivalised persons" in the household, using the McClements scale as explained in *Economic Trends*, December 1995, p. 57.

chants accumulated at a prodigious rate, it would seem, with their wealth growing far faster than that of professionals, shopkeepers, yeomen, or craftsmen. Marx might have been pleased with such estimates, were it not for the fact that even the middling groups gained in absolute real wealth and held their share of the population, instead of slipping down into the proletariat.[7]

[7] Though he refused to make a will, "Karl Marx, Gentleman, a Widower" left almost £300 in personal estate in 1883, according to the Principal Probate Registry. Frederick Engels, again a "Gentleman", left $25,265 a dozen years later. Other personal-estate probate entries (excluding real estate in each case) include £31,821 for Sir Isaac Newton in 1727, almost £10,000 for Sir Frederick Morton Eden in 1810, almost £300,000 for David Ricardo in 1823, and £129,542 for Charles Dickens in 1870 (Public Record Office, PROB3/26/66 and IR59).

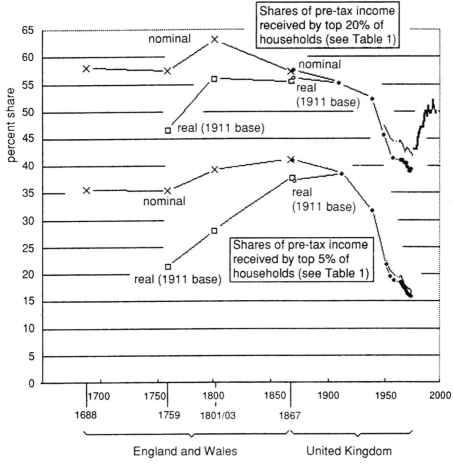

Fig. 1. Income inequality trends in the UK since 1688. (Sources: See text and the notes to Table 1.)

Yet the rise in wealth inequality vanishes when the personal wealth figures are weighted and combined into a size distribution for England and Wales. As Table 2 makes clear, the wealth share held by the top 5% of adults (approximately the top 10–11% of household heads) was high, but not clearly changing any time before this century. The lack of trend is consistent with the dramatic widening of class wealth gaps between 1810 and 1875, simply because the very richest groups (landed aristocrats and merchants) were a declining share of the adult population, and land was a declining share of national wealth and national income. The evidence on nonhuman wealth thus shows wide inequality gaps before 1914, but no clear trend.[8] Combining this trendless property distribution with the available estimates of human earnings or human capital still leaves an apparent net rise in income inequality between mid-eighteenth century (1740–1759 benchmarks) and the French War era (1801–1810), whether one sticks with an income measure or uses a total-wealth measure (Lindert, 1986).

The other main quantitative data base for judging movements in British income inequality before 1914 consists of series on the mean and dispersion of labor earnings by occupation. Jeffrey Williamson (1985, Chap. 3) has ambitiously pieced together the average male pay rates, intra-occupational earnings distributions, and employment weights for dozens of occupations for benchmark years from the late eighteenth century to the early twentieth. He finds that earnings inequality rose over the first half of the nineteenth century, peaking at the 1851 benchmark. After an apparent plateau, 1851–1881, earnings inequality began to drop, both within and between broad occupational classes. On these estimates, the rise and fall of earnings inequality look more dramatic for the economy as a whole than within nonagriculture, since the nonfarm/farm ratio of wage rates for common labor also peaked in 1851. The rise and fall of earnings within the nineteenth century contrasts with the lack of trend for overall income inequality shown in Table 1.[9]

---

[8] Relative to other countries, mid-Victorian Britain (1867–1875) stood out as a nation of extreme inequality in landownership, personal net worth, and pre-tax incomes (Lindert, 1987). We lack sufficient data to say definitively, however, whether Britain occupied the absolute top inequality position among major nations at the time.

[9] While carefully noting that earnings inequality and overall income inequality need not follow the same trends, Williamson felt that they just happened to rise and fall together in nineteenth-century Britain. This coincidence no longer holds, however, now that the present Table 1 (like Feinstein, 1988; Jackson, 1994; Lindert, 1994a) has adjusted the key 1867 income distributions to a household basis more comparable with earlier and later income distributions.

An earlier movement noted by Williamson (1985: pp. 47–49) also differs from a trend in overall income inequality implied by the social tables. He found that pay gaps narrowed from 1781 to 1805, before rising again. The narrowing of employee pay rates during the French Wars is a plausible counter-current in the presumably turbulent income movements of that era. Sudden wartime inflations often compress the pay ratio between higher- and lower-paid employee groups, because higher salaries tend to advance more steadily, less cyclically, than the wage rates of lower-paid groups.

The unusual compression of employee pay gaps around 1805 is consistent with the conclusion that overall inequality had widened considerably (that rise from 1759 to 1801–03 in Table 1). Those in the skilled manual trades and lower-paid professions, whose nominal pay failed to keep pace during the wartime inflation, were probably dropping down the *quantile ranks* as well, while farmers, yeomen, and farm laborers were probably rising. Even tenant farmers and yeomen on long-term leases must have shared some of the wartime jump in the residuals generated by farming. (The relative income of handloom weavers, a non-wage 3–4 % of the labor force, also peaked briefly in the French War era, on the eve of the weavers' infamous demise).

My overall impression of the changes from the mid-eighteenth century to the French War era is that top groups gained relative to all others, while many occupations reshuffled their relative positions in the lower income ranks. The identity of the fastest-gaining top groups is an uncertain mix of landed aristocracy and top merchants. The top-end gainers in the income distribution were the top 5% of households (Table 1), but the top 1% did not gain in income share, unlike the gain shown for the top 1% in the wealth distribution (Table 2). For much richer detail on the social and occupational identities of the richest individuals, see Rubinstein (1981, 1986).

Table 2

Wealth inequality trends in the UK, 1670–1989

| | Shares of aggregate marketable net worth England and Wales | | Great Britain | |
	Top 1% of households	Top 5% of adults		
1670	48.9	84.6		
1700	39.3	81.9		
1740	43.6	86.9		
1810	54.9	85.3		
1875	61.1	84.0		
	Top 1% of adults	Top 5% of adults	Top 1% of adults	Top 5% of adults
1911–13	69.0	87.0		
1923	60.9	82.0		
1924	59.9	81.5		
1925	61.0	82.1		
1926	57.3	79.9		
1927	59.8	81.3		
1928	57.0	79.6		
1929	55.5	78.9		
1930	57.9	79.2		
1936	54.2	77.4		
1938	55.0	76.9	55.0	77.2
1950	47.2	74.3	47.2	74.4
1951	45.8	73.6	45.9	73.8
1952	43.0	70.2	42.9	70.3
1953	43.6	71.1	43.5	71.2
1954	45.3	71.8	45.3	72.0
1955	44.5	71.1	43.8	70.8
1956	44.5	71.3	44.0	71.1
1957	43.4	68.7	42.9	68.6
1958	41.4	67.8	40.9	67.7
1959	41.4	67.6	41.8	67.9
1960	33.9	59.4	34.4	60.0
1961	36.5	60.6	36.5	60.8
1962	31.4	54.8	31.9	55.4
1964	34.5	58.6	34.7	59.2
1965	33.0	58.1	33.3	58.7
1966	30.6	55.5	31.0	56.1
1967	31.4	56.0	31.5	56.4
1968	33.6	58.3	33.6	58.6
1969	31.1	56.1	31.3	56.6
1970	29.7	53.6	30.1	54.3
1971	28.4	52.3	28.8	53.0
1972	31.7	56.0	32.0	57.2

Table 2

(continued)

	UK marketable personal net worth		UK personal net worth including all private and state pensions	
	Top 1% of adults	Top 5% of adults	Top 1% of adults	Top 5% of adults
1976	21	38	13	26
1977	22	39	14	27
1978	20	37	13	26
1979	20	37	12	25
1980	19	36	11	24
1981	18	36	11	24
1982	18	36	11	24
1983	20	37	11	24
1984	18	35	10	23
1985	18	36	11	25
1986	18	36	11	24
1987	18	37	11	25
1988	17	38	10	26
1989	18	38	11	26

The minimum age of independent adulthood varies in the estimates, as in society. For the pre-1900 estimates, this is assumed to be 20 years. Atkinson and Harrison assume that it dropped linearly from 23 years in 1923 to 20 years in 1953 and 18 years in 1973.
The sources are Lindert (1986) for 1688–1875; Atkinson and Harrison (1978: pp. 139, 159) for 1911–1913–1972; and Central Statistical Office, *Economic Trends*, November 1991 for the UK 1976–1989.
The 1911–13 figure originates from Daniels and Campion, and Atkinson and Harrison (pp. 143–146) warn that the Daniels and Campion measures are not fully comparable with later estimates.

While the occupational earnings data have thus become abundant for Britain in the nineteenth century, their use as a clue to overall income inequality trends is compromised by three drawbacks. The first, of course, is their omission of property incomes. Second, the occupations tend to slide around the income ranks, denying us a view of pay ratios between fixed percentile positions. Williamson has documented such rank-switching (Williamson, 1980, 1985: p. 11), but it remains a problem. Third, Jackson (1987) and Feinstein (1988) have pointed out defects in some of the pay series Williamson collected and presented, particularly those for the higher-paid services. When the most suspect series are removed, the nineteenth-century rise and fall are muted. It is hard to say there was any rise-fall pattern in pay gaps within the nonfarm sector across the nineteenth century. The revisions suggested by Williamson's critics do show a slight rise-and-fall pattern in the economy-wide ratio for skilled/unskilled pay from 1827 to 1851 to 1911 (Jackson, 1987: p. 567; Feinstein, 1988: p. 712). But the economy-wide rise and fall in earnings inequality now hinges almost solely on the nonfarm/farm ratio, and caveats abound.

To supplement these traditional inequality measures, we should briefly note the likely changes in five other sources of inequality before 1914: (1) difference in the cost-of-living trends for rich and poor; (2) unequal mortality; (3) difference in household composition; (4) male/female pay gaps; and (5) regional inequalities.

(1) Real inequality trends differ from nominal inequality trends whenever the cost of living moves differently for rich and for poor. Cost-of-living trends can indeed differ by income class even when everybody faces the same prices for individual commodities. In most settings this point does not matter much (e.g., for the US up to the 1970s, as shown in Williamson and Lindert (1980, Chap. 5), and for the UK since 1978 in Crawford (1996)). Yet it matters greatly in our judgment of English inequality trends in the 18th and 19th centuries, as argued elsewhere (Lindert, 1998). In that setting the rich spent a much lower share of their incomes on food than did the poor, and the rich also paid out a smaller share of their income in housing rents.[10] The relative price of food rose something like 25% 1760–1800, then fell back after 1815. Real housing rents quadrupled between 1760 and 1835, again relative to the overall cost-of-living index. The consumer goods that declined in real price were fuel and textiles-clothing. Thus the cost of living rose more, or fell less, for the bottom 80% of the income ranks than for the top 20% or top 5%, as sketched in the "real" inequality series of Table 1 and Fig. 1. Paying attention to this point re-introduces a noticeable rise in inequality, especially between the mid-eighteenth century and the early nineteenth.

(2) Mortality trends could change our perceptions of inequality trends in ways already introduced. If one chooses to view deaths in the family as deductions from the well-being of survivors in the same family and same income strata, then again inequality may have risen more sharply between the mid-eighteenth century and the mid-nineteenth than Table 1 has shown. The reason is that the chances of survival improved markedly for the upper classes, to judge from peers' family records, but only slightly for the nation as a whole. On the other hand, if we follow the inequality of lifetime consumption among individuals, then even the modest gains in life expectancy between 1688 and 1867 were enough to bring a net equalization. Again, as noted, the choice depends on the question asked.[11]

---

[10] A technical point of considerable importance here is that much of the top income households' housing was owner-occupied. The available data apparently do not impute income from owner-occupied housing as part of nominal income. Accordingly, it should also not be counted as part of the consumer bundle purchased by home-owning households. Thus, rent was a lower share of household income for the rich than for the poor, and the rapid rise in rents hurt lower-income purchasing power more than the purchasing power of the rich. This difference in housing weights and the difference in food weights explain why real inequality probably rose more between 1759 and 1801–03 than did nominal inequality. For a fuller discussion, see (Lindert, 1998).

This point seems to have been missed by the otherwise excellent coverage of recent UK class differentials in housing costs by Crawford (1996: pp. 89–90), who views the opportunity cost of wealth tied up in owner-occupied housing as a user-cost part of the cost-of-living deflator for income measures that failed to include the full value of that housing. Yet Crawford does usefully capture the capital-gain effects in his user-cost measure.

[11] On mortality trends by class and age group, see Hollingsworth (1977); Jackson (1994); Wrigley and Schofield (1981); Wrigley et al. (1997); Woods (1988–89, 1993); Williamson (1984); Lindert (1994a); Floud and Harris (1996).

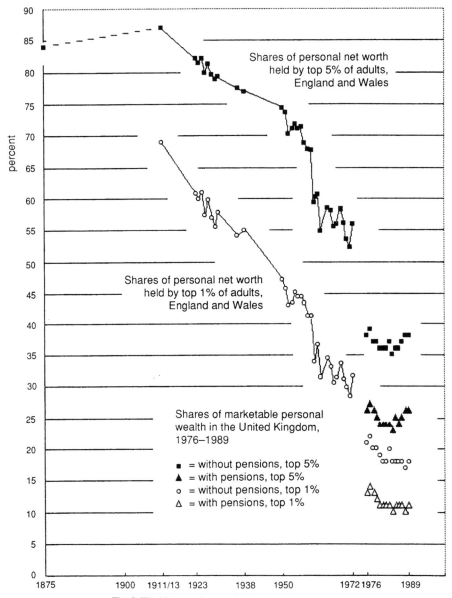

Fig. 2. Wealth inequality trends in the UK since 1875.

(3) Adjusting for the changing social gradient of household composition would give an upward tilt to the British inequality trend between 1688 and 1867. So far we have discussed only the distribution of household incomes. A popular alternative is to rank households by their income per capita, or per adult-consumption-equivalent, on the ground that larger household size dilutes consumption standards. While no such adjustment is presented here, we know the direction in which it would change the trend between, say, 1688 and 1867. Over these 179 years, household size fell more rapidly among high-income households than among low-income households. In 1688 household size had a slight positive correlation with household income, with the richest households including servants and with unrelated individuals making up a large share of the pauper host at the bottom of the ranks. Thus for 1688 the ratios of top to bottom incomes would be lower on a per-capita basis than on the per-household basis shown in Table 1. Two centuries later the correlation between household income and household size was less positive, and possibly negative. For 1867, the ratios of top to bottom incomes might have been higher on a per-capita basis than for total household income. There would be more of a trend toward inequality in income per capita (or per adult consumption equivalent) than Table 1 has revealed.

(4) Our view of early trends in Britain's male-female income differences is still obscured by the paucity of data on women's wage and salary rates.[12] The few quantitative studies available tend to focus on the classic 1780–1850 era (Horrell and Humphries, 1992, 1995; Lindert, 1994a; Feinstein, 1996b; and the literature cited there). For this era, there is a range of possibilities. It seems unlikely that women's real wage rates advanced faster than those of unskilled males and there are hints that they advanced slower than those male rates, or not at all, across the early nineteenth century. An overall income distribution featuring good data on women's wages might thus show a bit more trend toward inequality between 1780 and 1850 than is now evident.

(5) As for regional income inequalities, British history reveals two sharp turning points, though their implications for overall inequality are unclear. Before the late eighteenth century, the poorer regions tended to be in Northern England, Wales, and highland Scotland (Schofield, 1965; Hunt, 1986). By 1800, however, poverty had become a feature of the rural South and West. Northern England retained an income advantage over the rest of Britain (bar London) for over a century. World War I brought the other great turning point, and prosperity has been a southeastern specialty ever since. Famous as these two turning points are, they carry no obvious implications for a quantitative measure of national inequality trends.

---

[12] The phrase "wage and salary rates" is chosen over "wages and salaries" or "earnings" in order to set aside the changes in male/female income inequality that reflect differing trends in the annual labor hours and labor-force participation of women. As argued elsewhere (Lindert and Williamson, 1983: pp. 17–19; Lindert, 1991: p. 374), it seems wiser to focus on the wage-price of a unit of a woman's time as a measure of her earning potential. This approach strikes a compromise between the extremes of valuing women's unpaid time at zero and valuing it above the wage rate (as would be valid for women who actually choose to work zero hours for pay). Most of the literature still adheres to the former extreme view, interpreting non-participation in the labor force, or any reduction of hours worked, as a shift toward a use of women's time that is worth zero.

2.2. When did American inequality rise?

By 1929, and probably by 1914, income and wealth and earnings were as unequally distributed in America as in Britain. Had it been that way ever since Jamestown?

Lee Soltow has implied as much, consistently doubting any early rise in inequality (Soltow, 1971, 1984, 1989, 1992). If that is true, then the colonists' incomes were at least as unequal as the incomes back in Britain. Such inequalities may fit preconceptions about the colonial South, but they clash with most preconceptions about the middle or New England colonies. Were past observers wrong in thinking that migrants to these colonies set up a more egalitarian property system, free of the latifundistos that controlled the English and Irish countryside? A host of scholars have worked on this issue since the 1970s.

Most evidence fits our usual preconceptions, not Soltow's hypothesis, showing a relatively egalitarian America, outside the South, up to at least 1800. That evidence comes in indirect forms: wealth distributions, suggestive wage gaps, mortality trends, and other odds and ends. There are many studies to draw on, but none of them has the kinds of income distributions that were conjured up by Britains' early social tables and partial income-tax returns, since America did not have an income tax that reached below the top one percent until this century.

The best starting point is Alice Hanson Jones's pioneering estimation of the 13-colony distribution of net worth in 1774 from 939 probate records and supporting materials. Using an elaboration of estate-multiplier methods, Jones developed a distribution of wealth among the living from the wealth of the deceased, with results shown at the top of Table 3. While the sample is small, no clear defects in her estimates have been revealed.

To compare colonial inequality with English wealth inequality at similar dates, one can roughly equate the top 10% of household heads with the top 5% of all adults. Equating these two shares shows an unmistakable contrast between the mother country and Jones's portrait of the 13 colonies. The richest 5% of adults held 85–87% of net worth in England and Wales (1740 and 1810 in Table 2) but only 59% of net worth in the 13 colonies, even when America's slaves are counted both as holders of zero wealth and as other people's property.[13]

---

[13] Recently Lars Osberg and Fazley Siddiq (1988) have argued that slaves should be counted as having had *negative* net worth, equal to −£155 per slave household in 1774, because their freedom was denied them. On this basis they conclude that colonial wealth inequality was much greater than today's wealth inequality. The assumption and interpretation do not seem valid. They offer no defense of the large absolute value of £155 per slave household, which nearly equals the mean wealth of all households at the time. Why not £1 or £10,000, and what is such a valuation (of freedom?) doing in a distribution of capital excluding free people's ownership of their own human capital? And why choose a value so large that this arbitrary valuation of negative Southern wealth drives the whole conclusion about all 13 colonies? The conventional procedure followed here at least lends itself to familiar interpretations. In addition, their interpretation should have included the point that the time-trend would still follow a great rise from colonial egalité toward greater inequalities, starting from the relatively non-slave 1630 and rising for over a century, possibly rising all the way to 1860 (depending on what

While Jones's study is the only one to pull together estimates over all the 13 colonies, it is buttressed and extended by a host of local studies following the distributions of probated or assessed wealth across a century or more of colonial experience.[14] The flavor of the local-wealth results is shown by Fig. 3's trends from Boston and nearby Hingham, Massachusetts. The general trend seems to be upward in most cases, often dramatically so, suggesting that wealth might have been held even more equally in the seventeenth century than in the eighteenth. The appearance deceives, however. Most of the studies follow wealth trends in fixed places, usually near the seaboard of the New England and middle colonies. The inland frontier, however, was both more egalitarian and an ever-rising share of the total population. The westward drift of people was, in fact, so great that there appears to have been no trend at all in the wealth inequality of the New England and Middle colonies (Williamson and Lindert, 1980, 1981). For these colonies, wealth inequality back in the seventeenth century was probably not much different from that shown in Alice Hanson Jones's 1774 benchmark.

Yet there was one region where wealth inequality probably did rise across the colonial era—the region omitted from most of the studies of colonial wealth trends. In the South, the share of slaves in the overall population rose from near zero in 1630 to 40% in 1770. So great a rise in zero-wealth population, and in people who represented wealth for others, must have raised wealth inequality within the South over the century and a half ending in the Revolution, even though we lack earlier figures to compare with Jones's small Southern sample in 1774.[15]

But if colonial life outside the South was much more egalitarian than life in the early twentieth century, we have a nineteenth-century American puzzle: When did the Americans become so unequal? Did it happen before, during, or after the Civil War?

The wealth–inequality studies imply rising inequality over most decades of the century and a half from Alice Hanson Jones's 1774 benchmark to 1929. There was no sudden jump in wealth inequality, as far as we can tell. Still, there were episodes. The most likely short-run *troughs* in wealth inequality came near wars: the 1810s–1820s, the 1860s, and World War I. All other periods of a decade or longer probably brought rising inequalities.[16]

Table 3 and Fig. 3 sketch the net trend in nineteenth-century wealth inequality, using a few relatively reliable benchmark studies. The main pillar supporting both the antebellum and postbellum spans of the bridge is Soltow's pathbreaking (1975) study of census

---

negative values they would put on the net worth of slaves who had a higher real price in 1860 than back in 1774).

[14] For a list of relevant colonial wealth studies by Bruce Daniels, Allan Kulikoff, James Lemon, Gloria Main, Jack Main, Gary Nash, Daniel Scott Smith, and Gerard Warden, and others, see Williamson and Lindert (1981).

[15] The inequality trend implied by the rise in the slave share of the population across the colonial era was pointed out by Robert Gallman (1981: p. 133).

[16] For an extensive survey, see Williamson and Lindert (1981). A more recent contribution, one that follows individuals over time, is Steckel (1994).

Table 3

Wealth inequality in the US, benchmark measures, 1774–1989

	Net worth			Total assets		
	Percent shares held by			Percent shares held by		
	Top 1%	Top 10%	Gini	Top 1%	Top 10%	Gini
1774 (Alice Hanson Jones)						
All households	16.5	59.0		14.8	55.1	
Free households	14.3	53.2	0.694	12.6	49.6	0.642
All adult males	16.5	58.4		13.2	54.3	
Free adult males	14.2	52.5	0.688	12.4	48.7	0.632
Census samples (Lee Soltow):						
1860, all adult males				30.3–35.0	74.6–79.0	
1860, free adult males				29.0	73.0	0.832
1870, all adult males				27.0	70.0	0.833
1890, families (G.K. Holmes)	25.8	72.2				
Households: 1922	36.7			25.5		
(Wolff– peak = 1929	44.2			30.7		
Marley 1933	33.3					
series, as 1939	36.4			25.3		
revised 1945	29.8			20.7		
in Wolff 1949	27.1			18.8		
1994) 1953	31.2			21.7		
1962	31.8	58.7–73.0	0.731	22.1		
1965	34.4			23.9		
1969	31.1			21.6		
1972	29.1			20.2		
trough = 1976	19.9			12.7		
1979	20.5					
1981	24.8					
1983	30.9	60.1–77.9	0.739	28.6		0.703
1986	31.9					
1989	35.7					

The 1774 estimates are based on 919 probated estates, from Alice Hanson Jones (1977, Vol. 3, Table 8.1). These estimates follow the usual "GNP, not GDP" convention of focusing on residents' incomes and (here) wealth, not on wealth held (or income earned) in this country by residents of all countries. For a contrary view, see Carole Shammas's (1993) treatment of non-colonists' wealth in the 13 colonies. Counting the colonial wealth of British residents, Shammas raises the top 1% share of net worth to 18%.

Lee Soltow's spin samples of the census (1975: pp. 99, 103) consist of 13,696 men in 1860 and 9823 men in 1870, where men are males 20 and older.

The Holmes estimates are discussed in Williamson and Lindert (1981: p. 57).

The Wolff–Marley estimates are the W2 estimates of net worth and total assets (without household inventories) from their 1989 NBER chapter (pp. 806, 809, 811), as extended in Wolff (1995: pp. 62, 63). The more detailed update is Wolff (1994).

Figure 3's Wolff–Marley "augmented" series for the share of net worth held by the top 1% of households, which includes pensions and social-security wealth, is also from Wolff–Marley (1989: pp. 806–811) and Wolff (1995: pp. 62, 63).

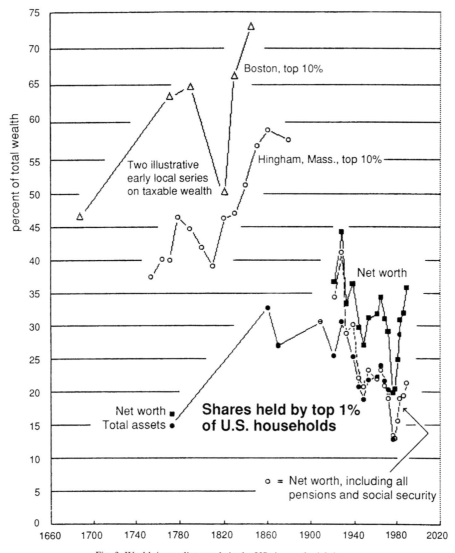

Fig. 3. Wealth inequality trends in the US since colonial times.

returns on the real and personal estates of males living in 1860 and 1870, plus returns on real estate alone for 1850.

For the period between 1774 and 1860, most local studies show the same kind of rise that Table 3 and Fig. 3 imply with their contrast between Alice Jones's 1774 and Lee Soltow's 1860. The changes across the Revolutionary and early federal years are hard to judge. One might have expected that top-rank shares of all wealth would have been raised by the confiscation of large properties from Loyalists whose primary resident was outside the colonies, but we lack good numbers on this.[17] Soltow has made a valiant attempt to plot the contours of early federal wealth by sampling 1798 census values of real estate. The data, however, are not up to the standard of his wealth samples from the 1850–1870 censuses. The 1798 census asked people to estimate "dwelling houses .... lands, lots, buildings, wharves, owned, possessed, or occupied" with no reporting of holdings under $100 or vacant lots over 2 acres (Soltow, 1989: p. 286 and passim). The data omit all non-land property and all human earnings. They also cast a fog by mixing tenancy with elements of ownership. If the data had been gathered only from households in their role as occupants, their consumption of housing could be used to conjecture about the income distribution. That was not done. On the other hand, the ownership data are incomplete, in that the holdings of the same person in different areas are not collated. Soltow struggled to interpret the ostensible rise in inequality from Alice Jones's 1774 to his 1798, saying it was true but probably smaller than he himself had estimated (1989: pp. 170–174). The best solution seems to be to agree that inequality may have risen a bit between 1774 and 1798, but not as much as his 1798 figures imply.

As a corollary, the widening of wealth gaps appears to have continued beyond 1798 all the way to the Civil War, aside from an 1810s–1820s dip suggested by a few local studies. The pre-war widening apparently owed little to compositional shifts in the population. True, there was a rise in immigration, an urbanization trend, and a continuing frontier settlement. Yet several accounting exercises show no major role for shifts in the age distribution, the urban share, or the share foreign born (Williamson and Lindert, 1981).

Beyond 1860, the wealth gaps remained wide, aside from temporary narrowing during the Civil War decade and during World War I. In either 1913 or 1929, American wealth inequality matched that in the UK.

Still, nonhuman wealth relates to only part of the income distribution, and one strains to find other indicators of relative income movements across the nineteenth century. One promising path is to collect occupational pay series, to suggest possible movements in the Lorenz curves for earnings and for total income, as several scholars have done (Williamson and Lindert, 1980; Margo and Villaflor, 1988; Goldin and Margo, 1992a; Margo, 1992). Jeffrey Williamson and I saw a pre-war surge in wage inequality between the 1820s and the mid-1850s, a timing that would suggest parallelism between wealth-widening and wage-widening. Margo and his co-authors challenged this view by introducing new data on civilian workers hired by the army in each of the major settled regions. In their data wage widening proved elusive between 1821 and 1856. It showed up for some regions but not others, under some summary measures but not others. This does indeed clash with the series used earlier, and casts some doubts on a pre-war surge

---

[17] The values of non-resident Loyalist estates available for confiscation as of the 1770s are sketched by Shammas (1993). We still need better post-Revolutionary numbers, however, on who acquired these assets.

in wage inequality. The doubts serve to repeat the question already posed in this section. If there was no pronounced widening of pay gaps before the Civil War, *when did* income inequality, like wealth inequality, reach the heights we can document for 1929? Nothing we know about the colonial economy suggests that income should already have been so highly unequal outside of the South, given that wealth was not nearly so unequal as it was to become in 1929. If the income gaps did not widen between the 1820s and the 1850s, then when did they?

The inequality of average regional incomes offers a better-data haven from the larger uncertainties about the income distribution.[18] We do know that the regional inequality in commodity product per capita rose across the nineteenth century. In this case, however, the shift was a single discrete event. The Civil War and emancipation cut Southern incomes relative to the rest of the nation between 1860 and 1880. The main reason for this widening was not wartime destruction, but a change with an unusual welfare twist: Slave emancipation cut black labor supply by 28–37%, as they used their freedom to reduce the work hours of children, women, and the elderly down to white norms (Ransom and Sutch, 1977). While it may have raised the inequality of conventional incomes across regions, emancipation is a change that lacks the welfare cost usually associated with a widening of regional income gaps, since people near the bottom of the income ranks were choosing to cut their incomes when given control over their own time. After the 1880 benchmark the wide gaps between the non-South and the South remained until 1940.

The nineteenth-century movement of male/female wage gaps in the United States was quite different from the widening trends that show up for the inequality of wealth and of regional incomes. Thanks to Claudia Goldin's (1990) pioneering work, we have a better quantitative history of the gender pay gap for America than for Britain. Goldin finds considerable narrowing of the male/female pay gap (i.e., a rise in women's relative pay) between the 1820s and the 1850s, further blurring the picture of this era as one of rising inequality. After the 1850s, the trends in the male/female pay-ratio were flatter until the late twentieth century.

To raise further the stakes in figuring out just when Americans became more unequal across the nineteenth century, consider a health-trend puzzle that hints at a widening of gaps in overall life expectancy up to about 1870. Several authors have found that stature and life expectancy both shortened from about 1790 to about 1870 (Kunze, 1979; Fogel, 1986; Steckel, 1995), even though real wage rates surely rose between these two dates, both for common laborers and for artisans. The worsening of health appears to have happened all across the country, north and south, rural and urban. By itself, the

---

[18] The underlying data here are Richard Easterlin's estimates of state and regional income, as reproduced in Fogel and Engerman (1971) and in the *Historical Statistics of the United States*, and as transformed into an inequality measure in the earlier article by Williamson (1965). The measurement of real, as opposed to nominal, regional income gaps is pursued with spatial cost-of-living indices in Coelho and Shepherd (1976) and Williamson and Lindert (1980, Chap. 5). The real gaps move like the nominal ones, albeit at lower levels of inequality. For a recent overview of the regional inequality motif, see Nissan and Carter (1993).

worsening mortality lowered average living standards, in the sense described in Section 1. In addition, if worsening health and earlier death visited the poor in particular, as Steckel's (1992, 1995) work implies, then we have another way in which the inequality of living standards widened before 1870. One should be cautious about the related belief that the rising inequality of life expectancy shows us a rise in the inequality of annual incomes. Other studies cast doubt on any reliable link between annual-income inequality and the level and inequality of mortality. The puzzle remains, however: What caused that long gradual worsening—and the presumably increasing inequality—of mortality?

In sum, we know that income inequality must have risen sometime between 1774 and any of these three competing peak-inequality dates: 1860, 1913, and 1929. The inequality of health and life expectancy also worsened between 1790 and 1870, and improved thereafter. Beyond this, the evidence on the rise of unequal America is only suggestive and incomplete.

3. When incomes leveled

The early twentieth century brought three related changes to Britain, to the United States, and to other high-income countries: (1) Governments redistributed more; (2) governments collected and published more income data; and (3) incomes became more equal even "before" taxes. Let us follow the third of these developments, carefully using the second and wondering about the role of the first. While the role of redistribution is automatically reduced by our following the convention of looking at the distribution "pre-fisc" income, it is still a significant force in shaping that distribution.

The timing of the equalization of incomes differed greatly between these two countries. Let us turn first to Britain, whose leveling era lasted longer and achieved more.

3.1. Britain

When did the leveling of British incomes start? There is strong reason to wonder, and there are some shaky data to satisfy our curiosity on events before 1938. We wonder primarily because we seek to know whether the leveling of market incomes antedated the confiscation of top property holdings by progressive taxation. Taken at face value, the rough estimates shown in Table 1 and Fig. 1 say that the equalization of fixed incomes did indeed antedate Lloyd George, since inequality was less pronounced in the revised-Bowley estimates for 1911 than for the revised-Baxter estimates for 1867. Intriguing as this possibility is, it cannot be considered a "finding" until far better data are available for the late nineteenth and early twentieth centuries.

Starting in 1938, and continuing through 1974, the Central Statistical Office produced its Survey of Personal Incomes (SPI) estimates of the distribution of before-tax income among tax units. From 1949 through 1984–85, it offered the alternative "Blue

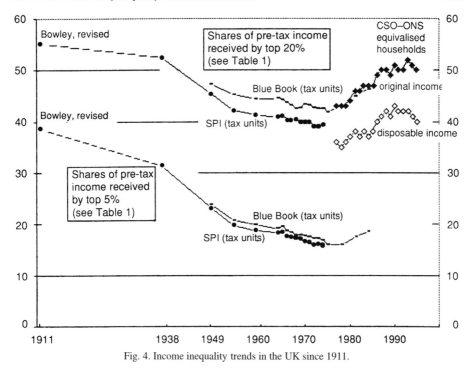

Fig. 4. Income inequality trends in the UK since 1911.

Book" series drawing on results of the Family Expenditure Survey, still sticking with the tax unit as the population base. Then, with data running from 1977, the CSO (now the Office of National Statistics) transformed the population unit to the consumption-equivalised household. This current series, however, presents shares only for quintiles, hiding our view of movements within each quintile. Subject to the much-discussed limitations of the various series (Royal Commission 1977: Chaps. 2, 3, 5; Atkinson and Micklewright, 1992; Atkinson, 1995, Chap. 1), Fig. 4 and Table 1 present Gini's and top-quantile shares to summarize the history they offer.

The gap between top-income groups and other Britons continued to narrow across the first three quarters of the twentieth century. There were important limitations to this movement, however. The top 5% definitely lost greatly in their income share, but there the leveling may have stopped. The very next group, the 80–95% group, did not suffer any erosion of income relative to those below them. Table 1's SPI estimates for taxpayer units imply that the average pre-fisc income of the 80–95% group *kept the same ratio* to that of the bottom 80% of taxpayers all the way through to the end of the leveling era around 1974:

Year	Mean-income ratio (80–95%/0–80%)
1867	2.03
1911 (SPI)	1.96
1938 (SPI)	2.34
1949 (SPI)	2.16
1964 (SPI)	2.04
<u>1974</u> (SPI)	<u>2.08</u>
1975 (Blue Book)	2.39
1984 (Blue Book)	2.76

This contrasts with the reverse movement from 1975 on, when the 80–95% group definitely shared in the top-rank gains. Furthermore, as far as we can tell from the especially poor figures on income in the bottom income ranks, the bottom 40% did not gain relative to the middle quintile after 1938 (no guesses should be ventured about movements below the median between the 1911 and 1938 benchmarks). Britain's leveling in pre-fisc income, then, may have conformed to a simple formula: The top 5% lost ground, and (at least after 1938) the gaining ranks were the next 55%, not the bottom 40%.

Trends in the inequality of *disposable* income, after taxes and transfers, probably had similar turning points, but with a greater net change and a different locus of equalization between income ranks. Fiscal redistribution brought more equalization after World War II than any time before. The fiscal redistribution, unlike the trends in pre-fisc inequality, clearly raised the share received by the bottom 40% of households.

The same three-quarters of a century saw a drop in the concentration of personal wealth into the hands of the top 5% of adults, as Table 2 and Fig. 2 have shown. To be more precise, that dramatic decline in wealth concentration came between the 1911–13 benchmark and about 1980—and then stopped. While the wealth figures require, and have received, very careful handling (Atkinson and Harrison, 1978; *Economic Trends*, November, 1991; Feinstein, 1996a), the existence of a decline can withstand even large errors in the estimates.

Britains' pay ratios, too, have shown some compression since the start of the twentieth century (Routh, 1965; Lydall, 1968; Phelps Brown, 1977). Despite the usual caveat about the trickiness of the link between pay ratios and inter-quantile earnings (or income) ratios, the twentieth-century pay data are rich enough—and the pattern of compression consistent enough across broad occupational groups—to establish that there was a net change, at least over the whole sweep of 75 years. So both wealth inequality and pay ratios (and presumably labor-earnings inequality) moved in harmony with the overall pre-fisc income distribution.

Probably very little of Britain's twentieth-century leveling took the form of a drop in regional inequality. There was, to be sure, that historic shift of relative prosperity from northern England to the southeast, particularly to the home counties, across World War I. This may not have implied a great reduction in income inequality, however. Rather, the regional inequalities seem to have moved only in sympathy with the aggregate unemployment rate. Given that Britain's unemployment has been highly regionalized in this century, a period of high unemployment tends to become a period of high regional inequality. Thus World War II brought a lasting drop in Britain's regional income inequalities (Williamson, 1965: p. 25), and the rising unemployment since the late 1970s has raised them.

Like nineteenth-century America, twentieth-century Britain poses a puzzle about trends in unequal mortality. The British mortality puzzle is this: Why, over three-quarters of a century of income leveling, did not mortality, even infant mortality, become more equal across the five main socio-occupational classes? In fact, the opposite happened, to judge from standardized mortality measures: Of the five census occupational classes, the highest (professional and managerial) had the greatest improvement in life expectancy, and the lowest (manual labor) had the least from the start of the century to the 1970s (Titmuss, 1943; Hollingsworth, 1979; Preston et al., 1981; Townsend et al., 1988; Hollingsworth et al., 1990; Lee, 1991; Wilkinson, 1996: Chaps. 3–5).

There are ways to discount the puzzle, but it resists elimination. Mere shifts in group sizes and inclusiveness do not seem to explain the puzzle, though there could have been some selectivity effect related to the rise in the top-class group's share of the population and the decline in the bottom group's share. It is also true that the absolute mortality rates, per 1000 per year, have converged, even though the inter-class ratios among them have diverged. Finally, one can switch to a focus on the inequality of lifetime consumption among individuals, as described in Section 1 of this chapter. Doing so makes the trend in life-expectancy egalitarian, simply by reducing absolute infant mortality.

Nonetheless, the puzzle remains: Why did not the inter-class mortality ratios also decline? While the debate continues, we need only to grant that something in twentieth-century health experience did not conform to movements in income inequality as one might have expected.

3.2. America

For the US, the shift to more equal pre-fisc incomes lasted only a quarter century, from 1929 to 1953, the year when Burns read Kuznets's book. Over that quarter century, it kept pace with the changes in Britain's pre-fisc inequality. Then it stopped altogether. Thus over the entire sweep from 1867 to 1974 Britain's leveling was greater. Britons were less equal than Americans around the 1870s. A century later the two countries' inequalities may have been similar before taxes and transfers, but the disposable incomes people could consume or save were probably less unequal in Britain.

The American change was nonetheless pronounced. Figure 5 and Table 4 plot what we know about American income inequality since income tax was introduced in 1913. The fuller Lorenz curves show that the decline at the top was shared by the whole top 20%, and there is no clear shift of relative incomes within the remaining 80%. America's wide lower income gaps—for example, between the middle quintile and the bottom—have stood out in international perspective throughout this century.

The income leveling of 1929–1953 was not a statistical lie, even though the main data set comes from income tax returns. To explain away the apparent decline in the top income shares, the pattern of hiding or mis-reporting income would have had to have twisted implausibly, and production-based data confirm that the aggregate underreporting of income is not peculiar to interest and profit incomes (Williamson and Lindert, 1980: pp. 86–88). Less direct confirmation of the change can be seen in shifts in America's occupations and living arrangements, particularly across the 1940s. Domestic servants, barbers, and beauticians declined as a share of the labor force, probably because higher-income customers found them less affordable (Stigler, 1956). Boarding and lodging stopped being a common practice, and people moved to their own homes with fewer persons per housing unit. While some of these changes were responses to the absolute growth of average incomes, the equalization of incomes probably brought more people over those occupational or home-ownership thresholds.

As with Britain, the compression in America's income distribution was paralleled by compression in its wealth distribution. For the same era studied by Kuznets, Robert Lampman (1962) found a reduction in top wealth shares. Since then both the estimates for those years and the experience of more recent years have changed. Edward Wolff and Marcia Marley (1989) have adjusted the estimates, and have presented variants with and without a valuation of pension entitlements. As shown in Table 3, the net wealth leveling from the 1929 peak to the 1950s still stands. Since the 1950s, there have been further gyrations in the top wealth share, with a trough in the late 1970s and a rise across the 1980s.

Another parallelism is that US occupational pay ratios and earnings inequality also declined between 1929 and 1953, mainly across World War II (Ober, 1948; Phelps Brown, 1977; Williamson and Lindert, 1980; Goldin and Margo, 1992b). While skilled/unskilled pay ratios, the main form of evidence here, are subject to the same caveats mentioned earlier in this chapter, their behavior over the leveling era is clear enough to withstand some roughness on the income positions each occupational average wage defines. The drop in those ratios also guides our search for underlying causes of the change in income inequality: Any explanation should incorporate changes in the market returns to different kinds of labor.

The parallelism also extends to America's inequalities among regions and between races, and perhaps to the gender gap in wage rates, though these three conformities are not equally close. Regional inequalities shrank across the 1940s in particular, coinciding with at least part of the equalization of incomes nationwide (Smolensky, 1963; Williamson, 1965; Amos, 1989; Fan and Cassetti, 1994). So did the gap between white

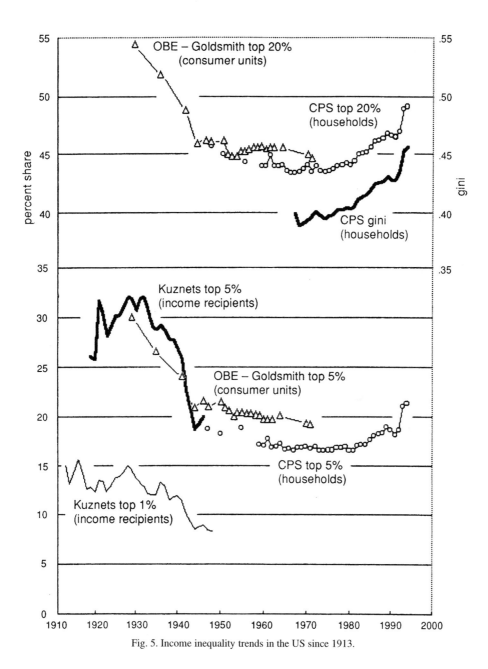

Fig. 5. Income inequality trends in the US since 1913.

Table 4
Measures of pre-fisc income inequality in the US, 1913–1994

Year	Kuznets Top 1% basic variant	Kuznets Top 5% economic var.	Year	OBE-Goldsmith consumer units Top 5%	Top 20%	Gini	Year	Current Population Survey (CPS) families plus unrelated individuals (households from 1967 on) Top 5%	Top 20%	Gini
1913	15.0		1929	30.0	54.4	0.49	1947	18.7	45.6	
1914	13.1		1935–36	26.5	51.7	0.47	1948			
1915	14.3						1949			
1916	15.6		1941	24.0	48.8	0.44	1950	18.2	45.0	
1917	14.2		1942				1951			
1918	12.7		1943				1952			
1919	12.8	26.1	1944	20.7	45.8		1953			
1920	12.3	25.8	1945				1954	18.8	44.3	
1921	13.5	31.7	1946	21.3	46.1		1955			
1922	13.4	30.4	1947	20.9	46.0	0.40	1956			
1923	12.3	28.1	1948				1957			
1924	12.9	29.1	1949				1958			
1925	13.7	30.2	1950	21.4	46.1	0.40	1959	17.1	43.9	
1926	13.9	30.2	1951	20.7	44.9		1960	17.0	44.0	
1927	14.4	31.2	1952	20.5	44.7		1961	17.7	44.9	
1928	14.9	32.1	1953	19.9	44.7		1962	16.8	43.9	
1929	14.5	31.9	1954	20.3	45.2	0.39	1963	16.9	43.9	
1930	13.8	30.7	1955	20.3	45.2		1964	17.2	44.1	
1931	13.1	32.0	1956	20.2	45.3	0.39	1965	16.6	43.6	
1932	12.9	32.1	1957	20.2	45.5		1966	16.7	43.4	
1933	12.1	30.8	1958	20.0	45.5		1967	16.5	43.4	0.399
1934	12.0	29.1	1959	20.0	45.6		1968	16.8	43.5	0.388
1935	12.1	28.8	1960	19.6	45.4		1969	16.8	43.7	0.391
1936	13.4	29.3					1970	16.9	44.1	0.394

1937	13.0	28.5
1938	11.5	27.8
1939	11.8	27.8
1940	11.9	26.8
1941	11.4	25.7
1942	10.1	22.5
1943	9.4	20.9
1944	8.6	18.7
1945	8.8	19.3
1946	9.0	20.0
1947	8.5	
1948	8.4	

1961	19.6	45.5	
1962	19.6	45.5	0.40
1963			
1964	20.0	45.0	
1965			
1966			
1967			
1968			
1969			
1970	19.2	44.9	
1971	19.1	44.6	

1971	16.7	43.5	0.396
1972	17.0	43.9	0.401
1973	16.6	43.6	0.397
1974	16.5	43.5	0.395
1975	16.6	43.6	0.397
1976	16.6	43.7	0.398
1977	16.8	44.0	0.402
1978	16.8	44.1	0.402
1979	16.9	44.2	0.404
1980	16.5	44.1	0.403
1981	16.5	44.4	0.406
1982	17.0	45.0	0.412
1983	17.1	45.1	0.414
1984	17.1	45.2	0.415
1985	17.6	45.6	0.419
1986	18.0	46.1	0.425
1987	18.2	46.2	0.426
1988	18.3	46.3	0.427
1989	18.9	46.8	0.431
1990	18.6	46.6	0.428
1991	18.1	46.5	0.428
1992	18.6	46.9	0.434
1993	21.0	48.9	0.454
1994	21.2	49.1	0.456

The Kuznets economic series (Kuznets, 1953: p. 635) is the variant he preferred, for reasons given in his introduction. He presented his basic series in order to reach back to 1913. Both series refer to income before taxes and to taxpaying units. Unlike the other series, the Kuznets series rank recipient units according to income per person.

The OBE–Goldsmith series start from estimates by Selma Goldsmith (1967, p. xiii) and the Office of Business Economics. These estimates mix different sets of primary data. For 1929 they combine tax returns with an independent Brookings Institution estimation of the entire income distribution. For 1935–36, and 1941, goldsmith adjusted the results of two household surveys. For later years the Census Bureau's CPS series were adjusted to the OBE-Goldsmith definitions of income and recipient unit.

The Census Bureau's CPS P-60 series refer to money incomes including cash transfers (but not in-kind transfers) from government.

The population unit for the estimates up to 1967 consists of families and unrelated individual liking alone. From 1967 on, the unit is households.

Up to 1993, the series is reported in CPS Series P60-184 ("Money Income of Households"). superceded in 1993 by P60-189 ("Income, Poverty, and Valuation of Noncash Benefits"). The overlapping data for 1993 suggest that various changes in measurement procedure raised the top 5% share by 1% of aggregate income, the top 20% share by 0.7%, and the gini by 0.007. The higher new-basis estimates are shown here.

and black average incomes, though this particular egalitarian trend continued at least through 1975 (Donaghue and Heckman, 1991; Bound and Freeman, 1992; Maloney, 1994). The male-female pay gap may also have improved sometime between 1930 and 1970, though the change looks small, especially in comparison with what followed in the 1980s (Goldin, 1990).

4. Rising inequality since the 1970s

The main creative contribution of the last two decades to the study of inequality trends has been to serve notice that we should spend at least as much time asking why there are episodic reversals between decades as we have spent on the long-run sweep across the centuries. If the Kuznets curve meant graduation from Marxian-classical linearity to a quadratic trend, then one should hope that the British and American experience of the last two decades leads modelers to take more than just the next step. Instead of just predicting a long-run cubic inequality curve, they should invest in an eclectic approach that finds different causes for movements in different epochs, as Atkinson (1997) has stressed. The obsolescence of the Kuznets curve, in any case, stands out clearly enough in these two countries' recent experience.

4.1. Britain

Britain's era of gradual leveling reversed around 1977, according to the various income and earnings series reported in Table 1 and Fig. 4. Since 1977 the top quintile of households gained at the expense of the bottom 40%. The turning point and the new trend are robust to choices of inequality measure, and are also not the result of shifts in age, household composition, fiscal policy, or industrial structure. By most measures, Britain's inequality rise was as great as that experienced by any industrialized country after 1977.[19]

Movements in Britain's overall wage-salary gaps paralleled those in household income (Atkinson and Micklewright, 1992; Katz et al., 1993). The top-wealthholder shares of all wealth, however, did not widen until an upturn from 1984 to 1991–92 (Table 2 and Banks et al., 1996).

There were important cross-currents related to gender. As far as rates of pay were concerned, women experienced a slight fall-back between 1978 and 1985, though it was not serious enough to erase their relative progress from 1973 to 1978 (Blau and Kahn, 1993: p. 106). On the other hand, the rise in married women's rates of participation and work hours was so great that it played a key role in restraining the overall widening in household income gaps shown by those income estimates in Table 1 and Fig. 4 (Borooah et al., 1995, 1996; Harkness et al., 1996).

---

[19] See Jenkins (1995) on both the alternative trend series and the decompositions by population group, and also Atkinson and Micklewright (1992: pp. 269–278 and Tables BE1-BI4), Johnson and Webb (1993), Smeeding and Coder (1995), Atkinson (1996, 1997), and Goodman et al. (1997) on the trends.

4.2. America

America's gaps in household income, already wide by international standards, have also been widening. The turning point came sometime between 1974 and 1980, depending on the specific measure chosen. As a general rule, it is the top 5% of households that have gained, and the bottom 60% that have lost, in relative shares.[20] Even within that favored top 5%, the biggest gains may have come at the very top. Studies of the compensation given to corporate Chief Executive Officers show that America's CEOs have extended their already substantial lead, both relative to CEOs in other industrialized countries and relative to US production workers (Crystal, 1993; Abowd and Bognanno, 1995). Measures of inequality in individual earnings, as distinct from household income, show that the widening extended all the way down the spectrum. Thus, for example, the pay ratio of the 90th percentile to the median and the ratio of the median to the 10th percentile both widened, both among men and among women (Blackburn and Bloom, 1987; Karoly, 1993: pp. 57–65; Freeman and Katz, 1995; Karoly and Burtless, 1995). Wealth inequality also jumped after 1980.

In fact, the rise in American inequality since the early postwar years may have advanced further, and may have started earlier, than implied by the top-group income shares and Gini's of Table 4 and Fig. 5. There is mounting evidence that the official figures shown there underestimate the incomes of the top 3–5% of households.

The official US Census figures miss two key developments in the top tail of the income distribution. First, they omit capital gains and stock options, which became a large share of top incomes in the 1990s. Second, they are subject to a serious "top coding" problem. As others have begun to point out (US Congress, 1992, 1993; Ryscavage, 1995; Mishel et al., 1997: pp. 417–421), the Census estimates value all household incomes in the top class at the *floor* of that top class. That floor was only $50,000 for 1967–1976, then $100,000 for 1977–1984, $300,000 for 1985–1992, and $1 million since 1993. The official CPS estimates imply that between 1980 and 1997 Bill Gates of Microsoft earned less than $8 million—from which he somehow accumulated a personal net worth valued over $36 *billion* in 1997 (*Newsweek*, Aug. 4, 1997: pp. 49–50). Worse yet, the published official CPS size distributions display even lower top-class cutoffs, frustrating any attempt to view what has happened within the top 5% of households.

Better clues about the true postwar movements in US income inequality are afforded by abandoning the top-income shares and Gini's in favor of inter-quantile income ratios that only dare measure incomes up to the 95th percentile, just below that top-5% darkness. Table 5 and Fig. 6 do so, showing a quite different view of the net change in inequality since 1929. At face value, it appears that households at the 95th- and 80th-percentile positions in 1995 could be as far above the median household, in ratio terms, as their counterparts back in 1929, thus erasing all the leveling of the 1929–1953 era. While changes in the basis of measurement pose dangers for such long-run comparisons,

[20] In addition to the series shown in Table 4 and Fig. 5, see Blackburn and Bloom (1987, 1994); Danziger and Gottschalk (1993, 1995); and Raj and Slottje (1994).

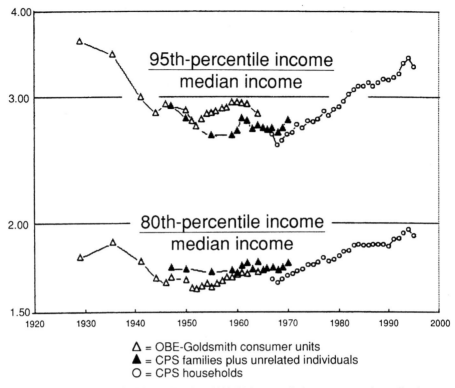

Fig. 6. An alternative view of US inequality since 1929: high-percentile incomes versus the median income.

there is a case for re-examining the whole basis of the income inequality measurements to see what share of the earlier income equalization has now been reversed.[21]

The overall rise of inequality since the 1970s has cast different moving shadows when viewed from a regional, racial, or gender standpoint. Among regions, it took the form of a 1978–1988 reversal in the continuing convergence of regional incomes-per-capita in the US. After that decade of widening, some narrowing of regional gaps resumed (Amos, 1989; Fan and Cassetti, 1994; Husted, 1991; Ram, 1992; Nissan and Carter, 1993; Sherwood-Call, 1996). On the racial front, the relative income position of blacks failed to make progress after 1975, especially for black males, though it did not retreat on the average (Oliver and Shapiro, 1995; Donoghue and Heckman, 1991; Freeman and Bound, 1992).

---

[21] The author thanks Claudia Goldin, Lawrence Katz, Lawrence Mishel, and the US Census Bureau for guidance on the mis-measurement of top US incomes. My attempts to produce better estimates of incomes above the 95th percentile with the help of tax-return data have been unsuccessful, leaving Table 5 and Fig. 6 as the best set of indirect clues.

Table 5

Incomes relative to the median income, US 1929–1995*

Year	OBE–Goldsmith 95th %ile	80th	20th	CPS, families plus unrelated individuals 95th %ile	80th	20th	CPS, households 95th %ile	80th	20th
1929	3.60	1.78	0.46						
1935.5	3.45	1.87	0.49						
1944	2.85	1.66	0.52						
1946	2.94	1.64	0.53						
1947	2.92	1.67	0.53	2.93	1.72	0.43			
1950	2.88	1.65	0.51	2.81	1.71	0.39			
1951	2.78	1.61	0.52						
1952	2.73	1.61	0.52						
1953	2.79	1.62	0.51						
1954	2.84	1.63	0.51						
1955	2.85	1.62	0.52	2.65	1.70	0.39			
1956	2.87	1.64	0.52						
1957	2.89	1.65	0.51						
1958	2.90	1.67	0.52						
1959	2.95	1.67	0.50	2.65	1.71	0.40			
1960	2.94	1.68	0.50	2.69	1.69	0.40			
1961	2.94	1.69	0.50	2.80	1.73	0.39			
1962	2.94	1.69	0.50	2.78	1.75	0.40			
1963				2.71	1.71	0.39			
1964	2.84	1.70	0.47	2.74	1.75	0.40			
1965				2.72	1.71	0.40			
1966				2.70	1.72	0.41			
1967				2.71	1.72	0.41	2.66	1.66	0.42
1968				2.68	1.71	0.42	2.56	1.64	0.43
1969				2.71	1.72	0.41	2.60	1.66	0.43
1970	2.79	1.70	0.49	2.79	1.74	0.40	2.65	1.68	0.42
1971	2.78	1.70	0.50				2.67	1.68	0.42
1972							2.74	1.70	0.42
1973							2.71	1.71	0.42
1974							2.78	1.74	0.44
1975							2.77	1.74	0.43
1976							2.79	1.75	0.43
1977							2.87	1.78	0.43
1978							2.83	1.75	0.42
1979							2.88	1.77	0.43
1980							2.91	1.77	0.43
1981							2.95	1.81	0.43

*Each figure is the ratio of the income at this percentile to the median 50th-percentile) income.

Table 5

(continued)*

Year	OBE–Goldsmith 95th %ile	80th	20th	CPS, families plus unrelated individuals 95th %ile	80th	20th	CPS, households 95th %ile	80th	20th
1982							3.03	1.82	0.42
1983							3.07	1.85	0.43
1984							3.10	1.86	0.43
1985							3.10	1.85	0.42
1986							3.14	1.85	0.42
1987							3.11	1.86	0.41
1988							3.15	1.86	0.42
1989							3.17	1.86	0.42
1990							3.16	1.84	0.42
1991							3.20	1.88	0.42
1992							3.23	1.89	0.41
1993							3.35	1.93	0.42
1994							3.40	1.95	0.42
1995							3.32	1.91	0.42

*Each figure is the ratio of the income at this percentile to the median 50th-percentile) income.

For the OBE–Goldsmith and families-plus unrelated series, the median income was estimated as the geometric average of the two nearest quintile border incomes (Y60 and Y40).

Y20, the border income at the top of the bottom quintile, is derived for 1929 by special assumptions. First, we accept Goldsmith's estimate that the bottom quintile received 3.5% of all consumer-unit income the second quintile received 9.0%. These estimates imply respective average quintile incomes of $409 and $1051. Where, between these, is the quintile border income Y20?

In 1935–36, the same OBE–Goldsmith estimates imply that the border was 0.541 of the way up from the bottom-quintile average income to the second-quintile average. But that was with heavy unemployment, which would drag down the bottom-quintile average a lot. So assume that in 1929, the border was exactly halfway between $409 and $1051, or $730.

America's gender pay gap has been particularly wide because the whole pay structure is more spread out in America. That is, gender pay gaps tend to be correlated with overall occupational gaps across industrialized countries, the main exception being the high relative pay for Australian women. Still, the 1980s and early 1990s brought a peculiar cross-current. American women swam upstream against the general rise in inequality, posting their best relative gains in pay per hour of any decade since the mid-nineteenth century (Goldin, 1990; O'Niell and Polachek, 1993; Blau and Kahn, 1995: pp. 106–107; Blackburn and Bloom, 1987; Cancian et al., 1993). This dramatic improvement in women's relative position came later than in other countries, and appears to have owed much to the rise of anti-discrimination enforcement across the 1980s.

5. The main sources of episodic inequality movements

Economists' attempts to explain such movements in income inequality generally pass the data through a group-decomposition filter, and then settle on choices of more exogenous underlying causes. The decomposition phase is of great value in channeling the search for underlying causes, because it multiplies the number of separate movements—changes in between-group inequalities, versus changes in within-group inequalities, versus inequality changes due to shifts in group weights—that any underlying theory must explain. When the decompositions are done, however, six kinds of causal forces usually are chosen for the task of explanation:

1. Population growth (demographic transition, migration);
2. The rate of skills growth per member of the labor force;
3. Biases in technological change;
4. Product-demand shifts (either domestic or global);
5. Labor-market institutions, including unions; and
6. Government fiscal redistribution.

The first four forces have been featured in most explanations of America's inequality movements. They have been emphasized over labor-market institutions and government redistribution, for the most part, because these fifth and sixth categories were smaller shares of American economic life, especially before 1933.

For example, Williamson and Lindert (1980) featured the first three forces in their interpretation of movements in US earnings gaps from 1839 through 1973. The rates of population growth and skills growth were negatively correlated and worked in combination. In particular, one reason why the leveling came in the period 1929–1948 was the combination of slower population growth and faster skills growth. Conversely, across the nineteenth century population grew faster, skills per worker grew slower, and the skilled/unskilled pay ratio widened. Imbalances in the factor-demand implications of technological (or total-factor-productivity) change played an important complementary role in explaining trend reversals in pay ratios.[22]

The recent debate on the causes of the wage widening in Britain and America since the 1970s is another case study, one that has featured demand and supply forces equivalent to (1)–(5) above. The competing views differ in the relative roles to be assigned to: (a) immigration (a part of (1) above); (b) slowdown in skills growth; (c) labor-saving technological bias; (d) shifts in domestic product demand (part of (4) above); (e) increasing import competition and out-sourcing of supply sectors (also a part of (4) above); versus (f) the decline of labor-union power ((5) above).

---

[22] The computable-general-equilibrium (CGE) exercises performed by Williamson and Lindert should be extended in a number of directions. First, the model should be complicated to include more than four factors of production and more than three output sectors, including input-output ratios between the output sectors. Second, it could incorporate forces that shift product demand, such as tariff policy and transportation costs, as Williamson (1974) did when analyzing growth rather than inequality. Third, it could be used to explain movements in the relative returns to non-human property, as O'Rourke et al. (1996) have done for international patterns of movements in land rents.

On the heavily-studied American experience since the 1970s, there seems to be an emerging consensus that the international parts of the story—immigration, out-sourcing, and trade competition—will explain part, but less than half, of the observed widening. Biased technological progress and the deceleration of skills growth across the 1980s combine to explain a large part of the recent widening.[23] Labor-market institutions, our force (5) above, do play a role in twentieth-century income movements, even in the US. Several writings by Richard Freeman (e.g., 1980, 1993) have shown that unionization trends shaped both the US wage compression of 1929–1953 and the more recent US wage widening. Blau and Kahn (1996) confirm that de-unionization and decentralized wage bargaining account for most of the peculiarity of the American income distribution relative to Europe.

The sixth force, government fiscal redistribution as an influence on the inequality of pre-fisc incomes, remains a singular challenge. It is always hard to trace effects of tax-transfer progressivity or regressivity back onto the pre-fisc distribution. We can test the premise, however, that the movements in pre-fisc inequality (equalization) seemed to follow trends toward regressivity (progressivity) of the fiscal structure. Crude tests of this sort can be sketched for Britain's pre-fisc income leveling up to the 1970s and for both countries' return to greater inequalities thereafter.

Could all of Britain's income leveling up to the 1970s have been the result of government fiscal redistribution?[24] That is possible, even though we are following measures of pre-fisc income here. Perhaps government took such a large confiscatory tax bite from the richest in society, year after year, as to reduce their share of nonhuman wealth and therefore of property income, bringing about the overall leveling we observe.

There are at least three reasons why fiscal redistribution probably does not explain all of the observed leveling of Britain's pre-fisc incomes since the late nineteenth or early twentieth century:

(a) The compression of occupational pay ratios could not have come from fiscal redistribution as such, and it was large enough that it must have accounted for a noticeable share of the income leveling.

(b) The income leveling occurred in many countries, some with more progressivity than Britain and some with less (Lydall, 1968; Lindert and Williamson, 1985; Phelps Brown, 1988).

---

[23] See Lawrence and Slaughter (1993); Murphy and Welch (1993); Berman et al. (1994); Wood (1994, 1995); Katz et al. (1995); Burtless (1995); Feenstra and Hanson (1995); Richardson (1995); and the whole January 1995 issue of the New York Federal Reserve Bank's *Economic Policy Review*.

[24] Bear in mind that the only government interventions being considered here are taxes and transfers, with no attention to industrial relations laws, incomes policies, and other less-budgetary tools of government.

Note also that the text here is considering the effect of taxation on income equalization, not its effect on wealth equalization. The fisc's share of the credit for wealth equalization might be different from its share of the income equalization. In particular, it could be that a greater share of the wealth equalization achieved by 1938 was due to taxation of high unearned incomes, and less to other forces, than for the income movements featured here.

(c) The historic decline in the income share of the top 5% seems to have started before the tax-transfer system took a particularly large bite from that top 5%. The early estimates by Lord Samuel (1919) imply that the top 5% paid only something like 10% average tax on unearned income in 1903–04 and only 5–7% on earned income, versus 5–9% for everybody else in the taxpaying ranks. By 1913–14 Lloyd George and others had raised the top-5% tax bite to 15% on unearned income and 7–8% on earned income, versus 5–7% on all other taxpayers. These differences would not seem large enough to have caused the declines in the top 5% share we observe. Granted, Barna (1945) has estimated that by 1937 the average tax take from the top 5% had risen greatly, to numbers like 40–60%, versus 20% for all other taxpayers. The CSO estimates for 1953 say something similar. These 1937 and 1953 snapshots do indeed imply a system that could radically re-shape the holding of property income. But if further study of interwar tax incidence confirms that the progressivity did not single out the top 5% much until the 1930s, the point will remain that much of the leveling had taken place before the linkage from differential tax rates to differential property accumulation could have taken effect.

Could Britain's widening pre-fisc inequalities since the 1970s have been the result of a prior regressive shift toward lighter taxation of the top income ranks? The recent history is difficult to read. There was indeed a long uneven decline in the progressivity of tax-transfer effects from 1949 to 1980, to judge from the usual kind of incidence calculations published in *Economic Trends*. One might imagine that this set the stage for the reversion toward higher property-income growth in the top ranks since the 1970s. Yet from 1980 to 1984, over the first half of the Thatcher government, the figures show a pronounced *rise* in progressive redistribution through government, placing the mid-Thatcher years alongside the Attlee years as the most progressive spells of the whole postwar era. The underlying reason, of course, is that the early-1980s return to progressivity was unintentional: Unemployment soared so much that fixed entitlement formulas raised the transfers toward the poor. It is only after 1984 that one sees a simultaneous combination of increasing regressivity and increasing pre-fisc inequality (Atkinson, 1996, 1997). If there is a longer-run feedback from regressivity to pre-fisc inequality in recent decades, only a more detailed calculation can quantify it.[25]

The 1980s US income widening might have been slightly augmented by a retreat from progressivity. While we again lack a detailed tracing of the feedback from regressivity trends to subsequent pre-fisc inequality, studies of the determinants of post-fisc inequality do show that regressivity and pre-fisc inequality marched together in America

---

[25] In the absence of detailed calculations about feedbacks from tax-transfer regressivity to pre-fisc income inequality, all we have are the kinds of studies that document the co-existence of the two movements, by decomposing the sources of change in *post*-fisc inequality. Thus for the UK between 1979 and 1988, Johnson and Webb (1993) estimate that the changes in the tax-benefit system account for 43% of the shift in post-tax-and-transfer income inequality, versus only 23% for the widening of earnings, 29% for the rise in unemployment, and 5% residual noise. As the text makes clear, that effect of the tax-transfer system must have come after 1984.

since the late 1970s. Gramlich et al. (1993: pp. 233–243) find that of the 6.8% rise in the post-fisc Gini for US family incomes between 1980 and 1990, a pre-fisc rise accounted for 5.0 points and a shift away from tax-transfer progressivity accounted for the remaining 1.8 points.

Thus in three cases—Britain's pre-fisc leveling, plus the widening of pre-fisc inequalities in both countries since the 1970s—the trends in fiscal progressivity (regressivity) were more or less followed by trends toward pre-fisc income leveling (widening). The timing is imperfect, however, and the underlying link awaits more detailed studies covering decades of data.

6. Lessons about long-run changes

In addition to spotlighting the six forces that shape most of the episodic swings in income inequality, the accumulated history of Britain and America also offers generalizations that span the sweep of the last three centuries. These generalizations yield predictions about the future experiences of the world's least developed countries. They also light the way to the next phase of research on what drives inequality in the long run.

6.1. The Kuznets curve as a Milky Way

First, it is evident that the Kuznets curve flickers. It cannot steadily illuminate all inequality history, any more than the Phillips curve reliably links unemployment to wage-price inflation. Best seen dimly in the distance without the distraction of competing light sources, the Kuznets curve is still visible as a convenient tendency related to the development process. It blurs into the background where Kuznets admitted he had the greatest doubts, namely in the early-modern settings where he thought inequality might have risen. As noted earlier, that is as we should have expected, since countries begin sustained development from radically different initial distributions, especially land distributions. The downslope of the inverted U stands out more clearly and predictably. So does the end of the downslope.[26]

6.2. The Robin Hood paradox

A final pattern that emerges over the centuries points toward a different path for future research on the determinants of inequality trends.

The pattern is this: Across time and across jurisdictions, redistribution toward the poor is least achieved where it is most warranted by the usual principles of welfare policy, such as cushioning the lowest absolute incomes most, redressing inequalities where they are the greatest, and encouraging labor- force re-entry. Elsewhere I have called this

---

[26] "Land" here should include mineral and forest rights. Bourguignon and Morrisson (1990) have rightly stressed the importance of mineral rights in explaining international differences in inequality and skewness.

the Robin-Hood Paradox, since the paradox suggests that Robin Hood's redistributive army is missing when and where it is most needed (Lindert, 1991: pp. 226–231). There is an immediate corollary for trends in redistribution and inequality: A rise in pre-fisc inequality will be accompanied by a shift toward fiscal regressivity, and an era of leveling will be an era of increasing fiscal progressivity.

The earlier and poorer the setting, and the greater the inequality, the stronger the case for taxing property to aid the poor. With a large share of the population near subsistence and in poor health, there is a good chance that giving aid will raise labor supply: the aid can improve workers' health and survival enough to outweigh any incentive to take more subsidized leisure. Yet the earlier and poorer the setting, the less that support was given.[27] With the advance of average incomes, and especially in the eras when pre-fisc inequality was also being reduced, aid to the poor became more generous. As we have seen, recent experience hints that the correlation might even hold when the trend is away from, not toward, pre-fisc equality. That appears to be the case in the US, though in Britain the temporal correlation was weakened by the temporary rise of redistributive spending from 1979 to 1984. Over space, the paradox also holds more often than not. Certainly in today's global international cross-section, progressive redistribution toward the poor correlates strongly with both average incomes and pre-fisc equality of incomes. Across sub-national jurisdictions, the same is often true. In twentieth-century America, particularly before the late 1960s, the poor have received more aid, even as a share of average incomes, in those states where poverty has been less severe. There are spatial exceptions to the paradox, however.[28]

How could pre-fisc inequality be correlated with a regressivity in taxes and transfers? Here we are triply challenged. First, there is that difficult task of quantifying the feed-back from the tax-transfer system to the pre-fisc Lorenz curve. A second challenge added here is to determine how pre-fisc inequality in turn affects society's willingness to redistribute between income ranks. Having received hints about a *simultaneous* relationship between redistribution and pre-fisc inequality, we must solve the problem of estimating them simultaneously. Correct appreciation of the influence of fiscal redistribution on pre-fisc inequality waits upon the simultaneous identification of the determinants of the redistribution itself.

---

[27] Here the text concentrates on trends in British and other European settings, where the earlier settings remained highly unequal and average incomes grew across the nineteenth century. In such settings the paradox predicts a drift toward poor relief. For early America, the trend predictions of the paradox are mixed: per-capita income growth across the nineteenth century would favor giving more to the poor, but the rise in inequality would cause less to be given.

[28] One exception relates to the distribution of poor relief across the parishes of England in the Old Poor Law era 1780–1834. In that case, tax-based poor relief was indeed most generous where poverty was greatest, namely in the rural Southeast. This pattern has been well explained by George Boyer (1985) as a reflection of differences in the lobbying power of labor-hiring landlords. In the southeast such landlords had dispropor-tionate power in local government, and outvoted the non-hiring family farmers, raising local poor rates so as to keep the poor around during the winter.

Before sending the task off to the econometric laboratory, however, one should formulate a strategy for dealing with a third research challenge, one related to political voice. Our usual hunches about the effect of income distribution on redistributive policies are in danger of colliding with the overall empirical pattern summarized by the Robin Hood paradox. The quickest way to see the third research challenge is to think of an unequal and underdeveloped society, like Britain before the 1830s or a Latin American country today. In such societies, incomes and socio-economic mobility are highly skewed. There is a wealthy elite far above the rest of the ranks, and the mean income far exceeds the median. Our usual theoretical priors are that such a skewed society is ripe for taxing the rich, with the median voter preferring a high rate of progressive taxation. So say most recent models of the redistributive process (e.g., Peltzman, 1980; Meltzer and Richard, 1981; Kristov et al., 1992; Alesina and Rodrik, 1994; Persson and Tabellini, 1994). If so, then why do we observe the opposite, with such less-developed and highly skewed societies yielding the least redistribution from rich to poor?

The answer must lie in the relationship of the income distribution to political voice. In fact, highly skewed societies are ones in which the wealthy elite retains a high share of political power as well as of wealth and income. The usual pressure-group models, such as median-voter models, should not be applied until they are cast in terms of the self-interests of those who actually have political voice. In the highly skewed societies, the median voter is often someone up in the top quintile of the income ranks. Thus, for Britain, the task is to re-examine how the self-interests of well-to-do swing voters were transformed by the Reform Acts of 1832, 1867, 1883–84, and beyond. For the task of understanding what is so different about America, it is essential to incorporate the peculiarly low rate of political participation of America's poor.

Here, surely, is a key to resolving the mysteries of how redistribution though government relates to overall inequality. Only when we have a tested working theory of the three-way relationship between income inequality, inequality of political voice, and redistribution through government, will we have a clear view of any of these three sides to the inequality issue.[29]

References

Abowd, J.M. and M.L. Bognanno (1995), International differences in executive and managerial compensation, in R.B. Freeman and L.F. Katz, eds., Differences and Changes in Wage Structures (University of Chicago Press, Chicago), pp. 25–66.

Acemoglu, D. and J.A. Robinson (1996), Why Did the West Extend the Franchise? Democracy, Inequality, and Growth in Historical Perspective, Manuscript, October.

Alesina, A. and D. Rodrik (1994), Distribution, politics, and economic growth, Quarterly Journal of Economics 109: 465–490.

[29] Some initial headway into the three-way relationship between income inequality, redistribution, and political voice has been made empirically by Lindert (1994b, 1996) and Barro (1996), and theoretically in a new model by Acemoglu and Robinson (1996).

Amos, O.M. (1989), An inquiry into the causes of Increasing regional income inequality in the United States, Review of Regional Studies 19: 1–12.

Atkinson, A.B. (1995), Incomes and the Welfare State (Cambridge University Press, Cambridge).

Atkinson, A.B. (1996), Seeking to explain the distribution of income, in John Hills, ed., New Inequalities : The Changing Distribution of Income and Wealth in the United Kingdom (Cambridge University Press, Cambridge), pp. 19–48.

Atkinson, A.B. (1997), Bringing income distribution in from the cold, Economic Journal 107: 297–321.

Atkinson, A.B. and A.J. Harrison (1978), Distribution of Personal Wealth in Britain (Cambridge University Press, Cambridge).

Atkinson, A.B. and J. Micklewright (1992), Economic Transformation in Eastern Europe and the Distribution of Income (Cambridge University Press, Cambridge).

Banks, J., A. Dilnot and H. Low (1996), Patterns of financial wealth-holding in the United Kingdom, in John Hills, ed., New Inequalities : The Changing Distribution of Income and Wealth in the United Kingdom (Cambridge University Press, Cambridge), pp. 321-346.

Barna, T. (1937), Redistribution of Incomes through Public Finance (Clarendon Press, Oxford).

Barro, R.J. (1996), Democracy and growth, Journal of Economic Growth 1: 1–28.

Berman, E., J. Bound and Z. Griliches (1994), Changes in the demand for skilled labor within U.S. manufacturing: evidence from the annual survey of manufactures, Quarterly Journal of Economics 109: 367–398.

Blackburn, M.L. and D.E. Bloom (1987), Earnings and income inequality in the United States, Population and Development Review 13: 575–609.

Blackburn, M.L. and D.E. Bloom (1994), Changes in the Structure of Family Income Inequality in the United States and Other Industrial Nations During the 1980's, National Bureau of Economic Research Working Paper No. 4754.

Blau, F. and L.M. Kahn (1995), The gender earnings gap: some international evidence, in R.B. Freeman and L.F. Katz, eds., Differences and Changes in Wage Structures (University of Chicago Press, Chicago), pp. 105-44.

Blau, F. and L.M. Kahn (1996), International differences in male wage inequality: institutions versus market forces, Journal of Political Economy 104: 791–837.

Borooah, V.K., P.P.L. McGregor and P.M. McKee (1995), Working wives and income inequality in the UK, Regional Studies 29: 477–487.

Borooah, V.K. and P.M. McKee (1996), How much did working wives contribute to changes in income inequality between couples in the UK? Fiscal Studies, 17: 59–78.

Bourguignon, F. and C. Morrisson (1990), Income distribution, development, and foreign trade, European Economic Review 34: 1113–1132.

Boyer, G.R. (1985), An economic model of the English poor law, circa 1780-1834, Explorations in Economic History 22: 129–167.

Burns, A. (1954), The Frontiers of Economic Knowledge (Princeton: Princeton University Press).

Burtless, G. (1995), International trade and the rise of earnings inequality, Journal of Economic Literature 33: 800–877.

Cancian, M., S. Danziger and P. Gottschalk (1993), Working wives and family income inequality among married couples, in S. Danziger and P. Gottschalk, eds., Uneven Tides: Rising Inequality in America (Russell Sage Foundation, New York), pp. 195–221.

Clark, G. (1991), In Search of the Agricultural Revolution: Southern England, 1611–1850, paper presented at the All-University of California Conference in Economic History, Davis, November 8–10.

Coelho, P. and J. Shepherd (1976). Regional differences in real wages: the United States, 1851–1880, Explorations in Economic History 13: 203–230.

Crawford, I. (1996), UK household cost-of-living indices, 1979–92, in John Hills, ed., New Inequalities : The Changing Distribution of Income and Wealth in the UK (Cambridge University Press, Cambridge), pp. 76–102.

Crystal, G. (1993), In Search of Excess: The Overcompensation of American Executives, Second edition (W.W. Norton, New York).

Danziger, S. and P. Gottschalk, eds. (1993), Uneven Tides: Rising Inequality in America (Russell Sage Foundation, New York).

Danziger, S. and P. Gottschalk (1995), America Unequal (Russell Sage Foundation, New York and Cambridge and Harvard University Press, London).

Donaghue, J. and J. Heckman (1991), Continuous versus episodic change: the impact of civil rights policy on the economic status of blacks, Journal of Economic Literature 29: 1603–1643.

Fan, C. C. and E. Cassetti (1994), The spatial and temporal dynamics of US regional income inequality, 1950–1989, Annals of Regional Science 28: 177–196.

Feenstra, R.C. and G.H. Hanson (1995), Foreign Investment, Outsourcing, and Relative Wages, NBER Working Paper No. 5121, May.

Floud, R. and B. Harris (1996), Health, Height, and Welfare: Britain 1700–1980, NBER Historical Paper No. 87. May.

Feinstein, C.H (1988), The rise and fall of the Williamson curve, Journal of Economic History 44: 699–729.

Feinstein, C.H. (1996a), The equalizing of wealth in Britain since the Second World War, Oxford Review of Economic Policy 12: 96–105.

Feinstein, C.H. (1996b), Conjectures and Contrivances: Economic Growth and the Standard of Living in Britain during the Industrial Revolution, University of Oxford, Discussion Paper in Economic and Social History No. 9 (July).

Fogel, R.W. (1986), Nutrition and the decline in mortality since 1700: some preliminary findings, in S.L. Engerman and R.E. Gallman, eds., Long-Term Factors in American Economic Growth (University of Chicago Press, Chicago), pp. 439–527.

Fogel, R.W. and S.L. Engerman, eds. (1971), The Reinterpretation of American Economic History (Harper and Row, New York).

Freeman, R.B. (1980), Unionism and the dispersion of wages, Industrial and Labor Relations Review 34: 3–23.

Freeman, R.B. (1993), How much has de-unionization contributed to the rise in male earnings inequality? in S. Danziger and P. Gottschalk, eds., Uneven Tides: Rising Inequality in America (Russell Sage Foundation, New York), pp. 133–163.

Freeman, R.B. and J. Bound (1992), What went wrong? The erosion of relative earnings and employment among young black men in the 1980s, Quarterly Journal of Economics 107: 201–231.

Freeman, R.B. and L.F. Katz, eds. (1995), Differences and Changes in Wage Structures (University of Chicago, Chicago).

Gallman, R.E. (1969), Trends in the size distribution of wealth in the Nineteenth Century: some speculations, in L. Soltow, ed., Six Papers on the Size Distribution of Wealth and Income (Columbia University Press, New York).

Gallman, R.E. (1981), Comment on chapters 1 and 2, in J.D. Smith, ed., Modeling the Distribution and Intergenerational Transmission of Wealth (University of Chicago Press, Chicago), pp. 128–136.

Goldin, C. (1990), Understanding the Gender Gap: An Economic History of American Women (Oxford University Press, New York).

Goldin, C. and R.A. Margo (1992a), Wages, prices, and labor markets before the Civil War, in C. Goldin and H. Rockoff, eds., Strategic Factors in Nineteenth Century American Economic History (University of Chicago Press, Chicago), pp. 67–104.

Goldin, C. and R.A. Margo (1992b), The great compression: the wage structure in the United States at mid-century, Quarterly Journal of Economics 107.

Goldsmith, S.F. (1967), Changes in the size distribution of income, in E.C. Budd, ed., Inequality and Poverty (Harper and Row, New York), with an update in Budd's introduction.

Goodman, A., P. Johnson and S. Webb (1997), Inequality in the UK (Oxford University Press, Oxford).

Gramlich, E.M., R. Kasten, and F. Sammartino (1993), Growing inequality in the 1980s: the role of federal taxes and cash transfers, in S. Danziger and P. Gottschalk, eds., Uneven Tides: Rising Inequality in America (Russell Sage Foundation, New York), pp. 225–250.

Harkness, S., S. Machin and J. Waldfogel (1996), Women's pay and family incomes in Britain, 1979–91, in John Hills, ed., New Inequalities: The Changing Distribution of Income and Wealth in the UK (Cambridge University Press, Cambridge), pp. 158–179.

Hollingsworth, J.R. (1979), Inequality in Levels of Health in England and Wales, 1891–1971, University of Wisconsin – Madison, Institute for Research on Poverty, Discussion Paper No. 581–579, November.

Hollingsworth, J.R., J. Hage and R.A. Hanneman (1990), State Intervention in Medical Care: Consequences for Britain, France, Sweden, and the United States, 1890–1970 (Cornell University Press, Ithaca).

Hollingsworth, T.H. (1977), Mortality in the British peerage families since 1600, Population, numéro special.

Horrell, S. and J. Humphries (1992), Old questions, new data and alternative perspectives: families' living standards in the industrial revolution, Journal of Economic History 52: 849–880.

Horrell, S. and J. Humphries (1995), Women's labour force participation and the transition to the male-breadwinning family, 1790–1865, Economic History Review 48: 89–117.

Hunt, E.H. (1986), Industrialization and regional inequality: wages in Britain 1760–1914, Journal of Economic History 46: 935–966.

Husted, T.A. (1991), Changes in state income inequality from 1981 to 1987, Review of Regional Studies 21: 249–260.

Jackson, R.V. (1987), The structure of pay in nineteenth-century Britain, Economic History Review 4: 561–570.

Jackson, R.V. (1994), Inequality of incomes and lifespans in England since 1688, Economic History Review 47: 508–524.

Jenkins, S.P. (1995), Accounting for inequality trends: decomposition analyses for the UK, 1971–86, Economica 62: 29–63.

John, A.H. (1989), Statistical appendix, in G.E. Mingay, ed., The Agrarian History of England and Wales, VI, 1750–1850 (Cambridge University Press, Cambridge), pp. 972–1155.

Johnson, P. and S. Webb. (1993), Explaining the growth in UK income inequality: 1979–1988, Economic Journal 103: 429–435.

Jones, A.H. (1977), American Colonial Wealth: Documents and Methods, three volumes (Arno Press, New York).

Jones, A.H. (1980), Wealth of a Nation to Be (Columbia University Press, New York).

Karoly, L.A. (1993), The trend in inequality among families, individuals, and workers in the United States: a twenty-five year perspective, in S. Danziger and P. Gottschalk, eds., Uneven Tides: Rising Inequality in America (Russell Sage Foundation, New York), pp. 99–164.

Karoly, L.A. and G. Burtless (1995), Demographic change, rising earnings inequality, and the distribution of personal well-being, 1959–1989, Demography 32: 379–405.

Katz, L.F., D.G. Blanchflower and G.W. Loveman (1995), A comparison of changes in the structure of wages in four OECD countries, in R.B. Freeman and L.F. Katz, eds., Differences and Changes in Wage Structures. Chicago: University of Chicago Press, pp. 25–66.

Kristov, L., P. Lindert and R. McClelland (1992), Pressure groups and redistribution, Journal of Public Economics 48: 135–163.

Kunze, K. (1979), The Effects of Age Composition and Changes in Vital Rates on Nineteenth-Century Population: Estimates from New Data (University of Utah Ph.D. dissertation, Salt Lake City).

Kuznets, S. (1953), Shares of Upper Income Groups in Income and Savings (Columbia University Press, New York).

Kuznets, S. (1955), Economic growth and income inequality, American Economic Review 45: 1–28.

Lampman, R.J. (1962), The Share of Top Wealth-Holders in National Wealth, 1922–1956. (Princeton University Press, Princeton).

Lawrence, R.Z. and M.J. Slaughter (1993), International Trade and American Wages in the 1980s: Giant sucking sound or small hiccup? Brookings Papers in Economic Analysis: Microeconomics, (2): 161–226.

Lee, C.H. (1991), Regional inequalities in infant mortality in Britain, 1861–1971: Patterns and hypotheses, Population Studies 45: 55–65.

Lillard, Lee A. (1977), Inequality: Earnings vs. human wealth, American Economic Review 67: 42–53.

Lindert, P.H. (1983), Some Economic Consequences of English Population Growth, 1541–1913, University of California – Davis, Agricultural History Center, Working Paper 14, August.

Lindert, P.H. (1985), Lucrens Angliae: The Distribution of English Private Wealth since 1670, University of California – Davis, Agricultural History Center, Working Papers 18 and 19, February.

Lindert, P.H. (1986), Unequal English wealth since 1670, Journal of Political Economy 94: 1127–1162.

Lindert, P.H. (1987), Who owned Victorian England? The debate over landed wealth and inequality, Agricultural History 61: 25–51.

Lindert, P.H. (1991), Toward a comparative history of income and wealth inequality, in Y.S. Brenner, H. Kaelble and M. Thomas, eds., Income Distribution in Historical Perspective (Cambridge University Press, Cambridge), pp. 212–231.

Lindert, P.H. (1994a), Unequal living standards, in Volume 1 of R. Floud and D. McCloskey, eds., The Economic History of Britain since 1700 (Cambridge University Press, Cambridge), pp. 357–386.

Lindert, P.H. (1994b), The rising of social spending, 1880–1930, Explorations in Economic History 31: 1–36.

Lindert, P.H. (1996), What Limits Social Spending? Explorations in Economic History 33: 1–34.

Lindert, P.H. (forthcoming), When did inequality rise in Britain and America? Journal of Income Distribution.

Lindert, P.H. and J.G. Williamson (1982), Revising England's social tables, 1688–1812, Explorations in Economic History 19: 385–408.

Lindert, P.H. and J.G. Williamson (1983), Reinterpreting Britain's social tables, 1688–1913, Explorations in Economic History 20: 94–109.

Lindert, P.H. and J.G. Williamson (1985), Growth, equality and history, Explorations in Economic History 22: 341–377.

Lydall, H.B. (1968). The structure of Earnings. Oxford: Oxford University Press.

Maloney, T.N. (1994), Wage compression and wage inequality between black and white males in the United States, 1940–1960, Journal of Economic History 54: 358–381.

Margo, R.A. (1992), Wages and prices during the antebellum period: a survey and new evidence, in R.E. Gallman and J.J. Wallis, eds., American Growth and Standards of Living before the Civil War (University of Chicago Press, Chicago), pp. 173–210.

Margo, R.A. and G.C. Villaflor (1987), The growth of wages in antebellum America: new evidence, Journal of Economic History 47: 873–895.

Meltzer, A.H. and S.F.Richard (1981), A rational theory of the size of government, Journal of Political Economy 89: 914–927.

Mishel, L., J. Bernstein and J. Schmitt (1997), The State of Working America 1996–97 (Economic Policy Institute, Washington).

Mookherjee, D. and A.F. Shorrocks (1982), A decomposition analysis of the trend in UK income inequality, Economic Journal 92: 886–902.

Murphy, K. and F. Welch (1993), Industrial change and the rising importance of skill, in S. Danziger and P. Gottschalk, eds., Uneven Tides: Rising Inequality in America (Russell Sage Foundation, New York), pp. 101–132.

Nissan, E. and G. Carter (1993), Income inequality across regions over time, Growth and Change 24: 303–319.

Ober, H. (1948), Occupational wage differentials, 1907–1947, Monthly Labor Review 67: 127–134.

Oliver, M.L. and T.M. Shapiro (1995), Black Wealth/White Wealth: A New Perspective on Racial Inequality (Routledge, New York).

O'Niell, J. and S. Polachek (1993), Why the gender gap in wages narrowed in the 1980s, Journal of Labor Economics 11: 205–228.

O'Rourke, K.H., A.M. Taylor and J.G. Williamson (1996), Factor price convergence in the late nineteenth century, International Economic Review 37: 499–530.

Osberg, L. and F. Siddiq (1988), The inequality of wealth in Britain's North American colonies: the importance of the relatively poor, Review of Income and Wealth 34: 143–163.

Peltzman, S. (1980), The growth of government, Journal of Law and Economics 23: 209–288.

Persson, T. and G. Tabellini. (1994), Is inequality harmful for growth? American Economic Review 84: 600–621.

Phelps Brown, E.H. (1977), The Inequality of Pay (University of California Press: Berkeley).

Phelps Brown, E.H. (1988), Egalitarianism and the Generation of Inequality (Clarendon, Oxford).

Preston, S.H., M.R. Haines and E. Pamuk (1981). Effects of Industrialization and Urbanization on Mortality in Developing Countries. International Union for the Scientific Study of Population, International Population Conference, Manila.

Raj, B. and D.J. Slottje (1994), The trend behavior of alternative income inequality measures in the United States from 1947–1990 and the structural break, Journal of Business and Economic Statistics 12: 479–487.

Ram, R. (1992), Interstate income inequality in the United States: measurement, modelling and some characteristics, Review of Income and Wealth 38: 39–48.

Ransom, R.L. and R. Sutch (1977), One Kind of Freedom (Cambridge University Press, New York).

Richardson, J.D. (1995), Income inequality and trade: how to think, what to conclude, Journal of Economic Perspectives 9: 33–55.

Routh, G. (1965), Occupation and Pay in Great Britain, 1906-1960 (Cambridge University Press, Cambridge).

Royal Commission on the Distribution of Income and Wealth (1977), Report No. 5, Third Report of the Standing Reference (HMSO, London).

Rubinstein, W.D. (1981), Men of Property (Rutgers University Press, New Brunswick, New Jersey).

Rubinstein, W.D. (1986), Wealth and Inequality in Britain (Faber and Faber, London).

Ryscavage, P. (1995), A surge in income inequality? Monthly Labor Review 118: 51–61.

Samuel, Lord (1919), The taxation of the various classes of the people, Journal of the Royal Statistical Society 82: 143–185.

Schofield, R.S. (1965), The Geographical Distribution of Wealth in England, 1334–1649, Economic History Review 18: 483–510.

Shammas, C. (1993), A new look at long-term trends in wealth inequality in the United States, American Historical Review 98: 412–432.

Shanahan, M. and Margaret Corell (1997), In Search of Kuznets's Curve: A Re-examination of the Distribution of Wealth in the United States between 1650 and 1950, Paper presented at the Third World Congress of Cliometrics, Munich, 10–13 July 1997.

Sherwood-Call, C. (1996), The 1980s divergence in state per capita incomes: what does it tell us? Federal Reserve Bank of San Francisco Economic Review 1: 14–25.

Smeeding, T.M. and J. Coder (1995), Income inequality in rich countries during the 1980s, Journal of Income Distribution 5: 13–29.

Smolensky, E. (1963), An interrelationship among income distributions, Review of Economics and Statistics 45: 197–206.

Smolensky, E. and Robert Plotnick. (1993), Inequality and Poverty in the United States, 1900 to 1990. University of Wisconsin – Madison, Institute for Research on Poverty, Discussion Paper 998–993 (March).

Smolensky, E., R. Plotnick, E. Evenhouse and S. Reilly (1994), Growth, inequality, and poverty: a cautionary note, Review of Income and Wealth 40: 217–222.

Soltow, L.C. (1968), Long-run changes in British income inequality, Economic History Review 21: 17–29.

Soltow, L.C. (1969), Evidence on income inequality in the United States, 1866–1965, Journal of Economic History 29: 279–286.

Soltow, L.C. (1971), Economic inequality in the United States in the period from 1790 to 1860, Journal of Economic History 31: 822–839.

Soltow, L.C. (1975), Men and Wealth in the United States, 1850–1870 (Yale University Press, New Haven).

Soltow, L.C. (1984), Wealth inequality in the United States in 1798 and 1860, Review of Economics and Statistics 66: 444–451.

Soltow, L.C. (1989), Distribution of Wealth and Income in the United States in 1798 (University of Pittsburgh Press, Pittsburgh).

Soltow, L.C. (1990), Inequality of wealth in land in Scotland in the eighteenth century, Scottish Economic and Social History 10, 38–60.

Soltow, L.C. (1992), Inequalities in the standard of living in the United States, in R.E. Gallman and J.J. Wallis, eds., American Economic Growth and Standards of Living before the Civil War (University of Chicago Press, Chicago), pp. 121–166.

Steckel, R.H. (1992), Stature and living standards in the United States, in R.E. Gallman and J.J. Wallis, eds., American Economic Growth and Standards of Living before the Civil War (University of Chicago Press, Chicago), pp. 265–308.

Steckel, R.H. (1994), Census manuscript schedules matched with property tax lists: a source of information on long-term trends in wealth inequality, Historical Methods 27: 71–85.

Steckel, R.H. (1995), Stature and the standard of living, Journal of Economic Literature 33: 1903–1940.

Stigler, G. (1956), Trends in Employment in the Service Industries (Princeton University Press, Princeton).

Summers, R. (1956), An econometric investigation of the size distribution of lifetime average annual earnings, Econometrica 24: 346–347.

Titmuss, R.M. (1943), Birth, Poverty, and Wealth: A Study of Infant Mortality (Hamish Hamilton, London).

Townsend, P., N. Davidson and M. Whitehead (1988), Inequalities in Health, consisting of the Black Report and the Health Divide (Penguin, London).

United Kingdom, Central Statistical Office, Various years, Economic Trends (HMSO, London).

United States Congress, House Ways and Means Committee (1992 [1993], The Green Book 1992 [1993] (GPO, Washington).

Usher, D. (1973), An imputation to the measure of economic growth for changes in life expectancy, in M. Moss, ed., The Measurement of Economic and Social Performance (Columbia University Press, New York).

van Zanden, J.L. (1995), Tracing the beginning of the Kuznets curve: western Europe during the early modern period, Economic History Review 48: 643–664.

Wilkinson, R.G. (1996), Unhealthy Societies: The Afflictions of Inequality. (Routledge, London).

Williamson, J.G. (1965). Regional inequality and the process of national development, Economic Development and Cultural Change 13, Part 2 (entire).

Williamson, J.G. (1974), Late Nineteenth-Century American Development (Cambridge University Press, Cambridge).

Williamson, J.G. (1980), Earnings inequality in nineteenth-century Britain, Journal of Economic History 40: 457–476.

Williamson, J.G. (1984), British mortality and the value of life, Population Studies 38: 157–172.

Williamson, J.G. (1985), Did British Capitalism Breed Inequality? (Allen and Unwin, Boston).

Williamson, J.G. and P.H. Lindert (1980), American Inequality: A Macroeconomic History. (Academic Press, New York).

Williamson, J.G. and P.H. Lindert (1981), Long-term trends in American wealth inequality, in J.D. Smith, ed., Modeling the Distribution and Intergenerational Transmission of Wealth (University of Chicago Press, Chicago), pp. 9–94.

Wolff, E.N. (1994), Trends in household wealth in the United States, 1962–83 and 1983–89, Review of Income and Wealth 40: 143–174.

Wolff, E.N. (1995), Top Heavy: A Study of the Increasing Inequality of Wealth in America (Twentieth Century Fund Press, New York).

Wolff, E.N. and M. Marley (1989), Long-term trends in U.S. wealth inequality: methodological issues and results, in R.E. Lipsey and H.S. Tice, eds., The Measurement of Saving (University of Chicago Press, Chicago), pp. 765–839.

Wood, A. (1994), North-South Trade, Employment and Inequality (Clarendon Press, Oxford).

Wood, A. (1995), How trade hurt unskilled workers, Journal of Economic Perspectives 9: 57–80.

Woods, R.I. (1988–89), The causes of rapid infant mortality decline in England and Wales, 1861–1921, Population Studies 42: 343–366, and 43: 113–132.

Woods, R.I. (1993), On the historical relationship between infant and adult mortality, Population Studies 47: 195–219.

Wrigley, E.A. and R.S. Schofield (1981), The Population History of England, 1541–1871 (Harvard University Press, Cambridge, Massachusetts).

Wrigley, E.A., R.S. Davies, J. Oeppen and R.S. Schofield (1997), English Population History from Reconstitutions (Cambridge University Press, Cambridge).

Chapter 4

HISTORICAL PERSPECTIVES ON INCOME DISTRIBUTION: THE CASE OF EUROPE

CHRISTIAN MORRISSON

Université de Paris I, Panthéon-Sorbonne

Contents

Handbook of Income Distribution, Volume 1. Edited by A. B. Atkinson and F. Bourguignon

Abstract

The evolution of income distribution over two centuries is an attractive topic because it allows one to test the inverse U-curve hypothesis using long series instead of cross-section data. In Section 1 the distribution trends in countries where global data are available, is considered, that is in four Scandinavian countries, the Netherlands, the German states and Germany, and in France. The inverse U-curve hypothesis is verified in four of them. Section 2 presents in a consistent framework, using the Theil indicator, all available information on inequality trends between agricultural and nonagricultural sectors and on inequality trends within each sector in European countries. Finally Section 3 throws light on the political and economic factors explaining the long-term evolution of distribution. The economic factors playing a key role are the market structures, the diffusion of education and saving, and dualism.

Keywords: income distribution, salary distribution, redistribution, intersectoral inequality, intrasectoral inequality, wealth distribution, dualism, factor shares

JEL codes. D30; D31; D33; H24; H55; J31; N33; N34

Studying the evolution of income distribution over one or two centuries represents an attractive attempt for all economists interested in income distribution issues. Instead of venturing flimsy suppositions, always debatable, about such an evolution from cross-section data on a group of countries (ranging from the poorest to the richest), economists can test the inverse U-curve hypothesis with secular series and understand the reasons for this evolution, or rebut this hypothesis and explain a permanent trend of inequalities reduction. Moreover, Kuznets was the first, in 1955, to make the hypothesis of increasing inequality in the first development and industrial takeoff phase and decreasing inequality as development continues. He attempted to explain this inverse U-curve by the dualism between two sectors (agricultural and nonagricultural) and by population transfer from one to the other. If this approach avoids the disadvantages of the cross-section analysis, it unfortunately presents other difficulties of great importance nevertheless. Indeed, available information on European countries in the eighteenth and nineteenth centuries is much less satisfactory than current data on some developing countries. Even for poor countries, nowadays one can find detailed national accountings, reliable enough national inquiries on household expenditures, and other statistics, allowing the estimation of income distribution with rather low margins of error or the construction of social accounting matrixes. Understandably most of this information was absent in Europe one or two centuries ago. As a result, one has to develop more or less hazardous estimates from scarce available data. However, pre-industrial economies were much simpler than developed economies. There were fewer sources of income and most households benefited from only *one* source of income (e.g., unskilled wage labor and land rent) whereas in industrialised and rich societies, members of the same household could receive simultaneously interest, dividends, wages and entrepreneurial income. This makes mapping from functional income distribution to income distribution by size more difficult. Finally, social transfers did not exist, income taxation was very limited and, in several countries, most people did not pay any direct taxes. These differences explain why it is easier to estimate a distribution of total income by social economic groups in eighteenth century France than it is now.

Frequently, this information has a tax origin. Pareto (1897) studied the income distribution from such statistics as early as the end of the nineteenth century. But the serious disadvantage of this information is that it does not take into account families who pay no taxes, who often represent the majority of families. On the other hand, a tax distribution can vary greatly from an income distribution if, for example, only principal income has to be declared (as for "capitation" in France), or if tax is proportional to rent (to the extent that the rent does not represent a constant percentage of income)—not to mention the most frequent bias, due to fraud and tax evasion.

Certainly, we sometimes have other data at our disposal, such as salary differentials according to qualification, distribution between salaries and capital incomes, or income and working population distribution between agricultural and nonagricultural sectors. But we are then confronted with a jigsaw puzzle of which the majority of pieces are missing. The information on salary differentials is not sufficient to estimate salary distribution. For example, a reduction of salary differentials can go hand in hand with a strong increase of the percentage of highly skilled wage- earners, so that distribution becomes more unequal despite this reduction.[1] Income and working population distribution between agricultural and nonagricultural sectors allow the computation of Theil's intersectoral contribution, i.e.:

$$T = T_a + T_b, \tag{1}$$

$$T_b = m_1 T_1 + m_2 T_2, \tag{2}$$

where T_a corresponds to the inequality between the two sectors, T_b is the total sum of inequalities within each sector, m_1 and m_2 are the shares of the two sectors in total income, and T_1 and T_2 are being the internal Theils for these two sectors.

[1] For a population divided into two groups (with no inequality within each group) and for

w_u = unskilled wage

w_s = skilled wage

w_a = average wage

if we assume a large increase in the percentage of skilled workers and a decrease of w_s/w_u, the two Lorenz curves may intersect and an increase of the Gini coefficient is possible (the upper part of the curve shifts up because w_s/w_a decreases and the lower part shifts down if w_a rises more than w_u).

But it is impossible to estimate the long-term evolution of T from T_a because the inequality inside the nonagricultural sector (T_2) can strongly increase during the first stage of industrialisation, as it did in France from 1830 to 1865. Given the scarcity of data, economists may have been tempted to deduce the evolution of T from a sole element. But one should be sensible and not make a statistic say more than it does. Our approach will be guided by this concern. In the first section, we consider distribution trends in countries only where global data permit. This will allow us to answer a crucial and controversial issue: does global inequality follow an Inverse U-curve during the growth and industrialisation process as it was assumed by Kuznets from time-series data on England, Germany and the US? Kuznets explained this relationship mainly by the shift of population from traditional to modern activities with average per capita income much lower in the former than in the latter sector (with a constant ratio between the two sectors average income and with agricultural population falling from 90% to 10%, we always observe an increasing and then a decreasing inequality). The second part will systematically check off the jigsaw pieces so as to spotlight constants and deduce patterns for the evolution of long-term distribution, using all available data, including scarce data which does not allow drawing general conclusions for that country. Finally, we will specify the factors that can explain this evolution.

1. Long-term evolution of national income distribution

An income distribution can be assessed from fiscal sources since the nineteenth century in only a few European countries. Such information is available for more than a century for the Scandinavian countries, The Netherlands and Germany. As regards France, like Sweden, because of a shortage of tax sources, one has to resort to the aggregation of data within the framework of a brief national accounting.

The same principles have been followed for each country:
- Reaching as far back in time as possible, to include distributions from the stage of industrialisation, i.e., over a period when the majority of the population still lived on agriculture. This information is necessary since the explanatory pattern of an Inverse U-curve proposed by Kuznets relies upon this structural change: the fall of agricultural employment (from more than 70% to less than 20%), with a constant average income differential between the two sectors.
- Interrupting our description in the 1970's (or 1960's). Indeed, we have observed since circa 1980, a net increase of inequalities in several industrialised countries that has already stirred up a great deal of literature. We have excluded this very recent phenomenon from our field of analysis as it is a different issue and is analysed by P. Gottschalk and T. Smeeding in Chapter 5. From the early 1960's, all countries in our study were industrialised countries with high levels of income, and what is of particular interest to us is the evolution of income distribution starting from the pre-industrial period.

Table 1

Denmark

	1870	1903	1915	1925	1939	1949	1952	1953	1955	1963
1st quintile					4.4	4.8	4.9	4.6	4.5	5
2nd quintile					9	10.5	10.2	10.2	10.6	10.8
3rd quintile					13.5	16.3	16.8	16.9	16.9	16.8
4th quintile					22.1	23.4	24.2	24.1	24.4	24.2
9th decile					15.8	15.5	15.4	16.2	16.2	16.1
Top decile	50	38		36	35.2	29.5	28.6	28	27.4	27.1
Top 5%	36.5	28		26	24.6	19.4	18	18	17.6	16.9
MEC	0.50	0.35	0.45	0.36	0.34		0.28	0.28		0.27

Sources: 1870 to 1925 : Zeuthen (1928); 1939, 1952: Bjerke (1956), table II, p. 107; 1953, 1963: UN (1967), table 6, 10; 1949, 1955 : Bjerke (1964), table 6, p. 285. From 1870 to 1963 : MEC: R. Sorensen (1993).
MEC : Maximum Equalisation Coefficient : percentage of population with income smaller or equal to average income, less percentage of total income received by this population.
Unit: taxpayer household.
Income: taxable income, with a deduction for wage-earners.
Note: in all following Tables 1–6, there is no adjustment taking into account for household composition in the fiscal statistics.

— As far as possible, we tried to collect consistent data and some statistics were rejected because they include a significant bias relative to other available statistics. We can refer to the same source in many countries such as Denmark, Norway, The Netherlands, Finland, Saxony and Prussia (from 1873 to 1913). The best example is that of The Netherlands where homogeneous and nearly similar statistics are available from 1914 to 1972. But unfortunately in other countries, such as France, we must compare heterogeneous statistics. There is a tradeoff between the consistency of statistics and the number and length of the series and some discrepancies between series are acceptable if we do not forget the margin of error.

1.1. Denmark

All studies of Denmark are based on the same source: tax statistics. These statistics include all persons[2] above 16 years of age (except married women and children below the age of 18 who have no income) and the income taxed is the available income, i.e., after deduction of income tax, of insurance premiums, and of interest for debt reimbursement.

[2] From Bjerke (1956) paper we know that a small number of income payers had a zero income in 1939. So the tax data seem to include all persons and are not limited to those filling tax returns and paying income tax. But the number of persons who do not pay taxes may be underestimated. We can only hope that this bias is relatively constant from one year to another.

These deductions carry a bias for a comparison with countries where income is measured before tax, but they do not change the evolution of distribution in Denmark. Furthermore, according to Bjerke, tax statistics do not present a significant bias or at least they compensate for one another.

If we prefer the estimate of distribution by quantile, we must combine three studies: the Zeuthen (1928) data for the early period, then the Bjerke's papers (1957 and 1964) and the UN study (1967) for the last years. On the other hand, a recent paper of Sorensen (1993) gave us, for the first time, a consistent view over the whole period (from 1870 to 1986), but Sorensen uses only the maximum equalisation coefficient (MEC) to measure income inequality. The MEC indicates the share of total income which has to be transferred from the population with income above the average income ($\bar{y}$) to other people in order to achieve an equal distribution. The MEC is equal to $A - B$ (with A = share of the population with income $\leq \bar{y}$ and B = share of the total income received by this population).

The evolution of income inequality from deciles or quantiles percentages or from MEC follow the same trend. We observe a very important fall from 1870 to the 1900s. The First World War was marked by heavy price increases. Wages could not keep up with inflation because they were fixed by collective agreements for five-year periods whereas inflation entailed a boom in profits. These rapid changes in functional income distribution explain a peak of MEC in 1915 but after the war, the distribution returned to the pre-war situation and we notice even a slight decrease in inequality. A net decline appears from 1939 to 1949 (the share of the top decile records a 5.7 points fall). This trend continues more slowly later on: from 1949 to 1963, the shares of quintiles 1 and 2 grow by 0.5 points and the share of the top decile decreases by 1.4 points. It was reported by Bjerke (1964) that, before the war, redistribution was carried out almost entirely by transfers to households, whereas, since 1945, the contribution of direct taxes to redistribution increased (40% in 1955). So, within one century, Denmark has passed from a very concentrated distribution to a weak inequality, to the detriment of the top decile and mainly of the top 5% (whose share was reduced to 16.9% instead of 36.5%, whereas the decrease of the second last 5% is limited to 3 points, from 13.5 to 10.2). Moreover, the fall of inequality continued during the 1970s and 1980s. According to Sorensen, the MEC has decreased by 27% between 1970 and 1986 (for all persons liable to taxation).

One question remains unanswered: has inequality increased from the beginning of the nineteenth century until 1870 or not? As Denmark registered a higher per capita income in 1870 than the three other Scandinavian countries, equal to that of France, a comparison with neighbouring countries is not valid. One could imagine applying Kuznets' hypothesis, an evolution in Denmark similar to that in France where inequality increased from 1830 to 1870 and decreased after, but we do not have any indication on income distribution in Denmark before 1870.

1.2. Norway

For Norway the income data are interesting and long standing (since 1840), but of limited scope. Indeed, we have Soltow's survey (1965) regarding 8 towns within 2 counties since 1840.[3] Those eight towns accounted for 8.4% of the country's urban population in 1960 (17% in 1860). One may think that this source reflects at best the evolution of inequality within the urban population, but we cannot deduce the evolution of the country since we do not have two other elements: the fluctuations of T_a (intersectoral Theil) and internal Theil for the rural population. Soltow has computed the Gini coefficient for each town, and then the average of these coefficients for each county (see Table 2 indicating the average for 2 counties). The fall of this average in the long-term is spectacular since it exceeds 50% between 1855 and 1963 (from 0.68 to 0.29).[4]

This trend is confirmed by another tax source indicating that the share of the richest 5% in urban and rural zones was cut almost in half from 1907 to 1948. The fall of the Gini coefficient for the 2 counties may look less impressive (-20%), but the two fluctuations are compatible because the reduction of inequality mainly concerns the top twentieth, while the Gini coefficient reflects the whole distribution. We have estimates only for two postwar years (1951 and 1963, with similar results); distribution in 1963 proves slightly unequal (Gini coefficient: 0.36), with a slightly lower inferior share for the fifth quintile than Denmark's share at the same date.

Soltow, by entitling his work *Toward Income Equality in Norway* has gone beyond available sources. Indeed, the fall of inequality in the urban environment since the middle of the nineteenth century seems highly probable. Such a fact does not go without saying: in 1850, Norway was still a poor country with an average income 35% lower than that of France, and barely more than half of Great Britain's. One could therefore think, if Kuznets' hypothesis applies, that growth and industrialisation occurred after 1850 and at first increased income inequality in towns between 1850 and the beginning of the twentieth century. This was actually not the case and the reasons were given by Soltow.[5] But if the Theil index is split up as follows:

$$T = T_a + m_1 T_1 + m_2 T_2, \tag{3}$$

---

[3] The archives of each town contain the name, the job, the income and the wealth of taxpayers and Soltow made the best of this data in his analysis of inequality decline for more than a century, after having corrected the data to take into account persons not subjected to tax. The measured income includes income in nature, fictitious rent for owners of their own housing and capital gains as well as pensions, while insurance premiums and wage-earner contributions to national insurance are excluded.

[4] Before 1900, Soltow had been able to collect fiscal statistics in only one to three towns by county and for 1840 in only one town (Kristiansand), such that the figures for the nineteenth century are less significant than those from 1900 onwards. Comparing Gini coefficients for each town from 1840 to 1900, the downward trend is verified in each, including in Kristiansand, and the rise observed between 1840 and 1855 is not significant because it results solely from a change in the sample composition.

[5] The main factors explaining the lessening inequality are the breakdown of monopoly power groups, the diffusion of property income among households, the elimination of seasonal unemployment (cf. Soltow, 1965).

Table 2

Norway

	1840	1855	1865–75	1885–90	1900–10	1920	1930	1938	1948–50	1963
Gini coefficient (2 counties)	0.57[a]	0.68	0.49	0.49	0.40	0.34	0.41	0.43	0.32	29[b]
Top 5% (rural sector)					27			20	14	
Top 5% (urban sector)					30			22	19	
1st quintile										4.5
2nd quintile										12.1
3rd quintile										18.5
4th quintile										24.4
9th decile										15.6
Top decile										24.9
Gini coefficient										0.36

[a] In one town only.
[b] In one county only.
Sources: 2 counties: Soltow (1965). Top 5% in rural/urban sector: Okonomisk Utsyn (Economic Survey), 1900–50, table 93. In 1963: UN (1967), table 6, 10.
Unit: Soltow: taxpayer. Other: taxpayer household.
Income : Soltow: primary income plus imputed rent, bonuses, pensions, income in kind and capital gains and losses (except from securities). Other: taxable income.

we know only that: $T_1 < T_2$ (inequality is lower in rural zones than in urban zones, (see Table 2), T_2 has dropped since the middle of the nineteenth century, at the same time as m_2 was increasing.

We deduce a net decrease of $m_1 T_1 + m_2 T_2$ because if the share of the urban sector doubles while T_2 decreases by half (as we observe in reality), then $m_2 T_2$ is a constant. The decline of $m_1 T_1$ is important because m_1 has dropped from more than 0.5 to 0.1–0.2 in one century.

An unknown element remains: T's evolution. We know that T_a must have increased during the second half of the nineteenth century because two necessary conditions were present. The first was that the population still predominant in the rural sector, shifted towards the urban sector. And the second condition being a higher average income in towns. But we cannot compute the consequences of these two opposite effects (T_a's rise and $m_1 T_1 + m_2 T_2$'s fall). It is only from a given threshold for the share of the urban population that both effects had the same impact.

1.3. Sweden

Income inequalities in Sweden were the subject of numerous studies, based either on tax data, salary differential data, or on land distribution data, ranging from a microeconomic approach (income inequality within a village), to a national approach. The synthesis of such studies is of particular interest because inequality first increased, from 1750 to 1850–90, before decreasing rapidly from the period between the wars up to 1960–70.

The period 1750–1850

In 1850, Sweden, with a per capita income that was barely more than half of the English income, was not yet committed to its industrialisation phase, even though trade had increased since the middle of the eighteenth century and there had been a significant rise in agricultural production. This period corresponds therefore to the prerequisite during which all conditions were present for a takeoff.

There are no sources regarding the entire income distribution during this period, but we have an ensemble of data at our disposal (see Appendix A) all attesting to the same phenomenon: a rise of inequality in rural zones as well as in towns, i.e., of T_1 and T_2 and therefore of $(m_1 T_1 + m_2 T_2)$.

The rise of $m_1 T_1 + m_2 T_2$ being certain, T_a's evolution between 1750 and 1850 remains to be taken into account. Contrary to other countries, it is very probable that average income differentials between rural zones and towns did not increase as rural zones have profited both from agricultural development and from the start of industrialisation. On the other hand, as urbanisation slowly progressed from a weak initial level, it is obvious that T_a recorded only a slight increase. But T_a's rise, associated with a more important rise of T_b, is sufficient to deduce that inequality increased sharply in the whole country between 1750 and 1850.

The period 1850–1910/14

It is difficult to estimate the evolution of inequality during this period since we only have information regarding salaries. A comprehensive study on salaries (Soderberg, 1991) indicates an upward trend until 1914 that inverted during the war.[6]

[6] The most comprehensive study on wages focuses on 10 series of wages from 1870 to 1950, with a series on labor wages in 7 industries, on agricultural wages (men and women) and on administrative staff. A measure of inequality is computed from the standard deviation of the logarithm of wage ratios (that are weighted by the share of each series in aggregate employment). We observe a rise of this indicator from 1870 to 1913, followed by a strong decrease during the First World War. The decomposition of this rise shows that the unegalitarian structural effect, due to a strong increase of the share of skilled personnel in employment (for example, the staff of the administrative personnel is multiplied by 5) more than compensated (at least with the inequality indicator chosen) the egalitarian effect of a reduction of wage differentials in several industries. Thus the ratio between the average salary of administrative personnel and the average salary of the aggregate wage-earners lowered from 5 to 2 between 1870 and 1940. Studies on metallurgy, on railroads, and on Stockholm's workers corroborate this reduction of differentials according to skill, but this does not question the findings of the previous study that took into account this phenomenon.

An estimate of salary distribution is insufficient to appraise the evolution of T_a and T_b. The estimate is only an indication of income distribution in towns. We can assume that the distribution of the other incomes, which is much more concentrated, has not changed much and that the contribution to global inequality of average income differentials between salaried and nonsalaried workers has not changed or changed very little.[7] By accepting these hypotheses, we would conclude that inequality in towns has risen. This finding is in accordance with a survey regarding income distribution in a middle sized town from 1870 to 1950 according to tax sources and statistics on salaries (Kaelble, 1986: p. 34): the rise of average income coincided with an increase of inequality. According to Soderberg (1987b), the share of high incomes in industrial towns would have remained stable while the share of low incomes would have dropped to the benefit of the intermediate group, i.e., skilled wage-earners who benefited from rather substantial wage increases.

In any case, to conclude that there was a rise of inequality for the whole population, we must assume that:

– inequality in rural zones has not fallen, and
– the value of T_a has not decreased significantly.

These two hypotheses are not unrealistic as industrialisation started approximately around 1870, and the share of the rural population was still high at that time. Sweden was, at least until 1900, in this first stage when, according to Kuznets' pattern, the decrease of the rural share entailed inequality.

Soderberg's (1991) findings come to the same conclusion: inequality would have increased from 1870 to 1914, this movement extending from 1920 to 1930, after a steep drop during the war. The maximum would have therefore been reached around 1910–1914, approximately at the end of the industrialisation phase. For Soderberg, this evolution conforms to Kuznets' curve, all the more because the decline of the agricultural share in employment was more rapid in Sweden than in Great Britain and in the US. It means that T_a increased rapidly from 1870 to the beginning of the twentieth century. Such a rise associated with a more unequal income distribution of urban incomes makes a progression of the inequality very probable, with the only uncertainty being the date when it reached its maximum between 1890 and 1913.

---

[7] This hypothesis appears plausible given that this period is marked by industrialisation. In other countries (Germany, France), we observe a rapid progression, during the same period, of the share of capital income in urban income distribution.

From 1914 to the 1970s

After the period 1914–1930 when inverse fluctuations followed one another,[8] we have at our disposal reliable national sources from 1930 to the 1970's, allowing observation of the rapid decrease of inequality over 40 years.

It is easy to retrace the evolution of income distribution since 1930. Table 3 indicates the evolution for 1935–1970, and similarly we know, according to Bentzel (1952), that the distributions from 1930 and 1935 are almost identical (the same share for quintiles 1, 2 and 3, with one point higher for quintile 5). Those data based on tax sources affect the whole population and are homogenous. They indicate an important and a continuous fall of inequality before the stabilisation that occurred about 1970 (see Table 3).[9] The evolution is again more marked if we refer to the net income distribution (after direct tax) since the share of quintiles 1 and 2 doubled (from 9.9% in 1935 to 20.4% in 1970) while the fifth quintile's share is reduced from 54.1 to 34% (cf. UN, 1957 and Schnitzer, 1974). The redistribution by an increasingly progressive tax system played a role as important as differential reduction of primary incomes and in 35 years, Sweden passed from a nonegalitarian society to one of the most egalitarian of Western Europe.[10]

Such changes are relevant for a long-term study. From 1750 to the end of the nineteenth century, it is certain that inequality strongly increased for different reasons over time. From 1930 to 1970, it decreased even more, and more notably if we refer to net income. As we see, the only inaccuracy concerns the date when the tendency inverts. The decade 1900–1910 appears to be the most plausible for several reasons. If we compare this evolution to that observed in France, we see that inequality in Sweden was strong in 1930, compared to that in France for 1890–1900, but inferior to the French maximum for 1860–1865 at the end of the accelerated industrialisation period (corresponding to 1900 in Sweden). Sweden rapidly developed its education and training of a skilled workforce, which reduced salary differentials. And the direct tax system had a redistributive impact as early as 1920. Whatever the uncertainties about this date of change, it remains that Sweden offers a clear example of Kuznets' curve between 1750 and 1970.

---

[8] The rising demand for labourers because of the war entailed a very strong increase in the average salary of the unskilled that continued until 1930 (Soderberg, 1991). From 1914 to 1920, farm laborers' wages benefited from the same effect, such that wage inequalities decreased. But from 1920 to 1930, agricultural wages decreased and wage differentials rose according to qualification. These fluctuations explain the variations of the indicator designed from 10 wage series: after a strong fall from 1914 to 1920, it recovers, from 1920 to 1930, to its pre-war level. But this does not allow us to draw any conclusion about the inequality for the aggregate income, because of scarce data on income distribution among nonwage-earners and on the contribution to inequality of the average income differential between wage-earners and nonwage-earners.

[9] Within 35 years, the share of quintiles 1 and 2 grew by half, while that of the fifth quintile dropped from 56.1 to 42.5%.

[10] For example, the average available income differential between the poorest 40% and the richest 20% went from 11 : 1 to 3.3 : 1.

Table 3

Sweden

	1935	1945	1948	1970	1992
1st quintile	10	2.4	3.2	5.4	4.9
2nd quintile		8.6	9.6	9.9	10.3
3rd quintile	12.7	15.3	16.3	17.6	18.3
4th quintile	21.2	23.1	24.3	24.6	24.7
9th decile	16.6	16.5	16.3	42.5	41.8
Top decile	39.5	34.1	30.3		

Sources: 1935 and 1948, UN (1957), table 3. This study gets the data from R. Bentzel, Inkomstfördelningen i Sverige, Uppsala, 1953. R. Bentzel used tax statistics (all incomes are taken into account, including transfers), and Schnitzer used the same source. 1970, Schnitzer (1974), table 3, 8. 1992, Statistical Yearbook of Sweden 1995 (1994).
Unit: taxpayer household. Income: taxable income (primary income plus transfers).

Table 4

Finland

	1881	1900	1966	1985
Lowest 60% (b)			37.4	46.1
7th–9th deciles (b)			38.2	36
Top decile (a)	39	50	25	
(b)			24.4	17.9
Top 5% (a)	31	40	15	

Sources: (a) Hjerppe and Lefgren (1974). (b) Uusitalo (1989). Income Distribution in Finland. Central Statistical Office of Finland, Helsinki.
Unit: (a) taxpayer household; (b) person.
Income: (a) taxable income; (b) disposable household income per equivalent adult.

1.4. Finland

We have limited information, but it cannot be neglected because it dates back to the end of the nineteenth century (cf. Table 4). The article of Hjerppe and Lefgren (1974) provides estimates for 1881, 1900 and 1966 on tax incomes after adjustment for households and incomes that are not taken into account. According to this article cited earlier, inequality would have clearly increased from 1881 to 1900, and decreased in the twentieth century. Nevertheless, it should be noted that this statistic concerns only the last decile and the last twentieth. This most important result (a large decrease of inequality since 1900) is confirmed by the M. Jäntti estimate (unpublished) concerning gross income distribution per tax unit (including only income above basic deduction). The Gini coefficient for this distribution has declined from 0.43 in 1921 to 0.30 in 1948.

The Finland Statistics Agency gives tax statistics for 1950–1969, but without any adjustment and the estimates for 1966 conflict with that of Hjerppe and Lefgren (the share of the top decile mounts to 32.7% instead of 25%). So, we prefer quoting Uusitalo's (1989) estimates for 1966 and 1985. This author considers distribution among persons of disposable household income per equivalent adult. Of course his definition of unit differs from that of Hjerppe and Lefgren (tax unit i.e., household), but the share of the top decile is the same (25% and 24.4%), and this consistency is necessary to build up a continuous series from 1881 to 1985 (cf. Table 4).

The assessment over a century would therefore show a rise of the inequality at the end of the nineteenth century, followed by a steep fall during the period between the wars up to 1985. The interest of this assessment is to test conformity with Kuznets's curve. Notice nevertheless that this assessment is fragile because it relies upon only one assessment in 1881, while we have at our disposal a wide range of evidence indicating an increase of inequality in Sweden during the nineteenth century.

1.5. The Netherlands

This country presents interesting information for two reasons: the existence of a homogenous and reliable source since 1914 for the national income distribution and the imposition of an income tax in Amsterdam as early as 1877, which gives us complementary information for the end of the nineteenth century. We have at our disposal a set of homogenous data for the period between 1914–1972 which are some of the most reliable data available in the long run.[11]

Table 5 indicates a steep fall in inequality since the share of the tenth decile was reduced to 32% instead of 42% in 1914, with an acceleration after the Second World War (−3.4 points from 1938–1939 to 1950–1952).[12] But this increase does not appear to benefit the bottom three quintiles: their share in 1972 (31%) was inferior to the figure for 1914: 33.4%. Note nevertheless that this last figure is only an estimate of nontaxable income. This share was reduced from 1920–1921 to 26%, when the uncertainty decreased because the number of taxable households increases. We can therefore wonder if the revenue distribution of 1914 is reliable for all households. On the other hand, figures for quintiles 3 and 4, and for the ninth decile clearly illustrate the phenomenon of trickle down, with strong increases, notably for the fourth quintile (from 13.8% to 22.2%) that has received two-thirds of what the tenth decile has lost in percentage alone.

Similarly, some income data in Amsterdam since 1877 allow us to conclude that the inequality was wide in this town from 1877 to 1890, before a moderate fall during the

---

[11] Income tax only covered the whole population since 1950, but we were able to estimate, from the origin, the exempted household incomes. On the other hand, we have adjusted tax series to estimate income before any deduction for children. As taxation law remained unchanged from 1914 to 1941, and because figures fluctuate very slightly from one year to another, we retained averages for two years, when it was possible, so as to obtain the safest series possible.

[12] This acceleration might even be underestimated. In a study (1976) Pen and Tinbergen concluded from many pieces that inequality has been cut by half since 1939 (I owe this information to Professor Hartog).

Table 5
The Netherlands

Year	Q1	Q2	Q3	Q4	D9	D10
1914		33.4		13.8	10.8	42
1915		29.2		13	10.2	47.6
1916		26.8		13.2	10.4	49.6
1917		26.3		14.2	11.1	48.4
1918		27.9		15.7	12.1	44.3
1919	14.5		10.5	17.1	12.3	45.6
1920	13.7		12.5	18.7	12.7	42.4
1921	12.3		13.2	20.1	13.6	40.8
1922	12.4		13	20.4	14.3	39.9
1923	12.7		13	20.1	14.4	39.8
1924	12.7		12.9	19.6	14.1	40.7
1925	13		12.9	19.5	13.9	40.7
1926	13		12.9	19.4	13.8	40.9
1927	13.1		12.8	19.2	13.7	41.2
1928	13.4		12.8	18.9	13.5	41.4
1929	13.6		13	19.1	13.5	40.8
1930	14.1		13	19.4	13.6	39.9
1931	14.6		12.3	19.8	14.3	39
1932	16.5		10.8	19.8	14.7	38.2
1933		27.8		19.7	14.7	37.8
1934		28.5		19.5	14.5	37.5
1935		29		19.2	14.4	37.4
1936		29		18.9	14.1	38
1937		28.8		18.8	13.9	38.5
1938		29		18.7	13.8	38.5
1939		28.8		18.9	13.7	38.6
1946	13.3		13.2	20.7	14.6	38.2
1950	5.2	9.2	16	20.6	14.3	34.7
1952	5	9.9	15.4	20.9	14.1	34.7
1953	5	9.8	15.6	20.9	14.2	34.5
1954	5.4	9.9	15.6	20.3	14.5	34.3
1955	5.9	9.6	15.6	21.4	14.4	33.1
1957	5	10.5	15.9	21.1	14.4	33.1
1958	5.5	10.3	15.6	21	14.2	33.4
1959	5.1	10.2	15.7	21.3	14.3	33.4
1960	5	9.9	16.3	21.3	14.3	33.2
1962	5	9.9	16	21.7	15.1	32.3
1963	4.6	9.7	15.8	21.4	15.3	33.2
1964	4.5	9.7	15.8	21.9	14.8	33.3

Table 5

The Netherlands – (continued)

Year	Q1	Q2	Q3	Q4	D9	D10
1965	3.3	9.4	15.6	21.7	14.6	35.4
1966	4.3	10.2	16.1	21.6	14.8	33
1967	4.6	10.5	16	21.5	14.8	32.6
1970	4.9	10.6	15.9	22	15.2	31.4
1972	4.3	10.8	16.4	22.2	14.8	31.5

Sources: Hartog and Veenbergen (1978).
Unit: taxpayer household.
Income: taxable income (primary income plus transfers).
Note: before 1940, incomes below the exemption level are omitted, but an adjustment takes into account these incomes. After 1940, such a correction could not be made, but there are few incomes below the exemption level.

last decade followed by a period of stability between 1900 and 1914.[13] From J. de Meere (1983), the Theil index declined from 1.2 (1880) to 1 (1895) before a drop in the 1920s (0.6 in 1929–1930)

One could object that the income distribution in Amsterdam is representative of distribution in only that town rather than representative of the entire country. But from 1877, the rate of urbanisation rose so much that the intrasectoral inequality depends especially on that urban environment. Under these conditions, we can conclude that inequality decreased in the Netherlands from the end of the nineteenth century, even if some exogenous shocks entailed temporary rises (e.g., the First World War caused a considerable rise of commercial profits while a lot of workers were reduced to unemployment.)

1.6. The German states and Germany

This case is of great interest for several reasons: the economic importance of this country, the existence of numerous statistics since the 1870's (the years that coincide with the acceleration of industrialisation), and finally, the contrasted variations during the period between wars.

The first question that arises obviously concerns the end of the nineteenth century: has the first stage of growth been marked by a rise of inequalities? To answer that question, we have at our disposal tax statistics for two important States, Saxony and Prussia. These statistics agree (see Appendix B) that inequality has clearly increased

---

[13] When the city of Amsterdam implemented an income tax, part of the population was also under the taxation threshold. But by using Theil's decomposing properties and data on these incomes, it is possible to outline the evolution of this inequality indicator between 1877 and 1939, and to compare it to Theil's value for national income distribution between 1914 and 1939. As both evolutions were very close during these 25 years, we can extrapolate from the series related with Amsterdam for 1877–1914.

from 1870 to 1900 before decreasing slightly from 1900, to the benefit of income filed in the intermediate deciles.

Tax data for Germany (or for Western Germany after 1945) enable one to outline the contrasted evolution since 1913. We indicate the fluctuations of percentages, but not the percentages themselves because there are discrepancies between one series and another, but as each is homogenous, this does not question the long-term evolution. The strong decrease of inequality between 1913 and 1926 parallels the same declines in other countries. However, this is the final result of contradictory fluctuations as shown by Dumke (1991): war increased inequalities, but the upheavals that occurred afterwards entailed a far more important decline. After 1926, the political and economic situation marked the evolution of the distribution with:

- a rise in favour of deciles 7–10 during the period of expansion (1926–1929);
- a fall of profits and unemployment during the crisis, which explains the fall of shares of the bottom deciles and tenth decile; and
- a rise of the share of the tenth decile from 1932 to 1936 because the policy of the new Nazi form of government favoured, from 1933, capital revenues (Jeck, 1968).

On the whole, these fluctuations partly compensate each other, however, the balance remains clearly negative for the first six deciles. Thus, there had been a distinct deterioration of the fate of this group between 1926 and 1936 to the simultaneous benefit of the intermediate and richest groups.

After the Second World War, inequality clearly decreased, to the detriment of the tenth decile, then after 1950, also to the detriment of the seventh to ninth deciles.[14] After 1968, it seems that the distribution in Western Germany no longer recorded substantial changes because the article of Hauser and Becker (1997) shows that there was near stability from 1973 to 1987.[15] If we refer to percentages, issued from adjusted tax statistics given by the Statistisches Bundesamt (1973), instead of variations, we can establish that the former are very close, in 1968, to the distribution of the Netherlands in 1972.

To venture an appraisal, excluding the upheavals of the interwar years for the sake of simplification, Germany offers us a clear example of the Kuznets' curve. It illustrates a widening inequality from 1870 to 1900, during the first stage of industrialisation and rapid urbanisation, and a narrowing in inequality from the beginning of the twentieth century, this trend being confirmed only after 1945. Besides, it is partly on the German statistics that Kuznets founded his diagram of the inverse U-curve.

---

[14] The UN estimates in 1957, and 1967, based upon the study of Professor Goseke, indicate very close fluctuations.

[15] In a more recent estimate, Hauser and Becker (1997) observe a small increase in inequality for the distribution of net income (after deduction of taxes and social security contributions and after adding social transfers of all kinds): the Gini coefficient has risen from 0.31 in 1973 to 0.33 in 1988.

Table 6a

Germany[a]

	1926/13	1928/26	1932/28	1936/32	1950/36	1968/50
Lowest 60%	+4.8	−4.8	−4.7	+1	+2.3	+5.1
7th–9th deciles	+0.7	+3.3	+6.9	−2.7	+2	−1.9
Top decile	−5.5	+1.5	−2.8	+2.3	−4.3	−3.2
Top 5%	−6.2	+1.5	−3.1	+2	−3.7	−1.2

Source: Statistiches Reichsamt (1939); Statistiches Bundesamt (1954, 1973), quoted by Kraus (1981).

	1950/36	1964/55
Lowest 60%	+2.5	+2.6
Top decile	−5	−2.6

Source: UN (1957, 1967).
[a] West Germany after Second World War.
Unit: taxpayer household.
Income: taxable income.

Table 6b

Saxony

	1874–76	1897–99	1913
1st & 2nd quartiles	20.9	20.3	19.7
3rd quartile	18.1	18.1	19.8
Top quartile	61	61.6	60.5
Top decile	43.3	44	42.9
Top centile	17.1	19.6	19.3

Source: Kaelble (1986).
Unit: taxpayer household.
Income: taxable income.

1.7. France

It is far more difficult to follow the evolution of income distribution in France than in Germany. One reason lies in the absence of reliable tax statistics covering the totality of households, including up to date information, since half of the households are not subjected to income tax. As a result, current estimation attempts from the capitation in the eighteenth century, then from the "cote mobilière" property tax in the nineteenth century or from income tax and budget inquiries, are always risky. This risk justifies resorting to disaggregated accounting data by group to check if these estimates are plausible. Moreover, France presents specificities compared to the countries already studied: industrialisation occurred much earlier at a time when statistical administration was poor

Table 6c

Prussia

	1873–75	1896–1900	1911–13
Top 5%	27.8	32.6	30.6

Source: Das Deutsche Volkseinkommen (1932), quoted by Kraus (1981).

	1873–80	1891–1900	1901–10	1911–13
Top 5%	28	32	32	31

Source: Mueller (1959), quoted by Kuznets (1963); income tax data were roughly corrected by Mueller for understatement.

	1913	1928
Lowest 60%	32	31
Top quintile	50	49
Top 5%	31	26

Source: Das Deutsche Volkseinkommen (1932), quoted by Kuznets (1963).

	1876–80	1896–1900	1911–13
Top 5%	28.4	32.6	30.6
top 1%	15.2	18.9	18

Source: Dumke (1991).

1875		1928	
% of population	% of income	% of population	% of income
6.75	29.2	4.10	24.20
15.45	21	6.50	14.10
19.90	17.80	31.70	32.60
56.90	32	57.70	29.10

Sources: Das Deutsche Volkseinkommen (1932), Engel (1878), quoted by Bresciani-Turoni (1939).

	1875	1892	1902	1908	1913	1928
P	78		84	80	79	
D		0.26		0.30	0.32	0.31

P: Ratio of the number of individuals with incomes below the average to the total number of income receivers.
D: The relative average deviation divided by 2 (or $= (a-1)^{a-1}/a^a$ with a from Pareto's definition).
Source: Bresciani-Turoni (1939).
Unit: taxpayer household.
Income: taxable income.

Table 7a

France: distribution of income between socio-economic groups in 1788

	% of population	% of income
Aristocracy, churchmen, middle class 'bourgeoisie')	9.6	48.7
Craftmen and traders	19.6	24.5
Farmers producing for market		
Small farmers	25.2	11.6
Workers-farmer		
Journeyman-farm labourer	45.6	15.2
Unskilled worker		
Domestic servant		

Unit: person.
Income: primary income.

Table 7b

France

	1780		1788	1864	1890	1929	1975
	a	b					
1st & 2nd quintiles	5	9.3	10/12	13–14	15	18	17
3rd & 4th quintiles	19	20.3			29	32.5	38
9th decile	16	14.8			11	13.5	16
Top decile	60	55.6	50/55	48–50	45	36	29

(a): Distribution of the "capitation" tax.
(b): After correction including non-monetary income.
Source: Morrisson and Snyder (1998).
Unit: 1780 and 1788: person; 1864: economically active person; 1890 to 1975: household.
Income: 1780 to 1890: primary income; 1929 and 1975: disposable income.

and the Revolution of 1789 had a major impact, but one difficult to measure on income distribution. The case of this country is of particular interest because it concerns, among the different countries of our sample, the first politically unified country and the first engaged in industrialisation.

As industrialisation began around 1830, we will attempt first to assess the evolution of income distribution before 1830, according to Morrisson and Snyder (1998). We have been able to estimate the inequality before 1789 (Tables 7a and 7b) from tax statistics and data on the income of socio-economic groups, and to show that it was very high (see Appendix C). France in the Ancien Régime was a very nonegalitarian country and this was not due to growth in the 1750s and the 1760s (in the agricultural sector as well as in exports and manufacturing). According to the rolls of capitation, inequality in tax distribution was the same since the beginning of the eighteenth century.

The Revolution of 1789 involved a decrease in inequality because of the abolition of feudal rights and of tithes and the redistribution of the land of the clergy and the nobility to the benefit of peasants and bourgeoisie. On the other hand, the noblesse de robe and the business bourgeoisie lost their wealth based on "charges" and their accruing income. If the Revolution first benefited intermediate groups through the sales of "biens nationaux" and civil servant recruitment, then there was also a good number of small peasants among buyers of "biens nationaux" and the real wage for workers in towns increased 30% between 1788 and 1817, while the per capita income did not vary. It is therefore probable that the share of the richest 5% clearly lowered: unfortunately, we do not have statistics of the Restauration to measure the scope of this phenomenon.

The take-off of the French economy dates from the years 1830–1840 to 1860–1870. Never had the pace of industrialisation and urbanisation been as rapid as during the nineteenth century. From 1840 to 1860, the stock of steam machinery increased five-fold, and manufactured goods exports tripled. From 1846 to 1866, the urban population increased 35%, while the rural population stagnated. Therefore, during this period, the real wage did not fluctuate (it was the same in 1860 as in 1835), while all capital incomes increased rapidly, their amount being multiplied by 2 or 3 in 30 years, as the case maybe. We can conclude that the share of the tenth decile was increased at the expense of the first deciles. From national accounts for 1864, we have been able to conduct an income breakdown by group and to estimate the proportion of quintiles 1 + 2 and the tenth decile, imputing to this decile, 80% of property income. Thus, we obtain figures very close to those in 1788, the sole difference owing to the fact that for the tenth decile, capital income in the nonagricultural sector predominated in 1864 instead of the landed estate income in 1788. This very strong inequality at the end of the first stage of indus-trialisation is entirely compatible with the two opposing movements that succeeded each other from 1788 to 1864 and have nearly compensated each other.

As early as the end of the nineteenth century, the question of income tax presented itself in political terms and as a result several assessments (in 1885, 1896, and then in 1907) were made of income distribution in order to estimate the possible yield of such a tax. After examination, we have retained the estimates indicated in Table 7b.[16]

We have only one estimate for the interwar period, that of Sauvy, concerning 1929. As this estimate focuses on income after income tax and monetary transfers, we have adjusted the 1929 distribution so as to obtain a homogenous series. For distributions of the nineteenth century, this adjustment is useless because of the absence of income tax and the negligible amount of monetary transfers.

The series thus formed (Table 7b) shows a very important fall in inequality between 1864 and 1975, since the share of the tenth decile almost decreased by half. This fall is also recorded with a similar evolution in other European countries in the twentieth cen-

---

[16] Estimates resulted from tax data on the "contribution mobilière" (and for Paris of a statistic on rents). Colson (1927) made a synthesis of these works and proposed a distribution that was withheld because it coincides with two independent assessments of income distribution by group from macroeconomic data for 1890, by Coste (1890) and Morrisson (1991).

tury. The most interesting fact is that this fall began as early as the 1870's. A net increase of the share of quintiles 1 and 2 (from 13 to 15% between 1864 and 1890) is confirmed by the evolution of farm workers and servants salaries (those people are numerous and range almost always among the poorest 40%).[17] Their real wages increased from 90 to 100% between 1864 and 1894, while the GDP per inhabitant progressed only 32%. If we consider only the period from 1820 to 1975, an evolution conforming to the Kuznets curve appears certain with a maximum at the end of the first stage of industrialisation in 1860–1870. But this period is juxtaposed in a way to the preceding (from 1700 to 1820), characterised by a very strong and stable inequality under the Ancien Régime, that the Revolution of 1789 and the First Empire clearly reduced; an evolution conditioned by political and not by economic factors, as was the case after 1820–1830. From 1820–1830 to 1860–1870, industrialisation and urbanisation have clearly entailed increasing inequality with a stagnation of wages, a surge of capital incomes and a concentration of wealth (cf. Daumard, 1973).

A first appraisal

Having gathered all available data on the long-term evolution of distribution, we can compare these results to verify the hypothesis of Kuznets's Inverse U-curve. Table 8 presents a three period division for six countries:
- — phase A is when inequality clearly increased (the share of the tenth decile increased 5 to 10 points),
- — phase B1 is characterised by weak decline, or stability, during which it is certain that inequality no longer progressed,
- — phase B2 is marked by an important fall (the share of the tenth decile is reduced by 12 to 20 points) that lead to the situation of the 1970's, where inequality was moderated or low, according to the country.

We have indicated the GDP per inhabitant (adjusted in terms of purchasing power parity) in order to see if these periods coincided with the growth phases.

For two countries, Denmark and the Netherlands, it is impossible to identify a phase A. But for the Netherlands, we can not reject the hypothesis of such a stage because the GDP per inhabitant was already high in 1890: $3110, and even in 1877 (with $2960), the first year for which the income distribution of Amsterdam is known. Given that the turning point between phases A and B, is situated between $1800 and $3000, inequality clearly could have previously increased in the Netherlands. Maddison (1981) argues that this was precisely the case in the eighteenth century, because of an increase of capital income linked to financial expansion while unemployment and poverty progressed because of industrial difficulties. This thesis is in some respect disputed by van Zanden (1995) who estimated the income distribution with a proxy: the rent of houses. If the ratio rent : income is constant, the Gini coefficient reached 0.56 in 1561, 0.63 in 1732 and 0.63 in 1808. Van Zanden explains the inequality increase during the seventeenth

---

[17] They represented in 1880, 28% of the working population.

Table 8

Income distribution and GDP/cap

	Germany		France		Sweden	
	Year	GDP/cap	Year	GDP/cap	Year	GDP/cap
A	1850	1,470	1830	1,350	1850	1,290
	1870	1,910	1870	1,860	1900	2,560
	1900	3,130				
B1	1900	3,130	1870	1,860	1910	2,980
	1914	3,230	1914	3,200	1930	3,940
B2	1920	2,990	1920	3,200	1930	3,940
	1970	11,930	1970	11,560	1970	12,720

	Netherlands		Denmark		Finland	
	Year	GDP/cap	Year	GDP/cap	Year	GDP/cap
A	?		?		1880	1,120
					1900	1,620
B1	1890	3,110	1870	1,930	1900	1,620
	1914	3,770	1900	2,900	1920	1,790
B2	1920	4,120	1900	2,900	1920	1,790
	1970	11,670	1970	12,200	1980	12,700

Note: We must exclude the two World Wars because these periods are characterised by sudden and very large variations of GDP/capita and of income inequality, while such variations resulting from the war are a short-term phenomenon. GDP/cap from Maddison (1995).
A: Increase of the share of top decile (from 40/45 to 50%).
B1: Stability or slight decrease (from 50 to 45/47).
B2: Large decrease (from 47 to 25/30%).

century by a rapid economic expansion (with a growth of international trade, of export industries and the accumulation of capital). On the contrary, the economic stagnation during the eighteenth century was coupled with a stabilisation of the income distribution (but with a slight decrease of the shares of the lowest 50% and of the top 5%). This increase of inequality during the seventeenth century cannot be explained by the Kuznets' pattern because it is pre-industrial growth. In fact, we cannot draw any conclusions on the evolution of distribution in the Netherlands during the A phase. We know only that inequality was high in 1808 and in 1877, but the estimates for these 2 years cannot be compared as they are based on very different methodologies. The main contribution of van Zanden's article remains this interesting hypothesis: a correlation between inequality and expansion in the pre-industrial economies.

In the four other countries, the succession of the three phases is evident, but the turning point goes from approximately $1800 for France and Finland to $3000 in Germany and Sweden. It remains that the concordance between the first stage of industrialisation and period A is confirmed: between 1850 and 1890, Germany experienced the industrial takeoff that occurred in France between 1830 and 1870. It is the same for Sweden where this takeoff occurred after that of Germany. It seems therefore that the turning point for the distribution takes place at the same moment of growth from a structural point of view.

However, the long-term evolution of distribution is not solely linked to industrial-isation as the cases of France and the Netherlands prove. In the former, a very large inequality marked the eighteenth century before the industrialisation stage, an inequal-ity that was clearly mitigated by the Revolution of 1789, that is to say, by political and noneconomical factors. For the Netherlands, factory development dates to the sev-enteenth century and not to the eighteenth. On the other hand, we observe that in all studied countries, the fall of inequality accelerated after each world war, while GDP per inhabitant may differ between two countries in the ratio 1 to 2 for the same year, because of a new political context. In this case, evolution corresponds to the pattern proposed by Kuznets, but not for the reasons that he mentioned, since it is the shock of the war that upset the political and social balance to the point that a strong and rapid reduction of inequality occurred; this exogenous shock coincided with a long-term trend, but it could have occurred during another stage or never have happened at all.

2. Intersectoral and intrasectoral inequalities

The study conducted in Section 1 can be completed by collecting other information on inequalities of income, salaries, wealth, or information on other countries.

To present them in a consistent framework, we used the Theil indicator and a division between agricultural and nonagricultural sectors.

$$T = T_a + m_1 T_1 + m_2 T_2. \tag{3}$$

That will lead us to successively appraise the evolution of T_a, T_1 and T_2 that is, inequality inside agricultural and nonagricultural sectors, and to induce the evolutions of T according to country. The purpose of such an approach is to offer both a substitute and a complement to Section 1 regarding national income distribution. With an indicator dividing the inequality into three elements, we can take into account a great deal of partial information and verify the likelihood of the global data of Section 1. Section 2 represents at the same time a transition between the descriptive study of the preceding section and the analysis of causes presented in Section 3, since analysing the inequality, using a decomposable indicator, provides a first glimpse at variables that can explain the evolution of inequality at the national level.

We must recall that there are other decomposable inequality measures which differ by the weight they give to internal inequality. The two extreme measures are the Theil indicator on the one hand and the mean logarithmic deviation (MLD) on the other. The inequality in sectors 1 and 2 is weighted by the percentage of income if we use the Theil and by the percentage of population with the MLD. So the analyses of the following pages must be qualified. If we refer to MLD instead of Theil, the evolution of total inequality will depend more on the evolution of inequality in agriculture and less on the evolution of inequality in the nonagricultural sector. This point can significantly alter the conclusions; for example, the effect of a large increase of inequality among urban incomes, due to industrialisation, will be lessened if we chose MLD instead of Theil.

The intersectoral inequality

Intersectoral inequality is computed from a percentage series of the population in agricultural and nonagricultural sectors, that is N_a and $N_{non\,a}$, and from the shares of each group in the total income, that is Y_a and $Y_{non\,a}$. According to Kuznets' hypothesis, the relationship between average incomes in both sectors would be constant during the development process. On the other hand, the share of agricultural population would continuously decrease and it would automatically result in a growing then decreasing T_a intersectoral inequality as per capita income increases, the maximal value of T_a being reached when N_a is situated between 0.6 and 0.5.

To test this hypothesis, we have computed long-term values of T_a for five countries (cf. Table 9): Germany, Denmark, France, Italy and Sweden. For the Netherlands, only figures since 1910 are available. Such an inverse U-curve is confirmed for Germany (maximum in 1895), France (in 1929), Denmark (in 1935). But in Sweden, the fall is continuous since 1870 and in Italy, T_a increased from 1870 to 1952. However, in Italy, as the agricultural share in employment went from 56% in 1906 to 41% in 1952, T_a should have decreased.

Kuznets's illustration relied on the hypothesis of a constant relative income differential between both sectors (for example, 2 to 1), the only variable being the population distribution between sectors. This hypothesis is invalidated by our data: in Italy, the ratio grew from 1.2 in 1870–1880 to 1.95 in 1952, and in Denmark, it went from 1.28 in 1870–1879 to 2.07 in 1930–1939. Furthermore, this ratio considerably fluctuates from one country to another: it has oscillated around 1.5 in France for two centuries while it was still exceeded in Germany by 2.3 from 1890 to 1950.

Given these differences between countries and the strong fluctuations of the ratio, in some countries, it is impossible that T_a fluctuates regularly in the same way in all countries as N_a declines. Moreover, even when T_a follows an Inverse U-curve, the maximum does not correspond to a N_a value included between 0.5 and 0.6. N_a values for this maximum in Germany and in France are equal to 36% and to 30% in Denmark. As a result, those maximums occurred in two cases after the first industrialisation phase. GDP per inhabitant reached $2810 in Germany in 1895, $5270 in Denmark in 1935 and $4400 in France in 1929. For Germany, T_a's maximum coincides with the end of phase A (see Table 8), but in Denmark and in France, it occurred in the middle of phase B2, so that it is impossible to impute to T_a a significant role in the evolution of inequality from phase A to phase B1. Similarly, in Italy or Sweden, the maximum of T_a in 1952 is not

Table 9

Inequality between the agricultural sector and the nonagricultural sector (T_a)

Germany	1865	1895	1910	1930	1935	1950
(a)	0.050	0.088	0.063	0.070	0.051	0.049
(b)	14%	22%	17%	24%		16%
Denmark	1875	1910	1935	1950		
(a)	0.007	0.026	0.044	0.004		
(b)			13%	2%		
France	1788	1880	1913	1929	1955	1979
(a)	0.034	0.015	0.019	0.025	0.005	0.005
(b)	5%	3%		8%		2%
Italy	1870	1880	1901	1906–10	1931	1950–54
(a)	0.006	0.002	0.033	0.037	0.036	0.046
Netherlands	1910	1950				
(a)	0.038	0.014				
(b)	10%	4%				
Sweden	1870	1910	1930	1950		
(a)	0.079	0.069	0.065	0.017		
(b)			15%	6%		

(a) T_a.
(b) T_a in percent of Theil (national income distribution).
Sources: Kuznets (1957) and country studies.

correlated to that of the global inequality indicator. In Sweden, phase A is completed circa 1900–1910, while T_a decreased from 1870 to 1910.

After having shown that T_a's evolution does not follow the diagram proposed by Kuznets, it remains to assess T_a's contribution to T in Table 9. This contribution is high in only one country, that is Germany, with a maximum of 24% in 1930 and figures always higher than 13%. On the other hand, this contribution fluctuates from 2% to 15% in Denmark, in Sweden and in Italy, and from 2% to 8% in France. If we exclude Germany, the intersectoral inequality played a less important role in European countries than in today's developing countries. Indeed, T_a/T values reached 40 to 60% in most sub-Saharan African countries. Around 1970, T_a/T reached 15% in Malaysia and in the Philippines, and 35% in Korea. Latin America is the only region where similar values as in Europe are observable: 9% in Colombia, 13% in Mexico.[18]

Thus, we have identified only one case conforming to Kuznets's sectoral shift pattern which is nevertheless important: Germany. In other countries, T_a's contribution to T is relatively low and its maximum does not correspond to the end of phase A so that fluctuations of T_a do not explain T fluctuations. This leads us to a comprehensive study of T_1 and T_2 as T mainly relies upon T_1 and T_2 fluctuations.

[18] See Lecaillon et al. (1984: p. 55).

The inequality inside the agricultural sector

We can evaluate inequality by distinguishing two groups: s for farm workers and p for farmers and/or owners:

$$T_1 = Tp/s + p_{1s}T_{1s} + p_{1p}T_{1p},\tag{4}$$

(with p_{1s} and p_{1p} being the shares of wage-earners and owners in the total income of the sector).

We will exclude the survey of T_{1s} because salary inequality is very low and constant within this group. Tp/s undoubtedly records a sharp decrease from the eighteenth century, or from the nineteenth century. For example in France, farm workers in 1788 accounted for nearly half of the population living on agriculture and only received 17% of incomes. In 1880 these ratios respectively went to 42% and 21%, and in 1913 to 37% and 25%.[19] Since 1945, the impact of Tp/s became increasingly weak, and was even nil in 1979 because the average salary was equal to the average income of farmers.

In Sweden, demographic growth involved (see supra) a strong rise of the proportion of wage-earners, 25% to 50% between 1750 and 1850, which increased the value of Tp/s given that the average income differential between farm workers and farmers did not decrease. Since 1850, Tp/s dropped because of the decrease in the number of farm workers and decreased again after 1930, because of a significant wage rise that caught up the average wage in the nonagricultural sector.

This example enlightens the demographic factor. During the eighteenth century and during a great part of the nineteenth century, both France and Sweden, recorded a manpower surplus in rural zones, which partly explains why the number of working days (200 per year in France) was much lower than in industry (or in today's agriculture). This surplus entails a very low salary level, which corresponds to a high value of Tp/s as this income differential with farmers goes hand in hand with substantial employment of farm workers (from a quarter to a half). Tp/s may have decreased in all countries for a century as the same factors played a role: surplus reduction until its disappearance and the fall of the percentage of journey-workers in the population living on agriculture.

The value of T_{1p} clearly depends on agrarian structures. These were very unequal in many countries during the eighteenth century. In Sweden, 0.5% of owners belonging to the nobility, owned one third of lands and in 1862, 2.5% held almost as much (29%). Soltow's estimate (1985) of rural zones in 1800 corroborates that land distribution, which was close to wealth distribution, is very unequal. Indeed, the Gini's coefficient reached 0.70. The same author also indicates that land distribution in Finland (in rural zones) was less concentrated (Gini = 0.55) because nobility ownership played a less important part in this country. In France, the share of the nobility, the clergy and the bourgeoisie (excluding lower middle class owners) accounted for approximately half of the land in the eighteenth century. But this group accounted only for 4 or 5% of the totality of owners and/or farmers. Moreover, we know according to the rolls of

---

[19] The Theils corresponding to these three cases are respectively 0.23, 0.10 and 0.03.

"capitation" that there are considerable income differentials between the microfarmers and the rich farm owners and/or farmers. Following the Revolution of 1789, and after the progress of the small landholders in the nineteenth century, the situation changed. After 1918, and especially after 1945, when tenant farming was regulated, rent accounted for a negligible proportion of agricultural incomes, so that income distribution (excluding salaries) corresponds to that of operating incomes. Even if this distribution is much more concentrated than the salaries distribution, the value of T_{1p} since 1945 was therefore much lower than during the eighteenth century.

We are able to conclude that there was a fall of T_1 since the eighteenth century because Tp/s's value, which was significant in the eighteenth and nineteenth centuries, appeared very weak while T_{1p} clearly decreased in all countries where agrarian structures were characterised by a concentration benefiting the nobility and/or the bourgeoisie. This decrease occurred at different speeds according to the country following its respective political history (revolution or no revolution) and with the evolution of labour markets for the low-skilled workforce in countries and in towns. Nevertheless, it has to be remembered that the decrease of T_1 coincides with drop of m_1 which rose for example from 0.50 to 0.05, so that the effect of this decrease on T became increasingly weak over time.

Inequality within the nonagricultural sector
According to the same approach, we can thus separate T_2 as following:

$$T_2 = Tp/s + p_{2s}T_{2s} + p_{2p}T_{2p}. \tag{5}$$

Contrary to T_{1s}, we cannot neglect the fluctuations of T_{2s}. Indeed, the fluctuations are important (but not regarding T_{1s}) and increasingly become more important as a country develops. In the most developed countries, m_2 approximately amounts to 0.95—which imputes a decisive role to T_2—and the share of wages in the nonagricultural sector (p_{2s}) can reach 0.70 to 0.80[20] so that salary inequality is becoming an important factor of the inequality inside nonagricultural sector.

Population and income distribution, in nonagricultural sectors, between wage-earners and nonwage-earners in the eighteenth and nineteenth centuries, indeed even until 1945, presents no difficulties. We have the wage-earners on one hand, for whom enterprise or property incomes play a negligible part, and on the other hand, nonwage-earners (that is a very heterogeneous group including the poorest free-lance workers who in today's developing countries have a lower income than that of most wage-earners—as well as the richest capitalists). We can therefore be satisfied, on an approximation basis, with the distribution of salaries and other incomes between wage-earners and nonwage-earners— a simplification that is increasingly debatable because the share of property incomes in the revenues of active salaried workers has increased.

---

[20] For example, the share of wages in the nonagricultural sector reached approximately 80% in Germany, the UK, The Netherlands, Norway and Sweden in 1964 (UN, 1967).

Table 10

France: Ts/p in the nonagricultural sector

1788	1880	1929	1955	1979
0.271	0.102	0.085	0.077	0.034

Having reconstructed the distribution between wage-earners and nonwage-earners for France, we have computed the evolution of Tp/s from two centuries (see Table 10). The value of Tp/s was very high in 1788 (0.27), which is not surprising: more than half of the nonagricultural population is salaried and receives only 17% of the incomes; the average income of nonwage-earners is 5.4 times higher than the average salary. Average salary is all the more lower because there are few skilled wage-earners and because the surplus of the labour force in rural zones provides a low-paid domestic workforce. For two centuries, the fall of Tp/s is significant and continuous. After each world war, the decrease of Tp/s is linked with the drop of property incomes.[21] Thus, from 1938 to 1950, the share of rents, interests and dividends reduced in France from 14.3% to 4.1%. Other countries have experienced comparable decline: in Norway, this share decreased from 8% to 3.4%, in Sweden from 5% to 2.3%; in The Netherlands—the amount of these incomes and of enterprise incomes also decreased: 43.7% in 1938 and 38.4% in 1950. As the distribution between wage-earners and nonwage-earners fluctuated little from 1938 to 1950, it is clear that Tp/s decreased little.

Nevertheless, a temporary rise of Tp/s in a period of accelerated industrialisation is possible. According to Dumke (1991), the share of capital incomes in the nonagricultural sector in Prussia progressed between 1850–1860 and 1910–1913, from 22.4% to 27.7%. We can not compute Tp/s because the distribution of agents between salaried and nonsalaried workers is not indicated. But Tp/s increased in principle because the percentage of wage-earners accrued while the share of salaries lowered.

As the situation of European countries in the eighteenth century and in the early nineteenth century is comparable regarding labour markets in towns (civil servant staffs are negligible, many wage-earners are servants, others are mostly low skilled and work as artisans or in factories and their salaries are very low), it is probable that the value of Tp/s was high, while it is low nowadays. Nevertheless, the two scenarios illustrated by France and Germany are possible: either a continuous fall, or an inverse U curve,

[21] It throws doubt on the hypothesis of a constant share of capital incomes. For example, in France, the share of property incomes dropped from 31% in 1880 to 9.6% in 1979, while the share mixed enterprise incomes were from 33% to 19%. Whatever the share imputed to capital in these enterprise incomes, it is clear that the amount of this share and of property incomes substantially decreased in one century.

but with a far weaker rise than the fall registered in the twentieth century, because of an accelerated industrialisation that involved an expansion of capital income.[22]

Salary distribution, T_{2s}, is usually the better documented subject. It is necessary, however, to avoid the confusion between salary differentials and salary distribution. Indeed, we know more often the differentials, and their reduction is sometimes assimilated to an equalisation of salaries, which can be inexact: if the percentage of very qualified wage-earners increases rapidly, a reduction of salary differentials is compatible with a higher Gini coefficient for salary distribution.

Regarding the secular fall of salary differentials, all sources agree (see Table 11). For example, in Germany, the premium qualification thus estimated ($W_1 - W_2/W_2$ with W_1 as average salary in iron and steel metallurgy and W_2 as average salary in textiles) decreased from 80% in 1910 to less than 40% in 1955 (Dumke, 1991); in France, the ratio between the salary of a senior executive and the salary of a labourer has been reduced by 7 or 8 : 1 to 5 : 1; and the relationship between the salary of a foreman and the salary of a nonskilled woman decreased from 3.7 : 1 to 2.3 : 1 between 1890 and 1980 (Morrisson, 1991). The public sector has known the same phenomenon: from 1875 to 1976, the salary treatment of a State counsellor went from 18 to 6.8 times that of an usher. The more the period is extended, the more spectacular the change: in 1810, the prefect of the Seine received 50 times the salary of a lower civil servant instead of 10 times at present (Jourdan, 1991). In Sweden, the average salary of the administrative personnel had been reduced to 1.5 times the average salary in 1950 instead of 5 times in 1850–1890.

However, this secular decreasing trend has been interrupted by temporary rises, notably when industrialisation caused the demand for skilled labour to grow rapidly. Thus, the beginning of iron and steel metallurgy in Sweden in the 1850–1860s can explain a rise of the wage ratio between wages in the metallurgy sector and for nonskilled workers (Soderberg, 1991), this ratio decreasing afterwards. In Germany, the premium qualification mentioned above increased between 1890 and 1910, following the second stage of industrialisation. In Belgium, salary differentials increased during the first stage of industrialisation in 1820–1850, because of a strong skilled labour demand in sectors like iron and steel metallurgy or mechanics (Scholliers, 1991). This unequal distribution obtained until 1880, then differentials rapidly narrowed thanks to the salary increase of low skilled personnel. Thus in Ghent, in textiles, the ratio between a mechanic's salary and that of an unskilled worker went from 1.6 in 1870–1880 to 1.15 in 1910. Temporary rises of salary differentials are possible in other circumstances. In Stockholm, after having been stable in the eighteenth century, the salary ratio between a carpenter and

---

[22] Any comparative analysis on Tp/s's evolution according to the country warrants caution because data can be nonhomogeneous. They are homogenous only if they are derived from surveys or from tax sources concerning individuals, but they are nonhomogenous if we use both this type of source and macroeconomic statistics on functional income distribution because in this case we include nondistributed profits that increase more rapidly than other incomes in the industrialisation period.

Table 11

Range of earnings in Germany, Belgium, France and Sweden

Germany	1910	1955
W_2/W_1	1.8	1.4
W_2 metalworker/W_1 textile worker		
Belgium (Gand)	1870–80	1910
W_2/W_1	1.60	1.15
W_2 skilled maintenance worker		
W_1 textile worker		
France	1890	1980
W_3/W_1	7.5	5
W_2/W_0	3.7	2.3
W_3 manager W_1 unskilled worker		
W_2 foreman W_0 unskilled worker (female)		
1st decile/top centile (civil servant)	18	6.8
Sweden	1890	1950
W_2/W_1	5	1.5
W_2/W_1: salary of administrative personnel to the overall average.		

nonskilled worker increased from 1800 to 1850, then decreased in the second part of the century. In France, the salary ratio between senior executives and workers increased from 1950 to 1959–1967 then fell and came back to its initial level in 1975 (Baudelot and Lebeaupin, 1979).

Our information regarding salary distribution (that depends both on differentials between salary levels and wage-earner distribution) is unfortunately less rich. It is, however, indispensable given that distribution is not necessarily correlated with salary differentials. The Swedish example illustrates this phenomenon: the inequality indicator for salary distribution progressed from 1870 to 1910, then (after a strong rise), from 1920 to 1930 before a decrease that put it back (in 1950) clearly below the level of 1870. Therefore, since 1870, the ratio of administrative personnel salary and average salary or the ratio of iron and steel metallurgy salary and average salary have not ceased to decline. But the very strong growth of the number of administrative personnel widened the inequality. Other salary differentials also contributed to the inequality: the ratio of farm labourer salary and average salary decreased until 1930, whereas farm labourers ranked at the bottom of the salary scale.

The previous ambiguity is essentially due to the fact that wage differentials may narrow at the same time as the changes in the occupational structure of the population widens inequality. This is shown in the following hypothetical example:

	Average wage (in index bases 100 for labour—employees)		Numbers of wage earners in %	
	1880	1980	1880	1980
Senior executives	825	345	3.5	10
Professionals and technicians	240	180	6.5	19.1
Workers and employees	100	100	90	70.9

According to these figures, akin to nineteenth century France, the Gini coefficient has decreased little (0.241–0.225) over a century whereas salary differentials had been strongly narrowed.[23]

Indeed, it seems that in all countries studied, the salary distribution towards 1970 was less unequal than in nineteenth century, but inequality may have increased in a rather long first period, and the extent of the fall after a century was very limited because of a structural qualification effect contributing to inequality.

The distribution of nonsalaried income, T_{2p}, always far more concentrated than that of salaries, has probably evolved for one or two centuries in the same direction as that of salaries. Soltow's study (1985) reveals a concentration of wealth, again greater in towns than in rural zones, in 1800 for Sweden and Finland alike, with Gini coefficients of 0.80 and 0.78. For example, in Sweden, the last twentieth controlled 58% of the wealth. It was the same in France where the last decile accounts for 80% of wealth in 1890 and where statistics on the "patente" (local tax) indicated a very strong concentration of merchants' incomes.

The current wealth concentration, always greater than that of income, is however a bit less strong, which leads us to think that the trend since the beginning of the century is a decreasing one. But previously, concentration in some countries increased. Studies in Daumard (1973) on patrimonies in Paris and Lyon reveal such a phenomenon from 1820 to 1900. In Prussia, capital tax statistics indicate the same tendency: this tax was paid only by 14% of taxpayers: among them, the richest 10% (that is 1.4% of the total population) who saw their share increase from 59% in 1896 to 63% in 1911 (Kaelble, 1986). Industrialisation involved an accelerated accumulation of riches, particularly to the benefit of manufacturers, large merchants, or bankers, while the lower middle-class (civil servants, professionals) or the aristocracy did not profit from the expanding wealth in France for example (Daumard, 1973). We have evidence "a contrario" (to

---

[23] We know that different rates of growth for staffs of various groups can have as important an impact as average income differentials between these groups. Furthermore the incidence of this demographic variable depends on the chosen inequality indicator.

the contrary) with the example of a town that industrialisation had little touched by the nineteenth century (Toulouse), where the wealth distribution did not change.

Indeed, this wealth distribution is only a proxy variable for our subject, that is, distribution of nonsalaried income in the agricultural sector. However, it is probable that wealth distribution influenced the distribution of nonsalaried incomes: the former experienced in some countries a concentration movement during the industrialisation stage, before slowly decreasing in the twentieth century with the progressive diffusion of capital.

A first appraisal

If we attempt to gather all elements of the jigsaw puzzle, we can thus summarise our results:

1. The value of T_a a is quite weak, (except in Germany), and it has clearly lowered, (except in Italy), since 1900.
2. The internal Theil for the agricultural sector (T_1) probably decreased since the beginning of the nineteenth century.
3. The evolution of the Theil for the nonagricultural sector (T_2) is complex because :

   − Tp/s in this sector can have either decreased since the beginning of the nineteenth century or have followed an Inverse U-curve as in Germany, and
   − values of the Theil for wages distribution (T_{2s}) and for property or entrepreneurial income (T_{2p}) are today lower than those in the early nineteenth century, but both can have equally followed an inverse U-curve.

It is difficult to deduce the fluctuations of T, given that:

1. If T a follows an inverse U-curve, the date of the peak varies significantly from one country to another.
2. Evolutions in the nonagricultural sector of Tp/s, T_{2s} and T_{2p} can be conformed to such a curve (to a different extent according to country) ; but the contrary (a continuing decrease for two centuries) is also possible.
3. The decrease of T_1 has a constant effect towards equality, but T_1 is balanced by an increasingly low coefficient.

As we have seen, various factors can contribute to the rise of T during the first phase of industrialisation, preceding a decrease in concordance with the inverse U-curve hypothesis. But on one hand, these factors occur with more or less intensity while T_1 continuously decreases, and on the other hand exogenous shocks (i.e., the French Revolution in 1789, First and Second World War) have had a significant impact on distribution. Therefore, many scenarios are possible, ranging from an inverse U-curve recording a sharp rise during phase A to a curve of limited scope, or even to a continuous decreasing trend of T starting in the early nineteenth century.

3. Factors explaining the long-term evolution of distribution

By choosing a long term approach, we exclude short-term changes of distribution correlated with the political or economic situation. Examples are easy to provide regarding this matter. In all countries studied, growth acceleration in the 1920's temporarily increased the share of capital incomes at the expense of labour incomes and also increased inequality; then recession involved a sudden collapse of profits so that inequality narrowed. During the First World War, profits, notably in trade, experienced a real expansion in the Netherlands which was a neutral country (see de Meere, 1983) while unemployment increased in the industrial sector due to supply difficulties. It resulted in a strong widening of inequality, which was immediately cancelled by the return to peace in Europe.

Excluding these cyclical shocks, we must first distinguish political factors from economic factors. Indeed for two centuries, political factors modified income distribution to a great extent independently of the economic context. Every time, it effected a change in the distribution of production factors, i.e., so to speak "upstream" of income distribution. The French Revolution in 1789 definitely modified the land distribution since neither the acquisitions obtained since 1789 nor the civil law code (which by abolishing the law of primogeniture was leading to the parceling out of landed property) were questioned after 1815. One could have objected that this political event itself resulted from the economic situation (increasing inequalities would have favoured the revolt). But this argument is debatable, as proved by Weir (1991): actual salaries of the poorest people in towns (unskilled workers or servants) remained stable in France in the 1770s and 1780s while they sharply decreased in neighbouring countries which did not experience revolutions. And it was precisely from this disadvantaged population that most demonstrators came. On the other hand, according to the rolls of "capitation", inequality did not deteriorate in the 1780's. Indeed, inequality was very large in France, as it was in other European countries.

The two world wars show the weight of political factors. On the one hand, the war can entail an inequality increase as in Denmark and the Netherlands : the dramatic rise in prices was not compensated by rising wages in the first years of the war, whereas the surge of foreign demand brought a boom in profits. Yet this was a short-term phenomenon and the level of inequality fell quickly to the level prevailing before the war. On the other hand, the war had a long-term and equalising effect in the fighting countries. If we retrace the evolution of distribution since 1900, what attracts attention is that in all countries, whatever the per capita income or the level of industrialisation, inequality dropped after each war. This drop occurred because during the war periods, and immediately after, governments had taken measures that changed the distribution of production factors. In each case, it concerns measures that amputate wealth and as a result reduce property incomes (cf. Table 12). For example, if rents are frozen and decrease by half in real value, this is equivalent to a 50% levy on real estate patrimonies. Similarly, if the States finance the war with monetary expansion so that the level of prices

Table 12
The share of dividend, interest and rent in household primary income

	1913	1926	1938	1950
Belgium			20	10.8
Finland[a]			14.3	3.9
Norway			10.5	3.2
United Kingdom			22.7	10.9
France	26.8	18.3	18.6	9
Germany[b] (4 lands)[c]	12.2	4		

[a] Dividend excluded.
[b] Land rent excluded.
[c] Baden, Bavaria, Saxony, Wurttemberg.
Sources: UN (1957), Chapter VIII. France: Morrisson (1991). Germany: Jeck (1968).

doubles, they levy a tax on bond holders that reduces their real value by half. In other cases, as in France after 1945, companies were nationalised by reimbursing a quarter of the share value to shareholders (17% for electric companies). The reasons for these measures are obvious: given the exorbitant cost of the war, these levies on patrimonies were unavoidable; moreover sacrifices asked of the population, on a human basis, were so important that a redistribution of wealth appeared necessary to compensate, at least marginally, these sacrifices. A rent freezing, associated with the right for the tenant and his children to remain in the premises, can be assimilated to a redistribution of real estate patrimony between owners and tenants.

It is significant that these measures had lasting distributive effects, during several decades, and that they always concerned the wealth distribution. This shows that government intervention to change income distribution is most efficient when it is addressed to wealth distribution rather than to income distribution. Such interventions are usually made in an exceptional political climate, such as a revolution or a war, and they correspond to an upheaval of political and social balance. The fact that such changes in wealth distribution have significant and more lasting impacts than measures directly affecting income distribution is not surprising. Wealth distribution is in a way located upstream and explains income distribution (see Bourguignon and Morrisson, 1998). Government intervention or shocks which affect income distribution directly by changing some macroeconomic variables have only short-run effects. For example the consequence of a cyclical shock like a bad harvest or of an increase of minimum legal wage soften after some years, while a change in wealth distribution will influence income distribution over several decades.

However, we must remind that political factors can also change directly and for a long time the income distribution. At first, a progressive income tax reduces income inequality. Before the First World War, the impact of direct taxes on inequality was nonexistent or unimportant, but in the 1920s and the 1930s direct taxation had already a significant effect in Scandinavian countries and in the UK. If we consider after-tax income instead of before-tax, the Gini coefficient was reduced by 11% in the UK (1938), 6% in Denmark (1939) and 4% in Sweden (1935).[24] After the Second World War, the political factors induce in some cases a large increase of taxation progressivity: in the UK, the Gini coefficient in 1949 was diminished by 19% instead of 11%. As the Gini coefficient before tax was nearly the same in 1949 (0.42 instead of 0.43 in 1938), in spite of a large decrease of the top decile's share, it is a reform of direct taxation which explains the decrease of the Gini coefficient after taxes (−10.5%). But the contrary happened in Denmark: the taxation progressivity only slightly increased (Gini reduction equals −9% versus −6% in 1939, whereas the before tax Gini was reduced by 12%). So the income equalisation results from a change in tax structure in the UK but from a change in gross income distribution in Denmark. Later, in the 1950s and the 1960s, the British tax structure has been copied in several European countries.

On the other hand, since the Second World War, the development of the welfare state has increased to a large extent public social expenditures, and if these transfers received by households are taken into account, the reduction of inequality induced by such transfers exceeds largely the reduction imputed to direct taxation. Of course this is true only for the 1960s or early 1970s. Since about 1980 we observe simultaneously in some countries, like the UK, an increase in gross income inequality and a decrease of redistribution by direct taxation and transfers.

Before moving on to the economic factors of an inverse U-curve, we first have to mention other economic factors that played a key role regardless of the industrial expansion.

The first factor is related to market structures. We are used to applying standard micro-economics based on market equilibrium to define income distribution.[25] But in the eighteenth century and even during the nineteenth century, the institutional framework was designed so as to guarantee rents to many interest groups except the unskilled workforce, like journeymen or labourers, who were the sole groups to be subject to market law. Soltow (1965) demonstrates how in Norway, this system of preferential rights involved a great inequality. Many entrepreneurs and merchants benefited from rights preventing competition. Until 1860, only merchants in towns could trade, so that the rural population had to come in town to do their shopping. A corporation system guaranteed monopolies in most activities; thus the musicians of a town could forbid the entry of the musicians of a neighbouring town. On the other hand, the well-off class benefited from a *de facto* quasi-monopoly of access to higher education and consequently to the liberal professions. This preferential system has been gradually removed in Norway from 1840–1850: regulations regarding corporations disappeared, free-trade was granted to everyone. Moreover, the abrogation in 1849 of the Navigation Act permitted Norwegians to have free maritime trade with England, so that their fleet rapidly developed

---

[24] UN (1957: Chap. 9).
[25] See Bourguignon and Morrisson (1998).

and generated many jobs. The French society of the Ancien Régime was organised according to the same pattern: many groups benefited from preferential rights granted by the State which guaranteed protected markets and rents. These rents disappeared with the suppression of corporations and "offices". But in the nineteenth century, part of the protectionist measures taken under the Restauration and the July Monarchy generated guaranteed incomes to manufacturers, because this policy went beyond the protection of infant industries.

There is a clear contrast between market structures during the eighteenth century compared with those around 1970. Most of guaranteed incomes benefiting the middle-class or the well-off disappeared. On the other hand, the State intervenes on the unskilled labour market by fixing a legal salary higher than its level of equilibrium and by compensating the unemployed. As long as the number of the latter remains low, such a policy reduces income inequalities. Other factors had the same effect because they modified the distribution matrix of production factors. This matrix is characterised in the eighteenth century by a very strong concentration. The vast bulk of physical and human capital was owned by 5 to 10% of the population, conversely 60 or 70% of the population had only one factor, the unskilled labour. However this concentration substantially decreased over two centuries for two reasons:

– The diffusion of education. Even if we refer to France, a country lagging behind Germany or Sweden, the diffusion of education clearly appeared before the scholar explosion which occurred in the 1960's. From 1850 to 1890, the annual number of people leaving secondary-school doubled, and was later multiplied by 10 between 1890 and 1955. If we reason on a stock basis, the stock of people leaving secondary-school accounts for 240,000 to 820,000 and the number of engineers tripled between 1890 and 1955.

– The diffusion of saving thanks to the increase of per capita income and to the creation of suitable institutions. The number of savings bankbooks in France is a good indicator of popular saving. The number of savings bankbooks per 1000 inhabitants grew in this country from 4 in 1835 to 40 in 1863, rising to 200 in 1907 and 300 in 1954. This evolution is significant: income inequality clearly increased during the first stage of industrialisation, i.e., in 1835–1863, but at the same time the number of savings bankbooks for 1000 residents was multiplied by ten which indicates the emergence of a financial popular saving. Both phenomena are not contradictory, because per capita income increased from 25 to 30% during this period. Then, despite an unfavourable economic situation during the 1870s and 1880s, the rise continued and as early as 1907, two-thirds of households possessed a savings bankbook (if we assume that the figure of 1954 corresponds to a saturation level). During the nineteenth century in other European countries, notably Germany and Switzerland, popular saving experienced considerable success favoured by the conjunction of several factors: inheritance legislation, growth of per capita income, the creation of suitable institutions and design of a socio-cultural framework stimulating savings.[26] Indeed the average amount is very small compared to the wealth of the richest 1 or 2%, but in the eighteenth century, the same families had no savings. During the twentieth century, and notably since 1945, these changes in the distribution of production-factors accelerated with the access to family housing ownership and with the diffusion of securities among 30% of the population or more instead of 5 to 10%.

All the factors we have reviewed have had a similar effect for two centuries, i.e., a continuous reduction of inequalities. But before the nineteenth century, other factors had the inverse effect. Soderberg (1987b) demonstrates how in Sweden, from the middle of the eighteenth century to 1820, inequality widened in rural zones because of demographic growth. Demographic growth led to an increase in the price of land and in the number of peasants without land. In a pre- industrial economy, the decline in arable land available per member of the labour force increases inequality, as we currently verify in LDCs.[27] The same demographic situation in France during the years 1760–1780 is responsible for a strong rise of wheat and land rent costs, which increased inequality in rural zones, like Sweden. But these phenomena belong to the past, because with industrialisation and population transfers from the country to the towns, such an inegalitarian mechanism can no longer function.

On the other hand, several studies have shown the inegalitarian effect of industrialisation in a first stage. The most comprehensive study focuses on Germany (Prussia before 1914), a particularly interesting case given that industrialisation occurred very rapidly, leading in a few years to deep structural changes. Dumke (1991) put forward two explanatory factors: the functional income distribution and the salary differentials. He chose as an indicator of inequality, the beta coefficient, which is the reverse of Pareto's alpha coefficient, and shows that the rise of beta from 1870 to 1895–1900, its stability between 1900 and 1914, and its fall after the war are correlated with the share of capital incomes and with the skill premium —that is, the average salary differential between iron and steel metallurgy and textiles/the average salary in textiles. According to Dumke, functional income distribution played a crucial role in these changes. By referring to the decomposition of T_2, (see above, Section 2), T_2 increases necessarily with P_{2p} (since T_{2p} is very superior to T_{2s}) and Tp/s also increases as the distribution of working population between wage-earners and capitalists does not change. After the war, capital incomes lowered, and due to 1923's hyperinflation a part of wealth disappeared. The skill premium was more or less stable from 1870 to 1914 but it rapidly lowered from 1914 to 1925 because of the labour force shortage during the war, then hyperinflation reduced salary differentials. But according to Dumke, the crucial factor remains the functional

---

[26] We can object that in the nineteenth century the share of landed properties (owned by households) in wealth decreased. But according to our information we know that land distribution is very nonegalitarian and that the vast majority of the agricultural workforce are journeyman without any property.

[27] See Bourguignon and Morrisson (1998).

distribution which tests the ratio between beta and the share of capital in national income for 1850–1913.

$$T_b = m_1 T_1 + m_2 T_2$$

$$\beta = \underset{(35.4)}{5337} + \underset{(3.7)}{0.24K} - 1 - \underset{(-5.3)}{0.029D_1} + \underset{(0.13)}{0.76D_2}, \quad R_2 = 0.92, \tag{6}$$

with $K - 1$ being the moving average share of the capital income over 3 years, D_1 is the dummy for 1850–1869, and D_2 is the dummy for 1892–1913.

Dumke focuses on the importance of the differential between the two variables, β and K, which proves that it is functional distribution change that entails change of income distribution. Even if the use of an indicator linked with Pareto's law can raise difficulties because adjustments with this law are not very satisfactory, it remains probable that functional distribution played a significant role, as is confirmed by other works. German economists who had immediately understood the difference between the first and the second stage of industrialisation (1895–1913) when inequality stabilised, sought to explain it. Thus Mueller and Geisenberger (1972) computed the correlation between the shares of the richest 1% or 5% and the share of capital income in Prussia and in other regions from 1891 to 1913. They obtained high correlation coefficients, which prove the crucial role of functional distribution.

Dumke wondered, finally, why functional distribution evolved along these lines. He shows that it cannot be explained by a bias in technical progress if we refer to a neo-classical production function, neither can it be an increase of monopoly power within the theoretical framework proposed by Kalecki. On the other hand, if we separate capital incomes by sectors, it appears that the capital share did not fluctuate in industry, while it doubled in agriculture, which explains the rise at the global level. This structural change in agriculture, results from the rapid transfer from a traditional agriculture to a capital-intensive agriculture using high-tech techniques. Functional distribution of agricultural incomes has therefore changed as capital replaced part of the workforce reoriented in industry. From 1890–1900, income inequality in Germany no longer increased, because the rise of the share of capital in agriculture became marginal; on the other hand, thanks to the existence of an ancient craft sector, with a well-skilled workforce, and thanks to rapid educational development, notably technical, during the nineteenth century, Germany had an abundant supply of skilled-labour at the end of this century, which avoided a rise of salary differentials.

For Dumke, the traditional model of a dual economy better explains the German case than the neoclassical pattern. In the mid-nineteenth century, the labour productivity in agriculture was much lower than in industry and the wage differential favoured migrations into towns. The State encouraged this migration, the urbanisation, a capital-intensive agriculture and an industrial development based upon iron and steel metallurgy. Such a strategy had an unegalitarian impact, but the State reduced this disadvantage by introducing very early on a social legislation; on the other hand, as early as the 1890's, the dualism disappeared, there was no longer a surplus of the workforce in agriculture and there was no longer salary differentials between the agricultural and the industrial sectors.

Soderberg (1991) also refers to the dualistic model to explain the labour income distribution in Sweden. He shows that agriculture continued to have a workforce surplus until approximately 1930, so that the ratio between agricultural salary and average salary decreased until 1914. This ratio benefited from a strong rise in 1914–1918 because of high workforce needs and decreased again after the war before increasing on a long term basis once the surplus disappeared. He views the lag of agricultural salary as the necessary factor for an intersectoral reallocation of work, by referring explicitly to Kuznets's diagram. Like Dumke, he assumes that in its early phase, industrialisation increases the need for a skilled labour force and can therefore increase salary differentials in industry, unless, as it is the case in Sweden, the development of education allows a rapid response to this new demand.

The same dualistic model appears relevant in France, where the actual salary of farm workers stagnated from 1830 to 1870, and then increased more rapidly than per capita income during the second period of industrialisation, with demographic stagnation specific to France helping the resorption of the workforce surplus in rural zones. The increase of inequality during the first period of industrialisation appears linked, like in Germany, with a change in the functional income distribution: the share of capital incomes, which is mainly retained by the tenth decile, increased rapidly from 1830 to 1865. But, contrary to Germany, the modernisation of agriculture did not accelerate simultaneously. The leading effect was the growth of the share of the non - agricultural sector where a strong inequality resulted from the distribution of income between capital and labour. A distribution disadvantageous for labour was linked to dualism: employment in the nonagricultural sector could rapidly increase without causing a salary rise because of the workforce surplus in rural zones.

Thus from one country to another, we again found the same mechanisms to explain an inverse U-curve since the beginning of industrialisation, functional income distribution and correlated dualism, as sources of inequalities. But these mechanisms are somehow superimposed on secular trends previously evoked. So that income distribution results from a group of factors which can have opposite effects. This is explained by Soltow's thesis (1965) on Norway according to which inequality has decreased during the whole period of industrialisation because equalisation factors have been preponderant. These factors are: the progressive disappearance of rents with liberalisation, the increasingly wider access to education, the development of unions and the reduction of underemployment in rural zones because of industrialisation. Industrialisation occurred in particular conditions in Norway because many factories were located in rural zones, which explains the originality of the evolution of the labour market in this country. Soltow's thesis is compatible with that of Dumke regarding Germany because the impact of opposite factors can be positive or negative according to conditions specific to each country concerning demography, industrial location, market structures, agricultural modernisation, or access to education. According to the nature of the final impact, authors insist on one group of factors or another. The analysis of income distribution evolution since the nineteenth century does not lead to the existence of a law like the inverse U-curve or to its rebuttal, but it has to review all factors playing a role in order to study each historical case by referring to a consistent and comprehensive theoretical framework.

Acknowledgements

I am grateful to T. Atkinson, F. Bourguignon and P. Lindert for many helpful comments and suggestions on earlier drafts of this paper.

Appendix A

Rural zones benefited from real development during this period for two reasons: agricultural progress was fostered by an increase in the ratio of wheat prices to manufactured goods prices and by the exploitation of iron and wood. Early industrialisation in Sweden was linked to these activities in rural areas, whereas in other countries, urbanisation and industrialisation were closely correlated. This entailed a clear improvement of the farmers situation as witnessed by the growth of demand in handicraft products (which explains demographic growth in small towns or townships) (see Soderberg, 1987b). But such an increase in the average peasant income was accompanied by widening inequalities. On the one hand according to several studies, land distribution became more concentrated,[28] but on the other hand, the inequality between farm labourers and farmers widened: the real wage of workers decreased due to a rise of wheat prices from 1732 to 1800. The nominal wage did not vary because of growth in the work force supply due to demographic growth and was followed by two opposite movements, an increase then a decrease, which compensated each other from 1800 to 1850. Moreover, because of demographic growth, the percentage of farm labourers in the agricultural population increased from 25% to 50% between 1750 and 1850. Bearing in mind this set of elements, it is certain that the share of quintiles 1, 2 and 3 clearly diminished in rural zones to the benefit of the richest 40%.[29]

Income distribution in towns followed the same evolution. According to Soderberg (1987a), agricultural price inflation benefited grain merchants, landowners and food producers. Conversely, in Stockholm, the number of craftsmen declined because of increasing bankruptcies and because their average income lowered. On the other hand

---

[28] See Winberg's study on several parishes (1800–1850), Soderberg's study on 2 parishes (1821–1862), Morel's study on 5 parishes (1770–1825), Enequist's study on one parish (1750–1824), and Isacson's study on one parish where inequality, after having dropped, increased from 1800 to 1850 (see Soderberg, 1987b).

[29] This gain of the two superior quintiles is entirely compatible with a decrease of the share of the last centile because of the drop of nobility's ownership from 1750 to 1862 (see Soderberg, 1987b).

from 1740 to 1800, real wages of unskilled workers and of skilled workers decreased in the capital even more than wages of farm labourers. From 1800 to 1850, the wages of skilled workers rose, but for unskilled wages this increase stopped in 1825 and was followed by a decrease. Such evolutions explain the lag of urban wages: in 1840, average salary, expressed in kilos of bread, is clearly lower in Stockholm than in most other great European towns, and in 1850, 34% of the Stockholm population was not subjected to tax because of very low incomes. This percentage is close (to the extent that a comparison is possible) to that estimated for the whole of France in 1790, when "active" and "passive" citizens were separated.

Appendix B

According to Jeck (see Kaelble, 1986: p. 30), Saxony's tax statistics covered total incomes better than Prussia's statistics. Moreover, Saxony was a more advanced State than Prussia in terms of industrialisation and urbanisation, which confers added interest to those statistics. Data by quartiles and data for the last decile and centile indicate an increase of inequality in the late nineteenth century (0.7 and 2.5 points) that especially benefited the last centile. Conversely, the share of the poorest 50% decreases by 0.6. Such a fall continues from 1897–1899 to 1913 (0.6 points), but we observe a clear trickle-down effect, since the share of the third quintile grows by 1.7 points while that of the fourth quintile decreases by 1.1 points. Thus, the late nineteenth century marks a turning point with the decrease of the shares of the fourth quintile, of the tenth decile and of the last centile between 1899 and 1913, to the benefit of intermediate incomes ranked in the third quartile.

The data for Prussia corroborates this widening in inequality from 1870 to 1900 and a weak decline at the beginning of the twentieth century. Certain series derive directly from published tax statistics, like those indicated by Kuznets (1963) for 1913 and 1928. But others have been adjusted for the underestimation of incomes or the omission of some households, as is the case in the studies of Mueller (1959) or Bresciani-Turoni (1939). Besides, as early as 1878, Engel adjusted this type of bias, which proves that the high reputation of German statisticians in Europe at this period was justified.

Whether we consider the shares of the last centile or of the last twentieth, the rise which occurred approximately around 1870 to 1900, is always very clear-cut, while the decrease from 1900 to 1913 is rather unimportant (1 or 2 points less for the share of the last twentieth). The share of the last centile is lower than in Saxony, which the observers of that time explained by Prussia's lag in industrialisation (and by its lag regarding industrial profit accumulation). As compared with Saxony, Bresciani-Turoni chose other inequality indicators: the percentage of the population having a lower income than that of average income and the D indicator correlated with Pareto's α. The first confirms both stages of widening and then of a narrowing in inequality. On the other hand, the second continues until 1913, but we know that Pareto's α indicator is more relevant for the distribution of high incomes than for that of total income. The article by Bresciani-

Turoni gives us additional evidence of the rise of inequalities between 1870 and 1900 with two distributions for 1875 and 1928 in Prussia. Because those distributions are close enough and because we know for certain that there had been a significant decrease from 1900 to 1928, there must have previously been a comparable rise so that both movements compensated each other. Moreover, several German specialists on that subject like Dumke (1991) or Kaelble (1986) present this rise as an undebatable phenomenon and focus their analysis on the explanation of this phenomenon.

Appendix C

From random samples of "capitation" rolls, from the beginning of the eighteenth century to 1790, we have assessed the distribution of this tax. This source raises two complex problems. The first is the relationship between taxation and income. When the "capitation" was created in 1695, the population breakdown between tax classes was made according to the social hierarchy and not according to income, so that there were very high income differentials within each class paying the same tax. But already in the early eighteenth century, local authorities were making their own appraisals and attempting to tax each taxpayer according to his income. We do not know, however to what extent this policy was a success. The second problem concerns the notion of "contributive capacity". According to the rolls, it is demonstrated that authorities referred to the monetary income. We have therefore adjusted tax distribution to obtain the income distribution by assuming that half of total income (for quintiles and 2) and the third (for quintile 3) is in kind. The distribution we obtain after adjustment proves very unequal since the share of the tenth decile exceeds 55%. It therefore appeared imperative to check if this estimate is plausible by decomposing the income of households in 1788 by groups. As Table 7a indicates, we obtain a three group division, where the first 10% of the population (nobility, clergy and middle class) receives approximately half of the incomes, an intermediate group (merchants, craftsmen, well-off peasants) that is 20% of the population, receives a quarter of incomes and the rest of the population (70%) lives in poverty with the last quarter. An estimate of Colquhoun, quoted by Soltow (1968), concerning income distribution by groups in England and Wales from 1801 to 1803 gives results close to our estimate. The classes that match the poorest socio-economic groups of Table 7a (with a yearly income per family equal or lower than 100 pounds) amounted to 70.2% of population and received 31.3% of national income. This share exceeds the share of poorest 70.8% in France: 26.8%. But if we take into account the decrease of inequality between 1788 and 1801, we can conclude that the share of the poorest deciles was roughly the same in France as in England in 1801.

It is impossible to go directly from this breakdown by group to income distribution because the "Ancien Régime" was a society of "ordres" where income was not a ranking criterion. Certain members of the nobility or the clergy could live in quasi-poverty; they still belonged to their "ordre". It is certain that the share of the tenth decile exceeds 49%. But conversely, the distribution estimate based upon capitation is perhaps too unequal.

For example, according to the evaluation of the electorate in 1790 (a very approximate estimate because of the limited facilities at the disposal of the "Constituante"), i.e., for the citizens who are able to pay a tax, it appears that the share of quintiles 1 and 2 would have reached 10 to 11% of households income. This distribution must be adjusted, by increasing for example the share of quintiles 1 and 2 up to 10–11% and by reducing the share of the last decile to 50–53%. It has to be noted that even after such an adjustment, we obtain a more unegalitarian distribution than any of those estimated for other countries during the nineteenth century.

References

Baudelot, C. and A. Lebeaupin (1979), Les salaires de 1950 á 1975, (Économie et statistique, Paris).

Bentzel, R. (1952), Inkomstfördelningen i Sverige (Industriens Utredninginstitut, Stockholm).

Bjerke, K. (1956), Changes in Danish income distribution 1939–1952. Income and Wealth, Series VI (London).

Bjerke, K. (1964), Redistribution of income in Denmark before and after the War. Income and Wealth, Series X (London).

Bourguignon, F. and C. Morrisson (1998), Inequality and development; the role of dualism, Journal of Development Economics.

Brenner, Y., H. Kaelble and M. Thomas (1991), Income Distribution in Historical Perspective (Cambridge University Press, Cambridge).

Bresciani-Turoni, C. (1939), Annual survey of statistical data: Pareto's law and the index of inequality of incomes, Econometrica 7: 107–133.

Bry, G. (1960), Wages in Germany 1871–1945 (Princeton University Press, Princeton).

Colson, C. (1927), Cours d'Économie Politique (Gauthier-Villars, Paris).

Coste, A. (1890), Étude sur les Salaires des Travailleurs et le Revenu de la France, Communication faite à la Société de Statistique de Paris (Guillaumin, Paris).

Daumard, A. et al. (1973), Les Fortunes Françaises au XIXe Siècle (Mouton, Paris).

de Meere, J. (1983), Long-term trends in income and wealth inequality in the Netherlands, 1880–1940, Historical Social Research 27: 8–37.

Dumke, R. (1991), Income inequality and industrialization in Germany 1850–1913: the Kuznets hypothesis re-examined, in Y. Brenner, H. Kaelble and M. Thomas, eds., pp. 117–148.

Engel (Dr.) (1875), Die Klassensteuer und Klassificirte Einkommensteuer und die Einkommensvertheilung im preussischen Staat in den Jahren 1852 bis 1875, Zeitschrift des Königlich-Preussichen statistischen Bureaus (Berlin), pp. 105–148.

Gustaffson, C. and H. Uusitalo (1990), Income distribution and redistribution during two decades: experiences from Finland and Sweden, in Inga Persson, ed., Generating Equality. The Swedish Experiment (Norwegian University Press, Oslo), pp. 323–343.

Hartog, J. and J. Veenbergen (1978), Dutch treat: long-run changes in personal income distribution, De Economist 126: 521–549.

Hauser, R. and I. Becker (1997), The development of the income distribution in the Federal Republic of Germany during the Seventies and the Eighties, in P. Gottschalk, B. Gustafsson. and E. Palmer, eds., Changing Patterns in the Distribution of Economic Welfare: an Economic Perspective (Cambridge University Press, Cambridge).

Hjerppe, R. and J. Lefgren (1974), Suomen tulonja kaufman kehityksesta 1881–1967, Kansantaloudellinen aikakauskirja 70: 97–119.

Jeck, A. (1968), The trends of income distribution in West Germany, in J. Marchal and B. Ducros, eds., The Distribution of National Income (Macmillan, London).

Jourdan, J.-P. (1991), Pour une histoire des traitements des fonctionnaires de l'administration au XIXe siècle, Histoire, Économie et Société 10: 227–244.

Kaelble, H. (1986), Industrialization and social inequality in the nineteenth century Europe (Berg, Leamington Spa).

Kraus, F. (1981), The historical development of income inequality in Western Europe and the United States, in P. Flora and A. Heidenheimer, eds., The Development of Welfare States in Europe and America, (Transaction Books, New Brunswick), pp. 187–236.

Kuznets, S. (1955), Economic growth and income inequality, American Economic Review 45: 1–28.

Kuznets, S. (1957), Industrial distribution of national product and labor force, Economic Development and Cultural Change 5: 1–111.

Kuznets, S. (1963), Distribution of income by size, Economic Development and Cultural Change 11: 1–80.

Lecaillon, J., F. Paukert, C. Morrisson and D. Germidis (1984), Income Distribution and Economic Development (ILO, Geneva).

Maddison, A. (1981), Les phases du développement capitaliste (Economica, Paris).

Maddison, A. (1995), Monitoring the world economy 1820–1992 (OECD, Development Centre, Paris).

Morrisson, C. (1988), Une révolution tranquille. L'égalisation des revenus en France depuis vingt ans, Commentaire, (Paris) 41: 203–212.

Morrisson, C. (1991), La répartition des revenus en France depuis 1880, in J.-C. Casanova et M. Lévy-Leboyer éds., Histoire Économique de la France 1880–1980 (Gallimard, Paris), pp. 131–155.

Morrisson, C. and W. Snyder (1998), Les inégalités de revenu en France depuis le début du XVIIIe siècle, mimeo (Paris).

Mueller, J. (1959), Trends in the distribution of income by size in Germany, 1873–1913, Meeting of the International Association of Research on Income and Wealth at Portoroz (Yugoslavia).

Mueller, J. and S. Geisenberger (1972), Die Einkommenstruktur in verschiedenen deutschen Ländern, 1874–1914 (Dunckler and Humblot, Berlin).

Pareto, V. (1897), Cours d'économie Politique, tome second (Pichon, Paris).

Schnitzer, M. (1974), Income Distribution: A Comparative Study of the US, Sweden, West Germany, the UK and Japan (Praeger, New York).

Scholliers, P. (1991), Industrial wage differentials in nineteenth century Belgium, in Y. Brenner, H. Kaelble and M. Thomas, eds., pp. 96–116.

Soderberg, J. (1987a), Real wage trends in urban Europe, 1730–1850: Stockholm in a European perspective, Social History 12: 155–176.

Soderberg, J. (1987b), Trends in inequality in Sweden 1700–1914, Historical Social Research: 21: 58–78.

Soderberg, J. (1991), Wage differentials in Sweden, 1725–1950, in Y. Brenner H. Kaelble and M. Thomas, eds., pp. 76–95.

Soltow, L. (1965), Towards Income Equality in Norway (University of Wisconsin Press, Madison).

Soltow, L. (1968), Long run in British income Inequality, The Economic History Review 21: 17–29.

Soltow, L. (1985), The Swedish census of wealth at the beginning of the nineteenth century, Scandinavian Economic History Review 33: 1–24.

Sorensen, R. (1993), Changes in the personal income distribution, in K. Persson, ed., The Economic Development of Denmark and Norway since 1870 (Elgar, Aldershot).

Statistical Yearbook of Sweden 1995 (1994), Statistics Sweden, Stockholm.

Uusitalo, H. (1989), Income Distribution in Finland, Central Statistical Office of Finland, Helsinki.

van Zanden, J.L. (1995), Tracing the beginning of the Kuznets' curve: Western Europe during the early modern period, The Economic History Review 48: 643–664.

Weir, D. (1991), Les crises économiques et les origines de la Révolution française, Annales E.S.C.: 917–947.

Zeuthen, F. (1928), Den Økonomisk Fordeling (Copenhagen).

United Nations (1957), Economic Survey of Europe in 1956 (Economic Commission for Europe, Geneva).

United Nations (1967), Incomes in Post-war Europe. A Study of policies, growth and distribution (Economic Commission for Europe, Geneva).

Germany: Statistisches Bundesamt, various years.

Germany: Statistisches Reichsamt, 1939, Die Einkommenschichtung im Deutschen Reich. Wirtschaft und Statistik.

Das Deutsche Volkseinkommen (1932) (Statistiches Reichsamt, Berlin).

Økonomisk Utsyn 1900–1950 (Copenhagen).

Chapter 5

EMPIRICAL EVIDENCE ON INCOME INEQUALITY IN INDUSTRIALIZED COUNTRIES

PETER GOTTSCHALK[a] and TIMOTHY M. SMEEDING[b, *]

[a]*Boston College;* [b]*Syracuse University*

Contents

* The authors wish to thank Esther Gray, Katherin Ross, Michael Förster and Peter Stoyko for their assistance, and Anthony B. Atkinson and Francois Bourguignon for comments on earlier draft. Smeeding also thanks the Ford Foundation and the MacArthur Foundation for their support. We assume full responsibility for any errors.

Handbook of Income Distribution: Volume 1. Edited by A. B. Atkinson and F. Bourguignon

Abstract

This chapter reviews the evidence on cross-national comparisons of annual disposable income inequality in over 20 wealthy nations. We begin by reviewing a number of conceptual and measurement issues which must be addressed by any cross-national comparison of survey-based household income data. With these caveats in mind, we present data on both the level of inequality during the early to mid-1990s, and in inequality trends since 1970. While most comparisons are made in terms of relative incomes within nations, we also make some real income comparisons at a point in time using purchasing power parities. The data indicate that a wide range of inequality exists across these rich nations during this decade, with the most unequal nation experiencing a level of inequality which is more than twice the level found in the most equal nation. Country specific trends in income inequality are more similar, although not universally so. The large majority of nations have experienced rising income inequality over the last decade or longer. This increase is not offset by changes in income mobility over this period, and follows a period of declining income inequality in most of these same nations.

Keywords: income inequality, cross-national comparisons

JEL codes. D31, C81

1. Introduction

This chapter reviews the empirical evidence on the level and trend in household[1] (family) income inequality in industrialized countries, primarily the OECD countries. How equally is income distributed across families in countries with very different labor market and social institutions? Has inequality increased in these countries as it has the USA? How do the recent changes compare to longer term trends in income inequality? Are the inequality levels of the 1990s appreciably different from those found in the 1970s or earlier?

Until recently, cross-national comparisons focused on differences in the standard of living of the average or typical person. The more recent literature on cross-national comparisons of inequality within each country allows direct comparisons of differences in the well-being of persons throughout the distribution. What is the relative income of a

---

[1] The unit of analysis for income sharing is the household (all persons sharing common living arrangements) though we sometimes interchangeably use the term family as well.

household at the 10th percentile compared to the median household in the same country? How does this household compare to a household in a different country at the same point in that country's distribution of household income? For example, do households below the 20th percentile in the US have a lower standard of living than comparable Swedish households?

This chapter builds on a number of chapters in this volume, particularly Chapter 2, which presents a detailed discussion of alternative measures of inequality. Our focus on household income is broader than the focus on distribution of earnings, in Chapter 7 although the two are closely related.[2] Our chapter is also closely related to Chapter 6, which focuses on the levels and trends in poverty in advanced countries. While poverty can change for a variety of reasons, changes in the distribution of household income are a key component in explaining differences in trends in poverty across countries during the 1980s.

The material presented in this chapter is largely descriptive. It presents the patterns that any theory of household income distribution would have to explain. We make no attempt to provide such a theory since modeling this complicated set of forces is well beyond the scope of this paper. A theory would have to address at least the following four cross-national differences:

1. differences in labor markets that affect earnings of individual household members;
2. difference sources of capital and in returns to capital;
3. demographic differences, such as the aging of the population and growth of single parent households, which affect both family needs and labor market decisions; and
4. differences across countries in tax and transfer policies that not only affect family income directly, but also may affect work and investment decisions.

Aggregating earnings across all individuals in a household and adding other sources of income takes us from the distribution of individual earnings to the distribution of family income. Ideally one would like to know how much of the change in inequality of total family income is caused by exogenous changes in each source of income. This would require a fully articulated model of behavioral responses. For example, if exogenous increases in inequality of male earnings led wives of low income husbands to work more, then this portion of the change in overall inequality would be caused by changes in the distribution of husbands' earnings, not wives' earnings. Structural models that include all behavioral links are well beyond the scope of existing empirical work. Researchers have, therefore, limited themselves largely to accounting exercises which decompose changes in overall inequality into a set of components.[3]

The inclusion of multiple income sources received by multiple individuals thwarts attempts to identify the causal links that led to variations across time and countries in the distribution of total post-tax and transfer household income. There is ample evidence that family members take account of all sources of income available to the household in

---

[2] Gottschalk and Smeeding (1997a) indicate that changes in the distribution of household incomes mirrored changes in the distribution of earnings in some, but not all, countries.

[3] For example, see Bourguignon and Martinez (1996).

deciding not only how much each member might work, but also how to structure living arrangements. Moreover, governments themselves react differently to market income changes via changes in redistribution (tax and transfer) policy, and via other policies (e.g., government employment).

Our focus is on a limited set of countries, particularly OECD and other advanced industrial countries. Both the level and trend in inequality in these industrialized countries may be quite different from those in the developing world discussed in Chapter 13, and in the economies making the transition from planned to market systems discussed in Chapter 14.

This chapter is divided into four main parts. Section 2 explores key measurement issues which the empirical literature must address. Section 3 presents evidence on cross-national differences in the *level* of inequality of household income across countries in the late 1980s and early 1990s. In Section 4, the focus shifts to *trends* in inequality of household income. This is followed by a comparison of mobility across countries and time. The chapter concludes with a summary of the results presented in the earlier sections.

2. Conceptual and measurement issues

Cross-national comparisons of income must confront two major issues. The first is conceptual. What measure would one ideally use to compare distributions of well-being across countries? The second issue moves from the ideal to the possible. What is the impact of using imperfect data to approximate this ideal? While both of these questions would have to be addressed even in a study of a single country, they take on a somewhat different role in cross-national studies.

2.1. Ideal measure

Ideally, one would want to compare the difference in the distribution of lifetime utilities of persons in different countries. Utility comparisons would reflect differences in leisure as well as all forms of potential consumption, including home production and publicly provided goods. Consumption would be appropriately adjusted for family size to reflect economies of scale in consumption. Utility comparisons would take account of differences in constraints faced both by people living in the same country and differences in constraints faced by people in different countries. For example, differences in the ability to smooth income across periods or differences in the allocation of income and leisure within the family would affect the distribution of lifetime utility both within and across countries.[4] At best, yearly post tax family income adjusted for family size is a proxy for this more fundamental concept.

---

[4] Utility will be lower for persons in families unable to smooth consumption, either because they live in countries with limited access to capital markets or because of unequal access to capital markets within a country. Similarly, differences in the allocation of resources within families will affect the distribution of

2.2. Impact of measurement error

Measurement error arises both from differences between the ideal and the measurable and from reporting error in the measurable. For example, post tax family income as reported by respondents may differ from the respondents actual income because of reporting error. The problem of measurement error is endemic to all income distribution studies, whether they focus on a single country or many countries. The question we ask in this section is whether the bias introduced by this measurement error is aggravated in cross-national studies. We start by focusing on differences in inequality across countries at a single point in time. We then turn to the impact of measurement error on differences in trends in inequality.

2.2.1. Level of inequality

To focus attention on the key elements consider the following simple errors component model for the jth percentile in country c:

$$m_c^j = d_c + v^j + e_c^j, \tag{2.1}$$

$$\ln P_c^j = \ln \pi_c^j + m_c^j, \tag{2.2}$$

where P_c^j is the measured percentile, π_c^j is the percentile for the ideal concept, m_c^j is measurement error, d_c is a country specific component that affects all deciles, v^j is a decile specific component common to all countries, and e_c^j is a decile and country specific component.

We start by considering the effects of measurement error on estimates of the $\ln(P_c^{90}/P_c^{10})$ in a single country, which we call the 90/10 or decile ratio for convenience. Since

$$\ln(P_c^{90}/P_c^{10}) = \ln(\pi_c^{90}/\ln \pi_c^{10}) + (v^{90} - v^{10}) + (e_c^{90} - e_c^{10}), \tag{2.3}$$

we see right away that measurement error that affects all deciles equally within the country cancel. For example, consumption of public goods unrelated to decile rank within the country will not bias the 90/10 ratio.

Now consider the effect of measurement error in a cross- national study. The object of interest is the difference in the 90/10 ratio between two countries l and k:

$$\ln(P_l^{90}/P_l^{10}) - \ln(P_k^{90}/P_k^{10}) = \ln(\pi_l^{90}/\pi_l^{10}) - \ln(\pi_k^{90}/\pi_k^{10})$$
$$+ (e_l^{90} - e_l^{10}) - (e_k^{90} - e_k^{10}). \tag{2.4}$$

lifetime utility across persons. And these may differ across countries. Finally, concepts different from utility might be appropriate for measuring well-being, e.g., Sen's (1992) concept of capabilities might be used instead of utility.

This illustrates the obvious, but sometimes overlooked point that decile specific errors that are common across countries do not affect cross-national comparisons of percentile ratios in a given year. For example, underreporting by respondents at the top or bottom of the distribution will not bias cross-national comparisons to the extent that this underreporting is common across countries.

The remaining measurement error in Eq. (2.4) reflects differences across countries at the 90th and 10th percentiles. Thus, the key measurement of concern to cross national studies is measurement error that differs *both* across deciles *and* across countries. For example, estimates of differences in inequality between two countries will be biased inasmuch as income underreporting is greater at the 10th than the 90th percentiles and this degree of differential under-reporting differ across countries.

While this simple notation illustrates that certain types of measurement error do not lead to bias in cross-national studies, we do not want to leave the impression that measurement error is not potentially important. Measurement error may be reduced by taking differences across countries but the signal to noise ratio may be increased. This can clearly be seen by comparing the signal to noise ratio for estimates of country specific inequality measures, $(S/N)_c$, as given on the right-hand side of Eq. (2.3),

$$(S/N)_c = \ln(\pi_c^{90}/\ln \pi_c^{10})/\{v^{90} - v^{10}) + (e_c^{90} - e_c^{10})\}, \tag{2.5a}$$

with the signal to noise ratio for differences across countries in these ratios, as given by the right-hand side of Eq. (2.4):

$$(S/N)_j - (S/N)_k = \{\ln(\pi_j^{90}/\pi_j^{10}) - \ln(\pi_k^{90}/\pi_k^{10})\}/\{(e_j^{90} - e_j^{10}) - e_k^{90} - e_k^{10})\}. \tag{2.5b}$$

Eqs. (2.5a) with (2.5b) shows that while taking differences across countries reduces noise (as shown in Eq. (2.4)) it may reduce the signal even more. Thus, differences in 90/10 ratios across countries, which eliminates decile specific errors that are common across countries (the v's in Eq. (2.3)), reduces the noise but the remaining noise may be large relative to what we are trying to measure, namely the *difference* in 90/10 ratios. Our distinction between measurement error that does and does not affect cross-national comparisons is, therefore, not meant to minimize the importance of measurement error but to focus attention on the relevant source of error.

2.2.2. Trends
Much of the recent literature has focused on differences across countries in trends rather than levels of inequality. Analyzing the biasing source of measurement error for these comparisons requires that we enter time explicitly into Eqs. (2.1) and (2.2).

$$\ln P_{ct}^j = \ln \pi_{ct}^j + m_{ct}^j, \tag{2.6}$$

$$m_{ct}^j = d_c + v^j + e_{ct}^j, \tag{2.7}$$

$$e_{ct}^j = g_{ct} + w_t^j + f_{ct}^j, \tag{2.8}$$

where g_{ct} is a time specific component that affects all deciles in country c, w_t^j is a time specific component that has differential effects across deciles, f_{ct}^j and is a component that is time, decile and component-specific.

The trend in the 90/10 in country c is given by

$$\ln(P_{ct}^{90}/P_{ct}^{10}) - \ln(P_{c,t+1}^{90}/P_{c,t+1}^{10}) = \ln(\pi_{ct}^{90}/\pi_{ct}^{10} - \ln(\pi_{c,t+1}^{90}/\pi_{c,t=1}^{10})$$
$$+ (e_{ct}^{90} - e_{ct}^{10}) - (e_{c,t+1}^{90} - e_{c,t+1}^{10}). \tag{2.9}$$

Following the logic of the previous section, differences across countries in trends will depend on g_{ct} and f_{ct}^j but not on w_t^j, since the latter is measurement error that differs across time and decile but not across countries. Again, taking cross-national differences reduces the absolute level of noise but has an ambiguous effect on the signal to noise ratio.

2.2.3. Summary
This section has shown that some but not all sources of measurement error affect cross-national comparisons of levels or trends in percentile ratios such as the decile ratio: The following generalizations emerge:

- Measurement error that is independent of decile rank affects neither level nor trend in inequality in a single country nor in cross-national comparisons of inequality.
- Measurement error that is common across countries does not affect cross-national comparisons of levels or trends in inequality; each country's decile ratio is biased but the difference in ratios is not.
- Cross-national comparisons of trends in decile ratios are not affected by measurement error that is either time invariant or time varying but common across countries.

2.3. Definitions and measures

The preceding section has shown that it is important to distinguish between different forms of measurement error. In this section we review the choices we need to make concerning the definition of income; the unit of analyses, income sharing rules, and the period of analysis in light of this discussion of measurement error.

2.3.1. Income definition
Many studies use a comprehensive definition of money income, which includes all forms of cash payment received by persons in the household or family. This measure of gross

income includes the earnings of all family members, property income, social insurance, universal cash transfers and public assistance. They also include "near-cash" income such as food stamps and rent rebates which are measured in currency terms. Many studies also examine the distribution of disposable income, which is equal to a gross income minus direct taxes and social contributions.[5]

The focus in the literature on the distribution of after tax disposable money income ignores two factors which directly affect family well-being and whose distribution may vary widely across countries. The first is the value of in-kind income. This includes both private goods and publicly provided goods. Among the most important private goods are imputed rent to owner-occupied housing, the value of home production, and employee fringe benefits, including paid time off. The latter are particularly important given large differences in benefits across countries. For example, the number of vacation days provided by employers differs substantially between the US and other OECD countries. Publicly provided goods include widely distributed goods such as medical care, education, transportation and police protection. Since there are likely to be large differences across countries both in the amount of in-kind income and the covariance between these sources of income and cash income, the omission of in-kind items is likely to affect distributional measures in country c at time t in as much as their omission affects deciles differently.[6]

Smeeding et al. (1993), Whiteford and Kennedy (1994) and Gardiner et al. (1995) find that the exclusion of non-cash income reduces measured inequality. Smeeding et al. (1993) and Whiteford and Kennedy (1994) find that the omission of non-cash income in the form of medical care, and education transfers and imputed rent from owned housing effect the level of inequality but not the ranking of nations. Gardiner et al. (1995) find fewer consistent effects.[7]

The second factor is indirect taxation. Mixes of direct and indirect tax vary substantially across nations (Atkinson et al., 1995, Table 3.6). If the distribution of taxes varies by type then the choice of which tax to include may affect the ranking of countries in a single cross-section. If the size or incidence of these taxes change over time, the choice of which to include may also affect the trends in inequality in different countries.

Estimates of indirect taxes paid (or non-cash benefits received) are normally based on imputations that require specific measures of consumption as well as income. Thus, surveys must measure both income and consumption. Moreover, these imputations depend on several assumptions upon which there is little or no agreement among economists. For example, consider the incidence of indirect taxes on rental housing, taxes on employers,

---

[5] These measures follow closely the guidelines set by the UN (1977) and other bodies. See Atkinson et al. (1995, Chap. 3, pp. 30–35) and Australian Bureau of Statistics (1997) for a discussion of remaining differences.

[6] The omission of in-kind income will lower the mean and will likely affect distributional measures.

[7] The study by Gardiner et al. (1995), experiments with different types of income definitions, poverty definitions, and different schemes for valuation of non-cash benefits for two countries—the UK and France. They find that depending on what is included and on how it is valued, the poverty rate rankings of these two nations can be reversed by a particular set of income and poverty definitions.

and taxes on corporations. These taxes may fall on profits, on workers, or on consumers. Thus, stockholders (who earn profits) and expenditures on taxed items must also be identified by the survey in order to impute such taxes. Limited experimentation with simulations (e.g., Bell and Rosenberg, 1993) indicates that including indirect taxes leads to higher levels of inequality but unchanged rankings of inequality for Germany, Sweden and the US.

2.3.2. Income data quality

Even if there were agreement on how to measure the value of in-kind benefits and indirect taxes, it would still be difficult to obtain comparable measures of income across countries since the types of survey data used to measure inequality are not uniform in nature, purpose or objective. For instance, consider Table 1 which shows some commonly used surveys for several OECD countries.[8] Some surveys are designed to collect income data; others are derived from income tax records; and still others come from special supplements to labor force surveys. Some datasets are based on income questions taken from expenditure surveys (as in the case of the UK); others are separate waves of longitudinal household panel data (e.g., Germany); and still others are taken, at least in large part, directly from government administrative data (e.g., Sweden, Finland and Denmark). Many nations have several types of income data. For instance, US data on income could come from income supplements to labor force surveys (such as the Current Population Surveys data used here), annual or subannual income surveys, Social Security records, household income panel data, or expenditure surveys. Since each type of survey is likely to have a somewhat different primary focus, these differences are likely to affect income reporting error.

It is well known that income is underreported in almost all surveys. If the under reporting is non-random, then both the degree of under reporting and the incidence across income groups will affect measures of inequality. One way of identifying the amount of under reporting is to compare aggregates in the micro data sets with those from National Income Accounts and other external data sources, which are presumed to be more accurate in the aggregate. Atkinson et al. (1995, Table 3.7) show that while wages and salaries are fairly accurately reported across countries, total income reported in the micro data sets vary widely across the small number of countries for which we have such comparisons.[9] Overall income comparisons of seven nations indicate that income surveys account for 77–93% of the aggregate amounts reported by external sources with five nations at 90% or above. We should hasten to point out that different nations have each made their own assumptions and imputations to compare aggregated microdata income component totals with adjusted administrative data. There has been

---

[8] Table 1 is taken from Smeeding and Weinberg (1998). Most of these datasets are included in the Luxembourg Income Study (LIS) database described below.

[9] See Atkinson et al. (1995). A group of these nations, the so-called Canberra Group, have joined to begin to set guidelines and standards for income distributional studies and to improve reporting of data quality comparisons and hopefully data quality itself. For more on this see Australian Bureau of Statistics (1997).

Table 1

Type of survey data and conceptual data quality

1.	Income or living standard survey[a]	US (unofficial), the Netherlands, Australia, Canada, Taiwan, Ireland, Italy, Switzerland, Japan
2.	Combination of survey and administrative records[b]	Finland, Sweden, Denmark
3.	Income tax records[c]	France, Norway
4.	Panel study[d]	Belgium, Germany, Luxembourg
5.	Labor force survey supplement[e]	US (official), Austria
6.	Expenditure survey[f]	UK, Spain

[a] Survey primarily aimed at measuring living standards or income. Secondary aims may include other items such as wealth, labor force status, expenditure, earnings, home ownership, finances, etc.

[b] Survey asks respondents for permission to access confidential comprehensive government registries and administrative data to get some income information. In Finland, additional information is obtained from interviews.

[c] Survey basis is from income tax records. Additional imputations are made for nontaxed income sources and related issues. Frame also used expenditure survey data.

[d] Dataset follows same persons over multiple years; cross-section data is taken as a "slice" of data for these persons for a given year.

[e] Primary survey objective is labor force participation, employment, unemployment, etc.; special supplement provides income data.

[f] Primary purpose of survey is expenditure data, but monthly/weekly income information is also gathered in some great detail.

Source: Atkinson et al. (1995, Table 3.3), updated and expanded.

no comprehensive cross-national study which has made such comparisons on a wholly consistent basis across countries.

Comparisons with aggregate totals give some idea of the magnitude of under-reporting, but they do not tell us whether, or not, under-reporting affects distributional measures. The latter require that under-reporting be correlated with income. If everyone under-reports their income proportionately then the mean of the distribution of income is lower but most measures of relative within-country inequality would be unaffected.[10] The impact of under-reporting in cross-national comparisons further requires that the bias in inequality measures be different in different countries. If they are not then differences across countries in inequality measures again will be unaffected by under-reporting.

Under-reporting is high for government transfers, property income, and self-employment income in all nations. Since transfers are more likely to be received by persons in the lower tail of the distribution, this under-reporting increases measured

---

[10] Note, however, that if the ratio of mean incomes to total national income differ across countries, purchasing power parity based comparisons of mean income will differ from comparisons of total national income.

inequality. On the other hand, under-reporting of property income tends to lower the income of families at the top of the distribution, which reduces measured inequality. Since these two sources of income have opposite effects on inequality, it is difficult to judge whether inequality is under- or over-estimated in a given country.[11] Identifying the bias caused by underreporting is even harder when comparing countries. Whether, or not, under-reporting affects cross-national comparisons depends on the degree to which under-reporting varies across countries. If the distribution of under-reporting were similar in all countries this would affect the level of inequality but not necessarily cross-national differences in inequality.

2.3.3. *Unit of analysis and sharing rules*

Well-being is affected by the resources available to persons in an income-sharing unit and the resulting economies of scale from joint consumption. The unit of analysis should, therefore, encompass all persons who share income or benefit from economies of scale. There are two obvious choices for the accounting unit: the household (which includes all persons in a common residence) and the family unit (which includes all persons in the residence related by blood or marriage.) Whether to use the household or family as the accounting unit depends the degree to which non-family members share income and/or benefit from economies of scale. For example, if three college students share an apartment, they are unlikely to be sharing income, but they are likely to benefit from economies of scale by having a common kitchen, livingroom, heat source, and having to pay only a small marginal cost for each extra bedroom. The fact that college students benefit from economies of scale but are unlikely to share resources, illustrates the problem of choosing an appropriate accounting unit. If one uses the family as the unit then each person is a separate accounting unit, which ignores economies of scale. Using the household as the unit of analysis, however, implies that the three people share their incomes fully.

The decision of whether to use the family or household as the unit of analysis is further complicated by differences in institutions across countries. For example, consider differences in the proportion of couples who are cohabiting (rather than being legally married) across OECD countries. Such couples are very likely to share income and benefit from economies of scale, so the household would be the more appropriate unit of analysis. But unless the dataset identifies cohabiting couples, one is left with the choice of treating them as unrelated individuals who do not share resources or treating all unrelated individuals, whether cohabiting couples or not, as sharing income.[12] Recently, analysts have begun to challenge this assumption and to show the different outcomes

---

[11] The self-employed are found at both ends of the distribution, again producing uncertain results.

[12] In the Luxembourg Income Study (LIS) datasets we use, cohabiting couples are treated as two families living in a single household in some nations. The data for Sweden, Norway and the Netherlands classifies unmarried couples living together of whatever gender as married. See footnote 15 for a more complete description of LIS.

which may occur if sharing within households (or families) is not equal (Jenkins, 1994; Sutherland, 1996).

Once one defines the unit that shares income and consumption and the sharing rule, it is necessary to adjust the unit's income for economies of scale. Equivalence scales have been developed to accomplish this adjustment by taking into account those household characteristics deemed to affect economies of scale and economies of scope as reflected by differences in household size and composition.

Buhmann et al. (1988) first proposed a single parametric approximation to equivalence scales which encompassed a wide range of scales in use:

$$\text{Adjusted Income} = \text{Disposable Income}/\text{Size}^E. \tag{2.10}$$

The equivalence elasticity, E, varies between 0 and 1; the larger is E, the smaller are the economies of scale assumed by the equivalence scale. Various studies make use of equivalence scales ranging from $E = 0$ (no adjustment or full economies of scale) to $E = 1$ (per capita income which implies zero economies of scale). Between these extremes, the range of values used in different studies is very large. These adjustments for household size can have a large effect on the level of measured inequality within and across nations.[13] However, using different equivalence scales preserves the general rank order of countries, albeit at different levels of inequality. Inequality rankings at a point in time are fairly robust to choice of equivalence scales (Atkinson et al., 1995, Tables 4.9 and 4.10; OECD, 1997, Annex 3) which illustrates our argument that factors which are not country-specific do not affect cross-national comparisons. Evidence for differences in trends within the US indicates that choice of equivalence scale may affect the level of measured inequality but not its trend (Karoly and Burtless 1995).

2.3.4. Period of analysis

The time period over which income is measured also affects measures of inequality. Inequality tends to decrease as the accounting period is lengthened since transitory fluctuations increase inequality in the current period but average out over longer periods. A standard economic model of utility maximizing agents with access to capital markets and full information implies that the appropriate accounting period is a lifetime, and that yearly measures of income overstate the degree of inequality. This, however, assumes that people have perfect foresight and can smooth out transitory fluctuations by lending or borrowing. Lifetime income may indeed be the proper measure for high income families who can either rely on savings or have access to capital markets to smooth transitory fluctuations, even with imperfect foresight. However, for low income or young families

---

[13] See Coulter et al. (1992) and Buhmann et al. (1988). An important and non-obvious lesson from these papers is that the relationship between inequality measures and elasticities is non-monotonic. Recently, the literature and equivalences adjustments in practice have moved beyond the one parameter equivalence scale to two parameter scales which include adjustments for types of individuals (e.g., by age) as well as for family size. See Jenkins and Cowell (1994) on this issue.

who have small savings and little access to capital markets, the appropriate accounting period may be a pay period or a month rather than a year. Thus, the use of an annual accounting period in most data sets (with monthly and weekly income in the UK being the largest exception) is likely to be too short for families that can smooth consumption over multiple years and too long for families that are severely credit constrained. Again, using the available rather than the ideal accounting period may affect inequality measures in each country but if the measurement error is the same in all countries this will not affect cross-country comparisons.

2.3.5. Summary

This brief review of measurement issues is designed to alert the reader to the types of choices and biases that exist in income inequality measures. As should be clear, the data with which we work are noisy and many of the results one obtains are affected by differences across surveys and over time. Sensitivity tests, which provide information on the differences that measurement choices produce, should also be conducted wherever possible. In some cases, our analyses suggest that results may not be affected greatly by many of the choices we have to make.[14] We proceed cautiously but believe that the weight of the evidence provides a fairly consistent picture of differences in levels and trends in inequality across a variety of countries.

3. Differences in inequality across OECD countries

In this section, we provide several alternative measures of inequality in OECD countries for the late 1980s or early 1990s. The following section sheds light on differences in levels of inequality as shown by Lorenz curves, decile ratios, and Gini coefficients. We begin with a brief description of the data we use in much of this paper.

3.1. Data and measurement choices

Our primary source of microdata is from the Luxembourg Income Study (LIS). The LIS datasets have been used here to compare the distribution of disposable income in 25 nations over a 20-year period, although not all periods are available for all nations.[15] This data overcomes some, but by no means all, of the problems discussed earlier. The LIS was created specifically to improve consistency across countries and the data is a collection of microdata sets obtained from the range of income and other surveys in various countries (e.g., see Table 1). The advantage of these data is that extensive effort has been made by country specialists to make information on income and household

---

[14] Further information on these topics may be found in Atkinson et al. (1995), Gottschalk and Smeeding (1997a), Burniaux et al. (1998), and in the technical material provided by many National Statistical Offices.

[15] For additional information please e-mail <LISAA@maxwell.syr.edu> or <caroline@post.ceps.lu> or visit the LIS homepage at Http://www-cpr.maxwell.syr.edu/lis-part//. The LIS website is also the website for the Canberra Group on household income statistics.

characteristics as comparable as possible across a large number of countries. A further advantage of the LIS is that it offers the only publicly available microdata sets for Denmark, Sweden, the Netherlands, Israel and Finland. Access to the microdata makes it possible to produce estimates based on individual household records, and to test the sensitivity of conclusions to alternative choices of units, definition and other concepts. For example, it is possible to check the robustness of findings to a series of adjustment for household size by applying a set of equivalence scales.

While the LIS overcomes some problems of comparability, several problems remain. As mentioned above, the underlying data were originally designed in different countries for a variety of purposes, and so they clearly depart from the ideal of a single survey instrument uniformly applied to all countries.[16] Attempts to make these datasets comparable has deficiencies as well as benefits. For example, not every variable is available on every dataset so some of the details in the original samples are lost. Another major drawback is that data are available only for a limited number of years due to both limited availability of surveys and costs of annually updating each nation's data. While the LIS offers the largest collection of microdatasets across a wide variety of countries, its drawbacks are potentially important. Therefore, whenever possible, we compare our results with those of country studies. The fact that these two sources of information are generally in agreement increases our confidence in the LIS.[17]

Our specific measure of income is household disposable income per equivalent adult, using an "intermediate" equivalence scale of the square root of household size.[18] This is a commonly used equivalence scale which increases at a decreasing rate with family size. Data are weighted by the number of persons in each family, so income is measured as (after tax and transfer) disposable personal income per adult equivalent. All of the nations have the same definition of disposable income with the exception of Austria where self-employment income is not counted in their survey. The samples generally exclude persons living in institutions such as pensions, hospitals and nursing homes; the homeless, military living in barracks and undocumented immigrants. Registered immigrants are included. Coverage in every country is 96% or more of the remaining civilian non-institutionalized populations (Atkinson et al., 1995, p. 17). No major population groups are omitted from any survey.[19]

---

[16] Even when a single survey, e.g., the European Community Household Panel, is carried out in multiple countries, robustness and comparability remain key issues (Verma, 1998).

[17] For example, of country studies of earnings inequality, see Freeman and Katz (1993). For income inequality see Gottschalk et al. (1996). For additional comparisons, see Gottschalk and Smeeding (1997a), Atkinson et al. (1995) and OECD (1997).

[18] Adjusted income is equal to disposable income/(family size)$^{1/2}$.

[19] This includes Japan where their Survey of Income Redistribution includes all but the institutionalized population as opposed to their Income and Expenditure Survey which until 1995 omitted single person units (Fukui, 1996).

3.2. Differences in the level of inequality

We start by examining differences in income inequality across countries in the late 1980s and early 1990s. We focus both on the relative differences (the 'various' percentile points and particularly the gap between the 10th and 90th percentile) within a country and how this translates into real differences across countries at different points in the income distribution. For example, how much less does a family at the 20th percentile in Sweden receive compared to the median Swedish family and compared to a family at the 20th percentile in the US?

3.2.1. Measuring and deploying the distribution of relative income

One of the key used in income distribution research is the choice of inequality measure and form of presentation. The literature employs Lorenz-based measures (e.g., Gini coefficients, Lorenz-dominance measures, Hasse diagrams) and other descriptive measures.[20] Due to differences in top and bottom coding of survey data by nations and surveys, selected measures of inequality may be sensitive to these limits. Some national datasets include negative incomes (e.g., losses for the self-employed), while others bottom code at zero or at some minimal positive level. Most surveys top-code income at some high figure to preserve confidentiality among high income recipients. The effects of top and bottom coding or truncation bias on the Gini coefficient are well known (see Fichtenbaum and Shahidi, 1988; Atkinson et al., 1995), and these boundaries need be tested for robustness of results.[21]

Our initial comparison of income distributions is based on Lorenz curves rather than summary measures, such as the Gini coefficient.[22] These plots allow us to see whether, or not, pairs of countries can be ranked by the standard dominance criteria.[23] Figures 1a–d present plots for the Nordic, Benelux and other European and Commonwealth countries. We also include data for the US on each graph in order to give a common

[20] See Cowell (Chap. 2, this volume) and Jenkins (1991) for compact and useful surveys of summary measures of inequality.

[21] For instance, Smeeding and Gottschalk (forthcoming, Table 1), show that while most OECD nations Gini estimates vary little with a top code of 10 times the median versus the amount reported on the survey, the Gini for Russia changes from 0.437 to 0.393 when a top code of 10 times the median in imposed. However, differences may still remain. For instance, Ryscavage (1995) addresses the effects of changing top-coding of income in the US *Current Population Survey* (CPS) on measures of inequality. In the CPS, both individual earnings *and* overall household income have been subject to different topcoding over time. These changes may have some effect on the trend in overall income inequality. Fortunately, the LIS topcode of ten times the adjusted median lies below the CPS topcode for 1994 and hence does not affect the estimates in Fig. 2. Moreover, this topcoding does not effect the P_{90} measure which produces a similar result in terms of cross-national rankings of the level of inequality.

[22] Data for these plots are presented in Appendix A to facilitate any comparison the reader may wish to make.

[23] See Cowell (Chap. 2, this volume) for properties of the Lorenz curves and dominance criterial As is well known, the vertical axis in these plots can be labeled either as the share of income received by the *p*th percentile or the mean of the truncated distribution, measured as a percent of the mean of the untruncated distribution.

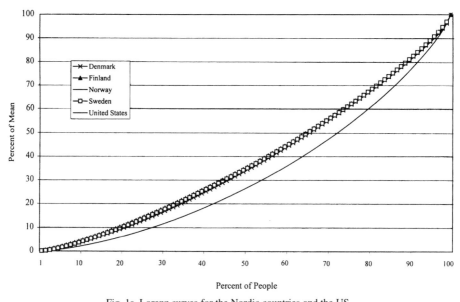

Fig. 1a. Lorenz curves for the Nordic countries and the US.

point of comparison. Figure 1a clearly shows that incomes are more equally distributed in all Nordic countries than in the United States. While the mean income for households below the 20th percentile was only 5.9% of the US mean, the comparable figures for the Nordic countries range from 9.4 to 11.0% of their country specific means. Because the Lorenz curves of Nordic countries cross, we cannot rank distributions within the region.

The Benelux countries in Fig. 1b likewise show substantial uniformity across countries with each having greater equality than the US. Among the the Benelux countries, the Netherlands is the least equal but the differences in inequality among Benelux countries are small compared to the differences between these countries and the US. Figures 1c and d show data for other European countries and some members of the British Commonwealth. There is less uniformity among these countries but the US is still more unequal than any of them. Figure 1c shows that Germany is more equal than Italy and France. Canada dominates Australia which dominates the UK. The UK and US, however, cannot be ranked since their Lorenz curves cross.

Another way to summarize this information is shown in Fig. 2 where several additional countries are represented. Nations from the Pacific Rim (Japan, New Zealand and Taiwan) have been added along with Southern Europe (Spain, Israel), Central Europe (Switzerland) and Ireland.[24] While not all of the points of the percentile distribution

---

[24] With the exception of New Zealand and Japan, all of the data in Fig. 2 is derived from the LIS. We thank Takahiro Fukui of the Japanese Statistics Bureau and the New Zealand Central Statistical Office for their help in preparing these estimates.

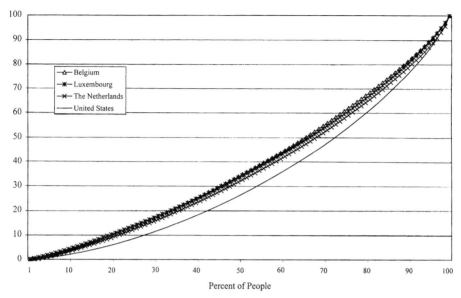

Fig. 1b. Lorenz curves for the Benelux countries and the US.

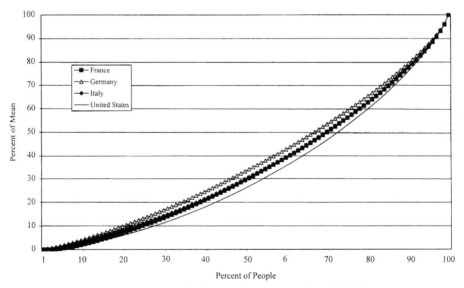

Fig. 1c. Lorenz curves for the other European countries and the US.

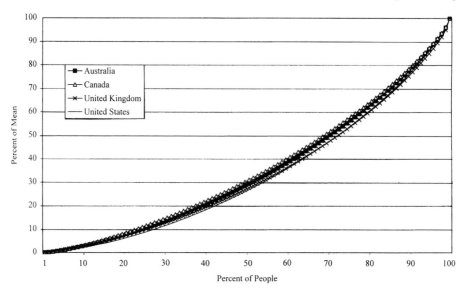

Fig. 1d. Lorenz curves for the Commonwealth countries and the US.

are laid out, and while the data are presented as percentiles of the median income (not of the mean income as in Figs. 1a to c), the obvious advantages of this presentation is its ability to summarize several nations in one picture and two summary measures of income distribution—the 90/10 ratio and the Gini coefficient. The bar chart and decile ratio also help to summarize the concept of "social distance" between persons at each end of the distribution of income. A person at the 90th percentile in the US has almost six and a half times the income of a person at the 10th percentile, while the distance is three times or less in the Nordic and Benelux countries.

Two additional features stand out in Fig. 2. First, the US continues to be very different at the bottom of the distribution. The second lowest P^{10} value found in Fig. 2 is 45 (Australia) compared to 34 in the US. At the other extreme, several nations P^{90} values are near that of the US, e.g., the UK and Ireland.

The second notable feature is the similarity in rankings based on the Gini coefficients and decile ratios.[25] For the most part, these rankings produce the same pattern of inequality with Nordic and Northern European nations having the least inequality, followed by Central Europe, Southern Europe and the Commonwealth, with the UK and US having the highest overall levels of inequality. The Pacific Rim nations (including Australia and the US), as well as Japan are all located toward the upper end of the inequality spectrum. Taiwan, in contrast, has below average inequality.

---

[25] The correlation between the percentile ratios and the Gini coefficient is 0.913.

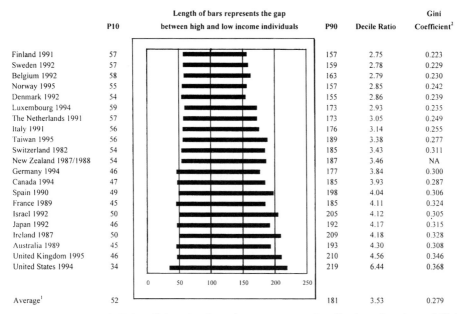

	P10	Length of bars represents the gap between high and low income individuals	P90	Decile Ratio	Gini Coefficient[2]
Finland 1991	57		157	2.75	0.223
Sweden 1992	57		159	2.78	0.229
Belgium 1992	58		163	2.79	0.230
Norway 1995	55		157	2.85	0.242
Denmark 1992	54		155	2.86	0.239
Luxembourg 1994	59		173	2.93	0.235
The Netherlands 1991	57		173	3.05	0.249
Italy 1991	56		176	3.14	0.255
Taiwan 1995	56		189	3.38	0.277
Switzerland 1982	54		185	3.43	0.311
New Zealand 1987/1988	54		187	3.46	NA
Germany 1994	46		177	3.84	0.300
Canada 1994	47		185	3.93	0.287
Spain 1990	49		198	4.04	0.306
France 1989	45		185	4.11	0.324
Israel 1992	50		205	4.12	0.305
Japan 1992	46		192	4.17	0.315
Ireland 1987	50		209	4.18	0.328
Australia 1989	45		193	4.30	0.308
United Kingdom 1995	46		210	4.56	0.346
United States 1994	34		219	6.44	0.368
Average[1]	52		181	3.53	0.279

Fig. 2. Decile ratios and Gini coefficient (numbers given are percent of median in each nation and Gini coefficient).
Source: Authors' calculations using the Luxembourg Income Study database; Japanese data courtesy of Isikawa (1996); New Zealand data comes from Atkinson, Rainwater and Smeeding (1995) Chap. 4.
[1] Simple average, excluding the US.
[2] Gini coefficients are based on incomes which are bottom coded at 1% of disposable income and top coded at 10 times the median disposable income.

These comparisons are similar to those made using the LIS based on earlier time periods with few exceptions (Gottschalk and Smeeding, 1997). Some of the remaining differences are probably due to use of different data sources (e.g., France, see Tables A2 and A3). The one notable change is that the most recent round of data finds Canada's unchanging inequality moving it closer to the middle range of countries.

3.2.2. Summary

The US has the least equal distribution of family income among all countries covered in this study. The Nordic and Benelux countries have the most equal distributions with the Commonwealth countries coming closest to the degree of inequality in the US. The largest differences between the US and the rest of the nations are in the lower part of the distribution of disposable income. Studies that decompose these differences indicate that greater earnings inequality and the relatively small level of social expenditures in the US account for much of the differences.[26] As a result, Canada which has a personal earnings distribution that is not very different from the US in the lower tail, manages to have substantially higher post tax and transfer family incomes at the bottom of the distribution. Other nations with a high proportion of low wage workers (e.g., Australia) also tend to do better than the US once other earners and the effect of direct taxes and income transfers are factored in.

3.2.3. Distribution of absolute income

Thus far we have examined differences across countries in relative incomes by focusing on Lorenz curves and Gini coefficients. We have compared the average income of households below the pth percentile relative to each country's mean. This properly measures the degree of inequality but ignores differences in real or absolute incomes across countries. While Swedish households below the 20th percentile may have incomes closer to the Swedish mean than the comparable low income household in the US, this does not necessarily mean that the low income households enjoy a higher standard of living in Sweden than in the US. The higher mean in the US may more than offset the higher degree of inequality.

In order to compare absolute levels of income we present generalized Lorenz curves which show the mean income of households below the pth percentile measured as a proportion of the US mean. This, however, requires an index with which to translate incomes in all countries into a common currency. The commonly used indices are based on purchasing power parity indices (PPPs), which were designed to compare GDP per capita across countries. These are a useful starting point but there are several issues raised in using these indices to compare income/needs ratios at different points in the distribution. One of the most difficult issue is exactly what index to use. As Förster (1998) has shown, the rankings of several countries depends on whether one uses PPP's for all goods, for private final consumption, or only for food and clothing.[27] The second issue is whether, or not, a single index is appropriate for all points in the distribution. Applying a single index assumes that the cost-of-living differences across countries for the average household is the same as for households at all points in the distribution. Third, the PPP constructed to compare GDP per capita may not be appropriate to compare after tax and transfer family money income when there are large differences across countries in the tax financed public provision of goods, such as education and health. While publicly provided goods are included in GDP they are not included in the money income received by households used in income distribution studies. For example, even if we had the ideal price indices to compare money incomes, this would still not solve the problem that most

---

[26] See Gottschalk and Smeeding (1997a) for evidence on the distribution of earnings. See Smeeding (1997) on low earnings, social expenditures and income inequality.

[27] Differences may also depend on the set of PPPs selected and their vintage. For instance, the Penn World Tables PPPs used here may differ from the World Bank PPPs and from the PPPs in the European Comparison Project (ECP) data provided by the OECD. Furthermore, OECD PPPs are rivised approximately every five years. Using different vintage of PPPs, e.g., 1989 estimates based on 1990 PPPs compared to the 1995 PPPs, also produces somewhat different results.

of the countries we examine have publicly provided health insurance and other publicly provided goods. While the exclusion of these goods also affect relative measures of inequality, the problem is particularly serious when making absolute comparisons.[28, 29]

An additional problem in trying to rank countries on the basis of absolute incomes at the pth percentile is that these rankings will depend on the percentile point chosen unless one country dominates another (i.e., income is uniformly higher at all points in one distribution than in the other). This is a particularly important problem for the countries we study since the higher mean income but greater inequality in the US seldom leads to unambiguous absolute rankings on the basis of dominance criteria.

With these issues in mind we proceed in two steps. We first provide a set of comparisons of generalized Lorenz curves, which allow visual comparisons at all points in the distribution. We then turn to a comparison with other studies and try to draw general conclusions based on the evidence currently at hand.

We use the PPP index created by Summers and Heston (1991), to transform the distributions in Fig. 1 into a common currency under the strong assumption that the PPP conversions reflect differences in purchasing power that are either equal at all points in the distribution or, if they are not, that these differences across percentile points are the same in all countries.[30] Figures 3a–d display generalized Lorenz curves which show the mean of the cumulative distribution up to the pth percentile measured as a proportion of the US mean (rather than as a proportion of the country specific mean as shown in Figs. 1a–d). Since almost all countries have lower mean equivalent income than the US, the plots for these countries cross the vertical axis below 1. Countries with higher absolute mean equivalent incomes than the US at the bottom of the distribution have generalized Lorenz curves that start above those for the US and then cross. The point where the two functions cross shows the percentile where the mean equivalent incomes of the truncated distributions are the same in the two countries. To the left of the crossover point, households in the US have lower incomes in spite of the higher overall mean in the US. For example, the data for the US and Sweden in Fig. 3a shows that the mean equivalent income of household below the 52nd percentile is the same

[28] If the distribution of publicly provided goods was the same as the distribution of market goods then their exclusion would not affect the ranking of countries when using relative measures. They would, however, affect absolute differences across countries as long as countries differed in the amount of public provision.

[29] Dowrick and Quiggin (1994) explore the role of differences in relative prices and tasks across countries and conclude that rankings of mean incomes of countries with GDP per capita that are less than 10% apart can be easily reversed.

[30] We use the Penn World Tables Mark 5.6 for our PPPs (Summers and Heston, 1991), which translates average incomes into a common currency. Figures 3a–d are calculated by using the ratio of the US consumer price index in the given year to US 1991 CPI and multiplying this factor by the PPP given by the Penn World Tables for 1991. This factor then produces a multiplier which is used to modify all percentile point (P) of the national distributions. This is the method suggested by Summers and Heston (1991) and others for use with aggregate data. A slightly different method was used in Gottschalk and Smeeding (1997a) with largely similar results.

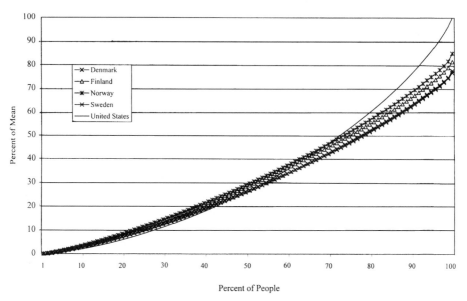

Fig. 3a. Generalized Lorenz curves for the Nordic countries and the US.

in both countries.[31] The value for $\ln(P^{50}_{\text{Sweden}}/P^{50}_{\text{US}})$ is equal to -0.19, indicating that the median family in Sweden has a level of spendable real equivalent income that is roughly 83% of the US median. However, families in the lowest 25% of the distribution have higher absolute equivalent incomes in Sweden. The crossover point for Finland is similar to that for Sweden, and for Denmark the crossover point is at the 70th percentile.

Figures 3b and c show generalized Lorenz curves for the Benelux (countries) and other European nations. In most cases the generalized Lorenz curves cut the curve for the US somewhere below the median, indicating that the median person in the US lives in a household with higher equivalent income than the median person in these countries, but persons in the lower tails of the distributions have higher absolute incomes than those in the United States in all countries other than France. For the Benelux nations, the crossover points range between the 33rd and 63rd percentiles (the Netherlands and Lux-embourg, respectively). France has lower income than the US at all points and Germany has a crossover point at the 45th percentile.

The Commonwealth nations (Fig. 3d) present a somewhat different picture. Australia cuts the US distribution at the 31st percentile, while the UK lies everywhere below the

[31] The points where the country specific plots cross the US plot and the horizontal axis should be viewed as rough indicators, not precise points since the intersection points will depend on the specific years in the LIS and other idiosyncratic differences in data discussed in the preceding footnotes. This caveat is particularly important when the two functions are flat. In this case small movements in either function will have a large effect on the crossover points. See Dowrick and Quiggin (1994).

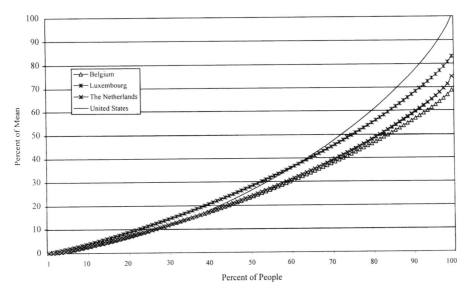

Fig. 3b. Generalized Lorenz curves for the Benelux countries and the US.

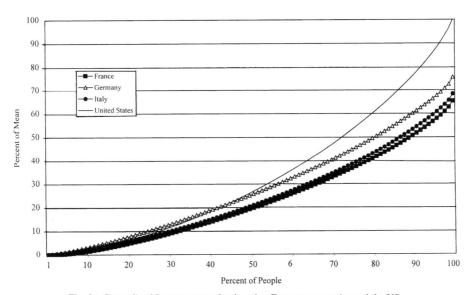

Fig. 3c. Generalized Lorenz curves for the other European countries and the US.

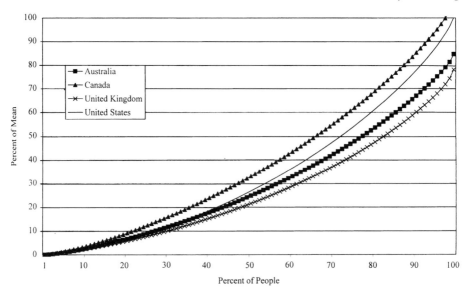

Fig. 3d. Generalized Lorenz curves for the Commonwealth countries and the US.

US. This means that real incomes are lower at all percentiles in the UK than in the US. Surprisingly these PPP conversions indicate that Canadians enjoy a higher income needs than the US at all points in the distribution (see also Wolfson and Murphy, 1998.)

3.2.4. Summary

Our data indicate a substantial gap in the real money incomes of US families in the bottom part of the income distribution compared to similarly situated families in the Nordic countries and in Luxembourg, Germany and Canada. Low income families in the US, however, have higher money incomes than comparable families in the UK and France. For the reminder of our countries the differences are too small to warrant even qualified statements.

Our results can be compared to several other studies that use different PPPs, different methods or different years.[32] For example, one early study (Atkinson, 1996) compares real income with the European Union. There is a general consensus across these studies that despite the lower mean income in the Nordic countries, incomes at the bottom of the distribution are higher, than in the US.[33] Luxembourg and Canada, likewise, stand out as countries that dominate the US at the bottom of the distribution. For other countries

---

[32] See Dalziger and Järtti (Chap. 6, this volume), Blackburn (1994), Förster (1993), Atkinson (1997b), Gottschalk and Smeeding (1997a) and Rainwater and Smeeding (1995).

[33] The single exception is Blackburn (1994) who shows poverty rates based on the US poverty line converted to Swedish kronor using PWT PPPs is twice as high in Sweden than in the US in the mid-1980s.

there is either insufficient consensus or an insufficient number of studies to warrant strong conclusions.

4. Differences in trends in inequality

Do the differences in inequality in OECD countries in the late 1980s and mid-1990s reflect convergence to a common level of inequality or are the less equal countries (the US, the UK and Australia) becoming even less equal? To answer these questions we start by comparing shorter term trends in inequality (from 1979 onwards). We then shift to longer term trends in inequality (from the 1950s through the 1970s) for a smaller number of nations.

4.1. Trend in income inequality: 1980 to 1995

Because the LIS data cover only two to four data points in each nation, we rely on published data from other sources to assess the trend in income inequality. While differences in units, income measures equivalence adjustments and other factors in different studies make it difficult to compare levels of inequality across studies, the trends will be comparable as long as differences across studies do not change over time.

The recent empirical evidence concerning trends in income inequality in different nations is summarized in Fig. 4. Countries are listed in order of yearly percentage changes in disposable income inequality (as measured by the change in the Gini coefficient) from largest to smallest change. Also shown is the absolute yearly change in the Gini over this same period.[34]

Inequality increased by more than 2% per year in one nation (the UK); and by 1% per year in three nations over this period (Sweden, the Netherlands and Australia); and from between 0.5–1.0% per year over this period in seven countries (Japan, Taiwan, the US, Switzerland, France, Germany and Norway). In four other nations (Israel, Canada, Finland and Ireland), the change was approximately zero, while in Italy inequality declined modestly.

The largest percentage changes in income distribution took place in two different countries, one that experienced large increases in earnings inequality, the UK, and one that did not, Sweden. Among the others, one had small increases in inequality of labor market income (the Netherlands), and the other (Australia), larger than average changes in earnings inequality.

---

[34] Percentage change may be misleading in cases such as Sweden or Denmark, where the base Gini is much lower than in other nations. Because we have data for different periods in different nations, we standardize by dividing by the number of years over which we measure the change. The raw data which underlies these changes and our sources for these data are presented in Appendix A2. In a few cases, notably France, Norway and Ireland, we interpolated the estimates from different time series. These are shown in Appendix A3. For many nations we have compiled three or four sets of estimates for the trend in inequality. However, because these estimates show largely the same trends, we use only the one set with the most recent estimates. The trends we find are very similar to those in OECD (1997).

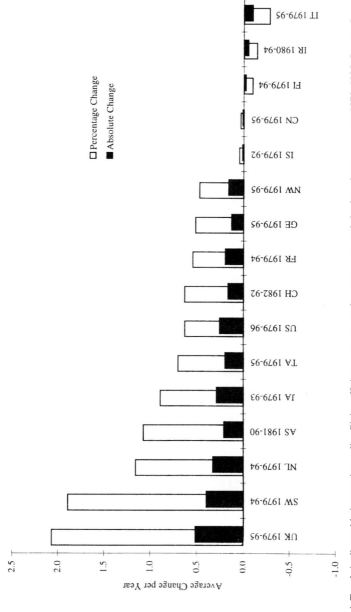

Fig. 4. Trends in disposable income inequality Gini coefficients percentage change per year and absolute change per year: 1979–1995. Source: See Appendix Tables A2 and A3.

While household income inequality increased in several countries, the timing of changes were also markedly different. In the UK income inequality fell through the mid-1970s but the Gini coefficient rose by more than 30% between 1978 and 1991, and has remained roughly constant since. This is more than double the decline in the UK from 1949 to 1976.[35] In Sweden all of the increases came since 1989; and in the Netherlands from the mid-1980s to the mid-1990s. While the large relative change in Gini in the UK might be ascribed to the fact that it started from a below average base year Gini, the absolute increase in inequality is also larger in the UK than in any other nation. The Swedish and Dutch distributions had relatively high percentage changes in their Ginis, in part because they began from a lower base Gini. But Sweden also experienced a large absolute change, second only to that found in the UK. Still, the Dutch and Swedish income distributions have remained considerably more equal than either Australia or the UK, while Australia and the Netherlands display a much smaller absolute change in their Ginis than did Sweden and the UK.

The US, Japan, Taiwan, France, Germany, Switzerland and Norway form another group of countries with moderate increases in family income inequality. Patterns of change in inequality differ across these nations as well. In the US, the largest increases in inequality occurred in the early 1980s and 1990s, peaking in 1994. In Japan and Taiwan, the largest changes were during the late 1980s, while in France, Germany and Norway, inequality did not increase until the early to mid-1990s. What is remarkable about the other five countries is that they have, so far, experienced little or no increases in the dispersion of family income. In Italy, measured income inequality has declined slightly since 1979, falling sharply between 1979 and 1991 and then rapidly increasing (see also Fig. 5c).

There also appears to be no clear relation between the trend over the 1980s and the overall level of inequality at the start of the period. Inequality increased in both the US and Australia, with a high level of inequality even before the increase, and in Sweden and the Netherlands, which started from much lower levels of inequality in the 1980s. Inequality fell by 4% in Italy but rose by 8% in France and Germany and by a third in the UK, all four occupying intermediate positions in the mid-1980s.[36] Nor is there a consistent country group story. Among the Nordic countries, Sweden (28%) experienced a rapid rise in inequality in the early 1990s, and Norway (8%) a more modest rise, while Finland (−1%) did not experience an increase. In Europe we find large secular increases in inequality in the UK and the Netherlands, but smaller increases in Germany, Switzerland and France, no increase in Ireland and a slight decline in Italy. Canada experienced no measurable increases in inequality of family income while the United States and Australia experienced much larger increases, despite similar

---

[35] Compare Karoly (1995) to Atkinson (1997a). See also Appendix A2 and Fig. 6.
[36] Changes shown in the bottom row of Appendix A2.

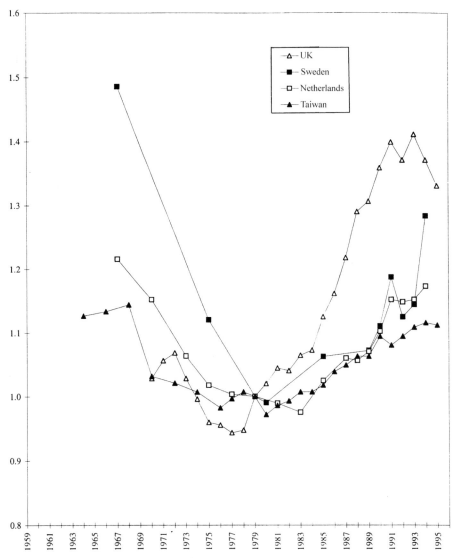

Fig. 5a. Relative Gini comparison (1979 = 100) in four nations. Source: See Appendix Table A2.

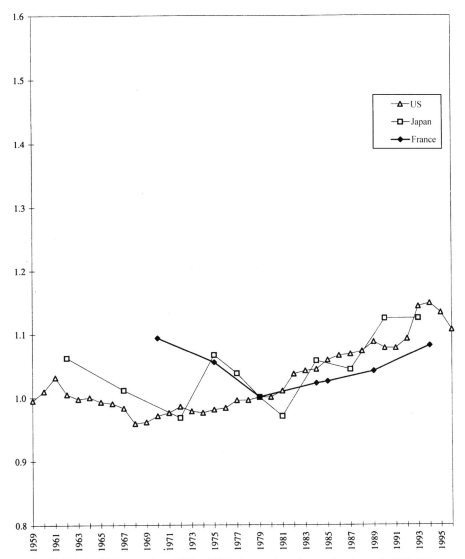

Fig. 5b. Relative Gini comparison (1979 = 100) in three nations. Source: See Appendix Table A2.

changes in earnings inequality.[37] Only in Japan and Taiwan do we find similar changes in similarly situated nations over roughly the same period.

---

[37] See also Card and Freeman (1993) on US and Canadian comparisons.

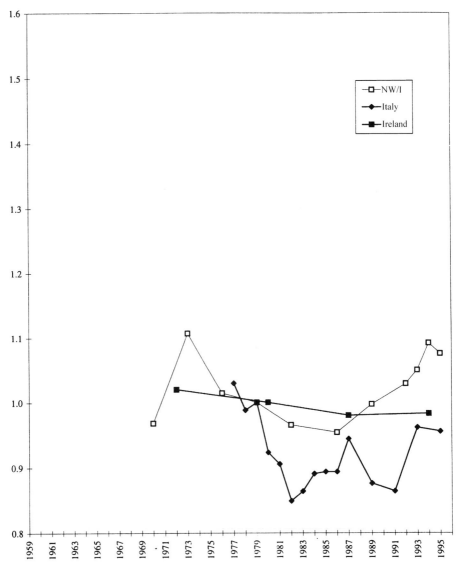

Fig. 5c. Relative Gini comparison (1979 = 100) in three nations. Source: See Appendix Table A2.

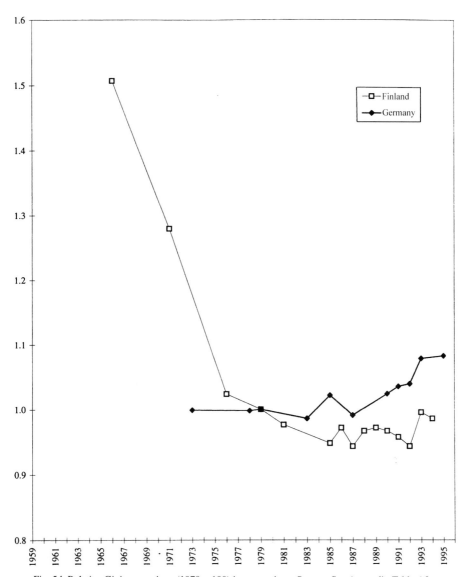

Fig. 5d. Relative Gini comparison (1979 = 100) in two nations. Source: See Appendix Table A2.

Whether, or not, the other countries will follow the trends in these nations is an open question. There is increased pressure from high unemployment and rising earnings inequality in most of the nations shown here (OECD, 1996), and very recent signs that they are having predictable effects in some nations (e.g., the Netherlands, Germany and France). Employment policy, tax and transfer policy, and other factors (e.g., increased labor force participation by married women) have so far prevented these market influences from showing up in the distribution of disposable income in some nations. Yet the pressures are building. At each stage of similar comparisons (e.g., Atkinson et al., 1995 for the early to late 1980s; Gottschalk and Smeeding, 1997 for the early 1980s through early 1990s) and now through the mid-1990s, an increasingly greater number of countries are exhibiting increases in inequality.[38] At the same time the nations which in the first comparison exhibited the largest rise in inequality (e.g., the US and UK) appear to be experiencing a plateau in those increases (see Table 6).

4.2. Longer term trends

Few nations have continuous annual data series which go back before the 1960s, and most that do have such series, have changed survey designs, income measures or other factors since that time.[39] Here, we present evidence for the US (1959–1995), the UK (1970–1995), Norway (1970–1995), Italy (1978–1995), Ireland (1971–1995), The Netherlands (1967–1994), Taiwan (1964–1995), France (1970–1994), Japan (1962–1993), Sweden (1967–1994) and Finland (1966–1994) (see Figs. 5a–d). We also present data for even longer trends for the US (1947–1995) and the UK (1949–1991) (Fig. 6).[40]

The historical literature on income distribution in the US and UK, suggests that income and wage inequality were both much more unequal in the early part of the century than in the 1960s or 1970s.[41] Atkinson (1997a) suggested that rather than continuous trends in income inequality, history is rife with various "episodes" of greater or lesser growth in inequality in many nations.[42] The 1960s and 1970s could be the aberration of low inequality with the 1980s and 1990s being more typical. Certainly the gains from the post-World War II economic recovery and boom during the 1950s and 1960s in the

---

[38] Burniaux et al. (1998, Table 2.2) reaches a similar conclusion. These find that beginning in the mid-1980s only Canada has not experienced at least a 2% increase in inequality.

[39] For a longer look at pieced together time series or older time series of estimates, see Lindert (Chap. 3, this volume) and Morrisson (Chap. 4, this volume) and Plotnick et al. (1998).

[40] We have gathered various series of inequality measures from national studies and from the Burniaux et al. (1998). These studies are based on one or more time series of data, interpolated at overlaps in some cases. See Appendices A2 and A3 for additional detail.

[41] This literature includes Williamson and Lindert (1980), Plotnick et al. (1998) and Goldin and Margo (1991), among others in the US and Lydall and Lansing (1959) and the Joseph Rowntree Foundation (1995) for the UK and US.

[42] When two or more episodes occur over the time period used to measure inequality, simply dividing by the number of years as in Fig. 4 may obscure both the magnitude and differences in trends. Hence, we present some of the trends not "smoothed" by this and technique in Fig. 6. The numerical estimates in Fig. 4 can be derived from the trends in Fig. 6.

US were more widely shared by the lowest income groups than were later changes. A similar pattern emerges for the UK[43] Was there also such a pattern in other nations?

Figures 5a–d provide some evidence of a U-shaped pattern in almost all other countries for which we have data. Each figure plots Gini coefficients for a set of countries, (with the Ginis benchmarked to 1.00 in 1979), and uses the same scaling on the vertical axes. The UK, Sweden, the Netherlands and Taiwan show very clear U-shaped profiles with the troughs coming in the late 1970s or early 1980s (Fig. 5a) and also for Norway and Italy, with troughs in the 1980s (Fig. 5c). Flatter U-shaped patterns are also apparent for the US, France and Japan (Fig. 5b) and for Ireland (Fig. 5c). Where the US stands out is in the timing of the change in inequality. While almost all other countries experienced a decline during the 1970s and a rise in the 1980s, the US reversal is a full decade earlier and quite continuous. The U- shape is just barely visible for Ireland (Fig. 5c), but seems clear for other nations in Figs. 5a–c. The lack of a U-shaped profile for Germany may be a result of our not having data prior to 1972, since it shows little change in inequality during the 1970s but a sharp increase since the mid-1980s (Fig. 5d). Finland is the only country to show a decline that is not followed by an upsurge in inequality during the 1980s and 1990s (Fig. 6d), although inequality in Finland has risen slightly since 1987.

The two nations with the longest pattern of comparable data on inequality are the US (1947–1996) and the UK (1949–1994).[44] Both series shown in Figs. 6a and 6b bear

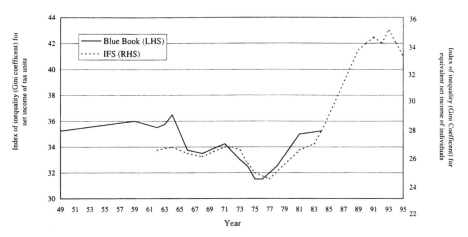

Fig. 6a. Change in income inequality in the UK. Source: Joseph Rowntree Foundation (1995), Förster (1998).

[43] Joseph Rowntree Foundation (1995).

[44] Data for each of these nations are from the US Census Bureau (Weinberg, 1996; US Bureau of the Census, 1997) and from the Joseph Rowntree Foundation Inquiry into Income and Wealth (Joseph Rowntree Foundation, 1995; Förster, 1998). Some Nordic countries may have even longer trends available, but were unobtainable by the authors or see for instance, Gustafsson and Johansson (1998) and Eriksson and Jäntti (1998).

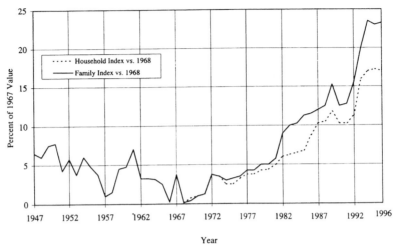

a remarkable resemblance with inequality in the UK in 1985 at the same level as 1949 and rising significantly since then before levelling out in the mid-1990s (see Fig. 6a). By the early 1980s, inequality in the US had reached 1948 levels and increased markedly before levelling out in 1994–1996. The figures in these two nations strongly suggested that the 1950s and 1960s in the US, and the late 1970s in the UK, were periods of unmatched equality.[45] The question which remains for others to answer is what were the economic demographic, institutional and policy forces which produced this pattern in each nation?[46]

5. Mobility

Thus far, we have focused on comparisons of yearly income distributions across time and countries. These, however, may be misleading since persons with low income in one year may move up the distribution in the following year. This suggests that if persons are able to smooth income across years, then a longer accounting period may be more appropriate.

The relationship between inequality of yearly income and inequality of income averaged over multiple periods depends on the full covariance structure of incomes. The relationship can be seen most easily by considering the variance of the log of average

[45] They also suggest that inequality has risen to new postwar heights in both of these nations. Only Japan also finds its current level of inequality at a post-war high. Sweden's rise in the 1990s still leaves it below the 1967 peak, as does Taiwan's rise compared to its 1967 peak (see Fig. 5a).

[46] For recent attempts at answering this question, see Burniaux et al. (1998) and Gustafsson and Johansson (1997).

income. Let, $f(Y_1, Y_2, \ldots, Y_K)$ be the joint distribution of log income across K periods. The variance of the average Y is given by:

$$
\begin{aligned}
\text{var}(\bar{Y}) &= \left[\frac{1}{K^2} \sum_{t=1}^{K} \text{var}(Y_t) + \sum_{t=1}^{K} \sum_{s \neq t} \text{cov}(Y_t Y_s) \right], \\
&= \frac{\overline{\text{var}}}{K} + \frac{K-1}{K} \overline{\text{cov}}.
\end{aligned}
\tag{5.1}
$$

where

$$
\overline{\text{var}} = \frac{1}{K} \sum^{k} \text{var}(Y_t),
$$

and

$$
\overline{\text{cov}} = \frac{1}{K^2 - K} \sum \sum \text{cov}(Y_s Y_t).
$$

The variance of multiple-period income $\text{var}(\bar{Y})$ is, therefore, a function of the average variance $(\overline{\text{var}})$ and the average of the covariances $(\overline{\text{cov}})$.[47] It can be shown that since correlations must lie between -1 and 1, the variance of multiple-period income can never be larger than the average variance of single-period income.

Equation (5.1) makes it clear that inequality of multiple year income depends on covariances as well as variances. Differences in mobility across countries may, therefore, affect comparisons of inequality based on multiple year income. Equation (5.1), however, also makes it clear that if mobility is to offset the impact of *increases* in inequality there must be a *change* in covariances. Increases in yearly inequality, as captured by increases in $\overline{\text{var}}$, must be offset by sufficiently large decreases in $\overline{\text{cov}}$ in order to keep $\text{var}(\bar{Y})$ from increasing. The extent of mobility, as captured by the level of $\overline{\text{cov}}$, is irrelevant to changes in inequality.

We first turn to a brief review of the evidence on cross- country differences in the amount of family income mobility. We then present the very limited evidence on changes in mobility. While the US has substantially more inequality than other OECD countries, it is not an outlier when it comes to mobility. Aaberge et al. (1996) compare income mobility in the US, Denmark, Norway and Sweden. In spite of their very different labor market and social institutions, these countries have remarkably similar income mobility. As a result, the ranking of countries remains unchanged when the accounting period is extended from 1 to 11 years. Likewise, Burkhauser et al. (1997) find income mobility in the US and Germany to be very similar. Evidence on earnings mobility reviewed in

---

[47] This term is an average covariance because the K by K covariance matrix has K^2 elements, K of which are variances.

OECD (1996) indicates that the US had the third lowest earnings correlation coefficient among eight countries (Denmark, Finland, France, Germany, Italy, Sweden, the UK and US) and was in the middle of the pack when countries are ranked by the proportion of persons staying in the same earnings quintile. Denmark and Finland have the most earnings mobility while Italy and Germany have the least.[48] Using the percentage reduction in inequality as a measure of mobility OECD (1997, Table 2.2) places the US again in the middle of the pack of six OECD countries.

In summary, the US is not an outlier in either earnings or family income mobility. In spite of very different social and labor market institutions the US has mobility patterns very similar to countries as diverse as the UK, Italy and Sweden. With similar mobility patterns the rankings of countries on measures of inequality are not very much affected by the length of the accounting period.

These cross-sectional comparisons are not germane to the question of trends in inequality. It is only if mobility *increased* that the *trend* in inequality could be offset by mobility. But obtaining trends in mobility requires very long panels. Since mobility itself requires income information for more than one year, changes in mobility require even longer periods. Therefore, the information on trends in mobility is very limited. Danziger and Gottschalk (1998), using over 20 years of data from the Panel Study of Income Dynamics, explored whether, or not, family income mobility changed in the US. They examined both changes in short-term mobility (changes in the probability of being in the same quintile in t and $t + 1$) and long-term mobility (changes in the probability of being in the same quintile in t and $t + 10$). None of their measures showed an increase in family income mobility. Likewise, Gottschalk and Moffitt (1995) found no evidence of increases in earnings mobility in the US. These studies, therefore, indicate that the rise in yearly inequality was not being offset by changes in mobility.

6. Summary and research implications

Our purpose was to summarize the empirical evidence on income inequality in OECD nations. Concerns about growing inequality in incomes (and also earnings and wealth inequality) have fueled social and political debates in many OECD countries. Over the past 15 years, new data resources (such as LIS) and the increased willingness of national statistical offices to furnish public-use data has provided the raw material to begin to answer some of the factual questions. And new international organizations and teams are now beginning to work improve comparability and to set practical guidelines for improved cross-national comparability.[49]

---

[48] Likewise, Burkhauser et al. found that the US has greater earnings mobility than German but similar family income mobility.

[49] These include the Canberra group (Household Income Steering Group) offices and international bodies working to improve data quality and comparability (Australian Bureau of Statistics, 1997).

While the data are by no means perfect, they produce some consistent patterns and provide answers to most of the questions posed at the beginning of this chapter. The range of income inequality in OECD countries is very wide at any point in time. The decile ratios in the most unequal country (US) is more than twice as large as that found in the most equal country (Finland) and the Gini coefficient more than half as large again.

Cross-national comparisons can be made in real as well as in relative terms. On a purely relative basis, lower income groups appear to be further from the median of the distribution in the US than in other nations.

While it is more difficult to make absolute comparisons, our data indicate that Americans at the bottom of the distribution have lower absolute as well as lower relative incomes. The higher mean does not offset the higher level of inequality, nor does income mobility in the US offset its higher level of inequality.

Income inequality has increased dramatically in a number of countries, particularly in the UK but also in the Netherlands, Denmark, Sweden, Australia and several other nations. While income inequality rose in 12 of the 17 nations examined from 1979 to 1995, this trend was not universal. In almost all countries inequality declined through the 1970s and started increasing in the mid-1980s through the mid-1990s. Thus, the increases we are seeing today are offsetting gains made during the 1960s and 1970s. Explanations of these trends and their periodicity should be high on the research agenda.

Peter Gottschalk and Timothy M. Smeeding

Appendix A1a.

Income[a] comparisons for the Nordic countries and the US

Percentile	US 1991 Nominal value	US 1991 As % of country median	Sweden 1992 Nominal value	Sweden 1992 Value in 1991 US[b]	Sweden 1992 As % of country mean	Sweden 1992 As % of US mean	Finland 1991 Nominal value	Finland 1991 Value in 1991 US[b]	Finland 1991 As % of country mean	Finland 1991 As % of US mean	Norway 1991 Nominal value	Norway 1991 Value in 1991 US[b]	Norway 1991 As % of country mean	Norway 1991 As % of US mean	Denmark 1991 Nominal value	Denmark 1991 As % of country mean	Denmark 1991 Value in 1991 US[b]	Denmark 1991 As % of US mean
5	2,403	0.6	32,824	3,545	1.2	1.0	30,919	5,071	1.7	1.4	46,987	4,934	1.6	1.3	31,261	1.2	3,439	0.9
10	3,734	2.0	48,833	5,274	3.7	2.8	38,374	6,293	4.2	3.4	60,051	6,305	4.0	3.4	47,104	3.6	5,181	2.8
15	4,691	3.8	57,926	6,256	6.6	5.0	43,477	7,130	7.1	5.8	68,391	7,181	6.8	5.8	55,468	6.3	6,101	4.9
20	5,515	5.9	64,637	6,981	9.8	7.5	47,593	7,805	10.3	8.4	75,163	7,892	10.0	8.5	61,590	9.4	6,775	7.3
25	6,272	8.4	70,190	7,580	13.3	10.2	51,037	8,370	13.8	11.3	80,985	8,503	13.4	11.4	66,720	12.7	7,339	9.9
30	6,997	11.3	75,059	8,106	17.0	13.1	54,082	8,869	17.6	14.3	86,112	9,042	17.1	14.6	71,396	16.3	7,854	12.7
35	7,683	14.5	79,393	8,574	21.0	16.1	56,868	9,326	21.5	17.6	90,741	9,528	21.1	17.9	75,812	20.2	8,339	15.7
40	8,351	18.0	83,405	9,008	25.2	19.4	59,469	9,753	25.7	21.0	95,014	9,976	25.2	21.5	80,090	24.4	8,810	19.0
45	9,014	21.8	87,173	9,415	29.7	22.8	61,889	10,150	30.1	24.6	99,026	10,398	29.6	25.2	84,170	28.9	9,259	22.4
50	9,674	26.0	90,709	9,797	34.3	26.4	64,206	10,530	34.7	28.3	102,883	10,803	34.1	29.1	88,106	33.6	9,692	26.1
55	10,341	30.6	94,111	10,164	39.1	30.1	66,468	10,901	39.5	32.3	106,662	11,200	38.9	33.1	91,879	38.5	10,107	29.9
60	11,021	35.6	97,472	10,527	44.2	34.0	68,693	11,266	44.6	36.4	110,374	11,589	44.0	37.4	95,576	43.7	10,513	33.9
65	11,715	41.0	100,838	10,890	49.5	38.1	70,912	11,630	49.9	40.7	114,087	11,979	49.2	41.9	99,200	49.1	10,912	38.2
70	12,425	46.8	104,227	11,256	55.2	42.4	73,167	11,999	55.4	45.2	117,837	12,373	54.7	46.6	102,806	54.8	11,309	42.6
75	13,159	53.1	107,673	11,629	61.0	46.9	75,459	12,375	61.2	49.9	121,686	12,777	60.6	51.6	106,426	60.8	11,707	47.2
80	13,938	60.0	111,223	12,012	67.3	51.7	77,839	12,766	67.4	54.9	128,193	13,460	70.6	60.1	110,083	67.1	12,109	52.1
85	14,775	67.6	114,990	12,419	73.9	56.8	80,379	13,182	73.9	60.3	129,924	13,642	73.3	62.4	113,855	73.7	12,524	57.3
90	15,713	76.1	119,167	12,870	81.1	62.3	83,195	13,644	81.0	66.1	134,569	14,130	80.4	68.4	117,921	80.8	12,971	62.8
95	16,839	86.1	124,072	13,400	89.1	68.5	86,585	14,200	89.0	72.6	139,976	14,698	88.3	75.1	122,624	88.7	13,489	68.9

[a] Income is adjusted disposable personal income measured at the household level. Incomes are adjusted by $E = 0.5$ where adjusted disposable personal income (DPI) = actual DPI divided by household size (s) to the power E: Adjusted DPI = DPI/s^E.

[b] Incomes were converted to US $ using PPPs derived from Penn World Table 5.6. The adjusted amounts were then inflated using the CPI-U-X1.

Appendix A1b.

Income[a] comparisons for the Benelux countries and the US

Percentile	US 1991		Belgium 1992				The Netherlands 1991				Luxembourg 1985			
	Nominal value	As % of country median	Nominal value	As % of country mean	Value in 1991 US[b]	As % of US mean	Nominal value	As % of country mean	Value in 1991 US[b]	As % of US mean	Nominal value	As % of country mean	Value in 1991 US[b]	As % of US mean
5	2,403	0.6	1,513	1.5	3,783	1.0	5,326	0.9	2,503	0.7	185,373	1.8	5,561	1.5
10	3,734	2.0	2,032	4.0	5,079	2.7	9,562	3.2	4,494	2.4	220,594	4.3	6,618	3.6
15	4,691	3.8	2,339	6.9	5,849	4.7	11,719	6.0	5,508	4.4	244,387	7.1	7,332	5.9
20	5,515	5.9	2,564	10.1	6,410	6.9	13,160	8.9	6,185	6.7	263,082	10.2	7,892	8.5
25	6,272	8.4	2,742	13.4	6,855	9.2	14,311	12.1	6,726	9.0	278,545	13.5	8,356	11.2
30	6,997	11.3	2,897	17.0	7,243	11.7	15,311	15.6	7,196	11.6	293,085	17.1	8,793	14.2
35	7,683	14.5	3,046	20.9	7,615	14.3	16,221	19.3	7,624	14.4	306,617	20.8	9,199	17.3
40	8,351	18.0	3,190	25.0	7,976	17.2	17,071	23.2	8,023	17.3	319,809	24.8	9,594	20.6
45	9,014	21.8	3,329	29.4	8,322	20.1	17,895	27.3	8,411	20.4	332,431	29.1	9,973	24.1
50	9,674	26.0	3,463	33.9	8,657	23.3	18,695	31.7	8,787	23.6	345,189	33.5	10,356	27.9
55	10,341	30.6	3,596	38.8	8,989	26.6	19,482	36.4	9,157	27.1	357,741	38.2	10,732	31.8
60	11,021	35.6	3,728	43.8	9,319	30.1	20,275	41.3	9,529	30.8	370,324	43.2	11,110	35.9
65	11,715	41.0	3,861	49.2	9,653	33.8	21,081	46.5	9,908	34.7	383,178	48.4	11,495	40.2
70	12,425	46.8	4,000	54.9	10,001	37.7	21,902	52.1	10,294	38.8	396,455	53.9	11,894	44.8
75	13,159	53.1	4,141	60.9	10,353	41.8	22,770	58.0	10,702	43.2	410,416	59.8	12,312	49.7
80	13,938	60.0	4,286	67.2	10,715	46.1	23,685	64.3	11,132	47.9	425,116	66.1	12,753	54.9
85	14,775	67.6	4,438	73.9	11,094	50.7	24,657	71.2	11,589	53.0	441,569	72.9	13,247	60.6
90	15,713	76.1	4,604	81.2	11,509	55.7	25,736	78.6	12,096	58.6	460,176	80.4	13,805	66.9
95	16,839	86.1	4,799	89.4	11,998	61.3	26,994	87.1	12,687	64.8	481,806	88.9	14,454	73.9

[a]Income is adjusted disposable personal income measured at the household level. Incomes are adjusted by $E = 0.5$ where adjusted disposable personal income (DPI) = actual DPI divided by household size (s) to the power E: Adjusted DPI = DPI/s^E.
[b]Incomes were converted to US $ using PPPs derived from Penn World Table 5.6. The adjusted amounts were then inflated using the CPI-U-X1.

Appendix A1c.

Income[a] comparisons for other European countries and the US

Percentile	US 1991 Nominal value	US 1991 As % of country median	Italy 1991 Nominal value	Italy 1991 As % of country mean	Italy 1991 Value in 1991 US[b]	Italy 1991 As % of US mean	France 1984 Nominal value	France 1984 As % of country mean	France 1984 Value in 1991 US[b]	France 1984 As % of US mean	Germany 1989 Nominal value	Germany 1989 As % of country mean	Germany 1989 Value in 1991 US[b]	Germany 1989 As % of US mean
5	2,403	0.6	4,759	1.2	3,141	0.8	4,017	0.3	767	0.2	8,064	1.5	4,097	1.1
10	3,734	2.0	6,303	3.3	4,160	2.2	12,254	1.9	2,341	1.3	10,749	3.9	5,460	2.9
15	4,691	3.8	7,233	5.6	4,774	3.9	17,966	4.2	3,432	2.8	12,349	6.7	6,273	5.1
20	5,515	5.9	7,957	8.3	5,251	5.7	22,179	7.0	4,236	4.6	13,567	9.8	6,892	7.4
25	6,272	8.4	8,582	11.1	5,664	7.6	25,541	10.0	4,878	6.6	14,558	13.2	7,396	9.9
30	6,997	11.3	9,174	14.3	6,055	9.8	28,332	13.4	5,412	8.7	15,418	16.7	7,832	12.6
35	7,683	14.5	9,750	17.7	6,435	12.1	30,821	17.0	5,887	11.1	16,199	20.5	8,229	15.5
40	8,351	18.0	10,333	21.5	6,820	14.7	33,133	20.9	6,328	13.6	16,948	24.5	8,610	18.5
45	9,014	21.8	10,913	25.5	7,203	17.4	35,299	25.0	6,742	16.3	17,658	28.7	8,970	21.7
50	9,674	26.0	11,487	29.8	7,581	20.4	37,376	29.4	7,139	19.2	18,351	33.2	9,322	25.1
55	10,341	30.6	12,063	34.5	7,962	23.6	39,398	34.1	7,525	22.3	19,032	37.8	9,668	28.6
60	11,021	35.6	12,641	39.4	8,343	26.9	41,390	39.1	7,905	25.5	19,709	42.8	10,012	32.3
65	11,715	41.0	13,234	44.7	8,734	30.5	43,397	44.4	8,289	29.0	20,400	47.9	10,363	36.2
70	12,425	46.8	13,842	50.4	9,135	34.4	45,441	50.1	8,679	32.7	21,106	53.4	10,722	40.4
75	13,159	53.1	14,474	56.4	9,553	38.5	47,543	56.1	9,081	36.6	21,841	59.2	11,095	44.8
80	13,938	60.0	15,141	62.9	9,993	43.0	49,736	62.6	9,500	40.9	23,127	68.4	11,748	52.5
85	14,775	67.6	15,865	70.1	10,471	47.9	52,093	69.7	9,950	45.5	23,478	72.2	11,927	54.5
90	15,713	76.1	16,661	77.9	10,997	53.2	54,739	77.5	10,455	50.6	24,418	79.5	12,404	60.1
95	16,839	86.1	17,608	86.9	11,621	59.4	57,877	86.5	11,054	56.5	25,541	87.7	12,975	66.3

[a]Income is adjusted disposable personal income measured at the household level. Incomes are adjusted by $E = 0.5$ where adjusted disposable personal income (DPI) = actual DPI divided by household size (s) to the power E: Adjusted DPI = DPI/s^E.

[b]Incomes were converted to US $ using PPPs derived from Penn World Table 5.6. The adjusted amounts were then inflated using the CPI-U-X1.

Appendix A1d.

Income[a] comparisons for the Commonwealth Countries

Percentile	US 1991		Australia 1989				Canada 1991				UK 1991			
	Nominal value	As % of country median	Nominal value	As % of country mean	Value in 1991 US$[b]	As % of US mean	Nominal value	As % of country mean	Value in 1991 US$[b]	As % of US mean	Nominal value	As % of country mean	Value in 1991 US$[b]	As % of US mean
5	2,403	0.6	3,297	0.9	2,815	0.8	5,138	1.1	4,311	1.2	1,925	1.1	3,100	0.8
10	3,734	2.0	4,959	2.7	4,235	2.3	6,987	3.0	5,862	3.2	2,535	2.8	4,081	2.2
15	4,691	3.8	5,976	4.9	5,103	4.1	8,330	5.3	6,989	5.6	2,903	4.8	4,674	3.8
20	5,515	5.9	6,787	7.4	5,796	6.2	9,459	8.0	7,936	8.5	3,195	7.1	5,144	5.5
25	6,272	8.4	7,501	10.2	6,406	8.6	10,414	11.0	8,738	11.8	3,469	9.6	5,585	7.5
30	6,997	11.3	8,148	13.3	6,858	11.2	11,264	14.3	9,451	15.3	3,739	12.4	6,020	9.7
35	7,683	14.5	8,758	16.6	7,479	14.1	12,056	17.9	10,115	19.0	4,010	15.6	6,455	12.2
40	8,351	18.0	9,346	20.3	7,981	17.2	12,819	21.7	10,755	23.1	4,286	19.0	6,900	14.8
45	9,014	21.8	9,926	24.2	8,477	20.5	13,550	25.8	11,369	27.5	4,562	22.8	7,345	17.8
50	9,674	26.0	10,505	28.5	8,971	24.1	14,264	30.2	11,967	32.2	4,843	26.9	7,797	21.0
55	10,341	30.6	11,089	33.1	9,470	28.0	14,971	34.9	12,560	37.2	5,128	31.3	8,256	24.4
60	11,021	35.6	11,690	38.1	9,983	32.2	15,684	39.9	13,159	42.5	5,420	36.1	8,726	28.2
65	11,715	41.0	12,306	43.4	10,509	36.8	16,414	45.2	13,771	48.2	5,720	41.2	9,209	32.2
70	12,425	46.8	12,940	49.2	11,050	41.6	17,154	50.9	14,392	54.2	6,032	46.8	9,712	36.6
75	13,159	53.1	13,600	55.3	11,614	46.9	17,923	57.0	15,037	60.7	6,363	52.9	10,245	41.3
80	13,938	60.0	14,293	62.0	12,206	52.5	18,730	63.5	15,715	67.6	6,720	59.6	19,819	46.6
85	14,775	67.6	15,042	69.4	12,846	58.7	19,600	70.6	16,444	75.2	7,113	67.1	11,451	52.4
90	15,713	76.1	15,864	77.5	13,548	65.6	20,569	78.5	17,257	83.6	7,547	75.3	12,150	58.8
95	16,839	86.1	16,828	86.7	14,371	73.5	21,702	87.4	18,208	93.1	8,062	84.9	12,979	66.3

[a] Income is adjusted disposable personal income measured at the household level. Incomes are adjusted by $E = 0.5$ where adjusted disposable personal income (DPI) = actual DPI divided by household size (s) to the power E: Adjusted DPI = DPI/s^E.

[b] Incomes were converted to US $ using PPPs derived from Penn World Table 5.6. The adjusted amounts were then inflated using the CPI-U-X1.

Appendix A2
Relative gini coefficients (1979 = 100)

Year	US	JA	UK	NW/I	FI	SW	GE	FR/I	CN	DK	NL	IT	IR/I	CH	IS	TA	AS
1959	0.9951																1.0730
1960	1.0097																
1961	1.0316																1.0280
1962	1.0049	1.0623															
1963	0.9976																1.0000
1964	1.0000																1.1263
1965	0.9927																
1966	0.9903					1.5071											
1967	0.9830	1.0111										1.2155					1.1333
1968	0.9586						1.4856										1.1439
1969	0.9611																
1970	0.9708		1.028	0.9682													1.0316
1971	0.9757		1.057						1.0934	1.0507							
1972	0.9854	0.9679	1.069			1.2796				1.0366		1.1519					1.0211
1973	0.9781		1.028	1.1069				0.9988		1.0366				1.0200			
1974	0.9757		0.996				1.1202			1.0225		1.0636					
1975	0.9805	1.0664	0.960						1.0549	1.0254							1.0070
1976	0.9830		0.956	1.0145		1.0237				1.0535		1.0177					0.9825
1977	0.9951	1.0373	0.944					0.9980		1.0197		1.0035	1.0296				0.9965
1978	0.9951		0.948							1.0338			0.9882			1.0000	1.0070
1979	1.0000	1.0000	1.000	1.0000		1.0000	1.0000	1.0000	1.0000	1.0000		1.0000	1.0000	1.0000			1.0000
1980	1.0000		1.020				0.9904			1.0085			0.9231				0.9719
1981	1.0097	0.9701	1.044			0.9763				0.9887	1.0000	0.9894	0.9053				0.9860
1982	1.0365		1.040	0.9653				0.9858		0.9944	0.9864		0.8491		1.0000	0.9930	1.0070
1983	1.0414		1.065							1.0225	0.9773	0.9753	0.8639				1.0070
1984	1.0438	1.0574	1.073			0.9479	1.0625		1.0220	1.0113	0.9955		0.8905				1.0175
1985	1.0584		1.125	0.9538		0.9716		1.0217	1.0250	1.0085	1.0045	1.0247	0.8935				1.0386
1986	1.0657		1.161			0.9431				1.0113	1.0045		0.8935			1.0188	1.0491
1987	1.0681	1.0438	1.218			0.9668		0.9909		1.0056	1.0182	1.0601	0.9438	0.9800			1.0632
1988	1.0730		1.290	0.9971		0.9716	1.0721	1.0240		1.0000	1.0545	1.0565					
1989	1.0876		1.307			0.9668	1.1106	1.0354		0.9915	1.0636	1.0707	0.8757				1.0632
1990	1.0779	1.1244	1.359			0.9573	1.1875	1.0394	1.0410	0.9915	1.1136	1.1025					1.0947
1991	1.0779		1.359			0.9431	1.1250			1.0056		1.1519	0.8639		1.0632		1.0807
1992	1.0925		1.367	1.0289		0.9953	1.1442	1.0787		1.0028		1.1484		0.9830		1.0063	1.0947
1993	1.1436	1.1250	1.339	1.0500		0.9858	1.2837	1.0827	1.0820	1.0085		1.1519	0.9615				1.1088
1994	1.1484		1.339	1.0920						0.9972							1.1158
1995	1.1338		1.310	1.0760						1.0056		1.1731	0.9556				1.1123
1996	1.1071																

Sources: US: US Census Bureau (1997); JA: Ishikawa (1996); UK: Goodman and Webb (1994) and as updated by Institute for Fiscal Studies (1999); NW/I: Interpolated series: See Appendix A3; FI: Uusitalo (1996); SW: Statistics Sweden (1997); GE: Hauser and Becker (1994); Gottschalk and Smeeding (1997b); FR/I: Interpolated series: See Appendix A3; CN: Statistics Canada (1996); DK: Aagerge et al. (1996); NL: Epland (1997); IT: Gottschalk and Smeeding (1997b); IR/I: Interpolated series: See Appendix A3; IT: Brandolini and Sestito (1997); IR/I: Interpolated series: See Appendix A3; CH: Stoyko (1997); IS: Gottschalk and Smeeding (1997a); TA: Gottschalk and Smeeding (1997a); AS: LIS (1998).

Appendix A3

	NW/I	NW	NW/2	FR/I	FR	FR/2	IR/I	IR	IR/2
1959									
1960									
1961									
1962									
1963									
1964									
1965									
1966									
1967									
1968									
1969									
1970	0.9682	0.9682		1.0934	1.0934				
1971									
1972							1.0200	1.0200	
1973	1.1069	1.1069							
1974									
1975				1.0549	1.0549				
1976	1.0145	1.0145							
1977									
1978									
1979	1.0000	1.0000		1.0000	1.0000				
1980							1.0000	1.0000	
1981									
1982	0.9653	0.9653							
1983									
1984				1.0220	1.0220	1.0000			
1985				1.0250		1.0032			
1986	0.9538	0.9538	1.0000						
1987			1.0043				0.9800	0.9800	1.0000
1988	0.9701								
1989	0.9971	0.9971	1.0470	1.0412	1.0412	1.0195			
1990			1.0299						
1991			1.0427						
1992	1.0289	1.0289	1.0385						
1993	1.0500		1.0598						
1994	1.0920		1.1026	1.0820		1.0584	0.9830		1.0031
1995	1.0760		1.0855						
1996									

Sources: NW/I: Interpolated series: Gottschalk and Smeeding (1997b), Epland (1997); NW: Gottschalk and Smeeding (1997b); NW/2: Epland (1997); FR/I: Interpolated series: Gottschalk and Smeeding (1997b), Förster (1998); FR: Gottschalk and Smeeding (1997a), Atkinson (1997b); FR/2: Förster (1998); IR/I: Interpolated series; Gottschalk and Smeeding (1997b), Atkinson (1997b); IR: Gottschalk and Smeeding (1997b); IR/2: Atkinson (1997b).

References

Aaberge, R., A. Björklund, M. Jäntti, M. Palmer, P.J. Pedersen, N. Smith and T. Wennemo (1996), Income Inequality and Income Mobility in the Scandinavian Countries Compared to the United States (Abo Akademi University, Turku, Finland).

Atkinson, A.B. (1993), What is happening to the distribution of income in the UK? Proceedings of the British Academy 82: 317–351.

Atkinson, A.B. (1996), Income distribution in Europe and the United States, Oxford Review of Economic Policy, Spring: 15–28.

Atkinson, A.B. (1997a), Bringing income distribution in from the cold, Presidential address to the Royal Economic Society, United Kingdom, mimeo, Oxford.

Atkinson, A.B. (1997b), Measurement of trends in poverty and the income distribution, DAE Working Paper No. MU9701, Amalgamated Series No. 9712 (University of Cambridge, Cambridge, UK), May.

Atkinson, A.B., L. Rainwater and T.M. Smeeding (1995), Income Distribution in OECD Countries: The Evidence from the Luxembourg Income Study (LIS) (OECD, Paris).

Australian Bureau of Statistics (1997), Papers and Final Report of the Canberra Group on Household Income Statistics (Australian Bureau of Statistics Canberra, Australia).

Bell, C. and C.B. Rosenberg (1993), Combining consistency with simplicity when estimating tax incidence: alternative assumptions and findings for three countries, Luxembourg Income Study Working Paper #102 (LIS, Luxembourg, September).

Blackburn, M.L. (1994), International comparisons of poverty, American Economic Review 84(2): 371–374.

Bourguignon, F. and M. Martinez (1996), Decomposition of the change in the distribution of primary family incomes: a microsimulation approach applied to France, 1979–1989, mimeo, May.

Brandolini, A. and P. Sestito (1997), La distribuzione dei redditi familiari in Italia, 1977–1991, Servizio Studi, Banca d'Italia.

Buhmann, B., L. Rainwater, G. Schmaus and T.M. Smeeding (1988), Equivalence scales, well-being, inequality, and poverty: sensitivity estimates across ten countries using the Luxembourg Income Study (LIS) database, Review of Income and Wealth 34: 115–142.

Burkhauser, R.V., A.D. Crews, M.C. Daly and S.P. Jenkins (1996), Where in the world is the middle class? A cross-national comparison of the shrinking middle class using kernel density estimates, Cross-National Studies in Aging Program Project Paper No. 26, All-University Gerontology Center, The Maxwell School (Syracuse University, Syracuse, NY).

Burkhauser, R.V., D. Holtz-Eakin and S. Rhody (1997), Labor earnings mobility and inequality in the United States and Germany during the 1980s, International Economic Review 38(4): 775–794.

Burniaux, J.-M., T.-T. Dang, D. Fore, M. Förster, M. Mirad'Ercole and H. Oxley (1998), Income distribution and poverty in selected OECD countries, Economics Department Working Paper No. 189, March (OECD, Paris).

Callan, T. and B. Nolan (1993), Income inequality and poverty in Ireland in the 1970s and 1980s, ESRI Working Paper No. 43 (ESRI, Dublin).

Card, D. and R. Freeman (eds.) (1993). Small Differences that Matter (University of Chicago Press, Chicago).

Concialdi, P. (1996), Income distribution in France: The mid-1980s turning point, in: P. Gottschalk, B. Gustaffsson and E. Palmer, eds., The Distribution of Economic Welfare in the 1980s (Cambridge University Press, Cambridge).

Coulter, F., F.A. Cowell and S.P. Jenkins (1992), Equivalence scale relativities and the extend of inequality and poverty, Economic Journal 102(1): 1067–1082.

Danziger, S. and P. Gottschalk (1995), American Unequal (Harvard University Press, Cambridge, MA).

Danziger, S. and P. Gottschalk (1998), Family income mobility—how much is there and has it changed? in J. Auerbach and R. Belano, eds., The Inequality Paradox Growth of Income Disparity (National Policy Association, Washington, DC).

Dowrick, S. and J. Quiggin (1994), International comparisons of living standards and tastes: a revealed preference analysis, American Economic Review 84(10): 332–341.

Epland, J. (1997), Income distribution, 1986–1995: why is inequality increasing? Economic Survey 3/97 (Statistics Norway, Oslo, Norway).

Epland, J. (1992), Inntektsfordelingen i 80-(Erene, Konimiske Analyser 2: 17–26.

Eriksson, T. and M Jäntti (1998). Explaining the distribution of income in the long run: changes in family structure and other socio-economic factors in Finland 1920–1992. Presented to the 25th General Conference of the International Association for Research on Income and Wealth (Cambridge, United Kingdom), 27 August.

Fichtenbaum, R. and H. Shahidi (1988), Truncation bias and the measurement of income inequality, Journal of Business and Economic Statistics 6(3): 335–337.

Förster, M. (1993), Poverty in OECD countries, OECD Social Policy Studies No. 10 (OECD, Paris).

Förster, M. (1998), Notes on PPP comparisons, mimeo (OECD, Paris).

Freeman, R. and L. Katz (1993), Rising water inequality: the United States vs. other advanced countries, in R. Freeman, ed., Working Under Different Rules (Russell Sage Foundation, New York), pp. 29–62.

Fukui, T. (1996), Outline of household income statistics in Japan, mimeo Statistics Bureau (Management and Coordination Aging, Tokyo, Japan), November.

Gardiner, K., J. Hills, J. Falkingham, H. Sutherland and V. Lechene (1995), The effects of differences in housing and health care systems on international comparisons of income distribution, Welfare State Programme Discussion Paper No. 110, STICERD (London School of Economics), July.

Goldin, C. and R. Margo (1991), The great compression: The wage structure in the U.S. at mid-century, NBER Working Paper No. 3817 (National Bureau of Economic Research, Cambridge, MA).

Goodman, A. and S. Webb (1994), For richer, for poorer, Institute for Fiscal Studies Commentary No. 42 (Institute for Fiscal Studies, London).

Gottschalk, P. and R. Moffitt (1995), Trends in the autocovariance structure of earnings in the U.S.: 1969–1987, July.

Gottschalk, P., B. Gustaffson and E. Palmer (1996), What's behind the increase in inequality? in The Distribution of Economic Well-Being in the 1980s (Cambridge University Press, Oxford).

Gottschalk, P. and T. Smeeding (1997a), Crossnational comparisons of earnings and income inequality, Journal of Economic Literature XXXV: 633–686.

Gottschalk, P.A. and T.M. Smeeding (1997b), Empirical evidence on income/inequality, Luxembourg Income Study Working Paper No. 154, Center for Policy Research, The Maxwell School (Syracuse University, Syracuse, NY).

Gustafsson, B. and M. Johansson (1997), In search for a smoking gun; What makes inequality vary over time in different countries? LIS Working Paper #172 (Luxembourg Income Study, Syracuse University, Syracuse, NY), November.

Gustafsson, B. and M. Johansson (1998). Was Sweden equal before the rapid growth of the welfare state? Findings from Microdata for the City of Göteborg. Presented to the 25th General Conference, International Association for Research in Income and Wealth, (Cambridge, United Kingdom), 27 August.

Hauser, R. and I. Becker (1993), The development of the income distribution in the Federal Republic of Germany during the seventies and eighties, Cross-National Studies in Aging Program Project Paper No. 14, All-University Gerontology Center, The Maxwell School (Syracuse University, Syracuse, NY).

Institute for Fiscal Studies (1999), Updated series for Goodman and Webb, as provided by A.B. Atkinson, 20 January.

Ishikawa, T. (1996), Data runs conducted by Ministry of Welfare, 26 November.

Jenkins, S. (1991), The measurement of income inequality, in L. Osberg, ed., Economic Inequality and Poverty (M.E. Sharpe, Inc., Armonk, NY), pp. 3–38.

Jenkins, S.P. (1994). Earnings distribution measurement: A distributional approach, Journal of Econometrics 61(1): 81–102.

Jenkins, S.P. and F.A. Cowell (1994), Dwarfs and giants in the 1980s: trends in the UK income distribution, Fiscal Study 15(1): 99–118.

Joseph Rowntree Foundation (1995), Inquiry into Income and Wealth, Volume 1 (Joseph Rowntree Foundation, York, UK).

Karoly, L.A. (1995), Anatomy of the United States Income Distribution: Two Decades of Change, mimeo (RAND, Santa Monica, CA), September.

Karoly, L.A. and G. Burtless (1995), Demographic change, rising earnings inequality and the distribution of personal well-being, 1959–1989, Demography 32(3): 379–405. Luxembourg Income Study (LIS) (1998), Authors' calculations from the Luxembourg Income Study database.

Lydall, H. and J. Lansing (1959). A comparison of the distribution of personal income and wealth in the United States and Great Britain, American Economic Review 149: 43–67.

Organization for Economic Cooperation and Development (1996), Employment Outlook (OECD, Paris), July.

Organization for Economic Cooperation and Development (1997), Employment Outlook (OECD, Paris), July.

Plotnick, R. and E. Smolensky, E. Evenhouse, and S. Reilly (1998), Inequality poverty and the Fisc in twentieth century America, Journal of Post-Keynesian Economies, 21(1): 51–76.

Rainwater, L. and T.M. Smeeding (1995), Doing poorly: the real income of American children in a comparative perspective, Luxembourg Income Study Working Paper No. 127, Center for Policy Research, The Maxwell School (Syracuse University, Syracuse, NY).

Ryscavage, P. (1995). A surge in growing income inequality, Monthly Labor Review, 118(8): 51–61.

Saunders, P. (1994), Rising on the Tasman tide: income inequality in Australia and New Zealand in the 1980s, SPRC Discussion Paper No. 49 (University of New South Wales).

Sen, A. (1992), Inequality Reexamined (Harvard University Press, Cambridge, MA).

Smeeding, T.M. (1996), America's income inequality: where do we stand? Challenge (September/October).

Smeeding, T.M. (1997), American income inequality in a cross-national perspective: why are we different, Luxembourg Income Study Working Paper, Center for Policy Research, The Maxwell School (Syracuse University, Syracuse, NY), February.

Smeeding, T.M. and P. Gottschalk (forthcoming), The international evidence on income distribution in modern economies: Where do we stand? in M. Bruno and Y. Mundlab, eds., Contemporary Economic Development Reviewed (MacMillan, London and New York).

Smeeding, T. and D. Weinberg (1998), Toward a uniform household income definition, Paper presented to the Canberra Group meeting on Household Income Measurement (Den Hague, the Netherlands), 10 March.

Smeeding, T.M., P. Saunders, J. Coder, S. Jenkins, J. Fritzell, A. Hagenaars, R. Hauser and M. Wolfson (1993), Poverty, inequality, and family living standard impacts across seven nations: The effect of noncash subsidies, Review of Income and Wealth 39(3): 229–256.

Statistics Canada (1996), Income after tax, distribution by size, Catalogue No. 13-210, Table VIII (Statistics Canada, Ottawa).

Statistics Sweden (1997), As provided by Kjell Janssons, September.

Summers, R. and A. Heston (1991), The Penn World Table (mark 5): an expanded set of international comparisons, 1950–1989, Quarterly Journal of Economics 105(2): 327–368.

Sutherland, H. (1996), EUROMOD: A New Microsimulation Project, mimeo (Cambridge, United Kingdom).

UN (1977), Provision Guidelines for the Distribution of Consumption, Income and Household Wealth (United Nations, Geneva).

US Census Bureau (1997), Money income in the United States: 1996 (US Government Printing Office, Washington, DC).

US Department of Commerce, Census Bureau (1995), Special tabulations of LIS disposable income, 1979–1993 (US Government Printing Office, Washington, DC).

US Department of Commerce, Census Bureau (1996), Money income in the United States: 1995, Current Population Reports, Series P-60, No. 193 (US Government Printing Office, Washington, DC).

Uusitalo, H. (1996), Changes in Income Distribution during a Deep Recession, mimeo (Finnish Trade Council), August.

Verma, V. (1998), Robustness and comparability in income distribution statistics, Paper prepared for the EU Think-Tank meeting on Poverty Statistics (Stockholm, Sweden), January.

Weinberg, D. (1996), A brief look at postwar US income inequality, Current Population Reports, Series P-60, No. 191 (US Census Bureau, Washington, DC), June.

Whiteford, P. and S. Kennedy (1994), The incomes and living standards of older people: a comparative analysis, Final Report, Vols. I and II, DSS 1211, Social Policy Research Unit (University of York, UK), August.

Williamson, J.G. and P. Lindert (1980), American Inequality: A Macroeconomic History (Academic Press, New York).

Wolfson, M. and B. Murphy (1998), New views of inequality trends in Canada and the United States, Monthly Labor Review 121(4): 3–23.

Chapter 6

INCOME POVERTY IN ADVANCED COUNTRIES

MARKUS JÄNTTI[a] and SHELDON DANZIGER[b]

[a]*Åbo Akademi University;* [b]*University of Michigan*

Contents

Handbook of Income Distribution: Volume 1. Edited by A.B. Atkinson and F. Bourguignon

Abstract

This chapter reviews definitional issues that arise in assessing the extent of, and change in, poverty in western industrialized countries, including the choice of resource, level of poverty line and appropriate adjustments for the size and type of the income-sharing unit. The chapter also reviews the existing empirical evidence and presents estimates using the Luxembourg Income Study database. The first-order iimpact of the public sector suggests that countries with similar rates of market income poverty can have very different poverty rates once taxes and transfers have been received. Cross-national evidence on longitudinal aspects of poverty suggests that much remains to be learned about the patterns of intra- and intergenerational poverty mobility and their covariates.

Keywords: Poverty measurement, poverty dominance, statistical inference, poverty orderings, poverty trends, taxes and transfers, integrational mobility

JEL codes. I32, D31, D63, H23, C43

1. Introduction

The living standard of the least well-off members of society—industrialized or not—concerns public policy and ethical interest. One way to examine differences between societies in this respect is to study the extent and severity of income poverty between countries and over time. While poverty can be thought of in many different ways, examining income poverty has a long tradition. This chapter reviews issues that arise in studying economic poverty in industrialized countries and examines evidence on their ranking according to poverty and its changes over time.

We review conceptual issues in Section 2. We discuss the measurement of resources, comparisons between different types of units, and what kinds of comparisons between different populations can be made. We also discuss the role of time, income sharing assumptions and the aggregation of poverty information. In Section 3, we discuss domestic evidence on poverty before turning to evidence drawn from the Luxembourg Income Study (LIS) on the incidence of relative poverty and its evolution over time. We then examine poverty orderings of countries using dominance criteria, studying the ordering by increasingly demanding conditions, and using both the poverty standard of each country and a common poverty line for all countries. We then move to examine in Section 4 the ordering of countries, using similar methods, for selected demographic subgroups of the population: children, the elderly and persons living in female-headed households.

In Section 5 we examine briefly the role of the public sector in terms of differences between market income and disposable income poverty rates, measured using the LIS. In Section 6 we examine longitudinal evidence on poverty, show some cross-national evidence on the patterns of intragenerational poverty mobility and persistence, and briefly discuss intergenerational poverty. A concluding section summarizes.

2. Conceptual and practical issues in the definition of poverty

We begin by addressing key conceptual issues concerning the measurement of poverty. These include the space of poverty measurement, poverty lines, the income definition, the income-sharing definition, and the method of aggregation. We discuss the types of poverty comparisons that can be made, with what type of evidence and data sources, including issues, such as purchasing power parities (PPP), deflators and choices of poverty lines in inter-country comparisons.

2.1. *A conceptual model of household income formation and poverty*

The process by which individuals form households and pool incomes involves several economic behaviors, including the labor supply of its members, their wage rates, educational attainments, unobservable characteristics, such as ability, motivation, etc., the mechanisms that affect mating behavior, fertility, and their responses to public policies (taxes, transfers, support of education, health care, etc.). Given all of these behaviors, the likelihood that a given individual in a given household will be poor is also affected by income- sharing patterns within the household, decision-making mechanisms, household production technology and the level of the poverty line (something that in turn is determined by a great number of factors).

No empirical economic analysis of income poverty can incorporate all of these behaviors. Any analysis takes many of the behavioral factors as given, either for analytical tractability or because of data limitations. For many questions, however, analysis of only some aspects of poverty will suffice. In particular, assessing the extent of poverty and its evolution over time requires the resolution of a different set of issues than evaluating how a policy change affected the likelihood of being poor.

Figure 1 sketches out some of these issues. We denote flows of persons (solid arrows) and money flows (uni- and bi-directional dashed lines) between parts of the population and social institutions. We have not incorporated the additional (and complicated) class of arrows that specify what kind of influences on behavior are present.

Population

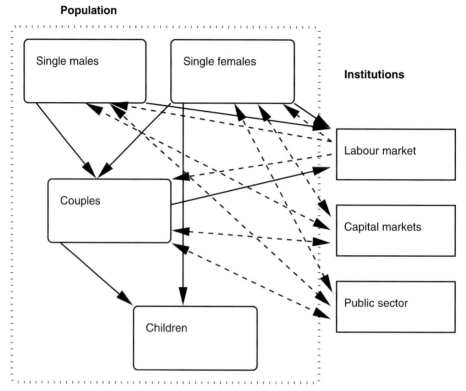

Fig. 1. Household formation and labor supply. Groups within the population and social institutions are drawn as boxes. Solid arrows denote flows of persons and uni- and bi-directional dashed arrow denote money flows.

The schema makes apparent that any aspect of policy, such as the tax system, can affect poverty in many ways. Economists often analyze the extent to which persons participate in the labor market and how certain factors affect that behavior. Two factors have been emphasized in numerous studies, namely how household members' labor supply is affected by money flows between individuals and households and the public sector. First, taxes flow from households to the public sector. Second, transfers flow from the public sector to households. Most studies focus on only one flow, say taxes, and how it affects the behavior of a population subgroup—-men, married men, married women, or so on. Other studies focus on the labor supply effects (or, say, job search effects) of transfers, such as unemployment benefits on unemployed men, or of welfare benefits on the labor force participation of single mothers.

Studies of the behavioral effects of public policies are reviewed in Section 5 and Chapter 9 of this volume. Such studies often document negative, often small, consequences on labor supply of high marginal tax rates or transfer payments. These studies, however, tend to neglect any assessment of the potential beneficial effects of social transfer payments. For example, Atkinson and Mogensen (1993) note that possible labor supply reductions that arise from redistributive taxes and transfers should be weighed against their enhancement of other goals, such as the avoidance of social exclusion Atkinson and Mogensen (1993) or the promotion of social cohesion and preservation of individual dignity (Barr, 1993).

2.2. Definitions of poverty

A recurring theme in poverty research is whether poverty should be defined as a relative or an absolute concept. Although the literature is voluminous (see, e.g., Sen, 1983, 1985; Townsend, 1985), a consensus has eluded us.

To fully distinguish between *relative* and *absolute* concepts of poverty requires substantial information. A relative view is typically one in which the rules for identifying the poor change as (some) other economic conditions change. Thus, one might assume that an absolute view of poverty would remain unchanged, regardless of any changes in economic conditions. However, many changes force us to redefine an absolute view of poverty, such as, changes in monetary systems, the industrial revolution and so on.

An "absolute" notion of poverty is fixed in terms of the relevant spaces at some point in time and, from that time on fixed in "absolute" terms in some space. If the relevant space is real income, then an absolute view implies a poverty line that is fixed in real terms (as well as one that holds constant a host of other things, e.g., equivalence scales). Although "absolute" is often treated as if it meant "fixed real income", a constant real income standard is not the only possible absolute notion. Indeed, this very point is made by Sen (1983) in discussing what it takes to enable the same functioning in two very different societies.

There are countless ways in which we could "fix" an absolute measure of poverty. For instance, the U.S. National Research Council (1995) suggests that the *rules* by which the poverty line, as well as the equivalence scales, were arrived at could be kept constant. This "absolute" poverty standard differs from the official US definition, which fixes the line in real terms, regardless of what the rules used to first define the line might imply under current conditions. However, in common parlance, a poverty concept is considered to be absolute as long as it does not vary with changes in real economic conditions.[1]

2.3. The space for poverty measurement

Poverty measurement requires criteria by which to: (i) *identify* who is poor, and (ii) *aggregate* the information. To identify the poor, the space(s) in which to define and

[1] For additional references and discussion, see, among others, Sen (1979, 1983, 1992), Hossain (1990), Atkinson (1989), Hagenaars (1986), Hagenaars and van Praag (1985), National Research Council (1995), Townsend (1979), Townsend (1985), van Praag (1993), Nolan and Whelan (1996b), Ringen (1987), Hagenaars and de Vos (1988) and Kapteyn, Kooreman and Willemse (1988).

analyze poverty must be specified. Economists typically analyze the space of income, expenditure or possession of certain material goods. Examples of the resource measure used to distinguish between poor and nonpoor households include these, singly or in combination:

1. (disposable cash) income
2. consumer expenditure
3. consumption
4. earnings capacity (Haveman and Buron, 1993b)
5. subjective poverty/perceived poverty (Hagenaars, 1986)
6. wealth
7. choice sets (Le Grand, 1991)
8. utility
9. capabilities (Sen, 1979, 1983, 1992; Hossain, 1990).

The selection of a definition of resources is related to two other issues: (i) which resources are relevant to economic well-being, and (ii) who is counted as being poor. Poverty is seen as being either *socially deprived* or as being *socially excluded*.

A decision about the choice of resources can be viewed in terms of the *space* for poverty measurement. Should poverty be defined in the space of income, earnings capacity or utility? Thinking in terms of the correct or ideal space for poverty measurement forces us to be consistent (or reveals the lack of consistency). It seems appropriate, for instance, to both *identify* the poor and *aggregate* the relevant information in the same space or explain why this is not done.[2] Second, to talk in terms of spaces also makes relevant what kind of ethical view we hold.

Our ideal choice of space might differ from the one we *can* empirically use. For instance, we might consider lifetime utility as the ethically-relevant choice for measuring poverty, but we might have to utilize a multi-year (but not lifetime) income average to implement our measure. The extent to which our orderings in the conceptual space correspond to those in the measured spaces is debatable.

The idea of well-being and poverty as capability (see, e.g., Sen, 1992) suggests that in comparing the well-being of individuals, we should analyze not only what they *have* (material goods, or income) but also what they *do*, and what they *can* do.[3]

Possession or control over material goods, services and income does not necessarily tell us what people can do with them. Ownership of a car enables certain types of *functionings*, such as travel to work or vacationing. Even if we *choose* not to use the car during our vacation, we could have done so. Sen defines this particular functioning as within our *capabilities*. If, however, we have no vacation, our having the car would make no difference. The functioning "vacation" would not be part of our capabilities.

---

[2] As a counter example, Haveman and Buron (1993a) examine the lower part of the distribution of earnings capacity, defining a different poverty space, but then define their aggregate poverty population as the same proportion of the population that is income poor.

[3] See Chapter 1 in this volume.

In this approach, what matters are our *potential* functionings. Social functionings are as central as private ones. A person whose resources prevent him from participating in society on a minimally acceptable basis has, in this sense, a limited set of capabilities.

The concept of functionings clarifies some aspects of the relative/absolute debate on the nature of poverty. The means to achieve some particular functioning generally varies with physical and social circumstances. A well-known example, due to Adam Smith, is the "ability to appear in public without shame".[4] This basic functioning required possession of very different material goods in the Roman Empire than in eighteenth century Britain. What in the space of functionings is absolute—to be without shame—is associated with material goods that vary with the social context. This absolute notion of functionings requires that the space of material goods be considered relative.

The achievement of functionings, thus defined, depends on the goods and services to which we have access, the society in which we live and our inherent abilities. These abilities may change over time and may depend on our resources and other functioning achievements. Literacy, for instance, is both a valuable functioning and a means to achieve other functionings. One possible adverse consequence of being poor is that it may diminish our capacity for functioning.[5]

According to Sen (1992), poverty is a state characterized by levels of capabilities that are, in the view of society, unacceptably low. What unacceptably low means is not defined precisely. That a person has low income is not a sufficient indicator of poverty. Income is one type of economic means to achieve higher levels of capabilities, and very low income can contribute to unacceptably low levels of capabilities. However, people with above average abilities may function well at low levels of income, while those with greater needs (e.g., for wheelchairs) may need higher incomes to achieve the same functionings. Analysis of income alone reveals only part of the extent to which people have capabilities below acceptable levels. An analysis of well-being based on the private possession of certain goods, such as automobiles, also requires consideration of the social context. For instance, possession of automobiles might increase without a corresponding increase in the number of persons having the functioning of travel to work, if the increased possession of automobiles just substitutes for declining public transport. In this case, only the same functionings can be achieved even though possessions have changed.

We now turn to the *space* in which poverty in practice is measured (Sen, 1983). Although poverty is a complex and multidimensional phenomenon, with some notable exceptions (e.g., Townsend, 1979; Mack and Lansley, 1985; Halleröd, 1995; Kangas and Ritakallio, 1995), most authors examine only income. Even the Dutch and Belgian "subjective" approaches (Deleeck et al., 1992; Hagenaars and van Praag, 1985) are ways

---

[4] The example is discussed, e.g., in Sen (1992: 115).

[5] Presumably, such problems become worse as the duration of poverty becomes longer. Long-term poverty would in this view be bad because poverty is by itself bad and being poor for a long time diminishes the individual's resources, such as the self-confidence, necessary to function well socially.

to revise the position of the poverty line and the cardinality of the equivalence scale, rather than ways to reflect the multi-dimensionality of poverty.

How might the choice of space matter in practice? Consider, for example, poverty measured in four different ways in Belgium and Ireland using the exact same data. In Fig. 2, from Deleeck et al. (1992), all four definitions are based on household income. Two definitions involve subjective approaches to determining the poverty cut-off (CSP and SPL), whereas the other two are based on a legislative definition (Legal) and the European Community standard—adjusted household income below half the overall mean (EC).[6] Not surprisingly, the level of poverty varies with definition. It is more disturbing, however, that the direction of change over time also varies with the definition.

In Belgium, for instance, poverty by the subjective poverty line (SPL) decreased between 1987 and 1989. According to another subjective line, derived using the Center for Social Policy (CSP) method, poverty increased. By contrast, in Ireland poverty increased as measured by the CSP method, but decreased relative to the administrative poverty definition (Legal). Thus, even controlling for population composition—the numbers are derived from the same samples—different methods may give different trends.

To the extent that poverty is multi-dimensional, the measurement dilemma becomes more difficult. In trying to determine who the poor are, does multi-dimensionality mean that *all* criteria have to be met or that *any* or *sufficiently many* must be met? In fact, few analysts begin with the formalized version of the "poverty is multi-dimensional" thesis, such as the notion of *capabilities* advanced by Sen (1983).[7] This is probably due to lack of suitable data.

Income is the most common space used in poverty studies and is the focus of this review. Income is in advanced economies an important resource that affects the size of people's possibility sets. Incomes are easy to measure and income information is readily available for long periods of time.

The cautious reader will prefer examining several indicators when they are available. We show, for instance, poverty rates for different fractions of median income and consumption expenditures in Finland in 1981 and 1990 (Fig. 3). Although for any particular poverty cut-off, the proportion of persons poor varies with the resource concept, in this particular comparison, poverty has decreased using both definitions.

2.4. Equivalence scales

Poverty assessments require a comparison of the well-being of households with varying structure, i.e., the choice of an equivalence scale. In theory, an equivalence scale simply accounts for economies of scale, e.g., a family with ten members does not need five times as many kitchens and bathrooms as a family of two persons. However, there is much dispute about the extent of economies of scale and how resources are transformed to generate well-being within different types of households.

---

[6] Deleeck et al. (1992: pp. 38–39) explain how the subjective approaches were implemented.

[7] See, however, Hossain (1990) for an analysis.

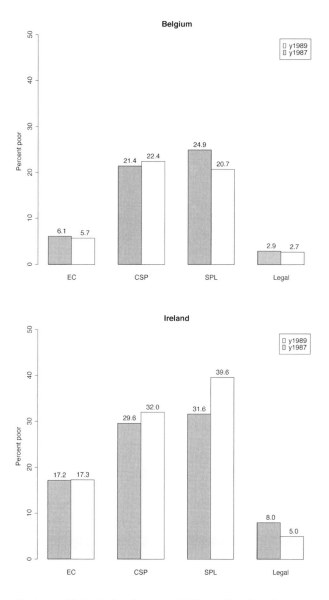

Fig. 2. Poverty in Belgium and Ireland using alternative definitions. Bars show the proportion of poor persons for following definitions. EC: OECD-adjusted income below half of mean income; CSP: Center for Social Policy Research subjective approach; SPL: the Leyden subjective poverty approach; Legal: income is less than the national income norm. Source: Deleeck et al. (1992).

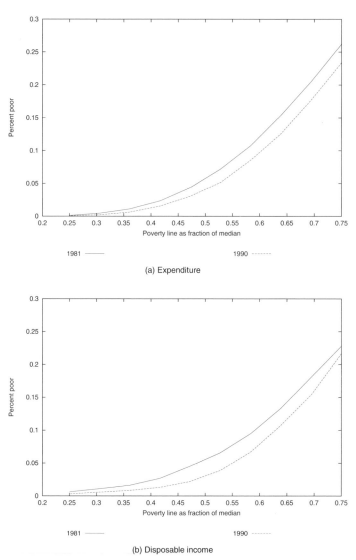

Fig. 3. Percent poor using disposable income and expenditure as resource concept, Finland, 1981 and 1990. Graph shows the head count ratio setting the poverty line at fractions of the median in 1981 and 1990 using either expenditure or disposable income as the resource variable. Source: Authors' calculations from Finnish Household Budget Survey microdata 1981 and 1990.

Let $F(y, s, x)$ be the joint cumulative distribution function of income y, family size s and a $(p \times 1)$ vector of other family characteristics x. The problem of finding the correct equivalence scale can be characterized as follows. An equivalence scale $e(u, s, x)$ for some utility value u for a family with characteristics (s, z) is defined by the cost $c(\ )$ of attaining the utility level u relative to the cost of attaining the utility level u in some reference household, indexed by 0:[8]

$$e(p, s, x, s_0, x_0; u) = \frac{c(s, x, p; u)}{c(s_0, x_0, p; u)}. \tag{1}$$

Although equivalence scales are defined in terms of some utility level (and therefore the scale can assume different values for other levels of utility), in most studies they are assumed to be constant across all characteristics other than (s, x). Given this very strong assumption, $F_e(y_e, s, x)$ is the distribution of equivalent income, where $y_e = y/e(s, x)$ for a scale e. Poverty comparisons can then proceed in terms of this new distribution function.

There are at least four different ways of obtaining equivalence scales:
1. nutritional and physiological studies;
2. expert judgments;
3. demand analysis;
4. population judgments (so-called subjective scales).

Often scales combine all these approaches. For instance, the US poverty line equivalence scale is based on nutritional studies, i.e., on the estimated cost of the food basket required for different types of families, combined with the fact that the average US family, according to the 1955 Household Food Consumption Survey, spent about one-third of its budget on food (National Research Council, 1995; p. 163).

There is no optimal method for deriving an equivalence scale. Indeed, without additional assumptions, there is no way of selecting the basis for choosing an equivalence scale, let alone the correct equivalence scale, out of the multitude that have been suggested.

For instance, full equivalence scales can not be identified from budget data on demands alone.[9] Rather, demand data reveal the cost of living index for a household relative to the reference household,

$$e(p, s, x; u) = \frac{L(s, x, p, p_0; u)}{L(s_0, x_0, p, p_0; u)} \frac{c(s, x, p_0; u)}{c(s_0, x_0, p_0; u)}, \tag{2}$$

where $L(\cdot)$ is the cost of living index defined by

$$L(s, x, p, p_0; u) = \frac{c(s, x, p; u)}{c(s_0, x_0, p_0; u)}. \tag{3}$$

---

[8] See Deaton and Muellbauer (1989) for a thorough treatment of the concept of the cost function.
[9] See Deaton and Muellbauer (1989) and, recently, Blundell (1998).

The first term in Eq. (2) is the relative level of living index, which can be identified from demand data alone, whereas the second term, the equivalence scale under the base price regime p_0 cannot be identified without additional information and/or assumptions.

Jenkins and Lambert (1993: p. 337) note that choosing an equivalence scale embodies three different assumptions (in addition to such choices as the space for welfare):

1. specification of the household or family characteristics that are relevant for differentiating between levels of need (e.g., household size and composition),
2. agreeing upon an ordinal ranking in terms of those characteristics, and
3. specifying the cardinal ranking of different households by need level, i.e., specifying how much more resources one household needs in order to attain the same level of well-being as another.

Many (or most) disagreements center around the third stage above, namely the cardinalization of the scales. It is, however, possible to explore the poverty ordering of two distributions without taking this final step.

Consider, for instance, the comparison of a two-parent, single-child family with a single-mother, two-child family. Based on household demand, children are, in general, assigned a lower weight than adults. Consequently the two-parent, three-person family needs more money income if its members are to be considered as equally well-off as the single-mother, three-person family. However, this single-mother family might be less well-off, even if it had as much money income (and therefore more income per equivalent adult) as the two-parent family, because two adults have more time for home production and child care than the single mother. We are not arguing that this is the case, just that one might disagree on the ranking of households according to needs, not only the cardinalization.[10]

Consider the simple but popular equivalence scale

$$y_e = \frac{y}{s^e}, \tag{4}$$

where y and y_e are income and equivalent income, s is family size and e is the elasticity of equivalent income w.r.t. family size, a parameter set by the researcher that lies between zero and one.[11] Equivalent income decreases monotonically in both family size and in the elasticity. As Coulter et al. (1992b) show, the extent of measured poverty, however, is not a monotonic function of the equivalence scale elasticity, but has a U-shaped pattern.

---

[10] These and related issues are discussed, for instance, by Danziger and Taussig (1979), Jenkins (1991), Jenkins (1994), Coulter, Cowell and Jenkins (1992b), Coulter, Cowell and Jenkins (1922a), Atkinson (1992), Atkinson and Bourguignon (1987), Nelson (1993), Fisher (1987), Buhmann, Rainwater, Schmaus and Smeeding (1988), Jenkins and Cowell (1994), Bradbury (1997), Deaton and Muellbauer (1989), Deaton (1992) and Rainwater (1990).

[11] This scale is used by e.g., Atkinson et al. (1995) along with numerous other studies.

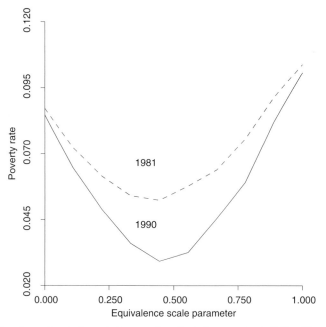

Fig. 4. Sensitivity of poverty rate to equivalence scale – Equivalence scale elasticity of income poverty in Finland, 1981 and 1990.

In Fig. 4, we demonstrate this phenomenon using data from the Finnish Household Budget Survey (HBS) for 1981 and 1990.[12] Note that although in both years the lines are U-shaped, the line drawn for 1981 is everywhere above that for 1990. The fact that the poverty index is not a monotonic function of the equivalence scale elasticity need not mean that changing the equivalence scale affects the assessed trend in poverty.

Two further popular scales are the scale (A),

$$y_e = y/\{1 + \beta(a - 1) + \gamma c\}, \qquad 0 < \gamma < \beta < 1 \tag{5}$$

and (B)

$$y_e = y/(a + \gamma c)^{\eta}, \quad 0 < \gamma, \quad \eta < 1. \tag{6}$$

The properties of these scales are discussed e.g., by Jenkins and Cowell (1994). The (A) scale in Eq. (5) commonly sets $\gamma = 0.5$ (i.e., children are considered to need half as much as the first adult) and $\beta = 0.7$ (i.e., an additional adult is considered to need 70% as much as the first adult). This corresponds to the so-called OECD-scale.

[12] Poverty is measured as the fraction of all persons whose equivalent disposable income is less than one half of equivalent median disposable income in the survey year.

A drawback is that this scale does not separate between two types of relativities: the needs of children relative to those of adults (how many children make up an equivalent adult?) and family size relativities (how much does a family's needs increase with the addition of an equivalent adult?). In the (B) scale in Eq. (6), γ specifies the needs of children relative to adults, whereas η reveals the increase in needs that the addition of an equivalent adult leads to.

2.5. Unit of analysis and intra-family distribution

Economists traditionally assume that the family acts as if it were a single utility maximizer and that all household members share the same level of well-being (Deaton and Muellbauer, 1989). In this case, the demand for goods is similarly affected by a change in nonlabor income, regardless of who in the household controls that source. Empirical tests (e.g., family labor supply) have tended to reject the hypothesis (see, e.g., Thomas, 1990; McElroy, 1990; Schultz, 1994).

Other models of family decision making have implications for the measurement of poverty—see Bergstrom (1996) for a review. In the bargaining model of family decision making (see, e.g., Browning et al., 1994; Bourguignon and Chiappori, 1994), the equal-sharing assumption emerges only as a special case, and the conceptual basis of equivalence scales derived from consumer expenditure surveys is called into question.

The abandonment of the equal sharing hypothesis complicates both the determination of the levels of income needed in different types of households to attain the same level of well-being (the "equivalence scale" question) and the assumption that levels of economic well-being are equal within a given household. Thus, some members of the household may be nonpoor, while others are poor, even though on average the household is nonpoor. It is also possible that some members in a non-poor household can be poor because of unequal sharing of resources.

Income inequality unequivocally increases in the absence of equal sharing. It is not clear what happens to poverty.[13] Unequal sharing in on-average non-poor households may push members into poverty, while unequal sharing in on-average poor households may allow some members to escape poverty.[14]

2.6. The relevant accounting period

Poverty measurement is sensitive to the choice of the time period over which resources are measured. Although most empirical studies use a calendar year as the accounting

---

[13] A criticism against using the head-count ratio is that it decreases for every poor person lifted out of poverty even if this were to happen at the expense of pushing an already poor person deeper into poverty, as will be the case for persons removed from poverty by unequal sharing within an on-average poor household. It is not possible, *a priori*, to determine which effect will dominate. Using more informative indices to measure the extent of poverty complicates the comparison further.

[14] See e.g., Danziger and Taussig (1979), Jenkins (1991), Jenkins (1994) and Haddad and Kanbur (1990) for discussion.

period, many researchers suggest that to be really poor requires deprivation for long periods of time.[15] On the other hand, viewing poverty as capability failure suggests that even short periods of poverty can be problematic.

It is often thought that temporary fluctuations in incomes are of little public concern. For example, some people receive their salary once a month and might, during a few days prior to receiving their next salary, have no money. This is not very likely to be a matter of great concern. Thus, for some "short" intervals it might not be bad to be poor in a single period, if one is nonpoor over most prior and subsequent intervals.

Using this rationale, many economists consider long-term economic (poverty) status to be the relevant concept. However, this does not resolve the issue as to the appropriate length of the "long-term", nor does it suggest that the "lifetime" of the individual is appropriate.

Because we have an intuitive understanding of what the word poverty means, some of what we know about poverty influences our research agendas. For instance, many economists claim that well-being should be evaluated over the long-run, because many of the poor in a given year and/or at a certain stage in their life (e.g., students) will over a longer time period not be disadvantaged at all.

Short-term poverty, however, can be extremely distressing or have long-lasting effects. While a person who experiences such a shortage will quite often in lifetime terms be nonpoor, some acute episodes may cause health problems, especially among young children, and frequent short-term spells of poverty may erode human capital. This suggests the study of the frequency of individuals' poverty spells, because the less resources they have, the more frequently they are likely to fall into poverty.

The emphasis on lifetime income rests on many implicit, but questionable, assumptions. For instance, saying that income averaged over several years is a better measure of individual well-being implicitly assumes symmetry and implies a form of risk-neutrality in well-being. Measuring poverty by average income implies that a loss of 10% compared to lifetime average income in one year can be compensated with an equally large gain in the next, or that being very poor for five years and nonpoor for five years is just the same as being poor and nonpoor in alternate years during a ten year period. This might be the case. However, if well-being is concave in money income, then the average of income over a period will overestimate actual well-being if those incomes vary from year to year.[16]

---

[15] See National Research Council (1995: pp. 285–298) for a discussion of *short-term* poverty. See also Ruggles (1990).

[16] See Duncan et al. (1993), Ruggles (1990) and National Research Council (1995).

2.7. Longitudinal aspects of poverty

Apart from the choice of accounting period, longitudinal aspects of poverty measurement deals with at least the following:[17]

- the duration of poverty spells
- the distribution of poverty spells across the population
- the impact of experienced poverty spells on the likelihood (and duration) of future spells.

The appropriate time period also has implications for cross-country poverty comparisons. For example, a population with the same value of a single time period poverty measure P_{t_1} as another population, but with a lower rate of multi-period poverty P_{t_1,t_2} might be better off if it has a lower rate of persistence of poverty, i.e., more movements into and out of poverty.

The *distribution* of poverty spells, apart from the level of poverty and the duration of poverty spells, is also of interest. Assume there are two populations with equal poverty rates, equal two-period poverty rates, but unequal distributions of the poverty spells. That is, in both populations, a fraction $P/2$ of the population enters the poverty population each year and stays there for two years. However, in one of them (A), the same individuals spend two years in poverty, two years out and then two years in again. There would only need to be four groups of people, each of size $P/2$, to keep the poverty rate and exit rate constant. A fraction $1 - 2P$ of the population can and, in our example, will never experience a poverty spell. In contrast, think of a population (B) consisting of $J > 4$ groups of equal size, all with positive probabilities q of entering the poverty population in period t such that the proportion poor is P in every period and the duration of every poverty spell is two years. After some number of time periods T, the distribution of poverty spells is more concentrated in A than in B, despite the fact that entry and exit as well as the level of poverty is constant across populations.

2.8. Poverty comparisons and sources

Let $P_{i,t}[F(y); z]$ be some measure of poverty in population (country) i at time t for some resource y and a poverty line (in the space of the resources y) z. If the purpose of poverty measurement is to rank different populations by the poverty measure P, comparisons can be made over various dimensions:

1. *within* a population at two different points in time;
2. *between* two populations at a single point in time;
3. compare the change in poverty between two points in time across two populations.

Meaningful comparisons depend on a number of assumptions about resources and the poverty line. As noted above, what is meant by "absolute" poverty is a comparison (in general) within a population across time, holding the value of z constant, assuming that the resources y can be compared across time. By contrast, a "relative" comparison

---

[17] See Ashworth, Hill and Walker (1994) for a lucid discussion.

of poverty rates does not keep the value of z constant, at least not in the sense that the resources y are comparable across time (by, e.g., simply deflating by a price deflator); with a relative measure the poverty standard gets indexed by t, z_t.

Several factors determine which comparisons are feasible, relevant and meaningful. For instance, the ranking of poverty changes (or, trends) across populations, a kind of a "difference in differences" approach, is one reliable way of comparing poverty across countries. The motivation is that comparing changes within countries over time abstracts (or differences out) factors that are constant or change only slowly *within*, but *not across* countries, such as differences in population structures or differences in sampling procedures. This argument depends not only on the *purpose* of the poverty comparison, but also on what type of poverty comparisons are made. For instance, if we adhere to a "strictly relativist" view, i.e., determine the poverty line $z_{i,t}$ separately for every country-year, the difference in differences argument might not apply because many things, including income above the poverty line, might change differently within countries. If the poverty cut-off is defined in terms of say median income, differences in the evolution in poverty may well be due not to changes in the circumstances of the poor but to changes among the nonpoor.

Furthermore, we could compare poverty in terms of

1. a common fixed poverty line, z applied to both countries at both points in time,

$$P_{i,t_1}(y; z) - P_{i,t_2}(y; z) \lesseqgtr P_{j,t_1}(y; z) - P_{j,t_2}(y; z),$$

a poverty line that is constant within country but different between countries (z_i, z_j)

$$P_{i,t_1}(y; z_i) - P_{i,t_2}(y; z_i) \lesseqgtr P_{j,t_1}(y; z_j) - P_{j,t_2}(y; z_j),$$

or

poverty lines that vary both between and within countries

$$P_{i,t_1}(y; z_{i,t_1}) - P_{i,t_2}(y; z_{i,t_2}) \lesseqgtr P_{j,t_1}(y; z_{j,t_1}) - P_{j,t_2}(y; z_{j,t_2}).$$

There is no consensus as to which approach either *in principle* or when implemented yields the most reliable results. For instance, assume that we apply a common poverty line across all countries over all time periods. We still must adjust the poverty change to take into account the differences in purchasing power and exchange rates across countries. Although purchasing power parities (PPP) are designed to facilitate such comparisons, it is not clear that the deflators used are the appropriate ones (Rainwater and Smeeding, 1995).[18]

PPPs have been designed to render comparable gross national products and other aggregate variables in the national accounts. Cross-national differences in consumption that is tax-financed, as opposed to household-expenditure financed, are not taken into account. We can not be certain whether differences in PPP-adjusted incomes reflect differences in the standard of living between average persons in different countries, or rather reflect differences in relative prices or in preferences. Dowrick and Quiggin (1994), analyzing disaggregated price and expenditure information from 60 countries,

---

[18] Moreover, there is question whether PPPs are appropriate for comparisons of well-being across countries. See Dowrick and Quiggin (1994) for a critical discussion.

found that the ranking of countries according to PPP-adjusted GDP is different from that obtained by comparing levels of welfare using the revealed-preference approach. Their results suggest that PPP-adjusted income can be a very poor measure of of economic well-being.

In this review, we take the view that poverty changes within a country, using similar methods, but not necessarily holding the poverty line constant, are the most plausible way to compare poverty differences across countries (or across studies within one country, for that matter).[19]

2.9. The poverty line

The choice of a poverty line, i.e., a point in the resource space which separates the poor from the nonpoor, involves choices about many issues, including the choice of the resource space, the particular view (absolute/relative) about poverty, the choice of an equivalence scale, and so on. Although some of these choices can be resolved by "objective" methods, much judgment is still required. Methods for dealing with uncertainty about the particular point in the resource space at which the poverty threshold lies are discussed below.

There is no unambiguous single correct poverty line for any population and time period. One can use systematic methods to determine several different poverty lines and base conclusions on them all. Or one can resort to the type of dominance methods discussed below and narrow the range of possible poverty lines.

2.10. Aggregation: the choice of poverty index

The literature on the aggregation of poverty information is, apart from the contribution of Watts (1968), inspired by the seminal article by Sen (1976). He demonstrated that poverty measurement consists of: (i) identifying the poor, and (ii) aggregating the poverty information. There are many detailed reviews of the aggregation issue, including Foster (1984), Seidl (1988), Ravallion (1994) and Sen (1997). Davidson and Duclos (1998) briefly review different dominance criteria and derive the asymptotic properties of many estimators of poverty indices and poverty curves (for dominance conditions).

Choosing a single index. Consider an income distribution that can be described by a cumulative distribution function (c.d.f.) $F(y)$, $y \in [0, \infty)$. Assume that the c.d.f. is strictly monotonically increasing and that the first and second moments exist. The poverty line is a positive constant z. A poverty index is a function $P(F; z)$ that is increasing in poverty, defined on F and $z \in Z$, where Z is the set of poverty lines. The head count ratio, the percentage of the population who are poor is given by

$$P_H = F(z) = \int_0^z \mathrm{d}F(y) = \int_0^\infty I[y < z]\,\mathrm{d}F(y), \tag{7}$$

[19] See Sen (1979) and Atkinson (1989) for discussion.

where $I[\cdot]$ is the indicator function, taking the value of one if the condition in the brackets is fulfilled and zero otherwise. The normalized poverty deficit (Atkinson, 1987) is defined by

$$P_D = \int_0^\infty I[y < z](1 - y/z)\, \mathrm{d}F(y). \tag{8}$$

Sen (1976) defines three basic axioms that a poverty measure (henceforth index) should satisfy:
1. the index should depend on poor incomes alone (Focus);
2. the index should be sensitive to the average income among the poor (Monotonicity);
3. the index should be sensitive to the distribution of income among the poor ([Weak] Transfer).

The head-count ratio fails to satisfy the Monotonicity and Transfer axioms; the normalized poverty deficit fails to satisfy the Transfer axiom. One can add additional axioms:
4. Symmetry (the poverty index is unchanged by a reordering of units); and
5. Replication invariance (the poverty index is unchanged by an identical proportional increase in the number of units with each income level).

Others have suggested additional or stronger requirements and poverty indices that satisfy them. Because comprehensive reviews of poverty indices are available (Seidl, 1988; Foster, 1984; Ravallion, 1994; Zheng, 1997), we do not review them here.

Most researchers accept Sen's axioms, but few empirical studies incorporate all of them. Poverty is usually measured as the proportion of the poor in the total population (the head count ratio), violating the second and third axioms. The head count ratio is easily interpreted and it is simple to rank distributions on the basis of the difference in the head count ratios.

Another debatable question w.r.t. the Focus axiom is the common practice, followed also here, to define the poverty line, z, to be some fraction of some functional (typically the mean or median) of the income distribution. For example, the official European Union method of measuring poverty uses a fraction of *average* income as the poverty line. This definition implies that a change in the richest person's income will affect poverty. But, it does not seem reasonable to let an increase in Queen Elizabeth's income raise the poverty line and our assessment of the extent of poverty in the UK.

Many poverty indices can be expressed in terms of poverty gaps g_y for income y and poverty line z as

$$g_y = \max\{z - y, 0\}. \tag{9}$$

Following Jenkins and Lambert (1997), indices that are defined in terms of g_y and that satisfy the Focus, Monotonicity, Transfer, Symmetry and Replication invariance axioms belong to the class of Generalized Poverty Gap (GPG) indices, a set denoted by $\mathcal{P}$.

Most poverty indices surveyed by Foster (1984) and Seidl (1988) are members of $\mathcal{P}$. Further, many indices in $\mathcal{P}$ form a subset $\mathcal{Q}$ that consists of indices defined in terms of relative poverty gaps Γ_y,

$$\Gamma_y = \max\{(z - y)/z, 0\} = \max\{1 - y/z, 0\}. \tag{10}$$

An important subset of $\mathcal{P}$ is the set of additively decomposable (AD) indices, which can be written as,

$$P_{AD}(F; z) = \int p_{AD}(y; z) \, dF(y), \tag{11}$$

where p_{AD} is a non-negative function of the poverty line and income. For decreasing and convex p_{AD}, the P_{AD} indices belong to $\mathcal{P}$. In Table 1, adapted from Jenkins and Lambert (1997), we list a few members of each class of indices.

Table 1
Membership of particular poverty measures in the classes $\mathcal{P}$ and $\mathcal{Q}$

Suggestion	$\mathcal{P}$	$\mathcal{Q}$	AD
Chakravarty (1983)	Yes	Yes	Yes
Clark et al. (1981)	Yes	Yes	Yes
Foster et al. (1984)	Yes	Yes	Yes
Hagenaars (1987) (Dalton type)	Yes	Some	No
Pyatt (1987)	Yes	Yes	No
Shorrocks (1995)	Yes	Yes	No
Watts (1968)	Yes	Yes	Yes

Source: Jenkins and Lambert (1997).

Dominance criteria. In order to avoid selecting a single index, researchers have examined under what conditions unanimous rankings can be achieved for larger classes of indices.[20] The general approach in these studies is to seek conditions under which poverty orderings can be arrived at despite differences in views on some particular choices.

For instance, methods for evaluating the order of two distributions are well-established when there is no agreement on the cardinal ordering of units w.r.t. needs (but an agreement exists vis-á-vis the order of unit types), the exact position of the poverty line in income space and which of the particular members of the family of additively decomposable poverty indices should be used for the comparison. These methods

[20] See Foster and Shorrocks (1988a, 1988b), Atkinson (1992), Atkinson and Bourguignon (1987), Jenkins and Lambert (1993) and Lambert (1997).

are not commonly used, perhaps because they become intractable when the number of comparisons increases.

The literature on poverty dominance provides methods for addressing three types of problems:

1. uncertainty concerning the position of the poverty line in the resource space (for (i) a common but uncertain line, for (ii) different and uncertain poverty lines)
2. uncertainty regarding the most appropriate choice of a particular poverty index among classes that satisfy generally acceptable conditions
3. uncertainty about the cardinal ranking of different types of households.

In many cases, several of these problems are dealt with simultaneously. The generality comes at a cost. Comparing poverty in terms a single index, using a fully cardinal equivalence scale and one known (or, in fact, even two separate, but known) poverty lines will lead to an ordering. Once sampling considerations are allowed for, the resulting ordering will almost surely be strict because asymptotically, the likelihood of a tie will go to zero. In the dominance approaches, the usual result is a partial ordering.[21]

*Dominance over a continuum of poverty lines (with one common line).*Define the binary relation **P**:

$$F\mathbf{P}G \text{ if and only if } P(G; z) \geq P(F; z) \qquad \text{for all} \quad z \in Z \tag{12}$$

and

$$P(G; z) > P(F; z) \qquad \text{for some} \quad z \in Z, \tag{13}$$

then **P** defines a strict partial ordering in poverty. If $F\mathbf{P}G$, we say that F poverty dominates G.

Foster and Shorrocks (1988a, 1988b) and Atkinson (1987) define criteria of dominance corresponding to levels of *stochastic dominance*. Foster and Shorrocks (1988a, 1988b) explore the properties of the parametric family P_α for $z \in [0, \infty)$, which is quite close to the problem of Lorenz dominance. Atkinson (1987) restricts interest to the AD class and a range of poverty lines $z \in [0, Z] = \mathbf{Z}$. This converts the question into one of *restricted* stochastic dominance. Atkinson (1987) also notes that lower degree dominance always implies higher degree dominance, but that the converse does not hold.

Atkinson (1987) derives the conditions which guarantee that the same ranking of a certain group of populations emerges regardless of which measure in the AD class is used. Denote the change in poverty on moving from distribution F to G by ΔP. If $\Delta P = P(G; z) - P(F; z) > 0$ for the poverty line z, there is more poverty in G than in

---

[21] See Foster and Shorrocks (1988a, 1998b), Atkinson (1987), Atkinson (1992), Atkinson and Bourguignon (1987), Jenkins and Lambert (1993), Jenkins and Lambert (1997), Jenkins and Lambert (1998b), Jenkins and Lambert (1998a) and Howes (1993). Shorrocks (1998) discusses connections between a few different approaches to examine profiles of the distribution of "bads".

F. The first condition is dominance according to the head count. If $\Delta P(z) > 0 \forall z \in Z$, i.e., the c.d.f. of one distribution is above the other in a certain range (or in other words, the head count of poverty is higher for all values of the poverty line in the set $\mathbf{Z}$), then we obtain the same ranking by all the measures in the AD class.

Atkinson's second condition states that if we can establish dominance by the aggregate poverty deficit, the ordering will be the same for all poverty measures in the AD class that satisfy the third requirement, i.e., for which p_{AD} is convex. Thus, if the normalized deficit for one distribution is lower than that for the other everywhere in the range $z \in Z$, then this will be true for all measures in the class AD. Given this condition, we know that if the poverty gap gives a conclusive ranking, more complicated measures will not provide any further information.[22]

Foster and Jin (1996) note that there are broad and appealing classes of poverty indices whose dominance conditions have not been studied. They derive dominance results for poverty indices that can be written as functions of the utility shortfall of the poor, based on the utility provided at the poverty level.[23]

Sequential dominance. Recall that the choice of equivalence scale can be divided into three stages: determining the characteristics that are needs-relevant, determining an ordinal ranking of units, and cardinalizing the ranking. Several authors have studied conditions under which poverty orderings are robust to the most controversial issue of the cardinalization of the differences in need (Atkinson and Bourguignon, 1987; Atkinson, 1992; Jenkins and Lambert, 1993).

Conditions for obtaining partial orderings do exist. The procedure involves checking for dominance within each population group sequentially, starting from the neediest. If, in each of these populations, one distribution dominates the other, any cardinalization of the ordinal ranking yields the same poverty ordering. An equivalent condition starts with a comparison of the neediest subpopulations and sequentially adds the next neediest group and checks for dominance only up to the next neediest group's poverty line. If, for every new group, one distribution dominates the other, all poverty indices and all equivalence scales within the specified class would yield the same ordering.

Dominance when poverty lines vary across distributions. Jenkins and Lambert (1997, 1998a,b) examine conditions under which poverty rankings can be obtained for the class of generalized poverty gap indices and possibly different poverty lines in two populations. They define poverty dominance using (censored) distributions of poverty gaps (see Eq. (9)) or normalized poverty gaps (see Eq. (10)). The latter turns out to

---

[22] Note the analogy with stochastic dominance results. First degree stochastic dominance is obtained if the 'zero' moments are unequal, no matter what the higher moments are; second degree dominance, if the means are unequal, etc. Thus, stochastic dominance of a higher degree may be obtained by merely checking for the lower order incomplete moments. In the present case, the head-count is the "zero" moment, the normalized deficit corresponds to the mean, and so on. See Fishburn (1980).

[23] See Hagenaars (1987) and also Spencer and Fisher (1992).

be useful for comparisons of poverty across distributions that arguably have different poverty lines—as will often be the case comparing two countries and even within a country across time.

The "TIP" curve is defined by

$$\mathrm{TIP}_g(p; F) = \int_0^{F^{-1}(p)} g(y; z)\,\mathrm{d}F(y), \tag{14}$$

using the non-normalized poverty gap and

$$\mathrm{TIP}_\Gamma(p; F) = \int_0^{F^{-1}(p)} \Gamma(y; z)\,\mathrm{d}F(y) \tag{15}$$

for the normalized gap. A TIP curve summarizes several aspects of poverty (see Fig. 5). At the point at which the graph of the cumulated (relative) poverty gap becomes horizontal, the proportion of the poor can be read off the horizontal and the (relative) poverty deficit off the vertical axis. The curvature of the TIP curve prior to that point visualizes information about the extent of inequality among the poor.

As shown by Jenkins and Lambert (1998a,b), if the TIP curve of a distribution F lies everywhere below that of distribution G, then the same ranking holds for all indices in the class $\mathcal{P}$ for the TIP curve defined on unnormalized gaps for a common poverty line, and $\mathcal{Q}$ for the TIP curve defined on the normalized gaps also for different poverty lines.

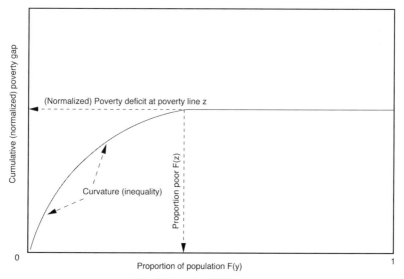

Fig. 5. Example of 'TIP' curve.

2.11. Measurement errors and poverty measurement

Non-sampling errors. Cowell and Victoria-Feser (1996) examine the robustness properties of poverty indices to *data contamination*, such as would occur if a subset of income
observations were erroneously coded. Taking the poverty line z to be a fixed constant,
they suggest that robustness (as measured by the boundedness of the *influence function*)
depends on the properties of the individual "poverty function" $p(z; y[; F])$. If this
function is "well-behaved", as it approaches the extremes of z and 0, the poverty index
will have a bounded influence function and therefore can be considered robust. Many
commonly-used poverty indices, such as the Sen index or the FGT class, are robust in
this sense. In many applications, the poverty line z is a fraction of some functional of
the income distribution itself—typically some fraction of the mean or the median. The
influence function and therefore the robustness of the poverty index depends also on the
robustness of the functional on which the poverty line is based. If that is the median,
the indices with well-behaved robustness properties remain robust. Nonrobust statistics,
however, in particular the mean, render the poverty index nonrobust, i.e., the influence
function is in such a case unbounded.

Howes (1996) discusses the impact of aggregation on inferring dominance relations
among distributions. Under plausible assumptions about the underlying distributions,
and for specific simulation examples, basing inferences of dominance on aggregated
data increases the likelihood of inferring that dominance is present, even when it is not.
Shorrocks and Subramanian (1994) discuss the possibility that the degree of confidence
with which a unit is considered to be among the poor can assume values other than zero
or one, suggesting fuzzy generalizations of many types of poverty indices.

Sampling issues. Poverty assessments using either (possibly several different) indices
or a particular dominance approach are most often conducted using samples drawn
from the actual populations being studied. This raises the issue of how close to the
population values the estimated indices can be expected to be. Most applications that
address statistical inference rely on classical inference.[24]

The most common approach to estimating the sampling variability of poverty indices
is to derive the asymptotic properties of the index under simple random sampling (SRS),
possibly with nonstochastic but varying sampling weights. Few data sets are, however,
drawn using SRS. An alternative is to employ re-sampling methods, such as a variant
of the jack-knife or bootstrap methods. These methods are robust w.r.t. to variations in
sampling design, the form of the index and, e.g., whether or not the poverty line is a
fraction of some functional of the income distribution (such as the mean or median),

The most straightforward case estimates a single poverty index from the class AD using randomly sampled data, and a fixed poverty line (not estimated using the same data).
Such estimators are means of simple functions of random variables and their sampling

---

[24] For a Bayesian approach, see Geweke and Keane (1996).

variance can be estimated using standard methods.[25] Data that are drawn from complex sampling designs warrant special attention. There exist well-developed methods for assessing the sampling variance of estimators in more complex designs.[26] Because AD indices for fixed poverty lines are just means of functions of random variables, they are applicable.[27]

The situation is more complicated when poverty statistics are based on sample estimates and also rely on an estimated fraction of the mean or median income. Preston (1995) derives the exact small and large sample distributions of the head-count ratio, again under SRS, when the poverty line is some fraction of the estimated median. The statistical properties of various estimators for poverty dominance are examined by Xu and Osberg (1998), Howes (1994a,b) and Jäntti (1992). Davidson and Duclos (1998) derive the sampling distribution under SRS for poverty deficit and TIP curves evaluated at a fixed set of points. The estimated versions of these variance–covariance matrices for empirical curves that are used for checking poverty dominance assist in performing statistical inference. The sampling distributions of several members of the class $\mathcal{P}$ arise as special cases.

These methods rely mostly on SRS. In more complex sampling settings, it may be very difficult to analytically find the variance (matrices) for estimators of poverty indices (curves). In such situations, sample reuse methods, in particular a bootstrap method, offer convenient and often the only practical options.[28]

3. Evidence about the extent of cross-sectional poverty

3.1. Changes in poverty within countries over time

3.1.1. Domestic sources
The most common way to examine poverty is to scrutinize changes over time within particular countries. Doing this avoids many comparability problems.[29] Even minor variations in definitions can in specific cases generate substantial differences in results. Although the differences can generally be traced to variations in particular choices among those issues raised in Section 2, they are often quite large. Deleeck et al. (1992), as discussed in Section 2, estimate the poverty head-count ratio in two waves of panel data for several EU countries, using four different definitions of poverty lines. Take

[25] See e.g., Kakwani (1993).

[26] See, for example, Pahkinen and Lehtonen (1995), Skinner et al. (1989) and Särndal et al. (1992).

[27] Malmberg (1988) and Bishop et al. (1997) discuss the sampling properties of the Sen (1976) poverty index proposed when the poverty line is a known constant and data are SRS. Jäntti and Nordberg (1992) discuss its estimation when the poverty line is a fraction of the median that is being estimated simultaneously with the poverty line. See also Davidson and Duclos (1998).

[28] See Efron and Tibshirani (1993) for an introduction to bootstrap methods and Xu and Osberg (1998) for an application to poverty measurement.

[29] See Mayer and Jencks (1993) for a discussion of comparability problems across time.

Ireland as a case in point. Unsurprisingly, different methods yield different levels of poverty (see Fig. 2). However, the head-count ratio *increased* using two subjective definitions, remained more or less unchanged by the European Union's below half-of-average definition and *decreased* by the definition that relies on administrative rules.

Such results suggest that definitions matter. Depending on the choices that are made, poverty levels and trends can be quite different within a country even using the exact same sample of data. Thus, it is important to choose an appropriate combination of equivalence scales and poverty lines.

We summarize in Table A.1 a number of poverty head count ratio estimates, based on a host of different studies from different countries, using many different combinations of methods. Inspection of these patterns suggests there is wide variance in poverty levels and trends across countries. On the basis of varying amounts of evidence per country, it would seem that poverty increased in the 1980s and early 1990s in Australia, Germany (West), Italy, Sweden, the UK and the US. The UK increase appears to be largest, followed by that in Australia. In Canada, Denmark, Finland and Spain, poverty decreased. There was little change in Greece, Norway and Portugal and the evidence is quite mixed for Belgium, France, Ireland, Luxembourg and the Netherlands.

Poverty rates across countries, from domestic sources as well as LIS, have been compiled by, e.g., Atkinson (1998) (European Union countries), and Bradshaw and Chen (1996) (the latter two mainly concerned with LIS). While the assessments in these studies vary somewhat, two conclusions are shared by them as well as our Table A.1 The country that stands out as having experienced a substantial increase in poverty is the UK. Further, there is little evidence of OECD-wide (or, advanced country wide) poverty trends in the many studies considered. This is in contrast with what has been observed about relative inequality (see, e.g., Gottschalk and Smeeding, 1997).

3.1.2. International sources (mainly LIS)

The Luxembourg Income Study (LIS) contains several years of data on about 20 industrialized countries from varying years since the late 1960s.[30] In Table 2, we show the level of relative poverty, as measured by the head count ratio, in the latest cross-section of LIS, along with information on poverty changes. Poverty is defined as 50% of the within-country within-year disposable median income. Incomes are pooled within the family and each member is assigned the equivalent disposable or market income, equivalized using the square root of family size. We show the percentage of persons who live in households with income per equivalent adult below this poverty line.[31]

The LIS single-point estimates of relative poverty suggest a grouping of countries with respect to poverty. The US has by far the highest poverty rate at 17.7% (and

---

[30] The Luxembourg Income Study is described, e.g., in Smeeding et al. (1990). See also http://lissy.ceps.lu

[31] We have examined the sensitivity of the LIS estimates to variations in equivalence scales. Our results do not appear to be sensitive to the choice of a common equivalence scale. In Table A.5 in the appendix we show the point estimates that underlie our trend assessments.

Table 2

Poverty rate and recent change in poverty using LIS data

Country	Latest year		Longest change		Latest change	
	Year	Poverty rate	Years	Time trend	Years	Change
Australia	1989	12.2	1981–1989	0.198	1985–1989	0.113
Austria	1987	3.4	n.a.		n.a.	
Belgium	1992	5.4	1985–1992	0.118	1988–1992	0.128
Canada	1991	11.3	1971–1991	−0.179	1987–1991	0.019
Denmark	1992	7.5	1987–1992	−0.586	n.a.	
Finland	1991	5.7	1987–1991	0.086	n.a.	
France	1989	9.5	1979–1989	0.203	1984.1–1989	−0.526
Germany	1989	5.6	1983–1989	6.456	1984–1989	−0.172
Ireland	1987	11.3	n.a.		n.a.	
Italy	1991	10.3	1986–1991	−0.024	n.a.	
Luxembourg	1991	4.7	1985–1991	0.117	n.a.	
Netherlands	1991	6.7	1983–1991	0.014	1987–1991	0.397
Norway	1991	6.6	1979–1991	0.209	1986–1991	−0.144
Spain	1990	10.2	1980–1990	−0.193	n.a.	
Sweden	1992	6.7	1967–1992	−0.286	1987–1992	−0.196
Switzerland	1982	8.3	n.a.		n.a.	
UK	1991	14.5	1969–1991	0.317	1986–1991	1.087
US	1991	17.7	1974–1991	0.118	1986–1991	−0.007

Numbers shown are the head count ratio using 50% of median adjusted disposable income as poverty line. Changes are measured by the slope of the regression of poverty rate on year. Table A.5 shows the point estimates that underlie the estimated trends.

Source: Authors' calculations from LIS database.

ranging from 16 to 18% over the years), followed by the UK, France and Australia. whose poverty rates vary between 13 and 15%. In addition, Canada, Ireland, Italy and Spain have poverty rates in excess of 10%. The Netherlands and the Nordic countries— Denmark, Finland, Norway and Sweden—have rates around 7%, and Belgium has the lowest point estimate at 5.4%.

Comparing the *level* of poverty across countries is controversial for many reasons, but comparing trends across countries is less so. If most problems of comparing poverty within a country at two points in time have been dealt with, remaining factors that induce differences in poverty levels across countries should be differenced out when trends are evaluated. Trend comparisons across countries are more reliable if they are found using similar definitions. It is not consistent, for example, to compare changes in the US official poverty with changes in the poverty rate in Sweden defined by the politico-administrative line.

In examining the within-country changes, the years the comparison is based on is constrained by LIS. It would be preferable to examine changes at similar stages of the business cycle, but this is not an option. We show in Table 2 the trend in poverty, as measured by the regression coefficient in a regression of the head count ratio in all LIS data sets for a country regressed against year, and the annual percentage point change between the two latest LIS years. If only two data points are available, the regression coefficient equals the annualized percentage point change in the head count rate of poverty (in that case, the regression coefficient is a *Wald* estimate).

Looking at both the time trend as measured over all the years in LIS and the latest change, the evidence does not suggest a common trend across countries. Poverty has increased in some countries and decreased in others. For instance, poverty increased over time in Belgium and the UK, the countries with the lowest and second highest poverty rates in the early 1990s. The increase in poverty in the UK from 1969 to 1991 was by almost a third of a percentage point per year. The increase in Belgium from 1985 to 1991 was around one tenth of a percentage point per year. For another pair of low and high poverty countries, in the early 1990s, poverty decreased in Denmark and Canada

In only two of our LIS countries is the direction of change of the longest time trend and the latest change different, namely in France and in Norway. In France, poverty increased, on average, by two tenths of a percentage point per year from 1979 to 1989, but decreased between 1984 and 1989 by half a point a year. In Norway, also, between 1979 and 1991, poverty increased by 0.2 percentage points per year, but decreased between 1986 and 1991.

Examining poverty dominance within countries reveals the robustness of the trend assessments obtained using single indices, such as the head count ratio. We illustrate this be showing in Fig. 6 three examples using the plot of the average cumulative poverty gap against the percentage of population, or the "TIP" curve (Jenkins and Lambert, 1997). If TIP curves do not cross, the same poverty ordering is obtained for all GPG indices (see Section 2.10). In two of the countries in LIS, Australia in 1981 and 1985 and the United Kingdom in 1986 and 1991, TIP curves cross and between the relevant years, robust conclusions cannot be drawn. By contrast, in Canada the estimated TIP curves do not intersect in any of the data sets in LIS. Rather, the TIP curves suggest a steady decline in poverty that is robust with respect to the choice of relative poverty line and poverty index.

3.2. Poverty orderings

Once a specific view of poverty is applied, poverty orderings of countries are possible. Because use of a head-count ratio below a single poverty line may be misleading, we examine the sensitivity of the poverty ordering by examining whether there are cases of poverty dominance by the head-count ratio for a range of poverty lines from 0 up to 60% of the current adjusted median disposable income. If we observe poverty dominance by

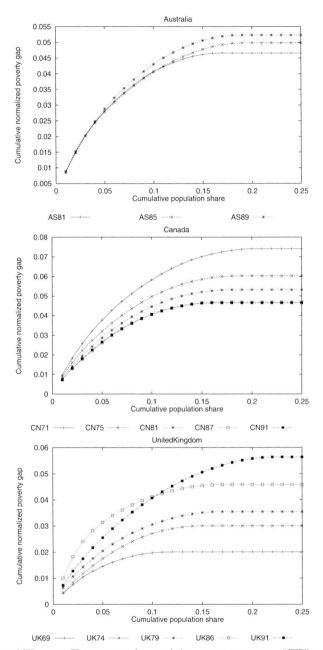

Fig. 6. Examples of TIP curves. The curves are the cumulative average poverty gap ("TIP" curves), using 60% of the current median income as poverty line, at different percentiles of the distribution of income. Source: Authors' calculations from the LIS database.

the head count, we know the order would be preserved for all lower poverty lines and all measures in the class AD.

Figures 7 and 8, as well as Tables 3 and 4, show first- (head count) and second-order (poverty gap) poverty dominance for relative poverty orderings for 16 advanced economies. In Table 3 we show, for the latest LIS data, the set of countries that it dominates (column 2) and the set of countries it is dominated by (column 3). This ordering of countries is also displayed as a Hasse diagram in Fig. 7.

First-order poverty dominance does not produce a "tight" ordering of countries. There are a large number of ties. For instance, the Netherlands is poverty dominated by Belgium, Finland, Germany and Austria and dominates in turn only France. However, in many cases, the lines cross and an unambiguous poverty ordering fails to materialize. Nonetheless, Fig. 7 produces a five-tier ranking, with Austria at the top, and Belgium, Finland, Germany and Norway having the second lowest level of poverty. France, Ireland and the US, in turn, have the highest. For example, the US dominates no other country, but is dominated by 13 of the 18 countries.

To what extent can we find dominance w.r.t the distribution of normalized poverty gaps? We restrict the class for which the orderings are to apply to that for which the poverty intensity function is strictly decreasing in income. As discussed in Section 2.10, if the normalized cumulative poverty gap for a distribution F is everywhere above that of another, say G, then F has a greater extent of poverty by all indices that are members of $\mathcal{Q}$. In other words, in order for country A to "TIP" dominate country B, the graph of the cumulative normalized poverty gap against the cumulative population share of country A must everywhere be below that of country B. In each case, we define the poverty line as 60% of the adjusted median within each country within each year.

In Table 4, we show the results of all pairwise comparisons of normalized poverty gap dominance. The proportion of comparisons that result in a dominance relation is considerably greater than it was using the poverty rate. We show in Table 4 for each country those it dominates and those it is dominated by according to the TIP-criterion. Again, the pattern of dominance orderings is illustrated using the Hasse-diagram (Fig. 8).

There are fewer ties than with first-order dominance. The ranking of many countries changes compared to the first-order case. Sweden, for instance, now dominates Canada and the UK, in addition to the four countries it first-order dominated. Also, Luxembourg and Norway are now among the countries that dominate Sweden (cf. Tables 3 and 4). The reduction in ties makes the Hasse diagram simpler, but increased the number of tiers, from roughly five to eight. France, Ireland and the US are still tied at the bottom of the diagram.

These comparisons of relative poverty rates and relative poverty gaps across countries do not account for differences in the real standard of living by country. Even though the US has a much higher poverty rate than, say, Norway, relative to the median standard of living in each country, some of the poor in the US may be better off than some of the nonpoor in Norway because of the higher median standard of living in the U.S.

Table 3

First-order poverty dominance using LIS data

Country	Dominates	Is dominated by
Australia	US	Austria Belgium, Finland, Germany, Italy, Luxembourg, Norway, Spain, Sweden, Switzerland
Austria	Australia, Belgium, Canada, Denmark, Finland, France, Germany, Ireland, Italy, Netherlands, Norway, Spain, Sweden, Switzerland, UK, US	
Belgium	Australia, Denmark, France, Ireland, Netherlands, Switzerland, US	Austria
Canada	US	Austria, Finland, Germany, Luxembourg, Norway
Denmark	France, Ireland	Austria, Belgium, Finland, Germany, Luxembourg, Norway
Finland	Australia, Canada, Denmark, France, Ireland, Italy, Netherlands, Spain, Sweden, Switzerland, UK, US	Austria
France		Austria, Belgium, Denmark, Finland, Germany, Luxembourg, Netherlands, Norway, Sweden, Switzerland
Germany	Australia, Canada, Denmark, France, Ireland, Italy, Netherlands, Spain, Sweden, Switzerland, UK, US	Austria
Ireland		Austria, Belgium, Denmark, Finland, Germany, Luxembourg, Norway, Sweden
Italy	Australia, US	Austria, Finland, Germany, Luxembourg
Luxembourg	Australia, Canada, Denmark, France, Ireland, Italy, Spain, Switzerland, UK, US	
Netherlands	France	Austria, Belgium, Finland, Germany
Norway	Australia, Canada, Denmark, France, Ireland, Switzerland, UK, US	Austria
Spain	Australia US	Austria, Finland, Germany, Luxembourg
Sweden	Australia, France, Ireland, US	Austria, Finland, Germany
Switzerland	Australia, France, US	Austria, Belgium, Finland, Germany, Luxembourg, Norway
UK	US	Austria, Finland, Germany, Luxembourg, Norway
US	Australia, Austria, Belgium, Canada, Finland, Germany, Italy, Luxembourg, Norway, Spain, Sweden, Switzerland, UK	

The poverty line is defined as 60% of the adjusted median in each country within each year.
Source: Authors' calculations from LIS data.

Table 4

Normalized poverty gap dominance using LIS data

Country	Dominates	Is dominated by
Australia	US	Austria, Belgium, Canada, Finland, Germany, Italy, Luxembourg, Norway, Spain, Sweden, Switzerland
Austria	Australia, Belgium, Canada, Denmark, Finland, France, Germany, Ireland, Italy, Netherlands, Norway, Spain, Sweden, Switzerland, UK, US	
Belgium	Australia, Denmark, France, Ireland, Netherlands, Switzerland, US	Austria, Finland, Luxembourg
Canada	Australia, France, US	Austria, Finland, Germany, Italy, Luxembourg, Norway, Spain
Denmark	France, Ireland, Netherlands	Austria, Belgium, Finland, Germany, Luxembourg, Norway, Sweden
Finland	Australia, Belgium, Canada, Denmark, France, Germany, Ireland, Italy, Netherlands, Norway, Spain, Sweden, Switzerland, UK, US	Austria, Luxembourg
France		Austria, Belgium, Canada, Denmark, Finland, Germany, Italy, Luxembourg, Netherlands, Norway, Spain, Sweden, Switzerland
Germany	Australia, Canada, Denmark, France, Ireland, Italy, Netherlands, Spain, Sweden, Switzerland, UK, US	Austria, Finland, Luxembourg
Ireland		Austria, Belgium, Denmark, Finland, Germany, Italy, Luxembourg, Norway, Spain, Sweden, Switzerland
Italy	Australia, Canada, France, Ireland, Spain, UK, US	Austria, Finland, Germany, Luxembourg
Luxembourg	Australia, Belgium, Canada, Denmark, Finland, France, Germany, Ireland, Italy, Netherlands, Norway, Spain, Sweden, Switzerland, UK, US	
Netherlands	France	Austria, Belgium, Denmark, Finland, Germany, Luxembourg, Norway, Sweden
Norway	Australia, Canada, Denmark, France, Ireland, Netherlands, Sweden, Switzerland, UK, US	Austria, Finland, Luxembourg
Spain	Australia, Canada, France, Ireland, UK, US	Austria, Finland, Germany, Italy, Luxembourg
Sweden	Australia, Denmark, France, Ireland, Netherlands, Switzerland, US	Austria, Finland, Germany, Luxembourg, Norway
Switzerland	Australia, France, Ireland, US	Austria, Belgium, Finland, Germany, Luxembourg, Norway, Sweden
UK	US	Austria, Finland, Germany, Italy, Luxembourg, Norway, Spain
US		Australia, Austria, Belgium, Canada, Finland, Germany, Italy, Luxembourg, Norway, Spain, Sweden, Switzerland, UK

The poverty line is defined as 60% of the adjusted median in each country within each year.
Source: Authors' calculations from LIS data.

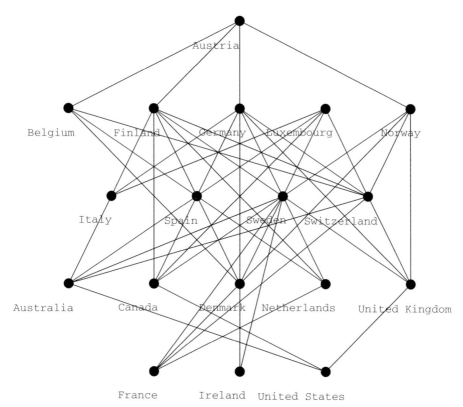

Fig. 7. Hasse diagram of first-order poverty dominance using LIS data. Fully relative poverty. The poverty line is defined as 60% of the adjusted median in each country within each year. Source: Authors' calculations from LIS data.

Addressing this issue requires a common metric in which to compare US to Norwegian incomes. A number of so-called Purchasing Power Parity (PPP) adjusted exchange rates have been developed for this purpose. Because such comparisons rely on average international prices, despite wide variation in relative prices across countries, Dowrick and Quiggin (1994) suggest that PPP-based welfare rankings are not firmly based in welfare economics. They propose that detailed price and consumption data be used to rank countries according to a revealed-preference approach instead, and present evidence which suggests PPP-based rankings are, indeed, inappropriate. Even if PPP-based approaches would yield well-motivated rankings, however, the commonly-used PPP adjustments are not designed for comparisons of real *disposable* income (as opposed

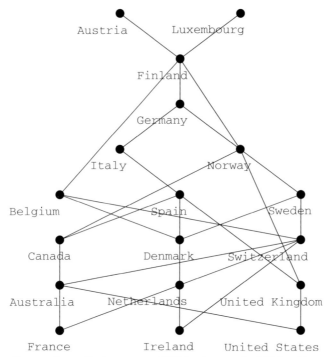

Fig. 8. Hasse diagram of normalized poverty gap (TIP) dominance using LIS data. The poverty line is defined as 60% of the adjusted median in each country within each year. Source: Authors' calculations from LIS data.

to real *national* incomes). Nonetheless, because we have no empirical alternative, we provide poverty orderings based on PPP-adjusted incomes as an illustration.[32]

In particular, we use the Penn World Tables Mark 5.6 data on PPP adjusted exchange rates for consumption in the year of the LIS data and deflate the resulting current-year US international dollar amounts to a common year's prices using the US Consumer Price Index (CPI).[33] The poverty line is then taken to be half of the US 1991 adjusted median disposable income (which choice leaves US. poverty unchanged, of course).

The Hasse diagrams of the real poverty first-order dominance ordering is shown in Fig. 9 and of the second-order or TIP dominance in Fig. 10. Because of its higher median standard of living, the US now ceases to be tied at the bottom of the ordering. Ireland now shares with France and Spain the bottom tie. The relative position of Canada improves substantially, as it is dominated only by Luxembourg in either ordering. Again, the TIP ordering results in fewer ties.

---

[32] See Section 2 for a discussion of real income comparisons.
[33] See Summers and Heston (1991).

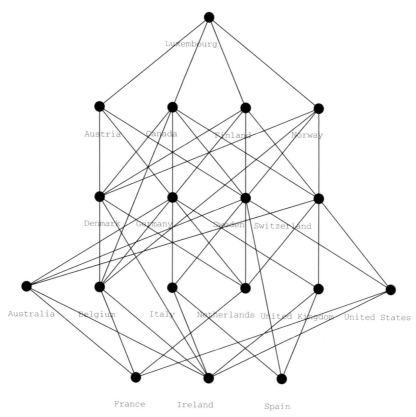

Fig. 9. Hasse diagram of first-order poverty dominance using LIS data. Real international income poverty using PPPs relative to US median. The poverty line is defined as 60% of the adjusted US 1991 PPP median in each country within each year. Source: Authors' calculations from LIS data.

These PPP results should be viewed with caution, as there are large differences in the extent to which households in different countries actually need to purchase certain items. For example, certain spending categories, such as on health care or college education, are largely privately funded in some countries and largely publicly funded in others. PPPs, developed for national accounts purposes rather than for comparisons of household well-being, do not take this into account. Despite this caveat, many of the countries ranking highly in the PPP ranking are those with extensively provided public services, such as Germany and the Nordic countries. And the US, despite its high level of real income, remains close to the bottom. In the TIP ordering (Fig. 10), it dominates only Ireland and France and it is dominated by nine countries.

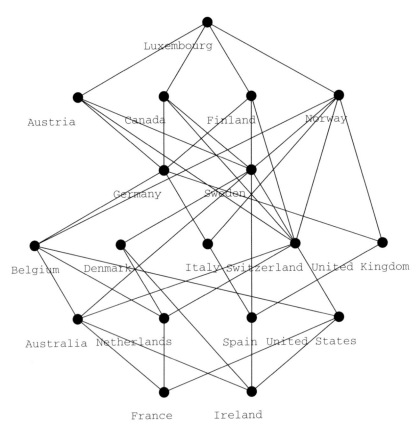

Fig. 10. Hasse diagram of normalized poverty gap (TIP) dominance using LIS data. Real international income poverty using PPPs relative to US median. The poverty line is defined as 60% of the adjusted US 1991 PPP median in each country within each year. Source: Authors' calculations from LIS data.

4. Decomposing poverty across population groups

4.1. Comparing poverty risks of different groups

Most studies that disaggregate poverty by various demographic characteristics do so with respect not to the individuals' characteristics, but those of the household head. For instance, a breakdown by age is typically a breakdown by the household head's age and so on.

Another troublesome aspect of sub-group poverty risks is the choice of the appropriate equivalence scales. Different assumptions about the economies of scale of household size, the consumption requirements and household production capacities of household members of different ages and sexes can dramatically affect the ordering of population groups by relative poverty risks. The choice of an equivalence scale is less likely to affect the assessment of changes in poverty rates across time, unless the population is undergoing rapid demographic change.

We examine the LIS poverty rates of

1. children
2. persons living in a household with an aged head, and
3. persons living in female-headed households/families

We examine both the poverty rates of these groups, how these change over time as well as their inter-country poverty ranking. We limit the analysis to these categories, not because they are the only meaningful ones, but because cross-sectional and trend differences for these groups reflect cross-national differences in the social welfare state that are often of interest.[34] Our purpose is to examine the level of and trend in poverty among groups traditionally thought to be at high poverty risk.

Demographic comparisons are also sensitive to the equal-sharing within household assumption. If sharing rules vary by family type within a country or across countries, our comparisons might be misleading. For instance, might single parents sacrifice and provide more than an equal share of income for their children than do other families?

The population of children consists of all persons below the age of 18 in the LIS data. The elderly are represented by persons who are more the 64 years old. Persons living in female-headed households are so identified if the LIS household has a female head or reference person. These decompositions are not mutually exclusive, as some children and elderly live in female-headed households.

4.2. *Poverty rankings of different demographic groups*

In Tables 5–7 we show for selected demographic groups poverty rates and poverty trends, as measured by the head-count ratio relative to one-half of the adjusted within-country overall median. The rates are the proportion poor in each subpopulation and the trend is measured, as in Table 2, by both the slope coefficient in a regression of each country's poverty rate against time (starting in 1900) and by the latest change.

We also examine the TIP poverty ordering up to 60% of the current overall median of different population subgroups using the latest wave in LIS. Poverty among children is defined by taking the adjusted income per equivalent adult in each household with

---

[34] Two reservations in the comparison of poverty across population groups should be noted. First, most data sets used to measure the extent of poverty gather information primarily about the "household head" and, the "spouse", if present. Rules about which household member is classified as the head vary between data sets, years and countries. In addition, if one attempts to assess, say, the excess risk of poverty due to unemployment, comparing poverty rates of persons in households whose heads are unemployed to those in the whole population will misclassify some households where a person other than the head is unemployed. That is, many breakdowns by the properties of the household head will misclassify households—the same would be the case if we were to compare poverty of the elderly and the non-elderly and we did not know the age of all persons living in the household.

children, allocating that to every child. The elderly are defined similarly. Poverty in female-headed households, by contrast, is estimated among all persons living in such units.

4.2.1. Children

The ordering of countries with respect to poverty among children, shown in Table 5, is broadly similar to that of all persons. The Anglo-Saxon countries have the highest rates according to this relative poverty ranking, central European ones populate the middle, and northern European and Nordic countries have relatively few children in poverty. Next we turn to the changes over time, both the long run changes, measured as above by the slope coefficient of the within-country regression of poverty rate against year, and of the latest change. There is, here as above, little evidence of an OECD-wide increase in poverty. In general, the direction of change in overall poverty and child poverty change is similar.

We also show, in Fig. 11, the Hasse diagram obtained when we check for TIP dominance. Austria and Luxembourg, in the overall ordering the dominating nations, are now much lower. France rises in this ordering. The Nordic and northern European countries tend to be found at or close to the top and the Anglo-Saxon countries near the bottom of this ordering.

4.2.2. Elderly

Another group traditionally at high risk of poverty, namely the elderly, are in the industrialized countries included in LIS no longer so exposed. The poverty risks of the elderly are, for the equivalence scale we have used, quite modest and, in many cases, lower than those of the overall population. The ordering of countries changes substantially for the elderly poverty ranking compared to both the overall and the child poverty rankings. The UK and the US, high overall poverty risk countries, are now quite similar to the northern European and Nordic countries. Only Ireland has double-digit elderly poverty; in most countries, between 5 and 8.5% of the elderly are poor. Thus, differences in ranks reflect very small differences in the likelihood that the average elderly is poor between these countries. The changes in elderly poverty very closely track the changes in overall poverty.

Our Hasse diagram (Fig. 6), that ranks countries using 60 rather than 50% of the current median and uses the TIP dominance criterion, somewhat re-shuffles the countries. Now Canada and Norway emerge at the top of the ordering, closely followed by Sweden and Luxembourg. The US and the UK have now dropped closer to the bottom.

The similarity across countries of the poverty rates for the elderly evaluated at the 50% of median line, and the changes in the ordering when examined at 60, are likely due to a similarity and a difference among the countries we study. All industrialized countries have implemented a public pension system that covers the elderly (Korpi and Palme, 1997). However, the generosity of the average pension and the spread about that

Table 5
Poverty rates and poverty trends for children

Country	Latest year		Longest Change		Latest Change	
	Year	Poverty rate	Years	Time trend	Years	Change
Australia	1989	14.8	1981–1989	0.103	1985–1989	0.320
Austria	1987	6.8	n.a.		n.a.	
Belgium	1992	4.3	1985–1992	0.048	1988–1992	0.198
Canada	1991	15.6	1971–1991	−0.077	1987–1991	0.214
Denmark	1992	5.1	1987–1992	0.091	n.a.	
Finland	1991	2.3	1987–1991	−0.135	n.a.	
France	1989	8.4	1979–1989	0.164	1984–1989	−0.345
Germany	1989	4.8	1983–1989	6.408	1984–1989	−0.322
Ireland	1987	13.8	n.a.		n.a.	
Italy	1991	13.5	1986–1991	0.398	n.a.	
Luxembourg	1991	5.4	1985–1991	0.035	n.a.	
Netherlands	1991	8.3	1983–1991	0.435	1987–1991	0.791
Norway	1991	4.9	1979–1991	−0.036	1986–1991	0.104
Spain	1990	12.3	1980–1990	−0.044	n.a.	
Sweden	1992	3.0	1967–1992	−0.075	1987–1992	−0.127
Switzerland	1982	4.3	n.a.		n.a.	
UK	1991	18.5	1969–1991	0.528	1986–1991	1.189
US	1991	24.1	1974–1991	0.322	1986–1991	−0.092

Numbers shown are the head count ratio using 50% of median adjusted disposable income as poverty line. Changes are measured by the slope of the regression of poverty rate on year. Each child (under 18) is counted once.

Source: Authors' calculations from LIS database.

mean varies substantially across countries, accounting for a divergence in rates when the poverty line is raised.

4.2.3. Female-headed households

The ranking of persons living in female-headed households by relative poverty rate, shown in Table 7, is much more similar to that found for children than that for the elderly. For all countries, the rates are much higher than for all persons. English-speaking countries have very high rates of poverty, central European ones lower and northern European ones are closest to the bottom, a pattern similar to that found for all persons. An interesting difference compared to earlier results is that Ireland has a comparatively low rate of poverty among the female-headed households.

The Hasse diagram of the TIP poverty ordering among persons living in female-headed households, shown in Fig. 13, is very complex, reflecting the large number of ties that the TIP dominance comparisons result in. We exemplify this by considering how Belgium, which has a rate of 12.4$ ends up in the bottom row, while Finland,

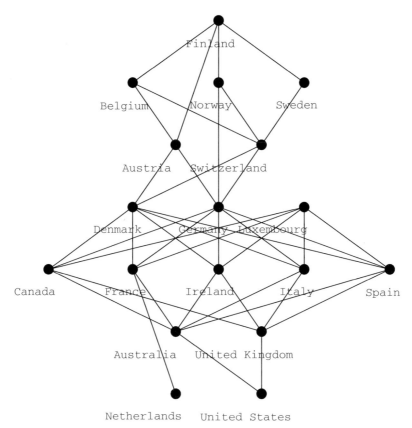

Fig. 11. Child poverty ordering. Hasse diagram of normalized poverty gap (TIP) dominance using LIS data. Fully relative poverty. The poverty line is defined as 60% of the overall adjusted median in each country within each year. Each child (under 18) is counted once. Source: Authors' calculations from LIS data.

which has a rate of 17.5% ends up near the top. It turns out that Belgium has in most pairwise comparisons a slight crossing with the other country close to the origin. Thus, even though Belgium has a low head-count ratio and a low average poverty gap, it ends up in the bottom row.

5. The impact of public policy on poverty

We now turn to research regarding the impact of public policy on the extent of poverty. We focus primarily on accounting models, as few behavioral models have been estimated with inter-country data.

Table 6
Poverty rates and poverty trends for elderly

Country	Latest year		Longest Change		Latest Change	
	Year	Poverty rate	Years	Time trend	Years	Change
Australia	1989	5.4	1981–1989	−0.446	1985–1989	−0.069
Austria	1987	1.2	n.a.		n.a.	
Belgium	1992	4.5	1985–1992	0.171	1988–1992	0.310
Canada	1991	8.3	1971–1991	−0.126	1987–1991	0.125
Denmark	1992	7.3	1987–1992	0.039	n.a.	
Finland	1991	6.0	1987–1991	0.118	n.a.	
France	1989	8.1	1979–1989	0.258	1984–1989	−0.732
Germany	1989	4.2	1983–1989	4.800	1984–1989	−0.113
Ireland	1987	11.5	n.a.		n.a.	
Italy	1991	5.0	1986–1991	−0.257	n.a.	
Luxembourg	1991	1.8	1985–1991	−0.226	n.a.	
Netherlands	1991	5.4	1983–1991	−0.087	1987–1991	0.009
Norway	1991	4.8	1979–1991	0.118	1986–1991	0.196
Spain	1990	7.9	1980–1990	−0.237	n.a.	
Sweden	1992	8.6	1967–1992	−0.346	1987–1992	−0.020
Switzerland	1982	2.7	n.a.		n.a.	
UK	1991	7.1	1969–1991	0.258	1986–1991	0.284
US	1991	8.4	1974–1991	−0.033	1986–1991	0.252

Numbers shown are the head count ratio using 50% of median adjusted disposable income as poverty line. Changes are measured by the slope of the regression of poverty rate on year. Each elderly person (over 65) person in the household is counted once.
Source: Authors' calculations from LIS database.

5.1. Measuring the impact of public policy on poverty

In thinking about how public policy affects poverty in advanced economies, we distinguish between two broad types of effects. The first starts with the simple notion that the disposable income y of a household is the sum of income obtained from "markets" (x) (labor and capital) less taxes paid (t) plus transfers received (b).

A "first order" approach to analyzing the impact of public policy defines it as the difference between poverty based on market income and that based on disposable income (by some measure P):

$$P_{i,t}[F(x); z] - P_{i,t}[F(y); z] = P_{i,t}[F(x); z] - P_{i,t}[F(x - t + b); z] = \Delta. \qquad (16)$$

This first-order definition is the wrong answer to the question "what is the impact of public policy on poverty", as the "real" impact is

$$P_{i,t}[\widetilde{F}(x); z] - P_{i,t}[F(y); z] = \widetilde{\Delta}, \qquad (17)$$

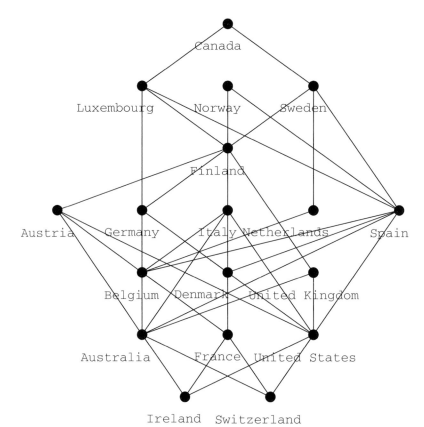

Fig. 12. Elderly poverty ordering. Hasse diagram of normalized poverty gap (TIP) dominance using LIS data. Fully relative poverty. The poverty line is defined as 60% of the overall adjusted median in each country within each year. Each elderly person (over 65) person in the household is counted once. Source: Authors' calculations from LIS data.

where $\widetilde{F}$ is the distribution of market income which would prevail without the public sector intervention in question or, more often, under some other public policies. A common view is that the first-order effect Δ overestimates the true effect $\widetilde{\Delta}$, because the quantity

$$P_{i,t}[F(x); z] - P_{i,t}[\widetilde{F}(x); z] = \Delta - \widetilde{\Delta} = \overline{\Delta}, \tag{18}$$

is assumed to be positive. That is, the difference in pre-public sector poverty assuming no behavioral responses vs. poverty after full behavioral response is assumed to be positive,

Table 7
Poverty rates and poverty trends for elderly

Country	Latest year		Longest Change		Latest Change	
	Year	Poverty rate	Years	Time trend	Years	Change
Australia	1989	41.6	1981–1989	0.316	1985–1989	−0.216
Austria	1987	28.9	n.a.		n.a.	
Belgium	1992	12.4	1985–1992	0.067	1988–1992	−0.438
Canada	1991	31.4	1971–1991	−0.921	1987–1991	0.290
Denmark	1992	18.1	1987–1992	−0.784	n.a.	
Finland	1991	17.5	1987–1991	0.661	n.a.	
France	1989	19.9	1979–1989	−0.463	1984–1989	−0.194
Germany	1989	16.9	1983–1989	17.373	1984–1989	−0.085
Ireland	1987	14.8	n.a.		n.a.	
Italy	1991	20.0	1986–1991	0.153	n.a.	
Luxembourg	1991	18.1	1985–1991	1.085	n.a.	
Netherlands	1991	15.6	1983–1991	0.868	1987–1991	1.581
Norway	1991	20.8	1979–1991	0.096	1986–1991	−1.468
Spain	1990	17.6	1980–1990	−0.247	n.a.	
Sweden	1992	15.4	1967–1992	−0.918	1987–1992	−0.274
Switzerland	1982	20.7	n.a.		n.a.	
UK	1991	32.5	1969–1991	0.017	1986–1991	3.792
US	1991	42.8	1974–1991	−0.025	1986–1991	−0.127

Numbers shown are the head count ratio using 50% of median adjusted disposable income as poverty line. Changes are measured by the slope of the regression of poverty rate on year. Every person living in a female-headed household is counted once.
Source: Authors' calculations from LIS database.

because some individuals work and save less in response to taxes and transfers than they would in their absence.[35]

We consider only the current behavioral effects of the public sector that operate via direct money flows. There are other ways in which public policy can affect poverty. For instance, beliefs about future policies regarding taxes can affect the willingness of persons to save and invest in either financial or human capital. Such longer term effects are, however, difficult to estimate, because policies change frequently during an individual's lifetime. Thus, policy changes that were enacted during the great depression

---

[35] Different tax-transfer mechanisms may have different effects on, say, labor supply. For example, benefits which are independent of market income, such as universal child allowances, have only income effects, whereas benefits that depend on market income will have both price and income effects. See Danziger et al. (1981) for estimates of these responses to the US transfer system.

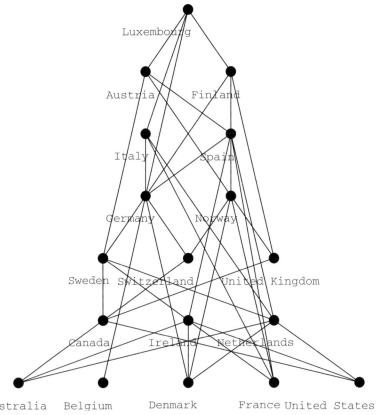

Fig. 13. Poverty ordering for persons living in female-headed households. Hasse diagram of normalized poverty gap (TIP) dominance using LIS data. Fully relative poverty. The poverty line is defined as 60% of the overall adjusted median in each country within each year. Every person living in a female-headed household is counted once. Source: Authors' calculations from LIS data.

may have current impacts because they induced people to alter their educational decisions or consumption patterns from what they would have been in their absence. Tracing out the influences of recent policy changes in order to construct a credible hypothetical distribution $\widetilde{F}$ is thus very difficult.

For practical purposes, models that revise first-order estimates of the impact of policy on poverty tend to isolate a single, often contemporaneous, policy parameter in constructing the measure $\widetilde{\Delta}$. It is not clear that this yields assessments of the public sector's role that are superior to those given by the first-order approach.

5.2. Empirical evidence on the impact of public policy on poverty

First-order effects. In Fig. 14 we show a basic measure of poverty reduction achieved by the public sector, the cross-plot of disposable and market income poverty rates. These are estimated from LIS using 50% of current adjusted disposable income as the income cut-off and showing the head-count ratio below that cut-off for both income variables.

The countries toward the top of the figure have a disposable income poverty rate that is most similar to the market income poverty rate; those toward the bottom redistribute the most, hence have a greater difference between these rates. The lines that are drawn through the origin divide the countries by the percentage reduction in poverty on moving from market to disposable income, with the lines corresponding to 0, 25, 50 and 75% reductions in poverty. The US, for example, has a market income poverty rate that is quite similar to that of Australia, Canada, the Netherlands, Italy, Denmark and Luxembourg. But its disposable income poverty rate is much higher because its system of taxes and transfers has such a small anti-poverty effect.

6. Poverty dynamics

We distinguish between two types of studies of poverty incidence across time, those that study the impact of a poverty spell in adulthood on future spells and those that study the impact of a poverty spell in childhood. The former are closely related to the study of poverty and income dynamics, whereas the latter are closely connected to the *intergenerational* transmission of poverty.[36]

6.1. Intra-generational poverty dynamics

Domestic sources. Research on the persistence of poverty requires longitudinal data on individual and/or household or family income. The prototype data set is the Panel Study of Income Dynamics (PSID) for the US (Morgan et al., 1992), in which annual data on family income has been collected starting in 1967. There are several good overviews of the US experiences, including Corcoran et al. (1985), Duncan et al. (1984) and Gottschalk et al. (1994).

A few studies discuss some of the theoretical issues, including labor market dynamics, mating and childbearing—see (Muffels, 1992), Jenkins (1998) and especially Burgess and Popper (1998).

Many studies analyze (most often male) earnings dynamics and are motivated by and explicitly address the persistence of low income and poverty, such as Geweke and Keane (1996) and Fritzell (1996). Rodgers and Rodgers (1993) develop a way of examining poverty persistence that relies on the additive decomposability of certain poverty

---

[36] There is considerable overlap between the two. For instance, intergenerational poverty could be studied by looking at the poverty status of the parents before the children were born, as well as studying the poverty status of the parents once the children are born.

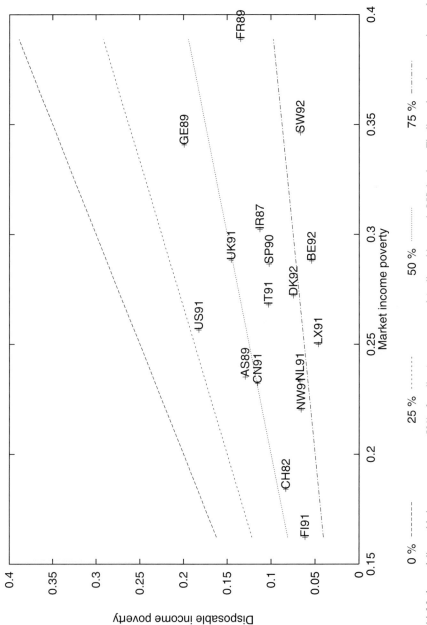

Fig. 14. Market and disposable income poverty at 50% of median (square root scale) adjusted income in LIS database. The lines show the proportionate decline in poverty due to taxes and transfers, from top to bottom: no reduction, 25, 50 and 75% reduction. Source: Authors' calculations from LIS data.

indices. Schluter (1997) provides evidence on poverty dynamics in Germany; Nolan and Whelan (1996a) use non-income measures of poverty in examining long- and short-run dynamics.

In Table 8 we show estimated poverty exit rates from a few national studies in Spain, the UK and the US. The US exit rates by Bane and Ellwood (1986) have served as a model for numerous other studies. The resource in all three countries is pre-tax income, but measured over different time periods. As Jarvis and Jenkins (1997: p. 131) point out, exit and re-entry rates should be examined together. High exit rates alone are compatible with income dynamics in which only a small part of the population shares all of the burden of poverty, with only short intervening spells on nonpoverty. This situation would be revealed by high re-entry rates.

Differences in following rules, income and household definitions, adjustments for needs and low-income cut-offs make it difficult to compare estimates such as the above. However, the similarity of UK and US exit and re-entry estimates is quite striking.

International sources. There are only a few *comparative* studies of poverty dynamics. Greg Duncan has, with a number of collaborators, prepared several of them. Duncan et al. (1993) analyze the extent to which families with incomes below 50% of the median in t have incomes above 60% of the poverty line in $t + 1$. These are more than "exit" rates, as the families are required to move some distance above the poverty line.[37]

The estimates are shown in Fig. 15, supplemented with data for Finland from Duncan et al. (1992). The relationship between the poverty rate and the escape rate is inverse. i.e., the countries in which a greater percentage of poor families exit out of poverty, are the countries that have lower rates of poverty.

Three-year cumulative survival rates for Canada, West Germany, the Netherlands and the US, also estimated by Duncal et al. (1993: p. 223), suggest a mobility ordering of countries similar to the one in Fig. 15. These results challenge the view that countries with large income differences and high poverty rates are the ones with the greatest mobility.

What kind of a relationship is to be expected between the probability of poverty exit and the poverty rate? Suppose that poverty outcomes between two consecutive years are independent and that the poverty rate is stable. It follows that the exit rate, $\Pr(y_{t_2} \geq z | y_{t_1} < z)$,

$$\Pr(y_{t_2} \geq z | y_{t_1} < z) = \frac{\Pr(y_{t_2} \geq z)\Pr(y_{t_1} < z)}{\Pr(y_{t_1} < z)} = 1 - \Pr(y < z). \tag{19}$$

---

[37] This explains why the US exit rate in Table 8 is so much higher than in Fig. 15.

Table 8

Poverty exit and re-entry rates in national studies

Country	Time period	Resource	Exit rate in period		Re-entry rate in period		Source
			First	Second	First	Second	
US	1971–81	Annual adjusted family income	0.45	0.29	n.a.	n.a.	Bane and Ellwood (1986)
US	1971–87	Annual adjusted family income	0.53	0.36	0.27	0.16	Stevens (1995)
UK	1991–94	Current adjusted family income	0.54	0.51	0.29	0.11	Jarvis and Jenkins (1997)
Spain	1991:2–92:4	Quarterly per capita family income	0.37 (0.21–0.45)	n.a.	n.a.	n.a.	Cantó-Sánchez (1996)

Spain: Poverty is defined in terms of half of median income. For quarterly exit rates, the average, min and max rates shown. Data stem from the Spanish Household Panel Survey (ECPF). UK: Poverty is defined w.r.t half of mean income. Data stem from the British Household Panel Survey. US: Poverty defined in terms of US official poverty line. Data stem from the Panel Study of Income Dynamics.

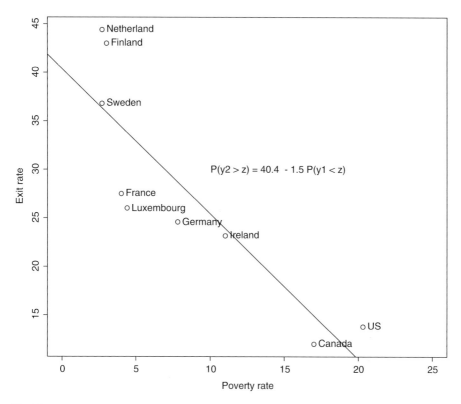

Fig. 15. Poverty and exit out of poverty. Poverty rates are measured as having adjusted income less than half of current median in t_1 and exit rates as the head count of those poor in year t with income higher than 60% of median. The solid line is the regression of exit rate on poverty. See Eq. (20) in text. Source: Duncan et al. (1992, 1993).

Thus, the slope of a regression of $\Pr(y_{t_2} \geq z | y_{t_1} < z)$ on $\Pr(y_{t_1} < z)$ would equal -1 if outcomes were independent and poverty stationary. Estimating this regression using the data for the nine countries in Fig. 15 yields

$$\Pr(y_{t_2} \geq z | y_{t_1} < z) = \underset{(3.3)}{40.4} \underset{(0.3)}{-1.5 \Pr(y_{t_1} < z)}, \, R^2(\text{adj}) = 0.72. \tag{20}$$

If we ignore that the income distribution is unlikely to be stationary, the extent to which the coefficient on $\Pr(y_{t_1} < z)$ is different from -1 could be used as a measure of the average persistence (in excess of independence) of two-year poverty.[38]

Deleeck et al. (1992) estimate two-year poverty and exit rates out of poverty for Belgium, Ireland, Lorraine and Luxembourg and the Netherlands. Exit rates are estimated (using the EC standard of poverty) to vary between 36% in Ireland and 59% in the Netherlands (p. 102). Exit rates for households with an unemployed head (in the first year) are always lower, sometimes only about one half of the exit rates of employed heads. An interesting finding is that the relative risks of entering poverty and staying there are fairly similar to the relative risks of being in poverty, as measured in a single-year cross-section. Thus, the correlates of poverty risks as assessed using cross-sections give, at least in these data, some indication of the correlates of poverty persistence.[39]

There is considerable mobility in the low end of the income distribution, and patterns of mobility do vary across countries. Recent studies of income dynamics question the traditional view that large differences in incomes are associated with high mobility. Further research, using longer and larger panels and looking at individuals, where possible, rather than households is needed to gain further and more robust insights into the cross-country patterns of longitudinal poverty.[40]

6.2. Family background and poverty

Domestic sources. Many studies measure the effects of family background on adult poverty outcomes for children in the US; they are reviewed by Corcoran (1995). These studies analyze actual patterns of "transitions" between childhood and adult poverty status, measured in a multitude of ways, including welfare receipt and low incomes. Researchers have addressed various explanations for the observed correlation of adult and child poverty outcomes, in particular the effect of environmental and social influences in childhood, such as experiencing a parental divorce, growing up in a high-poverty neighborhood, and so on.

---

[38] Let the event that $y_{t_1} < z$ be A and $y_{t_2} < z$ be B. From simple probability definitions it follows that the difference $\delta = \Pr(B|A) - \Pr(B)$ measures the extent to which there is more or less persistence than would be the case of A and B were independent. Suppose $\delta = \delta_0 + \delta_1 \Pr(B)$. Then $1 - \Pr(B|A) = (1-\delta_0) - (1+\delta_1)\Pr(B)$ and, for poverty persistence ($\delta_j \geq 0$) we would, indeed, observe the intercept less than one and the slope smaller than negative one. The regression in Eq. (20) was estimated using the nine countries' poverty rates (head count ratio of adjusted incomes below half of median) and exit rates (adjusted income more than 60% of median) measured in the following year.

[39] Some aspects of the Deleeck et al. (1992) results raise questions. For instance, only intact households are included, so that poverty spells of all individuals can not be assessed. Also, classifying people according to status in year 1 neglects the fact that they may change their status between the first and second wave. Moreover, the data sometimes cover two consecutive years (NL, Lo, Lu) and sometimes two years that are one year apart. This would, if exit rates were constant across countries, generate different exit rates as measured in the panel.

[40] For additional references and discussion, see Duncan et al. (1992), Duncan et al. (1993) and Burkhauser et al. (1998). See also Atkinson et al. (1992).

Table 9

Adult outcomes by childhood poverty in the US

Early adult outcomes	Childhood poverty status			
	Black		White	
	Poor	Nonpoor	Poor	Nonpoor
Mean schooling	12.3	12.9	11.1	13.5
Average family income (1980 USD)	16,980	22,778	22,141	33,655
Average ratio of income to needs	2.1	3.0	2.6	4.4
Percent who are poor as adults	24.9	9.6	9.3	1.2

Sample: Adults aged 27 to 35 yeas in 1988 from the PSID. Child outcomes are observed starting in 1968 for 3–13 years before age 17 and adult outcomes for 3–11 years after age 24. n = 969 (blacks) and 1306 (whites). Source: Corcoran (1995), Table 1, p. 247.

The US literature was made possible by two projects—the Panel Study of Income Dynamics (PSID) and the National Longitudinal Survey (NLS)—that collect longitudinal information on socio-economic phenomena at the individual and household level and that have been running long enough for both parents and children to be observed in adulthood.

Other countries have hitherto not gathered such data or have begun to do so only recently and, consequently, little is known about their actual transmission of poverty status across generations.[41] Studies in these countries have relied on data on the parents that have been recalled by the children in adulthood, a source that suffers from large and possibly non-random errors. Data on background factors, such as parental education, occupation, family structure during childhood and residential location, typically entered as covariates in explaining adult outcomes, are likely to suffer from less recall error than information about parental income. Explanations of poverty outcomes that make use of parental background information are, therefore, likely to be more reliable than actual patterns of income and poverty mobility.

Growing up in a poor household in the US is adversely associated with adult socio-economic outcomes. Educational attainment and average family income are worse and poverty risks are higher (Table 9). It would appear that race matters. While the outcomes for blacks are overall lower than for whites, growing up in poverty appears to be associated with larger differences compared to the nonpoor for whites. This is also evident in poverty transitions between generations (Table 10). Most studies that attempt to control for background factors in a multivariate context suggest substantial parental income influences on adult outcomes (Corcoran, 1995).

---

[41] There is at least one exception to this, the UK National Child Development Survey, which sampled all children born in Britain during a single week in 1951. Data on the parents was collected at the time of birth and the children have since been followed up at 5 occasions. Apparently these data contain only poor information about parental income.

Table 10

Transitions between childhood and early adult poverty

Childhood upbringing	Early adult outcomes		
Poverty status during childhood	Percent never poor	Percent poor 1–50% of year	Percent poor 51–100% of years
	Black		
Never poor	73.8	17.9	8.3
Poor 1–50% of years	63.3	17.0	19.8
Poor 51–100% of years	53.7	19.9	26.4
	White		
Never poor	89.8	9.0	1.2
Poor 1–50% of years	77.9	18.6	3.7
Poor 51–100% of years	75.9	14.3	9.3

Sample: Adults aged 27 to 35 years in 1988 from the PSID. Child outcomes are observed starting in 1968 for 3–13 years before age 17 and adult outcomes for 3–11 years after age 24. n = 969 (blacks) and 1306 (whites). Source: Corcoran (1995), Table 2, p. 248.

Some evidence on the intergenerational transmission of poverty is available from the UK. Namely, Atkinson et al. (1983) traced the adult children of the sample used by Seebohm Rowntree and associates in the 1950s in York (see Rowntree and Lavers, 1951). Using data of limited geographic coverage to gauge the bivariate distribution of parent-child income is subject to a number of limitations, as is using mainly single-year measures of income.[42] The authors discuss these limitations and also compare cross-sectional data from their resulting followed-up sample with nationally representative ones. While the data fall short of the ideal of a nationally representative panel with long-run income for both parents and children, Atkinson et al. (1983) carefully constructed income information and were very explicit about the possible shortcomings of the data. Moreover, the children were sampled through the follow-up at a stage in their life-cycle quite similar to that of their parents, which avoids the problem that the correlation of a young persons annual income with her long-run income may be quite low (see, e.g., Björklund, 1993). Examining patterns of intergenerational low income incidence is instructive. We show the 3×3 transition matrix for the followed-up sample in Table 11.

Given the differences in income definitions, sample design and coverage, and so on, it is not easy to compare these figures to US numbers. The odds of children of low income parents that remain low income rather than become comfortably off is 2.6. The odds that comfortably off children remain so rather than become low income is 1.7. While the odds of staying poor and comfortably off are quite high, there is also substantial movement across income classes.

[42] See Jenkins (1987 and Solon (1989).

Table 11

Intergenerational income transition matrices in the UK (York)

Parent	Children		
	Low income	Intermediate	Comfortably off
Low income	48.2	33.3	18.5
Intermediate	25.8	35.1	39.1
Comfortably off	26.5	29.1	44.1

Incomes are defined as family earnings, transfers, other income less taxes, national insurance contributions, other deductions and housing costs. These are then divided by the National Assistance (Parents, 1950) or Supplementary Benefit (Children, 1975–78) scale. The observations are classified as "low income" if they are below 1.4 times the NA/SB scale, "intermediate" if between 1.4–1.99 and "comfortably off" if they have more than twice the NA/SB scale. The overall sample size is 1430.

Source: Atkinson et al. (1983), Table 5.6, p. 81. See also p. 71 for the income definitions and pp. 46–52 for sample follow-up procedures.

Table 12

Generated intergenerational earnings mobility matrices in Sweden and the US

Father's income class	Son's income class			
	Poor <50% of median	Lower middle 50% of median to median	Higher middle median to 150% of median	Well-to-do ≥150% of median
		Sweden		
Poor	0.254	0.370	0.278	0.098
Lower middle	0.189	0.350	0.321	0.141
Higher middle	0.141	0.321	0.350	0.189
Well to-do	0.098	0.278	0.370	0.254
		United States		
Poor	0.403	0.252	0.197	0.148
Lower middle	0.296	0.249	0.232	0.223
Higher middle	0.223	0.232	0.249	0.296
Well to-do	0.148	0.197	0.252	0.403

The variance of five-year average earnings, standard deviations is 0.48 and 0.61 for fathers and 0.52 and 0.80 for sons in Sweden and the US; and $\rho = 0.20$ for Sweden and $\rho = 0.28$ for the US. The probabilities give the son's probability conditional on father's income class.

Source: Björklund and Jäntti (1997).

International sources. There exist no comparative studies that compare intergenerational poverty transitions. Indirect evidence can be inferred from work on intergenerational income correlations. As longer panel data have become available, studies that estimate the intergenerational correlation in earnings, most often of fathers and sons as young adults, have become more common.

Subject to stringent assumptions regarding functional form, estimates of the inter-generational correlations can be used to illustrate earnings outcomes. For example, in Table 12 we show the patterns of mobility between different earnings classes in Sweden and the United States, given estimated correlations and the assumptions that (a) the sons' long-run earnings variance is equal to that of the fathers' and (b) the data are drawn from a bivariate log-normal distribution. The results suggest a considerably higher "poverty" persistence in the United States relative to Sweden, a pattern that is accounted for by both the higher correlation and the higher cross-sectional variance.The assumptions that underlie the present numbers are strong. Moreover, the numbers in Table 12 refer to long-run earnings (measured quite early in the sons life). When longer panel data sets become available in other countries, further research can examine if findings such as the above persist when parametric assumptions are relaxed.

7. Summary

In this chapter, we have reviewed definitional issues that arise in assessing the extent of and change in poverty in western industrialized countries. Many issues must be resolved prior to (and after) analyzing empirical evidence on poverty, including the choice of resource, level of poverty line and appropriate adjustments for the size and type of the income-sharing unit. The specific choices that are made w.r.t these issues and a number of others influence the extent of measured poverty. The objective of assessing poverty is, however, often comparative: to compare the change in poverty over time within a country or across countries. We suggested that specific measurement choices are in that case less likely to affect a poverty ordering arrived at using the same methods than they are to affect the level in any country at a point in time.

We reviewed the existing empirical evidence and presented our own estimates using the LIS database, and demonstrated that the results are sensitive to the definitional issues discussed. Depending on how resources, poverty lines and equivalence scales are defined, for instance, poverty in Ireland increased a lot, a little, did not change or decreased a lot using the same data set between two years. Nonetheless, when we apply a consistent definition of poverty to the data sets available in LIS, we find that certain countries have poverty rates that are clearly higher (or lower) than those in other countries. However, there is little evidence for a uniform trend in poverty across countries—in recent years, poverty has increased in some countries and decreased in others.

Looking at the first-order impact of the public sector suggests that countries with similar rates of market income poverty can have very different poverty rates once taxes and transfers have been received. Longitudinal aspects of poverty have been most extensively studied where suitable data are available, most often in the US. Looking at cross-national evidence suggests that much remains to be learned about the patterns of intra- and intergenerational poverty mobility and their covariates. Given that longitudinal data that enable the study also on a cross-national basis of these issues are increasingly available, this is an area where our knowledge is likely to expand rapidly.

Appendix: Data sources

Data sources are listed in the following tables

Table A1

Poverty rates

Country	Years	Poverty rate	Resource	Poverty line	Equivalence scale	Reference
Australia	1981, 1985	12.5, 12.3	Disposable income	50% of median	Square root	Atkinson et al. (1995)
	1981, 1985, 1989	14.4, 15.7, 16.1	Disposable income	50% of average	OECD	Cantillon et al. (1996)
	1981.5, 1989.5	9.4, 15.0	Income AHC	Henderson poverty line	New York Budget Survey of 1954	Saunders (1997)
	1981.5, 1989.5	10.2, 16.4	Income BHC	Henderson poverty line	New York Budget Survey of 1954	Saunders (1997)
Austria	1987	6.7	Disposable income	50% of median	Square root	Atkinson et al. (1995)
Belgium	1985, 1988	2.9, 4.7	Disposable income	50% of median	Square root	Atkinson et al. (1995)
	1985, 1988, 1992	5.8, 6.2, 5.5	Disposable income	50% of average	OECD	Cantillon et al. (1996)
	1987, 1989	6.1, 5.7	Disposable income	50% of average income	OECD	Deleeck et al. (1992)
	1987, 1989	21.4, 22.4	Disposable income	CSP	Implied by CSP	Deleeck et al. (1992)
	1987, 1989	24.9, 20.7	Disposable income	SPL	Implied by SPL	Deleeck et al. (1992)
	1987, 1989	2.9, 2.7	Disposable income	legal	Implied by legal standard	Deleeck et al. (1992)
	1976, 1980, 1985	7.9, 7.6, 7.2	Disposable income	50% of average disposable income	OECD	O'Higgins and Jenkins (1990)
	1978–79, 1987–88	4.7, 7.4	Expenditure	50% of average	(1, 0.5, 0.3)	de Vos and Zaidi (1996)
Canada	1981, 1987	12.6, 12.2	Disposable income	50% of median	Square root	Atkinson et al. (1995)
	1975, 1981, 1987, 1991	10.2, 9.0, 8.1, 7.6	Disposable income	50% of average	OECD	Cantillon et al. (1996)
	1970, 1973, 1979, 1986	17.0, 10.6, 7.8, 7.1	Income	US poverty level (1985 PPP)	US poverty	Hanratty and Blank (1992)
Catalonia	1988	15.1	Disposable income	50% of average income	OECD	Deleeck et al. (1992)
	1988	31.3	Disposable income	CSP	Implied by CSP	Deleeck et al. (1992)
	1988	37.3	Disposable income	SPL	Implied by SPL	Deleeck et al. (1992)
Denmark	1987, 1992	8.9, 5.5	Disposable income	50% of average	OECD	Cantillon et al. (1996)
	1977, 1980, 1985	12.4, 13.0, 14.7	Disposable income	50% of average disposable income	OECD	O'Higgins and Jenkins (1990)
	1976, 1977, 1978, 1979, 1980, 1981, 1982, 1983, 1984, 1985, 1986, 1987, 1988, 1989, 1990	11.53, 11.35, 10.78, 10.15, 9.60, 10.20, 11.35, 10.87, 10.01, 10.17, 9.95, 9.06, 9.72, 9.62, 10.34	Disposable income	50% of adjusted median	OECD	Pedersen and Smith (1996)
EC	1973/77, 1978/81, 1984/85	12.8, 12.6, 13.9	Disposable income	50% of average disposable income	OECD	O'Higgins and Jenkins (1990)
Finland	1987	5.0	Disposable income	50% of median	Square root	Atkinson et al. (1995)
	1987, 1991	5.5, 6.4	Disposable income	50% of average	OECD	Cantillon et al. (1996)
	1966, 1971, 1976, 1981, 1985	20.1, 12.8, 5.1, 4.9, 2.9	Disposable income	Official (current national pension)	OECD	Gustafsson and Uusitalo (1990)
	1971, 1976, 1981, 1985, 1990, 1991, 1992, 1993	8.8, 5.1, 5.8, 3.5, 2.7, 3.6, 3.4, 3.2	Disposable income	50% of disposable median	OECD	Jäntti and Ritakallio (1996a)
	1981, 1985, 1990	4.9, 3.5, 2.5	Disposable income	50% of median	OECD	Jäntti and Ritakallio (1996b)
France	1979, 1984	8.2, 7.5	Disposable income	50% of median	Square root	Atkinson et al. (1995)
	1979, 1984	13.2, 11.9	Disposable income	50% of average	OECD	Cantillon et al. (1996)
	1975, 1979, 1985	19.9, 17.7, 17.5	Disposable income	50% of average disposable income	OECD	O'Higgins and Jenkins (1990)
	1984–85, 1989	12.4, 14.7	Expenditure	50% of average	(1, 0.5, 0.3)	de Vos and Zaidi (1996)
Germany	1984	6.5	Disposable income	50% of median	Square root	Atkinson et al. (1995)
	1978, 1983	8.2, 8.0	Disposable income	50% of average	OECD	Cantillon et al. (1996)
	1983, 1987, 1990	8.3, 7.7, 8.8	Income		1, 0.8, 0.45–0.9	Hauser and Becker (1993)
	1973, 1978, 1985	8.8, 6.7, 8.5	Disposable income	50% of average disposable income	OECD	O'Higgins and Jenkins (1990)
	1983, 1988	8.9, 9.7	Expenditure	50% of average	(1, 0.5, 0.3)	de Vos and Zaidi (1996)
Greece	1988	19.9	Disposable income	50% of average income	OECD	Deleeck et al. (1992)
	1988	42.6	Disposable income	CSP	Implied by CSP	Deleeck et al. (1992)
	1988	42.0	Disposable income	SPL	Implied by SPL	Deleeck et al. (1992)
	1974, 1981, 1985	26.6, 24.2, 24.0	Disposable income	50% of average disposable income	OECD	O'Higgins and Jenkins (1990)
	1982, 1988	18.1, 17.9	Expenditure	50% of average	(1, 0.5, 0.3)	de Vos and Zaidi (1996)
Iceland	1986, 1988, 1989, 1991, 1992, 1993, 1995	9.8, 9.5, 8.0, 9.0, 9.8, 10.5, 12.5				Olafsson and Sigurdsson (1996)

Table A1

(continued)

Country	Years	Poverty rate	Resource	Poverty line	Equivalence scale	Reference
Ireland	1987	10.7	Disposable income	50% of median	Square root	Atkinson et al. (1995)
	1973, 1980, 1987	15.9, 17.4, 21.2	Disposable income	50% of average	1, 0.6, 0.4	Cantillon et al. (1996)
	1987, 1989	17.2, 17.3	Disposable income	50% of average income	OECD	Deleeck et al. (1992)
	1987, 1989	29.6, 32.0	Disposable income	CSP	Implied by CSP	Deleeck et al. (1992)
	1987, 1989	31.6, 39.6	Disposable income	SPL	Implied by SPL	Deleeck et al. (1992)
	1987, 1989	8.0, 5.0	Disposable income	Legal	Implied by legal standard	Deleeck et al. (1992)
	1973, 1980, 1985	16.4, 16.9, 22.0	Disposable income	50% of average disposable income	OECD	O'Higgins and Jenkins (1990)
Italy	1975, 1980, 1984	10.6, 9.4, 11.7	Disposable income	50% of average disposable income	OECD	O'Higgins and Jenkins (1990)
	1985, 1989	18.6, 21.1	Expenditure	50% of average	(1, 0.5, 0.3)	de Vos and Zaidi (1996)
Lorraine	1987, 1989	9.7, 10.8	Disposable income	50% of average income	OECD	Deleeck et al. (1992)
	1987, 1989	26.6, 30.8	Disposable income	CSP	Implied by CSP	Deleeck et al. (1992)
	1987, 1989	29.1, 26.5	Disposable income	SPL	Implied by SPL	Deleeck et al. (1992)
	1987, 1989	5.7, 4.0	Disposable income	Legal	Implied by legal standard	Deleeck et al. (1992)
Luxembourg	1985	5.4	Disposable income	50% of median	Square root	Atkinson et al. (1995)
	1987, 1989	7.6, 7.6	Disposable income	50% of average income	OECD	Deleeck et al. (1992)
	1987, 1989	14.7, 14.5	Disposable income	CSP	Implied by CSP	Deleeck et al (1992)
	1987, 1989	23.2, 12.5	Disposable income	SPL	Implied by SPL	Deleeck et al. (1992)
	1987, 1989	6.4, 5.0	Disposable income	Legal	Implied by legal standard	Deleeck et al. (1992)
Netherlands	1983, 1987	6.6, 4.9	Disposable income	50% of median	Square root	Atkinson et al. (1995)
	1986, 1987, 1988	6.5, 8.3, 9.2	Disposable income	Legal poverty line	Those implied by legal poverty line	Dirven and Berghman (1992)
	1986, 1987, 1988	12.1, 12.7, 14.7	Disposable income	Subjective poverty line	Those implied by subjective poverty line	Dirven and Berghman (1992)
	1983, 1987, 1991	9.3, 8.3, 7.7	Disposable income	50% of average	OECD	Cantillon et al. (1996)
	1987, 1989	7.1, 7.2	Disposable income	50% of average income	OECD	Deleeck et al. (1992)
	1987, 1989	12.4, 10.9	Disposable income	CSP	Implied by CSP	Deleeck et al. (1992)
	1987, 1989	8.6, 15.9	Disposable income	SPL	Implied by SPL	Deleeck et al. (1992)
	1987, 1989	8.5, 7.2	Disposable income	Legal	Implied by legal standard	Deleeck et al. (1992)
	1977, 1981, 1985	6.6, 7.0, 7.4	EDI	50% of average disposable income	OECD	O'Higgins and Jenkins (1990)
	1980, 1988	4.7, 4.8	Expenditure	50% of average	Modified OECD (1, 0.5, 0.3)	de Vos and Zaidi (1996)
Norway	1979, 1982, 1984, 1985, 1986, 1987, 1988, 1990, 1991, 1992, 1993	5.2, 5.0, 3.3, 4.4, 4.9, 5.6, 6.5, 5.6, 5.7, 5.9, 6.3, 5.5	Disposable income	50% of median disposable income	OECD	Aaberge et al. (1996)
	1979, 1982, 1984, 1985, 1986, 1987, 1998, 1990, 1991, 1992, 1993	6.3, 6.2, 3.9, 4.9, 4.5, 5.0, 6.4, 5.8, 5.7, 5.7, 5.7, 4.5	Disposable income	50% of oerv-time average median	OECD	Aaberge et al. (1996)
	1979, 1982, 1984, 1985, 1986, 1987, 1988, 1990, 1991, 1992, 1993	5.5, 5.6, 4.3, 4.6, 5.2, 5.1, 5.5, 6.2, 6.4, 6.5, 7.1, 5.5	Disposable income	Legal pension	OECD	Aaberge et al. (1996)
	1979, 1982, 1984, 1985, 1986, 1987, 1988, 1990, 1991, 1992, 1993	5.1, 4.5, 3.4, 3.1, 3.7, 3.7, 4.0, 4.1	Net income	50% of median disposable income	OECD	Aaberge et al. (1996)
	1979, 1982, 1984, 1985, 1986, 1987, 1988, 1990, 1991, 1992, 1993	7.3, 7.3, 4.8, 3.3, 3.3, 2.5, 3.0, 3.9, 3.8, 3.9, 4.4, 4.1	Net income	50% of the over-time average medians	OECD	Aaberge et al. (1996)
	1979, 1982, 1984, 1985, 1986, 1987, 1988, 1990, 1991, 1992, 1993	5.0, 4.4, 3.1, 2.7, 2.8, 1.9, 2.0, 3.1,	Net income	Legal pension	OECD	Aaberge et al. (1996)
	1979, 1986	5.0, 7.3	Disposable income	50% of median	Square root	Atkinson et al. (1995)
	1979, 1986, 1991	4.8, 6.4, 5.3	Disposable income	50% of average	OECD	Cantillon et al. (1996)

Table A1

(continued)

Country	Years	Poverty rate	Resource	Poverty line	Equivalence scale	Reference
Portugal	1973/74, 1981, 1985	23.4, 27.8, 28.0	Disposable income	50% of average disposable income	OECD	O'Higgins and Jenkins (1990)
	1980, 1989	26.4, 24, 5	Expenditure	50% of national average	(1, 0.5, 0.3)	de Vos and Zaidi (1996)
Spain	1973, 1980, 1985	20.0, 20.5, 20.0	Disposable income	50% of average disposable income	OECD	O'Higgins and Jenkins (1990)
	1980, 1990	17.5, 15.9	Expenditure	50% of average	(1, 0.5, 0.3)	de Vos and Zaidi (1996)
Sweden	1981, 1987	5.4, 7.6	Disposable income	50% of median	Square root	Atkinson (1995)
	1975, 1981, 1987, 1992	5.2, 4.6, 6.3, 6.0	Disposable income	50% of average	OECD	Cantillon et al. (1996)
	1975, 1978, 1980, 1981, 1982, 1983, 1984, 1985, 1986, 1987, 1988, 1989, 1990, 1991, 1992, 1993	3.8, 2.7, 3.1, 3.5, 3.8, 3.9, 4.1, 4.6, 4.0, 4.3, 3.9, 4.4, 4.6, 4.8, 5.1, 5.2, 5.7	Disposable income	50% of disposable median	OECD	Gustafsson (1996)
	1975, 1978, 1980, 1981, 1982, 1984, 1985	11.8, 9.1, 8.0, 8.2, 9.8, 10.4, 8.6	Disposable income	Official (Soc. Ass. guidelines of 1985)	OECD	Gustafsson (1990)
Switzerland	1982	8.0	Disposable income	50% of median	Square root	Atkinson et al. (1995)
UK	1979, 1986	9.2, 9.1	Disposable income	50% of median	Square root	Atkinson et al. (1995)
	1974, 1979, 1986	11.4, 10.8, 13.0	Disposable income	50% of average	OECD	Cantillon et al. (1996)
	1978, 1982, 1985, 1988, 1991	6.8, 7.8, 10.7, 18.3, 20.4	Income (BHC)		0.61, 0.4, 0.09 −0.36	Goodman and Webb (1994)
	1975, 1980, 1985	6.7, 9.2, 12.0	Disposable income	50% of average disposable income	OECD	O'Higgins and Jenkins (1990)
	1985, 1988	12.8, 14.9	Expenditure	50% of average	(1, 0.5, 0.3)	de Vos and Zaidi (1996)
US	1979, 1986	16.6, 18.4	Disposable income	50% of median	Square root	Atkinson et al. (1995)
	1974, 1979, 1986, 1991	18.8, 18.6, 22.6, 22.6	Disposable income	50% of average	OECD	Cantillon et al. (1996)
	1959, 1960, 1961, 1962, 1963, 1964, 1965, 1966, 1967, 1968, 1969, 1970, 1971, 1972, 1973, 1974, 1975, 1976, 1977, 1978, 1979, 1980, 1981, 1982, 1983, 1984, 1985, 1989, 1990, 1991, 1992, 1993, 1994, 1995	18.5, 18.1, 18.1, 17.2, 15.9, 15.0, 13.9, 11.8, 11.4, 10.0, 9.7, 10.1, 10.0, 9.3, 8.8, 8.8, 9.7, 9.4, 9.3, 9.1, 9.2, 10.3, 11.2, 12.2, 12.3, 11.6, 11.4, 10.9, 10.7, 11.5, 11.9, 12.3, 11.6, 10.8	Money income	US poverty line	US poverty line	US Census Bureau (n.d.)
	1986, 1987, 1988,	10.4, 10.3, 10.7,				
	1970, 1973, 1979, 1986	10.1, 9.5, 9.0, 11.6	Income	US official poverty line	US poverty scale	Hanratty and Blank (1992)

Source: Authors' compilation based on the listed studies.

Table A2

Poverty rates of children

Country	Years	Poverty rate	Resource	Poverty line	Equivalence scale	Reference
Australia	1981, 1985, 1989	16.4, 17.0, 18.3	Disposable income	50% of average	OECD	Cantillon et al. (1996)
Australia	1982, 1986, 1990	14.0, 13.1, 14.0	Disposable income	50% of median disposable income	EI = $y/([\text{hh size}] \cdot 3.3 \times 0.99 \lvert \text{head's age} = 45 \rvert)$	Rainwater and Smeeding (1995)
Austria	1987	4.8	Disposable income	50% of median disposable income	EI = $y/([\text{hh size}] \cdot 3.3 \times 0.99 \lvert \text{head's age} = 45 \rvert)$	Rainwater and Smeeding (1995)
Belgium	1985, 1988, 1992 1992	4.7, 4.9, 4.9	Disposable income	50% of average	OECD	Cantillon et al. (1996)
Belgium	1985, 1988, 1992	3.4, 3.1, 3.8	Disposable income	50% of median disposable income	EI = $y/([\text{hh size}] \cdot 3.3 \times 0.99 \lvert \text{head's age} = 45 \rvert)$	Rainwater and Smeeding (1995)
Canada	1975, 1981 1987, 1991	16.5, 17.9, 18.1, 17.5	Disposable income	50% of average	OECD	Cantillon et al. (1996)
Canada	1971, 1975, 1981, 1987,	15.2, 14.6, 13.9, 13.6, 13.5	Disposable income	50% of median disposable income	EI = $y/([\text{hh size}] \cdot 3.3 \times 0.99 \lvert \text{head's age} = 45 \rvert)$	Rainwater and Smeeding (1995)
Denmark	1987, 1992	4.0, 3.6	Disposable income	50% of average	OECD	Cantillon et al. (1996)
Denmark	1987, 1992	5.3, 3.3	Disposable income	50% of median disposable income	EI = $y/([\text{hh size}] \cdot 3.3 \times 0.99 \lvert \text{head's age} = 45 \rvert)$	Rainwater and Smeeding (1995)
Finland	1987, 1991	3.4, 3.1	Disposable income	50% of average	OECD	Cantillon et al. (1996)
Finland	1987, 1991	2.9, 2.5	Disposable income	50% of median disposable income	EI = $y/([\text{hh size}] \cdot 3.3 \times 0.99 \lvert \text{head's age} = 45 \rvert)$	Rainwater and Smeeding (1995)
France	1979, 1984	12.8, 13.1	Disposable income	50% of average	OECD	Cantillon et al. (1996)
France	1979, 1984	6.4, 6.5	Disposable income	50% of median disposable income	EI = $y/(\text{hh size}) \cdot 3.3 \times 0.99 \lvert \text{head's age} = 45 \rvert)$	Rainwater and Smeeding (1995)
Germany	1978, 1983	4.9, 6.5	Disposable income	50% of average	OECD	Cantillon et al. (1996)
Germany	1985, 1989	4.0, 3.2, 4.8	Disposable income	50% of median disposable income	EI = $y/([\text{hh size}] \cdot 3.3 \times 0.99 \lvert \text{head's age} = 45 \rvert)$	Rainwater and Smeeding (1995)
Germany	1985, 1989	6.4, 6.8	Disposable income	50% of median disposable income	EI = $y/([\text{hh size}] \cdot 3.3 \times 0.99 \lvert \text{head's age} = 45 \rvert)$	Rainwater and Smeeding (1995)
Ireland	1973, 1980, 1987	15.7, 18.5, 26.0	Disposable income	50% of average	1, 0.6, 0.4	Cantillon et al. (1996)
Ireland	1987	12.0	Disposable income	50 % of median disposable income	EI = $y/([\text{hh size}] \cdot 3.3 \times 0.99 \lvert \text{head's age} = 45 \rvert)$	Rainwater and Smeeding (1995)
Israel	1979, 1986	8.2, 11.1	Disposable income	50% of median disposable income	EI = $y/([\text{hh size}] \cdot 3.3 \times 0.99 \lvert \text{head's age} = 45 \rvert)$	Rainwater and Smeeding (1995)
Italy	1986, 1991	10.8, 9.6	Disposable income	50% of median disposable income	EI = $y/([\text{hh size}] \cdot 3.3 \times 0.99 \lvert \text{head's age} = 45 \rvert)$	Rainwater and Smeeding (1995)
Luxembourg	1985	4.1	Disposable income	50% of median disposable income	EI = $y/([\text{hh size}] \cdot 3.3 \times 0.99 \lvert \text{head's age} = 45 \rvert)$	Rainwater and Smeeding (1995)
Netherlands	1983, 1987, 1991	7.0, 8.9, 9.2	Disposable income	50% of average	OECD	Cantillon et al. (1996)
Netherlands	1985	4.1	Disposable income	50% of median disposable income	EI = $y/([\text{hh size}] \cdot 3.3 \times 0.99 \lvert \text{head's age} = 45 \rvert)$	Rainwater and Smeeding (1995)
Norway	1979, 1985, 1991	4.5, 6.0, 8.2	Disposable income	50% of median	OECD	Aaberge et al. (1996)
Norway	1979, 1985, 1991	4.1, 3.4, 5.8	Net income	50% of median	OECD	Aaberge et al. (1996)
Norway	1979, 1986, 1991	4.4, 3.9, 3.9	Disposable income	50% of average	OECD	Cantillon et al. (1996)
Norway	1979, 1986, 1991	3.8, 3.8, 4.6	Disposable income	50% of median disposable income	EI = $y/([\text{hh size}] \cdot 3.3 \times 0.99 \lvert \text{head's age} = 45 \rvert)$	Rainwater and Smeeding (1995)
Sweden	1975, 1981, 1987, 1992	2.1, 4.5, 3.1, 2.6	Disposable income	50% of average	OECD	Cantillon et al. (1996)
Sweden	1967, 1975, 1981, 1987, 1992	3.3, 1.9, 3.9, 3.0, 2.7	Disposable income	50% of median disposable income	EI = $y/([\text{hh size}] \cdot 3.3 \times 0.99 \lvert \text{head's age} = 45 \rvert)$	Rainwater and Smeeding (1995)
Switzerland	1982	3.3	Disposable income	50% of median disposable income	EI = $y/([\text{hh size}] \cdot 3.3 \times 0.99 \lvert \text{head's age} = 45 \rvert)$	Rainwater and Smeeding (1995)
UK	1974, 1979, 1986	10.8, 10.7, 17.4	Disposable income	50% of average	OECD	Cantillon et al. (1996)
UK	1969, 1974, 1979, 1986	5.4, 7.0, 8.5, 9.9	Disposable income	50% of median disposable income	EI = $y/([\text{hh size}] \cdot 3.3 \times 0.99 \lvert \text{head's age} = 45 \rvert)$	Rainwater and Smeeding (1995)
US	1974, 1979, 1986, 1991	22.8, 24.1, 30.7, 30.3	Disposable income	50% of average	OECD	Cantillon et al. (1996)
US	1969, 1974, 1979, 1986, 1991	13.1, 17.3, 18.5, 22.9, 21.5	Disposable income	50% of median disposable income	EI = $y/([\text{hh size}] \cdot 3.3 \times 0.99 \lvert \text{head's age} = 45 \rvert)$	Rainwater and Smeeding (1995)

Source: Authors' compilation based on the listed studies.

Table A3

Poverty rates of elderly

Country	Years	Poverty rate	Resource	Poverty line	Equivalence scale	Reference
Over 65						
Australia	1981, 1985, 1989	29.9, 33.4, 32.5	Disposable income	50% of average	OECD	Cantillon et al. (1996)
Australia	1981, 1985	30.6, 33.9	Gross income	50% of median equivalent gross income	OECD	Phipps (1994)
Belgium	1985, 1988, 1992	11.3, 10.6, 10.6	Disposable income	50% of average	OECD	Cantillon et al. (1996)
Canada	1975, 1981, 1987, 1991	34.5, 24.6, 14.3, 8.6	Disposable income	50% of average	OECD	Cantillon et al. (1996)
Canada	1981, 1987	22.0, 12.8	Gross income	50% of median equivalent gross income	OECD	Phipps (1994)
Denmark	1987, 1992	25.9, 6.3	Disposable income	50% of average	OECD	Cantillon et al. (1996)
Finland	1987, 1991	10.1, 14.4	Disposable income	50% of average	OECD	Cantillon et al. (1996)
France	1979, 1984	16.0, 7.3	Disposable income	50% of average	OECD	Cantillon et al. (1996)
Germany	1978, 1983	20.9, 18.8	Disposable income	50% of average	OECD	Cantillon et al. (1996)
Ireland	1973, 1980, 1987	33.8, 24.4, 9.7	Disposable income	50% of average	1, 0.6, 0.4	Cantillon et al. (1996)
Netherlands	1983, 1987, 1991	6.4, 2.7, 7.2	Disposable income	50% of average	OECD	Cantillon et al. (1996)
Norway	1979, 1985, 1991	8.0, 2.9, 0.7	Disposable income	50% of median	OECD	Aaberge et al (1996)
Norway	1979, 1985, 1991	8.9, 3.2, 0.8	Net income	50% of median	OECD	Aaberge (1996)
Norway	1979, 1986, 1991	6.7, 16.4, 9.5	Disposable income	50% of average	OECD	Cantillon et al. (1996)
Sweden	1975, 1981, 1987, 1992	8.6, 0.9, 4.3, 4.9	Disposable income	50% of average	OECD	Cantillon et al. (1996)
Weden	1981, 1987	5.8, 11.4	Gross income	50% of median equivalent gross income	OECD	Phipps (1994)
UK	1974, 1979, 1986	34.4, 25.9, 13.3	Disposable income	50% of average	OECD	Cantillon et al. (1996)
US	1974, 1979, 1986, 1991	31.4, 28.9, 28.3, 26.1	Disposable income	50% of average	OECD	Cantillon et al. (1996)
US	1981, 1985	32.1, 29.3	Gross income	50% of median equivalent gross income	OECD	Phipps (1994)

Source: Authors' compilation based on the listed studies.

Table A4

Poverty rates of women

Country	Years	Poverty rate	Resource	Poverty line	Equivalence scale	Reference
Women						
Denmark	1976, 1980, 1985, 1990	12.93, 11.30, 11.67, 10.80	Disposable income	50% of median	OECD	Pedersen and Smith (1996)
Norway	1979, 1985, 1991	3.3, 4.0, 4.9	Net income	50% of median	OECD	Aaberge et al. (1996)
Norway	1979, 1985, 1991	2.6, 3.0, 4.0	Net income	50% of median	OECD	Aaberge et al. (1996)
UK	1971, 1976, 1981, 1988	9, 7, −5, 1	Household net (disposable) income	40% of average disposable income	McClements scale	Jenkins and O'Leary (1996)
UK	1971, 1976, 1981, 1988	7, 6, −2, −1	Household net (disposable) income	40% of current average disposable income	McClements scale	Jenkins and O'Leary (1996)
UK	1971, 1976, 1981, 1988	14, 11, 1, −1	Household net (disposable) income	50% of average disposable income in 1979	McClements scale	Jenkins and O'Leary (1998)
UK	1971, 1976, 1981, 1988	13, 11, 3, 5	Household net (disposable) income	50% of current average disposable income	McClements scale	Jenkins and O'Leary (1998)
UK	1971, 1976, 1981, 1988	13, 13, 5, 4	Household net (disposable) income	60% of average disposable income in 1979	McClements scale	Jenkins and O'Leary (1998)
UK	1971, 1976, 1981, 1988	14, 13, 8, 8	Household net (disposable) income	60% of current average disposable income	McClements scale	Jenkins and O'Leary (1998)
UK	1979, 1981, 1987, 1987, 1988.5 1990.5	5, −1, −2, −3, −8	Household net (disposable) income	40% of average disposable income in 1979	McClements scale	Jenkins and O'Leary (1998)
UK	1979, 1981, 1987, 1988.5 1990.5	5, −1, 1, 6, 6	Household net (disposable) income	40% of current average disposable income	McClements scale	Jenkins and O'Leary (1998)
UK	1979, 1981, 1987, 1988.5 1990.5	13, 3, 4, 6, 3	Household net (disposable) income	50% of average disposable income in 1979	McClements scale	Jenkins and O'Leary (1998)
UK	1979, 1981, 1987, 1988.5 1990.5	13, 3, 7, 9, 11	Household net (disposable) income	50% of current average disposable income	McClements scale	Jenkins and O'Leary (1998)
UK	1979, 1981, 1987, 1988.5 1990.5	16, 9, 7, 9, 8	Household net (disposable) income	60% of average disposable income in 1979	McClements scale	Jenkins and O'Leary (1998)
UK	1979, 1981, 1987, 1988.5 1990.5	16, 9, 10, 11, 12	Household net (disposable) income	60% of current average disposable income	McClements scale	Jenkins and O'Leary (1998)
Female head						
Australia	1981, 1985, 1989	39.4, 42.1, 42.5	Disposable income	50% of average	OECD	Cantillon et al. (1996)
Australia	1981, 1985	32.9, 34.9	Gross income	50% of median equivalent gross income	OECD	Phipps (1994)
Belgium	1985, 1988, 1992	9.0, 13.8, 9.9	Disposable income	50% of average	OECD	Cantillon et al. (1996)
Canada	1975, 1981, 1987, 1991	42.7, 35.4, 27.8, 26.9	Disposable income	50% of average	OECD	Cantillon et al. (1996)
Canada	1981, 1987	29.4, 26.1	Gross income	50% of median equivalent gross income	OECD	Phipps (1994)
Denmark	1987, 1992	20.2, 13.7	Disposable income	50% of average	OECD	Cantillon et al. (1996)
Finland	1987, 1991	15.9, 20.7	Disposable income	50% of average	OECD	Cantillon et al. (1996)
France	1979, 1984	23.4, 15.1	Disposable income	50% of average	OECD	Cantillon et al. (1996)
Germany	1978, 1983	28.7, 22.1	Disposable income	50% of average	OECD	Cantillon et al. (1996)
Ireland	1973, 1980, 1987	15.9, 17.4, 21.2	Disposable income	50% of average	1, 0.6, 0.4	Cantillon et al. (1996)

Table A4

(continued)

Country	Years	Poverty rate	Resource	Poverty line	Equivalence scale	Reference
Female head						
Netherlands	1986, 1987, 1988	17.2, 16.7, 15.0	Disposable income	Legal poverty line	Those implied by legal poverty line	Dirven and Berghman (1992)
Netherlands	1986, 1987, 1988	36.1, 38.0, 38.3	Disposable income	Subjective poverty line	Those implied by legal poverty line	Dirven and Berghman (1992)
Netherlands	1983, 1987, 1991	11.6, 10.9, 12.1	Disposable income	50% of average	OECD	Cantillon et al. (1996)
Norway	1979, 1986, 1991	10.7, 26.7, 17.6	Disposable income	50% of average	OECD	Cantillon et al. (1996)
Sweden	1975, 1981, 1987, 1992	13.9, 5.2, 13.1, 14.7	Disposable income	50% of average	OECD	Cantillon et al. (1996)
Sweden	1981, 1987	8.4, 17.1	Gross income	50% of median equivalent gross income	OECD	Phipps (1994)
UK	1974, 1979, 1986	36.7, 25.7, 15.7	Disposable income	50% of average	OECD	Cantillon et al. (1996)
US	1974, 1979, 1986, 1991	43.0, 36.8, 41.8, 40.0	Disposable income	50% of average	OECD	Cantillon et al. (1996)
US	1981, 1985	35.9, 38.2	Gross income	50% of median equivalent gross income	OECD	Phipps (1994)
Single mothers						
UK	1968, 1988	17.4, 4.1	Disposable income AHC	40% of 1988 average income	Those implied by the Supplementary Benefit System	Wright (1992)
UK	1968, 1988	38.5, 9.6	Disposable income AHC	50% of 1988 average income	Those implied by the Supplementary Benefit System	Wright (1992)
UK	1968, 1988	61.5, 23.7	Disposable income AHC	60% of 1988 average income	Those implied by the Supplementary Benefit System	Wright (1992)
US	1963, 1969, 1973, 1979, 1983, 1989	58.2, 48.3, 46.3, 41.3, 48.3, 43.8	Family income	US official	US official poverty	Cutler and Katz (1991)

Source: Authors' compilation based on the listed studies.

Table A5

Estimated poverty head count rates for all persons using LIS data

Country	Years	Poverty rates
Australia	1981, 1985, 1989,	10.6, 11.8, 12.2
Austria	1987,	3.4
Belgium	1985, 1988, 1992,	4.6, 4.9, 5.4
Canada	1971, 1975, 1981, 1987, 1991	15.0, 13.3, 12.3, 11.2, 11.3
Denmark	1987, 1992	10.4, 7.5
Finland	1987, 1991	5.4, 5.7
France	1979, 1981, 1984 (FR), 1984 (FB), 1989	8.2 , 7.3, 7.5, 12.0, 9.5
Germany	1983, 1984, 1989,	0.0, 6.5, 5.6
Ireland	1987	11.3
Italy	1986, 1991	10.4, 10.3
Luxembourg	1985, 1991	5.4, 4.7
Netherlands	1983, 1987 1991	6.6, 5.1, 6.7
Norway	1979 1986, 1991	4.3 7.3 6.6
Spain	1980, 1990	12.2, 10.2
Sweden	1967, 1975, 1981, 1987, 1992	15.3, 6.7, 4.0, 7.7, 6.7
Switzerland	1982	8.3
UK	1969, 1974, 1979, 1986, 1991	5.5, 9.1, 9.2, 9.1, 14.5
US	1974, 1979, 1986, 1991	16.0, 15.9, 17.7, 17.7

Numbers shown are the head count ratio using 50% of median adjusted Disposable income as poverty line.
Source: Authors' calculations from LIS database.

Table A6

Estimated poverty head count rates for children using LIS data

Country	Years	Poverty rates
Australia	1981, 1985, 1989	14.0, 13.5, 14.8
Austria	1987	6.8
Belgium	1985, 1988, 1992	4.1, 3.6, 4.3
Canada	1971, 1975, 1981, 1987, 1991	17.6, 14.9, 14.9, 14.8, 15.6
Denmark	1987, 1992	4.7, 5.1
Finland	1987, 1991	2.8, 2.3
France	1979, 1981, 1984 (FR), 1984 (FB), 1989	7.2, 6.9, 7.4, 10.1, 8.4
Germany	1983, 1984, 1989	0.0, 6.4, 4.8
Ireland	1987	13.8
Italy	1986, 1991	11.5, 13.5
Luxembourg	1985, 1991	5.2, 5.4
Netherlands	1983, 1987, 1991	4.8, 5.2, 8.3
Norway	1979 1986, 1991	5.2, 4.4, 4.9
Spain	1980, 1990	12.7, 12.3
Sweden	1967, 1975, 1981, 1987, 1992	5.8, 2.4, 4.8, 3.6, 3.0
Switzerland	1982	4.3
UK	1969, 1974, 1979, 1986, 1991	6.0, 8.0, 9.0, 12.5, 18.5
US	1974, 1979, 1986, 1991	19.4, 20.5, 24.6, 24.1

Numbers shown are the head count ratio using 50% of median adjusted Disposable income as poverty line.
Each child (under 18) is counted once.
Source: Authors' calculations from LIS database.

Table A7

Estimated poverty head count rates for elderly persons using LIS data

Country	Years	Poverty rates
Australia	1981, 1985, 1989	8.9, 5.6, 5.4
Austria	1987	1.2
Belgium	1985, 1988, 1992	3.3, 3.2, 4.5
Canada	1971, 1975, 1981, 1987, 1991	10.7, 9.5, 9.2, 7.8, 8.3
Denmark	1987, 1992	7.5, 7.3
Finland	1987, 1991	5.5, 6.0
France	1979, 1981, 1984 (FR), 1984 (FB), 1989	6.6, 5.8, 8.5, 11.7, 8.1
Germany	1983, 1984, 1989	0.0, 4.8, 4.2
Ireland	1987	11.5
Italy	1986, 1991	6.3, 5.0
Luxembourg	1985, 1991	3.1, 1.8
Netherlands	1983, 1987, 1991	6.1, 5.3, 5.4
Norway	1979, 1986, 1991	3.3, 3.8, 4.8
Spain	1980, 1990	10.2, 7.9
Sweden	1967 1975, 1981, 1987, 1992	18.9, 7.0, 1.6, 8.7, 8.6
Switzerland	1982	2.7
UK	1969, 1974, 1979, 1986, 1991	1.2, 3.0, 4.3, 5.7, 7.1
US	1974, 1979, 1986, 1991	7.9, 10.1, 7.2, 8.4

Numbers shown are the head count ratio using 50% of median adjusted Disposable income as poverty line. Each elderly person (over 65) person in the household is counted once.
Source: Authors' calculations from LIS database.

Table A8

Estimated poverty head count rates for persons in female-headed households using LIS data

Country	Years	Poverty rates
Australia	1981, 1985, 1989	39.1, 42.5, 41.6
Austria	1987	28.9
Belgium	1985, 1988, 1992	11.7, 14.1, 12.4
Canada	1971, 1975, 1981, 1987, 1991	48.3, 43.8, 35.2, 30.2, 31.4
Denmark	1987, 1992	22.0, 18.1
Finland	1987, 1991	14.8, 17.5
France	1979, 1981, 1984 (FR), 1984 (FB), 1989	18.7, 32.4, 14.4, 20.9, 19.9
Germany	1983, 1984, 1989	0.0, 17.4, 16.9
Ireland	1987	14.8
Italy	1986, 1991	19.3, 20.0
Luxembourg	1985, 1991	11.6, 18.1
Netherlands	1983, 1987, 1991	8.6, 9.2, 15.6
Norway	1979, 1986, 1991	20.4, 28.1, 20.8
Spain	1980, 1990	20.1, 17.6
Sweden	1967, 1975, 1981, 1987, 1992	41.2, 17.8, 8.0, 16.7, 15.4
Switzerland	1982	20.7
UK	1969, 1974, 1979, 1986, 1991	23.1, 30.4, 22.3, 13.6, 32.5
US	1974, 1979, 1986, 1991	45.2, 39.0, 43.5, 42.8

Numbers shown are the head count ratio using 50% of median adjusted Disposable income as poverty line. Every person living in a female-headed household is counted once.
Source: Authors' calculations from LIS database.

References

Aaberge, Rolf, Arne S. Andersen and Tom Wennemo (1996), Omfang, nivå og fordeling av lavinntekter i Norge, 1979–1993, in A. Puide ed., Den nordiska fattigdomens utveckling och struktur, number 1996:583 'TemaNord', Nordiskt ministerråd, chapter 2.

Ashworth, Karl, Martha Hill and Robert Walker (1994), Patterns of childhood poverty: new challenges for policy, Journal of Policy Analysis and Management 13: 658–680.

Atkinson, Anthony B. (1987), On the measurement of poverty, Econometrica 55: 749–764.

Atkinson, Anthony B. (1998), Poverty in Europe (Blackwell, Oxford).

Atkinson, Anthony B. (1989) Poverty and Social Security (Harvester & Wheatsheaf, Hemel Hempstead).

Atkinson, Anthony B. (1992) Measurement of poverty and differences in family composition, Econometrica 59: 1–16.

Atkinson, Anthony B., A.K. Maynard and C.G. Trinder (1983), Parents and Children: Incomes in Two Generations (Heinemann Educational Books).

Atkinson, Anthony B. and François Bourguignon (1987), Income distribution and differences in needs, in G. Feiwel, ed., Arrow and the Foundations of the Theory of Economic Policy (MacMillan, London).

Atkinson, Anthony B., François Bourguignon and Christian Morrisson (1992), Empirical Studies of Earnings Mobility, Fundamentals in Pure and Applied Economics (Harwood Academic Published, Chur).

Atkinson, Anthony B. and Gunnar V. Mogensen (1993), Welfare and Work Incentives. A North European Perspective (Clarendon Press, Oxford).

Atkinson, Anthony B., Lee Rainwater and Timothy M. Smeeding (1995), Income Distribution in the OECD countries: the Evidence from the Luxembourg Income Study,. Vol. 18 of Social Policy Studies (OECD, Paris).

Bane, Mary Jo and David T. Ellwood (1986), Slipping into and out of poverty: the dynamics of spells, Journal of Human Resources 21: 1–23.

Barr, Nicholas (1993), The Economics of the Welfare State, 2nd edition (Weidenfeld and Nicolson, London).

Bergstrom, Theodore C. (1996), Economics in a family way. Journal of Economic Literature 3: 1903–1940.

Bishop, John A., John P. Formby and Buhong Zheng (1997), Statistical inference and the sen index of poverty, International Economic Review 38: 381–387.

Björklund, Anders (1993), A comparison between actual distributions of annual and lifetime income: Sweden 1951–89, Review of Income and Wealth 377–386.

Björklund, Anders and Markus Jäntti (1997), Intergenerational income mobility in Sweden compared to the United States, American Economic Review 87.

Blank, Rebecca and Maria Hanratty (1993), Responding to need: a comparison of the social safety nets in Canada and the United States, in D. Card and R. Freeman, eds., Small Differences that Matter: Labor Markets in Canada and the United States (Chicago University Press, Chicago), pp. 191–232.

Blundell, Richard (1998), Equivalence scales and household welfare: what can be learned from household budget data? in S.P. Jenkins, A. Kapteyn and B. van Praag, eds., The Distribution of Welfare and Household Production, Chapter 16 (Cambridge University Press, Cambridge), pp. 364–380.

Bourguignon, François and Pierre-André Chiappori (1994), Income and outcomes: a structural model of intra-household allocation, in R. Blundell, I. Preston and I. Walker, eds., The Measurement of Household Welfare (Cambridge University Press, Cambridge).

Bradbury, Bruce (1997), Measuring poverty changes with bounded equivalence scales: Australia in the 1980s, Economica 64: 245–265.

Bradshaw, Jonathan and Jun-Rong Chen (1996), Poverty in the UK: a comparison with 19 other countries, Working Paper 147 (Luxembourg Income Study, Luxembourg).

Browning, Martin, François Bourguignon, Pierre-André Chiappori and Valérie Lechene (1994), Income and outcomes: a structural model of intrahousehold allocation, Journal of Political Economy 102: 1067–1096.

Buhmann, Brigitte, Lee Rainwater, Guenther Schmaus and Timothy Smeeding (1988), Equivalence scales, well-being, Inequality, and poverty: sensitivity estimates across ten countries using the Luxembourg Income Study (LIS) database, Review of Income and Wealth 34: 115–142.

Burgess, Simon and Carol Propper (1998), An economic model of household income dynamics, with an application to poverty dynamics among American women, Unpublished manuscript (University of Bristol).

Burkhauser, Richard V, Douglas Holtz-Eakin and Stephen E. Rhody (1998), Mobility and inequality in the 1980s: A cross-national comparison of the United States and Germany, in S.P. Jenkins, A. Kapteyn and B. van Praag, eds., The Distribution of Welfare and Household Production, Chapter, 6 (Cambridge University Press, Cambridge), pp. 111–175.

Cantillon, Bea, Ive Marx and Karel van den Bosch (1996), Poverty in advanced economies: trends and policy issues, Unpublished manuscript. Paper presented at the IARIW meetings in Lillehammer, Norway.

Cantó-Sánchez, Olga (1996), Poverty dynamics in Spain: A study of transitions in the 1990s, Discussion Paper 15 (Distribution Analysis Research Programme. London School of Economics).

Chakravarty, Satya Ranjan (1983), Ethically flexible measures of poverty, Canadian Journal of Economics 16: 74–85.

Clark, Stephen, Richard Hemming and David Ulph (1981), On indices for the measurement of poverty, The Economic Journal 515–526.

Corcoran, Mary (1995), Rags to rags: poverty and mobility in the United States, American Review of Sociology 21: 237–267.

Corcoran, Mary, Greg J Duncan, Gerald Gurin and Patricia Gurin (1985), Myth and reality: the causes and persistence of poverty, Journal of Policy Analysis and Management 4: 516–536.

Coulter, Fiona A.E., Frank A. Cowell and Stephen P. Jenkins (1992a), Differences in needs and assessment of income distributions, Bulletin of Economic Research 44: 77–124.

Coulter, Fiona, Frank Cowell and Stephen P. Jenkins (1992b), Equivalence scale relativities and the extent of inequality and poverty, The Economic Journal 102: 1067–1082.

Cowell, Frank A. and Maria-Pia Victoria-Feser (1996), Poverty measurement with contaminated data: a robust approach, European Economic Review 40, 1745–1760.

Cutler, David M. and Lawrence F. Katz (1991), Macroeconomic performance and the disadvantaged, Brookings Papers on Economic Activity 10: 1–74.

Danziger, Sheldon and Michael Taussig (1979), The income unit and the anatomy of income distribution, The Review of Income and Wealth 25: 365–375..

Danziger, Sheldon, Robert Haveman and Robert Plotnick (1981), How income transfer programs affect work, savings, and the income distribution: a critical review, Journal of Economic Literature 19: 975–1028.

Davidson, Russell and Jean-Yves Duclos (1998), Statistical inference for stochastic dominance and for the measurement of poverty and inequality, Working Paper 191 (Luxembourg Income Study, Luxembourg).

de Vos, Llass and M. Asghar Zaidi (1996), Trends in consumption-based poverty and inequality in the European Community, Working paper (Economics Institute, Tilburg).

Deaton, Angus (1992), Understanding Consumption (Oxford University Press, Oxford).

Deaton, Angus and John Muellbauer (1989), Economics and Consumer Behavior (Cambridge University Press, Cambridge).

Deleeck, Herman, Karel van den Bosch and Lieve de Lathouwer (1992), Poverty and the Adequacy of Social Security in the EC (Avebury, Aldershot).

Dirven, Henk-Jan and Jos Berghman (1992), The evolution of income poverty in the Netherlands. Results from the Dutch Socio-Economic Panel Survey, Unpublished manuscript.

Dowrick, Steve and John Quiggin (1994), International comparisons of living standards and tastes: A revealed preference analysis, American Economic Review 84: 332–341.

Duncan, Greg, Björn Gustafsson, Richard Hauser, Gunther Shmauss, Hans Essinger, Ruud Muffels, Brian Nolan and Jean-Claude Ray (1993), Poverty dynamics in eight countries, Journal of Population Economics 215–234.

Duncan, Greg et al., eds (1984), Year of Poverty, Years of Plenty (Survey Research Center, Institute for Social Research, University of Michigan, Ann Arbor, MI).

Duncan, Greg J., Björn Gustafsson, Richard Hauser, Gunther Shmaus, Stephen Jenkins, Hans Messinger, Ruud Muffels, Brian Nolan, Jean-Claude Ray and Wofgang Voges (1992), No pain, no gain? Inequality and economic mobility in the United States, Canada and Europe, Unpublished manuscript.

Efron, Bradley and Robert J. Tibshirani (1993), An Introduction to the Bootstrap, Monographs on Statistics and Applied Probability, Vol. 57 (Chapman & Hall, New York).

Fishburn, Peter C. (1980), Stochastic dominance and moments of distributions, Mathematics of Operations Research 5: 94–100.

Fisher, Franklin M. (1987), Household equivalence scales and interpersonal comparisons, Review of Economic Studies 54: 519–524.

Foster, James E. (1984), On economic poverty: a survey of aggregate measures, Advances in Econometrics 3: 215–251.

Foster, James E. and Anthony F. Shorrocks (1988a), Poverty orderings, Econometrica 56: 173–177.

Foster, James E. and Anthony F. Shorrocks (1988b), Poverty orderings and welfare dominance, Social Choice and Welfare 5: 179–198.

Foster, James E. and Y. Jin (1998), Poverty orderings for the Dalton utility-gap measures, in S.P. Jenkins, A. Kapteyn and B. van Praag, eds., The Distribution of Welfare and Household Production, Chap. 12 (Cambridge University Press, Cambridge), pp. 268–285.

Foster, James, Joel Greer and Erik Thorbecke (1984), A class of decomposable poverty measures, Econometrica 52: 761–766.

Fritzell, Johan (1996), Persistent low income. Unpublished manuscript (Stockholm University).

Geweke, John and Michael Keane (1996), An empirical analysis of male income dynamics in the PSID: 1969–1989. Unpublished manuscript (University of Minnesota).

Goodman, Alissa and Steven Webb (1994), For richer, for poorer: The changing distribution of income in the United Kingdom, 1961–91, Commentary 42 (Institute for Fiscal Studies, London).

Gottschalk, Peter, Sara McLanahan and Gary Sandefur (1994), The dynamics and intergenerational transmission of poverty and welfare participation, in S.H. Danziger, G.D. Sandefur and D.H. Weinberg, eds., Confronting Poverty: Prescriptions for Change, Chap. 4 (Harvard University Press and Russell Sage, Cambridge, MA), pp. 85–108.

Gottschalk, Peter and Timothy M. Smeeding (1997), Cross-national comparisons of earnings and income inequality, Journal of Economic Literature 32: 633–686.

Gustafsson, Björn and Hannu Uusitalo (1990), The welfare state and poverty in Finland and Sweden from the mid-1960s to the mid-1980s, Review of Income and Wealth 36: 249–266.

Gustafsson, Björn (1996), Fattigdom i Sverige. Föräandring åren 1975 till 1993, stuktur och dynamik, in A. Puide, ed., Den nordiska fattigdomens utveckling och struktur, number 1996:583, TemaNord, Chap. 2, Nordiskt ministerråd.

Haddad, Lawrence and Ravi Kanbur (1990), How serious is the neglect of intrahousehold inequality? Economic Journal 100: 866–881.

Hagenaars, Aldi, J.M. (1986), The Perception of Poverty, North-Holland, Amsterdam.

Hagenaars, Aldi J.M. (1987), A class of poverty indices, International Economic Review 28: 583–607. Hagenaars, Aldi J.M. and Bernard M.S. van Praag (1985), A synthesis of poverty line definitions, Review of Income and Wealth 31: 139–154.

Hagenaars, Aldi and Klaas de Vos (1988), The definition and measurement of poverty, The Journal of Human Resources 23: 211–221.

Halleröd, Björn (1995), The truly poor: direct and indirect measurement of consensual poverty in Sweden. Unpublished manuscript (Umeå University).

Hauser, Richard and Irene Becker (1993), The development of the income distribution in the Federal Republic of Germany (West) during the seventies and eighties. Unpublished manuscript. Published in German in Konjukturpolitik, Vol. 41, pp. 308–244.

Haveman, Robert and Lawrence Buron (1993a), Escaping poverty through work: the problem of low earnings capacity in the United States, 1973–88, Review of Income and Wealth 39: 141–157.

Haveman, Robert and Lawrence Buron (1993b), Who are the truly poor? Patterns of official and net earnings capacity poverty, 1973–1988, in D.B. Papadimitriou and E.N. Wolff, eds., Poverty and Prosperity in the USA in the Late Twentieth Century, Chap. 3 (St. Martin's Press, New York), pp. 58–89.

Hossain, Iftekhar (1990), Poverty as Capability Failure (Skrifter Utgivna av Svenska Handelshögskolan, nr 44, Helsinki).

Howes, Stephen (1993), Mixed dominance: a new criterion for poverty analysis, Working Paper 3, Distributional Analysis Research Program, London School of Economics.

Howes, Stephen (1994a), Asymptotic properties of four fundamental curves of distributional analysis.

Howes, Stephen (1994b), Testing for dominance: inferring population rankings for sample data. Unpublished manuscript (London School of Economics).

Howes, Stephen (1996), The influence of aggregation on the ordering of distributions, Economica 63: 253–272.

Jarvis, Sarah and Stephen P. Jenkins (1997), Low income dynamics in 1990s Britain, Fiscal Studies 18: 123–142.

Jenkins, Stephen P. (1987), Snapshots versus movies: 'lifecycle biases' and the estimation of intergenerational earnings inheritance, European Economic Review 31: 1149–1158.

Jenkins, Stephen P. (1991), Poverty measurement and the within-household distribution: an agenda for action, Journal of Social Policy 20: 457–483.

Jenkins, Stephen P. (1994), The within-household distribution and why it matters: an economist's perspective, Discussion paper series (Department of Economics, University College of Swansea).

Jenkins, Stephen P. (1998), Modelling household income dynamics. Unpublished manuscript (University of Essex).

Jenkins, Stephen P. and Frank A. Cowell (1994), Parametric equivalence scales and scale relativities, Economic Journal 104: 891–900.

Jenkins, Stephen P. and Nigel C. O'Leary (1998), The incomes of UK women: limited progress towards equality with men? in S.P. Jenkins, A. Kapteyn and B. van Praag, eds., The Distribution of Welfare and Household Production, Chap. 18 (Cambridge University Press, Cambridge), pp. 398–417.

Jenkins, Stephen P. and Peter J. Lambert (1993), Ranking income distribution when needs differ, Review of Income and Wealth 39: 337–356.

Jenkins, Stephen P. and Peter J. Lambert (1997), Three '*i*'s of poverty curves, with an analysis of UK poverty trends, Oxford Economic Papers 49: 317–327.

Jenkins, Stephen P. and Peter J. Lambert (1998a), Ranking poverty gap distributions: further tips for poverty analysis, Research on Income Inequality 8. JAI Press.

Jenkins, Stephen P. and Peter J. Lambert (1998b), Three '*i*'s of poverty curves and poverty dominance: Tips for poverty analysis, Research on Income Inequality 8. JAI Press.

Jäntti, Markus (1992), Poverty dominance and statistical inference, Research report 1992:7 (Stockholm University, Department of Statistics, Stockholm).

Jäntti, Markus and Leif Nordberg (1992), Statistical inference and the measurement of poverty, Meddelanden från ekonomisk-statsvetenskapliga fakulteten vid Åbo Akademi, Statistiska institutionen.

Jäntti, Markus and Veli-Matti Ritakallio (1996a), Ekonomisk fattgdom i Finland åren 1971 till 1993, in A. Puide, ed., Den nordiska fattigdomens utveckling och struktur, number 1996:583, TemaNord, Chap. 2, Nordiskt ministerråd.

Jäntti, Markus and Veli-Matti Ritakallio (1996b), Income distribution and poverty in Finland in the 1980s, in P. Gottschalk, B. Gustafsson and E. Palmer, eds., The Distribution of Economic Welfare in the 1980s (Cambridge University Press, Cambridge).

Kakwani, Nanak (1993), Statistical inference in the measurement of poverty, Review of Economics and Statistics 75: 632–639.

Kangas, Olli and Veli-Matti Ritakallio (1995), Different methods—different results? Approaches to multidimensional poverty, Themes from Finland 5/95 (National Research and Development Center for Welfare and Health).

Kapteyn, Arie, Peter Koreman and Rob Willemse (1988), Some methodological issues in the implementation of subjective poverty definitions, Journal of Human Resources 23: 222–242.

Korpi, Walter and Joakim Palme (1997), The paradox of redistribution and strategies of equality: welfare state institutions and poverty in Western countries, Working Paper 3/1997 (Swedish Institute for Social Research, Stockholm).

Le Grand, Julian (1991), Equity as an economic objective, in B. Almond and D. Hill, eds., Applied Philosophy: Morals and Metaphysics in Contemporary Debate, Chap. 17 (Routledge, London), pp. 183–195.

Mack, Joanna and Stewart Lansley (1985), Poor Britain (George Allen & Unwin, London).

Malmberg, Jan-Otto (1988), A.K. Senin köyhyysmitan estimointi, Master's thesis (University of Helsinki).

Mayer, Susan E. and Christopher Jencks (1993), Recent trends in economic inequality in the United States: income versus expenditures versus material well-being, in D.B. Papadimitriou and E.N. Wolff, eds., Poverty and Prosperity in the USA in the Late Twentieth Century, Chap. 5 (St. Martin's Press, New York), pp. 90–121.

McElroy, Marjorie B. (1990), The empirical content of Nash-bargained household behavior, Journal of Human Resources 25: 559–583.

Moffitt, Robert (1992), Incentive effects of the US welfare system: a review, Journal of Economic Literature: 30: 1–61.

Morgan, James N., Greg J. Duncan, Martha S. Hill and James Lepkowski (1992), Panel Study of Income Dynamics, 1968–1989 [Waves I–XXII] (Survey Research Center, Ann Arbor, MI).

Muffels, Ruud (1992), The elaboration of a behavioural model of transitions into and out of poverty. Unpublished manuscript (The Netherlands).

National Research Council (1995), Measuring Poverty: A New Approach (National Academy Press, Washington).

Nelson, Julie A. (1993), Household equivalence scales: theory versus policy? Journal of Labor Economics 11: 471–493.

Nolan, Brian and Christopher T. Whelan (1996a), The relationship between income and deprivation: a dynamic perspective, Revue Economiqué 47: 709–717.

Nolan, Brian and Christopher T. Whelan (1996b), Resources, Deprivation and Poverty (Clarendon Press, Oxford).

O'Higgins, Michael and Stephen Jenkins (1990), Poverty in the EC: 1975, 1980, 1985, in R. Teekens and B. Praag, van, eds., Analysing Poverty in the European Community (Eurostat News Special Edition 1-1990, Eurostat, Luxembourg), p. 187211.

Ólafsson, Stefá and Karl Sigurdsson (1996), Poverty in Iceland, in A. Puide, ed., Den nordiska fattigdomens utveckling och struktur, number 1996:583, TemaNord, Chap. 3, Nordiskt ministerråd.

Pahkinen, Erkki and Risto Lehtonen (1995), Practical Methods for Design and Analysis of Complex Survey (Wiley and Sons, New York).

Pedersen, Peder J. and Nina Smith (1996), Lavinkomster i Danmark, 1976–1990, in A. Puide, ed., Den nordiska fattigdomens utveckling och struktur, number 1996:583, TemaNord, Chap. 2, Nordiskt ministerråd.

Phipps, Shelley A. (1994), Poverty and labor market change: Canada in comparative perspective, Working Paper 108 (LIS, Luxembourg).

Preston, Ian (1995), Sampling distributions of poverty statistics, Applied Statistics 44: 91–99.

Pyatt, Graham (1987), Measuring welfare, poverty and inequality, The Economic Journal 97: 459–467.

Rainwater, Lee (1990), Poverty and equivalence as social constructions, Working Paper (Luxembourg Income Study).

Rainwater, Lee and Timothy M. Smeeding (1995), Doing poorly: the real income of American children in a comparative perspective, Working Paper 127 (Luxembourg Income Study).

Ravallion, Martin (1994), *Poverty Comparisons* (Harwood Academic Publishers, Chur, Switzerland).

Ringen, Stein (1987), The Possibility of Politics. A study in the Political Economy of the Welfare State (Clarendon Press, Oxford).

Rodgers, Joan R and John L. Rodgers (1993) Chronic poverty in the United States, Journal of Human Resources 28: 25–54.

Rowntree, Seebohm and G.R. Lavers (1951), Poverty and the Welfare State (Longman Green, London).

Ruggles, Patricia (1990), Drawing the Line. Alternative Poverty Measures and Their Implications for Public Policy (Urban Institute Press, Washington DC).

Särndal, C.-E., B. Swensson and Jan Wretman (1992), Model Assisted Survey Sampling (Springer Series in Statistics, Springer-Verlag, Berlin).

Saunders, Peter (1997), Economic adjustment and distributional change: income inequality and poverty in Australia in the 1980s, in P. Gottschalk, B. Gustafsson and E. Palmer, eds., Changing Patterns of Economic Welfare: An International Perspective (Cambridge University Press, Cambridge), pp. 60–83.

Schluter, Christian (1997), On the non-stationarity of the German income mobility: (and some observations on poverty dynamics), Discussion Paper 30 (Distributional Analysis Research Programme, London School of Economics, London).

Schultz, T. Paul (1994), Returns to human capital and economic development. Unpublished Unpublished manuscript (Yale University).

Seidl, Christian (1988), Poverty measurement: a survey, in D. Bös, M. Rose and C. Seidl, eds., Welfare and Efficiency in Public Economics (Springer-Verlag, Heidelberg), pp. 71–147.

Sen, Amartya (1976), Poverty: An ordinal approach to measurement, *Econometrica* 44: 219–231.

Sen, Amartya (1983), Poor, relatively speaking, Oxford Economic Papers 35: 153–169.

Sen, Amartya (1992), Inequality Reexamined (Clarendon Press, Oxford).

Sen, Amartya K. (1979), Issues in the measurement of poverty, *Scandinavian Journal of Economics* 81: 285–307.

Sen, Amartya K. (1985), A sociological approach to the measurement of poverty: a reply to Professor Peter Townsend, Oxford Economic Papers 37, 669–676.

Sen, Amartya K. (1997), On Economic Inequality, 2nd edn (Oxford University Press, Oxford).

Shorrocks, Anthony F. (1995), Revisiting the Sen poverty index, Econometrica 63: 1225–1230.

Shorrocks, Anthony F. (1998), Deprivation profiles and deprivation indices, in S.P. Jenkins, A. Kapteyn and B. van Praag, eds., The Distribution of Welfare and Household Product, Chap. 11 (Cambridge University Press, Cambridge), pp. 250–267.

Shorrocks, Anthony F. and S. Subramanian (1994), Fuzzy poverty indices. Unpublished manuscript (University of Essex).

Skinner, C.J., D. Holt and T.M.F. Smith (1989), Analysis of Complex Surveys (John Wiley and Sons, New York).

Smeeding, Timothy, Michael O'Higgins and Lee Rainwater (1990), Poverty, Inequality and Income Distribution in Comparative Perspective (Harvester Wheatsheaf, Hemel Hempstead).

Solon, Gary (1989), Biases in the estimation of intergenerational earnings correlations, The Review of Economics and Statistics 71: 172–174.

Spencer, Bruce D. and Stephen Fisher (1992), On comparing distributions of poverty gaps, The Indian Journal of Statistics 54: 114–126.

Stevens, Ann Huff (1995), Climbing out of poverty, falling back in: measuring the persistence of poverty over multiple spells, Working Paper 5390 (National Bureau of Economic Research).

Summers, Robert and Alan Heston (1991), The Penn World Table (mark 5): an expanded set of international comparisons, 1950–1988, Quarterly Journal of Economics 106: 327–368.

Thomas, Duncan (1990), Intra-household resource allocation, Journal of Human Resources 25: 635–664.

Townsend, Peter (1979), Poverty in the UK (University of California Press, Berkeley).

Townsend, Peter (1979), A sociological approach to the measurement of poverty — a rejoinder to Professor Amartya Sen, Oxford Economic Papers 37: 659–668.

US Census Bureau (n.d.), Current Population Reports: Consumer Income (P-60, US Government Printing Office, Washington, DC), various issues.

van Praag, Bernard M.S. (1993), The relativity of the welfare concept, in M. Nussbaum and A.K. Sen, eds., Quality of Life (Clarendon Press, Oxford), pp. 362–385.

Watts, Harold (1968), An economic definition of poverty, in D.P. Moynihan, ed., On Understanding Poverty (Basic Books, New York).

Wright, Robert E. (1992), Single-parenthood and poverty in Great Britain: what the data tell us. Unpublished manuscript (Stirling University).

Xu, Kuan and Lars Osberg (1998), A distribution-free test for deprivation dominance, *Econometric Reviews* 17: 415–429.

Zheng, Buhong (1997), Aggregate poverty measures, *Journal of Economic Surveys* 11: 123–162.

Chapter 7

THEORIES OF THE DISTRIBUTION OF EARNINGS *

DEREK NEAL[a] and SHERWIN ROSEN[b]

[a] *University of Wisconsin and The NBER;* [b] *University of Chicago and The Hoover Institution*

Contents

* We wish to thank participants from the Handbook of Income Distribution Conference in Florence, Italy, March, 1997. We owe special thanks to Francois Bourguignon, Jim Davies, Robert Gibbons, Lars Hansen, Daniel Hamermesh, Lawrence Katz, Boyan Jovanovic, Casey Mulligan, and Canice Prendergast.

Handbook of Income Distribution, Volume 1. Edited by A. B. Atkinson and F. Bourguignon

Abstract

Several empirical regularities motivate most theories of the distribution of labor earnings. Earnings distributions tend to be skewed to the right and display long right tails. Mean earnings always exceed median earnings and the top percentiles of earners account for quite a disproportionate share of total earnings. Mean earnings also differ greatly across groups defined by occupation, education, experience, and other observed traits. With respect to the evolution of the distribution of earnings for a given cohort, initial earnings dispersion is smaller than the dispersion observed in prime working years.

We explore several models that address these stylized facts. Stochastic theories examine links between assumptions about the distribution of endowments and implied features of earnings distributions given assumptions about the processes that translate endowments into earnings. Selection models describe how workers choose a career. Because workers select their best option from a menu of possible careers, their allocation decisions tend to generate skewed earnings distributions. Sorting models illustrate this process in an environment where workers learn about their endowments and therefore adjust their allocation decisions over time.

Human capital theory demonstrates that earnings dispersion is a prerequisite for significant skill investments. Without earnings dispersion, workers would not willingly make the investments necessary for high-skill jobs. Human capital models illustrate how endowments of wealth and talent influence the investment decisions that generate observed distributions of earnings.

Agency models illustrate how wage structures may determine rather than reflect worker productivity. Tournament theory addresses the long right tails of wage distributions within firms. Efficiency wage models address differences in wages across employments that involve different monitoring technologies.

Keywords: Human capital, selection, sorting, agency, comparative advantage, skewness

JEL codes. J2, J3

0. Introduction

Theories of earnings distributions have always had strong empirical motivations. The earliest empirical studies of wealth and income discovered a remarkable regularity that is found in all observed earnings distributions in large populations. Earnings distributions (and income distributions more generally) are always skewed to the right. Their density functions are asymmetric and display a long right tail and positive skewness measure (third moment about the mean). They are also leptokurtic (positive fourth cumulant) and have a "fat tail". Put differently, mean earnings always exceed median earnings. The top percentiles of earners account for a strikingly disproportionate share of total earnings.

Pareto (1897) and Bowley (1915) pioneered the assembly and empirical analysis of data on personal wealth and incomes. Later, extensive development of microeconomic data sources led to a more comprehensive development of the subject. Early work attempted to formulate the economic and statistical basis for fitting specific functional forms to empirical distributions. Were earnings capacities log-normally distributed, Paretian, or something else (Staele, 1943; Miller, 1955; Lebergott, 1959; Harrison, 1981)?

Various theories of the distribution of earnings address not only the fat tail of earnings distributions but also several other empirical observations. Earnings differ greatly across groups of workers defined by occupation, education, experience, and other observed traits. Earnings also vary within groups that are observationally similar. Further, earnings dispersion for a particular cohort of workers is greater among experienced workers than among workers who are beginning their careers. In a given cohort, much of the eventual inequality in lifetime earnings is not apparent until the workers are well into their careers.

Below, we describe four types of models that offer explanations for some or all of the observations. Stochastic theories begin with distributional assumptions about worker endowments and examine what kinds of stochastic structures might be consistent with observed earnings distributions. Selection models also begin with assumptions about the distribution of endowments but worker decisions concerning how to allocate their skills to specific tasks generate the overall distribution of earnings. Sorting models describe how workers change these allocations as they learn more about their endowments. Sorting contributes to the evolution of the distribution of earnings for a particular cohort. Human capital theory describes how workers acquire skills. It demonstrates that earnings inequality is a necessity in an economy where some activities require more costly investments than others. These models also illustrate how family resources and natural talents affect the skill investments that generate observed earnings inequality. Finally, agency theory approaches earnings inequality from an entirely opposite direction. Instead of describing how worker decisions and endowments generate a distribution of individual productivities that gives rise to a distribution of earnings, agency models describe how firms choose a distribution of earnings in order to elicit desired levels of individual productivity. Highly skewed wage distributions within firms can be an incentive device.

After discussing these models, we offer an evaluation of their relative contributions to our understanding of the main stylized facts about earnings distributions. We also comment on a specific shortcoming in the existing theoretical literature on earnings distributions.

1. The characteristic skew of earnings distributions

In the physical and biological worlds, distributions tend to be symmetric and bell-shaped. But in the social world, size distributions tend to be asymmetric and right-skewed. Thus, we begin with stochastic process theories and other models that focus specifically on generating earnings distributions with long right tails. We then turn to models that address skewness while generating richer behavioral implications.

From the central limit theorem, we know that normal distributions arise from sums of many independent and identically distributed components, irrespective of how the components themselves are distributed. To apply that argument to earnings and other long-tailed distributions in economics, it is necessary to hypothesize that a person's earning capacity is generated as a product of independent increments, as in

$$ y = \prod \epsilon_i, \tag{1.1} $$

where the ϵ_i's reflect the myriad factors that determine personal productivity (Roy, 1950). With enough independent ϵ-components, $\log(y)$ tends to the normal distribution whatever the distribution of the ϵ's (Aitchison and Brown, 1957). The distribution of the natural units (the antilog) has a long right tail. However, observed earnings distributions tend to have tails that are thicker and longer than the lognormal. For instance, the Pareto distribution has "infinite" second, third, and higher order moments and fits the upper tail of earnings distributions quite well.

1.1. Stochastic process theories

The stochastic process approach focuses on the "long-tail problem" (see especially the accounts of Steindl, 1968; Lydall, 1968; Pen, 1971). It builds up a "generating process" for the overall distribution from more elementary micro components. However, the components themselves have no behavioral content. A lognormal distribution is generated by a random walk in which the percentage change in a person's earnings is distributed independently of earnings itself. Such a process results in Eq. (1.1), but since an individual's earnings level is the product of random variables realized up to that time, such a process implies ever growing variance in the overall distribution of log earnings. Some stabilizing force that offsets the tendency for increasing variance is necessary for the process to converge to a stationary steady-state distribution.

Various economists devised different auxiliary stabilizing hypotheses to solve this problem (Kalecki, 1945; Rutherford, 1955; Simon, 1955; Wold and Whittle, 1957). Champernowne (1953, 1973) established the basic method. He replaced the random walk with a Markov chain where workers face identical, fixed transition probabilities of moving between exogenously defined (log) earnings classes. Markov chains also have the variance-increasing property unless the transition probabilities are appropriately restricted. Champernowne's theory controls the variance of earnings over time by restricting the average transition to be downward, toward lower incomes. Intuitively, the idea of intergenerational turnover of workers justified this restriction (such turnover is explicit in Rutherford, 1955): higher earning older workers drop out of the process at retirement and are replaced, in a sense, with lower earning new entrants. It is slightly astonishing that a simple specific form of Champernowne's restriction implies Pareto's law as the stationary distribution.

Singh and Maddala (1976) pursued a related hazard function approach. If $F(x)$ is the cumulative probability distribution of random variable x and $f(x)$ is its density, $1 - F(x)$ is called the survival function, and $h(x) = f(x)/[1 - F(x)]$ is its hazard (failure) rate. A decreasing hazard seems necessary to produce the kind of probability masses observed in the upper tails of earnings distributions. For example, the normal has a hazard that is strictly increasing in x, but the hazard of the Pareto distribution is strictly decreasing (it is $h(x) = \alpha/x$). The hazard of the lognormal is not monotone. It first increases and then decreases in x. Singh and Maddala produce a new class of distributions by specifying that the proportional hazard is logistic, or alternatively that the hazard itself follows a sech^2 law. These new distributions closely fit the overall distribution of family incomes.

1.2. Correlated increments and common factors

Another way to account for the extra concentration of mass in the tail (relative to the lognormal) is to allow the ϵ_i components in Eq. (1.1) to be positively correlated. The law of large numbers no longer applies, but it is intuitively clear why a multiplicative structure in Eq. (1.1) and positive correlation leads to a long right tail in the distribution of y. Think of Eq. (1.1) as a "production function" for earnings capacity, with the ϵ_i's regarded as "inputs". Then a person who has $100\lambda\%$ more of each component input earns $(1 + \lambda)^n$ times more money, where n is the number of different factors that determine individual productivity. The effect of λ is magnified many times over when n is large.

For instance, consider a statistical factor-analytic structure with a single factor λ, interpreted as generalized ability or "IQ". Suppose personal endowments of the specific ϵ-inputs follow $\epsilon_i = k_i(1 + \lambda)$, where k_i are independently distributed. The common factor λ induces positive correlation between ϵ_i and ϵ_j. Then Eq. (1.1) implies that personal productivity is $y = K(1 + \lambda)^n$, with $K = \prod k_i$. Even if λ is symmetric and normally distributed, the distribution of $K(1 + \lambda)^n$ has a long right tail, and the highest earners account for a disproportionate share of total earnings.

An example brings the point close to home. This kind of model accounts for the highly skewed distribution of journal publications among members of an academic profession. Remarkably few scholars produce the lion's share of academic publications: the median number of career publications in economics is one, while the mean is much larger (Lovell, 1973). The distribution of professional citations is even more concentrated (Leamer, 1981). Interpreting each ϵ_i as the probability of carrying through on one of the large number of steps needed to bring a research project to successful publication, scholars who are slightly better in each dimension are many times more likely to succeed overall.

When the ϵ_i's are interpreted as factors of production rather than as probabilities, it is natural to expect that some inputs are more important than others. A weighted specification is preferred, such as $y = \prod(\epsilon_i)^{\alpha_i}$, where the α_i's are fixed weights that affect marginal products. If $\sum \alpha_i > 1$, positive correlation among the ϵ_i's produces a long right tail in the y-distribution. A small common increment is magnified overall.

However, if $\sum \alpha_i \leq 1$ there is no magnification and skew cannot arise in this way. There is a sense in which a form of increasing returns to scale produces the characteristic skew of earnings distributions.

1.3. Scale-of-operations effects and superstars

Attempts to study the determinants of high earnings in terms of power and span-of-control (Simon, 1957; Lydall, 1959) are closely related to scale economies. What is at issue is a person's "scale of operations" (Mayer, 1960; Tuck, 1954; Reder, 1968). Most personal economic activity occurs on a small scale, but in some activities the size of a person's market can be noticeable, even relative to the economy as a whole. The term "scale of operations" comes from the tendency for extremely wealthy individuals, such as founders of large companies, to control vast amounts of capital and wealth. Scale economies account for this. For if person A can invest a dollar more efficiently than person B, person A can likely invest $1 billion better than person B and will end up controlling resources on a much larger scale. A small extra talent for control will command a large rent in the market equilibrium.

The executive labor market is a leading practical example of this effect. Control aspects of firms and management decisions contain "local public goods" elements because they affect the ways in which all resources within the organization are directed. Top level managerial decisions, such as what products to produce and how to produce and market them, affect the productivity of all resources employed by the firm. Just as a good soldier is not effective if fighting the wrong war, a talented and highly motivated worker is not socially productive if the organization is producing a good no one wants to purchase. Better decisions of this kind are worth a great deal when applied to a large organization. A person with a small edge in talent can have a very large marginal product.

The relevant theory describes how managerial talents are allocated to control functions in a market economy (Tuck, 1954; Grubb, 1985; Rosen, 1982)—how the executive labor market allocates talent. In essence, workers and the owners of the capital bid for the privilege of being managed by talented people. Thus, rents from greater capacity to make superior control decisions get transferred to managers. In equilibrium, more talented managers control larger or more valuable organizations. This is the principle reason that top-level managers and executives in large companies earn such high salaries (Rosen, 1992) and are typically found in the top percentiles of the earnings distribution.

The scale of operations effect extends to a broader array of services that have local public goods qualities for other reasons. In many transactions, the marginal costs of serving another customer are small. Though different customers are served simultaneously, access is rationed by price. The services of intellectual property often have these properties, especially when rendered through mass media. Use of the service by one person does not greatly diminish availability to others. An author who must personally tell his story to each person individually has much smaller chances of earning a high income than one who can, in effect, clone himself to many customers at a time by writing the story down once-and-for all and duplicating it, at negligible cost, to others as a book, cassette or compact disc. Similar considerations apply to entertainers, actors, television personalities and newscasters, musicians and composers, artists, intellectuals, software developers, and athletes (Rosen, 1981). Typically the chances of success in these endeavors are rather small, but the rewards of the successful can be enormous because relatively few people are needed to satisfy the entire market. The small chances of great success attract many entrants, and the "stars" who are successful ex post appear to dominate their fields. They earn enough to put them well into the upper tail of the earnings distribution (Frank and Cook (1995) present many examples).

However, the vast majority of workers in the top percentiles of the earnings distribution are not stars, superstars or chief executive officers because scale economies in the services they render mean that few people are required to produce them. There are simply not enough of them to make much of a dent in the upper tail, even in a large economy such as the US, where the incomes and activities of such people receive so much attention and publicity. Highly successful professional practitioners in law, medicine and other professions occupy the upper tail much more frequently. Here, technology sharply constrains one's personal volume of transactions. Doctors can see a relatively small number of patients per day, and lawyers can manage only a few cases at a time. Instead, the scale-of-operations effect works through total value. The most capable lawyers tend to be assigned to the largest claims, where a slight edge in talent can have huge financial effects on the value of resources in dispute (Spurr, 1987). Large claims bid up the fees of the most successful lawyers. The wealthiest people in need of medical services outbid others for access to the most capable physicians.[1]

Sattinger (1993) discusses the assignment of workers to machines or other indivisible units of capital. Jovanovic (1998) combines this assignment problem with a model of vintage capital. In his framework, lower costs of upgrading machines are associated with increased earnings inequality because skilled workers benefit most when new technologies are more readily available.

2. Selection theory

In 1951, Roy sketched the basic structure of selection, but economists did not widely recognize the importance of his work until the 1970's. Tinbergen's (1959) version is more elaborate (and more obscure),[2] so we follow Roy (1951) here. The microeconomic content of "the Roy model", as it is sometimes called, is minimal. It is based on a choice problem of the simplest kind. Its analytic interest lies in its aggregate market implications. By describing how different individuals sort across job categories in the

---

[1] Alfred Marshall (1947) briefly introduced this point 100 years ago.

[2] Specifically, Tinbergen specifies that tastes for different kinds of work follow a specific form that has never been pursued in the literature. Tastes have been treated in the literature on equalizing differences, but not specifically in the occupational or job choice literature.

economy at large, the model helps us understand the nature, determinants, and distribution of economic rents in labor markets. It also illustrates how selection may generate asymmetric, long-tailed densities for earnings distributions even when the distribution of potential earnings in each job is symmetric.

2.1. The Roy model

Consider an economy with n different types of jobs. Earnings are worker specific because worker productivity varies from job to job, and some workers are better at some jobs than others. Assume that supply and demand are equal in all job markets and examine the assignment of workers to jobs in market equilibrium. Let y_{ij} be the earnings capacity of worker i on job j. It is what worker i could earn in job j. Let y_i be the earnings actually observed for worker i. Maintaining the economic hypothesis that self-interested workers choose jobs that maximize their earnings, observed earnings for worker i are

$$y_i = \max(y_{i1}, y_{i2}, \ldots, y_{in}). \tag{2.1}$$

The model is completed by specifying a joint probability distribution $f(y_{i1}, y_{i2}, \ldots, y_{in})$ for earnings prospects in the population at large. Roy (1951) assumed that $f(y)$ is jointly normal. Mandelbrot (1962) assumed that $f(.)$ follows the Pareto–Levy form. The observed earnings distribution, $g(y)$, is the transformation of $f(y)$ implied by Eq. (2.1).

This simple model yields surprisingly complicated outcomes. The observed distribution $g(y)$ is a mixture of conditional distributions resulting from maximization. Note that if n is large, Eq. (2.1) suggests the extreme value distribution (the distribution of the first order-statistic) as a possible stationary distribution. The extreme value theorem, like the central limit theorem, proves that the first order-statistic of independent and identically distributed parents tends to a unique limiting distribution, independent of how the parents are distributed. The stationary distribution is a double exponential. It is skewed and leptokurtic, characteristic of the upper tail of earnings distributions.

Though this idea is insightful, the extreme-value theorem cannot be applied here because the component distributions of earning potential y_{ij} in each job are not identically distributed (they have different means and variances) and may not be independent. It proves necessary to work through all the conditioning information to derive the observed distribution $g(y)$. Mandelbrot (1962) shows that $g(y)$ follows the Pareto–Levy distribution if $f(.)$ is Pareto–Levy. In fact, this is the only case for which $g(y)$ is in the same family as its parent $f(.)$. Otherwise the conditional distributions which compose it are truncated, and $g(y)$ is a complicated mixture that is not easily described in closed form.

The model is best illustrated when there are two jobs ($n = 2$). Suppose $f(y_1, y_2)$ is normal (or lognormal), with means μ_1 and μ_2, variances σ_1^2 and σ_2^2 and covariance σ_{12}.

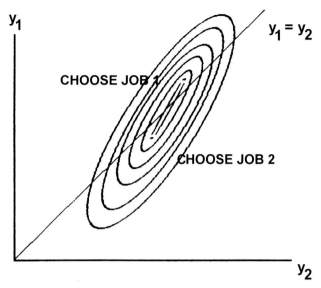

Fig. 2.1.

The correlation coefficient between earning capacities y_1 and y_2 is $\rho = \sigma_{12}/\sigma_1\sigma_2$. The assignment of workers to jobs is depicted in Fig. 2.1. The probability contours depicted assume $\mu_1 = \mu_2$, $\sigma_1 > \sigma_2$ and $\rho > 0$. Each person in the population is a point in the (y_1, y_2) plane. The probability mass there is proportional to the number of people in the population with those prospects. All workers along the 45° line $(y_1 = y_2)$ find the two jobs equally attractive. Earnings in job 1 exceed those in job 2 for all people above the line. They choose job 1 and $y_i = y_{i1}$. Similarly, all people in the region below the 45° line maximize earnings by choosing job 2, so $y_i = y_{i2}$ for them. Therefore the observed distribution $g(y)$ is the weighted sum of two truncated normals, one above the 45° line and the other below it. Maddala (1977) and Heckman and Honore (1990) present complete details of this model.

Economic rents enter this model both in the sense of relative talents ("producer" surplus or comparative advantage) and in the sense of absolute talents ("ability" rents and absolute advantage). In Fig. 2.1, workers with prospects along the equal earnings line represent the extensive margin between job types. Relative to their alternative, they receive zero surplus from their actual job choice. All others are inframarginal, and workers furthest from the 45° line (in either direction) receive the largest surplus from their choices. The length of the (y_{i_1}, y_{i_2}) vector provides a measure of general ability. Holding the ratio (y_{i_1}, y_{i_2}) constant, earnings rise with general ability.

With a little stretch, the variances and covariance in the probability contours can be given an economic interpretation. For instance, $\sigma_1 > \sigma_2$ implies a sense in which job 1 is more difficult than job 2. In this case, the outcome in job 1 is more dependent on who does the work. It offers more chances for talent to stand out. $\rho > 0$ means that a person whose earnings prospects are larger in job 1 is likely to have better than average prospects in job 2. For example, a one-factor structure of the type discussed above produces positive correlation between potential earnings in the two sectors and implies hierarchical selection. In Fig. 2.1 people with the highest earning prospects in both jobs tend to work in job 1. Those with lesser overall prospects tend to work in job 2. Notice that the relative variance condition is crucial to the order of the hierarchy. If $\sigma_1 < \sigma_2$ and $\rho > 0$, the probability contours cut the 45° line from above, and talented people are more often found in job 2.

The sign of the correlation coefficient is crucial to whether or not selection tends to be hierarchical. When $\rho < 0$, a person who is good at one job is likely to be below average in the other. The ellipses in Fig. 2.1 would be negatively sloped, and there would be positive selection in both jobs. Selection is not hierarchical in that case. Rather, people select jobs according to "comparative advantage". Selection on comparative advantage is empirically supported for the choice between high school and college education in some US data (Willis and Rosen, 1979). People choosing to stop school upon high school graduation are more likely to be attracted to blue collar jobs and those continuing through college are more likely to be found in white collar jobs. Willis and Rosen provide evidence that, on average, those who choose blue collar jobs are actually more productive in those jobs than more educated white collar workers would have been had they chosen blue collar work. This result is plausible to the extent that white and blue-collar jobs use much different kinds of talent and to the extent that different kinds of talent are negatively correlated. In such circumstances, the relevant concept of ability for earnings is clearly multidimensional. Single factor measures like IQ scores may be quite misleading.

Computational complexities of estimating selection models rise quickly in n, so these models have only been used for broad classification of job types. However, Garen (1984), who provides an approximation for selection bias in an educational choice model with a continuum of education levels, offers support for the multi-factor interpretation of selection according to comparative advantage. Heckman and Sedlacek (1985) expand the typical bivariate discrete econometric model to more alternatives, and recent applications of their methods reveal increasingly positive covariance in the earnings potential of individuals across occupations in the US data for the 1980's and 1990's (Gould, 1996), a period when earnings inequality in the US increased markedly. Perhaps selection on comparative advantage has become less important and selection according to absolute advantage more important over time. For instance, there is an alleged connection between increasing wage inequality and the information- processing content and computer intensity of work (Krueger, 1993).

Another possibility is that complementarities among qualities of workers have become more important for job assignments lately (Kremer, 1993: 1997). Worker complementarities are present when increasing stratification of worker types into more homogeneous groups raises their total productivity. Such an effect might arise from indivisibilities of tasks at the work-site. Increasing use of testing and other merit based methods for screening applicants to schools appear much more important now than in the past. However, much research remains to be done in this under-developed area.

2.2. *Selection on ability and stratification*

Figure 2.1 reveals that workers with similar earnings prospects choose the same type of job. When the number of job types n is large, one can examine interesting details of the assignments by thinking of talents as worker attributes that determine specific job productivity. Assume

$$y_{ij} = w_j \pi_{ij}, \tag{2.2}$$

where π_{ij} is the volume of the ith worker's output in the jth job, and w_j is the price per unit of worker output in job j (think of w_j as a piece rate). The choice criteria remains as in Eq. (2.1), so all pair-wise comparisons of w_j/w_k with π_{ik}/π_{ij} reveal a person's comparative advantage (Sattinger, 1975, 1993; Rosen, 1978). Furthermore, write

$$\pi_{ij} = \alpha_{1j}C_{1i} + \alpha_{2j}C_{2i} + \cdots + \alpha_{Kj}C_{Ki}, \tag{2.3}$$

where the C_{ki}'s are individual worker characteristics such as mathematical, motor, and verbal skills, etc., and the α_{kj}'s are the marginal products of those traits for the specific job. These marginal products generally vary from job to job. For instance, verbal skills are of greater value to a lawyer than to a carpenter, but manual dexterity is of greater value to a carpenter than to a lawyer. Combining Eqs (2.2) and (2.3),

$$y_{ij} = \beta_{1j}C_{1i} + \beta_{2j}C_{2i} + \cdots + \beta_{Kj}C_{Ki}, \tag{2.4}$$

where $\beta_{kj} = w_j \alpha_{kj}$ is the value of the marginal product of characteristic k in job j. Idiosyncratic random terms could be added to Eqs (2.2)–(2.3), but we ignore them here.

Applying the choice criterion in Eq. (2.1) to Eq. (2.4) reveals how people with similar C-endowments tend to choose the same type of job. Figure 2.2 illustrates the equilibrium stratification for 5 job types and two characteristics ($n = 5$, $K = 2$). Given job j, all people whose characteristics lie along the downward sloping line $C_1 = Y^*/\beta_{1j} - (\beta_{2j}/\beta_{1j})C_2$ would earn the same amount of money Y^* if they chose to work on job j. Draw such a line in the (C_1, C_2) plane for every job type and consider the inner envelope of the entire family of lines. This is the negatively inclined piecewise linear curve in the figure, after ordering job numbers by β_{2j}/β_{1j}. Rays from the origin through the corners of the envelope define regions where workers endowed with such traits maximize their incomes by choosing jobs 1, 2, ..., or 5. These partitions are completely deterministic when there is no randomness in Eq. (2.3). If specific random errors (noises) are present in Eq. (2.3), the partitions in Fig. 2.2 represent assignments in expected value. The partitions of the space of characteristics in Fig. 2.2 are open cones

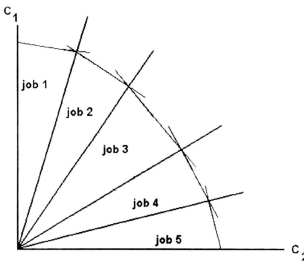

Fig. 2.2.

when the relations in Eq. (2.3) are homogeneous. However, if Eq. (2.3) has constant terms, the partitions can be closed and are much more complicated to describe.

Workers tend to choose jobs that highly value the personal characteristics they possess in relative abundance. The slope of each linear segment of the envelope in Fig. 2.2 is the ratio of marginal products α_{2j}/α_{1j} in Eq. (2.3). As illustrated, characteristic C_1 is highly productive in job 1 and C_2 is highly productive in job 5. Workers with relatively greater endowments of C_1 tend to choose job 1 and those with relatively greater endowments of C_2 tend to choose job 5. For instance, if C_1 is verbal skill and C_2 is manual dexterity, job 1 might be lawyer and job 5 might be carpenter. Both characteristics are equally important for productivity in job 3 and it tends to attract people with more balanced endowments. In this model, large earnings require large personal endowments of the C's. To the extent it is less probable to have large endowments of many characteristics than of only a few, high earners will tend to be more frequently found in occupations such as 1 and 5, which weigh only one characteristic strongly (Mandelbrot, 1962).

Prices, w_j, also affect the size of the partitions in Fig. 2.2. For instance, an increase in w_j reduces the intercept of the line that defines the facet and expands the width of the cone for which occupation j is optimal. Some persons who otherwise would have chosen neighboring occupations $j \pm 1$ now choose occupation j. The supply price of workers to jobs is always rising.

2.3. *Factor price equalization?*

The selection model contrasts with the Lancasterian combinable characteristics (hedonic) approach to product differentiation. Both place economic structure on a statistical factor-analytic model of personal earnings. In the hedonic approach, each worker supplies certain factors of production to employers, like strength and intelligence, etc. Equating demand and supply of each factor in an implicit aggregate factor market establishes market equilibrium prices and fixes the factor-loadings on the statistical structure. A worker's labor income is a fixed weighted sum of personal factor endowments (plus noise). If the number of factors is relatively small, the earnings distribution is compacted into a space of equally small dimensions. In effect, there are as many basic types of workers as underlying factors, and the earnings of every worker can be expressed as a linear combination of basic types (Welch, 1969)

This method rests on the crucial assumption that the total amounts of worker characteristics employed by a firm or sector of the economy are combinable and serve as its factors of production, independent of how the totals are obtained. It is a multivariate generalization of the old "efficiency units" assumption; e.g., a firm hiring two workers with half as many characteristics is the same as hiring one worker with twice as many. In essence, workers can unbundle their skills. Workers are allowed to allocate one type of skill to a given task while simultaneously allocating other skills to different tasks. In this form, the model is isomorphic to the theory of international trade, and the main question for its empirical relevance is whether or not there is "factor price equalization" across firms and industries. Unique prices imply that factor loadings are the same for all workers. But, if factor price equalization fails, the factor loadings are job specific, and the dimensionality economies afforded by the hedonic approach are lost.

Taking this model on its own terms, factor price equalization in labor markets is improbable. It fails if specialized factors are used in some firms but not in others. Further, because workers' skills are embodied, they cannot sell their skills in separate markets. An agent cannot sell brains to one employer while selling braun to another. This restriction limits the scope of arbitrage activities required to ensure unique factor prices in the labor market. The failure of factor price equalization makes the model in Fig. 2.2 more relevant (Rosen, 1983a; Heckman and Scheinkman, 1987).

3. Learning, sorting and matching

In the models discussed to this point, agents know their own productive capacities. We now review models where both workers and firms are uncertain about worker endowments. Both learn about the expected productivity of particular workers through successive observations of their performance. These models are dynamic extensions of selection and have implications for how the size distribution of earnings within a cohort evolves over time.

In simplest learning models, agents do not use information from the record of previous output when making subsequent allocation decisions. Information only influences wage rates. Since each observation of a person's output is an error-ridden measure of productivity, labor market competition implies that workers are paid their expected marginal products, given the information available. Thus wages for a given worker evolve as information accumulates over time. If the record is long enough, earnings in a cohort converge to the stationary distributions described in the stochastic models of Section 1.

More economically interesting information models introduce feedbacks from the data to future allocations along the lines of the selection models of Section 2. In sorting models, workers learn about their comparative advantage in various jobs and can switch jobs over time to better exploit their most valuable traits. In matching models, workers and firms gradually learn how productively they match with each other. If a realization is unfavorable, the relationship is terminated, and each side seeks a new match. Because workers keep good matches but abandon bad matches, wages grow, on average, as workers gain more information through work experience. Further, because workers leave poor matches, the wage distribution for a cohort becomes truncated over time, and wage distributions for experienced workers tend to be skewed relative to the distribution of wages among new workers.

Both matching and sorting models capture important aspects of individual careers. Without information about their relative aptitudes for different types of work, workers cannot make occupation choices that maximize their earnings. Thus, workers receive two forms of compensation from work experience. They receive their current earnings, and they receive information about their skills. This information affects future earnings because it informs future job choices.

Analyzing dynamic "Roy Models" requires putting more detailed structures on individual choices, and these structures make it more difficult to study the market equilibrium aspects of the problem. Little work has been done on how individual decisions based on gaining better personal information link up to overall market behavior. For instance, most learning models implicitly assume infinitely elastic demands for all types of skills. An exception is MacDonald (1982), who nests a learning model inside a supply and demand framework. MacDonald illustrates how learning generates sorting of workers across tasks in a general equilibrium context. The sorting process in his model also generates aggregate wage growth for a cohort and skewness in the size distribution of wages.

3.1. The basic learning model

Assume that two individual traits, X_i and θ_i, affect personal productivity of individual i at time t, y_{it}. All agents observe X_i. No one observes θ_i directly (workers have no private information). In each period, nature randomly assigns workers to firms. They are paid their expected marginal product as assessed at the beginning of the period, given X_i and their productivity history, $y_{it-1}, y_{it-2}, \ldots, y_{i0}$. The realization of worker output in each period is subject to an i.i.d. shock. Thus, output is a noisy measure from which to infer θ_i. Repeated observations of past performance allow inferences to become sharper over time. At each point, the worker's output y_{it} is an independent draw from the distribution $G(y_{it}|X_i, \theta_i)$.

Farber and Gibbons (1996) study how the distribution of wages evolves for a given cohort of workers in these circumstances. This problem is greatly simplified by the fact that true productivity does not vary over time. Consider a group of workers who share the same value of X_i. Since y_{it} is a random sample out of a fixed distribution, the mean wage for this group of workers does not change as the workers age. There is no cohort wage growth in large samples, and the mean wage in any period among these workers is always

$$E(w_{it}|X_i) = E(y_{it}|X_i) = E[(y_{it}|X_i, y_{it-1}, y_{it-2}, \ldots, y_{i0})|X_i]. \tag{3.1}$$

However, from well-known results on signal extraction in statistical decision theory, the variance of wages within each X_i class, and hence overall, increases with cohort experience. Simple as it is, this model produces the fundamental and important result that the distribution of wages is more compressed among young cohorts because there is not much information to differentiate one from another. Wage dispersion increases as work records reveal each worker's productivity more precisely.

Learning models are more interesting (and more difficult) when agents use acquired information to make real allocative decisions. The literature treats two kinds of problems. In one, workers use information to decide to invest in specific skills depending on what they learn about themselves (Jovanovic, 1979b). The implications for earnings distributions are perhaps not distinctive enough from the generic human capital models considered in Section 4 to warrant discussion here. In the other, matching and sorting models, workers base job mobility decisions on information gained from previous work experience. This kind of learning does not change skills per se. Rather, it changes perceptions of what skills one has and how they may be used more effectively. While these models occupy an important place in the literature on job mobility, their implications for individual wage growth also yield important insights concerning the evolution of the distribution of earnings for a particular cohort of workers.

A basic economic idea in information theory is that agents anticipate a priori how information gained currently and in the future will affect their subsequent decisions. For instance taking a low paying, low productivity job might have value in providing much information about the best sequence of subsequent jobs. The ability to change one's decision as information accumulates lends option value to choices. But this is very difficult to characterize analytically, and the structure of most work in labor economics minimizes this aspect of the problem.[3]

---

[3] Miller (1984) is an exception. Miller shows how workers sort across occupations when jobs differ with respect to both current expected returns and information content. In Miller's model, experience in a given job provides no information about expected productivity in other jobs, and given this form of independence across

3.2. Sorting by comparative advantage

Consider the following problem. There are N workers and J possible jobs. In each period output, y_{ijt}, of worker i on job j is

$$y_{ijt} = h(\theta_i, X_i, Z_j, \epsilon_{ijt}), \tag{3.2}$$

where θ_i are unobserved traits, and X_i are observed traits as before, Z_j is a set of job attributes, and ϵ_{ijt} is an idiosyncratic i.i.d. shock drawn from a known distribution $G(\epsilon)$. The function $h(.)$ is known, and outputs, y_{ijt}, are observed publicly. The "person effect" θ_i is an i.i.d. draw from a known distribution $F(\theta)$. Wage setting goes as before, and workers and firms are risk neutral. In the case where job characteristics are known, wages are given by

$$w_{ijt} = E(y_{ijt}|X_i, Z_j, y_{ijt-1}, \dots, y_{ij1}). \tag{3.3}$$

Workers choose the sequence of jobs that maximizes the expected present value of lifetime earnings, $\sum \beta^t w_{ijt}$, where β is the discount factor.

The solution is trivial when all traits of jobs and individuals are known: pick the job with the highest expected output and never switch. However, if some traits of jobs or individuals are unknown, then workers may sort across jobs based on their observed record of productivity in various employments. Sorting models describe how workers learn about their unobserved traits, θ_i, when these traits have different values on different jobs. Information helps allocate workers to these jobs more efficiently over time. By contrast, matching models describe situations where all learning is match-specific. Work experience on a particular job provides no information about the distributions of potential rewards associated with other jobs.

Matching models are easier to analyze, but sorting models may be more realistic. Nonetheless, both approaches tell the same basic story. As workers learn about their comparative advantages in different types of employment, or about the quality of their current job match, they sort away from things that they do poorly. This implies that, for a given cohort, average wages grow with experience. Further, in the sorting model below, the truncation of distributions associated with selection generates skewness in the distribution of wages.

The sorting model of Gibbons et al. (1997) nicely illustrates the main ideas while finessing many technical dynamic programming difficulties.[4] Here, the function $h(.)$ in Eq. (3.2) has the form

$$y_{ijt} = d_j + c_j(\theta_i + \epsilon_{ijt}). \tag{3.4}$$

jobs, he is able to use results from the literature on Dynamic Allocation Indices (or Gittins indices) to describe a tractable solution to the model. In models without this type of independence, tractable solutions are unlikely unless the information content of all jobs is the same.

[4] See Gibbons and Waldman (1998) for a related model dealing with promotion decisions. Kim (1998) and Ross et al. (1981) also provide variants of this type of model.

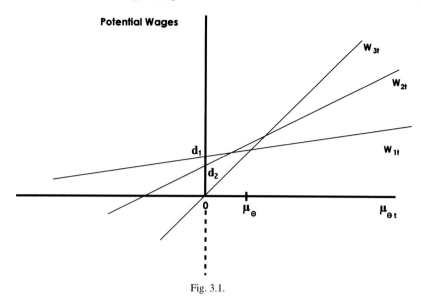

Fig. 3.1.

As in Section 2, this is a one-factor structure on "worker ability" θ_i, with factor loadings differing across job types. Here, the Z_j's in Eq. (3.2) are two parameters, c_j and d_j, and a known pair $\{c_j, d_j\}$ characterizes each job. Workers have one trait, θ_i. We ignore observed individual characteristics, X_i.

Coexistence of all types of jobs requires that if $c_j > c_{j'}$, then $d_{j'} > d_j$. Figure 3.1 illustrates three jobs. Job 1 requires almost no skill. It pays wages that vary little with worker ability. Job 2 offers higher returns to ability, and job 3 offers the highest returns to ability. The shocks, ϵ_{ijt}, come from a standard normal distribution. Individual ability, θ_i, also comes from a normal distribution with mean μ_θ and standard deviation σ_θ. Notice from the figure that if agents know θ_i, the analysis reduces to the deterministic factor model in Section 2, and sorting is strictly hierarchical: people with the highest values of θ_i choose job type 3 and those with the lowest values choose job type 1.

Hierarchial sorting simplifies the problem.[5] The problem is further simplified because the specified technology ensures that the information content of all jobs is the same and therefore does not affect job choice. Agents base posterior beliefs about the distribution of a worker's value of θ_i on the statistic

$$V_{ijt} = \theta_i + \epsilon_{ijt} = (y_{ijt} - d_j)/c_j. \tag{3.5}$$

---

[5] As noted in Section 2, if workers differ with respect to more than one skill, the presence of constant terms in Eq. (3.4) complicates sorting partitions.

Since the distribution of V_{ijt} is invariant across jobs j, the worker's optimal policy is to pick the job that offers the highest wage in each period. This is given by

$$\max_j w_{ijt} = C_j \mu_{\theta_{it}} + d_j, \tag{3.6}$$

where $\mu_{\theta_{it}}$ is the posterior mean of θ_i based on information available up to time t.

Consider a single cohort of workers. Assume these workers initially have the same expected ability, in the sense that their θ's come from the same distribution. The optimal policy described in Eq. (3.6) generates three implications for the evolution of the distribution of wages for this cohort. First, the distribution of wages becomes more dispersed as the cohort gains experience. Second, as workers sort across jobs in response to the information they receive, the average wage for the cohort as a whole increases with experience. Third, sorting across jobs generates skewness in the distribution of wages.

To understand how the sorting of workers across jobs creates wage growth in this model, note that since both θ_i and ϵ_{ijt} are normally distributed, $\mu_{\theta_{it}}$ is normally distributed across workers for $t > 1$. Further, the mean and median of $\mu_{\theta_{it}}$ equals μ_θ in each period. Consider the job choice of a worker with $\mu_{\theta_{it}} = \mu_\theta$ in Fig. 3.1. This worker chooses $j = 2$. If this were the only job in the economy, wages would be determined by

$$w_{it} = c_2 \mu_{\theta_{it}} + d_2, \tag{3.7}$$

and the variance of wages would increase with t, but the mean would remain unchanged at the starting wage, $w_{\text{start}} = c_2 \mu_\theta + d_2$. This is just a version of the pure learning model discussed in the previous subsection.

With more than one job, workers still begin their careers in $j = 2$, and all receive the same first period wage. But now, $\mu_{\theta_{it}}$ is not the only wage determinant that changes over time because workers have the opportunity to change jobs. Those who get favorable information and remain on $j = 2$ see their wage go up. Those who get unfavorable information and remain on $j = 2$ see their wage fall. However, the ability to change jobs convexifies the mapping from ability to wages, because those who learn they are much more capable move to $j = 3$, while those learning that their value of θ_i is quite small switch to $j = 1$, where ability is not so important. Those who switch from $j = 2$ to either $j = 1$ or $j = 3$ earn strictly more than they would have earned if they stuck with $j = 2$. Thus, the expected wage for a cohort of experienced workers exceeds the starting wage. Convexity of the market payoff to ability also imparts skew to the wage distribution. In sufficiently large samples, the median wage is constant. Therefore, the mean wage growth that results from sorting creates a growing gap between the mean and median wage.

The same logic applies in a model with an arbitrary number of jobs. As long as some workers sort away from their starting job, wages will grow on average with worker experience, and the distribution of wages will be skewed. In addition, since the variance of expected ability $\mu_{\theta_{it}}$ increases monotonically with t, the fraction of workers who have switched to new jobs increases monotonically with t. This implies that the gap between the mean and median wage of a cohort increases with experience. The truncation of distributions with sorting makes it difficult to say how the variance of wages changes with cohort experience. However, it can be shown that interdecile range measures of dispersion increase with t.[6]

To put models of this kind into perspective, bear in mind that much learning about individual talents (and preferences) occurs in school, prior to labor market entry. This is one of the reasons why all workers do not start work at the same wage on the same job. Instead, workers begin their careers on a range of jobs at a range of wages. The point here is that both of these ranges expand as workers gain experience. This model provides a useful description of how work experience yields information that affects the sorting of workers across jobs and how sorting affects the evolution of the distribution of wages for a given cohort of workers.

3.3. Matching models

In matching models, all learning is idiosyncratic to a particular worker-job match. Experience in one job provides no information about a worker's potential productivity in any other jobs. The following sketch draws heavily on Jovanovic's (1979a) model, which in turn resembles a search model. Worker i's productivity in job j at time t equals

$$y_{ijt} = \eta_{ij} + \epsilon_{ijt}. \tag{3.8}$$

Agents observe y_{ijt}, but do not observe its components. η_{ij} is the expected value of the match between worker i and job j, and ϵ_{ijt} is an i.i.d. realization of a normally distributed shock. The matches, η_{ij}, are i.i.d. draws from a normal distribution with mean μ_η and standard deviation σ_η. They are specific to workers and jobs jointly, not to either one separately as in sorting models. Again, workers are paid at the beginning of each period, before they produce output, and agents are risk neutral. There are enough firms competing for workers in all job categories that the labor market is competitive: the wage for worker i in job j equals the expected value of the match, η_{ij}, given past outputs.

As in search theory, the worker's optimum policy is to choose a reservation wage and switch jobs if the expected value of the current match, given all available information, falls below it. The reservation wage is a function of μ_η, σ_η, and tenure in the current job, τ. A job change in this model occurs when an agent draws a new η_{ij}. Average wages for a cohort grow with experience because workers and firms have the option to abandon bad matches. Further, the reservation wage policy ensures that, in the limit, the distribution

---

[6] For example, the 90–10 ratio increase with t because the variance of $\mu_{\theta_{it}}$ increases. As workers gain experience, both the 90th and the 10th percentiles of the $\mu_{\theta_{it}}$ distribution are moving farther away from the median μ_θ, which is constant over time. Since wages are a strictly monotonic function of $\mu_{\theta_{it}}$, the 90th and 10th percentiles of the wage distribution must also be moving farther away from the mean wage, w_{start}.

of wages is truncated. The left tail of the distribution is cut off at the reservation wage for a worker who knows η_{ij}.

3.4. Learning and general equilibrium

Most sorting and matching theory is partial equilibrium and does not analyze how the number of people engaged in an activity affect its returns. MacDonald (1982) embeds a sorting model in a market equilibrium context, and his results reinforce the predictions of basic sorting models. Wages grow, on average, with worker experience, and the sorting process tends to generate skewness in the distribution of wages.

MacDonald adapts the comparative advantage structure of Sattinger (1975) and Rosen (1978) to a learning environment in which workers learn their abilities over time. The structure of production is such that individual workers perform a large number of tasks arranged along a continuum, indexed by s; $0 \leq s \leq 1$. There are two types of workers, A and B, but neither firms nor workers know the type of a specific person. Workers of types A and B differ in their ability to perform the tasks. Type A workers have comparative advantage at one end of the spectrum, and type B workers have comparative advantage at the other end.

A fraction δ of all workers are actually type A workers. At the end of a period, each worker exogenously receives a piece of public information; an independent realization of a random variable X, where X takes one of two values. $X = a$, or $X = b$. The probability that $X = a$ is $\theta \geq \frac{1}{2}$ if the worker is an A. Likewise, the probability that $X = b$ is also θ if the worker is a B. All workers work for $N + 1$ periods and then stop. Thus, given the information technology, every worker belongs to one of $2N + 1$ information classes, where an information class is a group of workers with the same posterior probability of being of type A.[7] At any point in time, the supply of workers in a given information class is determined by the age distribution in the population.

MacDonald illustrates the determination of firm demands for workers from each information class in two steps. Given any set of workers from various information classes, the firm must determine the best way to assign workers to tasks. The solution to the assignment problem involves a set of critical tasks that define intervals on the task continuum, with one interval per information class. Because comparative advantage is ordered when there are only two types, the critical task intervals are ordered. Information classes are matched with these intervals according to the probabilities that workers in the class are of type A. These information classes correspond to conventional factors of production. Given an array of market wages for workers of various information classes, the firm must also choose the combination of optimally assigned workers that minimizes the cost of producing output. The solution yields the cost function and the

---

[7] Consider workers who vary with respect to experience, n. Denote x_n as the number of times $X = a$ in a work history with n periods. MacDonald shows that the number $k = n - 2x_n$ defines an information class. Workers who vary with respect to experience and x_n belong to the same information class if they share the same value of k. Figure 1 in MacDonald's paper shows that k may take on $2N + 1$ distinct values.

associated compensated factor demands. Markets clear when the demand for workers in each information class equals their availability in the population. Overlapping cohorts lead to a steady state equilibrium.

Equilibrium wages are positively correlated with worker experience in this model. As the market acquires more information about a given cohort of workers, these workers are, on average, assigned to tasks that more fully exploit their true comparative advantage, like the sorting model described above. However, the result is reinforced in this model by supply conditions. In this economy, young workers are found in information classes that contain relatively large stocks of workers, both within each cohort and in the labor market as a whole. Thus young workers have many substitutes. This is a second reason that young workers, on average, earn low wages.

For most interesting parameter specifications, the size distribution of wages in this model is skewed. If the skill endowments are such that neither A nor B has an absolute advantage at all tasks, the distribution of wages is always skewed. Further, in the benchmark case $\delta = 1/2$, mean wages exceed the median wage, regardless of initial skill differences between types A and B. Here, the median is constant, and mean wages grow with cohort age as workers are matched with tasks that better exploit their comparative advantage. However, if type A workers are more productive in all tasks, and $\delta \neq \frac{1}{2}$, then the distribution of wages may or may not be skewed. For example, if A workers are more productive in all tasks, and $\delta > \frac{1}{2}$, then median wages will grow with cohort experience because more than half of the workers in a cohort are actually "good" workers. In such a case, it is difficult to make general statements about the relative growth of cohort means and medians.

3.5. Summary

We have reviewed three types of models that highlight the role of information in determining wages. Simple learning models illustrate how wages should become more dispersed for a given cohort as the market gathers more information about cohort members. Sorting and matching models are an important part of the literature of wage growth and labor mobility, but the wage growth mechanisms described in these models also have implications for the evolution of the distribution of wages for a cohort. Sorting models provide the most direct contact with static theories of the distribution of earnings because they add a dynamic dimension to the literature on selection models. In both sorting and selection models, wage distributions are skewed relative to distributions of wage offers because workers sort to jobs where they have a comparative advantage. However, in sorting models, workers learn their comparative advantage only with time and experience. This implies aggregate wage growth for a cohort, and often implies that the distribution of wages for a cohort becomes more skewed as the cohort ages.

4. Human capital

In *The Wealth of Nations*, Adam Smith stated the central idea in modern human capital theory,

When any expensive piece of machine is erected, the extraordinary work to be performed by it before it is worn out, it must be expected, will replace the capital laid out upon it, with at least the ordinary rate of profits. A man educated at the expense of much labor and time ... may be compared to one of those expensive machines. The work which he learns to perform, it must be expected, over and above the wages of common labour, will replace to him the whole expense of his education with at least the ordinary rate of profits of an equally valuable capital.

Some wage inequality is a consequence of the fact that employments differ greatly with respect to the "difficulty and expense of learning the business". Because wages must compensate workers for the cost of learning their trade, wages would differ across employments even in a world where all workers possess the same initial skill endowments. The monetary value of the effort and time required to learn neurosurgery is great. If the wages of brain surgeons did not greatly exceed the wages of workers who learn their craft easily and quickly, we would observe a dire shortage of brain surgeons.

The two previous sections highlight how the market assigns people with heterogenous endowments to heterogeneous tasks and how assignments change as markets reveal information about workers' true endowments. Many models of human capital investment also highlight the role of heterogenous endowments, but the most important insight of the human capital approach is that patterns of investment in training help determine differences in productive capacities across workers. Here, investment costs drive earnings differences across groups of workers who have different levels of education, experience, or professional training.

4.1. Compensation for investments in training

Mincer (1958) is among the first modern economists to formalize Adam Smith's ideas concerning wage inequality and occupational training requirements. Suppose a worker who seeks to maximize his lifetime earnings is faced with two possible careers. The first requires d periods of training and pays a wage of W_0 per period. The second requires training for $d + s$ periods and pays a skilled wage of W_1 per period. Training requires no direct expense. The worker lives for n periods and discounts the future at rate r. A worker is indifferent between the two occupations if they offer the same lifetime earnings, or

$$\int_d^n W_0 e^{-rt}\, \mathrm{d}t = \int_{d+s}^n W_1 e^{-rt}\, \mathrm{d}t. \tag{4.1}$$

The ratio W_1/W_0 that leaves the worker indifferent between the two occupations is

$$k(d, s, n) = \frac{W_1}{W_0} = \frac{e^{-rn} - e^{-rd}}{e^{-rn} - e^{-r(d+s)}}, \tag{4.2}$$

k is the relative supply price of labor to the schooling-intensive occupation. It is increasing in s and decreasing in n. Though schooling has no direct cost, an increase in s postpones entry into the labor market and increases foregone earnings: k must increase for the worker to remain indifferent. Further, since an increase in work life, n, implies a longer working period in which to recover foregone earnings, k decreases.[8] Finally, k is an increasing function of d. Relative wage ratios and the rate of return to additional schooling should be larger for persons with 14 years of schooling than for those with 10 years, because when life is finite and independent of investment, a higher relative wage premium is required to cover the costs of schooling that occurs later in life. These last two effects are small when n is large.

As n goes to infinity, $k(d, s, n)$ ceases to be a function of d or n. In the limit (Mincer, 1974)

$$\ln W_1 = \ln W_0 + rs. \tag{4.3}$$

This is the clearest statement of how wages compensate for added training costs. Let s be the additional schooling required to perform job 1 instead of job 0. A worker is indifferent between the two jobs if the percentage difference between the wage for job 1 and the wage for job 0 is roughly equal to the product of r and s. If a group of workers, who are homogeneous with respect to talent and tastes, occupy a variety of occupations that require different levels of training or schooling, the distribution of wages for trained workers in this group is skewed relative to the distribution of schooling. For example, if the distribution of schooling is normal, the distribution of wages is lognormal.

Education and training means that wage inequality is not exclusively driven by heterogenous endowments and rents. Wage inequality results when some occupations require more training than others. Wage differences also must equalize the net advantages of work in other ways (see the survey in Rosen, 1986). For instance, some jobs are more onerous or dangerous than others. Some offer more earnings stability than others. Though these important factors affect measured inequality indexes, the scope of the subject is too broad to be included here. However, education and training deserve special emphasis for this survey because they are so important in determining personal productivity.

Mincer's approach is valuable because it illustrates an equilibrium condition that must be satisfied when workers acquire skills by investment. But, it does not tell us which workers invest in training and under what circumstances. We next review models of optimal investment in human capital to shed more light on the mapping between the distribution of individual traits and the distributions of wages and earnings.

So far, distinguishing between wage rates and total earnings has been inconsequential. In models discussed to this point, workers decide where to allocate their time, but,

---

[8] In societies where people work until roughly the end of their lives, increasing expected life span is associated with decreases in the relative supply price to training-intensive occupations. This effect has been important historically.

by assumption, workers allocate all of their time to some type of production. Further, in Mincer's original paper, while there is a training period, it is distinct from work, and once training is over, workers spend all their time producing goods. By contrast, in most human capital models, workers decide how to blend different activities at each point in time. Some models address the division of time between training and production. Others also address the consumption of leisure. In all cases, earnings, which equal incomes per unit of time, need not equal wages, which equal incomes per unit of time spent in goods production.

Having said this, we discuss the implications of human capital models in terms of actual earnings not wage rates or potential earnings. Links between the predictions of human capital models and empirical regularities in labor market data are more clear in earnings data than in wage data. Existing data often provide straightforward measures of actual earnings, but this is not always the case with hourly wage rates.[9]

4.2. Optimal investment

The most well known attempt to formulate a model that captures the implications of optimal investment in human capital for the distribution of labor earnings is Becker (1967),[10] who developed the useful graphical representation in Fig. 4.1. In Becker's model, workers supply labor inelastically and seek to maximize the present value of their lifetime earnings. Great simplification is achieved by reducing lifetime human capital investment to a static problem. Assume that human capital investment activities require complementary purchased inputs (e.g., books and teachers) as well as the student's time and that each investment activity combines time and purchased inputs in fixed proportions. Workers acquire human capital by progressing through a sequence of investments. Returns on successive investments must diminish at some point because the remaining work life is shortened and because the worker's opportunity cost of time increases with previous investments in human capital.[11]

The horizontal axis in Fig. 4.1 measures total lifetime expenditure on inputs purchased for human capital production. The downward sloping "demand" curve represents the marginal internal return on these expenditures. It equals $(PV_1 - PV_0 - C_1)/C_1$, where PV_1 and PV_0 are the present values of lifetime earnings with and without the marginal investment in human capital, and C_1 is the dollar value of purchased inputs

[9] For example, consider a college student who works for only three months in the summer and reports annual earnings of $5,000. Researchers commonly conclude that the student's summer earnings imply an annual wage rate or potential annual earnings of $20,000. Among other things, this conclusion rests on the assumption that the student receives no training on the summer job. If the student is working in an apprentice program or an internship, his actual earnings may grossly understate his earning potential which is based on the wage he could receive in a job that involved no training.

[10] This was later reprinted in Becker (1975).

[11] There may be regions of increasing returns if capital accumulation facilitates future learning. Below, we discuss assumptions concerning the way in which existing human capital affects the creation of new human capital. These assumptions are key to pinning down exactly how human capital theory links the distribution of talent and the distribution of earnings.

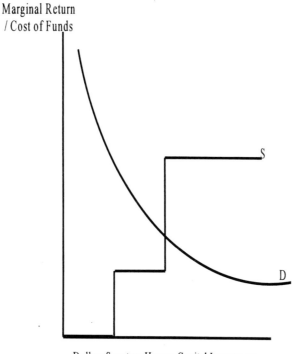

Marginal Return
/ Cost of Funds

S

D

Dollars Spent on Human Capital Investment

Fig. 4.1.

for the marginal investment.[12] Note that because $(PV_1 - PV_0)$ is the difference in the lifetime present values of two earnings streams, the marginal return in Fig. 4.1 is a net rate of return on the financial cost of investment, C_1. This rate of return incorporates the opportunity cost of foregone earnings.

The upward sloping "supply" curve traces out the opportunity cost of purchased inputs in human capital production. In most industrialized countries, elementary and secondary schooling are approximately free in terms of tuition costs, but investments in on-the-job training or post-secondary schooling require other inputs that families must pay for with their resources. For wealthy agents, the opportunity cost of funds spent on these purchased inputs is the market rate of interest. For poor agents, the price of these funds is the interest rate at which they can borrow to finance their human capital investments. The supply curve of funds for poorer agents is generally upward sloping but may have horizontal segments. Optimal lifetime investment is determined by the intersection of the supply and demand schedules.

[12] These present values are calculated for all individuals and investments using a common market interest rate.

Figure 4.1 pushes a number of important details into the background. Nonetheless, it is a useful general description of how ability and family wealth interact to determine the distribution of lifetime earnings. In a rough and ready way, the "demand" and "supply" representations in the figure correspond to the concepts of "nature and nurture" that dominate popular debates on inequality. The relevant concept of ability here is associated with returns from human capital investments. Assume that two workers, A and B, consider the same sequence of potential investments. Worker A is more able than worker B if A's marginal return from any particular human capital investment is always greater than B's. The demand curve for human capital by worker A is shifted up relative to worker B, and given the same supply conditions, worker A invests more than worker B. The effects of family circumstances and credit market imperfections work through the supply curve. Students with wealthier parents can finance their investments on better terms. Their supply curves are farther to the right than those of students from poorer backgrounds. Holding ability constant, students from wealthier families invest more.

Superimposing the demand and supply functions of all individuals on the same graph yields a cloud of points that describes the entire distribution of life-investment outcomes. For instance, the distribution of lifetime earnings tends to be more skewed when people have different talents (demand curves) and the same opportunities for financing investments (identical supply curves) than when people have identical talents but differ in their access to funds. Becker calls the first case "equal opportunity", because the terms of investment are independent of personal financial circumstances and family wealth. Those with large total investments in human capital also have high returns at the margin. But if all agents have the same ability and face different costs of funds, family wealth dominates investment outcomes: those with large total investments have low marginal returns because their marginal costs are low. Policies, like free education, that promote equal opportunity reduce the dispersion in supply curves.

This model has limited empirical content for understanding the details of observed earnings distributions because it deals with unobservable human capital concepts and does not impose enough structure to pin down the precise mapping from human capital wealth to observed earnings. This difficulty is transparent when one compares the model to the pure equalizing difference model of Mincer (1958). In Mincer's model, all persons have the same talent and tastes, and therefore, the present value of lifetime earnings is the same for everyone. Although there is considerable cross-section earnings inequality, there is no lifetime inequality. While available data provide evidence that lifetime earnings do vary greatly across individuals, Becker's model is too general to provide clear guidance concerning what portion of cross-section earnings inequality represents compensating differences on investment costs and what portion represents ability rents.

We need more specific models of human capital accumulation in order to precisely map talents and opportunities into life-cycle earnings profiles. The leading model of this kind is Ben-Porath's (1967) analysis of human capital investments as an intertemporal optimization problem. Workers seek to maximize the discounted present value of their lifetime earnings by allocating their time between investments in human capital and work and by choosing the optimal path of purchased investment goods over the life-cycle. The worker's problem is

$$\max_{s(.),i(.)} \int_0^T (w(v) - Pi(v))e^{-rv}\, dv$$

$$\text{s.t.} \quad w(t) = R(1 - s(t))k(t), \quad k'(t) = \beta(s(t)k(t))^{\gamma_1} i(t)^{\gamma_2}, \tag{4.4}$$

where $w(t)$ is the wage at t, $s(t)$ is the fraction of time spent training, $k(t)$ is the stock of human capital, $i(t)$ is purchased inputs used to produce human capital, R is the rental rate on human capital, P is price of purchased inputs, and r is the interest rate. $k(t)$ is "efficiency units" of human capital. Analysts typically assume that the equilibrium rental rate R and the price of purchased inputs P are constant over time. The expression for $k'(t)$ is the educational production function.

This is a standard control problem. The details of solution depend on the form of the production function. In this kind of model, the gross returns to using time either for direct production in the market or for investment in the production of human capital are increasing in the current stock of human capital. Ben-Porath's Cobb–Douglas form simplifies the problem immensely because it makes these two effects exactly offsetting and renders the optimal investment path of $k'(t)$ independent of $k(t)$. This property makes it possible to get closed form expressions for $w(t)$ and $k(t)$.

In the Ben-Porath framework, human capital $k(t)$ is used to produce both output and additional human capital. Therefore, one might treat the initial stock of human capital, $k(0)$, as an index of initial talent or ability. However, given this definition of ability, the Ben-Porath model does not yield the prediction that able workers invest more resources in human capital production. Both efficiency units of time investment, $s(t)k(t)$, and levels of purchased investment goods, $i(t)$, are independent of the current stock of human capital, $k(t)$. Workers with higher initial stocks of human capital have higher lifetime earnings, but they do not make larger investments in human capital production. Here, initial capital stocks are pure rents.

Becker's concept of ability is better captured by β, the scale parameter in Eq. (4.4). Consider two workers who begin their careers with identical human capital stocks, $k(0)$, but different values of β. Assume these workers make identical investments of purchased inputs, $i(0)$, and time, $s(0)$. The costs of these investments are the same in terms of forgone earnings and purchased inputs, but the high-β worker receives a greater return in terms of additional human capital, $k'(0)$. The worker with a higher β learns more efficiently, and it is easy to show that workers with more learning ability have higher lifetime disposable earnings. Further, for $t < T$, the more able worker invests more financial resources, $Pi(t)$, and more effective units of human capital, $s(t)k(t)$, in the production of human capital. Holding resource costs constant, workers who learn efficiently invest more in human capital and receive greater total returns from their investments. Thus, the

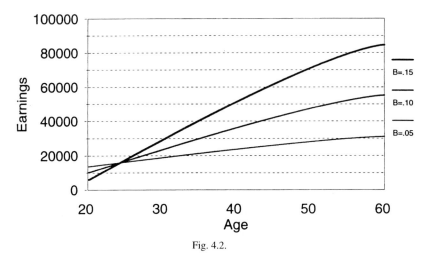

Fig. 4.2.

ability to learn appears to be closely related to Becker's notion of ability as a demand shifter.[13]

Lifetime accumulation of human capital also has implications for how the distribution of earnings for a particular cohort evolves over time. Figure 4.2 presents life-cycle earnings profiles for three workers in a Ben-Porath model with the same initial stocks of human capital but different learning efficiencies.[14] The dispersion in earnings for a given cohort is greater for mature workers than for young workers. Further, the increase in cohort earnings dispersion begins at a point well into the workers' careers. In fact, in this example, dispersion decreases over the first few years and then increases dramatically after the more able workers, who make large initial investments in training, catch up.

[13] The strong Markovian properties of Ben-Porath's functional specification afford so many analytical conveniences that its use has become routine. Alternatives are seldom considered. While convenient and simple, it is not necessarily descriptively accurate. For instance, the marginal costs of investment may be decreasing in $k(t)$. Then people who know more find it cheaper to invest. Initial stocks $k(0)$ as well as production function parameters affects optimum investment profiles and the effects of ability are more complex to describe. See Rosen (1976) for an example of this type. See Schultz (1975), Welch (1975) and Foster and Rosenzweig (1996) for extended discussion and evidence on how ability to learn affects productivity.

[14] The three values for β are 0.05, 0.10, and 0.15. The other parameters are $\gamma_1 = 0.2$, $\gamma_2 = 0.075$, $r = 0.03$, and $R/P = 4$. The initial capital stock is normalized to one. The relative price of human capital roughly equals the ratio of mean annual earnings for full-year workers who are twenty years old, male, and high school graduates ($16,300) to the mean cost of four quarters of college at a state university ($4,021) for the year 1994. The earnings data come from the March, 1995 Current Population Surveys, and the tuition data come from The Digest of Educational Statistics (1996). There are no available estimates of β, γ_1, and γ_2. However, Haley (1973) does provide estimates from a model without purchased inputs. Here, the parameters are chosen in order to get initial investments of time and purchased resources that roughly correspond to three investment levels: full-time college, part-time college or vocational training, and a modest level of on the job training. See Von Weizacker (1993) for a complete exposition of similar models and similar simulation exercises concerning the evolution of the distribution of earnings for a cohort.

This U-shaped relationship between cohort earnings variance and cohort age is an important theme in the literature on human capital (Mincer, 1974). In Fig. 4.2, all workers begin their careers with the same initial productive capacity, the same financial constraints, but different abilities to learn new skills. Because the most able worker will make the largest investments in training, she actually begins her career earning less than the other two. Thus, the figure illustrates that the dispersion of earnings for a cohort may initially decrease with age as efficient learners begin to make fewer training investments and start to catch up to the earnings levels of less able workers. At some point, the earnings of able workers overtake the earnings of less able workers, and in this scenario, experience-earnings profiles in the cohort fan out and the dispersion of earnings increases dramatically thereafter.

When workers differ in their ability to acquire skills, the location of young workers in the distribution of current earnings for their cohort misstates their position in the distribution of lifetime earnings because greater levels of investment depress their current earnings relative to less able workers.[15] Workers who learn more efficiently have both relatively steep earnings profiles and relatively high lifetime earnings. In contrast, among workers who differ only with respect to their initial stocks of human capital, $k(0)$, earnings profiles are parallel over the life-cycle,[16] and a worker's position in the distribution of current earnings is a perfect indicator of position in the distribution of lifetime earnings (Lillard, 1977; Lillard and Willis, 1978; Weiss and Lillard, 1978; Weiss, 1986).

It is difficult to incorporate capital market imperfections in models of optimal human capital accumulation. Borrowing constraints require a utility based framework because they break down the separation between maximization of wealth and utility. But one can still represent some imperfections by exogenous differences in costs and returns for human capital investments. While "equal opportunity" corresponds to an environment where every worker can borrow and lend at the same interest rate, r, and every worker can purchase inputs for human capital production at the same price, P, an environment where agents face different levels of r and P generates "noncompeting groups" of workers. The presence of such groups affects not only the shape of the cross-section earnings distribution but also how the distribution of earnings for a given cohort evolves over time.

Here are some examples.

(i) Government subsidies for both secondary and post-secondary education vary across countries and across regions within countries, and educational quality may differ among groups in the population. Both can be represented by interpersonal differences in P. Investment in human capital varies directly with R/P, the ratio of the rental rate on human capital to the price of purchased inputs in human capital

---

[15] For example, medical students appear "poor" on current earnings accounts, but are wealthy on human capital accounts.

[16] This result holds under the assumption that capital does not depreciate. In a model with skill depreciation, earnings profiles get closer together over the work life.

production. Persons facing low values of P invest heavily at the beginning of their careers and receive high earnings later in life.

(ii) Optimal human capital investment models usually are based on the idea of mutually exclusive time allocations between work and training. However, there is an equivalent alternative set up where work and learning are jointly produced on the job. In this learning-by-doing framework, learning opportunities differ across jobs, and jobs pay different wages as an equalizing difference. Workers choose the sequence of jobs that implements their optimal investment program (Rosen, 1972). Labor market discrimination and other barriers restrict access of some people to jobs with greater learning opportunities and better chances for advancement. This is equivalent to an increase in the marginal costs of learning, represented by a decrease in β or an increase in P. Either way, those affected reduce their investments, and consequently, their experience-earnings profiles are flatter.

(iii) Labor market discrimination can also cause rental rates (R) to differ across groups. This too reduces the marginal return to investment and restricts human capital accumulation incentives, again resulting in smaller lifetime earnings and flatter earnings profiles.[17]

4.3. Labor supply

Much earnings inequality is directly attributable to interpersonal differences in hours of work supplied to the market. This issue is important for empirical work and also bears on theory. The human capital models considered above treat labor supply as inelastic, independent of investment activities. However, one expects interactions because workers choose their investments and labor supply jointly. For instance, assuming that human capital investments do not affect the value of leisure, workers who expect to work more have greater incentives to invest in human capital because greater utilization of skills increases the rate of return to investment. In addition, those who invest more face higher costs of leisure at the margin and may substitute against nonmarket activities. Forces that determine the quantity and timing of leisure consumption can affect both the size distribution of earnings and the evolution of the distribution of earnings for a particular cohort.

Blinder (1974) was among the first to investigate these issues. He restricts his analyses to the pure effects of hours choices because he treats the path of wages as exogenous. Still, his work serves as a useful starting point. An agent's utility is a time- and goods-separable function of consumption and leisure. Workers borrow and lend at a fixed rate of interest, r, and face an exogenous life-cycle pattern of wages, $w(t)$. Each person

---

[17] The natural extension of these models is to introduce explicit intergenerational linkages. These issues of intergenerational mobility are crucial to the study of economic equality and are treated separately by Piketty in this volume.

maximizes utility by choosing optimal paths of consumption $c(t)$ and leisure $l(t)$ given their initial wealth, $M(0)$, and a concave bequest function, $B[M(T)]$:

$$\max_{c(t),l(t)} \int_0^T e^{-\rho t}[U(c(t)) + V(l(t))]\,dt + B(M(T))$$

s.t. $\quad c(t) + s(t) = rM(t) + w(t)(1 - l(t)),$

$$M'(t) = s(t), \quad M(0) = M_0, \quad 0 \le l(t) \le 1 \tag{4.5}$$

where $s(t)$ is savings at t, and ρ is the rate of time preference. To illustrate the solution assume $U(c(t)) = \log(c(t))$, and $V(l(t)) = \varphi \log(l(t))$ and $\rho = r$ for all workers. The first order condition for $l(t)$ is

$$l(t) = \frac{\varphi c(t)}{w(t)}. \tag{4.6}$$

When $\rho = r$, $c(t) = c(0)$ is a constant, and earnings are given by

$$E(t) = w(t) - \varphi c(0), \tag{4.7}$$

so actual earnings profiles, $E(t)$, and potential earnings profiles, $w(t)$—what the worker would earn if working full-time—are parallel. Because consumption $c(0)$ is an increasing function of lifetime earning potential, the gap between lifetime earnings and lifetime earning potential increases with earning potential. Thus, when the path of potential earnings is exogenous and leisure is a normal good, the consumption of leisure mitigates lifetime earnings inequality. Blinder (1974) demonstrates a similar result concerning overall income inequality. Workers who begin life with large initial asset endowments, M_0, consume more leisure over their lifetime. Nonearned income is a substitute for earnings.

If all workers have the same tastes, the positive relationship between wealth and consumption of leisure ameliorates overall income inequality due to individual differences in asset income and earning potential. However, all workers do not have the same tastes, and tastes for leisure may well be correlated with individual wage rates and assets. Blinder uses simulations to gauge what sources of individual heterogeneity contribute significantly to the observed inequality in labor incomes. His results suggest that individual differences in wage profiles are the most important factor in determining earnings inequality, but there is also an interaction between tastes and wages. If wages and preferences for leisure are negatively correlated, realized lifetime earnings inequality may be much greater than the underlying inequality in potential earnings. This finding is important because we expect tastes to influence earnings capacities. In Blinder's framework, correlations between potential earnings and tastes are simply correlations between worker endowments. However, in human capital models, earnings capacity is, in part, determined by tastes. Because workers with weak preferences for leisure forfeit relatively little in utility terms when they work, they have additional incentive to invest in market skills. In short, we expect future earnings capacity to vary inversely with current tastes for leisure.

Adding human capital investment to problem (4.5) yields a more complete model that analyses three uses of time: investment, $s(t)$, leisure, $l(t)$, and work time $(1 - s(t) - l(t))$.[18] We maintain the Ben-Porath technology for human capital investment in Eq. (4.4), but ignore bequests and purchased inputs, and write the instantaneous utility function as $u(c(t), l(t))$. Earnings capacities evolve as workers make investments in human capital. Assuming that the rate of time-preference equals the rate of interest, first order conditions for $c(t), l(t)$ and $k(t)$ satisfy

$$u_c(c(t), l(t)) = \lambda \tag{4.8}$$

$$u_l(c(t), l(t)) = \lambda R K(t), \tag{4.9}$$

$$\frac{R[s(t)k(t)]^{1-\gamma}}{\beta\gamma} = \int_t^T R(1 - l(\tau)) \exp(-r(\tau - t)) \, d\tau. \tag{4.10}$$

λ is the multiplier associated with the lifetime budget constraint. The right hand side of Eq. (4.10) is the discounted marginal value of a unit of current investment. The left-hand side is the marginal cost of additional human capital, $k'(t)$, in terms of forgone current earnings.

Equations (4.8) and (4.9) are the standard intertemporal substitution conditions, with earning capacity, $Rk(t)$, replacing the wage rate. It is clear from Eq. (4.9) that the marginal utility of leisure is inversely proportional to earnings capacity along the optimum path (over the life cycle). If the marginal utility of leisure is independent of current consumption, this implies that leisure varies inversely with earnings capacity over the life cycle. As in the standard Ben-Porath model, time spent investing, $s(t)$, declines monotonically with age. Thus, when we examine a cross-section of workers, part of the observed difference in earnings between experienced and inexperienced workers may reflect the fact that experienced workers not only enjoy higher earnings capacity because of previous human capital investments but also spend less time investing in human capital and consuming leisure. A similar result holds in Blinder's framework if one assumes that earnings capacity rises over time, but human capital models generate rising earnings capacities endogenously.

Further, while the model yields few general comparative dynamics results, it does provide a framework for discussing how differences in tastes for leisure across individuals may contribute to differences in the evolution of life-cycle earnings profiles. Take the special case where preferences are separable over both time and goods, and

---

[18] Examples include Heckman (1976), Ryder et al. (1976), and Blinder and Weiss (1976). Weiss (1986) provides a survey of life-cycle human capital models.

assume interior solutions for all $t < T$. Now, consider two workers with identical skill endowments but different tastes for leisure. Because worker A has a stronger preference for leisure, he begins his career by devoting more time to leisure than worker B. Worker B always invests more in terms of efficiency units of human capital, $s(t)k(t)$, because his weak tastes for leisure increase the returns from investments in market human capital. Therefore, over time, the earning capacity of B grows apart from the earning capacity of A. Since B always has higher earning capacity and weaker tastes for leisure, B always consumes less leisure than A.

Ignoring corner solutions, A always consumes more leisure than B. But, one cannot say that A always works less because A may spend less time training. As the workers age, differences in leisure consumption become more pronounced because earnings capacities continue to grow apart. However, differences in training must eventually diminish because training tends to zero for both workers as $t \rightarrow T$. Thus, differences in tastes for leisure lead to life-cycle patterns of leisure and training that eventually magnify earnings differences among experienced workers. Experienced workers with weak tastes for leisure have relatively high earnings capacities because of previous investments. For experienced workers, the combination of weak tastes for leisure and high earnings capacities reduces current leisure consumption and, at some point, must translate into both higher earnings and more labor supply.

While the exact life-cycle relationship between tastes for leisure and labor supply is ambiguous in general, it is clear that, holding ability constant, those with weaker tastes for leisure have higher discounted lifetime earnings.[19] Further, human capital models demonstrate that this result is more than a link between labor supply and tastes for leisure. There are two components to the link between tastes and earnings. Given earnings capacity, workers with weak tastes for leisure work more. But earnings capacity is not independent of tastes. Weak tastes for leisure enhance investment and therefore raise earnings capacity.

Adding labor supply considerations to human capital investment models extends the economic implications of these models. People with either weaker tastes for leisure (inferior opportunities for work outside the market) or lower costs of human capital production invest more. Thus economic development, decreasing fertility, and other factors affecting the labor force participation of women increase the demand for human capital investments and augment the future market supply of skill. What remains for future research is a better understanding of the demand for skilled labor and how such shifts in the supply of skill affect the equilibrium rental rate on human capital.

---

[19] If two workers have the same opportunities, the one with weaker tastes for leisure will enjoy more goods consumption. This requires higher lifetime earnings.

5. Insurance, agency and earnings

If firms could pay workers strictly on the basis of their own production, most incentive and labor relations problems between employers and employees would disappear. Pay would be contingent on a mutually acceptable outcome. Few labor contracts work this way because individual output is costly to assess at each point in time. Payments of salaries and wage rates for a worker's effort and time are the norm, and firms loosely structure the detailed duties and obligations of employees. Since workers typically have some degree of control and discretion over their work, they have opportunities to pursue their own interests instead of their employers' interests. Examples are shirking and taking malfeasant actions, such as theft of goods from the firm and accepting payments from outside contractors.

The economic theory of agency analyzes such problems by describing internal compensation mechanisms that resolve conflicts and align the interests of employer and employee. The literature on agency examines the scope and limitations of different payment schemes, such as piece rates, for eliciting desired worker behavior, but our interest in agency theory is restricted to its role in understanding the distribution of compensation in labor markets. In this regard, agency models provide an important contrast to the models reviewed earlier in this survey. In most theories of earnings distributions, competition ensures that individual earnings reflect individual productivity, and the chief aim of theory is to explain the distribution of individual productivity. The agency literature reverses things: methods of compensation affect the allocation of worker effort across tasks and therefore determine the distribution of individual productivity. Moreover, observed wage rates at any point in time may not reflect personal productivity at that point.

A related literature focuses on a different information problem. When firms can observe productivity, risk averse workers who are not privately informed of their personal productivity do not want to be paid strictly according to their ex post output. They want insurance against random factors that affect productivity but are beyond their control. This demand for insurance shapes compensation policies by weakening the links between pay and ex post performance.

Below we discuss implications of both agency models and models of earnings insurance for the distribution of earnings. We begin by describing the insurance components of wage payments. This is the starkest possible departure between personal pay and personal productivity: pooling risks introduces voluntary redistributions of income that tend to compress wage distributions. Next, we consider agency models where firms use policies that increase wage dispersion in order to elicit effort. Tournament models of competition for promotion and models of bonding and deferred compensation loosen the links between current productivity and current earnings.

We conclude with an examination of efficiency wage models that address monitoring problems. In these models, firms use wage premiums to elicit certain desired aspects of employee performance, but other nonwage aspects of pay, such as performance bonds are not present and labor markets do not clear. These models do not have clear implications for the overall distribution of earnings, but they do provide a possible explanation for observed differences in mean wages across sectors of the economy.

5.1. Attitudes toward risk

Worker preferences alone can give rise to voluntary redistribution in the presence of uncertainty. Friedman (1953) is the first to address earnings inequality in such terms (see also Kanbur, 1979). Risk averse workers have incentives to equalize their incomes when earnings have stochastic components. If ex post outcomes contain random elements and no one has private information, a group of ex ante identical risk averse workers who know the probability distribution of outcomes pool risks and insure each other. All agree ex ante to a binding contract in which everyone contributes their ex post earnings to a common fund. All receive the ex post mean, and ex post income is completely equal even though the distribution of ex post productivity might be dispersed.[20]

Full ability-insurance is not widely observed in the labor market as a whole due to moral hazard and adverse selection. People who turn out to be successful would be reluctant to share their windfalls with the less fortunate, and if they did, they would have little incentive to develop and exploit their skills. Further, people who thought themselves more talented ex ante would be reluctant to participate in such a scheme in the first instance.[21]

Harris and Holmstrom (1982) provide an interesting model of earnings insurance that is an elaboration of the simple learning model described in Section 3.1. The record of production gradually reveals a person's productivity, and there is market competition for workers. If workers and firms could write lifetime employment contracts, risk neutral firms could provide complete earnings insurance for workers. However, in the absence of such contracts, labor mobility limits the ability of firms to provide insurance. Ex post, highly productive workers have an incentive to leave a firm that pays each worker according to the ex ante expected productivity of all its workers. Nonetheless, even in an environment where workers are free to change firms, an employer can provide partial insurance by matching outside offers and guaranteeing that a worker's earnings never

---

[20] Friedman himself investigated the possibility that this kind of insurance is not observed because people are risk-loving rather than risk averse. Workers with Friedman–Savage preferences (risk-loving in a certain range) have incentives to increase the dispersion of income by gambling. Recently Bergstrom (1986) and others (see Freeman, 1996 and references therein) have shown that Friedman–Savage risk preferences occur when the marginal utility of material goods consumption interacts with the type of work a person does or with other indivisible life-circumstances, such as place of residence. However, these types of risk preferences need not be addressed by labor market mechanisms. Purely monetary side gambles are sufficient. After winners and losers settle these side bets, they can make their occupational and other indivisible choices deterministically (Rosen, 1996), just like the models in Sections 1–4.

[21] There is a certain awkwardness in the pure theory of insurance as applied to labor market contracts. Why should the arrangements flow through firms rather than being managed by third party insurance companies? One possibility is that the firm is better able to control the worker's work performance, on which the insurance is contingent.

fall below his starting wage, no matter what the subsequent record reveals about personal productivity.

Since the firm rationally expects to pay higher wages to successful workers later on, the starting wage must be less than the unconditional mean productivity in the group. But risk averse workers are willing to accept a lower starting wage for the privilege of being insured against subsequent wage cuts should their productivity record prove unfavorable. The difference between the guaranteed starting wage and mean productivity of the entry cohort represents an up-front insurance premium. It is payed by workers and is necessary to finance the insurance. Likewise, when a worker who performs well receives a new wage offer, the new offer is less than the worker's expected productivity given the new information. The worker's ability is still uncertain, and the worker is willing to accept a new wage somewhat below expected productivity in exchange for a guarantee that the new wage will never fall in the future. As the worker becomes more experienced, there is less uncertainty about his true ability, and it costs firms less to provide a guarantee against future wage cuts. Therefore, as a cohort of workers gains experience, those receiving wage increases pay smaller premiums for earnings insurance.

The predictions of this model are similar, but stronger than those of the sorting model in Section 3.2. In the sorting model, wages become more dispersed as the market learns more about individual abilities. Over time, average wages rise and the distribution of wages for a cohort spreads asymmetrically. Those who learn that they possess lower levels of ability mitigate their losses by switching to jobs where output is less sensitive to ability, while those who learn the opposite magnify their gains by switching to jobs that more fully exploit their talent. In the Harris and Holmstrom framework, learning also creates wage growth and asymmetric wage dispersion because the distribution is always truncated at the starting wage. But in addition, wages of individuals never fall, as they would in the pure sorting model. There is a kind of "downward wage rigidity".

In general, worker demands for insurance compress wages relative to the distribution of individual productivities, but, because workers and firms cannot write complete insurance contracts, the resulting compression is one-sided. Next, we turn to models of effort elicitation. These models also generate asymmetric wage distributions, but here the emphasis is on stretching the right tail of the distribution not truncating the left tail.

5.2. *Effort incentives and compensation in internal labor markets*

Wages differ substantially across job titles within firms. Not only are there substantial pay distinctions between rank and grade, but empirical work shows that wage jumps associated with promotions account for a high proportion of a worker's wage growth within firms, especially in white-collar jobs (Baker et al., 1994). At first blush, this is hard to reconcile with standard productivity theory. Though a person's job activities usually change after a promotion, one's inherent skills and productivity do not jump on promotion day. Evidently, firms tie wages to jobs as well as people.

Job transfers of existing personnel and promotions from within can be thought of as an internal labor market. A military organization, where outside recruitment occurs only at the lowest ranks and all higher level positions are filled by internal promotions, is the most familiar example. Other organizations recruit at all levels but fill most vacant positions through internal transfers. Private law firms promote associates to partnership status, academic departments grant tenure and change the rank of professors, and large firms draw many of their executive staff from lower ranking positions in the same firm.

The indivisibility of job assignments is the main reason for internal recruitment of personnel: there can only be one chief executive officer at a time. Promotion policies allow firms to learn worker capacities for more important jobs by observing performance on less important ones; and the workers gain specific knowledge of the firm's operations and procedures that enhance future productivity in such positions. Issues of testing and sorting naturally arise in the assignment of persons to positions in internal labor markets. Firms promote workers who surpass a certain threshold of performance. Raises associated with promotions provide incentives for performance, and holding the firm's wage structure constant, the levels of various performance thresholds also affect incentives.

Let x be a worker's productivity on the current job, with $x = \mu + \epsilon$, where μ is the worker's effort and ϵ is a random variable drawn with mean zero.[22] $C(\mu)$ is the cost to the worker associated with effort level μ. $C'(0) = 0$ and $C''(0) > 0$ for all μ. Normalizing the price of x at unity, the efficient choice of μ for a risk neutral worker occurs when the marginal cost of effort equals its marginal return, or $C'(\mu) = 1$. The probability of passing the promotion standard[23] is calculated from the distribution of ϵ as $p = p(\mu, s)$, where s is the pass threshold measured in units of x, and $p_\mu > 0$ and $p_s < 0$. The firm promotes those who pass to a job that pays wage W_1. Those who fail go to a lower paying job W_2.[24]

The expected return to the worker is

$$p(\mu; s)(W_1 - W_2) + W_2 - C(\mu). \tag{5.1}$$

The worker puts forth effort to satisfy the first order condition

$$p_\mu(\mu; s)(W_1 - W_2) = C'(\mu). \tag{5.2}$$

Comparative statics imply that μ is increasing in both $(W_1 - W_2)$ and s, when s is small. Therefore, combinations of the promotion bonus, $(W_1 - W_2)$, and the height of the bar, s,

---

[22] We also assume that the density, $g(\epsilon)$, is single-peaked at 0.

[23] If the cumulative distribution of ϵ is $G(\epsilon)$ and the worker is promoted if $x > s$ then $p(\mu; s) = 1 - G(s - \mu)$. Note that this is not necessarily concave in μ so first order conditions must be carefully checked for optimality. These complexities are ignored here.

[24] There is no mobility here. Workers and firms agree on a lifetime employment contract that gives the workers their reservation level of utility. If workers are free to leave in the second period, firms face additional participation constraints in choosing their wage structure.

can be found that achieve the efficiency condition $C'(\mu) = 1$. Firms pay increasing and convex costs to set their standards. With homogenous firms and workers, competition by firms for workers ensures an equilibrium combination $[(W_1 - W_2), s]$ that not only elicits efficient effort but also ensures that, given efficient effort, workers receive their opportunity cost and firms earn zero profits.[25]

$$pW_1 + (1 - p)W_2 = E(x) = \mu. \tag{5.3}$$

It is interesting that although the average wage equals average productivity, the actual wage almost never equals equals ex post realized productivity. For instance, the probability that a person's realized value of x equals either W_1 or W_2 is zero, if ϵ is continuous. Here, wage dispersion does not reflect ex post differences in personal productivity. Rather, wage dispersion elicits ex post productivity.

In many instances, it may be easy to rank workers on an ordinal performance scale but difficult or impossible for firms to rank workers on a cardinal scale. Even when it is clear that worker A is better than worker B, firms may not know how much better. Under these circumstances, firms make promotion decisions based on relative performance, such as head to head competition among lower ranking workers vying for higher level positions. The noise introduced by common-error components in measuring individual performance can be eliminated by comparing contestants with each other. The result is as a "tournament" (Lazear and Rosen, 1981; Nalebuff and Stiglitz, 1983; Green and Stokey, 1983; McLaughlin, 1988) or some other form of relative performance evaluation (Holmstrom, 1982).

In tournament theory, contestants vie against each other rather than against a fixed standard. This brings strategic considerations into the problem above, because the probability of promotion for each player depends on what others are doing. The efforts of all other contenders replaces s in the probability of winning function, and we must analyze wages as outcomes of a noncooperative game. Nonetheless, prizes exist that produce the socially efficient level of effort among ex ante homogeneous players.

The tournament literature provides other interesting results concerning the distribution of earnings within firms. Since more contestants competing for a fixed number of promotions adversely affects incentives (O'Keeffe et al., 1984), the age and experience distributions within a firm affect its internal wage policy. Further, analysis of sequential contests in promotion ladders reveals another reason why compensation is extraordinarily high in top level positions. In tournaments where contestants are eliminated from further contention after failing, the difference in rewards between adjacent ranks provides only part of the incentives to perform. There is substantial option value in the probability of contending for even larger prizes in better jobs down the line. But in the last rounds of the tournament, that option plays out. Maintaining performance incentives at this crucial stage requires that the option value be replaced by an extraordinary jump

---

[25] Although regions exist where effort declines with increases in the standard given $(W_1 - W_2)$, firms never set standards this high.

in wages at the top of the organizational chart (Rosen, 1986). Again, wages do not necessarily equal ex post personal productivity of persons who win such prizes but do affect the productivity of others in the organization.

5.3. Agency and performance bonds

Contests or tournaments constitute incentive schemes that magnify earnings dispersion within a firm for a particular cohort of workers. A given cohort of workers enters a contest and over time, their earnings grow apart as some win and some lose. However, a different class of agency models addresses earnings inequality across cohorts. Models of this type highlight the role of performance bonds and deferred compensation as monitoring devices.

The basic solution to agency problems is a performance bond, in which a worker is put in a position to lose something if shirking or malfeasance are detected by the firm. The threat of dismissal alone does not provide sufficient incentives if an alternative job with the same pay (utility) can be readily found, and paying wages in excess of opportunity costs just to prevent shirking essentially creates rents for workers fortunate enough to land such jobs. In agency theory proper, other components of pay are adjusted to eliminate these rents and achieve market clearing. These take the form of payments at the front (bonds) and back (pensions) of the contract. Section 5.4 discusses efficiency-wage models, where these extra market-clearing adjustments are not admissible.

Workers in positions to take malfeasant actions against the firm can be deterred by sufficient monitoring (Alchian and Demsetz, 1972), but, like police and lawyers, monitoring is expensive. A self-enforcing payment mechanism that induces workers not to take advantage of the firm may be less expensive and achieve the same result. Obviously this requires penalizing malfeasant behavior (the "stick" approach) or rewarding good behavior (the "carrot" approach), so that workers find it in their best self interest to behave as the firm desires them to behave (Lazear, 1995). Ross (1973) and Becker and Stigler (1974) established that an up-front performance bond and back loaded pension accomplish this.

Following Becker and Stigler (1974), consider the last period of job which pays a wage W_n and offers a chance at malfeasance worth x to the worker. Knowing that malfeasance can occur, the firm installs an imperfect monitor that detects malfeasance with probability p. The firm fires the worker if it detects malfeasance, and the worker may take a job elsewhere that pays V_n. The worker's expected return to malfeasance is $(1 - p)(W_n + x) + pV_n$. The return to honesty is W_n itself. Equating the two gives the minimum honesty-inducing wage

$$W_n = V_n + [(1 - p)/p]x. \tag{5.4}$$

Honesty requires paying a wage premium of $[(1 - p)/p]x$ that varies inversely with the probability of being caught.

Consider next a two-period job in which the wage paid in the second (last) period is given by Eq. (5.4), and thus, workers do not shirk in the second period. What wage is required to deter shirking in the first period? The present value of earnings in a job where the worker is deterred from malfeasance in both periods is $W_{n-1} + W_n/(1+r)$, where r is the discount rate. If the firm dismisses all malfeasant workers it detects in the first period, the expected present value of malfeasance is $(1-p)[W_{n-1} + x + W_n/(1+r)] + p[V_{n-1} + V_n/(1+r)]$. Equating present values gives the minimum payment needed to deter malfeasance in the first period as

$$W_{n-1} = V_{n-1} + [(1-p)/p][r/(1+r)]x. \tag{5.5}$$

Equation (5.5) generalizes to all contracts lasting an arbitrary number of periods.

Notice the difference between Eqs. (5.4) and (5.5). The wage premium needed to deter malfeasance is largest in the final period of the contract because the threat of termination has less deterrent value the shorter the remaining horizon. But, in every period of the contract, $W_t > V_t$. Since there are rents in every period, the expected present value of the job strictly exceeds that of the alternative. The difference in present values works out to be $[(1-p)/p]x$. To equalize present values and avoid job rationing, workers are obliged to post front money of $[(1-p)/p]x$. Shirking may be eliminated without job rationing under the following contract: (i) workers post a performance bond before work begins, (ii) wages at each period equal opportunity wages plus interest on the bond, and (iii) deferred pay at the end of the contract equals the bond itself.

There is an important general point in this example. Current wage rates alone are insufficient to achieve efficient incentive alignment in many agency problems. In this example, front and back-loaded payments, as well as wages are needed. In a sense, one price, the wage rate, has to do too many tasks (Lazear, 1995). The firm needs to attract applicants for the job and provide performance incentives once workers take the job. Generally more than one price is needed to accomplish more than one economic function. The bond creates a "price", as it were, for malfeasance.

Pensions and deferred pay represent significant components of total compensation in many jobs where malfeasance is of obvious concern. Examples include the military, police, judges, politicians and some civil servants. Of course pensions are of growing importance in total compensation for other reasons having to do with the tax advantages of saving for retirement in this way. Nonetheless, most private pension plans that are based on a person's previous wage record, greatly penalize departures from the firm prior to the standard retirement age and serve a deterrence function in this respect. The data do not support the up-front bonding aspects of the solution. Explicit performance bonds are seldom observed in labor markets. If x is large and p is small, large bonds might be necessary but infeasible for liquidity constrained workers. Further, workers would be reluctant to post performance bonds when firms have the opportunity to falsely claim malfeasance by workers and seize their bonds.

Lazear (1979) developed an important extension of the basic model by noting that deterrence does not require strict equality between the values of malfeasance and honesty in each period. Inequalities also work. In Lazear's model there is no explicit up front bond. Instead workers gradually post the equivalent of a bond by working for less than their full productivity to the firm when they are young. The firm breaks even because it pays them more than their direct productivity when they are older. In a sense, workers are building an implicit "equity" or "partnership" position in the early years and receiving "stakeholder" returns in the form of wage premiums and pensions in later years. In this model, wage-experience profiles are upward sloping for incentive reasons. The distribution of wages within a firm is more dispersed than it would be in an environment without monitoring concerns.[26]

Akerlof and Katz (1989) point out that the implicit bonding scheme proposed by Lazear does not work at the beginning of careers. At each point in time, the worker weighs the benefits of shirking against its expected cost, which equals the value of the implicit bond that the worker has already posted times the probability of detection. At the beginning of the employment relationship, the value of the implicit bond is zero, and the worker has nothing to lose by shirking. Implicit bonding by workers requires some mechanism that gets around this "start up" problem. For instance, the firm may offer entry level jobs where output is easily observed, with workers posting bond by being paid piece-rates below their marginal product. After posting the bond, the worker can then be promoted to more complex jobs where output and effort are not directly observed. For workers who begin their careers with few skills, minimum wage laws or other employment regulations may frustrate attempts to post bonds in this manner. Nonetheless, there are other degrees of freedom. Firms may engage in intensive direct monitoring until workers develop the human capital necessary to post a bond while working at the minimum wage. If bonds cannot be posted implicitly, upward sloping wage profiles still serve as an incentive device, but the market does not clear. Efficiency wage models explore these issues.

5.4. Efficiency wage models

Efficiency wage models come in several flavors, but most share the common feature that workers are not allowed to post bonds. We devote our attention to the shirking model.[27] The model of Bulow and Summers (1986) uses inter-industry differences in monitoring technologies to explain how wage levels of observationally similar workers

---

[26] In addition, the model provides a rationale for mandatory retirement. When the contract reaches a termination date set at the beginning of the contract, the wage being paid at that time is greater than the worker's opportunity cost, and the worker "prefers" to keep working. The firm must terminate the worker by mandatory retirement at that point else the ex ante scheme would go insolvent. This is one of the only economic theories of mandatory retirement that has been proposed.

[27] Shapiro and Stiglitz (1985) also provide a well known shirking model. Some efficiency wage models address asymmetric information about worker quality, turnover costs or the nutritional needs of workers in undeveloped countries. In all these cases, up front payments are not allowed and ex ante rents and nonprice rationing of jobs creates unemployment. Bonds are not so crucial in efficiency wage models based on the sociological concept of voluntary gift exchange.

differ across sectors of the economy in a cross-section. Firms in the "primary" sector are, by assumption, unable to effectively monitor their workers. Direct expenditures on supervision do not change the probability of catching a worker who is shirking. Firms in the "secondary" sector are able to monitor their workers perfectly at zero cost.

In the primary sector, firms catch workers who shirk with probability p. Primary sector firms cannot change p, and by assumption, workers cannot post performance bonds either implicitly or explicitly. Firms may fire shirkers if they catch them shirking, but firms have only one additional means to deter shirking. They can make dismissal more costly by paying wages above the going wage rate in the secondary sector.[28] The wage premium required to prevent shirking is an increasing function of total employment in the primary sector because a large primary sector makes it relatively easy for a dismissed worker to find a new primary sector job. This no-shirk function is depicted in Fig. 5.1. The intersection between it and the demand for primary sector workers determines sectoral employment and the wage premium enjoyed by primary sector workers. The model generates an equilibrium where identical workers in different sectors of the economy earn different wages. The relative demand for primary sector output determines both primary sector employment and the magnitude of the inter-sector wage gap.

Wage levels differ considerably across the industries of modern economies. Controlling for observed differences among workers in various industries eliminates some of the interindustry wage variability, but much remains.[29] This theory offers an explanation for the variance remaining after standardizing for measured skills. It is easy to imagine a generalization of the model where w^* represents the value of home production, and there are N no shirk conditions that correspond to N different industries with various degrees of monitoring problems. Such a model would generate a pattern of differences in wages across industries that reflects differences in monitoring technologies across various workplaces rather than inherent differences in worker skill. However, as an empirical matter, unobserved differences in skills of workers across industries appear to account for at least part of these wage differentials.[30]

Efficiency wage models of shirking problems generate a distribution of wages across sectors of the economy that reflects heterogeneity across firms with respect to monitoring technologies. In these models, workers are not allowed to post bonds, and because this option is shut down, firms use wage premiums as a mechanism to provide performance incentives. Complete market agency models involve either implicit or explicit performance bonds, and over a worker's entire tenure with a firm, the present value of his lifetime wages equals his opportunity cost. It is difficult to separate these models empirically because available data provide little information about monitoring technologies.

---

[28] The result is similar to the one presented above in our discussion of Becker and Stigler (1974). However, the Bulow and Summers model is static and does not address how time horizons interact with the threat of dismissal.

[29] See Krueger and Summers (1988).

[30] See Gibbons et al. (1997), Gibbons and Katz (1992), and Murphy and Topel (1990).

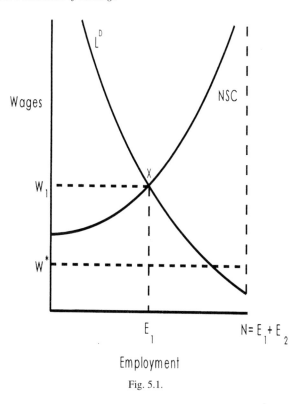

Fig. 5.1.

However, previous studies have not demonstrated a link between monitoring practices and inter- industry wage premiums.[31]

6. Conclusion

We began by noting that earnings distributions are always skewed. The right tail is much longer than the left. Selection and sorting models illustrate that when workers choose the job that best suits their skills, observed earnings do not include many of the worst outcomes from distributions of potential earnings associated with specific jobs. Insurance models describe how partial insurance contracts truncate wage distributions on the left, while tournament models illustrate how firms stretch the right tail in order to provide incentives. Human capital models can generate skewed distributions because individual endowments like learning ability, productive capacity and tastes for leisure can interact to generate considerable heterogeneity in investment behavior.

[31] See Neal (1993) and Leonard (1987).

Human capital models stand out because they tie observed differences in earnings across education and occupation groups to observed differences in skill investment. Human capital models also provide unique insights concerning how the distribution of earnings evolves for a particular cohort. Basic learning models as well as sorting models predict monotonically increasing earnings dispersion for a given cohort as the cohort ages. In human capital models, earnings dispersion can actually decrease with cohort age at the beginning of the life-cycle before increasing dramatically during middle age. When workers have the same initial productive capacities but different abilities to learn, earnings capacities grow steadily apart over the life-cycle even though observed earnings levels do not fully reflect this divergence in the early years. During later working years, investments are minimal, and earnings are closely tied to earnings capacities. This yields striking dispersion because capacities have grown apart for years.[32]

However, human capital models cannot generate the long right tails that we observe in modern earnings distributions. For instance, we cannot easily explain the salaries of top chief executives simply as the product of an exceptional talent for learning new skills. Rather, such earnings more likely reflect the optimal assignment of rare talents to a specific set of tasks. Models of scale economies and the span of control tell us why the persons assigned to such jobs earn such enormous salaries.

The literature on scale economies and span of control describes a link between technology and the distribution of earnings. Because technology determines the personal scale of a worker's operations, it affects the demand for skill and the distribution of ability rents. To the extent that recent advances in information technology have made it easier for talented individuals to have larger spans of control, the information revolution may be a driving force behind the recent explosion of earnings in the very top percentiles of the distribution. This feature of span of control models is quite unique among the models discussed in this survey. Most of the other models presented here generate earnings distributions entirely from supply decisions. They illustrate how the allocation of talents, time and energy generate and sustain earnings inequality. Selection models illustrate how workers supply their endowments to tasks that generate the highest earnings. Human capital models describe skill formation and demonstrate that inequality is necessary when different types of work require different levels of skill investment. Models of the investment process illustrate how talent and financial resources affect investment decisions and therefore demonstrate how human capital accumulation links initial endowments, family background, and realized inequality. Agency models focus on the supply of effort and describe wage inequality within firms as an incentive device.

---

[32] Most of the empirical work on this topic provides evidence on the evolution of the variance of log earnings for a particular cohort. Throughout the 1970s and early 1980s, several studies found evidence of a U-shaped relationship between the variance of log earnings and cohort work experience. Mincer (1974), Smith and Welch (1979), Hause (1980), and Dooley and Gottschalk (1984) address this topic. The U shaped relationship in log variances implies that the rate of increase in the dispersion of earnings levels is greatest during the prime working years and that the variance of earnings (measured in levels) is much greater during prime working years than during the initial years of a cohort's career.

None of these models say much about the determinants of labor demand or the elasticities of demands for different types of skill. This may be an important omission because much recent research explores potential "demand driven" explanations for the recent rise in wage inequality observed in many Western countries. A large empirical literature debates competing claims about the nature of labor demand and its response to changes in technology or trade barriers. We do not explore these issues here,[33] but we do note that most theoretical work on the distribution of labor earnings does not analyze the forces that shift or shape the demands for various types of market skills.

References

Aitchison, John and J.A.C. Brown (1957), The Lognormal Distribution, with Special Reference to its Uses in Economics (Cambridge University Press, Cambridge).

Akerlof, George A. (1982), Labor contracts as partial gift exchange, Quarterly Journal of Economics 47: 543–569.

Akerlof, George A. and Lawrence Katz (1989), Workers' trust funds and the logic of wage profiles, Quarterly Journal of Economics 525–536.

Alchian, Armen (1972), Production, information costs, and economic organization, American Economic Review 62: 777–795.

Alchian, Armen A. and Harold Demsetz (1972), Production, information costs, and economic organization, American Economic Review 62: 777–795.

Baker, George, Michael Gibbs and Bengt Holmstrom (1994), The internal economics of the firm: evidence from personnel data, Quarterly Journal of Economics 109: 881–919.

Becker, Gary S. (1967), Human capital and the personal distribution of income, W.S. Woytinsky Lecture, No. 1 (University of Michigan).

Becker, Gary S. (1975), Human Capital, A Theoretical and Empirical Analysis with Special Reference to Education, 2nd ed. (University of Chicago Press, Chicago and London).

Becker, G. and G. Stigler (1974), Law enforcement, malfeasance and compensation of the enforcer, Journal of Legal Studies 3: 1–18.

Ben-Porath, Yoram (1967), The production of human capital and the life cycle of earnings, Journal of Political Economy 75: 352–365.

Bergstrom, Theodore (1986), Soldiers of fortune? in Heller and Starr, eds., Essays in Honor of Kenneth Arrow, Vol. 2, Equilibrium Analysis (Cambridge University Press, New York), pp. 57–80.

Blinder, Alan S. and Yoram Weiss (1976), Human capital and labor supply: a synthesis, Journal of Political Economy 84: 449–472.

Blinder, Alan S. (1974) Toward an Economic Theory of Income Distribution (The MIT Press, Cambridge, Massachusetts, and London, England).

Bowley, Arthur Lyon (1915) Livelihood and Poverty (G. Bell and Sons, Ltd, London).

Bulow, Jeremy and Lawrence Summers (1986), A theory of dual labor markets with applications to industrial policy, discrimination, and Keynesian unemployment, Journal of Labor Economics 4: 376–414.

Champernowne, D.G. (1953), A model of income distribution, Economic Journal 63: 318–351.

Champernowne, D.G. (1973), The Distribution of Income between Persons (Cambridge [Eng.] University Press).

Dooley, Martin D. and Peter Gottschalk (1984), Earnings inequality among males in the United States: trends and the effect of labor force growth, Journal of Political Economy 92: 59–89

---

[33] Because the models described here do not address the elasticities of demand for various types of workers, they say little about how demographic changes affect the wage structure through changes in the relative supplies of various skills. Murphy and Welch (1992) and Katz and Murphy (1992) provide evidence concerning the relative importance of shifts in the demand and supply at different levels of worker skill.

Farber, Henry S. and Robert Gibbons (1996), Learning and wage dynamics, Quarterly Journal of Economics 111: 1007–1048.

Foster, Andrew D. and Mark R. Rosenzweig (1995), Learning by doing and learning from others: human capital and technical change in agriculture, Journal of Political Economy 103: 1176–1209.

Frank, Robert H. and Philip J. Cook (1995), The Winner-Take-All Society: How More and More Americans Compete for Ever Fewer and Bigger Prizes, Encouraging Economic Waste, Income Inequality, and an Impoverished Cultural Life (Free Press, New York).

Friedman, Milton (1953), Choice, chance, and the personal distribution of income, Journal of Political Economy 61: 277–290.

Garen, John (1984), The returns to schooling: a selectivity bias approach with a continuous choice variable, Econometrica 52: 1199–1218..

Ghez, G. and G. Becker (1975), The Allocation of Time and Goods Over the Life Cycle (NBER).

Gibbons, Robert, Lawrence Katz and Thomas Lemieux (1997), Learning, Comparative Advantage, and the Inter-Industry Wage Structure, mimeo (Universite de Montreal).

Gibbons, Robert and Michael Waldman (1998), A theory of wage and promotion dynamics inside firms, NBER working paper, # 6454.

Gibrat, Robert (1931), On Economic Inequalities, Chaps. 5–7 (Sirey, Paris) pp. 62–90.

Gould, Eric D. (1996), Essays on rising wage inequality, comparative advantage and the growing importance of general skills in the United States: 1966–1992, Ph.D thesis (Dept. of Economics, University of Chicago).

Green, Jerry and Nancy Stokey (1983), A comparison of tournaments and contracts, Journal of Political Economy 91: 349–364.

Grubb, David B. (1985), Ability and power over production in the distribution of earnings, Review of Economics and Statistics 67: 188–194.

Haley, William J. (1973), Human capital: the choice between investment and income, American Economic Review 6: 929–944.

Harris, Milton and Holmstrom Bengt (1982), A theory of wage dynamics, Review of Economic Studies 49: 315–333.

Harrison, Alan. (1981), Earnings by size: a tale of two distributions, Review of Economic Studies 48: 621–631.

Hause, John C. (1980), The fine structure of earnings and the on-the-job training hypothesis, Econometrics 48: 1013–1029.

Heckman, James (1976), A life-cycle model of earnings, learning, and consumption, Journal of Political Economy 84: S11–S44.

Heckman, James and Bo E. Honore (1990), The empirical content of the Roy model, Econometrica 58: 1121–1149.

Heckman, James and Jose Scheinkman (1987), The importance of bundling in a Gorman–Lancaster model of earnings, Review of Economic Studies 54: 243–255.

Heckman, James and Guilherme Sedlacek (1985), Heterogeneity, aggregation, and market wage functions: an empirical model of self-selection in the labor market, Journal of Political Economy 93: 1077–1125.

Holmstrom, Bengt (1982a) Managerial incentive problems – a dynamic perspective, in Essays in Economics and Management in Honor of Lars Wahlbeck (Swedish School of Economics, Helsinki).

Holmstrom, Bengt (1982b), Moral hazard in teams, Bell Journal of Economics 13: 324–340.

Jovanovic, Boyan (1979a), Job matching and the theory of turnover, Journal of Political Economy 87: 972–990.

Jovanovic, Boyan (1979b), Firm-specific capital and turnover, Journal of Political Economy 87: 1246–1260.

Jovanovic, Boyan (1998), Vintage capital and inequality, Review of Economics and Dynamics 1.

Kalecki, Michael (1945), On the Gibrat distribution, Econometrica 13: 161–170.

Kanbur, S.M. (1979), Of risk taking and the personal distribution of income, Journal of Political Economy 87: 769–797.

Katz, Lawrence F. and Kevin M. Murphy (1992), Changes in relative wages, 1963–1987: supply and demand factors, Quarterly Journal of Economics 35–78.

Kim, Dae Il (1998), Reinterpreting industry premiums: match specific productivity, Journal of Labor Economics, forthcoming.

Kremer, Michael (1997), How much does sorting increase inequality? Quarterly Journal of Economics 112: 115–139.

Kremer, Michael (1993), The O-ring theory of economic development, Quarterly Journal of Economics 108: 551–575.

Krueger, Alan B. (1993), How computers have changed the wage structure: evidence from microdata, 1984–1989, Quarterly Journal of Economics 107: 33–60.

Krueger, A.B. and L.H. Summers (1988), Efficiency wages and the inter-industry wage structure, Econometrica 56: 259–294.

Lazear, Edward P. (1979), Why is there mandatory retirement? Journal of Political Economy 87: 1261–1264.

Lazear, Edward P. and Sherwin Rosen (1981), Rank-order tournaments as optimum labor contracts, Journal of Political Economy 89: 841–864.

Leamer, Edward (1981), The hit parade of economics articles, in E. Tower, ed., Economics Reading Lists, Course Outlines, Exams, Puzzles and Problems, Vol. 14 (Eno River Press series).

Lebergott, Stanley (1959), The shape of the income distribution, American Economic Review 49: 328–347.

Leonard, Jonathan S. (1987), Carrots and sticks: pay, supervision, and turnover, Journal of Labor Economics 5: 136–152.

Lillard, Lee, A. and Robert J. Willis (1978), Dynamic aspects of earning mobility, Econometrica 46: 985–1012.

Lillard, Lee A. (1977), Inequality: earnings vs. human wealth, American Economic Review 67: 42–53.

Lovell, Michael C. (1973), The production of economic literature: an interpretation, Journal of Economic Literature 11: 27–55.

Lydall, Harold F. (1959), The distribution of employment incomes, Econometrica 27: 110–115.

Lydall, Harold F. (1968), The Structure of Earnings (Oxford University Press, London).

MacDonald, Glenn M. (1982), A market equilibrium theory of job assignment and sequential accumulation of information, American Economic Review 72: 1038–1055.

Maddala, G.S. (1977) Self-selectivity problems in econometric models, in P.R. Krishnaia, ed., Applications in Statistics (North-Holland, Amsterdam).

Mandelbrot, Benoit (1960), The Pareto–Levy law and the distribution of income, International Economic Review 1: 79–106.

Mandelbrot, Benoit (1962), Paretian distributions and income maximization, Quarterly Journal of Economics 77: 57–85.

Marshall, Alfred (1947) Principles of Economics, 8th edn. (Macmillan, New York).

Mayer, Thomas (1960), The distribution of ability and earnings, Review of Economics and Statistics 42: 189–195.

McLaughlin, Kenneth (1988), Aspects of tournament models: a survey, Labor Economics 9: 225–256.

Miller, Herman P. (1955), The Income of the American People (Wiley, New York).

Miller, Robert A. (1984), Job matching and occupational choice, Journal of Political Economy 92: 1086–1120.

Mincer, Jacob (1958), Investment in human capital and personal income distribution, Journal of Political Economy 56: 281–302.

Mincer, Jacob (1970), The distribution of labor incomes: a survey with special reference to the human capital approach, Journal of Economic Literature 8: 1–26.

Mincer, Jacob (1974), Schooling, Experience and Earnings (Columbia University Press for National Bureau of Economic Research, New York).

Moore, Henry L. (1911), Laws of Wages (Macmillan, New York).

Murphy, Kevin J. (1986), Incentives, learning, and compensation: a theoretical and empirical investigation of managerial labor contracts, Rand Journal of Economics 17: 59–76.

Murphy, Kevin M. and Robert H. Topel (1990), Efficiency wages reconsidered: theory and evidence, in Yoram Weiss and Gideon Fishelson, eds., Advances in the Theory and Measurement of Unemployment (St. Martin's Press, New York) pp. 204–240.

Murphy, Kevin J. and Finis Welch (1992), The structure of wages, Quarterly Journal of Economics 285–326.

Nalebuff, Barry J. and Joseph Stiglitz (1983), Prizes and incentives: toward a general theory of compensation and competition, Bell Journal of Economics 14: 21–43.

Neal, Derek (1993), Supervision and wages across industries, Review of Economics and Statistics 409–417.

O'Keeffe, Mary, W. Kip and Richard J. Zeckhauser (1984), Economic contests: comparative reward schemes, Journal of Labor Economics 2: 27–56.

Paglin, Morton (1975), The measurement and trend of inequality: a basic revision, American Economic Review 65: 598–609.

Pareto, Vilfredo (1897), Cours d'Economie Politique, Vol. II (Rouge & Cie, Lausanne).

Pen, Jan (1971), Income distribution: facts, theories, policies (Praeger, New York).

Reder, Melvin, (1968), The size distribution of earnings, in Marchal and Ducros, eds., The Distribution of National Income, Chap. 21, pp. 583–617.

Reder, Melvin (1969), A partial survey of the income size distribution, in Lee Soltow, ed., Six Papers on the Size Distribution of Income (NBER, distributed by Columbia University Press, New York).

Rosen, Sherwin (1972), Learning and experience in the labor market, Journal of Human Resources 7: 326–342.

Rosen, Sherwin (1976), A theory of life earnings, Journal of Political Economy 84: S45–S67.

Rosen, Sherwin (1978), Substitution and division of labor, Economica 45: 235–250.

Rosen, Sherwin (1981), The economics of superstars, American Economic Review 71: 845–858.

Rosen, Sherwin (1982) Authority, control, and the distribution of earnings, Bell Journal of Economics 13: 311–323.

Rosen, Sherwin (1983a), A note on aggregation of skills and labor quality, Journal of Human Resources 18: 425–431.

Rosen, Sherwin (1983b), Specialization and human capital, Journal of Labor Economics 5: 3–49.

Rosen, Sherwin (1986), The theory of equalizing differences, in Orley Ashenfelter and Richard Layard, eds., Handbook of Labor Economics, Vol. 1 (North-Holland, Oxford and Tokyo) pp. 641–692.

Rosen, Sherwin (1992), Contracts and the market for executives, in Lars Werin and Hans Wijkander, eds., Contract Economics (Blackwell, Cambridge, MA. and Oxford) pp. 181–211.

Rosen, Sherwin (1997), Manufactured inequality, Journal of Labor Economics 15: 189–196.

Ross, Stephen A. (1973), The economic theory of agency: the principal's problem, American Economic Review 63: 134–139.

Ross, Stephen, Paul Taubman and Michael Wachter (1981), Learning by observing and the distribution of wages, in Sherwin Rosen, eds., Studies in Labor Markets, pp. 359–386.

Roy, A.D. (1950), The distribution of earnings and of individual output, Economic Journal 60: 489–505.

Roy, A.D. (1951), Some thoughts on the distribution of earnings, Oxford Economic Papers 3: 135–146.

Rutherford, R.S.G. (1955), Income distributions: a new model, Econometrica 23: 277–294.

Ryder, Harl E., Frank P. Stafford and Paula E. Stephan (1976), Labor, leisure and training over the life cycle, International Economic Review 17: 651–674.

Sattinger, Michael (1993), Assignment models of the distribution of earnings, Journal of Economic Literature 31: 831–880.

Sattinger, Michael (1975), Comparative advantage and the distributions of earnings and abilities, Econometrica 43, 455–468.

Schultz, Theodore W. (1975), The value of the ability to deal with disequilibria, Journal of Economic Literature 13: 827–846.

Shapiro, C. and J.E. Stiglitz (1985), Equilibrium unemployment as a worker discipline device, American Economic Review 74: 433–444.

Simon, Herbert A. (1955), On a class of skew distributions, Biometrica 42.

Simon, Herbert A. (1957), The compensation of executives, Sociometry 20: 32–35.

Singh, S.K. and Maddala, G.S. (1976), A function for size distributions of income, Econometrica 44: 963–970.

Smith, James P. and Finis Welch (1979), Inequality: race differences in the distribution of earnings, International Economic Review 20: 515–526.

Spurr, Stephen J. (1987), How the market solves an assignment problem: the matching of lawyers with legal claims, *Journal of Labor Economics* 5: 502–532.

Staele, Hans (1943), Ability, wages and income, Review of Economics and Statistics 25: 77–87.

Steindl, Joseph (1968), Size distributions in economics, International Encyclopedia of Social Sciences, Vol. 14 (Macmillan and Free Press, New York) pp. 294–300.

Tinbergen, Jan (1959), On the Theory of Income Distribution, Selected Papers (North-Holland, Amsterdam).

Tuck, R.H. (1954), An Essay on the Economic Theory of Rank (Blackwell, Oxford).

Willis, Robert J. and Sherwin Rosen (1979), Education and self-selection, Journal of Political Economy 87: 7–36.

Weiss, Andrew (1990), Efficiency Wages: Models of Unemployment, Layoffs, and Wage Dispersion (Princeton University Press, Princeton).

Weiss, Yoram and Lillard, Lee A. (1978), Experience, vintage, and time effects in the growth of earnings: American Scientists, 1960–1970, Journal of Political Economy 86: 427–448.

Weiss, Yoram (1986), The determination of life cycle earnings, in Orley Ashenfelter and Richard Layard, eds., Handbook of Labor Economics, Vol. 1 (North-Holland) pp. 603–640.

Weizsacker, Robert K. von (1993), A Theory of Earnings Distribution (Cambridge University Press).

Welch, Finis (1969), Linear synthesis of skill distribution, Journal of Human Resources 4: 311–327.

Welch, Finis (1970), Education in production, Journal of Political Economy 78: 35–59.

Welch, Finis (1975), Human capital theory: education, discrimination, and life cycles, American Economic Review 65: 63–73.

Welch, Finis (1979), Effects of cohort size on earnings: the baby boom babies' financial bust, Journal of Political Economy 87: S65–S98.

Wold, Herman O. A. and P. Whittle (1957), A model exploring the Pareto distribution of wealth, Econometrica 25: 591–595.

Chapter 8

THEORIES OF PERSISTENT INEQUALITY AND INTERGENERATIONAL MOBILITY

THOMAS PIKETTY

CNRS-CEPREMAP, Paris, E-mail: thomas.piketty@cepremap.cnrs.fr

Contents

Handbook of Income Distribution, Volume 1. Edited by A. B. Atkinson and F. Bourguignon

Keywords: Income distribution, intergenerational mobility

JEL codes. D30, D31, D63

1. Introduction

This chapter aims to survey existing theories of persistent inequality across generations. That is, unlike other theory- oriented chapters in this Handbook, we are concerned with total economic inequality, both in wealth and in earnings, and we concentrate upon the intergenerational mobility dimension of total inequality. The questions we ask in this chapter are the following: what determines the degree of transmission and persistence of inequality across generations? What are the policy implications of the various existing theories?

Although the scope of this chapter is primarily theoretical, we will also offer a nonexhaustive, non-technical survey of existing empirical work about intergenerational mobility and persistent inequality between dynasties. Instead of presenting this body of empirical evidence in a separate section, we will refer to empirical studies when needed in order to confirm, contradict or illustrate the different theoretical models. Although existing evidence is scarce, we believe that such a straightforward confrontation between theories and empirical evidence is particularly needed in this field. The question of inter-generational mobility has always been one of the most controversial issues indeed, both in actual political conflicts and in academic writings by social scientists, and conflicting theories in this area have very often been motivated by conflicting qualitative perceptions of the extent of mobility (and conversely....). Before we describe the organization of the chapter and the main theoretical models of intergenerational mobility, it is useful to briefly recall some basic background about the controversies which characterize the history of this field.

1.1. The dimensions of conflict about intergenerational mobility

As a first approximation, one can say that controversies about intergenerational mobility have been dominated during most of the nineteenth and twentieth centuries by a violent conflict between what Erikson and Goldthorpe (1992) call the "liberal theory" of indus-trialization on the one hand, and the Marxist theory (and various socialist theories) on the other hand.[1] According to the "liberal theory", the industrial society is characterized by an irreversible commitment to technical and economic rationality, and therefore by high and rising rates of social mobility and equality of opportunity, as procedures of social selection become more and more rational. The Marxist theory basically says the

---

[1] See Erikson and Goldthorpe (1992: Chap. 1) and subsequent references. Erikson and Goldthorpe con-centrate on the post-World War II, academic section of this intellectual and political conflict, but similar controversies did already exist long before (at least since the industrial revolution).

opposite: capitalist societies are characterized by class reproduction, whereby a small number of capitalist dynasties reproduce themselves from generation to generation and a large and growing number of working-class dynasties is being exploited by capitalist dynasties from generation to generation.[2]

What is striking about these two conflicting viewpoints is that they combine conflicting empirical claims about mobility (is actual mobility low or high in industrial societies?) with conflicting theoretical claims about the working of the market system: are market economies characterized by rationality, efficiency and openness, or do they just perpetuate initial inequalities? Note also that the basic premise of both theories is that mobility should be high. In particular, the liberal theory implicitly assumes that allocative efficiency requires a high level of social mobility, presumably because the intergenerational correlation of ability and other efficiency-relevant individual characteristics is assumed to be low. Marxist and socialist theories obviously make this assumption as well, but they claim that the market system is unable to allocate individual talents as they should be and to achieve this high and efficient mobility level.

In its most extreme form, this conflict between liberal and Marxist theories of intergenerational mobility is by now well behind us. On the one hand, following the spectacular improvement of living standards in capitalist countries and the tragic failure of communist systems, nobody seems to support any longer the Marxist theory of mass proletarianization and class reproduction under capitalism. On the other hand, the optimist view of high and perpetually increasing mobility rates in market societies has proven to be excessively naive. During the past decades, sociologists in many countries have collected a large body of survey evidence about occupations and social status of parents and children, allowing them to compute mobility matrices and various other mobility measures. This type of data does not generally allow for easy and reliable comparisons of mobility measures over time and across countries, given the substantial variability of occupational categories and social status scales. It is remarkable however that all comparative empirical studies of social mobility rates, based upon different data sets collected at different points in time, have found very similar mobility matrices across industrial nations, and in particular no significant difference between Europe and the US.[3] This comparison between the US and various European countries has always played a central role in controversies about social mobility. At least since the time of Tocqueville, the "liberal theory" would seem to predict that a more open and market-oriented society such as the US should lead to significantly higher mobility rates. These empirical studies by sociologists also seem to show that there has been no significant

---

[2] In its most extreme dogmatic form, another version of the Marxist response is to dismiss the "bourgeois" question of mobility altogether (see Erickson and Goldthorpe, 1992: pp. 9–10).

[3] See, e.g., Lipset and Bendix (1959, 1966), Erikson and Goldthorpe (1985, 1992) and the references therein. See also the historical study by Kaelble (1985), who compares social mobility rates in various western cities over the 1840–1920 period, and finds no significant difference across western countries.

change in mobility rates over time, at least since World War II.[4] Comparative studies of educational mobility also suggest a high level of commonality and inertia of mobility rates, both over time and across countries.[5]

More recently, following the development of large panel data sets with economic variables spanning across several generations, economists have started to measure intergenerational mobility. These economic measures of intergenerational mobility should in principle offer more reliable cross-country and time-series comparisons. Preliminary results seem to confirm the sociologists finding about the absence of any distinctive US pattern: intergenerational correlation coefficients for both total income and labor earnings seem to be very similar across developed countries (see the recent survey of Bjorklund and Jantti (1998)). Overall, the relative consensus at the end of the twentieth century seems to be that commonality and inertia are the main characteristics of intergenerational mobility: mobility rates just do not seem to vary very much.

This relative consensus obviously does not imply that the issue of intergenerational mobility is no longer controversial. First, there are still some disagreements about whether the extent of mobility is that similar across countries. For example, Bjorklund and Jantti (1998) note that when discussing with their US colleagues, they "were struck by the strong belief that the US is a more open society with higher intergenerational mobility than Western European ones". Although there does not seem to exist any strong scientific evidence to confirm this "US exceptionalism" thesis, it is fair to say that there is sufficient uncertainty about these cross-country comparisons to explain how such disagreements can persist. Careful cross-country comparisons of mobility patterns are still in their infancy. Although we can be relatively confident that mobility rates do not differ enormously across comparable countries, it is by no means impossible that, as better data sets become available and more detailed comparative studies develop, we become able to identify interesting cross-country variations. For instance, a recent comparative study has found higher intergenerational educational and occupational mobility in the US than in Italy, which can be viewed as consistent with the liberal theory of mobility in industrial societies.[6]

Next, and most importantly, a relative consensus about the level of mobility in industrial societies obviously does not provide us with a consensus about a theory of intergenerational mobility. Many different theoretical models are consistent with a given level of mobility, and the kind of empirical evidence that would be needed in order

---

[4] See Erikson and Goldthorpe (1992), who offer the most complete comparative study of occupational mobility rates to date. Whether there was a significant increase in mobility rates before World War II is unclear: Lipset and Bendix (1959) conjectured that all countries reach a high mobility threshold as they industrialize; the historical study by Kaelble (1985) suggest that mobility rates did increase during the shift from family firms to large corporations, due to the emergence of a large class of nonowner business executives and associated upwardly-mobile careers (see Section 4.2 below).

[5] See Shavit and Blossfeld (1993).

[6] See Ichino et al. (1997). The authors conclude that higher mobility rates in the US could result from the higher mobility incentives implied by higher earnings inequality in the US, and that in any case that the Italian public school system seems to fail to deliver higher mobility.

to discriminate between these different models is even more uncertain and scarce than evidence about mobility levels. In particular, a relative consensus about actual mobility rates would not tell us very much about whether actual mobility is "high" or "low" and whether we should (and could) do something about it. This chapter will try to demonstrate that the issue of intergenerational mobility is still very controversial, but that disagreements between various existing theories span over many different dimensions, as opposed to the simple, one-dimensional conflict between liberal and Marxist theories referred to above. In the extreme form of the "liberal vs. marxist" conflict, things were indeed very simple: everybody agreed that mobility should and could be high, but the "right-wing" (i.e., pro-laissez-faire) view claimed that a mixture of free market and laissez-faire policies was sufficient to generate such an outcome, while the "left-wing" (i.e., pro-interventionist) view claimed that markets were so grossly imperfect that only a radical destruction of the free market system could make it happen. In practice, things can be more complicated.

First, there is no reason to believe that the socially-optimal level of intergenerational mobility should be high. If one believes that low intergenerational mobility is due to the high heritability of ability, and that the distortionary costs of welfare redistribution are very high, then it is perfectly reasonable to argue that public intervention should not try to interfere too much with the efficient functioning of the private choices and contractual arrangements made by families and markets, even though this laissez-faire process leads to little intergenerational mobility. Historically, this "conservative" type of right-wing view has been at least as widespread as the "liberal" type referred to above. Conservative right-wing views about mobility have been very influential not only in traditional societies, but also in advanced liberal societies such as the US, where there is long tradition of academic writing about the social efficiency of an "hereditary meritocracy" and the evils of egalitarian beliefs about individual abilities (see Herrnstein and Murray (1994) for the latest episode of this tradition). Although economists rarely use these terms to describe their theories, it is interesting to note that both types of laissez-faire theories are also present in the very important writings of Chicago economists about intergenerational mobility. On the one hand, Becker and Tomes (1986) interpret the high level of mobility that they observe in the US primarily in the liberal right-wing way (ability is moderately heritable and markets are highly efficient). On the other hand, Mulligan (1997) interprets the low level of mobility that he observes in the US primarily in the conservative right-wing way (persistent inequality derives from efficient parental and market choices, and there is not much one can do about it).[7]

Left-wing views are in a sense more homogenous: unlike right-wing views, they all share the basic premise that intergenerational mobility in the ideal society should be high. However they strongly disagree about what should be done in order to achieve this high and efficient mobility. Left-wing theories traditionally emphasize market imperfections and their inefficient, negative impact on intergenerational mobility. But there are

---

[7] See Sections 2-4 below, and especially Section 4.2.

different ways to analyze market imperfections: one can believe that markets have some imperfections that make inequality more persistent than it ought to be, without inferring from this claim that the only possible remedy is the abolition of private property and the market system altogether. At the very least, one needs to distinguish between "radical" left-wing views, of which Marxist and socialist theories of social mobility are the primary example, and "liberal" left-wing views, according to which market imperfections need to be corrected in a market-friendly manner.[8] In fact, left-wing, pro-interventionist theories of intergenerational mobility do not necessarily rely on any market imperfection at all. It is logically consistent to believe that observed mobility is the outcome of a market process that is basically efficient (in the Pareto sense), but that the distortionary costs of pure redistribution are relatively low, and that opportunities for consumption and welfare should be equalized between dynasties to a substantial extent.[9]

The very fact of locating the various views on a one-dimensional left vs. right scale can be in itself very misleading. For instance, it is not obvious how one would locate on such a one-dimensional axis the theory of social mobility developed in Plato's Republic.[10] On the one hand, Plato obviously does not believe that decentralized choices and the price system can set social priorities in the appropriate way. He recommends for instance that smart kids be taken away from their lower-class families, because the latter may not know how to raise them properly. This very activist view of mobility-enhancing policies would first seem to be very close to radical left-wing views, who have often advocated the need to socialize the education of children in order to counteract the family transmission and reproduction process. But on the other hand, Plato insists that bright lower-class kids are the exception rather than the rule, and that the ideal society should merely be characterized by a high degree of hereditary reproduction of rulers, warriors and producers. This makes Plato much closer to the conservative right-wing view of the "hereditary meritocracy" than to most left-wing views.

What this Plato example shows is not only that our modern concepts of right vs. left may not be very appropriate to classify the theories of the past. It also shows that there are deep reasons why the radical left and the conservative right are often much closer than what a one-dimensional classification would suggest. If we push it to the extreme (as historical experiments often did ...), the radical left's strong emphasis on market imperfections requires strong beliefs about the inequality of abilities between individuals: without the help of some enlightened elite, disadvantaged individuals are unable to interact in society and can easily be exploited, so that social justice and high mobility may require a very authoritarian hierarchical structure. Conversely, the conservative right's strong emphasis on the inequality of ability between dynasties can easily lead to question the capability of low-ability individuals to interact in society and on the

---

[8] See Sections 4–6 below.

[9] See Sections 2–3 below, and especially Sections 2.4 and 3.2.

[10] See, e.g., Merllié and Prévot (1991: p. 15) for an introduction to Plato's theory.

market place, which explains why the conservative right often advocates authoritarian, anti-market policies in some domains.[11]

1.2. Organization of this chapter

In order to distinguish as clearly as possible between the different dimensions of conflicts about persistent inequality and intergenerational mobility, the rest of this chapter will be organized as follows.

We will first deal with theoretical models of intergenerational mobility based upon Pareto-efficient markets (Sections 2 and 3). Section 2 concentrates on the process of (nonhuman) wealth transmission from parents to children, while Section 3 concentrates on the process of ability transmission. The assumption of efficient markets imply that policy intervention in these theoretical models is motivated solely by distributive justice considerations. That is, the only policy question is whether we should have a large redistributive tax on inheritance and/or labor earnings, so as to make consumption and welfare inequality less persistent than it would otherwise be. We will see that different theoretical models of the family transmission process have different implications regarding the distortionary costs of such redistributive policies, and that existing evidence does not allow us to discriminate very sharply between them.

We will then review the main existing theories of persistent inequality based upon market inefficiencies (Sections 4, 5 and 6). Section 4 deals with the intergenerational mobility consequences of imperfect credit markets. Section 5 discusses theories of persistent inequality based upon local segregation into unequal communities. Section 6 reviews theories of persistent inequality based upon self-fulfilling beliefs, and in particular the theory of discrimination. All of these theories imply that inequality is more persistent than what the simple family transmission of wealth and ability would imply if markets were perfect. Moreover, the extra persistence is inefficient, in the sense that appropriate corrective policies can raise intergenerational mobility and output at the same time. This attractive possibility obviously depends on the empirical relevance of these transmission mechanisms: if they do not account for a large fraction of persistent inequality, then we are back to the inequality/efficiency trade-off. As we will see, more empirical evidence is needed before we can give a precise estimate of how much these mechanisms contribute to the intergenerational transmission of inequality.

Finally, note that many other mechanisms of "inefficient inequality" have been explored by economists, although they are not covered in this chapter. For instance, the theory of employer monopsony implies that firms will pay wages below marginal products, even though this reduces labor supply, so that minimum-wage redistribution would be efficiency-improving.[12] More generally, the existence of mobility costs or firm-specific human capital can lead to hold-up problems and allow employers to pay wages below

---

[11] See especially Section 3.2 below.

[12] See, e.g., Card and Krueger (1995) for recent empirical research on local monopsony and the efficiency effects of minimum wages.

marginal products (or employees to charge wages above marginal products . . .), in which case salary scales and centralized constraints on wages can have positive distributive and efficiency effects at the same time.[13] Another important example is the keynesian theory, one popular version of which claims that redistributing purchasing power towards wage-earners can generate both a fairer distribution of income and positive expansionary effects for everybody.[14] All these theories play an important role in the way many people think about inequality and redistribution (rightly or wrongly), but they will be neglected in this chapter, because they do not deal explicitly with the issue of intergenerational mobility and persistent inequality across generations. In particular, we will assume throughout the chapter that wages are equal to marginal products, just as in the textbook model of competitive labor markets, so that fiscal redistribution is the only form of redistribution that can possibly be justified.

2. Persistent inequality and the family transmission of wealth

The most obvious channel explaining why inequality can persist across generations is the transmission of wealth from parents to children through inheritance. We first describe how inheritance contributes to raise inequality and to make it more persistent across generations (Section 2.1). We then show that most theoretical models of inheritance and inequality dynamics predict that wealth inequality and its effects on intergenerational mobility should indeed persist in the long-run (Sections 2.2 and 2.3). Finally, we use these theoretical models to analyze the prospects for raising welfare mobility through progressive inheritance taxation (Section 2.4).

2.1. The contribution of inheritance to the persistence of inequality

Consider a simple infinite-horizon model where each dynasty i lives during one period and has exactly one offspring.[15] Total income of dynasty i at period t can be written as the sum of two terms:

$$y_{it} = v_t a_{it} + r_t w_{it}. \tag{2.1}$$

The first term, $v_t a_{it}$, is the labor income of dynasty i at period t: it is the product of the wage rate v_t and of its productive ability parameter a_{it} (measured in efficiency labor units). The second term, $r_t w_{it}$, is the capital income of dynasty i at period t: it is the product of the interest rate r_t and of the wealth w_{it} transmitted by dynasty i from

---

[13] Thurow's (1975) theory of income distribution is largely based on the idea that there exist direct policy interventions on the labor market that would be both redistributive and efficiency-improving.

[14] See Murphy et al. (1989) for a modern modeling of how income distribution can affect demand composition and the level of economic activity.

[15] For a discussion of differential fertility behaviour, see Section 2.2 below. For a discussion of marriage, assortative mating and their effects on the persistence of inequality, see Section 5.3 below.

generation $t - 1$ to generation t. We note $G_t(w)$ the distribution of wealth inherited by generation t. This section concentrates on the process of (non-human) wealth transmission. The process of ability transmission, and in particular the possible impact of wealth inequalities on ability transmission (e.g., because of imperfect credit), will be analyzed in Sections 3–6 below. At this stage, we take as given some exogenous law of motion for abilities. Although most results of Section 2 can easily be generalized, for simplicity we will mainly consider the following cases: uniform labor earnings ($\forall i, t, a_{it} = 1$); random labor earnings with zero intergenerational transmission ($\forall i, t, a_{it} = 1 + \epsilon_{it}$, where ϵ_{it}, is an error term with zero mean, variance σ_ϵ^2 and zero serial correlation); random labor earnings with first-order serial correlation ($\forall i, t, a_{it} = 1 - \rho + \rho a_{it-1} + \epsilon_{it}$, where ρ is the intergenerational correlation of ability).

The first obvious implication of Eq. (2.1) is that as long as a_{it} and w_{it} are not negatively correlated, the inequality of total income will tend to be larger than the inequality of labor earnings. The standard deviation of total income is simply equal to the sum of the standard deviation of labor earnings and the standard deviation of capital income in case ability and wealth are uncorrelated, and it is even larger if the correlation is positive.[16] In practice, one does indeed observe that total income inequality is always larger than the inequality of labor earnings.[17]

If one further assumes the inheritance w_{it+1} left by dynasty i to generation $t + 1$ to be an increasing function $S(y_{it})$ of income y_{it}, then one obtains the following transition equation for total income:

$$y_{it+1} = v_{it+1} + r_{t+1} S(y_{it}). \tag{2.2}$$

Equation (2.2) shows that the second obvious implication of inheritance is that it tends to perpetuate the inequality of living standards across generations. For instance, Eq. (2.2) implies that even if the intergenerational correlation of labor earnings is assumed to be zero, the intergenerational correlation of total income is positive. More generally, Eq. (2.2) implies that the intergenerational income correlation will always be larger than the intergenerational earnings correlation, as long as the ability-wealth correlation is not negative. This second implication is also confirmed by recent empirical evidence. Mulligan (1997) uses the PSID to estimate these intergenerational correlations, and he finds that the correlation coefficients for consumption and total income fall in the 0.7–0.8 range, while the intergenerational correlation of earnings is about 0.5. These estimates are probably the most reliable estimates to date (see Section 4.2 below for a discussion of downward biases in previous estimates). Note that this is a very large

---

[16] Through this chapter, we will mostly refer to rudimentary measures of inequality and mobility such as standard deviations, coefficients of variation and intergenerational correlations, simply because they are very convenient in loglinear models. See, e.g., Cowell's chapter 2 in this Handbook for a survey of existing inequality measures.

[17] See, e.g., Davies and Shorrocks' chapter 11 in this Handbook. This simple fact shows that the main purpose of wealth accumulation is not to smooth life-time or integenerational earnings shocks (in which case income inequality should be lower than earnings inequality).

difference. For instance, an intergenerational correlation of 0.7 means that if parents of children i are five times richer (in total income) than parents of children j, then children i will be on average about 3.1 times richer (in total income) than children j. A correlation of 0.5 means that children of parents who are five times richer (in earnings) will be "only" about 2.2 times richer (in earnings).[18] This shows that inheritance is a very powerful mechanism to transmit inequality across generations, and this explains why the inheritance channel of inequality transmission has attracted so much attention.

2.2. The long-run dynamics of wealth inequalities with exogenous savings

From a theoretical viewpoint, should we expect these two properties (inheritance raises inequality and makes it more persistent across generations) to hold in the long-run? If the inheritance function $S(y)$ is concave and if there is no inequality of labor earnings ($\forall i\, a_{it} = 1$), then one can easily show that the answer is negative. As Stiglitz (1969) pointed out, the concavity of inheritance and the equalizing effect of labor earnings imply that wealth inequality will decline slowly over time and that each dynasty will eventually own the same steady-state wealth. To see this, assume that gross output is given by a standard, concave production function $f(k_t)$, where $k_t = w_t$ is the capital stock per labor unit, i.e., the average of w_{it} across all dynasties. Wealth depreciates at rate $\delta > 0$ (i.e., net output is equal to $f(k) - \delta k$). Dynastic and aggregate transition equations are given by:

$$w_{it+1} = S(v_t + r_t w_{it}) + (1 - \delta)w_{it}, \tag{2.3}$$

$$w_{t+1} = S(f(w_t)) + (1 - \delta)w_t. \tag{2.4}$$

Equation (2.4), together with the concavity of $S(y)$, imply that aggregate wealth w_t will converge to a unique long-run wealth level w_∞. In the special case where savings are linear ($S(y) = sy$), w_∞ is simply given by $sf(w_\infty) = \delta w_\infty$. The fact that the capital stock per labor unit converges to w_∞ implies that the interest rate r_t converges to $r_\infty = f'(w_\infty)$, while the wage rate v_t converges to $v_\infty = f(w_\infty) - r_\infty w_\infty$. Equation (2.3) then implies that all dynasties will converge to the same long-run wealth level $w_\infty = sv_\infty/(\delta - sr_\infty)$, irrespective of the initial wealth distribution $G_0(w)$. That is, initial wealth inequalities do not persist in the long-run.

However, this conclusion ceases to hold if any of the assumptions is relaxed. For instance, if inheritance behavior is better approximated by a convex savings function $S(y)$, i.e., if the savings rate of the poor is smaller than the savings rate of the rich, such as in the Kaldorian class savings model, then wealth inequalities will persist in the long-run (see Bourguignon (1981) for such an extension of the Stiglitz model). That is, the

---

[18] That is, $5^{0.7} = 3.1$, while $5^{0.5} = 2.2$. All the intergenerational correlation estimates referred to in this chapter are obtained by regressing the log of children's income (or consumption, or earnings) on the log of parental income (see Mulligan, 1997: Chaps. 6 and 7).

long-run distribution of wealth $G_\infty(w)$ will depend on the initial distribution $G_0(w)$. In general, there will exist multiple long-run wealth levels $w_{1\infty}$, $w_{2\infty}$, ..., $w_{n\infty}$, and the long-run wealth level of each dynasty can be expressed as a function of their initial wealth w_{i0}. In steady-state, wealthy dynasties have income and consumption levels that are permanently higher than those of poorer dynasties, although all dynasties have the same labor income.

Another reason why wealth inequalities might not decline over time is differential fertility behavior. If one assumes that dynasty i has $1 + n_i$ children, then Eq. (2.3) becomes:

$$w_{it+1} = S(v_t + r_t w_{it})/(1 + n_i) + (1 - n_i - \delta)w_{it}. \tag{2.4}$$

It is obvious from Eq. (2.4) that differential fertility behavior can have the same effects as convex savings functions: if poor dynasties tend to have more kids than wealthy dynasties, then wealth inequalities can persist in the long-run even if all dynasties have the same savings rate. This kind of analysis of how different savings behavior, family structure and inheritance patterns generate more or less persistent inequality has a long tradition in economics.[19]

Even in the absence of convex inheritance functions or differential fertility behavior, wealth inequalities persist in the long-run if we assume that labor earnings are unequally distributed. For instance, if abilities are perfectly transmitted across generations ($\forall t$, $a_{it} = a_i$), then the long-run wealth distribution amplifies the inequality of labor earnings: with linear savings, w_{it} converges toward $w_{i\infty} = sa_i v_\infty/(\delta - sr_\infty)$ (see Stiglitz, 1969: p. 394). The long-run standard deviation of total income is larger than that of labor earnings, and the multiplicity factor is an increasing function of the savings rate s. The intergenerational correlations of income, earnings and consumption are all equal to 1. If we assume abilities to be drawn at random at each generation ($\forall i, t, a_{it} = 1 + \epsilon_{it}$), then the transition equation $w_{it+1} = (1 - \delta)w_{it} + s(r_t w_i + v_t a_{it})$ implies that the wealth distribution $G_t(w)$ converges to a long-run distribution $G_\infty(w)$ with mean w_∞ (such as $sf(w_\infty) = \delta w_\infty$) and variance σ_w^2 given by:

$$\sigma_w^2 = s^2 r_\infty^2 \sigma_\epsilon^2/(1 - (1 - \delta + sr_\infty)^2). \tag{2.5}$$

Equation (2.5) shows that the long-run standard deviation of wealth is an increasing function of the savings rate and of the variance of shocks. In this model, the long-run standard deviation of total income is again larger than that of earnings, and the long-run integenerational correlation of total income is positive, although the intergenerational correlation of earnings is permanently equal to zero. More generally, if one assumes

---

[19] The concern about how the poor's high fertility might lead to persistent poverty dates back at least to Malthus and Ricardo. James Meade has also written extensively about the interplay between savings behavior, family patterns and inequality dynamics (see Atkinson (1980) and subsequent references). See Chu (1991) for a recent analysis of the effect of primogeniture on long-run inequality and mobility.

some positive heritability of abilities ($\forall i, t, a_{it} = 1 - \rho + \rho a_{it-1} + \epsilon_{it}$), then one can easily show that the long-run correlation between wealth and ability is positive,[20] so that the standard deviation and intergenerational correlation of total income are larger than the standard deviation and intergenerational correlation of labor earnings. That is, the two key properties pointed out in Section 2.1 hold in the long-run.

2.3. The long-run dynamics of wealth inequalities with dynastic utility functions

How would this analysis differ if one explicitly models inheritance behavior instead of taking as given some exogenous savings function $S(y)$? In general, there are different private motives that can contribute to explain the existence of inheritance. First, bequests might just be the unintended side-product of precautionary savings in a world of imperfect insurance. That is, each generation saves during its lifetime in order to self-insure against negative shocks to its earnings potential, and imperfections on the annuity market imply that accidental bequests are passed on to the next generation at the time of death. The exact form of the inheritance function $S(y)$ that one can derive from such a model depends on the specific structure of lifetime earnings shocks, risk aversion, the degree of insurance market imperfections, etc.[21] There does not seem to be any general presumption as to whether the resulting $S(y)$ function should be concave, linear or convex.

Next, bequests can be motivated by intergenerational altruism. There exists two different ways of modeling bequests and intergenerational altruism. Becker and Tomes (1979) and Atkinson (1980) are two often cited papers that explicitly incorporate intergenerational altruism in general-equilibrium, Stiglitz-type models. One can either assume that the bequest enters directly into the utility function of the parents, or that parents care about their children's utility per se. The first formulation depends entirely on the specific form of the parental utility function $U(c_{it}, b_{it+1})$. For instance, if the utility function over parental consumption and bequest has a Cobb–Douglas form ($U(c, b) = c^{1-s}b^s$), then the inheritance function is linear ($S(y) = sy$). The second formulation also depends on the specific way one assumes parents to care about future generations' utility levels. The following form of Beckerian dynastic utility function has become very popular among economic theorists:

$$U_{it} = \sum_{S \geq t} U(c_{is})/(1 + \theta_i)^s, \tag{2.6}$$

$\theta_i \geq 0$ is the rate of time preference: a low θ_i means that dynasty i is very altruistic towards its children, and conversely. Assume that each dynasty can perfectly forecast

---

[20] Simple computations give the following formula for the long-run covariance between wealth and ability: $\text{cov}(w_i, a_i) = sv_\infty \sigma_2^2/(1 - \delta + sr_\infty)$, with $\sigma_a^2 = \sigma_\epsilon^2/(1 - \rho)^2$.

[21] Note that in general the resulting $S(.)$ function might depend on wealth on w and not only on income y. See Davies and Shorrocks' chapter 11 in this Handbook for more on savings and inheritance behavior.

the ability parameters a_{it} of its future generations, or at least that each dynasty can purchase complete insurance contracts against such risks.[22] Under the assumption of perfect capital markets, utility maximization implies that the consumption level of future generations will not depend on their ability shock. For any dynamic process from which abilities are drawn, the trade-off between parental consumption and children's consumption leads to the following first-order condition:

$$U'(c_{it})/U'(c_{it+1}) = (1 + r_{t+1})/(1 + \theta_i). \tag{2.7}$$

This first-order condition has very strong impications for the dynamics of the wealth distribution. First, Eq. (2.7) implies that if some dynasties have a permanently higher θ_i than some other dynasties, then the consumption level of more altruistic dynasties will grow at a higher rate than the consumption level of less altruistic dynasties. In the long run, the relative consumption share of less altruistic dynasties goes to zero, and the most altruistic dynasties own all the wealth (Mayshar and Benninga (1996)). We will come back later to this extreme form of taste-based persistent inequality (see Section 3.2 below).

Next, in the case where all dynasties have the same rate of time preference ($\forall i \theta_i = \theta$), Eq. (2.7) implies that a necessary condition for the economy to be in a steady-state is $r_\infty = \theta$. With a concave, net-of-depreciation production function $f(k)$, this implies that the steady-state average wealth w_∞ per efficiency labor unit must be such that $f'(w_\infty) = r_\infty = \theta$. Conversely, any consumption distribution $G_\infty(c)$ that is consistent with an average wealth equal to w_∞ can be a steady-state, where "consistent" simply means that average consumption c_∞ is equal to long-run average output $f(w_\infty)$. In the special case with uniform labor earnings ($\forall i \, a_{it} = 1$), any wealth distribution $G_\infty(w)$ such that the average wealth is equal to w_∞, can be a steady-state. Dynasty i with long-run wealth $w_{i\infty}$ consumes $c_{i\infty} = v_\infty + r_\infty w_{i\infty}$ at each period. In the general case where productive abilities are drawn from some arbitrary dynamic process, dynastic long-run wealth may vary with the specific ability shock of each generation, but the important point is that each dynasty will converge towards a fixed consumption level. That is, irrespective of what the intergenerational correlation of labor earnings might be, the theoretical prediction of the dynastic utility model is that the long-run intergenerational correlation of consumption should be equal to 1. This theoretical prediction can be viewed as an extreme form of the more general prediction according to which the intergenerational correlation of consumption and total income should be higher than that of labor earnings.[23]

Mulligan (1997) has recently pointed out that this very strong theoretical prediction has strong implications regarding how we should model intergenerational altruism. Mulligan argues that since we do observe regression to the mean in consumption across

---

[22] That is, risks about the future ability parameters of its future generations.

[23] These steady-state results can be generalized to models with balanced growth, such as those surveyed by Bertola's chapter 9 in this Handbook.

generations (the observed intergenerational consumption correlation is less than 1; see
Section 2.1 above), it must be the case that altruism is not randomly distributed across
dynasties and that poor dynasties are on average more altruistic than wealthy dynasties.[24] Mulligan then develops a theoretical model of endogenous altruism where the
poor turn out to be more altruistic than the rich, so that the predicted intergenerational
correlation of consumption is less than 1. The basic idea of Mulligan's model is that
the amount of time spent per kid increases altruism: since rearing costs include time
costs, high wage rate dynasties will spend less time with their children and will love
them less. Note that this theory differs from the Becker–Barro (1988) theory of fertility
and quality/quantity trade-offs, according to which fixed monetary rearing costs induce
wealthy parents to choose to have more kids of lower average quality (i.e., less altruism
per kid). This allows Becker and Barro to predict regression to the mean in consumption
in the dynastic utility model, but Mulligan argues that the predicted positive relationship
between income and fertility is counterfactual. In contrast, Mulligan's model predicts
that wealthy dynasties have both less kids and less altruism per kid. Mulligan (1997)
concludes that his theoretical model is the only model that can simultaneously account
for all the observed facts.

Mulligan's reasoning is not entirely convincing, however. First, the dynastic utility model predicts a unitary intergenerational correlation of consumption only if we
assume perfect insurance markets. In practice, one can very well imagine why even
very altruistic parents cannot guarantee with absolute certainty that their children will
enjoy some fixed consumption level, irrespective of their labor earnings. Obvious moral
hazard reasons can easily explain why there must be some degree of regression to the
mean in consumption across generations in the dynastic utility model, with no need for
a theory of endogenous altruism. Next, regardless of this imperfect insurance issue, one
must bear in mind that the dynastic utility model described by Eqs. (2.6) is primarily a
convenient theoretical construction, rather than a well-documented explanation of how
people actually behave. Models with exogenous savings $S(y)$, which can be rationalized
by models of inheritance based upon precautionary savings or direct utility for bequests,
can easily explain why the intergenerational correlation of consumption is both larger
than the intergenerational earnings correlation and smaller than 1. More empirical evidence seems to be needed before we take too seriously the implications of Eq. (2.7) for
the theory of intergenerational altruism (see below).

2.4. "Active" vs. "passive" inheritance: the costs of redistribution

Most theories of justice would argue that it is unfair that two individuals with exactly the
same behavior and characteristics enjoy vastly unequal consumption and welfare levels,
simply because one individual received a large inheritance and the other did not. For

[24] If wealthy dynasties were more altruistic, then we would observe no regression to the mean and the
wealth distribution would diverge (just as in the case where some dynasties have a rate of time preference that
is permanently higher than that of other dynasties).

instance, according to Rawls' difference principle, we should try to improve as much as possible the prospects of the children who receive no inheritance.[25]

The obvious way to correct for the unfair persistence of inequality implied by the family transmission of wealth would be to tax inheritance and to redistribute the tax revenues to all individuals. If wealth inequalities tend naturally to decline over time, such as in the model with concave savings and uniform labor earnings, then the redistributive taxation of inheritance does not only redistribute income and welfare today: it also increases the rate at which wealth is equalized (Stiglitz, 1969: p. 392). More generally, in models where full equality of wealth is a steady-state, i.e., in models with uniform labor earnings (either with exogenous savings or with dynastic preferences), it is sufficient to redistribute wealth at a 100% rate at $t = 0$ in order to reach a permanent steady-state with no wealth inequality. However, in more realistic models with unequal labor earnings, the economy always returns to a steady-state regime of persistent wealth inequalities (see Sections 2.2 and 2.3 above). In these more realistic models, redistributive inheritance taxation needs to be permanent in order to reduce permanently the intergenerational transmission of inequality trough inheritance.

Such a permanent taxation of inheritance is likely to have some adverse effects on the level of bequests. The magnitude of these adverse effects depends crucially on how one models inheritance behavior. If inheritance is the unintended side-product of precautionary savings and life-cycle wealth accumulation, then inheritance taxation has obviously no effect on the level of pre-tax bequests. That is, the distortionary costs of redistributive inheritance taxation are negligible if inheritance is primarily a "passive" phenomenon. On the other hand, if inheritance is primarily motivated by intergenerational altruism and is the outcome an "active" choice process, then the distortionary costs are potentially large. Several empirical studies have shown that intergenerational transfers are at least partly motivated by intergenerational altruism: for instance, households do not seem to annuitize their wealth as much as they could.[26] However, economists vastly disagree about what part of total wealth accumulation and transfers can be explained by intergenerational altruism and what part can be explained by life-cycle accumulation and precautionary savings, i.e., about the relative importance of "active" and "passive" inheritance.[27]

Moreover, intergenerational altruism per se does not necessarily imply that the effect of taxation on pre-tax bequests is negative. If bequests enter directly into the utility function of the parents ($U_i = U(c_{it}, b_{it+1})$), then the effect of taxation on pre-tax bequests can be positive or negative, depending on whether the elasticity of substitution between parental consumption and bequest is smaller or larger than 1 (see Atkinson, 1980: p. 178 and subsequent references). In the special case of a Cobb–Douglas utility

---

[25] See, e.g., Sen's chapter 1 in this handbook for a survey of distributive justice theories.

[26] See, e.g., Bernheim (1991).

[27] See, e.g., Kessler and Masson (1989), Kotlikoff (1988) and Modigliani (1988) for conflicting empirical viewpoints.

function ($U(c, b) = c^{1-s}b^{s}$), the elasticity of substitution is equal to 1, and pre-tax bequests do not depend on the level of inheritance taxation.

However, if intergenerational altruism is better described by dynastic utility functions given by Eq. (2.6), then redistributive inheritance taxation has unambiguously negative effects on capital accumulation.[28] This is because when parents care about their children's consumption, inheritance taxation acts as a capital income tax, and capital income taxes are well-known to have negative accumulation effects in models with infinite-horizon, dynastic preferences. For instance, if all dynasties have the same rate of time preference θ and can perfectly insure against all future ability shocks, Eq. (1.7) implies that if inheritance is taxed at rate τ, then the long-run, pre-tax interest rate r_∞ will be shown that $(1 - \tau)r_\infty = \theta$. That is, the long-run capital stock per capita k_∞ will decline until the point where the after-tax rate of return is again equal to θ, i.e., the new long-run k_∞ will be such that $(1 - \tau)f'(k_\infty) = \theta$. It follows that long-run income depends negatively on the rate of redistributive inheritance taxation.

Some authors have used this simple result in order to conclude that the socially-optimal rate of all forms of capital taxation, and in particular of inheritance taxation, should be equal to zero (see, e.g., Lucas, 1990). This very strong conclusion seems excessive. First, as was already pointed out, the infinite-horizon, dynastic utility model is not the only available theoretical model, and the question of its empirical relevance usually receives far less attention than the careful derivation of its theoretical implications. Next and most importantly, even if higher tax rates on inheritance do imply lower long-run average wealth, which seems like the most likely case, this obviously does not imply that the socially-optimal tax rate should be equal to zero. In order to make a proper welfare analysis, one needs to compare the distortionary costs of inheritance taxation, as measured by the long-run fall in average income, with the redistributive gains. In the standard dynastic utility model, one can show that in the long-run, even zero-wealth individuals will loose more from the distortionary costs of the tax than they will gain from its redistributive impact.[29] But in a world of permanent growth in living standards, the interpretation of such a result is somewhat complicated: the low-wealth individuals who benefit from redistributive inheritance taxation in the short-run enjoy lower welfare levels than those who are affected by the distortionary effects of taxation in the long-run, and it is not obvious how one should balance the two effects. In other words, even if we knew with certainty that inheritance taxation, as it has been applied in the US during the

---

[28] Note that we have little direct empirical evidence as to whether intergenerational altruism is better described by utility for bequests, by dynastic utility functions, or by other mathematical representations. From a theoretical perspective, Bernheim and Bagwell (1988) and Abel and Bernheim (1991) have argued that if the dynastic model leads to a number of implausible implications if we take it too seriously, and therefore that we should be extremely cautious when we use it for policy purposes.

[29] If bequests are taxed at rate t and the tax revenues are used to finance a lump-sum transfer, then the long-run net income of a prolaterian dynasty with zero wealth is equal to $v_\infty + T_\infty$, i.e., the sum of the wave rate $v_\infty = f(k_\infty) - r_\infty k_\infty$ and the lump-sum transfer $T_\infty = tr_\infty k_\infty$. That is, $v_\infty + T_\infty = f(k_\infty) - (1 - t)r_\infty k_\infty = f(k_\infty) - \theta k_\infty$. It follows that the long-run net income of zero-wealth dynasties is maximized if $f'(k_\infty) = \theta$, i.e., if $t = 0$ (see Judd, 1985).

twentieth century, has caused an average income loss of 10% by 1998 (which we do not know), this would not automatically mean that total social welfare during the twentieth century would have been higher in the absence of all inheritance tax revenues. From a practical policy perspective, the only interesting question is the magnitude of the adverse effects of redistributive inheritance taxation and the speed at which these negative effects are produced, as compared to the size and timing of positive distributive effects.

Under special assumptions, one can show that the tax-induced decline in absolute wealth dispersion can be smaller than the fall in average wealth, so that redistributive inheritance taxation can actually lead to a long-run rise of relative wealth inequality. This paradoxical result (redistribution increases long-run inequality) has been given high prominence by Becker and Tomes (1979: pp. 1175–1178).[30] To see how it works, consider the model with linear savings and i.i.d. ability shocks (see Section 2.2 above). Equation (2.5) shows that the long-run standard deviation of wealth is an increasing function of the savings rate s. If we assume that s is a decreasing function of the inheritance tax rate t (for instance because the elasticity of substitution between parental consumption and bequests is larger than 1), then it follows that inheritance taxation leads to decline in the long-run standard deviation of wealth. However, long-run average wealth also declines ($w_\infty = s v_\infty / (\delta - s r_\infty)$). One way to measure long-run, relative wealth inequality is to compute the coefficient of variation of the long-run distribution of wealth:

$$CV(s) = \sigma_w^2 / w_\infty^2 = (\delta - s r_\infty) \sigma_\epsilon^2 / (2 - \delta + s r_\infty). \tag{2.8}$$

Equation (2.8) shows average wealth falls more rapidly than the standard deviation of s when s declines, so that $CV(s)$ is a decreasing function of s. Therefore inheritance taxation and lower savings rate can lead to a long-term rise of relative inequality. However, as Atkinson (1980: p. 178) has pointed out, this is again a theoretical result, and one can easily construct other theoretical models with different specifications of savings behavior where the standard deviation of wealth would decline more than the average wealth.

Overall, we just seem to have very little practical knowledge about the socially-optimal rate of redistributive inheritance taxation. After a quick review of how cross-country and time-series variations of tax progressivity might have affected observed intergenerational mobility, Mulligan (1997: p. 218) is led to the obvious conclusion: "much more research (...) are necessary to arrive at a strong conclusion regarding the unimportance of progressive taxes for intergenerational mobility".

---

[30] See also Stiglitz (1978).

3. Persistent inequality and the family transmission of ability

Intergenerational wealth transfers make consumption and welfare more persistent across generations than labor earnings. According to the best available estimates, the intergenerational correlation goes up from about 0.5 for earnings to about 0.7 for consumption and total income (see Section 2.1 above). However, although wealth transfers are a very powerful transmission mechanism, these figures show that the main component (at least 70%) of the intergenerational correlation of welfare is due to the persistent inequality of labor earnings, and any useful theory of intergenerational mobility must address this fact. Some theories attribute a large fraction of the intergenerational earnings correlation to market inefficiencies, and in particular to wealth transfers themselves (see Sections 4–6 below). In this section, we focus on theories based upon efficient markets, according to which persistent earnings inequality can be explained either by a combination of direct family transmission of productive abilities and efficient human capital investments (Sections 3.1 and 3.2), or by the family transmission of ambition and other tastes that are conducive to high productive ability (Section 3.3).

3.1. The transmission of productive abilities

In Section 2, we considered a simple model of ability transmission, where productive abilities were measured in labor efficiency units and were given by the following transition equation:

$$a_{it} = 1 - \rho + \rho a_{it-1} + \epsilon_{it}. \tag{3.1}$$

In order to introduce human capital investments and to distinguish between pure ability endowments and human capital investments, Eq. (3.1) can be broken down into two separate equations (see, e.g., Becker and Tomes, 1986):

$$e_{it} = 1 - \rho + \rho e_{it-1} + \epsilon_{it}, \tag{3.2}$$

$$a_{it} = A(e_{it}, h_{it}). \tag{3.3}$$

Equation (3.2) relates the pure ability endowment of generation t to that of the previous generation, where ρ measures the intergenerational correlation of ability endowments. Becker and Tomes (1979, 1986) emphasize that pure ability endowments should be interpreted in a broad sense. That is, Eq. (3.2) measures not only the genetic transmission of innate abilities, but also the cultural transmission of family characteristics through childhood learning and family interaction. The relative importance of genetic vs. cultural transmission has always been a very controversial issue. In fact, even Herrnstein and Murray (1994), who have often been accused of overestimating the importance of genetic transmission, recognize that from the few reliable adoption studies that we have, childhood family environment seems to be more important than genetic factors per se.[31] In any case, the relevant question from a policy perspective is whether one can do something about these early childhood environmental factors. If the inequality of ability endowments is primarily determined by childhood learning through interaction with the parents at a very early age, and if this nurturing process is associated with the personality and behavior of the parents rather than with material wealth per se, then there is not much one can do about persistent inequality of abilities, aside from mass adoption programs. In other words, if "culture" means nurture at the family level, then the nature vs. culture debate is almost irrelevant (see Becker and Tomes, 1986).[32]

The other key component of Eq. (3.1) is Eq. (3.3), which simply says that ability endowments e_{it} and human capital investments h_{it} translate into productive ability parameters a_{it} (measured in efficiency labor units). Becker and Tomes (1986) argue that ability endowments and human capital investments are likely to be complementary (i.e., $\partial^2 A / \partial e \partial h > 0$), so that allocative efficiency requires that high endowed ability kids benefit from higher human capital investments. Whatever the exact pattern of efficient investments might be, these efficient levels of human capital investments will be undertaken if one assumes credit and education markets to be first-best efficient. As Becker and Tomes (1986: p. S10) put it: "access to capital markets to finance investments in children separates the transmission of earnings from the generosity of resources of parents". That is, bright kids will always find sufficient credit on the market to finance their human capital investment as long as their investment is profitable, irrespective of their parental wealth. Becker and Tomes (1986) also introduce credit constraints into their framework, so that h_{it} can also depend on parental wealth w_{it} per se, but their conclusion is that credit constraints must be unimportant in the real world (see Section 4.2. below for an evaluation of their empirical argument).

This theory of efficient ability transmission has strong policy implications. First, it implies that public intervention should not try to interfere directly with the process of ability formation. If markets are efficient, then it is useless to finance public subsidies to human capital investments or to attempt to equalize opportunities in education, since all efficient investments were already made in the first place. Compensatory responses of parents would tend to undo their potential positive impact, so that such policies would have purely distortionary effects (Becker and Tomes, 1986: pp. S16–S17). In particular, such policies will not lead to higher mobility.[33] As Mulligan (1997: pp. 247–248) puts it,

---

[31] See Herrnstein and Murray (1994: pp. 410–413) and subsequent references, and especially the well-known French adoptions studies of Schiff et al. (1982) and Schiff and Lewontin (1986).

[32] The point is obviously that "culture" might also include socially-inefficient processes of inequality transmission, such as local segregation (see Sections 4–6 below).

[33] See also Conlisk (1974) for an early model showing under what conditions attempts to equalize educational opportunities can have negative effects, in the form of a decline of mobility rates. Conlisk's model is not based upon compensatory responses of parents, however: no choice process is formalized in the Conlisk model, which belongs to the class of what Goldberger (1989) refers to as the "mechanical" models of intergenerational mobility. Conlisk's result is based on the interpretation of equal opportunity policies as a reduction of the variance of random ability shocks (so that equalizing opportunities can reduce the probability of social ascent of bright poor kids).

"rather than reducing inequality, government subsidization of schooling may only have the effect of transferring resources from taxpayers to educators and richer families who are more likely to choose many years of schooling for their children". That is, the first implication of the theory of efficient ability transmission is that there is not much to do about the persistent inequality of abilities and labor earnings.

3.2. Efficient inequality and the costs of redistribution

However, the fact that we should not interfere with the efficient process of ability transmission does not imply that there should be no redistribution at all. If children are not responsible for the ability that they inherit from their parents, then even though we cannot redistribute productive abilities, it would seem to be fair to redistribute consumption and welfare, just as in the case of nonhuman wealth transmission (see Section 2.4 above). In the same way as in the case of redistributive inheritance taxation, the key question is that of the magnitude of the distortionary costs of a redistributive tax on labor earnings. Although a great deal of effort has been devoted to the empirical evaluation of these distortionary costs, economists vastly disagree about their magnitude.[34] In order to illustrate what these disagreements involve, Piketty (1995) developed a simple intergenerational mobility model where agents try to learn about the magnitude of the incentive costs of redistribution. Assume that labor income y_{it} of dynasty i at period t can take one of two positive values y_0 and y_1, with $y_1 > y_0 > 0$. The probability of obtaining a high income y_1 is given by the following equations:

$$\text{Proba}(y_{it} = y_1 | y_{it-1} = y_0, e_{it} = e) = \pi + \theta e, \qquad (3.4)$$

$$\text{Proba}(y_{it} = y_1 | y_{it-1} = y_1, e_{it} = e) = \pi + \Delta\pi + \theta e, \qquad (3.5)$$

$\theta > 0$ measures the extent to which individual achievement is responsive to individual effort e_{it}. Effort should be interpreted in a broad sense: it includes all actions that are within one's control and that can have an impact on achievement. $\Delta\pi > 0$ measures ex ante inequality between lower-class and upper-class children. For instance, if abilities are highly heritable, then $\Delta\pi$ should be large. Piketty (1995) assumes no market imperfection, so that the only redistributive policy that can possibly be justified is a redistributive tax on labor incomes y_0 and y_1. Effort is assumed to be private information, so that redistribution entails distortionary costs in the form of lower effort. One can easily show that distortionary costs are an increasing function of the income responsiveness of effort θ. It follows that the socially optimal rate of redistribution τ is low if economic success depends mostly on individual effort (θ high and $\Delta\pi$ low), and conversely that τ is high if economic success depends mostly on ex ante inequality (θ low and $\Delta\pi$ high).[35]

---

[34] See, e.g., Feldstein (1995) and Slemrod (1995) for some of the latest developments of this long-standing controversy.

[35] Piketty (1995) assumes a Rawlsian social welfare function (maximization of the expected utility of lower-class children), but the same qualitative property would hold with any utilitarian welfare function.

Piketty (1995) then assumes that dynasties use their own dynastic mobility experience to rationally update their probability beliefs μ_{it} about θ and $\Delta\pi$. One can show that this rational learning process will generally not result into complete learning of the true parameters (unless dynasties are sufficiently patient, so that they are ready to experiment during several generations effort levels which they believe to be inefficient in the short-run). In the long-run, "left-wing" dynasties believing that ex ante inequality is large and that the incentive costs of redistribution are low coexist with "right-wing" dynasties believing the opposite. Since they have stronger beliefs in individual effort, right-wing dynasties put in more effort and tend to be richer (whatever the true parameters might be). This implies that even though all dynasties have the same distributive objective, high-income individuals favor less redistribution than low-income individuals. This provides an example of a model where all agents agree about the aggregate mobility level, but disagree about how much incentives and mobility would be altered by redistribution, and therefore disagree about the socially-optimal level of redistribution. Just like economists, agents in this model would need large-scale social experiments in order to solve their disagreements. Unfortunately, reliable natural experiments are very difficult to design in the social sciences.

Some important ingredients are missing in the conflict over the socially-efficient level of redistribution described in the Piketty (1995) model. First, all right-wing dynasties in the model belong to the "liberal right-wing" type (see Section 1.1): they believe that the heritability of ability is low ($\Delta\pi$ low) and that market processes of social selection are highly responsive to individual effort (θ high).[36] This is because the model assumes that the incentive costs of redistribution are determined solely by the income responsiveness θ of children's effort input. That is, family choices are assumed not to be responsive to redistributive taxation: $\Delta\pi$ simply measures the mechanical transmission of inequality from parents to children, and a high $\Delta\pi$ means that the incentive costs of redistribution are low. However, as Becker's work on intergenerational mobility and the family has repeatedly emphasized, families do choose how much to invest in their children, and government intervention might tend to distort these choices. The theoretical models developed by Becker and his followers do not only describe how family wealth transfers might be adversely affected by government interference and redistributive taxation (see Section 2 above). Chicago economists also stress that families make many other choices, such as how much time they spend with their children, that might affect the labor earnings potential of future generations (and not only their capital income). For instance, Mulligan (1993) estimates that about 20% of the intergenerational transmission of earnings inequality can be attributed to the quality/quantity trade-offs made by parents.[37] A redistributive tax on future earnings might induce parents to spend less time

---

[36] All left-wing dynasties also belong to the "liberal" left-wing type.

[37] That is, Mulligan estimates (with PSID data) that the intergenerational earnings correlation would be about 20% lower if richer parents did not choose to have fewer kids of higher average quality (this is keeping everything else constant: as we already explained in Section 2.3, richer parents always tend to spend less time with their children than poorer parents in Mulligan's model; but the point is that if they did not choose to have

with their children and therefore to "produce" less productive ability, which might be detrimental to everybody in the long-run, in the same way as in the case of redistributive inheritance taxation (see Section 2.4 above). The potential sensitivity of nurturing and family choices to government policies implies that one can simultaneously believe that $\Delta\pi$ is high and that the socially-optimal, incentive-constrained level of redistribution is low. This corresponds to the "conservative right-wing" view referred to in Section 1.1.

In fact, this strong emphasis on the "active" family and how family choices might be distorted by all forms of government intervention, both by direct interventions on educational markets and by pure welfare redistribution, is the main contribution of Gary Becker and his followers to the study of intergenerational mobility. This is what Becker right responded to Goldberger (1989), who expressed some skeptical view about what Becker's contribution really was (as compared to standard mechanical models of intergenerational transmission). Becker (1989) summarized the main negative results about government interventions derived from his models, and explained to Goldberger that such results could not have been derived in a purely mechanical model. It is fair to say that Chicago economists have spent more energy in deriving the laissez-faire implications of their theoretical models rather than in trying to estimate empirically what the distortionary costs of activist policies really are. But one cannot deny that the introduction of utility maximization and active family behavior into the analysis of intergenerational mobility has important policy implications that purely mechanical models do not have.

The other important limitation of the Piketty (1995) model is that it seems to imply that left-wingers should be happy if the genetic component of inequality transmission was very important. That is, if the mechanical component of $\Delta\pi$ (i.e., the component that is beyond the family's control) is very high, then the incentive costs of redistribution are very low. In the extreme case where earnings inequality results entirely from genetic IQ inequality, then one can equalize consumption across dynasties at no incentive cost. However this theory would also imply that there is no hope of doing anything about the inequality of occupations and labor market status, whereas left-wing theories usually stress that such inequalities are due (at least in part) to market inefficiencies that can be corrected (see Sections 4–6 below). Moreover, a strong emphasis on IQ inequality often leads to questioning the ability of low-IQ segments of the population to make sensible choices. For instance, Herrnstein and Murray (1994) argue that one consequence of modernity is that "it has become much more difficult for a person of low cognitive ability to figure out why marriage is a good thing", and they recommend that we impose tough and simple rules on low-IQ individuals.[38] This illustrates how liberal, pro-market right-wing views about social inequality can easily shift to conservative, authoritarian and

---

fewer kids than poorer parents, they would spend even less time per child than they actually do, and inequality would be less persistent).

[38] "The old bargain from the man's viewpoint—get married, because that's the only way you're going to be able to sleep with the lady—was the kind of incentive that did not require a lot of intellect to process and had an all-powerful effect on behavior" (Herrnstein and Murray, 1994: p. 544).

anti-laissez-faire right-wing views:[39] If one's basic premise is that individual abilities are so unequally distributed that no policy can do anything about it, then one can easily be led to conclude that low-ability individuals have a limited ability to interact in society (including in markets), and that government policies should try to regulate their behavior, possibly in an authoritarian and anti-market manner. More generally, a strong emphasis on IQ inequality might also lead to question the relevance of Rawlsian and welfarist criteria of distributive justice: if the poor are so stupid, then why we should care about their consumption level? However, such non-welfarist arguments have become less and less popular over time, and incentive-based arguments against redistribution are usually produced as well. For instance, Herrnstein and Murray (1994: chapters 17–19) also argue that everybody (including low-IQ taxpayers) would gain if we chose to reward bright and successful children rather than to subsidize hopeless low-IQ neighborhoods and to encourage welfare dependency.

3.3. Taste-based persistent inequality

Sociologists have also been interested for a long time in the family transmission of productive abilities. The "reference group" theory formulated by Merton (1953) and Boudon (1973, 1974) has been particularly influential. The basic idea of the theory is that individuals tend to compare their social achievements to the "reference group" from which they come. As a consequence, agents with lower-class origins are less motivated to make human capital investments and to acquire high productive abilities, since they have less to prove to the outside world and they can easily maintain their initial social position. Conversely, agents with upper-class origins are more motivated and are able to maintain their initial social position. According to this theory, the intergenerational persistence of labor earnings inequality follows from the intergenerational transmission of ambition and taste for economic success. This theory can be formalized in a model where agents care about their "social prestige" or "social status" (defined as the public beliefs about one's ability), abilities are not directly observable, and earnings and labor market achievements act as a signal of one's ability.[40] In such a model, one can show that the status motive tends to amplify the persistence of inequality across generations.[41]

Although this sociological theory is very different from the Becker–Tomes or Herrnstein–Murray theories, the policy implications are fairly similar. Boudon (1973,

---

[39] See Section 1.1.

[40] It is interesting to note that economists who emphasize the role of private concern for relative status usually stress the rationale for government intervention arising from the status externality, whereas sociologists are mostly interested in the consequence for the intergenerational persistence of inequality (see Piketty, 1998). This probably reflects the fact that most economists are mainly concerned with the optimal size of monetary transfers and redistributive taxation, whereas sociologists are more interested in persistent occupational inequality per se.

[41] See Piketty (1998). More specifically, if agents with upper-class origins are expected to maintain the irinitial position with a very high probability, then the status motive will tend to magnify the inequality of ambition and effort levels and to make inequality more persistent.

1974) argues forcefully that there is nobody to blame for the low educational and economic performance of lower-class kids and the intergenerational persistence of inequality: this is just the unavoidable consequence of the family transmission of ambition. According to Boudon, the reason why for a given educational score at age 10, lower-class children tend to leave school earlier than upper-class children is not because of credit constraints, disadvantaged neighborhood environment or discrimination (see Sections 4–6), but rather because upper-class parents encourage their children not to leave school and reward educational achievements more than lower-class parents do. Boudon concludes that the only possible way to improve somewhat the educational achievements of lower-class kids would be to limit drastically the influence that parents have on their children, for instance by reducing their participation to school boards and class councils. This is not quite as tough to implement as mass adoption programs (see Section 3.1 above), but this means once again that the only possible way to do something about persistent inequality requires a major conflict between the government and the family, and therefore that we might prefer to be modest and accept the world as it is (as Boudon repeatedly suggests). In contrast, left- wing theories argue that market inefficiencies rather than the family are responsible for persistent inequality, and therefore that we do not need to initiate a fight against the family in order to reduce the persistence of inequality (see Section 4–6 below, and especially Section 6.2 on anti-"reference group" sociological theories).

If one is ready to assume that families can transmit their tastes across generations, then one can also construct other, more extreme taste-based theories of persistent inequality. For instance, if different dynasties are characterized by different rates of time preference in the model with dynastic preferences, then the most patient dynasties will become richer and richer, while the least patient dynasties will become poorer and poorer (see Section 2.3). The concern about how consumption and wealth will be distributed in the long-run between dynasties with heterogeneous preferences has a long tradition in economics, and can be found for instance in the writings of Rae, Ramsey and Irving Fisher.[42] Empirical evidence about time discount rates during one's lifetime seems to show that the poor do indeed discount the future at a substantially higher rate that the rich.[43] Assuming that this dynastic heterogeneity in "tastes" does explain a significant fraction of the intergenerational persistence of inequality, the policy implications are far from clear, however. The key question is where the heterogeneity of tastes comes from and whether it can be altered. If heterogeneous behavior and attitudes are due to some "culture of poverty", which is itself the consequence of neighborhood segregation or other socially-inefficient market processes, then activist redistributive policies are called for (see Sections 4–6 below). But if heterogeneous tastes come from direct family transmission and can be altered only at a very high cost, as in the "reference group" theory, then the only thing one can do is to redistribute consumption, the extent of which can

---

[42] See Mayshar and Benninga (1996) and subsequent references.

[43] See, e.g., Green et al. (1996) and Lawrence (1991) for recent evidence.

be severely limited by incentive considerations. If heterogeneous behavior comes from a dynastic learning process with limited experimentation, then the policy conclusions can be even more anti-redistribution. For instance, if one believes that persistent poverty is due to the fact that poor dynasties underestimate the returns to individual effort, then one may want to implement even less redistribution than would otherwise be the case (or even negative redistribution, from the poor to the rich), so as to induce the poor to experiment with high effort levels and to learn about the true returns to effort.[44] In other words, if poor dynasties are somehow responsible for their wrong behavior, then very little redistribution is called for.

4. Persistent inequality and the imperfect capital market

The simplest market failure theory of persistent inequality is the theory of imperfect credit: if credit markets are imperfect, then dynasties with little initial wealth face limited investment opportunities, and they remain poor. Credit constraints imply that the consequence of intergenerational wealth transfers is not only to make welfare and consumption inequality more persistent than earnings inequality (see Section 2): wealth transfers can also contribute to make earnings differentials more persistent across generations than they would otherwise be. We first briefly review why credit market imperfections might arise and describe the basic implications for the theory of intergenerational mobility (Section 4.1). We then ask the following question: what evidence do we have about the likely importance of credit constraints for intergenerational mobility? (Section 4.2). Finally, a number of theoretical contributions have recently explored some new implications of credit constraints for the dynamics of occupational structure, wealth inequality and intergenerational mobility, and we summarize the main ideas of these theories in Section 4.3.

4.1. Credit constraints vs. first-best credit

Credit or wealth constraints are said to arise whenever the opportunity to invest depends not only on the "technological" viability of the investment (rate of return, risk, ability of the entrepreneur, ...), but also on the initial wealth (or collateral) of the would-be entrepreneur per se. The idea of credit constraints is probably as old as capitalist economies. Although Marx and other nineteenth century socialist theorists do not refer explicitly to the concept of credit constraints, the belief that such constraints are pervasive in capitalist economies implicitly plays a central role in their analysis of the capitalist system. Their basic premise is that initial wealth and capital ownership per se are the key determinants of class reproduction and persistent inequalities on the workplace. This could not happen in a world with first-best credit, where initial wealth per se should be

---

[44] See Piketty (1995: p. 563, footnote 31).

irrelevant from the viewpoint of productive efficiency and should have no consequence on the distribution of earnings.

It is only recently however that formal theories describing precisely the microeconomic origin of credit constraints have been developed. It is by now well understood that the source of credit constraints is the commitment power of initial wealth: without a sufficient personal stake in the investment project, the would-be entrepreneur has no way no commit that he will reveal the truth to the lender (adverse-selection), nor that he will take the right actions to ensure that the lender will be paid back (moral-hazard).[45] Depending on the exact technological and informational parameters, this will result in equilibrium into some specific credit-rationing curve $k(w, r)$: $k(w, r) \geq w$ is the maximal capital investment a would-be entrepreneur with initial wealth w can undertake when the market interest rate is r, i.e., $k(w, r) - w$ is the maximal credit that lenders accept to offer. In contrast, with first-best credit $k(w, r)$ does not depend on w and is uniquely determined by technological opportunities alone. Note that credit constraints are likely to be particularly severe regarding children's human capital investments, since parents have a limited ability to commit on behalf of their children.

The first consequence of credit constraints is that unequal wealth may prevent some profitable investment from being undertaken. In other words, the inherited distribution of wealth $F(w)$ may not be output-maximizing. By allowing a larger number of able children and entrepreneurs to educate and invest, wealth redistribution can reduce inequality, raise the intergenerational mobility of earnings and increase output at the same time. This was first pointed out by Loury (1981), who introduced credit constraints into a Becker–Tomes (1979)-type model of intergenerational mobility. Limited borrowing ability thus provides the basic justification for redistributive public funding of education.[46] More generally, capital market imperfections imply that the usual results about the long-run efficiency costs of capital income taxation (see Section 2.4) are no longer valid: one needs to compare these efficiency costs not only with the distributive gains, but also with the efficiency gains resulting from previously unfinanced investments.[47] Credit constraints and the commitment value of initial wealth also imply that occu-

---

[45] See, e.g., Jaffee and Stiglitz (1990) and Bardhan and Bowles' chapter 10 in this Handbook for a survey.

[46] Public intervention in educational markets can obviously be justified by simpler considerations, such as the idea that young children and their ill-informed parents are unable to choose the education they need (for instance, illiterate parents may not be able to fully appreciate what literacy would bring to their children). Although modern economists usually dislike such "paternalistic" concerns and favor market-friendly policy interventions (see below), such concerns do play an important role in the way many people think about intergenerational mobility (see Section 1.1).

[47] Chamley (1996) shows that the efficient, long-run capital income tax rate can be positive in a model with imperfect capital markets. Note that this general result can be the consequence not only of credit market imperfections but also of insurance market imperfections: Aiyagari (1994) shows that imperfect insurance markets imply excessive precautionary savings, in the sense that a lump-sum transfer financed by capital income taxation can be welfare-improving. See Benabou (1997) for a recent attempt to quantify the efficiency gains of redistribution resulting from previously unfinanced profitable educational investments (he concludes that they are roughly comparable to the distortionary costs, and therefore the socially-optimal trade-off leads to "reasonable", interior solutions).

pational choice, i.e., who becomes a wage-earner, who becomes self-employed, etc., is partly determined by the distribution of wealth, even if the latter is unrelated to the distribution of productive abilities (Newman, 1991). Banerjee and Newman (1994) stress that these consequences of limited commitment power are the key economic implications of poverty: poor people have little to loose, and therefore have little credit and career opportunities. This implies that the contractual relationships governing the organization of production that emerge in equilibrium have no reason in general to be output-maximizing.[48] Again, the general implication is that appropriate corrective policies can have both positive distributive effects and positive efficiency effects.

But the explicit microeconomic modeling of credit constraints does not only allow modern economists to rationalize what older generations already knew. It also allows for a more balanced welfare analysis of capital market imperfections. First, the fact that wealth redistribution can be output-improving in the presence of credit constraints does not necessarily imply that wealth redistribution can be Pareto-improving. In general, market equilibria with credit constraints are second-best Pareto-efficient. For instance, it is well-known that sharecropping contracts are privately efficient: no policy can simultaneously raise the productivity of the tenant and the income of the landlord. The only way to raise productivity and output is to redistribute property rights away from the landlord. One cannot simply redistribute the higher output level so as to make everybody better off "after" the efficiency gains have been realized, since this would cancel the positive incentive effects of wealth redistribution, and private contracting could have done the same thing if that was incentive-compatible. This illustrates a more general lesson that can be drawn from microeconomic theory: incentive constraints apply both to private contracting and to activist policies. That is, the same informational and incentive reasons that imply the existence of credit constraints also imply that governments should be cautious before they try to make the credit market more efficient. This simple fact has been dramatically overlooked by radical "remedies" to credit imperfections, such as the abolition of private property, collective ownership or the centralization of credit. In contrast, modern theories of credit market imperfections suggest market-friendly corrective policies, such as a transparent system of educational subsidies or wealth transfers, with limited interference with how actual investments are being made by private individuals. If private individuals are short of cash rather than short of rationality, then governments should try to provide them with the former rather than with the latter.

---

[48] For instance, Legros and Newman (1995) consider a model where production can be organized either in partnerships, whereby agents with moderate wealth share the investment costs, or in "hierarchical" firms where one rich agent makes the investment and monitors low-wealth wage-earners. They show that hierarchical firms will tend to dominate in equilibrium even though partnerships lead to higher output (since there is no labor wasted in monitoring), simply because wealthy agents use hierarchical firms to extract a larger share of a smaller pie.

4.2.   What do we know about the importance of credit constraints for mobility?

What empirical evidence do we have about the extent to which credit constraints contribute to make inequality more persistent across generations? First, we do have extensive evidence showing that credit constraints do exist at the micro level. For instance, many empirical studies in developing countries have shown that redistributing the property of the land, or more generally securing the tenure of the land, can raise the incentives and productivity of poor farmers.[49] In developed countries, there is also extensive evidence that for given investment opportunities, firms' investment behavior depends heavily on their cash flows and retained earnings, although first-best credit would predict the opposite.[50] However, although these different pieces of empirical evidence of the micro level are suggestive, they obviously do not allow us to give a precise estimate of how much credit constraints are likely to affect aggregate intergenerational mobility at the macro level.

It is equally difficult to draw strong conclusions from traditional sociological studies about educational achievements and occupations across generations. For instance, the fact that, for given standardized test scores at age 10, lower-class children tend to leave school earlier than upper-class children does not necessarily imply that wealth constraints are binding. It is also consistent with the "reference group" theory of intergenerational mobility (see Section 3.2), or with the existence of some mismeasured endowed ability differential. Sociologists have also shown that for given educational achievements, upper-class children tend to reach higher-status and better-paid occupations than lower-class children.[51] This could be due to the fact that wealth constraints make it more difficult for low-wealth children to translate educational achievements into occupational outcomes. But this is also consistent with a post-school "reference group" theory, or with the fact that educational achievements are very difficult to measure and that the error term is correlated with parental status.

One empirical argument that has been put forward by Gary Becker is that since observed earnings mobility is so high, it must be the case that credit constraints are not very important. Until recently, the few existing studies by economists of the intergenerational correlation of earnings in the US usually found some very low estimates. For instance, Behrman and Taubman (1985: p. 147) estimate an intergenerational correlation of at most 0.2 and conclude: "the members of this sample come from a highly mobile society". Becker and Tomes (1986: p. 269) refer to a couple of similarly low estimates and reach the following conclusion: "The evidence suggests that neither the inheritability of (ability) endowments by sons nor the propensity to invest in children's human capi-

---

[49] See, e.g., Banerjee and Gathak (1996) for a recent empirical analysis of the productivity effects of land reform in West Bengal.

[50] See, e.g., Gilchrist and Himmelberg (1995) and Lamont (1997).

[51] See Goux and Maurin (1996) for recent evidence. In particular, Goux and Maurin show that, for given educational achievements, the effect of parental status on children is very strong all along one's occupational career (even more so that at the entry level).

tal because of capital constraints is large".[52] Becker's 1988 presidential address to the American Economic Association similarly concluded: "In every country with data that I have seen (...) low earnings as well as high earnings are not strongly transmitted from fathers to sons. (...) Evidently, abilities and other endowments that generate earnings are only weakly transmitted from parents to children" (Becker, 1988: p. 10).

However, these very low estimates of the intergenerational earnings correlation have been rejected by the more recent and reliable literature. Solon (1992) and Zimmerman (1992) have convincingly argued that previous estimates have been biased downwards by unrepresentative samples and measurement errors. The most important source of downward bias in previous studies derives from the use of single-year or short-run measures of earnings. The existence of large, short-run variations in earnings makes it impossible to estimate properly the true intergenerational correlation of life-time earnings based on such short-term measures. Solon and Zimmerman use better data sets than previous studies, correct for measurement errors by using multi-year income averages, and both estimate intergenerational earnings correlation coefficients in the 0.4–0.5 range. Mulligan (1997) further refines the Solon-Zimmerman approach to measurement errors and concludes that the correct estimate is likely to be at least equal to 0.5. Dearden et al. (1997) use a similar methodology with British data and also find an intergenerational earnings correlation in the 0.5–0.6 range. One must bear in mind that whether the intergenerational correlation is 0.2 or 0.5 has enormous consequences for actual mobility rates. If the intergeneration earnings correlation was equal to 0.2, as argued by Gary Becker and pre-Solon–Zimmerman estimates, this would mean that if parents are five times richer, then children will be on average less than 40% richer, and grand-children less than 7% richer. But if the correlation is equal to 0.5, as more recent and reliable studies seem to suggest, this means that if parents are five times richer, children will be more than 2.2 times richer, and the grand-children 50% richer.[53] To put it another way, a son whose father's status is in the fifth percentile has a 37% chance to rise above the median if the intergenerational correlation is 0.2, and a 17% chance to rise above the median if the intergenerational correlation is 0.5.[54]

In fact, some authors have pointed out a long time ago that simple raw estimates of intergenerational earnings correlation suffered from serious downward biases (see, e.g., Bowles (1972)). In the early 1980s, Atkinson (1981) and Atkinson et al. (1983) had already tried to correct for measurement errors and had found an intergenerational earnings correlation of 0.45 with British data. Becker's (1988) faith in very low estimates probably reflects when Bjorklund and Jantti (1998) describe about their US colleagues' faith in US exceptionalism (see Section 1.1 above).

Needless to say, one cannot conclude from the fact that intergenerational earnings correlation is pretty high that credit constraints are important. Low mobility might just

---

[52] The page number refers to the Becker (1991) reprint version of the Becker and Tomes (1986) article.

[53] $5^{0.2} = 1.38$ and $1.38^{0.2} = 1.066$, while $5^{0.5} = 2.23$ and $2.23^{0.5} = 1.495$ (see Section 2.1).

[54] See Solon (1992: p. 404). Note that this is assuming bivariate normally, which may overestimate the mobility chances of dynasties at the bottom and at the top of the distribution.

result from an efficient process of ability transmission in families and on human capital markets (see Section 3). For instance, Mulligan (1997) finds that the intergenerational correlation of earnings is at least equal to 0.5, but he agrees with Gary Becker about the fact that credit constraints must be unimportant in the real world. Mulligan's empirical argument is more sophisticated than that of Becker, however. Using PSID data, Mulligan (1997: Chap. 8) compares the intergenerational correlation of earnings and consumption of children who have received financial transfers from their parents at age 30 with that of children who did not receive such transfers, and finds that correlation coefficients are not significantly different between the two groups.[55] To the extent that the second group is more likely than the first group to suffer from wealth constraints, this can be taken as evidence that wealth constraints are not very important for mobility. Mulligan further concludes that since credit constraints are unimportant, they cannot possibly explain why consumption regresses to the mean across generations, and therefore that his model of endogenous altruism is the only model of intergenerational mobility that can simultaneously explain all the observed facts (see Section 2.3 above). Given that the available information used by Mulligan to identify credit-constrained dynasties can hardly have been viewed as satisfactory, such a strong negative conclusion about the importance of credit constraints seems premature. But Mulligan's empirical strategy is promising and clearly illustrates what the empirical work of the future should look like: the extensive use of richer and richer panel data sets should allow us to make progress on such issues.

Finally, note that it is by no mean impossible that the importance of credit constraints for intergenerational mobility does vary enormously over time and across countries. For instance, the historical study by Kaelble (1986) argues that the major change that occurred in the history of social mobility since the industrial revolution is the shift from the middle-size family firm to the large corporation. According to Kaelble, the consequence of the transition to "corporate capitalism" was that capital became less and less a precondition for the business career, which led to a slow decline of the business family and the emergence of a large class of non-owner business executives and of associated upwardly-mobile careers. Kaelble stresses the fact that this transition was very slow: he finds that the proportion of fathers of the business elite who were themselves businessmen was high and rising in all industrialized countries until the interwar years. Kaelble concludes that the initial effect of the industrial revolution on social mobility was probably a negative one, because of the transmission of property and land and crucial role of access to capital in the new world, and that the history of social mobility since the industrial revolution should be seen as a crisis and a subsequent response, rather than as self-sustained growth of mobility rates. From a completely different perspective, Herrnstein and Murray (1994: Chap. 1) also argue that capital barriers have become less and less important over time: they display some graphical evidence showing that IQ has

---

[55] Mulligan also uses information about the expectation of receiving such transfers.

progressively become more important than social origins per se in order to be admitted in top universities in the US over the course of the twentieth century.

4.3. Poverty traps vs. low-mobility traps

The simplest theoretical implication of credit constraints is the existence of poverty traps: dynasties with little initial wealth can remain poor forever. The following model, which is a slightly simplified version of the model of Galor and Zeira (1993), illustrates how it works.[56] Assume linear savings and a very extreme form of moral-hazard-induced credit-rationing: borrowers can always "take the money and run" at no cost, so that in effect the credit market completely collapses ($k(w, r) = w$). Further assume that each generation can either earn a subsistence income y or make a fixed investment I that yields a net return RI, with $RI > y$. Galor and Zeira (1993) choose to interpret the fixed investment I as a human capital investment, but this is obviously inessential. Credit constraints imply that at each period t, all agents whose initial wealth w_t is smaller than I earn y, while agents with $w_t \geq I$ earn RI, so that transitional equations can be written:

$$\text{If } w_{it} < I, \, w_{it+1} = (1 - \delta)w_{it} + sy, \tag{4.1}$$

$$\text{If } w_{it} > I, \, w_{it+1} = (1 - \delta)w_{it} + sRI. \tag{4.2}$$

If we assume the savings rate s to be small enough so that $sy + (1 - \delta I) < I$ and the rate of return R to be high enough so that $sRI + (1 - \delta)I > I$, then we have a poverty trap: poor dynasties starting with $w_0 < I$ earn a low income y and remain poor forever ($w_t \to w^0 = sy/\delta < I$), while rich dynasties starting with w_0 earn a high-income RI and remain rich ($w_t \to w^1 = sRI/\delta > I$). That is, if the initial distribution of wealth $F_0(w)$ is characterized by a mass $F_0(I)$ of poor dynasties and a mass $1 - F_0(I)$ of rich dynasties, then so will be the long-run distribution $F_\infty(w)$: initial wealth inequality persists in the long-run. This persistence would immediately disappear with first-best credit: everybody would invest I irrespective of one's initial wealth, and all dynasties would converge to the same wealth level, for any initial wealth distribution. This shows that the assumption of fixed costs or increasing returns is not sufficient to make the initial distribution relevant if it is not supplemented with the assumption of credit constraints. Conversely, poverty traps rely on a threshold effect and a technological nonconvexity and would not arise with credit constraints alone. Without the assumption of a fixed-size investment, poor dynasties could slowly accumulate by starting with small investment levels and eventually catch up with the rich. It is the combination of nonconvex technologies and credit constraints that produce nonconvexities in transition equations and the possibility of poverty traps. In effect, this combination gives rise to a dynamic model that is very similar to the Bourguignon (1981) model with a nonconvex savings function $S(y)$ described in Section 2.2. above.

[56] Freeman (1996) also offers a model of persistent inequality based upon borrowing constraints and a poverty trap.

The recent literature has explored more sophisticated dynamic implications of credit constraints. One important finding of the recent literature is that with credit constraints we actually do not need nonconvexities and threshold effects to conclude that credit constraints can have important long-run effects. Consider a model where agents can invest at any level according to a concave production function $f(k)$, but where moral-hazard in entrepreneurial effort leads to a credit-rationing curve $k(w, r)$ (see Section 4.1 above). Under natural assumptions, one can show that credit constraints become more and more binding as the market interest rate r goes up $(dk(w, r)/dr < 0)$.[57] Risks from investment are imperfectly insurable (because of moral-hazard), so that individual transitions $w_{it+1}(w_{it})$ are stochastic. With suitable concavity assumptions, one can ensure that individual transitions $w_{it+1}(w_{it})$ exhibit no threshold effect, i.e., that all dynasties can switch between any two wealth levels in a finite time with positive probability. If we assume that the market interest rate r is exogenously fixed, then this ergodicity property is sufficient to ensure global convergence, i.e., the fact that the long-run distribution $F_{\infty r}(w)$ does not depend on the initial distribution $F_0(w)$.

However things are different when the interest rate is endogenously determined by the supply and demand of capital. Note first that with credit constraints the equilibrium interest rate is not simply given by "the" marginal product of capital, since the latter varies across production units. In other words the equilibrium interest rate r_t now depends on the entire wealth distribution $F_t(w)$ at period t. One can then show that depending on the exact initial distribution $F_0(w)$ there will exist different possible long-run distributions $F_{\infty 1}(w)$, $F_{\infty 2}(w)$, associated with different long-run interest rates $r_{\infty 1}$, $r_{\infty 2}$, ... (see Piketty, 1997). The intuition is the following: initial distributions with a large population of low-wealth agents lead to a high demand for capital and to high interest rates, which in turn imply that it takes a long time for low-wealth agents to accumulate and rebuild their collateral, so that the initially large mass of poor agents is self-reproducing. Conversely, low initial interest rates lead to high wealth mobility, high accumulation and low equilibrium interest rates. Such a multiplicity will arise whenever an interest rate rise strengthens credit constraints more than it strengthens the accumulation of the rich, i.e., whenever $|dk(w, r)/dr|$ is large enough. The steady-states with higher interest rates have at the same time less wealth mobility and a lower aggregate output and capital stock. One key difference between this type of "low-mobility trap" and the poverty trap described earlier is that the latter can be eliminated once and for all by pushing all poor agents above the threshold, whereas the former is more perverse and requires continuous downward pressures on the interest rate (through fiscal or credit policy) in order to shift the economy to a lower interest rate, higher mobility development path.

This phenomenon of low-mobility traps is actually very general, and it has first been pointed out by Banerjee and Newman (1993) in a context that is slightly different

---

[57] For an endogenous derivation of such a curve, see Piketty (1997), whose moral-hazard credit model is an extension of that of Aghion and Bolton (1997).

from the Piketty (1997) model that we just described. Banerjee and Newman consider a dynamic accumulation/distribution model with a fixed exogenous interest rate r, but with an endogenous wage rate v_t playing a role that is similar to the endogenous interest rate in the previous discussion. In their model, the wage rate is the equilibrium market price of monitored labor. They consider a world where moral-hazard-induced credit constraints prevent poor agents from investing in large projects but where rich agents can use a technology to monitor poor agents working as wage earners. That is, unlike in the previous model where everybody was an entrepreneur, there are three possible occupations in their model: wage earners (who are too poor to make any investment on their own), self-employed (who finance and run their own investment) and entrepreneurs (who finance large investments and monitor wage earners). The equilibrium wage rate v_t is determined by the equality between the number of agents "choosing" to become wage-earners and the number of wage-earners required by entrepreneurs, and thus depends on the entire wealth distribution $F_t(w)$. One can easily see how this can generate long-run effects of the initial wealth distribution: an initially large mass of poor agents with no other option than becoming a wage-earner leads to a low wage rate and little upward mobility for wage earners, while an initially small mass of poor agents leads to high wage rates and high mobility between wage-earners and self-employed, which reproduces the forces leading to high wage rates. Depending on the initial distribution $F_0(w)$, the economy will therefore converge to different possible long-run distributions $F_{\propto 1}(w)$, $F_{\propto 2}(w)$, ... associated with different long-run wage rates $v_{\propto 1}$, $v_{\propto 2}$, ... Although the original Banerjee and Newman (1993) did assume a fixed cost technology (so as to simplify transitional dynamics), the Piketty (1997) model described above clearly shows that their central result would also hold with a standard, concave technology. If both models were combined, i.e., if both the interest rate and the wage rate depend on the wealth distribution, then the general conclusion would be that both long-run factor prices can depend on the initial wealth distribution. Note that this stands in great contrast with models based upon first-best credit, where equilibrium factor prices do not depend at all on the distribution of wealth.

Of course, whether this two-way interaction between the wealth distribution and equilibrium factor prices can be sufficiently strong in practice to generate such long-term effects depends on the empirical magnitude of credit constraints. Banerjee and Newman (1993) point out that historical evidence seems to suggest that this is plausible. Several historians have argued that the two different initial distributions of land in France and in Britain in the early 1800s in the aftermath of the French Revolution did generate persistently divergent development trajectories: the large population of British landless peasants pushed industrial wages down and fostered early industrial development, while the large population of small French landowners delayed the industrial revolution and had long-run implications for French economic development.[58] Such long-run effects

---

[58] See Banerjee and Newman (1993: p. 292) and subsequent preferences. Note that in the context of the Banerjee–Newman model, the UK trajectory would appear as a low wage, low output, "industrial trap". This controversial welfare interpretation can easily be modified by introducing learning-by-doing-type externalities

of the initial wealth distribution on mobility and development would be impossible to explain in a world of first-best capital markets, but can be accounted for by a Banerjee–Newman-type model.

This two-way interaction between the distribution of wealth and equilibrium factor prices implied by credit constraints can also generate other interesting and empirically plausible development patterns. For instance, Aghion and Bolton (1997) show that this interaction can generate trajectories characterized by a declining price of capital and an endogenous Kuznets curve. During the initial stage of development, little capital is available, the equilibrium interest rate is high and strong credit constraints imply that only the rich can invest and wealth, mobility is low and income inequalities tend to widen. The capital accumulation of the rich progressively forces the interest rate to drop, so that credit constraints become less binding, mobility rises and inequality begins to decline.

5. Persistent inequality and local segregation

The importance of local segregation into unequal communities for understanding intergenerational mobility has long been emphasized by sociologists.[59] Formal economic models of equilibrium segregation into unequal neighborhoods have been developed more recently, however. These models are important because they show under what conditions local segregation can be socially inefficient, which is the key question from a policy perspective. We first review the main contributions of these recent theoretical models (Section 5.1). We then analyze their empirical and policy implications (Section 5.2). Finally, we discuss the role of other levels of local segregation (Section 5.3).

5.1. Models of inefficient segregation into unequal neighborhoods

Consider first the following model due to Benabou (1993). Agents must choose to live in one of two spatially distinct neighborhoods and whether to obtain a low education (cost C_L) or a high education (cost C_H). These costs $C_L(x)$ and $C_H(x)$ depend negatively upon the fraction x of one's neighbors choosing to obtain a high education, reflecting the positive external effects of education on one's neighbors (in the classroom, as a role model, ...). Whether or not it is socially optimal to get all agents choosing a high education to live in the same neighborhood depends on the slope of the total educational cost function $C(x)$ given by the following equation:

$$C(x) = xC_H(x) + (1 - x)C_L(x). \tag{5.1}$$

in the large-scale, industrial sector, so that productivity and wages are eventually higher in the industrial development path.

[59] The scientific study of ghettos and residential segregation in the US sociological tradition dates back to the Chicago school of sociology in the interwar period, up to the more recent works of William Julius Wilson (see, e.g., Wilson, 1987).

If $C(x)$ is convex, then for any given optimal number of high-education agents, it is less costly to divide them equally between the 2 neighborhoods. Conversely, segregation is optimal if $C(x)$ is concave.

The key point is that whether segregation or integration will prevail in laissez-faire equilibrium depends on a different condition. Benabou shows that the condition for equilibrium segregation is the following:

$$C'_H(x) < C'_L(x). \qquad (5.2)$$

If condition (5.2) holds, i.e., if the marginal private benefits of having more educated neighbors are higher if one chooses high education, then integration is inherently unstable and market forces push towards stable segregation. The intuition is that if the two neighborhoods have initially a marginally different composition, this condition implies that high-education agents are ready to pay a marginally higher rent to live in the better neighborhood, which leads to more segregation, and so on. The reason why the conditions for social optimality and decentralized equilibrium are different is that high-education agents only take into account their marginal private benefits of moving to a better neighborhood and do not internalize the marginal costs they impose on their initial neighborhood by diminishing the fraction of high-education agents. The failure of the price system is that the housing market does not charge the true social costs of moving: market rents are the same for everybody, whereas a socially-optimal price system should charge a higher rent to high-education movers to a high-education area (or, alternatively, a lower rent to high-education movers to a low-education area). These two conditions also highlight which parameter configurations typically lead to inefficient segregation: if $C'_H(x) < C'_L(x)$ but both slopes are very close, then $C(x)$ will be convex if $C_H(x)$ and $C_L(x)$ are convex, i.e., if the benefits of living with educated people exhibit decreasing returns. Conversely if these returns are increasing segregation will be socially optimal, and so will be the decentralized equilibrium.[60] Note that unlike in the case of credit constraints (see Section 4.1 above), local externalities can make market equilibria inefficient in the Pareto sense: corrective policies cannot only raise total output but also raise everybody's welfare.

In the original Benabou (1993) model, all agents are ex ante equally endowed in human capital, which allows us to identify in a very transparent way the conditions for inefficient segregation. In a dynamic world however, human capital inequality and segregation reinforce each other over time, and segregation leads to lower intergenerational mobility than would otherwise be the case. The model and the conditions for inefficient segregation described above can easily be extended to such a setting. Moreover, Benabou (1996a) has also shown that even if it is less costly in the short-run to have segregated neighborhoods in order to produce more human capital ($C(x)$ concave), segregation may

---

[60] Assume for instance that $C_L(x) = (1 - a)C_H(x) - c$, with a sufficiently close to 0. Then $C''(x) = C''_H(x) - ad^2((1 - x)C_H(x))/dx^2$, which is arbitrarily close to $C''_H(x)$.

not be efficient in the long-run because it tends to amplify future human capital inequality, which can be harmful for total output . Under these conditions there can be a trade-off between minimizing the short-run costs of existing inequality through segregation and minimizing the long-run costs of inequality through mixing and integration. Again, the theoretical model allows us to identify the exact conditions that need to be empirically estimated: the values of the complementarity parameters of the local interaction process and of the global production function determine whether segregation is inefficient from the viewpoint of long-run growth.

In the Benabou model, the forces pushing towards segregation or integration are the pure forces of local externalities (peer effects) and the housing market. This framework can be extended in several directions. First, segregation could be supported by other institutions than a competitive housing market, such as the possibility for local communities to enact zoning regulations, so as to restrict access to their neighborhood to agents meeting specific criteria (income, age, landowner/tenant status, ...), which will in general exacerbate segregation (Durlauf, 1996; Fernandez and Rogerson, 1996). The effects on efficiency are unclear however, since such institutions might also allow communities to internalize the relevant local externalities.

Next, individual motives for segregation can be more complex than direct peer effects. If each community decides how much fiscal revenue to allocate to schools and the quality of schooling depends on the level of educational spendings, this creates an incentive to locate in a wealthy neighborhood, even if there is no direct peer effect at the neighborhood level. The local external effects $C_L(x)$ and $C_H(x)$ of the Benabou model can be interpreted as a reduced form of this "fiscal channel". Explicit models of this "fiscal channel" for local segregation can be found in Fernandez and Rogerson (1994) and Benabou (1996b). Whether segregation will take place and whether it is efficient then depend on the shape of the marginal benefits of having better-funded schools, just as in the Benabou model. For the same reasons as in the Benabou model, there is no reason to suspect that housing prices will lead to an efficient level of segregation. For instance, Fernandez and Rogerson (1994) estimate that the positive output efficiency effects of a switch from local educational finance to federal, redistributive educational finance would be substantial in the US.

Note also that the forces behind inefficient segregation always tend to be magnified by imperfect capital markets. For instance, if one adds to the Benabou model that agents are initially unequal and face credit constraints, then poor agents might be unable to move to a better neighborhood even if $C'_H(x) > C'_L(x)$, i.e., even if their marginal benefits of moving are higher (see Benabou, 1996b).

5.2. *The policy implications of local segregation*

The fact that intergenerational mobility depends not only on parental characteristics but also on the composition of the local neighborhood is well documented (see, e.g., Borjas (1992, 1995) on the effect of ethnic residential segregation). However the fact that segregation matters does not necessarily imply that segregation is socially inefficient. If $C(x)$ was concave (see Eq. (5.1) above), then it would be socially inefficient to try to raise intergenerational mobility by forcing unequal dynasties to live together in homogeneous neighborhoods. If $C(x)$ was concave, it would be more cost-effective to spend available resources to help educate credit-constrained children (Section 4), to fight discrimination (Section 6), or simply to redistribute consumption and welfare if one believes that credit constraints and discrimination are unimportant and markets are efficient (Sections 2 and 3).

It is very difficult however to measure empirically whether the conditions for inefficient segregation identified by the theoretical models are met in practice. One of the main difficulties is the fact that measured neighborhood effects may reflect a spurious correlation, induced by the possibility that the same factors which lead to particular location choices also lead to particular socioeconomic outcomes. Cutler and Glaeser (1997) have developed an ingenious empirical methodology in order to correct for these biases in the formation of racial ghettos, and they find that a one standard deviation decrease in segregation would eliminate one-third of the black-white differential in schooling and employment outcomes.[61] Although they do not compare these costs of segregation with the benefits of segregation enjoyed by well-off neighborhoods, their findings are suggestive.

A very skeptical empirical argument about local segregation has recently been developed by Kremer (1997). Kremer estimates with PSID data that a child's educational attainment can be expressed as 0.39 times the educational attainment of the child's parents, plus 0.15 times the average educational attainment in the census tract in which the child grew up, plus an error term with a standard deviation of 1.79 years of schooling.[62] Kremer concludes that moving from no educational segregation to complete educational segregation would increase the steady-state standard deviation of education by only 9% (from 1.95 years to 2.13 years),[63] and therefore that the magnitudes of the effects are just too small to justify much public concern about residential segregation. However, whether 9% of the steady-state standard deviation should be viewed as small or large is a matter of perspective: Kremer's estimate also imply if the parental persistence parameter was equal to 0 (instead of 0.39), then the steady-state standard deviation of education would decline by only about 8% (from 1.95 to 1.79), although a persistence parameter of 0.39 does mean substantial persistence of inequality across generations (see Section 4.2 above). To put it another way, Kremer's findings also indicate that moving from no segregation to complete segregation would increase the intergenerational persistent

---

[61] Cutler and Glaeser exploit variations across US cities in a number of exogenous factors that are likely to have an impact on the probability of having ghettos, such as the number of rivers and naturally divided neighborhoods.

[62] Mulligan (1993) estimates (also with PSID) data that about 10% of the observed intergenerations correlation of earnings can be attributed to residential segregation. Note however that he uses county-level averages to identify neighborhood effects, which may severely underestimate the true effects of finer local neighborhoods.

[63] $1.95 = 1.79/(1 - 0.39^2)^{1/2}$, and $2.13 = 1.79/(1 - 0.54^2)^{1/2}$. See Kremer (1997: p. 116).

parameter by about 40% (from 0.39 to 0.54), which most observers would view as a substantial effect. Moreover, linear estimates tend to underestimate the effects on mobility at the bottom and at the top of the distribution. Cooper et al. (1994) also use PSID data, but their methodology allows them to find that neighborhoods effects on mobility are highly nonlinear, and that for a given parental income group, intergenerational income correlations can vary by a factor of two depending on the average income of the parents' neighborhood. Finally, note that the key question raised by the theoretical models is not whether neighborhood effects on mobility are small or large, but whether they are larger for more disadvantaged children than for less disadvantaged children, i.e., whether $C(x)$ is convex or concave. The point is that if the conditions for inefficient segregation apply, then it is possible to raise output and intergenerational mobility at the same time, which would look like an interesting thing to do, even if the orders of magnitude were not enormous. From that viewpoint, the Cooper et al. (1994) findings about the strong nonlinearity of neighborhood effects would seem to indicate that Benabou's conditions for inefficient segregation are likely to be satisfied. If marginal changes in neighborhood composition produce large effects on the mobility prospects of kids at the very bottom of the distribution and moderate effects on the mobility prospects of middle-class kids, then integrated neighborhoods might well be socially efficient.

The theoretical models also raise the question of whether the peer effect channel or the fiscal channel of local interaction is most important. If residential segregation matters mostly because of its effect on local funding for education, then one does not need to force neighborhoods to be socially integrated in order to correct the negative effects of segregation: it is sufficient to redistribute educational resources across neighborhoods, for instance through a uniform national system of educational finance. However if local externalities operate mostly through the peer effect channel, i.e., via direct interaction between children who are in the same school, role models, etc.,[64] rather than educational finance per se, then more radical policies are necessary: one needs to intervene directly on the housing market, e.g., by subsidizing low-rent housing in wealthy neighborhoods, and/or to force children coming from unequal neighborhoods to go to the same school, e.g., via busing policies.[65] Such radical policies are very difficult to implement, because of their strong interference with what most parents consider as their purely private choices. This explains why low estimates of the effects of redistributing educational

---

[64] Roemer and Wets (1994) have recently proposed endogenizing peer effects in informational terms. They assume that agents are uncertain about the shape of the convex relationship between the level of human capital investment and the resulting market income, and that they learn about this relationship through linear extrapolation of the (human capital investment, market income) vector that they observe in their social neighborhood. They show that this can generate persistent inequality in human capital investment and market income between otherwise identical neighborhoods, which provides yet another example of a "self-fulfilling" theory of inequality (see Section 6).

[65] This opposition between educational finance and housing/busing policies should not be overestimated, however. In practice, some degree of local responsibility over educational finance can be beneficial for other reasons, so that even if local interaction operates only through the fiscal channel, it might be socially efficient to force neighborhoods to be somewhat integrated.

finance across neighborhoods have usually been interpreted as negative results from a policy perspective.[66] For instance, the conclusion of the Coleman (1966) report, who argued that financial transfers to the schools of disadvantaged neighborhoods had little effect on educational performance, was that there is not much to do about local segregation and persistent inequality.[67] However such results could also be interpreted as the proof that more radical housing and busing policies are necessary.

5.3. Other levels of segregation

Residential segregation is not the only level of segregation that can have tremendous consequences for intergenerational mobility. Other potentially important levels of local interaction include the family and the firm.

At the level of the family, it is obvious why positive assortative mating can contribute to make inequality more persistent across generations: if children's abilities depend on the characteristics of both parents, then the fact that men and women with similar characteristics tend to mate together makes intergenerational mobility lower than it would be under random matching. Kremer (1995) argues that a cumulative mechanism might exist along similar lines: if higher human capital inequality increases the incentives to marry with someone of similar human capital level, then higher human capital inequality between parents leads to higher human capital inequality between children, and so on. Kremer illustrates the relevance of these cumulative dynamics by contrasting the US case with that of Brazil.[68] However the key difference between residential segregation and assortative mating is that the housing price system is unable to internalize all relevant external effects (see the Benabou model in Section 5.1 above), whereas potential partners should in principle be able to internalize the effects of assortative mating on their children. Gary Becker has repeatedly argued that positive assortative mating is likely to be an efficient market outcome (see especially Becker, 1991: Chap. 4). Things can be different in models where marriage patterns result from private concern about relative status and some self-enforced social norm.[69]

If human capital acquisition is influenced by one's coworkers (just as by one's neighbors and one's parents), then skill segregation at the firm level can also contribute to make inequality more persistent. Kremer and Maskin (1995) have argued that higher human capital inequality can increase the incentives of high-skill workers to break away

---

[66] This is again another example of the "do nothing or hit the family" dilemma (see Section 3.2).

[67] Coleman's empirical results have however been challenged by more recent estimates using post-school wages rather than standardized tests (see, e.g., Card and Krueger, 1992).

[68] Whether marital sorting has recently increased in the US is controversial. Kremer (1997) finds the correlation between spouses' education has declined somewhat. However Meyer (1995) estimates that almost half of the total increase of US household income inequality during the past 20 years can be accounted for by the rise in the correlation between spouses' earnings (she also finds that almost 40% of the rise of this correlation can be attributed to the rise of divorce: marital sorting is on average higher for second marriages than for first marriages, probably because more information about potential partners' permanent attributes is available at the age of second marriages).

[69] See Cole et al. (1992) for such a model.

from low-skill workers and to work together. For instance, assume that there two possible human capital levels in the population, h_1 and h_2, with $h_1 > h_2$. If production requires two workers (one "manager" and one "assistant") and output is given by $Y = h_A h_M^2$ (where h_A is the assistant's human capital and h_M is the manager's human capital), then one can show that it will be efficient for high-human-capital agents to work together if and only if the human capital ratio h_1/h_2 is larger than some threshold $\lambda > 1$. Similar intuitions can be obtained with more general production functions (see Kremer and Maskin, 1995). Kremer and Maskin show that this process might be relevant to account for the recent evolution of wage inequality in western countries: they find that in almost every production sector the variance of the distribution of firm-level mean wages has increased much more rapidly than the mean variance of the firm-level distribution of wages. In the Kremer–Maskin model, equilibrium skill segregation between firms is efficient: forcing firms to be more integrated would diminish total output, and it would again be more efficient to have a purely redistributive tax on earnings and to let the market do its job. However, this need not be the case in general. In case the initial productivity of lower-skill workers in high-skill firms is very low, then wealth constraints might prevent lower-skill workers from joining such firms, even if the long-run productivity effects of interacting with high-skill workers were higher for them than for higher-skill workers. This illustrates once again the importance of distinguishing between local segregation as a general channel of inequality transmission and local segregation as a source of inefficient persistent inequality.

6. Persistent inequality and self-fulfilling beliefs

Can self-fulfilling beliefs alone generate persistent inequality across generations? One answer is given by the well-known model of statistical discrimination (Phelps, 1968; Arrow, 1973). We first review the basic mechanism and policy implications of the theory of discrimination (Section 6.1). A number of sociologists have also been interested in phenomena of self-fulfilling inequality, and we will briefly review these theories in Section 6.2.

6.1. The theory of discrimination

Assume that two social groups (say, the blacks and the whites) have the same distribution $G(c)$ of private costs c to become a qualified worker. These costs can measure the heterogeneity of tastes with respect to human capital investment, as well as the heterogeneity of investment potentials and abilities. If employers could perfectly observe whether a given would-be employee has made the investment or not, then there would exist a unique threshold c^* below which individuals would choose to invest. There would be no systematic inequality between the two social groups. Assume however that employers only observe a noisy signal θ of workers' qualification. Then under appropriate assumptions there exists a discriminatory hiring policy (θ_B, θ_W) which is self-fulfilling. This can be an equilibrium because if employers are expected to promote to qualified tasks black workers with a $\theta \geq \theta_B$ and white workers with a $\theta \geq \theta_W < \theta_B$, then this discourages black workers and induces them to become qualified less often than the whites (the threshold cost c_B is lower than c_W). This in turn validates employers' discriminatory priors. That is, persistent intergenerational inequality between two social groups with homogenous characteristics has been generated solely out of self-fulfilling beliefs. More generally, self-fulfilling discriminatory beliefs can make the inequality between social groups with initially unequal characteristics more persistent than it would otherwise be.

Although the development of this theory of statistical discrimination was primarily inspired by racial discrimination in the US, one can apply this same logic to other observationally distinguishable groups than blacks and whites. For instance, Acemoglu (1995) shows in a model where employers imperfectly observe whether unemployed have paid the cost to recover their skills that an equilibrium where unemployed do not incur this cost and are discriminated by employers can be supported by self-fulfilling beliefs. He then shows how this can justify policies of positive discrimination towards long-term unemployed, although such policies would seem inefficient in a model where the latter are simply less productive. More generally, persistent inequality through self-fulfilling beliefs can be generated between men and women, upper-caste and lower-caste dynasties, high-wealth and low-wealth dynasties, etc. Wilson (1987) has argued that residential segregation tends to increase labor market discrimination. The idea is that if employers can more easily associate a particular set of would-be employees to a specific, disadvantaged neighborhood, then self-fulfilling discriminatory beliefs can more easily develop. Since credit constraints also tend to make residential segregation more likely (see Section 5.1), this means that credit imperfections, local segregation and discrimination can operate together and lead to a cumulative process of socially-inefficient persistent inequality.

Assume that persistent intergenerational inequality is due to discrimination, at least in part. What would socially-efficient redistribution look like? First, note that statistical discrimination is grossly inefficient: first-best efficiency would require all individuals with similar characteristics to make the same investments. That is, corrective policies could simultaneously raise output and make inequality less persistent, just as in the case of credit constraints and residential segregation (see Sections 4 and 5). The ideal corrective policy would be to force employers to use the same testing requirements $\theta_B = \theta_W$ for every social group. This would immediately put an end to self-fulfilling discriminatory beliefs. The problem is that it might be difficult to observe the threshold θ which is applied by employers. This issue of optimal second-best anti-discrimination policies has recently been addressed by Coate and Loury (1993). Coate and Loury argue that direct anti-discrimination policies are in general not enforceable, and that in practice affirmative action policies look much more like quotas: employers must end up with the same distribution of black and white workers in their qualified and unqualified tasks. Coate and Loury then distinguish between two cases. First, they show that if initial discrimination is not complete, in the sense that a positive fraction of black workers ends up in qualified tasks, then quota-type policies are generally dominated by a policy of state-financed income subsidy to black workers promoted to qualified tasks, which would gradually eliminate discrimination. The intuition is that quotas can lead to "patronizing" hiring policies whereby employers reduce their standards θ_B so much in order to meet the quota that black workers have even less incentives to become qualified than in the previous situation. However, if we start from a situation where θ_B is so high that no black worker is allocated to qualified tasks (complete discrimination), then quota-type affirmative action is the only way to make progress. In any case, note that the optimal policy tool (race-specific income subsidies to promotion, or quotas) would be difficult to justify without a model of persistent inequality based upon self-fulfilling beliefs. Coate and Loury's analysis of corrective policies in the discrimination model also illustrates what may be the most important contribution of formal economic modeling to our understanding of inequality and redistribution. In the same way as in the case of credit constraints (see Section 4.1), formal economic modeling of discrimination makes transparent the fact that the informational imperfections that generate market failures and inefficient inequalities also apply to government and public policies, thereby making government intervention more difficult than it would otherwise be.

Whether unconventional policy tools such as quotas and other affirmative-action policies are appropriate depends however on whether one believes that statistical discrimination is an important source of inequality. For instance, Friedman (1962) argues that to the extent that discrimination does exist, i.e., to the extent that persistent earnings inequality does not simply derive from the "normal" family transmission of unequal abilities, discrimination is due primarily to consumers' tastes rather than to employers' discriminatory behavior. Friedman concludes that there is not much to do about discrimination per se: redistribution should rather take the form of a transparent redistributive tax on labor earnings, and the rates of such a negative income tax should be relatively low, so as to minimize the incentive costs of redistribution. Herrnstein and Murray (1994: Chaps. 19–20) argue that persistent racial inequality can easily be accounted for by the transmission of unequal cognitive abilities across generations, with no need for a theory of discrimination. They also argue that the average cognitive ability of blacks in top universities and top occupations is now lower than that of their white counterparts, which shows how inefficient affirmative action policies in higher education and on the workplace have been. Most labor economists seem to have a more balanced view of the empirical relevance of employers' discrimination. According to Freeman (1973, 1981), a large part of the narrowing of the black/white earnings gap since 1964 can be attributed to the Civil Rights movement and the development of affirmative action policies. Neal and Johnson (1996) also find evidence of current labor market discrimination, although they argue that the most important part of racial inequality in the US can be explained by a skill gap that can be measured by test scores at age 16, i.e., before labor market discrimination. It is true however that it is extremely difficult to distinguish empirically the effects of discriminatory beliefs from the many other channels through which unequal social and cultural attitudes can be transmitted across generations.[70]

6.2. Sociologists' theories of self-fulfilling inequality

Unlike economists, whose formal models of "self-fulfilling inequality" are to a large extent unconventional and do not reflect the way mainstream economists usually think about labor markets and earnings inequality, mainstream sociologists' theories have always emphasized the role of "beliefs" and related cultural attitudes in the generation of persistent inequality between dynasties. In particular, the very influential works of French sociologist Pierre Bourdieu all describe the various social processes through which individuals from lower-class backgrounds are being discouraged by the "dominant discourse" from making adequate mobility-enhancing investments, especially within the schooling system (see, e.g., Bourdieu and Passeron, 1964, 1970).[71] For instance, lower-class children can be discouraged by school teachers who tell them they have no chance of going to a good college and they should opt for a more "reasonable" school orientation. Lower class individuals can also be discouraged by bosses who tell them that they will never be sufficiently able to be a manager and that should better accept their life as a factory worker. More generally, lower class individuals can be discouraged by the general "dominant discourse" produced by politicians, opinion leaders and the capitalist system as a whole, according to which persistent inequality is basically efficient and lower-class dynasties should better accept their inferior role. According to Bourdieu, they can be discouraged to such an extent that they "internalize" entirely the low probabilities of social ascent enjoyed by their peers within the current structure of social inequality and adopt behaviors that validate the "dominant discourse".

There exists an obvious similarity between Bourdieu's theory and the theory of self-fulfilling discriminatory beliefs described above. In both cases, inequality is persistent simply because the elite expects inequality to be persistent, so that the poor are discouraged and validate the elite's expectation. One important difference is that the theory of statistical discrimination puts the blame exclusively on employers, which leads to a number of specific policy recommendations (see Section 6.1 above). In contrast, Bourdieu's theory tends to put the blame on the society as a whole, so that the set of appropriate policy tools is potentially enormous. For instance, Bourdieu implicitly suggests that one just needs to change the "dominant discourse", e.g., by writing books.

Note that the emphasis by sociologists on beliefs and non-economic sources of persistent inequality is not confined to "left-wing" theories. Indeed, most sociologists agree

---

[70] See Ichino and Ichino (1997) for a recent attempt to distinguish between persistent inequality due to the intergenerational transmission of cultural attitudes and persistent inequality due to discrimination, in the context of the inequality between southern and northern Italian workers (they use labor market data about north-south migrants).

[71] Other radical analysis of how the conservative ideology of the school system might contribute to make inequality more persistent than it would otherwise be have also been produced in the US (see, e.g., Bowles and Gintis, 1975).

that intergenerational inequality persists above and beyond the pure transmission of ability differentials, but they disagree about the extent to which this economically useless
inequality can be altered by policy. For instance, one of the main counter-arguments
to Bourdieu's theories is based upon the "reference group" theory, according to which
inequality is persistent simply because lower-class families transmit less ambition and
taste for economic success than upper-class families (see Section 3.3 above). It is interesting to note that the conflict between Bourdieu's theory and the reference group
theory is at the origin of the major, long-standing controversy within French sociology,
after the reference group theory had been advocated by Boudon (1973, 1974). To a large
extent, this conflict is still the major dividing line in the French community of academic sociologists, where scholars need to affiliate themselves either as pro-Bourdieu or
pro-Boudon. The conflict about the existence of efficient corrective policies is obvious:
both theories describe persistent inequality as a self-fulfilling phenomena, whereby poor
dynasties remain poor because of their lack of ambition, but Bourdieu puts the blame
on society and suggests that radical activism can easily raise social mobility, whereas
Boudon insists that there is nobody to blame for it, unless one is ready to destroy the
family institution.[72] As we have seen in the case of statistical discrimination, the parameters involved in these conflicting theories are extremely difficult (if not impossible) to
measure empirically, which may explain why these political conflicts are so persistent.

The claims made by radical sociologists should however not be dismissed on purely
a priori grounds. Needless to say, the idea that discourse and beliefs alone can have a
significant impact on "real" economic inequality sounds inherently suspicious to most
economists. Economists legitimately consider that redistributive taxation can at least
alleviate with certainty the "real" inequality of living standards, as compared to the uncertain outcomes of "beliefs politics". On the other hand, it is probably true for instance
that the dramatic improvement of the relative economic position of women during the
twentieth century, which probably constitutes the most spectacular redistribution that
has ever happened, has not happened through fiscal redistribution and economic policies
but rather through the evolution of beliefs and mental attitudes towards women. In the
same way, it is not impossible that the discourses of Gandhi have done more to modify
social attitudes toward lower-caste Indians and to improve their economic prospects than
any straight economic redistribution could ever have. It is also possible that all those
phenomena that noneconomists attribute to "discourse" or changing mental attitudes
towards others can actually be explained by some underlying "technological" evolution
of demand and supply, so that discourse is just a veil, but this needs to be proven rather
than assumed. The challenge for economists is to be able to recognize and measure the
relative importance of such channels of inequality transmission and at the same time
maintain the rigor and the intellectual standards of the discipline.

---

[72] See Section 3.3 and Piketty (1998). Note that the Piketty (1995) model of dynastic learning about the
income responsiveness of effort (see Section 3.2 above) offers another theory of self-fulfilling inequality where
there is nobody to blame (different dynasties just happen to have different experimentation trajectories).

References

Abel, A.B. and D.B. Bernheim (1991), Fiscal policy with impure intergenerational altruism, Journal of Political Economy 59: 1687–1711.

Acemoglu, D. (1995), Public policy in a model of long-term unemployment, Economica 62: 161–178.

Aghion, P. and P. Bolton (1997), A trickle-down theory of growth and development with debt-overhang, Review of Economic Studies 64: 151–172.

Aiyagari, S. (1994), Optimal Capital Income Taxation with Incomplete Markets, Borrowing Constraints and Constant Discounting, mimeo, Minneapolis.

Arrow, K. (1972), The theory of Discrimination, in O. Ashenfelter and A. Rees, eds., Discrimination on Labor Markets (Princeton University Press).

Atkinson, A.B. (1980), Inheritance and the redistribution of wealth, in G.A. Hughes and G.M. Heal, eds., Public Policy and the Tax System: Essays in Honour of James Meade (Allen and Unwin, London).

Atkinson, A.B. (1981), On intergenerational income mobility in Britain, Journal of Post-Keynesian Economics 3: 194–218.

Atkinson, A.B., A.K. Maynard and C.G. Trinder (1983), Parents and Children: Incomes in Two Generations (Heinemann, London).

Banerjee, A. and M. Ghatak (1996), Empowerment and efficiency: the economics of tenancy reform, mimeo, MIT.

Banerjee, A. and A. Newman (1993), Occupational choice and the process of development, Journal of Political Economy 101: 274–299.

Banerjee, A. and A. Newman (1994), Poverty, incentives and development, American Economic Review 84: 211–216.

Becker, G. (1988), Family economics and macro behavior, American Economic Review 78: 1–13.

Becker, G. (1989), On the economics of the family: reply to a skeptic, American Economic Review 79: 514–518.

Becker, G. (1991), A Treatise on the Family (Harvard University Press).

Becker, G. and N. Tomes (1979), An equilibrium theory of the distribution of income and intergenerational mobility, Journal of Political Economy 87: 1153–1189. (reprinted as chapter 7 of Becker (1991)).

Becker, G. and N. Tomes (1986), Human capital and the rise and fall of families, Journal of Labor Economics 4: S1–S39. (reprinted as supplement to chapter 7 of Becker (1991)).

Becker, G. and R. Barro (1988), A reformulation of the economic theory of fertility, Quarterly Journal of Economics 103: 1-25. (reprinted as supplement to chapter 5 of Becker (1991)).

Behrman, J.R. and P. Taubman (1985), Intergenerational earnings mobility in the United States: some estimates and a test of Becker's intergenerational endowments model, Review of Economics and Statistics 67: 144–151.

Benabou, R. (1993), Workings of a city: location, education, production, Quarterly Journal of Economics 108: 619–653.

Benabou, R. (1996a), Heterogeneity, stratification and growth: macroeconomic implications of community structure and school finance, American Economic Review 86: 584–609.

Benabou, R. (1996b), Equity and efficiency in human capital investment: the local connection, Review of Economic Studies 63: 237–264.

Benabou, R. (1997), What Level of Redistribution Maximizes Long-Run Output? mimeo, New York University.

Bernheim, D.B. (1991), How strong are bequest motives? evidence based on estimates of the demand for life insurance and annuities, Journal of Political Economy 99: 899–927.

Bernheim, D.B. and K. Bagwell (1988), Is everything neutral? Journal of Political Economy 96: 308–338.

Bjorklund, A. and M. Jantti (1998), Intergenerational mobility of economic status: is the United States different? Working Paper (Swedish Institute for Social Research, Stockholm).

Borjas, G.J. (1992), Ethnic capital and intergenerational mobility, Quarterly Journal of Economics 107: 123–150.

Borjas, G.J. (1995), Ethnicity, neighborhoods and human capital externalities, American Economic Review 85: 365–390.

Bourdieu, P. and J.C. Passeron (1964), Les héritiers (Les éditions de Minuit, Paris).

Bourdieu, P. and J.C. Passeron (1970), La reproduction (Les éditions de Minuit, Paris).

Boudon, R. (1973), L'inégalité des chances (Armand Colin, Paris).

Boudon, R. (1974), Education, Opportunity and Social Inequality (Wiley, New York).

Bourguignon, F.(1981), Pareto-superiority of unegalitarian equilibria in Stiglitz' model of wealth distribution with convex savings function, Econometrica 49: 1469–1475.

Bowles, S. (1972), Schooling and inequality from generation to generation, Journal of Political Economy 80: S219–S251.

Bowles, S. and H. Gintis (1976), Schooling in Capitalist America (Basic Books, New York).

Card, D. and A. Krueger (1992), Does school quality matter? Journal of Political Economy 100: 1–40.

Card, D. and A. Krueger (1995), Myth and Measurement: the New Economics of the Minimum Wage (Princeton University Press).

Chamley, C. (1996), Capital Income Taxation, Income Distribution and Borrowing constraints, mimeo (DELTA, Paris).

Chu, C.Y. (1991), Primogeniture, Journal of Political Economy 99: 78–99.

Coate, S. and G. Loury (1993), Will affirmative-action policies eliminate negative stereotypes? American Economic Review 83: 1220–1240.

Cole, H., G. Mailath and A. Postlewaite (1992), Social norms, savings behavior and growth, Journal of Political Economy 100: 1092–1125.

Coleman, J. (1966), Equality of Educational Opportunity, Report to the US Department of Health, Education and Welfare.

Conlisk, J. (1974), Can equalization of opportunity reduce social mobility? American Economic Review 64: 80–90.

Cooper, S., S. Durlauf and P. Johnson (1994), On the evolution of economic status across generations, American Statistical Association, Business and Economics Section, Papers and Proceedings 50–58.

Cutler, D.M. and E.L. Glaeser (1997), Are ghettos good or bad? Quarterly Journal of Economics 112: 827–872.

Dearden, L., S. Machin and H. Reed (1997), Intergenerational mobility in Britain, Economic Journal 107: 47–66.

Durlauf, S. (1996), A theory of persistent income inequality, Journal of Economic Growth 1: 75–93.

Erikson, R. and J.H. Goldthorpe (1985), Are American rates of social mobility exceptionally high? European Sociological Review 1: 1–22.

Erikson, R. and J.H. Goldthorpe (1992), The Constant Flux: A Study of Class Mobility in Industrial Societies (Clarendon Press, Oxford).

Feldstein, M. (1995), The effects of marginal tax rates on taxable income: a panel study of the 1986 tax reform act, Journal of Political Economy 103: 551–572.

Fernandez, R. and R. Rogerson (1994), Public Education and Income Distribution: A Quantitative Evaluation of School Finance Reform, NBER Working Paper 4883.

Fernandez, R. and R. Rogerson (1996), Income distribution, communities and the quality of public education, Quarterly Journal of Economics 111: 135–164.

Freeman, R. (1973), Changes in the labor market status of black Americans, 1948–1972, Brookings Papers on Economic Activity 1: 67–120.

Freeman, R. (1981), Black economic progress after 1964: who has gained and why? in S. Rosen, ed., Studies in Labor Markets (Chicago University Press).

Freeman, S. (1996), Equilibrium income inequality among identical agents, Journal of Political Economy 104: 1047–1064.

Friedman, M. (1962), Capitalism and Freedom (The University of Chicago Press).

Galor, O. and J. Zeira (1993), Income distribution and macroeconomics, Review of Economic Studies 60: 35–52.

Gilchrist, S. and C.P. Himmelberg (1995), Evidence on the role of cash flow for investment, Journal of Monetary Economics 36: 541–572.

Goldberger, A. (1989), Economic and mechanical models of intergenerational transmission, American Economic Review 79: 504–513.

Goux, D. and E. Maurin (1996), Meritocracy and social heredity in France: some aspects and trends, European Sociological Review.

Green, L., J. Myerson, D. Lichtman, S. Rosen and A. Fry (1996), Temporal discounting in choices between delayed rewards: the role of age and income, Psychology and Aging 11: 79–84.

Herrnstein, R. and C. Murray (1994), The Bell Curve: Intelligence and Class Structure in American Life (The Free Press).

Ichino, A., D. Checchi and A. Rustichini (1997), More Equal but Less Mobile? Education Financing and Intergenerational Mobility in Italy and the U.S., mimeo (Universita Bocconi and IGIER).

Ichino, A. and P. Ichino (1997), Culture, Discrimination and Individual Productivity: Regional Evidence from Personnel Data in a Large Italian Firm, CEPR Discussion Paper No. 1709.

Jaffee, D. and J. Stiglitz (1990), Credit rationing, in B. Friedman and F. Hahn, eds., Handbook of Monetary Economics, Vol. 2 (Elsevier Science Publishers).

Judd, K. (1985), Redistributive taxation in a simple perfect foresight model, Journal of Public Economics 28: 59–83.

Kaelble, H. (1986), Social Mobility in the Nineteenth and Twentieth Centuries: Europe and America in Comparative Perspective (St. Martin's Press, New York).

Kessler, D. and A. Masson (1989), Bequests and wealth accumulation: are some pieces of the puzzle missing? Journal of Economic Perspectives 3: 141–152.

Kotlikoff, L.J. (1988), Intergenerational transfers and savings, Journal of Economic Perspectives 2: 41–58.

Kremer, M. (1994), The Dynamics of Inequality: US vs Brazil, mimeo, MIT.

Kremer, M. (1997), How much does sorting increase inequality? Quarterly Journal of Economics 112: 115–140.

Kremer, M. and E. Maskin (1995), Segregation by Skill and the Rise in Inequality, NBER Working Paper 5718.

Lamont, O. (1997), Cash flow and investment: evidence from internal capital markets, Journal of Finance 52: 83–109.

Lawrence, E.C. (1991), Poverty and the rate of time-preference: evidence from panel data, Journal of Political Economy 99: 54–77.

Legros, P. and A. Newman (1996), Wealth effects and the theory of organisation, Journal of Economic Theory 70: 312–341.

Lipset, S.M. and R. Bendix (1959), Social Mobility in Industrial Society (University of California Press, Berkeley).

Lipset, S.M. and R. Bendix (1966), Class, Status, and Power: Social Stratification in Comparative Perspective, 2nd. edn. (The Free Press, New York).

Loury, G. (1981), Intergenerational transfers and the distribution of earnings, Econometrica 49: 843–867.

Lucas, R. (1990), Supply-side economics: an analytical review, Oxford Economic Papers 42: 34–45.

Mayshar, J. and S. Benninga (1996), Heterogeneity of Intertemporal Tastes and Efficient Capital Markets as Sources for Inequality: Extending a Theme by Rae and Ramsey with some Policy Implications, mimeo, Hebrew University.

Merllié, D. and J. Prévot (1991), La mobilité sociale (La Découverte, Paris).

Merton, R. (1953), Reference group theory and social mobility, in R. Bendix and S.M. Lipset, eds., Class, Status and Power (The Free Press, New York).

Meyer, C.(1995), Income Distribution and Family Structure, PhD dissertation (Department of Economics, MIT).

Modigliani, F. (1988), The role of intergenerational transfers and life cycle saving in the accumulation of wealth, Journal of Economic Perspectives 2: 15–40.

Mulligan, C. (1993), On Intergenerational Altruism, Fertility and the Persistence of Economic Status, PhD dissertation (Department of Economics, University of Chicago).

Mulligan, C. (1997), Parental Priorities and Economic Inequality (The University of Chicago Press).

Murphy, K.M., A. Shleifer and R.W. Vishny (1989), Income distribution, market size and industrialization, Quarterly Journal of Economics 104: 537–564.

Neal, D.A. and W.R. Johnson (1996), The role of pre-market factors in black-white wage differences, Journal of Political Economy 104: 869–895.

Newman, A. (1991), The Capital Market, Inequality and the Employment Relation, mimeo, Columbia University.

Phelps, E. (1968), The statistical theory of racism and sexism', American Economic Review **62**, 659–661.

Piketty, T.(1995), Social mobility and redistributive politics, Quarterly Journal of Economics 110: 551–584.

Piketty, T.(1997), The dynamics of the wealth distribution and the interest rate with credit-rationing, Review of Economic Studies 64: 173–189.

Piketty, T. (1998), Self-fulfilling beliefs about social status, Journal of Public Economics 70:1 115–132.

Roemer, J. and R. Wets (1994), Neighborhood Effects on Belief Formation and the Distribution of Education and Income, mimeo, UC Davis.

Schiff, M., M. Duyme, A. Dumaret and S. Tomkiewicz (1982), How much could we boost scholastic achievement and IQ scores? A direct answer from a French adoption study, Cognition 12: 165–196.

Schiff, M. and R. Lewontin (1986), Education and Class: the Irrelevance of IQ Genetic Studies (Clarendon Press, Oxford).

Shavit, Y. and H.P. Blossfeld (1993), Persistent Inequality: Changing Educational Attainment in Thirteen Countries (Westview Press).

Slemrod, J. (1995), Income creation or income shifting? Behavioral responses to the Tax Reform Act of 1986, American Economic Review 85: 175–180.

Solon, G. (1992), Intergenerational income mobility in the United States, American Economic Review 82: 393–408.

Stiglitz, J. (1969), Distribution of income and wealth among individuals, Econometrica 37: 382–397.

Stiglitz, J. (1978), Equality, taxation and inheritance, in W. Krell and A.F. Shorrocks, eds, Personal Income Distribution (North-Holland, Amsterdam).

Thurow, L. (1975), Generating Inequality: Mechanisms of Distribution in the US Economy (Basic Books, New York).

Wilson, W.J. (1987), The Truly Disadvantaged: The Inner City, the Underclass, and Public Policy (University of Chicago Press).

Zimmerman, D.J. (1992), Regression toward mediocrity in economic stature, American Economic Review 82: 409–429.

Chapter 9

MACROECONOMICS OF DISTRIBUTION AND GROWTH

GIUSEPPE BERTOLA*

Università di Torino and European University Institute

Contents

* I thank participants at the Handbook conference and Luigi Pasinetti for comments and conversations, A.B. Atkinson, Onorato Castellino, Giovanni Pavanelli, Josef Zweimueller, and especially François Bourguignon for comments on previous drafts, and Jessica Spataro for editorial assistance. I am most grateful to students at the Institut für Höhere Studien and at the European University Institute (especially Winfried Koeniger), who attended lectures based on this material and made many detailed comments. Financial support from C.N.R., M.U.R.S.T. and the Research Council of the E.U.I. is gratefully acknowledged.

Handbook of Income Distribution, Volume 1. Edited by A.B. Atkinson and F. Bourguignon

Abstract

This chapter reviews various interactions between the distribution of income across in-dividuals and factors of production on the one hand, and aggregate savings, investment, and macroeconomic growth on the other. Tractable models necessarily focus on specific causal channels within this complex web of interactions, and the survey is organized around a few relevant methodological insights. In a "neoclassical" economy where all intra- and intertemporal markets exist and clear competitively, all distributional issues should be resolved before market interactions address the economic problem of allocat-ing scarce resources efficiently, and the dynamics of income and consumption distrib-ution have no welfare implications. Other models, recognizing that market interactions need not maximize a hypothetical representative individual's welfare, let accumulated and nonaccumulated factors of production be owned by individuals with exogenously or endogenously different saving propensities, and feature interactions between the per-sonal and functional distribution of resources and macroeconomic accumulation. Fur-thermore, rates of return to savings and investments are generally heterogeneous when they are only partially (if at all) interconnected by financial markets, as is the case in overlapping generation economies, in models with binding self-financing constraints, and in models where financial market imperfections let individual consumption flows be affected by idiosyncratic uncertainty. The chapter also reviews models where distri-butional tensions, far from being resolved ex ante, work their way through distortionary policies and market interactions to bear directly on both macroeconomic dynamics and income distribution. Finally, it relates theoretical insights to recent empirical work on cross-country growth dynamics and on relationships between within-country inequality and macroeconomic performance.

JEL codes: O4, economic growth and aggregate productivity; O16, financial markets; saving and capital investment; D3, distribution; D72, economic models of political processes; E25, aggregate factor income distribution

1. Introduction

"Macroeconomics" and "distribution" are a somewhat odd couple of words, almost an oxymoron in some contexts. While macroeconomists find it convenient to characterize economic behavior in terms of a single "representative" agent's microeconomic problems, it is only too easy to point out that relationships among aggregate variables are much more complex when individuals' objectives and/or economic circumstances are heterogeneous, as must be the case if distribution is an issue. Any attempt to model economies inhabited by millions of intrinsically different individuals would of course find it impossible to obtain results of any generality. Hence, the distinguished strands of literature that do study interactions between macroeconomic phenomena and distributional issues need to restrict appropriately the extent and character of cross-sectional heterogeneity, trading some loss of microeconomic detail for macroeconomic tractability and insights.

This chapter reviews various interactions between the distribution of income across individuals and factors of production on the one hand, and aggregate savings, investment, and macroeconomic growth on the other. It would be impossible to cover exhaustively these and related aspects of the literature here. Many insightful reviews of the subject are already available, ranging from Hahn and Matthews (1964), through the contributions collected in Asimakopoulos (1988), to the surveys of recent research offered by Bénabou (1996c) and by the papers in the January 1997 special issue of the *Journal of Economic Dynamics and Control*. In fact, distributional issues are so complex and so central to economic theories of accumulation and value determination as to call for book-length treatments (such as Roemer, 1981; Marglin, 1984; Kurz and Salvadori, 1995 among the most recent). This necessarily limited survey makes only passing references to such deeper issues and mainly focuses on methodological aspects, with the aim of highlighting how appropriate modeling strategies make it possible to study macroeconomic dynamics without abstracting from distributional issues.

1.1. Overview

At both the aggregate and individual levels, income dynamics depend endogenously on the propensity to save rather than consume currently available resources and on the rate at which accumulation is rewarded by the economic system. In turn, the distribution of resources across individuals and across accumulated and nonaccumulated factors of production may determine both the volume and the productivity of savings and investment. Tractable models necessarily focus on specific causal channels within this complex web of interactions. The survey is organized around a few such methodological insights.

The models reviewed in Section 2 study, under suitable functional form assumptions, the interaction of macroeconomic accumulation with the distribution of income, consumption, and wealth distribution when savings are invested in an integrated market.

When all intra- and intertemporal markets exist and clear competitively—i.e., when the economy is "neoclassical" for short—then savings are rewarded on the basis of their marginal productivity in a well-defined aggregate production function. In that setting, however, all distributional issues are resolved before market interactions even begin to address the economic problem of allocating scarce resources efficiently, and the dynamics of income and consumption distribution have no welfare implications.

In earlier and more recent models, by contrast, the functional distribution of aggregate income is less closely tied to efficiency considerations, and is quite relevant to both personal income distribution and aggregate accumulation. Section 2.2.1 outlines interactions between distribution and macroeconomic accumulation when accumulated and nonaccumulated factors are owned by classes of individuals with different saving propensities. Not only Classical and post-Keynesian contributions, but also many recent models of endogenous growth let factor rewards be determined by more complex mechanisms than simple allocative efficiency. If factor rewards result from imperfect market interactions and/or policy interventions, aggregate accumulation need not maximize a hypothetical representative agent's welfare even when it is driven by individually optimal saving decisions. It is then natural to explore the implications of factor-income distribution for personal income distribution and for macroeconomic outcomes. The discussion of such models in Section 2.2.2 offers simple insights in balanced-growth situations, where factor shares are immediately relevant to the speed of economic growth and, through factor ownership, to the distribution of income and consumption across individuals.

The models reviewed in Section 3 recognize that rates of return to savings and investments are generally heterogeneous when they are only partially (if at all) interconnected by financial markets in potentially integrated macroeconomies. Under certainty, the scope of financial markets is limited by finite planning horizons in the overlapping-generations models considered in Section 3.1, and by self-financing constraints in models discussed in Section 3.2. If the rate of return on individual investment is inversely related to wealth levels, then inequality tends to disappear over time and reduces the efficiency of investment. If instead the large investments made by rich self-financing individuals have relatively high rates of return, then inequality persists and widens as a subset of individuals cannot escape poverty traps, and unequal wealth distributions are associated with higher aggregate returns to investment.

Section 3.3 reviews how idiosyncratic uncertainty may affect the dynamics of income distribution and of aggregate income. A complete set of competitive financial markets would again make it straightforward to study aggregate dynamics on a representative-individual basis, and deny any macroeconomic relevance to resource distribution across agents. While financial markets can be perfect and complete in only one way, they can and do fall short of that ideal in many different ways. In the models considered by Section 3.3.1, returns to individual investment are subject to idiosyncratic uncertainty which might, but need not, be eliminated by pooling risk in an integrated financial market. Section 3.3.2 discusses the impact of financial market imperfection for savings, growth, and distribution in the complementary polar case where all individual asset portfolios yield the same constant return, but nonaccumulated income and consumption flows are subject to uninsurable shocks and lead individuals to engage in precautionary savings.

Once theoretical mechanisms are identified that link distribution to growth and growth to distribution, it is natural to study how an economy's characteristics may endogenously determine both distribution and growth. Section 4 reviews models where distributional tensions, far from being resolved ex ante, work their way through distortionary policies and market interactions to bear directly on both macroeconomic dynamics and income distribution. Section 5 reviews empirical work on the cross-sectional dynamics of different countries' aggregate production and income, and on the relationship between within-country inequality, savings, and growth. A brief final section mentions related issues, neglected here for lack of space.

1.2. Preliminaries

The models reviewed below can be organized around a simple accounting framework. At the level of an individual (or a family), a discrete time dynamic budget constraint reads

$$\Delta k = y - c, \quad \text{or} \quad \Delta k = rk + wl - c, \tag{1.1}$$

where c denotes a period's consumption flow, and the contemporaneous income flow y accrues from l units of nonaccumulated factors of production, each rewarded at rate w, and k units of accumulated factors ("wealth"), each yielding r units of income.[1] As in most of the relevant literature, the factor l will be dubbed "labor" in what follows, and its level and dynamics (if any) will be treated as exogenous in all models reviewed below to better focus on the role of the accumulated factor k. This might include human capital and knowledge as well as physical and financial assets and evolves endogenously, as in Eq. (1.1), on the basis of individual decisions to save rather than consume a portion of income.

Any or all of the variables in Eq. (1.1) may bear a time index, and may be random in models with uncertainty. To address distributional issues, it is of course necessary to let consumption, income, and their determinants be heterogeneous across individuals. Heterogeneous income and consumption levels may in general reflect different (k^i, l^i) basket of factors owned by individuals indexed by i, and/or different reward rates r^i and w^i for factors which, while measured in similar units, are owned by different individuals.

---

[1] In Eq. (1.1) the reward rates r and w associate an income flow over discrete time periods to the factor stocks owned at a point in time; wealth, capital, income, and consumption are measured in the same units at all points in time. Continuous-time specifications more often yield elegant closed-form solutions, and avoid the need to specify whether stocks are measured at the beginning or the end of each period. Empirical aspects and the role of uncertainty, however, are discussed more easily in a discrete-time framework.

To address macroeconomic issues, let uppercase letters denote the aggregate counterpart of the corresponding lowercase letter, so that for example

$$Y \equiv \int_{\mathcal{N}} y^i \, dP(i), \tag{1.2}$$

where $\mathcal{N}$ is the set of individuals in the aggregate economy of interest and $P(\cdot)$, with
$\int_{\mathcal{N}} dP(i) = 1$, assigns weights to subsets of $\mathcal{N}$.[2] The set $\mathcal{N}$ may not be fixed, but its
variation over time need not be made explicit unless population growth, finite lives, or
immigration have a role in the phenomena of interest.

Heterogeneity of the nonaccumulated income flow wl may be accounted for by
differences in w and/or l across individuals. To better focus on endogenous accumulation dynamics, the models reviewed below take l as exogenously given. Hence, little
generality is lost by treating it as a homogeneous factor, and

$$L = \int_{\mathcal{N}} l^i \, dP(i), \tag{1.3}$$

denotes the amount of nonaccumulated factors available to the aggregate economy. Since
the relative price of c and Δk is unitary in Eq. (1.1), aggregating wealth as in

$$K \equiv \int_{\mathcal{N}} k^i \, dP(i), \tag{1.4}$$

measures the aggregate stock K in terms of foregone consumption. The definitions in
Eqs. (1.2), (1.3) and (1.4) readily yield a standard aggregate counterpart of Eq. (1.1),

$$\Delta K = RK + WL - C = Y - C. \tag{1.5}$$

Two points of interpretation deserve to be noted with regard to the relationship between
the definition of K and its economic interpretation as "aggregate capital". First, as the
individual-level budget constraint Eq. (1.1) features net income flows, so does Eq. (1.5),
hence the aggregate Y flow is obtained subtracting capital depreciation from every period's gross output flow. Second, it may or may not be possible to give a meaningful
economic interpretation to R, the aggregate rate of return on past accumulation. In the
models discussed in Section 2 below, all units of each factor are rewarded at the same
rate; then, $r = R$, $w = W$, and income distribution straightforwardly depends on factor-
ownership patterns and on R and W themselves. In the more complex and realistic
models reviewed in Section 3, however, unit factor incomes are heterogeneous across
individuals. At the same time as it introduces additional channels of interaction between

---

[2] If $\mathcal{N}$ has n elements, then the weight function $P(i) = 1/n$ defines Y as the arithmetic mean of individual
income levels y. The general notation in the text, where the relative size or weight $P(A)$ of a set $A \subset \mathcal{N}$ of
individuals can be arbitrarily small, conveniently lets the idiosyncratic uncertainty introduced in Section 3.3
average to zero in the aggregate.

distribution and macroeconomic dynamics, such heterogeneity also makes it difficult to give an economic interpretation to aggregate factor supplies and remuneration rates. As a matter of accounting, the conventions introduced in Eqs. (1.1)–(1.5) define R and W as weighted (by factor ownership) averages of their heterogeneous microeconomic counterparts,

$$R = \int_{\mathcal{N}} r^i \frac{k^i}{K} \, dP(i), \qquad W = \int_{\mathcal{N}} w^i \frac{l^i}{L} \, dP(i). \tag{1.6}$$

These aggregate factor prices, however, are ambiguously related to both income distribution and macroeconomic developments. In particular, the "capital stock" K as defined in Eq. (1.4) may not be the argument of an aggregate production function when not only the economy's aggregate wealth, but also its distribution influence the size of the aggregate production flow, as is the case in the models considered in Section 3 below.

2. Aggregate accumulation and distribution

The models reviewed in this section assume away all uncertainty and rely on economy-wide factor markets to ensure that all units of k and l are always rewarded at the same rate. This relatively simple setting isolates a specific set of interactions between factor remuneration and aggregate dynamics on the one hand, which depend on each other through well-defined production and savings functions; and personal income distribution on the other hand, which is readily determined by the remuneration of aggregate factor stocks and by the size and composition of individual factor bundles.

2.1. Neoclassical allocation and accumulation

Models where income distribution is determined in complete and competitive markets are familiar to most readers, and their benign neglect of distributional issues prepares the ground for more articulate models below. If firms employ units of accumulated and nonaccumulated factors in concave production functions $f(\cdot, \cdot)$, and take as given the prices at which factors can be rented from families, then the first order conditions

$$\frac{\partial f(k, l)}{\partial k} = r, \qquad \frac{\partial f(k, l)}{\partial l} = w, \tag{2.1}$$

are necessary and sufficient for profit maximization. The factor prices r and w might in general depend on the identity of the agents concerned, and the production function $f(\cdot)$ could itself be heterogeneous across firms. If factors can be allocated across firms so as to arbitrage marginal productivity differentials, however, all units of each factor must be rewarded at the same rate, hence $w = W$ and $r = R$. Since the two factors' marginal productivities are equal in all of their possible uses, the equilibrium allocation maximizes the aggregate production flow obtained from a given stock of the two factors, and defines an aggregate production as a function $F(K, L)$ of aggregate capital and labor. In the general case where firms' technologies are heterogeneous, the form of the aggregate production function depends on that of firm-level production functions and on the distribution of fixed factors across firms. If all firm-level functions have constant returns to scale, however, so does the aggregate production function, and aggregate factor-income flows coincide with total net output, since

$$F(K, L) = \frac{\partial F(K, L)}{\partial L} L + \frac{\partial F(K, L)}{\partial K} K = WL + RK, \tag{2.2}$$

for $F(K, L)$ a linearly homogeneous function.[3] Decreasing returns to scale at the firm level can be accomodated by including fixed factors in the list of (potentially) variable factors, and the rents accruing to them in aggregate income.

The level and dynamics of income flows accruing to each individual or family indexed by i are determined by the amounts k^i and l^i of factors it brings to the market, and by their prices R and W. For this survey's purposes, it will be convenient to treat each l^i as an exogenously given and (for simplicity) constant quantity.[4] A constant-returns production structure and competitive markets make it possible to disaggregate income not only across individuals, but also across factors:

$$Y = F(K, L) = \int_{\mathcal{N}} y^i \, dP(i) = R \int_{\mathcal{N}} k^i \, dP(i) + W \int_{\mathcal{N}} l^i \, dP(i). \tag{2.3}$$

2.1.1. Saving propensities and the dynamics of distribution
In the macroeconomic accumulation relationship

$$\Delta K = F(K, L) - C = \int_{\mathcal{N}} \left(y^i - c^i \right) dP(i), \tag{2.4}$$

the personal distribution of income is directly relevant to aggregate savings if individual consumption depends nonlinearly on individual income and/or wealth. If, for example, poorer individuals have a higher marginal propensity to consume than richer ones, then

---

[3] By the accounting conventions of Section 1.2, both firm-level and aggregate production functions are defined net of capital depreciation. This has no implications for the simple argument above, since the net production function is concave and has constant returns to scale if the gross production function does and, as is commonly assumed, a fixed portion of capital in use depreciates within each period.

[4] In more general models where the nonaccumulated factor is identified with labor, its individual and aggregate supply should depend endogenously on current and expected wage rates, on financial wealth and the structure of preferences. For a discussion of how models of labor/leisure choices may yield analytically convenient and realistic aggregate models under appropriate simplifying assumptions, see Rebelo (1991), and his references.

more equal income distributions are associated with a smaller ΔK and slower aggregate accumulation.[5] The potential relevance of consumption-function nonlinearities is obvious, but hard to make precise in the absence of precise theoretical foundations. It is insightful to focus for the moment on the case where Eq. (2.4) *can* be written in terms of aggregate capital and income only, regardless of how the same variables are distributed across individuals. If at the individual level savings $y^i - c^i$ depend linearly on y^i and k^i, i.e., if

$$c^i = \bar{c} + \hat{c}\, y^i + \tilde{c}k^i, \tag{2.5}$$

where the $\bar{c}$, $\hat{c}$ and $\tilde{c}$ are constant parameters, then

$$\Delta K = (1 - \hat{c})Y - \tilde{c}\, K - \bar{c}, \tag{2.6}$$

at the aggregate level, regardless of income and wealth heterogeneity.

While a linear consumption function in the form Eq. (2.5) lets aggregate savings be independent of distribution, the converse need not be true. The evolution over time of individual income and wealth depends endogenously on the parameters of individual savings functions, on the character of market interactions, and on the resulting aggregate accumulation dynamics. Following Stiglitz (1969), consider the implications of Eq. (2.5) for the dynamics of income and wealth distribution dynamics in a neoclassical economy where factor markets assign the same income to all units of each factor and all individuals own the same amount $\bar{l} = L$ of the nonaccumulated factor, so that all income and consumption inequality is due to heterogeneous wealth levels.[6] Using Eq. (2.5) in Eq. (1.1), the dynamics of individual i's wealth obey

$$\Delta k^i = (1 - \hat{c})y^i - \tilde{c}k^i - \bar{c} = (1 - \hat{c})\left(Rk^i + W\bar{l}\right) - \tilde{c}k^i - \bar{c}. \tag{2.7}$$

In an economy where R, W and $\bar{l}$ are the same for all individuals, the individual wealth level k is the only possible source of income and consumption heterogeneity. Suppressing the i index on k^i and normalizing Eq. (2.7) by individual wealth k, the dynamic evolution of any such heterogeneity is driven by wealth accumulation according to

$$\frac{\Delta k}{k} = (1 - \hat{c})R - \tilde{c} + \frac{(1 - \hat{c})W\bar{l} - \bar{c}}{k}.$$

---

[5] Stiglitz (1969) discusses the implications of nonlinear consumption functions. The empirical relevance of the idea that a more equal distribution of permanent income should be associated with higher aggregate consumption is explored by Blinder (1974). Its theoretical implications are studied in more detail by Bourguignon (1981).

[6] If l^i is permanently different across i, wealth accumulation tends to different asymptotic values and reinforces income inequality. Stiglitz (1969, Section 6) discusses such phenomena in the case where $\bar{c}$ is still the same for all individuals.

Heterogeneity tends to be eliminated and the economy's distribution converges towards equality if higher levels of wealth (and income and consumption) are associated with slower rates of accumulation, or if

$$(1 - \hat{c})W\bar{l} > \bar{c}. \tag{2.8}$$

If $\hat{c} = 1$ and $\bar{c} = 0$, both terms in Eq. (2.8) are identically zero, and wealth inequality remains forever constant in proportional terms. In this case, as in the models discussed in Section 2.2.1, all wage income is consumed, while savings are positive (as long as $\tilde{c} < 0$) and proportional to wealth. Condition (2.8) has straightforward implications for other familiar macroeconomic models which do rely on special cases of Eq. (2.5), i.e., on easily aggregated linear consumption functions. The textbook Solow (1956a) growth model assumes that savings are a constant fraction of income flows: with $\bar{c} = 0$ and $\hat{c} < 1$, condition (2.8) is satisfied as long as $W\bar{l} > 0$. Thus, a constant average savings propensity unambiguously tends to equalize wealth, income, and consumption across individuals.

The tendency towards equality would be even stronger if $\bar{c} < 0$, i.e., if the average savings rate was higher for poorer individuals, but it may be more appealing to assume that richer agents have a higher average propensity to save or bequeath wealth, i.e., that $\bar{c} > 0$ in Eq. (2.5), as in textbook Keynesian macroeconomic models.[7] If $\bar{c}$ is so large as to violate the inequality in Eq. (2.8), wealthier agents save a larger proportion of their income and, for given R and W, wealth inequality tends to increase over time. In a neoclassical economy, however, factor prices depend endogenously on aggregate accumulation. The rate of return $R = \partial F(K, L)/\partial K$ is a decreasing function of K and, as shown by Stiglitz (1969), this exerts a further equalizing force. If the aggregate economy converges to a stable equilibrium, in fact, net returns to accumulation tend to vanish, and the distributional impact of heterogeneous wealth levels and saving rates weakens over time. Formally, aggregate accumulation obeys

$$\Delta K = Y - C = (1 - \hat{c})F(K, L) - \tilde{c}K - \bar{c}, \tag{2.9}$$

and the aggregate economy approaches a stable steady state where $\Delta K = 0$ only if a larger stock of capital is associated with a smaller (and possibly negative) rate of

---

[7] A positive correlation between income levels and savings propensity can be rationalized in that and other contexts by consumption smoothing in the face of income fluctuations (see also Section 3.3.2 below). In a long-run framework of analysis, however, cross-sectional relationships between savings rates and income levels are not as easy to document by hard evidence as introspection and casual empiricism might indicate (see, e.g., Williamson 1991: p. 71, and his references).

accumulation in its neighborhood.[8] Using the stability condition $\partial(\Delta K)/\partial K < 0$ in Eq. (2.9) yields

$$(1 - \hat{c})\frac{\partial F(L, K)}{\partial K} - \tilde{c} < 0,$$

thus, $(1 - \hat{c})R - \tilde{c} < 0$ in the neighborhood of a stable steady state where $(1 - \hat{c})\left(RK + W\bar{l}\right) - \tilde{c}K - \bar{c} = 0$. Since these two relationships imply Eq. (2.8), aggregate convergence to a stable steady state is accompanied by cross-sectional convergence of individual wealth levels.[9]

2.1.2. Optimal savings and the distribution of consumption

The ad hoc consumption functions considered above usefully highlight mechanical interactions between distribution and macroeconomic growth. For the purpose of assessing welfare implications, however, savings behavior needs to be interpreted on the basis of its underlying motivations. For this purpose, individuals may be viewed as maximizing a standard objective function in the form

$$V(\{c_{t+s}\}) = \sum_{s=0}^{T} \left(\frac{1}{1 + \rho}\right)^s U(c_{t+s}), \tag{2.10}$$

and let the time horizon T (which may be infinite), the rate of time preference $\rho \geq 0$, and the increasing and concave period utility function $U(\cdot)$ are the same across individuals. Since savings yield the rate of return R_{t+1} between periods t and $t + 1$, the optimal consumption path satisfies first order conditions in the form

$$U'(c_t) = \frac{1 + R_{t+1}}{1 + \rho} U'(c_{t+1}), \tag{2.11}$$

for all $t < T$, and an appropriate transversality condition at the end of the planning horizon. In the above framework of analysis, aggregate savings were independent of resource distribution if, and only if, consumption is a linear function of income and wealth.

---

[8] When $\bar{c} > 0$ then the economy also features an unstable steady state, where production is absorbed by consumption even though returns to accumulation are high. Stiglitz (1969) notes that growth is associated with increasing inequality in the neighborhood of such a steady state, and that relatively poor individuals may decumulate wealth indefinitely (or, more realistically, until the budget constraint that is left implicit by ad hoc consumption functions becomes binding) even as the aggregate economy converges to its stable steady state. Bourguignon (1981) discusses the resulting "inegalitarian" steady state where a destitute class has no wealth.

[9] The stability condition is satisfied if the net rate of return R is negative and/or the propensity to consume out of wealth $\tilde{c}$ is positive. The net income flow R generated by each unit of capital can be negative if capital depreciates, and a positive $\tilde{c}$ also reflects of capital depreciation in the standard Solow growth model, where the average and marginal savings propensity is constant for *gross* rather than net income, to imply that the aggregate accumulation equation reads $\Delta K = (1 - \hat{c})[Y + \delta K] - \delta K = (1 - \hat{c})Y - \hat{c}\delta K$, or $\tilde{c} = \hat{c}\delta$ in the notation of Eq. (2.9).

In an optimizing setting, similarly straightforward aggregation obtains if preferences are "quasi-homothetic".[10] As a simple example, let the marginal utility function be

$$U'(c) = (c - \bar{c})^{-\sigma}, \tag{2.12}$$

where $0 < \sigma$. Using Eq. (2.12) in Eq. (2.11) yields

$$c_{t+1} = (1 - \xi_{t+1})\bar{c} + \xi_{t+1}c_t, \quad \text{where } \xi_{t+1} \equiv \left(\frac{1 + R_{t+1}}{1 + \rho}\right)^{1/\sigma}, \tag{2.13}$$

depends on R_{t+1} but is homogeneous across individuals who have the same utility function and discount rate, and earn the same rate of return on their savings. Dividing Eq. (2.13) through by each individual's consumption level,

$$\frac{c_{t+1}}{c_t} = (1 - \xi_{t+1})\frac{\bar{c}}{c_t} + \xi_{t+1}, \tag{2.14}$$

establishes that higher current consumption is associated with faster or slower consumption growth depending on whether, or not, $\bar{c} \gtreqless 0$, and whether, or not, $\xi_{t+1} \gtreqless 1$. Since the relationship (2.13) between individual consumption levels in adjoining periods is linear, a similar relationship holds at the aggregate level as well:

$$C_{t+1} = (1 - \xi_{t+1})\bar{c} + \xi_{t+1}C_t. \tag{2.15}$$

Hence, aggregate consumption is steady if and only if $\xi_{t+1} = 1$, which by Eq. (2.14) also implies that $c_{t+1} = c_t$ (all individual consumption levels are constant). To close the model, note that $\xi_{t+1} \gtreqless 1$ hinges on whether, or not, $R \gtreqless \rho$, recall that $R = \partial F(K, L)/\partial K$ by Eq. (2.1) in a neoclassical model, and consider the macroeconomic dynamics implied by Eqs. (2.15) and (1.5). If the macroeconomy is growing towards the steady state (i.e., $R > \rho$) and the required consumption level $\bar{c}$ is positive, then higher consumption levels are associated with faster consumption growth in the individual condition Eq. (2.13), and consumption inequality increases over time.[11]

The distribution of consumption and its dynamic evolution, however, have little economic significance in the "neoclassical" setting we are considering. On the one hand, the same functional form assumptions that make it possible to characterize aggregate dynamics as in Eq. (2.15) imply that the speed of aggregate growth depends

---

[10] For this class of preferences, also known as "extended Bergson" or "hyperbolic absolute risk aversion", marginal utility is proportional to a power of a linear function of consumption. Not only the constant relative risk aversion specifications considered here, but also other common specifications of utility (including constant absolute risk aversion and quadratic ones) belong to this class; see Merton (1971), Chatterjee (1994), and their references.

[11] This result, and symmetric ones under other combinations of assumptions, are derived by Chatterjee (1994).

only on aggregate variables, not on their distribution across individuals. If preferences lend themselves nicely to aggregation, as in Eq. (2.12), then macroeconomic dynamics can be interpreted in terms of representative-agent savings choices even as the economy features persistent and variable heterogeneity of individual consumption paths.

On the other hand, the dynamics of consumption distribution have no substantive welfare implications: if all individuals' savings earn the same rate of return, relative welfare remains constant over time even though, as in Eq. (2.13), relative consumption levels may diverge or converge. To see this, consider that equations in the form Eq. (2.11) hold for all individuals, and take ratios of their left- and right-hand sides for different individuals: for any $i, \; j \in \mathcal{N}$ and all t we may write

$$\frac{U'(c_t^i)}{U'(c_t^j)} = \frac{U'(c_{t+1}^i)}{U'(c_{t+1}^j)} \equiv \frac{\omega^j}{\omega^i}, \tag{2.16}$$

where ω^i differs from ω^j if individuals i and j enjoy different consumption flows, but neither ω^i nor ω^j depend on time. It is straightforward to show that conditions in the form of Eq. (2.16) are necessary and sufficient for maximization of a weighted sum of individual welfare functionals in the form Eq. (2.10) under an aggregate resource constraint. Formally, the market allocation of the neoclassical economy under consideration solves the social planning problem

$$\max \quad \int_{\mathcal{N}} \omega^i V(\{c_t^i\}) \, dP(i)$$

$$\text{s.t.} \quad \int_{\mathcal{N}} c_t^i \, dP(i) \leq F(K_t, L) + K_t - K_{t+1}, \; \forall t \geq 0,$$

and the dynamics of consumption inequality (if any) are just a byproduct of efficient once-and-for-all allocation of a maximized welfare "pie". In the context of the simple example above, convergence or divergence of cross-sectional consumption rates in the $\bar{c} \neq 0$ case reflects the fact that individuals who are relatively privileged in the initial allocation must remain so in all future periods. Since the elasticity of marginal utility is not constant when $\bar{c} \neq 0$, the market allocation adjusts relative consumption levels so as to keep marginal utilities aligned as in Eq. (2.16), and preserve the relative welfare weights of different individuals. Less tractable and more general specifications of preferences may not allow straightforward aggregation as in Eq. (2.15). Regardless of whether, or not, aggregate accumulation dynamics may be interpreted on a representative-individual basis, however, when intertemporal markets clear competitively then dynamic changes in the distribution of consumption and income flows across individuals have no implications for their welfare, which depends only on their initial endowment of factors of production. This perspective on distributional issues, of course, is very different from that suggested by real-life experience, and from that of models (outlined below) where market interactions are imperfect.

2.2. Factor income distribution and growth

In a market economy, each individual's entitlement to a portion of aggregate output is based on factor ownership, and the distribution of income and consumption flows is determined by the size and composition of each individual's bundle of factors. When competitive economic interactions yield an efficient allocation, initial factor endowments and equilibrium factor rewards determine each individual's income entitlements, and the welfare weights ω^i in the equivalent social planning problem characterized above. In reality, of course, the distribution of income across *factors* of production need not always reflect efficiency considerations, and the literature has often studied it in different frameworks of analysis.

To focus on factor-income distribution in the simple two-factor setting of the derivations above, let γ denote the fraction of consumable income Y that is paid to owners of L, the nonaccumulated factor of production. The remaining $(1-\gamma)$ fraction of aggregate resources is paid to owners of accumulated factors of production (i.e., past foregone consumption), and the two factors are remunerated according to

$$W = \gamma \frac{Y}{L}, \qquad R = (1-\gamma)\frac{Y}{K}, \tag{2.17}$$

where all quantities and the factor shares themselves may in general be variable over time. In the neoclassical economy characterized above, aggregate output Y is efficiently produced from available factors according to the production function $F(K, L)$, and W and R coincide with the aggregate marginal productivities of the two factors of production. The shares γ and $1-\gamma$ of the two factors are uniquely determined by the aggregate K/L ratio under constant returns, and are constant if the production function has the Cobb–Douglas form $Y = L^\gamma K^{1-\gamma}$. For this and more general convex functional forms, the reward rate R decreases over time in a growing economy where an increasing capital stock K is associated with a declining output/capital ratio Y/K for given L.

The role of factor-income distribution in determining individual savings, income distribution, and aggregate accumulation was far from explicit in the above derivations. A relationship between the factor composition of income and saving propensity is implicit in the linear specification (2.5): since inserting $y \equiv W\bar{l} + Rk$ in it yields

$$c = \bar{c} + \hat{c}(W\bar{l} + Rk) + \tilde{c}k = \bar{c} + \hat{c}W\bar{l} + \left(\hat{c}R + \tilde{c}\right)k, \tag{2.18}$$

the propensity to consume out of wealth (or out of accumulated income, Rk) does generally depend on the rate of return R and differs from that relevant to nonaccumulated income flows. Factor-income shares and the unit incomes they imply through Eq. (2.17) also have a subdued role in the determination of optimal savings. A higher rate of return

R on savings makes it optimal to plan faster consumption growth, but also lets it be financed by a smaller volume of savings, and the net effect on savings depends on the balance of these substitution and income effects.[12] The complex and ambiguous role of *R* and *W* in individual and aggregate optimal savings decisions, and the fact that factor incomes are viewed as a byproduct of efficient market allocation of available resources, lead "neoclassical" models of personal savings to pay little attention to issues of factor-income distribution.

2.2.1. Savings, accumulation and classes

A long and distinguished stream of earlier models, by contrast, viewed factor ownership as an essential determinant of individual savings behavior.[13] The logic of such models is simply stated. As above, let individuals be entitled to portions of the economy's aggregate income flow on the basis of factor ownership and, for simplicity, let consumption and income consist of a single, homogeneous good.[14] The owner of each unit of capital receives a return *R* and, as in Eq. (2.17), each unit of the nonreproducible factor *L* entitles its owner to *W* units of income. The factor(s) denoted by *L* may include land and other natural resources as well as labor. It is unnecessary to disaggregate *L* along such lines, however, if none of the income flows accruing to nonreproducible factors are saved. Accordingly, let both land-owning "rentiers" and "workers" consume all of their income, while the propensity to save is positive for owners of reproducible factors of production, or "capitalists". Such simple income-source-based characterizations of savings behavior is natural if sharp income-source heterogeneity across hereditary class lines has stylized-fact status, as it probably did in the early nineteenth century, and its implications are consistent with the assumed association between wealth and further accumulation: an individual can come to own more accumulated wealth than others because his past savings propensity was relatively high, and the classical assumption amounts to a presumption that such heterogeneity (whatever its source) persists over time.[15] At the theoretical level, the assumption that workers never save any portion

---

[12] For the quasi-homothetic preferences considered above, the marginal propensity to consume available resources is independent of their level and is a decreasing function of *R* if $\sigma < 1$, while income effects are stronger than substitution effect is if $\sigma > 1$. Under complete markets, consumable resources include the present discounted value of future nonaccumulated income flows, or "human wealth", and factor-income distribution affects individual saving decisions through such wealth effects as well as (ambiguously) through income and substitution effects.

[13] This section draws on Bertola (1993, 1994b, c). Space constraints make it impossible to survey properly a literature that spans physiocratic tableaus, Ricardian theory, and post-Keynesian growth models. Asimakopoulos (1988) offers a more extensive review of this material. Levine (1988) discusses Marxian theories of the distribution of surplus (the portion of net income in excess of what is necessary to reproduce the economy's capital and labor force).

[14] The models implicit in the work of Ricardo did feature multiple goods, and in particular a distinction between luxuries and basic consumption goods. The relationship of simpler post-Keynesian single-good macromodels to Ricardian theory is discussed in, e.g., Kaldor (1956: Section I) and Pasinetti (1960, footnote 24).

[15] A preference-based class structure can also feature a nonzero propensity to save out of labor income. Pasinetti (1962) lets a relatively low (but strictly positive) savings propensity apply to both the accumulated

of their resources may be rationalized by the classical notion of a "natural" wage rate which barely suffices to let the labor force subsist and reproduce but leaves no room for savings.[16] Once savings behavior is assumed to depend on income sources, aggregate accumulation is straightforwardly related to resource distribution. If $(1 - s^p)$ denote the portion of capitalists' income which is consumed, and capital depreciation is ruled out for simplicity, the aggregate capital stock evolves according to

$$\Delta K = s^p RK = s^p (1 - \gamma)Y, \tag{2.19}$$

where Eq. (2.17) is used to express R in terms of capital's factor share $(1 - \gamma)$. Since the savings propensity s^p is viewed as an exogenous parameter, the income share γ of nonaccumulated factors of production has a crucial role in determining the economy's accumulation rate. In turn, factor shares depend on the economy's dynamic behavior through the law of diminishing returns. As more capital is accumulated, relatively scarce nonaccumulated factors can command an increasing share of aggregate output if they are rewarded according to marginal productivity and earn inframarginal *rents* on intensive or extensive margins. A wage level higher than the "subsistence" one that would let the labor force reproduce itself may lead to faster population growth, implying that no rents accrue to labor in the long run (Pasinetti, 1960; Casarosa, 1982).[17] No such mechanism restrains the inframarginal rents paid to factors in fixed supply ("land"). As an ever larger share of the economy's resources is paid to landowners with low propensity to save, the economy tends to settle into a stationary state where capitalists' savings and investment just suffice to reproduce the existing capital stock. The capitalists' savings propensity determines not only the distribution but also the growth rate and ultimate level of aggregate income.

The idea that decreasing returns and increasing rents would prevent capitalists' savings from endlessly fueling accumulation could be acceptable to nineteenth-century economists who had not experienced prolonged periods of economic development. Later, long-run growth at approximately constant rates achieved "stylized fact" status (Kaldor,

and nonaccumulated income flows accruing to individuals belonging to the working class, and shows that the exact value of their propensity to save is irrelevant in the long run as long as it is lower than the aggregate one. Samuelson and Modigliani (1966) argue that it is more logically consistent to attach different savings propensities to income sources rather than recipients. In his comments, Kaldor (1966) acknowledges that high savings propensity "attaches to profits as such, not to capitalists as such" (p. 310).

[16] A subsistence approach to wage determination makes it natural for classical theories to suppose that wage payments precede production flows. Thus, wages are a portion of the economy's working capital, and the notion of "organic" composition of capital plays an important role in Marxian studies of factor-income distribution (see Roemer, 1981, for a critical review and formal results in this field). For simplicity—and consistently with Marglin (1984), Kaldor (1956) and Sraffa (1960)—the timing of wage outlays is the same as that of accumulated-factor income flows in this section's equations.

[17] Through Malthusian population dynamics, labor is an accumulated factor of sorts in a classical economy: while no part of workers' income is saved in the form of capital, faster population growth when wages exceed subsistence levels does contribute to extend the economy's production possibilities. The role of endogenous population dynamics in modern growth models is surveyed by Nerlove and Raut (1997).

1961), and theories of accumulation needed to account for technological progress. Given a constant stock of L (or in per-capita terms), constant proportional output growth and a constant savings rate are consistent with each other if the capital/output ratio is constant, and an index of technological efficiency enters the production function in L-augmenting fashion as in

$$F_t(K, L) = \tilde{F}(K, A_t L). \tag{2.20}$$

Denoting $A_{t+1}/A_t \equiv \bar{\theta}$, it is straightforward to derive the Kaldor (1956) link between growth and income distribution. If capitalists save a given portion s^P of their income flow and other agents' savings are negligible, then along a balanced growth path where $K_{t+1}/K_t = A_{t+1}/A_t = \bar{\theta}$, Eq. (2.19) implies $R = (\bar{\theta} - 1)/s^P$ and, in light of Eq. (2.17),

$$\bar{\theta} = 1 + s^P (1 - \gamma) \frac{Y}{K}. \tag{2.21}$$

This tight relationship between the propensity of capitalists to save, the economy's rate of balanced growth, and the aggregate share of accumulated factors of production, is given a precise causal interpretation by post-Keynesian theorists. If not only $\bar{\theta}$, but also the output/capital ratio Y/K is viewed as an exogenously given parameter, the capitalists' savings propensity s^P is consistent with only one value of γ, and hence determines the unique balanced-growth configuration of income distribution.

2.2.2. Factor shares in long-run growth

The neoclassical approach to the same issues lets factor incomes be determined by efficient market interactions and, as noted above, has looser implications for the relationship between factor income distribution and aggregate accumulation. Decreasing returns to accumulation, however, still play a role. Competitive determination of factor incomes is well defined only if the neoclassical aggregate production function has constant returns to K and L together. This implies that accumulation of K encounters *decreasing returns* if it is not accompanied by a proportional increase in L, and makes it hard for savings to sustain long-run growth even when they accrue from all income rather than from profits only. In fact, the growth rate of total production can be written

$$\frac{\Delta Y}{Y} \approx \frac{\partial F(K, L)}{\partial K} \frac{\Delta K}{Y} + \frac{\partial F(K, L) L}{\partial L} \frac{1}{Y} \frac{\Delta L}{L}, \tag{2.22}$$

by a Taylor approximation (which would be exact in continuous time). On the right-hand side of Eq. (2.22), the net savings rate $\Delta K/Y$ is multiplied by the marginal productivity of capital, $\partial F(K, L)/\partial K$, which under constant returns is a function of the capital/labor ratio only, and decreasing in it. In the canonical Cobb–Douglas specification, for example, $F(K, L) = K^\gamma L^{1-\gamma}$ with $\gamma < 1$, implies $\partial F(K, L)/\partial K = \gamma (K/L)^{\gamma-1}$. Thus, as capital intensity increases the economy's savings propensity is an ever less important driving force of growth. If, as in the Cobb–Douglas case,

$$\lim_{K \to \infty} \frac{\partial F(K, L)}{\partial K} = \lim_{K \to \infty} \frac{\partial F(K/L, 1)}{\partial (K/L)} \leq 0, \tag{2.23}$$

(with strict inequality if capital depreciates), then only the second term on the right-hand side of Eq. (2.22)—i.e., the competitive share of L times its proportional growth rate— remains relevant as capital intensity increases. Hence, the economy tends to settle in a steady state where aggregate income growth depends on the exogenous growth $\Delta L/L$ of nonaccumulated factors in Eq. (2.22), and is accompanied rather than generated by endogenous factor accumulation.

Even under constant returns, the limit in Eq. (2.23) may be strictly positive. If, for example, $F(K, L) = K^\alpha L^{1-\alpha} + BK$ with $0 < \alpha < 1$, then

$$\frac{\partial F(K, L)}{\partial K} = \alpha \left(\frac{K}{L}\right)^{1-\alpha} + B, \tag{2.24}$$

tends to $B > 0$ and, if this limit is larger than the rate of time preference, the economy features unceasing accumulation driven growth, as was already recognized by Solow (1956a) and recently modeled by Jones and Manuelli (1990). In a single-sector model where returns to scale are constant in the aggregate and returns to accumulation are bounded away from zero, however, nonaccumulated factors of production earn a vanishing share of aggregate production if they are rewarded at marginal-productivity rates. If the aggregate production function is that given in Eq. (2.24), for example, then the competitive income share of labor is

$$\gamma = \frac{\partial F(K, L)}{\partial L} \frac{L}{F(K, L)} = \frac{1 - \alpha}{1 + (K/L)^{1-\alpha} B},$$

and tends to zero as K grows endogenously towards infinity.

Recall that, in Section 2.1's framework of analysis, the intercept $\bar{c} \neq 0$ of individual consumption functions has a crucial role in determining distributional dynamics: with $\bar{c} > 0$, an economy that grows towards a steady state would feature increasing inequality, as the higher average savings propensity of richer individuals reinforces wealth inequality. In many interesting models, however, the economy is capable of sustaining endless growth—because of exogenous technological progress, as in Eq. (2.20), or because capital accumulation does not endogenously deplete returns to investment, as in Eq. (2.24). If aggregate consumption does tend to grow at a proportional rate in the long run, relative-consumption dynamics must eventually become irrelevant, as a finite "required" consumption level constitutes an ever lower proportion of each individual's total consumption. Asymptotically, a growing economy behaves as if $\bar{c} = 0$ in Eq. (2.12), or

$$U'(c) = c^{-\sigma}. \tag{2.25}$$

When preferences are in the form Eq. (2.25) and all savings earn the same rate of return R, the growth rate of consumption is constant across individuals and constant marginal utility ratios, as in Eq. (2.16), imply that ratios of consumption levels remain forever constant across individuals. Along a path of balanced long-run growth, savings behavior perpetuates whatever heterogeneity may exist across consumption and income levels.

In balanced growth, output and capital grow at the same rate as consumption,

$$\frac{K_{t+1}}{K_t} = \frac{Y_{t+1}}{Y_t} = \frac{C_{t+1}}{C_t} \equiv \theta :$$

optimal savings choices associate a larger rate of return R with faster consumption growth.[18] In light of Eq. (2.17), balanced growth at a constant rate is associated with a constant income share $(1 - \gamma)$ for accumulated factors, and a larger factor share for capital is associated with faster growth. This echoes the "classical" relationship between the two in Eq. (2.21), and in fact reflects a similar relationship between income sources and savings propensities. This is most clearly seen in the case where $\sigma = 1$ (the utility function is logarithmic) and the balanced growth rate is given by

$$\theta = \frac{1 + R}{1 + \rho} = \frac{1 + (1 - \gamma)\frac{Y}{K}}{1 + \rho}, \tag{2.26}$$

along the balanced growth path of standard optimizing models where agents have identical infinite planning horizons and utility functions. Consider the intertemporal budget constraint of an individual who owns k_t units of wealth and l units of the nonaccumulated factor of production at time t, when the latter is compensated by a wage rate W_t. Since R is constant in balanced growth, we can write

$$\sum_{j=0}^{\infty} c_{t+j} \left(\frac{1}{1+R}\right)^j = k_t(1 + R) + \sum_{j=0}^{\infty} l W_{t+j} \left(\frac{1}{1+R}\right)^j, \tag{2.27}$$

and, since a constant R implies a constant growth rate for both wages and individual consumption, inserting $c_{t+j} = c_t\theta^j$, and $W_{t+j} = W_t\theta^j$ in Eq. (2.27) yields

$$c_t = W_t l + (1 + R) \left(1 - \frac{\theta}{1 + R}\right) k_t = W_t l + (1 + R - \theta)k_t. \tag{2.28}$$

Across individuals, any difference in the amount of nonaccumulated income $W_t l$ is reflected one-for-one in different consumption levels, and the propensity to consume nonaccumulated-factor (or "labor") income is unitary just like the simple classical or

---

[18] Even when income effects associate a higher R with lower savings, in fact, a higher rate of return unambiguously makes it possible to consume more in the future.

post-Keynesian models outlined above. In fact, it is unnecessary (and would be suboptimal) to save any portion of the income flows accruing to nonaccumulated factors of production when their wages grow at the same rate as each individual's optimal consumption, as is the case along a path of balanced growth. Any individual who happens to own only l and no accumulated factors of production enjoys a stream of income that grows like W and like desired consumption, never saves, and never accumulates any capital.

By contrast, and again consistently with Kaldorian behavioral assumptions, a portion of capital income *must* be saved for individual consumable resources to keep up with individual desired consumption paths. Savings by an individual who owns k_t and l units of the two factors are given by

$$Rk_t + W_t l - c_t = (R - (1 + R - \theta)) k_t = (\theta - 1)k_t, \tag{2.29}$$

and hence directly proportional to wealth and accumulated-factor income. An individual who is a pure "capitalist", i.e., happens to own only an amount k of the accumulated factor of production, needs to save $(\theta - 1)k$ for his wealth and income to increase at the same rate θ as consumption across periods.

Since savings behavior perpetuates any initial heterogeneity in the factor composition of income, the economy can feature a stable class structure, and the functional and personal distribution of income are strictly related to each other and to the economy's growth rate. In optimization-based models, causal relationships among factor shares, savings propensities, and growth are not as easy to identify as in Kaldor's Eq. (2.21), because in Eq. (2.26) the growth rate θ and/or the output/capital ratio Y/K are variables rather than given parameters as in Eq. (2.21). Furthermore, savings propensities are attached to factor-income flows rather than to individuals belonging to different "classes", and the rate at which "profits" are saved is endogenous to preferences and distributional parameters.

Any balanced-growth path under optimal savings features relationships similar to Eq. (2.26) among factor income distribution, aggregate growth and the capital/output ratio. If factor markets are cleared by price-taking economic interactions and lump-sum factor redistribution can address distributional issues, of course, then such relationships need not have the same distributional implications as in the class-based models of savings outlined above. Furthermore, if decreasing returns to accumulation leave exogenous growth of the nonaccumulated factor L as the only source of long-run growth then equations like Eq. (2.26) simply determine the endogenous steady-state capital/output ratio. Interactions between factor income distribution and macroeconomic phenomena are more complex and interesting in models which, following Romer (1986), specify the economy's technological and market structure so that returns to aggregate accumulation are constant. If the reduced form of the aggregate production function $F(K, L)$ is $A(L)K$, where

$$\partial F(., .)/\partial K = A(L), \tag{2.30}$$

depends on L if nonaccumulated factors have a productive role but is constant with respect to K, the capital/output ratio for given L is also independent of K, and the proportional growth rate of output is constant if the aggregate savings rate and $A(L)$ are constant:

$$\frac{\Delta Y}{Y} = \frac{\Delta K}{K} = \frac{Y - C}{K} = A(L)\frac{Y - C}{Y}. \tag{2.31}$$

If nonaccumulated factors have a nonnegligible role in production, and accumulation does not encounter decreasing returns, aggregate returns to scale are not constant, but increasing. Since it is always conceptually possible to increase production by proportionately increasing all inputs or "replicating" identical microeconomic production units, decreasing returns to aggregate inputs can be ruled out on a priori grounds (Solow, 1956a). Replication arguments do not rule out increasing returns, however: as in Romer (1986, 1989, 1990), such *nonrival* factors as know-how, software, and other determinants of an economy's technological prowess can be simultaneously used in an arbitrary number of production units or processes, and need not increase in proportion to rival inputs to yield proportionately larger output at the aggregate or at the firm level. This makes it possible to rationalize increasing returns from first principles in many qualitatively realistic ways, and to model growth as endogenous to the economy's preferences, technology, and market structure. Intratemporal markets prices and factor payments for given K may be determined by competitive interactions if increasing returns are external to firms, as in Arrow's (1962) learning-by-doing model and Romer (1986). Inputs which are nonrival but excludable, such as patent-protected knowledge, imply increasing returns within each firm, and are naturally associated with market power in the models of Romer (1987), Grossman and Helpman (1991) and others. In general, isoelastic functional forms for technology and demand lead to "*AK*" reduced form functions which satisfy Eq. (2.30) when aggregate flows are measured as a price-weighted index of heterogeneous goods.[19]

For the present purpose of analyzing interactions between distribution and aggregate growth, the most relevant and general feature of this class of endogenous growth models is the simple fact that, under increasing returns, intertemporally efficient allocations cannot be decentralized in complete, competitive markets: since the sum total of marginal productivities exceeds aggregate production, the private remuneration of one or more factors of production must differ from its "social" counterpart. When the microeconomic structure of markets and production cannot be such as to guarantee that market equilibria are efficient then, as in class-based models of savings, the distribution of income flows across factors is obviously relevant to aggregate dynamics and, if factor ownership is heterogeneous, to resource distribution across individuals. Hence, aggregate growth and distribution hinge on policies, institutions, and politics (as in the models reviewed in Section 4 below) rather than on technological features only.

---

[19] Grossman and Helpman (1991) and Aghion and Howitt (1998) offer extensive and insightful reviews of these and other microeconomic foundations of endogenous growth.

As pointed out by Rebelo (1991), efficient market interactions between accumulated and nonaccumulated factors of production can support endogenous balanced growth in multisector growth models, as long as a "core" of accumulated factors reproduces itself without encountering decreasing returns.[20] Like in single-sector models of growth, savings propensities of individuals who happen to own accumulated and nonaccumulated factors in different proportions depend on income sources along such economies' balanced-growth paths because, again, an individual who owns no capital never needs or wants to accumulate any wealth. While aggregation of heterogeneous goods into homogeneous "capital" and "output" measures may be difficult from an accounting point of view (unless production functions satisfy separability conditions, as in Solow, 1956b), relative prices are unambiguously defined and easily interpreted as long as perfect, competitive markets support an efficient allocation (Dixit, 1977). Along the balanced growth equilibrium paths of multisector economies, taxes or other distortions which introduce wedges between factor incomes and marginal productivities affect the economy's growth rate, factor shares, and the relationship between the former and the latter in much the same way as in the simpler single-good models outlined above. Recent work on models of suboptimal endogenous growth under a variety of market imperfections has rekindled interest in distributional issues (see Section 4 below). If the distribution of income across factors owned by different individuals is allowed to play a substantive economic role, it unavoidably affects relative prices. From this survey's point of view, it may be interesting to note that factor-income distribution also affects the relative prices of capital and consumption in ways that are somewhat reminiscent of the Sraffa (1960) problem of how savings, investment, and "capital" might be measured in models where multiple capital goods are used in production and reproduction, and relative prices and the value of the aggregate stock of capital in terms of consumption generally depend on factor-income distribution.[21]

3. Investments, savings and financial markets

The interactions between inequality and growth reviewed in Section 2 arise from factor-reward dynamics, and from heterogeneous sizes and compositions of individual factor bundles. None of the models encountered above explains what might generate such heterogeneity in the first place, however, and by assuming that all individuals' savings are allocated to similar investment opportunities the models surveyed so far strongly restrict the dynamic pattern of cross-sectional marginal utilities and consumption levels. Regardless of whether the homogeneous rate of return $r = R$ appropriately reflects

---

[20] Externalities and other market imperfections do play an essential role in other multisector growth models, such as those of product and quality innovation proposed by Grossman and Helpman (1991) where growth is driven by production of K (which represents "knowledge" in these models) in a research and development sector which employs and compensates only labor, a nonaccumulated private factor of production.

[21] Marglin (1984) and especially Kurz and Salvadori (1995) offer recent extensive treatments of these matters.

"social" intertemporal tradeoffs, or is distorted by imperfect intratemporal markets or policy instruments, inequality is eventually stable and may tend to disappear along balanced growth paths.

The literature reviewed in this section allows for imperfections and/or incompleteness of the *intertemporal* markets where individual savings meet investment opportunities. In reality, financial market imperfections are presumably endogenous to microeconomic information and enforcement problems. What follows, however, focuses on the macroeconomic consequences rather than on the microeconomic sources of financial market imperfections, and aims at highlighting the basic mechanisms underlying many recent contributions also reviewed by Pagano (1993), King and Levine (1993), Bénabou (1996c), Greenwood and Smith (1997) and Levine (1997).

Realistic financial market imperfections introduce interesting interactions between distribution and macroeconomic phenomena, but also make it impossible to characterize the latter on a representative-individual basis. Under appropriate simplifying assumptions, however, macroeconomic models do feature meaningful linkages between resource distribution and aggregate dynamics when investment opportunities are heterogeneous. Most straightforwardly, the planning horizon of investment and savings differ across finitely-lived agents in the overlapping-generations models reviewed in Section 3.1 below. Furthermore, ex ante investment opportunities may differ across individuals with different wealth if self-financing constraints are binding (Section 3.2), and ex post returns in consumption terms may differ across individuals if idiosyncratic risk cannot be pooled in the financial markets (Section 3.3). Since no financial-market counterpart could ever exist for a representative individual, neither self-financing nor borrowing constraints could be binding in a homogeneous economy and, more generally, not only the structure of financial markets but also the extent of inequality is relevant to macroeconomic outcomes and to the evolution of income inequality.

3.1. *Finite lives*

In the models reviewed above, the dynamics of each individual's income and wealth evolve over the same infinite horizon that is applicable to macroeconomic dynamics. One obvious reason why investment opportunities differ across individuals is the simple fact that not all individuals can participate in intertemporal markets, because some of them are not yet alive when the financial market is supposed to clear. Many of the models reviewed in this and the next section indeed limit the time horizon of individual savings and investment problems, often for the sake of simplicity: since optimal consumption decisions across two periods are much more simply characterized than optimal forward-looking plans, an overlapping-generation structure recommends itself naturally to models which analyze explicitly other complex features of reality, such as uncertainty or politico-economic interactions.

Overlapping-generations models, however, are not just simpler versions of their infinite-horizon counterparts. When individuals have finite lifetimes within an infinite-horizon economy, aggregate income flows are distributed across generations as well as across factors and individuals. While redistributing disposable income from accumulated to nonaccumulated factors of production necessarily decreases the level and/or growth rate of income in infinite-horizon growth models, the same experiment is likely to increase the economy's savings propensity in a conventional Diamond (1965) overlapping-generations economy with two-period lifetimes. In that setting, all savings are performed by "young" agents who earn only (nonaccumulated) labor income and solve a maximization problem in the form

$$\max_{c^y} \quad U(c^y) + \frac{1}{1+\rho} U(c^o)$$

$$\text{s.t.} \quad c^o = (Wl - c^y)(1+R),$$

(3.1)

where c^y and c^o denote each agent's consumption when young and old respectively, and the rate of return R is the same for all individuals. The usual first-order condition

$$U'(c^y) = \frac{1+R}{1+\rho} U'(c^o),$$

(3.2)

and the budget constraint in Eq. (3.1) determine the two consumption levels. When utility is logarithmic ($U'(x) = 1/x$), income and substitution effects offset each other exactly and the individual savings rate

$$Wl - c^y = \frac{1}{2+\rho} Wl,$$

(3.3)

is independent of the return rate R. Factor-income distribution, however, matters for aggregate accumulation, because in standard overlapping generations economies all (non accumulated) income is earned by young individuals, who also perform all of the aggregate economy's savings—while old individuals consume not only all of their (accumulated factor) income but also their stock of wealth. Accordingly, aggregate savings are given by

$$\Delta K_t = \frac{1}{2+\rho} W_t L - K_t = \left(\frac{1}{2+\rho} \gamma \frac{Y_t}{K_t} - 1 \right) K_t,$$

(3.4)

and are increasing in the share γ of the nonaccumulated factor of production L in aggregate income.

To study the implications of this simple insight for macroeconomic dynamics, it is necessary to specify how the capital/output ratio and the factor share γ are determined by the economy's markets, policies, and technology. Uhlig and Yanagawa (1996) study a simple endogenous-growth economy where $Y_t/K_t = A(L)$ is constant, and discuss the effects of tax policies which shift disposable income from "capital" to "labor". Under the logarithmic specification of preferences above, aggregate savings are an increasing function of the share γ of nonaccumulated factors in aggregate income, and so is aggregate capital growth, since

$$\frac{K_{t+1}}{K_t} = \left(\frac{\gamma}{2 + \rho}\right) \frac{Y_t}{K_t}. \tag{3.5}$$

A lower rate of return on savings is likely to be associated with higher aggregate savings and to faster investment-driven growth also for more general specifications of preferences. For the opposite result to hold in a standard overlapping-generations model, in fact, the intertemporal elasticity of consumption substitution must be so high—i.e., σ must be so much lower than unity in the constant-elasticity case (2.25)—as to let substitution effects dominate not only the income effect, but also the effects of income redistribution across agents with different planning horizons.[22] The model's implications are not as sharp when young individuals can look forward to future wages. If agents still live for two periods, leave no bequests, and maximize loglinear objective functions, but are endowed with l^o units of labor in the second period of their life as well as with l^y units in the first, then consumption of the young is given by

$$c^y = \frac{1 + \rho}{2 + \rho} \left(W_t l^y + \frac{W_{t+1} l^o}{1 + R}\right). \tag{3.6}$$

Shifting functional income distribution towards capital decreases W in all periods, but even when the utility function is logarithmic (and income and substitution effects offset each other) a higher R tends to decrease consumption and increase savings via wealth effects, i.e., because the present value of future wages is smaller. More complex and realistic but qualitatively similar effects are featured by continuous-time models where lifetimes are exponentially distributed (Bertola, 1996).

As in infinite-horizon models, growth can be sustained if some of the accumulated factors' contribution to aggregate production "spills over" to owners of nonaccumulated factors, because of external effects and/or market imperfections; correspondingly, the private remuneration of savings will be lower than capital's contribution to future aggregate production. This, however, does not have the same normative implications as it would in the standard infinite-horizon model: a higher savings rate would increase the economy's growth rate and future income, but this cannot result in a Pareto improvement if the finitely-lived generations whose consumption is decreased is distinct from those

---

[22] A similar mechanism is at work when an infinite number of market participants lets asset prices deviate from their fundamental values (Grossman and Yanagawa, 1993). Like public debt or unfunded social security, asset bubbles transfer resources from the (saving) young to the (dissaving) old. As each generation finds it less necessary to rely on productive capital for consumption-smoothing purposes, investment-driven economic growth slows down.

which will enjoy the resulting income stream.[23] Jones and Manuelli (1992) and Boldrin (1992) show that standard discrete-time overlapping-generations models, where individuals own no capital in the first period of their lives, cannot sustain endogenous growth if factors are rewarded according to their marginal productivity. For intratemporal markets to support marginal-productivity-based income distribution, in fact, returns to scale to capital and labor together must be constant. As in the example (2.24) above, nonaccumulated factors must then earn a vanishing share of aggregate production if returns to accumulation are asymptotically constant. Neoclassical markets assign an ever smaller share of aggregate production to labor at the same time as the economy accumulates an increasingly large stock of capital, and it must eventually become impossible for young capital-poor individuals to purchase with their savings the aggregate capital stock from older, about-to-die individuals.[24]

3.2. Self-financed investment

All the models reviewed so far allow agents to access an integrated financial market which, ruling out arbitrage, offers the same rate of return to all individuals. Other models rule out access to financial markets, so that investment must equal savings not only at the aggregate but also at the individual level, or otherwise link intertemporal investment opportunities to individual circumstances (such as the availability of collateral) rather than to equilibrium conditions in the financial market. Such capital-market imperfections are most realistic for educational investments and other forms of human capital accumulation, since labor income can hardly serve as collateral and investment returns generally accrue to heirs who are not legally bound to honor debts incurred by their parents.

The macroeconomic relevance of self-financing constraints clearly depends on the extent of inequality across individuals. Identical agents would not trade with each other even when allowed to do so, and the aggregate economy's accumulation path would simply resemble each (representative) individual's in that case. If resource levels and investment opportunities are both heterogeneous across individuals, conversely, the relationship between the two bears on the dynamics of distribution. Inequality tends to disappear if technology and markets offer less favorable rates of return to relatively rich individuals, and tends to persist and widen if the opposite is the case.

---

[23] Since an overlapping-generations economy features infinitely many market participants, its competitive equilibrium is not necessarily Pareto-efficient. As shown by Saint-Paul (1992a), however, dynamic efficiency is guaranteed to obtain if the marginal productivity of capital is independent of accumulation, as is the case along a path of endogenous balanced growth.

[24] Jones and Manuelli also show that an overlapping-generations economy can experience unbounded endogenous growth if, as is possible in multisector models, the price of capital in terms of consumption and wages declines steadily over time. The growth effects of policy interventions which redistribute income towards the early stages of individual lifetimes are similar to those outlined above, and can even make endogenous growth possible for an economy whose income would reach a stable plateau under *laissez-faire* markets: once again, however, such growth-enhancing policies affect intergenerational distribution.

To isolate the role of self-financing constraints, it is useful to model investment opportunities as simply as possible. In the absence of financial market access, the accumulation constraint may be written in the form $k_{t+1} = f(k_t - c_t)$ at the level of each individual or family. Consumable resources are identified with wealth k_t (thus abstracting from any possible role of nonaccumulated sources of income) and, unlike the budget constraint Eq. (1.1) above, the function $f(\cdot)$ which maps foregone consumption at time t into future resources is nonlinear. Simplicity is also a virtue with regard to savings decisions in this setting. Many studies of financial-market imperfections consider two-period planning problems with logarithmic objective functions, abstracting from the complex and ambiguous effects of current and expected future returns in more general models. The role of different investment opportunity sets in determining relative and aggregate accumulation dynamics may also be highlighted in the even simpler case where the savings rate is exogenously given, as in the models of Bencivenga and Smith (1991) and Piketty (1997), so that the dynamics of each individual's wealth,

$$k_{t+1} = f(sk_t), \tag{3.7}$$

depend essentially on the shape of the function $f(\cdot)$.

3.2.1. Convex investment opportunities

Since finitely-lived individuals face a smooth tradeoff between time spent in education and working time, educational investment opportunities may be modeled by a standard decreasing-returns function $f(\cdot)$ with $f'(\cdot) > 0$, $f''(\cdot) < 0$. As a simple example, consider the relative-wealth dynamics implied by $f(x) = x^\alpha$, $0 < \alpha < 1$. Denoting with $x_t \equiv k_t^i / k_t^j$ the wealth of individual i relative to that of individual j, we have

$$x_{t+1} = \frac{f(sk_t^i)}{f(sk_t^j)} = \left(\frac{k_t^i}{k_t^j}\right)^\alpha = (x_t)^\alpha .$$

Since $\alpha < 1$, relative wealth levels tend to converge to the stationary configuration $x_t = x_{t+1} = 1$ of this recursion, hence to complete equalization and, in the absence of exogenous nonaccumulated income, complete stability of individual wealth levels. More general decreasing-returns functions such that

$$\lim_{x \to \infty} f'(x) = 0, \tag{3.8}$$

have similar implications. Relative wealth convergence is also implied by decreasing returns to individual accumulation in optimizing models, such as

$$\max \quad U(c_t) + \frac{1}{1+\rho} V(k_{t+1})$$

$$\text{s.t.} \quad k_{t+1} = f(k_t - c_t), \tag{3.9}$$

as long as the savings rate $s(k_t) = (k_t - c_t)/k_t$ does not depend too strongly on individual-specific investment returns (and certainly in the logarithmic case considered above). The two-period optimization problem Eq. (3.9) can be brought to bear on longer-horizon dynamics if the second-period utility $V(\cdot)$ is interpreted as a "warm glow" benefit of wealth bequeathed to one's descendants, along the lines of Andreoni (1989), or as the value function of an infinite-horizon optimization model. Of particular interest in the present context is the fact that if $V(\cdot)$ is the value function of an infinite-horizon model, then the dynamics converge to a unique steady state under the same conditions that would yield a well-defined competitive equilibrium for a neoclassical macroeconomy faced by the same problem as the individual considered (see, e.g., Chatterjee, 1994).[25]

Condition Eq. (3.8), in fact, is more than superficially related to Eq. (2.23). In neoclassical models where Eq. (2.23) is true, aggregate accumulation histories always converge to the same steady state level, while nondecreasing returns to accumulation would let an economy determine its own rate of long-run growth. Similarly, a cross-section of individual wealth levels may fail to converge if the return to investment and the savings rate eventually become constant as wealth increases. Under self-financing constraints, as noted by Chatterjee (1994), aggregate dynamics break down in a collection of side-by-side individual problems similar to that facing the representative individual or social planner of a neoclassical aggregate economy.

When savings are not allocated efficiently to investment opportunities by an integrated financial market, the level and dynamics of aggregate output are a function of all individual wealth levels $\{k^i\}$ rather than of the aggregate stock $K \equiv \int_{\mathcal{N}} k^i \, dP(i)$ only. As in Bénabou (1996c, d), interactions between distribution and aggregate dynamics can be analyzed in a parsimonious way if the form of individual production functions and of wealth distribution is appropriately restricted. If the accumulation technology at the individual level has a constant-elasticity form, as in $k_{t+1}^i = (k_t^i)^\alpha (k_t^i - c_t^i)^\beta$, then a constant investment rate s (as might be implied by optimization of similarly loglinear intertemporal objective functions) yields

$$k_{t+1}^i = (k_t^i)^{\alpha+\beta} (s)^\beta . \tag{3.10}$$

As long as $\alpha + \beta < 1$, the marginal return to individual i's investment is a decreasing function of individual resources k_t^i, and the next period's aggregate resources $K_{t+1} = \int_{\mathcal{N}} (k_t^i)^{\alpha+\beta} (s)^\beta \, dP(i)$ are smaller than they would be if the amount e^i invested in the production function $(k^i)^\alpha (e^i)^\beta$ did not need to coincide with that same individual's savings $k^i - c^i$. In general, the output loss due to inefficient allocation across decreasing-returns investment opportunities is an increasing function of the degree of heterogeneity

---

[25] If future wealth's contribution to utility has a "warm glow" interpretation, however, then multiple equilibria are possible. For example, Galor and Tsiddon (1997) let k_{t+1} depend on k_t as well as on $k_t - c_t$, and show that the recursion implied by optimal savings behavior can have multiple fixed points, depending on third-order and mixed derivatives. The resulting wealth dynamics are similar to those (reviewed below) generated by nonconvex investment opportunity sets, which are perhaps easier to interpret.

across individuals. For the constant-elasticity specification (3.10), a closed-form expression is available if, following Bénabou, $\log k^i \sim N(m, \Sigma^2)$ (i.e., initial wealth is lognormally distributed). As a function of the average level of wealth and of its dispersion, aggregate production in the second period is given by[26]

$$(s)^\beta \int_{\mathcal{N}} (k_t^i)^{\alpha+\beta} \, dP(i) = (s)^\beta \, E[(k_t^i)^{\alpha+\beta}] = s^\beta K_t^{\alpha+\beta} e^{(\alpha+\beta)(\alpha+\beta-1)\frac{\Sigma^2}{2}}, \tag{3.11}$$

and with $\alpha + \beta < 1$ less inequality (a lower value of Σ) reduces the extent to which self-financing constraints are binding, and increases output. If second-period resources could be redistributed, there would be no reason for inequality to reduce the economy's efficiency. The social planning problem

$$\max \quad \int_{\mathcal{N}} (k_t^i)^\alpha \left(e^i \right)^\beta \, dP(i)$$

$$\text{s.t.} \quad \int_{\mathcal{N}} e^i \, dP(i) = K - C = sK, \tag{3.12}$$

is solved if the marginal efficiency of investment is the same across all investment opportunities, i.e., if

$$e^i = \frac{(k^i)^{\frac{\alpha}{1-\beta}}}{\int (k^{i'})^{\frac{\alpha}{1-\beta}} \, dP(i')} sK$$

is invested in individual i's production function. The exponent of k^i is less than unity if $\alpha + \beta < 1$: to equalize marginal productivity across individuals, the amount invested increases less than proportionately to the initial endowment of individual i. When Pareto optimal redistribution of resources cannot be implemented at time $t + 1$ by financial markets, then taxation and subsidies come into play along the lines of models reviewed in Section 4 below.

The accumulation Eq. (3.10) implies that the relative wealth of any two individuals evolves according to

$$\frac{k_{t+1}^i}{k_{t+1}^j} = \left(\frac{k_t^i}{k_t^j} \right)^{\alpha+\beta} \tag{3.13}$$

and converges to unity if $\alpha + \beta < 1$ (hence, Σ converges to zero unless idiosyncratic shocks are added to each individual's accumulation equation). The aggregate expression

---

[26] These derivations make use of the fact that then $\log((k^i)^{\alpha+\beta}) \sim N((\alpha + \beta)m, (\alpha + \beta)^2\Sigma^2)$, and that, since $K_t = E[k_t^i] = e^{m+\Sigma^2/2}$, $e^{(\alpha+\beta)m+(\alpha+\beta)\Sigma^2/2} = K_t^{\alpha+\beta}$.

in Eq. (3.11) makes it straightforward to study the dynamics of aggregate consumption and/or of its distribution. The growth rate of capital is given by

$$\frac{K_{t+1}}{K_t} = s^\beta K_t^{\alpha+\beta-1} e^{(\alpha+\beta)(\alpha+\beta-1)\frac{\Sigma^2}{2}}, \tag{3.14}$$

and is a decreasing function of K_t for given Σ if $\alpha + \beta < 1$. Hence, long-run growth of aggregate consumption and capital cannot be endogenously determined by savings decisions under the same conditions that imply convergence of cross-sectional wealth levels. This coincidence of individual and aggregate convergence implications is not surprising, since this simple model of self-financed investment represents the evolution of a cross-section of individual wealth levels as a collection of atomistic accumulation problems similar to each other, and to their own aggregate counterpart.

More general models, however, need not feature convergence or lack thereof at both the individual and aggregate levels. In the present setting, if the market allocation were the one that solves the social planning problem (3.12) investment and production would be immediately and completely equalized in cross-section but, depending on the specification of utility functions, consumption may or may not converge across individuals under complete financial markets. Conversely, an economy can be capable of endless endogenous growth even as individuals within it converge towards each other. This is the case if, despite their inability to interact in financial markets, individuals engaged in self-financed accumulation programs interact with each other and influence aggregate growth through *non*-market channels: externalities and spillovers across saving programs can sustain aggregate growth even when each individual's savings would eventually cease to fuel his own income's growth if performed in isolation. As in Tamura (1991), models can be specified where Eq. (2.23) is violated at the aggregate level, so that economy-wide growth proceeds at an endogenous rate in the long run, but Eq. (3.8) holds at the individual level, to imply convergence in the cross-sectional distribution of wealth.[27] To illustrate the point in the present context, let the specification of individual accumulation constraints feature an aggregate knowledge spillover, as in

$$k_{t+1}^i = (k^i)^\alpha (k_t^i - c_t^i)^\beta K_t^{1-\alpha-\beta}. \tag{3.15}$$

This leaves Eq. (3.13) unchanged, but alters Eq. (3.14) to read

$$\frac{K_{t+1}}{K_t} = s^\beta e^{(\alpha+\beta)(\alpha+\beta-1)\frac{\Sigma^2}{2}}. \tag{3.16}$$

The aggregate growth rate is independent of the aggregate capital stock K_t, and hence does not tend to decline as production grows (its dynamics, if any, will instead reflect

---

[27] Barro and Sala i Martin (1997) and others studied models where growth is sustained by realistic knowledge spillovers, such as those generated by imitation of new inventions.

changes in the degree of wealth and income inequality, here denoted by Σ and kept constant for simplicity).[28]

3.2.2. Increasing returns to individual investments

In the neoclassical model of Section 2.1, factor remuneration on the basis of marginal productivity was a logical possibility only if production functions had nonincreasing returns. It was then natural to let the marginal productivity of capital be decreasing in the capital intensity of production, and possibly so strongly decreasing as to satisfy Eq. (2.23). When self-financing constraints make it impossible to trade accumulated factors of production on a competitive market, however, returns can be increasing at the level of individual production units.

To see how investment nonconvexities may lead to divergent wealth dynamics and segmentation, consider an economy where the individual savings rate s is again a given constant, but let investment opportunities feature an indivisibility similar to that studied by Galor and Zeira (1993) in an optimizing context. At time t, individual or family i consumes a fraction $1 - s$ of available resources, which consist of labor income w_t^i as well as of accumulated wealth k_t^i. The amount $s(k_t^i + w_t^i)$ that is saved at time t can earn a net rate of return R in the financial market, but part of it may be invested in an indivisible educational opportunity instead. Against payment of a given cost $\bar{x}_t$, purchase of education ensures that in the next period $w_{t+1}^i = w^S$, the labor income flow of a skilled worker, rather than the unskilled wage rate w^N. Hence, individual i's resources evolve according to

$$k_{t+1}^i + w_{t+1}^i = (1 + R)s(k_t^i + w_t^i) + w^N, \tag{3.17}$$

if the investment in education is not undertaken, and to

$$k_{t+1}^i + w_{t+1}^i = (1 + R)\left[s(k_t^i + w_t^i) - \bar{x}_t\right] + w^S, \tag{3.18}$$

if education is purchased.

Clearly, the indivisible educational opportunity is relevant only if it offers higher returns than financial investment,

$$w^S - w^N > (1 + R)\bar{x}_t, \tag{3.19}$$

in which case it would be efficient to educate all individuals if aggregate resources suffice to do so, i.e., if $s(K_t + W_t L) \geq \bar{x}_t$. If $s(k_t^i + w_t^i) < \bar{x}_t$ for some i and education must be self-financed, however, then some resources will inefficiently earn only the financial

---

[28] Convergence can occur within subeconomies, or neighborhoods, if the nonmarket interactions that allow aggregate growth to proceed forever occur within such units. Bénabou (1996a, b), Durlauf (1996), and others propose and study models of endogenous neighborhood choice and discuss their implications for the dynamics of distribution and of aggregate variables.

return R even as some opportunities for educational investment remain unexploited, because financial market imperfections make it impossible to reap the fruits of investment in others' education.

If $\bar{x}_t = \bar{x}$ is constant and $(1 + R)s < 1$, then the wealth paths of individuals who always earn different wages converge to heterogeneous steady states. In the case of poor individuals who cannot afford education and earn only w^N, wealth follows the dynamics in Eq. (3.17) and may always remain too low to afford education. Symmetrically, the wealth of individuals who are initially rich enough to afford education may always suffice to make education affordable for them. Thus, there exist configurations of parameters such that all individuals with initial resources below the critical level $\bar{x}/s$ never purchase education and, if their wealth is initially above the steady state level, become increasingly poor over time, while individuals whose resources are even only marginally higher than $\bar{x}/s$ follow a path of increasing wealth and consumption.

Such distributional dynamics can be embedded in more or less complex and realistic models of macroeoconomic dynamics. Galor and Zeira (1993) interpret their similar, more sophisticated model as a small open economy, where the rate of return on financial investment is given at the world level, and discuss possible interactions across individual problems in the case where the wage paid to unskilled workers depends on the amount of labor supplied to a sector which uses no internationally mobile capital. Other models feature dynamic interactions among individual-level savings and investment problems. The model of Aghion and Bolton (1997) determines interest rates endogenously, and features a "trickle down" mechanism by which aggregate growth eventually brings all individuals to take advantage of the more favorable opportunities afforded by their non-convex investment sets. In the context of the simple model above, any fixed $\bar{x}$ would similarly become irrelevant if aggregate wages grew along with aggregate capital. The poverty traps would not disappear, however, if the cost $\bar{x}_t$ of education grows in step with aggregate income and wages, as might be realistic if it is specified in terms of labor.

The prediction that equality is associated with better efficiency and faster growth under self-financing constraints can be overturned if investment projects are indivisible: in the context of the simple example above, if $s(K_t + W_t L) < \bar{x}_t$ (i.e., the aggregate economy is so poor as to be unable to educate all its members) then an egalitarian allocation of resources would make self-financing constraints binding for all individuals, and prevent all savings from earning the higher of the two rates of return in Eq. (3.19). Since the speed of further aggregate development depends on the initial distribution of resources under these circumstances, macroeconomic dynamics are generally path-dependent and may feature multiple equilibria. The point is relevant in the context of the model analyzed by Acemoglu and Zilibotti (1997), who abstract from distributional issues by assuming that all individuals are identical within each generation, and in many other models where individual returns are increasing in the size of investment, such as those proposed by Banerjee and Newman (1993) and Perotti (1993) where individual-level increasing returns interact with complex and realistic financial-market imperfections and endogenously determined redistributive policies.

3.3. Idiosyncratic uncertainty

The dynamics of individual and aggregate income, consumption, and wealth levels were deterministic in all the models above. In reality, random shocks are certainly relevant to the evolution of aggregate resources and of their distribution. Individual-level or "idiosyncratic" uncertainty, however, would be completely irrelevant if exchanging contingent securities in perfect and complete financial markets made it possible for individuals to smooth consumption not only over time, as in the models of Section 2, but also across different realizations of exogenous random events. As in Section 2.1.2, the equilibrium allocation under complete markets can be interpreted in terms of a social planning problem. Exchange of state- and time-contingent claims in financial markets ensures that different individuals' marginal utilities always remain proportional, as in Eq. (2.16), and the constants of proportionality ω_i depend on the individual i's endowment of factors of production. As shown by Cochrane (1991) in more detail, the specification that is most relevant for macroeconomic purposes—where utility functions are the same across individuals and have the isoelastic form Eq. (2.25)—implies that consumption levels should remain proportional to each other at all times. Thus, under complete markets, idiosyncratic events have no implications for aggregate dynamics, which can be analyzed on a representative-individual basis, or for distribution, which is determined once and for all by initial conditions.

In reality, of course, not all idiosyncratic (hence potentially insurable) risk is traded in perfect and complete markets, and any discussion of dynamic income inequality must explicitly allow for imperfect insurance.[29] For the purpose of characterizing the macroeconomic relevance of distribution dynamics, it will be helpful to assume that the economy of interest is populated by so many atomistic individuals that, by a law of large numbers, aggregate dynamics are deterministic if all uncertainty is idiosyncratic, yet uninsurable because financial markets fall short of completeness in one or more respects. The distributional implications of uninsurable idiosyncratic uncertainty are qualitatively straightforward, and perhaps most immediately illustrated in the context of the models with self-financed investment opportunities reviewed above, where idiosyncratic events may generate or regenerate inequality across individuals. In stochastic versions of models where, like in Section 3.2.2, self-financing constraints imply higher investment returns for poor individuals, wealth levels converge asymptotically to a distribution rather than to complete equalization; in steady state, ongoing random shocks offset the mean reversion induced by savings and investment returns (Loury, 1981; Benabou, 1996b). In models where, as in Section 3.2.2, indivisibilities and fixed costs imply locally divergent wealth dynamics, idiosyncratic shocks may or may not ensure that stochastic paths of wealth accumulation converge to a single ergodic distribution; if the

---

[29] In a complete-markets setting, in fact, income flows could hardly be defined and measured, since Arrow–Debreu market participants should own portfolios of contingent claims rather than bundles of production factors.

tendency towards segmentation is strong enough, initial conditions and one-time events can have long-run implications (see, e.g., Piketty, 1997).

The macroeconomic implications of idiosyncratic uninsurable uncertainty are more subtle. By definition, idiosyncratic events cancel out in the aggregate. As illustrated by the simple models outlined below, however, random investment opportunities affect individual behavior in ways that do bear on aggregate dynamics, and this is the case even when utility and savings functions obey the restrictions introduced and discussed in Section 2—so that a one-time redistribution of resources would leave unaltered the aggregate propensity to save in a certainty framework.

Assets available to each individual may yield idiosyncratic random returns, and the risk associated with investment in individual-specific assets may be uninsurable. Further, uncertainty about future nonaccumulated income is relevant to savings decisions whenever available assets' payoffs cannot isolate individual consumption from idiosyncratic events. In general, the microeconomic consumption/savings problem of an individual may feature uncertain returns to endogenously accumulated wealth, borrowing constraints, and/or random flows of nonaccumulated factor income in the dynamic accumulation constraint Eq. (1.1). Many of the relevant insights can again be obtained from a simple two-period specification. Consider the problem

$$\max_{c_t} \quad U(c_t) + \frac{1}{1+\rho} E_t[V(k_{t+1}; w_{t+1}, l_{t+1}, \ldots)]$$
$$\text{s.t.} \quad k_{t+1} = f(k_t - c_t; z_{t+1}) + w_{t+1}l_{t+1}, \qquad c_t \leq \bar{c},$$

where the realization of the z_{t+1} determinant of investment returns and/or the amount of nonaccumulated income $w_{t+1}l_{t+1}$ are random as of time t, and borrowing limits may impose an upper bound on current consumption. Under the usual regularity conditions, the necessary and sufficient condition for choice of c_t reads

$$U'(c_t) = \frac{1}{1+\rho} E_t[f'(k_t - c_t; z_{t+1})V'(k_{t+1}; \ldots)] + \mu_t, \tag{3.20}$$

where the Kuhn–Tucker shadow price μ_t is positive if the borrowing constraint is binding, and zero otherwise. As in simpler settings such as Eq. (3.9) above, the implications of more complex multiperiod problems are qualitatively similar, since the second term in the two-period problem's objective function can be interpreted as the value function of utility-maximization problems over longer planning horizons. What follows uses Eq. (3.20) to characterize individual savings behavior and its implications for aggregate accumulation and inequality in two complementary special cases: that where nonaccumulated income is certain (and, for simplicity, equal to zero), but returns to accumulation are partly or wholly individual-specific; and that where returns to accumulation are constant, but nonaccumulated income is subject to idiosyncratic shocks.

3.3.1. Uncertain returns to accumulation

Realized returns to accumulation may be heterogeneous across individuals not only because capital-market imperfections require partial or complete self-financing of investments, but also because they make it difficult or impossible to avoid exogenous rate-of-return risk. To focus on the latter phenomenon, consider the case where an individual's investment opportunity set offers stochastic constant returns, i.e., let

$$f(k - c; z_{t+1}) = (k - c)(1 + r(z_{t+1}^i)) :$$

unit investment returns depend on an exogenous "state of nature" realization z_t^i, but are independent of wealth and investment levels, implying that self-financing constraints (if any) would not affect distributional and aggregate dynamics through the mechanisms reviewed above under certainty.

In Eq. (3.20), the extent to which investment risk influences individual-specific returns and consumption growth depends on the degree of financial market completeness on the one hand, and on the proportion of individual savings channeled through risky assets on the other. When a "stock market" is open, access to less risky (hence more favorable) investment opportunities may or may not increase the savings rate, depending on the balance of income and substitution effects. The point can be illustrated simply in the case where nonaccumulated or "labor" income is absent and all period utility functions have the isoelastic form Eq. (2.25). Under these circumstances, Eq. (3.20) can be rearranged to read

$$\left(\frac{c_t^i}{k_t^i - c_t^i}\right)^{-\sigma} = \frac{1}{1 + \rho} E_t \left[(1 + r(z_t^i))^{1-\sigma}\right]. \tag{3.21}$$

The left-hand side of Eq. (3.21) is a decreasing function of c_t^i for all $\sigma > 0$. Its right-hand side is constant if $\sigma = 1$: as usual, savings are independent of the rate of return on investment under logarithmic utility and in the absence of nonaccumulated income, since income and substitution effects cancel each other and there are no wealth effects. When $\sigma \neq 1$, the effects of rate-of-return uncertainty depend on whether the function whose expectation is taken on the right-hand side of Eq. (3.21) is convex or concave. When the elasticity of intertemporal substitution is small ($\sigma > 1$), then $(1 + r)^{1-\sigma}$ is a convex function of r and, by Jensen's inequality, wider dispersion of investment returns around a given mean increases the right-hand side of Eq. (3.21). Hence, first-period consumption is decreased—and savings are increased—by higher rate-of-return uncertainty. If $\sigma < 1$ instead, lower rate of return uncertainty at the individual level increases each individual's savings rate: roughly speaking, when income effects dominate substitution effects then a more favorable investment opportunity set leads to lower savings.

The basic insight illustrated above is relevant in different ways to various models proposed in the literature. An overlapping-generations structure is convenient when the risk structure of returns is less than trivially endogenous to individual choices, and many models adopt it to study the implications for growth and distribution of (idiosyncratic) risk in investment returns and liquidity constraints. The simple results obtained in a two-period framework are qualitatively similar to those obtained in infinite-time horizon models. In the absence of nonaccumulated income dynamics, an infinite horizon program can be analyzed as a sequence of two-period problems in the form Eq. (3.9) if $V(\cdot)$ is viewed as a Bellman value function, whose functional form is the same as that of the period utility function $U(\cdot)$ if the latter belongs to the quasi-homothetic class of which Eq. (2.12) is an example (see, e.g., Merton, 1971). Continuous-time specifications of rate-of-return uncertainty yield closed-form solutions, which Obstfeld (1994) applies to the financial market integration issues of interest here.[30]

As only the mean rate of return matters for aggregate saving's contribution to future output and growth, when $\sigma > 1$ then forms of financial market development that simply allow individuals to pool idiosyncratic rate-of-return risk are associated with slower growth. In fact, since the savings rate satisfying Eq. (3.21) is the same for all individuals faced by the same ex ante investment opportunity set, aggregating across individuals yields

$$
\begin{aligned}
K_{t+1} &= \int_{\mathcal{N}} (k_t^i - c_t^i)(1 + r(z_t^i)) \, dP(i) \\
&= \left(\frac{K-C}{K}\right) \int_{\mathcal{N}} k_t^i (1 + r(z_t^i)) \, dP(i);
\end{aligned}
$$

and if realized returns are uncorrelated to individual wealth levels, then

$$
\int_{\mathcal{N}} k_t^i (1 + r(z_t^i)) \, dP(i) = \int_{\mathcal{N}} k_t^i \, dP(i) E_t[(1 + r(z_t^i))] \equiv K_t(1 + R),
$$

hence

$$
\frac{K_{t+1}}{K_t} = \left(\frac{K-C}{K}\right)(1 + R). \tag{3.22}
$$

The realized mean return R is a given parameter if all uncertainty is idiosyncratic, and idiosyncratic uncertainty has aggregate effects only through the savings propensity. If $\sigma > 1$, an economy without financial markets produces a larger amount of aggregate resources even as it distributes it more unevenly across its consumers/investors—whose

[30] Obstfeld (1994), like Devereux and Smith (1994) and Devereux and Saito (1997), emphasizes the implications of financial market integration in an international context, along the lines of the discussion in Section 5.1 below. Obstfeld also studies a more general case where utility is not additively separable over time and, as in Weil (1990), makes it clear that the effects of investment opportunities on consumption growth are mediated by σ in its role as the inverse of the intertemporal elasticity of substitution, rather than as the coefficient of relative risk aversion.

welfare is, however, lowered ex ante by consumption volatility, and quite imperfectly approximated by conventional output measures (Devereux and Smith, 1994, compute and discuss welfare measures).

If individuals can control the riskiness of their investment portfolios, risk pooling is generally relevant to the investment efficiency of any given volume of savings, or to the size of the aggregate return R in Eq. (3.22). Risky investments must be more productive (on average) than safe ones if they are ever undertaken. Hence, aggregate productivity is higher and growth is ceteris paribus faster when risk pooling makes it individually optimal to reduce the portfolio share of safe, low-expected-return assets, and increase that of (well diversified) high-return risky assets. Saint-Paul (1992b), Obstfeld (1994), Devereux and Saito (1997) formulate and solve models where this effect has a role.[31]

Distributional implications. Models where returns to accumulation are idiosyncrati-cally uncertain obviously rationalize ex post inequality over any finite horizon. In infinite-horizon models, inequality would simply increase without bounds if returns to invest-ment were continuously perturbed by idiosyncratic shocks, and were unrelated to wealth levels.[32] In general, financial markets offer better insurance against idiosyncratic income and consumption uncertainty, and a more efficient allocation of aggregate savings across investment opportunities. Across economies at different levels of financial development, accordingly, higher production and faster growth should be associated with more stable inequality. Recent work brings this insight to bear on time-series developments, allowing the evolution of financial markets to be endogenously related to growth and wealth dynamics. Greenwood and Jovanovic (1990), Saint-Paul (1992b), and other models surveyed by Greenwood and Smith (1997) let it be costly for individuals to access an intermediated financial market. The implications of costly access to the favorable investment opportunities offered by organized financial markets depend on distribution as well as on the level and expected growth rate of income, and are similar to those of the indivisibilities and fixed costs in individual investment opportunity sets reviewed in Section 3.2.2 above.[33] Depending on the distribution of resources, a more or less large fraction of the population may be able to afford participation when its costs are partly fixed at the individual's level. Since relative welfare levels are completely stabilized across those individuals who do participate in the financial market the dynamic paths of aggregate output and cross-sectional inequality are jointly determined and, as in the sim-pler setting discussed in Section 3.2.2, fixed participation costs may become irrelevant

---

[31] Similarly, a well-developed financial market lets savings be allocated more efficiently when new capital takes time to become productive and, as in the model proposed by Bencivenga and Smith (1991), individual portfolios are biased to more liquid but less productive assets when financial institutions ("banks") are not available to smooth liquidity risk across heterogeneous individuals; see also Greenwood and Smith (1997).

[32] Models like Bénabou's (1996c, d) feature uncertain returns to investment, but also self-financing constraints, which generate mean-reverting wealth dynamics as in Tamura (1991).

[33] The model of Acemoglu and Zilibotti (1997), in fact, features better diversification in a more developed economy because investment projects are indivisible, rather than because of assumptions regarding financial market set-up costs.

if growth "trickles down" so as to eventually lead all individuals to enter the financial market.[34]

3.3.2. *Liquidity constraints and uninsurable endowment risk*

Consider a two-period problem where the rate of return is certain, as in Eq. (3.1), but nonaccumulated income accrues in the second as well as in the first period:

$$\max \quad U(c_t^y) + \frac{1}{1+\rho} U(c_{t+1}^o) \tag{3.23}$$

$$\text{s.t.} \quad c_{t+1}^o = (W_t l_t^y - c_t^y)(1+R) + W_{t+1} l_{t+1}^o, \tag{3.24}$$

where l_t^y denotes the labor endowment of individuals who are young at time t, and l_{t+1}^o that of the same individuals when old at time $t+1$. Let $l_t^o = l_{t+1}^o = \cdots = l^o$ be constant over time, and similarly let $l_t^y = l_{t+1}^y = \cdots = l^y$ for all t; in a growing economy, of course, different market wage rates may reward the individual's given labor supply at times t and $t+1$. Consumption choices satisfy Eq. (3.20) with $V(\cdot) = \frac{1}{1+\rho} U(\cdot)$:

$$U'(c_t^y) = \frac{1+R}{1+\rho} E_t[U'\left((W_t l^y - c_t^y)(1+R) + W_{t+1} l^o\right)] + \mu_t. \tag{3.25}$$

If $U'(c) = c^{-\sigma}$, it is easy to verify that $W_t l_t^y - c^y > 0$ (savings are positive) if

$$\frac{W_{t+1}}{W_t} \frac{l^o}{l^y} < \left(\frac{1+R}{1+\rho}\right)^{\frac{1}{\sigma}} \equiv \xi. \tag{3.26}$$

This condition is trivially satisfied if $l^o = 0$, as in the standard overlapping-generations model Eq. (3.1). In more general models, however, the growth rate of wages may exceed the desired growth rate of consumption, at least over part of an individual's life: if the inequality in Eq. (3.26) is reversed, then young individuals would wish to borrow, and if they are not allowed to do so then $\mu_t > 0$ in Eq. (3.25). Under certainty, if exogenous earnings increase faster than desired consumption then binding liquidity constraints imply larger savings in the aggregate.

A further "precautionary" increase in savings occurs if future nonaccumulated income is random, future consumption is uninsurably uncertain, and the utility function has a positive third derivative (see Deaton, 1991 and Carroll, 1992, for recent discussion of such phenomena). Ljungqvist (1993, 1995) and Jappelli and Pagano (1994) explore

---

[34] The Greenwood and Jovanovic (1990) model predicts convergence to a stable distribution of welfare (and, since utility is logarithmic, of consumption and wealth). Some individuals' wealth levels may never become high enough to induce them to enter the financial market. Even in that case, however, all of the economy's wealth is asymptotically invested in the financial market, for individuals may remain out of it only if their wealth becomes negligible in relative terms.

the growth implications of precautionary savings in overlapping-generations settings. When endogenous growth is driven by productivity spillovers, then liquidity constraints may improve every individual's welfare if the distortion of consumption patterns over each generation's lifetime is more than offset by the faster consumption growth induced by external effects. Besides distorting intertemporal consumption patterns relative to what would be optimal for the given private rate of return on savings, in fact, liquidity constraints also reduce individual borrowing, hence increase aggregate savings. To the extent that each generation's savings affect its own wages through external effects (and the social return on savings is higher than the private one, as is plausible in an endogenous-growth model), higher savings may bring each generation closer to the truly optimal lifecycle pattern of consumption.[35]

The direction of the inequality in Eq. (3.26) depends not only on the lifetime pattern of labor endowments l_t^y, l_{t+1}^o and on the taste parameters ρ, σ, but also on the rate of return on savings R and on the growth rate of wages W_{t+1}/W_t, either or both of which are generally endogenous in macroeconomic equilibrium. The models of Laitner (1979a, b, 1992), Aiyagari (1994), Aiyagari and McGrattan (1995), and others study wealth accumulation in general-equilibrium settings with exogenous or endogenous growth, and focus on the macroeconomic implications of savings intended to provide a "precautionary" cushion against idiosyncratic bad luck. In the notation adopted here, the rate of return on wealth R is both constant over time and common across individuals, while the income stream $\{l_t^i W_t\}$ is random and exogenous to the individual's consumption and savings choices. In analogy to R, one may let $w = W$ be homogeneous across individuals, and ascribe all uncertainty to the individual- and period-specific endowment l_t^i of the nonaccumulated factor L. This also ensures that uncertainty does not become irrelevant in proportional terms if W_t grows over time.

Distributional implications. Across individuals who may lend or borrow (subject to solvency constraints) but bear uninsurable risk, inequality tends to increase over time. To see this, consider that Eq. (3.20) with $f'(\cdot) = 1 + R$ and—in the absence of liquidity constraints— $\mu_t = 0$ implies:

$$U'(c_t^i) = \frac{1+R}{1+\rho} \left(U'(c_{t+1}^i - \epsilon_{t+1}^i) \right), \qquad (3.27)$$

where ϵ_t^i denotes the unpredictable difference between the expected and realized marginal utility of individual i's consumption. If $R = \rho$, each individual's marginal utility follows the driftless process

$$U'(c_{t+1}^i) = U'(c_t^i) + \epsilon_{t+1}^i, \qquad (3.28)$$

[35] De Gregorio (1996) studies the interaction of such welfare-enhancing effects of financial market imperfections with the investment distortions implied by self-financing constraints.

and marginal utility differentials across individuals also have unpredictable increments over time if, as we assume, all uncertainty is idiosyncratic. Like the probability distribution of a random-walk process, the cross-sectional distribution of consumption and welfare levels tends to widen. As noted by Atkeson and Lucas (1992), such lack of mean reversion in relative welfare levels is a general feature of efficient allocations under private information, which prevents full insurance but does not reduce the desirability of consumption smoothing over time. The same efficiency considerations that imply stability of relative marginal utilities in the first-best setting of Section 2.1.2 imply unpredictability of marginal-utility shocks when the planner's welfare weights need to be revised so as to maintain incentive compatibility under asymmetric information.[36]

If welfare is bounded below, however, marginal utility processes follow a renewal process with a well-defined ergodic distribution. Heuristically, an upper bound on marginal utility imposes a reflecting barrier on the nonstationary process Eq. (3.28), and past experiences become irrelevant whenever the barrier is reached. Liquidity constraints do impose such lower bounds on consumption and welfare, and effectively truncate individual planning horizons at the (random) times when binding constraints make past accumulation irrelevant to future consumption and welfare.[37] If liquidity constraints are binding with positive probability (and bind at any given time for a finitely positive fraction of a large economy's population), then individual marginal utilities are increasing on average (and utility levels drift downwards) over time, or $R < \rho$ in

$$U'(c_t^i) = \frac{1+R}{1+\rho} \left(U'(c_{t+1}^i) - \epsilon_{t+1}^i \right).$$

Since financial markets offer less favorable lending opportunities to richer individuals when poor individuals find it impossible to borrow, consumption-smoothing individuals decumulate wealth on average when they are rich enough to self-insure, i.e., draw on assets so as to buffer the effects of exogenous income shocks on their consumption. This behavior implies that accumulated wealth, driven by a cumulation of stationary labor-income realizations, follows a nonstationary process with negative drift and a reflecting barrier at the lowest level consistent with borrowing constraints, and has a well-defined distribution in the long run. Since consumption cannot be sheltered forever from labor-income uncertainty, consumers with decreasing absolute risk aversion find it optimal to transfer resources from present (and certain) to future (and uncertain) consumption by "precautionary" or "buffer-stock" savings. To ensure homotheticity of the objective

---

[36] Finite individual lifetimes or planning horizons, of course, limit the extent to which wealth and welfare levels can drift randomly away from each other. Deaton and Paxson's (1994) empirical work supports the implication that consumption inequality should be increasing with age within consumer cohorts.

[37] The implications of binding liquidity constraints, in fact, are in many ways similar to those of finite lifetimes in overlapping-generation models (Laitner, 1979a). Tighter bounds on consumption and wealth dynamics than those required by simple solvency may reflect nonnegativity constraints on bequests, limited possibilities to use future labor income as collateral, and/or welfare lower bounds implied by redistribution policies (Atkeson and Lucas, 1995).

function and avoid a trending savings rate in a growing environment, the period utility function must take the isoelastic form (2.25).[38] While a perfectly insured consumer would have a constant propensity to save out of current resources if the period utility function $U(\cdot)$ has the form (2.25), in the solution of Eq. (2.10) savings are luxuries—i.e., a higher proportion of available resources is saved by richer individuals—if labor income is uncertain (Laitner, 1979a). This provides a better rationale for wealth-dependent savings rates than the positive $\bar{c}$ required consumption levels studied above in a certainty setting, since any finite $\bar{c}$ would become asymptotically irrelevant in a growing economy unless required consumption is specified in relative terms.[39]

For the canonical isoelastic specification (2.25) of preferences, savings propensities depend in intuitive and realistic ways on both the level and the factor composition of individual and aggregate income flows. The propensity to consume out of wealth is higher for richer individuals, who are less concerned with (heavily discounted) future consumption volatility; the propensity to consume out of nonaccumulated income depends, in accordance with permanent-income theory, on whether the current flow is above or below its long-run expected level. This class of models can rationalize an increasing income elasticity of savings without resorting to ad-hoc assumptions on the form of utility, which would imply increasing rates of accumulation and growth in a growing economy where all agents become richer over time. The empirical realism of these models can be enhanced in a variety of ways, most notably allowing for realistic lifecycle patterns of labor earnings and wealth as in Laitner (1992).

The macroeconomic implications of such microeconomic behavior are qualitatively straightforward, but somewhat difficult to study because closed-form solutions are not available. As each individual attempts to self-insure against idiosyncratic risk, aggregate accumulation is more intense for any given rate of return and expected accumulation rate. If this results in a higher aggregate wealth-to-output ratio, steady-state equilibrium is restored by a decline of the rate of return on savings along a neoclassical factor price frontier (as in the models of Laitner, 1979a, b, and Aiyagari, 1994); if the marginal and average return of wealth accumulation is constant instead, as in endogenous growth models, the higher propensity to accumulate capital increases the average growth rate of consumption and nonaccumulated factor incomes, and the latter restores equilibrium as a larger expected flow of future income makes it less necessary for individuals to rely on accumulation to boost future consumption levels. One of the models that Devereux and Smith (1994) specify and solve in an international framework of analysis is isomorphic

---

[38] Closed-form solutions for precautionary-savings problems are available if absolute, rather than relative, risk aversion is constant (see Caballero, 1991). Under a constant absolute risk aversion specification, however, assets do not behave as a buffer stock; consumption responds fully to income innovations, and this has inconvenient and unrealistic implications for aggregate analysis (Irvine and Wang, 1994).

[39] Rebelo (1992), Atkeson and Ogaki (1996), and their references formulate and solve models of this type and assess their empirical relevance. The Uzawa (1968) assumption that the discount rate ρ is an increasing function of current utility (and wealth) has the unintuitive implication of a decreasing wealth elasticity of savings, yet it is often adopted in macroeconomic applications where asymptotic stability of wealth accumulation is needed.

to a macroeconomic model where infinitely lived individuals can neither borrow nor lend, and can only use self-financed investment for consumption-smoothing purposes. Like in the overlapping-generations model of Jappelli and Pagano (1994), precautionary savings induced by additive ("labor income") uninsurable shocks can accelerate endogenous growth to the point that welfare is higher under financial autarchy than under perfect insurance.

4. Politics and institutions

In a neoclassical economy with complete competitive markets, one-time redistribution could and should resolve any distributional issues without compromising the efficiency of macroeconomic outcomes. The appropriate lump-sum redistribution instruments, however, are simply not available in the absence of complete intertemporal markets. At the same time as distortions (such as taxes, subsidies, and market imperfections) decrease the size of the economic "pie" available to a hypothetical representative individual or to a social planner with access to lump-sum redistribution, they also alter the way economic welfare is shared among individuals. Hence, distribution and macroeconomics interact not only through the channels surveyed in the previous sections, but also by influencing the extent to which distortionary policies are implemented in politico-economic equilibria.[40]

The point is relevant to any model where policy is allowed to play a role, but perhaps most relevant in this survey's context when taxes and other relative price distortions can affect an economy's endogenous rate of growth, i.e., when they alter private incentives to allocate resources to the sector or sectors where a "core" of accumulated factors can reproduce itself without encountering decreasing returns (Rebelo, 1991). Since many such models feature increasing returns, missing markets, or imperfectly competitive market interactions, policy interventions meant to offset *laissez-faire* inefficiencies and distortions play a prominent role in this context. Accordingly, recent work (also surveyed by Bénabou, 1996c, and Persson and Tabellini, 1998) has focused on the growth implications of distributional tensions.

To illustrate the macroeconomic impact of distortionary policies and the political mechanisms linking distributional tensions to equilibrium distortions, consider the simplest model encountered above, where individual savings decisions aim at maximizing

$$\log(c_t^i) + \frac{1}{1+\rho} \log(c_{t+1}^i), \tag{4.1}$$

---

[40] Related incentive mechanisms may also be relevant in some contexts. Even selfish individuals may be concerned with inequality when it is so wide as to make predatory activities preferable to market participation for poor individuals, and costly defensive activities necessary for richer individuals; Grossman and Kim (1996) and their references analyze in detail the microeconomic determinants and macroeconomic implications of predatory activity. Distributional issues are also directly relevant when individuals' relative standing bears on their economic welfare and their savings decisions, as in the model of Cole et al. (1992).

and specify the budget constraint in such a way as to account for individual resource heterogeneity and for taxation. Let individual i's first- and second-period consumption levels be given by

$$c_t^i = w_t^i - k_t^i, \quad c_{t+1}^i = (1 + (1-\tau)R)k_t^i + S,$$

where the exogenous endowment w_t^i and the portion k_t^i saved out of it are individual-specific, while the gross return on savings R, the tax rate τ applied to it, and the subsidy S are the same for all individuals. Taking both τ and S as given, the individually optimal consumption choice is

$$c_t^i = \frac{1+\rho}{2+\rho}\left(w^i + \frac{S}{1+(1-\tau)R}\right). \tag{4.2}$$

With a logarithmic utility function, the lower net rate of return implied by a higher tax rate τ has offsetting income and substitution effects. The subsidy, however, unambiguously increased first-period consumption, to an extent that depends on the wealth effect of the tax-determined rate of return.

Both τ and S can be negative (to represent an investment subsidy financed by lump-sum taxes), and the two policy instruments are related to each other through the government's budget constraint if the per-capita subsidy is financed by taxing the income RK_t, of capital in the second period, so that

$$S = \tau R K_t \tag{4.3}$$

for $K_t = \int_N k_t^i \, dP(i)$ the aggregate capital stock at the end of the first period. Since

$$k_t^i = w^i - c^i = \frac{w^i}{2+\rho} - \frac{1+\rho}{2+\rho}\frac{S}{1+(1-\tau)R},$$

aggregating, denoting $\int w_t^i \, dP(i) = W_t$, and using Eq. (4.3) yields

$$K_t = \frac{W_t}{2+\rho} - \frac{1+\rho}{2+\rho}\frac{\tau R K_t}{1+(1-\tau)R}.$$

Solving for the equilibrium level of K_t, we find that

$$K_t = \left(2+\rho+\frac{(1+\rho)\tau R}{1+(1-\tau)R}\right)^{-1} W_t.$$

Hence, a higher tax rate τ unambiguously reduces the aggregate capital stock in the second period. The insight is more general than the simple model considered here. Rate of return taxes only have substitution effects when their revenues are rebated in lump-sum fashion, and under any homothetic objective function individual savings choices can be aggregated to yield the same qualitative results as in the logarithmic case considered here (Persson and Tabellini, 1994). Quite intuitively, a positive tax rate on investment returns and a lump-sum consumption subsidy make savings less attractive, for each individual can to some extent rely on taxation of others' savings to finance future consumption. In equilibrium, individuals free ride on each other's choices to postpone consumption, and less capital is accumulated.

4.1. Political sources of distortionary taxation

It is of course far from surprising to find that taxing the income of an endogenously supplied factor, like k_{t+1}^i in this simple model, decreases private supply incentives and has negative effects on macroeconomic efficiency. Such effects would be present even in a representative-individual macroeconomy where $w^i = W$ for all i. Recent research aims at highlighting how such outcomes, while clearly undesirable from the representative individual's point of view, may be rationalized by explicit consideration of redistributive motives in the politico-economic process that presumably underlies policy choices in reality.

To illustrate the insight in the context of the simple model introduced above, note that the Euler equation implies

$$c_{t+1}^i = \frac{1 + (1 - \tau)R}{1 + \rho} c_t^i,$$

for the simple example's logarithmic objective function. Hence, maximized individual welfare may be written

$$\frac{2 + \rho}{1 + \rho} \log(c_t^i) + \frac{1}{1 + \rho} \log\left(\frac{1 + (1 - \tau)R}{1 + \rho}\right).$$

Using Eqs. (4.2) and (4.3), and neglecting irrelevant constants, individual welfare depends on the tax rate according to

$$V(\tau) = (2 + \rho) \log\left(w^i + \frac{\tau W R}{2 + \rho + R(2 + \rho - \tau)}\right) + \log\left(1 + (1 - \tau)R\right). \quad (4.4)$$

Each individual's welfare is increased by the tax and subsidy package's impact on the two consumption levels, represented by the first term on the right-hand side of Eq. (4.4). Differentiating this term, it is easy to show that the welfare effect of a higher τ is more positive for small values of w^i: intuitively, relatively poor individuals' consumption levels are subsidized by taxing the higher savings of richer individuals.

All individuals' welfare is also decreased by the distorted intertemporal pattern of consumption, represented by the last term in the expression above: differentiating, it is easy to show that the two marginal effects offset each other at $\tau = 0$ if $w^i = W$, i.e., if the welfare expression refers to a representative individual's welfare whose welfare is maximized by the savings choices implied by an undistorted intertemporal rate of transformation. For individuals with $w^i < W$, however, the level effect is larger than the slope effect at $\tau = 0$, and welfare is maximized at a positive level of τ. Hence, relatively poor individuals prefer strictly positive tax rates, because from their point of view the benefits of redistribution more than offset the welfare loss from a distorted intertemporal consumption pattern. Conversely, for those endowed with more resources than the representative individual ($w^i > W$) a policy of investment subsidization and lump-sum taxes would be preferable to the laissez-faire outcome.

As noted by Persson and Tabellini (1994), realistic skewness of income distribution associates higher inequality with a higher percentage of relatively poor individuals. For example, a democratic one-person-one-vote political process should generally result in redistribution-motivated distortions, because the median voter is poorer—to an extent that depends on the degree of inequality—than the average (representative) individual. Other political decision processes will also yield interior solutions for tax rate τ, as individuals (or coalitions of individuals) weigh the costs and benefits of redistribution and distortions from their own point of view.

The insight can be brought to bear on macroeconomic growth if the simple two-period model above is embedded within a longer-horizon aggregate economy. Persson and Tabellini (1994) let each generation's initial resources, denoted W in the derivations above, depend on the previous generation's savings decisions through external effects. Then, the simple insights afforded by the two-period savings decision carry over directly to aggregate dynamics, since all economic and political interactions occur within a closed set of individuals alive at the same time: a higher level of exogenous inequality is associated with more intense redistributive tensions and, in situations where distortionary taxation is used for redistributive purposes, with slower growth. Persson and Tabellini (1994) offer evidence in support of this simple and realistic insight. Further and more detailed empirical work (briefly reviewed in Section 5 below) is less supportive, and other theoretical models also suggest more complex linkages between inequality, redistribution, and economic performance.

4.2. Dimensions of heterogeneity and distribution

As in the simple model above, distortionary redistribution can be a political equilibrium outcome only if individual agents' endowments are cross-sectionally heterogeneous ($w^i \neq W$ for at least some i). In fact, identical individuals—like a hypothetical social planner—would never want to decrease economic efficiency. The extent and character of heterogeneity, however, need not be as immediately associated with the size distribution of income as in the model outlined above.

Bertola (1993) and Alesina and Rodrik (1994) study policy determination in models of endogenous growth which, like those outlined in Section 2.2.2, feature balanced paths of endogenous growth with no transitional dynamics. In these models, the speed of growth is directly related to the private rate of return on savings and investment decisions, hence to the portion of aggregate production accruing to accumulated factors of production. Explicit discussion of policy choices is particularly important in this context, because the underlying economic models allow for market imperfections and/or for an explicit role of government expenditure (and for increasing returns to scale at the aggregate level) in order to obtain constant returns to accumulation. Thus, policy intervention would generally be desirable even from a representative individual's point of view.

If ownership of accumulated and/or of nonaccumulated factors of production is not evenly spread across all individuals, however, then factor-income distribution affects not only the aggregate growth rate, but also the distribution of income and welfare across individuals. The extent of such heterogeneity and the character of political interactions are crucial determinants of policy choices and, through them, of macroeconomic growth outcomes.

To illustrate this point, consider a simple discrete-time version of the relevant models. If all individuals aim at maximizing logarithmic utility flows discounted at rate ρ over an infinite horizon, a constant rate of return R on savings implies that all consumption flows grow according to

$$\frac{c_{t+1}}{c_t} = \frac{C_{t+1}}{C_t} = \frac{1+R}{1+\rho} \equiv \theta,$$

and the welfare level of individual i can be written

$$\sum_{j=0}^{\infty} \left(\frac{1}{1+\rho}\right)^j \log(c_t^i \theta^j) = \log(c_t^i)\frac{1+\rho}{\rho} + \log(\theta)\frac{1+\rho}{\rho^2},$$

as of time t. The budget constraint, as in Eq. (2.28), implies that

$$c_t^i = W_t l^i + (1 + R - \theta)k_t^i, \tag{4.5}$$

for an individual who owns a constant number l^i of units of the nonaccumulated factor (each earning W_t at time t) and k_t^i units of the accumulated one at time t (earning a constant gross rate of return $1 + R$). If the output/capital ratio is a constant A, then using $W = \gamma A K_t / L$ and $R = (1 - \gamma)A$ in Eq. (4.5) yields

$$c_t^i = \left(\gamma A \frac{l^i}{L} + \frac{\rho}{1+\rho}(1 + (1-\gamma)A)\frac{k_t^i}{K_t}\right) K_t, \tag{4.6}$$

and makes it possible to write individual welfare as a function of the factor share γ of nonaccumulated factors of production. Disregarding irrelevant constants and the level of the aggregate capital stock K_t, which affects all welfare levels equally, the relevant expression reads

$$V(\gamma) = \log\left(\gamma A \frac{l^i}{L} + \frac{\rho}{1+\rho}(1 + (1-\gamma)A)\frac{k_t^i}{K_t}\right) + \log(1 + (1-\gamma)A)\frac{1}{\rho}. \quad (4.7)$$

Like the savings tax rate in the two-period model above, different values of γ affect consumption levels (in a way that depends on initial endowments) on the one hand, and the slope of (all individuals') consumption paths on the other.

The slope effect of a smaller γ is unambiguously positive: faster growth benefits all individuals' welfare, and is the equilibrium outcome in this model if a larger share of aggregate output is paid to accumulated factors of production. Faster investment-driven growth must be financed by lower consumption levels, however, and the impact of a smaller γ on initial consumption depends on the factor composition of individual income sources. For the representative individual, $l^i/L = k^i/K \equiv 1$ by definition, and welfare is maximized when $\gamma = 0$ and the private gross return $1 + R$ coincides with the aggregate transformation factor $1 + A$. Equally unsurprisingly, the welfare of an individual i who happens to own only nonaccumulated factors of production (so that $k^i = 0$) is far from being maximized by $\gamma = 0$, which implies zero consumption and an infinitely negative welfare level.

More generally, the preferred value of γ depends on the *relative* size of k^i and l^i. Heterogeneity of factor income sources may (but need not) be related to the size distribution of income that was relevant in the above model, for example because accumulated wealth is more unequal than other sources of income; when a political process leads to implementation of policies (such as taxes and subsidies) which bear on the after-tax income shares of the two factors, its outcome generally depends on the distribution of political power across constituencies (or "classes") with different income sources (Bertola, 1993).

4.3. The menu and timing of policies

The simple models outlined above illustrate the general insights that distributional tensions can have macroeconomic effects when they result in distortionary policies. Their results, of course, hinge on the details of politico-economic interactions on the one hand, and on the specific distortionary instrument used for redistributional purposes on the other. In models where distribution-motivated policy interventions unavoidably distort incentives, individuals trade their preference for a large share of the social pie against the size of the latter, and it may be possible to obtain and characterize interior politico-economic equilibria.[41] In practice, of course, more than one instrument is generally

---

[41] For well-defined voting equilibria to exist, it is generally necessary to limit the extent and character of heterogeneity across agents in such a way as to ensure that preferences over packages of different policy instruments are well-behaved (single-peaked).

available to pursue distributional objectives and, like imperfect and incomplete financial markets, political interactions can be specified in many different ways. While the simple illustrative models above can characterize sharply the distortionary effects of political interactions by focusing on simple policy instruments, more complex models recognize that many different policies may be separately or simultaneously implemented in reality.

While in the simple models outlined above distributional tensions clearly reduce aggregate efficiency, redistribution can have beneficial effects on representative-agent welfare when it substitutes missing markets. Human capital accumulation is most likely to be distorted by self-financing constraints and uninsurability, and is often targeted by policy interventions (see Glomm and Ravikumar, 1992, for a simple model of the implications of private or public education schemes for growth and distribution). In the models reviewed in Section 3.2.1 and studied in more detail by Bénabou (1996c, d), self-financing constraints prevent relatively poor agents (and the aggregate economy) from taking advantage of high returns from investment in their own education. When the status quo cross-sectional allocation of savings is distorted by self-financing constraints, a more equal distribution improves the efficiency of investment allocation, and is associated with higher output levels (or faster growth). Since inefficient investment patterns (whether caused by self-financing constraints, or by the incentive effects of redistribution-motivated policies) are unanimously disliked, politico-economic interactions will tend towards efficiency whenever it can be achieved independently of distribution.

As the efficiency benefits of redistribution depend on the extent of inequality, but only the relatively poor ones gain from the redistributive aspects of investment subsidies, political support for such redistributive policies as education subsidies is generally not a monotonic function of status quo inequality. In the models proposed by Bénabou (1996c, d), which introduce tractable specifications of tax and subsidy schemes in loglinear budget constraints in the form Eq. (3.10), the relative importance of efficiency-enhancing and redistributive effects in political interactions depends on the dispersion and skewness of income distribution, and on the distribution of political power across income levels. Furthermore, since policies that affect ex post inequality feed back into their own political sustainability in a dynamic environment, multiple equilibria are possible: at relatively low levels of inequality, political equilibrium entails efficiency-enhancing redistribution and smaller income dispersion increases future political support for more redistribution, while symmetric reinforcing effects can be featured by high-inequality, low-redistribution dynamic trajectories.

In general, when the menu of available policy instruments is so wide as to make it possible to target both efficiency and distribution, then aggregate outcomes are much less likely to be affected by inequality, and distributional issues can be separated from macroeconomic performance in much the same way as in the complete markets case. Most relevantly, investment efficiency can be preserved by appropriately targeted subsidies even as politico-economic determination of tax rates pursues distributional objectives. In the models studied by Bénabou (1996c, d), where the accumulated factor is human capital, efficiency can be pursued by education subsidies (or by state-financed education) rather than by progressive taxation schemes. Individual agents, regardless of their income level, unanimously agree that efficiency should be achieved. This objective does not interfere with heterogeneous incentives to redistribute income when the latter can be pursued by a separate instrument. Similarly, Bertola (1993) finds that capital-poor individuals would obviously vote against policies that increase the growth rate of the economy by reducing their share of aggregate income, but would favor policy packages that restore growth-rate efficiency by subsidizing investment. In general, a wider menu of potentially distortionary policy instruments makes it easier for redistribution-motivated policy interventions to preserve efficiency, and brings macroeconomic outcomes closer to those that would be realized if distributional issues could be resolved by lump-sum instruments.

While once-and-for-all choices from a wide menu of policies can in principle minimize the distortionary consequences of politically desirable redistribution, the kind of one-time redistribution that would support the textbook separation of efficiency and distribution is hardly feasible in realistic dynamic settings. In the extreme case where the menu of available policies indeed includes a lump-sum redistribution instrument—e.g., taxation of the first-period endowment w^i in the two-period model of Section 4.1— nothing should in principle prevent macroeconomic efficiency but, since each individual would simply want to appropriate as large a share of aggregate resources as possible, it would be impossible to characterize interior political equilibria. In more complex dynamic models, and in reality, only distortionary instruments are available: in any situation where binding, complete intertemporal contracts are not available, in fact, "lump sum" redistribution is generally feasible only at the beginning of time, and can hardly be discussed or implemented in real time. Like capital income taxation in the simple model of Section 4.1, threats of "one-time" expropriation in an ongoing dynamic environment and lax enforcement of property rights loosens the link between individual supply decisions and individual consumption levels and, in the models proposed by Tornell and Velasco (1992), Benhabib and Rustichini (1996) and others, slows down capital accumulation.

Dynamic interactions between policy choices and political sustainability are potentially much more complex than simple models make it, and so is the relationship between ex ante or ex post inequality and macroeconomic outcomes. When taxation is decided ex post, or when predatory activity is made possible by imperfect protection of property rights, then the rational expectation of redistributive pressure affects incentives to save and invest even when all agents face identical problems and no redistribution takes place ex post. Distributional tensions are present and distortionary even when agents are and remain homogeneous, for the simple *fear* of ex-post expropriation tends to remove incentives to save and invest (Bénabou, 1996c). Recent work by Krusell and Rios Rull (1992), Krusell et al. (1997) and Huffman (1996) applies such intertemporal insights to the analysis of political decision processes focused on simple policy instruments, drawing a useful parallel to time inconsistency issues in optimal taxation problems from a representative-agent's perspective. Numerical results are qualitatively consistent with the outcome of simpler equilibrium notions: as in the simple models of Sections 4.1 and 4.2, capital-poor agents are less inclined to reward investment (and speed up growth) than the representative agent. The resulting equilibrium tax rate is different, however, when policy choices are made every period within a dynamic framework of analysis rather than once and for all, as in the simpler models outlined above and in Bertola (1993), Persson and Tabellini (1994) and Alesina and Rodrik (1994); even identical individuals, in fact, should generally refrain from supporting first-best investment rewards if they think they can free-ride on their own future time-consistent choices.

Symmetrically, when taxation and redistribution policies are decided before the realization of exogenous income inequality is known, the observed intensity of ex post fiscal redistribution may mimic that which would be implied by intertemporal contingent contracts. In reality, of course, imperfect insurance reflects incomplete or asymmetric information and, unless tax-based redistribution can exploit superior sources of information, ex post redistribution meant to shelter individual consumption from undesirable fluctuations should generally worsen the economy's allocative efficiency at the same time as it reduces ex post cross sectional inequality.

Perhaps as a trivial example of how policy-based redistribution may improve *laissez-faire* efficiency, however, consider how different the role of taxes and subsidies would be if the expected value of an objective function similar to Eq. (4.1) were maximized under the constraints

$$c_t^i = w_t^i - k_t^i, \quad c_{t+1}^i = (1 - \tau)w_{t+1}^i + (1 + R)k_t^i + S, \tag{4.8}$$

where w_{t+1}^i is idiosyncratically random as of time t. If for some reason individuals find it impossible to stipulate insurance contracts, or if such contracts are even slightly costly to write and enforce, all would unanimously agree that $\tau = 1$, $S = E_t \left[w_{t+1}^i \right]$ is a welfare-increasing set of taxes and subsidies (and, since a nonrandom second-period consumption would eliminate precautionary savings, higher welfare would be associated with slower aggregate consumption growth). Less benign, but qualitatively similar implications for the role of redistribution can be drawn from models where individuals are not ex ante identical. If $E_t \left[w_{t+1}^i \right]$ is heterogeneous across individuals in Eq. (4.8), then those individuals who expect relatively large exogenous income flows will be opposed to complete equalization of second-period incomes. As long as their second period income is uninsurably uncertain, however, even the richest individuals will favor at least partial redistribution. In politico-economic equilibrium, the extent and character of redistribution will then depend not only on the dynamics of status quo inequality, but also on the aggregate economy's dynamics. As in the model of Wright (1996), in fact, the insurance properties of ex post redistributive taxation may be made more or less desirable by faster growth of average labor-income endowments. Since future taxes and subsidies play the role of otherwise nonexistent financial investment opportunities in this type of model, the sign of growth effects—like that of many others discussed above—depends on whether the intertemporal elasticity of substitution is larger or smaller than unity. If $\sigma > 1$ in the canonical specification (2.25) of preferences, then faster growth is associated with less ex-post redistribution in a politico-economic equilibrium where the character of the economy's safety net is decided once and for all, at a constitutional stage, by individuals whose income is currently high but who fear future bad luck.

5. Empirical evidence

Like all empirical work, tests of the theoretical mechanisms reviewed above and measures of their relevance are constrained by data availability. Studies of relationships between growth rates and income distribution across countries can rely on data collected for national income accounting purposes, and similar data are often available for smaller regional units. The relevant literature is reviewed in Section 5.1 below, while Section 5.2 summarizes the strategies and findings of recent research on relationships between economic inequality at the level of individuals or households within countries and country-level macroeconomic performance.

5.1. Convergence across countries

Each of the models reviewed in the previous sections has specific predictions as to divergence or convergence of incomes over time within a macroeconomic entity. Two basic mechanisms lead to convergence (divergence) across individuals: relatively rich individuals may save less (more) than poor ones and/or obtain lower (higher) returns on their investment in physical or human capital. As noted when discussing Eq. (3.8) above, many of the relevant insights are similar to those applicable to macroeconomic growth dynamics. Accordingly, the theories reviewed above can be brought to bear on cross-country evidence if each country's aggregate income dynamics are interpreted on a representative individual basis—so that, in terms of the notation used above, the index i refers to any or all of the indistinguishable individuals inhabiting each country. While such an interpretation is clearly less than fully satisfactory, ready availability of of the relevant aggregate—notably the Summers and Heston (1991) harmonized dataset and its updates—has generated an extensive body of literature, reviewed in this section.

The data indicate that growth rates of per capita income are hardly any faster on average in relatively poor countries than in richer ones (see, e.g., Canova and Marcet, 1995). Since country-level growth rates vary widely over time, measures of income inequality display substantial divergence in the post-war period.[42] A standard approach to the interpretation of cross-country growth dynamics views each country as a macroeconomy of the type encountered in Section 2.1, within which all savings earn the same rate of

---

[42] As argued by Pritchett (1997), cross-country inequality was likely much narrower in pre-industrial times, since recent growth rates cannot be extrapolated backward without violating reasonable lower bounds on subsistence income levels.

return (and measured inequality may or may not be evolving over time). Rates of return, however, are allowed to differ across countries, reflecting an absence or imperfection of financial market interactions across the borders of different jurisdictions. In the limit case where economies are completely closed to international capital flows, then each country's national income dynamics should be similar to those of individual incomes under self-financing constraints in Section 3.2 above, and a given technology should offer higher returns to accumulation in relatively capital-poor locations. The empirical fact that poor countries do not grow noticeably faster than rich ones is hard to interpret from the standpoint of models where investment must be self-financed. At the country level, in fact, the degree of concavity of self-financed investment functions like Eq. (3.7) is to some extent measurable if marginal productivities are well approximated by market rates of return. It is standard to view the income share of labor as an empirical counterpart to the share of nonaccumulated factors γ in Eq. (2.17), and investment in physical capital as the empirical counterpart of accumulation as in Eq. (1.5). While these variables are less easy to measure in practice than to define in the simple theoretical framework above,[43] a share of capital of about one third in aggregate income implies that transitional dynamics towards steady state output levels (or towards balanced growth) should be very fast indeed when only the capital intensity of production determines income inequality across countries.[44]

Under the maintained hypothesis that capital does not flow across countries and that individual countries' data provide independent observations of similar economic processes, lack of convergence may be viewed as supporting evidence for models of country-specific endogenous growth. As in Romer (1986) and the subsequent literature, macroeconomic models of growth predict that growth rates need not decrease over time if returns to capital accumulation are allowed to be asymptotically constant or increasing, and the measured share of capital—which, as in Section 2.2.2 above, is an important determinant of long-run growth rates—reflects less than perfectly competitive market interactions as well as the capital's aggregate productivity. When applied to cross-country observations, these models would indeed imply that differences in per capita levels of capital and production should persist indefinitely, in the sense that no mean reversion is expected while the distribution of per capita incomes widens over time if countries experience idiosyncratic shocks.

This oversimplified contrast between different interpretations of cross-country growth experiences leads naturally to considering more flexible models. Two interrelated strands

[43] E.g., because labor income has to be disentangled from profits and rents in the case of the self-employed, and because capital stocks have to be constructed from investment data and depreciation assumptions by perpetual-inventory methods.

[44] The calibration exercises of King and Rebelo (1993) indicate that observed time-series patterns of country-specific growth rates are much too smooth to be consistent with the observed income share of capital and with realistic elasticities of intertemporal substitution in consumption. In a cross-country context, rates of return to accumulation should not only differ dramatically across countries with different initial conditions, but also vanish very quickly.

of recent empirical work on convergence issues are particularly easy to relate to the models outlined in the previous sections.

Even when technology is the same across countries which self-finance their accumulation, neoclassical growth models can be consistent with evidence of persistent inequality if countries converge to different steady state capital stocks. An extensive body of empirical work—surveyed by Barro and Sala-i-Martin (1994), Barro (1997) and De La Fuente (1997)—detects a mild but nonnegligible negative effect of initial income on subsequent growth after controlling for savings rates, population growth rates, and other determinants of a neoclassical economy's steady state output.[45] The role of such controlling factors is of independent interest. In fact, empirical work which applies representative-individual specifications to aggregate data is most convincingly motivated when it is focused on phenomena which feature interesting variation and insightful theoretical implications across the borders of countries. The size of government budgets, the character of property rights protection, and other policy variables indeed play significant roles in those regressions.[46] The rate of "conditional" convergence towards country-specific steady states, while statistically significant, is slow, and again hard to interpret if accumulated factors are identified with physical capital.[47] However, the distinction between accumulated (or reproducible) and nonaccumulated factors which has played a key role throughout this chapter need not coincide with the standard definition of reproducible factors as physical capital. If a portion of measured labor income accrues to (accumulated) human capital rather than to raw labor, for example, then a larger share of aggregate income is paid to accumulated factors in the absence of external effects.[48] Mankiw et al. (1992) specify such an "augmented" model of growth convergence, estimate it using school enrollment data as a proxy for human capital accumulation, and find that once savings and population growth rates (but not technology) are allowed to be heterogeneous across countries the model is capable of interpreting the evidence if the output share of human capital is about one-third.

Furthermore, country observations certainly do not carry information about completely separate experiences. As originally pointed out by Feldstein and Horioka (1980), savings and investment rates covary strongly across countries, but factors and goods do flow across countries' borders (see Obstfeld, 1995, for references to recent contri-

---

[45] As pointed out by Carroll and Weil (1994), however, saving and growth rates are jointly endogenous in general, and the direction of causality may differ from that implicit in standard growth regressions.

[46] As noted by Barro (1997), the dynamics of the variables determining country-specific steady states are hard to characterize with available data; they may, however, be as important as the convergent dynamics emphasized by cross-sectional empirical work.

[47] Sala-i-Martin (1996a, b) finds similar rates of unconditional convergence across regions within the same countries, and argues that—since (omitted) conditioning variables should be less heterogeneous across regions than across countries—this offers additional support for conditional convergence specifications.

[48] Mulligan and Sala-i-Martin (1997) discuss how a measure of the relevant human capital may be constructed from wage and schooling data under the hypothesis that factor-income distribution reflects marginal productivities. Benhabib and Spiegel (1994) discuss various possible specifications for empirical counterparts of the theory's human capital stock.

butions). In the extreme case where countries belong to an integrated world economy, country i's per capita national income can be written in the form

$$y^i = Rk^i + Wl^i, \tag{5.1}$$

if k^i and l^i denote the per capita amounts of accumulated and nonaccumulated factors of production owned by its residents, and R and W denote factor prices in the world market. Since the expression in Eq. (5.1) coincides with the definition of an individual's income in the models of Section 2, those models yield the same implications for the dynamics of income across countries as they did above for the evolution of income inequality within a single macroeconomy. As in the model of Section 2.1.1, a common rate of return on heterogeneous wealth levels implies convergence if the propensity s to save out of total income is a given constant, since the proportional growth rate of national income is larger for countries who earn a lower portion of their income from accumulated factors. As long as complete specialization does not occur—hence in the single-good framework of the simplest macroeconomic models—unrestrained mobility of just one of the factors generally suffices to equalize the price of both. Further, trade can effectively substitute for factor mobility. Ventura (1997) models the world economy as a collection of fully integrated small open economies which, by trading intermediate inputs, can essentially rent each other's baskets of accumulated and nonaccumulated factors even in the absence of financial capital flows. In this setting, conditioning upon differences in productive efficiency (or, in the notation used here, on the available amount of nonaccumulated factors) yields empirically plausible convergence rates if the rate of return to aggregate accumulation is (mildly) decreasing along the transition to a steady state of endogenous or exogenous growth. Caselli and Ventura (1996) suggest that findings of "conditional" convergence may also be interpreted by a model similar to those reviewed in Section 2.1.2, allowing for heterogeneity in $\bar{c}$, and emphasize that incomes do converge towards each other when such "required consumption" parameters are negative. Smaller degrees of international integration are featured in other models, such as those proposed by Barro et al. (1995) where physical, but not human capital accumulation may be financed across country borders. Then, per capita domestic production differentials reflect differences in per-capita human capital levels, even if technologies are identical, and imply slow convergence of domestic production levels if the elasticity of production differentials with respect to (slowly) evolving human capital stocks is large.

The models underlying such interpretations of the empirical evidence rule out at least some economic interactions across countries, but maintain the assumption of identical technologies and homogeneous long-run growth rates. In reality, different technologies (or different per capita endowments of nonaccumulated factors) presumably do play an important role in determining cross-sectional inequality and income dynamics, and less than instantaneous technological spillovers across countries may explain much of the observed dynamics of per capital incomes.[49]

More generally, the extent to which optimal savings behavior and factor accumulation lead to convergence depends on the character of investment opportunity sets, hence on the extent of cross-country financial market integration. The various insights discussed above are in general as important at the cross-country level as in the income distribution models of Section 3 above. The empirical results of Durlauf and Johnson (1994), Quah (1996a, b) and others indicate that convergence is stronger within subsets of countries with similar income levels, suggesting that lack of overall convergence is the result of increasing polarization of income levels across groups of countries which *do* converge towards each other. These findings are consistent with a country-level interpretation of models where, like in Section 3.2.2 above, nonconvex investment opportunity sets generate poverty traps.

Obstfeld (1994), Devereux and Saito (1997), and others propose cross-country interpretations of models (reviewed in Section 3.3.1 above) of the growth and distributional implications of financial market integration. Again in an international framework of analysis, Devereux and Smith (1994) propose a model featuring both rate-of-return (as in Section 3.3.1) and endowment (as in Section 3.3.2) cross-country risk. Marcet and Marimon (1992) model international capital flows taking realistic information asymmetries and default risk into account, along the lines of closed-economy models of distribution discussed above. Ghosh and Ostry (1994) study the current account implications of precautionary-savings behavior; Ogaki et al. (1996) and their references study macroeconomic savings data in an optimizing framework of analysis, treating all individuals within each country on a representative-agent basis. Daniel (1997) points out that the role of precautionary savings in ensuring stability of income, wealth, and consumption distributions can be as important at the cross-country level as within closed economies: lower wealth levels make precautionary behavior a more important determinant of saving behavior, and poor countries tend to accumulate wealth faster than rich ones for the reasons outlined above.

5.2. *Growth and inequality within countries*

The closed-economy models of Sections 2 and 3 above featured many different channels of interaction between distribution across individuals and macroeconomic growth. In the context of the models reviewed in Section 5.1, the distribution of income across countries might in principle bear similarly on issues of worldwide growth. The extent of per capita inequality across countries, however, is only indirectly relevant to the arguably more important issue of inequality across individuals, and empirical work on growth

---

[49] Ciccone (1996) explicitly allows countries' production to exert external effects on each other, and can estimate the strength of these effects under the identifying assumption that external effects should be more important across neighboring countries.

and distribution prefers to relate country-specific growth performances to the relatively limited information available on income distribution within countries.

The relevant literature dates back to at least Kuznets (1955). Finding statistical evidence of decreasing inequality along the growth path of developed countries, Kuznets discussed how it might be interpreted along much the same lines as those of subsequent theoretical literature (and of this chapter)—arguing in particular how redistributive policies and finite lifetimes may offset theoretical mechanisms of wealth concentration—but privileged structural change as a source of U-shaped inequality dynamics along economic development paths,[50] while offering a lucid discussion of how data limitation may limit the progress of any such empirical work. While Kuznets's original U-curve intuition has remained somewhat elusive in available data, the subsequent literature, recently reviewed and extended by Bénabou (1996c), confirms that income distribution is far from unrelated to macroeconomic phenomena. The empirical evidence is far from settled (see Bénabou, 1996c; Aghion and Howitt, 1998, Chap. 9; Deininger and Squire, 1996a, b, for recent surveys and updates). It does indicate, however, that relatively high degrees of income inequality are tenuously associated, in cross-country growth regressions, with relatively low income levels and slow growth rates. This is perhaps suprisingly less ambiguous than the predictions of theoretical models, where higher inequality may be associated with faster or slower growth; and it is certainly interesting to find that measures of within-country inequality are not unrelated to macroeconomic growth performances, as would be implied by the neoclassical models of Section 5.2, where savings and investment rates are by construction independent of income and consumption inequality or, indeed, by the representative-agent view of country-level data implicit in Section 5.1's perspective on international income convergence.

Though the direction of causality is perhaps unavoidably difficult to ascertain in practice, this empirical evidence can in principle be brought to bear on those among the models reviewed above which identify specific causal links running from inequality to income growth—namely, on models of financial market imperfections from Section 3, and models of factor share determination and politico-economic interactions from Sections 2.2.2 and 4.

Extensive theoretical and empirical work on the role of financial markets in economic development has recently been reviewed by Levine (1997), and somewhat inconclusive evidence on the interaction of simple indicators of financial development with inequality is discussed by Bénabou (1996c). Some evidence is also available on the theoretical role of relative factor prices and factor shares. Lindert and Williamson (1985) argue that most of the variability in personal income distribution (across time and space) is due to variations in factor rewards rather than by variations in individuals' factor bundles, and Bourguignon and Morrisson (1990) find that land concentration and mineral resource endowments are closely associated with measures of inequality in cross-country data.

---

[50] The class of single-sector macroeconomic models reviewed here has no room for structural change, of course. Adelman and Robinson (1989) survey subsequent related work in the field of development economics.

While the dynamics of aggregate income and of inequality do not appear to be causally related in any obvious way, the evidence in Deininger and Squire (1996b) and Persson and Tabellini (1992) suggests that land ownership concentration appears unambiguously relevant to subsequent economic growth. If land ownership proxies for the distribution of wealth, such findings lend support to the idea that an inegalitarian wealth distribution exacerbates financial market imperfections, with particularly strong implications for accumulation of human capital and of other factors which are likely to face binding self-financing constraints. The empirical relevance of land as a source of income may also indicate that, as in the Classical framework of analysis and in the optimization-based models of Section 2.2.2, the role of factor income distribution in the determination of macroeconomic growth is to some extent independent of that of the size distribution of income.

As to politico-economic channels of causation from inequality to growth, it is difficult to disentangle ceteris paribus effects of inequality (even when pre-tax inequality is treated as an exogenous variable) from those of the distortionary policies that may, depending on the structure of political interactions, be equilibrium outcomes for different levels of inequality. The careful work of Perotti (1996) indicates that, across countries, before-tax inequality tends to be compounded rather than reduced by fiscal policies, contrary to what would be implied by models where (high) inequality causes slow growth via redistribution. These results are perhaps more indicative of theoretical models' simplicity than of the practical relevance of theoretical models. Distributional tensions do matter, but they presumably do so in many subtle ways, by creating institutional and market conditions more or less conducive to efficiency and to adequate incentives to private investment. As Bénabou (1996c) points out, when status quo inequality slows down growth by decreasing the efficiency of investment allocation, transfers and subsidies should indeed be conducive to more equal investment opportunities and faster growth. Moreover, the threat of expropriation is sufficient to reduce investment incentives and, if the status quo degree of inequality is preserved by the resulting low investment level, no actual transfers need be observed. The empirical literature in this field addresses this potential mechanism by introducing measures of politicol-economic instability and of property right enforcement in cross-sectional growth regressions (Alesina and Perotti, 1996).

6. Other directions of research

This chapter has focused on interactions of income and wealth distribution with growth and accumulation and, even within this already narrow scope, has necessarily neglected many relevant aspects of the literature. Of course, many other aspects of macroeconomic performance—such as inflation, which plays a prominent role in Barro's (1997) growth regressions—are theoretically and empirically related to growth, and to inequality (see e.g., Beetsma and Van der Ploeg, 1996, for an exploration of linkages between inequality and inflation). This brief concluding section outlines how recent and less recent research has addressed three sets of issues which, though eminently relevant to the subject matter, have found little or no room in this chapter.

First, almost all of the simple models and insights of the chapter have been framed in terms of a single-good macroeconomy, with only a passing reference at the end of Section 2.2.2 to ways in which relative prices, income distribution, and aggregate dynamics may be jointly determined in the context of multisector models with many output goods. Such issues are central to many classical models of long-run growth and value determination, of course, and may to some extent be analyzed abstracting from capital accumulation (as in Pasinetti, 1993). Recent contributions study the macroeconomic role of sectoral output composition in a representative-agent setting (Kongsamut et al., 1997), or in models where heterogeneous (Glass, 1996) or nonhomothetic (Zweimüller, 1995) preferences can make income distribution relevant to the speed of innovation-driven growth.

Second, the chapter has analyzed distribution and growth in a long-run setting, with only limited attention to transitional dynamics in Sections 2 and 5.1. It is of course difficult to isolate long-run, accumulation-driven dynamics from cyclical phenomena in empirical data, and all variables, parameters, and functions featured by the theoretical models above could in principle be allowed to depend on aggregate shocks. Realistic macroeconomic models would need to account for cyclical unemployment, for discrepancies between intended savings and investment, for monetary exchange technologies, and for price stickiness. Of course, it is extremely complex to model all or most of such features without relying on the representative agent paradigm. Cyclical dynamics have been studied in the context of models that, like those outlined in Section 2.2, took for granted a link between factor-income sources and savings propensities, without rationalizing consumption choices on a forward-looking basis; see, for example, Goodwin (1969) for a model of unemployment-based distributive dynamics and endogenous cycles. Many recent contributions exploring the role of incomplete financial markets in the "real business cycle" extension of neoclassical growth models could have been reviewed here but for space constraints. Interested readers should consult the methodological survey by Rios-Rull (1995), the empirically motivated analysis of Krusell and Smith (1997), and their references.

Finally, while wealth-driven inequality has played the most important role in this survey, earned-income inequality is far from unrelated to macroeconomic dynamics—and may be analyzed along much the same lines as those of this chapter if not only standard savings and investment choices, but also the accumulation of human capital and the introduction of new technologies respond to economic incentives and politically determined policies (see Aghion and Howitt 1998, chapter 9, for an introduction to these and other issues, and references to the literature).

References

Acemoglu, Daron and Fabrizio Zilibotti (1997), Was Prometheus unbound by chance? Risk, diversification, and growth, Journal of Political Economy 105: 709–751.

Adelman, Irma and Sherman Robinson (1989), Income distribution and development, in H. Chenery and T.N. Srinivasan, eds, Handbook of Development Economics, Vol. 2 (North-Holland, Amsterdam).

Aghion, Philippe and Patrick Bolton (1997), A theory of trickle-down growth and development, Review of Economic Studies 64: 151–172.

Aghion, Philippe and Peter Howitt (1998), Endogenous Growth Theory (MIT Press, Cambridge, MA and London, UK).

Aiyagari, S. Rao (1994), Uninsured idiosyncratic risk and aggregate savings, Quarterly Journal of Economics 109: 659–684.

Aiyagari, S. Rao and Ellen R. McGrattan (1995), The Optimum Quantity of Debt (F.R.B. of Minneapolis Research Dept. Staff Report 203).

Alesina, Alberto and Roberto Perotti (1996), Income distribution, political instability, and investment, European Economic Review 40: 1203–1228.

Alesina, Alberto and Dani Rodrik (1994), Distributive policies and economic growth, Quarterly Journal of Economics 109: 465–490.

Andreoni, James (1989), Giving with impure altruism: applications to charity and Ricardian equivalence, Journal of Political Economy 97: 1447–1458.

Arrow, Kenneth J. (1962), The economic implications of learning by doing, Review of Economic Studies 29: 155–173.

Asimakopoulos, Athanasios, ed. (1988), Theories of Income Distribution (Kluwer Academic Publishers, Boston, Dordrecht, Lancaster).

Atkeson, Andrew and Robert E. Lucas (1992), On efficient distribution with private information, Review of Economic Studies 59: 427–453.

Atkeson, Andrew and Robert E. Lucas (1995), Efficiency and equality in a simple model of efficient unemployment insurance, Journal of Economic Theory 66: 64–88.

Atkeson, Andrew and Masao Ogaki (1996), Wealth-varying intertemporal elasticities of substitution: evidence from panel and aggregate data, Journal of Monetary Economics 38: 507–534.

Banerjee, Abhijit V. and Andrew F. Newman (1993), Occupational choice and the process of development, Journal of Political Economy 101: 274–298.

Barro, Robert J. (1997), Determinants of Economic Growth: A Cross-Country Empirical Study, (MIT Press, Cambridge, MA).

Barro, Robert J. and Xavier Sala-i-Martin (1994), Economic Growth (McGraw-Hill, New York, London, Montreal).

Barro, Robert J. and Xavier Sala-i-Martin (1997), Technological diffusion, convergence and growth, Journal of Economic Growth 2: 1–26.

Barro, Robert J., N. Gregory Mankiw and Xavier Sala-i-Martin (1995), Capital mobility in neoclassical models of growth, American Economic Review 85: 103–115.

Beetsma, Roel M.W.J. and Frederick Van der Ploeg (1996) Does inequality cause inflation? The political economy of inflation taxation and government debt, Public Choice 87: 143–162.

Bénabou, Roland (1996a), Equity and efficiency in human capital investment: the local connection, Review of Economic Studies 63: 237–264.

Bénabou, Roland (1996b), Heterogeneity, stratification, and growth: macroeconomic implications of community structure and school finance, American Economic Review 86: 584–609.

Bénabou, Roland (1996c), Inequality and growth, in B.S. Bernanke and J.J. Rotemberg, eds., NBER Macroeconomics Annual 1996 (MIT Press, Cambridge and London), pp. 11–73.

Bénabou, Roland (1996d), Unequal Societies, NBER working paper #5583.

Bencivenga, Valerie R. and Bruce D. Smith (1991), Financial intermediation and endogenous growth, Review of Economic Studies 58: 195–209.

Benhabib, Jess and Aldo Rustichini (1996), Social conflict and growth, Journal of Economic Growth 1: 125–142.

Benhabib, Jess and Mark M. Spiegel (1994), The role of human capital in economic development: evidence from aggregate cross-country data, Journal of Monetary Economics 34: 143–173.

Bertola, Giuseppe (1993), Factor shares and savings in endogenous growth, American Economic Review 83: 1184–1198.

Bertola, Giuseppe (1994b), Theories of savings and economic growth, Ricerche Economiche 48: 257–277.

Bertola, Giuseppe (1994c), Wages, profits, and theories of growth, in Luigi L. Pasinetti and Robert M. Solow, eds., Economic Growth and the Structure of Long-Term Development (St. Martin's Press, New York; Macmillan Press, London), pp. 90–108.

Bertola, Giuseppe (1996), Factor shares in OLG models of growth, European Economic Review, 40: 1541–1560.

Blinder, Alan S. (1974), Distribution effects and the aggregate consumption function, Journal of Political Economy 83: 447–475.

Boldrin, Michele (1992), Dynamic externalities, multiple equilibria, and growth, Journal of Economic Theory 58: 198–218.

Bourguignon, François (1981), Pareto superiority of unegalitarian equilibria in Stiglitz's model of wealth distribution with convex saving function, Econometrica 49: 1469–1475.

Bourguignon, François and Christian Morrisson (1990), Income distribution, development and foreign trade: a cross-sectional analysis, European Economic Review 34: 1113–1132.

Caballero, Ricardo (1991), Earnings uncertainty and aggregate wealth accumulation, American Economic Review 81: 859–872.

Canova, Fabio and Albert Marcet (1995), The poor stay poor: non-convergence across countries and regions, CEPR D.P.1265.

Carroll, Christopher D. (1992), Buffer stock savings and the life cycle permanent income hypothesis, Quarterly Journal of Economics 107: 1–56

Carroll, Christopher D. and David N. Weil (1994), Saving and growth: a reinterpretation, Carnegie-Rochester Conference Series on Public Policy, pp. 133–192.

Casarosa, Carlo (1982), The new view of the Ricardian theory of distribution and economic growth, in M. Baranzini, ed., Advances in Economic Theory (Basil Blackwell, Oxford).

Caselli, Francesco and Jaume Ventura (1996), A Representative Consumer Theory of Distribution, mimeo (Harvard and MIT Cambridge, MA).

Chatterjee, Satyajit (1994), Transitional dynamics and the distribution of wealth in a neoclassical growth model, Journal of Public Economics 54: 97–119.

Ciccone, Antonio (1996) Externalities and Interdependent Growth: Theory and Evidence (W.P., University of California Berkeley).

Cochrane, John H. (1991), A simple test of consumption insurance, Journal of Political Economy 99: 957–976.

Cole, Harold L., George J. Mailath and Andrew Postlewaite (1992), Social norms, savings behavior, and growth, Journal of Political Economy 100: 1092–1125.

Daniel, Betty C. (1997), Precautionary savings and persistent current account imbalances, Journal of International Economics 42: 179–193.

De La Fuente, Angel (1997) The empirics of growth and convergence: a selective review, Journal of Economic Dynamics and Control 21: 23–73.

Deaton, Angus (1991), Saving and liquidity constraints, Econometrica 59: 1221–1248.

Deaton, Angus and Christina Paxson (1994), Intertemporal choice and inequality, Journal of Political Economy 102: 437–467.

De Gregorio, José (1996), Borrowing constraints, human capital accumulation, and growth, Journal of Monetary Economics 37: 49–71.

Deininger, Klaus and Lyn Squire (1996a), Measuring income inequality: a new database, World Bank Economic Review 10: 565–592.

Deininger, Klaus and Lyn Squire (1996b), New ways of looking at old issues: inequality and growth, Working paper, The World Bank; Journal of Development Economics, 57: 259–287.

Devereux, Michael B. and Makoto Saito (1997), Growth and risk-sharing with incomplete international assets markets, Journal of International Economics 42: 455–473.

Devereux, Michael B. and Gregor W. Smith (1994), International risk sharing and economic growth, International Economic Review 35: 535–590.

Diamond, Peter A. (1965), National debt in a neoclassical growth model, American Economic Review 55: 1126–1150.

Dixit, Avinash K. (1977), The accumulation of capital theory, Oxford Economic Papers 29: 1–29.

Durlauf, Steven N. (1996), A theory of persistent income inequality, Journal of Economic Growth 1: 75–93.

Durlauf, Steven and Paul Johnson (1994), Multiple regimes and cross-country growth behavior, Journal of Applied Econometrics 10: 365–384.

Feldstein, Martin and Charles Horioka (1980), Domestic savings and international capital flows, Economic Journal 90: 314–329.

Galor, Oded and Daniel Tsiddon (1997), The distribution of human capital and economic growth, Journal of Economic Growth 2: 93–124.

Galor, Oded and Josef Zeira (1993) Income distribution and macroeconomics, Review of Economic Studies 60: 35–52.

Ghosh, Atish R. and Jonathan D. Ostry (1997), Macroeconomic uncertainty, precautionary savings, and the current account, Journal of Monetary Economics 40: 121–139.

Glass, Amy Jocelyn (1996), Income Distribution and Quality Improvement, W.P. 96-18 (Ohio State University).

Glomm, Gerhard and B. Ravikumar (1992), Public versus private investment in human capital: endogenous growth and income inequality, Journal of Political Economy 100: 813–834.

Goodwin, Richard (1969), A growth cycle, in C. Feinstein, ed., Capitalism, Socialism, and Economic Growth (Cambridge University Press, Cambridge).

Greenwood, Jeremy and Boyan Jovanovic (1990), Financial development, growth, and the distribution of income, Journal of Political Economy 98: 1076–1107.

Greenwood, Jeremy and Bruce D. Smith (1997), Financial markets in development, and the development of financial markets, Journal of Economic Dynamics and Control 21: 145–181.

Grossman, Gene M. and Elhanan Helpman (1991), Innovation and Growth in the Global Economy (MIT Press, Cambridge and London).

Grossman, Gene M. and Elhanan Helpman (1994), Endogenous innovation in the theory of growth, Journal of Economic Perspectives 8: 23–44.

Grossman, Gene M. and Noriyuki Yanagawa (1993), "Asset bubbles and endogenous growth, Journal of Monetary Economics 31: 3–19.

Grossman, Herschel I. and Minseong Kim (1996), Predation and accumulation, Journal of Economic Growth 1: 333–350.

Hahn, Frank H. and R.C.O. Matthews (1964), The theory of economic growth: a survey, Economic Journal 74: 780–792.

Huffman, Gregory W. (1996), Endogenous tax determination and the distribution of wealth, Carnegie–Rochester Series on Public Policy 45: 207–242.

Irvine, Ian and Susheng Wang (1994), Earnings uncertainty and aggregate wealth accumulation: comment, American Economic Review 84: 1463–1469.

Jappelli, Tullio and Marco Pagano (1994), Saving, growth and liquidity constraints, Quarterly Journal of Economics 109: 83–109.

Jones, Larry E. and Rodolfo Manuelli (1990), A convex model of equilibrium growth: theory and policy implications, Journal of Political Economy 98: 1008–1038.

Jones, Larry E. and Rodolfo Manuelli (1992), Finite lives and growth, Journal of Economic Theory 58: 171–197.

Kaldor, Nicholas (1956), Alternative theories of distribution, Review of Economic Studies 23: 94–100.

Kaldor, Nicholas (1961), Capital accumulation and economic growth, in F.A. Lutz and D.C. Hague, eds., The Theory of Capital (St.Martin's Press, New York).

Kaldor, Nicholas (1966), Marginal productivity and the macro-economic theories of distribution, Review of Economic Studies 33: 309–319.

King, Robert G. and Ross Levine (1993), Finance, entrepreneurship, and growth: theory and evidence, Journal of Monetary Economics 32: 513–532.

King, Robert G. and Sergio Rebelo (1993), Transitional dynamics and economic growth in the neoclassical model, American Economic Review 83: 908–931.

Kongsamut, Piyabha, Sergio Rebelo and Danyang Xie (1997), Beyond Balanced Growth, NBER Working Paper No. 6159.

Krusell, Per, and José-Victor Ríos-Rull (1992), Vested interests in a positive theory of stagnation and growth, Review of Economic Studies 63: 301–329.

Krusell, Per and Anthony A. Smith, Jr. (1997), Income and wealth heterogeneity, portfolio choice, and equilibrium asset returns, Macroeconomic Dynamics 1: 387–422.

Krusell, Per, Vincenzo Quadrini and José-Victor Ríos-Rull (1997), Politico-economic equilibrium and economic growth, Journal of Economic Dynamics and Control 21: 23–73.

Kurz, Heinz D. and Neri Salvadori (1995), Theory of Production: A Long-Period Analysis (Cambridge University Press, Cambridge, New York, Melbourne).

Kuznets, Simon (1955), Economic growth and income inequality, American Economic Review 45: 1–28.

Laitner, John (1979a), Bequests, golden-age capital accumulation and government debt, Economica 46: 403–414.

Laitner, John (1979b), Household bequest behavior and the national distribution of wealth, Review of Economic Studies 46: 467–483.

Laitner, John (1992), Random earnings differences, lifetime liquidity constraints, and altruistic intergenerational transfers, Journal of Economic Theory 58: 135–170.

Levine, David P. (1988), Marx's theory of income distribution, in A. Asimakopoulos, ed., Theories of Income Distribution (Kluwer Academic Publishers, Boston, Dordrecht, Lancaster).

Levine, Ross (1997), Financial development and economic growth: views and agenda, Journal of Economic Literature 35: 688–726.

Lindert, Peter H. and Jeffrey G. Williamson (1985), Growth, equality, and history, Explorations in Economic History 22: 341–377.

Ljungqvist, Lars (1993), Economic underdevelopment: the case of a missing market for human capital, Journal of Development Economics 40: 219–239.

Ljungqvist, Lars (1995), Wage structure as implicit insurance on human capital in developed versus undeveloped countries, Journal of Development Economics 46: 35–50.

Loury, G. (1981), Intergenerational transfers and the distribution of earnings, Econometrica 49: 843–867.

Mankiw, N. Gregory, David Romer and David N. Weil (1992), A contribution to the empirics of economic growth, Quarterly Journal of Economics 407–437

Marcet, Albert and Ramon Marimon (1992), Communication, committment, and growth, Journal of Economic Theory 58: 219–249.

Marglin, Stephen A. (1984), Growth, Distribution, and Prices (Harvard University Press, Cambridge, MA and London).

Merton, Robert C. (1971), Optimum consumption and portfolio rules in a continuous-time model, Journal of Economic Theory 3: 373–413.

Mulligan, C.B. and X. Sala-i-Martin (1997), A labor income-based measure of the value of human capital: an application to the states of the United States, Japan and the World Economy 9: 159–191.

Nerlove, Marc and Lakshmi K. Raut (1997), Growth models with endogenous population: a general framework, in M.R. Rosenzweig and O. Stark, eds., Handbook of Population and Family Economics (North-Holland, Amsterdam).

O'Rourke, Kevin H., Alan M. Taylor and Jeffrey G. Williamson (1996), Factor price convergence in the late nineteenth century, International Economic Review 37: 499–530.

Obstfeld, Maurice (1994), Risk-taking, global diversification, and growth, American Economic Review 84: 1310–1329.

Obstfeld, Maurice (1995), International capital mobility in the 1990s, in Peter B. Kenen, ed., Understanding Interdependence: The Macroeconomics of the Open Economy (Princeton University Press, Princeton), pp. 201–260.

Ogaki, Masao, Jonathan D. Ostry and Carmen M. Reinhart (1996), Saving behavior in low- and middle-income developing countries: a comparison, International Monetary Fund Staff Papers 43: 38–71.

Pagano, Marco (1993), Financial markets and growth: an overview, European Economic Review 37: 613–622.

Pasinetti, Luigi (1960), A mathematical formulation of the Ricardian system, Review of Economic Studies 27: 78–98.

Pasinetti, Luigi (1962), Rate of profit and income distribution in relation to the rate of economic growth, Review of Economic Studies 29: 267–279.

Pasinetti, Luigi (1993), Structural Economic Dynamics (Cambridge University Press, Cambridge, New York, Melbourne).

Perotti, R. (1993), Political equilibrium, income distribution, and growth, Review of Economic Studies 60: 755–776.

Perotti, Roberto (1996), Growth, income distribution, and democracy: what the data say, Journal of Economic Growth 1: 149–187.

Persson, Torsten and Guido Tabellini (1992), Growth, distribution, and politics, European Economic Review 36: 593–602.

Persson, Torsten and Guido Tabellini (1994), Is inequality harmful for growth? American Economic Review 84: 600–621.

Persson, Torsten and Guido Tabellini (1998), Political economics and macroeconomic policy, in J. Taylor and M. Woodford, eds., Handbook of Macroeconomics (North-Holland, Amsterdam).

Piketty, Thomas (1997), The dynamics of the wealth distribution and the interest rate with credit rationing, Review of Economic Studies 64: 173–190.

Pritchett, Lant (1997), Divergence, big time, Journal of Economic Perspectives 11: 3–17.

Quah, Danny T. (1996a), Empirics for economic growth and convergence, European Economic Review 40: 1353–1375.

Quah, Danny T. (1996b), Twin peaks: growth and convergence in models of distribution dynamics, Economic Journal 106: 1045–1055.

Rebelo, Sergio (1991), Long-run policy analysis and long-run growth, Journal of Political Economy 99: 500–521.

Rebelo, Sergio (1992), Growth in Open Economies, Carnegie-Rochester Conference Series on Public Policy 36, pp. 5–46.

Ríos-Rull, José-Victor (1995), Models with heterogeneous agents, in T.F. Cooley, ed., Frontiers of Business Cycle Research (Princeton University Press, Princeton, NJ), pp. 98–125.

Roemer, John E. (1981), Analytical Foundations of Marxian Economic Theory (Cambridge University Press, Cambridge, London, New York).

Romer, Paul M. (1986), Increasing returns and long-run growth, Journal of Political Economy 94: 1002–1037.

Romer, Paul M. (1987), Growth based on increasing returns due to specialization, American Economic Review 77: 56–72.

Romer, Paul M. (1989), Capital accumulation in the theory of long-run growth, in R.J. Barro, ed., Modern Business Cycle Theories (Harvard University Press and Basil Blackwell), pp. 51–127.

Romer, Paul M. (1990), Endogenous technological change, Journal of Political Economy 98: S71–S102.

Saint-Paul, Gilles (1992a), Fiscal policy in an endogenous growth model, Quarterly Journal of Economics 107: 1243–1259.

Saint-Paul, Gilles (1992b), Technological choice, financial markets and economic development, European Economic Review 36: 763–781.

Sala-i-Martin, Xavier (1996a), Regional cohesion: evidence and theories of regional growth and convergence, European Economic Review 40: 1325–1352.

Sala-i-Martin, Xavier (1996b), The classical approach to convergence analysis, Economic Journal 106: 1019–1036.

Samuelson, Paul A. and Franco Modigliani (1966), The Pasinetti paradox in neoclassical and more general models, Review of Economic Studies 96: 269–301.

Solow, Robert M. (1956a), A contribution to the theory of economic growth, Quarterly Journal of Economics 70: 65–94.

Solow, Robert M. (1956b), The production function and the theory of capital, Review of Economic Studies 23: 101–108.

Sraffa, Piero (1960), Production of Commodities by Means of Commodities: Prelude to a Critique of Economic Theory (Cambridge University Press, Cambridge).

Stiglitz, Joseph E. (1969), Distribution of income and wealth among individuals, Econometrica 37: 382–397.

Summers, Robert and Alan Heston (1991), The Penn World Tables (Mark 5): an expanded set of international comparisons, 1950–1988, Quarterly Journal of Economics 106: 327–368.

Tamura, Robert (1991), Income convergence in an endogenous growth model, Journal of Political Economy 99: 522–554.

Tornell, Aaròn and Andrés Velasco (1992), The tragedy of the commons and economic growth: why does capital flow from poor to rich countries? Journal of Political Economy 100: 1208–1231.

Uhlig, Harald and Noriyuki Yanagawa (1996), Increasing the capital income tax may lead to faster growth, European Economic Review 40: 1521–1540.

Uzawa, Hirofumi (1968), Time preference, the consumption function, and optimum asset holdings, in J.N. Wolfe, ed., Value, Capital, and Growth: Papers in Honor of Sir John Hicks (Aldine Publishing Company, Chicago).

Ventura, Jaume (1997), Growth and interdependence, Quarterly Journal of Economics 107: 57–84.

Weil, Philippe (1990), Nonexpected utility in macroeconomics, Quarterly Journal of Economics 105: 29–42.

Williamson, Jeffrey G. (1991), Inequality, Poverty, and History (Basil Blackwell, Oxford and Cambridge, MA).

Wright, Randall (1996), Taxes, redistribution, and growth, Journal of Public Economics 62: 327–338.

Zweimüller, Josef (1995), Wealth Distribution, Innovations and Economic Growth, mimeo (I.A.S., Vienna).

Chapter 10

WEALTH INEQUALITY, WEALTH CONSTRAINTS AND ECONOMIC PERFORMANCE *

PRANAB BARDHAN[a], SAMUEL BOWLES[b] and HERBERT GINTIS[b]

[a] *University of California, Berkeley;* [b] *University of Massachusetts, Amherst*

Contents

Abstract

Where such behaviors as risk-taking and hard work are not subject to complete contracts, some distributions of assets (for instance the widespread use of tenancy) may preclude efficient contractual arrangements. In particular, the distribution of wealth may affect: (a) residual claimancy over income streams; (b) exit options in bargaining situations; (c) the relative capacities of actors to exploit common resources; (d) the capacity to punish those who deviate from cooperative solutions; and (e) the pattern of both risk aversion and the subjective cost of capital in the population.

Keywords: Efficient wealth redistribution, inequality and risk aversion, inequality and common pool resources, mutual monitoring and team production

JEL codes. D3, distribution; H1, structure and scope of government

* We would like to thank P. Jeffrey Allen, Jean-Marie Baland, Roland Bénabou, Timothy Besley, François Bourguignon, Michael Carter, Gregory Dow, Ernst Fehr, Karla Hoff, Eric Verhoogen and Elizabeth Wood for their helpful input in preparing this paper. We would also like to thank Jeffrey Carpenter, Jeff Dayton-Johnson, and Yongmei Zhou for research assistance and the MacArthur Foundation for financial support.

Handbook of Income Distribution, Volume 1. Edited by A.B. Atkinson and F. Bourguignon

1. Introduction

If costlessly enforceable contracts regulate all the actions of economic actors that affect the well being of others, competitive equilibria are Pareto efficient regardless of the distribution of wealth. However, where actions such as risk taking and hard work are not subject to such contracts, the assignment of residual claimancy over income streams and control over assets—that is, the distribution of property rights—will affect the feasibility, cost, and effectiveness of contractual provisions and other incentive devices that may be used to attenuate the incentive problems arising from contractual incompleteness. In this situation, as we will presently see, some distributions of assets support efficient or near-efficient competitive allocations, while others preclude efficient contractual arrangements. The widespread use of tenancy contracts governing residential and agricultural property is an example of the latter. Similarly, where contracts are incomplete or unenforceable, as is the case in labor and credit markets, the distribution of wealth matters for allocative efficiency.

Contractual incompleteness and unenforceability arise when actors have information that is either private (others do not have it) or is inadmissible in judicial proceedings and hence cannot be used to enforce contracts. Contractual incompleteness may also arise where appropriate judicial institutions are lacking, as in the case of sovereign debt among nations, or where potential users of commons-type resources cannot easily be excluded from access. In these cases the distribution of wealth may affect allocative efficiency by its impact on:

- residual claimancy over income streams and hence incentives for both an agent's own actions and the agent's monitoring of the actions of others;
- exit options in bargaining situations;
- the relative capacities of actors to exploit common resources;
- the capacity to punish those who deviate from cooperative solutions; and
- the pattern of both risk aversion and the subjective cost of capital in the population.

In this chapter we examine recent economic thinking about wealth effects on allocative efficiency in cases where information asymmetry, nonverifiability, or nonexcludablity of users, makes complete contracting infeasible.

It may be thought that the class of cases we are dealing with is not extensive, once the institutional setting is extended from one of competitive behavior governed by parametric prices to a more general environment in which private bargaining among small numbers of actors is feasible. Where property in assets may be readily traded and there are no impediments to efficient bargaining, inefficient assignments of control and residual claimancy rights over assets will be eliminated by voluntary exchange. This Coasean insight motivates the expectation that in competitive market economies, assets will be held by those who can use them most effectively, irrespective of their wealth.[1] If a tenant,

---

[1] Grossman and Hart (1986: p. 694) use this reasoning, for instance, to "explain asset ownership" while Hölmstrom and Tirole (1988) write that "contractual designs ... are created to minimize transactions

for example, could make better use of the land as owner, the land should be worth more to the tenant than to the landlord, and hence one might expect the tenant to buy the asset.

But the very informational asymmetries that make some assignments of property rights more efficient than others also systematically impede the productivity enhancing reassignment of property rights. In particular, nonwealthy agents may be credit constrained, and hence may not find it possible to acquire those assets for which their exercise of residual claimancy and control rights would allow efficiency gains.

Hence the Coasean reasoning may not apply. Competitively determined property rights assignments may be technically inefficient in the standard sense that there exist alternative allocations that produce the same outputs with less of at least one input and not more of any. These inefficiencies may be attenuated by a nonmarket transfer of assets from wealthier to less wealthy actors.[2]

However, potentially offsetting efficiency losses may result from egalitarian asset transfers where, as will generally be the case, they result in a transfer of control over productive risk taking from less to more risk averse agents. An important productivity enhancing aspect of high levels of wealth inequality is that assets are controlled by agents who are close to risk neutral, and who thus choose a more nearly socially optimal level of risk.[3]

Wealth concentrations may support productivity enhancing allocations in other ways as well, as for example, in attenuating free rider problems in the monitoring of corporate managers by owners (Demsetz and Lehn, 1985) or in more standard collective action problems (Olson, 1965). Similarly, the ethic of egalitarian sharing that pervades many simple societies may reduce incentives for individual investment, as the returns, should they materialize, will be shared while the costs will be individually borne (Hayami and Platteau, 1997). There can thus be no a priori conclusion concerning the efficiency effects of egalitarian asset redistribution.

The reader will note that in our argument, we have used the term "productivity enhancing" in place of the more familiar term "Pareto efficient". *We define a policy as productivity enhancing if the gainers could compensate the losers and still remain better off, except that the implied compensation need not be implementable under the*

---

costs .... This follows Coase's original hypothesis that institutions ... can best be understood as optimal accommodations to contractual constraints ... "

[2] Several recent studies suggest that some egalitarian redistributions can have positive efficiency effects. See the works cited above as well as Legros and Newman (1997), Moene (1992), Manning (1992), Mookherjee (1997) and Bénabou (1999). The underlying argument has many precursors including the early nutrition-based efficiency wage theories.

[3] We shall assume in this paper that the "socially optimal risk level" for individual projects is that which maximizes expected return. This is strictly true only if there are many individual projects and the returns to individual projects are uncorrelated, or if projects are correlated but there is some macroeconomic mechanism for smoothing returns across periods at zero cost.

Suboptimal risk choices in this sense are socially inefficient, but perhaps more important, such suboptimal risk choices can lead to dynamic inefficiencies if risk taking promotes the emergence and diffusion of new products and more advanced technologies. We do not model this effect here.

informational conditions and other incentive constraints in the economy. We will use this term for the following reasons.

Since we are analyzing distributions of assets (and hence of access to income and well being) the usual standard of Pareto efficiency will generally be inapplicable. A mandated transfer of an asset to an erstwhile employee that results in technical efficiency gains by reducing monitoring inputs, for example, is unlikely to represent a Pareto improvement without compensation from the gainer to the loser, and the required compensation, if implemented, would reverse the effect of the initial asset transfer and dampen the associated incentive effects. Indeed, were it a Pareto improvement, the transfer would be readily accomplished through private exchange, as long as bargaining over the assignment of property rights is unimpeded.

If the Pareto criterion is too stringent, the cardinalist alternative, based on "aggregate utility" is insufficiently so, for it may count an egalitarian redistribution as efficiency enhancing simply by dint of the diminishing marginal utility of income, even if the redistribution results in technical efficiency losses.[4] Transferring income from the rich to the poor could thus readily pass an efficiency test even if it were accomplished using very "leaky buckets" (to use Okun's expression for inefficient transfer mechanism). By contrast, commonly used net output measures avoid reference to individual utility altogether and thus preclude evaluation of welfare-relevant variations in work effort and risk, a serious shortcoming for an analysis in which these noncontractible but welfare-relevant behaviors play a central role. Similarly, the widely used joint surplus maximization criterion is applicable only where utilities are assumed to be linearly additive, requiring risk neutrality, and thereby failing to address the central questions concerning risk behavior and insurance.

The technical efficiency criterion—more output with less of at least one scarce input and not more or any—is uncontroversial if inputs are defined sufficiently broadly, but fails to give a decisive ranking in the case of most redistributions.

Finally, the usual "compensation" criteria, which consider a change efficient if the gainers could compensate the losers, are often inapplicable, since the improved incentives that account for the efficiency enhancing properties of the redistribution would be lost if compensation were actually made. For instance, if transferring land to a landless peasant is viable because it improves the wealth of the peasant and thus reduces the subjective costs of increased risk to which the peasant as landowner is subject, then obliging the peasant to compensate the former landlord may eliminate the effect of the transfer in reducing risk aversion, leaving the peasant worse off than prior to the transfer.

---

[4] Bénabou (1996: p. 13) addresses this problem by developing a measure of "pure economic efficiency which fully incorporates investment effects, labor supply effects and insurance effects but does not involve any interpersonal comparisons of utility.". He distinguishes between the intertemporal elasticity of substitution of individuals, which is incorporated in his measure, along with risk aversion, and society's possibly egalitarian evaluation of the appropriate interpersonal elasticity of substitution, which he treats separately as a normative, but not pure efficiency related, measure.

For these reasons we prefer the productivity enhancement criterion over the more traditional alternatives. Of course many productivity enhancing redistributions also satisfy the technical efficiency, joint surplus maximization, Pareto-efficiency, and other conventional criteria.

In Section 2 we take up the first of our major cases: credit market misallocations when some agents are risk neutral but wealth constrained. Contractual incompleteness here arises from asymmetric information concerning risk taking behavior, and unenforceability arises from limited liability restrictions. The main result is that because inferior projects will be funded and superior projects not implemented when some agents have limited wealth, a redistribution of assets may be productivity enhancing in the above sense. In Section 3 we consider the persistence of inefficient contractual relationships governing land (including insecurity of tenure, sharecropping, wage labor and others). The main result of this section is that given the incompleteness of credit markets and other aspects of agrarian social structures, the market assignment of residual claimancy and control rights will often not be to the parties that can make the best use of the land.

In Section 4 we take up the consequences of redistributive policies for risk taking and risk exposure when nonwealthy agents are risk averse. We identify both positive and negative effects. Increasing the wealth of the nonwealthy will support higher levels of risk taking among this group, but concentrating the wealth of this group in ownership of the assets with which they work will likely have the opposite effect. And a redistribution of residual claimancy and control from the wealthy to less wealthy individuals is likely to induce a reduction in the aggregate level of risk taking, with likely adverse consequences for innovation and efficiency in the long run. We consider the role of tax-subsidy policies and insurance against exogenous risk in attenuating these adverse efficiency consequences.

Section 5 extends the analysis of Section 2 to the problem of team production. We explore the allocative distortions that may arise when, for example, employee effort is not contractible because the relevant information is nonverifiable and production team members are wealth constrained. We investigate the allocative implications of a reassignment of residual claimancy and control rights to employees, along with the introduction of mutual monitoring. We show that an asset transfer to team members may be productivity enhancing even when teams are large.

Our final case, addressed in Section 6, addresses the relationship between wealth distributions and the provision of local public goods. We explore possible relationships between inequalities in initial endowments and the ability of a group of individuals to solve collective action problems on the local commons, where allocative inefficiencies may arise from problems of nonexcludability.

There are a number of ways that wealth inequalities may depress productivity that are not addressed in what follows. Perhaps most important is the possibility that high levels of inequality (of wealth or income) may induce political instability and insecurity of property rights, which in turn depress investment and productivity growth.[5] The fact that the poor suffer productivity-reducing nutritional and other health problems that might be attenuated by an egalitarian asset redistribution (Leibenstein, 1957; Dasgupta and Ray, 1986, 1987) is likewise not addressed.

We do not address processes of saving, human capital investment, bequests, or the political processes and policies that influence the time path of wealth redistributions, as these are dealt with elsewhere in this volume (see especially Piketty, Chapter 8). Thus, while we take account of the fact that the feasibility of an asset redistribution requires that it be supportable in a competitive equilibrium, we do not study the long term evolution of asset distributions under the influence of the forms of contractual incompleteness and public insurance and redistribution policies that we consider.[6] Finally, while we believe that the noncontractible effort, risk taking and other actions on which our argument hinges are critical to sustaining high levels of economic performance and that aligning incentives so that actors are residual claimants on the consequences of their actions may have a substantial impact on productivity, we do not address the size of the relevant effects.[7]

2. Wealth and efficiency when risk is noncontractible

This section uses a simple model to illustrate the result that nonwealthy agents are disadvantaged in gaining access to credit in that their projects may go unfunded even when less socially productive projects of wealthy producers are funded.

A series of recent papers following the early work of Loury (1981) have analyzed the credit limitations faced by the nonwealthy and their efficiency effects.[8] These models show that when it is impossible to write complete state-contingent contracts, the equity a producer commits to a project reduces adverse selection and moral hazard problems by signaling the project's quality and increasing the producer's incentive to work hard

---

[5] For the first relationship see Alesina and Perotti (1996), Barro (1996), Keefer and Knack (1995) and Pernotti (1996) and for the second all of the above plus Svensson (1993) and Venieris and Gupta (1986). However, one's concern that these cross-sectional results may provide little insight regarding relationships operating over time within countries is suggested by the failure of a measure of inequality to have the predicted negative coefficient in a country fixed effects model predicting investment (Benhabib and Speigel, 1997). In fact their coefficient is positive and significant.

[6] Robinson (1996) surveys the interactions between wealth distributions and political equilibria affecting macroeconomic policies, explicit redistribution, policies toward labor unions and the distribution of political rights.

[7] We refer to the relevant empirical literature throughout. Lazear (1996) studied a shift from hourly to piece rates in a large US company and found "extremely large" productivity effects. Similarly a study of the effects of changing from salaried management to management by a residual claimant (as well as changes in the other direction) in a large chain of US restaurants revealed strong residual claimancy effects (Shelton, 1957).

[8] See Stiglitz (1974), Gintis (1989), Stiglitz (1989), Banerjee and Jewman (1993), Rosenzweig and Wolpin (1993), Galor and Zeira (1993), Bowles and Gintis (1994), Barham et al. (1995), Hoff and Lyon (1995), Malherbe (1995), Hoff (1996b), Legros and Newman (1996), Aghion and Bolton (1997), Bénabou (1996) and Piketty (this volume).

and take the appropriate level of risk. However if there is a wealth constraint that limits agents' equity to their wealth holding, the nonwealthy may not be able to signal the quality of their projects and commit themselves to taking appropriate levels of effort and risk. Under these conditions, a redistribution of wealth from the wealthy to the nonwealthy may improve the efficiency of the economy fostering the substitution of more efficient production by the nonwealthy for less efficient production by the wealthy.

Are such credit constraints in fact operative? Several studies have shown that low-wealth producers in developing countries may be entirely shut out of credit markets or out of labor or land rental contracts that elicit high effort (Laffont and Matoussi, 1995; Carter and Mesbah, 1993; Barham et al., 1996; Carter and Barham, 1996; Sial and Carter, 1996). Other studies in low-income countries (Rosenzweig and Wolpin, 1993) show that net worth strongly affects farm investment, and low-wealth entails lower return to independent agricultural production (Rosenzweig and Binswanger, 1993; Laffont and Matoussi, 1995). Similarly, low net worth appears to depress labor market opportunities (Bardhan, 1984).

Turning to the advanced economies, Blanchflower and Osward (1998) found that an inheritance of $10,000 doubles a typical British youth's likelihood of setting up in business, and another British study (Holtz-Eakin et al., 1994a, b) found an elasticity of self-employment with respect to inherited assets of 0.52, and that inheritance leads the self-employed to increase the scale of their operations considerably. A third British study (Black et al., 1996) found that a 10% rise in value of collateralizable housing assets in the UK increases the number of startup businesses by 5%. Evans and Jovanovic (1989) find that among white males in the US, wealth levels are a barrier to becoming entrepreneurs, and that credit constraints typically limit those starting new businesses to capitalization of not more than 1.5 times their initial assets: "most individuals who enter self-employment face a binding liquidity constraint and as a result use a suboptimal amount of capital to start up their businesses" (810).[9]

Consistent with the hypothesis that the poor are credit constrained is the strong inverse relationship between individual incomes and rates of time preference. Hausman (1979) estimated rates of time preference from (US) individual buyers' implicit trade-offs between initial outlay and subsequent operating costs in a range of models of air conditioners. He found that while high income buyers exhibited implicit rates of time preference in the neighborhood of the prime rate, buyers below the median income level exhibited rates five times this rate. Green et al. (1996) elicited (hyperbolic) discount rates from high and low income respondents in the US using a questionnaire method. The low income group's estimated rates were four times the high income group. In both the Green et al. and the Hausman study the elasticity of the rate of time preference with respect to income was approximately minus one.

We present a simple model illustrating this phenomenon.

---

[9] See also Evans and Leighton (1989).

Consider a set of "producers", each of whom has access to an investment project the returns to which depend on the level of risk assumed by the producer. We assume the projects themselves cannot be exchanged among agents. Producers must therefore finance the project out of their own wealth or by borrowing. We assume all agents are risk neutral, and credit markets are competitive, in the sense that in equilibrium lenders receive an expected return equal to the risk free interest rate.

The results below are true if three conditions hold: (i) the level of risk assumed by a producer is private information and hence cannot be contracted for by a lender; (ii) any loan contract has a limited liability provision so that the promise to repay a loan may be unenforceable; and (iii) there is a minimum project size.

In this situation we show the following:

- socially productive projects of low-wealth producers may not be funded and hence may not be undertaken;
- Wealthy agents' relatively less productive projects may be funded in circumstances where less wealthy agents' relatively more productive projects are not funded;
- Wealthy agents will fund larger projects than less wealthy agents;
- If some producers are credit-constrained, a redistribution of wealth from lenders to such producers will be productivity enhancing; conversely if some but not all producers are size constrained, an asset transfer from a size constrained producer to a wealthier unconstrained producer may be productivity enhancing;
- If producers have projects of differing quality, there may exist a productivity enhancing asset transfer from a wealthy producer with a low-quality but profitable project to a credit-constrained producer with a high-quality project;
- If there are decreasing returns to scale, and if some but not all producers are credit-constrained, there exist productivity enhancing redistributions from wealthy to non-wealthy agents.

Consider a project for which the relationship between risk and expected return is $\phi(p)$, where $p \in [0, 1]$ is the probability of failure, a measure of the riskiness of the project, and $\phi(p)$ is the expected return net of all costs except capital costs of a project of unit size and quality. The riskiness of the project depends on the choice of technique (the type of seed planted, or the speed of operation of equipment) and level of effort or care taken by the producer. We assume $\phi(p)$ is inverted u-shaped, meaning $\phi'' < 0$ and $\phi'(p^*) = 0$ for some $p^* \in (0, 1)$.[10]

Suppose a producer with wealth **w** whose project of size $\alpha \geq 1$ requires capital $\alpha \mathbf{k} > 0$, which is fully depreciated in one period, and has expected return $\alpha\beta\phi(p)$,

---

[10] We take this to be the most plausible shape for the following reasons. First, production techniques that offer positive expected return are likely to involve a strictly positive level of risk. Hence, expected return is an increasing function of risk for low levels of risk. However, firms usually have access to production techniques that have very high returns when successful, but with a low probability of success (e.g., a firm may lower costs by not diversifying its product line, or by assuming the availability of particular production inputs). Such high-risk projects, which have low expected return, may be attractive to producers since lenders bear part of the losses in case of failure. Moreover, if producer effort reduces risk at a constant rate, and the cost of effort is convex, an inverted-U-shaped ϕ function may result independently of the choice of technology.

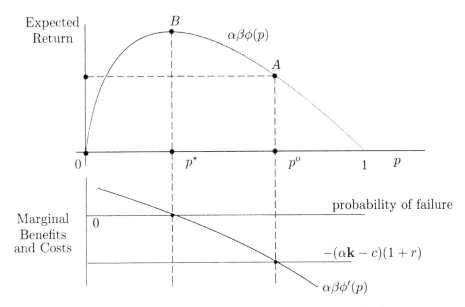

Fig. 1. Excessive risk in the credit market: the equilibrium risk level is p^*.

where $\beta > 0$ is a parameter representing the *quality* of the project. Expected returns $\alpha\beta\phi(p)$ are shown in the top panel of Fig. 1. Note that projects have minimum size of unity, but can be expanded with constant returns to scale above this minimum size.

Clearly p^* is the Pareto optimal risk level, since this maximizes the expected return to the project, and both producer and lender are risk neutral. We say the project is *productive* if

$$\beta\phi(p^*)/\mathbf{k} > 1 + \rho, \tag{1}$$

where $\rho > 0$ is the risk free interest rate. Thus a project is productive when the expected return per dollar of investment at p^* exceeds the return to a risk free security, and hence would be attractive to a risk neutral investor.

An *equity-backed loan* with equity c and interest rate r is a contract in which a producer with wealth $\mathbf{w}$ contributes equity $c \leq \mathbf{w}$ towards financing the project and the lender supplies the producer with the remainder $\alpha\mathbf{k} - c$. The producer then repays $(1+r)(\alpha\mathbf{k} - c)$ if the project is successful, and nothing otherwise. We assume the credit market is competitive and there is a perfectly elastic supply of risk neutral lenders at the risk free interest rate ρ. A producer can thus always obtain an equity-backed loan so long as the expected return to the lender is ρ.

We assume potential lenders know the producers' unit expected return schedule $\beta\phi(p)$, and can contract for particular levels of c and α, but the risk level p chosen by the producer is not subject to a costlessly enforceable contract, since the choice of technology and the effort level of the producer are both the private information of the producer. We thus have a principal-agent relationship in which the producer is the agent and the lender, who is the principal, knows that the interest rate r affects the agent's choice of noncontractible risk p. Given c, β and α, the producer chooses p to maximize the expected return minus the cost to the producer of financing the project, or expected profits which, recalling that nothing is repaid if the project fails, is

$$v = \alpha\beta\phi(p) - [(1-p)(\alpha\mathbf{k} - c)(1+r) + c(1+\rho)], \tag{2}$$

for which the first-order condition is

$$v_p = \alpha\beta\phi'(p) + (\alpha\mathbf{k} - c)(1+r) = 0. \tag{3}$$

The result is illustrated in the lower panel of Fig. 1, which reproduces Eq. (3). Note that the producer chooses p so that the marginal benefit from increased risk (namely, the benefits of increase likelihood of nonrepayment of the loan) or $(\alpha\mathbf{k} - c)(1+r)$, is equated to the marginal cost of increased risk $\alpha\beta\phi'$.

It is clear from Fig. 1 that if there is a positive level of borrowing, the chosen risk level p^o is excessively risky compared to p^*, which is Pareto optimal, given that both borrower and lender are risk neutral.

The producer's best response function $p^o = p^o(r)$, which is the solution to Eq. (3) for various values of r, is depicted in Fig. 2. This function is the locus of vertical tangent points on the producer iso-return schedules given by equating Eq. (2) to various levels of v. The producer iso-return loci are, by Eq. (3), positively sloped for $p < p^o(r)$ and negatively sloped for $p > p^o(r)$, as shown at points A through C.[11]

THEOREM 1. *The producer's best response function* $p^o = p^o(r; c, \alpha, \beta)$ *is an increasing function of* r, *shifts upward with an increase in project size* α, *and shifts downward with an increase in equity* c *or project quality* β.[12]

---

[11] This is true because totally differentiating the producer iso-profit equation

$$\alpha\beta\phi(p^o) - [(1-p^o)(\alpha\mathbf{k} - c)(1+r) + c(1+\rho)] = \underline{v},$$

we get

$$\left.\frac{dp^o}{dr}\right|_{v=\underline{v}} = \frac{(1-p^o)(\alpha\mathbf{k} - c)}{\alpha\beta\phi'(p^o) + (\alpha\mathbf{k} - c)(1+r)},$$

the denominator of which is zero for p^o, by Eq. (3).

[12] The proofs of this and subsequent theorems are not included in this chapter, but are available from the authors.

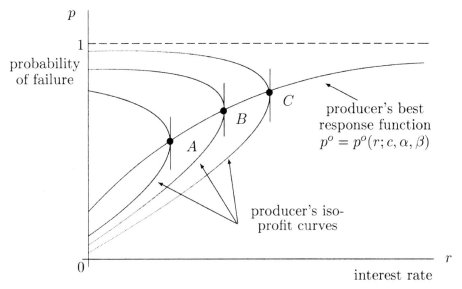

Fig. 2. The producer's best response function: risk taken as a function of the interest rate.

The intuition behind Theorem 1 is clear from Fig. 1. An increase in r raises the marginal benefit of risk taking and induces a higher level of risk, as does a larger project (for a given level of equity, c) for it shifts a larger fraction of the cost of failure to the lender. Conversely an increase in the quality of the project increases the marginal cost of risk taking and induces less risk.

Figure 3 illustrates Theorem 1 in a particularly simple, but not implausible, case. Suppose the gross return to a successful project with probability p of failure is just $\alpha\beta p$, so $\phi(p) = p(1 - p)$. Then the first order condition (3) becomes

$$\alpha\beta(1 - 2p) + (\alpha\mathbf{k} - c)(1 + r) = 0,$$

so rearranging the first order condition, the best response schedule is a linear function of r:

$$p^o = \frac{1}{2} + \frac{\alpha\mathbf{k} - c}{2\alpha\beta}(1 + r).$$

It is clear from this expression that an increase in project size α increases both the intercept and the slope of this linear function, an increase in project quality β shifts down both the intercept and the slope, and an increase in equity c shifts down the intercept and slope.

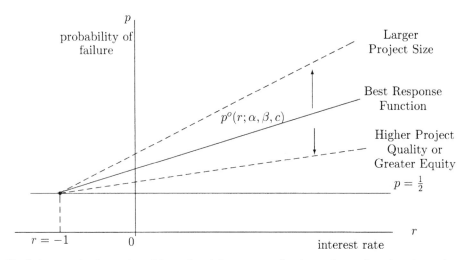

Fig. 3. An example: the reaction of the producer's best response function to changes in project size, project quality, and producer collateral when $\phi(p) = p(1 - p)$. The Pareto-efficient risk level is $p = 1/2$.

How is r determined? Because the credit market is competitive, any equilibrium (interest rate, failure rate) pair $(r, p^o(r))$ must lie on the lender iso-expected-return schedule

$$(1 + r)(1 - p^o(r)) = 1 + \rho, \qquad (4)$$

which is a hyperbola, increasing and convex to the p-axis. The equilibrium r in p-r space must be consistent with the producer's best response function. The equilibrium contract will thus be the intersection of the producer's best response function $p^o(r)$ and the lenders iso-expected-return schedule at expected return ρ (should such an intersection exist). Thus, using Eq. (4), we have

$$r = \frac{p^o(r) + \rho}{1 - p^o(r)}, \qquad (5)$$

Point B in Fig. 4 illustrates such an equilibrium. This figure superimposes the lender's iso-expected return schedule on part of Fig. 2.

We say an equity-backed loan is *feasible* if it offers a positive expected profit to the producer, and offers the lender an expected return at least as large as the risk-free interest rate. The nominal interest rate r required to induce a lender to participate in the contract will be a function of equity c, project quality β, and project size α, since these parameters affect the producer's choice of (noncontractible) risk. As we have seen, the producer's best response function depends on both the project size α and the amount of the producer's own wealth c in the project, differing values of these variables entailing

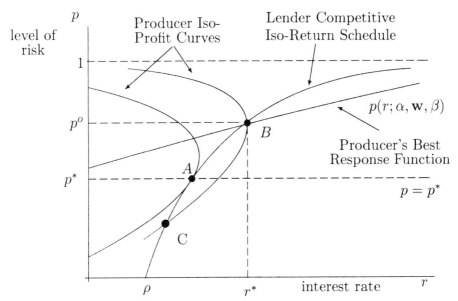

Fig. 4. Equilibrium choice of the nominal interest rate r and project risk p: the equilibrium is a point B. The Pareto optimum satisfying the lender's participation constraint occurs at point A, as compared to the equilibrium at B in the figure.

differing equilibrium levels of p and r as defined by Eq. (5). The producer thus varies α and c to maximize profits, taking account of the fact that his own best response function and hence the feasible interest rate r depends upon these variables.

The results presented below can be understood intuitively in terms of the following argument. First, since the producer is risk neutral and borrowing is more costly than self-financing (there are no incentive losses with self-financing), the producer always sets $c = \mathbf{w}$. Second, if the producer can choose the project size α without regard to the minimum size constraint $\alpha \geq 1$, there would be an optimal project size α^* and an optimal leverage ratio,

$$\lambda^* = 1 - \frac{\mathbf{w}}{\alpha^* \mathbf{k}},$$

namely one that balances the marginal benefits of borrowing (the ability to shift losses to the lender) against the marginal costs (the increased risk of failure occasioned by the producer's own choice of risk level under the incentive implied by the leverage ratio). Asset-poor producers, even if they are able to secure a loan, may be unable to implement λ^*, since for a poor producer it could be that $\alpha^* < 1$.

We say a project can be *fully financed* if a producer can obtain a loan to finance the project with no equity.

THEOREM 2. *There are productive projects that cannot be fully financed.*

The reasoning behind Theorem 2 is that because the producer's best response is to select $p > p^*$, the fact that the project is productive, i.e., that $\beta\phi(p^*) > \mathbf{k}(1 + \rho)$, does not insure that its expected return to the lender will equal or exceed $(1+\rho)$ when $p^o(r)$ rather than p^* is chosen by the producer. Thus, the best response function of a nonwealthy producer with a productive project need not intersect the lender's competitive iso-return locus. Such producers will not be financed. There will thus exist productive projects that cannot be fully financed.

We are interested precisely in those cases where projects cannot be fully financed. In this situation, among producers with projects of equivalent quality, there will be three types. One group, whom we call the *credit-constrained*, will be unable to finance even a project of minimum size. A second, the *unconstrained*, have wealth sufficient to finance projects above the minimum size. They select a project size, given their wealth, to implement the optimal leverage ratio $\lambda^* = 1 - \mathbf{w}/\alpha^*\mathbf{k}$. A third group, the *size-constrained*, are able to finance a project only at the minimum size, and with $\lambda > \lambda^*$. They would indeed prefer a smaller project, as this would entail a lower, more nearly optimal, leverage ratio which in turn would induce a lower level of risk and a higher return on the project. But this is technologically precluded by the minimum project size $\alpha \geq 1$. We have:

THEOREM 3. *Suppose a producer with wealth $\mathbf{w}$ has a productive project, and selects risk level p, equity $c \leq \mathbf{w}$, and project size $\alpha \geq 1$ to maximize profits, subject to offering a lender an expected return equal to the risk free interest rate ρ. Suppose r, c and α are contractible but p is not, and the project cannot be fully financed. Then there are wealth levels $0 < \underline{\mathbf{w}} \leq \overline{\mathbf{w}} < \mathbf{k}$ such that the following assertions hold:*

(a) for $\mathbf{w} < \underline{\mathbf{w}}$, there is no feasible equity-backed loan, so the producer cannot finance the project.

(b) for $\mathbf{w} \geq \underline{\mathbf{w}}$

   (i) there is a feasible equity-backed loan, the producer contributes equity $c = \mathbf{w}$, and the project is undertaken;

   (ii) the probability of failure p^o chosen by the producer exceeds p^*, so the choice of risk is not Pareto efficient;

(c) for $\underline{\mathbf{w}} \leq \mathbf{w} < \overline{\mathbf{w}}$ producers are size-constrained and

   (i) risk declines and project efficiency increases with increasing producer wealth;

   (ii) the rate of return on producer wealth, $\alpha\beta\phi/\mathbf{w}$, increases with increasing producer wealth;

(d) for $\mathbf{w} \geq \overline{\mathbf{w}}$ producers are unconstrained, the level of risk chosen and the rate of return is independent of wealth, and project size increases with producer wealth. Hence the total return on the project increases with producer wealth.

Part (a) is just an extension of Theorem 2: if zero wealth producers are credit-rationed, the same will be true of those with any wealth level insufficient to yield a best response function that intersects the lender's iso-return locus.

The two wealth bounds may be interpreted as follows. The lower bound is the level of wealth for which the producer's best response function is tangent to the lender's competitive iso-return schedule. The upper bound is the wealth level for which the minimal size project implements the optimal degree of leverage, given the producer's wealth (i.e., $\overline{\mathbf{w}} = \mathbf{k}\lambda^*$).

To see why the lender contributes as much equity as possible to the project (part b(i) of the theorem), note that given the credit market competitive equilibrium condition (5), the producer's objective function can be written

$$v = \alpha[\beta\phi(p(\alpha)) - \mathbf{k}(1 + \rho)], \tag{6}$$

where $p(\alpha)$ is the risk level chosen by the producer who obtains an equity-backed loan with collateral c and project size α. So the expected financial cost of the project, including the debt service and the opportunity cost of supplying equity, is $\alpha\mathbf{k}(1 + \rho)$ independent of how much of the producer's own wealth is invested. Since increasing c lowers p and $\phi'(p) < 0$ in the relevant region, the producer will set $c = \mathbf{w}$.

Part b(ii) holds because the lender pays some of the downside cost of the risk, and is clear from the producer's first order condition. Figure 4 illustrates this result. At the competitive equilibrium (point B) the producer's iso-profit curve has a vertical tangent, because it is a point on the producer's best response function—see Fig. 2. However the lender's iso-return schedule has positive slope at this point. Since mutual tangency of the iso-return schedules of producer and lender is the condition for Pareto efficiency, B is not Pareto efficient. The Pareto efficient point corresponding to the lender's participation constraint is at point A in Fig. 4, and always entail lower default probabilities and lower interest rates than the credit market equilibrium. The implied Pareto improvements are indicated by the lens-shaped region ABC. These points are infeasible, of course, as they are not on the producer's best response function. Note that the efficient contract locus is horizontal at level p^* (since agents are risk-neutral), and has no points in common with the producer's best response function.

Part (c) of the theorem is true on the same reasoning motivating part (a). For size-constrained producers, investing more wealth does not change the expected financial cost of the project, but it does raise the expected returns because it induces a lower nominal interest rate and hence a lower level of risk. Over the specified range of wealth, lowering the leverage ratio reduces the allocational distortion identified in b(ii), as is clear from Eq. (3) and Fig. 3.

The intuition behind part (d) is that $\mathbf{w} \geq \overline{\mathbf{w}}$ allows the producer to vary project size to implement the optimal leverage ratio, so increased wealth implies larger but otherwise identical projects.

Not surprisingly, wealthier producers may finance lower quality projects.

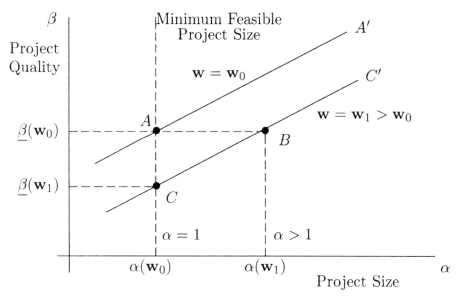

Fig. 5. Greater wealth allows larger or lower quality projects to be financed.

THEOREM 4. *For any wealth* **w** > 0, *there is a quality level* $\beta(\mathbf{w})$ *such that the pro-ducer's project will be funded when* $\beta \geq \underline{\beta}(\mathbf{w})$. *The minimum wealth level* $\underline{\mathbf{w}}$ *at which a producer's project can be funded decreases as the quality* β *of the project increases. Optimal project size is an increasing function of wealth* **w** *and project quality* β *for* $\beta \geq \underline{\beta}(\mathbf{w})$.

Theorems 3 and 4 are illustrated in Fig. 5. The locus AA' separates regions of feasible project (northwest and to the right of $\alpha = 1$) and infeasible project (southeast) for a producer of wealth $\mathbf{w}_0$, larger projects being fundable if they are superior quality. The locus CC' refers to a wealthier producer. It is clear that of two agents with projects of the same quality $\underline{\beta}(\mathbf{w}_0)$, the wealthier agent may have a larger project (of size $\alpha(\mathbf{w}_1)$ at point B) than the less wealthy (of size $\alpha(\mathbf{w}_0)$ at point A). Moreover, the wealthier agent can finance a lower quality project (of quality $\underline{\beta}(\mathbf{w}_1)$ at point C) than the minimum quality that can be financed by the less wealthy agent (which is of quality $\underline{\beta}(\mathbf{w}_0)$ at point A).

 An implication of Theorem 3 is that the rate of return to wealth increases in the level of wealth, as is illustrated in Fig. 6. Small wealth holders who are credit constrained receive ρ, while from Eq. (2) we see that the unconstrained receive an income of $v + c\rho$ giving them a rate of return of $v/\mathbf{w} + \rho$. Intermediate between these two cases, the size-constrained receive a return rising from the risk-free rate to the unconstrained rate $\alpha\beta\phi(p(\alpha^*))/\mathbf{w} > 1 + \rho$, as wealth increases from $\underline{\mathbf{w}}$ to $\overline{\mathbf{w}}$. Fig. 6 also illustrates the fact that the interest rate stipulated in the loan contract declines over the range $(\underline{\mathbf{w}}, \overline{\mathbf{w}})$

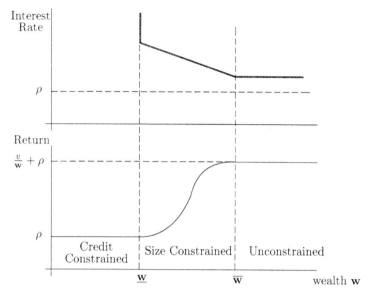

Fig. 6. Rate of return Increases with producer wealth.

and is constant for higher levels of wealth. Because expected rates of return are lower for the less wealthy, wealth inequalities may grow over time. Notice, however, that the technological nonconvexity constituted by the minimum project size $\alpha \geq 1$ is essential for the result: as Galor and Zeira (1993) point out, wealth constraints in credit markets alone do not bear this implication. If projects of any size were possible, those with limited wealth would have small projects with leverage ratios λ^*, earning the same expected rate of return as the wealthy.

Because we treat the wealth levels of individuals as exogenous and so do not take account of savings incentives and the long run evolution of the wealth distribution we will mention only in passing an important implication of Theorem 3. Individuals holding wealth over (or near) the size constrained range ($\underline{w}$, $\overline{w}$) have enhanced savings incentives, and may even benefit more from saving than do the wealthy (despite the fact that the average returns on wealth rise with wealth, as we have seen). The reason is that for wealthholders in this range increased wealth supports more nearly optimal contracts, and allows higher returns on wealth, thus providing additional savings incentives. Thus if the expected return to holding wealth $\mathbf{w}$ is $r(\mathbf{w})$ the incentive to add one unit to one's wealth is $r(\mathbf{w})+r'(\mathbf{w})\mathbf{w}$, where the second term may be sufficiently large that savings incentives for those in the size constrained range exceed those in the unconstrained range. If this is the case those in the size constrained range might over time save themselves out of their wealth constraints. Similar, though attenuated incentives exist for those whose low wealth leaves them credit constrained but for whom saving into the size constrained range is feasible. Thus we cannot say that wealth inequalities will grow overtime even when the return structure is as depicted in Fig. 7, an adequate treatment of this requiring not only endogenous savings decisions (above), but an account of the risk return choices of individuals at various wealth levels, a topic to which we will turn shortly.[13]

Not surprisingly, asset redistribution may be productivity enhancing under the conditions given.

THEOREM 5. *Suppose all projects are of the same quality. If some producers are credit-constrained, a redistribution of wealth from lenders to such producers will be productivity enhancing. If some producers are size constrained while others are unconstrained, an asset transfer from a size constrained producer to a wealthier unconstrained producer may be productivity enhancing.*

The first part of the theorem flows from the fact that lenders receive expected return $\alpha\mathbf{k}(1 + \rho)$, on an investment of $\alpha\mathbf{k}$, while a credit-constrained producer would receive expected return $\alpha\beta\phi(p) > \alpha\mathbf{k}(1+\rho)$ on this investment. The second part of the theorem follows from the result that the unconstrained select less risky (and hence Pareto superior) levels of risk. Suppose the transfer is large enough to reduce the size constrained producer to the status of an excluded credit constrained nonproducer. Then the effect of the transfer is simply to expand a project which will be operated in a less excessively risky manner, while eliminating a project being operated in a more risky manner.[14]

We now relax two simplifying assumptions. Suppose, first, that project quality, β varies among producers. We know from Theorem 4 that where both project quality and wealth differ among producers, there may exist superior projects which are infeasible due to the insufficient wealth of the producer, while inferior projects are funded. This result motivates an important result, consistent with our initial claim that productivity enhancing egalitarian asset redistributions are possible.

THEOREM 6. *Suppose individuals have projects of differing quality, and that some with productive projects are credit constrained while others are size constrained. Then there may exist an productivity enhancing asset transfer from a wealthy to a credit-constrained producer.*

The theorem follows trivially from the previous theorems. Under the stated conditions it will generally be possible to transfer wealth from an unconstrained producer with a

---

[13] Zimmerman and Carter (1997) calibrate a dynamic portfolio choice model of this process using data from three regions of Burkina Faso. Birdsall et al. (1996) develop a model of high powered savings incentives for poor credit constrained households.

[14] Note that voluntary exchange will not bring about this inegalitarian productivity enhancing change, since the wealthier agent does not want to borrow, even at the risk-free interest rate.

relatively poor project (one with $\beta = \hat{\beta}$) to an initially credit constrained producer with a superior project (one with $\beta = \tilde{\beta} > \hat{\beta}$). To see how this might work, imagine that a wealthless producer has a high quality project. If the amount transferred is sufficient to give the previously credit-constrained producer an amount of wealth at least as great as $\overline{w}$ without reducing the wealthy producer below this level, then the only effect of the transfer is to reduce the size of the inferior project by $\overline{w}/\lambda^*$ while introducing a superior project of equivalent size. The resulting increase in aggregate output is $\overline{w}(\tilde{\beta} - \hat{\beta})\alpha\phi(p(\alpha^*))$. The gains to the beneficiaries of the transfer obviously exceed the losses to the wealthy, and while it is not obvious how the losers could be compensated this is not required by our definition of a productivity enhancing asset transfer.

We now relax a second assumption. Suppose that each project faces a rising average cost schedule occasioned by the fact that while the minimum project size can be operated by the producer as residual claimant, larger project sizes require the employment of labor, occasioning a supervision cost. Specifically, suppose when the project size is $\alpha \geq 1$, the expected return schedule is

$$\alpha[1 - s(\alpha)]\beta\phi(p), \tag{7}$$

where $s(1) = 0$ where $s'(\alpha) > 0$ for $\alpha \geq 1$, and $s(\alpha) \geq 1$ for sufficiently large α. We have:

THEOREM 7. *Suppose there are decreasing returns to scale, given by the expected return schedule (7). Then if some producers are credit-constrained and other producers are sufficiently wealthy, there exist productivity enhancing redistributions from wealthy to nonwealthy agents.*

The intuition behind this theorem is as follows. For producer wealth $\mathbf{w}$ sufficient to secure an equity-backed loan, there is a profit maximizing project size $\alpha(\mathbf{w})$. Let $\mathbf{w}^*$ be the wealth level that maximizes the expected return per unit of capital $v(\alpha(\mathbf{w}), \mathbf{w})/k\alpha(\mathbf{w})(1+\rho)$. Then producers who have wealth $\mathbf{w} > \mathbf{w}^*$ can transfer $\mathbf{w} - \mathbf{w}^*$ to credit-constrained producers, which may allow them to operate at project size $\alpha(\mathbf{w}^*)$.

In sum, allocational distortions associated with loan contracts arise because limited liability protects borrowers from downside risks so that borrowers are not full residual claimants on the results of their actions. For the credit constrained the distortions are particularly great as their limited wealth induces them to assume a lower residual claimancy share than those with greater wealth. Those with sufficient wealth to assume full residual claimancy—by forgoing borrowing—adopt the Pareto efficient level of effort and risk choice. Where asset redistributions affect a redistribution of residual claimancy, as we have seen, they may attenuate or eliminate the above allocational distortions.

3. Land contracts

Among the most important, and studied, cases of contractual incompleteness and wealth effects on allocative efficiency concerns agricultural tenancy, whose harmful effects on productivity were famously lamented by Alexis de Tocqueville, John Stuart Mill and Alfred Marshall. In many poor countries the empirical evidence suggests that economies of scale in farm production are insignificant (except in some plantation crops, and that too more in processing and marketing than in production) and when accompanied by appropriate insurance and credit institutions, the small family farm may often be the most productive unit of production.[15] Yet the violent and tortuous history of land reform in these countries suggests that there are numerous roadblocks on the way to a more efficient reallocation of land rights. Why do the large landlords not voluntarily sell their land to small family farmers and use their market and bargaining power to acquire much of the surplus arising from this reallocation?

First the small farmer, as a nonwealthy agent, faces the disadvantages in credit and insurance markets described in Sections 2 and 4, and hence is often not in a position to buy or profitably rent more land.[16] Second, land as an asset may serve some special functions for the rich that the poor are less capable of using and therefore are not reflected in the prices offered by the latter. For example, holding land may offer some tax advantages or speculative opportunities or a generally safe investment vehicle for the rich (particularly, when nonagricultural investment opportunities are limited or too risky) that are not particularly relevant for the small farmer. Similarly, large land holdings may give their owner special social status or political power in a lumpy way, so that the status effect from owning 100 hectares, for instance, is larger than the combined status effect accruing to 50 new buyers owning two hectares each. Binswanger et al. (1995) point out that land is often used as preferred collateral in the credit market and thus serves as more than just a productive asset. The asking price for land then may be above the capitalized value of the agricultural income stream for even the more productive small farmer, rendering mortgaged sales uncommon—since mortgaged land cannot be used as collateral to raise working capital for the buyer.

For all these reasons land ownership does not pass from the large to the small farmer and, accordingly, the land market is very thin. In rich countries a large part of land transactions may be related to the life-cycle: the elderly sell land to buyers at an accumulating stage in their life-cycle. In the more inter-generationally close-knit families in poor countries such life-cycle related land transactions are rare. More often in poor countries land sales go the way opposite to what is suggested by the evidence of the

---

[15] See, for instance, Berry and Cline (1979) and Prosterman and Riedinger (1979, Chapter 2). For a more recent summary of the evidence and the methodological shortcomings of the empirical studies, see Binswanger et al. (1995). While there are many reasons for this regularity, among them are the agency problems we have stressed above (Shaban, 1987; Laffont and Matoussi, 1995).

[16] Mookherjee (1997), in a model with asymmetric information, thus generating potential informational rents for the supplier of unobserved effort, provides additional reasons why there will be no scope for mutually profitable land sales from landlords to tenants, or farm laborers.

more efficient small farmer: land passes from distressed small farmers to landlords and money-lenders. This tendency increases as the traditional reciprocity-based risk-coping mechanisms weaken, and farmers may have to depend more on land sales in times of crisis.

We will analyze how the initial wealth distribution affects static efficiency in the tenancy market. We point to the possibility of a "tenancy ladder" for tenants facing different wealth constraints. If risk neutral tenants are not wealth constrained, or if output does not depend strongly on tenant effort, the landlord will be able to devise a contract securing a Pareto efficient level of tenant effort, even where tenant effort is not verifiable. However,

- where tenants have little wealth or where expected output depends strongly on tenant effort, inefficient contracts will obtain, with the resulting degree of allocative inefficiency varying inversely with the wealth of the tenant;
- for this reason a transfer of wealth to asset poor tenants may be productivity enhancing, even if the amount transferred is insufficient to permit the tenant to become the owner.

We use a principal-agent model that emphasizes, along with moral hazard, a limited liability constraint, i.e., the tenant is liable up to his own wealth level $\mathbf{w} \geq 0$.[17] We abstract from risk sharing issues and assume both the tenant and the landlord to be risk neutral (we address questions of risk subsequently).

Consider a plot of land that requires an input of one unit of labor and yields an output of either H or $L < H$. The probability of the H-output depends on the tenant's effort, and without loss of generality we may let this probability of the good state simply be $e \in [0, 1]$, where e is the effort applied to the land by the laborer. Suppose the owner of the plot, the landlord, hires a tenant to supply the labor. We assume that effort e has disutility $d(e)$ to the tenant, where $d(e)$ is increasing and convex, with $d(0) = d'(0) = 0$.

Let us start with the benchmark case where e is fully observable. Given the convexity of $d(e)$, there exists a unique value of e that maximizes the combined payoff of the landlord and the tenant, $eH + (1 - e)L - d(e)$. Let us denote this first-best e as e^*. It is easy to see that the optimal level of effort will be that for which

$$d'(e^*) = H - L, \tag{8}$$

or the expected marginal product of effort equals the marginal disutility of effort. If e is fully observable, the landlord can offer the tenant a take-it-or-leave-it contract, which pays the latter's (given) reservation income $m \geq 0$ when e is observed to be e^*, and 0 if e is observed to be anything else.

But effort is not observable, so to motivate the tenant to supply an appropriate level of effort, the landlord offers the tenant a contract (h, l), under which the tenant pays the

---

[17] Early theoretical models in the literature with the limited liability constraint are those of Sappington (1983) and Shetty (1988). In a more recent paper Laffont and Matoussi (1995) use a dataset from the region of El Oulja in Tunisia to support their theoretical result that financial constraints have a significant impact on the type of tenancy contract chosen, and hence on productive efficiency.

landlord $H - h$ when H is realized and $L - l$ when L is realized, the tenant retaining the remainder of the output, h in the good state and l in the bad. We assume the tenant has wealth $\mathbf{w} \geq 0$, and is subject to limited liability, so the constraints $h + \mathbf{w} \geq 0$ and $l + \mathbf{w} \geq 0$ cannot be violated. Only the latter inequality is of interest, however, since under any incentive scheme chosen by the landlord h will be greater than l (see below). Thus to induce effort the landlord must design a contract that satisfies an incentive compatibility constraint (ICC), a participation constraint (PC), and a limited liability constraint (LLC). That is, given such a contract, which cannot require a payment by the tenant larger than his wealth $\mathbf{w}$ (LLC), the tenant chooses e as a best response (ICC), and receives an expected utility no lower than m (PC). The landlord thus varies h and l to maximize

$$\pi = \max_{h,l} e(H - h) + (1 - e)(L - l)$$

subject to

(PC) $\qquad\qquad\qquad eh + (1 - e)l - d(e) \geq m,$

(ICC) $\qquad\qquad e \in \arg\max_{\tilde{e}} \tilde{e}h + (1 - \tilde{e})l - d(\tilde{e}),$

(LLC) $\qquad\qquad\qquad\qquad l + \mathbf{w} \geq 0.$

The ICC must always hold as an equality, so it can be replaced by its corresponding first order condition, namely

$$h - l = d'(e). \tag{9}$$

This equality constraint can be used to eliminate the variable h, reducing the landlord's maximization problem to

$$\pi = \max_{l,e} e(H - l - d'(e)) + (1 - e)(L - l) \tag{10}$$

subject to

(PC) $\qquad\qquad l + ed'(e) - d(e) - m \quad \geq \quad 0,$

(LLC) $\qquad\qquad\qquad\qquad l + \mathbf{w} \quad \geq \quad 0.$

To solve this problem, we form the Lagrangian

$$\mathcal{L} = e(H - l - d'(e)) + (1 - e)(L - l) + \lambda(l + \mathbf{w})$$
$$+ \mu(l + ed'(e) - d(e) - m),$$

The first order conditions for this system are

$$H - L - d'(e) - (1 - \mu)ed''(e) = 0 \tag{11}$$
$$\lambda + \mu = 1 \tag{12}$$
$$\lambda(l + \mathbf{w}) = 0 \tag{13}$$
$$\mu(l + ed'(e) - d(e) - m) = 0. \tag{14}$$

We will see that depending on the tenant's wealth level, one or both of these constraints will be binding.

Suppose first $\mu = 0$, so the PC is not binding. Then Eq. (11) determines an effort level e_* such that

$$H - L = d'(e_*) + e_* d''(e_*), \tag{15}$$

and since $\lambda = 1$, $l = -\mathbf{w}$, so the contract stipulates that in the bad state the tenant surrenders his entire wealth to the landlord. The PC must also not be violated, so

$$\mathbf{w} \le \mathbf{w}_* \equiv e_* d'(e_*) - d(e_*) - m. \tag{16}$$

Thus for wealth in the range $[0, \mathbf{w}_*]$, the LCC constrains, the PC does not (the tenant enjoys a level of utility superior to his fallback position; i.e., he earns a rent, except at $\mathbf{w} = \mathbf{w}_*$), and effort is fixed at e_*. Finally the landlord's return is an increasing function of the tenant's wealth $\mathbf{w}$. This can be seen from Eq. (10), which by substituting $l = -\mathbf{w}$ now becomes

$$\pi = \mathbf{w} + L + e_*(H - L - d'(e_*)).$$

Comparing Eqs. (8) and (15) we see that $d'(e_*) < d'(e^*)$, so the convexity of $d(e)$ implies $e_* < e^*$. We conclude that the low wealth tenant's effort level is less than the Pareto optimal level—that which maximizes the joint surplus.

Suppose, by contrast, that $\lambda = 0$, so the LLC is not binding. In this case $\mu = 1$, the PC holds as an equality (the tenant receives his fallback). Then Eq. (11) implies $H - L = d'(e)$, so the effort level is just e^*, as in Eq. (8), where effort is fully observable and the joint surplus is maximized. We see that because the PC is satisfied as an equality (using Eq. (14)), the tenant's income in the low output state is now given by

$$l = m - e^* d'(e^*) + d(e^*),$$

and to satisfy the LLC we must have

$$\mathbf{w} \ge \mathbf{w}^* \equiv e^* d'(e^*) - d(e^*) - m. \tag{17}$$

For $\mathbf{w} \in [\mathbf{w}^*, \infty)$ effort is fixed at e^*, the low output state payment is fixed at $l = -\mathbf{w}^*$, and the LLC is not a binding constraint. Tenant wealth levels at least as great as $\mathbf{w}^*$ thus allow a contract supporting a Pareto optimal outcome.

The only remaining possibility in Eqs. (11)–(14) is that both λ and μ are nonzero. This case, in which both the LLC and the PC bind, represents a solution to the landlord's maximization problem only for $\mathbf{w} \in [\mathbf{w}_*, \mathbf{w}^*]$.[18] In this range, from the LLC we know that $l = -\mathbf{w}$ and from the PC we know that effort satisfies

$$\mathbf{w} = e_0 d'(e_0) - d(e_0) - m. \tag{18}$$

Notice here that $de_0/dw = 1/e_0 d''(e_0) > 0$, so $e_0(\mathbf{w})$ increases from e_* to e^* as $\mathbf{w}$ moves from $\mathbf{w}_*$ to $\mathbf{w}^*$. Also, l falls from $-\mathbf{w}_*$ to $-\mathbf{w}^*$ over this range, while h rises from $d(e_*) - \mathbf{w}$ to $d(e^*) - \mathbf{w}$.[19] The effect of the steepening payment gradient $h - l$ is to align tenant effort incentives more closely with the payoff to the landlord, approaching the Pareto optimal outcome as $\mathbf{w}$ approaches $\mathbf{w}^*$.

We thus have

THEOREM 8. **Tenancy ladders and inefficient contracts.** *Where tenant effort e affects expected output and is not contractible, and where the tenant's wealth level $\mathbf{w}$ is the maximum liability to which the tenant may be exposed by the terms of the landlord's output-contingent rental contract, there exist wealth levels $\mathbf{w}_*$ and $\mathbf{w}^* > \mathbf{w}_*$ such that the landlord's optimal contract has the following properties:*

(i) for $\mathbf{w} \geq \mathbf{w}^*$ the tenant chooses a Pareto optimal effort level e^*, the tenant's expected return equals the tenant's reservation position, and the landlord secures the entire surplus;

(ii) for $\mathbf{w} < \mathbf{w}_*$ the tenant chooses effort $e_* < e^*$ independently of $\mathbf{w}$, the tenant's expected return is superior to the reservation position and declining in the tenant's wealth, while the landlord's share of output is increasing in the tenant's wealth; and finally,

(iii) for $\mathbf{w}_* \leq \mathbf{w} \leq \mathbf{w}^*$, tenant effort is rising in tenant wealth (from e_* to e^*), the tenant's expected return equals the tenant's reservation position, and the landlord's absolute and relative share of the surplus of the project is rising in the tenant's wealth.

Figure 7 illustrates this theorem. Allocative efficiency rises with the wealth of the tenant because on efficiency grounds the payment gradient $(h - l)$ should equal the expected marginal product of effort $(H - L)$, but where the maximum penalty the landlord can impose on the tenant in the bad state is small, setting the payment gradient equal to the expected marginal product of effort can be accomplished only by raising h not by lowering l; because under these circumstances raising h not only enhances efficiency but

---

[18] This is because placing two constraints upon the landlord's choice cannot improve the landlord's payoff over the single-constraint alternatives available to him outside the range $[\mathbf{w}_*, \mathbf{w}^*]$.

[19] To see that h rises, we differentiate $d'(e_0(\mathbf{w})) - \mathbf{w}$ with respect to $\mathbf{w}$, getting $d''e_0' - 1 = 1/e_0 - 1 > 0$.

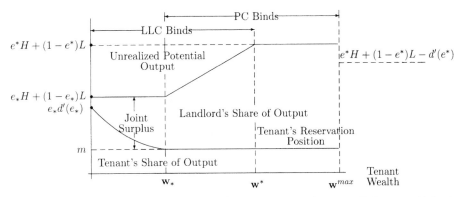

Fig. 7. Tenant wealth and allocative inefficiency. Efficient contracts require $\mathbf{w} \geq \mathbf{w}^*$. Lower wealth levels entail suboptimal effort and expected output and (for $\mathbf{w} < \mathbf{w}_*$) a smaller tenant share of the joint surplus.

distributes some of the efficiency gains to the tenant, the landlord's private incentives fail to implement the social optimum.

The intuition supporting Theorem 8, namely that tenant wealth attenuates allocative inefficiencies arising from contractual incompleteness, suggests that wealth limits will be more stringent where the noncontractible input effect is particularly powerful in inducing the good outcome, namely where $H - L$ is large, motivating

THEOREM 9. **Wealth constraints and noncontractible inputs.** *The wealth limits* $\mathbf{w}_*$ *and* $\mathbf{w}^*$ *defined in Theorem 8 vary with the importance of effort in determining outputs, namely, with* $H - L$.

The reason, which may be confirmed from Eqs. (11), (16) and (17), is that as $H - L$ increases, optimal effort is greater so the Pareto optimal payment gradient is steeper and hence the LLC is binding for higher levels of tenant wealth.

Finally, we have:

THEOREM 10. **Productivity enhancing redistributions to tenants.** *For the contract defined in Theorem 8, a redistribution of wealth from the landlord to a tenant with wealth* $\mathbf{w}' \in [\mathbf{w}_*, \mathbf{w}^*)$ *would enhance allocative efficiency.*

The reasoning, which may be confirmed by inspection of Eq. (18), is that over this range an addition to tenant wealth benefits tenants directly, while the induced increase in their effort (namely, $de/dw = 1/ed''(e)$) benefits the landlord, partially offsetting the cost of the transfer.

There is some wealth level $\mathbf{w}^{\max}$ for which the land in question will be worth more to the tenant as owner than to the landlord, taking account of the available credit and other considerations discussed at the outset. As owner, the tenant will of course implement the surplus-maximizing effort level.

It is possible, indeed likely in many cases, that the tenant's fallback position m will not be independent of the tenant's wealth—as in the case, for example, where the tenant's wealth is held in the form of a truck. If m varies with $\mathbf{w}$, and if the wealth level $\mathbf{w}_*$ is defined as before but with $m = m(\mathbf{w})$ where $m'(\mathbf{w}) > 0$, the tenant's share of output will rise with tenant wealth for $\mathbf{w} > \mathbf{w}_*$, with the landlord's share unambiguously declining for $\mathbf{w} > \mathbf{w}^*$ and with the effect of increased tenant wealth on the landlord's share being ambiguous over the range $\mathbf{w}_*$, $\mathbf{w}^*$, the sign depending on the strength of the $m(\mathbf{w})$ relationship. For $\mathbf{w} < \mathbf{w}_*$, the landlord's share is increasing in $\mathbf{w}$, so the landlord would prefer wealthier tenants.

In the model here we have discussed only the one-period game. In a multiperiod model there are interesting extra dimensions of the incentive effects under tenancy. The landlord may mitigate the problem of underapplication of the noncontractible input by using a threat of eviction when output is low.[20] The threat may be effective in our model with limited liability, since for $\mathbf{w} < \mathbf{w}_*$ the tenants earn some rent over and above their reservation income m, which they would lose if evicted. In a multiperiod model, apart from labor effort (and other current input choice), the incentive to invest may also be affected by the eviction threat. Such a threat may discourage long-term improvements on the land (that are often noncontractible).[21] One may add that the removal of the threat (say, through a land reform program that provides tenurial security) may also improve the bargaining power of the tenant, and investment may be encouraged because the tenant now expects to get a higher share of the additional output generated by that investment.

But as Banerjee and Ghatak (1996) point out, there are two ways in which eviction threats may also have a positive effect on the incentive to invest. First, just as eviction threats raise current labor effort because tenants care about the expected value of future rents from the work and the prospect of losing these rents induces them to work harder, similarly investment today raises the chances of doing well tomorrow and hence retaining the job day after tomorrow, thus they may respond positively to eviction threats. Secondly, if eviction threats raise current effort then that raises the chance of being around in the next period and this effect too is favorable to investment. All these put together make the net effect of eviction threats on investment rather ambiguous. The empirical evidence of Banerjee and Ghatak from a tenancy reform program in West Bengal (in the form of improvements in the security of tenure) suggests that the net effect of the program on the rate of growth of agricultural productivity is positive.

---

[20] This observation goes back to Johnson (1950) and has been formalized in Bardhan (1984) and Dutta et al. (1989).

[21] Classical economists have emphasized this adverse effect of tenurial insecurity on investment. John Stuart Mill, for example, regarded this as the major defect of metayage in France. This effect is formalized in Bardhan (1984) and Banerjee and Ghatak (1996).

One major limitation of limited liability models in the context of rural areas in poor countries is that some of the main results are driven by the assumption that the asset-poor cannot be penalized enough by the landlord for rent default in bad times. Apart from the linearity of the utility function assumed, which is clearly implausible when consumption is near zero, in long-term relationships of closed village communities landlords can sometimes get around this problem with a weather-dependent side-payment (credit) to the tenant to be paid back in better times. For a model of such tenancy-cum-credit contracts, see Kotwal (1985). Historical information on agricultural production under different weather conditions as well as information on production on neighboring farms may be used by the landlord in the design of an incentive contract in such cases. It should also be kept in mind that in a traditional village context the landlord has access to various noneconomic forms of punishing a defaulting poor tenant.

4. Wealth, risk aversion and insurance

An important impediment to policy measures to redistribute economic resources in favor of nonwealthy producers is that to have the desired incentive effects, assigning residual claimancy to producers also involves assigning them control rights over the relevant assets. Nonwealthy producers, however, tend to be more risk averse than wealthy and/or highly diversified nonproducers—for instance stockholders, entrepreneurs, or landlords.[22] As a consequence, there is generally a tradeoff between effective production incentives and socially optimal risk choices. We explore ways of attenuating this tradeoff, extending an approach suggested by Domar and Musgrave (1944) and Sinn (1995).

A number of empirical investigations document a high level of risk aversion on the part of the nonwealthy. Low wealth entails lower return to independent agricultural production, for instance, because farmers sacrifice expected returns for more secure returns. Rosenzweig and Wolpin (1993) find that low-wealth Indian farmers seeking a means to secure more stable consumption streams, hold bullocks, which are a highly liquid form of capital, instead of buying pumps, which are illiquid but have high expected return. The relevant effects are not small. Rosenzweig and Binswanger (1993: p. 75) find, for example, that a one standard deviation reduction in weather risk would raise average profits by about a third among farmers in the lowest wealth quartile, and virtually not at all for the top wealth-holders. Moreover, they conclude that the demand for weather insurance would come primarily, if not exclusively, from poor farmers. Nerlove and Soedjiana (1996) find a similar effect in Indonesia with respect to sheep.[23]

Thus because of risk aversion, a reassignment of property rights to low-wealth producers might be unsustainable if as a result producers' income streams are subject to high levels of stochastic variation. Carter et al. (1996) and Jarvis (1989) provide a vivid

---

[22] See Saha et al. (1994) and the many studies cite therein.

[23] See Hoff (1996a) for a discussion of this and related studies.

example: in the Central Valley of Chile three quarters of those families who received individual assignment of land rights under a land redistribution program in the 1970's sold their assets within a decade.

However, as Musgrave, Domar, and Sinn suggest, the availability of insurance can lead to increased risk-taking and willingness to hold risky assets. But the market for forms of insurance that promote risk-taking in production may be imperfect (Atkinson and Stiglitz, 1980). Shiller (1993) provides several contemporary applications, arguing that capital market imperfections even in the most advanced economies lead to the absence of insurance markets for major sources of individual insecurity and inequality. For instance, a major form of wealth insecurity in many families is the capital value of the family home, due to medium- to long-term fluctuations in average housing prices in a region. No insurance for such fluctuations is available, but Shiller suggests that this and other similar insurance markets can be activated through proper financial interventions. Along these same lines, Sinn (1995) argues that the welfare state in the advanced economies can be understood in part as a successful set of policy measures to improve the risk-taking behavior of the nonwealthy where private "social insurance" markets fail.

On the other hand, many attempts at preserving the small independent producer through extending credit availability and crop insurance have failed (Carter and Coles, 1997), though these failures may be due to forms of insurance that are not incentive compatible (Newbery, 1989). For instance, insuring individual crops reintroduces the same agency problems as sharecropping and wage labor. By contrast, as we show below, allowing producers to purchase insurance covering some general condition that is correlated with individual crop risk but that does not affect individual production incentives, can be effective in eliciting risk taking on the part of the nonwealthy without incurring efficiency losses. A crop insurance program in India, for example, based payments to individual farmers not on the output of their own plots but rather on average crop yields in larger agro-climatic regions to which they belong (Dandekar, 1985). Disaster insurance for crops in the US is similarly designed (Williams et al., 1993). Or insurance payments may be based on the exogenous source of the risk itself, if this is measurable. An example of this is rainfall insurance, whereby the producer pays a fixed premium, and receives a schedule of returns depending upon the average rainfall in the region over the growing season.[24]

In this spirit, we show below that under plausible conditions reducing the exposure of the nonwealthy to stochastic fluctuations independent of their productive activities can induce increased risk taking in production, and hence can help sustain otherwise unsustainable asset redistributions. General social insurance can also allow access to credit markets for wealth-poor agents who would be otherwise excluded. Platteau et al.

---

[24] Similarly, the taxation of agricultural income can be based on general growing conditions rather than measured farm output, thus combining insurance and revenue-producing goals. The idea is not new. The *Zabt* system of taxation, developed by the Mughal rulers of North India during the sixteenth century, based assessments on estimates of the productive capacities of the land rather than on actual harvests (Richards 1993: pp. 85ff).

(1980), Sanderatne (1986), Ardington and Lund (1995) provide some evidence for this phenomenon.

The model developed below shows that, exposed to the risk associated with residual claimancy, asset-poor producers

- may avoid buying projects that they could operate productively, even when they are financially capable of doing so, may sell rather than operate such projects that are transferred to them, and will choose suboptimal levels of risk for any project that they do retain and operate;
- there exists a class of productivity enhancing egalitarian asset redistributions that are sustainable as competitive equilibria but will not occur through private contracting even when loans are available to all producers at the risk-free interest rate;
- this class may be expanded by offering a fair insurance to nonwealthy asset holders that protects the producer against risk unassociated with the production process (e.g., health insurance, consumer goods price stabilization) or that protects independent producers against "industry risk" that is unrelated to the quality of their own decisions;
- while competitive profit maximizing insurers may supply some forms of insurance of this type, they will generally do so in a suboptimal manner.

Let us begin with a risk neutral employer who owns an asset and employs a worker. The worker receives a wage w, and the project uses nondepreciable capital goods with value $\mathbf{k}$. We assume the employer must supervise the worker to guarantee performance, with supervision costs $m > 0$. We also assume the project consists of a continuum of possible technologies of varying risk and expected return, with higher risk yielding higher expected return over some range. We summarize the choice of technology in an expected net revenue schedule $g(\sigma)$, which is a concave function of the standard deviation of revenue $\sigma > 0$, with a maximum at some $\sigma^* > 0$.[25]

We then write the employer's profits, net of the opportunity costs of capital, $p(\sigma)$ as

$$p(\sigma) = \sigma z + g(\sigma) - \rho \mathbf{k} - m - w \tag{19}$$

where z is a random variable with mean zero and standard deviation unity and ρ is the risk-free interest rate.

The employer, who is risk neutral, maximizes $\mathbf{E}p(\sigma)$, the expected value of profits, giving first-order condition

$$(\mathbf{E}p)_\sigma = g'(\sigma) = 0, \tag{20}$$

[25] This shape follows from two plausible assumptions. First, production techniques that offer positive expected return involve a strictly positive level of risk. Hence, expected return is an increasing function of risk for low levels of risk. Second, firms have access to production techniques that have very high returns when successful, but with a low probability of success (e.g., a firm may lower costs by not diversifying its product line, or by assuming the availability of particular production inputs). Hence, above a certain point expected return declines with increasing risk.

determining the expected profit-maximizing risk level σ^*. We further assume that the project is part of a competitive system with free entry, so profits must be zero in equilibrium. Since the employer is risk-neutral, this means the equilibrium wage rate w^* is given by

$$w^* = g(\sigma^*) - \rho \mathbf{k} - m. \tag{21}$$

Suppose the wage-earner considers becoming an independent producer by renting capital and undertaking production. To abstract from problems of credit availability, we assume that the productive equipment constituting the asset may be rented at a per-period cost $\rho \mathbf{k}$ where ρ is the risk-free interest rate. This is equivalent to assuming that the producer can borrow funds to purchase the asset at the risk-free rate. The independent producer's net payoff is then given by

$$y(\sigma) = \sigma z + g(\sigma) - \rho \mathbf{k}, \tag{22}$$

since being self-employed, the producer pays neither the wage nor the monitoring cost (we assume that the effort level of the producer remains the same). Indeed, the fact that the producer does not incur the monitoring cost captures our assumption that productive efficiency improves when the producer ceases being a wage-earner and becomes the residual claimant.

Suppose the producer has utility function $u(\mathbf{w})$, which is twice differentiable, increasing, and concave in wealth $\mathbf{w}$, and define

$$v(\sigma, \mu) = \mathbf{E}u(\mathbf{w}) = \int_{-\infty}^{\infty} u(\mu + \sigma z) \, dF(z), \tag{23}$$

where $F(z)$ is the cumulative distribution of z. Thus $v(\sigma, \mu)$ is the expected utility of the payoff $\mu + \sigma z$. We write the slope of the level curves $v(\sigma, \mu) = \bar{v}$ where $\bar{v} \in \mathbf{R}$.

$$s(\sigma, \mu) = -\frac{v_\sigma}{v_\mu}, \tag{24}$$

and we write the Arrow–Pratt risk coefficient for the agent as

$$\lambda(\mathbf{w}) = -\frac{u''(\mathbf{w})}{u'(\mathbf{w})}.$$

Then following Meyer (1987) and Sinn (1990), we know that $v(\sigma, \mu)$ behaves like a utility function where μ is a "good" and σ is a "bad". The level curves $v(\sigma, \mu) = \bar{v}$ are indifference curves which, in the case of decreasing absolute risk aversion, are increasing, convex, flat at $\sigma = 0$, become flatter for increasing μ when $\sigma > 0$, and become steeper for increasing σ. Movements to the north and to the west thus indicate both improved welfare and flatter indifference curves. These properties are illustrated in Fig. 8.

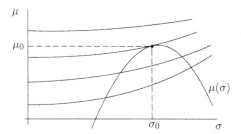

Fig. 8. Indifference curves of the decreasingly absolutely risk averse producer with utility function $v(\sigma, \mu)$.

We henceforth assume the producer exhibits decreasing absolute risk aversion, which means $\lambda'(\mathbf{w}) < 0$; i.e., the producer becomes less risk averse as wealth increases.[26]

The producer then chooses σ to maximize

$$\pi(\sigma) \equiv v(\sigma, \mu(\sigma))$$

where

$$\mu(\sigma) \equiv \mathbf{E}y(\sigma) = g(\sigma) - \rho\mathbf{k}, \tag{25}$$

giving the first-order condition

$$\pi_\sigma = v_\mu[g'(\sigma) - s(\sigma, \mu(\sigma))] = 0. \tag{26}$$

This indicates that the marginal rate of transformation of risk into expected payoffs, $g'(\sigma)$, must equal the marginal rate of substitution between risk and expected payoff, $s(\sigma, \mu)$. The producer's optimizing problem as residual claimant is depicted in Fig. 9 as choosing the highest indifference curve of $v(\sigma, \mu)$ that satisfies the constraint Eq. (25), which is just the tangency point at A, giving σ^o, which satisfies the first order condition Eq. (26). The producer's risk aversion implies $s(\sigma, \mu) > 0$, which by Eq. (26) requires that $\sigma^o < \sigma^*$, so the independent producer chooses a lower level of risk than the risk-neutral employer.

The tradeoff between the allocative gains and suboptimal risk losses that occur when the asset is assigned to the asset-poor producer is illustrated in Figure 9. This figure depicts both the pre-transfer allocation in which the employer chooses σ^* and pays w^*, and the post-asset-transfer situation indicated by point A. The allocative gain associated with the transfer is the increase in the expected return from w^* to the point D, or just m, the saving in monitoring input. The suboptimal risk loss is $D - F$, reflecting the fact that the risk averse producer prefers point A to point C on the risk-return schedule. There is no reason, of course, to expect the gains to exceed the costs.

[26] Virtually all empirical studies support decreasing absolute risk aversion. For a recent review of the literature, see Saha et al. (1994).

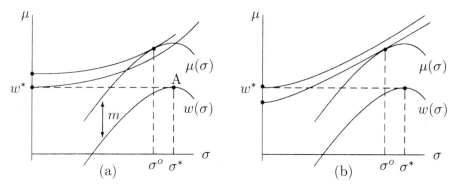

Fig. 9. The tradeoff between gain in expected return and lost in suboptimal risk taking.

To compare the producer's welfare as residual claimant as opposed to wage-earner, note that when the employer chooses σ, by Eq. (21) the equilibrium payoff to the employee occurs at the maximum point σ^* of the schedule $w = g(\sigma) - \rho\mathbf{k} - m$, as shown at point B in Fig. 10(a). Figure 10(a) shows the case where the producer is better off as residual claimant rather than working for the employer, since the indifference curve through $(\sigma^o, \mu(\sigma^o))$ is higher than the indifference curve through $(0, w^*)$. By contrast, Fig. 10(b) shows the case where the producer is better off working for the employer. Notice that in this case the producer has higher expected income as residual claimant than as wage-earner, but is exposed to an excessive level of risk. The differences between the two cases is the greater degree of risk aversion assumed in the second case, as is indicated by the steeper indifference locus. Competitive equilibrium for the first case implies that the producer acquires the asset and in the second that the producer work for the employer, so in both cases the competitive assignment of residual claimancy and control rights would appear to implement an efficient solution.

We now consider whether the analysis would be altered by an outright transfer of $\mathbf{k}$ to the employee, thus obviating the need to rent these assets. It might well be thought that the result would not change, as the producer's per period return from selling the asset $\rho\mathbf{k}$ is exactly the rental cost, so the asset transfer simply converts a direct cost (the cost of renting the capital) into an opportunity cost (the forgone cost of renting the capital to another agent), seemingly leaving the analysis unaffected. But this inference is unwarranted. Suppose the producer has wealth $\mathbf{w}$ independent from participation in production, and earns a secure income $\rho\mathbf{w}$ on this wealth. Then we find that

THEOREM 11. *If the producer preferences satisfies decreasing absolute risk aversion, the level of risk the producer assumes is an increasing function of wealth* $\mathbf{w}$.

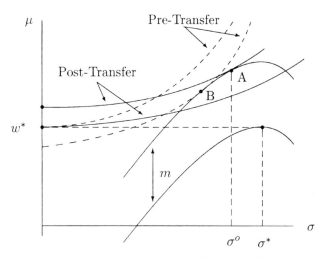

Fig. 10. Comparing wage earning and independent production. Note that in (a) the producer is better off as residual claimant, and in (b) the reverse is true.

This occurs because increasing the producer's wealth flattens the indifference curves in σ-μ space, so the optimal production point moves closer to the maximum on the risk-return schedule. To prove this formally, note that with wealth $\mathbf{w}$, Eq. (25) now becomes

$$\mu(\sigma) = \rho(\mathbf{w} - \mathbf{k}) + g(\sigma),$$

and the producer as before chooses σ to maximize $\pi(\sigma) \equiv v(\sigma, \mu(\sigma))$, giving the first order condition Eq. (26), which we totally differentiate with respect to $\mathbf{w}$ to obtain

$$\pi_{\sigma\sigma} \frac{d\sigma}{d\mathbf{w}} + \pi_{\sigma\mathbf{w}} = 0.$$

Now $\pi_{\sigma\sigma} < 0$ by the second order condition, and

$$\pi_{\sigma\mathbf{w}} = -\rho v_\mu s_\mu > 0,$$

since $s_\mu(\sigma_\mathbf{w}, \mu_\mathbf{w}) < 0$. Thus $d\sigma/d\mathbf{w} > 0$.

It follows that there exist wealth transfers of the following form: before the transfer, the producer prefers to work for an owner whose capital stock is $\mathbf{k}$. When an amount $\mathbf{k}$ of wealth is transferred to the producer, indifference curves become flatter, and in the new situation holding the productive asset and becoming an independent producer is the preferred alternative. The transfer is productivity enhancing because the increase in technical efficiency (elimination of m) is not offset by the output losses occasioned by the suboptimal risk level.

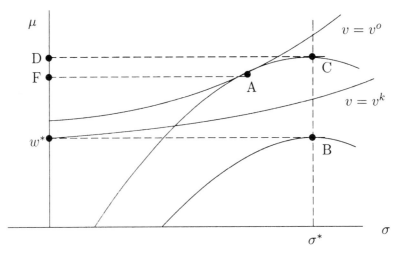

Fig. 11. Example of a productivity enhancing asset redistribution.

This is illustrated in Fig. 11. In this figure, the before-transfer indifference curves for the agent are the dashed curves. Clearly wage labor dominates independent production. After the transfer, indicated by the solid curves, the decrease in risk aversion of the agent renders independent production superior to wage labor.[27] Thus the transfer is sustainable. This result also demonstrates that the gains to the producer are sufficient to compensate the previous owner of the asset as the producer's returns to holding the asset exceed the opportunity cost $\rho \mathbf{k}$, which is identical to the required compensation.

An egalitarian wealth transfer may thus be productivity enhancing, although the compensation that rendered the transaction a Pareto improvement is not generally implementable, since a lump sum wealth transfer $\mathbf{k}$ to the former owner (or equivalently, an enforceable commitment of the producer to pay $\rho \mathbf{k}$ per period) would simply induce the producer to sell rather than operate the asset.

Credit market constraints played no part in this demonstration, as the producer was assumed to be able to borrow at the competitive risk-free interest rate ρ. However, if the asset poor do face credit constraints insofar as a transfer of wealth may alleviate these constraints a second class of productivity enhancing asset transfers may exist. To see this assume that the cost of borrowing to the producer is $r(\mathbf{w})$ where $\mathbf{w} \geq 0$ is the total collateralizable wealth of the producer, where

$$r'(\mathbf{w}) < 0 \quad \text{and} \quad \lim_{\mathbf{w} \to \infty} r(\mathbf{w}) = \rho. \tag{27}$$

---

[27] The utility levels corresponding to the dashed and the solid indifference curves are of course not the same. In particular, the dashed indifference curve through point $(0, w^*)$ corresponds to a lower utility level than the solid indifference curve through $(0, w^*)$, since in the latter case the agent has higher wealth.

It is simple to show (as in Bowles and Gintis, 1998c) that if a credit constrained worker with wealth $\mathbf{w}$ faces an interest rate $r(\mathbf{w})$ satisfying Eq. (27), and a fraction κ of the value $\mathbf{k}$ of the capital requirements of the project can serve as collateral on a loan, then for sufficiently large $\mathbf{k}$ the transfer of the capital good to the agent is productivity enhancing.

To see this why this is so, note that a producer with wealth $\mathbf{w}$ can acquire the capital good at per period cost of $r(\mathbf{w} - (1 - \kappa)\mathbf{k})\mathbf{k}$. The expected income μ_p for the work who purchases the asset is

$$\mu_p(\sigma) = g(\sigma) - r(\mathbf{w} - (1 - \kappa)\mathbf{k})\mathbf{k},$$

while the expected income μ_t for the producer who has acquired the asset by transfer is

$$\mu_t(\sigma) = g(\sigma) - r(\mathbf{w} + \kappa \mathbf{k})\mathbf{k}.$$

Choose σ_p^* and σ_t^* to maximize $v(\sigma, \mu_p(\sigma))$, and $v(\sigma, \mu_t(\sigma))$, respectively. The producer who is employed and receiving the wage w^* would not benefit from purchasing the asset if $v(\sigma_p^*, \mu_p(\sigma_p^*)) < v^*(0, w^*)$, which is clearly true for sufficiently large $\mathbf{k}$. The same producer having received the asset $\mathbf{k}$ by transfer would prefer to hold the asset if $v(\mu_t(\sigma_t^*), \sigma_t^*) > v^*(0, w^*)$. A productivity enhancing asset transfer thus requires that:

$$v(\sigma_p^*, \mu_p(\sigma_p^*)) < v^*(0, w^*) < v(\mu_t(\sigma_t^*), \sigma_t^*).$$

Suppose the first inequality is satisfied. Since

$$\mu_t(\sigma) - \mu_p(\sigma) = [r(\mathbf{w} - (1 - \kappa)\mathbf{k}) - r(\mathbf{w} + \kappa \mathbf{k})]\mathbf{k} > 0,$$

it is clear that, for sufficiently large $\mathbf{k}$, the second inequality will be satisfied as well at $\sigma = \sigma_p^*$, and hence a fortiori at $\sigma = \sigma_t^*$.

Thus where a wealth transfer will alleviate the credit market constraints faced by the wealth poor, productivity enhancing redistributions may exist even where the producers' risk aversion unaffected by the transfer. Hence wealth-related credit constraints and wealth-related risk aversion provide the basis for productivity enhancing asset redistributions. The two mechanisms are analogous in that in both cases the transfer of the asset reduces the costs associated with the assignment of residual claimancy and control rights to the wealth-poor, attenuating suboptimal risk taking and the costs of risk exposure in the first, and reducing the opportunity cost of ownership in the second.

Figure 12 illustrates a productivity enhancing redistribution to the credit constrained wealth-poor producer.

It follows that measures that render the producer less risk averse, or lessen the risk involved in production, lessen the risk allocation losses associated with the reassignment of residual claimancy and control rights to low-wealth producers. A producer who acquires the productive asset through an egalitarian redistribution policy, but who would

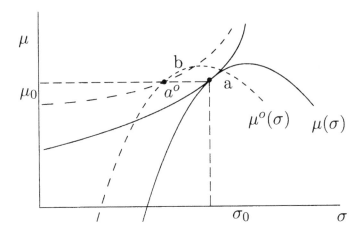

Fig. 12. A productivity enhancing redistribution where the producer faces a credit constraint.

otherwise prefer to sell this asset, could be induced by such measures to remain residual claimant on the use of the asset. In addition, such measures would reduce the losses from risk avoidance by producers willingly engaged in independent production. We shall suggest two plausible measures of this type. The first involves insuring producers against forms of risk exogenous to the production process, and the second involves insuring producers against public risk—risk correlated with the risk of independent production, but which is publicly observable.

Suppose the producer's wealth independent from participating in production, $\mathbf{w}$, has a stochastic element $\gamma \zeta$ of mean zero distributed independently from z, where $\gamma > 0$ is a constant. We call such a stochastic element *exogenous risk*, and we term a reduction in γ a *reduction in exogenous risk* (as opposed to the endogenous risk σz that chosen by the producer). Note that the total risk now facing the producer is $\sigma z + \gamma \zeta$ rather than simply σz in Eq. (23). Bowles and Gintis (1998c) show that under these conditions an economic policy measure that reduces the degree of uncertainty facing producers unrelated to the productive asset itself, for instance health insurance, consumer goods price stabilization, or business cycle stabilization, may induce nonwealthy producers to assume a higher level of risk exposure in production and thus increase the scope of application of productivity enhancing egalitarian redistributions.

A second measure with similar effects is insurance against public risk. Suppose the random variable η is positively correlated with the stochastic element z in production, and is publicly observable at the end of the production period, hence is contractible. We call η a *production-related public risk*. Average rainfall in the region over the growing season, for instance, is a form of production-related public risk. Consider a market for a fair insurance policy on production-related public risk that pays producers a premium l and obliges the producer to pay back an amount $b\eta$ at the end of the production period.

We call this a *public risk insurance policy*, and we call *b* the *payback rate*. Bowles and Gintis (1998c) show that

THEOREM 12. *There is a fair public insurance policy that induces the socially optimal level of risk-taking. Such a policy will not be purchased on a competitive insurance market, in which the producer can choose the payback rate to maximize expected payoff.*

The intuition underlying this result is that the socially optimal insurance policy induces risk neutral behavior by restricting the producer's choice to no insurance at all or more insurance than the producer would choose in a competitive environment. Profit maximizing producers would demand a lower level of insurance. The reason for the difference is that only when the degree of risk and the public signal are perfectly correlated does the insurance policy that renders the standard deviation of income invariant to the choice of risk level by the producer (inducing risk neutral behavior by the producer) also minimize the standard deviation of income (corresponding to the producer's desired fair insurance policy).

There are three reasons why the market in public risk insurance may fail. First the competitively determined insurance rate does not achieve the socially optimal outcome. Second, the market in public risk insurance is subject to adverse selection if $r_{z\eta}$ differs among producers and is not public knowledge. Third, a private industry selling public risk insurance may not be able to operate as approximately risk neutral, since the signal η is a macroeconomic variable that is perfectly correlated for all insurance purchasers, so insurance companies cannot use the law of large numbers to handle the volatility of their payouts. Moreover, if there is uncertainty concerning μ_η, or if μ_η shifts over time, the insurance companies' risk position becomes even more precarious. Thus government policy might be needed to implement this outcome.

Of course an analysis of the defects of the market solution to the independent producer's risk problem must be complemented by an analysis of the defects of the public sector as an insurance provider. In particular, in the absence of a mechanism guaranteeing their accountability, public decision-makers will choose the level and type of independent producer insurance to meet multiple objectives, of which fostering socially efficient production is only one.

5. Wealth constraints and residual claimancy in team production

Monitoring by peers in work teams, credit associations, partnerships, local commons situations, and residential neighborhoods is often an effective means of attenuating incentive problems that arise where individual actions affecting the well being of others are not subject to enforceable contracts (Whyte, 1955; Homans, 1961; Ostrom, 1990; Tilly, 1981; Hossain, 1988; Dong and Dow, 1993b; Sampson et al., 1997). Most explanations of the incentives to engage in mutual monitoring (Varian, 1990; Stiglitz,

1993) rely either on the small size of the interacting group, or on repeated interactions and low discount rates, allowing the Folk theorem to be invoked. Neither of these is completely satisfactory, since work teams are often large and the Folk theorem has little explanatory power.[28] Other treatments leave the incentive to engage in mutual monitoring unexplained (Arnott, 1991; Weissing and Ostrom, 1991).[29]

We provide an explanation of mutual monitoring in single shot interactions among members of large teams. The key conditions supporting mutual monitoring are (a) the fact that when members are residual claimants, shirking imposes costs on other team members, and contributing to production becomes a team norm, and (b) a fraction of team members are "reciprocators" who punish violators of team norms. We will provide evidence that under appropriate conditions reciprocators occur with sufficient frequency to sustain cooperative outcomes.

The problem of free riding in teams has been addressed by two standard models. The first, due to Alchian and Demsetz (1972), holds that residual claimancy should be assigned to an individual designated to monitor team members' inputs, thus ensuring the incentive compatibility for the (noncontractible) activity of monitoring itself, while addressing the members' incentive to free ride by the threat of dismissal by the monitor. They contrast this view of the "classical firm", as they call it, with an alternative in which team members are residual claimants and monitoring is performed, if at all, by salaried personnel. Alchian and Demsetz (1972: p. 796) correctly observe that group residual claimancy would dilute incentives, but simply posit the allocational superiority of the classical firm: "we assume that if profit sharing had to be relied on for all team members, losses from the resulting increase in central monitor shirking would exceed the output gains from the increased incentives of other team members not to shirk". As we will see, their invocation of the so-called "$1/n$ problem" to justify this assumption is not entirely adequate. Moreover, the classical firm they describe is not an accurate description of the way that conventional firms—except for the very smallest—handle the problem of monitoring, for monitoring is commonly done by salaried supervisors rather than residual claimants.

The second approach, pioneered by Hölmstrom (1982), demonstrates that in principal multiagent models one can achieve efficiency or near-efficiency through contracts that make individual team members residual claimants on the effects of their actions without conferring ownership rights on them. Contracts of this type typically impose

---

[28] The repeated game solution to the problem of sustaining cooperative behavior in teams has several weaknesses, including: (a) there are a multiplicity of equilibria, most of which do not exhibit high levels of cooperation; (b) subgame perfection (i.e., the credibility of threats to punish noncooperators) requires an implausible degree of coordination among team members.

[29] Dong and Dow (1993b) assume the team can impose collective sanctions on shirkers. This assumption is reasonable if shirking is easily detected and team members have more effective or lower cost forms of punishment than are available to a traditional firm. We do not make this assumption. Dong and Dow (1993a) assume shirking can be controlled by the threat of nonshirkers to exit the team. However the threat of exiting is credible only if team members have very high fallback positions—in Dong and Dow's model, this takes the form of independent production—which generally is not the case.

large penalties for shirking and require large lump-sum up-front payments on the part of agents, or they pay each team member the entire team output minus a large constant that, in the presence of stochastic influences on output, entail negative payments in some periods, or at best a substantial variance of income to team members. These arrangments are infeasible if team members have insufficient wealth. Moreover, where contributions (e.g., work effort) are continuously variable these incentive mechanisms support large numbers of Nash equilibria, thus rendering breakdown of cooperation likely.

These approaches do not explain how mutual monitoring works, but rather why it may be unnecessary. The limited applicability of the owner-monitor and optimal contracting approaches provides one motivation for exploring the relationship between residual claimancy and mutual monitoring in teams. Another motivation is empirical. There is some evidence that group residual claimancy is effective, by comparison with payments unrelated to group output, even in quite large teams (Hansen, 1997). Mutual monitoring based on residual claimancy appears to be effective in the regulation of common pool resources such as fisheries, irrigation, and grazing lands (Ostrom, 1990), in the regulation of work effort in producer cooperatives (Greenberg, 1986; Craig and Pencavel, 1995) and in the enforcement of noncollateralized credit contracts (Hossain, 1988). Experimental studies (Frohlich et al., 1998) provide additional support for the effects of residual claimancy in inducing lower supervision costs and higher productivity in (small) work teams. Furthermore, the fact that residual claimancy may provide incentives for monitoring even in quite complex settings and large groups is suggested by evidence that in the US home ownership is a significant predictor of participation in community organizations (Glaeser and DiPasquale, 1999) and local politics but, significantly, not national politics (Verba et al., 1995), as well as willingness to monitor and sanction coresidents who transgress social norms (Sampson et al., 1997).

Locating residual claimancy in teams can have positive incentive effects, since team members may have privileged access to information concerning the activities of other team members, and may have means of disciplining shirkers and rewarding hard work that are not available to third parties. As residual claimants, moreover, team members may have the incentive to use this information and exercise their sanctioning power, even if the team is large. Thus, while Alchian and Demsetz are surely correct in saying that residual claimancy in large teams does not substantially reduce the direct incentive to free ride, it may support superior means of sanctioning and hence discouraging free riding through mutual monitoring.[30] Monitoring is costly, however, and if the desire to monitor is not sufficiently widespread, we shall see, mutual monitoring will fail.

We will show that under certain conditions, residual claimancy by team members can provide sufficient incentives for mutual monitoring, and thus support high levels of team performance. A key element in our approach, one shared by recent contributions of Kan-

---

[30] Some models of mutual monitoring are presented in Varian (1990), Kandel and Lazear (1992), Weissing and Ostrom (1991), Dong and Dow (1993a, b), and Banerjee et al. (1994). Other models of incentives in teams include Hölmstrom (1982), McAfee and McMillan (1991), Legros and Matthews (1993), Rotemburg (1994) and Besley and Coate (1995).

del and Lazear (1992), Rotemburg (1994), Banerjee et al. (1994), and Besley and Coate (1995) is that our model is based on "social preferences" which, while unconventional, are well supported by recent experimental and other research.

We assume that though team members observe one another in their productive activity, they cannot design enforceable contracts on actions because this information is not verifiable (cannot be used in courts). In this situation we show that under appropriate conditions the assignment of residual claimancy to team members will attenuate incentive problems even when team size is large.

Two common characteristics of successful mutual monitoring are uncontroversial: the superior information concerning nonverifiable actions of team members available to other team members and the role of residual claimancy in motivating members to acquire and use this information in ways that enhance productivity. Less clear is whether, or not, residual claimancy motivates costly monitoring in large groups.[31]

A parsimonious explanation of mutual monitoring is provided, however, by the notion of *strong reciprocity*: the well-documented human propensity to cooperate with those who obey, and to punish those who violate social norms, even when this behavior cannot be justified in terms of self-regarding, outcome-oriented preferences (Campbell, 1983; Bowles and Gintis, 1998a). We distinguish this from *weak reciprocity*, namely reciprocal altruism, tit-for-tat, exchange under complete contracting, and other forms of mutually beneficial cooperation that can be accounted for in terms of self-regarding outcome-oriented preferences. The commonly observed rejection of substantial positive offers in experimental ultimatum games is consistent with this interpretation.[32] Moreover the fact that offers generated by a computer rather than another person are significantly less likely to be rejected suggests that those rejected offers at to cost to themselves are reacting to violations of norms rather than simply rejecting disadvantageous offers (Blount, 1995). More directly analogous to the team production case, however, are findings in n-player public goods experiments. These provide a motivational foundation for mutual monitoring in teams whose members are residual claimants, since these experiments show that agents are willing to incur a cost to punish those whom they perceive to have treated them or a group to which they belong badly.[33] In these

---

[31] The problem of motivating the peer-monitors would not arise, of course, if team members were sufficiently altruistic towards teammates. In this case members would simply internalize the benefits conferred on others by their monitoring. Rotemburg (1994) develops a model of this type. More generally, Robert Frank (1991: p. 168) writes: "Under [profit sharing] plans, the injury caused by an act of shirking affects not only the shareholders of the firm but also the shirker's co-workers. Individual workers who care about their co-workers will be reluctant to impose these costs . . . even when it is impossible for co-workers to observe the act of shirking". However were team members sufficiently altruistic in this sense to motivate mutual monitoring, there would be no initial free rider problem either.

[32] See Güth et al. (1982), Ostrom et al. (1992), Güth and Ockenfels (1993), Forsythe et al. (1994), Cameron (1995), Hoffman et al. (1998) and Falk and Fischbacher (1998). For an overview of the studies in this area, see Davis and Holt (1993) and Fehr et al. (1997).

[33] See Ostrom et al. (1992) on common pool resources, Fehr et al. (1997) on efficiency wages, and Fehr and Gächter (1998) on public goods. Coleman (1988) develops the parallel point that free riding in social networks can be avoided if network members provide positive rewards for cooperating.

experiments, which allow subjects to punish noncooperators at a cost to themselves, the moderate levels of contribution typically observed in early play tend to rise in subsequent rounds to near the maximal level, rather than declining to insubstantial levels as in the case where no punishment is permitted. It is also significant that in the experiments of Fehr and Gächter, punishment levels are undiminished in the final rounds, suggesting that disciplining norm violators is an end in itself and hence will be exhibited even when there is no prospect of modifying the subsequent behavior of the shirker or potential future shirkers.

The willingness to engage in costly punishment provides a basis for linking residual claimancy with mutual monitoring, even in large teams. An individual who shirks inflicts harm on the other members of the team if (and only if) they are residual claimants. Members may then see this violation of reciprocity as reason to punish the shirker. We should note that our model requires only that a certain fraction of team members be reciprocators. This is in line with the evidence from experimental economics, which indicates that in virtually every experimental setting a certain fraction of the subjects do not retaliate, either because they are self-interested, or they are purely altruistic.[34]

To see how mutual monitoring works, consider a team with n members ($n > 3$), each of whom can either Work, supplying one unit of effort, or Shirk, supplying zero units of effort. We assume the members of the team are equal residual claimants on team output, but there may be other residual claimants outside the team (e.g., equity-holders who do not engage in production, or a government that taxes output). For convenience, if we refer to i or j, we assume they are team members in $\{1, \ldots, n\}$ unless otherwise stated, and if we refer to both i and j, we assume $i \neq j$. Also we write $n_{-i} = \{k = 1, \ldots, n | k \neq i\}$. We assume agents have linear utility functions that are additive in costs and benefits.

Let σ_j be the probability that member j shirks, so $\sigma = \sum_{j=1}^{n} \sigma_j / n$ is the average rate of shirking. The value of team output net of nonlabor costs is the number of workers working times q, the average (and marginal) net product of effort, which we can write as $n(1 - \sigma)q$. Each member's payoff is then given by $(1 - \sigma)\alpha q$, where $\alpha \in [0, 1]$ is defined as the team's residual share. The loss to the team from one member shirking is αq. The gain to an individual from shirking is the disutility of effort, $b > 0$, which we assume is identical for all team members. We also assume $\alpha q > b$, otherwise universal shirking would be optimal.[35]

Consider a single team member j. Another member $i \in n_{-j}$ can either Monitor j at cost $c_i > 0$, or Trust j at zero cost. Member i imposes a cost $s_i > 0$ on j if i detects j shirking. This cost may involve public criticism, shunning, threats of physical harm and the like. We assume that acts of punishment, like work effort, are nonverifiable and hence not subject to contract. If j shirks and i monitors j, we assume the shirking will be

---

[34] For an especially clear example, see Blount (1995). Fehr and Schmidt (1997) provides a survey of rejection rates in ultimatum games.

[35] Most of the homogeneity assumptions we make can be dropped, at the expense of complicating the notation and the descriptions of the model.

detected with probability $p_{ij} \in (0, 1]$, where this *probability of detection* may vary with the spatial proximity of team members and the transparency of the production process, and other factors that we do not model here.

We model the incentive to monitor by supposing that i experiences a subjective gain $\rho_i(\alpha) \geq 0$ from disciplining a shirking member j, which occurs if j shirks, i monitors j, and j is detected.[36] The harm done by a shirker to team members is proportional to the degree of residual claimancy so it is reasonable to assume that the strength of the norm of cooperation increases with the degree of residual claimancy of the team. Thus $\rho_i(0) = 0$ and $\rho_i'(\alpha) \geq 0$ for all $i = 1, \ldots, n$. We call $\rho_i(\alpha)$ i's *propensity to punish shirkers*.[37] Note that some members may exhibit no propensity to punish; i.e., $\rho_i(\alpha) = 0, \alpha \in [0, 1]$.

If i monitors, the likelihood of detecting j shirking is $\sigma_j p_{ij}$, so the net cost of monitoring j over trusting j is $c_i - \sigma_j p_{ij} \rho_i(\alpha)$. Then if $\mu_{ij}, i \in n_{-j}$, the probability that i monitors j, is chosen to be a best response, we have

$$
\mu_{ij} \begin{cases} = 0, & c_i > \sigma_j p_{ij} \rho_i(\alpha) \\ \in (0, 1), & c_i = \sigma_j p_{ij} \rho_i(\alpha) \\ = 1, & c_i < \sigma_j p_{ij} \rho_i(\alpha). \end{cases} \tag{28}
$$

Let s_j^* be the expected punishment inflicted by all $i \in n_{-j}$ on j if j shirks. We have

$$
s_j^* = \sum_{i \in n_{-j}} p_{ij} \mu_{ij} s_i. \tag{29}
$$

Writing the direct gain to an individual from shirking as

$$
g = b - \frac{\alpha q}{n}, \tag{30}
$$

the expected gain to j from shirking, including the expected cost of punishment, is $g - s_j^*$. Therefore if σ_j is chosen as a best response, we have

$$
\sigma_j \begin{cases} = 0, & g < s_j^* \\ \in [0, 1], & g = s_j^* \\ = 1, & g > s_j^*. \end{cases} \tag{31}
$$

---

[36] In fact, we expect ρ_i to depend on αq, but since we do not vary q in our analysis, we suppress q in the argument. Note that, unlike a member's share of the firm's net revenue, the subjective gain from punishing does not decline with the size of the team. We motivate this assumption and discuss the effects of team size below. We assume $\rho_i(\alpha) < s_j$ for all $\alpha \in [0, 1]$, to avoid bizarre "*sado-masochistic*" optima in which team members cooperate by shirking, punishing, and being punished, the net psychic return to which is greater than the return to working.

[37] For simplicity we have assumed that a monitor's propensity to punish, ρ_i, is not affected by the propensities to punish or the observed rates of punishing of other members of the team. Replacing this with the assumption that punishing propensities are positively related opens the possibility of multiple equilibria, some involving high levels of punishing and some low. We explore this alternative below.

If $g < 0$ there is a unique, Pareto efficient, Nash equilibrium in which no members shirk and no member monitors.[38] In this case residual claimancy alone is sufficient to ensure efficiency. The more interesting case, however, is where group size is sufficiently large that residual claimancy alone does not entail incentive compatibility. We thus suppose in the rest of the paper that $b > q/n$, so that even with full residual claimancy assigned to the team as a whole, shirking is an individual best response in the absence of monitoring. In this case any Nash equilibrium involves positive shirking, since if $\sigma_j = 0$ for some j then by Eq. (28) $\mu_{ij} = 0$ for $i \in n_{-j}$. But then by Eq. (31), $\sigma_j = 1$, a contradiction. Thus we must investigate conditions under which $0 < \sigma_j < 1$ for some j in equilibrium, requiring

$$g = s_j^*.$$ (32)

We call such a situation a *working equilibrium*.

We say i is a *reciprocator* if $\rho_i(\alpha) > 0$. Suppose the fraction of reciprocators is f, so the remaining fraction $1 - f$ of team members are self-regarding—for these agents $\rho_i(\alpha) = 0$, and they never monitor or punish. Notice that if j is not a reciprocator, j has fn potential monitors, whereas if j is a reciprocator, j has $fn - 1$ potential monitors. In the a interest of simplicity of exposition, we will ignore this difference, assuming all agents face fn potential monitors.[39]

We say reciprocators are *homogeneous* if there are *parameters* p, c, s and $\rho(\alpha)$ such that if i is a reciprocator, then $c_i = c$, $p_{ij} = p$, $s_i = s$, and $\rho_i(\alpha) = \rho(\alpha)$. We have

THEOREM 13. *Suppose reciprocators are homogeneous, with parameters p, c, s and $\rho(\alpha)$. If $c > p\rho(\alpha)$, then the unique Nash equilibrium satisfies $\sigma_j = \sigma^* = 1$ and $\mu_{ij} = \mu^* = 0$ for all i, $j = 1, \ldots, n$; i.e., all members shirk and no member monitors. If $c < p\rho(\alpha)$ and $g > fnps$ the unique Nash equilibrium satisfies $\sigma_j = \sigma^* = \mu^* = 1$ for all i, $j = 1, \ldots, n$; i.e., all workers shirk and all members monitor. If $c < p\rho(\alpha)$ and $g < fnps$, then*

(a) there is a mixed strategy Nash equilibrium in which all members shirk with probability

$$\sigma^* = \frac{c}{p\rho(\alpha)}$$ (33)

and reciprocators monitor with probability

$$\mu^* = \frac{g}{fnps};$$ (34)

---

[38] This equilibrium is efficient because we have ruled out "sado-masochistic" optima.

[39] The effect of dropping this assumption is in all cases quite transparent, since in effect, the model is the union of n independent games, in each of which one agent is the worker and the other $n - 1$ agents are the monitors.

(b) the effect of residual claimancy on the incidence of shirking, $\partial \sigma^*/\partial \alpha$, is independent of team size and the fraction of reciprocators.

(c) the social welfare difference per team member between a first best world with no shirking and the equilibrium of this game is σq. This is declining in the degree of residual claimancy and is independent of team size and the fraction of reciprocators.

We note that while the fraction of reciprocators and the level of punishment they may inflict do not appear in Eq. (33), they are not unimportant in the determination of the level of shirking, for if f and s are sufficiently small, the condition $g < fnps$ is violated, and universal shirking occurs.[40] Notice also that, as one would expect, shirking declines with an increase in the propensity to punish shirkers, an increase in the probability of detecting shirking, or a decrease in the cost of monitoring.

The intuition behind part (a) of Theorem 13 is as follows. The equilibrium level of shirking, σ^*, equates the net benefits of monitoring and trusting, while the equilibrium level of monitoring equates the net benefits of working and shirking. Thus, when σ is greater than its equilibrium value Eq. (33), the expected benefits of monitoring, $\sigma p\rho$, exceed the costs c. Members who monitor with high probability will then receive higher payoffs than members who monitor with low probability, inducing some to increase their monitoring probability. As the monitoring probability increases, the gains to shirking decline, leading suppliers to reduce σ. This dynamic continues until Eq. (33) is satisfied. A similar dynamic occurs when σ is less than its equilibrium value. When μ is greater than its equilibrium value Eq. (33), the expected costs of shirking $f \mu nps$ exceed the benefits g. Suppliers who work with high probability will then be receiving higher payoffs than suppliers who shirk with high probability, inducing some to decrease their rate of shirking. As the shirking rate declines, the gains to monitoring decline, leading to a reduction in μ. This dynamic will continue until Eq. (34) is satisfied. A similar dynamic occurs when μ is less than the equilibrium value given by Eq. (34).

Behavioral traits such as a work ethic or a willingness to punish co-members for inflicting harm on the team are, of course, strongly norm governed and as such need not be proximately determined by the explicit optimization of any agent but rather may be the expression of behavioral rules. Thus the model underlying Theorem 13 may be interpreted as the basis of a dynamic treatment of work and punishment norms, with the updating of norms responding to the observed payoffs of others. For example, as our description of the intuition behind part (a) of Theorem 13 suggests, the determination of σ and μ may be represented as dynamic processes based on the differential replication of norms governing the working, shirking, monitoring and punishing behaviors we have modeled, the equilibrium values σ^* and μ^* simply representing outcomes that are stationary in the underlying dynamic. We do not develop this extension here.

---

[40] We have not investigated equilibria when $c = p\rho(\alpha)$ or $g = fnps$. This is because these cases are neither generic nor interesting.

It may be objected that it is plausible to treat $\rho(\alpha)$ as a decreasing function of team size, on the grounds that strong reciprocity may weaken when the team becomes larger, and thus the propensity to punish any given act of shirking would fall. Though this is possible, there is to our knowledge no clear evidence in support of this notion, and there are many "stylized facts" contradicting it. For instance, people are often observed to support their local sports team, their regional sports team, and their national sports team with equal commitment.

There are of course additional paths through which increasing team size might weaken the mutual monitoring mechanism. Increased n might lower the cost s a monitor can impose on a shirker, since the "average social distance" between a pair of workers can be expected to increase as the team becomes more numerous. The ability to detect shirking may also decline. It is clear from Eq. (33) that lowering p will indeed reduce the efficiency of the team, while Eq. (34) shows both mechanisms lead to an increase in the monitoring level required to prevent shirking. Since a change in μ does not affect the efficiency of the system, we will investigate only the former effect.

To model the relationship between team size and detection probability in a plausible manner, we will drop our homogeneity assumption. In its place we will assume that for any two team members i and j, either i can or cannot see j. Suppose that if j shirks and i inspects j, the probability of i detecting j shirking is p if i sees j, and is zero otherwise. Suppose in all other respects, the model is as described above. Then if there is an integer $k \geq 1$ such that as team size $n \geq k$ increases, each member sees exactly k other team members, then if $fkps > g$, our previous assertions hold with k substituted for n in the denominator of Eq. (34). The intuition behind this result is that as long as increasing team size does not reduce the number of team members that one may "see" the effectiveness of mutual monitoring does not decline as team size increases.

However large teams often do not have the informational homogeneity assumed above, since with increased size often comes a more refined division of labor in which there are specialized "work groups" whose members all see one another, and who are not seen by other team members. Members of such groups have an incentive to collude by agreeing that the reciprocators in the group will not monitor, and hence all are free to shirk without penalty. We call this a "shirking clique". Of course in a one-shot situation the promise not to monitor and punish is not credible, but it can be supported in a repeated game framework as a form of "tacit collusion". Teams can reduce the frequency of such behavior by rotating members among work groups, rendering the effective discount rate for the repeated game too high to support collusion, but such rotation may entail prohibitive organizational costs.

We conclude that under appropriate conditions, strong reciprocity can operate even in large teams, so that the allocative efficiency case for residual claimancy, and hence asset holdings by team members, is not necessarily weakened, unless the frequency of reciprocators is too low or the division of labor favors the widespread formation of shirking cliques.

If residual claimancy provides motives for mutual monitoring, the distribution of wealth may have allocational effects as in the more commonly treated cases of concerning human investment, agrarian tenancy, and entrepreneurship (Loury, 1981; Galor and Zeira, 1993; Laffont and Matoussi, 1995; Bowles and Gintis, 1998b). The reason is that some distributions (those in which team members are without wealth, for example) effectively preclude the assignment of residual claimancy to team members, because transferring residual claimancy over the income streams of an asset but not ownership itself to team members creates incentives for the team to depreciate the assets, the costs of which may more than offset any gains from mutual monitoring. Thus prohibitive costs may arise if residual claimancy is separated from ownership, and outright ownership may be precluded by borrowing limitations faced by zero wealth team members.

Thus a redistribution of wealth to team members may improve the allocational efficiency of the team. If, as in the case modelled, team members are risk neutral, such a redistribution must be potentially Pareto-improving, in the sense that the gains of beneficiaries of the redistribution exceed the amount necessary to fully compensate the losses of those whose wealth was redistributed. Such potentially Pareto improving asset redistributions to team members are necessarily egalitarian, assets being provided to the wealth-poor. The reason is that in the absence of borrowing limitations imposed by low wealth, the allocational gains associated with residual claimancy *via* mutual monitoring would be fully exploited by voluntary transactions among agents. Thus wealthy team members would not be precluded from becoming residual claimants and mutual monitors were this to improve allocational efficiency.

Where team members are not only poor but risk averse as well (the more probable case) this felicitous efficiency equity complementarity (rather than trade off) is still possible, but less likely.[41] The reason is that control rights over the use of the assets must accompany residual claimancy and ownership and, as we have seen in the previous section, risk averse team members would likely implement a socially suboptimal level of risk taking in decisions concerning investment and technical choice.

In Section 2 we surveyed the advantages of locating residual claimancy and hence asset ownership with agents making noncontractible production-related decisions with the resulting allocative efficiency prescription that where all agents are risk neutral those who control noncontractible actions should also own the results of those actions, thus requiring producers to hold the relevant assets. In this section we have asked under what conditions the logic of this prescription might be extended from the case of individual producers to team producers. We found that the mechanism of reciprocal fairness can operate even in large teams, so that even in large teams the allocative efficiency case for residual claimancy, and hence asset holdings by team members, is not necessarily weakened.

We saw in Section 2 that nonwealthy producers may be precluded from acquiring ownership of productive assets, and this obviously precludes nonwealthy members of

---

[41] We explore this case in Bowles and Gintis (1998c).

productive teams from acquiring the ownership needed to render mutual monitoring effective. One may then ask if the competitively determined assignment of residual claimancy and control are inefficient in the sense that a productivity enhancing re-distribution of assets of the type defined in the introduction might be possible. This question cannot be adequately addressed without dropping the assumption of general risk neutrality. Fortunately the results of Section 4 may be readily extended to the case of team production, suggesting that a reallocation of ownership to team members may be productivity enhancing even when the members are risk averse.

6. Initial asset inequality and cooperation on the local commons

One of the important, though somewhat neglected, ways in which asset inequality can affect economic efficiency is through influencing the likelihood of cooperation in the management of local public goods, varying from personal security and neighborhood amenities in urban residential settings to local commons situations. In particular, the daily livelihood of vast masses of the rural poor in many countries depends on the success with which common-pool resources (CPRs)—such as forests, grazing lands, in-shore fisheries, and irrigation water—are managed, and the environmental consequences of their management. A CPR is defined by Ostrom (1990: p. 30), as "a natural or man-made resource system that is sufficiently large as to make it costly (but not impossible) to exclude potential beneficiaries from obtaining benefits from its use". There are several documented examples of successful local-level cooperation on CPRs in different parts of the world—see Ostrom (1990) for many such examples—but there are also numerous cases of failure of cooperation. Understanding the factors that lead to success or failure of community management of these resources is critical.

CPR management is a collective action dilemma: a situation in which mutual coop-eration is collectively rational for a group as a whole, but individual cooperation may not be rational for each member. One factor that has not always been recognized as critical to the outcome of collective action dilemmas is heterogeneity among the players. Here our attention will, of course, be largely restricted to a single but potent kind of heterogeneity: asset inequality.

Olson (1965) hypothesized that inequality may be beneficial to the provision of a public good:

In smaller groups marked by considerable degrees of inequality—that is, in groups of members of unequal "size" or extent of interest in the collective good—there is the greatest likelihood that a collective good will be provided; for the greater the interest in the collective good of any single member, the greater the likelihood that member will get such a significant proportion of the total benefit from the collective good that he will gain from seeing that the good is provided, even if he has to pay all of the cost himself. (p. 34)

Inequality in this context can thus facilitate the provision of the collective good, with the small players free-riding on the contribution of the large player. Supporting this position, Bergstrom et al. (1986) show that, in a very general setting, wealth redistrib-utions that increase the wealth of a positive contributor to a public good will lead the latter to demand more (and therefore entail an increase the supply) of the public good.[42] These analyses of the supply of public goods are relevant to conservation among CPR users. Restraint in resource use is analytically equivalent to contributing to a public good. Following these studies, we would expect group heterogeneity to be conducive to the effective management of CPRs.

Nevertheless, field studies of CPR management have often shown that the relationship between inequality and collective action is more complex. Bardhan (1995) reviews the case study literature regarding the relationship between inequality and cooperation in locally-managed irrigation systems, primarily in Asia, and finds that while equality tends to favor successful local management in many cases, highly unequal traditional authority structures may also have served the efficient husbanding of resources. Baland and Platteau (1997) likewise summarize many relevant examples from the case-study literature; they focus more on forests, fisheries and grazing lands, and on African cases. In an econometric study of the determinants of cooperation in 104 local peasant committees in Paraguay, Molinas (1998) shows that there is a U-shaped relationship between inequality of land distribution and cooperative performance (in activities that include CPR management and provision of local public goods). With recourse to both theoretical analysis and empirical examples, Baland and Platteau show that inequality in resource-use entitlements has an ambiguous impact on the efficiency of the equilibrium outcome in the completely unregulated case. In regulated settings, inequality does not as a rule make common property regulation easier.

In the rest of this section we provide some simple and general theoretical arguments to analyze the effect of asset inequality on cooperation within a group, drawing on the model in Dayton-Johnson and Bardhan (1997). Although the model is couched in terms of a fishery, the qualitative results should be in principle transferable to the case of other CPRs. In a two-player noncooperative model we explore the necessary and sufficient conditions for resource conservation to be a Nash equilibrium, and we show that,

- contrary to the implication of the Olson hypothesis, increasing inequality does not, in general, favor full conservation. However,
- once inequality is sufficiently great, further inequality may push the players closer to efficiency.

Thus the theoretical model can generate a U-shaped relationship between inequality and economic efficiency.

In the preceding sections we have focused on a structure of incentives and constraints arising from a deliberately chosen contract. In contrast in this section the governing structure could be thought of more as a norm. The norm is viewed as self-sustaining if it is a Nash equilibrium in a simultaneous move game. The game is one of complete information. Markets are, however, incomplete because it is difficult to restrict access to

---

[42] Chan et al. (1996) report that when the Bergstrom-Blume-Varian model is tested in the laboratory, it correctly predicts the direction (though not the magnitude) of change in group contributions when income is redistributed toward positive contributors. It does not do so well in predicting individual behavior: individuals with low incomes overcontribute to the public good, and high income individuals undercontribute.

the commons (whereas market incompleteness in previous sections arises because some actions that affect the gains from exchange are private information).

Consider a lake in which fish are born in the Spring and are mature in the Fall. If two fishers have access to the lake, it is then efficient for them to cooperate in waiting until the Fall to harvest the fish. However it may pay one of the fishers to defect and harvest in the Spring, when there is no competition from the other fisher. Knowing this, it may be profitable for the second fisher to do the same. Moreover, if a nonwealthy fisher cannot compete effectively against a wealthy fisher, it may never pay the nonwealthy fisher to cooperate. Thus the efficient output may require a considerable degree of wealth equality. On the other hand with great wealth inequality, the efficient output can be approximated, simply because the poor fisher has the means to harvest only a small portion of the stock of fish in the Spring.

Suppose the fishers are $i = 1, 2$, and each fisher i is endowed with wealth $\mathbf{w}^i > 0$, representing the fishing capacity of the fisher's capital goods (boats, tackle, nets, and the like), measured in number of units of fish that can be obtained in a period. There are two periods $t = 1, 2$ (Spring and Fall), in each of which fisher i can apply some or all of his fishing capacity to farming the lake.

Let F be the stock of fish in the lake. In the first period, fisher i must choose to use some portion $\mathbf{k}^i$ of his capacity $\mathbf{w}^i$ in fishing, so $\mathbf{k}^i \leq \mathbf{w}^i$. Fishing yield is then given by

$$\phi^i = \begin{cases} \mathbf{k}^i & \text{for } \mathbf{k}^1 + \mathbf{k}^2 \leq F \\ \dfrac{\mathbf{k}^i F}{\mathbf{k}^1 + \mathbf{k}^2} & \text{otherwise.} \end{cases}$$

i.e., if the total take is less than F, fishers can fish to their capacity. Otherwise the fishers share F in proportion to the respective capacities they have applied to farming the lake.

Between Spring and Fall the stock of fish grows at rate $g > 0$, so that in period 2 the supply of fish is $(1 + g)(F - \phi^1 - \phi^2)$.[43] We assume the future is not discounted, so each fisher's utility is simply the total amount of fish he catches. Clearly then in any efficient outcome there will be no fishing in period 1.

In the second period, each fisher i again chooses to apply some portion of his capacity $\mathbf{w}^i$ to farming the lake. We make the following *commons dilemma assumption*:

$$\mathbf{w} \equiv \mathbf{w}^1 + \mathbf{w}^2 \geq (1 + g)F. \tag{35}$$

This assumption insures that the threat of resource degradation is sufficiently acute. Alternatively, Eq. (35) can be interpreted as a feasibility condition: the fishers are capable of harvesting the entire stock if they desire.

---

[43] If g were negative there would be no real dilemma. First period depletion of the resource would be an equilibrium and an optimum.

In the subgame consisting of the second period, both fishers will always fish to capacity, and will receive second period payoff

$$(1+g)(F - \phi^1 - \phi^2)\frac{\mathbf{w}^i}{\mathbf{w}},$$

where $\mathbf{w} = \mathbf{w}^1 + \mathbf{w}^2$ is the total wealth of the two fishers. However one fisher's period 1 action will enter the other fisher's period 2 payoff, and vice-versa. Thus we must concentrate on the fishers' actions in the first period. A strategy for each fisher is just a capacity choice $\mathbf{k}^i$ in the first period, so a strategy for the game is a pair $\{\mathbf{k}^1, \mathbf{k}^2\}$. We have:

THEOREM 14. *The strategy profile {0, 0} in which neither fisher harvests in the first period is a Pareto optimum.*

We call this situation a *first best*.

The goal of conservation in fisheries is to reduce fishing to some level so that the remaining stock at the end of every period is sufficient to guarantee the survival of the fish population. In our simple model, that level has been normalized to zero in the first period. The second period extends to the end of the fishers' relevant economic horizons.[44]

The following theorem notes the conditions under which the least efficient outcome is a Nash equilibrium.[45]

THEOREM 15. *If* $\mathbf{w}^i > (g)/(1+g)F$ *for* $i = 1, 2$, *then* $\{\mathbf{w}^1, \mathbf{w}^2\}$ *(i.e., complete resource depletion) is a Nash equilibrium.*

If the inequality in Theorem 15 holds, each fisher has sufficient capacity that if one fishes in the Spring, so little will remain in the Fall that the other fisher's best response is not to wait but also to fish in the Spring, sharing the undepleted catch. Note in particular that Theorem 15 holds when $\mathbf{w}^i > F$ for $i = 1, 2$, so each fisher can unilaterally harvest the whole lake. When is full conservation a Nash equilibrium?

---

[44] In this model we have abstracted from the problem of discount rates in order to focus more clearly on the incentives to conserve a resource. Formally, the discount rate would be subtracted from g, the rate of resource regeneration. If the discount rate is greater than g, first period depletion of the fishery is optimal, and conservation is not economically rational. Furthermore, as we have seen above, it is reasonable to suppose that each fisher's discount rate is a decreasing function of wealth. In this case, the more unequal the distribution of endowments, the more difficult it will be to sustain universal conservation of the resource. Taking account of a poor fisher's high rate of time preference is equivalent to the situation in which the poor fisher faces a low rate of growth of the stock and hence has little incentive to conserve.

[45] For proof of this and the subsequent theorems in this section, see Dayton-Johnson and Bardhan (1997).

THEOREM 16. *When both fishers have positive wealth, full conservation is an equilibrium of the model if and only if*

$$\mathbf{w}^i \geq \frac{\mathbf{w}}{1+g} \quad \text{for} \quad i = 1, 2.$$

To see why this is true, suppose fisher 2 conserves. Then for every unit fisher 1 harvests in the first period, he gives up $(1+g)\mathbf{w}^1/\mathbf{w}$ in the second period. Thus $(1+g)\mathbf{w}^1/\mathbf{w} \geq 1$ is the threshold above which fisher 1 will conserve, conditional on conservation on the part of fisher 2.

This theorem suggests the following corollary. Let

$$\Delta(\mathbf{w}) = \{(\mathbf{w}^{1'}, \mathbf{w}^{2'}) | \mathbf{w}^{1'}, \mathbf{w}^{2'} \geq 0 \quad \text{and} \quad \mathbf{w}^{1'} + \mathbf{w}^{2'} = \mathbf{w}\}$$

be the set of all distributions of $\mathbf{w}$. We say $(\mathbf{w}^{1'}, \mathbf{w}^{2'}) \in \Delta(\mathbf{w})$ is a *mean preserving spread* of $\{\mathbf{w}^1, \mathbf{w}^2\}$ if $|\mathbf{w}^{1'} - \mathbf{w}^{2'}| > |\mathbf{w}^1 - \mathbf{w}^2|$. We have:

COROLLARY 16.1. *If $(\mathbf{w}^{1'}, \mathbf{w}^{2'})$ is a mean preserving spread of $(\mathbf{w}^1, \mathbf{w}^2)$, then full conservation is an equilibrium with initial wealth $(\mathbf{w}^{1'}, \mathbf{w}^{2'})$ only if it is an equilibrium with initial wealth $(\mathbf{w}^1, \mathbf{w}^2)$. Also, for all $(\mathbf{w}^1, \mathbf{w}^2) \in \Delta(\mathbf{w})$ there is a mean preserving spread $(\mathbf{w}^{1'}, \mathbf{w}^{2'})$ such that full conservation is not an equilibrium with wealth $(\mathbf{w}^{1'}, \mathbf{w}^{2'})$.*

The Olson hypothesis that inequality enhances the prospects for collective action can be interpreted as a comparative static statement: increasing inequality for a given level of aggregate wealth makes full conservation more likely. The Corollary above suggests that this is not so. The second part of the Corollary states that, starting from any wealth distribution, there exists a less equal wealth distribution such that full conservation is not an equilibrium. In particular, if full conservation is an equilibrium under the initial distribution, then we know from Theorem 16 that $\mathbf{w}^i \geq \mathbf{w}/(1+g)$ for $i = 1, 2$. Then wealth can be taken from one fisher until $\mathbf{w}^i < \mathbf{w}/(1+g)$ for that fisher. Hence full conservation is no longer an equilibrium.

The Corollary to Theorem 16 shows that increased inequality does not necessarily lead to equilibrium conservation. Theorem 17, shows that under maximum inequality— that is, when one fisher holds all of the wealth—conservation is an equilibrium.

THEOREM 17. *If $g \geq 0$ then under perfect inequality ($\mathbf{w}^1 = 0$ or $\mathbf{w}^2 = 0$), full conservation is an equilibrium.*

In part, Theorem 17 reflects Olson's hypothesis that cooperation is more difficult in a group the larger the number of group members. In our fishery, conservation is an equilibrium outcome when the number of fishers with positive wealth is reduced to one. The above theorems consider only the conditions under which full conservation by both fishers is an equilibrium. The more realistic case in an unregulated fishery, and the case which may be closer to Olson's thinking, is the one in which changes in the distribution of wealth change the level of efficiency among a set of inefficient equilibria. This is considered in the following theorem. Theorem 18 says that if the distribution of wealth is sufficiently unequal already, then making it even more unequal can increase efficiency.

THEOREM 18. *Define* $F^*(\mathbf{w}^1, \mathbf{w}^2)$ *as the minimum amount of first period fishing among all Nash equilibria of the game when the distribution of endowments is* $(\mathbf{w}^1, \mathbf{w}^2)$*. Whenever* $\mathbf{w} > (1 + g)F$*, there exists* $(\hat{\mathbf{w}}^1, \hat{\mathbf{w}}^2) \in \Delta(\mathbf{w})$*, such that for all mean preserving spreads* $(\mathbf{w}^{1'}, \mathbf{w}^{2'})$ *of* $(\hat{\mathbf{w}}^1, \hat{\mathbf{w}}^2)$*, we have* $F^*(\mathbf{w}^{1'}, \mathbf{w}^{2'}) < F^*(\hat{\mathbf{w}}^1, \hat{\mathbf{w}}^2)$*.*

Indeed, the proof of Theorem 18 demonstrates that for the wealth distribution $(\hat{\mathbf{w}}^1, \hat{\mathbf{w}}^2) = (\mathbf{w} - gF/(1 + g), gF/(1 + g))$ and all mean preserving spreads of $(\hat{\mathbf{w}}^1, \hat{\mathbf{w}}^2)$, fisher 1 will conserve regardless of the other's behavior. The theorem also illustrates that the full conservation equilibrium under perfect inequality in Theorem 17 is a limiting case as inequality is increased. For distributions such as $(\hat{\mathbf{w}}^1, \hat{\mathbf{w}}^2)$, one fisher captures a sufficiently large share of the returns to conservation that he will unilaterally conserve. In particular, there exists an equilibrium in which the larger fisher conserves, the smaller fisher does not, and any mean preserving spread increases efficiency. If it were true that i's endowment were greater than $\mathbf{w}/(1 + g)$, then by Theorem 16, fisher i will always conserve if fisher j does. If it were true that is endowment were greater than $\mathbf{w}/(1 + g)$, then by Theorem 16, i would always conserve if j did. Thus any mean preserving spread of $(\hat{\mathbf{w}}^1, \hat{\mathbf{w}}^2)$, by reducing fisher i's capacity, will increase efficiency, since fisher j will play zero and more fishing will be deferred until the second period. This, then, is the commons analogue of the Olson public-goods hypothesis.

This situation is summarized in Fig. 13, which shows (assuming $g > 1$, which is clearly necessary for a cooperative equilibrium in the two-person case examined here) that as fisher 2's share increases from 1/2, full efficiency is maintained until his share reaches $g/(1 + g)$, at which point fisher 1 defects, reducing the total catch. Then as the share of fisher 2 continues to increase, the efficiency of the system increases apace, since fisher 1 is capable of harvesting a decreasing fraction of the fish stock in period 1. When fisher 2 owns all the wealth, full efficiency is restored.[46]

In fisheries worldwide, it has often been observed that large fishing companies with more opportunities to move their fleets elsewhere (compared to the small-scale local fishers) are much less concerned about conservation of fish resources in a given harvesting ground. This phenomenon of differential exit options depending on differential wealth levels extends also to other CPRs. On the other hand, there are cases where the poorer or smaller users may exercise an exit option.[47] In order to analyze such cases (Dayton-Johnson and Bardhan, 1997) extend the basic game presented above to the case when there is an exit option depending on a fisher's endowment level, $\mathbf{w}^i$; exit refers

---

[46] This figure is due to J.M. Baland, personal communication.

[47] For many examples of exit by the large and the small, see Baland and Platteau (1997).

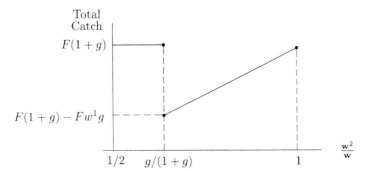

Fig. 13. Inequality and the efficiency of cooperation.

to investing or deploying one's capacity in another sector. In general, any comparative-static assertions about whether full conservation is a Nash equilibrium under different wealth distributions depends on the nature of the exit option function. In this connection Roland Bénabou has pointed out to us that, consistent with his discussion of "inequality of income versus inequality of power" in his paper (Bénabou, 1996), what matters is not inequality of wealth per se, but inequality of wealth relative to exit options and threats. If the value of one fisher's exit option grows faster than one-for-one with his wealth, then wealth inequality will foster rather than hinder cooperation.

If exit options are concave functions of wealth, increased wealth inequality does not, in general, enhance the prospects for full conservation. If full conservation is an equilibrium in a situation of perfect equality, then there is a mean preserving spread of the wealth distribution under which full conservation is not an equilibrium. Under the unequal distribution of wealth, it is the poorer fisher who finds it in his interest to play the exit strategy. But if the exit option functions are convex, it is the poorer fisher who has an interest in conditional conservation, while the richer fisher prefers the exit strategy. The nature of the exit option functions is ultimately an empirical question. In many situations, an exit option function could plausibly be linear beyond some level of wealth, but at lower levels of wealth it may be convex as a result of borrowing constraints.

The noncooperative model sketched above points to the nature of the complicated relationship between inequality and cooperation in an unregulated commons situation. One of the themes emphasized by many writers in the current policy discussion of the commons is that such problems are best described not always as prisoner's dilemmas, but rather that in many cases they may be problems of coordinating among multiple equilibria (Runge, 1981; Ostrom, 1990). This assertion is shared by our model: when the conditions of Theorem 16 are satisfied (i.e., $\mathbf{w}^i \geq \mathbf{w}/(1 + g)$ for $i = 1, 2$), both resource degradation (depletion of the fish stock in period 1) and full conservation (no fishing in period 1) are equilibria. However, under many parameter configurations, the problem is indeed a prisoner's dilemma: full conservation, though a Pareto optimum, is not an equilibrium.

One might presume that in real-world commons problems, economic actors often craft rules to regulate community use of common-pool resources. In the context of our noncooperative model of a fishery we may discuss one possible regulatory mechanism that takes the form of asset redistribution: fishers may decide to redistribute wealth before the game is played in order to secure Pareto optimal outcomes.[48] One is then interested in knowing whether a first-best outcome can be realized, particularly in cases where a first-best is not an equilibrium outcome of the unregulated game.

Theorems 15 through 17 above and their corollaries, regarding the basic model, are comparative-static results considering the effect on efficiency of changes in the wealth distribution. If we make the assumption that wealth can be redistributed, these results can be reinterpreted as statements about the effects of redistribution. Thus, Theorem 16 tells us that, for asset distributions which give each fisher positive wealth, full conservation is an equilibrium if and only if each fisher's share of total wealth is greater than $1/(1 + g)$. If g is at least one, then there always exists a wealth transfer (perhaps negative) from fisher 1 to fisher 2 such that full conservation is an equilibrium outcome. With the appropriate wealth transfer, full conservation can be supported as an equilibrium, even if it was impossible under the initial distribution. However, one may ask whether both fishers (in particular, the fisher who is asked to give up some wealth) would agree to such a transfer—or is this scheme of social regulation in fact Pareto optimal?

Let us say that the fisher who must cede some wealth to the other is fisher 2. If the fishers do not agree to transfer s between them, presumably the bad equilibrium will be played. In that case, fisher 2's payoff is $\mathbf{w}^2 F/\mathbf{w}$. If the transfer is effected and the good equilibrium results, fisher 2's payoff is $(\mathbf{w}^2 - s)(1 + g)F/\mathbf{w}$. Is the latter greater than the former? It is, as long as

$$ s < \frac{gw^2}{1 + g}. $$

This condition on the size of the transfer is always satisfied if the condition in Theorem 16 is satisfied post-transfer for fisher i.

In this section we have focused on particular mechanisms linking wealth inequality and economic performance.[49] The case study literature refers to a much richer variety of such mechanisms. In particular, social norms can be powerful enforcers of cooperative agreements, but this power may be attenuated in extremely unequal environments. Individuals may observe some cooperative norms, but only in relation to the set of individuals they regard as their peers. This perspective has its roots in the theory of

---

[48] In line with our earlier sections on land and on team production, we are assuming that credit market imperfections inhibit the operation of a market in boats and other assets in achieving first-best results.

[49] Most of the economics literature concentrates on problems of *sharing costs* in collective action dilemmas. Elster (1989) argues that problems of *sharing benefits* may frequently lead to the breakdown of collective action. The latter problem is usually one of income inequality rather than wealth inequality, although highly unequal initial asset distributions are likely to exacerbate the problem.

social exchange, one of whose founders, George Homans, comments: "The more co-hesive a group ... the greater the change that members can produce in the behavior of other members in the direction of rendering these activities more valuable". Public goods experiments by Kramer and Brewer (1984) eliciting levels of resource use in a commons tragedy situation found that common group identity (as opposed to within group heterogeneity) contributed strongly to conservation of the common resource.

This position receives some support from the experimental evidence. Indeed, con-trary to many conventional treatments, bargaining agents often fail to reach the Pareto efficient bargaining frontier for reasons initially surveyed by (Johansen, 1979). Initial inequality may be a cause of these bargaining failures. Socially beneficial cooperation often fails to materialize where the relevant actors cannot agree on and precommit to a division of the gains from cooperation. The resulting bargaining breakdowns are likely to occur where the bargaining power or wealth of the actors is particularly disparate. Experimental evidence suggests that subjects whose fallback positions are very different are less likely to come to agreements than are more equally situated subjects (Lawler and Yoon, 1996). Furthermore, the extent of cooperation and hence the average payoff in one-shot prisoner's dilemma games is inversely related to an experimentally manip-ulated social distance between the subjects (Kollock, 1997). The resulting bargaining failures may occur because inequality heightens informational asymmetries among the bargaining partners, because very unequal offers based on disparities in initial wealth or bargaining power are likely to be perceived as unfair and rejected, as in experimen-tal play of the ultimatum game (Camerer and Thaler, 1995; Rabin, 1993), or because changes in the rules of the game necessary to allow precommitments to ex post divisions of the gains to cooperation may be vetoed by the wealthy, who may fear the general redistributive potential of such institutional innovations.

It may also be that inequality affects the extent of enforceability of socially regulated solutions. The transaction costs for regulatory mechanisms may differ with the level of pre-existing inequality. These ideas are yet to be formalized.

7. Conclusion

The study of incomplete contracts prompted two reconsiderations of the relationship be-tween inequality and allocative efficiency. The first, a theoretical concern, has led many economists to reject the canon that allocational and distributional issues are separable and to recognize the stringency of the assumptions by which the Fundamental Theorem of Welfare Economics and the Coase theorem had initially established this separability result. The second, a more practical concern, has been to reconsider the policy relevance of the so called efficiency equality tradeoff. In the preceding pages we have surveyed some of the reasoning motivating both reconsiderations.

Where asymmetry or nonverifiability of information, or nonexcludability of users, makes contracts incomplete or unenforceable, and where for these and other reasons

there are impediments to efficient bargaining, we have shown that private contracting
will not generally assign the control of assets and the residual claimancy over income
streams of projects to achieve socially efficient outcomes.

Can a mandated redistribution of wealth from the rich to those with few assets—
perhaps in conjunction with other policies addressed to market failures arising from
contractual incompleteness, for example in insurance—do better? We have seen that
there are cases where such a redistribution will be sustainable in competitive equilibrium
and will allow the nonwealthy to engage in productive projects that would otherwise not
be undertaken, or to operate such projects in a more nearly socially optimal manner, or
will support a more socially efficient use of common property resources. The subjective
costs to the nonwealthy of increased risk exposure associated with residual claimancy
on a variable income stream may be attenuated both by the effect of the asset transfer
itself and by insurance against risks that are exogenous and public.

Thus mandated asset redistributions may rectify or attenuate the market failures
resulting from contractual incompleteness. But is there any reason to expect that the
indicated redistributions would be from rich to poor rather than the other way around? In
the pages above we have mentioned three cases in which highly concentrated assets may
contribute to allocative efficiency: in attenuating common pool resource problems, in
providing incentives for the monitoring of managers, and in inducing a socially optimal
level of risk taking. But in cases such as these, the asset will be worth more to the wealthy
than to the nonwealthy, and private contracting alone is sufficient to ensure an efficient
assignment or property rights, for the wealthy do not face the credit market disabilities
that sometimes prevent the nonwealthy from acquiring residual claimancy and control
rights. Thus the class of productivity enhancing asset redistributions is predominantly
from the wealthy to the asset poor.

The costs of mandated asset redistributions must also be carefully considered. The
social welfare gains from a producitivity enhancing asset redistribution accrue to the
recipients. As we have stressed, there may be no feasible means of recovering the costs
of the redistribution from the recipients without destroying the incentive effects upon
which the gains depend. Thus in general the government will be obliged to finance such
redistribution by increasing its revenue through taxation and other fiscal means. The
disincentive effects of such measures are well known and potentially severe (Buchanan
et al., 1980) but need not outweigh the allocative benefits of the redistribution (Hoff
and Lyon, 1995). Of course these disincentive costs fall on all forms of egalitarian
redistribution, including health and unemployment insurance, income transfers and job
creation programs, not just redistributions that are productivity enhancing.

It is clear, then, that distributional and allocational issues are thus inextricable, and
that while there can be no presumption that egalitarian redistribution will improve efficiency, the conventional presumption to the contrary must also be rejected.

Recognition of the importance of incomplete contracts has had another consequence
in economics: the revival of the classical economists' concern with "getting the institutions right". It is now commonplace to attribute national differences in economic

performance to differences in institutional structures, and to explain persistent economic backwardness by institutions that fail to align incentives in productivity enhancing ways. Many economists equate "getting the institutions right" with establishing unambiguous property rights, along with institutions for the unimpeded transfer of these rights. In this they follow Coase (1960: p. 19): "... all that matters (questions of equity aside) is that the rights of the various parties should be well defined ...".

But Coase himself stressed the crucial nature of his assumption of zero transaction costs, so we can set aside as utopian the possibility that property rights could be perfected to such an extent that all external effects are internalized through complete contracting. If incomplete contracts are thus unavoidable, we have shown that "what matters" for allocative efficiency includes who holds the property rights and not simply that the rights be well defined.

The reasons extend considerably beyond the cases we have considered above, but they may be summarized as follows. We know that differing initial distributions of assets may persist over long periods. Further the pattern of holdings may exercise a powerful influence on the viability of differing structures of economic governance, by which we mean the entire nexus of formal and informal rules governing economic activities. The effects of wealth differences on patterns of residual claimancy and control that we have stressed are examples. But so is the more comprehensive sharp contrast in the institutional structure of societies with yeoman as opposed to latifundia based agriculture (Engerman and Sokoloff 1997). While highly inefficient governance structures will not be favored in competition with substantially more efficient ones, the selection process is both slow and imperfect. Douglass North (1990: p, 113) comments that "economic history is overwhelmingly a story of economies that failed to produce a set of economic rules of the game (with enforcement) that induce sustained economic growth".

Thus institutions may endure for long periods because they are favored by powerful groups for whom they secure distributional advantage. For this reason inequality in assets may impede economic performance by obstructing the evolution of productivity enhancing institutions. In addition to the incentive problems on which we have focused, this may be true both because maintaining highly unequal distributions of assets may be costly in terms of resources devoted to enforcing the rules of the game and because at least under modern conditions inequality may militate against the diffusion of cultural norms such as trust that are valued precisely because they are often able to attenuate the problems arising from contractual incompleteness.

References

Aghion, Philippe and Patrick Bolton (1997), A theory of trickle-down growth and development, Review of Economic Studies 64: 151–172.

Alchian, Armen and Harold Demsetz (1972), Production, information costs, and economic organization, American Economic Review 62: 777–795.

Alesina, Alberto and Roberto Perotti (1996), Income redistribution, political instability, and investment, European Economic Review 40: 1203–1228.

Ardington, Elisabeth and Frances Lund (1995), Pensions and development: social security as complementary to programs of reconstruction and development, Southern Africa 12: 557–577.

Arnott, Richard (1991), Moral hazard and nonmarket institutions, American Economic Review 81: 180–190.

Atkinson, Anthony and Joseph Stiglitz (1980), Lectures on Public Economics (McGraw-Hill, New York).

Baland, J.M. and J.P. Platteau (1997), Wealth Inequality and Efficiency in the Commons (CRED, University of Namur).

Banerjee, Abhijit and Andrew Newman (1993), Occupational choice and the process of development, Journal of Political Economy 101: 274–298.

Banerjee, Abhijit and Maitreesh Ghatak (1996), Empowerment and Efficiency: The Economics of Tenancy Reform (MIT and Harvard University).

Banerjee, Abhijit V., Timothy Besley and Timothy W. Guinnane (1994), Thy neighbor's keeper: the design of a credit cooperative with theory and a test, Quarterly Journal of Economics 491–515.

Bardhan, Pranab (1984), Land, Labor and Rural Poverty: Essays in Development Economics (Columbia University Press, New York).

Bardhan, Pranab (1995), Rational fools and cooperation in a poor hydraulic economy, in Kaushik Basu et al., eds., Choice, Welfare, and Development: A Festchrift in Honor of Amartya K. Sen (Clarendon Press, Oxford).

Barham, Bradford, Steve Boucher and Michael Carter (1996), Credit constraints, credit unions, and small-scale producers in Guatemala, World Development 24: 792–805.

Barham, Vicky, Robin Boadway, Maurice Machand and Pierre Pestieau (1995), Education and the poverty trap, European Economic Review 39: 1257–1275.

Barro, Robert (1995), Democracy and growth, Journal of Economic Growth 1: 1–28.

Bénabou, Roland (1996), Inequality and Growth, NBER Macroeconomis Annual.

Bénabou, Roland (1999), Tax and Education Policy in a Heterogeneous Agent Economy: What Levels of Redistribution Maximize Income and Efficiency? (NBER Working Paper No. 7132).

Benhabib, Jess and Marc Speigel (1997), Cross Country Growth Regressions (C.V. Starr Working Paper No. 97-20, New York University).

Bergstrom, Theodore, Lawrence Blume and Hal Varian (1986), On the private provision of public goods, Journal of Public Economics 29: 25–49.

Berry, Albert R. and William R. Cline (1979), Agrarian Structure and Producitivity in Developing Countries (Johns Hopkins University Press, Baltimore, MD).

Besley, Timothy and Stephen Coate (1995), Group lending, repayment incentives and social collateral, Journal of Development Economics 46: 1–18.

Binswanger, H.P., K. Deninger and G. Feder (1995), Power, distortions, revolt and reform in agricultural and land relations, in Handbook of Development Economics, Vol. 3B (North-Holland, Amsterdam).

Birdsall, Nancy, Thomas Pinckney and Richard Sabot (1996), Inequality, savings and growth, Inter-American Development Bank, Office of the Chief Economist, Working paper.

Black, Jane, David de Meza and David Jeffreys (1996), House prices, the supply of collateral and the enterprise economy, Economic Journal 106: 60–75.

Blanchflower, David and Andrew Oswald (1998), What makes a young entrepreneur? Journal of Labor Economics 16: 26–60.

Blount, Sally (1995), When social outcomes aren't fair: the effect of causal attributions on preferences, Organizational Behavior & Human Decision Processes 63: 131–144.

Bowles, Samuel and Herbert Gintis (1994), Credit market imperfections and the incidence of worker owned firms, Metroeconomica 45: 209–223.

Bowles, Samuel and Herbert Gintis (1998), The Evolution of Strong Reciprocity, Working paper #98-08-073E (Santa Fe Institute).

Bowles, Samuel and Herbert Gintis (1998), Mutual Monitoring in Teams: The Effects of Residual Claimancy and Reciprocity, Work Paper #98-08-073E (Santa Fe Institute).

Bowles, Samuel and Herbert Gintis (1998), Risk Aversion Insurance, and the Efficiency-Equality Tradeoff, Working paper (University of Massachusetts).

Buchanan, James, Robert Tollison and Gordon Tullock (1980), Toward a Theory of the Rent-Seeking Society (Texas A&M University Press, College Station).

Camerer, Colin and Richard Thaler (1995), Ultimatums, dictators, and manners, Journal of Economic Perspectives 9: 209–219.

Cameron, Lisa (1995), Raising the Stakes in the Ultimatum Game: Experimental Evidence from Indonesia, Discussion Paper #345 (Department of Economics, Princeton University).

Campbell, Donald T. (1983), Two distinct routes beyond kin selection to ultra-sociality: implications for the humanities and social sciences, in Diane L. Bridgeman, eds., The Nature of Prosocial Development (Academic Press, New York), pp. 11–41.

Carter, Michael, Bradford Barham and Dina Mesbah (1996), Agro export booms and the rural poor in Chile, Guatamala and Paraguay, Latin American Research Review 31: 33–66.

Carter, Michael R. and Bradford Barham (1996), Level playing fields and *laissez faire*: post-liberal development strategies in inegalitarian agrarian economies, World Development 24(7): 1133–1150.

Carter, Michael R. and Dina Mesbah (1993), Can land market reform mitigate the exclusionary aspects of rapid agro-export growth? World Development.

Carter, Michael R. and Jonathan Coles (1997), Inequality-Reducing Growth in Latin American Agriculture: Towards a Market Friendly and Market Wise Policy Agenda (Inter-american Development Bank).

Chan, K.S., S. Mestelman, R. Moir and R.A. Muller (1996), The voluntary provision of public goods under varying income distributions, Canadian Journal of Economics 19: 54–69.

Coase, Ronald H. (1960), The problem of social cost, Journal of Law and Economics 3: 1–44.

Coleman, James S. (1988), Free riders and zeolots: the role of social networks, Sociological Theory 6: 52–57.

Craig, Ben and John Pencavel (1995), Participation and productivity: a comparison of worker cooperatives and conventional firms in the plywood industry, Brookings Papers: Microeconomics 121–160.

Dandekar, V.M. (1985), Crop insurance in India: a review 1976–1984-5, Economic and Political Weekly 20: A46–A59.

Dasgupta, Partha and Debraj Ray (1986), Inequality as a determinant of malnutrition and unemployment: theory, Economic Journal 96: 1011–1034.

Dasgupta, Partha and Debraj Ray (1987), Inequality as a determinant of malnutrition and unemployment: policy, Economic Journal 97: 177–188.

Davis, Douglas D. and Charles A. Holt (1993), Experimental Economics (Princeton University Press, Princeton).

Dayton-Johnson, J. and Pranab Bardhan (1997), Inequality and Conservation on the Local Commons: A Theoretical Exercise (University of California at Berkeley, CIDER Working Paper).

Deaton, Angus and Anne Case (1997), Large cash transfers to the elderly in South Africa, Economic Journal 108: 1130–1161.

Demsetz, Harold and Kenneth Lehn (1985), The structure of corporate control: causes and consequences, Journal of Political Economy 93: 1155–1177.

DiPasquale, Denise and Edward L. Glaeser (1999) Incentives and social capital: are homeowners better citizens? Journal of Urban Economics 45, 2: 354–384.

Domar, Evsey and Richard A. Musgrave (1944), Proportional income taxation and risk-taking, Quarterly Journal of Economics 58: 388–422.

Dong, Xioa-yuan and Gregory Dow (1993), Does free exit reduce shirking in production teams? Journal of Comparative Economics 17: 472–484.

Dong, Xioa-yuan and Gregory Dow (1993), Monitoring costs in Chinese agricultural teams, Journal of Political Economy 101: 539–553.

Dutta, B., D. Ray and K. Sengupta (1989), Contracts with eviction in infinitely repeated principal-agent relationships, in Pranab Bardhan, ed., The Economic Theory of Agrarian Institutions (Clarendon Press, Oxford).

Elster, Jon (1989), The Cement of Society (Cambridge University Press, Cambridge).

Engerman, Stanley and Kenneth L. Sokoloff (1997), Factor Endowments, Institutions, and Differential Paths of Growth Among New World Economics: A View from Econonic Historians of the United States, in Stephen Haber (ed.), How Latin America Fell Behind (Stanford University Press, Stanford).

Evans, David and Boyan Jovanovic (1989), An estimated model of entrepeneurial choice under liquidity constraints, Journal of Political Economy 97: 808–827.

Evans, David and Linda Leighton (1989), Some empirical aspects of entrepreneurship, American Economic Review 79: 519–535.

Falk, Armin and Urs Fischbacher (1998), A Theory of Reciprocity (Institute for Empirical Economic Research, University of Zurich).

Fehr, Ernst and Klaus M. Schmidt (1997), A theory of fairness, competition, and cooperation, Quarterly Journal of Economics 114.

Fehr, Ernst and Simon Gächter (forthcoming), Cooperation and Punishment, American Economic Review.

Fehr, Ernst, Simon Gächter and Georg Kirchsteiger (1997), Reciprocity as a contract enforcement device: experimental evidence, Econometrica 65: 833–860.

Forsythe, Robert, Joel Horowitz, N.E. Savin and Martin Sefton (1994), Replicability, fairness and pay in experiments with simply bargaining games, Games and Economic Behavior 6: 347–369.

Galor, Oded and Joseph Zeira (1993), Income distribution and macroeconomics, Review of Economic Studies 60: 35–52.

Gintis, Herbert (1989), Financial markets and the political structure of the enterprise, Journal of Economic Behavior and Organization 1: 311–322.

Green, Leonard, Joel Myerson, David Lichtman, Susanne Rosen and Astrid Fry (1996), Temporal discounting in choice between delayed rewards: the role of age and income, Psychology and Aging 11: 79–84.

Greenberg, Edward (1986), Workplace Democracy: The Political Efforts of Participation (Cornell University Press, Ithaca).

Grossman, Sanford J. and Oliver D. Hart (1986), The costs and benefits of ownership: a theory of vertical and lateral integration, Journal of Political Economy 94: 691–719.

Güth, Werner and Peter Ockenfels (1993), Efficiency by trust in fairness? Multiperiod ultimatum bargaining experiments with an increasing cake, International Journal of Game Theory 22: 51–73.

Güth, Werner, R. Schmittberger and B. Schwarz (1982), An experimental analysis of ultimatum bargaining, Journal of Economic Behavior and Organization 3: 367–388.

Hansen, Daniel G. (1997), Individual responses to a group incentive, Industrial and Labor Relations Review 51: 37–49.

Hausman, Jerry (1979), Individual discount rates and the purchase and utilization of energy-using durables, Bell Journal of Economics 10: 33–54.

Hayami, Yujiro and Jean-Philippe Platteau (1997), Resource Endowments and Agricultural Development: Africa vs Asia (Faculté Universitaires Notre-Dame de la Paix).

Hoff, Karla (1996), Comment on political economy of alleviating poverty: theory and institutions, in Timothy Besley, ed., Annual World Bank Conference on Development Economies, pp. 139–144.

Hoff, Karla (1996), Market failures and distribution of wealth: a perspective from the economics of information, Politics & Society 24: 411–432.

Hoff, Karla and Andrew B. Lyon (1995), Non-leaky buckets: optimal redistributive taxation and agency costs, Journal of Public Economics 26: 365–390.

Hoffman, Elizabeth, Kevin McCabe and Vernon L. Smith (1998), Behavioral foundations of reciprocity: experimental economics and evolutionary psychology, Economic Inquiry 36: 335–352.

Hölmstrom, Bengt (1982), Moral hazard in teams, Bell Journal of Economics 7: 324–340.

Hölmstrom and Jean Tirole (1988), The theory of the firm, in R. Schmalensee and R. Willig, eds., Handbook of Industrial Organization (North-Holland, Amsterdam).

Joltz-Eakin, Douglan, David Joulfaian and Harvey S. Rosen (1994), Entrepreneurial decisions and liquidity constraints, RAND Journal of Economics 25: 334–347.

Holtz-Eakin, Douglas, David Joulfaian and Harvey S. Rosen (1994), Sticking it out: entrepreneurial survival and liquidity constraints, Journal of Political Economy 102: 53–75.

Homans, George (1961), Social Behavior: Its Elementary Forms (Harcourt Brace, New York).

Hossain, M. (1988), Credit for Alleviation of Rural Poverty: The Grameen Bank in Bangladesh, International Food Policy Research Institute Report 65.

Jarvis, Lovell (1989), The unraveling of Chile's agrarian reform, 1973–1986, in William Thiesenhusen, ed., Searching for Agrarian Reform in Latin America (Unwin-Hyman, Boston), pp. 240–265.

Johansen, Leif (1979), The bargaining society and the inefficiency of bargaining, Kyklos 32: 497–522.

Johnson, D.G. (1950), Resource allocation under share contracts, Journal of Political Economy 58: 110–123.

Kandel, Eugene and Edward P./ Lazear (1992), Peer pressure and partnerships, Journal of Political Economy 100: 801–817.

Keefer, P. and S. Knack (1995), Polarization, Property Rights and the Links between Inequality and Growth (World Bank).

Kollock, Peter (1997), Transforming social dilemmas: group identity and cooperation, in Peter Danielson, ed., Modeling Rational and Moral Agents (Oxford University Press, Oxford).

Kotwal, A. (1985), The role of consumption credit in agricultural tenancy, Journal of Development Economics 18: 273–296.

Kramer, Roderick and Marilynn Brewer (1984), Effects of group identity on resource use in a simulated commons dilemma, Journal of Personality and Social Psychology 46: 1044–1057.

Laffont, Jean Jacques and Mohamed Salah Matoussi (1995), Moral hazard, financial constraints, and share cropping in El Oulja, Review of Economic Studies 62: 381–399.

Lawler, Edward J. and Jeongkoo Yoon (1996), Committment in exchange relations: test of a theory of relational cohesion, American Sociological Review 61: 89–108.

Lazear, Edward (1996), Performance Pay and Productivity, NBER Working paper #5672.

Legros, Patrick and Andrew F. Newman (1996), Wealth effects, distribution, and the theory of organization, Journal of Economic Theory.

Legros, Patrick and Steven A. Matthews (1993), Efficient and nearly-efficient partnerships, Review of Economic Studies 68: 599–611.

Leibenstein, Harvey (1957), Economic Backwardness and Economic Growth (Wiley, New York).

Loury, Glen (1981), Intergenerational transfers and the distribution of earnings, Econometrica 49: 843–867.

Malherbe, Paul (1995) Wealth, bargaining power, and control over firms: an approach based on contingent renewal (Department of Economics, University of Massachusetts).

Manning, Alan (1992), Imperfect labour markets, the stock market, and the inefficiency of capitalism, Oxford Economic Papers 44: 257–271.

McAfee, R. Preston and John McMillan (1991), Optimal contracts for teams, International Economic Review 32: 561–577.

Meyer, Jack (1987), Two-moment decision models and expected utility, American Economic Review 77: 421–430.

Moene, Karl Ove (1992), Poverty and land ownership, American Economic Review 81: 52–64.

Molinas, José R. (1998), The impact of inequality, gender, social capital, and external assistance on local-level collective action, World Development.

Mookherjee, Dilip (1997), information rents and property rights in land, in John Roemer, ed., Property Rights, Incentives, and Welfare (MacMillan, London).

Nerlove, Marc and Tjeppy D. Soedjiana (1996), Slamerans and Sheep: Savings and Small Ruminants in Semi-Subsistence Agriculture in Indonesia (Department of Agriculture and Resource Economics, University of Maryland).

Newbery, David (1989), Agricultural institutions for insurance and stabilization, in Pranab Bardhan, ed., The Economic Theory of Agrarian Institutions (Oxford University Press, Oxford).

Norman Frohlich, John Godard, Joe Opperheimer and Fred Starke (1998), Employee versus conventionally-owned and controlled firms: an experimental analysis, Managerial and Decision Economics 19: 311–326.

North, Douglass C. (1990), Institutions, Institutional Change and Economic Performance (Cambridge University Press, Cambridge).

Olson, Mancur (1965), the Logic of Collective Action: Public goods and the Theory of Groups (Harvard University Press, Cambridge, MA).

Ostrom, Elinor (1990), Governing the Commons: The Evolution of Institutions for Collective Action (Cambridge University Press, Cambridge).

Ostrom, Elinor, James Warker and Roy Gardner (1992), Covenants with and without a sword: self-governance is possible, American Political Science Review 86: 404–417.

Perotti, Roberto (1996), Income distribution, democracy, and growth: what the data say, Journal of Economic Growth 1, 2: 149–187.

Perotti, Roberto (1993), Political equilibrium, income distribution, and growth, Review of Economic Studies 60: 755–766.

Platteau, Jean-Philippe, J. Murickan, A. Palatty and E. Delbar (1980), Rural credit market in a backward area: a Kerala fishing village, Economic and Political Weekly 1765–1780.

Prosterman, Roy L. and Jeffrey M. Riedinger (1979), Land Reform and Democratic Development (Johns Hopkins University Press, Baltimore, MD).

Rabin, Matthew (1993), Incorporating fairness into game theory and economics, American Economic Review 83: 1281–1302.

Richards, John F. (1993), The Mughal Empire (Cambridge University Press, Cambridge).

Robinson, James (1996), Distribution and Institutional Structure: Some Preliminary Notes (Department of Politics, University of California at Berkeley).

Rosenzweig, Mark and Hans P. Binswanger (1993), Wealth, weather risk and the composition and profitability of agricultural investments, Economic Journal 103: 56–78.

Rosenzweig, Mark R. and Kenneth I. Wolpin (1993), Credit market constraints, consumption smoothing, and the accumulation of durable production assets in low-income countries: investment in bullocks in India, Journal of Political Economy 101: 223–244.

Rotemburg, Julio J. (1994), Human relations in the workplace, Journal of Political Economy 102: 684–717.

Runge, C.F. (1981), Common Property Externalities: isolation, assurance, and resource depletion in a traditional grazing context, American Journal of Agricultural Economics 63: 595–606.

Saha, Atanu, Richard C. Shumway and Hovav Talpaz (1994), Joint estimation of risk preference structure and technology using expo-power utility, American Journal of Agricultural Economics 76: 173–184.

Sampson, Robert J., Stephen W. Raudenbush and Felton Earls (1997), Neighborhoods and violent crime: a multilevel study of collective efficacy, Science 277: 918–924.

Sanderatne, Nimal (1986), The political economy of small farmer loan delinquency, Savings and Development 10: 343–353.

Sappington, David (1993), Limited liability contracts between principal and agent, Journal of Economic Theory 29: 1–21.

Shaban, Radwan Ali (1987), Testing between competing models of sharecropping, Journal of Political Economy 95(5): 893–920.

Shelton, John (1957), Allocative efficiency vs X-efficiency: comment, American Economic Review 57: 1252–1258.

Shetty, S. (1988), Limited liability, wealth differences, and the tenancy ladder in agrarian economies, Journal of Development Economics 29: 1–22.

Shiller, Robert J. (1993), Macro Markets: Creating Institutions for Managing Society's Largest Economic Risks (Clarendon Press, Oxford).

Sial, Maqbool and Michael Carter (1996), Financial market efficiency in an agrarian economy: microeconometric analysis of the Pakistani Punjab, Journal of Development Studies 32: 771–798.

Sinn, Hans-Werner (1990), Expected utility, μ-σ preferences, and linear distribution classes: a further result, Journal of Risk and Uncertainty 3: 277–281.

Sinn, Hans-Werner (1995), A theory of the welfare state, Scandinavian Journal of Economics 95: 495–526.

Stiglitz, Joseph (1974), Incentives and risk sharing in sharecropping, Review of Economic Studies 41: 219–255.

Stiglitz, Joseph (1989), Rational peasants, efficient institutions, and a theory or rural organization, in Pranab Bardhan, ed., The Economic Theory of Agrarian Institutions (Oxford University Press, Oxford), pp. 10–29.

Stiglitz, Joseph E. (1993), Peer monitoring and credit markets, in Karla Hoff, Avishay Braverman and Joseph E. Stiglitz, eds., The Economics of Rural Organization: Theory, Practice, and Policy (Oxford University Press, New York), pp. 70–85.

Svensson, J. (1993), Investment, Property Rights and Political Instability: Theory and Evidence (Institute for International Economic Studies, Stockholm University).

Tilly, Charles (1981), Charivaris, reportoires and urban politics, in John M. Merriman, ed., French Cities in the Nineteenth Century (Holmes and Meier, New York), pp. 71–73.

Varian, Hal R. (1990), Monitoring agents with other agents, Journal of Institutional and Theoretical Economics 46: 153–174.

Venieris, Y. and D. Gupta (1986), Income distribution and sociopolitical instability as determinants of savings: a cross-sectional model, Journal of Political Economy 94: 873–883.

Verba, Sidney, Kay Lehman Schlozman and Henry Brady (1995), Voice and Equality: Civic Voluntarism in American Politics (Harvard University Press, Cambridge).

Weissing, Franz and Elinor Ostrom (1991), Irrigation institutions and the games irrigators play: rule enforcement without guards, in Reinhard Selten, ed., Game Equilibrium Models II: Methods Morals and Markets (Springer-Verlag, Berlin), pp. 199–262.

Whyte, William F. (1955), Money and Motivation (Harper & Row, New York).

Williams, Jeffrey R., Gordon L. Carriker, G. Art Barnaby, and Jayson K. Harper (1993), Crop insurance and disaster assistance designs for wheat and grain sorghum, American Journal of Agricultural Economics 75: 435–447.

Zimmerman, Frederic and Michael Carter (1997), Dynamic Portfolio Management in Developing Countries (University of Wisconsin).

Chapter 11

THE DISTRIBUTION OF WEALTH *

JAMES B. DAVIES[a] and ANTHONY F. SHORROCKS[b]

[a]*Department of Economics, University of Western Ontario, London N6A 5C2, Canada;* [b]*Department of Economics, University of Essex, Colchester CO4 3SQ, UK and Institute for Fiscal Studies, 7 Ridgmount Street, London WC1E 7AE, UK*

Contents

* We should like to thank Andrea Brandolini, John Flemming, John Piggott, Edward Wolff and, most especially, Tony Atkinson and François Bourguignon, for their advice, comments and assistance. The first author also thanks the Social Sciences and Humanities Research Council of Canada for its support.

Handbook of Income Distribution: Volume 1. Edited by A. B. Atkinson and F. Bourguignon

Abstract

This chapter is concerned with the distribution of personal wealth, which usually refers to the material assets that can be sold in the marketpace, although on occasion pension rights are also included. We summarise the available evidence on wealth distribution for a number of countries. This confirms the well known fact that wealth is more unequally distributed than income, and points to a long term downward trend in wealth inequality over most of the twentieth century. We also review the various theories that help account for these feature. Lifecycle accumulation is one popular explanation of wealth differences, but inheritance is also widely recognised as playing a major role, especially at the upper end of the wealth range. A recurrent theme in work on wealth distribution is the relative importance of these two sources of wealth differences. We discuss the results of studies that assess the contributions of inheritance and lifecycle factors, and give attention also to a variety of related issues, such as the link between wealth status across generations, and the possible motives for leaving bequests.

Keywords: Wealth distribution, wealth inequality, portfolio composition, lifecycle saving, inheritance, bequests, intergenerational transfers

JEL codes. main: C81, D31, D91, E21, G11; secondary: D11, D12, D63, D64, J14)

1. Introduction

This chapter surveys what is known about the distribution of personal wealth and its evolution over time. We review the descriptive evidence as well as theoretical and applied research that attempts to explain the main features of wealth-holdings and wealth inequality observed in the real world.

There are many reasons for interest in personal wealth, and many ways in which the concept of wealth may be defined. If we were concerned with the overall distribution of economic well-being or resources, it would be appropriate to examine the distribution of "total wealth", that is, human plus nonhuman capital. But that is not our objective here. Instead, we exclude the human capital component and focus on material assets in the form of real property and financial claims. The term "wealth" will therefore usually refer to "net worth"—the value of nonhuman assets minus debts. Our aim is to examine the reasons for holding wealth, to document the observed differences in holdings across individuals and families, and to examine the causes of these observed differences.

One major reason for interest in wealth-holdings is that, unlike human capital, most real property and financial assets can be readily bought and sold. This allows nonhuman wealth to be used for consumption smoothing in periods when consumption is expected to be high (growing families) or income is expected to be low (retirement), and in periods of unanticipated shocks to either income or expenditure (the precautionary motive for saving). This consumption smoothing role is particularly important when individuals face capital market imperfections or borrowing constraints. Wealth may also be accumulated, or retained, for the purpose of making bequests. Additional noneconomic reasons for studying wealth include the power or social status which may be associated with certain types of assets such as privately-owned businesses. The pattern of wealth-holdings across individuals, families, and subgroups of the population, is therefore capable of revealing a great deal about both the type of economy in which people operate, and the kind of society in which they live.

The concept of net worth may appear to be straightforward, but should we deal with intangible assets which cannot be readily bought and sold? This category covers pension rights, life insurance, and entitlement to future government transfers (including "social security wealth"). Any attempt to include the rights to uncertain future benefits has to confront a variety of difficult valuation problems. For example, it is not obvious what discount rates should be used for these assets. Should they be risk-adjusted? Should a special adjustment be made for people who are borrowing constrained? Satisfactory answers to these questions require a considerable amount of painstaking work. It is therefore not surprising to discover that most applied work on wealth-holdings and wealth distribution confines itself to marketable wealth. When reviewing the empirical evidence, we use the term "augmented wealth" to refer to the broader concept which includes entitlements to future pension streams.

There are certain important "stylized facts" about the distribution of wealth which it is useful to highlight at the outset. These are:

1. Wealth is distributed less equally than labour income, total money income or consumption expenditure. While Gini coefficients in developed countries typically range between about 0.3 and 0.4 for income, they vary from about 0.5 to 0.9 for wealth. Other indicators reveal a similar picture. The estimated share of wealth held by the top 1% of individuals or families varies from about 15–35%, for example, whereas their income share is usually less than 10%.

2. Financial assets are less equally distributed than nonfinancial assets, at least when owner-occupied housing is the major component of nonfinancial assets. However, in countries where land value is especially important, the reverse may be true.

3. The distribution of inherited wealth is much more unequal than that of wealth in general.

4. In all age groups there is typically a group of individuals and families with very low net worth, and in a number of countries, including the US, the majority have surprisingly low financial assets at all ages.

5. Wealth inequality has, on the whole, trended downwards in the twentieth century, although there have been interruptions and reversals, for example in the US where wealth inequality has increased since the mid 1970s.

Possible explanations for these, and other, stylized facts will be investigated in this chapter. Section 2 begins with a review of simple models that try to account for the overall shape of the distribution of wealth. We also show how the accounting identity relating changes in wealth to earnings, rates of return, consumption and capital transfers provides a useful framework for investigating the proximate determinants of wealth inequality and its trend over time. Attention then turns to more detailed models of wealth-holdings, including numerous versions of the lifecycle saving model, and a variety of models concerned with bequest behaviour and the distributional impact of inheritance.

Section 3 reviews the descriptive evidence on wealth distribution in a number of countries, and discusses possible explanations for national differences and trends over time. The roles of asset prices, inheritance taxation, and other factors are examined. Then, in Section 4 we look at applied research which attempts to assess the contribution of different factors to the distribution and evolution of wealth-holding. These studies address a variety of questions, and use a variety of approaches, including decomposition procedures, simulation exercises, and conventional econometrics. But, in broad terms, all the research is linked by a common objective: to cast light on the reasons for wealth accumulation, and on the importance of inheritance vis-à-vis lifecycle saving as determinants of the level and distribution of wealth.

2. Theoretical approaches

Many different types of theories have been used to model aspects of wealth-holdings and wealth distribution. To a large extent they reflect the empirical evidence available at the time the theories were proposed. Prior to the 1960s, data on wealth were obtained primarily from estate tax and wealth tax records, with other evidence pieced together from small unrepresentative surveys and a variety of other sources. These tended to confirm the widely held view that wealth was distributed very unequally, and that material inheritance was both a major cause of wealth differences and an important vehicle for the transmission of wealth status between generations. There were also grounds for believing that wealth inequality was declining over time, and that the shape of the distributions exhibited certain statistical regularities which could not have arisen by coincidence. Early theoretical work on wealth distribution sought to explain these statistical regularities, and to understand the interplay of basic forces that could account for high wealth concentration and a declining trend over time.

More recently, research has shifted away from a concern with the overall distributional characteristics, focusing instead on the causes of individual differences in wealth-holdings. The change of emphasis was prompted in part by a recognition of the increasing importance of saving for retirement, and is reflected in the central role now assigned to the lifecycle saving model formulated by Modigliani and Brumberg (1954) and Ando and Modigliani (1963). The second major development has been the growth in the availability and sophistication of micro-data sets that offer not only estimates of the savings and asset holdings of individuals but also a range of other personal and household characteristics than can help account for differences in wealth.

This section reviews various models of wealth distribution and wealth differences, beginning with some of the early attempts to explain the overall distributional features and the evolution of wealth inequality. Section 2.2 discusses the simple lifecycle model and some of its many extensions, drawing out the implications for wealth accumulation over the course of the lifetime. Attention here is restricted to pure intra-generational models in which inheritances play no role. For the most part, Section 2.3 takes the opposite tack, suppressing interest in lifecycle variations and focusing instead on intergenerational links, especially those concerned with the motivation for bequests and the impact of inheritance.

The distinction between models of wealth accumulated for lifecycle purposes and models concentrating on the intergenerational connections reflects the theoretical literature on wealth distribution: very few contributions have attempted to deal simultaneously with both the lifecycle and inherited components of wealth. This is a major weakness of past theoretical work on wealth. While there may be some value in modelling lifecycle wealth in the absence of inheritance, it should be recognised that this exercise does not reveal the true pattern of lifecycle accumulation in the real world—since the real world also has inheritances. This rather obvious point is one which is often forgotten, particularly when attempts are made to assess the relative importance of accumulation and inheritance.

Current models of accumulation and bequests do not appear to capture the circumstances and motives of those who amass large fortunes in the course of their lifetimes. We look briefly at this issue in Section 2.4. Throughout, reference is made to relevant empirical evidence that has informed and influenced the development of the theories. Later, in Section 4, we consider in more detail some of the issues that have received most attention.

2.1. Simple models of wealth distribution

Early empirical work on personal wealth-holdings established two enduring features of the shape of the distribution of wealth. First, it is positively skewed, unlike the normal distribution, but roughly resembling a normal distribution when wealth is replaced by the logarithm of wealth. Second, the top tail is well approximated by a Pareto distribution, which yields a straight line graph when the logarithm of the number of persons with wealth above w is plotted against $\log w$. These two statistical regularities were observed not only for wealth-holdings, but also for many other skewed distributions such as those for incomes, the turnover of firms, and the size of cities (see, for example, Steindl, 1965, Appendix B).

The fact that these size distributions are approximated by the lognormal suggests that, by appealing to the Central Limit Theorem, they can be generated by a random walk of the form:

$$\ln W_t = \ln W_{t-1} + u_t, \tag{2.1}$$

where W_t is wealth at time t, and u_t is a stochastic component (Aitchison and Brown, 1957). Equation (2.1) contains the implicit assumption that the factors influencing changes in wealth over time operate in a multiplicative fashion, rather than additively. This became known as Gibrat's "law of proportionate effect", following Gibrat (1931).

As a model of wealth distribution, the simple random walk Eq. (2.1) has one major technical disadvantage: it predicts that wealth dispersion, as measured by variance of log wealth, increases over time without bound. It cannot therefore apply when wealth inequality is stable or decreasing. To overcome this problem it is necessary to introduce a mechanism which offsets the inequality increasing impact of the stochastic component. One simple solution is the formulation proposed by Galton (1889) in his study of inherited genetic characteristics, which yields

$$\ln W_t = \beta \ln W_{t-1} + u_t, \qquad 0 < \beta < 1, \tag{2.2}$$

with β indicating the degree of "regression towards the mean". Given appropriate constraints on the stochastic component u_t, this process can generate a stable lognormal distribution of wealth in which changes in wealth at the level of individuals exactly balance out to maintain equilibrium in the aggregate (see, for example, Creedy, 1985).

A number of other authors, including Champernowne (1953), Wold and Whittle (1957), Steindl (1972), Shorrocks (1973, 1975b), and Vaughan (1975, 1979), proposed alternative types of stochastic models capable of generating distributions of wealth with upper tails that are asymptotically Pareto. In broad terms, these models all assume that a variant of the law of proportionate effect applies at high wealth levels, where the expected change in wealth must be negative in order to prevent the top tail from drifting upwards over time. Equilibrium is maintained by some mechanism lower down the distribution—such as a pool of low wealth-holders in the case of Wold and Whittle (1957)—which stops wealth from converging to zero in the long run. As with the Galtonian specification Eq. (2.2), these models typically view the observed wealth distribution as the outcome of a stochastic process in which individual wealth movements net out to produce a stable aggregate configuration.

The simplest types of stochastic models lack an explicit behavioural foundation for the parameter values and are perhaps best viewed as reduced forms in which terms like the regression coefficient β and the random component u in Eq. (2.2) capture in some unspecified way the influence of factors such as the impact of wealth effects on consumption and the randomness of investment returns. Attempts to incorporate explicitly the relevant explanatory variables rapidly produced complex models that were difficult to solve analytically (Sargan, 1957; Vaughan, 1975, 1979; Laitner, 1979), and these technical obstacles have hampered further development of this line of research.

Meade (1964, 1975) offers another simple framework for analysing wealth distribution based on the accounting identity

$$W_t = W_{t-1} + E_t + r_t W_{t-1} - C_t + I_t, \tag{2.3}$$

where C_t and E_t are, respectively, consumption and earned income in period t, net of taxes and transfers; r_t is the average (net) rate of return on investments; and It represents net "inheritances" (gifts and bequests) received in period t. In the Meade formulation, inheritances are suppressed (or, more accurately, absorbed into the initial wealth level W_0), and consumption is assumed to depend on both income and wealth. This yields

$$
\begin{aligned}
W_t &= W_{t-1} + s_t(E_t + r_t W_{t-1}) - c_t W_{t-1} \\
&= (1 + s_t r_t - c_t) W_{t-1} + s_t E_t \\
&= (1 - \beta_t) W_{t-1} + s_t E_t,
\end{aligned}
\tag{2.4}
$$

where s_t is the average rate of saving from current income, c_t indicates the wealth effect on consumption, and $\beta_t = c_t - s_t r_t$ represents the "internal rate of decumulation out of wealth".

Equation (2.4) provides a convenient framework for investigating the forces leading to greater or lesser wealth inequality. Assuming for the moment that E_t, s_t and β_t are constant over time and across individuals, Eq. (2.4) has the solution

$$
W_t = W^* + (1 - \beta)^t (W_0 - W^*),
\tag{2.5}
$$

where $W^* = sE/\beta$. If β is negative, the initial wealth differences expand over time and wealth inequality grows without bound. Conversely, if β lies between 0 and 1, then wealth converges to the steady state level W^*, which depends only on savings from earned income and the internal rate of decumulation. Under the above assumptions, this implies that the distribution of wealth will be completely equalized in the long run. But once allowance is made for variations in earnings across individuals, the model suggests that long run differences in wealth will mirror the differences in earnings or income. As already noted, the tendency for the level of wealth inequality in the twentieth century to decline towards the lower level observed for incomes is one of the best documented findings of empirical studies of wealth distribution.[1]

The simple relationship between income inequality and the equilibrium level of wealth inequality is modified by variability in the values of E_t, s_t and β_t across individuals or over time. For example, as Meade (1964) points out, individual differences in the rates of return received on investments are likely to be a disequalizing influence, particularly so if the average rate of return increases with the level of wealth. Another possible consideration is the general equilibrium connections between the components contained in Eq. (2.4). Stiglitz (1969) bases his analysis on a similar model, but also links earnings and rates of return to average wealth via a simple neoclassical production

---

[1] It is interesting to note that the recent rise in wealth inequality in the US and, to a lesser extent, Sweden (see Fig. 1 below) have occurred during periods in which income inequality has grown. Wolff (1992) reports a regression of wealth inequality against income inequality in which the coefficient is not significantly different from one.

function. His analysis shows that if the savings rate s_t is constant, β is positive, and earnings are the same for all workers, then E_t and W_t converge to their steady state values, and wealth distribution is again completely equalized in the long run. Assuming a stable balanced growth path for the economy, Stiglitz demonstrates that a variety of saving functions (linear, concave, depending on income, or depending on wealth) produce the same result, but other factors, such as wage differences and class saving behaviour, have disequalizing effects over time.

In principle, the framework proposed by Meade, and captured in Eq. (2.4), could absorb the insights gained from subsequent work on lifecycle saving behaviour, which suggests how savings depend on current income and wealth, and how the parameters may adjust to, say, increases in life expectancy. The rich potential of Eq. (2.4) is also evident in the fact that it can be interpreted equally well in an intergenerational context, as is done by Atkinson and Harrison (1978), with W_t referring to the "lifetime wealth" of generation t, and the coefficient β capturing the impact of bequest splitting and estate taxation.

Returning to the accounting identity Eq. (2.3), and interpreting it in terms of the lifetime experience of a family (or individual) which begins at age 0 with zero wealth, implies that wealth at the end of age t is given by

$$W_t = \sum_{k=1}^{t}(E_k - C_k + I_k) \prod_{j=k+1}^{t} (1 + r_j). \tag{2.6}$$

From Eq. (2.6) it is clear that a family's wealth is determined by: (i) its age, and its history of; (ii) earnings; (iii) saving rates; (iv) rates of return; and (v) inheritances. A complete economic theory of wealth distribution needs both to determine the distributional impact of each of these five elements and to account for differences in the components across individuals and families. In principle, even the distribution of the population across age groups requires explanation, since fertility and mortality are in part economic phenomena. Although a complete theory of wealth distribution remains a distant objective, considerable progress has been made on many of the specific components. In the following subsections we review many of the relevant contributions, concentrating in particular on questions concerned with savings rates and inheritances. Theories of earnings distribution are considered in detail by Neal and Rosen in Chapter 7 of the Handbook, while fertility, mortality, and family formation are discussed in Rosenzweig and Stark (1997).

2.2. Lifecycle accumulation

The paradigm for intra-generational accumulation is the lifecycle saving model (LCM) pioneered by Modigliani and Brumberg (1954).[2] This now comes in several different

---

[2] The life-cycle model of Modigliani and Brumberg (1954) was developed contemporaneously with the closely related permanent income hypothesis of Friedman (1957). Insights from both these studies continue to have an important impact on current work.

variants, reflecting the degree of realism introduced into assumptions about institutions and about the uncertainties faced by savers. All versions of the model share the basic assumptions that: (i) consumers are forward-looking; (ii) their preferences are defined over present and future consumption, and possibly leisure time; and (iii) life is expected to end with a period of retirement. Extensions of the basic LCM allow individuals to be interested in the consumption of their offspring or in the size of their planned bequest. These are sometimes known as the "bequest-augmented LCM". The LCM can also be extended in many other ways—for example, by introducing capital market imperfections and/or borrowing constraints, and uncertainty in earnings, rates of return, or the length of life.

The simplest version of the LCM assumes there is no uncertainty; that everyone faces the same constant rate of return, r, and has the same length of life, T; and that there is no bequest motive. The consumer's problem is then:

$$\text{Max } U = U(C_1, \ldots, C_T), \tag{2.7a}$$

subject to:

$$C^L = \sum_{t=1}^{T} \frac{C_t}{(1+r)^{t-1}} \le \sum_{t=1}^{R} \frac{E_t}{(1+r)^{t-1}} = E^L, \tag{2.7b}$$

where C^L and E^L respectively denote lifetime consumption and lifetime earnings, and R is the retirement date. If there is a nonworking period at the end of life, minimal restrictions on the functional form of $U(\cdot)$ will ensure that saving is undertaken for the purpose of financing consumption in retirement. This is the key explanation offered by the LCM for personal wealth accumulation.

To simplify the exposition, leisure has been neglected in the maximization problem Eq. (2.7).[3] In other respects, the specification is too general to produce precise conclusions about patterns of saving behaviour. The solution to the problem does include, however, what Browning and Lusardi (1996) call the "central tenet" of the modern view of the LCM: that the consumer attempts to equalize the discounted marginal utility of expenditure in all periods.[4] In order to achieve this equalization, given diminishing marginal utility, consumers engage in "consumption smoothing". Retirement saving is one result. Another is that assets will fluctuate to keep consumption smooth. In addition, since earnings rise quickly in the initial working years, substantial net borrowing (i.e., negative net worth) is expected to be prevalent among young people. The fact that this is

---

[3] We note below those occasions when endogenous labour-leisure choices have important implications for wealth-holding.

[4] This goal can be achieved precisely in a world of certainty, but only in expectation when uncertainty is introduced.

not observed[5] suggests either that individuals cannot readily borrow against future earnings (often referred to as a capital market imperfection), or that they have precautionary reasons for saving, as discussed below.

To make more concrete predictions about saving behaviour, intertemporal utility is typically assumed to be additively separable:

$$U = \sum_{t=1}^{T} \frac{u_t(C_t)}{(1+\rho)^{t-1}},$$ (2.8)

where ρ is the rate of time preference. It is common to assume also that $u_t = u$, although intuition suggests that the instantaneous utility function is likely to change with age. Constant time preference is a requirement for consistent consumption planning over the lifetime (Strotz, 1956).

Various functional forms have been assumed for u. As discussed below, a quadratic function produces the certainty equivalent (CEQ) version of the LCM. Caballero (1991) and others use the constant absolute risk aversion (CARA) specification $u(C) = -e^{-\delta C}$, which, like the quadratic, yields closed form solutions under uncertain earnings. But the most popular specification by far is the constant relative risk aversion (CRRA) form given by:

$$u_t(C_t) = \frac{C_t^{1-\gamma}}{1-\gamma}, \qquad \gamma > 0, \quad \gamma \neq 1$$

$$u_t(C_t) = \log C_t, \qquad \gamma = 1$$ (2.9)

where γ is the coefficient of relative risk aversion.[6] When Eqs. (2.8) and (2.9) are incorporated into Eq. (2.7), the optimal consumption path satisfies

$$C_{t+1} = \left(\frac{1+r}{1+\rho}\right)^{1/\gamma} C_t = (1+g)C_t,$$ (2.10)

and planned consumption grows at a constant rate g, which is approximately (or, under continuous time, exactly) equal to $(r-\rho)/\gamma$.[7] From Eq. (2.10) it is evident that the intertemporal elasticity of substitution is $1/\gamma$.

---

[5] While surveys find some individuals at all ages with negative net worth, and a higher incidence among the young, the majority have positive net worth even at low ages. See, for example, Hubbard et al. (1995).

[6] The CRRA form is the only additively separable homothetic utility function. Many feel that it has intuitive plausibility, and not just analytical convenience, on its side. However, Attanasio and Browning (1995) find that it is decisively rejected in favour of a more general alternative.

[7] More generally, the hyperbolic absolute risk aversion (HARA) family formulated by Merton (1971)—which includes the CRRA, CARA and CEQ specifications as special cases—leads to a Euler equation similar to Eq. (2.10), but with an additional constant term.

Consumption in each period is proportional to the sum of wealth left over from the previous period and the present value of earnings over the remaining lifetime. In the initial period this gives:

$$C_1 = \frac{E^L}{\sum_{t=1}^{T}[(1+g)/(1+r)]^{t-1}}. \tag{2.11}$$

The propensity to consume rises with age, and is lower for individuals whose preferences generate a higher desired growth of consumption. The impact of the interest rate on the propensity to consume is positive or negative according to whether γ is greater or less than unity respectively.[8]

The prediction of a constant growth rate of consumption has a number of consequences for wealth-holding and wealth distribution. Consider, for instance, a situation in which earnings are constant up to retirement age and zero thereafter. Assume also that the interest rate and the planned consumption growth rate are both zero. Then the consumer will save a constant amount during each working year, and will dissave a constant amount during each retirement year, with accumulated savings falling to zero at the point of death. The net result is an age-profile of wealth which rises linearly with age until retirement, and then declines linearly to zero.

This very restrictive example highlights two important—and robust—implications of the LCM. First, the age-profile of wealth is expected to have a pronounced hump-shape, with the peak occurring at or near the date of retirement. Strictly speaking, this prediction is best tested against empirical estimates of wealth-holdings which include imputed pension rights. But a similar prediction holds for marketable wealth if pensions are treated as deferred earnings, as long as pension income is lower than earned income during working life.

The second implication is that substantial wealth inequality can arise between the richest members of society (those around retirement age) and the poorest (those just starting out on their working lives and those nearing death), even if everyone is completely equal in all respects other than age. Thus age differences alone are expected to account for a substantial proportion of observed wealth inequality. The significance of this point is that wealth variations due to age do not represent true differences in lifetime opportunities, and the resulting wealth inequality is therefore spurious from an equity perspective. The extent to which wealth inequality is attributable to age differences is a question which we consider in detail in Section 4.

More general consequences of the consumption path Eq. (2.10) are obtained if it is assumed that $r > \rho$, so that consumption is planned to grow at a constant positive rate. If earnings have the typical hump-shaped age-profile, individuals should typically

---

[8] Empirically, it is generally thought that γ exceeds unity by a significant amount. However, this does not necessarily mean that consumption is expected to decline with increases in the interest rate. E^L falls with r, generating a "human wealth effect" which is found to dominate in simulation exercises: see, for example, Summers (1981).

dissave for some period when young, but then save fairly heavily in middle years and, of course, dissave in retirement. However, as many researchers have pointed out, in the real world we find that: (i) most individuals and families are net savers when young; (ii) consumption tends to track earnings or income, also having a hump-shaped age-profile rather than an exponential one; and (iii) when family size is held constant, consumption falls on retirement and then declines further over time, producing less dissaving than the model suggests (Attanasio, 1998). Davies (1979, 1982) shows that taking account of family size in Eqs. (2.7) and (2.9) deals to a large extent with problems (i) and (ii) over the working lifetime (see also Attanasio et al., 1995). However, once children have left the home the CRRA specification (with $r > \rho$) predicts rising consumption as long as family composition remains constant. This runs contrary to what is observed. The downward jump in consumption on retirement can be explained by incorporating labour-leisure choice if goods and leisure are substitutes, since there should be substitution away from goods and towards leisure on retirement (Davies, 1988). The continued downward trend throughout retirement would follow if u_t varied with age in such a way that the marginal utility of consumption, at a given consumption level, decreased continuously over time.

Empirical evidence is not always in agreement on the main features of savings behaviour, a point well illustrated by the debate over whether individuals dissave in retirement, and if so to what extent. In the 1950s and 1960s a number of cross-section datasets appeared to indicate that mean wealth did not fall in retirement, or that mean savings remained positive.[9] This was viewed as a major challenge to the LCM, although Shorrocks (1975a) showed that the apparent lack of dissaving in the UK could be explained by compositional changes in an ageing population. More recent studies using panel data, for example the Retirement History Survey in the US, show significant dissaving in retirement (Hurd, 1997). This result is not always obtained. Alessie et al. (1997), for instance, find rising net worth in Dutch panel data between 1987 and 1991, and Jianako-plos et al. (1989) find that it is difficult to generalize about the results of going from cross section to panel data in the US. However, the broad consensus is that, after the first few years, private wealth (as well as social security wealth) declines in retirement. What remains in considerable doubt is the speed at which dissaving takes place: see, for example, Hurd (1997: table 9, p. 935).

As mentioned earlier, the simple LCM tends to predict that negative wealth-holdings will be common among the young. The fact that this is not borne out empirically suggests that liquidity constraints and/or precautionary saving behaviour should be taken into account. Other evidence points to the need to "augment" the LCM in other ways. White (1978), Darby (1979) and Kotlikoff and Summers (1981) all present calculations for the US which show that the aggregate savings rates and wealth-income ratios are much greater than those predicted by lifecycle saving alone. Although other researchers find the LCM to be more successful in this respect (see Hurd, 1997), most favour the

---

[9] More recent evidence of this type is considered by Mirer (1979) for the US.

introduction of bequest motives into the LCM—which would reduce dissaving among the retired—and the explicit recognition of various forms of uncertainty, such as those relating to rates of return, earnings, medical costs, and the length of life.

The simplest way of incorporating bequest motivation is to make U depend on terminal wealth W_T. This is sometimes referred to as the "warm glow" approach, since parents' satisfaction from making a bequest depends only on the size of transfer, and not on the characteristics of heirs, such as their incomes and needs. This approach might be defensible in modelling aggregate behaviour, but it is too crude an assumption for distributional analysis.[10] Alternative formulations of bequest motives are discussed in Section 2.3 below.

The effects of both uncertain rates of return and uncertain earnings received early analytical attention (e.g., Leland, 1968; Sandmo, 1970). However, more recent simulation-based work has tended to neglect uncertain rates of return, concentrating instead on earnings uncertainty and uncertain nondiscretionary expenditures like medical costs, which are formally equivalent to earnings uncertainty and can therefore be treated by similar methods.

The effects of uncertain rates of return are complex. On the one hand, introducing any form of uncertainty reduces the consumer's welfare and real income. If consumption is a normal good, this tends to increase saving. On the other hand, by increasing saving the consumer exposes himself to greater risk when returns are uncertain. In general the net effect is ambiguous. However, Lippman and McCall (1981) show that there is a clear cut result in the CRRA case: if $\gamma < 1$, the introduction of risky rates of return raises consumption and reduces saving; when $\gamma > 1$, saving rises. In the lifecycle simulation literature, γ is usually taken to be about 3 (Carroll, 1992; Hubbard et al., 1994), and some empirical work suggests even higher values (Mankiw and Zeldes, 1990). This suggests that introducing uncertain rates of return into the LCM might be a fruitful way of obtaining greater aggregate wealth, although, as mentioned earlier, this option has received little attention.

The simplest way to proceed when earnings are allowed to be uncertain is to use the certainty equivalent (CEQ) version of the LCM based on quadratic utility. This approach has been used recently to analyse the evolution of inequality in income, consumption, and wealth over the lifecycle. Deaton and Paxson (1994) show that the model predicts rising consumption inequality over the lifetime, as well as an increase in income inequality with age. These predictions are in accord with what is observed empirically. Davies (1996a) uses the CEQ approach to examine changes in wealth inequality with age.

---

[10] Under this approach none of the observed heterogeneity in bequest behaviour can be captured. Models which can help to explain, for instance, why parents with similar incomes might desire very different levels of bequest are needed in order to understand the complex patterns of bequest and inheritance.

Some of the important implications of the CEQ model for the distribution of wealth are brought out clearly in the case $r = \rho = 0$, where consumption simply equals wealth plus expected future earnings, divided by the length of the remaining lifetime:

$$C_t = \frac{W_{t-1} + E\left[\sum_{k=t}^{R} E_k\right]}{T - t + 1}. \tag{2.12}$$

Earnings have a permanent and transitory component, and may be written as $E_t = E_t^p + \epsilon_t$, where t has zero mean and a finite variance. Much recent work finds the permanent component of earnings to be highly persistent. Abstracting from the deterministic part of the age-earnings relationship, the earnings process in the US is approximated by a combination of white noise and a random walk (Carroll, 1992; Hubbard et al., 1994). This suggests $E(E_k^p) = E_t^p$, $k = t, \ldots, R$. Under that assumption Eq. (2.12) yields:

$$C_t = \frac{W_{t-1} + (R - t + 1)E_t^p + \epsilon_t}{T - t + 1}, \tag{2.3}$$

which indicates that the propensity to consume out of permanent earnings is much greater, and the propensity to save less, than out of current wealth or transitory earnings.

The result of an earnings process with highly persistent shocks is that earnings inequality tends to grow over the working lifetime. The wealth which has been built up by saving out of past permanent components of earnings will correspondingly become more unequal over time. However, as Davies (1996a) points out, empirical studies find that wealth inequality initially declines with age, and while it usually increases later, this increase does not begin until the later years of the working lifetime. The initial decline in wealth inequality can be mimicked by the CEQ model if transitory earnings are not merely measurement error. The high propensity to save out of transitory earnings, combined with the assumption that everyone begins life with zero wealth, means that wealth inequality will be dominated at low ages by saving (and dissaving) out of transitory earnings. Transitory earnings tend to "average out" over time, so that this source of wealth inequality declines with age.

While valuable insights are gained from the CEQ model, its prediction that earnings uncertainty does not affect saving is widely regarded as unrealistic and untenable. There is much empirical evidence that consumers save more in response to earnings uncertainty; in other words, they exhibit precautionary saving (Browning and Lusardi, 1996: pp. 1835–1838). As shown by Kimball (1990), any additive intertemporal utility function with a positive third derivative for u (such as a CRRA function), or what he terms "prudence", will produce precautionary saving.

The quantitative impact of earnings uncertainty on saving has been investigated by a number of authors. Skinner (1988) and Zeldes (1989) investigate the effects of assuming prudence, but do not include liquidity constraints or impatience—features which have subsequently received much attention. While Skinner and Zeldes obtain higher—that is, more realistic—levels of aggregate saving, they do not predict the frequent incidence of low positive wealth-holding at all ages which is a prominent feature of wealth distribution in the US and many other countries. Deaton (1991) accounts for the latter with an infinite horizon model incorporating a high rate of time preference (impatience) and liquidity constraints, as well as prudence.[11] In Deaton's model, when their earnings are high, savers accumulate a buffer stock of assets which, like the observed assets of many actual consumers, may be quite small. These assets are run down when earnings are low.

Carroll (1992) shows that liquidity constraints are unnecessary to obtain buffer stock behaviour if consumers are impatient and prudent, and if there is a finite probability of complete earnings interruptions, which he claims is the case for some individuals in the US. Since "earnings" must be interpreted broadly (that is, to include transfer payments), this argument would not apply in countries which have more comprehensive income maintenance systems.

Hubbard et al. (1994, 1995) claim that while buffer stock models predict the observed low wealth-holding of many individuals, they cannot generate sufficiently high values for mean saving for retirement. Their model produces both these features, by retaining the assumptions of prudence and liquidity constraints, but also adding uncertain medical costs, uncertain lifetimes, and means-tested transfer payments and other social benefits. The latter strongly discourage low income individuals and families from saving since most assets must be exhausted before an individual qualifies for means-tested benefits.

Uncertain lifetime is readily incorporated in the LCM. Taking the CRRA approach, the objective function becomes:

$$EU_t = \sum_{k=t}^{T} \frac{(1 - \phi_k) C_k^{1-\gamma}}{(1+\rho)^{k-t}(1-\gamma)}, \tag{2.14a}$$

where T is now interpreted as the maximum length of life, and ϕ_k is the probability of death before period k.

In order to characterize behaviour when the individual has the objective function Eq. (2.14a), it is necessary to specify the nature of insurance markets. In a perfect insurance market with actuarially fair annuities, all individuals completely annuitize their wealth. In that case Eq. (2.14a) is maximized subject to the constraint:

$$\sum_{k=t}^{T} \frac{(1 - \phi_k) C_k}{(1+r)^{k-t}} \leq W_{t-1} + \sum_{k=1}^{R} \frac{(1 - \phi_k) E_k}{(1+r)^{k-t}}. \tag{2.14b}$$

---

[11] Use of an infinite horizon means that Deaton's model steps outside the LCM framework. Its predictions about buffer stock saving behaviour may nevertheless have relevance for the situation of young consumers, whose planning is dominated by concerns about earnings fluctuations rather than the need to save for retirement.

As shown by Yaari (1965), planned consumption again follows the consumption path Eq. (2.10), growing at the constant rate g (approximately equal to $(r - \rho)/\gamma$).[12]

It is usually argued that annuity markets are sufficiently imperfect that the above solution does not apply.[13] If imperfections are severe, annuities may have such low rates of return that rather than annuitizing all of their wealth, individuals may not buy annuities at all. It is widely believed that this is broadly the situation in practice (Friedman and Warshawsky, 1988). In this case the individual again maximizes Eq. (2.14a), but subject to Eq. (2.7b) and a nonnegative wealth constraint. The solution to this problem yields a nonconstant growth rate of consumption, g^u, in periods of positive wealth-holding:

$$g^u = \frac{r - \rho - \pi_t}{\gamma}, \tag{2.15}$$

where $\pi_t = (\phi_{t+1} - \phi_t)/(1 - \phi_t)$ is the mortality hazard in period t: that is, the probability of death conditional on having survived to age t.

Under Eq. (2.15) the age-profile of consumption, and therefore the age-profiles of saving and wealth, are predicted to be quite different from those in a world of certainty. As is well-known, the mortality rate initially rises with age, and does so at an accelerating pace. Beyond some age (about 80 for males in the dataset used by Davies, 1981, for example) the mortality rate begins to decline towards a stable lower level. Assuming CRRA preferences and applying Eq. (2.15), this mortality pattern means that the growth rate of consumption will fall at an accelerating rate over the working lifetime and early retirement, but then rises at advanced ages. If $r - \rho$ is sufficiently small, this can produce a realistic hump-shaped age-profile of consumption, or a profile which is predominately hump-shaped, but with a rising trend in later years of retirement.

The recognition of uncertain lifetimes also leads to more realistic age-profiles for saving and wealth-holding. In particular, the rate of dissaving in retirement may be lower than in the case with a fixed lifespan. In the absence of state or occupational pensions, no rational consumer would ever run assets to zero. This simple result suggests that introducing uncertain lifetimes will produce higher aggregate savings in simulation exercises, possibly eliminating the need to introduce a bequest motive. Davies (1981) shows that this is indeed the case with a wide range of reasonable values for the parameters r, ρ, and γ, and realistic patterns of earnings and mortality. However, Davies' results also indicate

[12] Although the growth rate is the same as under certainty, the overall consumption profile may shift up or down.

[13] Both moral hazard and adverse selection have an effect on annuity markets, and these problems seem to be much more severe than for life insurance. Possible explanations include: (i) people take better care of themselves once they have an annuity, but are less inclined to take the opposite action when they are covered by life insurance (i.e., moral hazard is more severe under annuities); and (ii) the likelihood of unusually high life expectancy is largely private information, but poor health is often ascertainable and verifiable by an insurance company (i.e., adverse selection is more severe under annuities).

that it is wrong to disregard the effect of pensions, because if pensions are included and if γ is not too high, uncertainty about the length of life can cause faster decumulation.[14]

Over the course of the twentieth century, state and occupational pensions have tended to become more widespread and more generous. This does not necessarily mean that the need to save privately for retirement has declined, since retirement ages have also been falling and life expectancy has increased. However, these pension trends do imply that individuals may rationally run their private wealth to zero at some point during retirement.[15] As Leung (1994) points out, this provides another possible explanation for the low marketable wealth of part of the population.

Despite the ambiguous effect of uncertain lifetime on the rate of decumulation in retirement in the presence of pensions, it is interesting to note that, with uncertain earnings, medical costs and lifetime, Hubbard et al. (1994, 1995) generate age- profiles of consumption and wealth-holding, aggregate saving rates, and overall wealth-income ratios which are all close to those observed for the US. Thus it is not *necessary* to include intentional saving for bequests in order to replicate the aspects of wealth-holding of interest to those concerned with just consumption behaviour. However, intentional bequest behaviour is likely to be required in order to explain the shape of the upper tail of the wealth distribution, intergenerational wealth mobility, and the size distribution of inheritances. These are important issues for those interested in the distribution of wealth.

2.3. Intergenerational issues

Models of inheritance should ideally take account of demographic factors such as patterns of fertility and marriage, as well as factors which are more strictly economic. In contrast to lifecycle models, they should also analyse the evolution of the distribution over many generations. To do this it is helpful to begin with pure intergenerational models, which abstract from the relationship between inheritance and lifecycle saving, as well as the interaction between material inheritance and transfers in human form.

A useful point of departure is to consider how patterns of marriage, fertility, estate division, and taxation affect the evolution of wealth distribution in a world of pure accumulation, that is, one in which wealth grows at the rate of interest, and there is no consumption. The simplest case is that of a society in which all individuals marry, have children, and leave to their children (and no others) a total bequest equal to the amount they themselves inherited. In such a society the current distribution of inherited wealth depends only on the wealth distribution of the previous generation, together with patterns of marriage, fertility, estate division, and taxation. Blinder (1973) notes that in a world where all families have two children, of whom one is a boy and the other a

---

[14] Davies' pensions decline with age at an annual real rate of 2.25%, reflecting the imperfect indexation of pensions in the early 1970s in Canada. When pensions are constant in real terms throughout retirement, γ must be quite high to yield the result that uncertain lifetime increases saving. This is one reason for the differences in the results obtained by Leung (1994) and Davies (1981).

[15] Indeed, Leung (1994) shows that if they live long enough, people covered by pensions *must* exhaust their private wealth completely.

girl (i.e., in the absence of differential fertility and population growth), and where estate taxation is either absent or proportional, the distribution of (relative) inherited wealth remains unchanged over time if either (a) mating is completely assortative (children married partners from families with identical wealth) and all families at a given level of wealth divide estates in the same way between their son and daughter, or (b) the members of one gender inherit nothing.[16] In all other cases the distribution becomes more equal over time, with the speed of equalization depending on the correlation of parental wealth between spouses and the way in which estates are divided. The most rapid equalization occurs with completely random mating and equal estate division.

More general assumptions have been explored by Meade (1964), Stiglitz (1969), Pryor (1973), Atkinson and Harrison (1978), and Atkinson (1980). These authors show that, although imperfect correlation of spouses' inheritances has a powerful equalizing effect on the distribution of inherited wealth, other forces may have the opposite effect. For example, inherited wealth becomes steadily more concentrated over time under primogeniture (the practice of passing all wealth to the eldest son) if each family has more than two children, including at least one son, and all children marry (Atkinson, 1980: p. 48).[17] In addition, if the wealthy consistently have fewer children, inherited wealth can become continuously more unequal even in the presence of some sharing of estates among siblings and imperfect sorting of marital partners by parental wealth.

As Blinder (1973) points out, evidence for the US suggests that differential fertility is not particularly marked, and the correlation between spouses' family background characteristics, although positive, is low. Furthermore, unequal division of estates is relatively unusual in the US, and is also far from the norm in the UK, although it may be slightly more prevalent there. It is therefore likely that the patterns of marriage, fertility, and estate division in advanced Western societies tend toward equalization of the distribution of wealth over time. Complete equalization does not occur if rates of return on saving are positively correlated with the level of wealth, which will be the case if wealthier individuals choose riskier portfolios or have preferential access to advantageous investment opportunities. Against this, progressive tax systems tend to make after-tax rates of return lower for the wealthier. The net effect is difficult to judge.

The sensitivity of results to the pattern of lifetime saving becomes clear in the work of Pryor (1973) and Blinder (1976). Pryor simulated processes of marriage, fertility, saving over the lifetime, estate taxation and bequest division. In his model everyone marries and has two children. A normal distribution of earned income in each generation is assumed. Two different models of lifetime saving are considered: one in which the

---

[16] Shorrocks(1979) examines how altruistic parents may condition their division of estates between sons and daughters on the anticipated bequest behaviour of in-laws. Where there is no gender preference, any fixed ratio of son' to daughters' bequests could be supported. In contrast, even mild gender preference could lead to an equilibrium with primogeniture.

[17] The intuition is simple. Primogeniture maintains the same wealth distribution in each generation *among those with positive wealth*, but the proportion of positive wealth-holders is decreasing over time because of population growth.

bequest is proportional to income, and another in which bequests are proportional to income in excess of some threshold. Proportional saving out of income reduces the simulated inequality of income found after 30 generations have passed. The kinked bequest function, however, leads to an increase in income inequality after 30 generations, in the absence of primogeniture. (With primogeniture the effect is negligible.) The nature of lifetime saving therefore has important implications for the evolution of the distribution of wealth. This conclusion is echoed in the simulation exercise of Blinder (1976) who replaced the ad hoc lifetime saving models of previous authors with a bequest- augmented lifecycle model based on an explicit representation of preferences. Blinder found that, even with equal division of estates and random mating, the force of inequality coming from lifetime saving was strong enough to produce a rising trend in the inequality of inherited wealth over time.

In the last few decades considerable interest has been shown in models of intergenerational transfers rooted in an explicit specification of parental preferences and opportunities. The crucial distinction is between models in which transfers are made for reasons of altruism (see, for example, Becker and Tomes, 1976), and those in which they represent a quid pro quo for "attention" supplied by potential heirs. Models of the latter type are said to feature "exchange" or "strategic" bequests (Bernheim et al., 1985; Cox, 1987).

The Beckerian approach assumes that parental preferences are given by:

$$v = v(c^p; c_1, \dots, c_n),\tag{2.16}$$

where n is the number of children, c^p is parental lifetime consumption, and c_i is the lifetime consumption of child i.[18] Parents spend x_i on human capital investment in child i, and provide bequests b_i, $i = 1, \dots, n$. Children's earnings equal the product of the human capital rental rate, w, and their human capital, h_i, which is generated using inputs of x_i according to a production function which depends on the child's own characteristics:

$$e_i = wh_i(x).\tag{2.17}$$

Higher ability children have higher h_i for any given x_i. If the first derivative of h_i is also higher, and if parents make efficient investments, it can be shown that in equilibrium more able children will have greater earnings than less able children.

With this structure, and assuming a zero interest rate for convenience, the consumption of parents and children is given by:

$$c^p = e^p - \sum_{i=1}^{n}(x_i + b_i),\tag{2.18a}$$

---

[18] The amounts of "lifetime" consumption include only consumption in the adult phase of the lifecycle. Consumption of young children living at home with their parents is included in c^p.

$$c_i = e_i + b_i, \qquad i = 1, \ldots, n, \tag{2.18b}$$

where e^p is parental lifetime earnings. The parent's problem may be written:

$$\underset{b,x}{\text{Max}} \, v \left(e^p - \sum_{i=1}^{n} (x_i + b_i); e_1 + b_1, \ldots, e_n + b_n \right) \tag{2.19}$$

subject to $\quad x_i, b_i \geq 0, \qquad i = 1, \ldots, n.$

Suppose that capital markets are perfect and that parents can borrow against their children's earnings (relaxing the requirement that $b_i \geq 0$). In this case, Eq. (2.19) decomposes into two problems. The first is to choose the efficient level of investment in each child, x_i^*.[19] The corresponding earnings level for the child is e_i^*. The second part of the problem is to maximize Eq. (2.19) with respect to the b_i's, taking the e_i^*'s as given. If parental preferences treat children symmetrically, this produces the well-known result:

$$e_1^* + b_1 = \cdots = e_n^* + b_n. \tag{2.20}$$

In other words, under altruism parents plan to equalize completely the children's incomes net of transfers.[20]

As we discuss in Section 4 below, while some authors have found evidence of a negative impact of children's earnings on bequests, nothing like fully compensatory bequest behaviour has been observed in practice, where bequest division has been studied..

Davies (1986) analyses the equilibrium impact of bequests and estate taxation on overall inequality in the Becker model with perfect capital markets. He shows that a linear redistributive tax on bequests *increases* long-run inequality. The reason is that it interferes with the intergenerational sharing of luck, which in equilibrium leads total incomes within a generation to be distributed more equally than earnings. In other words, the institution of bequest reduces equilibrium inequality in the simple altruistic model, and policies which interfere with the bequest process are likely to increase inequality. This conclusion has been widely regarded as unrealistic (see, for example, Bevan, 1979; Atkinson, 1988; Wilhelm, 1997), and can be avoided by abandoning the assumption that parents can borrow against their children's future earnings (i.e., the perfect capital market assumption), or by incorporating nonaltruistic motives for bequests.[21]

The Becker model produces more interesting insights, and no longer predicts fully compensatory bequests in all cases, if we recognise that parents may end up at a corner

---

[19] Since there is no labour-leisure choice, with a perfect capital market parents choose x_i to maximize $e_i - x_i$. This occurs when $\partial e_i / \partial x_i = 1$. With a positive interest rate, r, the corresponding condition is $\partial e_i / \partial x_i = 1 + r$.

[20] Shorrocks (1979) points out that in a more realistic version of the model parents should take into account the bequests which their children's spouses can be expected to receive. In general this will invalidate Eq. (2.20).

[21] Bevan (1979) performs an intergenerational simulation in which negative bequests are not allowed. He finds that the existence of bequests may either raise or lower consumption inequality.

solution where $b_i = 0$. This will occur if parents do not find it optimal to set x_i high enough to achieve $e_i = e_i^*$. If parental income is low, or if the required expenditure is too great, they may only be willing to fund the efficient level of investment if b_i is negative. But, while some children may be trusted to repay parents for investments in their human capital, in modern societies this cannot usually be enforced. Thus, it is possible that some children will fail to achieve their efficient level of earnings, and will receive zero bequest. In general, bequests will no longer perfectly compensate for differences in earnings. Also, since zero bequests will be more common in families with low income parents, one would expect the incidence of bequests to rise with parental income, and to rise in a nonlinear manner. For example, if parental income and children's ability were perfectly correlated, bequests would be zero up to some threshold parental income, and increasing beyond that point. This prediction may help to explain why even many older people report not having received any significant bequest in their lifetime, and why Menchik and David (1983) found the estimated income elasticity of bequests to be less than one for the bottom 80% of the population, but considerably greater than one for the top 20%.[22]

An important aspect of the Beckerian analysis is its simultaneous consideration of human and nonhuman transfers. Thinking about transfers in this way yields the following insights:

1. It provides an explanation for the empirical observation that many families, perhaps the majority, never receive significant inheritances, and that bequests are a luxury.

2. It suggests that inheritances may not be as disequalizing as one might have thought, despite their high concentration. If material transfers and human capital investments are substitutes to some extent, as the theory suggests, then within a family those children who get larger bequests will tend to receive smaller investments in the form of human capital.

3. It indicates how the actions of parents may reduce the degree of intergenerational income mobility which would occur "naturally" if all children received efficient investments in their human capital, and if there were no inheritances.

4. It highlights the fact that changes in educational systems, opportunities, and finance may have an important impact on saving and wealth accumulation.

The altruistic model does not perform well when we consider the optimal timing of intergenerational transfers. With perfect capital and insurance markets, both parents and children are indifferent between lifetime gifts and bequests. However, if children are often liquidity constrained as young adults, they will prefer to receive their transfers earlier rather than later. The fact that parents provide a large fraction of their total transfers in the form of bequests is therefore a challenge to the altruistic model.

---

[22] Menchik and David (1983) used a longitudinal Wisconsin tax-filter dataset to construct estimates of parents' lifetime earnings, and estimated a spline relationship between lifetime income and the size of estate. They found elasticities ranging from insignificant negative values to +0.7 for the bottom 80% of parents, but elasticities ranging from 2 to 4 for the top 20%.

It should also be noted that it is possible to extend the altruistic model to allow parents to care not only about their children's consumption, but also about "attention" they may receive from children (see Cox, 1987; Davies, 1996b). Examples of attention include phone calls, letters, and visits, as well as the provision of more essential services during periods of ill health or infirmity. In an altruistic model, with the child behaving nonstrategically, the parent would pay the child for attention at a normal supply price—for instance, the child's wage rate. The total transfer to the child would then be composed of expenditures on attention, plus a gratuitous component, b_i^g.[23] This result has interesting implications. For example, in families where b_i^g is relatively small, the behaviour of b_i could be dominated by b_i^a, so that, for example, the observed correlation between b_i and e_i might be positive, holding parental income constant, despite parents being altruistic.

Bernheim et al. (1985) propose an alternative, strategic model of interactions between parents and their adult children. They set out a simple noncooperative game in which parents with two or more children could, it is claimed, credibly threaten to disinherit any child who did not accept a "forcing contract" specifying the amount of services they had to provide.[24] This approach generates the same outcome as that obtained when altruistic parents purchase attention from children who act nonstrategically. In both cases, all rents from parent-child interaction accrue to the parents.

Cox (1987) suggests that it might be more realistic to consider a model in which both parents and children have some bargaining power. One way to do this is via a cooperative bargaining approach such as Nash bargaining. Another is to model the relationship between parents and their children as a repeated game with an uncertain horizon (the parents' lifetime): see Kotlikoff and Spivak (1981) and Davies (1996b). Under the latter approach, parents show cooperation by holding some bequeathable wealth, and children cooperate by providing attention. Either side could defect, but would be punished. Under some, but not all, conditions, the threat of punishment can be sufficient to maintain cooperation.

The repeated game approach produces interesting insights. For example a parent-child pair may initially be in a region where cooperation cannot be supported because the actuarial value of the expected bequest is too small to induce attention from the child. However, as the parent ages, or perhaps as a result of parental ill health, the parent's mortality probability may rise sufficiently to allow cooperation to be maintained. This provides a possible explanation for the empirical observation that attention increases when parental health declines, and does so more if parents' bequeathable wealth is higher (Bernheim et al., 1985).

---

[23] The observation that even altruistic parents may purchase attention from their children implies that an exchange of gifts and bequests for child services is not only to be obtained in a strategic model. There is a tendency in the literature to treat signs of exchange as evidence against the altruistic model and in favour of a strategic alternative.

[24] It is questionable whether the threat to disinherit is credible. A parent who felt the slightest degree of altruism toward his children would be tempted to reinstate the disinherited child on his deathbed.

Regardless of whether or not exchange relationships between parents and adult children require a strategic explanation, one may ask why a higher incidence of bequests is not observed.[25] Parental desire for attention is presumably widespread. Adding an altruistic motivation for transfers would seem to suggest that sizeable bequests should be quite common. This is not the case in practice. The explanation may lie in the fact that much exchange between parents and children is not recorded, because it takes place via small gifts or in nonpecuniary form. While these forms of exchange are more difficult to observe, they may nevertheless have important effects on the wealth-holdings of a large portion of the population.

Little attention has been given to the impact of exchange and strategic bequest behaviour on wealth inequality. However, some implications can be noted. First, if children are simply paid for attention at their usual wage rates then bequests should be treated as part of their lifetime earnings and the analysis, in lifetime terms, is equivalent to assuming a world in which inheritances do not exist. But the fact that bequests are received later than earnings, and are subject to greater uncertainty, may affect lifetime expenditure patterns, especially if children face capital market constraints. This will have complex effects on the evolution of wealth inequality over the lifecycle which would need to be studied by simulation. In addition, if attention is a luxury good, higher income children will receive a larger proportion of their lifetime income in the form of bequests. This is likely to mean that bequests have an apparently disequalizing effect on lifetime income and wealth. An even more disequalizing impact could be generated by a model in which children shared some of the rents from interaction with their parents, assuming again that these interactions are relatively more important in wealthier families.

2.4. Self-made fortunes

There is one category of people for whom the current theories of lifetime accumulation and bequest behaviour seem quite inadequate: those who have made sizeable fortunes during the course of their lifetimes, largely, or exclusively, as a result of their own efforts. Very often they continue working even though they have amassed enough wealth to live forever in extreme luxury. Moreover, bequests to children and grandchildren do not appear to be strong motives. Two prominent examples, Bill Gates and Warren Buffett, have both announced their intention to leave the bulk of their fortunes to charity. While such people are, by definition, rare, their fortunes are sufficiently large to have an impact on wealth inequality.

A number of authors have stressed the need to provide a separate model for this type of person. Atkinson (1980) draws attention to the different bequest intentions of those who have obtained substantial wealth through entrepreneurship. Masson and Pestieau (1996) and Arrondel and Leferrere (1996) refer to "capitalist" bequest motives. Little has been done to develop a formal model of the bequest intentions of those with large

---

[25] Even in their relatively high income sample of retired academic faculty and staff, Laitner and Juster (1996: p. 897) report that only 41% had received, or expected to receive, any substantial transfer.

self-made fortunes. But the fact that many past fortunes have ended up in charitable foundations named after their benefactor suggests that a prime motivation may be a desire to see the continuation of their name in the public arena. This might be expressed as a "desire for immortality". It seems less than adequate to capture this objective simply in terms of the utility derived from terminal wealth.

Current theories are also inadequate in explaining how self-made fortunes are generated. Casual empiricism suggests that they are linked inextricably with entrepreneurial activity, and that, although ability and ambition play a part, the size of the fortune depends largely on "being in the right place at the right time"—in other words, luck. In effect, social and technological developments create opportunities for fortunes to be made, which specific individuals exploit with varying degrees of success.

Shorrocks (1988) presents a simple model of this kind of situation. There are two types of opportunities to make fortunes. One requires entrepreneurial time, but no capital: for instance, panning for gold in a river. The other requires time and a substantial amount of capital: for example, sinking a shaft for a gold mine, or prospecting for off-shore oil. High-capital risks offer a greater expected return, but to gain access to them, individuals must first succeed as low-capital entrepreneurs. This drives down the expected return from low-capital risks to a point below the wage that entrepreneurs would receive if employed. It becomes unattractive to pool risks, and hence low-capital entrepreneurs gamble everything on one activity. If successful, however, individuals have an incentive to diversify in order to retain access to the advantageous high-capital opportunities.

This approach highlights several important influences on wealth-holdings at the top of the distribution. First, it draws attention to the social forces and technological developments which create the opportunities for fortunes to be made. Recently in the UK, for instance, a number of large fortunes can be traced to the privatisation of publicly owned enterprises during the 1980s and 1990s. The approach also draws attention to the significance of capital market imperfections, an issue that plays a central role in the recent work on persistent inequalities reviewed by Piketty in Chapter 8 of the Handbook. The idea that prospective entrepreneurs with little initial capital must first establish a track record of success before being allowed access to finance for larger scale ventures is one that chimes well with real world practice, and one that could provide the basis of a model of self-made fortunes.

3. Empirical evidence on wealth inequality

Four sources of data have been used to estimate the distribution of wealth: household surveys of assets and debts, wealth and estate tax records, and investment income data. Other information on the very richest families is provided by independent estimates of the wealth of named individuals. We review each of these data sources in turn, discussing the problems that need to be addressed in order to produce reliable evidence on the pattern of wealth-holdings. We also summarise the evidence on wealth inequality for a range of countries, using the share of wealth owned by the richest groups in the population, or the value of the Gini coefficient, to represent the degree of concentration. This is followed by a discussion of the portfolio composition of wealth-holdings. The section concludes with a review of the factors which may account for differences in wealth distribution across countries and for the observed variations in wealth inequality over time.

It should be stressed at the outset that comparisons of wealth distributions present numerous difficulties. To begin with, the precise concept of wealth is open to question. The most widely applied definition is *net marketable wealth* or *net worth*—the total value of all assets which the owner can sell in the market, less any debts. Because contributions into pension schemes are a substitute for other forms of lifecycle saving, this concept of wealth is often expanded to include the capitalized value of entitlements to pensions, including state pensions; following Wolff (1995), we refer to this as *augmented wealth*. Other empirical studies have applied narrower concepts such as gross assets or financial wealth. Generally speaking, the precise definition used in empirical work reflects the availability of data and a desire for comparability with other data sets, rather than a judgement about the ideal concept of wealth which, in any case, depends on the purpose for which the data are subsequently employed.

A second major distinction is between the distribution of wealth across households (or families), and the distribution across individuals. Again, the choice is dictated primarily by the source of data rather than by an opinion about the most appropriate economic unit: as far as we are aware, there is no consensus on this issue. As will become apparent, other factors, such as the year in which the data are collected and the refinements applied to the raw data, may also significantly effect the estimates of wealth concentration. For all these reasons, wealth distribution data tend to be less homogeneous and more variable in quality than, say, income distribution data, and need to viewed with more than the usual degree of caution.

3.1. Household surveys

Household surveys of assets and debts are a valuable source of data on wealth distribution, but the information obtained is typically less reliable than that for income. There are two main reasons for this. First, the distribution of wealth is so heavily skewed that, even with fairly large sample sizes, sampling error may significantly affect estimates of dispersion. Consider, for example, a country with 10 million families, 500 of which have wealth in excess of $20 million. With a random sample of 15,000 families, there is about an even chance of including one or more of these wealthy families. If none of them are captured in the survey, the upper tail of the sample distribution will be too short. In other cases, for instance when a "centi-millionaire" family is sampled, the tail will be too long. So the raw data from a sample survey which does not over-sample at the top end cannot be expected to provide an accurate snapshot of the pattern of wealth-holdings among the very rich.

Nonsampling errors are also serious, and affect much more than the upper tail of the distribution. They fall into two main categories: *differential response and misreporting*. The problem of differential response is due to the refusal (or inability) of households to answer either all parts of the survey ("survey nonresponse"), or one or more specific questions ("item nonresponse"). Item nonresponse is more tractable than survey nonresponse since it can be combatted by careful imputation of missing amounts (Juster and Kuester, 1991: pp. 51–54.). Survey nonresponse would not cause difficulties if the response rate was uncorrelated with wealth-holding, but the evidence strongly suggests that the response rate is lower for better-off families. Furthermore, the pattern of nonresponse in wealth surveys is more pronounced than in surveys of income. For example, Projector and Weiss (1966: Table 15, p. 52) reported an overall response rate of 83% in the 1962 Survey of Financial Characteristics of Consumers (SFCC) in the United States, but a response rate of just 37% for families with incomes above $100,000. In the high-income sampling frame of the 1977 Canadian Survey of Consumer Finances, the response rate was about 45% (Oja, 1980: p. 342). Kennickell et al. (1998: p. 23) report that the response rate to both the 1992 and 1995 SCF's differed considerably between the representative subsample and the "list sample", which focuses on those with high incomes. The response rates across the two surveys were 70% in the representative sample, but only 34% in the list sample. Differential response according to income or wealth can be partly overcome by standard weighting techniques; but if no family with wealth over $10 million ever consents to an interview, there is no way that this omission can be corrected by re-weighting the sample.

The second form of nonsampling error is *misreporting*, which most often takes the form of under-reporting both assets and debts, either by failing to report ownership of certain assets (which may not be known to the person completing the survey), or by undervaluing those items which are recorded. The extent of under-reporting varies widely across the different types of asset. At one extreme, US studies have found that respondents on average report the value of owner-occupied houses to within four percentage points of the appraisal by real estate experts (Kain and Quigley, 1972). At the other extreme, it has been estimated that respondents under-report bank balances by up to 50–60% (Davies, 1979: pp. 248–251). For other categories of assets, such as consumer durables and privately owned businesses, undervaluation may not be due to ignorance, forgetfulness or deliberate under-reporting, but may instead reflect the ambiguous nature of the assessment—for example, whether the asset is valued as a "going concern" or on a "sell-up" or "realization" basis.

The net impact of nonsampling errors is revealed by comparing the raw aggregate figures derived from surveys with independent estimates of the balance sheet totals for the household sector, a practice now widely adopted in order to assess the reliability of wealth survey data.[26] While the balance sheet figures are themselves prone to certain types of error, they are generally regarded as more accurate, and this has prompted refinements of the survey data designed to eliminate, or significantly reduce, the discrepancy with the balance sheets.

The difficulties that arise in deriving estimates of wealth distribution from sample surveys have been addressed in a number of ways. One method of dealing with the sampling error problem is to pool information for several years, assuming that suitable data are available. Another common strategy is to adopt a dual sampling frame at the survey design stage. A high-income frame consisting of families or individuals known to have income above some cutoff on the basis of income tax, census, or other data is added to the usual sampling frame. This approach was followed in wealth surveys in the US by both the 1963 SFCC and recent Surveys of Consumer Finances (SCF). The same method was used in the 1977 (but not the 1984) Canadian SCF.

While comparisons between aggregate survey figures and independent balance sheet estimates indicate the scale of the problems associated with response bias and under-valuation, the exact contribution of each of these factors is difficult to gauge. As a consequence, attempts to reconcile the two sets of data need to make assumptions about the source of the discrepancies. It may be thought, for example, that lower response rates for wealthier households account for the low average wealth values typically observed in survey data. This may be partially rectified by re-weighting the sample using whatever additional information is available, although the sampling problems discussed above limit the extent to which this problem can be solved completely. Alternatively, it might be assumed that the entire gap is due to under-reporting; in other words, that sampling problems can be neglected and there is no response bias. As the degree of underestimation varies considerably across asset and debt types, it is natural to assume—as a first approximation—that the percentage degree of under-reporting for any particular asset or debt is the same for all wealth-holders. In order to gauge the possible impact of the errors involved, it is clearly advisable to offer calculations based on a range of alternative assumptions. Exercises of this type are reported by Davies (1979) for Canada, by Wolff (1987b, 1994) and Wolff and Marley (1989) for the US, and by Leipziger et al. (1992) for Korea.[27]

Numerous wealth surveys are in use around the world; here we mention only some of those that have attracted the greatest attention. Recent estimates of the overall wealth

---

[26] See, for example, Avery et al. (1988) for the US; Davies (1979) and Oja (1986) for Canada; Brandolini and Cannari (1994) for Italy; and Leipziger et al. (1992) for Korea.

[27] Davies (1979) explored a number of alternative procedures for aligning the 1970 Canadian SCF with independent household balance sheet figures, allowing for both under-reporting and differential response by wealth level. Wolff (1987b) adjusts the asset holdings of respondents in four different US wealth surveys to reconcile the figures with balance sheet information. In both studies, the net result was a small increase in the estimates of wealth concentration. Using 1988 household survey data collected by the Korean Development Institute, Leipziger et al. (1992) suggest that adjustments based on balance sheets would substantially increase estimates of wealth concentration in Korea, due to the fact that land is probably undervalued by a significant margin, and that land holdings are distributed very unequally.

distribution in the US are available from the short-panel Survey of Incomes and Program Participation (SIPP), the Panel Study of Income Dynamics (PSID) which has followed respondents over many years, and the Survey of Consumer Finances (SCF) which is now conducted every three years for the Federal Reserve Board.[28] SIPP provides considerable asset detail but performs less well than the PSID and SCF in terms of comparisons with independent balance sheets, and in other respects (Curtin et al., 1989). Its relatively poor performance appears to be due in part to the fact that it does not over-sample high income families. In contrast, the PSID asks a small number of questions about broad asset categories, but comes closer to the balance sheet totals, perhaps achieving better responses because of the long relationship with its respondents. The PSID may be particularly useful for those who need a good wealth variable to use as a regressor in empirical studies. The SCF provides the best information on the upper tail of the distribution, and allows comparisons of changes in wealth distribution over time.

SCF's yielding overall estimates of the distribution of wealth in the United States were conducted in 1983, and triennially since 1989. (See Avery et al., 1984, 1988; Weicher, 1995; Kennickell et al., 1998.) In addition, they can be compared with the 1962 SFCC, which employed a similar methodology. The SCF does not have a large sample—for example, the overall sample size in 1995 was 4299; but it includes a special high-income frame intended to represent roughly the top 1% of the population, and does well in comparisons with the Flow of Funds household balance totals (Curtin et al., 1989; Avery, 1989). A comprehensive range of marketable assets is covered and, for the 1983 SCF, estimates were also provided for the present value of social security benefits and private pensions for workers above age 40. Comparisons across years indicate that overall wealth inequality changed little between 1962 and 1983, but rose after 1983: see Wolff (1994, 1995) and Weicher (1995).[29]

There has been much interest in the distribution of wealth in Japan, in part because of the belief that the stock market and real estate booms of the 1980s fuelled a considerable increase in wealth inequality—a trend causing concern in a country widely regarded as relatively equal. The concern about possible increases in wealth inequality was reinforced by a perception that bequests were becoming increasingly important as the population aged rapidly and wealthy cohorts began to die.

---

[28] Other surveys provide longitudinal evidence on wealth of the elderly. These include the National Longitudinal Survey of Mature Men (NLS) which was conducted from 1967 to 1983, the Retirement History Survey (RHS) running from 1969 to 1979, and the Health and Retirement Survey (HRS) which began in 1992–1993. Juster and Kuester (1991) find that the estimates of wealth distribution from the NLS and RHS suffer from biases due to the lack of oversampling of high income families and other limitations. The HRS appears to provide more reliable estimates (Juster and Smith, 1997).

[29] There is some disagreement about the magnitude of the increase in wealth inequality between 1983 and 1989. Wolff (1994) reports a 5 percentage point increase in the share of the top one half percent of wealthholders, and a rise of 0.04 in the Gini coefficient. Weicher (1995) presents calculations based on alternative weighting schemes, and slightly different procedures. He does not report the share of the top groups, but claims that the increase in the Gini coefficient was no more than 0.027.

Although Japan has several alternative sources of wealth data, until recently they all suffered from limited coverage and other problems, as documented by Bauer and Mason (1992). The annual Family Saving Survey (FSS) excluded unattached individuals and nonfinancial assets. Unattached individuals were included in the National Survey of Family Income and Expenditure (NFIE), but this survey omitted those primarily engaged in agriculture, as well as merchants, private and corporate administrators, and professionals. Farm households were covered in the Farm Household Economic Survey (FHES). Full coverage of the population was achieved in the Financial Asset Choice Survey (FACS), conducted biannually since 1988 by the Institute for Posts and Telecommunications Policy (see Campbell and Watanabe, 1996a).

As Bauer and Mason point out, special difficulties affect the measurement of financial assets in Japan. In order to avoid high income and bequest taxes, many investors shelter their assets in holding companies, whose value tends to be underestimated due to the methods used to price shares in these companies. This problem needs to be borne in mind, since the main conclusions from Japanese survey data are that (a) wealth inequality is lower in Japan than in other countries such as the US or UK, and (b) most wealth inequality is due to inequality in holdings of land and housing (Mizoguchi and Takayama, 1984; Tachibanaki, 1989; Takayama, 1991). Takayama (1992) uses the NFIE, and finds a Gini coefficient of 0.52 and a share of the top 5% of 25%; Tachibanaki (1989) uses the FSS together with supplementary data to obtain a Gini of 0.58 (see Bauer and Mason, 1992: pp. 416–417). Campbell and Watanabe (1996b) find higher proportions of both wealthy and poor households, and higher mean net worth, in the 1994 FACS compared to the 1994 NFIE or FSS, but they do not report summary inequality measures.

Given the similarities between Japan and Korea, it is interesting to note that Leipziger et al. (1992) also report a Gini value of 0.58 for gross wealth inequality in Korea in 1988. This estimate was based on an income and wealth survey of 4291 households conducted by the Korean Development Institute (KDI), and fitted a truncated Pareto distribution to the upper tail in order to overcome the problems of sampling and differential response rates. Leipziger et al. review the wide range of supplementary information available for Korea, including inheritance and estate tax records, the distribution of financial assets across households, and, most importantly, detailed data on the distribution of land holdings. They even attempt to use share register information on named individuals to estimate the top tail of the distribution of equity in public companies. An aggregate balance sheet constructed from independent sources suggested that the raw KDI data underestimate average household wealth by at least 36%, and perhaps by as much as 73%, depending on the true aggregate value of land holdings. Reconciling the survey data with middle range estimates of land values, and assuming that nonresponse and undervaluation each accounted for roughly half of the missing wealth, produced estimates of 19, 37 and 48% respectively for the share of the top 1, 5 and 10% of wealth-holders. The single most important determinant of wealth concentration in Korea is undoubtedly land ownership: for the year 1988 it is estimated that the top 25% of landowners (comprising 11% of the adult population) owned over 90% of the total land value (Leipziger et al., 1992: p. 46).

Other countries which have had a variety of sample surveys of wealth-holding going back to the 1960s or earlier include Canada, Australia, France and Italy. Canada's Survey of Consumer Finance provided information for 1964, 1970, 1977 and 1984.[30] These surveys had reasonably large sample sizes (about 14,000 in 1984, for instance), but did not over-sample high income families except in 1977. The unadjusted 1984 results indicate shares of the top 1, 5, and 10% of families equal to 17, 38, and 51%, respectively, and a Gini coefficient of 0.69. Davies (1993) points out that this survey does not match the balance sheet totals well, and does not capture the upper tail of the Canadian wealth distribution. After reviewing various external sources of information, Davies concludes that the true shares of the top 1 and 5% in 1984 were approximately 22–27% and 41–46%, respectively.

Australia had a few early isolated wealth surveys, but they did not over-sample at the top end, and are not considered to have been reliable in the upper tail (Piggott, 1984). Dilnot (1990) supplemented the figures for housing wealth in the 1986 Income Distribution Survey (IDS) with estimates of nonhousing wealth generated by the investment income method (see Section 3.4 below). He obtained shares of the top 1, 5, and 10% of 20, 41, and 55% respectively. Baekgaard (1997) refines Dilnot's methods and obtains results suggesting a much lower level of concentration. His shares of top 1, 5, and 10% for the 1986 IDS are just 13, 32, and 46%. For France, Kessler and Wolff (1991) report a Gini of 0.71 for gross wealth in the 1986 INSEE survey, and shares of 26 and 43% for the top 1 and 5% of households.

Information on wealth-holdings in Italy is available from the Bank of Italy's Survey of Household Income and Wealth, conducted annually from 1965 to 1984, and biannually from 1987 onwards. Many researchers have used these data to investigate savings behaviour, intergenerational transfers, and the motives for bequests (see, for example, Ando et al., 1994), but only one unpublished study has looked at wealth inequality. Brandolini et al. (1994) report top wealth shares for 1987, 1989 and 1991, with the share of the top 1% declining over this period from 13 to 9%, and the share of the top 10% falling from 45 to 39%. These data include adjustments for nonreporting of assets and undervaluation, but sample selection bias means that about 30% of net worth, and about 50% of financial wealth, is excluded from the estimates. Brandolini et al. draw attention to the relatively low share of financial assets in Italy (especially holdings in pension and insurance funds), and to the almost negligible degree of indebtedness, both of which are attributed to the backwardness of the credit and insurance markets. Applying standard decomposition procedures, they suggest that real property accounts for around 80% of wealth inequality as measured by either the Gini coefficient or the variance.

---

[30] There was no Canadian wealth survey between 1984 and 1999. Statistics Canada conducted a new Survey of Financial Security in April–June 1999. It is expected to increase asset coverage relative to the SCF, including pension equity for example.

In recent years, further evidence on wealth-holding has become available in new household surveys conducted in Germany, Sweden, the Netherlands, Britain and Ireland. These new data sources have many strengths including, in some cases, a panel design (see, for example, Alessie et al., 1997, for the Netherlands). However, the surveys have been used primarily to investigate poverty, savings behaviour, labour supply, income mobility and other income related household topics. Information on wealth has not been studied in detail, and the evidence has tended to be reported in the form of means, medians, inter-quartile ratios, and standard deviations, rather than the shares of the top wealth groups or standard measures of inequality. For these reasons it is often difficult to fit the new results into an overall picture of the degree of wealth concentration across countries.

The German Socio-Economic Panel (GSOEP) was used by Burkhauser et al. (1997) to contrast wealth inequality in Germany in 1988 with US data derived from the 1988 PSID. They report a Gini value of 0.69 for net worth in Germany compared to 0.76 for the US. Bager-Sjögren and Klevmarken (1996) make use of the panel characteristics of the Swedish HUS survey to estimate wealth inequality and wealth mobility over the period 1983–1992. They obtain Gini values for net wealth in the range 0.52 to 0.59, which is lower than the figure expected on the basis of wealth tax information. This may reflect the deficiencies of the HUS data, including a small sample size (just 1150 households in 1992), the omission of individuals above age 75, and the need to impute data for a high number of incomplete records (59% of the sample).

Nolan (1991) analyses data on 3294 Irish households obtained from the 1987 Survey of Income Distribution, Poverty and Usage of State Services, which included questions on property (including farms), and certain types of financial assets and debts, but not consumer durables or life insurance-based investments. Comparison with various sources of external information led Nolan to conclude that the survey data provide reasonable estimates of the wealth of the bottom two thirds of the distribution, whose holdings are not recorded in the estate duty statistics. However, the survey is not regarded as a reliable guide to asset holdings at the top end of the wealth scale. This may well account for the small share of the top 1% observed in the raw sample data, which is very low by international standards, and also low in comparison with earlier estate-based estimates of wealth concentration in Ireland. According to Nolan, making allowance for missing wealth is likely to raise the share of the top 1% from 10 to 13–14%, and the share of the top 10% from 42 to 48%. One special feature of the Irish data is the significance of farming land, which accounts for half the wealth of the richest 1% of households.

3.2. Wealth tax data

A number of European countries levy wealth taxes. Estimates of the distribution of wealth can be derived, and coverage of the population is sometimes greater than under estate taxes. However, some assets (e.g., consumer durables) are missing and others are generally under-valued. Perhaps for these reasons, estimates of wealth distribution from this source have been made for relatively few countries.

In the 1975 data for Sweden used by Spant (1987), about 5000 families were selected at random from the wealth tax records, and a further 3000 added from a high wealth sampling frame. Spant made various adjustments in order to correct for missing and undervalued assets. His estimates of the shares of the top 1, 5, and 10% in net wealth at market prices were 17, 38, and 54%, respectively. Lindh and Ohlsson (1998) report corresponding estimates for more recent years which show that wealth inequality decreased between 1975 and 1984, then rose, with shares of the top 1, 5, and 10% reaching 20, 41, and 58% in 1992. On the basis of Danish tax records for 1975, Spant (1982) estimates the proportion of net wealth owned by the top 1, 5, and 10% in Denmark to be 25, 48 and 65%. This suggests that wealth inequality was higher in Denmark than in Sweden, at least during the 1970s. But the Danish survey did not over-sample the rich, and is considered less reliable than comparable Swedish data.

A major feature of the wealth tax information for Sweden is the length of time over which comparable estimates can be made for the distribution of wealth. The series reported in Spant (1987) show a continuous downward trend in net wealth inequality over the period 1920–1975, with the share of the top 1% falling from 50% in 1920 to 21% in 1975, and the share of the top 10% declining from 91 to 60%. However, these data refer to the wealth valuations declared in the tax returns, rather than true market values. Converting the data for the period 1920–1975 to the market value basis used since 1975 produces the long-term trend in the share of the top 1 % shown in Figure 1 below. It is evident that wealth inequality in Sweden has declined significantly over the last century, with the rise after 1984 only restoring inequality to about its level in 1970.

It is interesting to note that the 31 point drop in the share of the top 10% in Sweden between 1920 and 1975 is almost all accounted for by the 29 point decline in the share of the top 1%; indeed, over the full 55 year period, the share of those just below the top of the wealth distribution either remained constant or actually increased. The tendency for long run changes in wealth inequality in this century to be due almost entirely to a reduction in the share at the very top of the distribution is echoed in the estate-based figures for the UK (see Section 3.3 below), and was noted by Atkinson and Harrison (1978: chap. 6).

Table 1 summarises the evidence on household wealth inequality for a range of countries with survey or wealth tax data. To assist comparability across countries, the mid 1980s was chosen as the target time frame. Inequality appears to be lowest in Australia, Italy, Korea, Ireland, Japan and Sweden, with Gini values of 0.5–0.6 and shares of the top 1% of 20% or less. It has an intermediate value in Canada, Denmark, France, and Germany, where the share of the top 1% ranges up to 26%, and appears greatest in the US, where the Gini value is about 0.8 and the share of the top 1% of families exceeds 30%. Due to differences in definitions and procedures across countries, this ranking is necessarily rough. However, some confidence in the ranking is warranted, since it is broadly consistent with the careful assessments of international differences offered by a

Table 1

Selected survey and wealth tax data on the distribution of wealth across households

			Percentage wealth share of top *x* percent of households			Gini value	
			1	5	10		
USA	1983	(a)	35	56	–	0.79	Net worth
USA	1983	(a)	33	55	–	0.78	Adjusted net worth
France	1986	(b)	26	43	–	0.71	Gross assets
Denmark	1975	(c)	25	48	65	–	Net worth
Germany	1983	(d1)	23	–	–	–	Net worth
Germany	1988	(d2)	–	–	–	0.69	Net worth
Canada	1984	(e)	17	38	51	0.69	Net worth
Canada	1984	(e)	24	43			Adjusted net worth
Australia	1986	(f1)	20	41	55	–	Net worth
Australia	1986	(f2)	13	32	46	–	Net worth
Italy	1987	(g)	13	32	45	0.60	Net worth
Korea	1988	(h)	14	31	43	0.58	Net worth
Korea	1988	(h)	19	36	48	–	Adjusted net worth
Ireland	1987	(i)	10	29	43	–	Net worth
Japan	1984	(j)	–	25	–	0.52	Net worth
Sweden	1985	(k1)	16	37	53	–	Adjusted net worth
Sweden	1985	(k2)	11	24	–	0.59	Adjusted net worth

Note: "adjusted net worth" is net worth aligned to balance sheet totals.
Sources: (a) Wolff and Marley (1989). (b) Kessler and Wolff (1991). (c) Spånt (1982), using wealth tax records.
(d1) Börsch-Supan (1994). (d2) Burkhauser et al (1997). (e) Davies (1993). The figures for adjusted net worth
are the midpoint of the estimated range. (f1) Dilnot (1990). (f2) Baekgaard (1997). The Dilnot and Baekgaard
figures include imputations based on the investment multiplier method. (g) Brandolini et al. (1994). Figures
are partially adjusted, but not aligned to balance sheet totals. (h) Leipziger et al. (1992). (i) Nolan (1991).
(j) Takayama (1992). (k1) Lindh and Ohlsson (1998), using wealth tax records. (k2) Bager-Sjögren and
Klevmarken (1996), using HUS data.

number of other researchers, including Harrison (1979), Kessler and Wolff (1991), and
Wolff (1996).

3.3. Estate multiplier estimates

Estate tax records provide information similar to that recorded in wealth surveys, but the
data refer to individuals rather than households, and to an unusual population: decedents
sufficiently wealthy to pay (or to be assessed for) estate tax. Those who die comprise
a nonrandom sample of the population. Most obviously, their age distribution differs
from that of the general population. If mortality rates depended on gender and age
alone, this problem could be overcome by re-weighting the sample by the reciprocal
of the corresponding age-gender mortality rate (the "mortality multiplier"), so that, for

example, one decedent from a group with a 5% mortality risk is deemed to have been drawn from a sample of 20 similarly endowed living individuals. However, evidence on death rates by occupation and income suggests that mortality is higher for less wealthy individuals, substantially so at older ages. This means that the less wealthy are over-sampled in the estate tax records of any particular age group, and that different mortality multipliers need to be applied at different wealth levels. Atkinson and Harrison (1978: chap. 3) discuss in detail the construction and application of mortality multipliers, and investigate the theoretical impact of using multipliers graduated according to wealth level.

A related problem arises because those who die are more likely to have been in poor health prior to death. They may have been unable to work, or incurred larger than average expenditures for health and nursing care, or been more aware of the need to mitigate the impact of estate taxes. For all these reasons, the wealth of decedents may be lower than living persons with similar personal characteristics and life histories. However, it is difficult to assess the impact of this effect.

There are also a number of reasons why the estate tax records may be incomplete, and the reported values inaccurate. Those with estates below the tax threshold may not be required to file a tax return, and information on such individuals may be omitted entirely from the data. This is known as the problem of "missing persons". The problem of "missing wealth" is principally due to tax concessions which cause certain types of property to be omitted from the reported valuations. Well-known examples are property settled on a surviving spouse (with no power to dispose of the capital) and discretionary trusts. Interestingly, for at least one asset category—life insurance—"missing wealth" can be negative. The valuation of life insurance policies in the estates of decedents corresponds to the amounts assured, which typically exceeds—sometimes by a large margin when young—the value of the same policies in the hands of the living. If no adjustments are made, this factor will tend to inflate the estate-based estimates of the relative wealth of smaller (and younger) wealth-holders (Shorrocks, 1981). As with survey data on wealth, independent balance sheet figures have been used routinely to assess the magnitude of the problems associated with missing persons and missing wealth: see in particular the detailed study by Revell (1967).

Considerable effort has been spent attempting to overcome these problems in order to produce reliable estimates of wealth distribution, one major attraction being the long period of time over which quality data are often available. Much of the early pioneering work in the field was carried out in Britain and the US, where wealth distribution figures have been provided intermittently over a long period of time (see, for example, the reviews of Atkinson and Harrison, 1978; Lampman, 1962). More recently, researchers have been able to build upon this earlier work to produce a consistent series of wealth concentration figures for most of the twentieth century. In Britain this series is continued on a broadly comparable basis in the annual "Series C" estimates by the Inland Revenue,

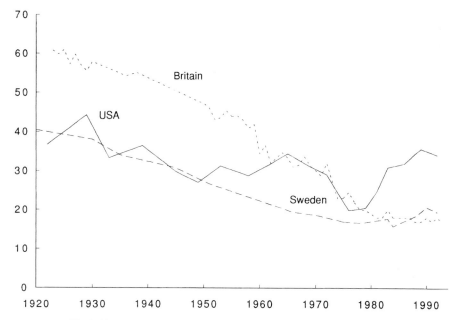

Fig. 1. Shares of net worth held by the top 1% of wealth-holders: 1920–1993.

which incorporate several additional refinements, most notably adjustments to reconcile the raw data with personal sector balance sheets.[31]

Atkinson and Harrison (1978) and Atkinson et al. (1989) report estimates of wealth concentration in England and Wales for the period 1923–1981. These show a pronounced downward trend in inequality, with the share of the top 1% declining, on average, by 0.7 percentage points per year (see Fig. 1).[32] The share of the top 1% of individuals in 1923 was 61%; by 1981 it had fallen to just 23%. Subsequent Inland Revenue "Series C" estimates for the UK suggest that wealth inequality in Britain has been relatively stable since 1980, with the shares of the top 1, 5, and 10% of wealth-holders averaging 18, 36 and 49%, respectively.[33]

---

[31] A summary of the results of the reconciliation exercise is published annually in *Inland Revenue Statistics*.

[32] The data series for the US refers to households and is taken from Table 1 of Wolff (1996). Data for Sweden are reported by Lindh and Olhsson (1998). The taxable wealth figures for the period 1920–1975 have been proportionately scaled to match the market value figures in 1975. Data for Britain refer to England and Wales during 1922–1938, to Great Britain for 1938–1977, and to the UK from 1977 onwards: see Atkinson et al. (1989), Good (1991) and Inland Revenue (1996).

[33] Major changes to the estimation procedure were implemented in 1989, leading to revised estimates for the period 1976–1988. The net effect was to reduce the share of the top 1% by 2–3 points, and the share of the top 10% by 3–6 points, except for 1976 where the share of the top 10% was revised downwards from 60 to 50%. See Good (1991) for a detailed discussion of these changes.

The Inland Revenue also publish two additional series of figures on wealth concentration. "Series D" broadens the concept of wealth to include the capitalized value of private (mainly employment-related) pension rights, while "Series E" extends the coverage to state pension rights. As expected, pension rights are distributed more equally than marketable wealth, so the net effect is a significant reduction in the estimates of the top wealth shares. Figures for recent years suggest that the share of the top 1% of wealth-holders is reduced from about 18 to 14% when private pension rights are included, and to about 11% when entitlements to state pensions are also added.

For the US, Wolff and Marley (1989) revise the earlier estimates of Lampman (1962) for the period 1922–1953, and those of Smith and Franklin (1974) and Smith (1984, 1987) for the period 1958-1976. Applying the narrow definition of wealth used by earlier authors, Wolff and Marley show that the share of the top 1% of individuals fell from 37% in 1922 to 17% in 1976, an average annual rate of decline of 0.36%—roughly half the rate of decline observed in UK. According to these estate multiplier estimates, by the 1970s the concentration of wealth in Britain and the United States was strikingly similar. The most rapid period of decline in the US was from 1939 to 1949; inequality increased a little from 1949 to 1972, and then fell sharply between 1972 and 1976 as a result of a drop in the value of corporate stock. Recent evidence, mostly from surveys, suggests that the period since 1976 has seen an increase in concentration that has taken the share of the top 1% in marketable wealth back to the level observed in the 1930s (see Fig. 1).

Wolff and Marley extend their concept of wealth to include trust funds and the capitalized value of pension rights. These modifications do not greatly affect the overall change in inequality from 1922 to 1976, but they do produce a hump in the mid 1960s (Wolff and Marley, 1989: Fig. 15.3, p. 787). Going further, and adding in an estimate of social security wealth, reduces the share of the top 1% in 1976 to just 14%, and almost eliminates the increase in inequality recorded previously for the period from 1949 through to the late 1960s. Adopting an augmented wealth concept also attenuates the increase in wealth inequality observed in recent years. When state and occupational pension rights are included, the share of the top 1% of households in 1989 is estimated to be 21%, exactly the same as the figure in 1969 (Wolff, 1995: p. 79).

The estate multiplier technique has also been applied in a number of other countries. Piggott (1984) reviews the evidence for Australia, which includes figures for wealth inequality in Victoria from 1860 to 1974 reported by Rubinstein (1979), and estimates of the top wealth shares for Australia as a whole for the period 1967–1977 by Gunton (1975) and Raskall (1977, 1978). Calculations for New Zealand for the period between 1893 and 1939 are given by Galt (1995), and for 1966 by Easton (1981). Lyons (1972, 1975), Chesher and McMahon (1977), and Chesher (1979) produce estimates for Ireland in 1966, and figures for France in 1977 are given by Fouquet and Strauss-Kahn (1984).

Table 2 summarises the most recent data on wealth concentration obtained from careful analysis of information on estates. Comparability across countries is handicapped by different wealth concepts, estimation procedures and time periods. However, the broad conclusions of the studies cited above are that the distribution of wealth in New Zealand

Table 2

Estate multiplier estimates of the distribution of wealth across adult individuals

			Percentage wealth share of top *x* percent of individuals			Gini value	
			1	5	10		
Marketable wealth							
UK	1966	(a)	33	56	69	0.81	Adjusted net worth
UK	1976	(a)	24	45	60	0.76	Adjusted net worth
UK	1985	(a)	18	36	49	0.65	Adjusted net worth
UK	1993	(a)	17	36	48	0.65	Adjusted net worth
US	1965	(b)	34	–	–	–	Adjusted net worth
US	1976	(b)	19	–	–	–	Adjusted net worth
US	1981	(b)	30	–	–	–	Adjusted net worth
New Zealand	1966	(c)	18	45	60	–	Net worth
Australia	1967–1972	(d)	22	45	58	–	Net worth
Ireland	1966	(e)	30	57	–	–	Net worth
France	1977	(f)	19	47	65	0.81	Net worth
Augmented wealth (including pension rights and social security entitlements)							
UK	1976	(a)	14	27	37	0.46–0.53	Adjusted net worth
UK	1985	(a)	11	25	36	0.48	Adjusted net worth
UK	1993	(a)	10	23	34	0.48	Adjusted net worth
US	1976	(b)	13	–	–	–2	Adjusted net worth
US	1981	(b)	20	–	–	–	Adjusted net worth

Note: "adjusted net worth" is net worth aligned to balance sheet totals.
Sources: (a) Inland Revenue (1987, 1996), Series C and E. (b) Wolff and Marley (1989). (c) Easton (1981). (d) Raskall (1977, 1978). (e) Chesher and McMahon (1977). (f) Fouquet and Strauss-Kahn (1984).

and Australia has been more equal than that in either the US or UK throughout the twentieth century; that the degree of concentration in Ireland in the mid 1960s was similar to that in UK; that wealth concentration is lower in France than in UK or the US; and that wealth inequality in the US has recently overtaken that in the UK. These findings tally with the evidence from sample surveys, and are consistent with the conclusions drawn in the previous international comparisons undertaken by Harrison (1979) and Wolff (1996).[34]

---

[34] Measured wealth inequality will decrease if all adults are paired up into family couples whose wealth-holdings are not perfectly correlated. For this reason, the distribution of wealth across households is expected to be more equal than the distribution across adult individuals (see Royal Commision, 1975: pp. 95–96). However, comparison between the figures in Tables 1 and 2 for the US, France, Australia and Ireland provide little, if any, support for this prediction, except possibly for Ireland.

3.4. The investment income method

The fourth way of estimating the distribution of some types of assets is the investment income method, also known as the income capitalization method. As pointed out by Giffen (1913), if data are available on investment incomes, say from income tax records, then the corresponding asset values can be estimated by dividing the investment income figures by the appropriate rate of return. For some assets, such as savings accounts and government bonds, the rate of return can be measured with some degree of accuracy, and is also fairly uniform across wealth-holders. In other cases, however, for example corporate shares or real estate, rates of return vary considerably across investors, and perhaps between wealth ranges, reducing the reliability of the investment income method.

The investment income procedure has been applied in a number of countries. Atkinson and Harrison (1978) carefully examine its usefulness in the British context, and conclude that, although the results are less reliable than those of the estate multiplier approach, they provide a valuable check on the latter. Before World War II the method was quite popular in the US, as discussed by Harrison (1979: pp. 18–20). Walravens and Praet (1978) provided the first wealth inequality estimates for Belgium using this method, finding shares of the top 1, 5, and 10% in 1969 equal to 28, 47, and 57%, respectively. As noted earlier, Dilnot (1990) used the procedure to impute nonhousing wealth to the Australian 1986 Income Distribution Survey (IDS) data. His results indicate less wealth inequality than found for the 1967–1977 period by the estate multiplier method (see Piggott, 1984).

The sensitivity of wealth distribution estimates to differences in assumptions and procedures is illustrated by the revised figures for Australian wealth inequality obtained in the study by Baekgaard (1997). Like Dilnot, Baekgaard presents estimates based on the 1986 IDS. He adds business assets and superannuation (pension rights) to the assets considered by Dilnot, makes use of new estimates of balance sheet aggregates, and divides some assets into finer categories before applying the investment income multipliers. The result is a significantly lower level of concentration than that estimated by Dilnot. The share of the top 1%, for example, falls from 20% to 13% (excluding pensions). Baekgaard applies similar techniques to the 1993–1994 Household Expenditure Survey (HES), and finds shares of the top 1, 5, and 10% of 14, 32, and 46%, omitting pensions. Including pensions reduces these shares to 12, 29, and 43% respectively.

3.5. Direct wealth estimates for named persons

The final method of estimating wealth-holdings uses publicly available information on ownership of real estate, corporate equity, art treasures and other valuable items to assess the wealth of the very richest individuals and families. In the US for many years, *Forbes Magazine* and *Fortune* have conducted such an exercise in order to provide lists of the very wealthy, and to comment on the way that fortunes are made and dissipated. A similar exercise for residents of the UK has been carried out annually since 1989 by *The Sunday Times* (see Beresford, 1990).

This type of data presents special difficulties: the assets covered in the estimates are restricted to those most easily identified in public records; the asset valuations involve a considerable degree of guesswork; and the criteria used to decide which people should be included are somewhat arbitrary. Individuals can enter and exit the lists depending on the country chosen as their principal residence, or on whether their holdings are combined with those of related family groups outside their immediate family.

The Sunday Times data (available on the internet) illustrate these problems. The Queen of England was ranked in first or second place in the UK during each of the years 1989–1994, but then vanished from the top 10 wealth-holders when the royal art collection was excluded from her personal wealth. In 1998 she ranked equal 94th. Other individuals seem to have experienced spectacular year-on-year changes in their fortunes, mainly as a result of revaluing their holdings in private companies. The appearance of Robert Maxwell, the publisher, in the 1991 list of the top 10 wealth-holders in Britain, just months before events following his death revealed massive debts, is testimony to the difficulty of accurately estimating the wealth of named individuals.

While information obtained in this way is clearly limited in its population coverage, it is potentially a useful supplement to the standard sources of data, which invariably fail to capture the very top end of the wealth distribution. *The Sunday Times* figures, for instance, suggest a rapid rise in the wealth of the top 100 families during the decade to 1998, a trend not yet reflected in the UK estate data. The fact that the data form, in effect, an annual panel, and that the personal details of the individuals concerned are often well known, also offers opportunities to study wealth mobility from year to year, and the degree to which high wealth status is transmitted between generations. For instance, *The Sunday Times* of April 19th 1998 claims that 31% of the top wealth-holders in Britain inherited their wealth, compared to 57% a decade earlier. Whether this claim bears close scrutiny, and whether the finding has wider implications for wealth inequality in the UK, remains to be seen: academic researchers have been slow to exploit the potential of evidence on the wealth of named individuals.[35]

3.6. Portfolio composition

In addition to reporting estimates of overall wealth inequality, many studies have reported evidence on the concentration of holdings of specific types of assets, and on the way that asset portfolios vary by age, gender and wealth level. There are several reasons why this disaggregated evidence might be important. First, while certain assets like cash simply represent stores of potential consumption, others convey additional advantages. Private homes and extensive land holdings, for instance, often generate a sense of attachment and pride that goes beyond the satisfaction of owning a valuable

---

[35] This kind of data has not been neglected entirely. Piggott (1984) mentions evidence on Australia's wealthiest "One Hundred" reported in *Business Review Weekly*, Leipziger et al. (1992) provides estimates of the wealth of the top shareholders in Korea; and Davies (1993) uses data on named individuals to produce the revised estimates of the top wealth shares in Canada shown here in Table 1.

asset. Similarly, direct equity holdings in stock market companies, and especially in private businesses with a small number of stock-holders, carry with them some degree of control over the lives of those associated with the firms, and hence some degree of social status not associated with bank balances, or indirect holdings in mutual funds. Information on the concentration of share-ownership in individual companies, and in all companies viewed collectively, is therefore likely to be relevant in assessing the type of society in which people live.

The second reason for interest in portfolio patterns is that observed differences across individuals are a potentially valuable source of information on household behaviour and personal preferences, for example with regard to risk.[36] Furthermore, the rates of return on different types of assets have often diverged quite markedly over long periods of time. So, to the extent that individuals continue to hold the same physical assets and the same financial securities over time, portfolio data and asset price series can help account for changes in the distribution of the value of wealth-holdings.

Using UK estate data for 17 types of assets and debts, Shorrocks (1982) examines the way that age, gender and wealth level influence the composition of individual portfolios. Although gender differences were statistically significant, the age and wealth pattern was found to be qualitatively similar, and suggested that the 17 asset/debt components cluster naturally into five broad categories: (i) Cash and savings accounts, which increase with age as a percentage of total assets, but decrease with wealth level; (ii) Bonds and stock market equity, whose portfolio proportion increases with both wealth and age; (iii) Assets and debts associated with private businesses, which decline with age and increase with wealth; (iv) Illiquid personal assets, such as life insurance policies and household goods, whose share declines with age but shows little variation with wealth; and (v) Property assets and debts, whose share falls with age and has an inverse U-shape relationship with wealth.

The tendency for the portfolio share of corporate equity to increase with wealth, and for housing to be most important for the middle classes, is echoed in many other empirical studies: see, for example, Projector and Weiss (1966) and Wolff (1994) for data on the US; Beach et al (1981: Table 88) for Canada; and Nolan (1991: Table 9.3) for Ireland. The implications for the impact of asset price changes on wealth distribution are clear. A rise in equity prices will disproportionately benefit the higher wealth groups, and hence increase wealth inequality. In contrast, the impact of a uniform rise in property values on wealth concentration is ambiguous, since it increases the relative wealth of those in the middle of the distribution, reducing the gap with those at the top while simultaneously widening the differential over those at the bottom.

Simple theoretical models of portfolio behaviour tend to predict that individuals will hold nonzero quantities of all assets in their portfolio, but this is patently not true in practice. For example, King and Dicks-Mireaux (1982) report that only 18% of a sample

---

[36] Arrondel et al. (1994) suggest that portfolio composition can help to identify bequest intentions: households with bequest motives will tend to hold less liquid assets and more real assets then households owning assets for precautionary purposes.

of Canadian households held more than 6 of the 12 identified types of assets, and less than 1% held more than 9.[37] The composition of portfolios by value therefore depends to a large extent on the number and type of assets in which individuals choose to invest. King and Leape (1984) comment on the overall lack of diversification observed in a sample of wealthy Americans, over half of whom owned no corporate equity. They also draw attention to the pronounced age effect on the average number of assets held, which exhibits a classic hump-profile over the lifetime, peaking in the age range 40–60 and then declining significantly in retirement years.

Detailed investigation of individual portfolio behaviour poses many difficult econometric problems. Some progress is evident in the studies by Dicks-Mireaux and King (1984), Leape (1987), and King and Leape (1998), as well as recent work by Halliassos and Bertaut (1995), Blake (1996), Hochguertal and van Soest (1996), Hochguertel et al. (1997), Poterba and Samwick (1997), and Attanasio et al. (1998). Other studies, including Feldstein (1976a) and King and Leape (1986), have looked at the impact of taxation on the choice of portfolio. However, the implications of this work for the level and distribution of wealth-holdings remain largely unexplored.

3.7. *Explaining national differences and changes over time*

Wealth distribution figures for different countries, or different years, inevitably prompt speculation about the causes of the observed differences. Variations in wealth inequality across countries are often seen as resulting from different social traditions, general economic environments (including tax regimes and the incentives for entrepreneurial activity), and the relative importance of inheritance vis-à-vis life-cycle accumulation. For example, the incidence of owner-occupied housing differs considerably across countries. Until quite recently, one explanation offered for the high concentration in wealth in Britain was the large stock of public housing. Kessler and Wolff (1991) account for the lower concentration of wealth in France compared to the US partly in terms of the lesser importance of corporate share ownership in France, which is due to the greater share of productive capital in the hands of the public sector. As regards the impact of inheritance, faster growing economies are likely to have a higher share of aggregate wealth associated with lifetime accumulation and are therefore expected to show less wealth inequality. The greater egalitarianism of bequest practices in North America and Australia compared to Britain or Europe has also been seen in the past as a contributory factor. While some aristocratic families in Britain continue to practice primogeniture to this day, equal division of estates is the general rule in North America and Australia, even for wealthy families.

---

[37] Sample surveys often reveal a surprisingly large number of households who claim to have little or no financial wealth of any kind. For example, 40% of a Korean sample fit into this category (Leipziger et al., 1992: p. 35). The corresponding proportion in the UK varied between 27 and 50% over the period 1973–1993 (Banks and Tanner, 1996: Table 9).

Several explanations have been proposed for variations in wealth concentration over time, in particular the downward trend in wealth inequality observed over the past century.[38] The fact that most of the reduction in inequality has been due to the fall in the share of the top 1% suggests that estate and inheritance taxes could be influential. Wealth taxes have never raised significant amounts of revenue compared to other sources of government income, but they may have had an indirect effect by encouraging the spread of wealth ownership (or *nominal* wealth ownership) within the wealthiest families. For this reason, inequality in the distribution of wealth across families may not have declined to the same degree as across individuals. High rates of estate taxation have also led to the routine use of tax shelters, such as family trusts, by high wealth families. The growth of tax avoidance measures suggests that current estimates of wealth concentration may not be directly comparable with estimates produced for earlier years in this century, and that some of the observed downward trend may be attributable to this (spurious) factor.

Another likely explanation for the downward trend in wealth inequality is the growth in savings for lifecycle purposes, accumulated in the form of real estate as well as financial assets. In Britain, for instance, there has been a marked spread of "popular assets", such as owner-occupied homes, consumer durables and, more recently, private pension fund assets, among middle and lower income households. This factor can be viewed as changing the wealth distribution via a net increase in the quantity of assets held by households. Changes in the wealth values can also result from changes in asset prices, and this will affect overall wealth inequality if the composition of individual portfolios varies systematically with wealth level, as the empirical evidence indicates. Asset price movements therefore offer a further explanation of changes in wealth concentration, particularly during stock market or housing booms or slumps. As already noted, a rise in stock market values is expected to increase wealth inequality, while a rise in house prices is likely to have a more ambiguous impact, reducing the wealth shares at both ends of the distribution.

The quantitative significance of the possible causes of changes in wealth inequality over time has been examined in most detail for Britain—by Harrison (1976), Atkinson and Harrison (1982), Harbury and Hitchens (1983), and Atkinson et al. (1989), all of whom use regression techniques. These studies show that a time trend explains much of the decline in shares of top groups in Britain, perhaps reflecting the underlying trends in lifecycle saving and inheritance practices discussed above. However, all of these studies also find that asset prices have a significant effect on the shares of the top wealth-holders. For example, Atkinson et al. (1989) decompose the substantial reduction from 31 to 21% in the share of the top 1% of individuals between 1972 to 1981. They find that the rise of share prices over this period boosted the top share by 5 percentage points. Acting in the opposite direction were a 2 point reduction due to the time trend and a 12 point decline due to the spread of popular assets. Atkinson and Harrison (1982) and Harbury

---

[38] See Chapter 3 of the Handbook for a discussion of trends in wealth inequality in Britain and the US over a longer period.

and Hitchens (1983) also report a regression, omitting the time trend, in which the rate of estate taxation proves to be highly significant (along with share prices). Inclusion of a time trend, however, robs the estate tax rate of its significance. While it is difficult to distinguish the effect of estate taxation from other secular factors reflected in the time trend, progressive estate and income taxation remains a plausible explanation for some of the decline in wealth inequality experienced in twentieth century Britain.

A different methodology was used by the Royal Commission on the Distribution of Income and Wealth (1979) to examine the change in UK wealth inequality from 1960 to 1972. They looked at each asset and debt component of the top wealth groups, decomposing the change in value into a price and quantity effect. In the period 1960–1972, the effects of a rise in house prices and in ordinary share values roughly cancel out, so asset price changes had little overall impact on wealth inequality. The 6 percentage point reduction in the share of the top 1% of wealth-holders was therefore attributed to lower than average growth in the quantities of assets held, in particular the quantity of life policies (which were commonly tied to mortgages, and used on maturity to repay housing loans). In contrast, almost all of the 1972–1976 reduction in top wealth shares was due to price effects resulting from a steep rise in house prices and a slump in the stock market.

Spant (1987) examines the influence of asset price changes on wealth inequality in Sweden between 1975 and 1983, a period during which real share prices rose considerably, but house prices declined. Overall, Spant estimates that price changes accounted for a 20% increase in wealth for the wealthiest 0.2% of Swedish households. In his view, this was the principal reason for the rise in the share of the top 1% of households from 17 to 20%.

Another episode during which changes in asset prices had a major impact on wealth distribution was the real estate and stock market boom of the late 1980s in Japan. In this case the price changes all contributed to an increase in inequality, and their impact was large. Using his 1984 data, Takayama (1991) simulated the effects up to 1987 and projected a rise in the Gini coefficient from 0.53 to 0.68.

The situation during the 1980s in the US appears more mixed. Weicher (1995: pp. 14–15) shows that the increase in the prices of stocks, bonds, investment real estate, and unincorporated businesses tended to raise the Gini coefficient for wealth by 0.03 between 1983 and 1989. However, over the same period there was a decline in the value of owner-occupied housing and farms, which exerted a slightly stronger, downward influence on inequality. Taken together, therefore, price changes would indicate a slight *decline* in the Gini coefficient over this period, although, as discussed earlier, the Gini value actually rose. Wolff (1992) uses a different, regression-based approach which suggests that growing income inequality and an increase in stock prices relative to house values contributed about equally to the rise in wealth inequality during the 1980s.

The overall conclusion is that long term factors such as lifetime accumulation behaviour, the cumulative impact of tax policies, and changing bequest practices appear to have important effects on the evolution of wealth inequality. However, the impact of the individual factors is difficult to identify within the general downward time trend, and further research will be required in order to assess with precision the significance of the individual contributions. Over shorter periods it is evident that asset price changes can cause sizeable deviations from trend.

4. Applied work on the determinants of wealth distribution

This section reviews further applied research that has improved our understanding of the factors which combine to explain the distribution of wealth. A range of techniques have been used in this work, including wealth-accounting or decomposition methods, simulation exercises, and conventional econometrics. We look in turn at four categories of contributions: (i) micro simulations of wealth accumulation and inheritance; (ii) empirical work on intergenerational wealth mobility; (iii) assessments of the aggregate significance of lifecycle saving and inherited wealth; and (iv) empirical research on the determinants of bequests. Overall, (i)–(iii) agree in assigning an important role to inheritance in determining the distribution of wealth, particularly its long upper tail. This makes clear the relevance of the research reviewed under category (iv).

4.1. Simulation studies

All versions of the lifecycle saving model predict that wealth will vary with age. If these age-related differences are quantitatively important, then a substantial portion of observed wealth inequality may be due to the fact that people are sampled at different points of their lifetimes. In an extreme scenario in which wealth depended only on age, differences in wealth-holdings would not represent differences in lifetime opportunities, and would be a purely demographic phenomenon, of no more interest or concern for public policy than differences in age.

To determine whether this is a plausible approximation to the real world, a number of authors have examined the distributions that would be observed in simple egalitarian societies where all wealth differences are due to age. Atkinson (1971), for example, considers a society in which everyone works for 40 years, retires for 10 years, and then dies. In a benchmark case, population and earnings both grow at a constant rate of 2% per annum, desired consumption grows at 3%, and the real interest rate is 4.5%. Under these assumptions, the shares of the top 1, 5, and 10% of wealth-holders would be 2, 10, and 20% respectively. In contrast, Atkinson estimated the actual shares of wealth (including state pensions) in Britain at the time to be 22, 41, and 52%.[39] Uniform inheritances received by all at age 50 and passed on unchanged at death, and an allowance for "propertyless women" raise the top shares to 3, 17, and 33% respectively, still far

---

[39] These figures are very close to the "Series E" estimates for the UK in 1971 (see Inland Revenue, 1987), but much higher than the Inland Revenue estimates for 1976 onwards (see Table 2 in Section 3). The share of the top centile in 1993, for example, is estimated to be only 10%.

short of the estimated actual shares. Atkinson went on to establish that wealth inequality within age groups is similar to wealth inequality across the whole population, before concluding that "lifecycle factors are not a major explanation of the observed inequality of wealth-holding in Britain".

Subsequent studies along similar lines examine more elaborate examples of pure lifecycle societies where other influences (apart from inheritance) are modelled. Oulton (1976) includes differences in earnings and rates of return, and derives expressions for the coefficient of variation (CV) and the variance of log wealth. He found that age and earnings differences together produce a CV equal to about 10% of the actual figures. Davies and Shorrocks (1978) extended Oulton's analysis to other inequality measures and used an alternative estimate of actual wealth inequality. Age and earnings differences were found to account for 60 or 82% of actual wealth inequality as measured by the Gini coefficient or variance of logarithms, and from 45 to 89% of wealth inequality using Atkinson's index with a range of parameter values. In their egalitarian society, the shares of the top 1, 5, and 10% of wealth-holders are 6, 17, and 27%, respectively. These figures can be raised to about 9, 28, and 45% by allowing uniform inheritance and propertyless women as in Atkinson (1971).[40]

Flemming (1976) also introduces unequal earnings into Atkinson's simple model, finding that the results can account reasonably well for the shape of the wealth distribution except in the upper tail. Interestingly, his top shares—5.5 and 16.5% for the top 1 and 5%—are almost exactly those obtained by Davies and Shorrocks (1978) using the Oulton model. This suggests that the differences between Oulton (1976) and Flemming (1976) are in large part a matter of how inequality is measured, and how the results are interpreted.

A similar exercise was performed for Canada by Wolfson (1977). In addition to differences in age, earnings, and savings propensities, his model includes unequal rates of return and a demographic sub-model determining family formation, divorce, remarriage, and mortality over the lifecycle of the cohort. Together, these factors appear to explain much of the observed wealth inequality, but not the concentration found in the extreme upper tail. Wolfson's base run, for example, yields a Gini coefficient exceeding the estimated actual value, but the share of the top centile is only 11%, compared to an estimated actual figure of 20% from the 1970 Canadian SCF.

The general inability of pure egalitarian models to reproduce the extreme upper tail of wealth-holdings suggests the need to add a realistic distribution of bequests. Flemming (1979) examined the possible consequences of inheritance through illustrative calculations which suggested an important role for both accidental and voluntary bequests. Wolfson (1977, 1979) and Davies (1982) construct full simulation models to explore these issues. Beginning in 1970, Wolfson simulates the process of bequest over the next 30 years by modelling the mortality of all cohorts, and dividing the wealth of

---

[40] It is interesting to note that the predicted share of the top 10% of wealth-holders in this version of an egalitarian society is actually above the recent Series E estimates by the Inland Revenue, which have ranged from 33–36% over the period 1979–1993 (Inland Revenue, 1996).

decedents among their heirs.[41] Under various assumptions, the distribution of wealth predicted for the year 2000 was found to be very similar to that observed in 1970. If, instead, inheritances were outlawed, by the year 2000 the shares of the top 1 and 5% would fall from 20 and 41% to 14 and 36% respectively. Thus Wolfson's work attributes considerable wealth inequality to lifecycle factors, but also leaves substantial room for the role of inheritance.

Davies (1982) assumes that parental preferences depend on the expected lifetime incomes of children as well as on their own consumption and the number of children. Inheritances are derived for an initial generation by applying assumptions about mortality rates, estate division and other factors to an adjusted version of Statistics Canada's 1970 SCF wealth distribution. Parameter values were chosen to ensure that the predicted distribution of wealth among the living was similar to the observed Canadian distribution. The role of lifecycle factors was then assessed by running the model with its benchmark parameter values, but setting inheritances to zero. This exercise produced predictions of 9, 30, and 46%, respectively, for the shares of the top 1, 5, and 10%, compared to the actual figures for Canada of 20, 43, and 58%. In the absence of inheritances, a simulated Gini coefficient of 0.66 is obtained, compared to the estimated actual value of 0.75. The results of other simulation exercises suggested that the effect of earnings differences in Canada was somewhat less than in Britain in the 1970s, and was roughly the same magnitude as the impact of unequal rates of return or age differences. Finally, allowing a small variation across families in the rate of time preference had a strong impact on the degree of simulated wealth inequality.[42]

As mentioned in Section 2, enhanced versions of the LCM have become popular vehicles for explaining observed patterns of consumption, saving, and wealth-holding. Laitner (1992) investigates a steady state model incorporating both lifecycle saving and altruistic bequests with liquidity constraints. He finds realistic wealth-income ratios and a high incidence of gifts inter vivos. Hubbard et al. (1994, 1995) and Huggett (1996) both model uncertain earnings and uncertain lifetime with imperfect annuity markets, and find that it is possible to achieve realistic overall saving rates in this way—that is, without including an explicit bequest motive.[43] Huggett (1996) explores the implications for the overall distribution of wealth, as well as for the age-wealth profiles and wealth

---

[41] An alternative approach was used by Blinder (1974), who used survey data collected by the Survey Research Center of the University of Michigan in 1960 to set up a distribution of inherited wealth. (Blinder did not report the results of his lifecycle simulation for the distribution of wealth, focusing instead on the distribution of lifetime income.) While the 1960 SRC data, and later survey data (see, e.g., Barlow et al., 1966) indicate a highly unequal distribution of inheritances, they are subject to problems of differential response and under-reporting.

[42] The recent simulation study by Fuster (1997) incorporates both inheritances and lifecycle saving, and analyses the effect of social security on wealth distribution.

[43] Gokhale et al. (1998) have explored a model with uncertain lifetime but certain earnings, in which the distribution of accidental bequests among heirs is modelled. Preliminary results indicate that considerable wealth inequality can be created by such a bequest process.

inequality within age groups.[44] His simulation generates an overall Gini coefficient close to that estimated by Wolff (1987b) on the basis of the 1983 SCF, but the simulated Gini coefficient values within age groups are less than the true figures, and the share of wealth held by the top centile is only about half the estimated actual figure. These deficiencies again suggest the need to pay further attention to modelling bequests. Huggett recognises the value of exploring the implications of "deeper models of the family", but also recommends modelling entrepreneurship.[45]

While all this work is of interest, there are several reasons why it falls short of conclusively establishing the quantitative impact of lifecycle factors on wealth inequality. First, little can be deduced from models that omit bequests and inheritances from consideration. Even if a model of a pure egalitarian society is capable of exactly replicating the wealth distribution observed in practice, this would have to be set against the fact that a pure inegalitarian society—with wealth determined entirely by inheritance—is also capable of generating the observed wealth distribution. The models which include both lifecycle saving and inheritance, and which succeed in reproducing the observed wealth distribution, address this problem. But it seems likely that more than one such model will be capable of achieving this objective, so there is an identification problem that can only be resolved by appealing to other evidence on wealth-holding. At the present time, there is no consensus on what that other evidence should be.

A further difficulty concerns the allocation of inequality contributions to factors which combine together in complex ways. One commonly used procedure is to compute the marginal impact of each factor, in other words the reduction in inequality that would result from eliminating the factor concerned. But it is very unlikely that these marginal contributions will sum to the observed degree of inequality. In the context of wealth distribution, such calculations could lead to the conclusion that lifecycle factors and inheritance each account for, say, 80% of wealth inequality. If that were the case, the results could well be interpreted as indicating that inheritance was relatively unimportant (because most of the observed wealth inequality can be "explained" by lifecycle factors), or that inheritance was the dominant influence, or that the two sources were equally significant. Whether any of these conclusions are correct remains open to question.

4.2. Intergenerational wealth mobility

As well as investigating the determinants of cross-section wealth inequality, economists have also examined the processes governing wealth mobility. This sometimes refers to

---

[44] In a related exercise, Huggett and Ventura (1998) investigate the determinants of the higher saving rate in the US among higher income households. They find that heterogeneity of preferences or temporary earnings shocks are not necessary to explain the difference in saving rates. The most robust explanation is provided by two factors: age and permanent income differences on the one hand, and the social security system on the other.

[45] Venti and Wise (1998) report on a very recent empirical exercise using US data which raises the possibility of decomposing wealth inequality at retirement into contribution from earnings, inheritances, health shocks, and other lifetime influences.

mobility among members of the same generation over short periods of time (see, for example, Jianakoplos and Menchik, 1997; Bager-Sjögren and Klevmarken, 1996), but more often concerns mobility across successive generations. The topic is partly motivated by an independent interest in mobility as a social phenomenon both positively and normatively distinct from inequality. However, studies of intergenerational wealth mobility are also of interest for the light they shed on the likely importance of inheritance in explaining wealth inequality; it is generally thought that a higher degree of intergenerational wealth mobility indicates a lesser role for inheritance as a determinant of wealth.

Wedgwood (1928, 1929) pioneered a method of studying intergenerational wealth mobility. Taking a sample of 99 estates in 1924–1925 worth at least £200,000, and a further sample of 140 estates in 1926 worth between £10,000 and £200,000, Wedgwood tried to establish the extent to which the wealth of these rich decedents was due to inheritance, by tracing the wills of their parents and other close family relatives. This proved unsuccessful for more than half of the female decedents. Overall, however, he identified predecessors in 169 cases, including 83 of the 99 people with estates over £200,000. Analysis of the subsample of male decedents led him to conclude that:

of the *men* in the upper and middle classes at the present day, about one third owe their fortunes almost entirely to inheritance (including gifts *inter vivos*), another third to a combination of ability and luck with a considerable inheritance of wealth and business opportunity, and the remaining third largely to their own activities. (Wedgwood, 1929: p. 163)

In other words, one-third could be classed as "inheritors", and one third as "self-made". The remaining one-third were in an intermediate category.

Concentrating for the most part on the relationship between the estates of fathers and children, Wedgwood's methods were later refined and reapplied to data from 1956–1957, 1965, and 1973 by Harbury (1962), Harbury and McMahon (1973), and Harbury and Hitchens (1976, 1979). The results largely echo Wedgwood's earlier findings, although there is some evidence of a decline over time in the relative importance of inherited wealth among the top wealth-holders (Harbury and Hitchens, 1979: chap. 3).

Menchik (1979) reports the results of a similar study which used data on residents of Connecticut who left estates worth at least $40,000 when they died in the 1930s and 1940s. However, instead of tracing their predecessors, Menchik looked forwards, tracing the children of the initial decedents who had themselves died by 1976. He managed to identify the estates left by 300 children who died in Connecticut, and found that 75% of them were worth at least $50,000 (in 1967 dollars).

All these wealth mobility studies suffer from the fact that the starting samples of decedents are drawn from the upper tail of the wealth distribution. The degree of relative immobility they display is not necessarily an accurate reflection of the value for the population as a whole. Menchik (1979) tried to correct for the sample selection bias. He found that, while the intergenerational correlation of terminal wealth for his sample was 0.5, correcting for sample selection yielded a coefficient of 0.8. By way of comparison, the best estimates of the intergenerational correlation coefficient for earnings in the US indicate a figure of 0.6 (Solon, 1992; Zimmerman, 1992).

Interest in intergenerational inheritance in the UK has resurfaced in connection with the growth of owner-occupation since the end of the war. House price inflation, particularly during the 1980s, meant that housing equity became the most important component of personal wealth, and prompted speculation about the economic and social consequences when this valuable and widely spread asset was passed on to the next generation. In a major public speech in 1988, Nigel Lawson, the Chancellor of the Exchequer, welcomed the fact that Britain was about to become "a nation of inheritors". Others pointed to the distributional effects of the transfer of housing wealth if those at the lower end of the income and wealth spectrum failed to share in this bonanza (Hamnett, 1991).

Holmans and Frosztega (1994) analyse the long run effects of housing inheritance, and emphasise the significance of the age at which inheritance is received. If only two generations are alive at any given time, inheritances tend to be received early in life. In this case, bequests of housing stock effectively provide the younger generation with a debt-free home. In contrast, the "three-generation model" envisages houses being passed to the middle generation, many of whom will have already acquired significant housing equity. This would be likely to lead to the sale of the property, with consequent effects on the housing and financial asset markets, on debt repayment, and on consumer expenditure.

Results from a specially commissioned UK survey in 1989–1991 suggest that, while there is considerable variation in the age at which inheritances are received, the three-generation model conforms reasonably well with the evidence, which shows 80% of inheritors to be above age 30, an age at which most first-time house buyers have already bought their home. The second generation beneficiaries of past house price inflation will therefore tend to be those with substantial assets of their own, although Holmans and Frosztega claim that the impact on the distribution of wealth will be relatively modest. Their findings may contain lessons for Japan which, until recently at least, shared a similar concern towards the potential adverse distributional consequences for the next generation of past rises in property values.

4.3. The aggregate importance of inherited versus lifecycle wealth

In the 1970s, a number of simulation studies based on the life-cycle model found that the implied aggregate saving rate was substantially less than real-world levels (White, 1978; Darby, 1979). This is sometimes cited as evidence that inherited wealth must be quantitatively important in aggregate terms. However, the results of such simulations can be quite sensitive to assumptions on taste and other parameters, the earnings process, the length of the working and retirement periods, and the treatment of family size effects. As Davies and Shorrocks (1978) point out, very little can be deduced about the quantitative significance of the lifecycle component of saving until (at a minimum) one has first built a complete model capable of replicating the main features of saving and wealth behaviour observed in the real world. Davies (1982), Hubbard et al. (1994, 1995) and Huggett (1996) provide examples of models which pass the latter test, and suggest that substantial amounts of aggregate wealth can be generated from pure life-cycle behaviour.

A separate line of research performs wealth decomposition exercises which measure the impact of inheritance on current wealth by summing either past inheritances or past life-cycle saving. To clarify some of the issues involved—and to highlight an important source of divergent opinions—we recall the accounting identity Eq. (2.6) for the wealth of a family aged t:

$$W_t = \sum_{k=1}^{t}(E_k - C_k + I_k) \prod_{j=k+1}^{t}(1 + r_j), \tag{4.1}$$

which can be rewritten as

$$W_t = \sum_{k=1}^{t} S_k R_k + \sum_{k=1}^{t} I_k R_k, \tag{4.2}$$

where $S_k = E_k - C_k$ denotes savings from earned income at age k, and $R_k = \prod_{j=k+1}^{t}(1 + r_j)$ indicates the returns to investments over a number of years.

Equation (4.2) offers a decomposition of wealth into self-accumulated (or "life-cycle") and inherited components. It is, however, somewhat arbitrary, since it implicitly assumes that all the investment income from inherited wealth is saved, and that all consumption occurs out of earnings. It is equally valid to write (4.1) in the form:

$$W_t = \sum_{k=1}^{t}(E_k - C_k + r_k W_{k-1}) + \sum_{k=1}^{t} I_k, \tag{4.3}$$

and to identify the first term, which cumulates forward all saving out of income, with lifecycle saving, and the second component with inheritance. Assuming positive rates of return to investment, the difference between the two decompositions is seen to lie in the smaller contribution of inheritance in Eq. (4.3) compared to Eq. (4.2).

Equation (4.3) might be thought to yield a lower bound to the contribution of inheritance, since it includes savings from returns on invested inheritances in the "lifecycle" component; but if one goes further, as in the Meade Eq. (2.4), and assumes that some portion of inherited wealth is consumed directly, and that this consumption exceeds the saving from interest on inheritances (i.e., $\beta > 0$ in Eq. (2.4)), then the contribution of inheritance to current wealth would be smaller still. The fact that one can generate different wealth decompositions depending on the way in which lifecycle saving is defined, and the way consumption depends on earnings, investment income, and wealth, illustrates again the need to consider the issue within the framework of a complete model of saving behaviour. The failure to recognise this fact is one of the inherent limitations of pure accounting approaches to the decomposition of wealth into its various contributory influences.

The best known application of the accounting approach is the study by Kotlikoff and Summers (1981), who use Eq. (4.2) to decompose wealth into its lifecycle and inherited components. The present value of inherited wealth in the US was estimated in two different ways. One method sums the amounts received as gifts or bequests by the current generation. This yielded a figure for the present value of inheritances equal to 46% of current household wealth.[46] A second exercise, which they considered more reliable and whose results have been more controversial, cumulates the difference between after-tax labour earnings and consumption expenditure in the US over time, in order to get an independent estimate of aggregate lifecycle wealth. This yielded a figure of 19% of current wealth due to past lifecycle saving. The residual, totalling 81% of current wealth, is attributed to inheritance.

The idea that 81% of current wealth is inherited is firmly dismissed by Modigliani (1988a, 1988b), who argues instead that about 80% is due to lifecycle saving, and only 20% to inheritance.[47] Modigliani (1988a: p. 28) suggests that the 61% point gap between the Kotlikoff and Summers figure and his own estimate can be broken down as follows:

 (i) 14% of wealth is accounted for by the fact that Kotlikoff and Summers treat household expenditure on durable goods as consumption rather than as saving. This has the effect of reducing the lifecycle saving component, thereby inflating the residual inheritance term.

(ii) 31.5% of wealth is due to capitalization of inheritances; in other words, to the fact that Kotlikoff and Summers use the decomposition Eq. (4.2) instead of Eq. (4.3).

(iii) 15.5% of wealth is due largely to parental support for dependent children over the age of 18, which Kotlikoff and Summers treat as a form of bequest, on the grounds that it represents investment in their human capital.

It seems reasonable to accept part of Modigliani's criticisms, by agreeing not to treat all expenditures on dependents over 18 as bequests, and by recognizing lifecycle saving in the form of durables. This position is consistent with that of Blinder (1988), who carefully reviews both sides of the debate. On this basis, inherited wealth accounts for perhaps 20–30% of total wealth in the US if it is not capitalized, and for about 50–60% if it is. The earlier comments regarding Eqs. (4.2) and (4.3) indicate that the capitalization issue turns on the marginal propensity to save out of investment income (including capital gains). A broad brush figure of one half yields a final estimate of 35–45% for the contribution of inheritance to aggregate wealth, which we believe to be a reasonable rough estimate.

---

[46] Kotlikoff and Summers (1981) reported a share of 52%, but this contains an error corrected in Kotlikoff and Summers (1988).

[47] Ando and Kennickell (1987) also find a high share of lifecycle wealth in the US—between 80 and 85% of net worth. Like Kotlikoff and Summers, they cumulate estimates of past lifecycle saving. However, their lifecycle accumulation covers all saving out of disposable income, not just saving out of labour income.

The conclusion that Modigliani's estimate of the importance of inheritance needs to be revised upward receives support from a variety of other evidence:

1. Modigliani (1988a) and Hurd and Mundaca (1989) review sample survey evidence which indicates that inherited wealth accounts for 20% or less of total wealth (without capitalizing). But it is well-known that sample surveys are subject to nonresponse and under-reporting, and that these are particularly severe for the very rich (for whom inheritance is more important). Taking recall bias into account as well, it seems clear that the survey evidence yields a lower bound on the importance of inheritance.

2. The direct estimate by Kotlikoff and Summers (1981) of the contribution of inherited wealth (46%) is at the margin of the 35–45% range we consider most reasonable.

3. Wolff (1997) performs a simulation based on US cross-section data from the 1960s to the 1990s which generates estimates of life-cycle saving and inheritances (the latter obtained by applying age and gender specific mortality rates to the observed distribution of wealth among the living), and residual estimates of gifts inter vivos. He concludes that approximately one third of the wealth individuals accumulate by retirement (or, indeed, over the whole lifetime) comes from each of these three sources. That is, about two thirds of wealth comes from gifts or bequests.

4. Laitner (1992) presents a model incorporating both life-cycle saving and inheritances, based on an altruistic bequest motive and including liquidity constraints, which uses US data. He obtains shares of inherited wealth ranging from 58 to 67%.

5. Lord and Rangazas (1991) and Lord (1992) present simulation models for the US including both life-cycle saving and inheritance, modelling the latter as altruistic in the first article and as based on exchange in the second. While they find that the existence of bequests does not raise aggregate saving rates greatly, the bequest share in overall wealth centres around one half, looking across their various runs and taking the midpoint between the two capitalization procedures.

6. Studies for other countries indicate a greater share of inherited wealth (see, for example, Kessler and Masson, 1989, for a review of French studies). Canadian evidence is perhaps of particular interest, given the similarities between Canada and the US. Davies and St-Hilaire (1987: pp. 107–108) apply an accounting approach to Canadian data, finding a 35% share for inherited wealth without capitalizing, and a 53% share when inheritances are capitalized. In an approach which takes behavioural impacts into account, Davies (1982) finds that equilibrium wealth declines 42% in his simulations if bequests are outlawed. These figures are again consistent with our estimate of a 35–45% share of inherited wealth when account is taken of saving out of investment income.

7. Gale and Scholz (1994) used 1983 SCF data on gifts inter vivos, trust accumulations, and life insurance payments to children to estimate "intentional transfers" in the US. They estimate that such transfers plus bequests account for at least 51% of net worth.

Overall, work on the aggregate importance of intergenerational transfers reinforces what has been learned through simulation studies of lifecycle accumulation and empirical studies of wealth mobility. The conclusion that, as economists and others have long believed, processes of inheritance play an important part in explaining the distribution of wealth, finds significant support in the work which has emerged from the debate sparked by Kotlikoff and Summers.

4.4. *Empirical studies of transfer behaviour*

There has now been a considerable amount of empirical work on the determinants of gifts and bequests at the micro level. Much of this work has focused on testing the altruistic model of transfers, and some of it has tested the exchange model as well.[48] Discriminating between these models has important implications for the distribution of wealth. As we saw in Section 2, transfers have a strong equalizing aspect in the altruistic model which is absent under exchange. In addition, private transfers have a tendency to offset public transfers under altruism, which would suggest, for example, that the effects of the rise in social security wealth on the distribution of wealth in this century is more apparent than real. However, there is more to learn about transfer behaviour than simply whether it is based on altruism or exchange. For example, the degree to which bequests are typically divided equally or unequally, and the size of the (parental) income elasticity of demand for bequests, are important for long run analysis of the evolution of wealth distribution, as we saw earlier. The empirical literature on transfer behaviour helps to provide answers to these questions. In view of the emphasis placed on borrowing constraints and precautionary saving in the recent literature on consumption behaviour, it is also interesting to know whether transfers are timed to alleviate liquidity constraints on the part of recipients.

Some of the studies have looked at gifts, others at bequests. There are important differences in terms of possible transfer motivation and the significance of the behaviour for the distribution of wealth. For bequests, there is a question of whether transfers are intentional. Bequests can be "accidental", that is merely the unintended consequence of the desire by the living to hold assets in bequeathable form (which could arise due to imperfect annuity markets, or a "capitalist" motive for accumulation). Gifts and bequests may also differ in their implications for saving and wealth-holding. Most obviously, in order to make a bequest a donor may hold substantial bequeathable wealth for a long period of time. A programme of gifts, in contrast, will likely give lower wealth for retirees and greater net worth for younger people, which could reduce wealth inequality relative to a no-transfer world even if gifts are not altruistically motivated.

Since gifts are clearly intentional, their relative size compared with bequests is itself an interesting question. It puts a lower bound on the importance of intentional transfers.

---

[48] As shown by Cox (1987) these two models can be obtained as alternative regimes of a single model in which parents are altruistic towards their children. Such parents may be at a corner where they do not desire to make gratuitous transfers, but still make payments to children in exchange for services. This is the exchange regime. However, parents who are sufficiently well-off, or whose children need more help, will make additional transfers, yielding the altruistic regime.

Using survey data from the President's Commission on Pension Policy (PCPP), Cox and Raines (1985) find that three quarters of transfers are in the form of gifts. Even given the likelihood that bequests are underestimated in this survey, this is impressive evidence that much of the intergenerational transfer flow is intentional. Using the 1983 SCF data, Gale and Scholz (1994) estimate that in excess of 38% of transfers were in clearly intentional form (gifts, trust accumulation, and life insurance payments to children).[49]

Hurd (1987) attempts to throw light on whether bequests are intentional by comparing rates of decumulation of bequeathable wealth in retirement by people with and without children. Using the Longitudinal Retirement History Survey (LRHS) over 1969–1979, he finds that rates of decumulation are not significantly lower for people with children. In part this might be explained by the fact that some childless retirees have reasons for making intentional bequests, for instance to friends, relatives, or charities. Hurd (1989) implemented a model using the same data (but restricted to single parents) in which the demand for bequests was estimated. Statistically significant desired positive bequests were only found in one specification, and were small.

Bernheim (1991) argues that evidence of a desire for intentional bequests can be found in patterns of demand for life insurance in the US. He looks at the life insurance and annuity holdings of individuals and families in the LRHS, and finds that demand for term life insurance is greater among those who are "over-annuitized" by high social security entitlements. This higher demand increases the value of wealth left at death, which is by definition an act of intentional bequest.

Other evidence also appears to suggest that a significant portion of the population has an intentional bequest motive. Laitner and Juster (1996) examine a sample of retirees covered by the US academic pension plan, TIAA-CREF. They find that 46% of those with children report that leaving an estate is "very important" or "quite important". Interestingly, 23% of retirees without children also regard leaving an estate as important. Laitner and Juster also point out that 73% of joint annuity holders with children select a guaranteed annuity. This ensures that, if both parents die within a specified number of years (10, 15, or 20), some wealth will be left for heirs. Again, as in the case of Bernheim (1991), we have what are by definition intentional bequests.

While there is therefore evidence that some parents make intentional bequests, studies like Laitner and Juster (1996) which draw on attitudinal questioning find that the importance placed on bequests ranges greatly across families. That families may be quite heterogeneous in their bequest behaviour is also a conclusion from the literature which has tested alternative models of intentional bequests.

The two leading approaches to explaining intentional transfer behaviour are the altruistic and exchange-based models. As noted in Section 2, a simple model assuming equal

---

[49] Gale and Scholz estimate that adding in gifts omitted from the SCF would raise intentional transfers by about one third.

parental altruism towards all siblings makes a number of strong testable predictions. These may be summarized as follows:

1. Transfers will not occur in all families or for all children. The probability that a child will receive a transfer should increase with parental income and decline with the child's earnings.
2. In families where transfers are made, a child's transfer should increase with parental income and decrease with child's earnings. The latter point implies that gifts and bequests should *compensate* if a child's earnings are low relative to the parent or siblings.

And, in view of these first two points:

3. The incidence of equal division of transfers between siblings should be low.
4. Across families, total transfers should decline with children's average earnings.
5. Total transfers should rise with parental income. The relationship is expected to be nonlinear, with most parents at low incomes leaving nothing and the incidence of positive bequests rising sharply at higher income levels. (This prediction rests on the plausible assumption that low income parents cannot force negative transfers on their children.)

Exchange-based models also predict that the likelihood of a transfer being received, and the amount, should be positively related to parental income. However, the exchange model differs in allowing a positive impact of child's earnings on the amount of transfer received. It also predicts that transfers should increase with the services provided by the child to the parent, which are generally referred to as "attention".

The simplest way to test the altruistic model is to look at patterns of estate division. Assuming that compensatory transfers are not exclusively undertaken by means of gifts, altruism predicts unequal division of estates. The results of Menchik (1977, 1988), Wilhelm (1996) and others, however, indicate that equal division is the dominant practice, at least in the United States.[50] Menchik (1988) reported exactly equal division in 84% of estates in a study based on probate records from Cleveland, Ohio.[51] In his data based on federal estate tax returns, Wilhelm (1996) finds equal division in 69% of estates with two or more heirs. Approximately equal division (within 2%) occurs in 77% of the estates.

While the incidence of equal division of estates is high, it is interesting to know what determines the division of bequests in the 15–25% of unequal cases. Tomes (1981) found a significant negative impact of recipient's income on bequest. Further, he found that impacts of parental schooling on child's schooling and bequests were also in line

[50] Wedgwood (1928, p. 48) reported contrary evidence for the wealthiest families in Britain during the early part of the twentieth century. More recent UK data analysed by the Royal Commission (1977: chap. 8) showed unequal division in half the cases examined, but the degree of unequal division was not systematically related to the size of the estate, as might be expected if primogeniture was widely practiced by the wealthy. Horsman (1978) found a higher frequency involving roughly equal division (about 75%). None of his cases of unequal division was clearly linked to primogeniture, although almost all favoured male heirs.

[51] Menchik's sample was drawn from the same frame as that used by Tomes (1981). Tomes relied on reports by heirs of the amounts they had received rather than using the probate records. His finding of equal division in only 21% of cases is a reflection of the degree of reporting error by respondents.

with predictions from the altruistic model. Wilhelm (1996) finds a significant (although small) negative impact of recipient's income on bequest in cases where estates were divided unequally. A small compensatory effect could be explained either by a minority of parents behaving in line with the simple altruistic model, or by altruistic forces being present in most families but largely offset by other influences—for example the need to avoid work disincentive effects on heirs.

Frequent equal division of estates would be consistent with altruism if compensatory behaviour were accomplished instead via gifts inter vivos. Considerable attention has focused on the study of gifts. Until recently, this work appeared to show that altruism was eclipsed by exchange (Cox, 1987; Cox and Rank, 1992). However, more recent studies have found evidence suggesting some altruistic motivation for gifts.

Cox (1987) studied the determinants of gifts using data collected by the President's Commission on Pension Policy (PCPP) in the US. He found that while the probability of receiving a gift was negatively related to recipient's income, conditional on a gift occurring the amount received *increased* with the donee's income. This rejects the altruistic model but is consistent with exchange-based transfers. It could be, for example, that higher income children charge a higher "price" for their services, and that parents' demand for these services is inelastic. Cox also found that, ceteris paribus, a family with more children receives less transfers from other families. This runs counter to altruism—since more children spell greater needs—but agrees with the exchange model, where more children imply the likelihood of supplying fewer services to other families. Finally, female headed families received larger transfers, and families with a married head received smaller transfers, ceteris paribus. The latter findings are consistent with the notion that unmarried children and women supply more attention.

Direct observations of parental income are not provided in the PCPP data, so Cox (1987) relied on mean income in the recipient's neighbourhood as a proxy for parental income. Since this is an imperfect measure, it is possible that the positive impact of recipient's income on the gift amount is spurious. It could reflect correlation between recipient's income and unmeasured components of parental income. Cox and Rank (1992) provide a check on this using the National Survey of Families and Households (NSFH), which does have a direct measure of parental income. Results are similar to those of Cox (1987). However, independent studies using other datasets have disputed these findings.

Altonji et al. (1992) studied the degree of altruistic linkage between parents and their "split-off" adult offspring in the Michigan Panel Study of Income Dynamics (PSID). They looked at the extent to which the food consumption of either parents or children moved in sympathy with income shocks to the other party. The altruistic model predicts a strong sympathetic movement, reflecting adjustments in underlying transfers. Altonji et al. found that although the induced changes in consumption were in the predicted direction, they were small. This may indicate that only a minority of parents operate in the altruistic regime, or that other influences (for instance, the need to avoid work disincentive effects on recipients) limit altruistic behaviour.

Altonji et al. (1997) use the transfer supplement to the 1988 PSID to examine the determinants of attention and transfers between parents and children. Like Cox (1987) and Cox and Rank (1992), they find that parental income has a positive impact on the probability and amount of transfer. However, in contrast to Cox, the child's income is negatively related to the transfer amount. Further evidence of a negative effect is provided by Rosenzweig and Wolpin (1993, 1994), who find that parental assistance to young people attending college is substantial, and increases as the child's income declines. McGarry and Schoeni (1995), McGarry (1996), Dunn and Phillips (1997), and Dunn (1997) all report similar results.

Dunn (1997) is able to control for a variety of biases that may have affected earlier work by using panel data from the National Longitudinal Survey of Labor Market Experience (NLS). Not only does this dataset provide direct measures of parental income, but its panel aspect makes it possible to control for fixed effects. An investigation of the response of transfers to transitory as well as permanent incomes is performed. As set out by Cox (1990), both altruism and exchange suggest that the likelihood and amount of transfers should be positively related to both the permanent and current income of parents. Also, the likelihood of transfer should be negatively related to the child's permanent and current income. Only with respect to the amount of transfer is there a difference in prediction, with altruism predicting a negative impact of permanent income, and exchange allowing a positive effect. Under both altruism or exchange, the transfer amount should be negatively affected by current income, since it is efficient to make transfers to the child when liquidity constraints are binding for the child, which is more likely to occur when the child's current income is low.

Like Cox (1990), Dunn (1997) finds that parents time their transfers to correspond with periods when the child's current income is low. Thus gifts are likely to have a significant impact on relieving the liquidity constraints faced by the young. This effect has interesting implications for saving behaviour, implying less need for precautionary saving, for example. Dunn (1997) finds that transfer amounts are negatively related to the child's permanent income, as well as current income, which is consistent with altruism.

Returning to bequests, it may be noted that altruism has implications for wealth distribution even if transfers on death are never used to achieve inter-sibling compensation. Compensation relative to the parent, rather than other siblings, could still be a goal pursued via bequests.

There is evidence that total transfers are positively related to parental income and negatively related to children's average earnings across families. In other words, bequests do seem to be used to achieve some smoothing of resources between parents and children. Wilhelm (1996) finds such effects in his tax return data, although the significant negative impact of children's average earnings in his results is not large. As mentioned earlier, Laitner and Juster (1996) present results based on a survey of retirees covered by the US academic pension plan, TIAA-CREF. While the sample is not representative of the US population, it is of special interest since it focuses on a group which would be likely to make voluntary nonhuman transfers on the basis of the altruistic model.

(Lower income families will often be at a corner solution where all transfers are made in human form.) For the sample as a whole, the altruistic model does not predict behaviour well. But for the half of households who intend to leave estates, behaviour is in accordance with some degree of altruism. In these households, bequeathable wealth is highest for those with the lowest assessment of their children's likely earnings, and levels of retirement-age net worth are higher by several hundred thousand dollars per household than for families where bequest is not considered important.

Further evidence on bequest behaviour which is consistent with a role for altruism is provided by Menchik and David (1983) who studied a sample of decedents in Wisconsin from 1960–1964. Inheritance records were matched with income tax returns from the period 1946–1964, making possible a very good study of the relationship between lifetime income and estate left on death. (Unfortunately, there was no information on heirs' incomes.) Menchik and David, who used a spline relationship, found that the elasticity of demand for bequests increased with income. In fact, it was below unity for the bottom 80% of the population, but in the range 2–4 for the top 20%. Such a pattern is predicted by the altruistic model, as noted earlier.

Exchange models predict that gifts and bequests should be positively related to the amount of "attention" supplied by children, as measured by the frequency of visits, telephone calls, letters, etc. However, Tomes (1981) found that the attention provided had a significant negative effect on the size of bequest received by a child. He also estimated an OLS "supply of visits" equation, finding an insignificant negative coefficient on inheritance received.

Bernheim et al. (1985) argue that Tomes' equations are misspecified because they fail to take into account the simultaneous determination of attention and bequests. They find that parents' bequeathable wealth has a significant positive effect on attention supplied by children in two stage least squares estimates using the LRHS. Nonbequeathable wealth has an insignificant impact on attention.

In summary, empirical work on transfer behaviour has found that at least half of intergenerational transfers are intentional since they are made in the form of gifts, life insurance payments and the like. There is also evidence that bequests are to some extent intentional. It is therefore interesting to ask why parents make intentional transfers. Broadly speaking, the evidence indicates that both altruism and exchange may contribute to the explanation, although the models investigated so far do not explain the bulk of the variation in transfers. Parents make larger gifts to children with lower earnings, and appear to save more for bequest if their children are on average lower earners. These observations suggest that altruism has some role. On the other hand, both gifts and bequests appear to increase with the amount of attention children give their parents, providing evidence of exchange. There is a high frequency of equal division of bequests, and the income elasticity of demand for bequests on the part of parents is low for most of the population, but in excess of unity for about the top fifth. Finally, we learn that gifts are more likely to be given, and are larger, when children are suffering temporarily low incomes or are investing in education. Whatever the underlying purpose of transfers, they appear timed for the maximum effect, providing reassurance that the economic approach to the analysis of transfer behaviour is worth pursuing.

5. Summary and conclusions

This chapter began by noting some of the most important facts about personal wealth-holdings: the distribution of wealth is more unequal than income, and has a long upper tail; financial assets and inherited wealth are both more concentrated than wealth as a whole; many households never accumulate much private wealth, even in rich countries; and wealth inequality has been on a downward trend for most of the past century. These are the kinds of evidence on wealth-holdings which we have tried to document and explain in the course of our survey.

Progress in explaining wealth distribution was first made via stochastic models, which accounted for the fact that the distribution of wealth is approximately lognormal, and its upper tail is approximately Pareto. Other early theoretical contributions used simple models of savings and inheritance behaviour to understand the interplay of basic forces that lead to high wealth concentration and a declining trend over time. This concern with the overall features of wealth distribution has been largely abandoned in recent research, which focuses instead on the causes of individual differences in wealth-holdings.

One reason for the change of emphasis is a recognition of the growing importance of wealth-holdings acquired for retirement purposes. This is reflected in the central role now assigned to the lifecycle saving model (LCM), and the numerous ways in which the LCM has been refined and extended. When allowance is made for uncertainty, liquidity constraints, precautionary saving, and the effects of social security and means-tested benefits, the LCM is able to account for such observed features as the low positive saving of many households and the slow rate of dissaving in retirement. In simulation exercises, the model is able to generate overall wealth inequality similar to that observed, but not the high concentration of wealth in the upper tail. Differences in ages, earnings, returns to investments, and saving rates, all appear to make significant contributions to inequality in lifecycle wealth.

Inheritances and other forms of intergenerational transfers can be incorporated within the LCM framework by including a bequest motive, although most of the behavioural models of intergenerational transfers abstract from the detailed pattern of lifetime consumption. Much work has been done in an altruistic framework, which captures not only gifts and bequests, but also parental investments in the human capital of children. The altruistic model correctly predicts that gifts and bequests will be relatively more important in wealthier families, but its prediction that intergenerational transfers will strongly compensate for earnings differences between siblings is not borne out in practice. Alternative models, emphasizing exchange between the generations and strategic behaviour, are also consistent with money transfers being relatively more important at higher income levels, but avoid the unrealistic prediction of strongly compensatory transfers. Other evidence showing that gifts are strongly (and positively) correlated with periods when children's earnings are temporarily low, supports the view that intentional transfers are important, and suggest that, whatever their motivation, transfers help to alleviate liquidity constraints on the young.

The implications of behavioural models of intergenerational transfers for the distribution of wealth have received little attention, although it seems likely that altruistic motives cause inheritances to have an equalizing impact on wealth inequality, while the reverse is true for exchange or strategic motives. Other theoretical studies with less explicit behavioural foundations have examined the effect of differential fertility, assortative mating, and the pattern of estate division on long-run wealth inequality, and have shown that equal division of estates, and low correlation in the wealth of husbands and wives, can be powerful forces acting towards wealth equalization in the longer run.

Empirical evidence on wealth-holdings is sometimes obtained from estate or wealth tax records, although these sources are becoming less important. Survey information on wealth-holdings is now available in many countries, and wealth details are being recorded in an increasing number of panel datasets. Surveys are very valuable sources of data, but they frequently suffer from under-reporting of assets and higher nonresponse rates among the wealthy. For this reason, estate and wealth tax data probably yield more reliable information on the upper tail of the distribution. Estimates of the wealth of named individuals provides another potentially valuable source of data on the very richest families, but they have not been given much attention to date by academic researchers.

The deficiencies of survey data on wealth mean that the results need to be treated with caution. But the weight of evidence strongly supports many long-standing beliefs. All studies agree that wealth is more highly concentrated than income, even when pension entitlements are included in the definition of wealth (augmented wealth in our terminology). Data constructed for the US, UK and Sweden confirm the long run decline in wealth inequality over the period 1920–1975. After 1975 the evidence is more mixed, and wealth inequality in the US seems to have moved upwards along with income inequality. Another widespread empirical finding is the high proportion of families that claim to have little or no financial wealth of any kind. It also appears that asset portfolios, even those of the wealthiest households, are not very diversified

Corporate stock is held disproportionately by the wealthiest families, so wealth inequality is expected to rise during stock market booms. In contrast, middle class families are expected to benefit most from increases in house prices. Both of these predictions are confirmed by the data, and may account for part of the recent rise in wealth concentration in the US. The reasons for the general downward trend in wealth inequality in the twentieth century are more difficult to determine with precision, but the spread of "popular" assets (especially houses and consumer durables) seems to have been an important factor. More equal estate division and progressive taxation may also have been influential.

A recurring theme in wealth distribution analysis concerns the importance of self-accumulated wealth relative to inherited wealth. We have reviewed a number of sources of evidence on this issue, including survey data on inheritances; simulations of wealth distribution which incorporate both life-cycle saving and inheritance; and studies of intergenerational wealth mobility. On the basis of this evidence, we conclude that inheritance probably accounts for about 35–45% of aggregate wealth in the US. Simulation studies indicate that a version of the lifecycle saving model which incorporates uncertain earnings, uncertain lifetime and liquidity constraints (but not intentional bequests) can reproduce the observed shape of the wealth distribution over most of its range, but accounts for only about half the share of wealth held by the top centile. This suggests that intentional bequests remain an essential ingredient in any credible explanation of the long upper tail of the wealth distribution, a conclusion corroborated by other evidence such as the finding that about half of the wealthiest people in the UK and US owe a great deal to inheritance.

While we have attempted to cover most of the important issues concerning the distribution of personal wealth, a number of topics have been omitted or given short shrift. Some of these relate to subject matter covered in detail elsewhere in the Handbook. Others reflect gaps in the literature. For example, we have touched upon estimates of the distribution of wealth which incorporate private pensions and social security wealth, but have not given this topic the attention it deserves. Estimates of private pension wealth require detailed information about pension entitlements which typically differ across, and even within, employers. Information on contributions and benefits is more readily available for state pension schemes, but estimating social security wealth presents its own special difficulties. Not the least of these is the fact that longevity rises significantly with income and wealth. Thus while it often appears that social security benefits are strongly redistributive, this is offset by the lower expected benefit period for low income retirees. Detailed analysis of the distributional implications of social security wealth would also need to embrace the large and controversial literature on the impact of social security schemes on private saving which began with Feldstein (1974). Taking account of the induced change in intergenerational transfers would complicate the analysis still further, so this topic presents a major challenge for researchers in the future.

Another area we have tended to neglect is the economic links between wealth distribution and demographic factors relating to mating, fertility, mortality, and family formation and dissolution. The individual chapters in Volume 1A of the Handbook of Population and Family Economics (Rosenzweig and Stark, 1997) provide excellent introductions to these topics, although here again the implications for wealth distribution have only been studied in a fairly cursory manner. One interesting line of future enquiry is the evolutionary modelling of bequest behaviour which has been provided by some economists (e.g., Chu, 1991; Bergstrom, 1994), building on the insights of anthropologists and biologists. This work points out that male offspring of higher income groups may get higher bequests if sons on average produce more grandchildren than daughters. This difference in reproductive fitness may occur where there is formal or

informal polygyny, conditions which have prevailed in almost all human societies, with the notable exception of the West in the last two centuries. Primogeniture may well be the optimal estate division policy when there are increasing returns in the process which converts bequests into grandchildren.

There is clearly a need for much more research on most of the topics we have covered. This applies to description, theory, simulations, and conventional empirical work. Measuring the distribution of wealth will always be subject to error and uncertainty, but this can be reduced in the case of surveys by research on the determinants of nonsampling error, by over-sampling the wealthy, and by careful alignment with independent balance sheets. Adoption of a common framework in different countries, along the lines that have been developed for income distributions, would improve the scope for comparative studies. Where possible, we also strongly encourage official agencies to provide consistent annual estate multiplier estimates of wealth inequality. The availability of such data in the UK has facilitated econometric and other studies which cannot be undertaken in the US, for example, where estate multiplier estimates are only available for isolated years. Another underutilised resource is the lists of the wealthy provided by journalists and others, which could be used more regularly to check and, if necessary, revise estimates of wealth-holdings in the extreme upper tail.

Although the lifecycle model has been extensively developed, and some progress has been made in linking the LCM with intergenerational models, important weaknesses remain. Most models assume riskless investment and a uniform rate of return. The riskiness of investment needs to be recognised, and its contribution to wealth inequality assessed more carefully. The acquisition of great fortunes by entrepreneurs and investors is another feature which needs to be modelled, since such explosions of individual wealth are clearly an important source of renewal for wealth inequality.

Some important recent secular trends pose challenges for research on the distribution of wealth. Up to the mid 1970s the downward trend in wealth inequality seemed relentless, and was mainly attributable to a decline in the observed share of the very rich. More recently, however, the shares of the richest groups in the population appear to have stabilised (Sweden, UK) or began to rise (US). We do not as yet have a good understanding of the reasons for this, although growing income inequality, rising share prices, the impact of social programs, and increasing use of tax avoidance measures, are all candidate explanations. The contributions of important demographic trends such as rising divorce rates, declining retirement ages, and rising longevity are also poorly understood, although the last two factors are certain to become more significant in future years. It seems likely that interest in wealth-holdings and wealth distribution will increase as the consequences of rising demand for assets for lifecycle saving purposes is seen more clearly in asset markets and changing asset prices.

References

Aitchison, J. and J.A.C. Brown (1957), The Lognormal Distribution (Cambridge University Press, Cambridge).

Alessie, R., A. Lusardi and T. Aldershof (1997), Income and wealth over the life cycle: evidence from panel data, Review of Income and Wealth 43: 1–32.

Altonji, J., F. Hayashi and L. Kotlikoff (1992), Is the extended family altruistically linked? American Economic Review 82: 1177–1198.

Altonji, J.G., F. Hayashi and L.J. Kotlikoff (1997), Parental altruism and inter vivos transfers: theory and evidence, Journal of Political Economy 105: 1121–1166.

Ando, A. and F. Modigliani (1963), The "life cycle" hypothesis of saving: aggregate implications and tests, American Economic Review 53: 55–84.

Ando, A., L. Guiso and I Visco (eds.) (1994), Saving and the Accumulation of Wealth: Essays on Italian Household and Government Saving Behavior (Cambridge University Press, Cambridge).

Ando, A. and A.B. Kennickell (1987), How much (or little) life cycle is there in micro data? The cases of the United States and Japan, in R. Dornbusch, S. Fischer and J. Bossons, eds., Macroeconomics and Finance: Essays in Honor of Franco Modigliani (MIT Press, Cambridge), pp. 159–223.

Arrondel, L. and A. Laferrere (1996), Capitalist versus family bequest: an econometric model with two endogenous regimes, Discussion paper 96-06 (DELTA, Paris).

Arrondel, L., S. Perelman and P. Pestieau (1994), The effect of bequest motives on the composition and distribution of assets in France, in T. Tachibanaki, ed., Savings and Bequests (University of Michigan Press, Ann Arbor), pp. 229–244.

Atkinson, A.B. (1971), The distribution of wealth and the individual life cycle, Oxford Economic Papers 23: 239–254.

Atkinson, A.B. (1980), Inheritance and the redistribution of wealth, in G.M. Heal and G.A. Hughes, eds., Public Policy and the Tax System (Allen and Unwin, London).

Atkinson, A.B. (1988), Comment on Chapter 5, in D. Kessler and A. Masson, eds., Modelling the Accumulation and Distribution of Wealth (Clarendon Press, Oxford), pp. 144–145.

Atkinson, A.B., J.P.F. Gordon and A. Harrison (1989), Trends in the shares of top wealth-holders in Britain, 1923–1981, Oxford Bulletin of Economics and Statistics 51: 315–332.

Atkinson, A.B. and A.J. Harrison (1978), Distribution of Personal Wealth in Britain (Cambridge University Press, Cambridge).

Atkinson, A.B. and A.J. Harrison (1982), The analysis of trends over time in the distribution of personal wealth in Britain, in D. Kessler, A. Masson and D. Strauss-Kahn, eds., Accumulation et Répartition des Patrimoines (CNRS and Economica, Paris), pp. 557–574.

Attanasio, O.P. (1998), Consumption demand, Working Paper No. 6466 (National Bureau of Economic Research).

Attanasio, O., J. Banks and S. Tanner (1998), Asset holding and consumption volatility, Working paper No. 98/8 (Institute for Fiscal Studies, London).

Attanasio, O.P., J. Banks, C. Meghir and G. Weber (1995), Humps and bumps in lifetime consumption, Working Paper 95/14 (Institute of Fiscal Studies, London).

Attanasio, O.P. and M. Browning (1995), Consumption over the life cycle and over the business cycle, American Economic Review 85: 1187–1137.

Avery, R.B. (1989), Comment, in R.E. Lipsey and H.S. Tice, eds., The Measurement of Saving, Investment, and Wealth (University of Chicago Press, Chicago), pp. 839–844.

Avery, R.B., G.E. Elliehausen, G.B. Canner and T.A. Gustafson (1984), Survey of Consumer Finances, Federal Reserve Bulletin, pp. 679–692.

Avery, R.B., G.E. Elliehausen and A.B. Kennickell (1988), Measuring wealth with survey data: an evaluation of the 1983 Survey of Consumer Finances, Review of Income and Wealth 34: 339–370.

Baekgaard, H. (1997), The distribution of household wealth in Australia: new estimates for 1986 and 1993, National Centre for Social and Economic Modelling (NATSEM), University of Canberra, mimeo.

Bager-Sjögren, L and N.A. Klevmarken (1996), Inequality and mobility of wealth in Sweden 1983–1984 to 1992–1993, mimeo, Uppsala University.

Banks, J. and S. Tanner (1996), Savings and wealth in the UK: evidence from micro-data, Fiscal Studies 17: 37–64.

Barlow, R., H.E. Brazer and J.N. Morgan (1966), Economic Behavior of the Affluent (Brookings Institution, Washington, D.C.).

Bauer, J. and A. Mason (1992), The distribution of income and wealth in Japan, Review of Income and Wealth 38: 403–428.

Beach, C.M., D.E Card and F. Flatters (1981), Distribution of Income and Wealth in Ontario (Ontario Economic Council and University of Toronto Press, Toronto).

Becker, G.S. and N. Tomes (1976), Child endowments and the quantity and quality of children, Journal of Political Economy 84: S143–S162.

Beresford, P. (1990), The Sunday Times Book of the Rich. Britain's 400 Richest People (Weidenfeld and Nicolson, London).

Bergstrom, T.C. (1994), Primogeniture, monogamy and reproductive success in a stratified society, University of Michigan, mimeo.

Bernheim, B.D. (1991), How strong are bequest motives? Evidence based on estimates of the demand for life insurance and annuities, Journal of Political Economy 99: 899–927.

Bernheim, B.D., A. Shleifer and L.H. Summers (1985), The strategic bequest motive, Journal of Political Economy 93: 1045–1077.

Bevan, D.L. (1979), Inheritance and the distribution of wealth, Economica 46: 381–402.

Blake, D. (1996), Risk aversion and portfolio insurance: An analysis of financial asset portfolios held by investors in the United Kingdom, Economic Journal 106: 1175–1192.

Blinder, A.S. (1973), A model of inherited wealth, Quarterly Journal of Economics 87: 608–626.

Blinder, A.S. (1974), Toward An Economic Theory of Income Distribution (MIT Press, Cambridge, MA).

Blinder, A.S. (1976), Inequality and mobility in the distribution of wealth, Kyklos 29: 607–638.

Blinder, A.S. (1988), Comments on Chapter 1 and Chapter 2, in D. Kessler and A. Masson, eds., Modelling the Accumulation and Distribution of Wealth (Clarendon Press, Oxford), pp. 68–76.

Börsch-Supan, A. (1994), Savings in Germany—Part 2: Behavior, in J.M. Poterba, ed., International Comparisons of Household Saving (University of Chicago Press, Chicago), pp. 207–236.

Brandolini, A. and L. Cannari (1994), Methodological appendix: The Bank of Italy's survey of household income and wealth, in A. Ando, L. Guiso and I. Visco, eds., Saving and the Accumulation of Wealth: Essays on Italian Household and Government Saving Behavior (Cambridge University Press, Cambridge).

Brandolini, A., L. Cannari and G. D'Alessio (1994), The composition and distribution of household wealth in Italy, 1987–1991, Bank of Italy, mimeo.

Browning, M. and A. Lusardi (1996), Household saving: micro theories and micro facts Journal of Economic Literature 34: 1797–1855.

Burkhauser, R.V., J.R. Frick and J. Schwarze (1997), A comparison of alternative measures of well-being for Germany and the United States, Review of Income and Wealth 43: 153–172.

Caballero, R.J. (1990), Consumption puzzles and precautionary savings, Journal of Monetary Economics 25: 113–136.

Caballero, R.J. (1991), Earnings uncertainty and aggregate wealth accumulation, American Economic Review 81: 859–871.

Campbell, D.W. and W. Watanabe (1996a), The 1994 Financial Asset Choice Survey: an assessment, Discussion Paper No. 1996-07 (Institute for Posts and Telecommunications Policy, Tokyo).

Campbell, D.W. and W. Watanabe (1996b), A comparison of household asset/saving surveys in Japan, Institute for Posts and Telecommunications Policy, Tokyo, mimeo.

Carroll, C.D. (1992), The buffer-stock theory of saving: some macroeconomic evidence, Brookings Papers on Economic Activity 2: 61–135.

Champernowne, D.G. (1953), A model of income distribution, Economic Journal 63: 318–351.

Chesher, A.D. (1979), An analysis of the distribution of wealth in Ireland, Economic and Social Review 11: 1–17.

Chesher, A.D. and P.C. McMahon (1977), The distribution of personal wealth in Ireland: The evidence re-examined, Economic and Social Review 8: 61–65.

Chu, C.Y.C. (1991), Primogeniture, Journal of Political Economy 99: 78–99.

Cox, D. (1987), Motives for private income transfers, Journal of Political Economy 95: 508–546.

Cox, D. (1990), Intergenerational transfers and liquidity constraints, Quarterly Journal of Economics 105: 187–217.

Cox, D. and F. Raines (1985), Inter-family transfers and income redistribution, in M. David and T. Smeeding, eds., Horizontal Equity, Uncertainty, and Measures of Well-Being (University of Chicago Press, Chicago), pp. 393–421.

Cox, D. and M.R. Rank (1992), Inter-vivos transfers and intergenerational exchange, Review of Economics and Statistics 74: 305–314.

Creedy, J. (1985), The Dynamics of Income Distribution (Blackwell, Oxford).

Curtin, R.T., F.T. Juster and J.N. Morgan (1989), Survey estimates of wealth: An assessment of quality, in R.E. Lipsey, and H.S. Tice, eds., The Measurement of Saving, Investment and Wealth (University of Chicago Press, Chicago), pp. 473–548.

Darby, M.R. (1979), Effects of Social Security on income and the capital stock (American Enterprise Institute, Washington, D.C.).

Davies, J.B. (1979), On the size distribution of wealth in Canada, Review of Income and Wealth 25: 237–259.

Davies, J.B. (1981), Uncertain lifetime, consumption, and dissaving in retirement, Journal of Political Economy 89: 561–577.

Davies, J.B. (1982), The relative impact of inheritance and other factors on economic inequality, Quarterly Journal of Economics 47: 471–498.

Davies, J.B. (1986), Does redistribution reduce inequality? Journal of Labor Economics 4: 538–559.

Davies, J.B. (1988), Family size, household production and life cycle saving, Annales d'Economie et de Statistique 9: 141–166.

Davies, J.B. (1993), The distribution of wealth in Canada, Research in Economic Inequality 4: 159–180.

Davies, J.B. (1996a), Wealth inequality and age, Working paper, University of Western Ontario.

Davies, J.B. (1996b), Explaining intergenerational transfers, in P.L. Menchik, ed., Household and Family Economics (Kluwer, Norwell, Massachusetts), pp. 47–82.

Davies, J.B. and A.F. Shorrocks (1978), Assessing the quantitative importance of inheritance in the distribution of wealth, Oxford Economic Papers 30: 138–149.

Davies, J.B. and F. St-Hilaire (1987), Reforming Capital Income Taxation in Canada: Efficiency and Distributional Effects of Alternative Options (Economic Council of Canada: Ottawa).

Deaton, A. (1991), Saving and liquidity constraints, Econometrica 59: 1221–1248.

Deaton, A. and C. Paxson (1994), Intertemporal choice and inequality, Journal of Political Economy 102: 437–467.

Dicks-Mireaux, L. and M.A. King (1984), The effects of pensions and social security on the size and composition of household asset portfolios, in Z. Bodie and J. Shoven, eds., Financial Aspects of the US Pension System (University of Chicago Press, Chicago).

Dilnot, A.W. (1990), The distribution and composition of personal sector wealth in Australia, Australian Economic Review 1: 33–40.

Dunn, T.A. (1997), The distribution of intergenerational income transfers across and within families, Economics Department and Center for Policy Research, Syracuse University, mimeo.

Dunn, T.A. and J.W. Phillips (1997), The timing and division of parental transfers to children, Economic Letters 54: 135–137.

Easton, B.H. (1981), The New Zealand Income Distribution (NZIER and Allen and Unwin, Auckland, New Zealand).

Feldstein, M. (1974), Social Security, induced retirement, and aggregate capital accumulation, Journal of Political Economy 82: 905–926.

Feldstein, M. (1976a), Personal taxation and portfolio composition: an econometric analysis, Econometrica 44: 631–650.

Feldstein, M. (1976b), Social security and the distribution of wealth, Journal of the American Statistical Association 71: 800–807.

Flemming, J.S. (1976), On the assessment of the inequality of wealth, in: Selected Evidence Submitted to the Royal Commission: Report No. 1, Initial Report on the Standing Reference (Royal Commission on the Distribution of Income and Wealth, HMSO, London), pp. 34–70.

Flemming, J.S. (1979), The effects of earnings inequality, imperfect capital markets, and dynastic altruism on the distribution of wealth in life cycle models, Economica 46: 363–380.

Fouquet, A. and D. Strauss-Kahn (1984), The size distribution of personal wealth in France 1977: a first attempt at the estate duty method, Review of Income and Wealth 30: 403–418.

Friedman, M. (1957), A Theory of the Consumption Function (Princeton University Press, Princeton).

Friedman, B. and M. Warshawsky (1988), Annuity prices and saving behavior in the United States, in Z. Bodie, J. Shoven and D. Wise, eds., Pensions in the U.S. Economy (University of Chicago Press, Chicago).

Fuster, L. (1997), Is altruism important for understanding the long-run effects of Social Security? Universitat Pompeu Fabra, mimeo.

Gale, W.G. and J.K. Scholz (1994), Intergenerational transfers and the accumulation of wealth, Journal of Economic Perspectives 8: 145–160.

Galt, M.N. (1995), Wealth and its distribution in New Zealand, 1893 to 1939, Australian Economic History Review 35: 66–81.

Galton, F. (1889), Natural Inheritance (Macmillan, London).

Gibrat, R. (1931), Les Inégalités Économiques (Sirey, Paris).

Giffen, R. (1913), Statistics (Macmillan, London).

Gokhale, J., L.J. Kotlikoff, J. Sefton and M. Weale (1998), Simulating the transmission of wealth inequality via bequests, Boston University, mimeo.

Good, F.J. (1991), Estimates of the Distribution of Personal Wealth, Economic Trends, October 1991 (London: HMSO), pp. 137–157.

Gunton, R. (1975), Personal Wealth in Australia, unpublished PhD thesis (University of Queensland).

Halliassos, M. and C.C. Bertaut (1995), Why do so few people hold stocks? Economic Journal 105: 1110–1129.

Hamnett, C. (1991), A nation of inheritors? Housing inheritance, wealth and inequality in Britain, Journal of Social Policy 20: 509–535.

Harbury, C.D. (1962), Inheritance and the distribution of wealth in Britain, Economic Journal 72: 845–868.

Harbury, C.D. and P.C.McMahon (1973), Inheritance and the characteristics of top wealth leavers in Britain, Economic Journal 83: 810–833.

Harbury, C.D. and D.M.W.N. Hitchens (1976), The inheritance of top wealth leavers: Some further evidence, Economic Journal 86: 321–326.

Harbury, C.D. and D.M.W.N. Hitchens (1979), Inheritance and Wealth Inequality in Britain (George Allen and Unwin, London).

Harbury, C.D. and D.M.W.N. Hitchens (1983), The Influence of Relative Prices on the Distribution of Wealth and Inheritance in E.N. Wolff, ed., International Comparisons of the Distribution of Household Wealth (Clarendon Press, Oxford), pp. 248–275.

Harrison, A.J. (1976), Trends over time in the distribution of wealth, in A. Jones, ed., Economics and Equality (Philip Allan, Oxford), pp. 66–86.

Harrison, A. (1979), The Distribution of Wealth in Ten Countries, Royal Commission on the Distribution of Income and Wealth, Background Paper No. 7 (HMSO, London).

Hochguertel, S. and A. van Soest (1996), The relation between financial and housing wealth of Dutch households, Discussion paper No. 40 (VSB-CenER Savings Project, Tilburg University).

Hochguertel, S., R. Alessie and A. van Soest (1997), Saving accounts versus stocks and bonds in household portfolio allocation, Scandinavian Journal of Economics 99: 81–97.

Holmans, A.E., and M. Frosztega (1994), House Property and Inheritance in the UK (HMSO, London).

Horsman, E.G. (1978), Inheritance in England and Wales: the evidence provided by wills, Oxford Economic Papers 30: 409–422.

Hubbard, R.G., J. Skinner and S.P. Zeldes (1994), The importance of precautionary motives in explaining individual and aggregate saving, Carnegie-Rochester Conference Series on Public Policy 40: 59–125.

Hubbard, R.G., J. Skinner and S.P. Zeldes (1995), Precautionary saving and social insurance, Journal of Political Economy 103: 360–399.

Huggett, M. (1996), Wealth distribution in life-cycle economies, Journal of Monetary Economics 38: 469–494.

Huggett, M. and G. Ventura (1998), Understanding why high income households save more than low income households, University of Western Ontario, mimeo.

Hurd, M.D. (1987), Savings of the elderly and desired bequests, American Economic Review 77: 298–312.

Hurd, M.D. (1989), Mortality risk and bequests, Econometrica 57: 779–813.

Hurd, M.D. (1997), The economics of individual aging, in M.R. Rosenzweig and O. Stark, eds., Handbook of Population and Family Economics, Vol 1B (North-Holland Elsevier, Amsterdam), pp. 891–966.

Hurd, M.D. and B.G. Mundaca (1989), The importance of gifts and inheritances among the affluent, in R.E. Lipsey, and H.S. Tice, eds., The Measurement of Saving, Investment and Wealth (University of Chicago Press, Chicago), pp. 737–758.

Inland Revenue (1987), Inland Revenue Statistics 1987 (HMSO, London).

Inland Revenue (1996), Inland Revenue Statistics 1996 (HMSO, London).

Jianakoplos, N.A. and P.L. Menchik (1997), Wealth mobility, Review of Economics and Statistics 79: 18–31.

Jianakoplos, N.A., P.L. Menchik and F.O. Irvine (1989), Using panel data to assess the bias in cross-sectional inferences of life-cycle changes in the level and composition of household wealth, in R.E. Lipsey and H. S. Tice, eds., The Measurement of Saving, Investment, and Wealth (University of Chicago Press, Chicago), pp. 553–640.

Juster, F.T. and K.A. Kuester (1991), Differences in the measurement of wealth, wealth inequality and wealth composition obtained from alternative US wealth surveys, Review of Income and Wealth 37: 33–62

Juster, F.T. and J.P. Smith (1997), Improving the quality of economic data: lessons from the HRS and AHEAD, Journal of the American Statistical Association 92: 1268–1278.

Kain, J.F. and J.M. Quigley (1972), Note on owner's estimate of housing value, Journal of the American Statistical Association 67: 803–806.

Kennickell, A.B., M. Starr-McCluer and A.E. Sunden (1998), Family finances in the US: recent evidence from the Survey of Consumer Finances, Federal Reserve Bulletin 83: 1–24.

Kessler, D. and A. Masson (1989), Bequest and wealth accumulation: are some pieces of the puzzle missing? Journal of Economic Perspectives 3: 141–152.

Kessler, D., and E.N. Wolff (1991), A comparative analysis of household wealth patterns in France and the United States, Review of Income and Wealth 37: 249–266.

Kimball, M.S. (1990), Precautionary saving in the small and the large, Econometrica 58: 53–73.

King, M.A., and L. Dicks-Mireaux (1982), Asset holdings and the life cycle, Economic Journal 92: 247–267.

King, M.A. and J.I. Leape (1984), Household portfolio composition and the lifecycle, Paper presented at the conference on Modelling the Accumulation and Distribution of Personal Wealth, Paris, September 1984.

King, M.A. and J.I. Leape (1986), Wealth, taxes and portfolio composition: An econometric study, Paper presented at the International Seminar on Life-Cycle Theory, Paris, June 1986.

King, M.A. and J.I. Leape (1998), Wealth and portfolio composition: theory and evidence, Journal of Public Economics 69: 155–193.

Kotlikoff, L.J. and A. Spivak (1981), The family as an incomplete annuities market, Journal of Political Economy 89: 372–391.

Kotlikoff, L.J. and L.H. Summers (1981), The role of intergenerational transfers in aggregate capital accumulation, Journal of Political Economy 89: 706–732.

Kotlikoff, L.J. and L.H. Summers (1988), The contribution of intergenerational transfers to total wealth: a reply, in D. Kessler and A. Masson, eds., Modelling the Accumulation and Distribution of Wealth (Clarendon Press, Oxford), pp. 53–67.

Laitner, J. (1979), Household bequest behaviour and the national distribution of wealth, Review of Economic Studies 46: 467–483.

Laitner, J. (1992), Random earnings differences, lifetime liquidity constraints, and altruistic intergenerational transfers, Journal of Economic Theory 58: 135–170.

Laitner, J. and F.T. Juster (1996), New evidence on altruism: a study of TIAA-CREF retirees, American Economic Review 86: 893–908.

Lampman, R.J. (1962), The Share of Top Wealth-holders in National Wealth, 1922–1956 (Princeton University Press, Princeton, NJ).

Leape, J.I. (1987), Taxes and transaction costs in asset market equilibrium, Journal of Public Economics, 33: 1–20.

Leipziger, D.M., D. Dollar, A.F. Shorrocks and S.Y. Song (1992), The Distribution of Income and Wealth in Korea (The World Bank, Washington).

Leland, H.E. (1968), Saving and uncertainty: the precautionary demand for saving, Quarterly Journal of Economics 82: 465–473.

Leung, S.F. (1994), Uncertain lifetime, the theory of the consumer, and the life cycle hypothesis, Econometrica 62: 1233–1239.

Lindh, T. and H. Ohlsson (1998), Self employment and wealth inequality, Review of Income and Wealth 44: 25–42.

Lippman, S.A. and J.J. McCall (1981), The economics of uncertainty: selected topics and probabilistic methods, in K.J. Arrow and M.D. Intriligator, eds., Handbook of Mathematical Economics Vol. 1 (North Holland, Amsterdam), pp. 211–284.

Lord, W.A. (1992), Saving, wealth, and the exchange-bequest motive, Canadian Journal of Economics 25: 743–753.

Lord, W. and P. Rangazas (1991), Savings and wealth in models with altruistic bequests, American Economic Review 81: 289–296.

Lyons, P.M. (1972), The distribution of personal wealth in Ireland, in A.A. Tait and J.A. Bristow, eds., Ireland: Some Problems of a Developing Economy (Gill and Macmillan, Dublin).

Lyons, P.M. (1975), Estate duty wealth estimates and the mortality multiplier, Economic and Social Review 6: 337–352.

Mankiw, N.G. and S.P. Zeldes (1990), The consumption of stockholders and nonstockholders, Working Paper No. 3402 (National Bureau of Economic Research).

Masson, A. and P. Pestieau (1996), Bequest motives and models of inheritance, Discussion paper 96-20 (DELTA, Paris).

McGarry, K. (1996), Inter vivos transfers and intended bequests, University of California at Los Angeles, mimeo.

McGarry, K. and R.F. Schoeni (1995), Transfer behavior in the Health and Retirement Survey: measurement and the redistribution of resources within the family, Journal of Human Resources 30: S184–S226.

Meade, J.E. (1964), Efficiency, Equality and the Ownership of Property (Allen and Unwin, London).

Meade, J.E. (1975), The Just Economy (Allen and Unwin, London).

Menchik, P.L. (1977), Primogeniture, equal sharing and the US distribution of wealth, Quarterly Journal of Economics 44: 299–316.

Menchik, P.L. (1979), Inter-generational transmission of inequality: an empirical study of wealth mobility, Economica 46: 349–362.

Menchik, P.L. (1988), Unequal estate division: is it altruism, reverse bequest, or simply noise? in D. Kessler and A. Masson, eds., Modelling the Accumulation and Distribution of Wealth (Clarendon Press, Oxford), pp. 105–116.

Menchik, P. and M. David (1983), Income distribution, lifetime savings and bequests, American Economic Review 73: 672–689.

Merton, R.C. (1971), Optimum consumption and portfolio rules in a continuous-time model, Journal of Economic Theory 3: 373–413.

Mirer, T.W. (1979), The wealth-age relation among the aged, American Economic Review 69: 435–443.

Mizoguchi, T. and N. Takayama (1984), Equity and Poverty Under Rapid Economic Growth: The Japanese Experience, Economic Research Series No. 21, The Institute of Economic Research, Hitotsubashi University (Kinokuniya Company Ltd., Tokyo).

Modigliani, F. (1988a), The role of intergenerational transfers and life cycle saving in the accumulation of wealth, Journal of Economic Perspectives 2: 15–40.

Modigliani, F. (1988b), Measuring the contribution of intergenerational transfers to total wealth: conceptual issues and empirical findings, in D. Kessler and A. Masson, eds., Modelling the Accumulation and Distribution of Wealth (Clarendon Press, Oxford), pp. 21–52.

Modigliani, F. and R. Brumberg (1954), Utility analysis and the consumption function: an interpretation of cross-section data, in K.K. Kurihara, ed., Post-Keynesian Economics (Rutgers University Press, New Brunswick NJ).

Nolan, B. (1991), The Wealth of Irish Households: What Can We Learn from Survey Data? (Combat Poverty Agency, Dublin).

Oja, G. (1980), Inequality of the wealth distribution in Canada, in Economic Council of Canada, Reflections on Canadian Incomes (Economic Council of Canada, Ottawa), pp. 341–364.

Oja, G. (1986), The wealth of Canadians: a comparison of Survey of Consumer Finances with National Balance Sheet estimates, Labour and Household Surveys Analysis Division Staff Reports, Statistics Canada.

Oulton, N. (1976), Inheritance and the distribution of wealth, Oxford Economic Papers 28: 86–101.

Piggott, J. (1984), The distribution of wealth in Australia—a survey, Economic Record 60: 252–265.

Poterba, J.M. and A.A. Samwick (1997), Household portfolio allocation over the life cycle, Working Paper No. 6185 (National Bureau of Economic Research).

Projector, D.S. and G.S. Weiss (1966), Survey of Financial Characteristics of Consumers (Board of Governors of the Federal Reserve System, Washington, D.C.).

Pryor, F. (1973), Simulation of the impact of social and economic institutions on the size distribution of income and wealth, American Economic Review 63: 50–72.

Raskall, P. (1977), The Distribution of Wealth in Australia, 1967–1972 (Planning Research Centre, University of Sydney).

Raskall, P. (1978), Who got what in Australia: the distribution of wealth, Journal of Australian Political Economy 2: 3–16.

Revell, J. (1967), The Wealth of the Nation. The Balance Sheet of the United Kingdom 1957–1961 (Cambridge University Press, Cambridge).

Rosenzweig, M.R. and O. Stark (1997), Handbook of Population and Family Economics (North-Holland, Amsterdam).

Rosenzweig, M.R. and K.I. Wolpin (1993), Intergenerational support and the life-cycle incomes of young men and their parents: human capital investments, co-residence and intergenerational financial transfers, Journal of Labor Economics 11: 84–111.

Rosenzweig, M.R. and K.I. Wolpin (1994), Parental and public transfers to young women and their children, American Economic Review 84: 1195–1212.

Royal Commission (1975), Royal Commission on the Distribution of Income and Wealth. Report No. 1, Initial Report on the Standing Reference (HMSO, London).

Royal Commission (1977), Royal Commission on the Distribution of Income and Wealth. Report No. 5, Third Report on the Standing Reference (HMSO, London).

Royal Commission (1979), Royal Commission on the Distribution of Income and Wealth. Report No. 7, Fourth Report on the Standing Reference (HMSO, London).

Rubinstein, W.D. (1979), The distribution of personal wealth in Victoria 1860–1974, Australian Economic History Review 19: 26–41.

Sandmo, A. (1970), The effect of uncertainty on saving decisions, Review of Economic Studies 37: 353–360.

Sargan J.D. (1957), The distribution of wealth, Econometrica 25: 568–590.

Shorrocks, A.F. (1973), Aspects of the distribution of personal wealth, PhD thesis (University of London).

Shorrocks, A.F. (1975a), The age-wealth relationship: a cross-section and cohort analysis, Review of Economics and Statistics 57: 155–163.

Shorrocks, A.F. (1975b), On stochastic models of size distribution, Review of Economic Studies 42: 631–641.

Shorrocks, A.F. (1979), On the structure of inter-generational transfers between families, Economica 46: 415–426.

Shorrocks, A.F. (1981), Life insurance and asset holdings in the United Kingdom, in D. Currie, D. Peel and W. Peters, eds., Microeconomic Analysis (Croom Helm, London), pp. 139–168.

Shorrocks, A.F. (1982), The portfolio composition of asset holdings in the United Kingdom, Economic Journal 92: 268–284.

Shorrocks, A.F. (1988), Wealth holdings and entrepreneurial activity, in D. Kessler and A. Masson, eds., Modelling the Accumulation and Distribution of Wealth (Clarendon Press, Oxford), pp. 241–256.

Skinner, J. (1988), Risky income, life cycle consumption, and precautionary savings, Journal of Monetary Economics 22: 237–255.

Smith, J.D. (1974), The concentration of personal wealth in America, 1969, Review of Income and Wealth 20: 143–180.

Smith, J.D. (1984), Trends in the concentration of personal wealth in the United States, 1958–1976, Review of Income and Wealth 30: 419–428.

Smith, J.D. (1987), Recent trends in the distribution of wealth in the US: data, research problems, and prospects, in E.N. Wolff, ed., International Comparisons of the Distribution of Household Wealth (Clarendon Press, Oxford), pp. 72–89.

Smith, J.D. and S.D. Franklin (1974), The concentration of personal wealth, 1922–1969, American Economic Review 64: 162–167.

Solon, G. (1992), Intergenerational income mobility in the United States, American Economic Review 82: 393–408.

Spant, R. (1982), The distribution of household wealth in some developed countries. A comparative study of Sweden, Denmark, France, Germany, United Kingdom and the United States, in D. Kessler, A. Masson and D. Strauss-Kahn, eds., Accumulation et Répartition des Patrimoines (CNRS and Economica, Paris), pp. 529–553.

Spant, R. (1987), Wealth distribution in Sweden: 1920–1983, in E.N. Wolff, ed., International Comparisons of the Distribution of Household Wealth (Clarendon Press, Oxford), pp. 51–71.

Steindl, J. (1965), Random Processes and the Growth of Firms (Griffin, London).

Steindl, J. (1972), The distribution of wealth after a model of Wold and Whittle 39: 263–280.

Stiglitz, J.E. (1969), Distribution of income and wealth among individuals, Econometrica 37: 382–397.

Strotz, R.H. (1956), Myopia and inconsistency in dynamic utility maximization, Review of Economic Studies 23: 165–180.

Summers, Lawrence H. (1981), Capital taxation and accumulation in a life cycle growth model, American Economic Review 71: 533–544.

Tachibanaki, T. (1989), Japan's new policy agenda: coping with unequal asset distribution, Journal of Japanese Studies 15: 345–369.

Takayama, N. (1991), Household asset and wealth holdings, in Public Pensions in the Japanese Economy, Manuscript (The Institute of Economic Research, Hitotsubashi University, Tokyo).

Takayama, N. (1992), The Greying of Japan: An Economic Perspective on Public Pensions (Kinokuniya Company Ltd. for Oxford University Press, Tokyo).

Tomes, N. (1981), The family, inheritance, and the intergenerational transmission of inequality, Journal of Political Economy 89: 928–958.

Vaughan, R.N. (1975), A study of the distribution of wealth, PhD thesis (University of Cambridge).

Vaughan, R.N. (1979), Class behaviour and the distribution of wealth, Review of Economic Studies 46: 447–465.

Venti, S.F. and D.A.Wise (1998), The cause of wealth dispersion at retirement: choice or chance? American Economic Review 88: 185–191.

Walravens, J. and P. Praet (1978), La distribution du patrimoine des particuliers en Belgique—1969, unpublished manuscript presented at the CREP-INSEE international meeting on Wealth Accumulation and Distribution, July 1978.

Wedgwood, J. (1928), The influence of inheritance on the distribution of wealth, Economic Journal 38: 38–55.

Wedgwood, J. (1929), The Economics of Inheritance (George Routledge & Sons: London).

Weicher, J.C. (1995), Changes in the distribution of wealth: Increasing inequality? Federal Reserve Bank of St. Louis Review 77: 5–23.

White, B.B. (1978), Empirical tests of the life cycle hypothesis, American Economic Review 68: 547–560.

Wilhelm, M.O. (1996), Bequest behavior and the effect of heirs' earnings: testing the altruistic model of bequests, American Economic Review 86: 874–892.

Wilhelm, M.O. (1997), Inheritance, steady-state consumption inequality, and the lifetime earnings process, Manchester School 65: 466–476.

Wold, H.O and P. Whittle (1957), A model explaining the Pareto distribution of wealth, Econometrica 25: 591–595.

Wolff, E.N. (ed.) (1987a), International Comparisons of the Distribution of Household Wealth (Clarendon Press, Oxford).

Wolff, E.N. (1987b), Estimates of household wealth inequality in the U.S., 1962–1983, Review of Income and Wealth 33: 231–256

Wolff, E.N. (1992), Changing inequality of wealth, American Economic Review 82: 552–558.

Wolff, E.N. (1994), Trends in household wealth in the United States, 1962–1983 and 1983–1989, Review of Income and Wealth 40: 143–174.

Wolff, E.N. (1996), International comparisons of wealth inequality, Review of Income and Wealth 42: 433–451.

Wolff, E.N. (1997), Wealth accumulation by age group in the US, 1962–1992: the role of savings, capital gains and intergenerational transfers, New York University, mimeo.

Wolff, E.N., and M. Marley (1989), Long-term trends in US wealth inequality: methodological issues and results, in R.E. Lipsey and H. S. Tice, eds., The Measurement of Saving, Investment, and Wealth (University of Chicago Press, Chicago), pp. 765–844.

Wolfson, M. (1977), The causes of inequality in the distribution of wealth: a simulation analysis, Ph.D. thesis (Cambridge University).

Wolfson, M. (1979), The bequest process and the causes of inequality in the distribution of wealth, in J.D. Smith, ed., Modelling the Intergenerational Transmission of Wealth (NBER, New York).

Yaari, M.E. (1965), Uncertain lifetime, life insurance, and the theory of the consumer, Review of Economic Studies 32: 137–150.

Zeldes, S.P. (1989), Optimal consumption with stochastic income: deviations from certainty equivalence, Quarterly Journal of Economics 104: 275–298.

Zimmerman, D.J. (1992), Regression toward mediocrity in economic stature, American Economic Review 82: 409–429.

Chapter 12

REDISTRIBUTION *

ROBIN BOADWAY[a] and MICHAEL KEEN[b]

[a]*Queens University, Ontario, Canada;* [b]*International Monetary Fund, Washington DC; University of Essex, UK; Institute for Fiscal Studies, UK*

Contents

* Helpful comments and advice from François Bourguignon, Sanjit Dhami and Jeremy Edwards are acknowledged with thanks. Views expressed are not necessarily those of any institution with which we are affiliated.

Handbook of Income Distribution: Volume 1. Edited by A. B. Atkinson and F. Bourguignon

Abstract

This paper reviews some of the central issues that arise in thinking about the motives for, politics of, constraints on and measurement of, redistribution. Amongst the themes are: the potential usefulness of apparently inefficient policy instruments in overcoming the self-selection constraints on redistribution and limiting the damage that ill-intentioned policymakers can do; the continued (perhaps increased) ignorance as to the effective incidence of many key taxes and benefits; and, while there are circumstances in which redistribution may plausibly generate efficiency gains, the likelihood that some trade-off between equity and efficiency is inescapable.

Keywords: Redistribution, equity, incidence, tax-transfer policy

JEL codes: D3, D6, D7, H2, I3

1. Introduction

One good reason for being interested in the distribution of income, the topic of this Handbook, is because one might want to change it. The term itself has become unfashionable in many parts of the world, but much of what governments do is manifestly redistribution of one kind or another. Private individuals also undertake large amounts of redistribution themselves. Whatever the labels they go by, distributional issues are, and will remain, the lifeblood of social and political debate, and of much economic analysis.

This paper reviews the rationale, nature and extent of redistribution, by which we shall simply mean an unrequited transfer of resources from one person to another. This is a vast canvas, so vast that—even in such a long paper as this—many issues are inevitably left unaddressed. Redistribution among regions within a federation is not considered, for example, and nor is redistribution among countries. Nor do we deal at any length with intra-generational redistribution within the family.[1] Some issues we cover only briefly, especially if good treatments are already available. Moreover, the perspective is mostly theoretical: the theoretical advances over the last twenty years or so have been more profound, arguably—and as yet—than the empirical ones.

The paper starts by considering the motives for redistribution (Section 2). Amongst these is the exercise of greed and compulsion, leading to a focus in Section 3 on the politics of redistribution. Section 4 then considers the limits to the redistribution that can be achieved in practice, and Section 5 considers the issues that arise in trying to measure the distributional impact of public sector policies. The concluding section highlights some of the central themes that emerge from this review.

2. Motives for redistribution

One can distinguish three broad rationales for redistribution:
- the pursuit of social justice as an ethical imperative;
- the achievement of mutually advantageous efficiency gains; and
- the exercise of self-interest through the coercive power of the state.

The conceptual distinction between these motives is less sharp, however, than it may at first seem. The notion that ethically acceptable decisions are those that would be taken, ex ante, behind a veil of ignorance as to one's own position in society, for example, leads readily to the adoption of an objective—maximization of the expected utility of a representative citizen—that is much the same as that to which a naive concern with efficiency would lead. And even if it involves redistributing away from themselves, for those with power to impose the implications of their own ethical preferences on others with different views is no less an exercise of coercive power than is expropriation of

---

[1] Thus we use the terms "individual" and "household" synonymously. The classic reference on the allocation of resources in the family is Becker (1981). For a recent survey, see Bourguignon and Chiappori (1992).

resources directly to those in power. In practice, of course, any measure of redistribution will rarely reflect the operation of just one of these motives.

Though the distinctions between them thus quickly become blurred, these three motives nevertheless provide a useful organizing framework within which to assess some of the main approaches to the analysis of redistribution. The rest of this section focusses on the first two broad classes of motive, leaving the third until the next section.

2.1. Redistribution as social justice

One might view a concern with distributional issues as a matter of ethical preference that transcends—or at least, is not explicitly modeled as part of—the determinants of economic behaviour. It is as if people have two distinct personalities, with their self-interested selves essentially disjoint from their ethical selves, a perspective adopted by Arrow (1951a). Such an approach might be defended simply on the lines of analytical convenience: our self-interested preferences guide our day-to-day participation in the market economy, while our ethical ones apply to our participation in collective decision-making. Such a split personality is made very sharply by the device—introduced by Vickrey (1945), subsequently and independently developed by Harsanyi (1955) and used too by Rawls (1971)—of attaching ethical significance to the choices people would make about social arrangements behind a hypothetical "veil of ignorance" as to which of all possible people they will become. Even to conceive of such an exercise requires that one be able to dissociate one's self-interested self from one's selfless self, with the latter best equipped to make ethical judgements.[2]

Within this class of approaches, different views are taken as to what constitutes social justice. The most common—still, indeed, the dominant approach to the normative economic analysis of redistribution—is the *welfarist* one (a term due to Sen, 1970a), according to which the social desirability of alternative social states is to be assessed in terms of some Bergson–Samuelson Social Welfare Function $W(U_1, \ldots, U_N)$ defined over the utility levels U_i, $i = 1, \ldots, N$ of the population under study. This function is naturally taken to be both anonymous (permuting utilities across individuals has no effect on social welfare) and Paretian (nondecreasing in all arguments). Tighter ethical judgements, and restrictions on the kind of interpersonal utility comparisons one is willing to make, impose further structure on the form of one's $W(\cdot)$: see, for example, Boadway and Bruce (1984).

The potentially powerful implications of the welfarist approach were recognized by Edgeworth (1881) over a century ago, and later stated most generally by Dasgupta et al. (1973). Suppose that all N members of the population have the same strictly concave utility function $U(Y)$ defined over lump sum income Y. Then the maximisation of any S-concave social welfare function—meaning, roughly, one that is increased by replac-

---

[2] Some would argue that ethical behaviour (honesty, altruism, etc.) can be viewed as being ingrained through an evolutionary process akin to the biological evolution of physical traits. For an outline of this approach, see Frank (1989).

ing each individual's utility by a weighted average of all utilities[3]—requires setting $Y_i = (1/N) \sum_k Y_k$, $\forall i$: that is, complete equalisation of incomes.[4] Note that the case for redistribution of *income* that thus emerges is quite distinct from any concern with the distribution of *well-being*: one arrives at complete equalisation of incomes even in the utilitarian case $W = \Sigma U_i$, in which government cares not about the distribution of utility but only its total. What ultimately drives redistribution in this case is not so much a concern for equality of utilities as a diminishing private marginal utility of income combined with identical utility functions.

This welfarist approach lends itself well to the applied analysis of distributional issues. Each individual—and, more particularly, each policymaker—can be conceived of as having a distinct social welfare function, and perhaps too distinct cardinalisations of utility. For any given preferences, and given a complete specification of how the economy functions, it is then in principle a straightforward matter to compute an optimal distribution of income.

For marginal reforms, in particular, welfarism provides an elegant and practicable analytical framework. Differentiating with respect to the lump sum income of the ith person gives a distributional weight $\beta_i \equiv (\partial W/\partial U_i)\partial U_i/\partial Y_i$ that enables one to compare and aggregate real income gains to different units: the higher is β_i the greater is the social gain from an increase in i's real income, and redistributing \$1 from individual k to individual i raises social welfare if and only if $\beta_i > \beta_k$. These distributional weights have proved a convenient way of introducing distributional concerns into applied welfare analyses. These have been widely used in cost-benefit analysis (Drèze and Stern, 1987) and have enabled an appealing approach to the identification of desirable tax reforms. Ahmad and Stern (1984), in particular show how the restriction that $\beta_i > 0$ for all households i can be used to identify Pareto-improving reforms; Mayshar and Yitzhaki (1995) show how the further restriction that the β_i fall with income enable reforms to be identified that increase social welfare for all concave $W(\cdot)$. Results of this kind hold the prospect of narrowing the range for dispute over sensible directions of reform, since all can subscribe to the same judgement even though they may differ in the precise form of their social preferences. Methodologically, this approach of exploring the implications of social welfare functions that appear in the analysis as something of a *deus ex machina* sits well with economists' preferred view of themselves as giving dispassionate advice on emotive issues: it enables one to analyse the consequences of alternative distributional judgements without endorsing any.

Though it has thus proved empirically valuable, welfarism has powerful critics. One line of attack sees it as too permissive in attaching no significance to the process by which the economy reaches its final state. No importance is attached, for example, to

---

[3] More precisely (and introducing the convention of indicating vectors by bold type) an S-concave function is one such that $F(P\mathbf{x}) \geq F(\mathbf{x})$ for all bistochastic matrices P (all square matrices, that is, with $P_{ij} \geq 0$, $\sum_i P_{ij} = \sum_j P_{ij} = 1$, $\forall i, j$.

[4] This of course ignores the possible incentive effects of taxation; Section 4 looks at the limits to redistribution these create.

any property rights that might stand in the way of redistribution. An extreme libertarian position would regard as illegitimate—a denial of social justice rather than a potential contribution to it—redistribution that violates property rights that have been legitimately acquired. Such a view, associated with Nozick (1974), leaves little scope for redistribution. Nor, conversely, is any independent importance attached to equality of opportunity, a dimension explored by Roemer (1996) and Fleurbaey and Maniquet (1998). Even in a minimalist state, however, distributional issues cannot be entirely avoided: for the basic functions of the nightwatchman—such as maintaining law and order—create efficiency gains that must somehow be shared across the members of the economy (Inman, 1985).

The second line of criticism of the standard welfarist approach, urged most forcefully by Sen (1985, 1992), sees it as too narrow: it focusses only on individuals' utilities, and moreover sees these as reflecting only real incomes in a somewhat narrow sense. It is possible, for example, to imagine redistribution going hand in hand with political repression (as perhaps in some formerly communist countries); one might wish to attach importance to the latter as well as to the former. A range of social concerns beyond material well-being—Rawlsian "primary goods"— may also matter. One such is liberty; and Sen (1970b) shows very starkly how even the apparently minimally liberalist notion that individuals should be allowed to make the final decision on some issues, such as what books they themselves read, may lead to Pareto inefficient outcomes.[5] Importance might also be attached, in and of itself, to whether people deal honestly with one another, or to whether they behave corruptly. Moreover, what matters in evaluating alternative economic arrangements may not be income in the usual sense but some rather wider notion of the quality of life enjoyed. This underlies Sen's notion of capabilities and functionings. The idea is that poverty is not simply an inadequacy of income; it is a lack of basic capabilities to function as a human being. Functioning involves being able to take part in activities such as clothing, feeding and housing oneself, participating in community activities, appearing in public without shame, avoiding morbidity, and so on. Alleviating poverty then involves generating minimally acceptable capabilities, which in turn requires that resources be tied to personal circumstances (such as age, gender, health status) and social circumstances (physical and social environments, epidemiological factors, public health characteristics). This approach has been developed into an alternative to the standard approach to distributional analysis described above. The relative difficulty of measuring capabilities, however, has meant that this alternative approach has not yet had the impact on practical distributional analysis that the standard distributional weights have done.

---

[5] Sen's celebrated example concerns two persons, prudish person 1 and racier person 2, and their joint decision as to whether 1, 2 or neither should read *Lady Chatterly's Lover*, called options x, y and z, respectively. Person 2's preference ordering is $z > x > y$, while 1's is $x > y > z$. Thus, x Pareto dominates y. But, Sen argues that liberalism would suggest that z is preferred to x (1 should not be forced to read the book), while y should be preferred to z (2 should be allowed to read it); so, y should be preferred to x on liberal grounds, which contradicts Pareto domination.

These two—the welfarist and capabilities approaches—are of course not the only possible approaches to social justice and its distributional consequences, though they are currently the most influential. One alternative with a strong historical pedigree, for example, is the notion that all should suffer equal sacrifice in financing government, a precept discussed fully in Musgrave (1959). Though this does not in itself call for redistribution—no sacrifice is needed if there is no public expenditure to be financed—it clearly is a distinct principle of distributive justice. And it has some strong implications. With such a view of the world it is far from obvious, for example—even in the absence of incentive effects—that taxes ought to be progressive.[6]

2.2. Efficient redistribution

One of the ideas most deeply ingrained in thinking about economic policy is the notion of an inherent trade-off between equity and efficiency. Efficiency-enhancing policies increase the size of the economic pie; redistribution, on the other hand, cuts the pie more fairly but in the process causes it to shrink.[7] This stark contrast view is reflected in Musgrave's (1959) influential distinction between three roles of government: stabilization, allocation and distribution. Allocative efficiency and distributive justice were seen as inherently conflicting objectives, and for clarity of purpose, at least, best kept distinct.

In recent years, however, there has been increasing interest in the possibility that redistribution and efficiency might not always conflict, but that in some circumstances, it might be possible to have both: to make the pie larger by cutting it more fairly. At a policy level, this new view of redistribution was lent special force by the observation—at least until recently—of economic success going hand in hand with improved distributional equity in some of the tiger economies (Kanbur, this volume, Chapter 13). At a theoretical level, it was fed too by a recognition that in a second-best world redistributing income might act on additional constraints in such a way as to generate efficiency gains. This section explores the possibility that redistribution might actually improve the efficiency with which the economy operates.

There is a semantic point of some importance here. The term "efficiency gain" is used in the literature in at least three different senses, to mean: a Pareto improvement; a potential Pareto improvement, meaning that all could gain if appropriate compensation were paid; an increase in total output, or some other such measure of aggregate activity. An efficiency gain in the first sense clearly implies also a gain in the second, but beyond

---

[6] It is straightforward to show, for example, that equal absolute sacrifice in financing some fixed level of public expenditure(requiring $U(Y - T(Y)) - U(Y) = \kappa$ for all Y and some κ) implies an increasing average tax rate if and only if the income elasticity if the marginal utility of income exceeds unity in absolute value. (This follows on setting the derivative of the utility difference to zero, multiplying by Y and rearranging to find that $T'(Y) > T(Y)/Y$ iff $U'(Y)Y$ is decreasing in Y).

[7] Having succumbed to one cliché, we should for completeness refer to another: Okun's (1975) notion that money transferred from rich to poor is carried in a "leaky bucket": "[s]ome of it will simply disappear in transit" (p. 91).

that the links between the three notions of efficiency gain are tenuous. Clearly too each has rather different ethical status. All, however, are potentially of interest.

2.2.1. Altruism

One case in which redistribution can obviously be Pareto-improving is that in which transferors are altruistically inclined towards recipients (early recognition of this is in Sen (1967), Hochman and Rogers (1969) and Thurow (1971)).

Indeed such altruism carries the possibility that some redistribution—though not, perhaps, enough—will be undertaken voluntarily. Historically, charity has been a major source of support of the poor, and voluntary giving remains sizeable in many developed countries: around 2 to 3% of GNP in the US, for example. Altruistic donations are perhaps even more important in developing countries, being a major source of support within families, extended families and even communities. Much of the international aid flowing from developed to developing countries presumably reflects altruism, at least in large part. More important for our purposes, altruism has potentially profound implications for the need for, and the effectiveness, of redistribution by the public sector.

The simplest view of altruistic redistribution sees the well-being of the recipients as a public good from which the donors derive pleasure. Imagine, for example, an economy comprising a single poor person, whose welfare $U^p(C_p)$ depends only on their consumption C_p, and N rich individuals, each of whose welfare $u^r[C_r, U^p(C_p)] \equiv U^r(C_r, C_p)$ also depends positively on that of the poor. To see the scope and limits of voluntary redistribution in such a context, consider the properties of a symmetric Nash equilibrium in which each rich person i chooses their gift to the poor, g_i, so as to maximise their own utility $U^r(Y_r - g_i, Y_p + g_i + G_{-i})$, taking as given the contributions $G_{-i} \equiv \sum_{k \neq i} g_k$ of all others; denote the solution by $g_i^* \geq 0 \ \forall i$.

This noncooperative equilibrium is indeed Pareto-superior to that without redistribution: the poor person is clearly better off, and so too is each rich person (they have revealed themselves to benefit by contributing, and benefit also from the gifts of the other rich).

But the equilibrium is also easily seen to be Pareto inefficient: all, rich and poor alike, could gain if each rich person were to give slightly more. This inefficiency is an immediate implication of viewing the income of the poor as a public good, for there then arises a standard free-rider problem: each rich person ignores the benefit that their gift to the poor conveys to other rich people, and so each ultimately gives too little.

This inefficiency creates scope for a Pareto-improvement through compulsory redistribution.[8] There is, however, an important limitation on what can be achieved: in this model, a limited amount of redistribution is liable to prove entirely ineffective, having no effect on the final well-being of the poor. The reason is straightforward: each rich person cares only about their own consumption and that of the poor person, and their ability to offset a redistributive tax levied on them by reducing their own voluntary transfers means

---

[8] The discussion focuses on the direct transfer of resources; an alternative response to the inefficiency is to subsidize private gifts, as often indeed often occurs through the tax deductibility of charitable donations.

that such a tax has no effect on the opportunity set they perceive. To see this formally, denote by T the tax imposed on each rich person, proceeds of which are redistributed to the poor. Imagine that all rich people except the ith respond to the introduction of this tax by reducing their gifts by the full amount of the tax, to $g^{**} = g^* - T$. The problem of the ith rich person is then to choose g_i to maximise $U^r(Y_r - g_i - T, Y_p + g_i + \sum_{k \neq i} G^{**}_{-i} + NT) = U^r(Y_r - \tilde{g}_i, Y_p + \tilde{g}_i + \sum_{k \neq i} G^*_{-i})$, where $\tilde{g} = g_i + T$. This is of exactly the same form as the problem in the absence of intervention, and so has the solution $\tilde{g}_i = g^*$, implying $g_i = g^*_i + T$: thus if all others reduce their gifts by the amount of the tax, so too will person i.

This ineffectiveness of redistribution clearly requires the altruistic link to be operative for all the rich: the inability of the rich to extract transfers from the poor means that compulsory redistribution which is taken so far that the voluntary gifts of the rich fall to zero will indeed affect the final income of the poor. The implication is powerful, nevertheless. Pareto improving redistribution does not merely require public intervention: it requires enough redistribution to crowd out private transfers. A little redistribution may have no effect.

This result bears an obvious resemblance to Barro's (1974) version of Ricardian equivalence in the sense that it predicts the neutrality of government transfers. But there is a major difference: in Barro's model, the allocation dictated by the dynastic utility function of the "representative" agent is fully efficient (see Piketty, this volume, Chapter 8, for an explicit treatment of the dynastic model). Altruism is kept within the dynastic family, so that the effects of all transfers are fully internalised. There is then no reason to regret the ineffectiveness of public policy: there is no inefficiency to be addressed. Inefficiency re-emerges, however, with a recognition that the socio-biological facts of life render the Barro dynastic family untenable: each child has parents from two separate families, so that all families are inextricably linked through future inter-marriage. The implication, developed by Bernheim and Bagwell (1988), is that a parent caring for his or her own offspring indirectly cares for the descendants of all contemporary parents. Thus, the altruistic bequest again becomes like a public good, and its level of provision inefficient. Too little saving will be done for future generations (perhaps none) a point that was recognized some time ago by Marglin (1963) and Sen (1967). Though this in turn suggests a case for public intervention, policy is again liable to be ineffective. Pursuing the argument to its limits, Bernheim and Bagwell (1988) provide a general statement of the considerable power of altruism to generate policy ineffectiveness. In particular, the ineffectiveness of policy continues to apply—until gifts cease to be made—if transfers to the poor are financed not by lump sum taxes on the rich but by distorting taxes on their labour supply (see their Example 2); and it applies too if the government makes no transfers to the poor but instead subsidies the gifts of the rich (Andreoni, 1990). The ineffectiveness of redistribution in models of altruism as enjoyment of a public good is in this sense rather general. To have effect, public redistribution must drive out private charity.

Returning to the model of redistribution as contribution to a public good, two implications for the situation of the poor deserve emphasis.[9]

The first is that the poor may find that any increase in their own pre-tax income Y_p is largely offset by a reduction in the gifts that the rich are willing to make to them. For they face an implicit marginal tax rate whose magnitude is determined by the preferences of the rich. In the limit, if the income elasticity of demand of the rich for the net income of the poor is zero,[10] then the poor face an effective marginal tax rate of 100%. In effect, the rich then care only about raising the poor to some minimum level of income, and then tax away any excess that the poor acquire by reducing their gifts. Such a situation gives rise to the *samaritan's dilemma* (Buchanan, 1975): knowing that their donations might induce the poor not to earn income, should the rich nonetheless promise to bring the poor up to some minimum level? We return to this question below.

A second striking implication is that an increase in the number of the rich can actually leave the poor worse off: not only may the net income of the poor deviate further from its first-best level (from the perspective of the rich) as the number of the rich increases—reflecting the intensification of the free-rider problem—the gift of each rich person may actually fall, and moreover by so much as to more than offset the increase in the number of people making the gift.[11]

The view of altruistic redistribution as the enjoyment of a public good thus has extremely strong implications. Some, indeed, appear to be inconsistent with practical experience. The model also predicts, for example—the well-known theorem of Warr (1983), further developed by Bergstrom et al. (1986)—that a redistribution of income amongst rich donors will have no effect on the final income of the poor; this runs counter to empirical evidence cited by, for instance, in Hochman and Rogers (1973). The model also implies that all rich contributors will enjoy the same level of utility, irrespective of any difference in their private incomes.[12]

So apparently implausible are the implications of this simple model of altruism that there has been much interest in developing alternatives. One such is to suppose that donors derive utility not only from the well-being of the recipient but also from the act of

[9] Both follow from routine comparative statics on the necessary condition for g_i, evaluated at a symmetric equilibrium,

$$U_Y(Y - g, Ng) + U_G(Y - g, Ng) = 0,$$

together with the second order condition $U_{GG} - U_{YY} < 0$. It is assumed too that the income elasticities of demand for both private consumption and consumption of the poor are strictly positive.

[10] So that $U_{YY} - (U_Y/U_G)U_{GY} = 0$.

[11] This is the case, for instance, if $U_{YG} = 0$ and initially $N = 1$ (here treating the number of rich people as a continuous variable).

[12] Intuitively, since all enjoy the same consumption of the poor, and the income elasticity of demand for the net income of the poor is strictly positive, the rich can all be content with their gift only if they all have the same net income. (More formally, the result can be seen by differentiating the necessary condition with respect to Y to find that the equality can hold for distinct net incomes only if $U_{YY} - (U_Y/U_G)U_{GY} = 0$.) See Itaya et al. (1997).

giving itself. In this view the ith rich person has utility $U^r(C_r, C_p, g_i)$, the appearance of g_i reflecting the *warm glow* of giving. This formulation blunts many of the stark implications of the public good approach: public redistribution will not be fully offset even when gifts are operative, for example, because the rich are no longer indifferent between \$1 that they give to the poor themselves and \$1 that the government gives; and the implicit marginal tax rate on the poor will be lower, since even if their gift becomes less needed the rich will be reluctant to forgo the distinct pleasure they derive from giving. Further implications are developed by Andreoni (1990).

The picture of redistribution as motivated by a selfless altruism is in many ways a happy one. So beguiling is it, indeed, that its lack of intrinsic ethical worth deserves emphasis. For example, in Section 4.8 we briefly review the literature on redistribution in federal systems, due originally to Boskin (1973) and Pauly (1973). This grounds redistribution in the supposition that the rich in each local jurisdiction are altruistically inclined towards the mobile poor; in one contribution that we shall later focus on, Wildasin (1991), for instance, characterizes policies that are "optimal" in the sense of maximising the welfare of the rich. But it is all too easy to forget—as Wildasin does not—that this is a narrow and conceivably repugnant sense, there being no reason for wanting to order society according only to the wishes of the rich, however well-intentioned they might happen to be. Indeed in a wider context altruism can clearly have a dark side. It may be racially or sexually biased. The altruism of the rich and powerful towards their own children may perpetuate inequalities of opportunity. The task of policy then quite possibly becomes not to facilitate the exercise of altruism but, on the contrary, to prevent it.

Note too that what looks like altruism may reflect a sharp self-interest: transfers may be made to the poor to forestall violence or theft (Sala-i-Martin, 1997).

2.2.2. *Social insurance*

Some people have bad luck. That bad luck can take many forms, including becoming unemployed or disabled, having poor health, having more children to finance than expected, having fewer children to look after one than planned, choosing a feckless partner; the list is depressingly long. If they have not been able to arrange appropriate insurance themselves, such ill-fortune creates an evident case for redistribution—from the lucky to the unlucky—on the grounds of social justice encountered earlier. Moreover, it may be that the prospect of such ex post redistribution will raise the expected utility of all, including those who in the event will prove to be lucky. In this sense social insurance may prove efficiency-enhancing. Indeed, as was noted long ago by Vickrey (1945) and hinted at above, one very general kind of bad luck—being born with low intrinsic ability to earn—can be seen as providing a very general basis for systematic redistribution across differing income levels: behind the veil of ignorance, people would prefer a system of redistribution amongst the living that would effectively insure them against the risk of being born with low ability.

Insurance market failure. The question, of course, is why individuals are unable to purchase such insurance for themselves. This may seem evident enough in the case of innate ability, since the outcome of the uncertain event is presumably publicly revealed at the time an individual reaches sufficient maturity to enter contracts. Even in this case, however, parents may be able to purchase insurance on their offsprings' behalf. For the narrower risks, prominent amongst the reasons for potential failure of insurance markets are asymmetries of information between insurance companies and those wishing to buy insurance. These asymmetries are conventionally grouped into two kinds: adverse selection (those wishing to buy insurance being better informed as to the likelihood of the event occurring to them than the insurance company can be) and moral hazard (insurance companies being unable to observe actions taken by the insured that affect the likelihood of the insured peril occurring or the size of the damage). The precise implications of these asymmetries are typically quite model-specific, sensitive to such matters as the conjectures insurers have as to whether actions they take which make contracts offered by others unprofitable will result in those contracts being withdrawn. In the broadest terms, however, the implication is that insurance markets may fail to exist, and if they do exist may reach equilibria that could be improved upon by a government with no better information than is available to private companies.[13]

Consider, for example, a possible market in which individuals can buy insurance against the possibility of becoming unemployed. Suppose that there are two types of workers, differing only in the probability of losing their job. Figure 1 illustrates. In the absence of any insurance, each consumes at point α, enjoying a wage of w when employed and nonlabour income of κ if not. The two types have the same (von Neumann–Morgenstern) preferences, and are risk-averse, so that their level curves of expected utility are convex to the origin as drawn, and differ only in so far as the probability of unemployment differs between them: specifically, the indifference curves of the group with the higher risk of being unemployed are steeper (the intuition being that since they are more likely to find themselves unemployed they are willing to forgo more consumption when employed for a marginal increase in consumption when unemployed). The line $\alpha\alpha$, the fair-bet line for the low-risk persons, shows the set of points at which the expected consumption of a low risk individual would be the same as at the endowment point α. Thus it represents the set of contracts which would exactly break even if taken up only by the low risks, with all points below that line — offering less consumption to the policy-holder in both states of nature — making strictly positive profit if taken up only by the low risk. Similarly, $\alpha\beta$ is the set of contracts that break even if taken up only by the high risks, while $\alpha\gamma$ is the set that would break even if taken up by all.

In an ideal world, each type of consumer would be able to fully insure themselves against unemployment. If an individual's type were costlessly observable, one would indeed expect competition to lead to this outcome, with contracts offered at both A and

---

[13] The material in this subsection is largely standard, and dealt with at more length by, for example, Atkinson (1991), Barr (1993) Hirshleifer and Riley (1992) and Mas-Colell et al. (1995).

(a) No pooling equilibrium

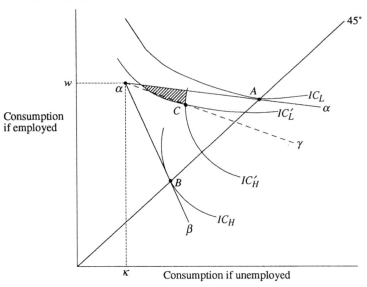

(b) Possibility of a separating equilibrium

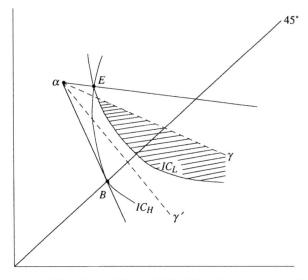

Fig. 1. Insurance market issues. (a) No poling equilibrium. (b) Possibility of a separating equilibrium.

B: low risks buy the former, high risk the latter, and neither faces any consumption uncertainty. Suppose, however, that risk-type now becomes unobservable. Then all high risks will try to buy contract *A*; but that means both types are buying *A*, and since *A* lies above $\alpha\gamma$ the contract makes a loss. Adverse selection thus prevents competitive markets attaining a first-best outcome.

What then will be the laissez faire outcome when insurance companies cannot observe type? The answer depends on the assumed form of market conduct. Suppose, following Rothschild and Stiglitz (1976), that each firm takes as given the set of contracts offered by other firms and can observe the total quantity of insurance each individual purchases. It is then easy to see that there cannot be a "pooling" equilibrium in which both types buy the same contract. If there were, for profits to be zero, it would have to be at a point like *C* in Fig. 1(a). But since the indifference curve of the low risk type through this point (IC'_L) is flatter than that of the high risk (IC'_H) there exists an area like that shaded in the picture such that any contract in this area would be purchased by the low risk but not by the high and, being below $\alpha\alpha$, would make a profit.

The only possibility is then of a separating equilibrium in which the two types buy different contracts, illustrated in Fig. 1(b). Such an equilibrium must constrain the contract for the low risks to be no more attractive to the high risks than the contract designed for the latter. The high risks are fully insured at point *B*. The contract bought by the low risks must then be along αE so that it is not bought by the high risks. But if the zero profit line for pooled contracts is $\alpha\gamma$ there can then be no equilibrium: any contract in the shaded area shown would attract the low risk away from *E* (or anything to the left of it) and the high risks away from *B*; and, being below $\alpha\gamma$, any such contract will make a profit. In this case there thus exists no equilibrium. In other cases, however, there does exist a separating equilibrium. Suppose, for example, that the zero profit line for pooled contracts were $\alpha\gamma'$. Then the shaded area vanishes, and contracts *B* and *E* do indeed constitute a separating equilibrium.

What then are the implications for public policy? While governments, by virtue of being able to elicit information from households in a mandatory way, may become better informed than private insurers, the interesting case is that in which government is no better informed. When it exists, the above separating equilibrium is constrained efficient: a general result in models of this sort. But if no equilibrium exists, a Pareto gain can be obtained by introducing a compulsory scheme of pooled insurance with all persons required to purchase a common amount. Redistributive objectives will have been satisfied since the unlucky will benefit at the expense of the lucky. But, this will be partly at the expense of a system in which low risks are cross-subsidising high risks.

On the other hand, if, unlike in the above model, private insurers are unable to monitor individual purchases of insurance (say, because they can spread purchases among more than one insurer), a pooling equilibrium can exist. Higher risk persons will purchase more insurance than lower risk ones at the common premium. In such a setting, compulsory provision of insurance in equal amounts to all can be implemented so that the lower risk households are better off, while high risks can be better or worse off (Johnson, 1977).[14]

It is thus conceivable that a redistributive scheme of social insurance can generate an efficiency improvement. The same may be true if the state is able to reap scale economies in the provision of insurance (a point which, as Atkinson (1991) reminds us, was given some importance in the Beveridge report), if the costs of administering a compulsory state scheme are less than those of a competitive scheme (as argued by Arrow, 1963) or if there are economies of scope in running insurance schemes of this sort in tandem with the tax collection system.

Much of what governments do—pensions, unemployment and sickness benefit—does indeed look so like the provision of compulsory insurance, with benefits payable at similar rates to all and subject to a test not of current means but rather of past contributions, that it is naturally labeled social insurance. Such measures are now often rationalised by reference to the kind of informational arguments above. Quite how persuasive an interpretation this is, however, remains unclear. Atkinson (1991) notes, in particular, that such models typically have the feature that it is the low risks who fare worst under market provision, just as in the example above it is they that bear some residual risk, with the high risks being completely insured. This seems a puzzle, since casual observation suggests that the concern which has often driven compulsory insurance schemes has been that it is the high risk that are hardly done by, not the low risk. This suggests that more work is still to be done on the relationship between insurance market failure and state provision. Perhaps—though this is not the case in the model above—it is precisely the adverse externality experienced by the low risks in the laissez faire equilibrium that galvanises them into supporting compulsory state provision. Or perhaps it is the case, for example, that the high risks also face a liquidity constraint that prevents them taking out the full insurance that would otherwise be available to them, so confounding the potential inefficiencies of insurance markets with capital market imperfections of the kind discussed below.

Risk-taking and investment. The model just analysed was one of pure adverse selection: people had no economic decisions to make. In practice, they face a myriad of choices that affect both their future incomes and the risks to which they are exposed. And a key concern in discussion of the welfare state has been precisely with the likely impact that the provision of insurance will have on such decisions. Will it lead people to save too little, for instance, and will it induce them too take too much risk (knowing there is a safety net to catch them if they fall)?

---

[14] This result depends critically on the ability of households to choose their quantities of insurance freely. Dahlby (1981) shows that if a Rothschild–Stiglitz equilibrium exists, a necessary, but not sufficient condition for compulsory insurance to be Pareto-improving is that households be free to purchase voluntary supplements. Moreover, if an equilibrium in the sense of Wilson (1980) exists, compulsory insurance can never be Pareto improving.

The potential trade-off between the desire to provide insurance and the desire to preserve appropriate incentives to work and save was raised and explored by Eaton and Rosen (1980) and Varian (1980). Sinn (1995, 1996) emphasises that redistribution may have beneficial effects on risk-taking. To see the considerations at work, it is useful to combine both sets of concerns into a single model.[15]

Consider then a two-period world in which a large number of (ex ante) identical individuals must take two decisions before the uncertainty is resolved. For one, they invest an amount x in acquiring human capital, yielding them $x + \lambda\theta$ in period 2, where θ is stochastic with (for simplicity) all realisations negative.[16] Clearly the choice of x will be affected by, but does not in itself affect, the uncertainty faced. The second choice variable does: by spending an amount e on risk prevention activities in the first period—studying harder or longer to enter a safer profession (a doctor rather than an actor) perhaps—the stochastic component of second period income is affected through $\lambda(e)$, with $\lambda' < 0$, $\lambda'' > 0$. Note that e affects both the uncertainty of second period income, its variance being $\lambda^2\text{var}(\theta)$, and expected second period income, $x + \lambda(e)\bar{\theta}$ (where $\bar{\theta} \equiv E[\theta]$). Preferences are described by a von Neumann–Morgenstern utility function $u(C_1) + v(C_2)$ over consumption in the two periods, with both u and v increasing and strictly concave. For definiteness, it is further assumed that $v''' = 0$.

If individuals could insure fully, all would optimally share equally in second period income. Assume a large number of identical individuals (their number normalised to one), then aggregate second period income is $x + \lambda\bar{\theta}$, and the first-best problem reduces to that of maximising $u(w - x - e) + v(x + \lambda(e)\bar{\theta})$, with necessary conditions

$$x : \ -u' + v' = 0, \tag{1}$$

$$e : \ -u' + \lambda'\bar{\theta}v' = 0. \tag{2}$$

To explore the effects and optimal design of redistributive taxation as a response to imperfections of the insurance market, suppose now, at the opposite extreme, that individuals are for some reason unable to buy any insurance. The only insurance is that implicitly provided by the government, which taxes second period income at rate t and returns the proceeds $t(x + \lambda(e)\bar{\theta})$ as a poll subsidy; there are no taxes or subsidies in period 1. People take the poll subsidy as independent of their actions, so that the typical individual's necessary conditions are:

$$x : \ -u' + (1 - t)E[v'] = 0, \tag{3}$$

$$e : \ -u' + (1 - t)\lambda'E[v'\theta] = 0, \tag{4}$$

[15] This is essentially an extension of that in Varian to capture Sinn's concerns by allowing for a decision on the extent of risk-taking.

[16] It may seem odd that the return to human capital is negative. But this is only for simplicity: it would be straightforward, but notationally burdensome, to ensure a strictly positive return in all states.

which implicitly define investment and risk-avoidance decisions as functions $x(t)$ and $e(t)$ of the tax rate.

The no-intervention equilibrium—that with $t = 0$—is clearly inefficient. Specifically, it can be shown that the level of risk-prevention e is higher in the absence of intervention than it is in the first-best:[17] the absence of insurance makes people too cautious. It also leads them to invest too little in their human capital: x is lower in the no-intervention equilibrium than in the first-best.[18]

Consider then the effects of the redistributive tax scheme. Solving Eqs. (3) and (4) for $x(t)$ and $e(t)$ and substituting into lifetime expected utility gives the effect of tax increase on maximised expected lifetime welfare $V(t)$ as:

$$\frac{V'(t)}{E[v']} = -\lambda(e)\frac{\text{cov}[v', \theta]}{E[v']} + t\bar{\theta}\lambda'e' + tx'. \tag{6}$$

This shows clearly the three effects at work. The first is an insurance effect: the presence of the tax reduces the uncertainty of net income, since the government cushions some of the loss if things turn out badly but also shares in the gain if they turn out well. Since $\text{cov}(v', \theta) < 0$, this effect of increasing the tax rate is unambiguously beneficial.

---

[17] To see this, note first that Eqs. (1) and (2) give

$$\lambda'(e^F)\bar{\theta} = 1 \tag{F.1}$$

the superscript indicating the first-best. Noting that Eqs. (3) and (4) imply $E[v'] = \lambda' E[v'\theta]$ when $t = 0$, using the definition of a covariance and rearranging one finds

$$\lambda'(e(0))\bar{\theta} = 1 - \lambda'(e(0))\left(\frac{\text{cov}(v', \theta)}{E[v']}\right) < 1. \tag{F.2}$$

From (F.1) and (F.2), $\lambda'(e(0)) > \lambda'(e^F)$, and it follows from the convexity of $\lambda(\cdot)$ that $e(0) > e^F$.

[18] Evaluating Eq. (3) at $t = 0$ gives

$$0 = -u'(w - x(0) - e(0)) + E[v'(x(0) + \lambda(e(0))\theta)]$$
$$= -u'(w - x(0) - e(0)) + v'(x(0) + \lambda(e(0))\bar{\theta})0 \tag{F.3}$$
$$< -u'(w - x(0) - e^F) + v'(x(0) + \lambda(e^F)\bar{\theta}) \tag{F.4}$$

$$\tag{5}$$

the second equality using the assumption that $v''' = 0$, and the third the observation that the right of (F.3) is decreasing in e combined the result above that $e(0) > e^F$. Comparing (F.4) with Eq. (1) gives

$$-u'(w - x^F - e^F) + v'(x^F + \lambda(e^F)\bar{\theta}) < -u'(w - x(0) - e^F) + v'(x(0) + \lambda(e^F)\bar{\theta})$$

and the conclusion that $x^F > x(0)$ follows on noting that $-u'(w - x - e) + v'(x + \lambda\bar{\theta})$ is decreasing in x.

Indeed if this were the only effect at work it would be optimal to set the tax rate at 100%. But there are also the induced effects on x and e to be considered. Note that these matter only for their effects on revenue: since individuals make their investment and risk-avoidance decisions to maximise their own welfare, the only welfare effect of policy-induced changes in these variables is through the external impact on redistributed tax revenues.

Thus the second term in Eq. (6) captures the effect of redistribution-cum-insurance on risk-taking. Given a further assumption that $u'' = 0$, it can be shown[19] that $e'(t) > 0$. This effect is therefore beneficial whenever $t > 0$. The intuition follows from the earlier observation that the absence of insurance tends to lead to an excessively high e. Social insurance can mitigate a tendency towards excessive caution that insurance market failure might otherwise create. The third effect in Eq. (6) is that on the acquisition of human capital. This is beneficial, again when $t > 0$ if social insurance tends to counteract the tendency towards under-investment in the absence of insurance. The sign of $x'(t)$, however, is uncertain.

Even in this simple model, with all its restrictions, there are few simple results on the nature of the optimal social insurance scheme: one cannot even show that the optimal tax rate is strictly positive. Balancing the insurance effects of social insurance schemes against their impact on risk-taking and incentives to work and save is a daunting task, as indeed experience makes all too clear.

One implication of the impact of social insurance on risk-taking is of particular interest. Insofar as it encourages risk-taking, an increase in the tax rate may actually increase post-tax inequality: the variance of net income, $(1-t)^2\lambda(e(t))$, may be increased more by the induced reduction in e (and consequent increase in λ) than it is reduced by the direct impact of a higher t. Indeed in Sinn's rather different model this must be true at an optimum so long as that optimum has the feature that more inequality raises average income (an eminently plausible feature, since otherwise by reducing inequality one could increase average income, suggesting that one is unlikely to have started at an optimum). Social insurance, commonly thought of as a response to underlying inequality, may thus serve, perfectly reasonably, to increase it.

The samaritan's dilemma and time consistency. Alternative explanations for some types of social insurance rely on time consistency arguments. One such applies the samaritan's dilemma argument to the public sector. Suppose that society has as a policy objective coming to the aid of the least well-off members of society. How well-off one is in the future depends in some measure upon one's actions undertaken at the present, such as saving to finance future consumption and unexpected contingencies, taking preventative measures to mitigate possible adverse outcomes, and human capital accumulation. If society cannot commit not to provide support to those who encounter bad luck, then

[19] By somewhat involved comparative statics on Eqs. (3) and (4), making use of the assumption that $v''' = 0$.

people will undertake too little in the way of self-insurance to protect their future well-being. In these circumstances, public provision of insurance can be welfare-improving.

An early formal treatment of the issues is that of Bruce and Waldman (1991). They construct a simple model with a representative poor person with no initial income, and a representative rich person. In the first period, the rich person transfers part of their income to the poor through the government to satisfy an altruistic urge. The poor can consume part and invest part, where the investment can be interpreted generally to include human capital investment or financial investment. Second-period consumption by the poor then depends upon the investment undertaken in the first period as well as further transfers provided by the rich. If the government acting for the rich can commit to a sequence of transfers announced at the beginning of the first period, the poor will choose an efficient amount of investment in the first-period and redistribution itself will be Pareto-optimal. But, if such commitment is not possible, the poor will have an incentive to under-invest in the first period in the expectation that in the second-period the government cannot avoid making an altruistic transfer to make up for the adverse consequences of low first-period investment. The time-consistent (sub-game perfect) equilibrium with cash transfers will be inefficient: either the poor will simply underinvest in the first period and obtain an excessive transfer in the second period, or the rich will ensure that second-period altruism is nonoperative by transferring and consuming an excessive amount in the first-period. But, Bruce and Waldman then show that if the government is able to make part of its transfers in the form of investment in the first period, full efficiency can be obtained even in the absence of commitment.

Coate (1995) extends the Bruce–Waldman argument by allowing private altruistic transfers to exist alongside government ones. In this case, even if the government can fully commit to second period policies, the fact that private donors cannot might still induce the poor to under-invest or, as in the Coate analysis, under-insure for the future. (The argument relies on private altruism being operative enough, despite there being a potential free-rider problem if there are a large number of rich.) Again, in-kind transfers of income insurance can restore efficiency.

Similar arguments can be used to justify mandatory public pensions (Kotlikoff, 1987) and mandatory education and training (Boadway et al., 1996). It may be, indeed, that it is the samaritan's dilemma which provides the most persuasive rationale for some of the major transfer schemes observed in developed countries (Stiglitz, 1999).

In the case of unemployment insurance, the time inconsistency of government policy can take another form. If the probability of unemployment is given, private insurers might be able to satisfactorily insure against the chances of individual workers being laid off (excepting for the purposes at hand the possible difficulties of coping with moral hazard problems). But, the probability of unemployment is not randomly determined; it is at least partly under the control of government. In these circumstances, governments might find it irresistible, given private unemployment insurance, to rachet up the unemployment rate thereby exploiting private insurance companies to the advantage of workers. (This is analogous to the central bank being unable to commit to keep inflation rates low.) Given this, private unemployment insurance markets may not exist, and governments may have to become the suppliers of unemployment insurance (Boadway and Marceau, 1994).

2.2.3. *Dynamic inefficiency and intergenerational redistribution*

We have already encountered one sort of efficiency argument for intergenerational transfers, that arising from altruism for the well-being of future generations. As with static altruism arguments, intergenerational altruism gives rise to a free-rider problem, though one which is somewhat more subtle than the static case. For, even if one cares directly only for one's own heirs, indirectly one cares for the heirs of all of one's contemporaries because of the chain of connectedness that arises through the intermarriage of descendants in the future. As we have seen, while this can render small amounts of public intergenerational redistribution ineffective, efficiency improvements can come about once public transfers are large enough to crowd out private bequests.

There is, however, a potential further source of inefficiency in a dynamic setting that might be addressed by redistributive transfers, and that is dynamic inefficiency. The argument is as follows. Suppose income per capita grows at the rate g per period. An on-going intergenerational transfer from younger to older cohorts which yields an implicit rate of return of g to each cohort on the taxes paid when they are young can be sustained in the long run. If g exceeds the market rate of return, say, r, instituting such a transfer makes all cohorts better off as long as the plan stays in effect, and as long as g continues to exceed r. Should such a situation exist in perpetuity, such a transfer will be Pareto-improving. Thus, an economy such that $g > r$ forever is said to be *dynamically inefficient* (Starrett, 1972). Conversely, economies with $r > g$ are dynamically efficient: any intergenerational transfer scheme will make some cohorts better off and some worse off.

The possibility of using intergenerational transfers to achieve dynamic efficiency gains has naturally led to considerable interest in the literature. But, the policy consequences are likely somewhat limited. First, evidence suggests that for much of recent history, rates of return on investment r have exceeded rates of growth in per capita incomes g (Abel et al., 1989). Second, even if g did exceed r, it would have to do so forever for dynamic inefficiency to be established.[20] Obviously, that is something that no one can predict. Third, the dynamic inefficiency result applies only in an infinite-horizon economy. If, for any reason, one views the economy as having a finite horizon, the phenomenon of dynamic inefficiency disappears: for the last generation is required to make a transfer to its predecessors but has no successors to receive a transfer from itself.

Once the prospect of dynamic inefficiency is discounted, intergenerational transfers become like movements along an intergenerational Utility Possibilities Frontier. Some persons are made better off, and some worse off, and more conventional rationales for

---

[20] Actually, g only has to exceed r on average forever, roughly speaking (Balasko and Shell, 1980).

redistribution apply: social insurance/justice motives come to the fore. In a static setting, social insurance was designed to consummate a form of insurance against bad luck at birth that households were not in a position to purchase for themselves. In an intergenerational context, it is recognized that not all bad luck at birth is "insurable" across a single cohort. Some cohorts are unlucky in the aggregate: they may face wars, natural catastrophes, demographic shocks, etc. But, good and bad risks might be insurable over time, that is, across generations. If so, governments could use intergenerational transfers as a policy device for smoothing out real incomes across generations (Gordon and Varian, 1988).

There is some evidence that intergenerational transfers are used to some extent to do so. Wars are financed by at least partly by debt; some major public pension schemes were introduced in the wake of the Great Depression, and so on. However, engineering social insurance schemes across generations encounters obstacles not faced by their static counterparts, which themselves are formidable. Governments last for relatively short periods of time, and there are obvious problems with current governments committing future ones to abide by intergenerational social insurance schemes. At best, the argument for social insurance based on intergenerational risk sharing can provide moral guidance rather than operational advice.

2.2.4. Nonconvexities: the case of efficiency wages

We saw in Section 2.1 above that concavity of the utility function implies that aggregate utility can be increased by equalising lump sum incomes. In the same way, nonconvexity of the technology can imply the existence of efficiency gains from redistribution: as first noted by Guesnerie (1975), with increasing returns some competitive equilibria may Pareto dominate others.

One especially powerful example of the potential significance of nonconvexities is provided by the analysis of land reform in the presence of efficiency wages by Dasgupta and Ray (1986, 1987). Suppose that a worker's effective labour supply is related to their consumption—which for simplicity we take to be identical with their income—by the relation $\lambda(C)$ shown in Fig. 2: greater consumption improves productivity, and at low levels does so at an increasing marginal rate. Workers derive this income from two sources: selling their labour at wage rate w, and receiving (lump sum) receipts from their landholdings of κ. If land holdings differ across workers, so too will the efficiency wage: the wage, that is, which minimizes the per unit cost of effective labour supply, $w/\lambda(w + \kappa)$. (Thus the efficiency wage of a landless labourer, for example, is given by the inverse of the slope of the line OA in Fig. 2). Since the efficiency wage decreases with the level of land-holding, those with low landholdings are disadvantaged in the labour market. Indeed it may well be that some of those with lowest land holdings are unemployed: their marginal product when paid their efficiency wage may be less than that efficiency wage. For those with large land holding, in contrast, the efficiency wage may be below their reservation wage, in which case the employment decision hinges on the comparison between their marginal product and that reservation wage.

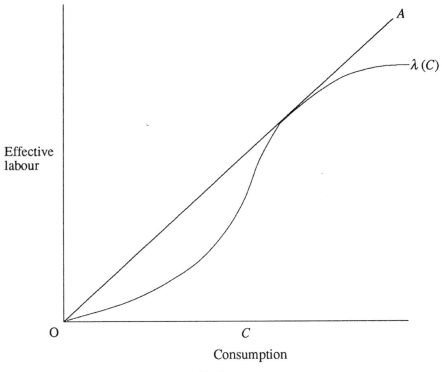

Fig. 2.

In such circumstances redistribution may lead to an increase in total output. Consider the effects of transferring land from a worker with a large initial land holding, for whom the reservation wage exceeds the efficiency wage, to a worker with a low initial land holding, who is currently unemployed. For the former, so long as the efficiency wage remains below the marginal product there is no change in employment. The induced reduction in the efficiency wage of the poorer worker, however, may be sufficient to bring them into employment. It is thus perfectly possible that redistribution of this kind will increase total output. In practice, egalitarian land reforms do indeed seem, at least in some prominent cases, to have led to an expansion of aggregate output.[21]

Note, in passing, that these results illustrate and emphasize the importance of distinguishing between the alternative notions of efficiency mentioned earlier. For while redistribution here generates an increase in total output it can never generate a Pareto

---

[21] Alesina and Rodrik (1994), for example, cite evidence that growth is faster the more equal the distribution of land, and refer to a widespread view that faster growth in Southeast Asia than in South America reflected there having been land reform in the former but not the latter. See also Kanbur (this volume, Chapter 13).

improvement: in attempting to share out the additional output, so as to ensure that all share in the gain, one inescapably undoes the productivity gain that generated it.

The efficiency wage model has one further striking implication for the potential effects of redistributing to the poor, shown by Ravallion (1984). Consider an individual currently paid exactly their efficiency wage. We have seen that redistributing towards such an individual (modelled as an increase in κ) would reduce the wage w that they are paid in equilibrium. It turns out, however, that the wage will actually fall by *more* than the amount of the transfer, so that their total income $w + \kappa$ actually falls.[22] Diagrammatically, the result can be seen by constructing a picture similar to Fig. 2, but with w on the horizontal axis. Increasing κ then shifts the λ curve uniformly to the left by the amount κ, and it can be seen that the new tangency with a ray from the origin will imply a wage that falls by more than the transfer increases. Intuitively, the employer could choose to reduce the wage so as to exactly offset the increased transfer; but this reduced wage means that the labour cost saved by an increase in the worker's efficiency is also reduced, so that it benefits the employer to cut the wage still further. Paradoxically, redistributing towards the poor in this case ultimately leaves them worse off.

In the argument above, the nonconvexity acted to favor redistribution towards the poor: in the presence of increasing returns, such transfers may help the poor escape from low-level equilibria (a feature which also operates in some of the models of pre-existing distortions that we discuss next). In some contexts, however, nonconvexities may point towards redistribution away from the poorest. In the framework above, for example, two poor workers may both have such high efficiency wages as to be unemployed, for example, but a disequalizing transfer of the land owned by one to the other might reduce the efficiency wage of the recipient by enough to make her employable. A similar harsh reality arises in the context of famine relief: minimizing mortality may require a policy of triage, with available resources concentrated on the better off, who stand some chance of survival, rather than shared with those so malnourished as to be beyond hope (Ravallion, 1987).

2.2.5. Capital markets, incentive constraints and other pre-existing distortions

These cases of efficiency-improving redistribution are instances of a more general observation: when there are constraints which prevent the economy attaining a first-best outcome, the utility possibilities frontier may be upward-sloping over some of its range.[23] As a simple example, it is straightforward to show that in a two-person economy with

---

[22] Minimising $w/\lambda(w + \kappa)$ requires that $\lambda - w\lambda' = 0$, the second order condition being $\lambda'' < 0$. Hence $w'(\kappa) + 1 = \lambda'/w\lambda'' < 0$.

[23] Consider for instance the problem of maximising the welfare of person A in a two-person economy, subject only to the constraint that person B achieve utility of at least $\bar{U}$ and the resource constraint $F(\mathbf{x}_A + \mathbf{x}_B)$. By the envelope theorem, the sign of the slope of the utility possibilities frontier is given by that of the multiplier λ in the Lagrangean $L = U_A(\mathbf{x}_A) + \lambda\{U_B(\mathbf{x}_B) - \bar{U}\} + \mu F(\mathbf{x}_A + \mathbf{x}_B)$. From the first order conditions—assuming there is some good i that has strictly positive marginal utility to both individuals—one finds $\lambda = (\partial U_A/\partial x_{Ai})/(\partial U_B/\partial x_{Bi}) > 0$. But adding a further constraint $G(\mathbf{x}_A, \mathbf{x}_B) \geq 0$ means—unless $G(\cdot)$ depends only on the sum of the two consumption vectors—that positivity of λ is no longer assured.

pre-existing commodity taxes it is possible for an unrequited transfer from one to the other to leave both better-off. (Piketty provides an extended treatment of these issues in Chapter 8 below.)

More powerful examples arise in the context of capital markets, which are afflicted by many of the same informational problems as insurance markets. Lenders' informationally-constrained responses to the possibilities that borrowers will default on their loans or simply abscond with the funds, are likely to lead to levels of investment that depart from the first-best. Differing models give differing predictions as to whether there will be under- or over-investment (de Meza and Myles, 1987): lenders may ration investments below the first best, for example, or borrowers may borrow excessively to take advantage of being able to default if things go badly. In either event, however, a redistribution of wealth towards borrowers is likely to move investment closer to the first best, so increasing aggregate income: incentive problems will be mitigated insofar as greater wealth enables (or obliges) investors to rely more heavily on their own funds rather than borrowed funds tainted with lenders' mistrust Effects of broadly this kind are analysed by Aghion and Bolton (1997) and Piketty (1997). Analogous issues in the accumulation of human capital are addressed by, in particular, Hoff and Lyon (1995)— who shows that lump sum redistribution may be a superior policy to the apparently better-targeted one of taxing or subsidising loans directly—and Galor and Zeira (1993). Banerjee and Newman (1993) consider similar effects in relation to occupational choice. Access to one's own resources may also ease the hold-up problem on relationship-specific investments: the reluctance, that is, of partners to finance investments which will leave them, ex post, at the mercy of the other party (Hoff and Lyon, 1995). There is an evident link, of course, between capital market imperfections and long run growth, and indeed these have been a focus of much of the recent work in this area. Indeed a recurrent lesson from endogenous growth models has been the potentially beneficial effects of redistribution in improving growth prospects by overcoming capital market imperfections.

The literature now abounds with other cases in which a pre-existing distortion creates a potential for Pareto-gain from redistribution: between two countries in a three-country world (Bhagwati et al., 1983);[24] between regions of a federation (Boadway and Flatters, 1982); between countries differing in their productivities in the provision of some international public good (Ihori, 1996).

So pervasive are such examples that it is worth emphasising that even when redistribution leads to an efficiency gain over some range, some trade-off is likely to remain at end of day. Altruism, for example, means that the utility possibilities frontier is upward-sloping over part of its range; but there will generally also be a range of options available on the downward-sloping part. In that sense, it is important to remember, conflict equity and efficiency often ultimately inescapable.

---

[24] The distortion here being the absence of an optimal tariff against some third country.

2.3. Redistribution as expropriation

A third motive for redistribution is simple greed: self-interested individuals may possess, and certainly have an incentive to acquire, the power to redistribute towards themselves. More generally, of course, all practical measures of redistribution, however motivated, emerge from some political arena; and it is to the broader topic of how politics can shape the outcome that we now turn.

3. The politics of redistribution

Unless it is Pareto improving, redistribution is ultimately an exercise of coercion and sovereign power and in that sense is an inherently political matter. Indeed Stigler (1970) asserts the understanding of redistribution to be the principal task of political economy.

In primitive societies redistribution is above all a matter of transfers extracted by a ruling elite, with the losers prevented from withdrawing by physical threat. The question is what limits the extent of redistribution in such a kleptocracy. The key point here is that even a self-serving despot can find it optimal to adopt policies that are far from outright appropriation. One reason for this is the threat of insurrection if redistribution towards the elite is taken too far. Thus Usher and Engineer (1987) and Grossman and Noh (1994) characterise despotic redistribution in terms of an extraction of surplus tempered by the possibility of revolution. Another brake on expropriation, emphasised by McGuire and Olsen (1996), is provided by the despot's interest in allowing enough resources to be channeled into productive uses to allow the base of her tax revenues to be sustained. Thus it was that the bandits in the *Seven Samurai* habitually left the villagers enough to sow next year's crop; and thus it was, perhaps, that the slave-masters of the south took a rational interest in the maintenance of their property (Fogel and Engerman, 1974). Indeed, one can view the historical emergence of social insurance as an attempt by entrenched elites to prevent insurgence by the poor.

In what follows, however, we focus on redistribution in societies that have attributes of democracy. Confiscation by physical force is excluded: compulsion is exercised through the rule of law, and those rules have democratic features. We consider in turn three forms of democratic decision-making: democracy in its purest form; representative democracy, bringing in a role for politicians; and the influence of interest groups.

3.1. Direct democracy

By this we simply mean a situation in which no agent—no politician, bureaucrat, or lobbyist—comes in any substantive way between the preferences of the citizenry and the selection and implementation of policy. Collective decision-making is simply a matter of applying some rule to the expressed wishes of the citizenry. Any politicians or civil servants required to write the policy into law or implement it are merely the faithful ciphers of the citizenry, able to commit to pursuing the policy decided upon and making no more than a reasonable call on resources in doing so.

The questions immediately arises as to the rule that society will, and should, choose for moving from individual preferences to the selection of a collective policy. This is the subject matter of social choice theory, which we make no attempt to survey here: see, for example, Mueller (1989) and, for an account with a view to issues of public economics, Inman (1985). There are many rules that one could imagine being used to make decisions on distributional matters. Unanimity has occupied a central place in libertarian treatment of optimal voting rules. Or one might conceive of a super-majority—a majority, that is, of some number over 50%—being needed for compulsory redistribution. The literature on distributional politics, however, has focused almost exclusively on just one choice rule: decision on the basis of a simple majority. This methodological feature has had such a marked impact on the literature as to require some discussion in itself.

3.1.1. Majority rule

In their treatise on collective decision-making, Buchanan and Tullock (1962) refer to the selection of a voting rule as the constitutional stage to be evoked, at least conceptually, from behind the veil of ignorance. Citizens will trade off the expected benefits from increasing the size of majority required to pass legislation—reducing the chance that they will be in the losing group when votes are taken on issues with distributive consequences—against the increased costs of decision-making. They envisaged there being some sort of consensus about the size of majority that would trade off these benefits and costs, but what that would be was left unexplained. The case for majority rule based on the Buchanan-Tullock calculus was provided in axiomatic form by May (1952) and later Rae (1969), and recounted by Inman (1985) and Mueller (1989). More pragmatically, the apparent prevalence of majority rule in democracies—albeit as a matter of voting in legislatures rather than of literal direct democracy—provides an obvious reason for interest in majority rule. More loosely, one might invoke majority rule—as do Alesina and Rodrik (1994)—as a simple way of capturing the idea that even despots cannot ignore the mass of opinion. Analytical convenience too, doubtless has some part in explaining the popularity of the approach.

Notice, however, that the mere specification of majority rule does not completely characterize the voting rule, for the question then remains as to precisely who it is that may vote. There may be important technical restrictions on the franchise: most particularly, future generations cannot themselves vote today on policy decisions that must be made today and which can powerfully affect their welfare. Even putting such issues aside, the extent of the franchise is itself a matter for choice and, hence, for explanation. Historically, major extensions of the franchise have been associated with real fear amongst the previously enfranchised that democracy will result in their expropriation: thus De Tocqueville warned of the "tyranny of the majority", and Lord Derby saw the 1867 Reform Bill that he and Disraeli brought into being—a substantial extension of the franchise—as "a leap in the dark".[25] For present purposes, however, we simply follow the literature in assuming that all economically relevant agents are enfranchised.

Majority rule is thus widely assumed. Modelling it requires some notion of equilibrium. The most natural is that of a *Condorcet winner*: an option which cannot be defeated in a majority vote by any other feasible alternative. The well-known paradox of voting, however, is that there may exist no such option: preferences (and the relative numbers who hold them) may be such that a majority prefer some option a to another b, b to c and yet a not beating, but rather being beaten by, c. Everything being beaten by something else in pairwise votes, the ordering implied by majority rule is intransitive. Under majority rule there is no guarantee that a best element will exist.[26]

There are various ways out of this dilemma (Sen, 1977), such as relaxing the axioms underlying the approach, or allowing the collective decision rule to use richer information than just household orderings. For the purpose of legitimizing majority voting, restrictions on the domain of preferences are most relevant. The literature has sought restrictions on preferences that will preclude such intransitivities. Here there arises an important distinction as to whether one or several dimension of policy issue are at stake.

In the one-dimensional case—meaning that the policy options from which selection is to be made can be described in terms of a single parameter—a well-known sufficient condition[27] for the existence of a Condorcet winner is that every individual's preferences be *single-peaked*: that is, that there be some ordering of options such that each individual has only one local optimum. The Condorcet winner is then easily characterised: ordering voters by the location of their preferred point, the Condorcet winner is the option most preferred by the median voter (Black, 1948).

Establishing that preferences are (or are not) single-peaked is thus the typical first-step of much analysis from a political economy perspective. It turns out that single-peakedness can be problematic even in rather simple models, and examples of this will be encountered below. But the failure of single-peakedness is not necessarily a disaster, for single-peakedness is a special case of a more general sufficient condition for the existence of a Condorcet winner: Sen's (1966) condition of value-restricted, which indicates the extent to which voter preferences must be sufficiently similar to avoid intransitivity. Sen's condition requires that among all combinations of three alternatives, voters must agree that some alternative is not worst, or some is not best, or some is not in the middle.[28] In practice, this may not be an easy property to check. A less powerful condition, but one whose economic content may be more relevant for

---

[25] Quoted in Blake (1966, p. 474).

[26] This is but one instance of Arrow's Impossibility Theorem: no collective decision rule based on individual preference orderings alone and respecting certain widely supported properties (including the Pareto principle) will yield a complete and transitive ordering of alternatives for all possible preferences of voters.

[27] Note no preference restriction can in itself be *necessary*: if a majority of the citizenry have the same preferences then majority rule will be transitive however weird the preferences of the minority.

[28] Pattaniak and Sen (1969) formalised this notion of value restriction into the following axiom on preferences: if for any three alternatives x, y, z some individual's preference ordering is $xPyPz$, then any other individual for whom zPx must also have $zPyPx$.

redistribution issues is the Gans and Smart (1996) notion of *single-crossing* (which, as discussed below, differs from, but is related to, the well-known Mirrlees–Spence single-crossing property). A sufficient (but not necessary) condition for value restriction—and hence a sufficient condition for the existence of a Condorcet winner—is that there exist some ordering of individuals (or, more precisely, preference types) and some ordering of options, such that if one person prefers *a* to *b* (respectively, *b* to *a*) then so do all those higher (lower) in the ordering. It is immediate, moreover, that single-crossing in this sense again implies that the median voter is again decisive.

Matters are much less straightforward in the multi-dimensional case. As Plott (1967) showed, there may exist no Condorcet winner even if all have single-peaked preferences along every dimension of policy: see the summary in Atkinson and Stiglitz (1980). There do exist restrictions that will yield transitivity of majority rule—Bucovetsky (1991), e.g.—but they are tight. One would certainly not expect them to be satisfied in contexts of redistribution. The reason is easily illustrated. Consider the problem of sharing a pie of size unity between three individuals A, B and C. The set of possible allocations of the pie is then described by the three-dimensional unit simplex, shown in Fig. 3. At point A, for example, individual A receives all of the pie—her bliss point—whilst along the axis BC she receives none. Assuming that individuals care only about their own share, indifference curves are parallel lines approaching each individual's bliss point. It is readily shown that for any allocation another may be found which defeats it in a majority vote, so voting cycles are endemic. For example, α beats β in a majority vote, and β beats γ; but γ beats α. Cycling is likely to be pervasive in direct voting over redistribution.

Reflecting these profound methodological differences, models in which the underlying issue space is multi-dimensional commonly have decisions taken through representative democracy, with citizens voting over candidates rather than policy bundles. With only two candidates, the paradox of voting disappears—at least from immediate view. For the disappearance may be illusory, since there will typically exist no Nash equilibrium in the platforms offered by the two candidates. Intransitivity may thus manifest itself.

Unidimensionality is thus a great convenience in addressing voting problems, though even then single-peakedness is far from assured. For the US, there is some reassuring evidence that politics is a largely uni-dimensional business, particularly in recent years: senators voting records suggest that they line up on issues in roughly the same order (Alesina and Rodrik, 1994). In other historical contexts, however, there is evidence of two or more dimensions being relevant: see, for instance, the discussion in Roemer (1998). In any case, it is clear that, reducing complex distributional issues to one-dimensional problems is largely a matter of brute force.[29]

---

[29] Alternatively, some of the problems of multi-dimensional voting can be avoided by supposing that voting occurs sequentially issue by issue. The voting paradox is avoided, but the order of voting becomes crucial and ultimately arbitrary.

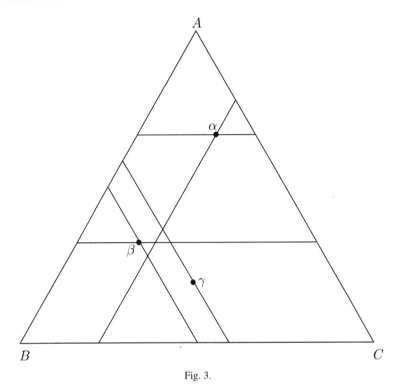

Fig. 3.

One dimensional models of this kind have thus been hugely influential in analysing the politics of redistribution; we now review some of the principle applications of this kind.

3.1.2. Income tax

The archetypal policy instrument for redistribution is a system of taxes and transfers related to pre-tax income. As such, the politics of the progressive income tax has been a leading case in positive analyses of redistribution.

The framework in which the issue is naturally posed is that of the optimal tax literature. We suppose then that people have entirely self-regarding preferences of the form $U(C, L)$, where C denotes the consumption of some composite commodity and L is the amount of labour supply. Individuals differ only in their pre-tax wage w, whose distribution, described by distribution function $F(w)$ on support Ω, is common knowledge but each individual's wage being their own private information. The government announces a tax schedule $T(Y)$ and each individual then chooses their labour supply to maximise $U(Y - T(Y), L)$, where $Y \equiv wL$ denotes gross income. To focus on redistributional issues, we take as given the amount that the government must raise for spending on goods and services; and for simplicity we take that amount to be zero. The problem addressed in the optimal tax literature is then that of characterising the schedule T which maximises some social welfare function or—along the lines discussed in Section 4—that of characterising the set of Pareto efficient schedules. Here our concern is with the schedule that will emerge in political equilibrium; and so, inevitably, with the prior question as to whether there will exist an equilibrium.

Linear income tax. Suppose first that for some reason—perhaps administrative, perhaps the need to eliminate arbitrage opportunities—only linear income taxes are used, those, that is, comprising a constant marginal tax rate t and a poll subsidy α. The policy choice to be made may thus appear two-dimensional, but the government's revenue constraint

$$\alpha = t \int_\Omega wL[(1 - t)w, \alpha] \, dF(w), \tag{7}$$

implies a relation between t and α which reduces the policy space to that of the single parameter t. Denoting by $v[(1 - t)w, \alpha]$ the indirect utility of a consumer with pre-tax wage w and assuming for simplicity that there are no income effects on labour supply, the welfare that a type-i enjoys at tax rate t is then $\Gamma(t; w_i) \equiv v[(1 - t)w_i, t \int wL[(1 - t)w] \, dF(w)]$. Differentiating, using Roy's identity and normalising the marginal utility of income to unity gives

$$\frac{\partial \Gamma(t, w_i)}{\partial t} = \bar{Y} - Y_i - t \int_\Omega w^2 L_w^c \, dF, \tag{8}$$

where $\bar{Y}$ denotes mean gross income and L_w^c the compensated effect of the net wage on labour supply. Intuitively, at unchanged behaviour, type-i persons gain more from the increased poll subsidy than they pay in taxes if their income is below the mean; but the reduction in the labour supply of others induced by the increased marginal tax rate is harmful in reducing the tax base and hence the subsidy.

Consider then the existence of a Condorcet winner. Here the first question is whether $\Gamma(t; w)$ is necessarily single-peaked in t. Itsumi (1974) and Romer (1975) show by example that it is not. A sense of the difficulty is immediate from Eq. (8): it would suffice for single-peakedness that $\Gamma(t, w)$ be strictly concave in t, but it is evident that concavity will turn, inter alia, on second derivatives of the labour supply function, upon which theory places few restrictions.[30]

As discussed above, there may still exist a Condorcet winner even if single-peakedness fails. Roberts (1977) shows that for value restriction to hold in this model, and hence

---

[30] Nor is it hard to envisage particular circumstances in which single-peakedness may fail to apply. Imagine, for example, an individual who earns less than the average ($y < \bar{y}$) when the tax rate is low, but then finds herself earning more than the average as further tax increases cause the less able to cease work entirely, and who then ceases to work ($y = 0$) as the tax rate rises still further though others do still choose to continue work (so that α continues to rise with t). Recalling Eq. (8), for such a person Γ might be increasing at low t, then falling and then rising again.

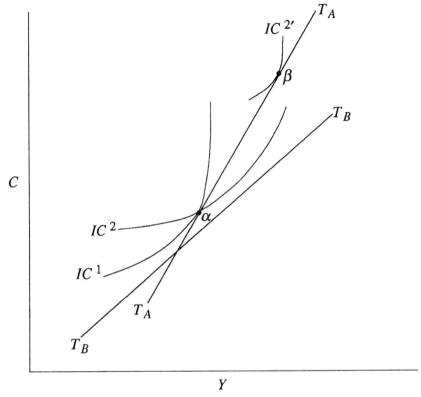

Fig. 4.

for majority rule to be transitive, it is sufficient that preferences satisfy a condition he calls *hierarchical adherence*: that for any pair of individuals one earns more than the other under all linear tax schedules. More recently, Gans and Smart (1996) show that a sufficient condition for hierarchical adherence is the Mirrlees–Spence single-crossing condition widely used in the context of analysing optimal taxation and screening models more generally: this is the condition that the level curves of $U(C, Y/w)$ in (C, Y)-space are steeper for less able individuals,[31] for which it is sufficient that consumption be normal.[32]

---

[31] Note that, confusingly, the Mirrlees–Spence single-crossing property is conceptually quite different from the Gans–Smart notion of single-crossing described in connection with majority rule in Section 3.1.1 above (which is rather the property that for all $t \neq t'$ there exist a unique $\hat{w}$ such that $\Gamma(t, w) - \Gamma(t', w)$ changes sign at $\hat{w}$). The essence of the Gans–Smart result being described here is that single-crossing in the Spence–Mirrlees sense implies single-crossing in the Gans–Smart sense.

[32] Meltzer and Richard (1981) note that normality of x is sufficient for hierarchical adherence, though not the link with the Mirrlees–Spence condition.

That this condition guarantees the existence of a Condorcet winner is shown in Fig. 4. This illustrates the choice between two linear schedules, A and B, represented by $T_A T_A$ and $T_B T_B$ respectively. Suppose that person 1 prefers A to B, as shown. The Spence–Mirrlees condition—that 2's indifference curve through 1's preferred point a be flatter than 1's indifference curve at that point—implies that 2's preferred position on schedule A is northeast of α, at a point like β; but then for 2 to prefer schedule B would require that $IC^{2\prime}$ cut IC^1 at least twice, which the Spence–Mirrlees condition precludes. Thus if 1 prefers A to B so do all those higher in the ability distribution than 1.[33] The schedule most preferred by the person of median ability will muster a majority against any other, and so will be a Condorcet winner. In these circumstances Eq. (8) implies that the equilibrium marginal tax rate under majority rule is given by

$$\frac{t}{1-t} = \frac{\bar{Y} - Y_m}{\int_\Omega w L \eta^c \, dF}, \tag{9}$$

where a subscript m relates to the median and $\eta^c[(1-t)\omega]$ denotes the compensated elasticity of labour supply with respect to the net wage $(1-t)w$.

The most immediate property of the equilibrium tax is that it is positive, provided only the distribution of labour income is positively skewed—which we presume to be the case.[34,35] More generally, Eq. (9) does not represent a closed form solution for t since elements on the right-hand side themselves depend on it. But inspection suggests that the equilibrium tax system under majority rule will be more progressive (t higher):

- The more skewed the distribution of income. It is natural to take an increase in skewness to be synonymous with an increase in inequality, but this is not necessarily correct: one can have an unambiguous increase in inequality (in the Lorenz sense) combined with a reduction in skewness. Nevertheless many—like Alesina and Rodrik (1994)—interpret skewness as a metaphor for inequality. On this interpretation, greater inequality leads to more intensive attempts at redistribution.
- The less responsive is labour supply. A higher value of η^c in the denominator on the right of Eq. (9) points to a lower tax rate on the left; and, more subtly, higher values of t also serve to close the gap between $\bar{Y}$ and Y_m in the numerator on the right.

Clearly, the form of Eq. (9) reflects voters' awareness of a fundamental equity-efficiency trade-off in this model, the median voter being constrained in the amount of redistribution she can have go her way by the reduction is the size of the pie available for redistribution as t increases. We shall find an analogous trade-off at work when we

---

[33] Notice too that this argument shows that the Mirrlees–Spence condition implies that for any linear tax all those with higher ability than 1 will also earn higher income, verifying our claim in the text that it implies hierarchical adherence.

[34] Neal and Rosen (this volume, Chapter 7) report evidence on, and possible explanations for, such skewness.

[35] This clearly reflects our assumption that labour supply is independent of lump sum income; it is sufficient for the conclusion to holds more generally that leisure be normal and aggregate uncompensated labour supply increasing in the net wage.

analyse the optimal linear income tax in a welfaristic context in Section 4: the beneficial effects of increasing t to mitigate inequality being offset by efficiency losses due to a labour supply.

Aumann and Kurz (1977) take a somewhat different tack to describe how a majority voting equilibrium might emerge in a linear income tax setting.[36] They assume that voter citizens participate in a multi-person cooperative game with side payments. Voters form into two coalitions—winning and losing ones—which then engage in Nash bargaining to determine the tax rate. The outcome is tempered by the presumption that those in the losing coalition can threaten to destroy their endowment rather than having it confiscated by the majority. The bargaining process ensures that an equilibrium exists, but it is one with a relatively high tax rate.

Nonlinear income tax. Far more fundamental than the linear tax case is that in which taxes may be nonlinear. This is the natural setting in which to pose some of the most critical issues in the positive analysis of redistribution. Director's Law, for example—the notion that redistribution will run from the extremes to the middle class—is not well-captured by a linear redistributive scheme. Nor can the contrast between universality and means-testing be captured with great richness without allowing for nonlinearity: the essence of means-testing being the targeting of benefits on the poor by means of schemes that impose especially high marginal tax rates on them.

It is a weakness of the literature that little progress has been made in characterising the outcome of voting over nonlinear tax schedules. This reflects the technical difficulty of the problem. Without some restriction on the set of nonlinear schedules over which people vote it is clear that there can in general be no Condorcet winner: for any schedule there will be another, preferred by a majority, in which a previous loser and a winner exploit another winner to the benefit of both.

One approach is to impose essentially arbitrary restrictions on the set of nonlinear schedules over which votes are taken. Gans and Smart (1996), for example, consider the case in which attention is confined to equal-revenue tax schedules that can be ranked according to Lorenz dominance. Hemming and Keen (1983) have shown that if one tax schedule Lorenz dominates another and so exhibits more progressivity, they will single cross each other (yet another distinct use of that term). There will be a critical level of income such that those above (below) have lower (higher) net income under the more progressive tax than under the less progressive tax. It is then easily seen that the Spence–Mirrlees single-crossing property implies that among all such tax schedules the Gans–Smart single-crossing holds; and thus that there exists a majority winner.

But the restriction on the set of admissible schedules underlying this result has no deep rationale. An alternative approach is taken by Roell (1996), who confines voting to those schedules that are most preferred for some voter, perhaps on the grounds that elected citizens cannot commit to pursuing other than self-interested policies. Even in

---

[36] Inman (1987) provides a particularly accessible account of their analysis.

this case the existence of a majority winner does not seem to be assured, though Roell is able to establish existence for the case in which the income elasticity of demand for leisure is zero. One very striking result does emerge, however, from the characterisation of the tax schedules that each voter will selfishly prefer. The voter's only concern with others in this context is as a source of revenue for redistribution to themselves. In considering this problem, of course, each voter must pay attention to the incentive effects of the tax schedule. This, Roell shows, leads each (under plausible conditions) to prefer a negative marginal tax rate—that is, an earnings subsidy—at levels of income below their own. The intuition follow from an observation of Stiglitz (1980) on the shape of the optimal tax schedule in the two-person self-selection model (discussed in Section 4.2): if redistribution runs from poor to rich—perverse in the two-person case, but the relevant comparison here, with each voter regarding all others, including those poorer than themselves, as resources to be exploited—the optimal marginal tax rate on the better-off individual is strictly negative. Loosely speaking, the negative marginal tax rate provides a way of transferring income to the better-off while at the same time inducing a higher level of effort by those better off that will reduce the incentive for the poor to mimic. We return below to the crucial role that the shape of the marginal tax schedule plays in mitigating the incentive to mimic, that is, in inducing incentive compatibility in the choice of a tax schedule which separates individuals according to productivity.

3.1.3. Redistribution and growth

The basic majority voting model has been applied in dynamic settings of endogenous growth models, most prominently by Bertola (1993), Alesina and Rodrik (1994), and, in a framework closer to the above, by Persson and Tabellini (1994a). (See also the overview by Bertola in Chapter 9 below.) The latter consider an overlapping generations model in which the currently young, once they learn their own endowment, vote over a proportional tax on capital income to be imposed next period, with the proceeds being paid to their generation when old as a lump sum subsidy. Each individual then faces essentially the same trade-off as in Eq. (8) above.[37] Preference restrictions imposed by Persson and Tabellini (1994a) imply single-peaked preferences, so the equilibrium tax on capital is that preferred by the person with the median endowment. Exactly as above, the tax rate is strictly positive so long as the distribution is positively skewed. Instead of reducing labour supply, however, this tax reduces capital accumulation (with only a substitution effect at work, because the proceeds are redistributed as a lump sum) which in turn reduces the growth rate (because of the beneficial effect of capital on next period's wage rate).[38] Hence their central conclusion is reached: inequality incites intensified redistribution, which retards growth. Alesina and Rodrik's central point is

---

[37] To which Eq. (7) of Persson and Tabellini (1994a) is essentially identical.

[38] This is not in itself cause for any adverse reflection on the political equilibrium: growth maximisation is generally not an appropriate objective in these models, any more than maximising aggregate output is in the model of labour taxation above.

essentially the same, though it is developed in a model in which redistribution is less explicit: tax revenues finance public infrastructure which boosts wages. They find that unless the policy chosen is that preferred by those who hold only capital, not labour, then policy will not maximise growth.

Further theoretical developments and the sizable empirical literature that has emerged in this area are reviewed by Bénabou (1997) and Bruno et al. (1998). Empirically, the suggestion which emerges is that higher levels of initial inequality (especially of land) are associated with, if anything, *lower* growth rates. But this may reflect factors other than redistribution. For example, if economies of scale in mass goods are important in spurring growth—along the lines of Murphy et al. (1989)—then inequality may retard growth for quite different reasons. Indeed Bénabou finds that the literature has failed to establish any strong direct effect of redistribution—measured variously by the shares of public expenditures, such as education, health, welfare or transfers, in GDP, or different marginal and average tax rates—on growth, concluding that redistribution is if anything positively related to growth.

Causation could indeed run the other way: from growth to redistribution. Wright (1996) develops a model of majority voting over social insurance schemes in which, with some permanence in policy decision, individuals vote today knowing that even if they have a favorable income draw this period, they (or their descendants) may not in the future. So they trade-off income today against buying insurance tomorrow. This turns on relative risk aversion: Wright shows that if relative risk aversion is less than unity, then faster growth rate will lead to more transfers to the poor and higher taxes on the rich.

3.1.4. Intergenerational redistribution
Redistribution between generations can take many forms, and can run in either direction. Taxes paid by the currently young may help to finance health or residential care for the currently aged; taxes paid by today's workers may finance the education of tomorrow's. Much of the discussion of intergenerational redistribution has been cast, however, in the context of pension provision—"social security", as the term is used in North America (usage being rather wider elsewhere)—though it is recognised that this is a metaphor for intergenerational redistribution more generally. The focus then is on the extent of intergenerational redistribution towards the elderly that one might expect through the adoption of pay-as-you-go (PAYG) pension schemes: schemes, that is, under which transfers to the currently old are financed not by the past contributions of the old themselves but rather by transfers from the currently young. This issue suffices to raise the tension between two key forces likely to shape the extent of intergenerational redistribution more widely.

The first—originally emphasised by Aaron (1966) and developed more explicitly by Browning (1975), Townley (1981) and Boadway and Wildasin (1989)—is the incentive that the relatively old have to extract transfers from the relatively young, and the consequent possibility of a political equilibrium in which the social security system is too large in terms of the ex ante welfare of each generation but is nevertheless supported ex post by a majority of voters. To see how this can arise, consider a simple overlapping generations economy inhabited by selfish people who live for several periods, working when young and retired when old, and a simple pay-as-you-go social security scheme in which the pension in each period is financed by the taxation (at a time-invariant rate) of contemporaneous labour income. Imagine too that (pre-tax) factor prices are exogenous (perhaps tied down in world goods markets) and do not change over time, so that each new generation faces essentially the same fundamentals as its predecessors. Finally, suppose that the social security system is to be decided, once and for all, by a single majority vote. In deciding how to vote, each generation balances the loss it suffers from paying a higher tax rate during whatever remains of its working life against a gain in terms of a higher pension. Then the youngest generation, in looking to maximise its own lifetime utility, effectively seeks to maximise the utility of each generation to come; in that sense, it prefers the scheme which is socially optimal. For each older generation, however, part of the working life has already gone, and so the impact of taxation at such earlier points in the life cycle is ignored. For the retired indeed, the working life is over and all that matters is the impact on pension paid. With the adverse effect of a tax increase during the working life partially ignored, the preference of each older generation is thus tilted toward a higher tax rate than the youngest generation would prefer. So long as the median voter is not to be found amongst the very youngest group, majority voting can thus be expected to lead to a social security scheme larger than is optimal. Thus Aaron shows, for example, that even if $r > n$, so that an unfunded scheme lowers steady state welfare—a PAYG scheme may be adopted in a majority vote.[39]

Notice that even though we have assumed the vote to be once-and-for-all, our assumptions imply that the same scheme would be confirmed if for some reason another once-and-for-all vote had to be taken. What is important to the argument is thus not simply the (in)frequency of voting. Rather the starkness of the conclusion reflects two features of the model. One is the incompleteness of the franchise, with future generations of necessity excluded from the vote: if the untold masses of the unborn generations were able to participate in the vote described above, their interest would align with that of the youngest living generation, and the efficient scheme would be adopted. The other source of the over-provision result is the assumption that it is possible to commit today to tax and benefit rates in the future. For unless the retired are in an absolute majority, they will require political support from the older workers to sustain a PAYG scheme; and those workers will only support the scheme if they themselves believe that succeeding generations will support them in future.

---

[39] An example may help. Suppose that individuals live for three periods, providing some fixed amount of labour in the first period and being retired in the last two. Denoting the tax payable when working by τ and the benefit received when retired by B, the net social security wealth in the first period of life is $-\tau + B\Lambda(r)$, where $\Lambda(x) = (1+r)^{-1} + (1+r)^{-2}$. With population growth at the rate n, the budget constraint for the scheme is that $B\Lambda(n) = \tau$. Since $\Lambda(x)$ is decreasing, the young will support $t > 0$ only if $r < n$, so that the no-tax position is dynamically inefficient. The retired however, look simply to increase B and so (in this simple set up) always prefer $t > 0$. So long as the retired outnumber the workers (requiring that $n(1+n) < 1$), there will be majority in favour of $t > 0$.

This brings us to the second general key force in intergenerational politics, Tullock's (1997) credibility problem: since workers are typically more numerous than the retired, why do they not renege on any promise they have made—or which the now-old previously made for them—to support the retired? The prospect thus arises of there being too little redistribution towards the old rather than too much. Even if $r < n$, for instance, the possibility that the next generation will renege may prevent the adoption of a Pareto-improving social security scheme.

Early attempts to address this issue simply presumed some ad hoc link between contributions today and benefits tomorrow: see, for example, Hu (1982) and Verbon (1987). More recently, the focus has been on identifying potential devices whereby the credibility problem may be overcome. Sjoblom (1985) envisages an efficient outcome being supported by punishment strategies to penalise generations that fail to support the old of their time; Kotlikoff et al. (1988) describe a reputation mechanism for overcoming such problems. Tabellini (1991) points out that altruism of the young towards the old may also generate political support for payment of pensions by enough of the young to create a winning coalition: in particular, the poor young may support taxes to pay pensions to the elderly, since the bulk of those taxes will be borne by the better-off of their own generation. That in turn raises the possibility that each generation will make inadequate provision for its own old age in the knowledge that tomorrow's young will choose to support them, a samaritan's dilemma of the kind discussed in Section 2. Forced saving may emerge as a means to precommit against excessive redistribution to the old.

3.1.5. Public provision of private goods: ends against the middle

Many governments spend considerable resources on providing private goods at prices that are substantially below marginal cost, and often zero. Basic health and education services, for example, have many characteristics of private goods yet are often provided free. The implicit redistribution this entails raises two sets of questions. First, can the public provision of private goods be an efficient way of pursuing distributional objectives? We address this in Section 4. Second, what are the political forces that sustain such redistribution? That is our concern here.

The issue was first addressed by Usher (1977), who considered the likely political support for a system under which the public sector uses a proportional income tax to acquire the entire supply of some private good, which it then makes available to all citizens in uniform quantity. Those with income below the mean benefit financially from the scheme, receiving more as an implicit subsidy on the private good than they pay in taxes. Assuming all to have the same preferences, the right skewness of the income distribution then implies that there will indeed be majority support for the scheme. Against this, however, Usher emphasises the potential role of heterogeneity of preferences in creating political support for private purchasing.[40] Wilson and Katz (1983) extend the approach to the analysis of public subsidies for the purchase of private goods.

---

[40] This conflict between the redistributive effect of public provision and the inefficiency of uniform provision is emphasised and explored in a normative context by Weitzman (1977).

These analyses assume that the public sector becomes the sole provider of the private good. In many contexts, however, consumers are left the alternative of purchasing the private good for themselves instead of—or perhaps as a top-up to—the rationed amount on offer from the public sector. Parents may be allowed to take their children out of the state sector and into fee-paying private schools, for example, or to buy private medical insurance. In opting out, however, one cannot opt out of paying the taxes which finance the benefits of those who remain in. Epple and Romano (1996a, 1996b) show that this can have profound effects on the nature of the political equilibrium.

Consider, to fix ideas, the case in which the government will provide some fixed amount of education to each voter, financing this by a proportional tax on their exogenous incomes (the only respect in which they differ), while allowing all to opt out entirely and purchase whatever amount of education they please in the open market. Using the government's budget constraint to eliminate one of its two choice variables—writing the per capita provision level as a function of the tax rate, say—the issue space is one-dimensional. But preferences may fail to be single-peaked over this dimension even though the underlying utility function is perfectly well-behaved. Take an individual with a relatively strong liking for the good at issue. At low tax rates, and hence low levels of provision, she may choose to opt out, in which case further increases in the tax rate are clearly unwelcome; but as the tax rate rises she now opts in, and over some range is likely to support further tax increases.

Failure of single-peakedness precludes the usual easy invocation of the median voter theorem. Recall, however, that the median voter will still be decisive if the single-crossing condition discussed above holds. Epple and Romano (1996a) show that it does indeed hold if the marginal willingness to be taxed in order to pay for public provision does not increase with income.[41] But that marginal willingness might equally well increase with income, in which case the existence of a Condorcet winner becomes problematic. If a majority voting equilibrium does exist, however, it has a striking property: the level of public provision is determined by the balance between a coalition of rich and poor on the one hand and a solid phalanx of middle-income voters on the other. The intuition behind this "ends against the middle" property—which has evident similarity to Director's Law—is straightforward: the poor would rather have cash than education, and the rich would rather buy their preferred, higher level of education for themselves.

The insight is an appealing and powerful one. Pestieau (1998), for example, arrives at a similar result in pension provision. Indeed it seems likely to emerge from a range of problems in which voting is over the provision of private goods in something like uniform quantity to all: the poor are so poor that they would rather not be forced to pay for the good, while the rich are so rich that they would rather buy their own preferred quantity. In this identity of interests may lie an understanding of the closely related phenomena of Directors' Law and, by the same token, Disraelian Tory democracy.

---

[41] More precisely, the condition is that the increase in the tax rate that just leaves the consumer indifferent after an increase in the level of per capita public provision on offer decreases with the level of income.

3.2. *Representative democracy*

Policy is rarely determined by the entire citizenry meeting in plenary. Rather democracy works principally through the election of officials. Such representative democracy presumably offers advantages over direct democracy in terms of transactions costs, and perhaps too in some of the strategic advantages of delegation. Persson and Tabellini (1994b) argue, for example, that if politicians are unable to commit themselves to pursue policies other than those which they themselves prefer—an issue to which we return below—then one way in which voters may be able to mitigate the time inconsistency problem in the taxation of capital income is by delegating tax-setting to politicians less inclined to tax capital than would be the median voter under direct democracy. Thus one might expect the institution of representative democracy in itself to lead to systematically less redistribution away from capital. It is in the context of representative democracy that political parties have a role to play. Downs (1957) argues that representation, especially by political parties, allows intensities of preference to be registered in ways that direct democracy does not. Political parties can put together a platform which implicitly amounts to vote trading, thereby allowing the collective decision rule to take account of more than simply preference orderings. He argues that this induces economic efficiency in political outcomes, including in those involving redistribution. Our concern here, however, is not to rationalise the prevalence of representative democracy but to explore its implications for distributional policies.

Representative democracies create a role for politicians, whose interests may now have a distinct impact on the outcome. One question that immediately arises is who in society—and how many of them—will emerge as politicians. Almost all of the literature simply assumes from the outset that elections are fought between only two candidates, essentially arbitrarily chosen. Osborne and Slivinski (1996) and Besley and Coate (1997) seek to endogenise the set of candidates by conceiving of each citizen deciding whether to run for office in order to implement their most preferred policy and, perhaps, enjoy some spoils of office. But since the implications for this richer approach for matters of redistribution remain as yet unclear, we here follow the well-trod route of simply supposing there to be two candidates, "left" (L) and "right" (R).[42]

The central questions are: How much redistribution would one expect to observe? And how much divergence would one expect between the policies pursued when in office by distinct parties?

The two candidates, we suppose, play Nash in their promises. The winner is the one with a majority. Given this, two broad sets of considerations shape the answers. The first is the degree to which politicians care not only about being in office—and we assume

---

[42] Both Besley and Coate (1997) and Osborne and Slivinski (1996) find that under plurality rule—victory going to the candidate with most votes—under quite weak conditions the equilibrium has only two candidates standing (so to some degree confirming a conjecture known as Duverger's Law). But this provides no support for the usual practice of simply assuming only two candidates: in these models, endogenous candidates cannot commit to pursuing any policy other than their most preferred, so that the equilibria are quite different from those studied in most two-candidate models.

throughout that they derive some "ego-rents" (that is, some psychic enjoyment, with no resource cost) merely from being elected—but also about the policy that they propose and (or, if defeated, that their opponents) implement. This is important because of its effect on the credibility of promises made to the electorate: politicians known to have their own preferences on policy may find it hard to commit themselves to policies other than those they prefer themselves. The strength of policy preferences thus shapes—but does not entirely determine, since reputational and other devices may also play a role—the extent to which candidates can credibly trim their own position in pursuit of electoral support. The second key consideration is the nature and extent of asymmetric information between voters and candidates: as Downs (1957) emphasised, candidates may be unsure exactly how many votes a particular policy will attract, and voters may not know exactly what policy preferences the candidates hold.

3.2.1. Office-seeking

Suppose first that politicians are entirely apolitical, in the sense that their sole concern is with being elected: they are prepared to, and credibly can, promise any feasible policy in order to get elected. The outcome in the one dimensional case—voting over a linear income tax, for example—is easy to see. Suppose that voters' preferences are known to the candidates and, for simplicity, are single-peaked. Then the same logic as led to the adoption of the preferred policy of the median voter under direct democracy implies that in equilibrium both candidates will offer the policy most preferred by the median voter: this is an instance of Hotelling's Principle of Minimum Differentiation. It has the obvious but important implication that the results for direct democracy above can also be interpreted as applying to a representative democracy in which there are (exogenously) two apolitical candidates. If candidates are uncertain about voters' preferred positions—but have the same distribution over the possibilities (perhaps having access to similar opinion polls or similar experience on doorsteps) then there will again be convergence to a common platform, though to exactly what is less clear.

More novel possibilities arise in voting over multi-dimensional issues. And indeed it is here that representative democracy comes into its own, reducing the dimensionality over which votes must actually be cast. Consider the case of lump-sum redistributive taxes, the extreme form of nonlinear taxes. For this case in isolation there is clearly no equilibrium. This reflects the empty core of the redistribution pie problem noted earlier, where each candidate can always find some schedule that a majority will prefer to whatever schedule is offered by his opponent. But individuals may vote not only over the extent of self-interested redistribution, but also over a range of other matters: foreign policy, domestic governance, charisma, and so on. These might in turn be summarised as matters of party loyalty. One such approach to redistribution in representative democracy—developed by Coughlin (1986), and Lindbeck and Weibull (1987, 1993)—is to suppose that party loyalties are private information, though candidates know their distribution in the population: and know their distribution, we shall suppose, conditional on pre-tax/transfer income. Suppose, for example, that individual i will vote for candidate L rather than R iff $U(Y_i + T_{Li}) > U(Y_i + T_{Ri}) + \gamma_i$, where T_{Si} denotes the transfer that party S commits to make to each individual with income Y_i if elected, γ_i denotes i's intrinsic preference for party R (presumably reflecting aspects of R's platform that do not directly affect i's net income—ideology in a broad sense). This leads to a simple model of probabilistic voting, with candidates unsure exactly how individual voters will choose to vote but able to evaluate the impact of their policy announcements on total support received.

Suppose then that the distribution of γ amongst those with pretax income Y_i is given by the distribution function $\Phi(\gamma_i; Y_i)$ (the conditioning on Y being to allow for the possibility that party loyalties may differ systematically across income groups). Each party, assume, seeks to maximise the expected number of votes it receives,[43] so that L chooses (T_k) to maximise $\Sigma_k N_k \Phi(\gamma_k : Y_k)$, or:

$$\Sigma_k N_k \Phi\left(U(Y_k + T_{Lk}) - U(Y_k + T_{Rk}); Y_k\right),\tag{10}$$

subject to the budget constraint $\Sigma_k N_k T_{Lk} = 0$, N_k being the number of voters with pre-tax income Y_k. It is straightforward to show that each party offers the same pattern of transfers (T_k) in equilibrium: since there is nothing they can do to affect party loyalties, each must look only to serving voters' self-interest.[44] The common first-order condition gives

$$\phi(0; Y_k)U'(Y_k + T_{Sk}) = \kappa, \qquad \forall k, \quad S = L, R.\tag{11}$$

where $\phi = \partial\Phi/\partial\gamma$ denotes the density of γ_k. Then an income group k has post-tax/transfer income above the average only if its $\phi(0; Y_k)$ is above the average. This quantity is the proportion of individuals with income Y_k who are indifferent between the parties, in the sense that they would be equally happy voting for either if they offered the same tax schedule; it is thus a measure of the "waveringness" of group k. The implication of Eq. (11) is thus that it is not the groups which show most party loyalty that are receive the most generous transfers, but those who show least loyalty. Indeed the outcome is exactly as if government maximised a social welfare function of form $W \equiv \Sigma\phi(0; Y_k)N_k U_k(Y_k + T_k)$: a utilitarian social welfare function, that is, but with the key difference that groups are weighted not by the number of their members but by their waveringness.

<hr/>

[43] An alternative is to suppose that politicians seek to maximise the probability of their securing a majority. Only in special cases will the two objective functions lead to the same conclusion: Lindbeck and Weibull (1987) show, for example, that Eq. (11) below continues to hold in this alternative case iff $\Phi(0 : Y)$ is independent of Y. (See also Grossman and Helpman, 1996). Neither approach is intrinsically preferable to the other, and indeed a more general approach would accommodate both: politicians may care both about being elected and their majority when in office. The modelling choice is essentially arbitrary, but for present purposes nothing critical appears to turn upon it.

[44] That this is the only equilibrium is established in Lindbeck and Weibull (1987, 1993).

Notice that the equilibrium tax structure implied by Eq. (11) is not even necessarily progressive, nor—weaker still—need the transfer even fall with pre-tax income. Concavity of U points towards equalisation, so that if $\phi(0; Y)$ is independent of Y, one obtains complete equalization, as in Section 2.[45] But this effect can be dominated by the tendency to inegalitarianism if the poor are sufficiently determined in their views.[46] One further implication, emphasised by Lindbeck and Weibull (1987) and Dixit and Londregan (1996), is of particular interest. Suppose, for some unexplained reason, that high income persons choose to be affiliated with one party, and low income persons with the other. Then ϕ_k has inverse-U shape over before-tax income. So Eq. (11) implies that middle-classes will be especially favoured: in this special case, Director's Law thus emerges again.

3.2.2. The role of ideology

Consider now the case in which politicians care not only about office but also about policy.

One key issue then is whether or not they can commit to adopt policies other than those they most prefer themselves. Suppose first that they can; for there are indeed devices—the desire for re-election, party discipline (retiring politicians penalised if have broken implicit contract)—that may serve such a commitment purposes.

Reverting to the one-dimensional case, in the absence of uncertainty, there will again be convergence of both candidates to the position of the median voter. Whatever their own preferences, both left and right propose and implement, for example, the linear income tax preferred by the median voter: intuitively, it is always preferable to implement a policy proposed by one's opponent than have the opponent implement that same policy. Matters are different, however, if there is uncertainty as to the preferences of the electorate. In this case each party will adopt a platform somewhere between its own preferred policy and the distinct policy offered by the opposition. For suppose, to the contrary, that each offered the same policy in equilibrium. Then each would perceive an advantage from shifting policy towards its preferred point: for since the initial policy maximised the probability of election given the opponent's policy, such a change has no first-order effect on the probability of being elected but since (for at least one candidate)

---

[45] Mueller (1989), drawing on Coughlin (1984) also discusses how models in which voter support is uncertain and in which candidates maximise their expected votes, can lead to a unique egalitarian majority equilibrium in the case where voting is over redistribution of a fixed amount of resources.

[46] The ambiguity remains even when incentive effects are admitted and attention confined to linear tax schedules. In this case the equilibrium tax rate can be shown, using Eq. (8), to be

$$\frac{t}{1-t} = -\frac{\text{cov}[\phi_k^*(0), Y_k]}{\int_\Omega \omega l \eta^c \, dF},$$

where $\phi_k^* \equiv \phi_k / \Sigma_i \phi_i$. From Eq. (27) below, the outcome is thus as if the maximisation were of a social welfare function $\Sigma \phi_k(0) \Omega(t, w_k)$; and the marginal tax rate will be positive if, on average, low earners are also waverers.

that common platform is away from its preferred policy such a policy shifts raises the politician's welfare if elected. Policy preference on the part of politicians thus sustains a partial divergence of platforms, a point emphasised by Alesina (1988). In the context of probabilistic voting along the lines above, Lindbeck and Weibull (1993) show that[47] each politician announces a policy somewhere between that which maximises $\Sigma_k \phi_k(0) u$ and that which is preferred in their own preferences. The ideological component of voters' preferences in the probabilistic voting model above—captured by the exogenous constant γ—plays no real role in shaping the outcome. Recent contributions have given it a more purposive role.

Dixit and Londregan (1998) put more flesh on γ, and allow party platforms to influence it, by supposing that voters differ in the relative weights that they attach to (particular measures of) equality and efficiency in the design of tax policy. Thus parties can influence voter's intentions not only through the effects on voters' own incomes but also by the wider distributional policy they propose. Politicians themselves are assumed to care not only about holding office but also about the distributional position they adopt: party platforms will therefore diverge. In the equilibrium of such a game, it emerges, given the parameterization Dixit and Londregan adopt, that each party offers a tax schedule characterized by a single marginal tax rate (differing across parties in reflection of their differing distributional positions) but with group-specific intercept terms (reflecting the attempt to capture the votes of groups according to the waveringness of their ideological preferences ϕ_i as discussed above, and again in Section 3.3 below). Not surprisingly, the party more to the left ideologically (that is, putting more weight on equality relative to efficiency) will propose the higher marginal tax rate.

The ideological differences between parties might, however, be on matters quite distinct from redistributional policy: on race or religion, say. Roemer (1998) considers how such matters might affect party platforms on issues of redistribution. There immediately arises the problem of multidimensionality raised earlier: there generally will not exist a Nash equilibrium. Roemer addresses this by proposing a distinct equilibrium concept. Parties are assumed to comprise three types: opportunists, who care only about office; militants, who care only about the platform that is proposed; and reformists, who care about the expected utility of their client group.[48] This leads to the concept of equilibrium as a pair of platforms such that in neither party do all three types agree to a deviation given the policy proposed by the other. In such a setting, Roemer (1998) shows how parties temper their redistributional policy to secure support along the other dimensions of policy: a working-class anti-clerical party, for instance, may offer less than full redistribution to the poor in order to secure support from better-off, anti-clerical voters.

The same equilibrium concept is applied in Roemer (1999) to the pure redistribution problem in which the two competing political parties are identified with the interests of particular income groups. The Left party prefers outcomes most favourable to a par-

---

[47] This is for the case in which the number of policy options is finite.

[48] Thus the objective function in Dixit and Londregan (1998) is a weighted average of the militant and opportunist objectives.

ticular low-income voter, and a Right party sides with a high-income voter. The policy space is restricted to quadratic tax schedules, which implies using the government budget constraint that two parameters must be chosen, an outcome which would preclude a Condorcet winner in the standard electoral competition for votes. Again, equilibria are defined as those policy platforms such that there are no alternative platforms which would be weakly Pareto preferred by party militants, opportunists and reformers. Then, all such equilibria involve progressive income tax systems.

All this assumes that politicians can commit themselves. Suppose they cannot. If voters know the candidate politicians' types, matters are straightforward. It may be, however, that a politician's type—their preferred progressivity of the tax system, for concretenesss—is their private information. A politician who believes her true type to be unpopular with the voters then has an incentive to disguise that type; similarly, a politician who believes her type to be popular has an incentive to take actions that will credibly signal that type. These issues are considered by Dhami (1997), the framework being one in which voters are uncertain of an incumbent's type—the progressivity of their preferred linear income tax—and term limits mean that the incumbent, if re-elected, cannot run for office again (and so will simply set their preferred tax rate). As one would expect, one possible outcome is a separating equilibrium in which the incumbent finds it worthwhile pursuing a sufficiently extreme policy during their first period in office that their type cannot be mistaken. In the presence of term limits, distributional policy may thus change even though the politician in power does not, a conclusion which finds some echo in the finding of Besley and Case (1995) of greater fiscal volatility in US states with gubernatorial term limits.

3.2.3. The spoils of office

So far we have considered candidates preferences for tax-transfer policies as they affected the welfare of the electorate. But policymakers (politicians/bureaucrats) may have an opportunity to extract resources or rents for themselves, as emphasised in the earlier discussion on kleptocracy. One well-known instance of this is the Leviathan view of government, as posited by Brennan and Buchanan (1980). In the simplest case, the policymaker has as their only objective the extraction of surplus from society. Less starkly, one can envisage policymakers also giving some weight to citizens' well-being, either because of fear of insurrection or a real sense of social justice. Either case is of some interest for our purposes, since the Leviathan tendencies leading a policymaker to divert resources to herself has implications too for extent of redistribution amongst citizens.

To see the forces at work, suppose the policymaker diverts an amount C of the revenue obtained from a linear income tax to herself. The government revenue constraint becomes:

$$\alpha + C = t \int_{\Omega} wL[(1-t)w, \alpha] \, dF(w). \tag{12}$$

Consider the general case in which the policymaker derives well-being not only from C, but also—a reflection of concerns of the kind just mentioned—from some weighted sum of utilities, $\sum_i \lambda_i u_i$, where $\lambda_i \geq 0$ with strict inequality for some i. The policymaker's problem is then to choose t and C to maximise an objective function given by $\mu(C, \sum_i \lambda_i \Gamma(t, C, w_i))$ where $\mu(\cdot)$ is strictly increasing in both arguments and $\Gamma(t, C, w_i) \equiv v[(1 - t)w_i, t \int \omega L[(1 - t)w, \alpha] dF(w) - C]$ denotes indirect utility for a household of type i. Assuming there to be no income effects on labour supply, the necessary condition on t is easily seen to reduce to $\sum_i \lambda_i \Gamma_t(t, C, w_i) = 0$. If, following our earlier analysis, there are no income effects on labour supply,[49] Γ_t is independent of C, and the solution for t is exactly as for maximisation of $\sum_i \lambda_i u_i$. Since the policymaker will set $C > 0$, the conclusion is that concern with rent extraction will leave t unchanged but the poll subsidy α lower, so that the concern with rent extraction means a systematic bias towards less progressive taxation than would otherwise be the case.[50] To understand why, it helps to think of the policymaker solving her problem in two stages. In the first, she takes C as given and chooses (t, α) to maximize the social welfare part of her utility function, subject to the revenue constraint implied by using that particular C in Eq. (12). In the second, she identifies the full optimum by repeating the exercise for all C. What drives the result is that the constancy of the welfare weights λ and quasi-linearity of household preferences imply that the optimal marginal tax rate at the first stage is unaffected by the revenue constraint (as can be seen from Eq. (27) below). Thus the efficient extraction of surplus takes the form of poll tax.

3.3. Interest groups

Many measures with redistributive content appear to be "particularist" or "tactical" in the sense that the gains are targeted towards a rather narrowly-defined group. This in turn both reflects and encourages interest groups or lobbies—we use the terms synonymously— to solicit such benefits for their own members. It is to these politics of "pork-barrel" that we turn in this section.

The connotations of pork barrel and lobbying, of course, are bad. It is as well to remember, however, that lobbies may represent groups whose interests might be widely recognised as more than mere special pleading: lobbies may represent single-parent families, or the aged for example, just as they might represent such easy bogies as farmers, lawyers or the arms industry. In any event, our concern here—as in most of the literature—will not be with the distributional worthiness of the beneficiaries of lobbying activities (which may include, not least, policymakers themselves). Nor do we consider the formation of lobbies, but rather take their existence as given.[51] Instead we focus on two prior issues on which the literature has focussed:

---

[49] Then $v[(1 - t)w, b] = b + h((1 - t)w)$ for some increasing $h(\cdot)$.

[50] This ties in with, though with reasoning somewhat different, the Brennan and Buchanan (1980) argument for requiring progressive tax structure as a check on revenue maximisation.

[51] Olsen (1965, 1982) provides a wide-ranging analysis of the incentives to form interest groups, and their consequences for redistribution and growth. His analysis is based on the notion that interest groups exist

- Which kinds of lobbies should one expect to be most successful in winning pork barrel for their members? Does it help to be small, for example, and so able to spread the cost of any redistribution over a large number of others; or is it better, on the contrary, to have many members and so be able to deliver more votes? Do policymakers reward those with ideological commitments similar to their own, or do they on the contrary attempt to buy support from their natural opponents?

- Will tactical redistribution be delivered in an efficient manner, or will inefficient methods of redistribution be used? At first sight, many forms of redistribution observed in practice appear to be inefficient. A popular example is provided by the Common Agricultural Policy of the European Union. This traditionally benefits farmers by maintaining food prices (to both consumers and producers) above world prices. But exactly the same benefit could be delivered to farmers by simply subsidising their production whilst allowing consumers to trade at world prices: with the benefit to consumers from an increase in consumer surplus more than outweighing the cost of financing the subsidy. Other apparently inefficient policies would include, for example, using entry barriers to support the incomes of professionals (rather than simply paying them a lump sum) and favouring local suppliers in procuring goods for public sector use. The "Virginia" view—see Tullock (1967) and Buchanan (1980)—is that there is indeed a distinct tendency for particularist redistribution to come in inefficient forms. The "Chicago" view on the other hand—see Stigler (1982) and Becker (1983)—is that there are incentives tending towards the use of efficient instruments. What appear to be inefficient tools will often turn out, on close inspection, to be second-best efficient, a phenomenon that will recur when we consider redistributive policy instruments in the face of self-selection and commitment problems in Section 4.

Note that there is a link here with the literature on rent-seeking, though the focus there tends to be somewhat different. Rent-seeking refers to the resources and effort devoted to obtaining a share of the rents that are generated by government legislation or regulation—the creation of a monopoly supplier, the protection of products through tariffs, taxes and subsidies, the granting of licenses, and so on. The distortions are typically taken as given and attention is then focused on whether the rents that they create will be dissipated in the competition to enjoy them. Rent-seeking is a risky business: only some rent-seekers will be successful. They will devote resources until the cost just equals the expected utility of the lottery. Such resource expenditures are pure waste, and may dissipate a substantial part of the rent being competed for. Indeed, if rent-seekers are risk-neutral and symmetric, and if there is free entry, the dissipation will be complete. Here, in contrast, the endogeneity of the distortions is of the essence, and (implicitly) the real resources used in their creation are taken as given (in a sense that will become clearer later).

largely to exploit common interests, and the consequent free-rider problems will influence the types of groups that will form and be successful.

It is on these two issues that we concentrate. Though the distinction[52] ultimately proves rather strained, it helps organise ideas to distinguish between two approaches to the formal analysis of these issues, differing in the proximate motivation attributed to the lobbies.

The first approach attributes to lobbies only what Grossman and Helpman (1996) call an "electoral motive": their sole concern is assumed to be with the probability of (re-)electing a policymaker whose interests are favourable to its own. In particular, the lobbies take as given the platforms announced by electoral candidates (and believe they will be implemented if elected).

The question then arises as to what the lobbies have to offer that might affect the electoral outcome. And here it is natural to begin with the case in which all they have to offer is their members' votes. This takes us back to the model of probabilistic voting in the preceding section, from which one can extract a little more in terms of the kinds of groups that are likely to be favoured. Suppose, following Dixit and Londregan (1996), that the utility function in Section 3.2 is of the form $U_i(C) = \frac{\theta_i}{1-e}C^{1-e}$. Solving Eq. (11) then gives the share in total consumption of the typical member of group j as

$$\frac{C_j}{\sum N_i y_i} = \frac{\pi_j}{\sum N_i \pi_i}, \tag{13}$$

where Dixit and Londregan call $\pi_j \equiv [\phi_j(0)\theta_i]^{1/e}$ a measure of the "clout" of group j. The lobbies that do best are thus those with the greatest clout. Other things equal, two things tend to place a lobby in a strong position. The first is an ideological indecisiveness, in the sense of a high value of $\phi_i(0)$, the reason being as discussed above. The second is a high degree of venality, in the sense of a relatively large value of θ_j: for θ indicates the weight placed on consumption relative to ideology, and a high value means that a vote is more easily bought.

Three other implications of Eq. (13) are of interest. The first is that the poor are inherently advantaged in this game of pork-barrel, irrespective of their clout. To see this, note that if two groups have the same clout then they will end up with the same per capita consumption; and hence the per capita tax will be lower for the poorer group. The reason is simple: the greater marginal utility of income of the poor makes their votes cheaper to buy. The second striking implication is that the size of a lobby has no bearing on its clout. Small interest groups are relatively cheap to buy, but they also have few votes to offer: the two effects cancel, leaving the political power of a lobby independent of its size. There is an indirect effect of the size of a lobby on the per capita consumption of its members operating through the denominator of Eq. (13), but it is still clout that is critical. Suppose, for example, that all in group i and j have the same per capita income; then an increase in the membership N_j of lobby j combined with a reduction in the size of i will benefit the now-larger group j if and only if it has the greater clout. The third is

[52] Which is also made by Rodrik (1995).

that both parties offer the same program to the electorate: ideology (which drives voters' intrinsic preferences for the parties) plays no role in the redistribution they offer.

The simplicity of the solution in Eq. (13)—in particular, its first-best Pareto-efficiency—reflects the assumption that lump sum taxes are available to the policymaker. Hettich and Winer (1988) examine the choice between distorting taxes in a similar model of probabilistic voting. The characterisation of equilibrium policy is conceptually straightforward: the vote-maximising politician will seek to equate across alternative tax instruments the number of votes expected to be lost per dollar of additional revenue. Though the implied tax structure may be complex, it shares two important properties with that in Eq. (13). First, it will be Pareto efficient relative to the instruments available (so long as each lobby group has some positive probability of voting for the party being examined): for it would otherwise be possible to attract more votes from some group without forgoing votes from another. The implication is thus that when only distorting taxes are available the equilibrium tax system will be second best Pareto efficient. Second, all parties again offer the same tax structure.

Inefficient policies may emerge in equilibrium, however, if the government is unable to commit to its future redistribution policies. The argument there is developed by Dixit and Londregan (1995) in the context of support to declining industries. The efficient response to such a decline is likely to involve workers reallocating to higher income occupations, with any compensation deemed appropriate or judicious paid as a lump sum. Once workers move, however, they are liable to find themselves in a new interest group. Ex post, policymakers will simply arrange transfers to that group in line with Eq. (13) above. Thus any private income gains associated with moving to an interest group with higher income may ultimately be taxed so heavily that the net gain falls short of the cost of moving; then forward-looking voters will not make the move, but instead remain in the declining sector and take such transfers as Eq. (13) generates. Suppose, to take an extreme case, that the efficiency-enhancing action requires moving between two groups that have the same clout; then unless the government is able to commit to distinguish ex post between those who moved and those who did not, those who move will experience no private gain from doing so. The economy is thus locked into an inefficient policy by the inability of government to commit itself to allow those who move to enjoy sufficient of the efficiency gains they create in doing so. Note though that this problem is not particular to a world of pork-barrel. Exactly the same time consistency problem arises whenever governments are unable to commit themselves not to redistribute away the private benefits that individuals are able to reap from decisions that enhance overall efficiency: such as investments in education, an example we shall return to in Section 4.

The lobby groups envisaged in the discussion so far have been very passive: all they do is vote. One generally thinks of lobbies as seeking to exercise power in other ways too. A more proactive way in which they might pursue their electoral motive is by contributing to the campaign funds of political parties. For by sending costly messages to rationally uninformed voters—that is, who would otherwise not find the cost of informing themselves worthwhile in terms of the gain from any conceivable change in their voting behaviour—lobbies may affect the distribution of electoral outcomes. It may be, for example, that they are able to provide (perhaps misleading) information on the consequences of policy choices that voters would otherwise not find it worthwhile obtaining for themselves or their contributions themselves convey information to voters as to the magnitude of the income transfers at stake in choosing between alternative policies (Pyne, 1997).

This potential use of campaign contributions to affect election outcomes is at the heart of an influential approach to the analysis of lobbies developed by Magee et al. (1989). Suppose there are just two parties and two lobbies, with lobby i contributing, if at all, only to party[53] i, $i = 1$, 2. The probability of party 1 being elected is taken to be some function $\pi(c_1, c_2, \theta_1, \theta_2)$ of the campaign contributions c_i of the two lobbies and the actions θ_i of the two parties. The function π is not derived from first principles, but instead assumed to satisfy plausible restrictions. In particular, π is increasing in c_1 and decreasing in c_2. Politicians choose policies θ and are concerned only to maximise the probability of winning office. Lobby i derives utility $U_i(\theta) - c_i$ from policies enacted, and so chooses its contributions to maximise expected utility $\pi U_i(\theta_1) + (1 - \pi)U_i(\theta_2) - c_i$. Lobbies play Nash against one another, and in doing so take declared policies θ_i as given; that is, contributions are determined after platforms. Parties play Nash against each other, as first movers relative to the lobbies. In the basic formulation of the model, each party recognises that its own policy may affect the contributions of its own lobby, but takes as given the contributions of the other.

The principal prediction of this framework is that the presence and activities of the lobbies may well involve the parties offering distinct policies even though they have no ideological commitments; and, most important for present purposes, they can be expected to sacrifice efficiency to the particularist interests of the lobbies. Suppose, for example, that there is some policy θ^* which maximises the sum of utilities, so that a fully efficient solution requires both parties to commit to θ^* and both to make zero contributions. And suppose too, to bring out the distinctive consequences of lobbying, that if contributions were fixed at zero each party would find it optimal to offer the efficient policy, implying that (taking π to be differentiable, for simplicity)

$$\frac{\partial \pi(0, 0, \theta^*, \theta^*)}{\partial \theta_1} = 0. \tag{14}$$

In these circumstances it is clear that the efficient polices cannot be sustained in the equilibrium of the model above. For each party would then find it optimal to deviate by offering a policy close to θ^* but more attractive to its own lobby: the change in policy itself will have no impact on the probability of election, from the property just described,

---

[53] This can indeed be shown to be the case, under weak restrictions: the only return to contributions is changing the probability of election, so that contributing to both is merely to some degree self-defeating. In a wider context, of course, contributing to both may be optimal if, for example, past contributions, buy access to politicians in office.

but it will induce positive contributions from lobby 1—which now finds it worthwhile to seek the election of that party rather than its opponent—and thus the probability of election increases. More generally, any tendency towards reduced political support consequent upon deviating from an efficient policy may be more than compensated for by the political support that can be bought from the increased contributions of the favoured lobby.

This presumption of inefficiency, however, depends crucially on the assumption that each party takes the contributions of the other party's lobby as given in making its decisions. Clark and Thomas (1995) show that once this impact is taken into account the efficient solution will indeed be sustained in equilibrium. Intuitively, any departure from efficiency must damage the other lobby even more than it benefits the favoured lobby, and thus the other lobby has a greater incentive to campaign against the party proposing the deviation than its supporters have to lobby for it. Thus efficiency comes to predominate despite the willingness of politicians to serve the interests of particularist groups.

This brings us to the second broad approach to the analysis of interest groups: that which sees them as deliberately attempting to affect the policy of a government in office. Elections and electoral concerns are relegated to the background in modelling this influence motive. One interpretation of these models is that they are reduced forms in which the appearance of interest groups ultimately reflects their impact on electoral outcomes. A more coherent rationale would rest on a view that elections are ultimately bought, a view put forcefully by Becker (1983), who rationalises a neglect of voting on the grounds that "voter preferences are frequently not a crucial *independent* force in political behavior [but] can be manipulated and created through the information and misinformation provided by interested pressure groups" (p. 392). This may be more plausible for relatively narrowly defined particularist redistribution rather than programmatic redistribution. In any event, the key feature of these models is that interests seek to affect the distribution over policy outcomes other than by affecting electoral outcomes.

One simple way of modelling this is to posit some essentially ad hoc influence function by which resources spent by lobbies—on advertising, political contributions, or simple bribes—tilt policy in their direction. From such a framework Becker (1983), in a pioneering contribution, developed two influential sets of arguments.

First, he too arrived at a presumption—albeit a carefully qualified one—that efficient methods of redistribution (and its financing) will tend to be used. The reason is similar to, though distinct from, those that emerge from the electoral motive stories: beneficiary interest groups can expect to encounter less political resistance if their handouts are financed by an efficient tax structure, and if the amount that must be raised is reduced by distributing the benefits in efficient ways. An important qualification to this argument, as emphasised by Becker, is that the total amount of support is taken as given; we return to this below.

The second implication is that it is advantageous for a lobby group to have relatively few members: for then the tax rate levied on the rest of society will be relatively low (as will the associated deadweight loss), implying, one might suppose, relatively low political resistance.[54] This is in stark contrast, of course, to the implication of the model of probabilistic voting above that size is of no importance. The advantage that the poor enjoy of being cheap to support is no longer offset by the disadvantage of having relatively few votes at their disposal. This conclusion does indeed seem consistent with the casual observation of the support often enjoyed by such relatively small groups as farmers in the developed countries, workers in declining industries. In practice, however, it is not entirely clear that this is independent of electoral consideration, since such groups may often be large relative to voting constituencies even though small relative to the population as a whole. The role of smallness too will be returned to later.

An alternative approach to capturing a direct influence of lobbies on policy is to suppose that their interests enter into the objective function of policymakers with a particularly heavy weight. Like the influence function, this "political support" function is obviously something of black box. The common agency approach to the analysis of interest group pressures—developed by Grossman and Helpman (1994), and further refined and applied by, in particular, Dixit (1996) and Dixit et al. (1997)—takes as its point of departure precisely the attempt to model explicitly the way in which interest groups may influence policy. The essence is to see the policy maker as a single agent responding to, in the interest groups, many principals.

Consider for example the lobbying by firms for publicly financed subsidies on their inputs. Suppose there are M sectors in the economy, with the typical sector i comprising N_i individuals each with access to a technology $f_i(x)$ for producing good i from an imported input x and some fixed factor owned by that individual. Prices of all goods are fixed on world markets, and normalised at unity. Purchases of sector i are subsidised at rate s_i, and these subsidy rates are potentially the object of lobbying as are, for expositional purposes, lump sum subsidies a_i payable to members of each sector. Profits of the typical member of sector i are then $\pi_i(s_i) \equiv \max_x\{f_i(x) - (1 - s_i)x\}$, giving total income

$$Y_i \equiv \pi_i(s_i) + a_i - c_i(\mathbf{s}, \mathbf{a}) - \frac{1}{N}\left\{r(\mathbf{s}) + \sum_{j=1}^{M} N_j a_j\right\}, \tag{15}$$

where $c_i(\mathbf{s}, \mathbf{a})$ denotes the contribution that i makes to the policymaker (whether as campaign contribution or other inducement, legal or not)—which, note, are conditional on the policy pursued—whilst $r \equiv \sum N_j s_j Y_j(s_j)$ denotes total revenue (campaign contributions, it is assumed, being necessarily retained by the policymaker), $N \equiv \sum N_j$ denotes the total population and it is assumed that any revenue requirement is raised by a uniform poll tax. The utility of individual i is then $U(Y_i)$, with U concave.

---

[54] Olsen (1965) argued that size was a disadvantage in interest group formation for another reason. The fewer the members, the easier it is to overcome free-rider problems that inevitably accompany interest groups lobbying for a common interest.

The policymaker cares both about the contributions received and the sum of utilities, with linear preferences between the two described by the objective function

$$G(\mathbf{s}, \mathbf{a}) \equiv \sum_{i=1}^{M} c_i(\mathbf{s}, \mathbf{a}) + \beta \sum_{i=1}^{M} N_i U(Y_i). \tag{16}$$

We assume that the policymaker values contributions more than citizens' well-being, in the sense that she would prefer to receive a dollar in contributions than have a dollar given to any citizen: thus we confine attention to circumstances in which

$$1 \geq \beta U'(Y_i), \quad \forall i. \tag{17}$$

The interest groups choose their contribution schedules so as to maximise $U(Y)$.

For the moment, suppose lump sum transfers are impossible, so that $a_k = 0, \forall k$. The first-order condition for the government's choice of s_k is then

$$\sum_{i \in L} N_i \frac{\partial c_i}{\partial s_k} + \beta \sum_{i=1}^{M} N_i U'(Y_i) \left(\delta_{ik} x_k - \frac{\partial c_i}{\partial s_k} - \frac{1}{N} \frac{\partial r}{\partial s_k} \right) = 0, \quad \forall k, \tag{18}$$

where L denotes the set of sectors organised into lobbies (which we take to be given exogenously, and unchanging), δ_{ik} is the Kronecker delta and use has been made of the relation $\pi_k'(x_k) = x_k$. To characterise the optimal choice of schedule by the lobbies, note that lobby i will set its schedule so that the policy choice it induces maximises $G + U(Y_i)$: for since the contribution schedule effectively enables side payments to be made between i and the policymaker, it would otherwise be possible to make both better off by choosing differently. And since we have just seen that policy is chosen to maximise G, it must be therefore be the case that it maximises the utility of each active lobby. Thus

$$\delta_{ik} x_k - \frac{\partial c_i}{\partial s_k} - \frac{1}{N} \frac{\partial r}{\partial s_k} = 0, \quad \forall k \in L. \tag{19}$$

Combining Eqs. (18) and (19) gives[55]

$$x_k \left(\gamma_k - \alpha_L + \beta(1 - \gamma_k) U'(Y_k) - \beta \sum_{i \notin L} \alpha_i U'(Y_i) \right)$$

---

[55] Condition Eq. (20) below is exactly the necessary condition for maximising an objective function of the form $\sum_i \sigma U(Y_i)$, where $\sigma = \gamma_i / U'(Y_i^*) + (1 - \gamma_i)\beta$, Y^* denotes the value of income at the optimum and γ_i is as defined below. The outcome is thus as if the policymaker sought to maximise a political support function in which (by our assumption that $\beta \lambda < 1$) those organised in lobbies receive especially high weight.

$$= s_k x_k' \left(\alpha_L + \beta \sum_{i \notin L} \alpha_i U'(Y_i) \right) \quad \forall k. \tag{20}$$

where γ_k takes the value unity (zero) if sector k is (not) organised as a lobby, $\alpha_i \equiv N_i/N$ and $\alpha_L \equiv \sum_{i \in L} \alpha_i$ denotes the proportion of the population in organised sectors. Also denoting (minus) the elasticity of demand for the input by E_k, one finds from Eq. (20) the equilibrium subsidy to sector k to be given by

$$\frac{s_k}{1 + s_k} = \frac{1}{E_k} \left(\frac{1 - \alpha_L - \beta \sum_{i \notin L} \alpha_i U'(Y_i)}{\alpha_L + \beta \sum_{i \notin L} \alpha_i Y'(Y_i)} \right), \tag{21}$$

if k is organised and

$$\frac{s_k}{1 + s_k} = \frac{1}{E_k} \left(\frac{\beta(U'(Y_k) - \sum_{i \notin L} \alpha_i U'(Y_i)) - \alpha_L}{\alpha_L + \beta \sum_{i \notin L} \alpha_i U'(Y_i)} \right), \tag{22}$$

if it is not.

An immediate implication of Eq. (21), given the assumption in Eq. (17), is that all organised groups receive a positive subsidy. The position of the unorganised is less clear-cut: some of them may also receive subsidies, their marginal utility of income being so high that the policy-maker's interest in their well-being justifies favouring them. It is sufficient, however, for all unorganised groups to find their input being taxed in order to subsidise the organised groups, that all such groups have the same marginal utility of income.

Within the set of organised groups the only characteristic that affects the size of the subsidy is the elasticity of demand: the lower this is, the higher is the subsidy. For a lower elasticity means a lower deadweight loss, and hence a greater welfare gain for both the group concerned and, thereby, the policymaker.

The size of an interest group, on the other hand, has no impact on the subsidy that it receives in equilibrium. What matters instead is the size of all active lobbies taken together, α_L. The intuition, it seems, is that since all particularist benefits are ultimately paid for by the unorganised, and since the policymaker weights all individuals equally—in terms of both their welfare and their cash contributions—so it is simply the collective size of the organised groups that determines the rate at which each is subsidised.

The final welfare of any interest group i depends, however, not only on the subsidy rate s_i that it is able to attract but also on the resources $c_i(\mathbf{s}, \mathbf{a})$ it spends in the process. This in turn is tied down by the condition that the payoff to the policymaker be the same as it could obtain by dealing with all active lobbies except the ith: the payoff can be no less, otherwise the policymaker would indeed deal only with those others; and it can be no more because otherwise the interest group could change its contribution schedule so as to leave the marginal incentives facing the policymaker unchanged but the level of contributions lower. Thus the welfare of any interest group will generally depend on the extent and nature of other organised interest groups. One might expect, in particular, the final benefit to any lobby to be smaller—and the net gain to the policymaker greater— the more active groups there are. For suppose, at one extreme, that only one lobby is active in the subsidy game above. Then since in the absence of that lobby all subsidies would be zero, the payoff to the policymaker must be just as in the no-intervention case. Thus the policymaker derives no benefit from the activities of the interest group, with the contribution received exactly offset by the welfare losses of the nonorganised groups. All the gains go to the lobby. At the other extreme, if all groups are organised then Eqs. (21) and (22) imply that all subsidies are zero in equilibrium. If any one group were to be eliminated, however, it would find itself facing a positive tax in order to finance the others. Thus each group will make some contribution simply to avoid being made the victim of all others: all citizens—organised and not—would be better off it the organised could commit not to make any contribution, with all the rents created by their ability to do so being captured by the policymaker.

This reminds us that the analysis takes as given—as indeed we have done through-out—the existence of organised interest groups. One might naturally think of taking this game back one stage further to consider entry decisions by lobbies, though it seems this has not yet been done in this framework.

Consider next the issue of whether one would expect inefficient policies to be used in a world of the kind just described if efficient policies are technically feasible. This can be addressed by now allowing the lump sum transfers **a** to be deployed. Proceeding as above, the condition analogous to Eq. (20) reduces to

$$\gamma_k - \alpha_L + \beta(1 - \gamma_k)U'(Y_k) - \beta \sum_{i \notin L} \alpha_i U'(Y_i) = 0 \quad \forall k, \tag{23}$$

which, combined with Eqs. (21) and (22), implies that $s_k = 0, \ \forall k$. Thus only the efficient policy is used in equilibrium. This does not mean, however, that the availability of efficient instruments is Pareto-improving. Organised interest groups may prefer that the policymaker be restricted to using the inefficient subsidy system. Take, for example, the extreme case in which all groups are organised, so that each must in effect pay protection money in order not to be exploited by the others. Then since lump sum taxes provide a more efficient means of expropriation, groups may well find themselves having to pay more protection money as a consequence. The same effect may be at work when not all are organised.

More strikingly still, one can show that at least one unorganised group is certain to prefer an equilibrium in which only the inefficient instrument is available (and used) to one in which efficient lump sum transfers can be made.[56] The intuition is essentially

[56] To see this note first that Eq. (21) implies that $\beta U'(Y_i^{*A}) = 1$ for all $i \notin L$, where the superscript $*A$ refers to an optimum when lump sum transfers a are available. (This follows on setting $\gamma_k = 1$ in Eq. (23) to find $1 - \alpha_L - \beta \sum_{i \notin L} \alpha_i U'(Y_i^{*S})$ and using this to evaluate Eq. (23) for $\gamma_k = 0$). Since it is easily seen from Eq. (23) that $s_k > 0$ for some k implies the existence of some $i \notin L$ such that $\beta U'(Y^{*S}) < 1$ (the superscript

the same as just given for the lobbies, the only difference being that it is sure to apply for at least one group: a restriction to inefficient policies can reduce vulnerability to expropriation.

There is indeed a general principle here: when policy-making is not entirely benevolent, a restriction to the use of inefficient instruments may be socially beneficial. An early instance of this, for reasons quite distinct from those in the model of common agency above, was developed by Rodrik (1986).[57] The argument there is that since free-rider problems are likely to impede the formation of lobbies to seek tariffs (whose benefits are a public good to all firms in the protected sector) more effectively than they impede the formation of lobbies to seek firm-specific subsidies (whose benefits are akin to a private good), a commitment to deploy only tariffs may render the economy less vulnerable to special-pleading. The same principle is present too in the prescription of Brennan and Buchanan (1980) that the citizenry may wish to restrict a revenue-maximising Leviathan to the use of inefficient instruments as a means of limiting the extent to which revenue can be extracted from them: one might, for example, require commodity taxes to be uniform even though there would be efficiency gains from appropriate differentiation. Indeed Brennan and Buchanan would on these grounds require Leviathan to impose a tax schedule that is progressive: for it is well-known that such a schedule is (which cannot have a zero marginal tax rate at the top) cannot always be revenue-maximising.

If one is to explain the apparently widespread use of inefficient means for tactical redistribution in terms of the benefits that a commitment to the use of such instruments conveys on the otherwise vulnerable, some explanation of how such commitment is achieved in practice is needed. One might perhaps rationalise nondiscrimination rules in tax legislation as to some degree serving to commit against the use of firm-specific measures of the kind that may be most vulnerable to lobbying. Beyond that, however, it seems one must look to extra-legal commitment devices. And here it is unclear, for example what mechanisms are at work to penalise politicians who replace inefficient instruments with efficient.

It remains to consider one further view, not captured in any of the models described so far but apparently widely held, as to why inefficient policies may be pursued: because the losers find their losses from inefficient policies opaque and harder to perceive than they would under a system of lump sum transfers. A formal treatment of such "optimal obfuscation"[58] is provided by Coate and Morris (1995). Voters, it is assumed, are uncertain about both the type of politicians' seeking their vote—whether they are "good" in the sense of caring only for the citizens' well-being or "bad" in the sense of having a political support function that reflects the interests of some lobby—and the social return on some public project—which is certain, however, to benefit the special interests. Rather than simply pay lump sum transfers to the interest group and thereby

---

S indicating the regime in which only the distortionary subsidies s are available), there thus exists some $i \notin L$ such that $U'(Y^{*L}) > U'(U^{*S})$, and the result then follows from concavity.

[57] See also Wilson (1990).

[58] The term originates, it seems, with Magee et al. (1989).

reveal their type, bad politicians, it is shown, may implement the particularist project even when they (though not the voters) know it to be socially undesirable.

The notion of optimal obfuscation is reminiscent of, though distinct from, the argument of Becker (1983) and Stigler (1982) touched on above, also apparently widely held, that small lobbies tend to be successful because the cost of the support is spread over so many people that the cost to each is so small—perhaps even unnoticed—as not to warrant any action. Both raise the same counterargument (powerfully argued by Breton (1993): exploitation of an ill-informed majority by a minority creates an opening for a political entrepreneur to make the majority aware of the position and reap the reward of their electoral support. This then raises a range of issues concerning the ability of political entrants to discover the underlying truth—the true social return to the project, in the Coate-Morris model—and credibly convey it to the electorate, who will be aware that the entrant has an incentive to misrepresent the true position. It is thus by no means obvious that the entrepreneurial flair of politicians can be relied on to eliminate inefficient redistributive policies in democracies. Indeed if they could, the problem would become that of explaining why one does not observe more oppressive redistribution away from minorities.

4. Constraints on redistribution

In an ideal world, policymakers would have the luxury of choosing among allocations along the economy's first-best utility possibilities frontier (UPF). The first-best UPF represents the Pareto-efficient utility combinations achievable when the only constraints are the resources available and the technologies for converting resources into goods and services. In a first-best world, the decentralization of economic decisions to competitive markets has well-known desirable characteristics, summarized in the *Two Fundamental Theorems of Welfare Economics* (Arrow, 1951b). The first theorem states that competitive markets are Pareto-efficient regardless of the pattern of ownership of the economy's resources. The Second, more relevant for our purposes, says that, given convex preferences and technology, any Pareto-efficient allocation of resources can be achieved by a suitable reallocation of endowments (that is, lump sum income) among households in the competitive economy. The redistribution problem facing a welfarist policymaker is then to choose a pattern of lump-sum transfers of income so as to achieve the desired point on the UPF.

The choice among various utility combinations depends upon the precise form of the policymaker's social welfare function. For the purposes of this section, we restrict ourselves to considering Pareto-efficient outcomes, those chosen from the relevant UPF. The rationale for this is based on the role of economist as scientific policy advisor rather than as an analyser of actual political decision-making, the latter hat having been worn in the preceding section. We focus on the considerations that determine the alternative utility allocations from which the policymaker might choose, eschewing any attempt to evaluate one versus the other using interpersonal utility comparisons. The analysis will not be completely value-neutral, however, for we typically take for granted both the welfaristic perspective and the Pareto principle. And, typically we illustrate our points using relatively mild restrictions on the ordering of alternatives. In particular, we shall usually suppose that the policymaker's objective function is quasi-concave in individual utilities, an assumption that allows us to concentrate on that portion of the UPF which involves redistribution from the better-off to the less well off. Recall that a quasi-concave social welfare function encompasses degrees of aversion to inequality ranging from zero (utilitarianism) to infinite (maximin).

4.1. First-best redistribution

As a benchmark, it is useful to consider how optimal redistribution policies can vary in an ideal first-best world according to context. Consider first the case in which household incomes are fixed but can vary from one household to another. Household utility depends only on income, which can be used to purchase a composite commodity. If all households had identical strictly concave utility functions and if the policymaker had any quasi-concave social welfare function, then—essentially for the reason discussed at the outset of Section 2—optimal redistributive policy would imply full egalitarianism regardless of the degree of inequality aversion.

Next, suppose that utility functions differ among households such that some households receive more utility from a given level of income than others, and also have a higher marginal utility at any income level. Some persons, say the disabled, are less efficient "utility generators" than others. Thus, if person A is a better utility generator than person B, $U_A(Y) > U_B(Y)$ and $U'_A(Y) > U'_B(Y)$ for all incomes Y. In this case, as Sen (1973) observed, optimal redistributive policy depends critically upon the degree of aversion to utility inequality. Under a utilitarian social objective function, all that matters is the sum of utilities, so more income goes to the more efficient utility generators. The result is an unequal distribution of both incomes and utilities. At the other extreme, under a maxi-min social objective function, the point of equal utilities on the UPF will be chosen, with more income going to the less efficient utility generators. For less extreme values for the aversion to inequality, some utility inequality will be tolerated alongside some income inequality, though less than under utilitarianism.

For future purposes, one feature of these outcomes should be noted. To implement the optimal redistributive scheme, policymakers must know which utility function is attached to each household. If not, households cannot be relied upon to report truthfully on their utility functions. Any attempt to invoke an unequal distribution of incomes will be incentive-incompatible: under utilitarianism, persons will all prefer to tell the policymaker that they are highly efficient utility generators, and vice versa for maxi-min (Dasgupta and Hammond, 1980). Given this inability to identify utility functions with individuals, the government can do no better than to equalise incomes, a policy which had been proposed by Lerner (1944) because it maximized expected social welfare. The requirement that income redistribution policies be incentive-compatible when governments have imperfect information is the key limit to redistribution that we focus on later in this section.

Once income is allowed to be variable, matters become murkier still. Suppose, following the standard example used in the optimal redistributive taxation literature (Mirrlees, 1971), that household incomes come from variable labour supplies, with different households able to generate different amounts of income per unit of labour supplied. Let utility functions be the same for all households, with leisure and consumption both normal goods. In this case, the maxi-min objective function still generates equal utilities in the first best. Since their wage rate is higher, higher ability persons supply more labour and earn more income, but since they must reach the same utility level as lower ability persons, they also consume more. The amount of (lump-sum) taxes they pay will be higher, but their average tax rate (taxes divided by income) can be higher or lower depending on the form of the utility function. That is, the tax system need not be progressive (Sadka, 1976).[59] This is rather surprising, given that the maxi-min social objective function puts extremely high weight on egalitarianism.

The opposite extreme of utilitarianism is equally surprising. As Mirrlees (1974) showed, in this case (and so long as leisure is a normal good) higher ability persons end up with *lower* utility levels than lower ability persons. The reason is that because they are more efficient at producing output, they are required to supply much more labour. The tax system is in a sense highly redistributive, completely reversing the rankings of utility.[60] One the other hand, it may or may not be progressive depending again on the

---

[59] Formally, in the maxi-min optimum with identical preferences, all individuals achieve the same utility level: $U(C_i, L_i) = \bar{U} \; \forall i$. By utility maximization, individual's i's consumption-labour choice satisfies $w_i = -U_L/U_C$. The indifference curve associated with the equilibrium utility level $\bar{U}$ implicitly defines a relationship between C and L, say, $C = g(L)$. Then, by differentiation of the utility function along an indifference curve, we obtain $w_i = -U_L(C, L)/U_C(C, L) = g'(L)$. The average tax rate for person i is given by

$$T_i/Y_i = \frac{w_i L_i - C_i}{w_i L_i} = 1 - \frac{g(L_i)}{g'(L_i)L_i} = 1 - \frac{1}{E(L_i)},$$

where T_i is a lump-sum tax and $E(L_i)$ is the elasticity of the indifference curve. Thus, the tax is progressive iff $E(L)$ is increasing along the indifference curve, which Sadka shows will be the case if the elasticity of consumption of leisure for consumption is less than or equal to one.

[60] The proof is as follows. Let $C(w)$ and $L(w)$ be consumption and labour supply for a type-w individual. Then the change in utility as skills increase is given by $dU/dw = U_C C_w + U_L L_w$ where C_w and L_w are uncompensated price derivatives. In a utilitarian optimum $U_C = k$ for all w, and $U_L = -w U_C$ by consumer maximization. Totally differentiating these two conditions and solving, one obtains:

$$C_w = \frac{U_C U_{CL}}{D}; \qquad L_w = -\frac{U_C U_{CC}}{D},$$

where $D = U_{CC} U_{LL} - U_{CL}^2 > 0$ by the second-order conditions. Substituting these back into the expression for dU/dw, one obtains:

$$\frac{dU}{dw} = \left(\frac{U_C U_{CL} - U_L U_{CC}}{D} \right) U_C.$$

Since the numerator is negative if leisure is normal, $dU/dw < 0$.

curvature of indifference curves.[61]

The upshot of this discussion is that, even under ideal first-best conditions, there is no presumption about how progressive the redistributive lump-sum tax structure should be, or even if it should be progressive at all. Traditionally, most analyses of optimal redistributive policy have presumed that distortionary taxation must be used. Thus, the process of redistribution induced inefficiencies, forcing redistributionally minded policymakers to choose from points along a second-best, or *n*th-best, UPF. The expectation was then that, whatever the form of the social objective function, the progressivity of the tax system will be even less that it would have been under first-best redistributive taxation.

But why must distortionary taxation be imposed? Recent literature has suggested that rather than being imposed externally, distortionary taxes are optimal instruments in a second-best world in the sense that they enlarge the utility possibilities available to the policymaker. This literature stresses that what prevents the government from redistributing along the first-best UPF—equivalently, what causes a violation of the Second Theorem of Welfare Economics—is imperfect information. The government cannot directly discern the better-off from the less well-off, so must induce individuals to reveal their true types through their behaviour. According to this view, to which we turn next, the choice of redistributive tax is a problem in mechanism design. The use of distorting taxes turns out to be an "efficient" way to induce truthful revelation.[62]

4.2. Imperfect information as a limit to redistribution

The well-being of individuals depends on the set of circumstances facing them—their preferences, the state of their health, the effort they exert, their attitude toward risk, their productivity, and so on. Some of these are likely to be private information to the individual, and this inhibits the government from pursuing its welfaristic objectives. It does not preclude redistribution entirely because the government may be able to observe behavioural and other characteristics of individuals that are correlated with these underlying circumstances. But, imperfect information restricts the utility possibilities, or the efficiency-equity trade-off, available to the government.

The standard way to illustrate this uses the optimal income tax framework for redistribution due to Mirrlees (1971).[63] Differences among households are confined to one characteristic, their ability, which, given the linear production technology and the

---

[61] Using techniques similar to above, Sadka (1976) shows that the tax will be progressive if the elasticity of the curve along which the marginal utility of income is constant is less than or equal to one; but if that elasticity is large enough the tax will be progressive. The intuitive interpretation of this elasticity is not apparent.

[62] The importance of an imperfectly informed government was recognized by Vickrey (1945) and Van Graaff (1957), and formalized by Mirrlees (1971, 1974). The role of distorting taxation in such a setting out carefully in Nichols and Zeckhauser (1982) and analyzed as a problem of mechanism design by by Roberts (1984).

[63] While Mirrlees solved the optimal income tax problem and drew attention to its implications, Vickrey (1945) had actually set down the formal problem facing the imperfectly-informed government.

assumption of perfect substitutability among different ability-types of labour, can be normalized to be the household's wage rate w. For purposes of exposition, we assume a discrete distribution, following Guesnerie and Seade (1982), Stern (1982) and Stiglitz (1982). In fact, we can often simplify the distribution to one with only two ability-types with wage rates $w_2 > w_1$. Though the government cannot observe individual wage rates, it can observe incomes, $Y \equiv wL$. Given an income tax function $T(Y)$, it then also knows consumption $C = Y - T(Y)$. Through its choice of an income tax structure, the government is able to offer any relationship between consumption and income, including highly nonlinear ones, subject to its budget constraint being satisfied.

Since the government cannot observe each person's ability, it cannot make a person's tax payment contingent on their ability-type. It can only make it contingent on their income, which can be manipulated by the taxpayer. The redistribution problem is thus a classic revelation mechanism design problem. Taxpayers will only be induced to choose the (C, Y) combination intended for them—that is, to reveal their ability-type—if they prefer that (C, Y) over those intended for other ability-types. This is the source of an *incentive compatibility* or *self-selection constraint* that limits the extent of redistribution possible. Intuitively, higher-ability persons can earn a given income with less effort than can lower-ability persons. As the government attempts to redistribute income from better-off to worse-off persons using income as the indicator, at some point before income equality is reached the higher-ability persons will prefer the income-consumption bundle intended for the lower-ability persons over that intended for themselves; that is, they will be tempted to *mimic* lower-ability persons. At that point, the self-selection constraint binds and further redistribution becomes impossible. In principle, a self-selection constraint must be satisfied between all pairs of ability-types.

More formally, recall the definition of the utility function for a person of type i: $V^i(C, Y) \equiv U(C, Y/w_i)$. As mentioned, indifference curves in C, Y-space are positively sloped and exhibit increasing marginal rates of substitution, and assuming that consumption and leisure are normal, the Mirrlees–Spence single-crossing property applies:

$$-\frac{V_Y^i(C, Y)}{V_C^i(C, Y)} < -\frac{V_Y^j(C, Y)}{V_C^j(C, Y)} \qquad \forall w_i > w_j, \tag{24}$$

for any bundle C, Y. Geometrically, at any consumption-income bundle, the slope of an indifference curve, $dC/dY|_{V^i}$, is less for a higher-ability person than for a lower-ability one. The choice of an optimal nonlinear income tax structure is equivalent to the choice of consumption-income bundles for the various types of persons. The general problem of a planner whose objective function is welfaristic and satisfies the Pareto principle can be written:

$$\max \quad W\left(V^1(C_1, Y_1), V^2(C_2, Y_2), V^3(C_3, Y_3), \cdots V^n(C_n, Y_n)\right), \tag{25}$$

subject to

$$\sum_{i=1}^{n} N_i (Y_i - C_i) \geq R, \tag{B}$$

$$V^j(C_j, Y_j) \geq V^j(C_i, Y_i) \qquad \forall i, j, \tag{SS}$$

where N_i is the number of type i persons. The first constraint (B) is the government budget constraint, where R is some given revenue requirement. The second constraints (SS) are the self-selection constraints that must be satisfied among all pairs of households: each person must weakly prefer the bundle intended for them over any one else's bundle to preclude mimicking.

This problem can be used to trace out all Pareto-efficient combinations of household utilities by taking the objective function to be a weighted sum of utilities with weights being allowed to vary. But, for redistribution policy purposes, we may be interested in the set of Pareto-efficient allocations associated with an objective function that gives rise to some desire for redistribution from the better-off to the less well-off. For this purpose, the function $W(\cdot)$ can be taken to be quasi-concave in utilities.

Consider first the case in which there are two ability-types ($n = 2$). The single-crossing property implies that at most only one of the two self-selection constraints (SS) will be binding, and it is straightforward to show that with any quasi-concave social welfare function, the constraint applying to a type 2 person—$V^2(C_2, Y_2) \geq V^2(C_1, Y_1)$—will bind.[64] Moreover, $V^2(C_1, Y_1) > V^1(C_1, Y_1)$ since a given income corresponds to less labour supply for the higher wage household. Thus all allocations satisfying the self-selection constraint must satisfy $V^2(C_2, Y_2) > V^1(C_1, Y_1)$. Therefore, the second-best UPF, unlike the first-best one, will include only points such that type 2's are better off than type 1's.

Figure 5 illustrates some relevant features of the solution for the two ability-type case. For simplicity, we suppose there are identical numbers of the two types, and the government has no net revenue requirements ($R = 0$). Panel (a) depicts three allocations. The first one (L_1, L_2) is the laissez faire allocation where $C_i = Y_i$ for each household. Naturally, type 2's are better off than type 1's and (SS) is not binding in either direction. Imagine now the government implementing redistributive lump-sum (nondistorting) taxes contingent on incomes. This can occur until the allocation (S_1, S_2) is reached. At that allocation, the self-selection constraint on household 2 just becomes binding ($V^2(C_2, Y_2) = V^2(C_1, Y_1)$), and lump-sum redistributions can be carried no further. But further redistribution can be achieved beyond this point if distortionary taxes are allowed. The allocation (O_1, O_2) represents one such allocation, and one

---

[64] As we saw earlier, the first-best outcome under a quasi-concave social welfare function will leave the low-ability person no worse off than the high-ability person. Since in the laissez faire the low-ability person is worse off, redistribution must go from the high-ability to the low-ability person. The self-selection constraint will become binding before equal utilities are achieved.

which satisfies the above planning problem for a planner with a quasi-concave social welfare function. It can be implemented by an infinite number of tax schedules, or C, Y-schedules, a representative one of which is shown in panel (a). As can be seen, the marginal tax rate—one minus the slope of the C, Y-schedule—is discontinuous at the point O_1, and more generally in the multiple-type case at all allocations chosen by households other than the most able (except in the limit when the distribution of types in continuous). When we speak in what follows of the marginal tax rate, we simply mean the implicit marginal rate defined by the slope of the taxpayer's indifference curve at that point: more precisely, $T'(Y) = 1 + V_Y/V_C$.

Several features of this optimal income tax allocation are worth noting. The marginal tax rate applying to type 2's is *zero*, while that applying to type 1's is between zero and 100%.[65] Intuitively, the use of distortionary taxation allows the government to relax the self-selection constraint on type 2's in the following way. Begin at the lump-sum allocation (S_1, S_2) where the self-selection constraint just binds with lump-sum taxes. Since the opportunity cost of additional income is higher for type 1's than type 2's (reflecting the higher labour supply required to generate a given income), distorting income slightly downwards for type 1's by imposing a positive marginal tax, but reducing their after-tax income so their utility does not change makes the mimicking households worse off. Thus, the self-selection constraint is relaxed and redistribution can be pushed further. This is an important insight, for it shows that distortionary taxation need not be imposed as an exogenous constraint on the problem; it arises naturally as an optimal form of policy in a world of imperfect information. Moreover, as we shall see below, its role as a device for relaxing self-selection constraints induces us to look to other forms of distortionary policy which might serve the same purpose, an insight first noted by Nichols and Zeckhauser (1982).

In this pure-redistribution two-person case, the tax system is obviously progressive: high-ability types pay positive taxes, while low-ability types receive a subsidy. But, if the government has a revenue requirement sufficient to induce both persons to pay taxes,

---

[65] Formally, the Lagrangian for the government problem is

$$\mathcal{L} = W\left(V^1(C_1, Y_1), V^2(C_2, Y_2)\right) + \lambda[N_1(Y_1 - C_1) + N_2(Y_2 - C_2)] + \gamma[V^2(C_2, Y_2) - V^2(C_1, Y_1)],$$

The first-order conditions on C_2 and Y_2 yield $-V_Y^2/V_C^2 = 1$ (implying a zero marginal tax rate on type 2's). Those on C_1 and Y_1 yield

$$-\frac{V_Y^2}{V_C^1} = \frac{-\gamma \hat{V}_Y^2 + \lambda N_1}{\gamma \hat{V}_C^2 + \lambda N_1},$$

where a hat refers to a household of type 2 when mimicking a type 1. Since, by the property of diminishing marginal rate of substitution, $0 < -\hat{V}_Y^2/\hat{V}_C^1 < 1$, this entails that $0 < -V_Y^2/V_C^1 < 1$, implying a positive implicit marginal tax rate on type 1's.

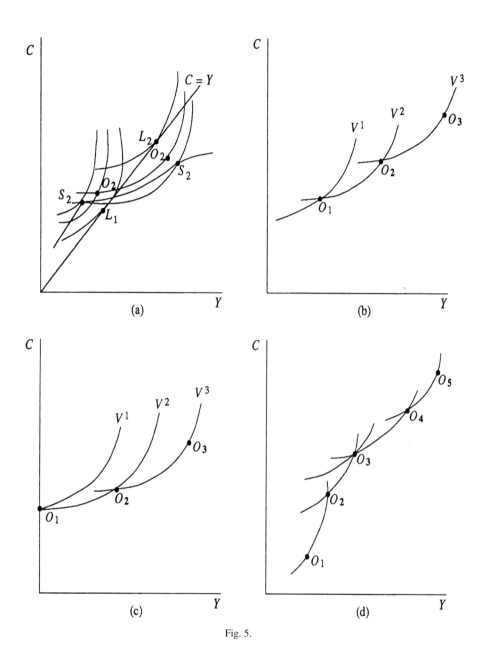

Fig. 5.

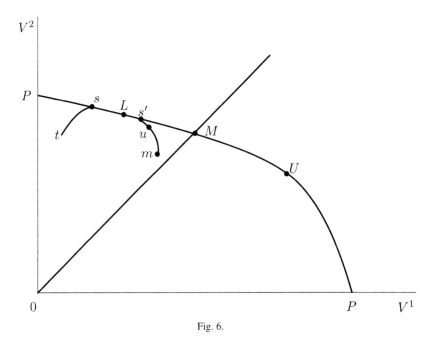

Fig. 6.

there is no guarantee that the tax schedule is a progressive one. As in the first-best case, average tax rates may rise or fall with incomes.

Optimal tax allocations like (O_1, O_2) are obviously Pareto-inferior to at least some allocations on the first-best UPF. The informationally constrained, or second-best, UPF labelled tm is compared with the first-best UPF labelled PP for the two ability-type case in Fig. 6. There is a range $s's$ around the laissez-faire allocation L which coincides with the first-best UPF. In this range, the self-selection constraints are not binding. In the range ts', redistribution goes from the low-ability types to the high-ability types, and the self selection constraint is binding on the low-ability types only. The point t is the "maximax" point, the allocation that maximizes the welfare of the high-ability types. More relevant for our purposes is the range sm along which the self-selection constraint is binding for the high-ability types. For it is along this range that the solution must lie if a quasi-concave objective function is used. Since the self-selection constraint precludes any allocation which makes the low-ability types as well off as the high-ability types, the second-best UPF lies everywhere above the equal-utility locus, so neither the first-best utilitarian outcome U nor the first-best maximin outcome M can be achieved. The points u and m are the informationally constrained utilitarian and maximin allocations, and the range enclosed by them are all those that would be obtained from a quasi-concave objective function.

The analysis extends in a straightforward way to the multiple-ability case. Panel (b) in Fig. 5 illustrates a typical case in which individuals are fully separated by ability-type. They line up by ability level, with self-selection constraints binding between each ability-type and the next lowest one (except for the lowest ability-type). Consumption, income and tax liabilities all rise with ability. A further complication arises in the multi-ability type and that is that partial pooling or bunching can occur whereby adjacent groups of ability-types choose the same C, Y–bundle (Guesnerie and Seade, 1982). In the bunching case, the self-selection constraints are also binding for adjacent ability-types, while consumption, income and tax liabilities are weakly increasing in abilities.[66]

It may be optimal for one or more ability-types at the bottom not to be working, in which case they are also bunched, receiving the same C with $Y = 0$, so tax payments are negative.[67] Panel (c) of Fig. 5 illustrates this case. It should be intuitively obvious that the lower the ability of the lowest income household, the more likely are there to be nonworking households at the bottom. In the extreme, if the lowest ability types are completely nonproductive ($w = 0$), as is often assumed (e.g., Mirrlees, 1971), there will necessarily be at least one ability-type not working at the bottom. And the lower the revenue requirements, the more likely is it that the nonnegative income constraint will bind: reductions in the revenue requirement would cause the entire pattern of consumption-income allocations to shift to the left.

These results for discrete distributions have been presented for the case of a government with nonnegative aversion to inequality, where redistribution goes from higher to lower ability persons. But, political economy considerations of the sort discussed in the previous section suggest that such schedules may not reflect those that would be chosen by decisive voters. As mentioned, Roell (1996) has supposed that voting might take place among the set of tax schedules most preferred by the self-interested members of the electorate, and one might expect higher income voters to prefer redistribution to go towards rather than away from themselves. A voter of ability type i will prefer the tax schedule that maximises $V^i(C_i, Y_i)$ subject to a revenue constraint and the relevant self-selection constraints; in other words, one which extracts as much revenue from the other voters as possible. Panel (d) in Fig. 5 depicts the most preferred tax schedule for

---

[66] The circumstances under which bunching occurs has been studied for the continuous distribution case by Ebert (1992). In this case, each household faces the same continuous C, Y budget constraint. Incentive compatibility requires that each household maximizes its utility by choosing the point on the constraint intended for their ability type. The incentive compatibility constraints imposed on the problem must include both the first-order necessary conditions for the household's choice of C, Y bundle and the second-order sufficiency conditions. The latter turn out to require that incomes be nondecreasing. (See Myles (1995) for a careful exposition of this.) Bunching occurs when the second-order conditions are violated. Apparently, it is prone to occur at the bottom when the wage rate of the least able person is very low (Mirrlees, 1971) or when the welfare weights are relatively high on the lowest ability persons (Lollivier and Rochet, 1983), or at any point in the distribution when the density function of abilities is sharply decreasing (Ebert, 1992). Weymark (1986) has extended the analysis of the determinants of bunching to the discrete case.

[67] Formally, a nonnegative income constraint must be imposed on all households. When it is binding on some households, these households will have zero incomes. Given that incomes are nondecreasing in abilities, these will be the lowest ability households.

a middle-ability person in a five-ability world. For all persons above person 3, self-selection constraints are binding downward as above: redistribution goes from higher to lower ability persons. The top person has a zero marginal tax rate, while the next one faces a positive marginal tax. But, for persons of types 1 and 2, the self-selection constraints bind in the opposite direction since the poor redistribute to the less poor. The poorest person faces a zero marginal tax rate, while the tax for the second poorest is negative. As Roell's analysis indicates, the class of such most-preferred tax schedules may or may not satisfy the Smart–Gans single-crossing property.

These results tend to go through in the case in which there is a continuum of abilities, the case taken by Mirrlees (1971) and Tuomala (1990). There is still a zero marginal tax rate at the top, reflecting the absence of a self-selection constraint applying for the most able person. Marginal tax rates in the interior are all positive and less that 100%. In the absence of bunching at the bottom, the marginal tax rate for the lowest ability person is zero (Seade, 1977). If, however, there is bunching at the bottom, the marginal tax rate facing the household at the end of the bunching interval is positive. Intuitively, since a positive marginal tax rate creates a deadweight loss the only purpose it can serve is to raise revenue from those higher up the distribution for redistribution to those below. But at the bottom of the distribution there is no-one further down to redistribute to, and so no equity gain to offset against the efficiency loss. If the poorest do not work, however, there is no such efficiency loss, leaving only the revenue-raising advantage of the positive marginal tax rate. As in the discrete case, utility is increasing with ability (reflecting the self-selection constraints), as are consumption, income and tax liabilities, except in the bunched intervals. But the analysis is very complicated and little in general can be said about the pattern of optimal tax rates, either marginal or average. That is because closed-form solutions for the optimal tax problem are generally not available except under special assumptions. For example, Diamond (1998) shows that if preferences are quasi-linear in consumption, an explicit expression for the marginal tax rate can be derived in terms of the elasticity of labour supply, the distribution of ability types, and the form of the social welfare function. For this case, he finds that above some critical skill level, the pattern of marginal tax rates is U-shaped if the density of skills is single-peaked, the elasticity of labour supply is constant and skills follow the Pareto distribution above the modal skill level, with the minimum marginal tax rate occurring at the mode. But even here, average tax rates not specified.

Given the paucity of analytical results, simulation analyses have played a central role in developing a firmer sense of the likely nature of optimal nonlinear tax schedules. Mirrlees (1971), in his classic study, calculated the optimal tax structure for the special case of a utilitarian social welfare function, Cobb–Douglas preferences in consumption and leisure, and a lognormal distribution of abilities. He found, famously, that the optimal schedule is then not very progressive: it approximates a linear tax with a relatively low marginal rate. Others have found that reasonable changes in specification can readily lead to greater progressivity. Stern (1976), simulating the optimal linear tax (characterised in Eq. (27) above) found the optimal marginal rate to be sensitive to the elasticity of substitution in consumption between consumption and leisure (which the Cobb–Douglas assumption restricts to unity): the easier the substitution—and hence the more elastic the labour supply—the lower the optimal marginal rate, which is as our earlier discussion would lead one to expect. Atkinson (1973) found that increasing the aversion to inequality of the social welfare function substantially changed Mirrlees' qualitative results (there being no aversion to inequality in utility in the utilitarian case considered by Mirrlees, of course): for example, with a maximin social welfare function the optimal tax is no longer roughly linear, and a much larger proportion of people at the bottom end of the ability distribution are optimally idle. This suggests that the progressivity of the optimal income tax depends critically on the inter-personal value judgements incorporated into the government's objective function.

Modifications of this classic Mirrlees–Stiglitz optimal income tax framework naturally modify the conclusions. One result which is of some importance for redistribution, and which is sensitive to the assumptions, is that the marginal tax rate for lower ability households should be positive. There are a number of model variations in which negative marginal tax rates, or wage subsidies, at the bottom are optimal, either to increase labour supply by low-skilled persons or to induce them into the labour force. These include: (i) if the government's objective is nonwelfaristic and relatively little weight is put on the leisure of the poor (e.g., if the aim is to reduce a poverty index involving consumption) (Oswald, 1983; Kanbur et al., 1994); (ii) if there are labour market distortions, such as efficiency wages or union power, which induce involuntary unemployment (Keen, 1997); (iii) if skilled and unskilled labour are complementary inputs in the production process (Allen, 1982); (iv) if there is a minimum amount of income that must be earned to enter the workforce (Boadway et al., 1999); (v) if there are differences in productivity among workers in the market and nonmarket sectors (Beaudry and Blackorby, 1997); or, (vi) simply if there are other tax-transfer programs which have an implicit positive tax rate on labour, such as a indirect tax on consumption.

4.3. Restricted instruments: linear taxes

To implement the optimal nonlinear income tax is a daunting task. Although the policymaker cannot identify households by ability-type, other informational requirements are highly demanding, including knowing household preferences and the distribution by types. Moreover, the setting is highly simplified relative to the real world: the economy is static, asset wealth is nonexistent, households are homogeneous except for ability, there is no uncertainly, and so on.Although progress has been made to incorporate various of these elements into the optimal income tax formulation on a piecemeal basis, the kinds of tax structures obtained from the theory are typically much more complex than those used in the real world. policymakers simply do not fine-tune the tax structure to elicit truthful revelation the way the theory suggests they should.

Rate structures are typically relatively crude: many countries have piecewise linear tax systems with relatively few tax brackets of successively increasing marginal tax rates. These may be supplemented with indirect commodity tax systems with some differentiation of rates among major commodity groups (food, alcohol, luxuries, etc.). Why tax structures should be linear, piecewise or not, is not well understood. Simplicity itself may be a virtue, especially when administrative and compliance costs are taken into consideration, a point stressed by Slemrod (1990). Whatever the reason, the seeming inability of the policymaker to use other than relatively simple linear tax structures itself restricts the redistribution that can be achieved. We can summarise briefly some of the features of linear tax structures as they affect the redistributive potential of the tax system.[68]

The most restrictive linear redistributive tax structure is one which relies entirely on differential commodity taxes. The early optimal tax literature characterised how the standard Ramsey tax rules would have to be revised to take account of distributive concerns (Diamond and Mirrlees, 1971; Feldstein, 1972). Indeed the conflict was stark: roughly speaking, efficiency considerations suggested taxing goods in relatively inelastic demand, which tended to include those whose income elasticities of demand were relatively low, while distributional concerns suggested the opposite (Atkinson and Stiglitz, 1972). The summary statement was by Diamond (1975), who formulated a "many-person Ramsey tax rule" which illustrated explicitly the equity-efficiency trade-off involved. In particular, per unit tax rates t_i on commodity X_i ($i = 1, \ldots, N$) should satisfy the following conditions:

$$\frac{\sum_i t_i \sum_h S_{ik}^h}{H \bar{X}_k} = \sum_h \frac{b^h}{H} \frac{X_k^h}{\bar{X}_k} \quad k = 1, \cdots, N,$$

where S_{ik}^h is the substitution effect between X_i^h and X_k^h for household h, H is the number of households, $\bar{X}_k$ is average household consumption of commodity k, and b^h is the net social marginal valuation of income going to household h, $b^h = W_h' \alpha^h / \lambda + \sum_i \partial X_i^h / \partial M^h$, where W_h' is the derivative of the social welfare function with respect to household h's utility, and λ is the Lagrange multiplier on the government revenue constraint. The left-hand side is analogous to Ramsey's proportional reduction (in compensated demands) rule, which in the single household case is the same for all commodities. Here, the proportionate reduction in compensated demands is smaller for commodities which tend to be more important for households with a high social valuation of income, reflecting the equity concern.

Apart from the part played by the many-person commodity tax rule in the development of the optimal tax literature, what possible interest might there be in it? Its main relevance would seem to be to the case of developing countries where, for administrative reasons, indirect taxes remain the mainstay of the revenue system. Although

---

[68] Of course, although the rate structures themselves are relatively simple, the definition of the base and the structure of credits and exemptions can be relatively complex. These can be a source of differentiation among taxpayers which can enhance the extent of redistribution even for very simple rate structures. There has been surprisingly little analysis of this in the literature.

the indirect tax systems of such countries undoubtedly stray widely from many-person Ramsey optimality, the latter may nonetheless serve as a useful benchmark. Indeed, Ahmad and Stern (1984, 1991) have used the framework as a basis for determining welfare-improving tax reforms in India and Pakistan, starting from a tax system which is demonstrably different from an optimal one. Perhaps more to the point for our purposes, Sah (1983) has demonstrated just how impotent a system of indirect taxes is likely to be as a redistributive device. He shows analytically that, under the optimal indirect tax system, the proportional gain in real income (as measured by the expenditure function at a representative set of prices) to the worst-off households is always less than the ratio of the maximum share of the budget among commodities for that household to the minimum average budget share among commodities across all households. That can be very small indeed: even for very large income differences among households, this ratio is of the order of 1.01–1.13 for the case of typical demand functions for the UK estimated using the Linear Expenditure System of demands.

The Sah analysis, like those of Diamond and Ahmad and Stern, is for a particularly restrictive form of linear taxation—indirect commodity taxes. Once households can be taxed directly, the redistributive potential of linear taxes can be enhanced. Consider the above many-person commodity tax setting. Suppose we expand the policymakers instruments to include a poll tax or transfer on each household. As Atkinson and Stiglitz (1980) show, the policymaker can now combine the optimal indirect tax with a poll subsidy and obtain a general linear progressive tax system: a system of taxes on commodities combined with a lump-sum payment to all taxpayers. In the simplest case of one good and leisure, this is equivalent to a linear progressive income tax.[69]

The trade-off between efficiency and equity comes out particularly clearly for this case. Choosing the parameters of a linear income tax (exactly as in Section 3.1.2) so as to maximize a social welfare function $W[V^1, \ldots, V^H]$, for indirect utilities $V^i \equiv [(1-t)w^i, \alpha]$, subject to a revenue constraint:

$$\int t Y_w(\alpha, t) \, dF(w) = \alpha, \tag{28}$$

one finds from the first-order conditions that:

$$\frac{t}{1-t} = \frac{-\text{cov}[b, Y]}{\int Y \varepsilon_{LL} \, dF(w)}, \tag{29}$$

where $b_w \equiv W' v_w / \lambda + tw \partial L / \partial \alpha$ is, as above, the net marginal social value of an additional unit of income and ε_{LL} is the compensated elasticity of supply of labour (Sheshinski, 1972; Atkinson and Stiglitz, 1980). The numerator involves equity considerations, it being larger the more concavity there is in the social welfare function.

---

[69] In a multi-commodity world, the optimal commodity tax structure will be uniform—so that only a linear income tax is needed—if leisure and all other goods are separable, with linear Engel curves from the former (Deaton and Stern, 1986).

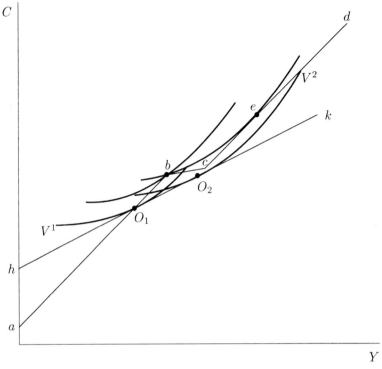

Fig. 7.

The denominator is the efficiency term; it tends to make the optimal tax rate lower the more elastic is the compensated labour elasticity. Simulation results on the optimal linear income tax are reported by Stern (1976).

The assumption that the government can deploy only a linear income tax substantially restricts the utility possibilities open to the government. Moreover, it does not allow the government to exploit its redistribution objectives to the fullest, given the information that is assumed to be available to it. To see this, consider Fig. 7, which depicts linear progressive income tax options for the two ability-type case. The common budget constraint is hk, where the two ability-types choose allocations O_1 and O_2. Changing the budget constraint to the piecewise linear one $abcd$, where the segments ab and cd are both $45°$, allows household 2 to choose the preferred point e and household 1 to choose the preferred point b, while raising the same amount of tax revenue and not violating the self-selection constraint. This is a strict Pareto improvement. The source of the inefficiency of linear taxation is that all self-selection constraints are bound to be slack, indicating that an opportunity to improve the efficiency-equity tradeoff is not being exploited.

Variants of the simple linear progressive income tax can improve the efficiency of redistribution by expanding the UPF. Thus, Fair (1971) allows the income tax to be of a polynomial form. More recently, Sheshinski (1989) and Slemrod et al. (1991) considered the extension to the two-bracket piecewise linear case. But, while these extensions relax the constraints on redistribution, the qualitative features of the linear case remain. In particular, the self-selection constraints remain slack, indicating a lost opportunity to exploit Pareto-improving tax structure changes.

We return then to the Mirrlees–Stiglitz optimal nonlinear income tax, that which is optimal given the information available to the planner. But, as we have seen, because of the demands of incentive-compatibility, redistribution options are severely restricted relative to those available in the full-information first-best allocations. Can we do better than that? It turns out that once we leave the soothing world of the first-best, where lump-sum redistribution is the norm, and enter the world of the second-best where the policymaker is encumbered by imperfect information, not only is distortionary nonlinear taxation "efficient", so too may be a myriad of other nonstandard policy instruments, and for somewhat similar reasons.

4.4. Self-selection and nonstandard instruments

We have emphasised that nothing precludes the policymaker from implementing nondistorting redistributive taxes in a world with a discrete number of ability-types. But, increasing the marginal tax rate above zero serves to relax the self-selection constraints and thereby expands the equity-efficiency trade-offs available to the policymaker. This insight turns out to have much broader potential implications. If distortionary income taxation can relax the self-selection constraints, perhaps other distortionary policy instruments can as well, policy instruments that would not be used in a first-best world. There have been several examples of this in the literature. Some of them are as follows.

4.4.1. Public goods
So far we have assumed that revenue requirements are fixed, possibly at zero. Suppose now that in addition to redistributing from the better-off to the less well-off, the government requires revenue to finance a Samuelsonian public good, say G, where household preferences may now be written $V^i(C_i, Y_i, G)$. In a first-best world, it is well-known that the amount of G chosen would be that which satisfies the Samuelson conditions, $\sum_i V_G^i / V_C^i = p$, where p is the producer price of G in terms of C, which for simplicity we take as given.[70] Suppose though that the policymaker is imperfectly informed and must raise revenues using an optimal nonlinear income tax. The problem for the

---

[70] We have chosen C to be the numeraire good here, but could have chosen leisure. In a first-best world that is of no consequence: a Samuelson rule will apply in either case. But, when distortions exist, the choice of numeraire affects the form of the optimality rule for public goods. For a discussion, see Boadway and Keen (1993).

redistribution-minded policymaker in the two ability-type case now becomes (Boadway and Keen, 1993):

$$\max_{C_i, Y_i, G} \quad W(V^1(C_1, Y_1, G), V^2(C_2, Y_2, G)),$$

subject to

$$N_1(Y_1 - C_1) + N_2(Y_2 - C_2) \geq pG,$$

$$V^2(C_2, Y_2, G) \geq V^2(C_1, Y_1, G)).$$

The necessary conditions for this problem yield the standard optimal nonlinear tax structure as discussed above, plus

$$N_1 \frac{V_G^1}{V_C^1} + N_2 \frac{V_G^2}{V_C^2} = p + \frac{\gamma \hat{v}_c^2}{\lambda} \left[\frac{\hat{V}_G^2}{\hat{V}_C^2} - \frac{V_G^1}{V_C^1} \right],$$

where, as before γ and λ are the Lagrange multipliers on the self-selection and revenue constraints, and "hat" indicates a type-2 person mimicking a type 1. This condition reduces to the Samuelson condition, $\sum_i MRS_{GC}^i = p$, iff the mimicker's marginal evaluation of the public good relative to consumption equals that for the type 1 person being mimicked, $\widehat{M}RS_{GC}^2 = MRS_{GC}^1$. This will be the case if G and C are separable from leisure in the utility function (since a mimicker obtains the same G and C as the person being mimicked, but has more leisure time). If G is complementary with leisure, in the sense that its marginal valuation rises with leisure, $\sum_i MRS_{GC}^i > p$, so there is a tendency to under-provide the public good; and vice versa for the substitute case.

The intuition for this result is apparent and instructive. Suppose we start at an optimal nonlinear tax allocation such that the Samuelson condition is satisfied, and assume that $\widehat{M}RS_{GC}^2 < MRS_{GC}^1$, so G and leisure are substitutes in the above sense. Increase G incrementally and adjust taxes so that $dT^1 = MRS_{GC}^1$ and $dT^2 = MRS_{GC}^2$. This leaves V^1 and V^2 both unchanged, and keeps the government budget balanced. But mimickers are now worse off since they value the increment in G at less than MRS_{GC}^1, the additional tax levied. Thus, increasing G beyond the Samuelsonian optimal point relaxes the self-selection constraint and enables the policymaker to engage in further redistribution.[71]

4.4.2. Indirect taxation

The mix of direct and indirect taxes has long been an important policy issue. The informational approach to optimal redistributional policy uncovers a role for differential

---

[71] This result can be further interpreted as implying that the marginal cost of public funds is less than unity. In contrast, under linear income taxes, the marginal cost of public funds will typically exceed unity when taxes are linear (Browning, 1976; Usher, 1986).

commodity taxes in relaxing the incentive constraints. Suppose that low-ability persons allocate their chosen income differently among goods than does a higher-ability mimicker. Then, using the same intuition as above, the self-selection constraint can be relaxed by imposing relatively high tax rates on goods that make up less of the low-ability household's consumption bundle, and relatively low ones (e.g., subsidies) on more preferred goods in such a way as to leave the household's welfare unchanged. This will make a high-ability mimicker worse off, relaxing the self-selection constraint and enabling more redistribution through the income tax to take place. Roughly speaking, as Edwards et al. (1994) and Nava et al. (1996) show, this requires imposing relatively high tax rates on goods that are more complementary with leisure, a result reminiscent of the famous Corlett and Hague (1953) Theorem. If goods are weakly separable from leisure in the utility function, differential commodity taxation will be of no avail since households and their mimickers will differ only in leisure taken: they will allocate their identical incomes the same way across commodities (Atkinson and Stiglitz, 1976).

4.4.3. Quantity controls

If introducing price distortions can be welfare-improving by relaxing self-selection constraints, perhaps quantity controls can as well. In a seminal contribution, Guesnerie and Roberts (1984) showed that in a second-best economy with linear price distortions, imposing incremental quantity controls, either rationing or forced consumption, would generally be welfare-improving. In particular, if the distortions were commodity taxes, welfare would be improved by forcing a consumer to increase consumption of a good, assumed to be nonretradeable, whose consumption the tax system had discouraged, or to force a consumer to consume less of a good which the tax system had encouraged.[72] They subsequently suggested that this result could be used to condone the use of minimum wages, which are a form of labour market rationing (Guesnerie and Roberts, 1987).

The Guesnerie–Roberts analysis applied for linear tax distortions. As we have pointed out, linear tax regimes are inefficient in the sense that they do not exploit all the information available. The issue then arises whether quantity controls can still be welfare-improving when optimal nonlinear taxes are in place. A series of papers have argued that they might be. It has been shown that in-kind transfers, such as education and health care, can enhance social welfare even when optimal nonlinear taxation is in place (Blackorby and Donaldson, 1988; Boadway and Marchand, 1995; Blomquist and Christiansen, 1995). The in-kind transfers can be made anonymously available to all with the possibility of private supplementation, or the use of publicly provided goods may be mutually exclusive with private provision so that users of the former have to

---

[72] More precisely, let $d_n^h = -\sum_\ell t_\ell S_{n\ell}^h$ be the so-called index of discouragement of commodity n for individual h, where $S_{n\ell}^h$ is the compensated elasticity of demand for commodity n with respect to the price of good ℓ. If $d_n^h > 0$, a quantity control which forces individual h to increase their consumption of commodity n above that voluntarily chosen would be welfare-improving, and vice versa for $d_n^h > 0$.

"opt in".[73] Another example concerns workfare, the requirement that transfer recipients perform some work. Given that the opportunity cost of working is less for low-ability persons than for potential mimickers, this might be expected to relax the self-selection constraint restricting redistribution to low-ability households. This turns out to be the case, at least as long as the productivity of workfare is not too low (Besley and Coate, 1992; Brett, 1998). Finally, it has been shown that minimum wages, supplemented by unemployment insurance, can be welfare-improving as well even when the optimal non-linear income tax is in place (Marceau and Boadway, 1994). This literature on the use of public expenditures and pricing controls for redistributive purposes is still in its infancy. But, it is also somewhat suggestive and potentially relevant given the widespread use by governments of these type of policy instruments as well as other related ones, such as mandated private sector purchases (Summers, 1989).

4.5. Altering the information assumptions

The Mirrlees–Stiglitz model illustrates the implications for redistributive policy of the government not knowing certain features of the economy and of its inhabitants. It presumes that the government is ill-informed in one key respect—it knows only the aggregate distribution of household characteristics—but well-informed in another—it knows household preferences and can accurately observe incomes. Other informational assumptions are possible. If the government does not know even the aggregate distribution (or household preferences), there is an element of aggregate uncertainty to be resolved on top of the standard redistributive problem. But the nature of the limit to redistribution itself does not change.

On the other hand, the government may know more than just the aggregate distribution of abilities. For example, it may have access to a signal or "tag" that is correlated imperfectly with underlying characteristics.[74] If so, the government can condition redistribution instruments according to the tag obtained by a person. Since tagging is imperfect, its use can involve both type I errors (failing to tag deserving persons) and type II errors (tagging undeserving persons). Segmenting the population into tagged and untagged groups allows the government to apply a separate redistributive tax-transfer system within each group, as well as redistribution from the untagged to the tagged group. The result is that more redistribution is made to the less well-off within the tagged group, but at the expense of less redistribution to the deserving who are mis-

---

[73] The conditions under which in-kind transfers are welfare-improving are similar to those under which preferential commodity taxation would be called for, leading to the question as to whether optimal commodity taxation alongside income taxation would eliminate the usefulness of in-kind transfers. But, Boadway et al. (1998) have shown that, even when optimal commodity taxation is allowed for, the use of in-kind transfers can still be welfare-improving.

[74] The idea of improving the ability of redistribution programs to target people by the use of a tag was proposed by Akerlof (1978) and applied to disability programs by Diamond and Sheshinski (1995) and Parsons (1996). For an extended discussion of it in the context of redistributive programs in developing countries, see van de Walle and Nead (1995).

takenly not tagged. If the tagging is costless, society is necessarily better off by its use since it expands the utility possibilities available. But if it is costly, the benefits of the additional information must be set against the costs. Moreover, as some observers have pointed out, the use of tagging may also raise questions of political feasibility (e.g., Sen, 1995). The more targeted are transfers towards the truly needy, the less support might be forthcoming from the excluded middle classes who constitute the bulk of voters. How telling this might be in the debate between those who would advocate targeting as a way of improving the efficiency of distribution and those who would opt for more universal schemes is surely a ripe item for future research.

The use of targeting also raises issues of the institutional delivery of redistributive programs. In principle, the tagging could be done through the tax system so that the program took the form of a (nonlinear) negative income tax system, albeit one where the amount of the transfer was determined not only by income but also by other observable characteristics. But, in practice, most redistributive transfers are not delivered through the tax system, but through welfare agencies. Presumably, the reason is that the relevant tags are not readily observable to the tax collecting agencies, and the system of self-reporting that tax systems rely on is not suitable. Instead, the tagging is done by social workers who, through their own effort and the use of administrative resources, determine the category of eligibility into which applicants fall. In such a system, not only is the accuracy of the tag endogenous and dependent upon resources devoted to it, it is also dependent upon the effort and preferences of social workers. There is thus a conventional agency problem involved in the tagging process, whose costs must be factored into determining not only whether tagging should be done, but also how many categories of targeting should be used (Boadway et al., 1999).

4.6. Cheats and liars

The standard optimal redistributive tax theory just discussed assumes that the otherwise ill-informed government can observe all taxpayers' incomes. But, income tax liabilities are typically based on self-assessment by taxpayers, so the accuracy of this procedure relies on the taxpayers truthfully reporting their incomes. The extent to which truthful reporting occurs depends not only on the standards of behaviour of the community,[75] but also on the monitoring and sanctioning activities of the tax authorities. In theory, one might suppose, following Becker (1968), that penalties for evading taxes could be set high enough to eliminate it at minimal cost to the administration. In practice, such maximal sanctions are rarely observed for tax evasion, let alone for other criminal acts. Various arguments have been put forward for the absence of maximal sanctions: there may be errors in conviction; sanctions may be costly to impose and the costs may increase with the level of sanction; criminals may be able to engage in costly avoidance activities which reduce the probability of being caught; there may be imperfect

---

[75] Gordon (1989) and Bordignon (1993) study how social norms affect taxpayer honesty in reporting their incomes.

information about the probability of apprehension or about whether acts are subject to sanctions; if law enforcement is general so that all crimes are deterred with the same probability, and if there is a limit to the maximal sanction so that the general probability of apprehension is not too small, it may be optimal to use less than maximal sanctions for lower gain crimes to prevent over-deterrence of these crimes; if criminals are risk averse, and if some crimes are "good" ones in the sense that the private gain to the criminal exceeds the social cost, it might not be optimal to impose a maximal sanction with a small probability of detection; and, there may be purely ethical arguments against the state imposing maximal sanctions. Whatever the reason, it is typically simply assumed in most of the tax evasion literature that there is some limit to the penalty for tax evasion, a limit that is below the maximal sanction.[76]

The presence of tax evasion that this implies is a further limit to redistribution. At the simplest level, for a given probability of detection and penalty, the incentive to evade increases with the marginal tax rate: the expected benefit from reporting one less pound of income is the tax revenue saved if not caught. This suggests that the revenue responsiveness of an increase in the tax rate will be reduced by the presence of evasion, so that the MCPF is increased (Usher, 1986). This would seem to increase the efficiency costs of redistribution, and thereby further worsen the efficiency-equity trade-off. More formal treatments of optimal redistributive policy in the presence of tax evasion exist in the literature. Marhuenda and Ortuño-Ortín (1997), building on the model of Chandar and Wilde (1998), investigate the form of tax and auditing functions which induce truthful self-reporting of incomes to the tax authorities when incomes are exogenous, penalty function satisfy certain social norms, and the government objective is to redistribute income. In particular, it is assumed that: (1) penalties cannot exceed agents' true incomes; (2) audited agents who are dishonest pay at least the same amount in taxes and penalties as honest agents of the same income level; and (3) the "punishment fits the crime" so the penalty function is continuous and related to the severity of the crime (rather than being a maximal sanction in the sense of Becker (1968)). They find, surprisingly, that even when incomes are fixed, average tax rates are decreasing with income, that is, the tax system is not progressive.[77]

---

[76] The issue is discussed in more detail in Cowell (1990). It is also possible that admitting some tax evasion may be useful for other reasons, as Stiglitz (1987) argues. For one thing, inducing some tax evasion by low-ability households could relax the self-selection constraint if it makes it more costly (in expected terms) for higher-ability ones to mimic them. But, this requires low-ability persons to be less risk-averse, which may not be plausible. Alternatively, allowing some tax evasion is analogous to imposing random taxation. This might be efficient if the government aggregate revenue function is not concave in the tax rate, something which is a distinct possibility in second-best problems.

[77] One problem with the analyses of both Marhuenda and Ortuño-Ortín and Chandar and Wilde is that they assume tax liabilities must be nonnegative. This would seem to rule out an equal lump-sum payment to all taxpayers, which could turn a tax system from regressive to progressive even if marginal tax rates were decreasing. Cremer et al. (1990) analysed the optimal linear income tax in a similar setting in which the penalty was fixed, but audit probabilities could vary with reported incomes. The optimal audit and linear tax system which induces truth-telling is one in which audit probabilities increase with reported incomes up to a cut-off level. Beyond that, there is no audit. The tax system has piecewise linear marginal tax rate: up to the

Cremer and Gahvari (1996) investigate the more general case of the optimal non-linear income tax along with penalty structures and audit strategy when incomes are endogenous. The penalty is constrained not to exceed a taxpayer's income. The government must induce the truthful reporting of income as well as satisfying the standard self-selection constraints. The form of the income tax structure for the two ability-type case they investigate is similar to the standard case where incomes can be observed: the marginal tax rate at the top is zero, while that for the low-ability types is zero as long as the self-selection constraint is binding. But, the self-selection constraint may not be binding: redistribution may be limited not by the fact that high-income persons can mimic the true income of the low-ability persons, but by the fact that high-wage persons must be precluded from reporting their incomes to be that of the low-ability persons even though they earn more. If so, the marginal tax rate is zero for both persons. In any case, there is no auditing at the top, since with a zero marginal tax rate there is no saving in tax payments from misreporting incomes. Only low-ability persons are audited. Moreover, honest reporting should be rewarded, so those audited and found to be honest should pay lower taxes than those not audited. Unfortunately, as in other optimal income tax problems, little can be said about the progressivity of the tax. But, given that the inability to observe true income further constrains government, presumably the progressivity of the tax is lower than in the standard optimal income tax case.

The under-reporting of income is not the only form of illegal behaviour associated with the tax system. In some settings, tax administrators themselves may engage in corrupt practices. Tax collectors may collude with taxpayers to under-report income, with the gain being shared by the two parties (Besley and McLaren, 1993; Flatters and MacLeod, 1995). Or, if their own income depends in part on the revenue they collect, tax collectors may credibly engage in extortion by demanding payments from taxpayers under threat of over-reporting their income. Hindriks et al. (1998) show that, for a quite realistic class of tax, penalty and incentive schedules, the distributional impact of such practices is clear-cut: the effective tax system—taking account not only of tax payments but also bribes and penalties—is unambiguously less progressive, in the sense of implying a less equal distribution of net income, than the statutory tax system. Moreover, since the potential gain from understating income by one pound increases with the level of income under a progressive tax system, in order to implement such a scheme honestly it may be necessary to offer inspectors an incentive payment that increases with the tax they collect, a cost of progressive taxation quite distinct from those usually emphasized.

4.7. Time consistency

Our discussion so far has concentrated mostly on various forms of imperfect information as the reasons why the economy's second-best UPF shrinks relative to the first-best one. But, once one takes the principal-agent view of government's relationship to its

audit cut-off, the marginal tax rate is positive, but beyond that it is zero. Thus, at least over the lower part of the income range, the tax will be progressive.

citizens seriously and allows for a sequencing of decisions, another important source of restriction on the UPF arises. In an intertemporal world, if the government is restricted to using distortionary tax instruments, second-best policies are time-inconsistent: even the second best UPF is not attainable.[78] The intuition for this is straightforward. Suppose households decide both how much wealth to accumulate at the beginning of a sequence of periods and how much labour to supply in each of the periods. The government might calculate its sequence of optimal tax rates on, say, labour and capital incomes at the beginning of the first period, taking account of the responsiveness of household savings and labour supply decisions. If the government announced these tax rates, households acted on them and the government stuck by its announcement, the second-best optimal tax allocation would result. But, once households have taken their savings decisions, if the government could re-optimize, it would recognize that wealth so accumulated was now fixed. It would prefer to renege on its announced second-best policies, increasing taxes on capital income and reducing taxes on labour income, which is still variable. The second-best policies would not be time-consistent (sub-game perfect). Notice that this is not a consequence of irrationality on the government's part: a fully rational government could not prevent itself from reneging on announced second-best optimal tax rates.

In contemplating equilibrium responses to the time-inconsistency of second-best policies, it is natural to focus on policies that are time-consistent: policies, that is, which the government will not find it ex post optimal to renege on. In a simple economy with homogeneous consumers, optimal time-consistent policy equilibria will be clearly welfare-inferior to second-best ones. They will involve relatively high rates of tax on capital income, rates that are rationally anticipated by households and lead to lower wealth accumulation than in the second-best optimum (Fischer, 1980). In an economy with heterogeneous agents in which the government has a redistributive motive, time-consistent tax policies are also likely to restrict the equity-efficiency trade-off significantly. Such tax policies will tax wealth owners "too much", and that is likely to lead to excessive redistribution given the government's goal: if past accumulated wealth is highly unequally distributed, an egalitarian government cannot prevent itself from imposing highly redistributive taxes on it. But, the end result of this may well be welfare-reducing because the redistributive tax policy, being anticipated by households, will induce a reduction in wealth accumulation. Boadway et al. (1996) construct a model in which wealth accumulation takes the form of human capital investment, with different individuals able to obtain differing returns from a given amount of such investment. Because the government cannot avoid taxing the returns to human capital investment in a highly redistributive way, the time-consistent outcome can actually be Pareto-inferior to the laissez faire allocation.

As in the case where the limits to redistribution result from binding self-selection constraints, the problem of time inconsistency may induce the government to search for

---

[78] This was demonstrated by Hillier and Malcomson (1984) and Calvo and Obstfeld (1988). An early application to tax policy was by Fischer (1980), followed by Rogers (1987).

otherwise unconventional policy instruments. We have seen (in Section 2.2.2) how, in the context of the samaritan's dilemma, it can rationalize mandatory insurance and pension schemes. Clearly too there are potential implications for taxes on saving and investment. Given that time inconsistency results in too little wealth accumulation, governments may resort to up-front incentives for saving or investment, or even quantity controls. Indeed, a cursory glance at real world policies reveals not only that capital tax rates are much higher than optimal tax reasoning might suggest, but also that they tend to be accompanied by policies that mitigate their effects, such as investment tax credits and subsidies, incentives for human capital investment and retirement savings (including mandating these types of wealth accumulation) (Kotlikoff, 1987), tax holidays (Vigneault, 1996; Wen, 1997), and lax enforcement of capital income tax evasion (Boadway and Keen, 1998; Renström, 1998).

4.8. Interjurisdictional mobility

Mobility of households across jurisdictional borders poses a constraint on redistribution in a decentralized federation or an economic union (a recent survey being provided by Cremer et al. (1996)). The basic argument was put by Boskin (1973) and Pauly (1973). Suppose there are several jurisdictions, say local governments, each populated by some "rich" and some "poor" persons. If the rich are altruistic towards the poor, they will agree collectively through their local government to make transfers to the local poor financed by taxes on themselves. If persons were not mobile across localities, the efficient amount of redistributive transfers would be made in each jurisdiction (and would differ according to local preferences). Now suppose the poor are mobile across jurisdictions: they will respond to different transfer levels offered by different local governments. If local jurisdictions take into account the effect of their transfer policies on the number of poor in their own jurisdiction, they will have an incentive to reduce the level of transfer payments to the poor. The movement of one poor person to another jurisdiction will result in a saving of the transfer that would be made to the poor person, but, since the poor person will obtain a transfer in the destination jurisdiction, there will be no corresponding reduction in altruistic benefit. Thus, there will be a tendency to free ride on neighbouring jurisdictions, and the Nash equilibrium will result in too low a level of transfers from an efficiency point of view. The lower the cost of moving, the more responsive will migrants be to transfer differences among jurisdictions, and the greater will be the severity of the free-riding problem. The argument applies whether or not altruism applies only to the poor located within one's jurisdiction. It also applies more generally for local government objective functions other than those based on altruism.

It may be, however, that while labour mobility may make redistribution harder it may also make it less necessary: it enables individuals to self-insure by moving elsewhere in the face of unanticipated shocks (Wildasin, 1998). Moreover there do exist models in which a reduction in the extent of redistribution brought about by labour mobility is actually socially desirable.[79] The general presumption, however, has been that free-riding is likely to lead to less redistribution than is desirable; and much attention then focussed on the question as to how to redress this bias.

The most obvious is to assign redistribution to some level of government that over-arches the range of mobile labour. This is a classic prescription for the allocation of tax powers in a federation (Musgrave, 1959; Oates, 1972).

An alternative approach builds on the observation that the tendency to compete away transfers to the poor is a form of inter-jurisdictional externality that can be corrected by a matching grant from higher to lower levels of government. Wildasin (1991) constructs a model of a central government and several lower-level jurisdictions, each of which are populated by some immobile taxpaying households and some mobile poor households. The poor supply a fixed amount of labour and obtain market income from the value of their marginal product. The taxpayers own fixed factors in their jurisdiction of residence and obtain market incomes equal to their rent, which in turn depends upon the number of poor workers. The taxpayers care about their own consumption and the per capita consumption of the poor in their jurisdiction. Each lower-level jurisdiction acts in the interests of the local taxpayers and makes transfers to the poor to satisfy their altruistic objectives. Since the poor are mobile, there will be an interjurisdictional externality associated with local redistribution: an increment in transfers by one jurisdiction will induce an inflow of poor from other jurisdictions, reducing the wage and consumption of the local poor and increasing them in other jurisdictions. In a Nash equilibrium, each jurisdiction will ignore the benefit its transfers yield for taxpayers in other jurisdictions, and so will under-redistribute. Wildasin shows that when the poor are perfectly mo-bile, optimal central government policy is to subsidize local jurisdictions' transfers by matching grants whose rates are such that in equilibrium *all* jurisdictions make the same transfers to each poor person (despite the fact that they may have different degrees of altruism). This requires higher subsidy rates for jurisdictions with lower transfers, and vice versa. In this way the redistribution function can be efficiently decentralized to the lower-level jurisdictions.

Boadway et al. (1998) obtain a related result in an explicitly federal context. Both both central and lower-level governments engage in redistributive activities, using a linear progressive tax on earned income. The two levels of government are assumed to share the same objective function. It emerges when there are two income-classes of persons, redistribution can be fully decentralized to the states provided the federal

---

[79] Janeba and Raff (1997) show that this can be the case, for example, in a voting model with more distinct jurisdictions than ability types. Each jurisdiction, suppose, can levy a linear income tax on its residents. Preferences are assumed to be such that—amongst the class of linear tax schedules—expected utility (behind the veil of ignorance) is maximized by zero taxation. Such an outcome is realised if labour can move, since in equilibrium there is only one ability type within each jurisdiction (and hence no redistribution). But if labour cannot move—and ability types are not fully sorted by region in the initial situation—then a standard median voter story means that some redistribution will occur.

government makes appropriately differential per capita lump-sum transfers to the two states.

These approaches to the problem all presume, however, some over-arching federal authority. Matters are evidently more difficult in circumstances such as that of the European Union, with no central authority mandated to act in such matters. One approach which has been suggested in such a context is that taxation (and entitlement to benefit) be determined not by residence but by nationality (Sinn, 1989). Only the US and the Philippines have sought to tax their citizens wherever in the world they happen to reside; doing so obviously raises considerable practical difficulties (the information-sharing requirements are likely to be formidable), and wider difficulties too concerning the right to renounce one's nationality (Pomp, 1989). Though not entirely far-fetched—arrangements are already in place to pay pensions to nationals who retire in other member states, for instance—this seems a distinct prospect.

It is not only the mobility of labour that jeopardizes redistribution. The more dramatic developments in recent years has been the increased mobility of capital: and with residence-based taxes proving increasingly hard to enforce (being weakened by evasion and avoidance which some jurisdictions find it in their interests to promote) and source-based taxes looking vulnerable to downward tax competition, the pressures towards lower taxation of capital is pronounced. The distributional implications of this are not entirely clear—recipients of capital income include pensioners with low lifetime incomes, for instance—but the effects may clearly be substantial.[80]

4.9. Altruism and intergenerational redistribution

As noted earlier, while altruism can provide some rationale for redistribution it also constrains the amount of redistribution that can be achieved: see Section 2.2.1.

5. Measuring redistribution

The previous two sections have emphasised some of the factors tending to compromise the extent to which the objectives of redistribution can be achieved in practice. Not only are there significant limits to the utility possibilities, or the possibilities for achieving other nonwelfaristic objectives, that can be achieved because of informational and other restrictions, but also the political process itself may conspire to confer high weight on the amount of redistribution preferred by selected groups in society. How these tensions resolve themselves is an empirical matter, and there is a disparate literature that attempts to measure the amount of redistribution that occurs in the real world. We cannot do full justice to that literature, given the many methodologies that can be used and the many

---

[80] There is a large literature (surveyed in Keen (1996)) on the implications of, and possible responses to, current pressures on capital income taxation. For a dissenting view on the likelihood of capital taxes vanishing, Mintz (1994).

countries and time periods to which the methodologies can apply. Our purpose is limited to outlining the main procedures that have been applied.[81]

5.1. Methodological issues in assessing redistribution

By its very nature, the measurement of the amount of redistribution implicit in existing or alternative fiscal policies is a counterfactual exercise. It involves measuring how a given set of policies affects different classes of households compared with those of some benchmark policy that is in some sense distributionally neutral. Quite what that might mean is far from obvious. One approach is to take as counterfactual a situation in which there is simply no government. There is an evident difficulty in applying this concept of *absolute incidence*. For the fiscal system includes not only the tax-transfer system, whose redistributive effect we take it one is most interested in measuring, but also public expenditure on goods and services. The latter will also affect real incomes to some degree, but since the goods are typically unpriced and have varying degrees of publicness associated with them, their redistributive effect is hard to measure. (Indeed if it were easy to measure the value consumers place on them, public provision would hardly be warranted).

An alternative approach—that of *differential incidence*—is to conceive of holding constant the observed levels of public expenditure but instead financing that provision in a distributionally neutral way. The difficulty of defining a distributionally neutral tax-transfer system replaces the difficulty of measuring the distributive effects of public expenditures on goods and services. Some apparently see appeal in taking the benchmark system to be an equal per capita tax—a poll tax—levied on all households; just as all typically pay the same price for each unit of a private good, so perhaps we should see it as natural that all pay the same price for public services. The failure of the poll tax in the UK, however, suggests that many see taxes of this kind as far from equitable. A much more common notion of distributional neutrality is that of a proportional tax system: one, that is, which takes the same share of income from all households. Such a system is the only one with the feature that the Lorenz curves of before-tax income, after-tax income and tax payments all coincide.

5.1.1. Progressivity comparisons

It is the notion of a proportional tax as being distributionally neutral, combined with the appeal of the Lorenz criterion, that underlies the standard definition of a progressive tax as one characterized by an average tax rate that everywhere increases with pre-tax income, since that ensures—as a corollary of a result expanded on below—that whatever the distribution of pre-tax income, post-tax income will be distributed more equally (in the Lorenz sense); and tax payments will be distributed less equally.

---

[81] Attention is confined too to the evaluation of redistribution by the public sector so that we do not consider, for example, the extent and effect of charitable gifts, bequests and the like. For a discussion of this aspect of redistribution, see Rose-Ackerman (1996).

One wants of course to go further than statements about the existence of redistribution or—the aspect we focus on here—of progressivity in the tax schedule.[82] One would like to make statements to the effect that redistribution is greater under one system than another, or that one tax is more progressive than another. The natural way to approach this is by looking for Lorenz dominance across the relevant distributions. Opinion differs, however, as to whether it is the distribution of tax payments or of after-tax incomes that should matter for progressivity comparisons. How progressive. for example, is capital gains tax? Payments are generally heavily concentrated amongst high income groups; but they are also sufficiently low that the tax has relatively little effect on the distribution of after-tax incomes. These two views of progressivity can give different answers: it may be, for example, that a reform generates a more equal distribution of net income but the Lorenz curves for net income cross. This though is a rather sterile dispute. The more fundamental questions are how to make comparisons when Lorenz curves cross and whether there are conditions under which one can be sure they will not. On the former, much attention has been given to the development of global measures of progressivity that will enable a complete ordering of schedules.

An answer to the latter question is provided in a result variously derived by Fellman (1976), Jakobsson (1976) and Kakwani (1977). This shows that, whatever the distribution of underlying income Y, the Lorenz curve of a schedule $a(Y)$ Lorenz dominates that of $b(Y)$—assuming both schedules to be everywhere strictly positive—if and only if the elasticity of a everywhere exceeds that of b. Thus one tax is more progressive than another in the sense of inducing a less equal distribution of tax payments iff it has a greater "liability elasticity" (elasticity, that is of tax payments with respect to pre-tax income) at all income levels. Similarly it is more progressive in the sense of generating a Lorenz-dominating distribution of net income iff it has a lower "residual income elasticity". Comparing the distribution of tax payments and net income under a schedule $T(Y)$ with that of a proportional tax $t \cdot Y$, for instance, one finds the former to be unambiguously more progressive if the marginal tax rate exceeds the average, so that the average rate is everywhere increasing: exactly the definition of progressive tax given earlier.

In many contexts of course these elasticity conditions will not hold; the distributional impact of taxation will then depend on the underlying pre-tax distribution. Moreover, the application to the distribution of tax payments requires an unappealing assumption that the tax payments are always strictly positive. This is clearly not the case; as a consequence, that result cannot be applied to such basic questions as whether an increase in tax allowances leads to an increase in progressivity: for a key aspect of such a reform is that it takes some people out of tax altogether (an apparently progressive move), whilst at the same time conveying an absolute benefit that is greatest to those facing the higher marginal tax rate (which is apparently regressive). Keen et al. (1998) extend the Feldman–Jakobsson–Kakwani result to deal with such situations. The effect

---

[82] An excellent account of the concept and measurement of progressivity is provided by Lambert (1993).

of increasing tax allowances is seen to depend on a condition not previously encountered in this area: for such an increase to increase progressivity (in terms of the distribution of tax payments), it is sufficient[83] that the log of the tax schedule is everywhere log concave: for then the proportionate reduction in tax liabilities implied by an increase in the allowance falls with the level of pre-tax income.

Unambiguous progressivity comparisons cannot be made if these conditions fail. There may nevertheless be instances in which distributional inferences can be made from the shapes of tax schedules conditional on the distribution of pre-tax income. Hemming and Keen (1983) show, for example, that if two schedules raise the same revenue and cross only once then the net income distributions they induce can be Lorenz-ranked. Extensions of this result to multiple crossings are discussed in Lambert (1993).

All this assumes, however, that there are no behavioural responses to taxation. If there are, then—as Allingham (1979) shows by example—one schedule may be more progressive than another in the Feldman–Jakobsson–Kakwani sense and yet lead to a less equal distribution of net income.

5.1.2. Incidence and deadweight loss

Behavioural responses also mean that the impact of taxation on a household's real income cannot be inferred from the amount of tax that it actually pays.[84] Consider for instance the evaluation of the differential incidence of a system composed entirely of indirect taxes. Actual tax paid in the observed economy is $(Q - P).'X(Q, U)$, where Q and P are the vectors of consumer and producer prices respectively (so that $T = Q - P$ is the vector of commodity taxes in specific form), and $X(Q, U)$ is the vector of Hicksian demand functions; U is the level of utility attained in the taxed equilibrium, so that, characterizing preferences by an expenditure function $E(Q, U)$ and indirect utility function $v(Q, Y)$, we have $U = v(Q, E(Q, U))$ Denote by T^* the taxes paid in the counterfactual situation in which the same revenue is raised as in the observed situation but by a proportional tax on income; and suppose too that this means a tax on endowment income, so that T^* is a lump sum tax. Assuming pre-tax endowment income to remain unchanged, so that $E[P, v(P, Y - T^*)] = Y - T^*$, it is readily seen that

$$E[P, v(P, Y - T^*)] - E[P, v(P)] = \{(Q - P)' \cdot X(Q, U) - T^*\} + L(Q, U), \quad (30)$$

where $L(Q, U) \equiv E(Q, U) - E(P, U) - (Q - P)' \cdot X(Q, U)$. The real income loss that an individual experiences from paying the observed indirect taxes rather than trading at current producer prices and instead paying the benchmark proportional tax is thus the sum of two effects. The first is simply the change in the amount of tax paid. The second, L, is a measure of the deadweight loss from the tax system:[85] it indicates the

---

[83] And necessary too if the result is to hold for all initial positions.

[84] By "pays" we refer not to legal liability—the question of formal incidence—but the amount by which the value of an individual's consumption bundle at consumer prices exceeds the value at producer prices.

[85] The desirable properties of this particular measure are shown by Kay (1980).

excess of the amount that the consumer would be willing to pay in order to trade at producer rather than consumer prices over the amount of tax they would thereby save. It is readily seen that $L \geq 0$, the equality holding only if there are no substitution effects in consumption. More generally, calculating comparative tax payments under actual and benchmark situation will understate the real income loss that an individual suffers from taxation. Some households, for example, who pay more tax under the proportional tax system may actually enjoy such a reduction in deadweight loss that they are actually better off than under the initial system. How this bias will affect of overall picture of the impact on the distribution of real income depends on how deadweight loss varies with the level of the endowment, about which there are few general results. It is clear, nevertheless, that focussing simply on tax payments may give a misleading impression.

But the pattern of tax payments—defined as above, rather literally, as the difference between the value of a household's observed net trades $\mathbf{X}(Q, U)$ at consumer and producer prices—may nevertheless be a matter of considerable interest in its own right. For in measuring the excess of the value of the resources they provide over the resource cost of servicing their demand, it indicates precisely an individual's net contribution to the economy. As argued by Hicks (1946) and pursued by Dilnot et al. (1990), this seems to be a quantity that people care about; the latter give the example of the lack of sympathy likely to be extended to a multi-millionaire who notes that although he paid no tax this year, it had been a considerable inconvenience to arrange his affairs so as to bring about this outcome. It is a quantity, moreover, whose calculation requires absolutely no assumption about the shifting issue to which we turn shortly: it depends only on prices and quantities in the initial situation, not those of any counterfactual equilibrium. Indeed we shall see that common incidence assumptions are tantamount to simply measuring tax payments thus defined; and in this sense a concern with the distribution of tax payments as such may provide a more coherent rationale for many incidence studies than does the concept of differential incidence itself.

A key assumption underlying Eq. (30)—though not of course the argument for an intrinsic interest in tax payments as such—is that producer prices are the same when the consumer trades at those prices as when he trades at consumer prices. Though perfectly coherent in itself, there is an evident problem in maintaining this assumption when assessing the redistributive impact over the entire set of consumers: if in practice distorting taxes were removed, producer prices would generally change from their level in the taxed equilibrium, to P^* say. Proceeding as before, and allowing too for the possibility that the value of the endowment may change (from Y to Y^*)—perhaps because the individual sells part of the endowment at producer process, perhaps through asset price effects—one now finds that the change in real income in moving to the counterfactual state is

$$E[P^*, v(P^*, Y^* - T^*)] = \{(Q - P)' \cdot \mathbf{X}(Q, U) - T^*\} + \{Y^* - Y\} + L(Q, U). \quad (31)$$

Detailed incidence studies of the kind discussed below often focus on the amount by which the cost of an individual's observed consumption attributable to facing the prices of the taxed state rather than counterfactual equilibrium exceeds the tax they would pay under the counterfactual system. This is precisely the amount $(Q - P)' \cdot X(Q, U) - T^*$ in Eq. (31): which is seen to understate the welfare loss suffered by the household by the amount of the deadweight loss plus the reduction in the value of the endowment induced by the tax system.

In practice, excess burdens are accounted for to varying degrees in incidence studies. Those which are based on fully specified general equilibrium models of the sort discussed below automatically take account of excess burdens in calculating real income effects. Of course, the magnitude of these excess burdens will be model-specific. Those which rely more on assigning tax and transfer burdens to income classes according to some assumed rules of shifting typically ignore excess burdens: they assign all taxes and transfers to income classes, no more.

In any event, implementation, whether with a view to a full welfare analyses or for calculation only of pseudo tax payments, requires estimation of the prices P^* and endowment incomes Y^* of the counterfactual equilibrium, which brings us into the area of incidence analysis. This is a vast topic, much of it excellently surveyed by Atkinson (1994), Atkinson and Stiglitz (1980), Kotlikoff and Summers (1987), and Jha (1998). Here we focus only on recent developments in the analysis of incidence under various forms of imperfection, which may prove to have significant implications for assessing the distributional impact of the tax-benefit system.

5.1.3. Imperfect markets, unemployment and tax incidence

Recent years have seen especially striking progress in two broad areas of incidence analysis. One is the analysis of intertemporal issues; we review work on this in Section 5.3. The other, on which we focus, is the analysis of shifting issues in imperfect markets.

Imperfect product markets. Commodity taxes can have surprising effects once one leaves a world or perfect competition: they may be "over-shifted", with consumer prices increasing by more than the amount of the tax; and they may even increase profits. The intuition behind these results—established by Seade (1985) and Stern (1987), but anticipated by Cournot (1838) and analysed by Musgrave (1959)—is straightforward. The possibility of over-shifting follows quickly from the the monopolist's first order condition: $(Q - T - MC)/Q = 1/\epsilon(Q)$, where $\epsilon(Q)$ is the elasticity of demand and $\epsilon < 1$ for a maximum. Assuming marginal cost MC to be constant, a tax increase dT is marked up by the factor $1 - (1/\epsilon)$ to produce an even greater increase in Q. The possibility that a tax increase may even lead to higher net profits arises from its effect in bringing about a coordinated contraction in the output of all firms, a contraction that their isolated self-interest fails to produce. That is, it enables firms to deal with the externality that each imposes on the other when it expands its output; profits increase if this gain through mitigation of external effects (which cannot arise in the monopoly case) dominates the direct effect of a higher tax rate.

Product quality also becomes an issue once the assumption of perfect competition is relaxed. Differential indirect tax structures may then have implications of product quality that in turn have distributional consequences. Predominantly ad valorem taxation, for example, is likely to lead to lower product quality than is predominantly specific: under specific taxation, the producer need only raise the consumer price by $1 to recoup the cost of a $1 quality improvement; under a 50% ad valorem tax, on the other hand, it must raise the consumer price by $2. Myles (1988) establishes, moreover, the surprising result that a utilitarian may wish to subsidise a high quality good consumed by the better off; the intuition being that since the rich choose to purchase the higher quality goods but the poor do not, there must be a point at which the marginal utility of income of the rich exceeds that of the poor.[86]

The empirical work to which these theoretical developments lead has not found strong evidence of over-shifting (Besley and Rosen, 1999; Baker and Brechling, 1992): instead it seems that taxes are shifted to the consumer by roughly 100%, so tending to confirm what has long been a standard assumption in incidence analyses. The tentative finding of Keen (1998) that specific and ad valorem taxes on cigarettes have significantly different effects suggests that, in that market at least, quality and imperfect competition are phenomena of real importance.

Unemployment. Tax incidence analyses in the spirit of Harberger (1964) assume market clearing, and so cannot address tax effects operating through the level of unemployment. This precluded, until quite recently, consideration of an obviously important channel for public policy to have distributional consequences. Not before time, the area is now one of considerable activity, and one in which considerable progress has been made (by, amongst others, Atkinson (1994), Lockwood and Manning (1993) and Sørensen (1998)). Two results give a flavour of the consequences of explicitly modeling unemployment for assessing the distributional effects of public policy:

- Nonstandard instruments—such as wage subsidies or a minimum wage— may become optimal (a point touched on in Section 4.4.3 above);
- Progressive taxation is good for employment. This result is robust against alternative specifications of the bargaining process (Koskela and Vilmunen, 1996) the underlying intuition being quite simple: greater progressivity makes increasing the post-tax wage more expensive in terms of the gross wage, tilting the balance in employee-firm negotiations towards higher employment rather than higher wages.

Incidence analysis in developing countries. The pervasiveness of distortions in some developing countries, although reduced by programs of structural adjustment, continue to raise particular issues for incidence analysis. For example, in the presence of quotas the incidence of a tariff may not be on consumers, even for a small country: instead the

---

[86] To see this, picture two curves showing utility as a function of income, one conditional on consuming the lower quality good the other conditional on consuming the higher. The point then follows from the observation that the latter cuts the former from below.

incidence may be on the holders of the quota rents. Thus a tariff even on a necessity could quite plausibly turn out to have a progressive effects, rather than a regressive one. Shah and Whalley (1991) provide many such examples arguing that presumptions on incidence conventional for developed countries may be quite inappropriate in the more distorted circumstances often found in developing ones.

5.1.4. The treatment of expenditure, and the contributory principle

The framework in Section 5.1.3 is deceptively simple. It is readily extended to nonlinear taxes by working in terms of virtual prices and defining lump sum income to include virtual income. It deals neatly with public goods: by holding their provision constant, it avoids the need to allocate the benefits across households. In practice, however, much public expenditure is not of that form, and the question of how it should be treated in incidence studies is problematic.

Transfers are naturally thought of as simply negative taxes. But this may be inappropriate if they are perceived simply as a return to individuals from their past contributions. By the same token, payroll and other taxes that are perceived as buying entitlement to future benefits—pensions, health care, education—are not taxes in the normal sense of being unrequited by the government. Payments into actuarially fair social insurance schemes might thus be excluded from the analysis of redistribution. Implementation faces two difficulties. First, assessing the fairness of such schemes is a difficult matter; this has been carefully addressed in the literature on intergenerational accounting addressed below. Second, it is unclear how to proceed if—as seems to be the case in the US, for example—contributors perceive the benefit entitlement purchased by their contributions to be bigger than it is. Practice differs in this area.

Tricky issues arise in connection with the provision by the government by goods that are largely private in nature, such as education, health care, some social services. These are generally either ignored, or their value imputed to recipients at cost: treated, that is, as a negative tax of that amount. In some cases, however, it may be hard to identify the true beneficiary of public provision. Take for example the case of education. To the extent that education increases future earnings ability, the beneficiary would appear to be the child, not the parent to whom, under standard procedures, the benefit would be allocated. In a Ricardian world, however, parents may be able to reap this gain for themselves by reducing their bequest to their children. This in turn may be easier for the rich, who plan to make bequests than for the poor who do not. Public provision may thus entitle the currently rich and the children of today's poor, a point that will not be picked up by the standard allocation procedure.

5.2. Fiscal incidence modelling strategies

There are two broad approaches to measuring the incidence of fiscal systems—data-based and model-based approaches. In the data-based approach, one uses disaggregated data on the sources and uses of income by income class of household, and attributes the net burden of the various tax and transfer components to income class using assumptions about burden shifting. Neither the behaviour of households and firms nor relative price changes are taken explicitly into account, except through the shifting assumptions. The model-based approach constructs a general equilibrium model of the economy and calibrates it to actual data. It then lets the workings of the model determine the incidence pattern of various fiscal measures. This approach usually adopts a differential incidence approach to avoid having to deal with the general equilibrium effects of public expenditures, while the data-based approach can measure either absolute or differential incidence. The following summarizes the variants of these approaches.

The tax-transfer system and the Lorenz curve. The statistical agencies of many countries routinely calculate tables of the size distribution of income. These show the proportion of the income earned by each of the five quintiles or ten deciles of the income distribution. For OECD countries, the pre-tax and transfer income distribution shows more than 40% of the income going to the top quintile, and less than 5% to the lowest quintile, a pattern which seems to be reasonably similar across countries and through time, although there is some evidence of income becoming less equally distributed in recent years.

These tables, whose data refer to points on the Lorenz curve, are then adjusted in two ways to account for redistributive effects of government policies. First, transfer payments to households are added to income, and second, direct taxes are taken out. These changes typically show that direct personal taxes and transfers serve to even out income distributions to differing degrees in different countries.

These studies, although relatively straightforward to calculate and easy to interpret, are somewhat limited descriptions of fiscal incidence. Only direct taxes and transfer applying to households are included. And, the shifting assumptions are relatively crude: all taxes and transfers are assumed to be borne by those who are pay or receive them. It is not surprising that they typically show that the tax-transfer system is relatively progressive.

Detailed data-based fiscal incidence studies. The shortcomings of the above approach are addressed in much more detailed fiscal incidence studies which include a much broader spectrum of taxes and transfers, and which use different incidence assumptions for the various tax sources. Standard studies using this approach include: Pechman and Okner (1974), Musgrave et al. (1974) and Browning and Johnson (1979) for the US; Nicholson and Britton (1976) and, annually, the Central Statistical Office for the UK; and Gillespie (1980) and Vermaeten et al. (1995) for Canada. These studies tend to focus mainly on tax incidence and include the five main tax sources—the personal income tax, the corporate income tax, sales and excise taxes, payroll taxes, and property taxes. For each tax, the burden is allocated across income classes according to shifting assumptions which draw on standard theoretical and empirical analyses. It is commonly assumed that personal income and payroll taxes are borne by the income earners, sales taxes are borne by consumers and allocated according to consumption patterns across income groups, and corporate and property taxes tend to be allocated to capital earners, partly those in taxed sectors and partly capital income earners more generally. Results based on these types of assumptions typically show that the pattern of tax incidence is roughly proportional to income, a finding that belies the progressive tax as an important instrument in government's redistribution arsenal.

The proportionality result is a consequence of the mix of taxes and of the presumed incidence applying to each tax type. There has been some controversy in the literature about the assumptions adopted and their consequences for incidence. Some of the more important sources of controversy are as follows.

Perhaps the factor that most accounts for the absence of progressivity in the tax system is the assumption that sales and excise taxes are borne in proportion to consumption patterns out of income. Because low-income persons consume a much higher proportion of their incomes than do high-income persons, especially for highly taxed goods, these taxes tend to be very regressive. Browning and Johnson (1979) have advocated that the incidence of sales and excise taxes ought to be based on factor incomes rather than consumption. They argue that because transfers to households are typically indexed for the price level, the effect of increases in the price level due to sales and excise taxes for low-income persons will be undone by compensating increases in transfers. When sales and excise taxes are allocated according to factor incomes, they turn out to be progressive rather than regressive.

Another reason why standard incidence assumptions might understate the true progressivity of the tax system is because of the way savings are treated. Sales and excise taxes are assumed to apply only to current consumption, and not to savings. Income taxes apply to savings to the extent that savings are done out of after-tax income. Once one views savings as future consumption, these incidence assumptions are more questionable. Sales and excise taxes do not apply to savings, but they do apply to the future consumption it yields. As well, savings generate capital income which itself will be subject to various taxes in the future. Taking all these into account will cause the tax system to appear more progressive than standard estimates would indicate.

The standard treatment of payroll taxes also contributes to the lack of measured progressivity. Not only do payroll tax rates apply just to earnings and not capital income, they also usually have an upper limit. But, it might be argued that payroll taxes should be omitted from incidence calculations because they are earmarked for particular social insurance programs that benefit contributors: any adverse effects on incidence should be offset by benefits received.

Whalley (1984), in a provocative piece, has shown that if incidence calculations are adjusted to take account of all the above arguments, the result will be a relatively progressive tax system rather than one which is merely proportional. By the same token, he has suggested a number of defensible adjustments that could be made in the opposite direction to make the tax system appear to be highly regressive. Most of these adjustments have to do with the interpretation of taxes on capital income. The standard analysis assumes that taxes on corporate income are borne by capital, either in the corporate sector or more generally. But, there are a number of reasons why this may not be appropriate. Corporations may be able to shift the burden of their taxes forward to consumers, or perhaps more likely backward to other factors, especially labour. This might be especially true in a small open economy. Taxes on personal capital income might also not be borne by asset owners, given the ease with which capital may be shifted abroad to avoid taxation, or shifted into untaxed assets (housing). It might even be argued that the part of labour income that is attributable to human capital accumulation will not be borne by the household, given that accumulating human capital is a substitute for accumulating assets with taxable capital income. Whalley shows that taking into account these considerations, the incidence of the tax system, in his case the Canadian one, can be made to appear very regressive. One is left with a very agnostic view of the true pattern of tax incidence. Almost as agnostic, indeed, as Edwin Cannan was when expressing his doubts about the possibility of evaluating tax burdens to a Select Committee of the House of Commons over seventy years ago:

I think that enquiry is a will-o'-the-wisp myself. I cannot help it if the House of Commons has asked you to do it.[87]

Whalley's results indicate just how sensitive fiscal incidence studies are to the shifting assumptions made. One could add other concerns to those expressed by Whalley. Incidence studies ignore the existence of unemployment and the policy responses to it, such as unemployment insurance. They also do not take account of the effects of nontax instruments such as minimum wage laws, quantity controls in sectors like agriculture, and industrial subsidies, all of which have distributive effects. Perhaps most important, most studies concentrate largely on the tax side. As we have discussed above, it is becoming widely recognized that public expenditures are to a large extent devices for redistribution. Expenditure programs in areas of health, education, welfare and social insurance are ultimately motivated by redistributive goals. The extent to which these program succeed in redistributing real income remains elusive.

Some studies have included expenditures in their estimates of fiscal incidence, notably Gillespie (1980) for Canada, Le Grand (1982) for the UK and, more recently, van de Walle and Nead (1995) for developing countries (where public services form the bulk of redistribution policies, given the absence of comprehensive progressive tax systems). The methodology is analogous to that used to measure (absolute) tax incidence. Some assumption must be made about the incidence of the benefits of individual spending programs. For example, in studies in van de Walle and Nead, the actual costs of public services are allocated to income classes according to estimates of service usage. Obviously, this is a rather crude procedure, identifying as it does benefits with costs and ignoring any surplus that might be obtained by households. Nonetheless, the results are at least suggestive and in accordance with what one might expect. These studies find that public spending is at least mildly progressive in the sense that it is yields higher benefits for the poor when measured as a percentage of individuals' initial incomes, although it is

---

[87] Quoted by Prest (1955).

regressive when it is measured in absolute value. But this broad overall incidence pattern masks important differences across public services. For example, public spending on primary and often secondary education is progressive, while it is regressive when spent on tertiary education. Likewise, primary health care centres are usually more pro-poor than hospital services, and in the former communist countries of Eastern Europe pension schemes are generally regressive while family allowances are progressive.

The expenditure side of the budget includes not only spending on goods and services but also transfers. Even though transfers are equivalent to negative taxes so might be treated analogously to taxes, including them in incidence calculations is the exception rather than the rule. This may be partly because they are typically delivered as separate programs rather than through the tax system. In many cases, they are at least partly taken account of in defining the income base to include transfers received. As Whalley (1984) has shown, the tax system is much more progressive when measured as a proportion of income including transfers than when transfers are excluded. Clearly, the neglect of the expenditure side of the budget in fiscal incidence studies is a major shortcoming, despite the fact that public spending is an important part of redistributive policy. Indeed, its neglect is even more striking in model-based incidence studies discussed below.

A striking feature of most incidence studies is the apparently limited amount of redistribution they achieve. This might reflect both the theoretical limits to redistribution (Section 4) and the constraints imposed by the political system (Section 3). Goodin and Le Grand (1987) argue more generally that the nonpoor inevitably benefit substantially from the welfare state. Using historical evidence from Australia, the UK and the US, they argue that middle class support is needed to introduce major welfare state expenditures; that such programs will either be universal in focus, such as social insurance programs intended to alleviate insecurity, or if meant for the poor, will be infiltrated by the nonpoor; and that, when under threat, welfare programs benefiting mainly the poor will be the most vulnerable. Indeed, for many social programs, the nonpoor may benefit more than the poor. The nonpoor are politically powerful so can manipulate the political agenda. They are better educated and able to exploit the administrative rules to their own ends. Their superior personal resources and flexible work schedules enable them to gain better access to public services. And, they are more able to make themselves appear to be poor so as to gain access to targeted programs. Goodin and Le Grand argue that inevitable middle class involvement in the welfare state is especially important in programs designed to achieve "secondary" income redistribution, that is, to change the "primary" income distribution obtained from participation in the market. They argue that a sensible strategy might instead be to focus redistribution policy on primary incomes by such instruments as employment policy, enhancing human capital investments, child care, the removal of barriers to employment by certain demographic groups, and even minimum wages. These forms of intervention might induce less involvement of the middle classes.

Microsimulations. The fabulously increased ease with which household-level micro-data can be manipulated has produced, from the 1980s, a different kind of micro-based study. This focusses not on the infrequent exercise of assessing the overall incidence of the tax system but on more routine evaluation of specific reforms: changes in the tax rate structure of income and payroll taxes for instance or in the tax treatment of the family. In this way it is possible to bring together detailed information on actual households of the kind to be affected by the reform—moving beyond the hypothetical stylized case—with detailed information on often enormously complex tax-benefit structures.

Most applications of such methods continue to assume away behavioural effects. This is clearly problematic, not least because the very purpose of the reform may be to induce particular kinds of labour supply or other effects. Over this same period, equally dramatic developments have been made in the development of microeconometric methods designed precisely to recognize behavioural effects and incorporate them into the welfare analysis. Packages have been constructed that bring together the flexibility of micro-simulation analyses, able to handle a wide range of potential reforms, and the ability to incorporate behavioural responses. No doubt these capabilities will develop still further in the coming years.

These exercises continue to rest, however, on the same crude incidence assumptions as the incidence analyses described above; they largely neglect, that is, the general equilibrium consequences of the reforms they address.

Computable general equilibrium incidence models. A major deficiency of the data-based fiscal incidence studies is their treatment of the interaction between the fiscal system and the market economy. By simply positing how various taxes are shifted, they do not explicitly take account of the complicated way in which relative prices and incomes might be influenced by distorting taxes. Computable general equilibrium models make the tax system a component of a fully-specified model of the market economy and allow incidence to be determined endogenously through the working of the economy. They thus avoid the need to assume rather arbitrary shifting assumptions.

Of course, this benefit is obtained at a cost. Computable, or applied, general equilibrium models may not be able to take advantage of the highly disaggregated data reflecting the complicated details of the fiscal system that are used in data-based incidence studies. Moreover, in place of the arbitrary shifting assumptions, one must select an almost equally arbitrary economic model along with parameters for technologies and tastes. One might argue that the choice of parameters can be made in a relatively informed way. Econometric estimates of elasticities of substitution in production and of systems of demand may be available. As well, the variables can be chosen so that the model can be calibrated to replicate the real world. And, sensitivity analysis can readily be carried out on the key variables in the model.[88]

---

[88] The use of computable general equilibrium models for policy analysis is outlined and defended in Shoven and Whalley (1984).

Nonetheless, it is now well-known that the results of computable general equilibrium models can be very model-specific. This is illustrated by the work of Cox and Harris (1985) in their study of the effects of free trade on the Canadian economy. Contrary to the standard computable general equilibrium model with perfectly competitive industries operating with constant returns to scale, they treated the manufacturing industries as being imperfectly competitive, with economies of scale arising from fixed costs. They estimate the annual welfare gains from multilateral trade liberalization to be in the range of 8 to 10% of GNP, an order of magnitude greater than estimates obtained from models with perfect competition (which were generally less than 1%). Much of the gain is attributed to intra-industry rationalization to take advantage of economies of scale.

There is also an issue of interpreting the results of computable general equilibrium simulations. Incidence studies involve comparing the allocation achieved under the existing fiscal system with that of a benchmark case. The computation assumes that the existing capital stock and labour supply can be reallocated costlessly among alternative uses. Presumably the calculation cannot be thought to show what would, in fact, happen if the fiscal system were changed from the existing one to the benchmark case: the adjustment to a new equilibrium would take time, during which capital and labour supplies would have changed. The comparison must be viewed as hypothetical, comparing the economy as it is with what it might have looked like had a different tax system been in place some time ago. The fact that calculating the effects of moving from an existing general equilibrium allocation to an alternative one cannot be interpreted as describing what would actually happen if the tax system were to change makes it difficult to draw policy implications from the exercise.

The use of general equilibrium analysis to study the incidence of taxes had its genesis in the seminal work on the corporate tax by Harberger (1962), later synthesised and extended to other taxes by Mieszkowski (1969).[89] The original interest was in the effect of taxes on the functional distribution of income, essentially its effect on capital versus labour income. Harberger had argued that although the corporate tax was essentially a tax on the corporate sector of the economy, its incidence in general equilibrium fell capital in general, given the parameter values he used.

The use of computable general equilibrium models to study the incidence of taxes by income class has been quite limited. Most analyses have had more limited objectives, such as studying the effects of individual taxes or of particular tax reforms.[90] That reflects the difficulties in modelling economies to include the vast array of taxes in existence. One notable exception is Piggott and Whalley (1985), who compared the general equilibrium allocation of the UK tax system in 1973 with a benchmark system raising the same revenues with a proportional sales tax on all goods and services. In addition

---

[89] This work studied the general equilibrium effects of differential changes in the tax system using comparative static analysis, and extrapolated it to discrete changes using linear approximations. Harberger's work was replicated by Shoven and Whalley (1972) using computable general equilibrium techniques and the results were found to be qualitatively virtually the same.

[90] A summary of several studies may be found in Shoven and Whalley (1984).

to finding relatively large excess burdens from the tax system (6–9% of GDP, or almost one-quarter of government revenues), they find that the tax system is quite progressive, much more so data-based methodologies have generally suggested. In particular, the benchmark tax system leaves the top decile of the income distribution 25% worse of than the existing system, and the bottom decile 20% better off.

5.3. Intertemporal issues

5.3.1. Lifetime perspectives on tax incidence
The data-based fiscal incidence studies discussed above rely on annual income for classifying households. But, it is well-known that annual income distributions are heavily influenced by persons in extreme income positions for short periods of time. For example, lower income groups contain persons temporarily out of work as well as retired persons whose incomes might be much lower than their consumption. Higher income groups contain persons at the peaks of their earnings periods. It has been estimated that up to one half of inequalities in annual earnings can be attributed to variations of income over the life cycle (Lillard, 1977; Blomqvist, 1981). That being the case, basing fiscal incidence on annual income statistics can be misleading. An alternative procedure is to calculate tax incidence on the basis of lifetime rather than annual incomes.

Different fiscal instruments will affect households differently in different periods of the life cycle. Sales and excise taxes are paid throughout the life cycle, while payroll taxes and property taxes are not. Income taxes also have an uneven lifetime profile, made more pronounced by their progressive nature. As well, transfers received tend to be concentrated in periods of low annual income. On a lifetime basis, they are likely to be much less progressive. The treatment of saving must also reassessed in a lifetime context. If households are life-cycle savers, sales and excise taxes are paid on both current consumption and savings and, as mentioned above, are likely to be less regressive on that account: Poterba (1989) finds, for example, that the distribution of excise payments in the US looks much less regressive when households are ordered by consumption than when they are ordered by income. But, if a high proportion of household savings is for bequests as some evidence suggests, sales and excise taxes might still be regressive on a lifetime basis. The overall impact of these life-cycle effects for fiscal incidence based on lifetime incomes are not obvious.

Measuring fiscal incidence on a lifetime basis is a very demanding task. Longitudinal lifetime income and tax profiles must be constructed on the basis of annual cross-sectional data, and that requires information on lifetime earnings, savings and inheritance and bequest patterns. An ambitious lifetime fiscal incidence study was undertaken by Davies et al. (1984) for the Canadian economy. Applying similar shifting assumptions to the five major tax types as above, they find that overall tax incidence is only mildly progressive, not unlike those found in annual studies. As well, the extent of progressivity varies relatively little as different shifting assumptions are adopted. These results reflect that fact that individual tax types which are progressive using annual data (e.g., income, corporate and property taxes) are less so using lifetime data, and the same for those which are regressive (sales and excise taxes and payroll taxes).

5.3.2. *Intergenerational redistribution*

Looking at fiscal incidence on a lifetime basis raises a further issue which has had considerable attention, and that is the effect that a fiscal program has on the lifetime real incomes of different age cohorts. As emphasised by Kotlikoff (1984), almost all fiscal measures have an intergenerational impact. The liabilities for income, consumption and payroll taxes differ systematically across the life cycle, so any change in the tax mix will induce intergenerational redistribution. For example, increasing sales taxes at the expense of payroll taxes will redistribute from older to younger cohorts. Transfers tend to occur especially in old age, implying that public pension schemes that are financed out of current taxes will tend to redistribute from younger to older cohorts. Expenditures on public goods and services also have obvious age-specific benefits. And, deficit financing by the government is equivalent to a transfer from the future to current taxpayers.

Merely identifying the generational impact of these various policy measures is not sufficient to indicate the extent of intergenerational redistribution that ultimately occurs. Two mitigating effects must be considered. First, intergenerational redistribution imposed by the government may be partially offset by changes in private intergenerational transfers (bequests). Though the theoretical basis for full Ricardian neutrality has been considerably undermined by the critique of Bernheim and Bagwell (1988) as discussed earlier, nonetheless saving for future generations may have some characteristics of the voluntary provision of a public good for which the Warr (1983) neutrality theorem applies. Moreover, to the extent that bequests are involuntary and related to the accumulation of wealth for precautionary purposes, some offsetting of public intergenerational transfers might occur. Second, net intergenerational redistribution is considerably dampened in the long run when each cohort is a recipient from previous generations as well as a transferer to following ones. In the steady state, the only net redistribution that occurs is that which is made possible by growth in per capita incomes. In other words, most of the intergenerational redistribution that occurs happens during the transition. The implications is that estimates of intergenerational incidence may need to be done over relatively long periods of time.

Two lines of research into the intergenerational impact of budgetary policies have been pursued, corresponding to the model-based and the data-based approaches to fiscal incidence described above. In each case, the focus has been mainly on identifying intergenerational redistributive effects rather than intragenerational ones.

In the first, dynamic overlapping-generations models are used to simulate the effect of fiscal policy changes that reallocate tax burdens across generations. In the seminal work, Summers (1981) constructed a simple single-sector neo-classical growth model with continuously overlapping generations of representative households. Households of different cohorts supplied identical quantities of labour over their fixed working lives and decided only how to reallocate it to a lifetime consumption profile using capital markets. Wage rates rose proportionately over time due to technical progress. In this setting, Summers simulated the steady state effects of replacing the existing system of taxes on wages and capital income in the US with a tax on wages alone, and with a tax on consumption alone, in both cases to finance a given stream of government expenditures. Removing the tax on capital income would eliminate the only distortion in the tax system, and presumably stimulate savings. The two tax substitutions would also affect savings by affecting a pure intergenerational transfer. Thus, since a wage tax imposes tax liabilities earlier in the life-cycle than a combined wage and capital income tax, substituting the former for the latter amounts to an ongoing intergenerational transfer from the young to the old, analogous to unfunded public pensions. This tends to reduce savings. On the other hand, substituting a consumption tax for an income tax will have the opposite effect of transferring from the old to the young, increasing savings. Summers obtained rather large effects from his simulations. In his base-case scenario, the wage tax substitution increased the capital-output ratio by 42%, per capita lifetime consumption by 13% and lifetime utility by 5% in the steady state. The consumption tax effects were even larger: the capital-output ratio rose by 54%, per capita lifetime consumption by 16%, and lifetime utility by 12%.

In retrospect, the source of these dramatic increases was apparent. In Summers' economy, the capital stock was well below its "Golden Rule" optimum. That is, the steady-state rate of interest was 10.5% compared with a rate of growth in income of 3.5%: the implicit return on an additional pound of investment was well in excess of the implicit rate of return on an additional pound of intergenerational transfer from the young to the old, so households would be made better off by reducing the latter and stimulating savings instead. And, since the amount of stimulation of savings was that much greater for the consumption tax than for the wage tax, the welfare effects were correspondingly larger.

Summers' work was influential both in academic work and policy discussion, for it suggested that a move away from capital income taxation would reap immeasurable benefits. But, the approach was not without problems. For one thing, some of the assumptions built into the model tended to bias the simulated effects on savings. These included the absence of a labour-leisure choice, which would make both a consumption and a wage tax distortionary; the assumption of no bequests, either intentional or unintentional; the assumption of perfect capital markets, especially the absence of liquidity constraints which would imply that increased wage taxes might reduce consumption rather than savings; the assumption of an exponentially increasing wage profile over the life cycle; the assumption that taxes were proportional rather than progressive; the assumption of an exogenous retirement date and length of life; and the assumption of perfect foresight among households.

Much of the subsequent literature addressed these issues,[91] but one further issue was of overriding importance—the restriction of simulated intergenerational redistributive

---

[91] See the summary in Boadway and Wildasin (1994).

effects to steady-state ones. Much of the welfare gain in the steady state can be attributed
to an increase in the capital stock. Since the adjustment to a higher capital stock entails
forgoing current consumption, those generations alive while the bulk of the adjustment
takes are liable to suffer losses. To the extent that is true, some of the long-run welfare
gains will be offset by short-term welfare losses. Indeed, if the increased savings is due
to an intergenerational transfer rather than an elimination of the distortion on capital
markets, the gain to generations in the long run is simply a redistribution from current
generations and cannot be viewed as an efficiency gain. Thus, simulating the temporal
time pattern of intergenerational redistributive effects would seem to be mandatory. This
is precisely what has been reported in Auerbach and Kotlikoff (1987).

Auerbach and Kotlikoff construct an dynamic overlapping-generations model in which
all agents have perfect foresight, and use it to simulate the effects of tax substitutions
on the time path of resource allocation beginning from an initial steady state, and on the
welfare of all cohorts along the path. Though similar in structure to Summers' model,
their model also addresses some of the shortcomings mentioned above: labour supply
and retirement ages are endogenous, the age-earnings profile is strictly concave, and
taxes are progressive.[92] As well, the policy simulations include not only tax substitutions analogous to those of Summers, but other fiscal policies with intergenerational
impacts, such as public pensions and deficit finance. Not surprisingly, in the case of the
tax reform simulations, tracing out both the short-run and long-run consequences of the
tax substitutions considerably tempers the impact of the Summers results. Switching
from an income tax to a wage tax still produces some increase in the capital stock in the
long run, and to a consumption tax a larger increase. But, the transitional analysis reveals
that not all age cohorts share in the benefits of this. In the case of the consumption tax,
cohorts who are young during the transition as well as all future cohorts obtain gains
in lifetime utility, but older cohorts are made worse off. When a wage tax is substituted
for an income tax, the effects are the opposite. Younger and future generations are made
worse off by the change, despite the fact that the capital stock has risen. (With variable
labour supply there is now a distortion introduced by wage taxation.) Older generations
are made better off.

The companion simulations that Auerbach and Kotlikoff conduct on changes in
public pensions and deficits show comparable effects. An increase in unfunded public
pensions entails an intergenerational transfer from the young to the old which is analogous to, say, a substitution of a wage tax for a consumption tax. And, both are analogous
to the substitution of deficit for tax financing of government expenditures. This leads
them to the view that the budget deficit as conventionally reported by governments is
a misleading indicator of the impact of the budget structure on the economy and on
the well-being of various generations. The implicit liability created by unfunded social
security or by tax reforms that change the timing of tax liabilities over the life cycle

---

[92] One shortcoming that Auerbach and Kotlikoff share with Summers is the neglect of intragenerational
effects. In both studies, all households of a given cohort are identical.

are indistinguishable in their economic effects from the budget deficit. This has led the authors to propose an alternative form of reporting, on which stresses the full impact of budgetary policies on different generations—*generational accounting*.[93]

Like the above simulation models, generational accounting focuses exclusively on the effect of fiscal policies on representative members of different generations. But, as with data-based incidence studies, it does so by assigning net benefits to various cohorts using some presumed notion of burden-bearing without taking account of behavioural or relative price changes. The methodology is straightforward, and is based upon the intertemporal budget constraint unavoidably faced by government:

$$\sum_{s=0}^{T} A_{t,t-s} + \sum_{s=1}^{\infty} A_{t,t+s} = \sum_{s=t}^{\infty} \frac{G_s}{(1+r)^{t-s}} - W_t,$$

where $A_{t,k}$ is the present value at time t of the remaining net tax payments of persons in cohort k (its "generational account"), G_s is government expenditures on goods and services in year s, W_t is the stock of government wealth in year t, and r is the discount rate, assumed to be constant. The first term on the lefthand side reflects the generational accounts of all cohorts currently living, while the second is for future generations. Implementing the notion of generational accounting involves calculating for some presumed future path of budgetary policies the values of $A_{t,k}$ and G_s that satisfy this budget constraint. Auerbach et al. (1991) propose calculating generational accounts for the case where current policies, both tax-transfer policies and expenditure policies, are kept intact into the future. Based on these policies, and using forecasts of population and average taxes and transfers for each cohort, generational accounts are calculate for all cohorts currently live. Next, values for the righthand side terms are calculated, again based on projections of current policies into the indefinite future. Then, the sum of generational accounts for future generations is obtained simply from the budget deficit. Finally, the average lifetime net tax burden to be faced by future generations is calculated, assuming that the net tax payment rises at the rate of productivity growth for the economy (which itself must be assumed). In effect, the net liabilities of the government as of today are amortized over all future generations: they all share in the paying debt.

Auerbach et al. (1994) report generational accounts as of 1991 for males and females separately. They find that, among the currently alive generations, older generations (those 60 and over) will have negative generational accounts: they will be net recipients of transfers. Younger generation will have positive accounts, with the peak being for those aged 30 for males and 25 for females. Males have systematically larger generational accounts than females of similar age. Significantly, representative members of future generations have much higher generational accounts than the youngest member of the current generation. In the case of both males and females, the generational accounts

---

[93] See Auerbach et al. (1991) for the initial contribution. Subsequent summaries may be found in Kotlikoff (1992) and Auerbach et al. (1994). See also the critical view of Haveman (1994).

of future cohorts are over twice as high as those of the current newborns, reflecting what they refer to as a current bias in government budgets.

Generational accounts are clearly in their infancy, and the magnitudes reported by Auerbach et al. are likely to be controversial. They are based on projections that assume that current policies are likely to remain in effect forever, but that the debt will be spread equally over all generations yet to be borne. Nonetheless, they do serve to complement existing budgets and incidence estimates by highlighting the intergenerational biases built into existing policies.

5.4. Explaining redistribution

There has been strikingly little empirical work seeking to explain observed patterns of redistribution. But the list is growing, and some instructive stylised facts beginning to emerge, albeit in some cases still tentatively. Here we simply indicate some of the issues and broad findings.

- Redistribution tends to be greater the wider the franchise: see, for instance, Metzler and Richard (1981) and Lindert (1994, 1996). This is doubtless as one would expect, though quite why the initial elite should decide to widen the electorate may not always be as obvious as it seems.[94]

- Demographics play a powerful role. Lindert (1994, 1996) shows how the development of pension schemes, for example, was related to greying of the population.

- Attention has recently been drawn to a strong positive correlation between openness and government size. Rodrik (1998) attributes this to the greater vulnerability of open economies to uninsured shocks, creating a greater social insurance role for government. Alesina and Wacziarg (1998) argue instead that the correlation reflects rather a positive correlation between openness and size, with scale economies causing the share of government to be lower in large economies. Or the correlation might reflect the administrative advantages that openness offers in levying taxes.[95]

- Attitudinal data suggests a considerable dose of self-interest in the support for redistribution. There is evidence, for example, that public health care is supported most strongly by those likely to become recipients, as for unemployment benefit too.

- Perhaps most intriguingly, there are recurring signs that redistribution tends to be greater the *less* underlying pre-tax inequality there is. First noted by Peltzman (1980), the effect is noted too by Bénabou (1997), Lecallion et al. (1984), Persson (1995) and emphasized in this volume by Lindert (2000), who dubs this the "Robin Hood paradox". At a more introspective level, the combination in both the US and UK of increased inequality and reduced political support for redistribution suggests the same pattern.

---

[94] There has been surprisingly little theoretical work on the role of the franchise and redistribution, and this has been reflected in omission of the topic from this survey. Such work is beginning to emerge however: see Acemoglu and Robinson (1997).

[95] While Rodrik addresses and rejects this, the administrative advantages will extend beyond the trade taxes that he focusses on (extending, not least, to VAT).

Causation is evidently a concern here. Greater redistribution leading to paradoxically more inequality could be explained in terms of risk-taking induced by social insurance, along the lines discussed in Section 2.2.2. As an empirical regularity, however, redistribution does appear to be negatively related to prior inequality. Such a link is not easily explained. It runs exactly counter to the implication of the standard models of linear taxation described above. An increase in inequality would be expected to reduce the median wage relative to the mean, so leading to more progressivity in the voting model of Section 3.1.2. In the optimal linear income tax model of Section 4.3, one would again expect an increase in pre-tax inequality to be associated with more redistribution, not less.

It is not entirely easy to see how the link might run the other way. Persson (1995) attempts an explanation in terms of interdependent preferences. Peltzman's explanation runs in terms of diminished commonality between middle and lower income groups as inequality increases. Perhaps the explanation—building on the importance of self-interest in motivating redistribution—is that it is not increased inequality at any moment which matters but rather the extent to which low spells of low income are concentrated amongst particular groups. The more concentrated such spells are, the less inclined those least subject to such spells will be to support schemes that would protect them if they did fall on hard times.

6. Conclusions

Such a long paper should not be burdened with a long conclusion. There are, however, a few themes that merit some emphasis and comment.

- The recent literature has shown that policy instruments widely criticized as being inefficient—such as in-kind welfare support, production subsidies, minimum wages—may have a proper place in the government's armory of redistributive tools. They may enable a weakening of the self-selection constraints that limit the amount of redistribution which can be achieved, and they may restrict the damage that ill-intentioned policymakers can do.

  These arguments, however, must be applied with care. Just as the results of the new trade literature, establishing potential benefits from trade restrictions, are recognized to hold the potential for abuse, so too may these justifications for nonstandard policy instruments. Some private interests are evidently served, for example, by arguments for public provision of private goods, or even for a minimum wage.

- The politics of redistribution are complex. Empirical work has given rise to Director's Law, that much redistribution is to the centre; and Disraelian conservatism in the UK has long built on the supposed natural conservatism of the working poor. Recent theoretical analyses have begun to explain why it might indeed be that high and low income groups find themselves allied against middle groups in the public provision of private good: the poor would rather do without, the rich would rather fend for themselves.

Understanding of these and related positive issues—such as the widespread perception that it is easier to sustain political support for universal rather than means-tested programs—is hampered by the lack of progress in understanding the technically challenging issue of voting over nonlinear tax schedules.

- It is still the case that very little is known about the effective incidence of some—perhaps most—key taxes. Understanding of the distributional impact of, for example, the corporate tax, dividend tax and capital gains tax has not progressed greatly (from a low base) over the last twenty years or so. Much policy advice continues to be based on naive incidence assumptions: that major welfare reforms will leave the level and distribution of pre-tax wages unchanged, for instance. Moreover, theoretical developments over this period have expanded the range of our ignorance by showing that the competitive analyses previously developed do not even bound the possible outcomes under when markets are imperfect. More positively, advances in the understanding of imperfect labour markets provide a real gain in the applicability of incidence analysis, and it may be that the empirical work that these theoretical advances have started to foster will generate real advances on the perennially troublesome issue of effective incidence.

- Much empirical work on redistribution over the last two decades or so has focused on microdata, exploiting the enormous technological advances over the period. Recent work from a more macroperspective, however, has raised a range of intriguing issues.

  One such is the question of how redistribution affects growth. Another is the apparent regularity that more equal societies apparently redistribute more (an observation that also seems consistent with the casual observation that increased inequality in the UK and US during the 1980s has been associated with a turn of political tide against redistributive programs). This runs exactly counter to the predictions of our standard models. Finding a coherent explanation—which may require exploiting microlevel data—may bring a deeper understanding of the underlying rationale for redistributive programs.

- The relationship between equity and efficiency considerations is much more complex than the traditional view of an unavoidable trade-off. Capital market and other imperfections provide quite coherent reasons to suppose that redistribution may in some circumstances increase growth: equity and efficiency may go together. Happy though such an outcome is, eyes should not be closed to the likelihood that, beyond some point, the two will indeed conflict. The range of conflict between equity an efficiency may be narrower than previously thought; but it has not gone away. And it is ironic that economists have produced reasons to suppose that redistribution may be good for growth at precisely the time that voters in so many countries have been persuaded of exactly the opposite.

References

Aaron, A.A. (1966), The social insurance paradox, Canadian Journal of Economics and Political Science 32: 371–376.

Abel, A., G. Mankiw, L. Summers and R. Zeckhauser, (1989), Assessing dynamic efficiency: Theory and evidence, Review of Economic Studies, 56: 1–20.

Acemoglu, D. and J. Robinson (1997), Why did the West extend the franchise?: Democracy, inequality and growth in historical perspective, MIT Working Paper No. 97-23.

Aghion, P. and P. Bolton (1997), A theory of trickle-down growth and development, Review of Economic Studies 64: 151–172.

Ahmad, E. and N. Stern (1984), The theory of tax reform and Indian indirect taxes, Journal of Public Economics 25: 259–298.

Ahmad, E. and N. Stern (1991), The Theory and Practice of Tax Reform in Developing Countries (Cambridge University Press, Cambridge, UK).

Akerlof, G.A. (1978), The economics of "tagging" as applied to the optimal income tax, welfare programs, and manpower training, American Economic Review 68: 8–19.

Alesina, A. (1988), Credibility and policy convergence in a two-party system with rational voters, American Economic Review 78: 796–805.

Alesina, A. and R. Wacziarg (1998), Openness, country size and government, Journal of Public Economics 69: 305–321.

Alesina, A. and D. Rodrik (1994), Distributive politics and economic growth, Quarterly Journal of Economics 109: 465–490.

Alesina, A. and H. Rosenthal (1995), Partisan Politics, Divided Government and the Economy (Cambridge University Press, Cambridge, UK).

Allen, F. (1982), Optimal linear income taxation with general equilibrium effects on wages, Journal of Public Economics 17: 135–143.

Allingham, M. (1979), Inequality and progressive taxation: An example, Journal of Public Economics 11: 273–274.

Andreoni, J. (1990), Impure altruism and donations to private goods; A theory of warm-glow giving, Economic Journal 100: 464–477.

Arrow, K.J. (1951), Social Choice and Individual Values (Yale University Press, New Haven, CT).

Arrow, K.J. (1951), An extension of the basic theorems of classical welfare economics, in Proceedings of the Second Berkeley Symposium (University of California Press, Berkeley), pp. 507–532.

Arrow, K.J. (1963), Uncertainty and the welfare economics of medical care, American Economic Review 53: 942–973.

Atkinson, A.B. (1973), How progressive should income tax be, in M. Parkin and A.R. Nobay, eds., Essays in Modern Economics (Longman, London).

Atkinson, A.B. (1991), Social insurance, Geneva Papers on Risk and Insurance 16: 113–131.

Atkinson, A.B. (1994), The distribution of the tax burden, in J.M. Quigley and E. Smolensky, eds., Modern Public Finance (Harvard University Press: Cambridge, MA), pp. 13–49.

Atkinson, A.B. and N. Stern (1974), Pigou, taxation and public goods, Review of Economic Studies 41: 119–128.

Atkinson, A.B. and J.E. Stiglitz (1972), The structure of indirect taxes and economic efficiency, Journal of Public Economics 1: 97–119.

Atkinson, A.B. and J.E. Stiglitz (1976), The design of tax structure: Direct versus indirect taxation, Journal of Public Economics 6: 55–75.

Atkinson, A.B. and J.E. Stiglitz (1980), Lectures in Public Economics (McGraw-Hill, Maidenhead, UK).

Auerbach, A.J. and L.J. Kotlikoff (1987), Dynamic Fiscal Policy (Cambridge University Press, Cambridge, UK).

Auerbach, A.J., J. Gokhale and L.J. Kotlikoff (1991), Generational accounting: A meaningful alternative to deficit accounting, in D. Bradford, ed., Tax Policy and the Economy, Vol. 5 (MIT Press, Cambridge, MA), pp. 55–110.

Auerbach, A.J., J. Gokhale and L.J. Kotlikoff (1994), Generational accounting: A meaningful way to evaluate fiscal policy, Journal of Economic Perspectives 8: 73–94.

Aumann, R.J. and M. Kurz (1977), Power and taxes, Econometrica 45: 1137–1161.

Baker, P. and V. Brechling (1992), The impact of excise duty changes on retail prices in the UK, Fiscal Studies 13: 48–65.

Balasko, Y. and K. Shell (1980), The overlapping generations model, I: The case of pure exchange without money, Journal of Economic Theory 23: 281–306.

Banerjee, A.V. and A.F. Newman (1993), Occupational choice and the process of development, Journal of Political Economy 101: 274–298.

Barr, N. (1993), The Economics of the Welfare State (Oxford University Press, Oxford).

Barro, R.J. (1974), Are government bonds net wealth? Journal of Political Economy 82: 1095–1117.

Beaudry, P. and C. Blackorby (1997), Taxes and employment subsidies in optimal redistribution programs, Discussion Paper No. 97-21, Department of Economics, University of British Columbia, Vancouver, Canada.

Becker, G.S. (1968), Crime and punishment: An economic approach, Journal of Political Economy 76: 169–217.

Becker, G.S. (1981), A Treatise on the Family (Harvard University Press, Cambridge, MA).

Becker, G.S. (1983), A theory of competition among pressure groups for political influence, Journal of Political Economy XCVIII: 371–400.

Bénabou, R. (1996), Inequality and growth, NBER Macroeconomics Annual (MIT Press, Cambridge, MA), pp. 11–74.

Bergstrom, T.C., L. Blume and H. Varian (1986), On the private provision of public goods, Journal of Public Economics 29: 25–49.

Bernheim, B.D. and K. Bagwell (1988), Is everything neutral? Journal of Political Economy 96: 308–338.

Bertola, G. (1993), Factor shares and savings in endogenous growth, American Economic Review 83: 1184–1198.

Bertola, G. (2000), Macroeconomics of Distribution and Growth, this volume, Chapter 9.

Besley, T. and A. Case (1995), Does electoral accountability affect economic policy choices? Evidence from gubernatorial term limits, Quarterly Journal of Economics 110: 769–796.

Besley, T. and S. Coate (1992), Workfare versus welfare: Incentive arguments for work requirements in poverty-alleviation programs, American Economic Review 82: 249–261.

Besley, T. and S. Coate (1997), An economic model of representative democracy, Quarterly Journal of Economics 112: 85–114.

Besley, T. and J. McLaren (1993), Taxes and bribery: The role of wage incentives, Economic Journal 103: 119–141.

Besley, T. and H. Rosen (1999), Sales taxes and prices: An empirical analysis, National Tax Journal LII: 157–178.

Bhagwati, J.N., R. Brecher and T. Hatta (1983), The generalized theory of transfers and welfare: Bilateral transfers in a multilateral world, American Economic Review 73: 606–618.

Black, D. (1948), On the rationale of group decision-making, Journal of Political Economy 56: 23–34.

Blake, R. (1966), Disraeli (Methuen, London).

Blackorby, C. and D. Donaldson (1988), Cash versus kind, self selection and efficient transfers, American Economic Review 78: 691–700.

Blomquist, S. and V. Christiansen (1995), Public provision of private goods as a redistributive device in an optimum income tax model, Scandinavian Journal of Economics 97: 547–567.

Blomqvist, N.S. (1981), A comparison of distributions of annual and lifetime income: Sweden around 1970, Review of Income and Wealth 27: 243–264.

Boadway, R. and N. Bruce (1984), Welfare Economics (Basil Blackwell, Oxford).

Boadway, R.W. and F.R. Flatters (1982), Efficiency and equalization payments in a federal system of government: A synthesis and extension of recent results, Canadian Journal of Economics 15: 613–633.

Boadway, R. and M. Keen (1993), Public goods, self-selection and optimal income taxation, International Economic Review 34: 463–478.

Boadway, R. and M. Keen (1998), Evasion and time consistency in the taxation of capital income, International Economic Review 39: 461–476.

Boadway, R. and N. Marceau (1994), Time consistency as a rationale for public unemployment insurance, International Tax and Public Finance 1: 107–126.

Boadway, R. and M. Marchand (1995), The use of public expenditures for redistributive purposes, Oxford Economic Papers 47: 45–59.

Boadway, R., N. Marceau and M. Marchand (1996), Investment in education and the time inconsistency of redistributive tax policy, Economica 63: 171–189.

Boadway, R., N. Marceau and M. Sato (1999), Agency and the design of welfare systems, Journal of Public Economics 73: 1–30.

Boadway, R., M. Marchand and M. Sato (1998), Subsidies versus public provision of private goods as instruments for redistribution, Scandinavian Journal of Economics 100: 545–564.

Boadway, R., M. Marchand and M. Vigneault (1998), The consequences of overlapping tax bases for redistribution and public spending in a federation, Journal of Public Economics 68: 453–478.

Boadway, R.W. and D.E. Wildasin (1989), A median voter model of social security, International Economic Review 30: 307–328.

Boadway, R. and D. Wildasin (1994), Taxation and savings: A survey, Fiscal Studies 15: 19–63.

Bordignon, M. (1993), A fairness approach to income tax evasion, Journal of Public Economics 52: 345–362.

Boskin, M.J. (1973), Local tax and product competition an the optimal provision of public goods, Journal of Political Economy 81: 203–210.

Bourguignon, F. and P.-A. Chiappori (1992). Collective models of household behaviour: An introduction, European Economic Review 36: 355–364.

Brennan, G. and J. Buchanan (1980), The Power to Tax: Analytical Foundations of a Fiscal Constitution (Cambridge University Press, Cambridge, UK).

Brennan, G. and J. Buchanan (1977), Towards a constitution for Leviathan, Journal of Public Economics 8: 255–273.

Breton, A. (1993), Toward a presumption of efficiency in politics, Public Choice 77: 53–65.

Brett, C. (1998), Who should be on workfare? the use of work requirements as part of an optimal tax mix, Oxford Economic Papers 50: 607–622.

Browning, E.K. (1975), Why the social insurance budget is too large in a democracy, Economic Inquiry 13: 373–388.

Browning, E. (1976), The marginal cost of public funds, Journal of Political Economy 84: 283–298.

Browning, E.K. and W.R. Johnson (1979), The Distribution of the Tax Burden (The American Enterprise Institute, Washington).

Bruce, N. and M. Waldman (1991), Transfers in kind: Why they can be efficient and nonpaternalistic, American Economic Review 81: 1345–1351.

Bruno, M., M. Ravallion and L. Squire (1998), Equity and growth in developing countries: Old and new perspectives on the policy issues, in V. Tanzi and K-Y. Chu, eds., Income Distribution and High Quality Growth (MIT Press, Cambridge, MA).

Buchanan, J.M. (1980), Rent seeking and profit seeking, in J.M. Buchanan, R.D. Tollison and G. Tullock, eds., Toward a Theory of the Rent-Seeking Society (Texas A&M Press, College Station, Texas), pp. 3–15.

Buchanan, J.M. and G. Tullock (1962), The Calculus of Consent (The University of Michigan Press, Ann Arbor, Michigan).

Bucovetsky, S. (1991), Choosing tax rates and public expenditure levels using majority rule, Journal of Public Economics 46: 113–131.

Calvo, G.A. and M. Obstfeld (1988), Optimal time-consistent fiscal policy with finite lifetimes, Econometrica 56: 411–432.

Chandar, P. and L.L. Wilde (1998), A general characterization of optimal income tax enforcement, Review of Economic Studies 65: 165–183.

Clark, D. and J. Thomas (1995), Probabilistic voting, campaign contributions, and efficiency, American Economic Review 85: 254–259.

Coate, S. (1995), Altruism, the samaritan's dilemma, and government transfer policy, American Economic Review 85: 46–57.

Coate, S. and S. Morris (1995), On the form of transfers to special interests, Journal of Political Economy 103: 1210–1235.

Corlett, W.J. and D.C. Hague (1953), Complementarity and the excess burden of taxation, Review of Economic Studies 21: 21–30.

Coughlin, P. (1984), Expectations about voter choices, Public Choice 44: 49–59.

Coughlin, P. (1986), Elections and income distribution, Public Choice 50: 27–91.

Cournot, A. (1960, originally published 1838), Researches into the Mathematical Principles of the Theory of Wealth (Frank Cass, London).

Cowell, F.A. (1990), Cheating the Government: The Economics of Evasion (MIT Press, Cambridge, MA).

Cox, D. and R. Harris (1985), Trade liberalization and industrial organization: Some estimates for Canada, Journal of Political Economy 93: 115–145.

Cremer, H., V. Fourgeaud, M. Leite-Monteiro, M. Marchand and P. Pestieau (1996), Mobility and redistribution: A survey, Public Finance 51: 325–352.

Cremer, H. and F. Gahvari (1996), Tax evasion and optimal general income tax, Journal of Public Economics 60: 235–249.

Cremer, H., M. Marchand and P. Pestieau (1990), Evasing, auditing and taxing: The equity-equity-compliance tradeoff, Journal of Public Economics 43: 67–92

Dahlby, B.G. (1981), Adverse selection and Pareto improvements through compulsory insurance, Public Choice 37: 547–558.

Dasgupta, P. and P. Hammond (1980), Fully progressive taxation, Journal of Public Economics 13: 141–154.

Dasgupta, P. and D. Ray (1986), Inequality as a determinant of malnutrition and unemployment: Theory, Economic Journal 96: 1011–1034.

Dasgupta, P. and D. Ray (1987), Inequality as a determinant of malnutrition and unemployment: Policy, Economic Journal 97: 177–188.

Dasgupta, P. A.K. Sen and D. Starrett (1973), Notes on the measurement of inequality, Journal of Economic Theory 6: 180–187.

Davies, J., F. St-Hilaire and J. Whalley (1984), Some calculations of lifetime incidence, American Economic Review 74: 633–649.

de Meza, D. and D.C. Webb (1987), Too much investment: A problem of asymmetric information, Quarterly Journal of Economics 102: 281–292.

Deaton, A. and N. Stern (1986), Optimally uniform commodity taxes, taste differences and lump-sum grants, Economics Letters 20: 263–266.

Dhami, S. (1997), Political economy of tax policy under asymmetric information, mimeo, University of Toronto.

Diamond, P.A. (1975), A many-person Ramsey tax rule, Journal of Public Economics 4: 335–342.

Diamond, P. (1998), Optimal income taxation: An example with a U-shaped pattern of optimal marginal tax rates, American Economic Review 88: 83–95.

Diamond, P.A. and J.A. Mirrlees (1971), Optimal taxation and public production, II: Tax rules, American Economic Review 61: 261–278.

Diamond, P. and E. Sheshinski (1995), Economic aspects of optimal disability benefits, Journal of Public Economics 57: 1–23.

Dilnot, A., J.A. Kay and M.J. Keen (1990), Allocating taxes to households: A methodology, Oxford Economic Papers 42: 210–230.

Dixit, A.K. (1996), The Making of Economic Policy (MIT Press, Cambridge, MA).

Dixit, A.K., G.M. Grossman and E. Helpman (1996), Common agency and coordination: General theory and application to government policy-making, Journal of Political Economy 105: 752–769.

Dixit, A.K. and J. Londregan (1995), Redistributive politics and economic efficiency, American Political Science Review 89: 856–866.

Dixit, A.K. and J. Londregan (1996), The determinants of success of special interests in redistributive politics, Journal of Politics 58: 1132–1155.

Dixit, A.K. and J. Londregan (1998), Ideology, tactics, and efficiency in redistributive politics, Quarterly Journal of Economics 124: 497–529.

Dixit, A.K. and V. Norman (1980), Theory of International trade (Cambridge University Press; Cambridge, MA).

Downs, A. (1957), An Economic Theory of Democracy (Harper and Row, New York).

Drèze, J. and N. Stern (1987), The theory of cost-benefit analysis, in A.J. Auerbach and M. Feldstein, eds., Handbook of Public Economics, Volume II (North Holland, Amsterdam), pp. 909–989.

Eaton, J. and H.S. Rosen (1980), Optimal redistributive taxation and uncertainty, Quarterly Journal of Economics 95: 357–364.

Ebert, U. (1992), A reexamination of the optimal nonlinear income tax, Journal of Public Economics 49: 47–73.

Edgeworth, F.Y. (1881), Mathematical Psychics (Routledge and Kegan Paul, London).

Edwards, J., M. Keen and M. Tuomala (1994), Income tax, commodity taxes and public good provision: A brief guide, Finanzarchiv 51: 472–497.

Epple, D. and R.E. Romano (1996a), Ends against the middle: Determining public service provision when there are private alternatives, Journal of Public Economics 62: 297–325.

Epple, D. and R.E. Romano (1996b), Public provision of private goods, Journal of Political Economy 104: 57–84.

Fair, R.C. (1971), The optimal distribution of income, Quarterly Journal of Economics 85: 551–579.

Feldstein, M.S. (1972), Distributional equity and the optimal structure of public prices, American Economic Review 62: 32–36.

Fellman, J. (1976), The effects of transformations on Lorenz curves, Econometrica 44: 869–881.

Fischer, S. (1980), Dynamic inconsistency, cooperation and the benevolent dissembling government, Journal of Economic Dynamics and Control 2: 93–107.

Flatters, F. and W.B. MacLeod, (1995), Administrative corruption and taxation, International Tax and Public Finance 2: 397–417.

Fleurbaey, M. and Maniquet, F. (1998), Optimal income taxation: An ordinal approach, CORE, Université Catholique de Louvain, mimeo.

Fogel, R.W. and S.L. Engerman (1971), Time on the Cross: The Economics of American Negro Slavery (Little, Brown, Boston).

Frank, R.H. (1987), If *homo economicus* could choose his own utility function, would he want one with a conscience? American Economic Review 77: 593–604.

Galor, O. and J. Zeira (1993), Income distribution and macroeconomics, Review of Economic Studies 60: 35–52.

Gans, J.S. and M. Smart (1996), Majority voting with single-crossing preferences, Journal of Public Economics 59: 219–237.

Gillespie, W.I. (1980), The Redistribution of Income in Canada (Gage Publishing, Ottawa).

Goodin, R.E. and J. Le Grand (1987), Not Only the Poor: The Middle Classes and the Welfare State (Allen and Unwin, London).

Gordon, J.P.F. (1989), Individual morality and reputation costs as deterrents to tax evasion, European Economic Review 33: 797–805.

Gordon, R.H. and H.R. Varian (1988), Intergenerational risk sharing, Journal of Public Economics 37: 185–202.

Grossman, G.M. and E. Helpman (1994), Protection for sale, American Economic Review 84: 833–850.

Grossman, G.M. and E. Helpman (1996), Electoral competition and special interest politics, Review of Economic Studies 63: 265–286.

Grossman, H.I. and S.J. Noh (1994), Proprietary public finance and economic welfare, Journal of Public Economics 53: 187–204.

Guesnerie, R. (1975), Pareto optimality in nonconvex economies, Econometrica 43: 1–29.

Guesnerie, R. and K. Roberts (1984), Effective policy tools and quantity controls, Econometrica 52: 59–86.

Guesnerie, R. and K. Roberts (1987), Minimum wage legislation as a second best policy, European Economic Review 31: 490–498.

Guesnerie, R. and J. Seade (1982), Nonlinear pricing in a finite economy, Journal of Public Economics 17: 157–180.

Harberger, A.C. (1962), The incidence of the corporation income tax, Journal of Political Economy 70: 215–240.

Harberger, A.C. (1964), Taxation, resource allocation, and welfare, in J. Due, ed., The Role of Direct and Indirect Taxes in the Federal Revenue System (Princeton University Press, Princeton), pp. 25–70.

Harsanyi, J.C. (1955), Cardinal welfare, individualistic ethics and interpersonal comparisons of utility, Journal of Political Economy 73: 309–321.

Haveman, R. (1994), Should generational accounts replace public budgets and deficits? Journal of Economic Perspectives 8: 95–111.

Hemming, R. and M.J. Keen (1983), Single-crossing conditions in comparisons of tax progressivity, Journal of Public Economics 20: 373–380.

Hettich, W. and S.L. Winer (1988), Economic and political foundations of tax structure, American Economic Review 78: 701–712.

Hicks, U. (1946), The terminology of tax analysis, Economic Journal 56: 38–50.

Hillier, B. and J.M. Malcomson (1984), Dynamic inconsistency, rational expectations, and optimal government policy, Econometrica 52: 1437–1452.

Hindriks, J., M. Keen and A. Muthoo (1998), Corruption, extortion and evasion, Journal of Public Economics, forthcoming.

Hirshleifer, J. and J.G. Riley (1992), The Analytics of Uncertainty and Information (Cambridge University Press, Cambridge, UK).

Hochman, H.M. and J.D. Rodgers (1969), Pareto optimal redistribution, American Economic Review 59: 542–557.

Hochman, H.M. and J.D. Rodgers (1973), Utility interdependence and income transfers through charity, in K.E. Boulding, ed., Transfers in an Urbanized Economy (Wadsworth, Belmont, CA).

Hoff, K. (1994), The second theorem of the second best, Journal of Public Economics 45: 223–242.

Hoff, K. and A.B. Lyon (1995), Nonleaky buckets: Optimal redistributive taxation and agency costs, Journal of Public Economics 58: 365–390.

Hu, S.C. (1982), Social security, majority voting equilibrium and dynamic efficiency, International Economic Review 23: 269–287.

Ihori, T. (1996), International public goods and contribution productivity differentials, Journal of Public Economics 61: 139–154.

Inman, R.P. (1985), Markets, government and the new political economy, in A. Auerbach and M.S. Feldstein, eds., Handbook of Public Economics, Vol. 2 (North-Holland, Amsterdam), pp. 647–777.

Itaya, J.D., de Meza and G.D. Myles (1997), In praise of inequality: Public good provision and income distribution, Economics Letters 57: 289–296.

Itsumi, Y. (1974), Distributional effects of linear income tax schedules, Review of Economic Studies 41: 371–382.

Jakobsson, U. (1976), On the measurement of the degree of progression, Journal of Public Economics 5: 161–168.

Janeba, E. and H. Raff (1997), Should the power to redistribute income be (de-)centralised? An example, International Tax and Public Finance 4: 453–461.

Jha, R. (1998), Modern Public Economics (Routledge, London).

Johnson, W.R. (1977), Choice of Compulsory Insurance Schemes under Adverse Selection, Public Choice 31: 23–35.

Kakwani, N. (1977), Application of Lorenz curves in economic analysis, Econometrica 45: 719–727.

Kanbur, R. (2000), Income Distribution and Development, this volume, Chapter 13.

Kanbur, R., M.J. Keen and M. Tuomala (1994), Optimal nonlinear income taxation for the alleviation of income poverty, European Economic Review 38: 1613–1632.

Kay, J.A. (1980), The deadweight loss from a tax system, Journal of Public Economics 13: 111–120.

Keen, M. J. (1996), The welfare economics of tax coordination in the European Community: A survey, in M. Devereux ed., The Economics of Tax Policy (Oxford University Press, Oxford), pp. 189–214.

Keen, M. (1997), Peculiar institutions: A British perspective on American tax policy, National Tax Journal 50: 779–802.

Keen, M.J. (1998), The balance between specific and ad valorem taxation, Fiscal Studies 19: 1–37.

Keen, M.J., H. Papapanagos and A.F. Shorrocks (1998), Tax reform and progressivity, Economic Journal, forthcoming.

Koskela, E. and J. Vilmunen (1996), Tax progression is good for employment in popular models of trade union behaviour, Labor Economics 3: 65–80.

Kotlikoff, L.J. (1984), Taxation and savings: A neoclassical perspective, Journal of Economic Literature 22: 1576–1629.

Kotlikoff, L.J. (1992), Generational Accounting (The Free Press, New York).

Kotlikoff, L.J. (1987), Justifying public provision of social security, Journal of Policy Analysis and Management 6: 674–689.

Kotlikoff, L.J. and L. Summers (1987), Tax incidence, in A.J. Auerbach and M.S. Feldstein, eds., Handbook of Public Economics, Vol. 2 (North-Holland, Amsterdam), pp. 1043–1092.

Kotlikoff, L.J., T. Persson and L.E.O. Svenson (1988), Social contracts as assets: A possible solution to the time consistency problem, American Economic Review 78: 662–677.

Lambert, P.J. (1993), The Distribution and Redistribution of Income: A Mathematical Analysis (Edward Elgar, Aldershot).

Le Grand, J. (1982), The Strategy of Equality (Allen and Unwin, London).

Lecaillon, J., F. Paukert, C. Morrison and D. Germedis (1984), Income Distribution and Economic Development (International Labor Organization, Geneva).

Lerner, A.P. (1944), The Economics of Control (Macmillan, New York).

Lillard, L.A. (1977), Inequality: Earnings vs. human wealth, American Economic Review 67: 42–53.

Lindbeck, A. and J.W. Weibull (1987), Balanced-budget redistribution as the outcome of political competition, Public Choice 52: 273–297.

Lindbeck, A. and J.W. Weibull (1993), A model of political equilibrium in a representative democracy, Journal of Public Economics 51: 195–209.

Lindert, P. (1994), The rise of social spending 1880-1930, Explorations in Economic History 31: 1–37.

Lindert, P. (1996), What limits social spending? Explorations in Economic History 33: 1–34.

Lindert, P. (2000), Three Centuries of Inequality in Britain and America, this volume.

Lockwood, B. and A. Manning (1993), Wage-setting and the tax system: Theory and evidence for the UK, Journal of Pubic Economics 52: 1–29.

Lollivier, S. and J.-C. Rochet (1983), Bunching and second-order conditions: A note on optimal tax theory, Journal of Economic Theory 31: 392–400.

Magee, S.P., W.A. Brock and L. Young (1989), Black Hole Tariffs and Endogenous Policy Theory (Cambridge University Press, Cambridge, UK).

Marceau, N. and R.W. Boadway (1994), Minimum wage legislation and unemployment insurance as instruments for redistribution, Scandinavian Journal of Economics 96: 67–81.

Marglin, S.A. (1963), The social rate of discount and the optimal rate of investment, Quarterly Journal of Economics 77: 95–112.

Marhuenda, F. and I. Ortuño-Ortín (1997), Tax enforcement problems, Scandinavian Journal of Economics 99: 61–72.

Mas-Colell, A., M.D. Whinston and J.R. Green (1995), Microeconomic Theory (Oxford University Press, Oxford).

May, K.O. (1952), A set of independent, necessary and sufficient conditions for simple majority decision, Econometrica 20: 680–684.

Mayshar, J. and S. Yitzhaki (1995), Dalton-improving indirect tax reform, American Economic Review 85: 793–807.

McGuire, M. and M. Olsen Jr. (1996), The economics of autocracy and majority rule: The invisible hand and the use of force, Journal of Economic Literature XXXIV: 72–96.

Meltzer, A.H. and S.F. Richard (1981), A rational theory of the size of government, Journal of Political Economy 89: 914–927.

Meltzer, A.H. and S.F. Richard (1983), Tests of a rational theory of the size of government, Public Choice 41: 403–418.

Mieszkowski, P.M. (1969), Tax incidence theory: the effects of taxes on the distribution of income, Journal of Economic Literature 7: 1103–1124.

Mintz, J.A. (1994), Is there a future for capital income taxation? Canadian Tax Journal 42: 1469–1503.

Mirrlees, J.A. (1971), An exploration in the theory of optimum income taxation, Review of Economic Studies 38: 175–208.

Mirrlees, J.A. (1974), Notes on welfare economics, information, and uncertainty, in M. Balch, D. McFadden and S. Wu, eds., Essays on Equilibrium Behavior under Uncertainty (North-Holland, Amsterdam), pp. 243–258.

Mirrlees, J.A. (1990), Taxing uncertain incomes, Oxford Economic Papers 42: 34–45.

Mookherjee, D. and I. Png (1989), Optimal auditing, insurance, and redistribution, Quarterly Journal of Economics 104: 399–415.

Mueller, D. (1989), Public Choice II (Cambridge University Press, Cambridge, UK).

Munro, A. (1992), Self-selection and optimal in-kind transfers, Economic Journal 102: 1184–1196.

Murphy, K.M., A. Schleifer and R.W. Vishny (1989), Income distribution, market size, and industrialization, Quarterly Journal of Economics 104: 537–564.

Musgrave, R.A. (1959), The Theory of Public Finance (McGraw-Hill, New York).

Musgrave, R.A., K.E. Case and H.B. Leonard (1974), The distribution of fiscal burdens and benefits, Public Finance Quarterly 2: 259–311.

Myles, G.D. (1988), Some implications of quality differentials for optimal taxation, Economic Journal 98: Conference Issue 148–160.

Myles, G. D. (1995), Public Economics (Cambridge University Press, Cambridge, UK).

Nava, M., F. Schroyen and M. Marchand (1996), Optimal fiscal and public expenditure policy in a two-class economy, Journal of Public Economics 61: 119–137.

Neal, D. and S. Rosen (2000), Theories of the Distribution of Earnings, this volume, Chapter 7.

Nichols, A.L. and Zeckhauser, R.J. (1982), Targeting transfers through restrictions on recipients, American Economic Review 72: 372–377.

Nicholson, J.L. and A.J.C. Britton (1976), The redistribution of income, in A.B.Atkinson, ed., The Personal Distribution of Income (Allen and Unwin, London), pp. 313–334.

Nozick, R. (1974), Anarchy, State and Utopia (Basic Books, New York).

Oates, W.E. (1972), Fiscal Federalism (Harcourt Brace Jovanovich, New York).

Okun, A.M. (1975), Equality and Efficiency (The Brookings Institution, Washington).

Olsen, M. Jr. (1965), The Logic of Collective Action (Harvard University Press, Cambridge, MA).

Olsen, M. Jr. (1982), The Rise and Decline of Nations: Economic Growth, Stagflation, and Social Rigidities (Yale University Press, New Haven, CT).

Osborne, M.J. and Slivinski, A. (1996), A model of political competition with citizen-candidates, Quarterly Journal of Economics 111: 65-96.

Oswald, A.J. (1983), Altruism, jealousy and the theory of optimal nonlinear taxation, Journal of Public Economics 20: 77–87.

Parsons, D.O. (1996), Imperfect "tagging" in social insurance programs, Journal of Public Economics 62: 183–207.

Pattanaik, P. and A.K. Sen (1969), Necessary and sufficient conditions for rational choice under majority decision, Journal of Economic Theory 1: 178–202.

Pauly, M.V. (1973), Income redistribution as a local public good, Journal of Public Economics 2: 35–58.

Pechman, J.A. and B.A. Okner (1974), Who Bears the Tax Burden? (The Brookings Institution, Washington).

Peltzman, S. (1980), The growth of government, Journal of Law and Economics 23: 209-287.

Persson, M. (1995), Why are taxes so high in egalitarian countries? Scandinavian Journal of Economics 97: 569–580.

Persson, T. and G. Tabellini (1994a), Is inequality harmful for growth? American Economic Review 84: 600–621.

Persson, T. and G. Tabellini (1994b), Representative democracy and capital taxation, Journal of Public Economics 55: 52–70.

Pestieau, P. (1998), The political economy of social security reform, mimeo, University of Liège.

Piggott, J.R. and J. Whalley (1985), U.K. Tax Policy and Applied General Equilibrium Analysis (Cambridge University Press, Cambridge, UK).

Pigou, A.C. (1947), A Study in Public Finance: 3rd edn (Macmillan, London).

Piketty, T. (1997), The dynamics of the wealth distribution and the interest rate with credit rationing, Review of Economic Studies 64: 173–189.

Piketty, T. (2000), Theories of Persistent Inequality and Intergenerational Mobility, this volume, Chapter 8.

Plott, C.R. (1967), A notion of equilibrium and its possibility under majority rule, American Economic Review 57: 787–806.

Pomp, R.D. (1989), The state, the individual and the taxation of economic migration, in J.N. Bhagwati and J.D. Wilson, eds., Income Taxation and International Mobility (MIT Press, Cambridge, MA).

Poterba, J.M. (1989), Lifetime incidence and the distributional burden of excise taxes, American Economic Review 79: 325–330.

Prest, A.R. (1955), The statistical calculation of tax burdens, Economica 22: 234–245.

Pyne, D. (1997), Microfoundations of influencing public opinion: Lobbying and voting for trade policies, mimeo, University of York.

Rae, D.W. (1969), Decision-rules and individual values in constitutional choice, American Political Science Review 63: 40–56.

Ravallion, M. (1984), How much is a transfer payment worth to a rural worker? Oxford Economic Papers 36: 478–489.

Ravallion, M. (1987), Towards a theory of famine relief policy, Journal of Public Economics 33: 21–39.

Rawls, J. (1971), A Theory of Justice (Harvard University Press, Cambridge, MA).

Reinganum, J.F. and L.L. Wilde (1985), Income tax compliance in a principal-agent framework, Journal of Public Economics 26: 1–18.

Renström, T.I. (1998), Tax evasion as a disciplinary mechanism for fiscal policy, in H. Shibata and H. Ihori, eds., The Welfare State, Public Investment and Growth (Springer, Tokyo), pp. 84–111.

Roberts, K.W.S. (1977), Voting over income tax schedules, Journal of Public Economics 8: 329–340.

Roberts, K.W.S. (1984), The theoretical limits to redistribution, Review of Economic Studies LI: 177–195.

Rodrik, D. (1986), Tariffs, subsidies, and welfare with endogenous policy, Journal of International Economics 21: 285–299.

Rodrik, D. (1995), Political economy of trade policy, in G. Grossman and K. Rogoff, eds., Handbook of International Economics (North-Holland: Amsterdam) pp. 1457–1494.

Rodrik, D. (1998), Why do more open economies have bigger governments? Journal of Political Economy 106: 997–1032.

Roell, A. (1996), Voting over nonlinear income tax schedules, mimeo, ECARE.

Roemer, J. (1996), Egalitarian Perspectives: Essays in Philosophical Economics (Cambridge University Press, Cambridge, UK).

Roemer, J.E. (1998), Why the poor do not expropriate the rich: An old argument in new garb, Journal of Public Economics 70: 399–424.

Roemer, J.E. (1999), The democratic political economy of progressive income taxation, Econometrica 67: 1–19.

Rogers, C.A. (1987), Expenditure taxes, income taxes and time-inconsistency, Journal of Public Economics 32: 215–230.

Romer, T. (1975), Individual welfare, majority voting and the properties of a linear income tax, Journal of Public Economics 4: 163–185.

Rose-Ackerman, S. (1996), Altruism, nonprofits, and economic theory, Journal of Economic Literature 34: 701–728.

Rothschild, M. and J.E Stiglitz (1976), Equilibrium in competitive insurance markets, Quarterly Journal of Economics 90: 629–650.

Sadka, E. (1976), On progressive income taxation, American Economic Review 66: 931–935.

Sah, R.K. (1983), How much redistribution is possible through commodity taxes? Journal of Public Economics 20: 89–101.

Sala-i-Martin, X. (1997), Transfers, social safety nets and economic growth, IMF Staff Papers 44: 81–102.

Seade, J.K. (1977), On the shape of optimal income tax schedules, Journal of Public Economics 7: 203–235.

Seade, J.K. (1985), Profitable cost increases and the shifting of taxation: Equilibrium responses of markets in oligopoly, University of Warwick Discussion Paper No. 260.

Scotchmer, S. and J. Slemrod (1989), Randomness in tax enforcement, Journal of Public Economics 38: 17–32.

Sen, A.K. (1966), A possibility theorem on majority decisions, Econometrica 34: 491–499.

Sen, A.K. (1967), Isolation, assurance and the social rate of discount, Quarterly Journal of Economics 81: 112–124.

Sen, A.K. (1970a), Collective Choice and Social Welfare (Oliver and Boyd, Edinburgh).

Sen, A.K. (1970b), The impossibility of a Paretian liberal, Journal of Political Economy 78: 152–157.

Sen, A.K. (1973), On Economic Inequality (Clarendon Press, Oxford).

Sen, A.K. (1977), Social choice theory: A re-examination, Econometrica 45: 53–89.

Sen, A.K. (1985), Commodities and Capabilities (North-Holland, Amsterdam).

Sen, A.K. (1992), Inequality Reexamined (Harvard University Press, Cambridge, MA).

Sen, A.K. (1995), The political economy of targeting, in D. van de Walle and K. Nead, eds., Public Spending and the Poor (Johns Hopkins University Press, Baltimore), pp. 11–24.

Shah, A. and J. Whalley (1991), The redistributive impact of taxation in developing countries, in J. Khalilzadeh and A. Shah, eds., Tax Policy in Developing Countries (World Bank, Washington DC), pp. 166–187.

Sheshinski, E. (1972), The optimal linear income tax, Review of Economic Studies 39: 297–302.

Sheshinski, E. (1989), Note on the shape of the optimum income tax schedule, Journal of Public Economics 40: 201–215.

Shoven, J.B. and J. Whalley (1972), A general equilibrium calculation of the effects of differential taxation of income from capital in the US, Journal of Public Economics 1: 281–321.

Shoven, J.B. and J. Whalley (1984), Applied general-equilibrium models of taxation and international trade, Journal of Economic Literature 22: 1007–1051.

Sinn, H-W. (1989), Tax harmonization and tax competition in Europe, European Economic Review 34: 489–504.

Sinn, H-W. (1995), A theory of the welfare state, Scandinavian Journal of Economics 97: 495–526.

Sinn, H-W. (1996), Social insurance, incentives and risk-taking, International Tax and Public Finance 3: 259–280.

Sjoblom, K. (1985), Voting for social security, Public Choice 45: 225–240.

Slemrod, J. (1990), Optimal taxation and optimal tax systems, Journal of Economic Perspectives 4: 157-178.

Slemrod, J., S. Yitzhaki, J. Mayshar and M. Lundholm (1996), The optimal two-bracket linear income tax, Journal of Public Economics 53: 269–290.

Sørensen, P.B. (1998), Public finance solutions to unemployment problems, paper presented at the 54th Congress of the International Institute of Public Finance, Cordoba, Argentina.

Starrett, D. (1972), On golden rules, the "biological rate of interest", and competitive efficiency, Journal of Political Economy 80: 276–291.

Stern, N. (1976), On the specification of models of optimum income taxation, Journal of Public Economics 6: 123–162.

Stern, N. (1982), Optimum taxation with errors in administration, Journal of Public Economics 17: 181–211.

Stern, N. (1987), The effects of taxation, price control and government contracts in oligopoly and monopolistic competition, Journal of Public Economics 32: 133–158.

Stigler, G.J. (1970), Director's law of public income redistribution, Journal of Law and Economics 13: 1–10.

Stigler, G. (1982), Economists and public policy, Regulation 6: 13–17.

Stiglitz, J.E. (1982), Self-selection and pareto efficient taxation, Journal of Public Economics 17: 213–240.

Stiglitz, J.E. (1987), Pareto efficient and optimal taxation and the new new welfare economics, in A.J. Auerbach and M. Feldstein, eds., Handbook of Public Economics, Vol. II (North-Holland, Amsterdam), pp. 991–1042.

Stiglitz, J.E. (1999), Taxation, public policy, and the dynamics of unemployment, International Tax and Public Finance 6: 239–262.

Summers, L.H. (1981), Capital taxation and accumulation in a life cycle growth model, American Economic Review 71: 533–544.

Summers, L.H. (1989), Some simple economics of mandated benefits, American Economic Review, Papers and Proceedings 79: 177–183.

Tabellini, G. (1991), The politics of intergenerational redistribution, Journal of Political Economy 99: 335–357.

Thurow, L.C. (1971), The income distribution as a pure public good, Quarterly Journal of Economics 85: 416–424.

Townley, P.G. (1981), Public choice and the social insurance paradox: A note, Canadian Journal of Economics 14: 712–717.

Tullock, G. (1967), The welfare costs of tariffs, monopolies and theft, Western Economic Journal 5: 224–232.

Tullock, G. (1983), Further tests of a rational theory of the size of government, Public Choice 41: 419–421.

Tullock, G. (1997), Economics of Income Redistribution (Kluwer Academic, Boston).

Usher, D. (1977), The welfare economics of the socialization of commodities, Journal of Public Economics 8: 151–168.

Usher, D. (1986), Tax evasion and the marginal cost of public funds, Economic Inquiry 24: 563–586.

Usher, D. and M. Engineer (1987), The distribution of income in a despotic society, Public Choice 54: 261–276.

van de Walle, D. and K. Nead (1995), Public Spending and the Poor: Theory and Evidence (Johns Hopkins University Press, Baltimore).

Van Graaff, J. de (1957), Theoretical Welfare Economics (Cambridge University Press, Cambridge, UK).

Varian, H.R. (1980), Redistributive taxation as social insurance, Journal of Public Economics 14: 49–68.

Verbon, H.A.A. (1987), The rise and evolution of public pension systems, Public Choice 52: 75–100.

Vermaeten, A., W.I. Gillespie and F. Vermaeten (1995), Who paid the taxes in Canada, 1951–1988? Canadian Public Policy 21: 317–343.

Vickrey, W. (1945), Measuring marginal utility by attitudes towards risk, Econometrica 13: 215–236.

Vigneault, M. (1996), Commitment and the time structure of foreign direct investment, International Tax and Public Finance 3: 479–494.

Warr, P.G. (1983), The private provision of a public good is independent of the distribution of income, Economics Letters 13: 207–211.

Weitzman, M. (1977), Is the price system or rationing more effective in getting a commodity to those who need it most? Bell Journal of Economics 8: 517–524.

Wen, J.-F. (1997), Tax holidays and the international capital market, International Tax and Public Finance 4: 129–148.

Weymark, J.A. (1986), Bunching properties of optimal nonlinear income taxes, Social Choice and Welfare 3: 213–232.

Whalley, J. (1984), Regression or progression: the taxing question of tax incidence? Canadian Journal of Economics 17: 654–682.

Wildasin, D.E. (1991), Income distribution in a common labor market, American Economic Review 81: 757–774.

Wildasin, D.E. (1998), Factor mobility and redistributive policy: Local and international perspectives, in P.B. Sorensen, ed., Public Finance in a Changing World (MacMillan Press, London), pp. 151–192.

Wilson, C. (1980), The nature of equilibrium in markets with adverse selection, Bell Journal of Economics 11: 108–130.

Wilson, J.D. (1990), Are efficiency improvements in government transfer policies self-defeating in political equilibrium? Economics and Politics 2: 241–258.

Wilson, L.S. and M.L. Katz (1983), The socialization of commodities, Journal of Public Economics 20: 347–356.

Wright, R. (1996), Taxes, redistribution, and growth, Journal of Public Economics 62: 327–338.

Chapter 13

INCOME DISTRIBUTION AND DEVELOPMENT

RAVI KANBUR*

Cornell University

Contents

* This paper was essentially completed in late 1996 and reflects the literature up to that time. I am grateful to Rajshri Jayaraman for research assistance in preparation of this paper.

Handbook of Income Distribution: Volume 1. Edited by A. B. Atkinson and F. Bourguignon

Abstract

This paper is a review of the post-war literature on income distribution and development. It argues that the literature has cycled from one consensus to another, responding to emerging policy issues and new analysis. On the basis of the review, the paper identifies five areas that will command the attention of analysts in the coming two decades: (i) country case studies rather than cross-country regression analysis; (ii) the phenomenon of increasing inequality; (iii) different levels of disaggregation, particularly distribution between broadly defined groups; (iv) intra-household allocation; and (v) alternative modes of redistribution in face of inequality increasing tendencies.

Key words: Inequality, poverty development, income distribution, growth and distribution, intra-household inequality

JEL codes: D30, D31, D63, O15, 049

1. Introduction and overview

The second half of the twentieth century has seen remarkably differentiated patterns of development in economies considered "poor" or "underdeveloped" in 1950. The focus of this paper is the interaction between these development processes and their accompanying distributional changes. The experience provides a rich set of variations with which to test different theories of development. It has also been used to draw policy inferences on the best way to influence or manage the process of development and distribution. The literature has cycled from one consensus to another—the latest being the position that it is possible to have both growth and equity. This paper will argue that such a consensus may be premature, that the trade off between growth and equity is ever present and needs to be negotiated by each society in the context of its own socio-political framework.

1.1. Some ground clearing

The topic of income distribution and development is vast, and there have been many surveys of it (e.g., Frank and Webb,1977; Lecaillon et al., 1984; Adelman and Robinson, 1988; and most recently, see the excellent and comprehensive review by Lipton and Ravallion, 1995). In order to keep this paper manageable, and to avoid undue repetition of what is already compiled in other surveys, it is necessary to limit and define the scope of this survey.

The relationship between the level and growth of per capita income (or consumption) and its distribution is the object of examination in this paper. We will, therefore, eschew broader notions of development, and broader notions of distribution. There has been much discussion of the limits to growth, and the impact of growth on cultural values and society, the implication being that increases in per capita national income do not necessarily capture all dimensions of national well-being. While accepting this in principle, we will retain our focus on income, noting only that whenever people vote with their feet, it seems always to be in the direction of economies with higher per capita income! By distribution we will mean the distribution of command over commodities, as conventionally measured by income or consumption. Thus, we will not venture into broader conceptions of the standard of living, which incorporate such notions as "capabilities". These issues are treated elsewhere in this volume, and do not necessarily illuminate the line of argument we wish to pursue.

However, when we look at the evolution of the distribution of income or consumption we will consider the *whole* distribution. In other words, we will be interested in inequality, which measures dispersion across the whole distribution, as well as poverty, which focuses on the lower end of the distribution. Again, we will not go into the technicalities of measuring inequality or poverty—these are covered elsewhere in this volume. Nor will we discuss the data problems in developing countries, which are discussed, for example, in Lipton and Ravallion (1995).

Since we will be discussing the evolution of inequality, poverty and growth together, it is as well at this stage to consider the relationship between them. It is purely a matter of accounting, that any pattern of change in individual incomes will have associated with it a change in the mean of distribution, a change in measures of inequality, and a change in measures of poverty. In general, these changes need bear no relation one to the other. A restriction in the pattern of individual income changes can put more structure on the relationship between mean, inequality and poverty—again, in an accounting sense. Thus, if all incomes change proportionately, mean independent measures of inequality such as the Gini coefficient will remain unchanged, and all standard measures of poverty will fall. On the other hand, if incomes change so as to leave the mean unchanged but move the Lorenz curve out uniformly, then most reasonable inequality measures will increase, as will a wide class of poverty measures which are sensitive to distribution among the poor (the behavior of the proportion of population below the poverty line, the head count index, is ambiguous).

Using these accounting properties, a number of authors (e.g., Kakwani, 1994) have offered methods for decomposing distributional change into a growth component and an inequality component, and poverty change into growth and inequality components. These decompositions are useful as far as they go, but they carry the danger of mechanistic extension. Thus, for example, from calculations which show by how much poverty will fall if incomes increase proportionately, this being christened the "growth effect", it is easy to slip into using distributional neutral growth as the norm—or, rather to assume that distributionally neutral growth is policy neutral also. In fact, even to achieve distributional neutrality may require considerable policy intervention. More to the point, such macrolevel reduced form relationships between growth, inequality and poverty, miss policy and country specificities which we will emphasize in this paper.

In certain circles, it is common to view poverty as the overriding policy concern, and to treat inequality as being relevant only in so far as it affects poverty, in interaction with growth. The accounting procedures discussed above are the technical counterpart to this focus on poverty. In this paper we will look at the interactions between growth processes and both poverty and inequality. The reason for not treating inequality as a mere adjunct is, firstly, that even if poverty were the policy concern, the evolution of inequality may nevertheless give valuable clues about the development process and, secondly, that inequality is indeed a major policy concern. As we will discuss, the political economy of development and growth processes is much influenced by what happens to incomes in the middle of the distribution, and exorbitant increases in the very highest incomes, even though they have no effect on measures of poverty, have strong political consequences. At the same time, distribution and redistribution across socio-politically relevant groups turns out to be a key feature of the development process which influences policy choice—whether, or not, measured poverty or inequality changes one way or the other.

Thus, although we will spend some time in this paper reviewing the standard literature on the aggregate relationship between growth and distribution, our object throughout will be to drive for policy implications in the actual socio- political context of a given economy.

1.2. Overview

Post-war thinking on the interactions between development and distribution has gone through several phases. In the immediate post-war period, the focus was on rapid growth and industrialization (Rosenstein-Rodan, 1943; Mahalanobis, 1963). This is not necessarily because of a lack of concern with poverty and the poor. Rather, it was thought to be the best and quickest way of reducing poverty. To quote Rosenstein-Rodan: "It is generally agreed that industrialization of international depressed areas ... is *the* way of achieving a more equal distribution of income between different areas of the world by raising incomes in depressed areas at a higher rate than in the rich areas".

In fact, many writers in the 1950s discussed the distributional consequences of growth explicitly. Most famously, Kuznets (1955) put forward his "inverted-U hypothesis", that inequality first increases and then decreases as per capita income rises. This hypothesis, and the literature surrounding it, will be discussed later in the paper. But the surplus labor model of Lewis (1954) also had implications that inequality would initially increase, as labor started to move from the low income traditional sector to the high income modern sector. Writing 30 years after his justly celebrated paper, Lewis (1983) once again emphasized why development and distribution might conflict—at least in the short run:

... development theorists have always maintained that growth is an inegalitarian process. This was so in the classical models of Smith, Ricardo and Marx. Theorists since the Second World War approached the subject differently, via the behavior of different sectors of the economy, but reached the same conclusion .... Development must be inegalitarian because it does not start in every part of an economy at the same time. Somebody develops a mine, and employs a thousand people. Or farmers in one province start planting cocoa, which grows in only 10% of the country. Or the Green Revolution arrives to benefit those farmers who have plenty of rain or access to irrigation, while offering nothing to the other 50% in the drier regions.

Of course in the longer term these benefits might spread more equally, but Lewis' (1983) characterization informs one of the central tenets of this paper, that the *short-run* distributional consequences of growth processes need to be actively managed.

The 1960s and 1970s saw the culmination of concerns on the distributional consequences of fast growth, fed by the experiences of such countries as Brazil, where Fishlow (1972) argued that distributional worsening may even have been such as to increase poverty despite rapid growth. The Indian Third Five Year Plan explicitly took on distributional objectives. The President of the World Bank, Robert McNamara (1973), moved the focus of that institution away from heavy infrastructure towards rural areas and the urban poor. The World Bank's document 'Redistribution With Growth' (Chenery et al., 1974) is perhaps the best summary of development of thinking at that time, reflecting concern that growth of the type seen by Rosenstein-Rodan (1943), and promoted by the international community, might not benefit the poor because of its distributional pattern, and that active intervention was required to manage the distributional consequences of growth processes. Much of the discussion of "targeting" of transfers for poverty alleviation also comes out of this literature, and we will discuss this later on in the paper.

However, almost as soon as the "Redistribution With Growth" consensus was attempted, it gave way to a new development in thinking which, far from warning about possible conflicts and tradeoffs between growth and distribution, argued that both more growth and more equity were possible. There were four distinct strands in the literature which brought us to this point by the end of the 1980s. First was the large body of empirical work on the Kuznets hypothesis, which will be reviewed in this paper, which failed to find a systematic relationship between growth and inequality in the cross-section data. The second was the equally large body of work on the possible consequences of "structural adjustment" in the highly distorted economies of Africa and Latin America. It was argued that these distortions (e.g., exchange rate overvaluation) and other government interventions (e.g., large state owned enterprises) were both inefficient and inequitable. Policy reform in these dimensions would therefore not only raise national income but reduce inequality and poverty. This strand of the literature will be closely examined in this paper, but there can be no doubt that the focus on policy reform in the debt crisis decade of the 1980s was one of the reasons for decline in attention to growth-equity tradeoffs. The third strand in the literature was the phenomenal "growth-with-equity miracle" of East Asia. These economies, particularly with their development in the 1970s and 1980s, seemed to provide a clear demonstration that there need be no conflict—one could have more national income and more equity. This literature will also be examined in this paper, but one line of argument emphasized the role of equitable *initial conditions*—in terms of the distribution of land and of human capital—in ensuring that the proceeds of growth were distributed equally. This investigation of the East Asian story, which continued into the1990s (see World Bank, 1993) inspired and coincided with the fourth strand—a theoretical literature which helped to rationalize why equitable initial conditions might not only distribute growth equally but also facilitate higher growth than would otherwise take place. The fourth strand was the theoretical development of arguments about complementarities between reducing inequalities and increasing growth, which will be discussed later in the paper.

The World Bank's (1990) World Development Report and the UNDP's (1990) Human Development Report capture the consensus that seemed to rule at the start of the last decade of the twentieth century. As Kanbur (1994) notes, it is remarkable how similar these two documents are in asserting that not only is growth necessary for poverty reduction but that growth and equitable distribution of growth can indeed go hand in hand—all that is needed are the right policies. The World Development Report, in particular, put forward a two-pronged strategy which seemed to resolve the conflicts highlighted in the earlier literature—the two prongs being labor-demanding growth based on private sector incentives, and public investment in basic education, health and infrastructure, these two prongs to be supported by social safety nets to protect the very poor and vulnerable. In their survey, Lipton and Ravallion (1995) argue that "While there are differences in emphasis, there now appears to be broad agreement on these basic elements of a poverty reduction strategy".

And yet, in the 1990s, a new wave of thinking has questioned the consensus that there is, essentially, no tradeoff between growth and equity. While much of the focus of this literature is on the short run, it has a pedigree going back to the 1950s and the work of Kuznets (1955) and Lewis (1954), and it is based on an examination of some uncomfortable evidence on the consequences of policy reform in Africa and Latin America, and even more recent evidence that, after two decades or more of growth accompanied by greater equity, inequality has begun to widen in some East Asian economies (Ahuja et al., 1997). There is a possibility, therefore, that a consensus based on the experience of the 1970s and 1980s may indeed be inappropriate for the twenty-first century. We will examine this phase of the literature in greater detail in subsequent sections.

An overview of the literature on development and distribution thus reveals four distinct phases. The first, from the 1940s to the 1950s saw growth and industrialization as the key to poverty reduction, and did not pay much attention to distributional consequences. The second phase, from the mid-1950s to the mid-1970s, emphasized possible conflicts between growth and distribution, and the need for intervention to manage the process. The third phase, from the mid-1970s to the early 1990s, led to the currently dominant consensus that if only policy can be engineered appropriately, there need be no conflict between fast growth and distribution, in the short or long run. The fourth phase of the literature may be about to begin, and we would like to emphasize this phase in this paper. We predict that in the coming decade analysts and policymakers will rediscover the possibility of the conflicts and tradeoffs highlighted in the 1950s and 1960s, as the short-run consequences of growth strategies and growth paths currently being followed, in the context of emerging global conditions, become clearer.

Throughout the four phases of thinking on development and *within-country* distribution, there has been an overlapping literature on *between-country* gaps in per capita income. The central issue has been one of whether per capita incomes were converging or diverging. This literature will also be reviewed in this paper, and we will argue that while the literature provides some interesting theories, and interesting tests, of development processes, its policy implications are unclear. If convergence is confirmed, say, should this give comfort to a poor country—simply to wait for convergence to take it to the levels of richer countries? We think not—countries can indeed accelerate or decelerate their growth though policies (including distributional policies), and there is no law of nature which determines a growth path.

Section 2 starts with distribution within countries, and examine theories of relationships between development and distribution, and the evidence for such relationships. Section 3 moves to a discussion focussing, in particular, on the impact effects of policy reforms and alternative growth strategies. Section 4 considers three further aspects of distribution—national convergence, intra-household inequality and inter-group inequality, arguing that moving one level below and one level above the household introduces interesting dimensions to the way in which we think about development and distribution. Section 5 concludes the paper.

2. Distribution and the process of development

Perhaps the dominant strand in the income distribution and development literature is one which can be labeled "Kuznetsian" after one of the most famous contributions to the topic (Kuznets, 1955). The approach, in this strand of the literature, might be described as aggregative and reduced form in nature, because in its theoretical mode the ultimate interest is in deriving a relationship between measures of economy-wide income distribution and per capita incomes as the process of development evolves; and in its empirical mode the focus is on estimating this economy-wide relationship. The empirical literature sees the estimated relationship either as a test of a development process postulated, or as a stylized fact to be explained or taken into account in policy making. A central part of this approach is the attempt to either derive or test for the "Kuznets hypothesis" (which some have elevated to the Kuznets "law") that as per capita rises inequality first worsens and then improves. We will review the literature surrounding the Kuznets hypothesis, arguing that it is inconclusive—and for good reason. However, we will argue that this Kuznetsian literature, obsessed and focused as it is on the aggregative, reduced form relationship between inequality and per capita income, tends to overlook the rich texture of actual relationships between these two, which can be revealed by detailed case studies of development process—advice which was given by Kuznets (1955) himself, but is ignored by the literature which bears his name.

2.1. The theory of development and distribution

Theoretical analysis of the interaction between development and distributions spans the full range from broad discussion to mathematical modelling, and from analysis which traces the link from development to distribution, to analysis which examines the linkage in the other direction. The classic analyses of Lewis (1954) and Kuznets (1955) take the approach of broad (though sophisticated) discussion as opposed to mathematical modelling, and focus on the impact of development on distribution, viewing the changes in distribution as an integral part of the development process.

Thus, the Lewis (1954) paper, which outlines a development process in which growth and accumulation starts up in a modern enclave in the economy, traces the distributional consequences of this process and the impact of the distributional evolution on development in turn. As is well known, in the Lewis model there are two sectors—the modern/urban/industrial sector in which capitalists hire labor at a given wage and reinvest the profits from production; this investment leads to even greater demand for labor, drawn from the traditional/rural/agricultural sector, from which it is hypothesized that labor can be supplied indefinitely at a fixed wage. While these assumptions pertain, growth continues as the result of investment, capitalist profits grow while wages are stagnant and inequality worsens. If it is further assumed that there is a fixed wage premium in the modern sector, inequality as between wage earners will worsen for a time as well—since some workers will now be earning higher wages. One can continue to complicate the model further, for example, by introducing unemployment or underemployment in the modern sector to go with the wage premium being earned by those employed (Todaro, 1969), but the basic analysis remains the same. The process of development, at least initially and possibly for a considerable length of time, leads to a widening of income disparities, so long as the impact on the traditional sector is not felt though rising wages and incomes there. As Lewis (1983) notes:

> This failure of response is also one reason why development widens inequality: incomes rise in the enclave, while all around in the traditional sectors incomes may remain the same. The differences can be astonishingly wide: the average income in the cocoa region may be five times as high as the average income of surrounding provinces—a degree of difference which could not persist very long in a developed country, where labor would be flowing rapidly to the richer region and capital flowing rapidly to the poorer.

What Lewis has in mind in the above is the eventual exhaustion of the surplus labor pool in the traditional sector and subsequent increases in the wages in that sector. If nothing else happens, such as technical progress in the modern sector which can utilize labor more efficiently even at the higher wages, or technical progress in the traditional sector which can continue to release more labor, the initial impact of wage increases will be to reduce profits of capitalists in the modern sector and thus, given the accumulation assumptions a reduction in the rate of growth. This shows how complex the relationship between per capita income, or growth in per capita income, and inequality can become even in this very simple setting.

In the surplus labor phase of the Lewis (1954) model, inequality will rise with per capita income. Once the surplus labor phase ends, increases in per capita income will continue, but with narrowing inequality. This pattern is nothing other than the inverse-U hypothesized by Kuznets (1955) which we will come to presently. What about growth and inequality? In the simplest Lewis model, with no technical progress, diminishing returns in the modern sector will continually reduce profits and hence accumulation and growth—thus, decreasing rates of growth will coincide with increasing inequality. It should then be clear that the introduction of technical progress will lead to even more complex and indeterminate effects—depending on exactly how the technical progress is modelled.

Thinking through the complex consequences of the simple Lewis (1954) model is a good antidote to the somewhat simplistic conclusions that are sometimes drawn from another classic paper in the literature—Kuznets (1955). In keeping with the nature of the discourse in the 1950s, Kuznets focussed on intersectoral shifts of population as a defining characteristic of the development process. Unlike the Lewis (1954) paper, however, he did not model the origins of this transfer, concentrating instead directly on the implications of this population transfer on the distribution of income, under various assumptions:

An invariable accompaniment of growth in developed countries is the shift away from agriculture, a process usually referred to as industrialization and urbanization. The income distribution of the total population, in the simplest model, may therefore be viewed as a combination of the income distributions of the rural and of the urban populations. What little we know of the structures of these two component income distributions reveals that: (a) the average per capita income of the rural population is usually lower than that of the urban; (b) inequality in the percentage shares within the distribution for the rural population is somewhat narrower than in that for the urban population .... Operating with this simple model, what conclusions do we reach? First, all other conditions being equal, the increasing weight of urban population means an increasing share for the more unequal of the two component distributions. Second, the relative difference in per capita income between the rural and urban populations does not necessarily drift downward in the process of economic growth; indeed, there is some evidence to suggest that it is stable at best, and tends to widen because per capita productivity in urban pursuits increases more rapidly than in agriculture. If this is so, inequality in the total income distribution should increase.

The above quotation from Kuznets (1955) is important for several reasons. First, it illustrates the nonformal style of reasoning which was prevalent in the 1950s—indeed, much of the recent literature is devoted to formalizing these basic insights. Secondly, and relatedly, it highlights a particular approach which starts from stylized facts and processes and drives for distributional implications. It is interesting that the subsequent literature, which models development processes more formally and in greater detail, often judges itself by whether or not it can produce "Kuznets-like" results. Thirdly, and finally, note that the focus of attention in this Kuznetsian discourse is to explain or derive a widening in the distribution of income as development starts. This is to be set against the subsequent focus of the Kuznetsian literature on whether or not there was a "turning" point where, eventually, inequality would start decreasing with development. Interestingly, as we shall discuss presently, the empirical evidence on the basis of which Kuznets (1955) launched his discussion, long- run data for the UK, Germany and the

US, all showed declining inequality with increasing per capita over time. It was to incorporate this finding that Kuznets continued the process discussed in the quote, arguing that eventually population shifts on its own would tend to decrease inequality, *and* that various policy measures and interventions would begin to reduce inter- and intra-sectoral inequality—hence the observed decline, the only tendency for which he had evidence.

This last point highlights a duality in the literature which persists to this day. Most authors want their discussion, or their models, to speak to the short- and long-run time path of income distribution as development proceeds. They want, indeed, to be able to explain both in a simple framework. Thus, in the Lewis framework the prediction is that until the surplus labor phase ends inequality will increase. In the Kuznets framework there is a similar tendency to try and capture 50 or more years of distributional evolution in the "inverted-U"—inequality first (in the short run) increases with development and then (in the long run) decreases beyond a "turning point". It cannot be overemphasized how important, and how (ultimately) damaging is this need to capture all aspects in one, aggregative reduced form relationship. In particular, as we shall see in the review of the empirical literature, there is a tendency to try and capture the *whole* inverted-U in the data. And, when this attempt is unsuccessful, to throw out *any* relationship between growth and distribution—even in the short run. The fact that in the long run, or in a cross-section with wide variation in per capita income, where structural and policy variations can swamp other effects, no relationship is found between growth and distribution is *not* a reason to believe that one might not exist in the short run. And, as we shall argue in the next section, the existence or otherwise of a reduced form relationship may have very little to say to policy makers—certainly in the short run.

As noted earlier, the theoretical literature which followed Lewis (1954) and Kuznets (1955) is in one sense nothing other than various attempts at formalizing their insights. In fact, in a strange way the framework set out by the originators may have by now become a straightjacket which inhibits fresh thinking, as every new attempt to model development and distribution does so with at least half an eye on whether or not the model can, in principle, generate an inverted- U relationship between inequality and development, while most empirical work keeps returning to the question of whether or not there is an inverted-U pattern to be discerned in the data.

A formalization of the implicit distributional process in the Kuznets (1995) paper is presented in Anand and Kanbur (1993a), following on from early attempts by Robinson (1976) and Fields (1980). Modelling the national income distribution as the population weighted sum of two sectoral distributions, Anand and Kanbur (1993a) trace through the implications of shifts in the population weights under various "Kuznetsian" assumptions. Thus, for example, it can be shown that if the sectoral distribution whose population share increases "first-order dominates" (in the sense of Hadar and Russell (1969)) the other distribution, the population shift will lead to a first-order dominating shift in the national distribution. Such a change would be preferred by all social welfare functions which are increasing in individual income. Similarly, for second-order dominance, so that population shift will lead to a national income distribution which is preferred by all social welfare functions which are increasing, symmetric and quasi-concave in individual incomes. This analysis can then be specialized to the behavior of Lorenz curve, and specific inequality indices. Anand and Kanbur (1993a) derive the relationship between per capita income and six inequality indices for the pure population shift case, and specify conditions for there to be a "turning point" leading to the famous Kuznets inverted-U.

These relationships are then tested on cross-section data (see later discussion), but an equally important issue is the incorporation of movements and processes that go beyond pure population shift. Consider, for example, the implications of superimposing on the change in sectoral population shares a change in sectoral means. For inequality measures that are invariant to a proportional change in all income, it should be clear that the key determinant will be the behavior of the ratio of the sectoral means relative to the population shift. In the Kuznets (1955) quote given above, the assumption is that the ratio of the means widens, at least in the initial stages. Ahluwalia (1976) extends this assumption as follows:

> The assumptions(s) of ... equal growth rates in sectoral incomes (is) obviously unrealistic. In fact, we would expect ... mean income differences to change systematically with development. Interestingly, there are plausible reasons for supposing that these changes may reinforce the U-shaped pattern in overall inequality ... The ratio of mean incomes between sectors may also follow a U- shaped pattern with intersectoral differences widening in the early states .... These differentials can be expected to narrow in the later stages of development ...".

Anand and Kanbur (1993a) show that while the heuristic argument that the above pattern of mean changes would reinforce the inverted-U prediction may appear plausible, the interactions between the effects of population shift and means shift on measures of inequality can be quite complex. Just as there is no guarantee that even in the pure population shift case there will be an inverted- U, whether or not a given pattern of mean shift reinforces the argument cannot be guaranteed—it depends on conditions which may, or may not, be met in practice.

The "Kuznets process", as christened and formalized by Anand and Kanbur (1993a) is a useful device as far as it goes, but it is somewhat mechanical, with very little economic modelling of the underlying process. Lewis (1954) is of course an early attempt at modelling the development process, although it can be argued that the focus of attention was not so much the distributional consequences but the dynamics of capital accumulation and labor shift from traditional to modern sector. Lewis (1954, 1983) himself drew some distributional implications of this process and Anand and Kanbur (1985) extended the basic model to incorporate rural-urban migration decisions in the spirit of Todaro (1969). It is shown that each enriching of the basic Lewis (1954) surplus labor model, by modelling economic decision making complicates the relationship between development and distribution, making it increasingly difficult to draw out sharp conclusions—let alone a relationship as specific as the Kuznets inverted-U.

In another strand of the theoretical literature, the formal modelling of growth and distribution owes much to attempts to enrich the famous Solow neoclassical model of economic growth. In the basic model, with identical agents, the economy achieves a steady state equilibrium path where per capita income is constant, its level depending on technology and preferences. If the economy starts with per capita income below this level, it can be shown that per capita income will increase monotonically. Hence, the possibility that if we could move from the assumption of identical agents and introduce heterogeneity, there may well be a pattern in the time path of inequality as per capita income increases. Stiglitz (1969) is an example of an early modelling effort in this direction. But such modelling has really taken off in the last decade, incorporating other advances in the literature such as the introduction of endogenous growth or the analysis of political and voting equilibrium. Interestingly, a feature of growth and distribution models in the last decade has been to emphasize causal links *from* distribution to growth. In fact, many of the models determine growth and distribution in equilibrium simultaneously. There are a large number of papers in this tradition, and we illustrate the type of analysis involved by focussing on a few recent efforts which cover a range of interesting issues.

Galor and Tsiddon (1996) is an example of a paper which combines a number of elements that have emerged in the recent literature, and attempts a fairly comprehensive approach at deriving an aggregative relationship between distribution and growth. The basic building block is a eoclassical growth model with endogenous technological progress. Output is a function of capital and human capital, and the overall efficiency of production is a function of the total human capital of the labor force. In addition, it is assumed that while all individuals are born with identical preferences, an individual's level of human capital depends on the parental level of human capital: this in turn affects their own decision to invest in education, and so on. Fairly standard assumptions are invoked on consumption preferences, but with the earlier assumptions it is easy to see how a distributional dynamic can be set in motion—the amount of investment in human capital increases with the parental level of human capital, and also with the overall efficiency of technology which in turn depends upon total human capital.

Given the nonlinearities and feedback built into the assumptions, it should not be too difficult to see why, unlike as in the basic Solow growth model, there may be multiple locally stable steady state equilibria to which dynasties converge, leading to inequality even in the long run. Suppose that the economy wide technological externality kicks in only after some critical level of human capital has been reached so that, up to this point, the key influence on dynamics is the parent-to- child human capital externality. Then Galor and Tsiddon (1996) show that under certain conditions the economy polarizes to two dynasties, rich and poor. But when the global technological externality kicks in, it can cause a qualitative change in the nature of the dynamical system which, again under certain assumptions, leads to a unique steady state equilibrium to which both dynasties converge. Of course, what we have here is the Kuznets inverted-U: inequality first increases and then decreases. In this model, and in models like it, it is possible to do comparative static exercises by changing the initial distribution of human capital, and combine this with the dynamic analysis to argue as follows:

... for some initial distribution of human capital the model can demonstrate that at the early stages of development, an increase in the aggregate level of investment in human capital may not be feasible unless the distribution of human capital (and consequently the distribution of income) is unequal. Inequality enables members of families from the highly educated segments of society to overcome the gravity of a low stable equilibrium and to increase their investment in human capital. Thus, inequality may be essential in order to increase the aggregate level of human capital and output during the early stages of growth. As the investment in human capital of the upper segments of society increases and income inequality widens, the accumulated knowledge trickles down to the lower segments of society via a technological progress in production ... investment in human capital becomes more beneficial to members of all segments in society. In particular, members of the less educated segments, who initially invested relatively little in the formation of human capital, find it beneficial to increase their investment. Due to diminishing returns to the family-specific external effects, the rate of investment (at a certain stage) becomes higher among members of the lower segments of society. Thus, in accordance with the Kuznets hypothesis, during the early stages of development, output growth is associated with increased income inequality whereas in the later stages output growth is accompanied by a more equal distribution of human capital and income.

We have quoted at length from the Galor and Tsiddon (1996) paper because it illustrates very well some features of the burgeoning literature on growth and distribution based on neoclassical endogenous growth models. First, particular types of interlinkages and externalities drive the dynamics of inequality, accumulation and growth. Thus, nonlinearities and interlinkages in savings functions could generate some of these results directly in the standard Solow growth model with heterogeneous agents—indeed, such results are to be found in Stiglitz (1966). But the results are very sensitive to key assumptions. While Galor and Tsiddon (1996) draw the conclusion that "a relatively poor economy which values equity as well as prosperity may face a difficult trade-off between equity in the short run and equity and prosperity in the long run" other papers derive the pure result that equitable distribution of assets unambiguously raises growth rates (e.g., Banerjee and Newman, 1993). Second, notice the "Kuznetsian" drive to generate an aggregative relationship between growth and inequality and, indeed, satisfaction at having derived an inverse-U shape for this reduced form relationship. Thirdly, notice the paucity of real world policy implications—is the recommendation to engineer an increase in inequality at the start of the development process?

The recent explosion of work on political economy models also provides a channel for thinking about the relationship between growth and distribution. A good example is the paper by Alesina and Rodrik (1994). Once again, the basic model is one of endogenous growth. Output depends on capital, labor and a public good, which is financed through a proportional capital tax. Individuals differ in their endowment of capital and labor. Given identical, time separable, isoelastic utility of consumption, it can be shown that all capital endowments grow at a common rate which depends upon the proportional tax rate. Each individual will have a different view on what the common tax rate should be, since the tax revenue will deliver a common benefit but cost individuals in proportion to their capital ownership—those with a low share of capital income will prefer a higher tax rate. Using the median voter theorem one can investigate the relationship between distribution and growth. As the ratio of the median to the mean wealth rises, i.e., this measure of equality increases, the median voter is more and more concerned about capital taxation—the actually voted for tax rate will thus be lower, and the growth rate higher.

The basic story developed by Alesina and Rodrik (1994) is present in many papers in the recent literature, in more or less elaborate form. Thus, Perotti (1993) has a model in which individuals invest in their education, but all individuals benefit indirectly through an externality. Imperfect capital markets means that some individuals will invest more than others in education, and hence will have higher income in the next period. The economic structure is thus similar to that of Galor and Tsiddon (1996). In a very poor economy, under certain conditions, only a very unequal distribution may give enough resources to those at the upper end to invest in education and thus generate the econo- mywide externality to in turn generate growth. The issue then is the preference of the median voter over redistributive taxation. Once again, it should not be surprising that Perotti (1993) drives for a Kuznets inverted-U, and expresses some satisfaction that his model can generate such an aggregative reduced form relationship.

There has thus been a veritable explosion of theoretical work trying to generate a re- lationship between growth and distribution. Under various assumptions, different types of relationships can be derived—even the Kuznets inverted-U, indeed, most papers seem to set themselves the goal of demonstrating that such a shape is possible in their models. We will discuss the policy significance of all this later in the paper. For now we turn to the empirical evidence on development and distribution.

2.2. Econometric testing

Given the obsession of the theoretical literature with the Kuznets inverted U, it should not be surprising that the dominant strand of the empirical literature is that which at- tempts to estimate and test for, with different degrees of complexity and sophistication, the reduced form relationship between measures of inequality and measures of per capita income (a selection of these studies include Saith, 1983; Cumpano and Salvatore, 1988; Tsaklogou, 1988; Clarke, 1993; Anand and Kanbur, 1993b; Jha, 1995; Ram, 1995; and Ravallion, 1997). Given data constraints, most of the variation in observations is provided by cross-country observations—time series data does not stretch back very far for most developing countries, and very few intertemporal observations are typically available. We will argue that the "Kuznetsian" empirical literature, although moving towards a consensus still presents a wide array of results from which support can be drawn for a range of competing hypotheses.

We start by considering the truly vast literature which looks at data across countries (with, perhaps, a small number of intertemporal observations for some countries). The issue of comparability and quality of distributional data strikes one immediately as being a central issue. Kuznets (1955) himself emphasized requirements for the quality of dis- tributional data which seem to have been forgotten by some of the subsequent literature. A very widely used source is the compilation by Jain (1975), and the dataset in Paukert (1973), for example, is used by Persson and Tabellini (1994) to test propositions on the impact of inequality on growth—a dataset which Deininger and Squire (1996a) do not give very high marks to.

In fact, Deininger and Squire (1996a), following on from Fields (1989a, b), set out a series of criteria which distribution data should satisfy:

(1) the unit of observation has to be either the household or the individual. In other words, the generation of "synthetic" distributions from national accounts and applying distributions from other "similar" countries would run foul of this criterion;

(2) the coverage of the population has to be comprehensive. Thus, for example, if only the urban household distribution of income is available, it is not permissible to translate this directly into the national distribution. The same is true if the data is restricted only to the economically active, to wage earners, etc.; and

(3) the measurement of income (or expenditure) has to be comprehensive. For example, income from self-employment and production for auto-consumption should be included.

These criteria are similar to those used by Fields (1989a, b) and by Anand and Kanbur (1993b) to trim down the compilation in Jain (1975) and other sources up to the 1970s. Deininger and Squire (1996a) perform a considerable service to the literature by first assembling an up-to-date set of Gini coefficients and other distribution measures reported in the literature. From the more than 2600 such observations, they went back to primary sources to assess the quality and comparability applying the three criteria above. This led to a database of 682 observations for 108 countries. If the same criteria had been applied to Fields (1989a, b), his 105 observations would have been reduced to 73 observations for 36 countries. Similarly, Paukert's (1973) 55 observations would have been reduced to 18 for 18 countries, and Jain's (1975) 405 observations would have been reduced to 61 for 30 countries. In fact, Anand and Kanbur (1993b) do an even more stringent stripping of the Jain (1975) dataset to arrive at 38 observations for 18 countries.

Even for the Deininger and Squire (1996a) dataset, 35% of the observations are not calculated directly from the primary source but quoted by a reliable secondary source. Ravallion and Chen (1997) conduct a similar quality and comparability exercise, but base their calculations only on surveys that were *directly* available to them. This gives rise to a dataset for 67 countries of which 42 have at least two surveys since 1980, giving 64 "spells" of growth and distribution change. For example, they only make intertemporal comparisons when both observations are based on nationally representative household surveys which use the same indicator (income or expenditure). They also ensure that measures of inequality are household size weighted. Deininger and Squire (1996a) also recognize these problems, and that such stricter criteria will further reduce their number of observations.

It would be somewhat tedious to keep track of the data problems of individual studies as we go through our assessment of the empirical literature on growth and distribution. Suffice it to say that *most* econometric estimation in this area is subject to the criticism that the dataset underlying it is not of very high quality. We have already noted Persson and Tabellini's (1994) reliance on Paukert (1973). But even studies which have made attempts at weeding out problematic data points can be subjected to criticism. Alesina and Rodrik (1994) in a test of their model discussed earlier in this paper use the dataset of Fields (1989a, b) who, according to Deininger and Squire (1996b) "uses quality standards that are similar to ours—the only difference being his inclusion of distributional data that refer to the wage earning population only". However, even the dataset used by Deininger and Squire (1996a) to test the Kuznets hypothesis does not satisfy the stricter criteria of Ravallion and Chen (1996).

These data shortcomings cast a dark cloud over the whole "Kuznetsian" approach of seeking an aggregative, reduced form relationship between distribution and development in cross-sectional data. However, leaving these data problems to one side, what sort of a picture merges from this mountain of econometric work? Let us start by examining the Kuznets curve literature. As noted earlier, Kuznets discussed long-run, time series, data for the UK, US and Germany. He did not have, at that time in the immediate post-war period, any data of note from developing countries. A major boost to examining the relationship for developing countries was given by the work in the mid-1970s leading up to the World Bank's "Redistribution With Growth" volume Chenery et al. (1974), in particular the compiliation of cross-country data in Jain (1975) and the econometric work of Ahluwalia (1976). The same period saw other work and other compilations of data (e.g., Paukert, 1973). The Ahluwalia (1976) paper is important in having set the framework for much of the later discussion. Quite simply, Ahluwalia regressed inequality (actually, a measure of equality—the income share of the bottom 40% of the population) against per capita income and per capita income squared for a cross-section of countries (he also included regional dummies to capture the uniformly higher inequality in Latin America and the uniformly lower inequality in the then socialist economies of Eastern Europe). He found a confirmation of the Kuznets inverted-U through testing for the sign of the coefficient on the quadratic term in per capita income.

This finding, and other similar results at the time, set off an enormous industry examining the relationship between inequality and per capita income, with studies using different datasets, different inequality measures, and different econometric methodologies. Thus, for example, Anand and Kanbur (1993a) derived the functional form of the relationship between inequality and per capita income for six inequality indices, based on an explicit modelling of the intersectoral population shift process implicit in Kuznets (1955). They then estimated these specific functional forms (which differ from inequality index to inequality index) for the *same* dataset as Ahluwalia (1976). They found that the estimates "differ vastly in goodness-of-fit, in turning point, and in the predicted behavior of inequality in the long run". For some of the cases, the statistical significance of the coefficient did not support a turning point at all. For most, the restrictions implied by the "Kuznets process" of intersectoral shifts was rejected. Anand and Kanbur (1993b) is a more direct investigation of the robustness of the Ahluwalia (1976) results, focussing on their sensitivity to choice of dataset and functional form. It is argued that we must test alternative functional forms against each other, since some support the inverse-U and others do not. After an exhaustive set of tests it is concluded that for datasets of higher quality than used by Ahluwalia (1976), and for functional forms which are supported by the data, the inverse-U is not supported.

Throughout the 1980s and 1990s, an extraordinarily large number of studies have attempted to confirm or reject the inverse-U. While a consensus seems to be developing that the evidence for such a relationship is not strong, in even the latest studies one finds differing points of view. One of the most recent tests is that by Deininger and Squire (1996c) based on their newly developed dataset, Deininger and Squire (1996a). They estimate a relationship between the Gini coefficient and the per capita income and the inverse of per capita income. They also include a dummy for socialist countries. For the "pure" cross section, where they use averages whenever they are multiple observations for a country, they do indeed find an inverse-U. But the result does not stand up to robustness tests, as might be expected from Anand and Kanbur (1993a,b). Among the variations they try are to estimate the model in decadal differences than in levels. This does not provide support for the Kuznets curve (the same as in Ravallion, 1995). They also find, matching the recent work of Fields and Jakubson (1995) that sometimes there is evidence of a U rather than an inverted U—a result also found in Anand and Kanbur (1993b). As they conclude: "Together, these results offer virtually no support for an increase of inequality at low levels of income and a decrease at higher income levels as suggested by Kuznets' inverted-U relationship". This statement by Deininger and Squire (1996b) seems to us to capture the emerging consensus and the weight of recent work. But it would be appropriate to point out that there continue to be studies which do indeed offer support for the Kuznets curve. One recent paper, which emphasizes econometric techniques is that by Ogwang (1994), who uses the dataset developed by Ram (1988). This dataset also emphasizes data quality and comparability, but Ogwang's (1994) contribution is on functional form, in the framework of nonparametric regression. Using the kernel method he estimates the relationship between inequality and per capita income and finds support for the Kuznets inverted-U.

Fairly clearly, large and cross-country variations in key variables such as policy and initial conditions might be explaining some of the weak relationship between inequality and per capita income. Bruno et al. (1995) take one country for which relatively long-run time series on inequality are available—India—and try to estimate a Kuznets relationship. For 33 observations spanning 1951 to 1992, they conclude that: "There is no sign that growth increased inequality, including during the period of higher growth in the 1980s. On running the Anand-Kanbur test equation appropriate to the Gini index one obtains, not an inverted-U but an ordinary U, though for most of the range of the data inequality falls as average income increases. However, if one takes first differences of the above equation (so that it is the change in the Gini index between surveys which is regressed on the change in average income and the change in its inverse) then the relationship vanishes. There is no sign in these data that higher growth rates in India put any upward pressure on overall inequality".

Let us turn now to the literature which tests the relationship *from* distribution *to* growth. As Bruno et al. (1995) point out, not only are all the standard data problems from the Kuznets literature still present, but, "the noisy inequality variable is now on the *righthand side*, so there must be a general presumption that standard estimators will give biased results". These problems have not stopped a crop of recent studies claiming to support a negative effect of initial inequality on subsequent growth, which is consistent with at least some of the models in the "endogenous growth-policy economy" tradition, as discussed earlier in the section. But Fishlow (1996) reports that with a Latin American dummy, there is no such relationship. Deininger and Squire (1996b) use their dataset to estimate growth as a function of initial inequality and other variables. They find that while the effect of initial income inequality on growth is not robust, initial land inequality is indeed associated with low growth.

2.3. The country case study approach

Despite the huge amount of resources devoted to the development-distribution relationship in the Kuznetsian approach, it has to be said that the harvest is meager. This is so whether we look straightforwardly for a relationship between inequality and development, or for its implications for the nature of underlying development processes, or (as we shall argue in the next section) for its policy implications. An alternative to the Kuznetsian approach is to examine in great detail the development experience of individual countries, telling an overall story which incorporates a range of influences, including policy. A number of such studies are available, and we will illustrate this method by recounting the argument in an excellent recent paper by Chu (1995).

By all accounts, Taiwan's post-war experience has been one of growth with equity. It is one of the economies of East Asia that managed to achieve extraordinarily high rates of growth with extraordinarily (by international standards) low levels of inequality and, indeed, declining inequality. One might, of course, take an aggregative reduced form approach to this and try to estimate a Kuznets curve on the 20 or so distributional observations available (indeed, some of these observations are present in the Kuznetsian literature reviewed earlier), but the usual problems would attend such an exercise, and it is unclear that we would learn more from it than from the earlier Kuznetsian literature. However, Chu (1995) weaves together a compelling account of how Taiwan managed to attain high growth and equity, building on the earlier pioneering work of authors such as Ho (1978), Fei et al. (1979) and Kuo (1983). It is a tale worth retelling in some detail, and we follow Chu (1995) closely in doing so.

The "initial conditions" for Taiwan's post-war miracle came about as a result of its particular history. Before the war, when Taiwan was under Japanese colonial rule, much of the land was owned by sugar companies, which were in turn owned by the Japanese. About one tenth of all cultivated land in the 1930s was owned by them. There was also considerable Japanese ownership of large areas of cultivated land. After the war, when Taiwan was returned to Nationalist Government in China, the Government expropriated all property belonging to the Japanese and thus became, at a stroke, the largest landlord. After their defeat by the Communists and their arrival in Taiwan, the

Kuomintang enacted major land reforms through rent reduction, sale of public land and compulsory sale of private land.

Chu (1995) divides the development of Taiwan into three phases: (i) the 1950s and early 1960s; (ii) 1964–1980; and (iii) 1980 to the present. The first phase was that of rapid agricultural development and import substitution. Although distributional data are sparse and unreliable for this period, an account can be pieced together from various sources. Inequality of income among farm households was low and fell from a Gini of 0.2860 in 1952 to a Gini of 0.1790 in 1967. Clearly, the land reform was central to this trend, as well as to growth. Ho (1978) argues that land improvement and agricultural education both benefitted from land reform. Chu (1995) also argues that, moreover, smaller land holding households had a higher percentage of members involved in off-farm employment, and the Gini of wage income was particularly low. Finally, with the network of roads and broad spread of factory employment, and a relatively free labor market, an even income distribution was consolidated. Data on distribution within farm households is almost nonexistent, but Kuznets (1980) argued that the ratio of per capita farm household income to the national average rose from 54.88 in 1952 to 56.20 in 1962. However, the fact that the population share of nonfarm sector was rising would, Kuznets (1980) argued, be a factor in increasing overall inequality. Chu (1995) also argues that one would expect, given rapid expansion of import-substituting industry in the 1950s, that capitalist income would increase and thus contribute to greater inequality—however, this would be counteracted by the fact that there was a considerable degree of nationalization of large enterprises, and that the small and medium enterprise sector played a key role in industrial expansion. For what the data are worth, Taiwan's Gini coefficient fell from 0.558 in 1953 to 0.440 in 1959 and 0.321 in 1964. But what is important in Chu's (1995) analysis is the finely textured appreciation of the many different factors, some pulling in opposite directions, which contributed to this decline. Far better, in our view, to conduct this type of analysis than to feed the aggregative Ginis into an attempt to test a reduced form relationship between per capita income and inequality.

By the mid-1960s, agriculture's share in national output had fallen to under 30%, and the import substitution strategy was running out of steam. As is well documented in a host of retrospective studies, the Government introduced policies to encourage export expansion—including export processing zones, tax rebates on imports for export manufacture, and exchange rate alignment. With these changes, Taiwan plugged into the still buoyant US import demand at a time when Japanese labor costs were beginning to increase. From 1964 to 1970 the Gini coefficient of household income fell from 0.321 to 0.294 and then to 0.277 in 1980. Chu (1995) follows earlier work by Fei et al. (1979) in carrying out a detailed decomposition analysis and concludes as follows:

In 1964-80, inequality started at a low level due to initial conditions set in the 1950s and early 1960s. It stayed low and is suspected to have declined further. This has been shown to be mainly the result of low and shrinking inequality of wage income, which in turn was due mainly to the popular participation in employment in the export-driven, labor-intensive manufacturing industries. As before, the labor market was accessible: as before, strong demand more than offset the rapidly rising labor force, the result was mass employment or very low unemployment .... More specifically, the shrinking wage income inequality among households is suspected to reflect the shrinking inequality among individual workers/income receivers. The latter has been shown to be attributable to the fall in marginal returns to education and to working in the cities. Supply of workers was rising fast, that of higher education workers rose faster due to significant improvement in education. Demand for all types of labor rose faster than supply, that for low-skill (low education as a proxy) labor rose even faster. Consequently, average wage rate rose, and that of the low-education workers rose faster, resulting in narrow wage differentials.

During the 1980s and 1990s, the total supply of labor in Taiwan fell, although the share of population aged 6 or above receiving secondary education or above increased to 44% in 1980 and 65% in 1985. The increase in unskilled wages, which was a centerpiece of decreasing inequality, combined with currency appreciation in the late 1980s (to which the phenomenal export surplus contributed) hit labor-intensive exports. In fact, the economy started the process of upgrading to skill-intensive products domestically, and overseas investment in labor intensive plants in cheap labor economies such as Malaysia, Thailand, Mauritius and Bangladesh. One would expect the skilled–unskilled wage ratio to respond to such a change in demand—the average wage of those with college education as a ratio of those with primary education or less declined from 2.24 in 1976 to 1.72 in 1980, but rose to 1.80 by 1986–1987. Latest figures indicate that the trend has continued. At the same time, the share of capital and property in total income increased, which was linked to the increasing importance of larger private enterprises, and the steep escalation of land values. However, according to Chu's (1995) detailed decomposition analysis, the major factor explaining increasing household inequality in the 1980s and 1990s—one which is missing from nearly all studies in the "Kuznetsan" tradition—is the pattern of household formation. Household size fell from 5.85 in 1970 to 4.84 in 1980 and 4.10 in 1993.

Once again, for our purposes, Chu's (1995) analysis is interesting not only for its own sake but as a contrast to the Kuznetsian aggregative, reduced form approach. With this alternative approach one gets a much better sense of the links between development processes and their distributional consequences (for broader illustrations of the case study approach, see Wade, 1990; Oshima, 1994; and Jung, 1992). From 1980 onwards the Gini coefficient in Taiwan *rose*, from 0.277 in 1980 to 0.312 in 1990 and 0.316 in 1993, during a period when per capita income has kept on increasing at very high rates by international standards. Thus, running a straightforward time series regression between the Gini coefficient and per capita income for Taiwan would give the exact inverse of the Kuznets curve—inequality decreased from 1953 to 1980 and then increased to the present. But it should be clear that whether or not a U or an inverse-U exists for this country over time is quite beside the point, and a focus on this would divert attention away from a far richer discussion of the exact nature of the processes of development and their distributional consequence, and the policy implications of this experience.

The trends identified by Chu (1995) as the driving forces behind Taiwan's inequality in the 1980s and 1990s have begun to appear in some East Asian "miracle countries", certainly by the mid-1990s. Thus, for example, trends in income and wage inequality have tended to turn upwards (see Ahuja et al., 1997). The stories, while having their own peculiarities, all contain skyrocketing land values and increasing returns to skilled labor. The similarities with developments in the US (e.g., Freeman and Katz, 1994) over the last 15 years, particularly on the skilled/unskilled wage differential, should be apparent. Paradoxically, therefore, a detailed examination of the very latest trends in the East Asian miracle countries, whose experience in the 1960s, 1970s and 1980s contributed to the current consensus that growth and equity might be simultaneously achievable, are beginning to raise questions about whether this is true in the emerging conditions of the 1990s and of the next century. They also raise questions about the policy mix needed not only in the East Asian countries, but about the policy lessons for other developing countries. The next section turns to a discussion of the role of policy in the relationship between income distribution and development.

3. Distribution, development and policy

3.1. Policy and the Kuznetsian literature

The Kuznetsian literature's drive for deriving and estimating an aggregative, reduced form relationship between inequality and development has a strong tendency to minimize the role of policy—indeed, to treat the distribution/development relationship as a law. For example, this tendency is always present, no matter how hedged, in both supporters and critics of the inverted-U relationship. Supporters of the inverted-U relationship draw one of two inferences. The more left-leaning commentators view it as a warning that growth will have disruptive short-run distributional effects, with increasing inequality and perhaps even poverty. The more conservative commentators view the relationship as vindicating a drive for growth—since inequality will eventually fall, all the better to accelerate growth and get over the "hump" of the inverted-U. Those who do not find an inverted-U in the data use this finding typically to argue against those who are seen as warning against growth because of its distributional consequences—since there is no systematic relationship, no law which decrees that inequality must increase as growth accelerates, policies for accelerating growth can safely be followed (and these policies, as we shall see, may well entail inducing greater equity). These commentators add that even if inequality increased with growth, the net effect on poverty may still be positive. Thus, for example, Deininger and Squire (1996b) conclude their analysis as follows:

First, while policy makers should certainly pay attention to the distributional consequences of different policy options the fear of a systematically negative effect of economic growth on the distribution of income is ill-founded. Second, unequal distribution of assets, more than income, can be an impediment to rapid growth, implying that redistributive policies could enhance growth. Third, while redistributive policies have the potential to benefit the poor both directly and indirectly, they will do so only if redistribution does not jeopardize productive investment. This disqualifies conflict-ridden redistributive policies of the past and implies that, if countries want to implement redistributive policies, their ability to devise mechanisms that would at the same time maintain or increase investment incentives may well be decisive for the final success of such programs.

We will return presently to the second and third conclusions above, with which we largely agree, but consider the first conclusion that policy makers need not fear any systematic negative effects of growth on distribution. The problem with this conclusion is not whether it is valid or not, although in the previous section we have pointed to alternative positions in the literature, but that it is not particularly useful for a policy maker because it does not bear any relation to specific policy instruments. Does it really imply that growth can be maximized without fear of distributional worsening? If not, then which policy combinations are better than others? And, as Ravallion's (1996) analysis shows, about one fifth of the spells he studied were cases in which poverty was rising, some in cases with positive growth.

It seems to us far better to focus directly on policies, or combinations of policies, which will generate growth without adverse distributional effects, rather than rely on the existence or nonexistence of an aggregative, reduced form, relationship between per capita income and inequality. In this section we will consider three main types of policies—macroeconomic adjustment and liberalization, asset redistribution, and targeted public expenditures. As we shall see, the impact of each of these can be very country specific, depending on particular conditions in place and the realm of the politically feasible.

Let us approach the question of whether or not there is a "trade-off" between growth and equity through the policy space as follows. Imagine the evolution of growth and distribution to be determined by buttons on a policy instrument panel. Pressing each button can be thought of as implementing a particular policy (tariff reform, reducing fiscal deficits, reorienting public expenditure, etc.) which can be as specific and detailed as necessary. The panel can be thought of as being large enough to include all feasible policy options. Pressing combinations of buttons constitutes a policy package, and its impact on the economy is determined by the model of the economy (which for the moment we can think of as a black box under the panel). We can now ask two questions:

(1) Does there exist a (sufficiently broad, if necessary) set of policy instruments such that, if implemented, the economy will eventually achieve both higher per capita income and higher equity?

(2) Does there exist a (sufficiently narrow, if necessary) set of policy instruments such that, if implemented, the economy will, in a sufficiently short time horizon, get higher per capita income only at the expense of greater inequality and perhaps even greater poverty?

The answer to both questions, for reasonable models of the economy, is surely yes. Those who say that policy makers should not worry about the adverse effects of growth on distribution often, implicitly, have in mind configurations of policy adjustment which can deliver equity with growth over the medium run. Those who urge caution are essentially concerned that in reality, and in the short run, the range of feasible policy choices may not be broad enough to counteract the adverse distributional effects of growth. Let us return, for example, to the insightful discussion of Lewis (1983), who argued that growth typically starts in enclaves and is thus by its nature inegalitarian. Indeed, he argued that growth in the enclave might even immiserize the surrounding area because:

> The development enclave may be predatory on the traditional sectors. It may, for example, as so often in Latin America and Africa, drive people off their lands, reduce them to serfdom, or put taxes on them to force them to work for wages. It may, as Stalin did to the Russian farmers, seize their food to feed the towns; or, as Latin American elites do, turn the terms of trade against the countryside through import substitution policies …. Products of enclaves may compete with and destroy traditional trades …. Office machinery destroys clerical jobs; household equipment destroys domestic services; railways destroy porterage; the Green Revolution impoverishes those farmers who cannot use its inputs for lack of water.

Now, of course Lewis was well aware that with sufficient policy adjustment, and sufficient time, these forces could be overcome. The issue, though, is the time horizon and the range of policy instruments available. To take another example, consider the implications of reducing an excessive fiscal deficit, without which inflation will scupper the chances of investment and long-run growth, and may have long-run inequitable consequences. Clearly, the reduction in fiscal deficit can be achieved in many different ways—the short-run consequences of these different methods will be very different on short-run growth and equity. Too fast a contraction may itself adversely affect investment and growth. And the pattern of expenditure reduction can be pro-poor or not. It should be clear, therefore, that an assertion that there is no systematic relationship between growth and inequality in country level data is cold comfort to a policy maker faced with difficult policy choices, whose short term (and long term) consequences he will have to live with. Direct analysis of these policy choices is needed, and we consider some of these policies in what follows.

3.2. Macroeconomic and external sector adjustment

As noted in Section 1, from the late 1970s onward, the literature on growth and distribution took a particular turn, brought on by the debt crisis in Latin America and Africa, and the severe macroeconomic and trade distortions which this crisis revealed. These countries were diagnosed as having excessive fiscal deficits, severely misaligned exchange rates, restrictive trade policies and patterns of public expenditure which were inefficient and inequitable. We will return presently to patterns of public expenditure. But the focus on fiscal prudence and openness was enhanced by the growing realization that these were precisely the foundations of the growth with equity miracle of the East Asian economies—discussed for the case of Taiwan in the previous section. Despite the fact that these countries generally had a period of successful import substitution before they switched to export based growth strategies, it was judged that the import substitution policies in Africa and Latin America had largely failed, being both inefficient and inequitable because unlike in East Asia, they were not preceded or accompanied by policies promoting equitable agricultural growth such as land reform. This is the current mainstream view, and has been confirmed not only by detailed country case studies for East Asia but also by cross country analysis in the Kuznets tradition. Thus, Bourguignon and Morrison (1990) find that the presence of protection worsens income distribution, while Barro (1991) and Sachs and Warner (1997) are among the many authors who find that measures of trade distortion are associated with lower growth.

Accepting that a movement towards greater openness is desirable from the point of view of efficiency in the medium run, what are the distributional consequences of policy reform which moves the economy in this direction? Let us conduct the following stylized exercise (adapted from Kanbur, 1992) for an economy with an overvalued exchange rate which undertakes a devaluation (an earlier analysis is present in Knight (1976)). What this does is to increase the relative price of tradeables to nontradeables. The immediate impact effect of this is to increase the profitability of tradeable goods production and decrease that of nontradeable goods production. Thus, entrepreneurs in the tradeable goods sector benefit while those in the other sector lose. At this, first, stage the effect on inequality and poverty depends on the relative characteristics of the distribution of income within the entrepreneurial class in each production sector. At the next stage, if we assume that factors are immobile between sectors in the short run, factor prices will be bid up in the tradeable goods sector. The impact in the nontradeable sector will depend on how flexible factor prices are in that sector. If they are downwardly inflexible in the very short run, some factors will become unemployed, causing the distribution of factor income to worsen. As factor prices in this sector begin to decline with the pressure of excess supply of factors, overall factor incomes will fall relative to these in the tradeable goods sector—the impact of this on overall distribution will depend on differences in mean factor income and in factor income inequality in the two sectors. Finally, in the next phase, as factors migrate across sectors in search of higher returns, output in the tradeable goods sector will expand and that in the nontradeable goods sector will contract (which was the objective of the devaluation in the first place) but, if the conditions of the Stolper–Samuelson theorem hold, the relative return to the factor which is used more intensively in the tradeable goods sector will rise.

Much of the analysis of external sector liberalization typically jumps straight to the last stage, and looks for the distributional consequences of an increase in the return to the factor used more intensively in the tradeable goods sector. Thus, if we consider a model with labor and capital as the two factors of production, and characterize tradeables (exports and import-competing production) as labor intensive then, clearly, returns to labor will rise relative to capital. This is argued to be the mechanism for greater equity in the labor-intensive export processing booms in the East Asian economies. It has also been argued to be the mechanism which would ensure that external sector liberalization in African and Latin America, a central plank in their adjustment programs after the debt crisis, would indeed be equitable.

We will return presently to this claim, but notice the many intermediate stages— during different lengths of the "short run". It can be argued that this "short run" can be quite long in calendar time, especially in economies which do not have well developed infrastructure and well functioning factor and product markets to facilitate rapid adjustment, and it is precisely these effects which are relevant to policy makers and politicians. In the very first phase, entrepreneurs in the tradeable goods sector will benefit and those in the nontradeable goods sector will lose. Who are these entrepreneurs? The picture is complicated, and differs from country to country. The tradeable goods sector covers a wide range of situations in Africa, for example. It includes the small holder primary export sector, the mineral exporting sector, and the newly emerging nontraditional sectors such as finance or the export of cut flowers. Since in many countries the producer price of commodity exports is controlled by the government and decided on a year to year basis, the impact depends on how much of the price increase the government decides to pass though to the small farmers and, to the extent that it does not, what it does with the higher revenue. In the mineral sector, there are typically long-run contracts which specify the extent of pass through, often automatic, so that it is the mineral companies which largely benefit. And the main beneficiaries of a sudden improvement in the profitability of non-traditional exports will be those who have the capital, the skill and the contacts to take advantage of the opportunity opened up. Thus, in the tradeable sector some already rich people will benefit, although many poor farmers may also do so. On the nontradeable side, there are similar differences. Not all nontradeable production is concentrated in large, inefficient, state protected enterprises. Domestic service, or the production of food crops, is a nontradeable production (often carried out by women). Similar complications can be illustrated for the following phases. Certainly, if unemployment is created in the nontradeable sector this will add to inequality.

Faced with these complications, the literature has resorted to three types of analysis. There is, indeed a huge literature. A selection of the studies include Addison and Demery (1985), Azam et al. (1989), Bourguignon et al. (1991), Bourguignon et al. (1991), Cornia et al. (1987), Glewwe and Hall (1994), Grootaert (1995), Huppi and Ravallion (1991), Lenaghan (1992), Maasland and Van der Gaag (1992), Pinstrup-Andersen (1989), Ravallion and Huppi (1991), Ribe et al. (1990), Sahn and Sarris (1991) and Streeten (1987). The first is straightforwardly to look at outcomes on inequality and poverty before and after an adjustment package is put into place. This is very useful, and it is after all the final outcome which matters, but it does not help understand the processes involved, particularly since adjustment packages are themselves quite complex, and exogenous factors are changing all the time. The second type of exercise is to develop specialized, and highly stylized, frameworks to trace through the impact of different policy measures. Thus, for example, in Kanbur (1987a,b) the national distribution is decomposed into two subdistributions, and it is assumed that the impact of income change is uniform (additively or multiplicatively) within each subdistribution, although of course different across the subdistributions (incomes increasing in one, and decreasing in the other). Then, using the subgroup decomposable class of poverty indices of Foster et al. (1984), the impact on national poverty of various patterns of income change is analyzed (a similar analysis could, in principle, be carried out for decomposable inequality measures). Interpreting the two distributions as tradeable and nontradeable incomes, and using stylized empirical data Kanbur (1990) argues that trade liberalization is unlikely to increase poverty in the Côte d'Ivoire. The third and final type of exercise is one which models the structure of and interactions in the economy in far greater detail (e.g., Demery and

Demery, 1991; Thorbecke, 1991; Bourguignon et al., 1991a; in a general equilibrium framework. Such exercises also provide insights, particularly on the consequences of price rigidity in one sector—not surprisingly, the distributional consequences are worse Bourguignon et al. (1991). They also allow the evaluation of alternative policy packages. The difficulty, however, is that with a complicated general equilibrium framework the intuitive reasoning behind the results gets lost or, if one does succeed in providing an intuitive explanation, it is essentially by suppressing many of the complications and feedback effects (Kanbur, 1990).

The evidence on the impact of macroeconomic adjustment and external sector liberalization on inequality and poverty is mixed. Horton et al. (1997) and Berry et al. (1996) are among those who review the recent literature. For Africa, lack of data is a particular problem, since analysis requires at least two comparable household surveys which span a period of adjustment. For six such countries (Côte d'Ivoire, Kenya, Nigeria, Tanzania, Ghana and Ethiopia), Demery and Squire (1995) compare the change in percentage of population below the poverty line with the change in a weighted score of macropolicy variables (including fiscal deficit and exchange rate misalignment). In five out of these six countries, macropolicy improved and the incidence of poverty fell. In the sixth (Côte d'Ivoire), macroworsened and the percentage of poor rose. For Latin America, Morley (1994) has argued strongly that adjustment and the climb out of recession improved poverty—poverty increased in 55 out of the 58 cases of recession and it fell in 22 out of 32 recoveries. Moreover, inequality worsened during recessions and improved during the recoveries which followed adjustment. However, Berry (1995) has questioned the empirical basis of these results. He finds that income distribution worsened in Argentina, Chile, Colombia, the Dominican Republic, Ecuador, Mexico, and Uruguay, and he argues further that trade liberalization has a significant causal influence. In fact, for Africa, Demery and Squire (1996), while arguing that national income increased and poverty fell with policy reform in Africa, also note that relative inequality did increase with policy reform.

The evidence on increasing inequality raises a question which we note here but will deal with in detail later. The results on poverty (and on inequality) are the aggregation of a myriad of income changes, combining the fortunes of winners and losers. If the losing groups are sizeable, it is cold comfort that the winning groups (or, at least, their winnings) are even greater in number, so that overall poverty falls. Moreover, among the winners will be some who are very rich, and among the losers will be some who are very poor. Much of the politics of policy reform, and NGO perceptions of the consequences of reform (Watkins, 1995), are driven solely by the losers from reform. Thus, relatively well off civil servants and unionized workers may lose, as may selected groups of extremely poor people. Aggregation, while useful, loses these effects and may contribute to misperceptions and miscommunication among those who advocate reform on the basis of aggregative long term effects and those who have to deal with its disaggregated short term consequences.

Returning to the effects of trade reform on inequality, one strand of the literature has looked at skilled/unskilled wage differentials. Wood (1995) confirms Chu's (1995) analysis for Taiwan, that wage inequality increased. He also arrives at the same finding for Hong Kong, but not for Korea and Singapore. Here the relative supply of skilled workers increased rapidly enough to keep the differential in check. This highlights the importance of taking supply and demand side factors together. Again, Robbins (1995a, b) finds widening differentials for Chile, Costa Rica, Colombia, the Philippines and Argentina. A widening of differentials in Mexico after trade liberalization has been identified by a number of authors (Feenstra and Hanson, 1996; Revenga and Montenegro, 1995; and Alarcon and McKinley, 1995). In developed countries, there is a similar debate about the role of openness in driving a remarkable increase in wage inequality (Atkinson, 1995; Freeman, 1995).

We have already touched on how an opening up of the economy may influence wage differentials. If the two factor model is interpreted as one with skilled and unskilled labor, and we characterize more developed countries with having a greater relative supply of the former, then an opening up will lead to imports of unskilled labor intensive production into the developed countries from the developing countries. This will increase wage inequality in developed countries but should decrease it in developing countries (holding factor supply constant). We certainly seem to be seeing the increasing of inequality in developed countries, but its converse, decreasing inequality in developing countries, is not yet apparent in the data. As argued earlier, some of this may come simply from short run (which can be quite long) rigidities as the economy works its way through various phases of adjustment. However, Wood (1994) has argued that in a model with three types of labor the complications may survive even in the long run. He postulates a model in which labor either has no education, or basic education, or high education. He further characterizes labor-intensive manufactured exports from developing countries as requiring at least basic education. Thus, expansion of these types of exports will increase the return to those with basic education. This narrows the gap between them and those with higher education, but increases the gap vis-à-vis those with no education. The net effect is indeterminate.

The experience of Taiwan, described in the previous section, is one of an economy where almost the entire workforce had basic education by the time of the export boon of the late 1960s to the early 1980s. Thus, the policy of opening up led to higher growth *and* greater equity. But in Latin America and in Africa, and in some countries in South-East Asia, those with a sufficiently high level of education to benefit from a growth strategy of light manufacturing are quite small in number. These groups will benefit, but others will be left behind. One is beginning to see this in statistics, but behind the statistics are real people (Richburg, 1996):

The economic turning point for the Philippines ... came in 1992, when Fidel Ramos, the general who saved former president Corazon Aquina from a half-dozen coup attempts, won the presidency in his own right .... Ramos developed a plan called Philippines 2000, whose cornerstone is to lure foreign investment to designated industrial enclaves, managed by the Export Processing Zone Authority ... Cavite is home to one of the oldest zone authority enclaves .... JRA, Philippines, which makes Jordache jeans for sale in U.S. department stores, transferred to Cavite from Manila three years ago .... JRA employs 350 workers (who) can earn as much as $480 a month, which is more than school-teachers or government office workers make .... Romeo Gil M. Santos, 38 a production manager who considers himself lucky to have a job with JRA .... The factory is so well known for good wages and benefits, he said, that the demand for jobs far exceeds the number of openings .... Santos is experienced in the garment business .... Workers without previous experience in the garment business have little chance of getting a job with JRA.

Armando Rodriquez does not know how to operate machines. Rodriquez, 38, is a fisherman and owns a small boat. He remembers the days when bay fishing was good and he could earn about $120 a month in the peak season. But that was long ago ... Armando Rodriquez feels little effect of the export processing plants on his own life. 'The zone authority helps, because it is able, to provide jobs, especially for my sister', he said. 'But we small fisherfolk feel threatened, especially if the (authority) is going to expand and cover other areas ... '.

Interestingly enough, the East Asian tigers, who based their growth with equity miracle on labor-intensive exports and universal education, are themselves feeling the strain as investment moves to new areas of cheap labor surplus such as the Philippines or Bangladesh. Demand for unskilled labor has started to fall relative to supply, leading to a situation similar to that in the US industry in these countries is moving to upgrade to more skill intensive products. Robbins (1995a) and Leamer (1995) are among those who have developed analyses which suggest that such processes, which interact strongly with capital inflows, may widen skill differentials unless the supply of highly skilled labor also increases. Whether it is in the East Asian tigers, or in the poor economies of South-East Asia, Africa, and Latin America, education policy—or policy to deal with the distribution of human capital—turns out to be key, and we turn to an examination of this and other distribution policies.

3.3. Redistributive policies: land, education and transfers

In the face of possible short and long-run distributive consequences of alternative growth policies, and theoretical and empirical argument that equitable distribution of assets, in particular, can be the foundation of economic growth, a considerable literature had developed on distributive policies. In this section, we will focus on policies towards land, towards education, and on the role of transfers and the targeting of policies towards the poor.

The distribution of physical and human capital emerges from the theoretical and empirical literature as the key to the distributional consequences of growth, and as a determinant of growth itself. In the Kuznets curve literature, where the primary focus is on estimating a relationship between inequality (or poverty) and per capita income, measures of inequality in physical and human capital turn out to be significant explanatory variables, even when no clear conclusions can be drawn on the independent influence of the level or growth of income. Thus, Bourguignon (1994), Bourguignon and Morrison (1990), Papanek and Kyn (1986) and Jung (1992) are examples of innumerable studies which find that equality, and growth, benefits from universal basic education, and from a wide spread of secondary education. In addition, as noted earlier in this section,

Deininger and Squire (1996b) is the latest in a long line of studies to emphasize the role that land inequality plays in holding back growth, equity and poverty reduction, a position that was also advanced in the consensus attempted by the World Bank in its 1990 World Development Report.

An examination of the empirical literature on the consequences of land redistribution shows the difficulties of implementing such reforms in practice. There is, of course, the basic political economy problem that in most countries where the land distribution is highly unequal, the landed elites tend to control the political process. The land redistribution in Taiwan and Korea occurred under very special war-related circumstances. The literature is replete with examples of attempts at redistribution which were circumvented in practice by the elites (see Bardhan, 1984). Some particular method of land reform, such as restrictions on tenancy, can actually harm the poor in the absence of effective ownership ceilings because landlords will, quite simply, take land out of the renting market, thereby reducing a source of income for the landless poor. As noted by Chu (1995) there were effective ownership restrictions in Taiwan, enforced by mandated selling at below market prices by those above the ceiling. Moreover, since a large proportion of land was in public ownership, sales could be controlled by the government. But the key here was the fact that the Nationalist government (perhaps in response to developments in mainland China in the 1940s and 1950s) was determined to achieve an equal land distribution. Attempts in Latin America to collectivize farming have failed (Thiesenhusen, 1989). In Africa, the distribution of landholding at independence was highly unequal in many Eastern and Southern African countries but relatively equal in Western Africa. In Zimbabwe, for example, almost two decades after a government committed to land redistribution took over, land inequality remains acute, and the source of highly unequal distributional outcomes. At the same time, the Ujaama experiment of collective farming in Tanzania is generally recognized to have been a failure.

Lipton and Ravallion (1995) argue that even if effective land redistribution can be effected, its impact on distributional outcomes may not be as large as might appear at first sight.

The rural poor usually do overlap substantially with those who own and or operate little or no land. But there are exceptions. Rural teachers, shopkeepers, and artisians are often welloff though landless; in parts of West Africa rural nonfarm employment, not occupancy of farmland, appears to predict lower risk of poverty (Hill, 1972; Reardon et al., 1992). Conversely, households that own and operate as much as 3 or 4 hectares of bad land can be very poor; in Western India, they are no likelier to escape poverty than are the landless (Visaria, 1980; Lipton, 1985). In better farming areas, lack of land is a clear *correlate* of poverty, but it is an imperfect one; this constrains the prospects of reducing aggregate rural poverty by land based redistributions. (Ravallion and Sen, 1994)

The above also highlights the large variations in the possible impact of land redistribution—from the very high man-land ratios in South Asia to conditions approaching "land surplus" in parts of Africa, from good quality irrigated and intensely cultivated land dedicated to single crops to poor quality, rainfed land with multiple cropping, from historically highly unequal distributions to areas where distribution is already relatively equal, from countries coming out of experiments in large scale collectivist farming, to countries where most land is already privately owned, and so on. Add to this the political economy constraints, and the fact that land is by no means a perfect correlate for income, and we can see why the literature, while agreeing on the importance and efficacy of land reform in theory, is much less bullish on the practicalities of such reform.

In fact, there is a far greater consensus in the literature on the importance, and the feasibility, of improving the distribution of education (and health) in the population (see Anand and Ravallion, 1993). There is now almost total consensus that universal basic education is a necessary condition for sustained equitable growth. Special emphasis is put on girls education, since this in turn reinforces not only the health of children but also the equality of intra-household distribution, an issue we shall take up in the next section. In fact basic education is distributed quite unequally in most poor countries. The adult literacy rate, for example, is close to 100% in the industrialized countries. In the newly industrializing countries of East Asia, it is also high—97.6% in Korea, 90.3% in Singapore, 93.6% in Thailand and 82.2% in Malaysia. But in Nigeria this figure is 12.8%, in Burkina Faso 18.0%, in Pakistan 36.4 and 50.6% in India (see UNDP, 1996). With these figures, it should be clear why a strategy based on exports whose manufacture requires labor with basic education (Wood, 1994) would be equitable in Korea but inequitable in Burkina Faso or Pakistan. Clearly, for all countries that fall below it, as rapid a move as possible to universal basic education has to be the priority.

Not surprisingly, once we move beyond basic education to the secondary and tertiary levels, inequalities increase. The implications of inequalities in high levels of skill, in those countries specializing in skill-intensive production and exports, are worrying. Countries like Taiwan, as their unskilled labor- intensive export strategy comes face-to-face with huge pools of equivalent but lower wage labor in mainland China, Vietnam, and so on, have to move to skill intensive production. But higher levels of education are distributed much more unequally than basic education. Unless Taiwan accelerates the equalization of higher levels of education, the required growth strategy will be disequalizing.

Thus, the redistributive policies needed in the area of education vary from country to country. In the poorest countries, equalization of basic education is needed to ensure equitable, labor intensive manufactures based growth. In the newly industrializing countries, the urgent need is to upgrade labor force skills and education to the next highest level. This is not the place to discuss the technicalities of implementing education policy in developing countries. Suffice it to say that in most countries in Africa, Latin America and south East Asia, public expenditure on basic education is disproportionately low. In Burkina Faso, 32% of public expenditure on education is on the tertiary level, and in Egypt it is 37% compared to 30% in Hong Kong, 16% in Malaysia and only 7% in Korea (UNDP, 1996). While efficiency of such expenditure is clearly important, figures like those for Burkina Faso and Egypt are not consistent with a policy to equalize basic education. (There is a large literature on allocation of public expenditure e.g., Foxley, 1979; Meerman, 1979; Selowsky, 1979; Selden and Wasylenko, 1994; etc.)

While accelerating skill upgrading in the population is a key policy, this is not something that can be achieved overnight, or even quickly enough to match the pace of change in labor demand. But for the poorest countries, with very large numbers of people with minimal or no education, it may take quite some time to approach even moderate spread of basic education. As discussed earlier, in the meantime a light manufactures exports led strategy will then lead to greater inequality, and perhaps even immiserization of those with no education. This suggests that policy should first and foremost target those with no education, and with little prospect of crossing over into the ranks of the educated over a five to ten year horizon. This seems to be the analytical basis of the call from many NGOs (for example, Watkins, 1995) for a focus not on an outward oriented, export based growth strategy but one which targets increasing food production yields ("food self-sufficiency"), particularly by women. This, together with basic education, health and infrastructure targeted at rural areas is the core of their proposed strategy for equitable growth, particularly in Africa. While overall growth may indeed be lower (though this point is not fully conceded) its pattern will benefit the poor.

For the newly industrializing countries, there remains the prospect that, over a five to ten year horizon, while those with higher levels of education will benefit, those with lower or no levels of education may lose out. In Taiwan and Korea unskilled unemployment is on the rise, causing social tensions in its wake—a phenomenon well known from OECD countries in the last ten years. And the fact has to be faced that there may be a significant number of people who cannot be retrained or retrained quickly enough, to meet the new realities. For these people, transfers of income must form an important component of survival. An analytical framework for thinking through this problem in its most general form is provided in Kanbur and Tuomala (1994). Using the Mirrlees (1971) model of optimum income taxation, they ask—what happens to the extent and nature of the *optimal* degree of redistribution (i.e., redistribution which takes into account incentive effects) when *inherent* inequality (in the Mirrlees model, the inequality of underlying labour productivity) increases? The answer, perhaps obvious, is that the optimum income tax system becomes more progressive, taxing the better off at higher rates to support the less well off. Changes in the global trading and production environment, discussed throughout this paper, can be interpreted as having increased inherent or underlying inequality in developed, newly industrializing and developing countries. Thus, one of the policy responses should be a greater willingness to redistribute through the tax and transfer system. There is a huge literature on appropriate targeting of public expenditures and transfers so that they do indeed reach those less well off, prompted by many failures of the 1960s, 1970s and 1980s, where expenditures ostensibly intended for the poor ended up in the hands of the nonpoor (e.g., Cornia and Stewart, 1995; Cox and Jimenez, 1994; Datt and Ravallion, 1993, 1994; Foxley, 1979; Grosh, 1994; Hammer et al., 1994; Meerman, 1979; Ravallion, 1993; Van de Walle, 1994).

The Mirrlees (1971) model of optimal nonlinear income taxation is, in fact, a prototype model of income based targeting, except that it also deals integrally with the issue of raising revenues. Among the best recognized results from this paper, and the literature that followed it, are that (under certain conditions) marginal tax rate should be zero at the top and the bottom end of the distribution, and that the marginal tax rates fall over the bulk of the income range. The US literature of the 1960s and 1970s on the negative income tax is in this tradition, facing explicitly the tradeoff between providing sufficiently high transfers to the poor and the high marginal tax rates that this would necessitate further up the income distribution if the government's budget constraint were to be met. Akerlof (1978) was one of the first to point out this tension could be eased somewhat if the government could distinguish individuals not only by their income but by other easily observable and monitorable characteristics. The information base of the government would expand, and the overall effect on social welfare was bound to be beneficial. Immonen, Kanbur et al. (1998) are among those who follow this tradition of combining targeting by income relation and targeting by contingent or group characteristics. It is shown in Immonen et al. (1998) that allowing for such group specific income tax schedules can make significant gains compared to the case where no group differentiation is allowed. Moreover, the group specified schedules can have very different properties from the single schedule case. Thus, for example, one of the stylized findings of calculations based on the Mirrlees (1971) model (see Tuomala, 1990), is that with the usually assumed range of overall revenue requirement of 10–30%, marginal tax rates tend to fall over a large part of the distribution. However, Immonen et al. (1998) show that with two groups the tax schedule for the poorer group can display increasing marginal tax rates over a significant range. This is attributed to the fact that in the optimum a relatively large transfer is required for the poorer group, and we can thus interpret the problems as choosing an optimal nonlinear schedule for this group with a large *negative* revenue requirement, a range of parameters not considered by the earlier, Mirrlees-inspired, literature.

Kanbur and Keen (1989) derive results for the two group case by restricting attention to the class of linear income tax schedules. However, it can be argued with the administrative weaknesses in most developing countries, *any* form of income contingent transfer is problematic if not infeasible. A literature has thus developed on targeting of income and expenditure transfers which rely solely on observable characteristics of individuals or household—every unit with the same characteristic is treated identically, and indeed given a uniform transfer. The basic analytics of this framework are developed in Kanbur (1987a) for the case of two group distributions, and an overall budget for disbursement. It is assumed that any budget allocated to a group will raise all incomes in the group in *identical* fashion—this can be an additive increase, or multiplicative increase. Rules of thumb are then derived for reallocation of budget based only on observable summary statistics of group distribution (the actual analysis is carried out for poverty indices, but the application is much broader). This type of "indicator targeting" is sometimes used in practice in its pure form, but more often it is used indirectly—for example, by targeting the housing renovation budget to poorer areas, or restricting supplementary feeding programs to particular districts, or restricting transfers to those above (or below) a certain age (Grosh, 1995). While the details differ, the basic framework, and trade-offs, are very similar. Ravallion and Chao (1989) apply this framework to a simulation exercise showing how much improvement in targeting of a given transfer budget there would be if, instead of being divided equally among the rural population, it were optimally targeted to different categories of land holding. They find some improvement, but still significant leakage because land holding is not a perfect correlate of low living standards.

Food subsidies have always been an enormously popular method of attempting to target the poor. Fairly obviously, the efficacy of this method depends on which items are being subsidized. Besley and Kanbur (1988) derive rules for targeting these subsidies if the objective is poverty minimization—under various conditions. For example, one of the key indicators turns out be the ratio of the consumption by the poor of a commodity to the total consumption of that commodity in the economy. Commodities for which this ratio is higher should attract a higher subsidy. The intuition behind this is as follows. A unit reduction in the price of a commodity is equivalent to a transfer of purchasing power in proportion to the consumption of that commodity. Thus, total consumption of that commodity is proportional to the budgetary cost of the subsidy while the consumption of the poor is proportional to the impact on poverty (the latter relation is exact for certain measures of poverty). Hence, the "poverty reduction per unit of budgetary cost" is proportional to the proposed ratio. Of course, in practice it turns out that food subsidies are not allocated according to this or similarly motivated rules.

Another method of making transfers which has received attention in the literature is based on employment. Ravallion (1991) and others have examined the efficacy of Employment Guarantee Schemes in the Indian state of Maharashtra and elsewhere. The schemes in India date back from the Famine codes of the British colonial era. The idea is that instead of simply making unconditional transfers, or transfers based on socio-demographic characteristics, a public works scheme will be set up at which labor will be hired at a given wage rate. Obviously, only those for whom income in alternative time-use is lower than this wage will turn up. If it is assumed that these are the poor group, then the scheme targets through self selection. Of course, the targeting is not perfect. For example, the old and the infirm will not benefit from an employment based scheme. But as Ravallion's (1991) survey shows, in practice such schemes will target the poor relatively well, and create local infrastructure in addition. However, one of the lessons from all these experiences is on the importance of administrative capacity to manage such schemes.

Thus, if, as we have argued in this paper, there is sometimes a tendency for the growth process to accentuate inequality or even immiserize certain groups in the population, even if only in the "short run", targeting of transfers in cash and kind may be one policy response. On the face of it, this seems quite attractive—simply identify (directly or indirectly) those who are poor or adversely affected by the changes in question, and target either transfers or income raising interventions to them. But, as Besley and Kanbur (1993) warn, targeting should not be seen as a panacea—or, at least, it should not be seen as costless. They identify three principal problems. First, implicit in the notion of targeting is the feature that as the individual or household gets better off the benefit is withdrawn. This is true whether the transfer is in cash, in kind, or in terms of help with productive inputs (e.g., credit for farmers, school scholarships for children from poor households, etc.). It is also true whether the targeting is based directly on measures of the standard of living, or on group characteristics based on indicators. To different degrees, the basic feature that for targeting to be effective benefits have to be withdrawn rapidly as the poverty threshold is crossed will mean, in effect, high marginal tax rates on the poor. The trade off between incentive and targeting effects will have to be managed, as shown in Kanbur et al. (1994).

The second problem highlighted by Besley and Kanbur (1993) is that of administrative costs and capacity. The more sophisticated and "fine" a targeting system, the greater its requirements in terms of administrative input. Anand and Kanbur (1991) discuss the administrative problems caused by the reform of Sri Lanka's rice ration system in the late 1970s. Before the reforms, there was a general rice ration, delivered through the public distribution system which had been set up during the war and functioned quite well. But, because this general subsidy had a high rate of leakage to the poor, it was decided to target the rice ration only to those households with income below a certain level. Thus, rolls had to be developed and maintained on eligible households. For a start, the criteria themselves were more complex than a simple income level—there were different income levels for different household sizes. And there was the issue of "cleaning out" the rolls every year—an administrative and political nightmare. Ultimately the new scheme was introduced and did function, but such detailed engineering would be even more problematic in a country without such a high level of administrative competence as Sri Lanka is recognized to have.

The third problem with targeting as a panacea is political. There are good political reasons why transfers are not finely targeted to the poor in most societies—including developed ones. The Sri Lanka case is again instructive. As Anand and Kanbur (1991) note, after the reforms which retargeted the rice ration budget to the poor, this budget itself declined (the value of the subsidy was allowed to be eroded by inflation) without eliciting any of the protest that earlier attempts to reduce the generalized subsidy had given rise to. Quite simply, those above the (low) income threshold which cut off the subsidy were no longer interested in the level of the subsidy—the poor were left to their own political devices. Besley (1997) discusses this political economy dimension of targeting, and he points out the limits of fine targeting as a redistributive device when the overall degree of redistribution in the economy is itself subject to a political game.

4. Beyond national income distributions

Up to now we have more or less restricted ourselves to the national income distribution. But many of the issues in the realm of income distribution invite us to go beyond the national income distribution in different dimensions. First, while the focus in this paper, and indeed in the literature, has been the distribution of income (or consumption) between households or individuals, many important aspects of the political economy of the development process concern distribution across racial, ethnic or regional groups. Second, there has been a great increase in attention paid to *intra-household* distribution, including distribution by gender. And third, going from a lower to a higher level of aggregation, an important strand of the literature addresses the issue of the global distribution of income, in particular, the gaps in per capita income between nations. We will discuss these three extensions to the core literature on income distribution and development in this section.

4.1. Inter-group distribution

The core literature on Income Distribution and Development is strangely silent on interracial or inter-ethnic dimensions of distribution as development proceeds, while the daily political discourse in many countries, particularly in Africa, has this as a constant topic of discussion and tension. The recent ethnic strife in Central Africa, which is recognized to be at least in part based on distributional struggle, or the acknowledged success of Malaysia's active management of interethnic distributional issues, should raise some questions on why so little attention is paid in the analytical literature to these issues.

One reason, it seems to us, is the inexorable pull in the literature towards an individualistic Utilitarian social welfare function which sees social welfare simply as an (additive) aggregate of individual well-being derived from consumption. With this overall framework, it is not surprising that inter-group issues are seen primarily and merely as contributing to a discussion of interpersonal distributional issues, rather than being important in their own right. Thus, for example, Anand (1983) and others decomposed aggregate, national inequality in the interpersonal distribution of income in Malaysia into its "within ethnic-group" and "between ethnic-group" components for data from the 1970s. The ethnic dimension of distribution between Malays, Chinese and Indians came to the fore when the country was torn apart by race riots in the late 1960s, and the government formulated its New Economic Plan to foster growth and stability. From the three group decomposition of standard inequality indices such as the Theil index, it was possible to distinguish between the "between group component" of inequality (i.e., the interpersonal inequality that would remain if incomes within each group were equalized) and the "within group component" (i.e., the inequality that would remain if the mean of the three groups were equalized at the national mean through proportional scaling). Through such an "analysis of variance" it turned out that the between group component of inequality was "only" around 15%. It was these quantitative magnitudes that led Anand (1983) and others to argue that the dominant component of the government's strategy had to be within group inequality and not, as was the case in the New Economic Plan, between group differences.

The point is, of course, that such a focus on the interpersonal distribution misses one of the central factors in Malaysia's success in the last quarter century. After the race riots of the late 1960s, ethnic harmony has been restored and social stability is one of the key factors mentioned by foreign investors to explain their choice of Malaysia over other destinations where labor costs are lower. Social stability and racial harmony are indeed important components of the social infrastructure that any society has to offer, and this breaks down once the interracial differences—the *average* differences between groups—go beyond a critical threshold. What this threshold is varies from society to society—but the fact that it exists cannot be denied.

The effect of ethnicity on growth and distribution is most discussed in Africa, where the overlay of nation states on intersecting tribal jurisdictions give a high degree of ethnic fragmentation. Bates (1981) is an example of a political science based analysis. Easterly and Levine (1997) use an ethnic fragmentation variable in a cross-section econometric study of growth in Africa and find the variable to be significant. But a richer analysis of the interplay between ethnicity, growth and distribution is possible only with a case study approach, and several papers in the political science literature do this. We will highlight one such paper (Austin, 1996) which illustrates well the nature of this approach, and its contrast with the standard focus on interpersonal distribution. Austin's focus is development, distribution and ethnicity leading up to the mass killings of 1994 in Rwanda, an attempted genocide of the Tutsi minority by the Hutu majority. He considers two views in the literature of the importance of ethnicity in sub-Saharan Africa:

One is the argument that ethnicity is 'primordial', meaning that it is an original and permanent feature of African societies, with the implication that economic variables are neither a cause of ethnic conflict nor, potentially, a means of reducing it. At the other extreme is the view that ethnicity is of no causal importance in itself, being simply a channel through which other causes (economic included) operate. If that is so, it follows that ethnic tensions could be reduced or even eliminated by the creation of appropriate economic conditions. The argument of this (paper) is that both views are mistaken, and specifically that they are mistaken *because they are ahistorical*. Rather, we should recognize the historicity of ethnicity, in the double sense that ethnic identities are "constructed" in particular historical contexts, and are therefore malleable; but, on the other hand, that they are malleable only in ways constrained by the very paths through which they evolved. The operational implications of this are correspondingly double- edged. On the 'optimistic' side, ethnic divisions do change, and, more specifically, the risks of ethnic war can be reduced by economic policy. But, more 'pessimistically', they cannot be changed easily, because past experiences and the perceptions of these experiences condition present responses to new policies and incentives. Applying these to Rwanda yields the propositions (a) that it is worth specifically trying to devise economic incentives for interethnic cooperation, but, (b) that these are unlikely to be very effective unless certain political conditions are met which would increase trust between different ethnic groups.

For our purposes, the interaction between distribution and ethnic conflict, for which Austin (1996) supplies more than enough evidence, is the most important conclusion to draw from his analysis. He shows that while there is not much evidence of major disparities, on average, between Hutus and Tutsi's in the rural areas of Rwanda, the fears of a land grab by Tutsi's in the wake of a victory by their rebel (RPF) army, motivated individual and group acts of murder by the Hutus of their Tutsi neighbors in their local areas. Thus, growing rural poverty exacerbated an ethnic conflict which already had deep historical roots. In urban areas, the ethnic distribution of public sector jobs had always been divisive. There were explicit programs to redistribute these jobs under different regimes in favor of Hutus. The fear of these jobs disappearing if there should be a Tutsi victory, or improving the prospect of promotion or advancement for oneself or one's relatives by literally eliminating Tutsis in jobs, seems to have been the reason why a large number of lower level Hutu civil servants (including teachers) participated in the massacres in the capital and smaller towns.

What about future policy? The Rwanda case is illustrative, in extreme form, of the problem of growth and distribution faced by many if not most African countries. The countries desperately need growth in order to oil the wheels of ethnic compromise. But if the "standard" measures such as openness, privatization of state-owned enterprises, land distribution, etc., have impact effects which are ethnically differentiated, then the very social equilibrium which policy makers are trying to sustain may be disrupted. There are two points to be made here—first, that the real issues faced by policy makers on the ground are not so much the impact of growth inducing policies on measures of inequality and poverty in the interpersonal distribution of income but whether their impact is likely to be acceptable to the social and ethnic consensus. Second, there may well be a *short term* tradeoff between fast growth and ethnic equilibrium, depending on the specifics of the case. Thus, Malaysia's spectacular growth performance in the last decade, based primarily on a surge of foreign investment, is based on the social equilibrium fashioned through redistribution in the decade before of sluggish growth. For Rwanda, Austin (1996) warns us to be careful about the interethnic aspects of privatization policy, for example:

In principle, if state monopolies merely become private monopolies without effective regulation, the result may be a further opportunity for the appropriation of rents. If the state itself remains an ethnic monopoly, those rents are likely to accrue exclusively to be selected members of the dominant ethnic group. Indeed, precisely this is alleged to have happened in privatizations carried out in the terminal period of the old regime (Prunier, 1995). Even foreign ownership would not necessarily solve the inter-ethnic problem in employment unless the companies have incentives to avoid discrimination. Whatever the form of ownership, there must be a strong case for the introduction of ethnic monitoring of employment.

Austin makes a similar case for a range of policies, and the parallels with the policy discussion in Malaysia in the late 1960s and early 1970s should be clear.

We have argued that extensive use of standard measures of inequality and poverty, which are built up from individual income/consumption, and which are "decomposable", assists the easy slide into a neglect of inter-group inequality in the current literature. Foster and Sen (1996) have recently challenged the reasonableness of the axiomatic foundations of decomposability, which essentially posit an excessive degree of independence of supposedly irrelevant outcomes elsewhere in the distribution. These axioms, while leading to a convenient class of measures which have become the work horse of the theoretical and empirical literature, go against basic institution and considerable evidence which suggest that individuals do indeed pay special attention to outcomes for their particular racial, ethnic or regional group—perhaps because this embodies a prediction of their own prospects in an uncertain world. The literature on inequality and poverty measurement now needs to axiomatize group dependence, and develop corresponding measures. Such a development would help the broader literature focus on the undoubted importance of intergroup distribution in the interactions between income distribution and development.

4.2. Intra-household distribution

The most commonly used procedure for constructing an income or consumption distribution is as follows. From a household survey, a measure is constructed of total consumption (or income) for each household. While there may be data on income earned or time-use patterns by individuals, consumption data is typically collected at the household level. If a household has total income y and number of members n, this is treated as n observations of consumption y/n each. Many exercises also take into account differing consumption needs by using adult equivalent scales. However, the basic feature of the construct should be clear—total household consumption is divided equally among all members of the household adjusting for need.

This basic assumption has been questioned in recent years from a number of different directions, starting with the pioneering work of Sen (1983), which looked at vastly different outcomes by gender within the household, at different ages. The figures, which range from food consumption to hospitalization to mortality rates, confirm a significant gender bias, at least in South Asia. A huge literature has developed to substantiate and extend this work, a selection of the papers includes: Alderman et al., 1995; Bardhan, 1982, 1985; Haddad et al., 1995; Browning, 1992; Chen et al, 1981; Dasgupta, 1987; Garcia, 1991; Greenhalgh, 1985; Haddad, 1991; Haddad and Kanbur, 1990, 1992; Kanbur and Haddad, 1994; Harriss, 1990; Louat et al., 1993; Standing, 1985; Svedberg, 1990; Thomas, 1990).

As an example, consider Haddad and Kanbur (1990), which uses *individual* level calorie-intake data from a special survey conducted in the Philippines. The data problems and issues are discussed in the paper. The basic argument is that since we have individual level data we can calculate "true" measures of inequality and poverty, and then compare these with what we would have got had we gone the traditional route of calculating total consumption at the household level. Not surprisingly, the traditional method will always understate inequality and poverty as measured by "Lorenz-sensitive" measures. But by how much? Haddad and Kanbur (1990) show that the understatement can be significant—about 30–40% for this dataset. However, what about use of the conventional approach for targeting—for ranking different socio-demographic groups by their inequality and poverty? Here, it is shown that such rankings do not change when based on household characteristics—thus, for example, the ranking of groups by region or by primary crops grown does not change dramatically when comparing the "true" situation with that which would be revealed under the conventional method of collecting consumption data only at the household level. However, the relative rankings of groups by individual characteristics, e.g., men versus women, is indeed sensitive to what type of data is used—indicating that intra- household inequality has a strong gender dimension.

Another cut at the issue of intra-household allocation is through tests of the "income-pooling" restriction. In the standard neoclassical model of the household, which maximizes a common utility function, consumption patterns should depend only on total household income and not on who earns that income. If, however, intra-household allocation patterns are determined by bargaining between different parties, we would expect that the income pooling restriction would not hold. While there is still some room for debate because the econometric results can be interpreted in different ways, Alderman et al. (1995), in their review, argue that the consensus is moving away from the "unitary" model of the household to the "collective" model.

Once one allows departures from the "unitary" model of the household, there are profound implications for policy. Among other things, it opens up the question as to whether it is the household or individuals within a household who are the targets of transfer policies. In many developed countries there is a perennial debate as to whether child benefit should be paid through the tax system (so that it would typically be the father who brings home the money) or through the social security system (so that it would typically be the mother who picks up the money at the social security office), a debate which would be meaningless if income-pooling were the norm. The evaluation of supplementary feeding programs in developing countries which target undernourished children at the feeding stations has to be tempered with the realization that the extra glass of milk at the station could mean a glass of milk less at home for the child. Employment guarantee schemes have to worry about the differential impact of male and female hiring on the allocation of resources to women and children in the household.

As an important example of how gender bias in the intra-household allocation of resources can affect policy analysis, consider the literature discussed in the previous section on structural adjustment and distribution. There, it was argued that measures such as a devaluation, which increase the profitability of tradable goods production relative to nontradable goods production, will have a beneficial effect on poverty because the incidence of poverty in the nontradable goods sector was lower than that in the tradable goods sector. But the empirical basis of this claim, as in Kanbur (1990), are standard household surveys which collect information on consumption only at the household level. Thus, typically households are classified by occupation or activity of the head of the household or, for farm households, the dominant source of income. This would be reasonable if income pooling was the norm. But it is not, and add to this the fact that there are significant differences between men and women in farm activity—in many African countries, men control the cash crop plot and women control the food crop plot. The former is typically an exportable such as cocoa, while the latter is nontradable such as roots and tubers. Moreover, childbearing and child rearing, the quintessential nontraded activity, is largely the domain of women. With these structural characteristics, we might expect some negative impact of the standard macrolevel terms of trade adjustments on women. The framework developed in Kanbur (1987a, b) and elsewhere cannot accommodate the possibility of such effects, which have been highlighted by many NGOs (Watkins, 1995).

Thus, the area of intra-household resource allocation without income pooling is one of the most exciting new areas in the analysis of income distribution and development. Once income pooling is abandoned, a number of interesting theoretical, empirical and policy issues arise which the literature has only just begun tackling.

4.3. Global distribution

Having worked on income distribution within a country, it might be tempting to analyze the evolution of income distribution in *the world as a whole*. The overall distribution of income in the world is conceptually simply a population weighted sum of national distributions. Thus, overall inequality depends upon inequality within each country, the population shares, and per capita incomes across countries. Overall poverty can be derived applying a common poverty line across the global distribution (e.g., Chen et al., 1994). Such exercises are fraught with methodological and data problems, ranging from establishing income comparability across different countries, through the conceptual basis of a common poverty standard for all countries, to the comparability of disparate household surveys across countries (plus the fact that some countries do not have any worth using).

But, nevertheless, there seems to be a demand in international policy circles for such work—at least for global numbers on "the poor". Lipton and Ravallion (1995) summarize the sorts of results that can be obtained:

Recent estimates following this methodology indicate that about one-fifth of the population of the developing world in the mid-1980s had a real consumption level less than India's poverty line of about $23 per month in 1985 U.S. prices (adjusted for cost-of-living differences between countries). At a more generous poverty line of $31 per month—one dollar per day—the head-count index of poverty increases to about one in three. There are no strictly comparable earlier estimates, but the proportion of people poor has probably fallen since the mid-1970s, while the absolute number of poor has probably increased. However, these aggregates hide great regional diversity, for example, while the proportion who are consumption poor has declined in much of Asia it has probably increased in sub- Saharan Africa and Latin America during the 1980s. (World Bank, 1990; Chen et al., 1994)

It is unclear what exactly the policy implications are of such estimates of global income distribution. As for poverty, its calculation is dominated by assumptions and adjustment to measures of per capita income—technical adjustments to the China data can, and do, swing the estimates around considerably. But the influence of per capita income is behind another standard issue in the "global income distribution" literature—that on whether or not per capita income converge or diverge. There is considerable controversy on the theory of such evolution, on the empirical evidence for it, and on what it might mean for policy.

In the standard Solow neoclassical model of growth, the economy tends to a steady state of constant per capita income, with a negative relationship between per capita income and the growth rate on the path to the steady state. Thus, if all countries followed this model with the same technology, savings and population growth assumptions, there would be *absolute convergence* towards the common steady state per capita level of income. The *conditional convergence* hypothesis predicts the same outcome of a negative relationship between per capita income and growth rate in per capita income, and the consequent convergence to the same per capita income in the long run, but only for those countries which have the same preferences, technologies, rates of population growth, government policy, etc. But Galor (1996) argues that both of these hypotheses are related to the unique and globally stable steady state equilibrium in the standard neoclassical growth models, so that the long-run evolution of the economy is determined independently of initial conditions. If the dynamic system had multiple, locally stable, equilibria, then in order to converge to the same steady state countries would have to have not only the same technologies, etc. but also not be too different in their initial conditions. This is christened the *club convergence hypothesis*. In this framework, countries can indeed diverge in the long run, and transitory shocks (and policy) can alter the long-run equilibrium. As Galor (1996) notes:

Once the neoclassical growth models are augmented so as to capture additional empirically significant elements such as human capital, income distribution, and fertility, along with capital market imperfections, externalities, nonconvexities, and imperfectly competitive market structure, club convergence emerges under broader plausible configurations. The incorporation of human capital formation into basic growth models provides an environment in which club convergence is a viable theoretical hypothesis under plausible scenarios. Countries that are identical in their structural characteristics but differ in their initial level or distribution of human capital may cluster around different steady state quilibria in the presence of social increasing returns to scale from human capital accumulation (e.g., Lucas, 1988; Azariadis and Drazen, 1990), capital market imperfections (e.g., Galor and Zeira, 1993), parental and local effects in human capital formation (e.g., Benabou, 1996; Durlauf, 1996; Galor and Tsiddon, 1994), imperfect information (e.g., Tsiddon, 1992) and nonconvex production function of human capital (e.g., Becker et al., 1990)

There is considerable empirical literature on whether or not per capita income levels in fact converge over time. Kuznets (1966, 1971) had already discussed this issue. In the 1980s, the work of Baumol (1986) and others drew considerable interest. In the 1990s, Barro (1991), Barro and Sala-I-Martin (1992, 1995), Mankiw et al. (1992) are among the best known papers in a large and growing literature. In a recent paper, Pritchett (1997) argues that the following eight facts characterize the pattern of growth rates in the last century or so: (i) massive divergence in absolute and relative per capita income; (ii) steady and near equal growth rates amongst the leaders in the long run; (iii) the currently poor countries have had very low growth historically; (iv) in the modern period, some countries that began poor in 1960 continued to stagnate; (v) but other countries who started poor had extremely rapid growth; (vi) growth rates have varied dramatically across developing countries; (vii) growth over time for individual developing countries has also been highly variable; and (viii) growth rates in developing countries have not been characterized by persistence.

These stylized facts obviously reject simple absolute convergence. They also indicate support for the club convergence hypothesis. Certainly, getting the structural features right can change the growth prospects for a country—the "conditioning" variables in standard regression tests are the usual ones such as physical and capital accumulation rates. So can "initial conditions" which include, for example, the initial distribution of land holdings. It is possible to understand the development of Taiwan, discussed earlier in the paper, in terms of the fortuitous initial condition of a relatively equal land distribution, as the result of the war, and continual policy adjustment, which kept the country on an equitable growth path. Perhaps the most worrying aspect of early discussions of, and seeming support for, "convergence" was the tendency to sideline policy—if "convergence" was the norm, there was nothing that could be done but accept lower growth rates for the leaders, and perhaps all the laggards had to do was to wait for "convergence" to pull them up. The theoretical and empirical literature of the last two decades has laid to rest such simplistic tendencies. Convergence has not come to the rescue of the poor countries who have stagnated since 1960. On the other hand, there are very clear policy reasons for why those countries which have grown rapidly have done so. In short, there is no underlying law for the world distribution of income to either equalize or disequalize—whether this happens or not is very much the aggregate effect of a myriad of policy decisions taken at the country level.

5.   Conclusion: directions for the the next decade

The literature on income distribution and development ends the twentieth century in a vibrant state, with the new conditions of the time raising new questions, and old questions anew. We would like to highlight the following promising directions for the next decade from this review of the literature.

5.1.   Country case studies

We have shown that the literature of the last three decades is dominated by an approach which drives for an aggregative, reduced form relationship between measures of inequality and measures of development, often tested with data from a cross-section of countries. We have argued that such exercises are useful as far as they go, but they have severe limitations either as tests of alternative hypotheses on the development process itself, or as indicators of what policy responses are appropriate. A superior approach is one which looks at country experiences in their historical and policy detail, and approaches the issues of policy directly and specifically—relying on cross country regressions of inequality on per capita income or growth to support or contradict a policy "tradeoff" between the two does not seem to have been very productive.

5.2.   Increasing inequality

By the late 1980s and early 1990s, it seemed as though the literature had approached a consensus, towards the view that growth with equity was definitely a feasible option. The experience of East Asia, and analysis of the macroeconomic distortions in Africa and Latin America, seemed to suggest that it was possible to have more growth and more equity. But, it seems, that no sooner had the consensus been formulated than it began to be questioned by developments, not least in East Asia. Skill-biased technical progress, and vast increases in the global supply of unskilled labor as the result of greater openness, have together begun to widen inequality in many countries—even if poverty continued to decline. The analysis of these new trends, and the possible policy responses to them, will keep the literature active in the years to come.

5.3. Disaggregation

Many of the key policy issues in the area of income distribution and development show themselves in very *disaggregated* fashion. Thus, if overall measured poverty falls as development proceeds, but this is the aggregation of improvements and deteriorations in poverty across the country, quite often the real policy story—or certainly an important component of it—is the plight of those immiserized by the process. The literature needs to focus more on these disaggregated effects. Similarly, if overall inequality in the inter-personal distribution of income remains unchanged, or even it improves the real policy consequences may flow from charges in various intergroup distributions of income—for example, movements in the ratios of ethnic mean incomes in an ethnically divided society. The individualistic tendency in inequality measurement, which is reinforced by the use of convenient decomposable inequality measures, skates over these intergroup issues which will demand increasingly greater attention.

5.4. Intra-household allocation

Until the mid-1980s, the intra-household and gender dimension of income distribution and development had not received sufficient attention in the analytical literature. But in the last decade, driven to some extent by growing policy concerns, considerable work on this topic has begun. Analytically, the area spans work on intrahousehold allocation, models of discrimination, disaggregated measurement of inequality and poverty, and intergenerational transmission of disadvantage. The policy importance is given by the fact that many policy instruments may have a gender differentiated impact, and gender based targeting may be a key policy approach to enhancing not only distribution but also growth.

5.5. Alternative modes of redistribution

If it is true that globalization and technical progress will create strong forces for in-creasing inequality in the early decades of the next century, it stands to reason that redistribution will come to the fore in the policy discussion, just as it did in the 1960s and 1970s. The task of the analytical literature will be to learn from the mistakes (and successes) of extensive attempts in these decades to redistribute, and to provide pol-icy makers with a framework for discussion and with rankings of alternative forms of redistribution—particularly where transfers are concerned. These issues will not go away—indeed, they may reappear in even stronger form in the next decade.

These five areas—country specific analysis, new inequality trends, disaggregated approaches, intra-household allocation and alternative forms of redistribution—stand out as requiring further research in the coming decade. There is every prospect, then, that the literature on distribution and development will continue to excite and interest economists in the years to come.

References

Addison, T. and L. Demery (1985), Macroeconomic stabilization, income distribution and poverty a preliminary survey, Overseas Development Institute Working Paper No. 15 (ODI, London).

Adelman, I. and S. Robinson (1988), Income distribution and development, in H. Chenery and T.N. Srinivasan, eds., Handbook of Development Economics, Vol. I (North-Holland, Amsterdam).

Ahluwalia, M.S. (1976), Inequality, poverty and development, Journal of Development Economics 3: 307–342.

Ahuja, V., B. Bidani, F. Ferreira and M. Walton (1997), Everybody's Miracle? Revisiting Poverty and Inequality in East Asia (The World Bank, Washington DC).

Alarcon, D. and T. McKinley (1995), Widening wage dispersion under structural adjustment in Mexico, Discussion Paper No. FC1995-4 (University of Toronto, Toronto).

Alderman, H. and P.-A. Chiappori, L. Haddad, J. Hoddinott and R. Kanbur (1995), Unitary versus collective models of the household: is it time to shift the burden of proof? World Bank Research Observer 10: 1–19.

Alesina, A. and D. Rodrik (1994), Distributive politics and economic growth, Quarterly Journal of Economics 109: 465–490.

Akerlof, G. (1978), The economics of 'tagging' as applied to the optimal income tax, welfare programs and manpower planning, American Economic Review 68: 8–19.

Amos, O.M. Jr. (1988), Unbalanced regional growth and regional income inequality in the latter stages of development, Regional Science and Urban Economics 18: 549–566.

Anand, S. (1983), Inequality and Poverty in Malaysia (Oxford University Press, Oxford).

Anand S. and R. Kanbur (1985), Poverty under the Kuznets process, Economic Journal (suppl) 95: 42–50.

Anand S. and R. Kanbur (1991), Public policy and basic needs provision in Sri Lanka, in J. Drèze and A.K. Sen, eds., The Political Economy of Hunger, Vol. III: Endemic Hunger (Clarendon Press, Oxford), pp. 59–92.

Anand, S. and R. Kanbur (1993a), The Kuznets process and the inequality-development relationship, Journal of Development Economics 40: 25–52.

Anand S. and R. Kanbur (1993b), Inequality and development: a critique, Journal of Development Economics 41: 19–43.

Anand, S. and M. Ravallion (1993), Human development in poor countries: on the role of private income and public services, Journal of Economic Perspectives 7: 133–150.

Atkinson, A.B. (1995), Income Distribution in the OECD Countries: evidence from the Luxembourg Study (OECD, Paris).

Aturupare, H., P. Glewwe and P. Isenman (1994), Poverty, human development and growth: an emerging concensus? HRO Working Paper No. 36 (The World Bank, Washington DC).

Austin, G. (1996), The effects of government policy on the ethnic distribution of income and wealth in Rwanda: a review of published sources, mimeo (London School of Economics, London).

Azam, J.-P., G. Chambas, P. Guillaumont and S. Guillaumont (1989), The impact of macroeconomics policies on the rural poor, UNDP Policy Discussion Paper (UNDP, New York).

Azariadis, G. and A. Drazen (1990), Threshold externalities in economic development, Quarterly Journal of Economics 105: 501–526.

Banerjee, A.V. and A.F. Newman (1993), Occupational choice and the process of development, Journal of Political Economy 101: 274–298.

Bardhan, K. (1985), Women's work, welfare and status, Economic and Political Weekly 20: 51–52.

Bardhan, P.K. (1982), Little girls and death in India, Economic and Political Weekly 17: 1448–1450.

Bardhan, P.K. (1984), Land, Labor and Rural Poverty (Columbia University, New York).

Barro, R. (1991), Economic growth in a cross section of countries, Quarterly Journal of Economics 106: 407–443.

Barro, R. and X. Sala-i-Martin (1992), Convergence, Journal of Political Economy 100: 223–251.

Barro R. and X. Sala-i-Martin (1995), Economic Growth (McGraw-Hill, New York).

Bates R. (1981), Markets and States in Tropical Africa (University of California, Berkeley).

Baumol, W.J. (1986), Productivity growth, convergence and welfare: what the long run data show, American Economic Review 76: 1072–1085.

Becker, G., K.M. Murphy and R. Tamura (1990), Human capital, fertility and economic growth, Journal of Political Economy 98: 512–537.

Benabou, R. (1996), Equity and efficiency in human capital investment: the local connection, Review of Economic Studies 63: 237–264.

Bennett, L. (1991), Gender and Poverty in India, Country Study (The World Bank, Washington DC).

Berman, E., J. Bound and Z. Griliches (1994), Changes in the demand for skilled labor within U.S. manufacturing: evidence from the annual survey of manufactures, Quarterly Journal of Economics 109: 267–397.

Berry, A. (1995), The social challenge of the new economic era in Latin America, Centre for International Studies Discussion Paper FC1995-8 (FOCAL, Toronto).

Berry, A., S. Horton and D. Mazumdar (1996), Globalization, adjustment, inequality and poverty, mimeo (University of Toronto, Toronto).

Besley, T. (1997), Political economy of alleviating poverty: theory and institutions, in M. Bruno and B. Pleskovic, eds., Proceedings of Annual Bank Conference on Development Economics, 1996 (The World Bank, Washington DC), pp. 117–134.

Besley, T. and R. Kanbur (1988), Food subsidies and poverty, Economic Journal 98: 701–719.

Besley, T. and R. Kanbur (1993), Principles of targeting, in M. Lipton and J. van der Gaag, eds., Including the Poor (The World Bank, Washington DC), pp. 67–90.

Birdsall, N. and J. Behrman (1991), Why do males earn more than females in urban Brazil: earnings discrimination or job discrimination? in N. Birdsall and R. Sabot, eds., Unfair Practices: Labor Market Discrimination in Developing Countries (The World Bank, Washington DC), pp. 147–169.

Bourguignon, F. (1994), Growth, distribution and human resources, in G. Ranis, ed., En Route to Modern Growth: Essays in Honor of Carlos-Diaz Alejandro (Johns Hopkins University, Baltimore), pp. 43–70.

Bourguignon, F., J de Melo and A. Suwa (1991), Modeling the effects of adjustment programs on income distribution, World Development 19: 1529–1544.

Bourguignon, F. and C. Morrison (1990), Income distribution, development and foreign trade: a cross-sectional analysis, European Economic Review 34: 1113–1132.

Bourguignon, F., C. Morrison and A. Suwa (1991), Adjustment and the rural sector: a counterfactual analysis of Morocco, mimeo (OECD Development Centre, Paris).

Browning, M. (1992), Children and household economic behavior, Journal of Economic Literature 30: 1434–1475.

Bruno, M., M. Ravallion and L. Squire (1995), Equity and growth in developing countries: old and new perspectives on the policy issues, Policy Research Working Paper No. 1563 (The World Bank, Washington DC).

Campano, F. and D. Salvatore (1988), Economic development, income equality and Kuznets' U-shaped hypothesis, Journal of Policy Modeling 10: 265–280.

Chen, L., E. Huq and S. D'Souza (1981), Sex bias in the family allocation of food and health care in rural Bangladesh, Population and Development Review 7: 55–70.

Chen, S., G. Datt and M. Ravallion, (1994), Is poverty increasing in the developing world? Review of Income and Wealth 40: 359–376.

Chenery, H., M. Ahluwalia, C. Bell, J. Duloy and R. Jolly (1974), Redistribution with Growth (Oxford University Press, Oxford).

Chu, Y.-P. (1995), Taiwan's inequality in the postwar era, Working Paper No. 96-1 (Sun Yat Sen Institute, Taiwan).

Clarke, G.R.G. (1995), More evidence on income distribution and growth, Journal of Development Economics, 47: 403–427.

Cornia, G.A., R. Jolly and F. Stewart, eds. (1987), Adjustment with a Human Face, 2 Vols (Oxford University Press, New York).

Cornia, G.A. and F. Stewart (1995), Two errors of targeting, in D. van de Walle and K. Nead, eds., Public Spending and the Poor: Theory and Evidence (Johns Hopkins University, Baltimore), pp. 350–386.

Cox, D. and E. Jiminez (1995), Private transfers and the effectiveness of public income redistribution in the Philippines, in D. van de Walle and K. Nead, eds., Public Spending and the Poor: Theory and Evidence (Johns Hopkins University, Baltimore), pp. 32–346.

Dasgupta, M. (1987), Selective discrimination against female children in rural Punjab, India, Population and Development Review 13: 77–100.

Datt, G. and Ravallion, M. (1993), Regional disparities, targeting and poverty in India, in M. Lipton and J. van der Gaag, eds., Including the Poor (The World Bank, Washington DC), pp. 91–114.

Datt, G. and Ravallion, M. (1994), Transfer benefits from public-works employment: evidence for rural India, Economic Journal 104: 1346–1369.

Deininger, K. and L. Squire (1996a), A new data set for measuring income inequality, World Bank Economic Review 10: 565–591.

Deininger, K. and L. Squire (1996b), Does inequality matter? Reexamining the links between growth and inequality, mimeo (The World Bank, Washington DC).

Deininger, K. and L. Squire (1996c), New ways of looking at old issues: inequality and growth, mimeo (The World Bank, Washington DC).

Demery, L and Demery, D. (1991), Poverty and macroeconomic policy in Malaysia 1979–87, World Development 19: 1615–1632.

Demery, L. and L. Squire (1996), Macro economic adjustment and poverty in Africa, World Bank Research Observer 11: 39–59.

Drèze, J. and A.K. Sen (1989), Hunger and Public Action (Oxford University Press, Oxford).

Durlauf, N.S. (1996), A theory of persistent income inequality, Journal of Economic Growth 1: 75–93.

Easterly, W. and R. Levine (1997), Africa's growth tragedy: policies and ethnic divisions, Quarterly Journal of Economics 112: 1203–1250.

Feenstra, R.C. and G.H. Hanson (1996), Foreign investment, outsourcing and relative wages, in R.C. Feenstra, G. Grossman and D. Irwin, eds., Political Economy of Trade Policy: Papers in Honor of Jagdish Bagwati (MIT Press, Cambridge, MA), pp. 89–127.

Fei, J.C.H., G. Ranis and S.W.Y. Kuo (1979), Growth with Equity (Oxford University Press, New York).

Fields, G. (1980), Poverty, Inequality and Development (Cambridge University Press, New York).

Fields, G. (1989a), Changes in poverty and inequality in developing countries, World Bank Research Observer 4: 167–185.

Fields, G. (1989b), A compendium of data on inequality and poverty for the developing world, mimeo (Cornell University, Ithaca).

Fields, G. (1994), Data for measuring poverty and inequality changes in the developing countries, Journal of Development Economics 44: 87–102.

Fields, G. and G. Jakubson (1994), New evidence on the Kuznets curve, mimeo (Cornell University, Ithaca).

Fishlow, A. (1972), Brazilian size distribution of income, American Economic Review 62: 391–402.

Fishlow, A. (1996), Inequality, poverty and growth: where do we stand? in M. Bruno and B. Pleskovic, eds., Annual World Bank Conference on Development Economics, 1995 (The World Bank, Washington DC), pp. 25–39.

Foster, J., J. Greer and E. Thorbecke (1984), A class of decomposable poverty measures, Econometrica 52: 761–766.

Foxley, A. (1979), Redistributive Effects of Government Programmes: The Chilean Case (Pergamon, Oxford).

Frank, C.R. Jr. and R.C. Webb, eds. (1977), Income Distribution and Growth in the Less-developed Countries (The Brookings Institute, Washington DC).

Freeman, R.B. (1995), Are your wages set in Beijing? Journal of Economic Perspectives 9: 15–32.

Freeman, R.B. and L.F. Katz (1994), Rising wage inequality: the United States vs other advanced countries, in R.B. Freeman, ed., Working Under Different Rules (Russell Sage, New York), pp. 29–62.

Galor, O. (1996), Convergence? Inferences from theoretical models, Economic Journal 106: 1056–1069.

Galor, O. and D. Tsiddon (1994), Human capital distribution, technological progress and economic growth, CEPR Working Paper No. 971 (CEPR, London).

Galor, O. and D. Tsiddon (1996), The distribution of human capital and economic growth, Tel Aviv Sackler Institute for Economic Studies No. 18/96 (Sackler Institute, Tel Aviv).

Galor, O. and J. Zeira (1993), Income distribution and macroeconomics, Review of Economic Studies 60: 35–52.

Garcia, M. (1991), Impact of female sources of income on food demand among rural households in the Philippines, Quarterly Journal of International Agriculture 30: 109–124.

Glewwe, P. and G. Hall (1994), Poverty and inequality during unorthodox adjustment: the case of Peru, 1985–1990, Economic Development and Cultural Change 42: 689–717.

Greenhalg, S. (1985), Sexual stratification: the other side of 'growth with equity' in East Asia, Population and Development Review 11: 265–314.

Grooteaert, C. (1995), Structural change and poverty in Africa: a decomposition analysis for Côte d'Ivoire, Journal of Development Economics 47: 375–401.

Grootaert, C. and R. Kanbur (1990), Policy Oriented Analysis of Poverty and the Social Dimensions of Structural Adjustment, for the Social Dimension of Adjustment Project (The World Bank, Washington DC).

Grosh, M.E. (1995), Towards quantifying the tradeoff: administrative costs and targeting accuracy, in D. van de Walle and K. Nead, eds., Public Spending and the Poor: Theory and Evidence (Johns Hopkins University, Baltimore), pp. 450–488.

Hadar, J. and W.R. Russell (1969), Rules for ordering uncertain prospects, American Economic Review 59: 25–34.

Haddad, L. (1991), Gender and poverty in Ghana, IDS Bulletin 22: 5–16.

Haddad, L. and R. Kanbur (1992), Intra-household inequality and the theory of targeting, European Economic Review 36: 372–378.

Haddad, L. and R. Kanbur (1990), How serious is the neglect of intra-household inequality? Economic Journal 100: 866–881.

Haddad, L., R. Kanbur and H. Bouis (1995), Intra-household inequality at different welfare levels: energy intake and energy expenditure data from the Philippines, Oxford Bulletin of Economics and Statistics 57: 389–409.

Hammer, J.S., I. Nabi and J.A. Cercone (1995), Distributional impact of social sector expenditures in Malaysia, in D. van de Walle and K. Nead, eds., Public Spending and the Poor: Theory and Evidence (Johns Hopkins University, Baltimore), pp. 521–554.

Harriss, B. (1990), The intrafamily distribution of hunger, in J. Drèze and A.K. Sen, eds., The Political Economy of Hunger, Vol. I (Oxford University Press, Oxford), pp. 351–424.

Hill, P. (1972), Rural Hausa: A Village in a Setting (Cambridge University Press, Cambridge).

Ho, S. (1978), Economic Development of Taiwan, 1860–1970 (Yale University Press, New Haven).

Horton, S., R. Kanbur and D. Mazumdar (1997), Inequality and developing country labor markets, in Y. Mundlak, ed., Contemporary Economic Issues, Vol. 2, Labor, Food and Poverty (Macmillan, London).

Horton, S., R. Kanbur and D. Mazumdar, eds. (1994), Labor Markets in an Era of Adjustment, 2 Vols (The World Bank, Washington DC).

Huppi, M. and M. Ravallion (1991), The sectoral structure of poverty during an adjustment period: evidence for Indonesia in the mid-1980s, World Development 19: 1653–1678.

Immonen, R., R. Kanbur, M. Keen and M. Tuomala (1998), Taxing and tagging: the optimal use of categorical and income information in designing tax/transfer schemes, Economica 65: 179–192.

Jain, S. (1975), Size Distribution of Income: A Compilation of Data (The World Bank, Washington DC).

Jayaraman, R. and P. Lanjouw (1998), Rural living standards in India: a perspective from village studies, Policy Research Working Paper No. 1870 (The World Bank, Washington DC).

Jha, S. (1995), More evidence on the Kuznets curve, mimeo (University of Washington, St. Louis).

Jha, S. (1996), The Kuznets curve: a reassessment, World Development 24: 773–780.

Jung, J.H. (1992), Personal income distribution in Korea, 1963–1986: a human capital approach, Journal of Asian Economics 3: 57–71.

Kakwani, N. (1994), Poverty and economic growth, with application to Côte d'Ivoire, Review of Income and Wealth 39: 121–139.

Kakwani, N. (1995), Income inequality, welfare and poverty, and illustration using Ukranian data, Policy Research Working Paper No. 1411 (The World Bank, Washington DC).

Kanbur, R. (1987a), Measurement and alleviation of poverty, IMF Staff Papers 36: 60–85.

Kanbur, R. (1987b), Structural adjustment, macroeconomic adjustment and poverty: a methodology for analysis, World Development 15: 1515–1526.

Kanbur, R. (1990), Poverty and the social dimensions of structural adjustment in Côte d'Ivoire. Social Dimensions of Adjustment in sub-Saharan Africa (The World Bank, Washington DC)

Kanbur, R. (1991), Projects versus policy reform, in S. Fischer, D. deTracy and S. Shekhar, eds., Proceedings of the World Bank Annual Conference on Development Economics, 1990 (The World Bank, Washington DC), pp. 397–413.

Kanbur, R. (1994), Poverty and development: the Human Development Report (1990) and the World Development Report (1990), in R. van der Hoeven and R. Anker, eds., Poverty Monitoring: An International Concern (St. Martin's Press, London), pp. 84–94.

Kanbur, R. and L. Haddad (1994), Are better off households more unequal or less unequal? Oxford Economic Papers 46: 445–458.

Kanbur, R. and M. Keen (1989), Poverty, incentives and linear income taxation in A. Dilnot and I. Walker, eds., The Economics of Social Security (Oxford University Press, Oxford), pp. 99–115.

Kanbur R., M. Keen and M. Tuomala (1994), Labor supply and targeting in poverty alleviation programs, World Bank Economic Review 8: 191–211.

Kanbur, R. and M. Tuomala (1994), Inherent inequality and the optimal graduation of marginal tax rates, Scandinavian Journal of Economics 96: 275–282.

Knight, J. (1976), Devaluation and income distribution in less-developed countries, Oxford Economic Papers 28: 208–227.

Kuo, S.W.Y. (1983), The Taiwan Economy in Transition (Westview Press, Boulder, CO).

Kuznets, S. (1955), Economic growth and income inequality, American Economic Review 45: 1–28.

Kuznets, S. (1966), Modern Economic Growth: Rate, Structure and Spread (Yale University Press, New Haven).

Kuznets, S. (1971), Economic Growth of Nations: Total Output and Production Structure (Belknap Press, Cambridge).

Kuznets, S. (1980), Notes on income distribution in Taiwan, in L.R. Klein., M. Nerlove and S.C. Tsiang, eds., Quantitative Economics and Development: Essays in Memory of Ta-Chung Lui (Academic Press, New York), pp. 255–280.

Leamer, E. (1995), A trade economist's view of U.S. wages and "globalization", mimeo (University of California, Los Angeles).

Lecaillon, J., F. Paukert, C. Morrison and D. Germidis (1984), Income Distribution and Economic Development: An Analytic Survey (ILO, Geneva).

Lenaghan, T. (1992), Adjustment and the poor in Africa, Development Alternatives 3: 8–17.

Lewis, W.A. (1954), Economic development with unlimited supplies of labor, Manchester School of Economics and Social Studies 22: 139–181.

Lewis, W.A. (1983), Development and distribution, in M. Gersovitz ed., Selected Economic Writings of W. Arthur Lewis (New York University Press, New York), pp. 443–459.

Lipton, M. (1985), Land assets and rural poverty, World Bank Staff Working Paper No. 744 (The World Bank, Washington DC).

Lipton, M. and M. Ravallion (1995), Poverty and policy, in J. Behrman and T.N. Srinivasan eds., Handbook of Development Economics, Vol. III (North-Holland, Amsterdam), pp. 2551–2657.

Lipton, M. and J. van der Gaag, eds. (1993), Including the Poor (The World Bank, Washington DC).

Louat, F., M. Grosh and J. van der Gaag, eds. (1993) Welfare implications of female headship in Jamaican households, LSMS Working Paper No. 96 (The World Bank, Washington DC).

Lucas, R.E. Jr. (1988), On the mechanics of economic development, Journal of Monetary Economics 22: 3–42.

Maasland, A. and J. van der Gaag (1992), World Bank-supported adjustment programs and living conditions, in V. Corbo, S. Fischer and S.B. Webb, eds., Adjustment Lending Revisited: Policies to Restore Growth (The World Bank, Washington DC), pp. 40–63.

Mahalanobis, P. (1963), The Approach of Operational Research to Planning in India (Asia, Bombay).

McNamara, R.S. (1973), Address to the Board of Governors at the Nairobi Meeting (The World Bank, Washington DC).

Mankiw, G., D. Romer and D. Weil (1992), A contribution to the empirics of economic growth, Quarterly Journal of Economics 107: 407–437.

Meerman, J. (1979), Public Expenditure in Malaysia: Who Benefits and Why? (Oxford University Press, New York).

Mirrlees, J. (1971), An exploration in the theory of optimum income taxation, Review of Economic Studies, 38: 175–208.

Morley, S.A. (1994), Poverty and inequality in Latin America: Past evidence, future prospects, Policy Essay 13 (ODC, Washington DC).

Ogwang, T. (1994), Economic development and income inequality: a nonparametric investigation of Kuznets' U-curve hypothesis, Journal of Quantitative Economics 10: 139–153.

Oshima, H.T. (1994), The impact of technological transformation on historical trends in income distribution of Asia and the West, Developing Economies, 32: 237–255.

Papanek, G. and O. Kyn (1986), The effect on income distribution of development, the growth rate and economic strategy, Journal of Development Economics, 23: 55–65.

Paukert, F. (1973), Income distribution at different levels of development: a survey of evidence, International Labor Review 108: 97–125.

Perotti, R. (1993), Political equilibrium, income distribution and growth, Review of Economic Studies, 60: 755–776.

Persson, T. and Tabellini, G. (1994), Is inequality harmful for growth? American Economic Review 84: 600–621.

Pinstrup-Andersen, P. (1989), The impact of macroeconomic adjustment: food security and nutrition, in S. Commander, ed., Structural Adjustment and Agriculture (ODI, London).

Prichett, L. (1997), Divergence, big time, Journal of Economic Perspectives, 11: 3–17.

Prunier, G. (1996), The Rwanda Crisis 1959–1994: History of a Genocide (Hurst, London).

Quibria, M.G., ed. (1993), Rural Poverty in Asia: Priority Issues and Policy Options (Oxford University Press, New York).

Ram, R. (1988), Economic development and income inequality: further evidence on the U-curve hypothesis, World Development 16: 1371–1376.

Ram, R. (1995), Economic development and inequality: an overlooked regression constraint, Economic Development and Cultural Change 43: 425–434.

Ram, R. (1997), Reply to the comment on Rati Ram's test of the Kuznets hypothesis, Economic Development and Cultural Change 46: 191–195.

Ravallion, M. (1991), Reaching the rural poor through public employment: arguments, experience and lessons from South East Asia, World Bank Research Observer 6: 153–175.

Ravallion, M. (1993), Poverty alleviation through regional targeting: a case study for Indonesia, in K. Hoff, A. Braverman and J. Stiglitz, eds., The Economics of Rural Organization: Theory, Practice and Policy (Oxford University Press, Oxford), pp. 453–467.

Ravallion, M. (1996), Can high inequality developing countries escape absolute poverty? mimeo (The World Bank, Washington DC).

Ravallion, M. (1997), A comment on Rati Ram's test of the Kuznets hypothesis, Economic Development and Cultural Change 46: 187–190

Ravallion, M. and K. Chao (1989), Targeted policies for poverty alleviation under imperfect information: algorithms and applications, Journal of Policy Modeling, 11: 213–224.

Ravalllion, M. and S. Chen (1997), What can new survey data tell us about recent changes in distribution and poverty? World Bank Economic Review 11: 357–382.

Ravallion, M. and M. Huppi (1991), Measuring changes in poverty: a methodological case study of Indonesia during an adjustment period, World Bank Economic Review 5: 57–82.

Ravallion, M. and B. Sen (1994), Impacts of rural poverty of land-based targeting, World Development 22: 823–838.

Reardon, T., C. Delgado and P. Matlon (1992), Determinants and effects of income diversification amongst farm households in Burkina Faso, Journal of Development Studies 28: 264–296.

Revenga, A. and C. Montenegro (1995), North American integration and factor price equalization: is there evidence of wage convergence between Mexico and the United States? mimeo (The World Bank, Washington DC).

Ribe, H., S. Carvalho, R. Liebenthal, P. Nicholas and E. Zuckerman (1990), How adjustment programs can help the poor, World Bank Discussion Paper No. 71 (The World Bank, Washington DC).

Richburg, K. (1996), Free trade helps lift world poor, Washington Post, 29 December 1996, A, 1: 2A12.

Robbins, D. (1995a), Earnings dispersion in Chile after trade liberalization, mimeo (Harvard University, Cambridge, MA).

Robbins, D. (1995b), Schematic summary of findings for country wage and employment structure studies, mimeo (Harvard University, Cambridge, MA).

Robinson, S. (1976), A note on the U-hypothesis relating income inequality and economic development, American Economic Review 66: 437–440.

Romer, P.M. (1986), Increasing returns and long-run growth, Journal of Political Economy 94: 1002–1037.

Rosenstein-Rodan, P. (1943), Problems of industrialization in Southern and Eastern Europe, Economic Journal 53: 202–211.

Sachs, J. and A. Warner (1997), Fundamental sources of long-run growth, American Economic Review 87: 184–188.

Sahn, D.E. and H. Alderman (1995), The effect of food subsidies on labor supply, in D. van de Walle and K. Nead, eds., Public Spending and the Poor: Theory and Evidence (Johns Hopkins University, Baltimore), pp. 387–410.

Sahn, D.E. and A. Sarris (1991), Structural adjustment and rural smallholder welfare: a comparative analysis, World Bank Economic Review 5: 259–289.

Saith, A. (1983), Development and distribution: a critique of the cross-country U hypothesis, Journal of Development Economics 13: 367–382.

Samorodov, A.T. (1992), Transition, poverty and inequality in Russia, International Labor Review 131: 335–353.

Selden, T.M. and Wasylenko, M.J. (1994), Measuring the distributional effects of public education in Peru, in D. van de Walle and K. Nead, eds., Public Spending and the Poor: Theory and Evidence (Johns Hopkins University, Baltimore), pp. 154–186.

Sen, A.K. (1983), Resources, Values and Development (Blackwell, Oxford).

Sen, A.K. (1997), On Economic Inequality, 2nd edn. (Clarendon Press, Oxford).

Selowsky, M. (1979), Who Benefits from Government Expenditure? (Oxford University Press, New York).

Singh, A. (1994), Global economic changes, skills and international competitiveness, International Labor Review 133: 167–183.

Standing, H. (1985), Women's employment and the household: some findings from Calcutta, Economic and Political Weekly 20: WS23–38.

Stiglitz, J. E. (1969), Distribution of income and wealth among individuals, Econometrica 37: 382–397.

Streeten, P. (1987), Structural adjustment: a survey of issues and options, World Development 15: 1469–1482.

Svedberg, P. (1990), Undernutrition in sub-Saharan Africa: is there a gender bias? Journal of Development Studies 26: 469–486.

Thiesenhusen, W.C., ed. (1989), Searching for Agrarian Reform in Latin America (Unwin Hyman, Boston).

Thomas, D. (1990), Intra-household resource allocation: an inferential approach, Journal of Human Resources 25: 635–664.

Thorbecke, E. (1991), Adjustment, growth and income distribution in Indonesia, World Development 19: 1595–1614.

Todaro, M.P. (1969), A model of labor migration and urban employment in less developed countries, American Economic Review 59: 138–148.

Tsaklogou, P. (1988), Development and inequality revisited, Applied Economics 20: 509–531.

Tsiddon, D. (1992), A moral hazard trap to growth, International Economic Review 33: 299–321.

Tuomala, M. (1990), Optimal Income Tax and Redistribution (Clarendon Press, Oxford).

UNDP (1990), Human Development Report (Oxford University Press, New York).

UNDP (1996), Human Development Report (Oxford University Press, New York).

van de Walle, D. (1994), The distribution of subsidies through public health services in Indonesia 1978–87, World Bank Economic Review 8: 279–309.

van de Walle, D. (1994), Incidence and targeting: an overview of implications for research and policy, in D. van de Walle and K. Nead, eds., Public Spending and the Poor: Theory and Evidence (Johns Hopkins University, Baltimore), pp. 585–619.

van de Walle, D. and Nead, K., eds. (1994), Public Spending and the Poor: Theory and Evidence (Johns Hopkins University, Baltimore).

Visaria, P. (1980), Poverty and living standards in Asia, Population and Development Review 6: 189–223.

Wade, R. (1990), Governing the Market: Economic Theory and the Role of the Government in East Asian Industrialization (Princeton University Press, Princeton).

Watkins, K. (1995), The Oxfam Poverty Report (OXFAM, Oxford).

Wood, A. (1994), North-South Trade, Employment and Inequality: Changing Fortunes in a Skill-driven World (Clarendon Press, Oxford).

Wood, A. (1995), Does trade reduce wage inequality in developing countries? mimeo (IDS, Sussex).

World Bank (1990), World Development Report (Oxford University Press, New York).

World Bank (1993), The East Asian Miracle (Oxford University Press, New York).

Chapter 14

INCOME DISTRIBUTION, ECONOMIC SYSTEMS AND TRANSITION *

J.S. FLEMMING[a] and JOHN MICKLEWRIGHT[b]

[a]*Wadham College, Oxford;* [b]*UNICEF International Child Development Centre, Florence*

Contents

* We are grateful to Alessandra Cusan of UNICEF ICDC for very able and patient research assistance, to Aline Coudouel, Gáspár Fajth, Péter Galasi, Thesia Garner, Alexandre Kolev, Judit Lakatos, Sheila Marnie, Albert Motivans, Gyula Nagy, Barry Reilly, Olga Remenets, Jan Rutkowski, Kitty Stewart, and Jiri Večerník for their help in various ways in assembling and interpreting data on the transition period, and to the editors for comments. Sections 2.2–2.5 draw heavily on joint work by Atkinson and Micklewright (1992).

Handbook of Income Distribution: Volume 1. Edited by A. B. Atkinson and F. Bourguignon

Abstract

We consider the differences in income distribution between market and planned economies in two ways. First, using benchmarks from the OECD area we review evidence from the countries of Central and Eastern Europe and the former Soviet Union during the socialist period. Second, we look at the transitions currently being made by the latter. In each case we review available data and the problems they present before considering in turn: (i) the distribution of earnings of full-time employees; (ii) the distribution of individuals' per capita household incomes; and (iii) the ways in which the picture is altered by nonwage benefits from work, price subsidies and social incomes in kind. For the socialist period we are able to consider long series of data, often covering several decades, and we can thus show the changes in the picture of distribution under the socialist system. We also emphasise the diversity across the countries concerned. For the period of transition, itself incomplete, the series are inevitably shorter but we are able to avoid basing conclusions on evidence drawn from single years. The picture during transition, like that under socialism, is varied. Russia has experienced very sharp increases in measured inequality to well above the top of the OECD range. The Czech Republic, Hungary and Poland have seen more modest rises. We note the lack of a satisfactory analytic framework in the literature that encompasses enough features of the transition, a framework which would help interpretation of the evidence.

Keywords: Transition, economic systems, Central and Eastern Europe

JEL codes: D31, P2, P5

1. Introduction

Other chapters in this handbook consider long runs of data for several countries. In a number of cases these reveal significant and essentially permanent shifts in the interpersonal inequality of earnings or income. Such shifts are sometimes associated with major events such as wars or revolutions. This chapter considers such an event—the collapse of communist central planning in Central and Eastern Europe—which is, as we show, having substantial effects on income inequality in several of the countries. We are not in a position to document fully the extent of the changes, as the process of transition is incomplete, let alone their durability. Nor do we consider poverty, although we refer to changes in national income which, together with increasing relative inequality, would imply very serious increases in the successor states of the Soviet Union and several other countries in the region.

While for some purposes our sample includes all fifteen post Soviet Republics of the former Soviet Union as well as Poland, Hungary, and former Czechoslovakia, we concentrate mainly on these three (or four after the separation of the Czech and Slovak

Republics) and Russia (or earlier the whole Soviet Union). We thus exclude China and Vietnam and take a narrower view of "transition" than one might of "emergence".

The transitions of the formerly centrally planned economies into more conventional market economies have considerable implications for the distribution of income. Trading and middle-man activity is legal while private property ownership is also permitted. In the transition itself market disequilibrium is likely to prevail—generating large positive (and negative) quasi-rents. Social institutions of redistribution and support through taxation and social services may break down or need to be radically recast. Keeping track of such a process, of which this chapter offers an account, is a major challenge. After some conceptual preliminaries we begin, however, in Section 2, with a reassessment of the starting point in the socialist economies relative to well-documented capitalist ones. This is not merely a recapitulation of what was already known but a reconsideration in the light of new data and analyses emerging from within the previously controlled and censored communities.

The process of transition now in train is, however, not only incompletely documented, but is so far from complete in itself that we cannot identify clearly what it is a transition to—nor is it likely to be easy to recognise when it is over. In as much as the transition is to a social market economy characteristic of Western Europe, one needs also to recognise that that represents a moving target. Not only have measures of earnings inequality changed under the impact of changing technology and competition from newly industrialising countries, but institutions and redistributive policies have also changed with privatisation, pressure to reduce tax rates and the ageing of the population.

Within the transition economies themselves there was in many cases a sharp break as controlled prices and trading arrangements were swept away—on 1 January 1990 in Poland, 1 January 1992 in Russia and so on. It is very important to recognise that however clean that break, it never represented a shift from a socialist to a capitalist (or from a controlled to a market) *equilibrium.*

Through the 1980s macroeconomic disequilibria were intensifying throughout the COMECON area. In particular excess demand, which was normal under central planning, increased, adding to monetary overhangs, black market premia on foreign exchange rates, and other indicators. These disequilibria increase the complexity of systems' comparisons. How, for instance, should the accumulating stocks of private money balances be valued?

The disequilibrium, which varied in intensity across the region, being least in Czechoslovakia and least repressed in Hungary, did not disappear immediately when prices were liberalised and stabilisation programmes adopted. Relative to what had gone before, the disequilibrium of the last days of communism was largely monetary (though with the usual fiscal roots). The liberalised economies faced not only stabilisation problems but also those of industrial and financial restructuring. This affected the labour market, and hence the distribution of earnings, at many levels. It seemed likely that patterns of participation by sex and age would tend to converge on Western patterns. The sectoral structure of economic activity was likely to shift radically away from heavy industry towards services. A new financial sector would be called for and the massive state enterprises were likely to be reorganised into smaller and more specialised units capable of competing internationally. Such a process of adjustment, with all its implications for the distribution of income, is bound to take time. The most that we can hope to do is to develop a framework for the analysis, recognising the key features of the varied starting points and range of possible, and shifting, destinations.

As various authors have shown, and is confirmed in Section 2 below, there was by no means a single "socialist" model distribution of income, even within the COMECON area on which we concentrate. Measured inequality was much less in Czechoslovakia, for instance, than in Russia. The extent and form of privileges for the nomenklatura elites varied markedly and presented different degrees of difficulty for the statistician. These variations tempted some commentators, who had focused on particular socialist states, to conclude either that they were much more, or much less, equal than those of Western Europe.

In market economies with pretensions to internal competition, we expect payments to factors and their owners to relate to the market valuation of the contribution of each input to output, the value of which is determined in a relatively free market. We then expect this distribution of pre-tax incomes to be translated into a distribution of post-tax and net real income by a tax/benefit system of social security contributions and benefits, and of direct and indirect taxation.

Many Western social security systems include elements, such as the British National Health Service, involving benefits in kind, but factor payments are overwhelmingly in money. This was much less true of socialist societies in which access to many social facilities, including housing, was, ostensibly at least, often linked to employment and the work-place. In both cases valuation of such benefits in kind is problematic. The scale of the problem, and its occurrence at the pre-tax rather than post-tax level, makes it a much bigger problem in the case of the socialist economies. Moreover the problem accumulates since cost of provision, in which wages have been very large, is a natural starting point for valuing the services which are themselves a component in labour compensation.

Not only was payment in cash supplemented by extra payment in kind but the cash itself did not give a simple command over goods—the supply of which to individuals was frequently subject to constrained availability at controlled prices. This raises a number of questions, many of which impinge primarily on the measurement of the price of a consumer goods basket. Obtaining rationed goods might involve extensive periods of queuing. How should that be regarded, as an input other than work-place time, or as a cost of consumption additional to the cash price of the goods in question? Such factors are important if there are privileged agents with access to shops in which goods are more readily available, who have to wait less long for consumer durables, or who have privileged access to education, health, foreign travel or other services, such as those of a dacha.

Moreover, out of equilibrium, when money wages might exceed the "price" of the basket of rations, how should the unspendable excess cash be valued? By reference to returns on savings deposits? The prospect of rations being increased at some future date? Or the price of goods on the black market?

Along with rationing and privileged access to goods and services goes an incentive to obtain goods beyond one's ration or access to privileges to which one is not entitled. This corruption and black market operation is relevant for two distinct reasons. First, if the black market is extensive enough it may supply a set of market prices and, in the extreme, the rationed quantities available at a lower official price become a per capita subsidy (a negative poll tax) if everyone enjoys the same rations. Second, corruption also means that officials may have significant income sources over and above their basic salaries as well as expenditures over and above those at officially controlled prices of some of their purchases. Of course, supplementary and second incomes of moonlighting or cultivation of gardens are not confined to senior officials but permeate many layers of different societies, including those in the West.

Partly for these reasons the adequacy of official data for a full picture varied even while socialist economies appeared to be sustainable. With the breakdown of these regimes the data problem has become worse, both as far as macro- and microeconomic data are concerned. For both, the new smaller private enterprises are important, and machinery for collecting statistical returns from them has taken time to build. Under central planning data on many things passed from enterprises to branch ministries—and the centre—as an administrative matter. For the new situation a very different procedure is necessary.

In the context of economic and systemic transformation it is obviously desirable to be able to track the changing pattern of distribution; all the problems of static systems' comparisons of Section 2 are made even more difficult in the process of transition examined empirically in Section 4. Price jumps have big effects on real balances—should they be taken into account? Privatisation involved the issuing of vouchers to citizens or to employees. How should these be valued and does their distribution constitute a part of household income? These, and many similar questions, while important in principle, are rendered less relevant in practice by the fact that change in the early 1990s was much more rapid than the establishment of procedures for tracking some of the consequences.

Section 3 picks up the conceptual theme with which Section 2 opens. Whereas the comparison of mature systems may rely on the concepts of static equilibrium analysis, the transition cannot. As a comparator, Section 3.1 considers the consequences of the rapid liberalisation of a previously seriously distorted market economy—by reference to a two sector model. This analysis highlights the importance of the ex post substitutability of capital and labour and also of the degrees of heterogeneity and mobility of the labour force. It is suggested that market-clearing real wages would be liable to fall severely in realistic cases and in practice that serious unemployment would emerge. The scope for mitigating these effects by policy intervention is discussed in Section 3.2, while

actual policies adopted to control wages and in response to unemployment are reported
in Section 3.3, social services and taxation in Section 3.4 and restitution in Section 3.5.

Section 4 picks up the data story from Section 2 with subsections on data sources
(Section 4.1), the distribution of individual earnings (Section 4.2), inequality of household incomes (Section 4.3), and the distributional impact of remaining subsidies,
nonwage income from employment, and social expenditures in kind from the state
(Section 4.4). Section 5 concludes.

2. Income distribution in socialist countries

In a market economy we can, as already indicated, look at the distribution of earnings,
of property income, of wealth, of benefits in kind (typically as part of the education
and health systems), and of cash transfers by way of taxes paid and benefits received
by way of old age pensions, sick pay, unemployment benefits etc. In Section 2.1 we
present some conceptual issues relating to the measurement of original and final income
in nonmarket economies and some features of the allocation of labour under socialism,
before examining data sources, which turn out to be relatively plentiful, in Section 2.2.
We then look in turn at evidence on the distribution of earnings (Section 2.3) and of
household incomes (Section 2.4) in Central Europe and the former Soviet Union. The
section concludes (Section 2.5) by considering what the evidence implies about the distribution of economic welfare and how the picture is changed when consumer subsidies
and income in kind are taken into account.

2.1. Labour income in market and socialist economies

Typically the distribution of earnings is a dominant element in the over-all distribution.
Earnings differentials reflect variations in hours of work and in hourly rates (which may
in part reflect differences in shift length). We also need to take account of deferred
pay represented by contributions to occupational pension schemes. This is not an easy
matter when pensions are related to terminal salaries rather than a return on contributions
previously made. Pay differentials in market economies are generally taken to reflect
differentials in education, training and skills captured in the concept of human capital.
The value of any particular skill at a point in time being determined by the interaction
of supply and demand. Changes in education systems and access to capital to finance
periods of training will affect the effective supply of the more difficult-to-acquire skills.

All of these factors contribute to earnings inequalities by age, sex, marital and occupational status discussed by Neal and Rosen in Chapter 7. Accumulation and inheritance
of real and financial assets contribute to the distribution of wealth. Using either actual or
imputed returns to wealth means that one can combine labour and property income into a
single income distribution. Whether this is preferable to presenting the joint distribution
of earnings and wealth is questionable for several reasons. If actual property income

is used it is liable to be misleading. £1 of dividend income on a low yielding growth stock is very different in security etc., from £1 of interest income from the bonds of a near bankrupt company. More systematically, few surveys take the effect of inflation on yields on property into account.

In one idealised model, investment in human capital might be driven by students themselves with access to good information and a ready supply of finance obtainable on the security of the human capital being acquired. This would allow returns to human capital to be equated with those on its other forms only if very high personal debt ratios were acceptable or if equity-type claims on human capital could be sold. Neither condition has ever come near to being met (see Chapter 8 by Piketty).

If the conditions of market efficiency are to be met then intervention is necessary to get the right education and training to the right people—intervention which may take externalities as well as private returns into account—an intervention which is, in principle, as plausible in a socialist as in a market economy. Russia in fact developed proportionately more specialist schools for young musicians, gymnasts and mathematicians than was typical of Western Europe.

In addition to rewards for cultivated human capital, there are, in market economies, rents earned by "stars", not only in sports and entertainments but also in certain professions. Some such rents, as to the tallest basketball players, have a physical and objective basis in the number of points they can score. Even then the top scorer may earn a premium disproportionate to the margin of points. In cultural areas there is no objective scale for the margin by which the "best" operatic tenor outperforms the second best. To some extent it is a matter of fashion and taste how far audiences regard one as a substitute for the other and what premiums they are prepared to pay to hear "the best"—or the best paid (see Rosen, 1981). Socialist economies were not immune from these pressures for three reasons: they were anxious not to appear too philistine, they needed to motivate performers, and they needed to prevent their emigrating in the course of foreign tours promoting the national culture of the socialist state.

In many socialist countries there was a formal structure of pay norms across industries with higher rewards for those involving muscle power, such as mining or heavy engineering, and much lower rewards for activities such as medicine or education which were physically less demanding—and often disproportionately employed women. Within hierarchies there was also a prescribed graduation based on qualifications, seniority and responsibility—applicable to fringe benefits as well as to basic pay—not very different from Western organisations of a comparable scale in the 1960s and 1970s. As has already been mentioned, although the arts, and sports (when not undertaken through the military), were not rated highly in the structure of industrial pay norms, there was flexibility to pay large differentials for internationally mobile stars or winners of Lenin prizes or other such distinctions.

On one view, labour allocation under socialism was quite different from that in a market economy. This view appears to be given support by the description of allocation of labour resources in urban China:

Since 1957 the state labour bureaux have exercised a virtual monopoly over the allocation of urban labour. The scope for individual expression of preferences is very limited, even in the 1980s: job assignments are made normally without regard to the wishes of either employer or employee .... The initial assignment to a job is very important: the first job is often the last .... Without official consent—rarely granted—a change of employing unit is practically impossible. (Knight and Song, 1990: p. 9)

But our concern in this chapter is not with the form of socialism that emerged in China. In the case of the Soviet Union, Marnie notes similar rigid controls on labour allocation in the 1930s but she goes on to explain that the post-war period was very different:

Although the Soviet literature never referred to a "labour market", labour allocation was in fact predominantly achieved through market mechanisms. Since the mid 1950s workers in the Soviet Union have been free to quit their jobs at will. Only a small share of jobs are centrally allocated; otherwise employees are free to choose their job, skill, or profession, as well as the region where they work ... and, although a state employment service has existed since the 1960s, it has never had a monopoly over the allocation of labour (1992: pp. 38–39).

This picture serves also as a reasonable description of the allocation of labour in many other Eastern European countries under socialism, although there was some notable variation within the region.[1] Yugoslavia's form of economic organisation with worker managed firms is an obvious outlier. On this different view, the allocation of labour in these countries and in post-war USSR may be seen in terms of departures from a market allocation, rather than as a totally different system.

One significant difference was in the degree of centralised wage determination, but it was argued by various authors that in view of the relative freedom enjoyed by workers in their choice of job, the setting of differentials was in part concerned to provide incentives similar to those in a market economy, as noted above. For example, Phelps Brown (1977) reports that wage differentials were set with regard to incentives to invest in human capital, to enter occupations with unpleasant conditions, to bear responsibility, to work hard on the job, and to move to industries or areas selected for an expansion of employment. The desire to overcome labour shortages, such as those for skilled labour, may have meant that wage differentials departed less than might be expected from those which would have characterised a market economy at the same level of development.

However, some departures there certainly were. Numerous authors have drawn attention to the differences in differentials by industry and occupation between economic system—influenced in part by the reward to muscle power that has just been noted. A good example, that illustrates the impact of change of system directly, is provided by movements in differentials by sector in Czechoslovakia between 1948 and 1953 associated with the Communist take-over. These are shown in Table 1. The favourable position under socialism of manual workers relative to nonmanual workers that is implied by these sorts of figures was frequently documented in the literature.

---

[1] The separation rate in manufacturing in the USSR in 1989 of about 18% exceeded that in Japan, France, Italy, Sweden and the Netherlands, with voluntary quits being the single largest cause of separations (IMF et al., 1990: Volume II, Chart 2 and Table IV.6.5). The separation rate in Hungary in the mid-1980s exceeded 20% (*Hungarian Statistical Yearbook*, 1987: Tables 4.4 and 4.8).

Table 1
Earnings by sector in Czechoslovakia in 1948 and 1953 relative to the national average (%)

	1948	1953
Manufacturing	92.7	108.0
Construction	101.2	115.2
Transport	109.4	110.3
Trade/Catering	102.5	90.0
Health/Social Welfare	120.9	92.2
Education and Culture	124.7	90.0
Banking and Insurance	134.7	104.3

Source: Večerník (1991: p. 238).

Any reasonable account of the operation of labour markets under socialism would combine elements of the different views. And it is clear that the mix would vary between countries and across time. As a result, it is not surprising that simple conclusions about "the" distribution of earnings under socialism are elusive. The picture can be expected to vary substantially from country to country and between different periods—as it does in capitalist countries.

When looking at earnings inequality one has to decide on the relevant population. Is it those in employment or those who are seeking employment? And if so how should they be identified? Or should one consider the whole population—perhaps of "working age". If one considers the population of working age comparisons may be affected by relatively arbitrary differences in what constitutes "working age". Even if this difference did not exist differences in participation rates can become very important. The socialist economies had much higher female participation rates at nearly all ages. This makes for a more equal personal distribution of income. Evaluating that difference, however, depends enormously on the explanation of the differential participation.

Conscripting housewives without providing care for their children could equalise income but not necessarily even the lowered level of welfare. Virtual conscription, for fear of being called a "parasite", with child care of uncertain quality, leaves comparisons difficult to make. Is relatively low participation of mothers in much of Western Europe—although much higher than it was—due to inadequate access to childcare (by whatever criterion) or due to choice in an affluent society (though that is difficult to square with trends in societies said to be getting richer)? Similarly, variations in age-specific partic-ipation rates may reflect healthy investment in human capital or study as superior only to unemployment. Early retirement may be an affordable luxury or a statistical gimmick designed to reduce recorded unemployment.

Recorded unemployment was very much lower in all centrally planned economies even than the rates below 5% achieved in the 1950s in much of the OECD area. Since 1975 rates in the West have been nearer to 10% while rates in the COMECON area showed little change while that institution, and central planning, lasted. As many of the transition economies have specified Western European models as their goals, the transition seems likely to be associated with manifold increases in recorded unemployment quite apart from the rises of rates into the high teens in the early disequilibrium stages of the transition process. Any profile of income inequality over the transition must take into account the higher incidence of unemployment and the adequacy, or otherwise, of unemployment compensation.

To some extent the contribution of open unemployment to income inequality may be associated with a decline of reported inequality of earnings among the employed if the latter included people on zero-hours or drawing minimum wages that were only 10% of the average—as has been reported of the USSR. On the other hand in several countries, particularly in Central Europe, the introduction and extension of market forces is increasing the inequality of earnings as incentive mechanisms play a growing rôle and as abnormal quasi-rents are earned on skills now in very short supply—supply which will presumably respond to the (temporary) reward.

In both market and planned economies taxes, subsidies, transfers and benefits in kind mean that one has to distinguish between the distribution of gross or ("original") income and that of net income, expenditure or consumption. Even if we are particularly concerned with the latter it may be interesting to know whether country A's more equal distribution of net income arises from greater original equality or more radical intervention. Unfortunately it is difficult to invoke this distinction especially when making comparisons across systems. Ideally, and consistently with the Diamond and Mirrlees (1971) prescription for production efficiency, there might be no taxes or subsidies impinging on pre-tax incomes. In practice there are many in all economies, from trade taxes on intermediate goods to excise duties levied at the wholesale stage or subsidies paid to "producers".

Socialist economies typically made more interventions at this stage, including the effects of price and wage controls, which sometimes made explicit personal income taxes redundant. Thus it is likely that reported "original" incomes were more influenced by policy in socialist than in market economies so that the identified contributions of policy to the determination of the net distribution is likely to be understated. Socialism was in principle particularly inimical to private wealth holding and its passing between generations in the form of inheritance which is, potentially, an important influence on income distribution in several ways. Obviously inherited wealth is one source of property income. Parental income or wealth can be used to buy human capital for the next generation and parental influence may affect children's access to earning opportunities.

Direct intergenerational transfers were typically relatively small in socialist economies as accumulation of personal assets was less significant. The successful manager's dacha was not bought but occupied on employment related terms—more of an annuity than a freehold. The blocking of significant monetary bequests may merely have increased the importance of parental influence in securing places in the right schools, universities, and enterprises. At times, preference for the children of workers and peasants may have limited or even eliminated the scope for parental influence but that does not seem to have been typical of Eastern Europe or the USSR since 1950.

2.2. *Data sources on income distribution under socialism*

The newcomer to the empirical investigation of income distribution in socialist countries may be surprised by the amount of evidence that exists on the subject. Surely the state suppressed discussion of the extent of inequality, with the result that information on the distribution of earnings and of household incomes was not available?

Statements over the years by Western and Soviet writers alike bore witness to the lack of available information on the distribution of income in the USSR. For example, the discussant of a paper on Soviet income distribution that was presented at a 1964 meeting of the International Economic Association noted ironically that he wished the author could have given his readers some idea of the extent of the size distributions of earnings and household incomes (Marchal and Ducros, 1968: p. 236). And in his 1984 survey article on income inequality under state socialism, Bergson concluded that "the Soviet government apparently prefers to withhold rather than to release information" (1984: p. 1091). Can, then, the distribution of income under socialism in Eastern Europe be investigated in any serious way?[2]

Data on the distribution of earnings and of household incomes *were* collected in the USSR in great quantities in the post-war period and in other communist countries too.[3] The Soviet Family Budget Survey (FBS), with its origins in surveys of the 1920s, was in continuous operation in the post-war period, and by the break-up of the Union in 1991 had a sample of some 90,000 households. Regular enquiries into the distributions of earnings and household incomes in Czechoslovakia and Hungary began in the late 1950s or early 1960s.

The problem facing scholars of the USSR was the lack of *availability* of the data, the results from which were indeed systematically suppressed. Researchers were forced to work with what few scraps were available and in doing so displayed considerable powers of detection and ingenuity.[4] Notable use was also made of surveys of Soviet emigrés in the 1970s (much of this work is collected together in Ofer and Vinokur, 1992).

It would be wrong, however, to suppose that the situation in the USSR was representative of that in all of the Soviet bloc. The statistical offices of several countries in Eastern Europe had a long tradition of publication as well as data collection. From at least the 1960s onwards, the Polish, Hungarian and Czechoslovak statistical yearbooks contained considerable information on the distribution of earnings and of household in-

---

[2] Following the convention in much of the literature on the socialist period, we use "Eastern Europe" to refer to all of Central and Eastern Europe and the former Soviet Union.

[3] The situation in Poland, Hungary, Czechoslovakia and the USSR is documented in Atkinson and Micklewright (1992), which we draw on here, and a substantial amount of data for these countries is contained in an appendix to their book.

[4] A good example is the reconstruction of the Soviet earnings distribution by Wiles and Markowski (1971) from a graph with no scale in a Russian language publication.

comes. Statisticians in these countries published their results on occasion in international journals.[5] Moreover, the period of *glasnost* saw a sharp change in Soviet publication policy, resulting in greatly increased availability of data for the USSR in the late 1980s.

A second preconception surrounding distributional data under state socialism is that the quality of available information was low. Using Britain as a yardstick, Atkinson and Micklewright summarise the data on the distribution of earnings in the Eastern European countries they cover as suggesting that "the similarities [with British data] are more striking than the differences" (1992: p. 55). There were exclusions from the coverage of Eastern European sources, including the armed forces and, typically, full-time employees of the Communist Party. Those working in the private sector were often excluded—the numbers concerned varied greatly from country to country, being very small for example in Czechoslovakia but more important in Poland. Those in small enterprises were often excluded. Coverage of agricultural employment, an important sector in most countries, was typically far from complete. And the earnings data in most countries relate only to full-time workers and just to those working a full month.

These exclusions are important to note, but may be no worse than in Western countries. The French *Declarations Annuelles de Salaires* was estimated in 1982 to cover only three-quarters of all full-time workers due to a number of exclusions including employees in agriculture and state and local authorities (Bourit et al., 1983: p. 29). The Portuguese *Quadros de Pessoal* excludes those working in public administration by design and about 15% of firms fail to provide information (Cardoso, 1997: p. 22). The German *IAB* data based on social security registers excludes civil servants (Steiner and Wagner, 1996). The British New Earnings Survey lacks data on about 15% of full-time and a substantially higher fraction of part-time employees (Atkinson and Micklewright, 1992: p. 53); one reason for this shortfall in coverage is the exclusion, as in the Eastern European countries, of many workers changing jobs around the time of the survey. The European Union earnings enquiry of 1995 had a host of exclusions (Eurostat, 1998), including persons working in small firms—a more important restriction than in socialist countries given the different distribution of firm size in market economies.

The quality of data on household incomes in socialist countries is less straightforward to relate, with substantial variation from country to country and between different sources within country.[6] The methodology of collecting household income data is more complicated than that of data on individual earnings. This is true whatever the prevailing economic system and it is salutary to consider the degree of success achieved by the British Family Expenditure Survey (FES), a long-running enquiry of high international standing. After allowance for the average level of nonresponse to the FES (just under 30% at that time), the shortfall in income aggregates recorded in the survey for 1977 from those shown in the national accounts was 6% for earnings, 9% for social transfers, a quarter for self-employment income and occupational pensions, and as much as a

---

[5] The article in *Econometrica* by Éltetö and Frigyes (1968) is one example.

[6] A number of countries collected data on incomes through more than one survey. We give examples of the methodologies rather than trying to be comprehensive.

half for investment income (Atkinson and Micklewright, 1983). The last two types of income should not figure prominently in socialist countries, and the example cautions against judging data collected under socialism against some unattainable ideal.

Survey coverage displayed considerable variation. Examples of good practice were provided by the Hungarian income survey, held every five years from 1963 to 1988, and the Czechoslovak microcensus, of which there were eight between 1958 and 1988. Sample design in these surveys followed standard international methodology of multi-stage sampling intended to give each household an equal probability of selection (with the sole exclusion in Czechoslovakia of households with a member in the armed forces or the police). Response to these surveys was very good, with rates of 97% in Czecho-slovakia in 1988 and 91% in Hungary in 1983. Achieved sample sizes were large—100,000 households in Czechoslovakia and 20,000 in Hungary.

The other end of the spectrum is represented by the USSR Family Budget Survey (FBS), to which we referred earlier. The operation of the survey was shrouded in mystery for many years but sufficient was known for it to be the subject of considerable criticism by Western and Soviet scholars alike. McAuley (1979) argued that "statistics from this source have been rejected by many, perhaps a majority, of Soviet economists and statisticians as worthless" (p. 51).

The sample design of the FBS was a major source of complaint, being "subject to a great many different biases, often severe and cumulative, [so that] the survey is highly unrepresentative of the population as a whole" (Shenfield, 1984: p. 3). The survey had a quota sample of families of persons working in state enterprises and collective farms, the quotas over-representing heavy industry and under-representing the services. One implication of the survey design is that households had a probability of selection pro-portional to their number of workers in covered sectors. Some pensioner households were added to the sample in 1979 but it seems clear that pensioners remained under-represented (Atkinson and Micklewright, 1992: p. 267). Once in the survey respondents were asked to participate indefinitely—the survey was a panel with no planned rotation, implying an ageing sample and a further loss of representativeness. The reasons for the sample design were partly ideological, with the quotas reflecting a bias towards the "productive sectors". Shenfield (1984) notes too that the development of probabilistic survey sampling in the 1930s and 1940s, for example the work of Mahalanobis in India, never penetrated the USSR in the Stalin era.

The Polish budget survey was somewhere in the middle of the spectrum in terms of coverage, especially in its early years. Prior to 1973, the sample design had similarities to that of the Soviet FBS with the survey restricted to households of employees in the state sector, but in this year the survey changed to a territorial basis (a sampling frame of addresses rather than enterprises). However, households working in the private nona-gricultural sector (about 10% of the labour force in 1989) continued to be excluded. And response was well below the level of the Czechoslovak and Hungarian surveys mentioned earlier (no doubt in part due to the greater burden of participation in a budget survey), averaging 65% at first interview during 1982–1989 and only 40% or less prior to 1982 when rotation was introduced into the survey's panel design (Atkinson and Micklewright, 1992: p. 260; Kordos, 1996). By the 1980s the sample size was about 30,000 households.

The concern about quality of data on household incomes in socialist countries extends beyond the issue of survey coverage. Is the relationship between the state and its citizens one that encourages accurate reporting of incomes? In particular, the view is often expressed that Eastern European data covered only "official" income and that "second" or "hidden" economy income was missing from the data. This is a genuine concern in view of discussion of the size of the unofficial economy, especially towards the end of the 1980s. The growth of the second economy in Hungary was discussed by many authors. Official estimates put aggregate illegal income in the USSR at some 9% of GDP in the late 1980s (*Vestnik statistiki*, 1990: No. 6). Other estimates were significantly higher. Estimates based on a sample of Soviet emigrés suggest that up to a third of the urban population's income came from illegal sources, although the representativeness of the sample may be open to doubt (Grossman, 1987).

The questionnaires of household surveys in Eastern Europe typically allowed all forms of incomes to be reported but the success with which information on nonofficial income was collected is a matter for real debate. Under-reporting of this income is a serious qualification of the data collected. The success of statistical offices in capitalist countries in persuading respondents to reveal legally obtained income that has not been declared for income tax purposes may be an analogous problem.

Some aspects of the statistical offices' work was made easier by the nature of the socialist state. In all the surveys described above, earnings data provided by respondents were verified with their employers—something not possible in many nonsocialist countries on grounds of confidentiality and a practice that has had to be abandoned in the transition. We have already noted the absence of some private income sources under socialism that appeared seriously under-represented in British data. The less complex systems under socialism of cash transfers from the state, aiding the work of survey statisticians, should also be noted, although the more developed systems of consumer price subsidies that in part substituted for cash transfers in turn raise issues of interpretation of the income data that we return to below.

Other aspects of data quality stem in part from the level of development of the socialist countries and in particular the importance of agriculture. Agriculture in the early 1980s accounted for 30% of employment in Poland, 20% in the USSR and Hungary and over 10% in Czechoslovakia (ILO, 1984: p. 89, and 1987: p. 63). Notwithstanding collectivisation and the creation of state farms, many agricultural households consumed their own produce. The evidence suggests that "private plots" were often very important for nonagricultural households as well. Such consumption represents income and should be included in the calculations along with incomes in cash.

The USSR Family Budget Survey required respondents to continuously record consumption of their own produce in diaries which were regularly monitored by interviewers. It is clear that monitoring of this type is very onerous for respondents but it is likely to be more accurate than collecting information by recall, which is the practice in many Western countries, for example in the Living Standards Measurement Study (LSMS) surveys sponsored by the World Bank. The Polish and Hungarian statistical offices followed different practices but clearly took the subject seriously (Atkinson and Micklewright, 1992: Sources and Methods). However, the Czechoslovak microcensus excluded this form of income.[7]

To summarise, the data sources available in pre-reform Eastern Europe appear to have been mixed in quality—just as in capitalist countries. Data on the distribution of earnings compares favourably with Western sources while surveys on household incomes display considerable variation, the data from the former USSR being of much lower quality than those from several Central European countries.

2.3. The distribution of earnings in socialist labour markets

A number of authors over the years have looked in detail at the size distribution of earnings under socialism and at the comparison with that in capitalist countries. The field owes a great deal to the study by Lydall (1968), in which he carefully assembled evidence for a wide range of countries for the period around 1960. To facilitate comparisons across countries, he defined a "standard distribution", which related to the earnings of adult males, in all occupations, in all industries except farming, working fulltime and for the full period. Earnings were defined to be money income from employment before tax or other deductions (Lydall, 1968: p. 60).

The Eastern European countries covered by Lydall were Czechoslovakia, Hungary, Poland and Yugoslavia. These same countries (particularly the first three) were often the focus of later authors too and it must be acknowledged that extensive evidence on the distribution of earnings (or of household incomes) over time is hard to find for Albania, Bulgaria and Romania. Lydall found that the least unequally distributed earnings were those in Czechoslovakia and Hungary, which appeared distinctly different from the Western European countries. Yugoslavia and Poland found their place among the group of Western countries with less inequality, such as Denmark and Sweden and, at that time, the UK. The data of Lydall were analysed further by Pryor (1973), who made explicit allowance for other systematic reasons why earnings dispersion may be expected to vary across countries, in particular that earnings inequality declined with the level of development and increased with the size of population. Allowing for these, he concluded that there was on average a six percentage point difference in the Gini coefficient.

By contrast, Redor (1992), with more recent evidence, reached the conclusion that, comparing Western and Soviet-type economies:

---

[7] The dual price systems in socialist economies—a low official price at which goods have limited availability and a higher market-clearing price for private trade—had direct consequences for interpretation of income data, but it was also relevant for the valuation of income in kind. Practice differed across countries, and the system applied by the Polish and Hungarian statistical offices seems reasonable. However, official state prices were used in the USSR budget survey, thus under-recording the income of agricultural households and others with private plots and as a result probably overstating income inequality.

there appears to be no systemic difference between the earnings dispersions of wage earners as a whole. Although at the beginning of the 1980s the US is the country with the highest earnings dispersion, both Western and Soviet-type economies occupy the ranks that follow. (1992: p. 60).

The evidence regarding the Soviet Union, in particular, is rather mixed. Pryor's figures for 1959 show the fifth percentile (from the top) in the Soviet Union as earning more relative to the median than the corresponding group in the US, the UK and other Western European countries (except France). More recent evidence was summarised by Bergson as showing:

a rather striking similarity in [earnings] inequality, as measured, between the USSR and Western countries. Inequality in the USSR fluctuates in the course of time, but only rarely does any particular percentile ratio fall outside the range delineated by corresponding measures for Western countries. (1984: p. 1065).

At the same time, he developed further the normalisation for differences in the stage of development and population size, and this led him to conclude that, allowing for such conditioning factors, "inequality in the USSR in the early seventies may have been somewhat low by western standards" (1984: p. 1092).[8]

It is clear, therefore, that there were indeed differences *between* socialist countries of the Soviet bloc and that earnings inequality may have changed over time. These observations were the starting point for the work by Atkinson and Micklewright (1992), on which we draw here, that tried to put together consistent time-series on earnings inequality in Czechoslovakia, Hungary, Poland and the USSR, up to the end of the socialist period. Following Lydall, they defined a standard distribution to help comparison across countries, but, unlike him, focused on men and women together and included where possible agricultural employment (but not self-employment); their figures refer to monthly earnings of full-time workers before deductions and including any bonuses (Atkinson and Micklewright, 1992: p. 79).

Figure 1 shows the decile ratio (the ratio of the 90th to the 10th percentile) estimated by Atkinson and Micklewright for each of their four countries from the late 1950s to the late 1980s.[9] A benchmark was provided by the authors for these series with the analogous figures for Great Britain (the UK excluding Northern Ireland) for 1968–1990. Like some of the Eastern European figures, the decile ratio in Britain displayed considerable variation over time, with a minimum value of 2.87 in 1977 and a maximum of 3.65 in 1968. The average value was 3.20.

Czechoslovakia stands out in its low level of earnings distribution and the impression from Fig. 1 is of considerable stability. Over 1959-1990 the decile ratio varied between 2.30 and 2.53—well beneath the range for Britain. As it was put by Večerník, "all the basic features of the structure of earnings inequality were established in the initial post-war period and firmly fixed for the future" (1991: p: 238). But he went on to say that the

---

[8] Bergson's normalization follows the concept of the Kuznets curve, which is the subject of some debate—see Chapter 13 by Kanbur.

[9] It should be noted that these estimates were made from grouped data (and not microdata), raising issues of interpolation.

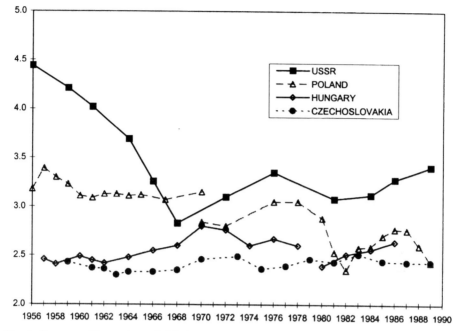

Fig. 1. Gross monthly earnings of full-time workers: decile ratio, 1956–1989. Source: Atkinson and Micklewright (1992), Tables CSE1, HE1, HE4, PE1, PE4, UE1, UE2.

stability in the distribution hid changes in the returns to human capital, which declined sharply in the late 1970s and early 1980s, and a shift in the age-earnings profile in favour of older workers.

Next in the ranking comes Hungary, with a decile ratio above that for Czechoslovakia from the early 1960s onwards but still below the range for Britain. The figures for Poland display yet more variation, although in part this is associated with a change in the definition of the series in 1970. Prior to this year the decile ratio is at about the average level of that in Britain for 1968–1990. The later period saw some sharp changes, especially in the 1980s with the changing fortunes of the Solidarity trade union movement.

Top of the ranking comes the USSR. Only at the end of the 1960s does the decile ratio dip beneath 3.0 (associated with an increase in the minimum wage on the occasion of the 50th anniversary of the 1917 revolution) and for much of the period it is above the average British value. There is substantial variation, reflecting the mixed findings of earlier authors. And there was a steady increase in inequality in the 1980s, the decile ratio rising from 3.08 in 1981 to 3.41 in 1989.

Two former socialist countries shown in Fig. 1 split apart in the 1990s. Were the points of departure for the constituent republics similar in terms of earnings inequality? In the case of the two halves of the Czech and Slovak Federation the starting point was almost identical. The decile ratios for the two republics in 1989 were both 2.14 and the Gini coefficients both 0.20 (Atkinson and Micklewright, 1989: Table CSE5). Nor had there been differences of any size in the recent past—the overall degree of inequality in earnings had been similar for a long time (we will see below that the story was rather different for household incomes).

In the case of the USSR, the sheer size of the country leads one to expect that the picture may not have been as for the Czech and Slovak Federation. Wiles (1974) suggested that the Union was formed of "a group of egalitarian regions, the averages of which history has separated" (p. 54). This would imply that inter-regional differences in earnings accounted for a substantial amount of the overall inequality and would help explain why the USSR comes top of the ranking in Fig. 1. But it would also be the case that the starting points in terms of earnings inequality for the now independent states were fairly similar *and* that they were lower than for the USSR as a whole.

Average earnings certainly did vary by republic; as a percentage of those in Russia in 1989 average earnings varied from 69% in Azerbaijan to 104% in Estonia (Atkinson and Micklewright, 1992: Table UE4). Figure 2 sheds some light on intra-republic inequality, showing the decile ratio for each Soviet republic in 1986. The range is substantial, from 2.86 in Moldova to 3.46 in Armenia, but it is difficult to detect clear regional group-ings, with the exception that the three nonRussian Slav republics—Belarus, Ukraine and Moldova—are at the bottom of the ranking. And although the variation is quite substantial, it is notable that even Moldova, with the lowest recorded dispersion, displays a greater degree of inequality than found in Czechoslovakia, Hungary or Poland at any point in the 1980s.

To this point we have compared recent evidence from the Eastern European countries with that from Britain only. Figure 3 introduces several other Western countries into the comparison and in the case of the Eastern countries concentrates on those that will be the focus in Section 4 when we turn to the transition period of the 1990s. The evidence on the other Western countries is again for gross earnings of all full-time workers, but in other respects it is not fully comparable either with Britain or with the Eastern European countries, referring, for example, in the case of Canada and France to annual earnings.[10] The evidence for the Eastern European countries refers to 1986 or 1987, thus avoiding any changes in earnings inequality right at the end of the socialist period. The Western evidence refers in most cases to 1990.

The diagram shows the top and bottom deciles relative to the median, with the decile ratios given in brackets after each country's name. As already implied by Fig. 2, Russia displays a markedly higher degree of earnings inequality than the other Eastern Euro-pean countries. Figure 3 shows that this greater inequality arose at both ends of the distribution, although more notably at the top. The low level of Czech inequality results,

---

[10] We have eschewed data for a number of other OECD countries given in the same sources that were even more obviously not strictly comparable.

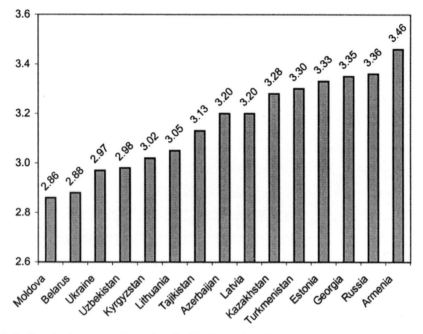

Fig. 2. Decile ratio of gross monthly earnings for full-time workers: Soviet republics, 1986. Source: Atkinson and Micklewright (1992), Table UE5.

in particular, from a difference at the top—the bottom decile as a percentage of the median is virtually the same as in Hungary.

Among the Western countries, France and Germany have distributions that are more compressed at the bottom end than any of those in the Eastern countries. And the top decile in Germany as a percentage of the median is the same as that in Hungary, with the result that the overall degree of inequality as measured by the decile ratio is effectively the same as in the Czech Republic.[11] Australia appears very similar to Poland, at both ends of the distribution. The overall degree of inequality in France is substantially less than that in Russia. Only the USA and Canada dominate Russia in terms of overall dispersion and in Canada even the top decile as a percentage of the median is the same as for Russia, the differences between the distributions appearing at the bottom. The shape of the distribution in Britain appears very similar to that in Russia.

---

[11] The German data refer only to full-year workers, which probably reduces the degree of inequality relative to that in the Eastern European sources. But the picture given of Germany as a country with earnings inequality at a level similar to that in the Eastern countries with low earnings dispersion bears out that found with earlier data by some other authors. Redor, for example, reports a decile ratio of 2.3 for Germany in 1978 (Redor, 1992: Table 3.2). The results comparing sources for the mid 1980s of Steiner and Wagner (1996) for the 80th and 20th percentiles indicate that earnings inequality is slightly lower in social security register data than in the household survey data used for Germany in Fig. 4.

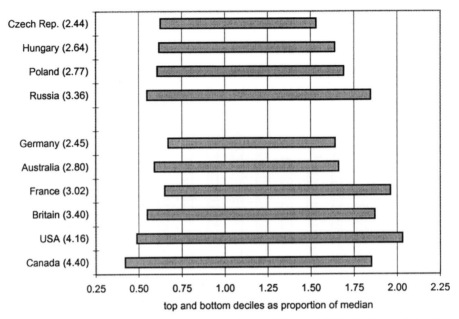

Fig. 3. Quantile ratios of earnings for full-time workers: East and West, end 1980s. Decile ratio in brackets. Earnings are gross. Sources: Hungary (1986), Poland (1986), Russia (1986) and Britain (1990): Atkinson and Micklewright (1992), Tables 4.1, UE5, BE1; Czech Republic (1987): data supplied by the former Czechoslovak Federal Statistical Office (as in Atkinson and Micklewright, 1992, Table CSE5, and results calculated in same way); Canada (1990), France (1990), Germany (1989): OECD (1993; Table 5.2); Australia (1990), USA (1993): OECD (1996a: Table 3.1).

The comparison of the Eastern with the Western countries is undoubtedly sensitive to choice of year and to definitional issues. Nevertheless, the data in Fig. 3 reflect the message coming from work of different scholars over the years. In the late socialist period, earnings inequality in several Central European countries for which data were most readily available was towards the lower end of the range in Western countries, but not outside it. And in the case of Russia (and, on the evidence of Fig. 2, some other former Soviet republics too), earnings inequality was already at a level well up in the range found in Western countries.

2.4. Inequality of household incomes under socialism

The movement from evidence on inequality of earnings to that on household incomes involves a number of factors, and these may change the view obtained of the level of inequality under socialism compared to that under capitalism. It may also alter the picture of how inequality changed over time under socialism. This is illustrated by Fig. 4, which shows the decile ratio for the distribution of individuals by household per capita income

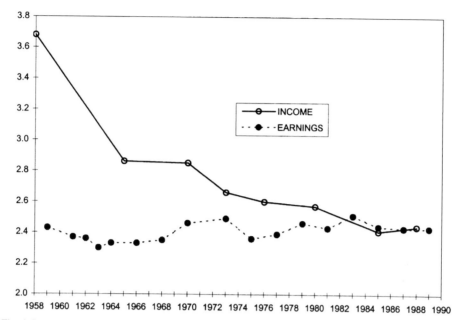

Fig. 4. Decile ratios for full time workers' earnings and for the individual distribution of per capita income: Czechoslovakia, 1958–1989. Source: Atkinson and Micklewright (1992), Tables CSE1 and CSI1.

in Czechoslovakia for 1958–1988, together with the ratio for earnings of employees that was focus of the previous section. Measured inequality of household incomes declined notably over the period, particularly between 1958 and 1965. Whereas the decile ratio of per capita incomes was one and a half times that of earnings in 1958, the difference between the two had disappeared by the 1980s. Switching from the unit of the employee to that of the household and including other sources of income has changed the picture of stability in Czechoslovakia obtained from the earnings data for full-time workers.

Under capitalism we would expect this movement to increase the measured degree of dispersion, due in particular to the presence of significant investment income, the existence of unemployment, and lower labour force participation rates than under socialism. None of this can be expected to be fully averaged out by moving to the unit of the household—indeed the opposite may be the case. Atkinson and Micklewright (1992) find that the move from earnings of employees to per capita income of individuals leads to a rise in the Gini coefficient in the UK in 1985 of four percentage points. In Hungary and the USSR in the mid 1980s, however, there was effectively no change, as in Czechoslovakia at this time, although Poland proves the exception to the rule where the Gini rose by three points, more or less as in the UK. Pyror (1973) concluded that the existence of property income raises the Gini coefficient in developed capitalist countries by between three and six percentage points compared to that under communism, although he went on to argue that this may not be the most important source of differences between the two systems. Some factors are common to both systems, notably the presence of cash transfers, although the design and hence redistributive impact of these may not be the same (and of course varies under capitalism).

The suggestion is, therefore, that the move to household incomes may lead to more clear water between capitalism and socialism. As with the evidence on earnings of employees, however, writers over the years have differed in their conclusions about the degree of measured inequality in household incomes under the two systems.

Lydall (1979) concluded that there was little difference between the shape of the distribution of household incomes in the UK and that in Czechoslovakia, Hungary and Poland. Morrisson (1984) reached a similar conclusion in a comparison which included in addition Bulgaria, Yugoslavia and the USSR, as well as a number of other Western countries, although it should be noted that his estimates included an approximate adjustment for the nonmonetary privileges of the elite under communism (but not capitalism). Using data mainly from the early or mid 1970s, Poland and the USSR were found by Morrisson to have a relatively higher degree of inequality with Gini coefficients of 0.31 in both cases, but more or less on a par with Canada (0.30) and the USA (0.34). (The figures refer to the individual distribution of per capita household income.) The Gini for Hungary was estimated to be 0.24, compared with 0.25 in both Sweden and the UK. Only Czechoslovakia, with a Gini of 0.22, was considered by Morrisson to stand out as having a more egalitarian income distribution than those in advanced Western countries. The ranking of the USSR accords with the conclusions of Bergson in his much-quoted survey of evidence about income inequality under Soviet socialism: "Income inequality in the USSR is commonly assumed to be less than that in the US. That is doubtless so, though not by so wide a margin as sometimes imagined" (1984: p. 1073).

The view that there was less inequality in pre-reform Eastern Europe than in Western countries was supported by the results of Wiles (1978). Using data for the late 1960s and early 1970s, and the decile ratio of per capita income as his measure of dispersion, he ranked (in ascending order) Bulgaria, Poland, Hungary, the USSR and Czechoslovakia, all of them firmly behind (again in order) Sweden, West Germany, the UK, Italy, Canada and the USA. This finding was in line with the conclusion of Pryor (1973) that holding other things constant, including level of development, the Gini coefficient of "total income inequality is at least 0.10 less in the East than in the West" (p. 88).

One reason for the differing views may be that the situation in the Eastern European countries changed over time so that the comparison depends on the particular year chosen. The distributions of the different components of household incomes may change, as may household formation. Figure 4 shows that the data from the late 1950s or the 1960s give a different picture of inequality of household incomes in Czechoslovakia than do the data from the 1980s. We consider changes for other countries below and return also to the issue of comparison with the West using more recent data.

Before doing so, however, an important issue concerning adjustment of the data on household incomes needs to be made clear. The data on income distribution from communist countries typically refers to household incomes per capita. The per capita adjustment for differences in household size is one not often made in official publications of Western income distributions, where an adjustment that instead embodies some economies of scale is usually made. Wiles, in his article referred to above, points out that Western data are often expressed in terms of total household income unadjusted for differences in household size, implying infinite scale economies, noting also that the Western data often refer to the distribution of *households* and the Eastern data to the distribution of *individuals*, that is households weighted by their sizes. The appropriate adjustment is a matter for judgement and the per capita scale may be more appropriate for socialist societies on account of the lower fixed costs of a household due to subsidised prices of housing and fuel (Atkinson and Micklewright, 1992).

The sensitivity of results to the method of presenting the data is illustrated by the following estimates of the decile ratio for Hungary in 1987 and the UK in 1985:[12]

	Household distribution of total household income	Individual distribution of per capita income
Hungary	5.43	2.82
UK	5.09	3.86

Not only do the orders of magnitude of the two measures differ greatly, making vital the use of the same definition for comparisons, but the ranking of income inequality in the two countries differs on the two measures. Hungary appears more equal than the UK when using the definition of the distribution commonly used in the East, but less equal when using the definition commonly used in the West.[13] Similar findings were noted by Bruinooge et al. (1990) in their comparison of income inequality in Hungary in 1982 with that in the Netherlands.[14]

We now turn to changes over time in the distribution under socialism, looking at the same countries that were the focus in our discussion of earnings. Figure 5 shows the Gini

[12] The figures are taken from Atkinson and Micklewright (1992: Tables HI3 and BI3).

[13] Note that an argument could be made for using different equivalent scales when making comparison between systems. If economies of scale in household size really do differ sharply between economic system then this could be taken into account when trying to produce comparable distributions of economic welfare.

[14] The same issue arises for comparisons of targeting under socialism and capitalism. Milanovic (1995) considers the incidence of social benefits in cash and in kind under both economic systems. The concentration of cash incomes on the lower part of the distribution appears far better in market economies than in socialist economies (Milanovic, 1995: Table 17-2). However, the data for the market economies refer to the distribution of total household income, unadjusted for differences in household size, while that for the socialist economies is for per capita income. In the same volume, Jarvis and Micklewright (1995) show that the incidence of family allowance in pre-reform Hungary differed sharply between these two distributions, being much less well concentrated on the poor when total household income is used. This would appear to suggest that Milanovic's finding would be even stronger if the distributions in market and socialist economies were defined in the same way, but it is pension expenditure that dominates the cash benefit figures and here the result could go the other way.

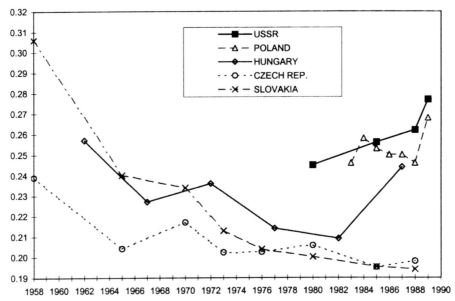

Fig. 5. Gini coefficient for the individual distribution of per capita household income, 1958–1989. Source: Atkinson and Micklewright (1992), Tables HI1, PI1, UI1, CSI5 (results for 1964–1985 for the Czech Republic and Slovakia calculated in the same way from data supplied by the former Federal Statistical Office).

coefficient for the individual distribution of per capita household income for Hungary, Poland and the USSR, and for Czechoslovakia, distinguishing in this instance between the Czech and Slovak republics.[15] The Polish and Soviet data refer only to the 1980s although the series for Hungary, like that for Czechoslovakia, covers three decades.[16] The sources for the data were described in Section 2.2 and the warning made there about the source of the Soviet data, the Family Budget Survey, must be repeated here—this was a low quality source with a large question mark over its degree of representativeness.

   The most striking feature of the diagram is the reduction in income inequality in Slovakia from the late 1950s to the late 1970s, the Gini coefficient falling by 0.1— a very substantial change. The Gini in the Czech half of the Federation was nearly 7 percentage points below that in the Slovak half in 1958. At this time there were

[15] The Gini coefficient for Czechoslovakia as a whole is given for each year in Atkinson and Micklewright (1992: Table CSI1).

[16] The Soviet evidence for earlier years is sparse but includes the important work by McAuley (1979) for 1967, drawn on by several later authors including Bergson (1984) and Morisson (1984), and that of Ofer and Vinokur (1992) who used data collected from samples of emigrés in the early 1970s. Atkinson and Micklewright argue that the differences in sources and the uncertainty surrounding their use are too great to allow strong statements about trends in the USSR up to 1980, concluding that all one can say is that the degree of inequality displayed by the Family Budget Survey data for 1980 is "fairly similar" to that found in the earlier work (1992: p. 131).

therefore sharp differences in income distribution between the two republics but by the mid 1970s recorded inequality was effectively the same. The reduction in intra-republic inequality in Czechoslovakia over 1958–1988 was accompanied by a big catch-up in average income by Slovakia. The ratio of average per capita income between the two republics fell from 70% in favour of the Czechs in 1958 to a differential of only 10% from 1976 onwards (Atkinson and Micklewright, 1992: Table CSI4).

In the mid-1960s recorded inequality in Hungary was at about the level of that in Slovakia, and movements in the Gini at this time were similar to that in the Czech lands. By 1982 the Gini had fallen to 0.21, the same figure as for Czechoslovakia as a whole in 1980. The difference in experience between the two countries in the mid-1980s was striking. While inequality in Czechoslovakia was effectively unchanged, there was a sharp increase in Hungary, with the Gini coefficient rising by three and a half percentage points between 1982 and 1987. Rising inequality during this period in Hungary is consistent with the relaxation of central planning in the 1980s and we have seen earlier that earnings inequality increased at this time.[17]

The series for Poland starts only in 1983 so the impact of the Solidarity trade union in the early 1980s cannot be seen. The incomes policy package of Solidarity following the Gdansk Accord of 1980 was described by Flakierski as "one of the most egalitarian programmes ever defined in a socialist country" (1991: p. 96) but although a separate series for worker households shows a sharp drop in inequality between 1981 and 1982, there was a rise again in 1983 (Atkinson and Micklewright, 1992: Fig. 5.7). Figure 5 shows that recorded inequality in the population as a whole at this time was clearly greater than in both Hungary and Czechoslovakia. With the exception of a jump in 1989, inequality in Poland during the period shown did not exhibit any great changes and the Gini in 1987 was effectively the same as that in Hungary.

Figure 5 shows inequality in the Soviet Union rising throughout the 1980s, starting from the same level in 1980 as displayed by Poland for 1983—a Gini coefficient of just under 0.25. The value by 1989 was some three percentage points higher. The question mark over the Soviet data reduces any confidence that can be placed in the comparison of the level of inequality with that in the other countries, but the changes over time during the decade may be more robust to deficiencies in the source. Putting such concerns to one side, the evidence of Fig. 5 is that inequality of household incomes in the USSR at the end of the 1980s was, like that of earnings, higher than in Hungary and Czechoslovakia.

Did socialism reduce regional disparities in incomes across the USSR as we have seen occurred in Czechoslovakia? And what was the degree of disparity in income *within* each republic at the time of the break-up of the Union? McAuley (1979) analysed changes in available data on average incomes by republic in the 1960s and concluded that there had been "little if any" (p. 99) reduction in regional differences. Evidence for

---

[17] Éltető (1997) discusses in detail the changes in income distribution in Hungary over the 1970s and 1980s, comparing these with those for earnings. He notes that the correlation between an employee's earnings and the per capita income of his or her household was only 0.35 in both 1977 and 1982, a reminder of the difference between the two income concepts.

the 1980s is given by Atkinson and Micklewright who note that seven out of the eleven nonBaltic republics had failed to make any significant progress relative to Russia and that a number had fallen further behind, notably in Central Asia where the four core republics in 1988 had average per capita income of less than two-thirds of the Russian figure.

Questions concerning the differences within republics are harder to answer. The only data readily available are for the end of the 1980s and come once again from the Soviet budget survey, which had a small sample size in several republics (less than 1500 households in five cases). With these caveats, some clear patterns emerge from the results for 1989 given in Table 2.[18] There was substantial variation in the degree of measured inequality in individual republics. The European Slavic republics of Ukraine and Belarus, and to a lesser extent Moldova, appear to have had less measured inequality in 1989, with Gini coefficients at about the same level as that shown in Fig. 5 for Hungary in 1987. The position of Ukraine and Belarus relative to the other republics reflects what was found earlier for earnings. The five Central Asian countries, on the other hand, all had Ginis that were four or five percentage points higher than for these two Slavic republics, which is a sizeable difference. The Baltic and Caucasian republics had varied results (Azerbaijan appears to have been the most unequal republic in the Union). The Gini shown for Russia is very similar to that for the USSR as a whole.[19]

We finish by considering for the 1980s the question that many scholars had addressed for earlier years—whether measured inequality of income was lower in pre-reform Eastern Europe than in the OECD countries (as then defined). Our ability to answer this question is greatly enhanced by the work on income inequality in the OECD countries by Atkinson et al. (1995). Their analysis, based on the use of microdata sets in the Luxembourg Income Study (LIS), provides results under a variety of definitions—including the distribution by individuals with the per capita equivalence scale, the definition most commonly used in Eastern Europe. Table 3 compares the Gini coefficients given in Fig. 5 with those for per capita income in 16 of the 24 countries that formed the OECD in the mid-1980s.

The comparison does not of course provide "the" answer to the question of how the distribution of income differed between socialism and capitalism. Income inequality has

---

[18] The value of the available information depends on the publication from which it is taken. In the Family Budget Survey report for 1989 used by Atkinson and Micklewright, the bottom range of the data for five republics contained a third or more of the distribution in each case. The estimates in Table 2 are based on more detailed data, although the top decile still lies in an open top interval for several republics.

[19] The greater inequality in the Central Asian republics combined with their lower average incomes resulted in a far higher proportion of the population in this region below what had become by the end of the 1980s the conventional all-Union poverty line, a monthly income of 75 rubles per capita. The four core Central Asian republics all had a third or more of the population beneath this level, compared with only 5% in Russia and 6% in the Ukraine. It might be thought that much larger household sizes coupled with a per capita adjustment of incomes has much to do with this but Marnie and Micklewright (1994) show that even with the distribution of household size present in Ukraine, the proportion of households below the 75 ruble line in Uzbekistan, the largest Central Asian republic, would only have fallen in 1989 by a third, indicating that low total rather than per capita household incomes was the principal explanation.

Table 2

Individual distribution of per capita household income in the Soviet republics, 1989

	Gini	Decile ratio
Slav republics		
Ukraine	0.23	2.7
Belarus	0.23	2.7
Moldova	0.25	3.1
Russia	0.27	3.1
Baltic republics		
Latvia	0.26	3.0
Lithuania	0.26	3.0
Estonia	0.28	3.2
Caucasian republics		
Armenia	0.25	3.1
Georgia	0.28	3.5
Azerbaijan	0.31	4.1
Central Asian republics		
Kyrgyzstan	0.27	3.5
Turkmenistan	0.28	3.5
Kazakhstan	0.28	3.5
Uzbekistan	0.28	3.5
Tajikistan	0.28	3.6

Source: Estimation using data in Atkinson and Micklewright (1992: Table UI3) with the bottom range split between 0–50 and 50–75 rubles drawing on a table from *Solsia'noe razvitie SSSR 1989*, p. 119 (which by contrast combines higher ranges that are split in the source used by Atkinson and Micklewright). The Pareto assumption was used to interpolate within intervals and in the top interval.

varied over time in the West, as well as in the East, and comparisons made in a different period could give a different picture—as the earlier literature reviewed above suggests. Rather, the comparison should be seen as showing how the starting point for the Eastern European countries when entering the transition process compared with the situation at that time in the OECD area.

Czechoslovakia and Hungary in the mid 1980s were just below the bottom of the OECD range. Poland and Russia were certainly above the most equal OECD country, Finland, but very much at the level of the other Nordic countries and Belgium. In all other OECD countries the Gini coefficient was higher than in the Eastern countries and in most cases by a sizeable margin. The means differ by seven percentage points. The figure for the US was far higher than that for Russia, suggesting that the earlier comparisons of the US with the USSR for the 1970s by, for example, Bergson, were not a good guide to a Russo-American comparison for the 1980s.

Table 3

Gini coefficients for the individual distribution of per capita income, Eastern Europe and OECD in the mid 1980s

		0.20	Czechoslovakia
		0.21	Hungary
Finland	0.22		
Sweden	0.24		
		0.24	Russia
		0.25	Poland
Norway	0.25		
Belgium	0.25		
Luxembourg	0.27		
Germany	0.28		
Netherlands	0.28		
Canada	0.32		
Italy	0.32		
UK	0.32		
Australia	0.33		
France	0.33		
Portugal	0.33		
Ireland	0.36		
Switzerland	0.36		
USA	0.37		

Mean OECD = 0.30   Mean E. Europe = 0.23

Source: Czechoslovakia (1985), Hungary (1982), Poland (1985): Atkinson and Micklewright (1992, Tables 5.1 and HI3); Russia (1985): estimates based on grouped data (nine ranges with top and bottom classes containing less than 10% each) in *Argumenty i fakty*, No. 20, 1990 (Pareto assumption used to interpolate within intervals and in the top interval.); Figures for all OECD countries (1984–1987) were estimated from the piece-wise linear (resulting in a slight under-estimate) Lorenz curves implied by the quantile shares given in Atkinson et al. (1995: Table 4.10), other than that for Portugal (1980/81) which was taken from (Rodrigues, 1993: Table 3).

Suppose that as a result of the transition process, an Eastern European country with a pre-reform income share of the bottom quintile given by the average of the figures for the four countries in the table—10.7%—were to move to a distribution of income with a share of the bottom quintile given by the OECD average—8.1%. (These shares are taken from the same sources as the Gini coefficients.) Average real income would need to rise by one third for the income of the bottom quintile to merely stand still in absolute terms.

2.5. Benefits in kind, subsidies and "fringe" benefits

Was the distribution of households' incomes in Eastern Europe under socialism a good guide to the distribution of their economic well-being? Can the data be interpreted in the same way as those from market economies when we take into account the existence of subsidised prices, rationing, nonwage remuneration from work, and social benefits in kind? These questions are of interest not only for the historical comparison of income distribution in Eastern Europe under socialism with that in Western countries, but also for establishing the starting point for the transition process for the former socialist countries and hence for interpreting changes in measured income inequality in the 1990s and beyond.

The problem facing the researcher was described by Bergson in the context of the USSR:

In the appraisal of equity, incomes that are compared, while expressed in monetary terms, are supposed to represent commensurate differences in real incomes. Income, that is, should ideally be received in a monetary form, and be freely exchangeable for goods and services at established prices that are uniform for all households in any market area. (Bergson, 1984: p. 1057)

The implications of departures from this ideal have been of frequent concern to those writing on the distribution of income under socialism. But at the same time, it must be remembered that, as Bergson went on to put it, "the ideal is hardly realised anywhere". To return to the comparison at the end of the previous section, the quintile shares in OECD countries would also need adjustment. The main difference in type between economic system, as opposed to degree, concerns the availability of goods, although even here there have been periods in Western economies where queues have developed, especially in the housing market.

We begin with social benefits in kind, expenditure by the state on education and health. These are well developed in many market as well as socialist economies. At the end of the 1980s, expenditure by the state on education and health in Hungary, Poland, Czechoslovakia and Yugoslavia represented between 12 and 16% of household income (Milanovic, 1995: Table 17-6). This compares to a range of 13–22% (and a mean of 17%) at the beginning of the 1980s in the seven OECD economies considered by Smeeding et al. (1993: Table 2).

The typical analysis of the distributional impact of social benefits in kind proceeds by imputing a share of total state expenditure to each household and then summarises the impact across the distribution of income with the device of the concentration curve (or coefficient). Putting aside the far from trivial question of how to value the state's expenditure, at least two methodological issues arise.

First, the incidence of benefits in kind can be expected to be sensitive to the equivalence scale that is adopted when adjusting cash incomes for differences in households' needs. The per capita adjustment may be expected to put households with children further down the distribution than do other equivalence scales and, as a result, expenditure on education may appear more concentrated on the lower part of the distribution than would otherwise be the case. Milanovic (1995) for Eastern Europe and Smeeding et al. (1993) for OECD economies use different concepts of income and therefore their results cannot be directly compared: the former looks at incidence across the per capita income distribution while the latter considers incomes unadjusted for differences in household size.

Second, the issue arises of how to attribute the expenditure to households, especially in the case of health. Official calculations in the UK impute health expenditure to households on the basis of information from other sources on average usage of medical services by age and sex. This could be seen as attributing to each household the insurance premium that would be paid in a system of private provision. By contrast, calculations made in Hungary in the 1980s attributed health expenditure to households in survey data on the basis of their recorded usage of medical services in that same survey. This procedure is no doubt one reason why the Hungarian calculations display considerable dispersion of expenditure on social benefits *within* income groups (Atkinson and Micklewright, 1992: Fig. 6.5).

The results of Milanovic (1995: Table 17-7) for Hungary, Poland, Czechoslovakia and Yugoslavia at the end of the 1980s all display negative concentration coefficients for education expenditure. Households in the lower part of the distribution receive more than their equal share of the benefit in kind, implying a strong equalizing effect.[20] This confirms the conclusions of earlier authors based on less detailed data. Morrisson (1984), for example, cites evidence from Hungary for the 1970s which suggested that the inclusion of in-kind social benefits reduced the Gini coefficient for household incomes by two percentage points, as in the UK, the US and France.[21] Of course, as for cash incomes, the distribution of social benefits may change over time. (This issue is the focus of the analysis for the UK by Sefton, 1997.)

The distributional impact of consumer price subsidies in pre-reform Eastern Europe attracted a lot of attention. The size of the explicit consumption subsidies varied substantially across time and countries, as they do in market economies. The same is true of producer subsidies from which of course consumers often derived indirect benefit. In 1988, consumer subsidies represented about 5% of GDP in Hungary and 10% in Poland, figures which represent a potential for considerable leverage on inequality. This may be compared with a figure for subsidies in Britain as a percentage of net household income of less than 4% in the mid-1970s and only 1% in the early 1990s.

Newbery (1995) reports on the work for Hungary in the mid-1970s by Szakolczai (1979), who argued that the then consumer price system had a poor redistributive effect; Newbery's conclusions using the same data are rather different: "production and

---

[20] It is notable, however, that the equalising impact of education expenditure varies considerably with the level of education, expenditure on kindergarten and primary levels being much more concentrated on the lower part of the distribution than expenditure on secondary and vocational education.

[21] In the case of education, a similarity in the incidence East and West is consistent with the view that educational access under socialism was characterised by some of the same social class differences as that under capitalism (UNICEF, 1998; Micklewright, 1999).

consumption price distortions appear to have been remarkably effective at redistributing purchasing power" (pp. 850–851). Analyses for Poland and Hungary in the late 1980s revealed that poorer households received a less than equal share of total state expenditure on consumer subsidies—the concentration coefficients were positive (Atkinson and Micklewright, 1992; Milanovic, 1995). (Newbery points out that policy on the use of the price system as a redistributive tool may well have been consciously changed over time.) But the distribution was less unequal than that of cash incomes, implying an equalising effect. (This is the situation where the concentration curve is between the Lorenz curve and the line of equality.) The picture for individual subsidies, however, varied considerably.

The valuation of subsidies in these analyses attributes state expenditure on the basis of observed consumption. (Newbery's methodology is an exception.) This contrasts with the appropriate theoretical concept, the equivalent variation of the price subsidy—the amount of income that would be required to keep the household at the same level of utility if the subsidy were to be abolished. But the standard illustration of the amount of the equivalent variation may need adjustment if subsidies go hand in hand with rationing, since a household's observed expenditures may represent a mix of purchases at a lower subsidised price and a higher market price (Atkinson and Micklewright, 1992; Cornes, 1995). Nor should analysis focus only on the effect of explicit subsidies, ignoring the impact of other forms of price regulation and indirect tax. When the state owns all sales outlets and stands to bail-out any in financial trouble, the distinction between a price control and a price subsidy is blurred. As was put by the IMF and others, "in an economy where practically all commodity and factor prices are administered, the economic concepts of subsidies and taxes can become so broad as almost to lose their meaning, insofar as administered prices, wages, interest rates and the exchange rate all deviate from market-clearing values" (IMF et al., 1991: vol. 1, p. 267).

Housing was a good where subsidies varied considerably across the socialist countries, and where state intervention has also been common in market economies. In part this was linked to big variations in the pattern of housing tenure. Bulgaria and Hungary, for example, were countries where owner-occupation was at a surprisingly high level by the end of the socialist period, although this does not imply that there were no housing subsidies for the households concerned—low interest mortgages from the state were a prominent feature. Three-quarters of the total housing stock at this time was occupied by owners in Hungary (Pudney, 1995) with the same figure found in urban areas in Bulgaria (Renaud, 1991).

In contrast, the Soviet Union "maintained the dominant features of a centrally planned housing system for the longest time and in their most traditional forms" (IMF et al., 1991: vol. 3, p. 317) and this was associated with substantial over-crowding as indicated by standard measures. The state owned two-thirds of the housing stock, and almost 90% in large cities such as Moscow and St. Petersburg (Buckley and Gurenko, 1997). Levels of rent in the 1980s were still largely determined by regulations from the

1920s. This was an extreme case, but state sector rents in Bulgaria and in Czechoslovakia dated from the 1960s (Renaud, 1991).

In Hungary, subsidies to public-sector rents in the 1970s were estimated to have had a regressive impact, re-enforcing the picture of inequality obtained from cash incomes alone (Dániel, 1985) with the same true of all housing subsidies in 1989 (Dániel, 1997), including those to owner-occupiers (taking the value of subsidies as merely being the explicit expenditures in the state budget).[22] In the USSR, by contrast, analysis based on data on Soviet emigrees referring to urban households in the 1970s showed rent subsidies reducing inequality (Alexeev, 1990), the upper-bound of the market-clearing price being estimated as the average rent per square metre in the data for accomodation rented—illegally—from private individuals.

The illicit subletting of public housing was a result of the housing shortages in the USSR. Places in the housing queues might be sold (again illicitly) with the result, according to Alexeev (1988), that the rent subsidy received by some high income households living in low-rent public housing represented in part a return on their investment. (Alexeev's results have subsequently been questioned by Buckley and Gurenko (1998), who argue that income had little impact on housing demand at the end of the Soviet period.)

The existence of "fringe" benefits—nonwage benefits from work—in pre-reform Eastern Europe also received a lot of interest from writers concerned with inequality under socialism. Much of this focused on the rewards going to the nomenklatura— superior housing, cars, holiday homes, access to imported goods. At the same time, noncash benefits were far from being limited to the elite. For example, many enterprises provided nurseries and kindergartens that were highly subsidized, and, in some countries, housing. Enterprise provision of goods and services played an important role in a shortage economy. Where enterprises could obtain supplies of scarce consumer goods, through barter with other producers, they were able to give their workers access to goods that would otherwise have been unobtainable. Competition for scarce labour through cash wages that was restricted by centralised wage determination could occur instead through fringe benefits.

In the West, substantial fringe benefits are available to top managers in the private sector. This aspect of remuneration from work in market economies has received much less attention than has the nomenklatura's benefits in socialist economies. (See also Chapter 5 by Gottschalk and Smeeding.)

Access to goods in short supply that could not be obtained elsewhere at *any* price seems an important difference in nonwage benefits under socialism. The existence of severe shortages in consumer goods clearly varied across country and time. For example, while reports of shortages of many consumer goods in the USSR in the 1970s abound, most consumption goods seem to have been in reasonable supply in Hungary in the late

---

[22] Dániel's earlier study attempted to allow for variations in quality as well as size of housing and employed a variety of different assumptions regarding valuation of the subsidy.

1980s. The distributional implications of shortages depends on how these shortages are overcome. Effective rationing could be highly egalitarian and even if secondary markets develop "the tendency towards dampening of real relative to monetary income differentials should be mitigated" (Bergson, 1984: p. 1058) albeit not eliminated. However, queues may be subject to manipulation—not all buyers are treated equally in the face of shortages as the discussion of public housing and of nonwage benefits indicates.

Social benefits in kind, subsidies and fringe benefits certainly do alter the light in which income data under socialism should be viewed. The same is true for income data in market economies and in the case of social benefits in kind the light is probably altered in much the same way. Milanovic (1995) surmises that subsidies and fringe benefits broadly speaking cancel out in their impact on inequality under socialism, but that the latter dominate in market economies, with the result that the generally higher inequality of cash incomes in OECD economies understates the true comparison. The evidence is insufficient for any such general conclusion and the picture, as for cash incomes, undoubtedly varied across time and between countries. What is certainly true is that the impact on economic well-being of these factors is important and needs monitoring during the transition alongside changes in cash incomes.

3. Distribution in transition—theory

No aspect of transition is tightly defined. We have seen above that there were significant differences in the starting points of the socialist economies of Central and Eastern Europe. There is also no unique endpoint for transition and there are several Western models between which there is room for choice but all of which also represent moving targets. The transition itself could also take many different forms as the experience of China and its regions demonstrate, as do the differences between Central Europe and the CIS. In this section we focus on several aspects of the transition relevant to the evolution of income distribution within the process itself.

While there are several theoretical models of, for instance, the reallocation of labour between sectors in a liberalised—but previously distorted—economy (see, for example, Flemming, 1993) and between a state owned and a private-sector characterised by distinct wage setting processes (see, for example, Aghion and Blanchard, 1994) they generate little inequality, except through unemployment, as labour is, essentially, assumed homogeneous. The first approach concentrates on the effects of the relative price changes associated with liberalisation which the latter ignore to concentrate on the effects of privatisation, which may itself be endogenous. According to the first approach instantaneous changes in relative product prices have implications for both factor prices and resource allocation—which can be expected to evolve together. This process could be influenced by a variety of interventions including employment subsidies or transitional protection. It is also likely that any tendency for the market clearing real wage for some category of labour to fall sharply would set up interactions with either the old or the new structure of income support possibly including formal or informal minimum (real) wages.

Nearly all socialist economies (with the exception of Czechoslovakia) embarked on the process of transition with a substantial monetary overhang. Thus where prices were liberalised they jumped, sometimes by factors of two or three. To the extent that monetary overhangs had accumulated from a flow of excess demand under controlled prices, there was a danger of continuing inflation and a need for stabilisation policies. Both of these interacted, as did the price jump itself, with income determination and income support processes. Several countries experimented with taxes on wage increases while apparently high ratios of pension or other benefits to wages were eroded by rapid inflation and lags in uprating benefits.

Unemployment itself was a virtual novelty, challenging the administration to devise and implement procedures, criteria, and structures for delivering benefits. Socialist economies distributed many social services through places of work. With the prospect of declining participation, smaller enterprises and higher labour turnover, higher unemployment, as well as separation of the state from production, this becomes less appropriate. The transfer of these services from enterprises to, say, municipalities, is a major undertaking which is likely to impinge on the support and services supplied. The fiscal system also needs to be rebuilt with personal and corporate direct taxation as well as the widespread adoption of Value Added Taxes often in incomplete forms (especially in the CIS).

Finally, the process of administrative reform has a number of implications for income distribution. It may be that the existence of abnormal quasi-rents would in any case bring protection racketeers into existence, certainly the incompleteness of liberalisation leaves underpaid bureaucrats in a position to make life difficult for new ventures unless they are paid off. Many aspects of the modern market economy are typically regulated whether financially, environmentally or in land use, not to mention by tax officers. It is not clear that either the bureaucrats of the former branch ministries or the staff of the communist enforcement agencies were very promising material for these *market* regulatory rôles. Assuming that new structures have to be developed, it is quite possible that the transition from central planning to market regulation will not be monotonic but will involve a period in which there is not much central effort at control while there remain sufficient vestiges of the old controls for corruption of the nomenklatura as well as the criminality of the so-called "mafia".

3.1. Transitional adjustment and the distribution of earnings

Some light on the consequences of rapid liberalisation of a heavily distorted centrally planned economy may be thrown by considering the effects of the rapid elimination of distortions in a (competitive) market economy. The parallel between the two situations is not very close for two reasons. First, the interventions under central planning included enterprise-specific ones with no obvious parallel in a market economy distorted by product-specific border or excise taxes or subsidies. Second, the distorted market economy has the market mechanisms and institutions in place to respond to changed price signals which may not be true of the formerly centrally planned economies.

What would happen if major distortions were eliminated overnight? Clearly, by assumption, relative prices would change radically at the enterprise level as well as at the consumer level. This will be true both of inputs, such as energy which was underpriced throughout COMECON, as well as of outputs. Thus value-added margins change sharply—some widening while others narrow. Resources should shift from sectors in which margins have narrowed to those in which they have widened. To the extent that this occurs, output at world prices will be increased thereby.

A number of commentators (see, for example, McKinnon, 1991; Hughes and Hare, 1992) argued that significant sectors of the centrally planned economies were subtracting value at world prices. These would find themselves facing negative value-added margins on liberalisation. If they could not change their input/output ratios very quickly, or change their product design or quality, the cessation of such activities would also raise world price GDP at the same time as releasing labour and other inputs for use elsewhere. In the very short run the scope for redeploying that labour would depend on the technical nature and flexibility of the capital employed in the rest of the economy— particularly where value added margins were widest. If capital were flexible, labour could be redeployed promptly without its physical or, in an open economy, its value marginal product being seriously depressed. In this case world price GDP could rise considerably and immediately, and with it, possibly, the market-clearing real wage (at the same prices).

At the other, and arguably more realistic, extreme, opportunities for ex post substitution of labour for capital in the high value-added-margin sectors are virtually nonexistent. Redeployed labour drives its marginal (physical) product down very rapidly before it has added much to world-price GDP. In this case the market-clearing real wage may fall sharply on liberalisation if labour is homogeneous and the market competitive, as in Fig. 6A. If it is not, in the short run, there may be marked differentials unrelated to previous patterns and not strongly related to long-term steady state differentials under the new regime—see Table 4.

There may of course exist some sectors, such as certain services or subsistence agriculture, in which the physical product of labour does not fall significantly as numbers rise. The living standard thus afforded would then play an important, albeit transitional, rôle in determining the distribution of income. If the relevant level was low relative to prevailing norms, whether dictated by social convention, formal minimum wages or a reservation wage driven by social security benefits, those not employed in organised sectors would join the ranks of the unemployed or possibly of those recorded as nonparticipants—see Fig. 6B.

Apart from the value of their leisure or the fruits of gardening or other possibly "grey" activity, output falls in such cases relative to those in which subsistence sectors act as residual employers and a fortiori relative to those in which the market clearing real

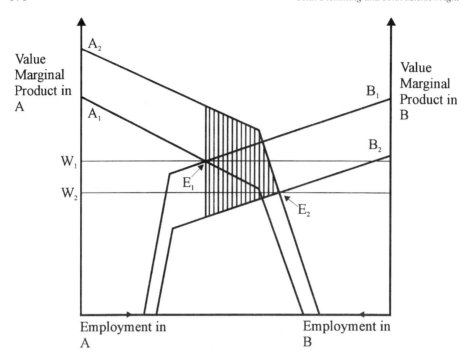

Fig. 6A. Two sector model of the labour market with homogeneous labour. The bends in the functions A and B relate to capacity levels. (The steeper segments might be vertical at least over some ranges.) Up to that point additional employment is on older/inferior vintages of equipment—beyond it more labour is applied to that equipment. E_1 is the initial (distorted) equilibrium. If distortions are removed (and other repercussions allowed, e.g., in the exchange rate) one curve rises, as $A_1 \rightarrow A_2$, and one falls, as $B_1 \rightarrow B_2$. If the shifts are large enough for the two flatter segments no longer to intersect, the new equilibrium at E_2 may be associated with a sharply reduced market clearing real wage (falling from W_1 to W_2). The shaded area is the addition to world price GDP as labour is redeployed from B to A.

Table 4

Impact of rapid liberalisation of a distorted market economy in which labour markets clear

| | | Capital/labour substitutability (ex post) | |
		High	Low
	Homogeneous and mobile	Market-clearing real wage tends to rise	Market-clearing real wage falls
Labour		Real wage dispersion remains low	
	Heterogeneous/immobile	Real wages tend to rise	Real wages tend to fall
		Real wage dispersion rises	Real wage dispersion tends to rise

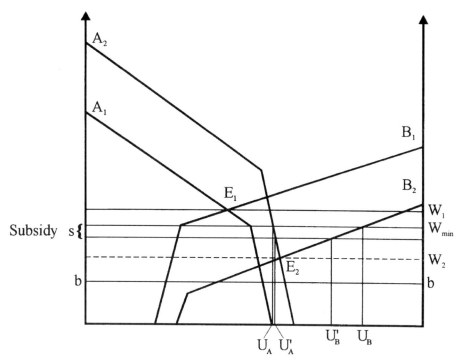

Fig. 6B. Two sector model of the labour market with homogeneous labour. Removal of the distortion shifts *A* and *B* as in Fig. 6A. At E_2 the wage W_2 is lower than the minimum wage $W_{\min}$. This gives rise to unemployment $U_A - U_B$. An employment subsidy s, paid to employers and leaving employees' net real pay unchanged at $W_{\min}$, would raise output, reduce dole payments (at the rate b) and reduce unemployment from $U_A - U_B$ to $U'_A - U'_B$. Alternative effects of the subsidy on wages and earnings are considered in the text.

wage falls little if at all. The implications for income distribution depend crucially on the cash income of the unemployed and nonparticipants. This might arise either under an explicit unemployment compensation scheme or under the terms of a more general social security safety net.

As has been stressed above, the process of transition is a dynamic process of re-source reallocation as well as a politico-economic process of reform, restructuring and institution-building, of which the former is the more amenable to economic analysis. At the new structure of liberalised relative prices, abnormal quasi-rents will accrue to the owners of some types of physical plant and machinery and also to the owners of certain types of human capital. These abnormal returns should induce the expansion of the supplies of the relevant types of capital thus bidding down their abnormal temporary rentals.

If the labour market were to clear at a relatively low average real wage while world price GDP actually rose (by an amount represented by the shaded area in Fig. 6A), there would clearly be a large increase in average profits and there might be a presumption that this shift in the factoral distribution of income would be favourable to investment. The investment would obviously tend to be concentrated in areas where returns were highest. How far this would extend to investment in any form of human capital would, as always, depend on the structure of the capital market and the appropriability of the returns. Low real earnings for most people would limit investment by households, while investment by profitable enterprises in training current or prospective employees might be deterred by their scope for migration to other employers. Limitation of investment in human capital to the children of workers themselves earning high quasi-rents would both slow down the process of adjustment and reinforce a cumulative deterioration in the distribution of income and wealth.

3.2. The scope for mitigating measures

The effect of the changed structure of value added margins on the distribution of earnings depends not only on the homogeneity or heterogeneity of labour skills but also on labour mobility between enterprises, industries and locations and also on the degree of competition in the market. Mobility was reduced in socialist states by the bureaucratic mechanisms for allocating accommodation—often linked to employing enterprises. The intensity of labour market competition immediately after liberalisation is very hard to assess although crucial for certain types of possible policy interventions.

Suppose that labour is homogeneous and labour market competition sufficiently intense to establish a single real wage. Suppose further that there were significant sectors subtracting value (at world prices) under the old regime, that capital is sector specific and has (ex post) virtually fixed coefficients and that there is no subsistence service or agricultural sector but a social security system which establishes a de facto minimum reservation real wage. This is clearly a recipe for post-liberalisation unemployment as well as a uniformly low real wage. A tax on profits used to subsidise employment would make some additional positive value added activities financially viable. It would thus raise employment and real (world price) GDP. It would not raise wages since the factors determining the reservation wage are unchanged. As long as the subsidy was smaller than the social security payments previously made to the unemployed, net government revenue and/or investible profits would actually rise.

The process can be illustrated by the following example:

If employment is n, the minimum wage $\underline{w}$, the subsidy s and the dole (unemployment benefit) b, an increase (ds) in the pre-existing rate of subsidy (s) raises employment by dn, it raises output by dn times labour's marginal product $(\underline{w} - s)$

(its net cost to employers). Thus output rises by $(\underline{w} - s)dn$ and household income by $(\underline{w} - b)dn$ and the total of profits plus government revenue minus dole payments (as the intramarginal subsidy boosts profits), by $(b-s)dn$, which is positive as long as $s < b < \underline{w}$.

Although the remarkably favourable effects of a profits-tax-financed employment subsidy in the model are sensitive to the subsidy's effect on the take-home pay of the marginal employee, it does not require perfect competition. It is shown in Appendix A that while labour sharing in the quasi rents raised by the subsidy and an effective minimum wage linked to average earnings make more demanding the conditions for incremental subsidisation to be so beneficial, it is by no means impossible that these conditions should be met.

In practice no transition economy implemented any such scheme, possibly because they were reluctant to take any risks with revenue at a time when raising revenue was seen as an essential element in a stabilisation package. In principle, if there were a single economy making the transition, many of the effects of a temporary employment subsidy could be achieved by a suitable structure of temporary protection.

For many of their client states, the international financial institutions recommend the tariffication of inherited distortions which should then be phased out over a number of years—see John Williamson's "Washington Consensus" (Williamson, 1997). An exception was, however, made for the European transition economies for reasons that have never been clear.

A programme of this sort would, however, have confronted several problems:

- that of converting the often opaque distortions of central planning and state trading into equivalent transparent border taxes;
- that of the initial enthusiasm of the central European transition economies for free trade (Messerlin, 1992);
- the complication of there being several transition economies, trade between which should not have been distorted simply because each of them was unready for free trade with the West; and
- the problem of making the timetable for phasing out the border taxes credible.

The last problem might be mitigated in several ways. The countries could have agreed amongst themselves in a trade treaty involving mutual commitments to phase out such transitional protection. Or its phasing out could have been a condition of World Bank or IMF assistance, or of access to EU markets under the Europe Agreements of the early 1990s. At that time the transition economies had very low formal tariffs. A declining ceiling could still have been imposed in a treaty and would have limited the scope for government concession to subsequent sectoral lobbying. The risk of such concession appears to have been underrated relative to those of an initially more protective regime initiated by government which might, by taking control and anticipating the lobbying pressure, have been better placed to resist it.

3.3. Wage controls and unemployment

In practice, intervention in labour markets was directed more to the restraint of inflation than to the support of employment. Wages were in several countries subject to controls and in others to taxes (such as the *Popiwek* in Poland) related to the rate of increase of nominal wage rates, enterprise wage bills or of average earnings. The latter offered an incentive to retain relatively low paid staff on the books to restrain the growth of the average. In Russia the excess of the average earnings over some multiple of the minimum wage was taxed as profits. This has the effect of converting the profits tax into a tax on value added (profits plus wages) less a per capita allowance per employee.

In Russia and other parts of the former Soviet Union enterprises kept some employees on the books at the minimum wage which might be only 10–25% of the average. There is some dispute as to how far this practice increased during the transition. It could be explained in several ways, in particular as reducing the taxation or as enabling those essentially unemployed to retain employment status which might be important to establish eligibility for a variety of social benefits (Standing, 1996).

The emergence of open unemployment called for administrative innovations to establish and operate unemployment benefit offices and labour exchanges. While the benefits scheme was operated consistently and fairly restrictively in the Czech Republic, a significant part of the fluctuation of registered unemployment in Poland in 1991–1993 has been attributed to variations in the application of eligibility standards. Effective replacement rates were also liable to wide variations with fluctuations in inflation rates and operating procedures. (See, for example, Boeri, 1994, 1995; Burda, 1993, 1995; Boeri and Edwards, 1998). One explanation offered initially for the continuing low level of open unemployment in Russia was that claims offices were so far apart as to be virtually inaccessible to many people (not only in rural areas).

3.4. Reforming delivery of social services and collection of taxes

Some of these issues should be modified as the rôle of enterprises in the provision of social services, always greater in the former Soviet Union than in Central Europe, diminishes, to be replaced (in practice often only partially) by a clearer and more transparent provision by agencies of central or local government. This switch is not easily achieved as the transfer of funds and responsibilities is difficult to synchronise across competing enterprises in different regions and sectors, and the agencies concerned may be unenthusiastic about their new role.

Of equal or greater import for the distribution of income is the direct tax system and also the system of indirect taxes and border taxes on consumer goods. On IMF and World Bank advice, Valued Added Taxation has been widely adopted in transition economies although the speed with which the reforms were claimed to have been introduced was such as to raise doubts as to the adequacy of the administrative machinery in fact in place. In Russia, in particular, there are grounds for doubting how quickly input tax was made recoverable as opposed to crude adjustments being made to cascading sales taxes.

While under central planning there were features of the pricing system that could be interpreted as commodity taxes (possibly at enterprise-specific rates) personal income taxes were even less well developed, particularly in the Soviet Union. Developing reporting, assessment and collection systems was not at all straightforward, as mentioned above. There are grounds for doubting the availability within the previous bureaucracy of personnel qualified for the collecting of taxes in a market economy. The scope for corruption is obvious and there is continuing evidence of failure to collect revenue in Russia and the rest of the CIS (EBRD, 1998). Such failures relative to approved budgets either lead to monetary financing and inflation or to public expenditure cuts often in the form of arrears of wages. As monetary controls have tightened, the problem of arrears and their impact, not well documented, on the distribution of income have increased.

3.5. Restitution

Appropriability is not a problem only in the case of returns to human capital, considered at the end of Section 3.1. In many transition economies property rights were initially ill-defined and difficult to enforce. Moreover protection racketeers might cream off quasi-rents and, if monopolistic, mafiosi discourage the adjustment process as the scope for their activities would be smaller in any long-term equilibrium.

Another uncertainty about property rights in a number of Central European transition economies arose from the decision to return real property to its former owners (or their descendants).[23] Uncertainty as to who had the best claim was liable to deter any incumbent or claimant from improving or even maintaining the disputed assets. In such cases the property was often vested in the incumbent with other claimants being made eligible for monetary compensation for their former expropriation. Interests in property by those who had, for instance, lent on its security were nowhere recognised.

Given the alternative of distributing the value uniformly amongst citizens of what had, in the interim, become state property, it is clear that policies of restitution—often of estates to emigré aristocrats—do not make a positive contribution to the equality of distribution of income and wealth. Nor, being related only to expropriation and restitution to the living, is restitution focused on compensating the most acute victims of communism.

One argument used to justify restitution was that the new regimes were pledged to respect private property and could demonstrate that commitment most effectively by

---

[23] Restitution of land to indigenous peoples is an issue in several other regions such as the USA, Canada, Australia and New Zealand. This usually relates to underdeveloped land in government ownership although in some cases (e.g., Australia) it may have been leased to graziers.

returning to its previous owners, or their descendants, property taken by communists. This is not a very convincing argument. If the re-establishment of private property is a unique event, its security under the new regime is not enhanced by restitution which is only relevant to the future to the extent that further expropriation is a possibility. At the same time restitution to emigré aristocrats in particular might have had the effect of alienating people from the new regime. The fact that restitution appears not to have been unpopular suggests that people either did not recognise the value of the assets in question, or were so alienated from the socialist regime they saw as having been the owners of the assets that they did not realise that what was being given back was, or could have been, theirs.

4. Distribution in transition—evidence

The annual *Transition Report* of the European Bank for Reconstruction and Development (EBRD) documents the changes in the Eastern European economies. Some of these changes are shown in Table 5 in the form of unweighted average values for groups of countries. The first column gives the value in 1997 (the last year for which we have data on the distribution of earnings or incomes) of the EBRD's "transition index", which is intended to summarise countries' cumulative progress from a planned to a market economy. The index takes into account a variety of dimensions of transition, including price liberalisation, privatisation, restructuring, competition policy, and reform of financial institutions.

The most advanced countries in 1997, in terms of the EBRD's judgement of progress in the transition, were those in Central Europe and the Baltics. All the countries in these two groups had a value of the transition index greater than 3.0 and on average the private sector accounted for over two-thirds of GDP. The four other groups of countries, three of which are formed by the countries of the Commonwealth of Independent States (CIS), had made less progress and retained higher public sector shares of output. The least progress of all had been made by the Central Asian republics, although the group average hides substantial variation (Kazakhstan and Kyrgyzstan had values of the transition index and private sector shares of output at about the average level for South East Europe, while Tajikistan and Turkmenistan were well behind).[24]

One expectation might be that inequality changes most in the countries which make the greatest progress away from the planned economy and where private activity accounts for the majority of output. To the extent that the state compressed the distribution of income pre-reform, surely a greater retreat of the state from the organisation and control of economic activity will be associated with a larger rise in inequality?

---

[24] There is substantial variation in some other groups too, notably the Western CIS where Russia was at this time much further advanced than the other three. By 1998 Russia had slipped back on the transition index to the level of Ukraine, following government controls on the economy introduced during the financial crisis of the summer (EBRD, 1998: Chart 2.2).

Table 5

Indicators of transition

	EBRD transition index	Private sector share of GDP, 1997	Change in real GDP, 1989–1997	Average annual inflation, 1991–1996	Average registered unemployment, 1991–1996	Government expenditure as share of GDP, 1996
		(%)	(%)	(%)	(%)	(%)
Central Europe	3.4	68	−1	34	10.6	46
SE Europe	2.7	59	−30	179	17.3	37
Baltics	3.2	67	−37	254	4.9	38
Western CIS	2.4	46	−50	775	1.3	38
Caucasus	2.4	50	−63	1926	3.1	19
Central Asia	2.2	41	−42	758	1.6	24

Note: Central Europe is the Czech Republic, Hungary, Poland, Slovakia and Slovenia; South East Europe is Albania, Bulgaria, FYR Macedonia and Romania; The Baltics are Estonia, Latvia and Lithuania; Western CIS is Belarus, Moldova, Russia and Ukraine; Caucasus is Armenia, Azerbaijan and Georgia; Central Asia is Kazakhstan, Kyrgyzstan, Tajikistan, Turkmenistan and Uzbekistan. The figures in the table are all unweighted averages of the data for each country. Source: EBRD (1997: Table 2.1) for the transition index and private sector share, EBRD (1998: Table 3.1 and country annexes) for GDP change and government expenditure share, and UNICEF (1998: Annex Tables 10.9 and 10.12) for inflation and unemployment.

Other factors suggest that any simple relationship between the extent of economic reform and the change in inequality will not be found. First, the withdrawal from direct organisation of economic activity by the state does not necessarily imply an indifference to the distributional implications of a more liberalised economy. Governments may try to redistribute income from those gaining to those losing as a result of economic liberalisation. Electoral pressure, a new constraint to the state's activity, may be one motive for this. A result of such redistribution may be that inequality of gross earnings widens faster than the distribution of household incomes.

Second, a continued dominant role for the state does not mean that the governments in the countries concerned will follow the same distributional objectives as before. The evidence reviewed earlier from the pre-reform period demonstrated that substantial changes in the distribution of earnings and household incomes took place during the socialist period as governments altered their distributional stance. Such alterations may continue, both among democratically-elected governments and among those that are a continuation of the previous regime. Table 5 shows that the slow reformers saw the largest falls in output over 1989–1997. (The extent to which this represents cause and effect is of course the subject of debate.) Groups within the population may differ sharply in their political leverage and hence in their ability to protect their living standards from the implications of these changes. For example, workers in energy industries, where output is now traded on world market prices, may be able to secure increases in their wages relative to the average. The huge rates of inflation shown in Table 5, experienced in particular by the slower reformers, will have permitted sharp changes in relative wage rates and in the relationship between state transfers and wages.[25] State transfers are an important element of government expenditure, which the last column in the table shows to vary substantially in terms of the share of GDP, and in particular to be much lower in the Caucasus and Central Asia than elsewhere.

A further complication is that the evidence on distributional changes refers to *measured* income inequality, as in the pre-reform period. Transition has seen a sharp reduction in consumer price subsidies, and on the evidence of the pre-reform period this will have had a regressive impact. Measured changes in the distribution of household incomes may provide a lower bound on changes in the distribution of economic welfare, and the importance of this may well vary across the groups of countries identified in Table 5, fast reformers cutting out subsidies more quickly. We consider some evidence on the distributional impact of remaining subsidies at the end of the section.

As in the discussion of the pre-reform period, we look first at evidence on changes in the distribution of earnings, before turning to household incomes. Throughout this discussion we consider only changes in *relative* incomes. The comparison of income growth with change in income inequality of course underlies much of the discussion of the change from planned to market economy, but it is too early to assess the consequences of incomplete transitions. (By 1997, measured output in only one country, Poland, exceeded the level achieved in 1989.) An investigation of this issue remains a task for the future.

4.1. Data sources in transition

Transition towards a market economy and, in many cases, to a more open society has important consequences for available sources of distributional data and the interpretation to be put on them. The household budget survey of the former Socialist Republic of Salubria may continue in the now democratic, mixed-economy, Salubrian state—but this does not mean that the data are collected as before or that they can be interpreted in the same light. Or the Salubrian statistical office may abandon its previous survey methodology completely. These changes affect the use of the available data to judge the impact of transition on income inequality.

Some issues will be obvious from our earlier discussion of data from the pre-reform period, including the comparison made with sources in Western countries. Transition has seen sharp increases in the share of private activity, poorly covered by many pre-reform surveys. There are more small firms, which are often excluded from employer earnings enquiries; there are more self-employed, a group often not included in pre-reform budget surveys and whose income is hard to measure if now included. Unemployment has made household incomes more variable over the year with the result that annual income is

---

[25] Inflation rates vary enormously within the groups of countries shown in Table 5 and the period chosen misses, for example, the hyper-inflation in Poland in 1990.

harder to measure than before. Systems of social security benefits have become more complex, including increased use of means-testing, and as a result are more difficult to survey. The introduction of personal income tax may provide a disincentive to accurately report incomes to household surveys. And a change in the relationship between the citizen and the state may of itself change willingness to cooperate with enquires by the state statistical office.

These changes should have reduced the quality of data that are collected. On the other hand, price liberalisation means that the data that do exist should more accurately represent the distribution of economic welfare than before, although this in turn reduces comparability with the pre-reform period. In each case the changes reflect the differences between one economic and political system and another.

Other changes are less obvious and are a feature of the *process* of transition. They may again be expected to reduce the quality of the data or their comparability with those from earlier years. Reductions in public expenditure as output has fallen will have cut statistical office budgets, which may reduce the quality of the work undertaken and the regularity with which data are collected. A common problem has been the loss of staff, lured away by higher private sector wages. Rampant inflation, which Table 5 shows has occurred especially (but not only) in parts of the former Soviet Union, results in various problems for surveying. Data on annual incomes may be rendered meaningless.[26] The phenomenon of arrears in wage payments and social security benefits, again common in the former Soviet Union, is an associated problem. Arrears represent a command over resources for the individual to whom they are owed but inflation greatly reduces their value. The introduction of progressive income tax may be coupled with a grossing-up of "first economy" earnings so as to leave net earnings unchanged, leading to a one-off spurious rise in earnings inequality.

The importance of these problems varies from country to country, as the examples of inflation and wage arrears illustrate. The same is true of the ability of statistical offices to cope with the challenges faced. The offices in many of the republics of the former Soviet Union have been in a particularly weak position, exacerbating the problems stemming from a poor inheritance of surveying tradition. Separate offices in each republic existed prior to the break-up of the Union but they had little autonomy. The Family Budget Survey seems to have continued much as before in many republics during the first half of the 1990s, becoming an even less suitable source for the study of income distribution—its multiple weaknesses exposed ever more severely by the change in economic system.[27]

To set against this there have been some positive developments in sources, often as a result of technical assistance from international organisations. The World Bank

---

[26] If surveying is continuous through the year and no adjustment is made of the monthly figures, the annual amounts will be dominated by the data for the last quarter.

[27] For example, the part of the survey relating to Uzbekistan was laudably expanded by the Republic's statistical office from 3000 to 4250 households in 1992 with the aim of improving the representativity of the quotas relating to each sector of the economy. However, the quotas were still unrepresentative of their target population (Falkingham and Micklewright, 1997: Table 3.1).

has been instrumental in developing completely new surveys in several former Soviet republics, using conventional methods of sample design and survey conduct, based on its Living Standard Measurement Study (LSMS) methodology (Oliver, 1997). A prominent example is the Russian Longitudinal Monitoring Survey (RLMS), conducted by the University of North Carolina (Mroz et al., 1997)—a survey of several thousand households, of which seven rounds had been held by the end of 1996 (with the first in 1992).[28] Other examples include surveys in Azerbaijan (1995), Kazakhstan (1996), Kyrgyzstan (1993), and Ukraine (1995).

The new data have enabled some important insights, but these surveys did not necessarily result in quick improvements in the capacity of statistical offices in the countries concerned (Falkingham and Micklewright, 1997).[29] (The main purpose of several of the surveys was to collect data for World Bank staff to carry out one-off assessments of poverty and of targeting of state spending.) However, clear progress has been made in some cases, for example the new official budget surveys in Belarus, Latvia and Lithuania (Martini et al., 1996; Lapins and Vaskis, 1996; Sniukstiene et al., 1996) and the LSMS-type survey carried out by the Kyrgyz statistical office in 1996 (National Statistical Committee of the Kyrgyz Republic, 1997). Even in Russia, where resistance to change appears to have been strong, revisions started to be made during 1996 to the sample design of the Family Budget Survey (Frolova, 1998).

The more advanced Eastern European statistical offices were better placed to react quickly to some of the problems of data collection posed by the change of economic system. The Hungarian statistical office began to include the self-employed in the country's budget survey in 1989; in 1992 the Polish statistical office extended the sample of its budget survey to households of the nonagricultural self-employed (the agricultural self-employed had already been included)—the survey in 1991 had excluded from coverage about 15% of all private households (Kordos, 1996: p. 1128). The same household type was included in the Czech and Slovak budget surveys in 1993. This was a negligible group in 1989 but by 1992 it represented 6% of households in the Czech Republic and 4% in Slovakia (Garner, 1998: p. 296). Users of Czech or Slovak budget survey data, or of Polish data, from the early 1990s are therefore faced with a changing sample coverage—an increasingly important group (likely to have disproportionately high or low incomes) is first excluded and then included in the survey.[30]

Coverage and representativeness have also changed due to varying survey response rates, and a fall in the willingness of households to participate in official surveys seems

---

[28] The availability of the RLMS microdata through the internet (www.cpc.unc.edu/rlms) provides a striking contrast with the situation regarding data in the Soviet period.

[29] Analyses of distributional issues with surveys sponsored by the World Bank in former Soviet republics include Mroz and Popkin (1995), Newell and Reilly (1996), Ackland and Falkingham (1997), Falkingham (1997), Commander et al. (1999) and the papers in Klugman (1997). An example using a survey from outside the former USSR is the work on Albania by Alderman (1998).

[30] Garner reports that the household types covered by the Czech and Slovak budget surveys (both quota samples) represented about 95% of all households in each republic in 1989, but that by 1992 the figures had dropped to 90 and 84% (1998: p. 296).

to have been characteristic of the transition. For example, response to the Czech micro-census fell 20 percentage points between 1989 and 1997, from 96% to 76% (Večerník, 1998). In Hungary, response to the budget survey fell from an average of 78% in the three surveys in 1983–1987 to 61% in the annual surveys in 1993–1995, with a figure of only 33% achieved during the latter period in the capital, Budapest.[31] Frolova (1998) reports declining response to the Family Budget Survey in Russia.[32]

The changing nature of the data, and of the interpretation that should be put on them, make it difficult to arrive at simple conclusions from the available evidence on the impact of transition on income distribution. As was put by the 1996 *World Development Report*, devoted to transition, "comparisons across countries and over time are very approximate" (World Bank, 1996: p. 67).

The *World Development Report* went on to argue that "some clear patterns emerge ... inequality has risen throughout the region". In the case of the Czech Republic, the evidence in the Report recorded a rise in the Gini coefficient of per capita household income of about seven percentage points between 1988 and 1993—a sizeable change. The sources were not given, but investigation reveals that the data from the two years came from very different surveys. The data for 1988 refer to information on annual income, collected in the official microcensus which covered some 60,000 households (the source we used in Fig. 5). Those for 1993 relate to income in January of that year, collected through a survey with a quota sample of some 1700 adults, conducted by the Institute of Sociology.[33] Like was not being compared with like (we show the consequence below).

Even when the sources concerned appear to be the same, there are good reasons for being cautious about accepting the evidence at face value. The uncertainties that surround the data make particularly valuable evidence on changes over time from different sources. Do the changes in earnings inequality recorded in a country's employer enquiry correspond with those suggested by the budget survey or some other source? Do independent surveys of household incomes corroborate the patterns in official sources? We try in what follows to collect evidence of this type so that a more robust picture of changes can be obtained.

---

[31] We are grateful to Judit Lakatos of the Hungarian Central Statistical Office for this information. It should be noted that the shortfall in response in Hungary and the other countries we refer to is not just due to refusal to participate. For example, Lapins and Vaskis (1996) point to the deficiencies in available sampling frames in the early transition period as a major factor in the 30% nonresponse rate to the new Latvian budget survey.

[32] By contrast, response to the Polish budget survey has increased sharply, apparently as a result of a reduction in the period for which households are asked to participate from three months to one month (Kordos, 1996: Tables 1 and 2).

[33] The Institute of Sociology of the Academy of Sciences conducted a series of such surveys of "Economic Expectations and Attitudes" from 1991. The surveys are an important initiative but their author, Jiri Večerník, has been careful to note that the income questions are not as detailed as in the microcensus. (Respondents to the EEA surveys were asked five simple questions about their own income and that of all other household members.) And he comments "it is clear that the quality of our surveys' data could not be the same as with statistical surveys. Results could serve as preliminary information only" (Večerník, 1993: p. 32). Results from the EEA surveys and other Czech sources, covering a range of issues, are given in (Večerník, 1996).

Where possible, we compare *series* from before and after the end of the period of the planned economy, so as to avoid conclusions that hinge unduly on comparisons made for single years. The data series from the transition period are, of course, rather short, and by definition reflect an unfinished process—but it is that process which is of most interest, rather than a particular point along the way. As we noted at the start of the chapter, the study of transition is not one of comparing *equilibria* before and after the end of socialism.

4.2. *The distribution of earnings in transition*

How has the size distribution of earnings changed in economies in transition? Labour markets in Central and South-Eastern Europe have been characterised by substantial unemployment, sectoral shifts in employment and rapid growth in the private sector, and rising returns to education and skill (Allison and Ringold, 1996; Rutkowski, 1996a).

The picture in many of the republics of the former Soviet Union is rather different, reflecting in part their slower pace of economic liberalisation. One important difference has been the lower rates of open unemployment in the first half of the 1990s, with adjustment in the labour market to the large falls in output and changes in terms of trade being largely in terms of price rather than quantity—at least in terms of formal shedding of labour. This difference is reflected in the registered unemployment rates shown in Table 5, although these data undoubtedly understate the true level of unemployment in many former Soviet republics, where the incentive to register as unemployed has often been low. For example, unemployment in Russia as measured by the standard ILO/OECD criteria of search and availability for work was nearly 5% in late 1992 and over 9% by the end of 1995, compared to less than 1% and little more than 3% respectively, according to the official register.[34]

We start with Central Europe. In the case of former Czechoslovakia, we have data from the transition period only for the Czech Republic. A series of data for the distribution of earnings in Slovakia appears not to exist (or at least is not readily available) and this is particularly unfortunate given the natural interest in the different experiences of the two halves of the former federation after their separation in 1992.[35] (We saw earlier that the distribution of earnings in the two republics was very similar at the end of the 1980s.)

Figure 7 shows for 1980–1997 the decile ratio, and the ratios of the top and bottom deciles to the median, for the distribution of monthly gross earnings for men and women taken together (full-time workers). The estimates for the 1980s are the same as those in Fig. 1 (except in the case of the Czech Republic although the source here is the same,

[34] The figures on ILO/OECD basis are from the labour force survey for 1992Q4 and 1995Q4, given in the OECD CCET labour market database.

[35] Rutkowski (1996a: p. 54) gives information on the distribution of earnings in Slovakia in 1993 but the data come from a labour force survey and are not therefore comparable in nature with those from an employer earnings enquiry given for 1989 (Jan Rutkowski pointed out to us that the 1993 data do not refer to the public sector only as stated in his paper).

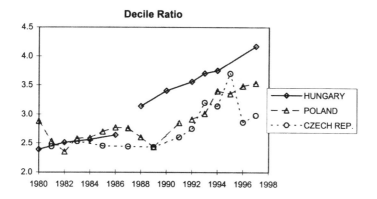

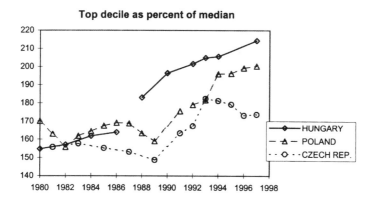

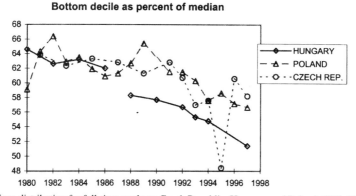

Fig. 7. Earnings distribution for full-time workers: Czech Republic, Hungary, and Poland, 1980–1997. Source: see Fig. 1 and Appendix B (except 1988 for Hungary, which is from Atkinson and Micklewright, 1992: Table HE1).

the Fig. 1 results referring to all of Czechoslovakia) and are included so that changes during the 1990s can be viewed in relation to any that occurred in the previous decade. (The reader should note that the scale in this and other graphs covering the 1990s is not necessarily the same as in those earlier in the chapter for the socialist period alone.)

The data for the 1990s are a continuation of the same series of employer enquiries from the pre-reform period, and in this sense there is comparability across the two decades. However, the coverage of the enquiries and the definitions of the included earnings may have changed during transition. We noted earlier that the introduction of progressive personal income taxation will lead to a break in the series if accompanied by grossing-up of earnings to leave net pay unchanged. In Hungary this occurred in 1988 which is why the figure for this year was not included in Fig. 1. The same occurred in Poland in 1992.[36] The extent to which measured earnings inequality rose as a result of the changes is difficult to judge and we have dealt with the problem by merely indicating in the diagram a break in the series (the effect in Hungary appears to be much larger than in Poland). In all three countries there have been growing exclusions from coverage, the importance of which are again hard to gauge. The data for the enquiries in Hungary and the Czech Republic exclude firms with less than 50 and 25 employees respectively. The Polish enquiry excludes private sector firms with less than 6 employees.

The decile ratio for Hungary shows a steady increase from 1988, reaching 4.17 in 1997. This continues a trend that was already present over 1980–1986 but at a rate that is over two and a half times faster. To help put this into perspective, the average annual increase in Hungary during 1980–1986 was the same as in Britain during 1980–1990, a period in which inequality is considered to have risen quite rapidly (Atkinson and Micklewright, 1992: Table BE1). By this yardstick the widening of the distribution in Hungary over the 1990s was indeed fast. A look at the lower parts of the diagram shows that the rise in inequality in Hungary was driven more or less equally by changes at either end of the distribution.

The story in Poland for the 1990s is similar. The decile ratio rises rapidly at much the same annual rate as in Hungary (again driven by changes at either end of the distribution), although it was only in 1994 that its value exceeded those in 1976–1978 shown in Fig. 1.

The figures for the Czech Republic, however, show much greater variation and the changes at each end of the distribution during the 1990s are more complicated. The decile ratio for 1996–1997 was below that in 1993–1995. We have not established the reasons for the changes but the overall pattern shows the danger of focusing on individual years during the transition period—just as earlier we noted the danger of taking a single year when studying the socialist period.

The exclusion from the data of persons working for small firms may affect both the level of measured earnings inequality at any one time and its speed of change. In the case

---

[36] Personal income tax was introduced in the Czech Republic in 1993 but in a manner that apparently led to no effect on measured earnings inequality (we are grateful to Jiri Večerník for this information). Information on coverage of the Czech and Polish enquires is taken from Večerník (1995) and Rutkowski (1996b).

of Hungary, the employer enquiry does in fact include these persons, although they are kept separate by the statistical office in the analysis. We have the data for 1993 and the number of employees concerned was considerable—over 20% of all full-time workers were in firms with less than 50 workers. Not surprisingly, their earnings differ from those of employees of larger firms and when we include these individuals in the calculations the decile ratio rises from 3.70 to 4.01. It seems a safe bet that the ratio including the smaller firms' workers in 1997 would be at least 4.5.

In all three countries, there is also information from household survey data on the distribution of earnings. Pudney (1994a,b) compares results from the same employer enquiry data for 1988–1992 used in Fig. 7 (for firms with more than 50 employees) with those based on budget survey for 1989 and 1991. He finds that the two sources tell the same story for the change in inequality, but that the level is substantially higher in the budget survey data.[37] By contrast, Večerník (1995) finds a notably larger rise in earnings inequality between 1988 and 1992 in Microcensus data for the Czech Republic than is recorded in the employer enquiry used in Fig. 7. And labour force survey data for Poland show very little change in the dispersion of monthly earnings over 1992–1996 (Newell and Socha, 1998); the decile ratio was 2.69 at both the beginning and end of the period, compared to a rise from 2.91 to 3.48 in the employer data in Fig. 7. All these results again show the danger in taking the estimates from one set of data as being definitive.

Hungary, Poland and the Czech Republic are countries that were well advanced on the process of economic reform by the mid-1990s. The changes in Hungary began long before 1989; Poland always had a substantial private sector; the Czech Republic had by 1995 the largest private sector share of GDP of any economy in transition. Russia, by contrast, has been a slower reformer (although faster than several others). How did measured earnings inequality change in this country where the transition process had further to go by the late 1990s? Figure 8 shows how the decile ratio and the top and bottom deciles relative to the median evolved in Russia over 1981–1997, again based on data on monthly earnings for full-time workers from employer earnings enquiries (the same source as in Fig. 1 for the USSR).

The changes in measured earnings inequality in these data are extraordinary, dwarfing those recorded for Hungary, Poland and the Czech Republic. In the last year of the Soviet Union, 1991, the data for Russia show a jump in the decile ratio from 3.4 to 4.3, restoring it to the level shown by Fig. 1 for the end of the 1950s—or about that for Hungary in 1997. In 1992, the first year of price liberalisation, the decile ratio in Russia

---

[37] A further source is the annual panel survey of 2000 households started by the research institute, TARKI, in 1992. Péter Galasi kindly calculated for us the decile ratio of monthly earnings of full-time employees in the TARKI panel who worked a full month (the same definition of sample and time period to that in the employer enquiry data). The TARKI data refer to net earnings and not surprisingly in view of deductions due to a progressive income tax, these data show a substantially lower level of earnings dispersion than do the employer enquiry data that refer to gross amounts (although if an estimate of the tax paid by each individual is added back into the data, a substantially higher decile ratio for gross earnings is found). The change in the decile ratio showed by the TARKI panel is more erratic than in the employer enquiry but broadly speaking moves up at the same speed.

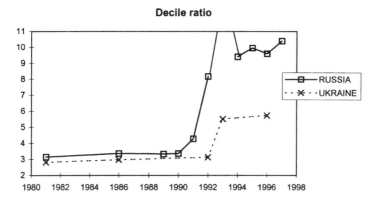

Decile ratio

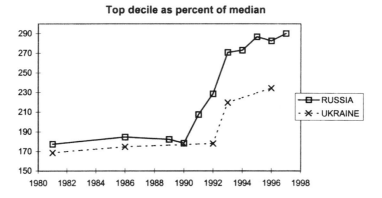

Top decile as percent of median

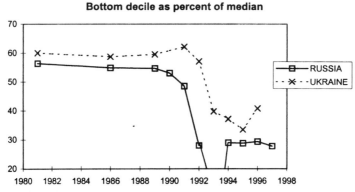

Bottom decile as percent of median

Fig. 8. Earnings distribution for full-time workers: Russia and Ukraine, 1981–1997. Source: Atkinson and Micklewright (1992: Table UE5) and Appendix B.

leaps to over 8, and, incredibly, almost doubles again the next year to over 15—off the top of our graph—before falling back to about 9 or 10 in 1994–1997, a level far above that in any OECD country.[38] The bottom part of Fig. 8 shows that the rise in inequality has been driven, broadly speaking, by similar changes at both ends of the distribution, as in the Central European countries. The bottom decile halved relative to the median over 1989–1997 while the top decile rose by 60% . Put another way, the fall in the bottom decile would have been sufficient alone to push the decile ratio to 6.5, while the rise in the top decile alone would have driven it up to 5.3.

What has been the cause of this dramatic widening of the Russian earnings distribution? The changes seem almost to defy credibility.

The first issue to consider is indeed whether, or not, the rise in dispersion recorded in these data is spurious in some sense. Is it found in other datasets that provide an alternative source of information to the official employer enquiry? One might expect the Russian enquiry to have deteriorated in quality and representativeness more than those in the Central European countries considered earlier. (The Russian enquiry is meant to cover both state and private employers but we have no knowledge of its coverage in practice during the 1990s.) Or is the definition of "full-time" work meaningful in any Russian dataset from this period? Are there large numbers of persons in the data who are officially employed full-time but who do little or no work, and who are paid accordingly? What is the treatment in the data of wage arrears, which grew notably in importance in Russia in the first half of the 1990s?

We have no other data for Russia that span both the break-up of the USSR and the liberalisation of prices in 1992. However, the Russian Longitudinal Monitoring Survey (RLMS), a household survey referred to in our earlier discussion of sources, provides information from the second half of 1992 onwards, each round of the survey containing several thousand employees who should form a representative sample of all workers. Table 6 gives quantile ratios from three rounds of RLMS for earnings paid in the previous month (if positive) in the respondent's main job. These show a level of inequality of a similar order of magnitude to those in the employer enquiry, especially for 1994–1995 when the ratios of top and bottom deciles to the median, as well as the decile ratio, correspond quite well in the two sources.

The results in Fig. 8 for the mid-1990s therefore appear to be repeated in a quite different dataset. But do either the employer enquiry or the RLMS really refer to full-time earnings? Russian enterprises often sought to minimise lay-offs during the period in question, putting employees on leave with no or minimal pay or on short-time work. By mid-1994, 22% of the labour force were apparently in one of these categories (Standing, 1996: p. 82). Those on short-time work (which seems to have been much the more common of the two) probably enter the employer enquiry data (we have no information about those on leave), implying that the dispersion shown in Fig. 8 is biased upwards.

---

[38] In each year both top and bottom deciles lie in closed intervals containing only a few percent of the distribution, so the results cannot be very sensitive to the method of interpolation. The only exception is in 1997 when the top decile lies in an open interval containing 14% of the distribution.

Table 6

Quantile ratios of monthly earnings for full-time workers in the Russian Longitudinal Monitoring Survey (RLMS)

RLMS wave	Q_{90}/Q_{10}	Q_{90}/Q_{50}	Q_{10}/Q_{50}
1992 (round 1—Jul/Sept)	6.3	2.50	0.40
1994 (round 5—Nov/Dec)	9.8	2.95	0.30
1995 (round 6—Oct/Nov)	9.2	2.75	0.30

Note: Interviewing in each round of RLMS is conducted over two or more months and respondents are asked the earnings paid in the previous month. Before calculating the quantiles, in each case we have adjusted the data for changes in average earnings between the months covered. Source: Calculations were made from microdata. Sample size was 5386 in 1992, 2505 in 1995, and 2201 in 1995. We restricted the samples to those working as an employee in their main job, with earnings paid in the last month, and with hours worked in the last month of 140 hours or more.

On the other hand, the results from the RLMS in Table 6 are restricted to individuals who reported working at least 140 hours in the previous month in the job in question, and should therefore be largely free of this problem. (It is of course possible that some respondents are not actually working the hours that they report.) It should also be re-membered that the rise in dispersion shown in Fig. 8 is not just on account of changes at the bottom of the distribution—there was a sharp increase in inequality at the top as well.

The issue of wage arrears further complicates matters, and underlines the difference between an employer enquiry and a survey of employees. RLMS data show that by late 1996, a half of all working-age adults were owed money by their primary employer, with "these delinquent payments being equal, on average, to one month's expenditures for an average household" (Mroz et al., 1997: p. 14). Arrears are said to be the main cause for the rise in the number of respondents reporting employment but no earnings for the previous month, from 6% of the labour force in 1992 to 21% in 1996. The employer earnings enquiry seems to ignore the distinction between arrears and payment—the figures reported to the statistical office apparently include both earnings actually paid and those still owed to workers. The RLMS figures refer to payments received, but the data do not allow the identification of either partial payments made in the last month or payments that included arrears from earlier pay-periods. Both of these would lead to upward bias in the recorded dispersion.

Notwithstanding all these difficulties, it is difficult to dismiss the levels of recorded earnings dispersion in Russia in the mid-1990s as a mere aberration of the data. A substantial part of the inequality in full-time earnings recorded in the available data for Russia seems to be genuine, especially when viewed in the light of accounts of wage determination during the transition.

Mikhalev and Bjorksten (1995) and Standing (1996) both emphasise the contrasts between wage setting in the "budgetary" sector (enterprises and institutions paid from the state budget), in state-owned enterprises, and in the private sector, composed partly of privatised former state enterprises and partly of new private firms. Centralised wage setting remained only in the budgetary sector, where wage indexation was carried out by periodic increases in the minimum wage to which the wage tariff scale was fixed. The minimum wage was changed twice in 1992, three times in 1993, but only once in 1994. Substantial erosion of wages in the budgetary sector relative to other sectors occurred both between these changes and over the period 1991–1994 as a whole, when the minimum wage dropped from about 25 to 8% of the average wage. Few workers were actually *paid* at the level of the minimum pre-transition—the importance of the minimum wage in Russia comes from its link with other wage rates and social security benefits.[39]

State-owned enterprises gained financial autonomy in 1992 with managers free to set wages as desired, subject to some limited union influence (see also Commander et al., 1995). And by mid-1994 medium or large-sized enterprises employing 85% of the industrial labour force had been privatised (Standing, 1996: p. 11). The effect on wages depended on the nature of each enterprise's business—workers in enterprises operating as natural monopolies, notably in energy extraction and supply, saw big rises in relative wages. Wages in light manufacturing, hit by a sharp reduction in demand for output, fell relative to others. The private sector, important in trade and financial services, emerged as the sector with the highest average wages. Survey data for different months in the first half of 1994 record average private sector wages consistently about double those in state-owned enterprises (Mikhalev and Bjorksten, 1995: Table 15). Summarising the situation, Standing argues that "the wage system that emerged in the early and mid-1990s could be characterised as one of the most flexible conceivable" (1996: p. 113) and reports evidence from employer surveys of increasing determination of wages according to individual performance[40] (see also Layard and Richter, 1995).

Was the increase in Russian earnings dispersion associated with much movement by different groups around the distribution, or are those doing well before and after 1991 the same people? The evidence is mixed. Workers in energy extraction and supply did relatively well after 1991 but also benefited from the bias towards the "productive" sector pre-reform. Standing, however, argues that interindustry wage differentials were changing by the mid-1990s (1996: p. 143). There seems agreement about some groups. Mikhalev and Bjorksten report that "a striking development is that professionals and engineers who have traditionally been underpaid in Russia have lost more ground in recent years" (1995: p. 22), noting that many are found in the budgetary sector.

[39] The link with state transfers is a feature in common with other transition countries, including several in Central Europe. Standing and Vaughan-Whitehead (1995) argue that it has led to a reduction in the importance of the minimum wage in the region's labour markets as governments have used minimum wage policy as a way of controlling expenditure on state transfers. (The minimum wage in Hungary, for example, declined from 65% of the average wage in 1989 to 35% by mid-1994.)

[40] He also argues that the excess-wage tax applied to enterprises in Russia in the wake of price liberalisation provided an incentive for managers to retain very low paid employees so as to reduce the average wage, a possibility we noted in Section 3.

By way of comparison with Russia we include in Fig. 8 what is more limited data for Ukraine, the second most populous former Soviet republic. Ukraine provides a comparator which has been one of the slowest reformers among all the former socialist countries and where macroeconomic collapse has been even deeper than in Russia. The differences in the figures for 1992 between Russia and Ukraine are striking. From then on dispersion rises sharply in Ukraine although we are only able to track adequately the changes from year to year at the bottom of the distribution.[41] Both bottom and top decile stay somewhat closer to the median than in Russia (especially the top decile) but the decile ratio by 1996 is 5.7, well above the level for the Central European countries in Fig. 7. (We have no information about the quality or coverage of the Ukraine data during the 1990s, which, like those from the 1980s, come from an employer enquiry.)

How do the levels of earnings inequality in the 1990s in the countries we have considered compare with those in other industrialised countries? The 1997 values of the decile ratio from the employer enquiries in our five transition countries were (to one decimal place):

Czech Republic	3.0
Poland	3.5
Hungary	4.2
Ukraine (1996)	5.8
Russia	10.4

The figures for Ukraine and, especially, Russia are well in excess of those found in OECD countries, although for these two cases there is considerable uncertainty about what the data actually measure. Looking back at Fig. 3, the level in Hungary is at about that in Canada or the US and well above those in Western Europe (and we argued that the true value in Hungary was higher). The value for Poland just exceeds that in Britain, a country with one of the highest levels of earnings inequality in the European Union (Eurostat, 1998). The Czech Republic has a value equal to that for France in 1990 and above those in the same year for Australia and Germany.

4.3. Inequality of household incomes in transition

How do the changes in inequality of households' incomes compare with those of employees' earnings? As with the pre-reform data, the change in the unit of observation and the inclusion of other sources of income may alter the picture considerably, and it is notable that the share of labour market earnings in total household income declined across a range of countries in the first half of the 1990s; Milanovic (1999) reports falls of 10–20%.

---

[41] We do not estimate the top decile in 1991, 1994 or 1995 since in these years it lies in an open interval, containing a quarter of the distribution in 1991 and 1994 and over 40% in 1995.

The impact of emerging unemployment may reinforce that from higher earnings dispersion if job losses are concentrated in households where other members are in the lower part of the earnings distribution. And if job losses are correlated across household members, the impact on household income inequality will be larger still. (An analysis of the changing numbers of workless households in transition economies, along the lines of the work by Gregg and Wadsworth (1996) for OECD countries, would be of considerable interest.) An increased importance of self-employment and capital income can be expected to have the same effect. On the other hand, redistributive taxation and cash transfers may pull back the rise in overall income inequality beneath that of earnings.

As with the discussion of earnings, we look first at Central Europe. Figure 9 shows Gini coefficients in the 1990s for the Czech Republic, Hungary, and Poland, together with those for the 1980s shown earlier in Fig. 5. The data for the 1990s, as for the earlier decade, refer to income per capita, although this adjustment may now be harder to defend due to the reduced importance of subsidies for housing and fuel. The sources are the same as before in the Czech Republic and Poland (the official microcensus and budget survey respectively) although coverage may well have changed—we pointed out the extension of the Polish survey to full coverage of the self-employed in 1992 and the fall in response in the Czech microcensus during the 1990s. In the case of Hungary, the source for 1987–1997—the official budget survey—differs from that used in Section 2— the official income survey. The Gini coefficient for the overlapping year, 1987, differs by over 3 percentage points. Hungarian statisticians stress that the income survey was the superior source at this time.

Hungary stands out as registering only a modest rise in dispersion of individuals' per capita incomes, a change in the Gini of 3 percentage points over 1989–1997, (or 4 from 1987) which may be compared with that for employees' earnings over 1988–1997 of 8 points. There was even a fall between 1989 and 1991, whereas the rise for earnings was continuous. And the average annual increase over 1991–1997 was little more than that for 1982–1987.

Growth in income inequality was more marked in Poland, with the Gini rising 6 points in the eight years from 1989, although here too it fell initially—when earnings inequality was rising—and the increase to 1997 was again less than that for employees' earnings. The Czech Republic also registers a 6 point rise in the per capita income Gini, between 1988 and 1996 (as does the Gini for earnings), with the rate of increase the same as that for Hungary over 1991–1997.

Do other sources for the three countries give similar results to these? In the case of Poland, nothing can be done—the budget survey appears to be the only regular source of information on household incomes. We are unable to see, for example, whether the jump in inequality shown in 1993 is shared by another dataset.[42]

---

[42] Figure 7 shows only modest growth in earnings inequality in this year, and totals for different headings of state social expenditures in cash show no sharp differences from 1992 (Rutkowski, 1998, Annex 1).

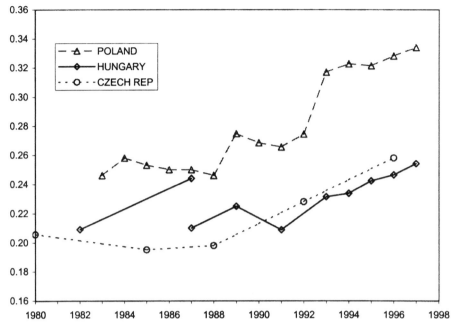

Fig. 9. Gini coefficient for the individual distribution of per capita income: Czech Republic, Hungary and Poland, 1980–1997. In the case of Hungary, results for 1982–1987 are from the income survey (as in Fig. 5) and those for 1987–1997 are from the budget survey. Source: See Fig. 1 and Appendix B (except for the budget survey figure for Hungary for 1987 which is from Milanovic, 1998: Table A4.3).

Figure 10 shows results based on alternative sources for Hungary and the Czech Republic (these again refer to annual income per capita). For Hungary, our other source is the TARKI household panel survey.[43] This source shows a notably higher level of income inequality than the budget survey—the Gini coefficient is 7–8 percentage points higher, which is a big difference. The ranking reflects that of the income and budget surveys in 1987 (see also Andorka et al., 1996). But it is comforting to see that the two sources give a reasonably similar picture of the changes between the early and mid 1990s—a rise in the Gini of about 3 percentage points.

For the Czech Republic, the budget survey is an alternative source to the microcensus. It has the attraction of providing information annually, allowing changes over time to be tracked more carefully, and of the data being collected through the year rather than through recall. But its sample design (a quota panel sample with no planned rotation) may well lead to inferior coverage, especially in the early 1990s. For 1993–1997 we show our own estimates of the per capita Gini based on interpolating the distribution from grouped data, but for 1989–1993 we draw on what are undoubtedly superior esti-

[43] See footnote 37.

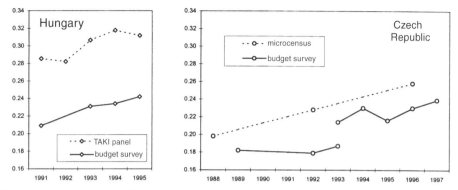

Fig. 10. Alternative estimates of the Gini coefficient for the individual distribution of annual per capita income: Hungary and the Czech Republic in the 1990s. Source: Hungary: (a) TARKI panel results from Galasi (1998: Table 1) (Galasi's table refers to the year of interview but since the annual income data cover the 12 months to March we have given his results as referring to the year prior to interview), (b) budget survey results as in Fig. 9; Czech Republic: (a) budget survey results for 1989–1993 from Garner (1998: Table 13.1) and Garner and Terrell (1998: footnote 30) and those for 1993–1997 from Appendix B, (b) microcensus results as in Fig. 9.

mates by Garner (1998) and Garner and Terrell (1998) who use the survey microdata and in addition re-weight to improve their representativeness. The figures for the overlapping year, 1993, illustrate the sensitivity of results to the precise methods used.

The budget survey shows a smaller rise in income inequality than the microcensus. The Garner/Terrell results show essentially *no* change in income inequality to 1992, and a rise of just a half percentage point over 1989–1993. Our estimates for the later period show a change of a two and a half points over 1993–1997. Neither the budget survey nor the microcensus support the finding from the 1996 *World Development Report* that we referred to earlier of a 7 percentage point rise in the Gini coefficient in the Czech Republic between 1988 and 1993, a finding based on taking two quite different sources for the two years.

Although the alternative sources for Hungary and the Czech Republic do show some differences, the broad picture is not dissimilar. The early phase of transition in the first part of the 1990s in these countries and in Poland saw small or even no increases in income inequality at a time when the earnings distribution was definitely widening, followed by larger increases.[44] (The microcensus results for the Czech Republic are an exception, in that they show a steady increase, but there are only two observations in the period under review.) Looking back at Table 3, the last values shown in Fig. 9 for Hungary (0.25) and the Czech Republic (0.26) are at the high Scandinavian or low Benelux level for the late 1980s—towards the lower end of the OECD range, although the alternative source puts Hungary near the average. That for Poland (0.33), is around

[44] This is broadly in line with the conclusions of Boyle Torrey et al. (1996) who use microdata from a variety of sources for the three countries up until 1992.

the level at that time for Australia, Canada, France, Italy, Portugal and the UK—above the OECD average.

Garner and Terrell (1998) provide a careful analysis of different components of household income in the Czech Republic using budget survey data for the early transition period. (They also cover Slovakia, where the picture turns out to have been similar.) Decomposing the changes in the Gini coefficient, they show that increased inequality of labour earnings was largely compensated for by changes to the tax and, especially, the transfer system.

The importance of changes in state transfers can also be seen in Poland, although here the story told in Milanovic (1998) and Rutkowski (1998) is rather different to the Czech one. The equalising impact in 1995 of all cash transfers taken together was less than in 1989. The figures are dominated by expenditures on state earnings-related pensions that rose sharply, from 7% of GDP in 1989 to 16% in 1994–1995, becoming more concentrated on higher parts of the income distribution (Rutkowski, 1998: Tables 3.7 and A1-1). The equalising effect of other state transfers, however, increased. The same picture of contrasting impacts of changes in pensions and other cash transfers is found for Hungary over 1987–1993 (Milanovic, 1998: Table 4.2) although in this case the changes for pensions were more modest. (Jarvis and Pudney, 1995, however, draw attention to the reduction in progression in personal income tax in Hungary since its introduction in 1988.)

We turn now to Russia. Fig. 11 shows the Gini coefficient for per capita income calculated from the official Family Budget Survey (FBS), which has many deficiencies, and the Russian Longitudinal Monitoring Survey (RLMS), used earlier to look at earnings, a source that should provide much more reliable estimates. The FBS figures refer to annual income, although it is unclear what this means given the enormous inflation experienced in several years. The RLMS figures refer to income over one month. (There are almost certainly other significant differences between the definitions of income in the two sources.)

The FBS series shows a huge jump in the Gini between 1992 and 1993 of 11 percentage points. After a further slight rise in 1994, it falls back somewhat in 1994–1997 to around 0.38, effectively the value for the USA shown in Table 3, the OECD maximum. The RLMS figures are substantially higher, by 4 percentage points in 1993–1994, rising to over 10 points in 1996. (The difference is at its greatest in 1992, the year of price liberalisation, when the FBS data may be particularly suspect.)[45] Income inequality

---

[45] Other figures from the FBS show a higher level of income inequality for 1992 than that in Fig. 11. Our own estimate, based on tabulated FBS data labelled "average of quarterly figures", is much higher (0.36). Doyle (1996) estimates the Gini for per capita income from tabulated data for five different months in 1992 and reports a 9 point increase between March and August. (If the normal practice of the Russian statistical office were followed to produce these data, the monthly figures would in fact represent income cumulated during the year to the month in question, but unadjusted for price changes.) The RLMS figure for 1992 refers to the summer, after liberalisation had begun.

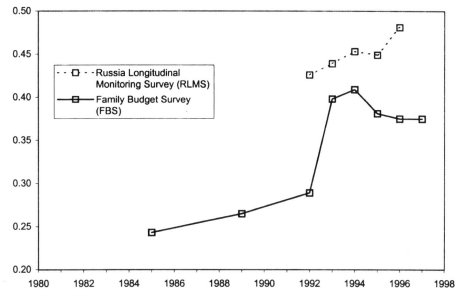

Fig. 11. Gini coefficient for the individual distribution of per capita income: Russia, 1985–1997. Source: See Appendix B for FBS figures. RLMS results refer to monthly income and are from Commander et al. (1999: Table 5, rounds 1 and 4–7).

in Russia, judged by this source, was well above the top of the OECD range by the mid-1990s.

One obvious concern is the implication of price differences across regions, which are substantial. In December 1995, average food prices faced by the 10% of the population living in the most expensive regions exceeded those for the 10% living in the cheapest regions by well over 50%.[46] Moreover, inflation rates have varied substantially between regions, especially over the most rapid period of price change, 1992–1993.[47] Does this mean that the dispersion of nominal incomes is much greater than that of real incomes? (The same question would apply in our earlier analysis of earnings.) It transpires that adjustment of household incomes in the RLMS for differences in regional prices results in only small differences to the estimated level of income inequality and the calculations in Fig. 11 are in fact already based on incomes adjusted for differences in regional price inflation.

---

[46] This calculation is based on data on the cost of a 19 good food basket for one city in each of Russia's 88 regions (excluding Chechnya). (Eleven autonomous regions that contain only 2% of the population are excluded from the calculation.) The distribution of prices is then calculated weighting the cost of each city's basket by its region's population. We are grateful to Kitty Stewart for this information.

[47] The highest measured rate of consumer price inflation over the 12 months from December (Kalmykia Republic in the Volga region) was two and a half times the lowest (St. Petersburg) (Stewart, 1998: Appendix A).

The huge rise in income inequality in Russia comes as no surprise in the light of what happened to the distribution of earnings, shown earlier. But as in Central Europe, there were other factors involved. Milanovic decomposes the change in the Gini coefficient between 1989 and 1994 (1998: Table 4.2). The increased dispersion of earnings is certainly the main factor driving higher inequality but the changes in all other headings have a re-inforcing effect: pensions, other cash transfers, and non wage private sector income. The marked difference between the nature of the sources used for the two years—FBS in 1989 and RLMS in 1994—may affect the results, but analysis of RLMS alone for 1992–1996 by Commander and Lee (1998) gives a picture of the determinants of inequality in transition which is not inconsistent with that painted by Milanovic. In particular, Commander and Lee note the failure of public policy to counteract the effect of a greater dispersion of labour income:

> even at the outset of transition, the redistributive effect of public policy appears to have been significantly smaller in Russia than in Central Europe. Furthermore, over the course of transition, the evidence strongly suggests that with respect to transfers, there has been an unambiguous shift toward greater proportionality (p. 16).

Pensions formed the major part of expenditures on cash transfers throughout the period. While in 1992 their effect was to reduce overall income inequality, by 1996 the opposite was the case.[48] This switch is as in Poland, but in Russia expenditure fell as a share of national income rather than rose—from nearly 7% of GDP in 1992 to 4.5% in 1996 (with the real value of the average pension falling by almost half). Spending on other transfers also fell relative to GDP and, for example, the proportion of families receiving family allowance payments in 1996 was less than half that in 1992 (Commander and Lee, 1998: p. 7).[49]

How does the level of income inequality that emerged in Russia in the 1990s compare with that in other former Soviet republics? A variety of estimates can be found for the latter, some based on surveys that seem to be descendants of the old Soviet FBS and some on the new surveys described in our discussion of sources. Milanovic (1998: Table 4.1) reports Gini coefficients for per capita income from the early part of the transition (1993–1995) for 10 other countries. The value for Ukraine in 1995 was much the same (0.47) as those in Russia based on RLMS for the mid-1990s. That for Kyrgyzstan in 1993 was higher (0.55). The other countries all had Ginis of less than 0.4 although only one (Belarus in 1995 with 0.28) had a value below 0.3, the OECD average shown in Table 3. While Russia and one or two other republics may be at the upper end of the range for the now independent states (a range larger than that at the end of the Soviet period), it

---

[48] This is not to say that transfers became unimportant at the lower end of the distribution—the share of transfers in total income continued to be at its highest in the lower quintiles.

[49] One striking feature of incomes in Russia during 1992–1996 was the change in the importance of different sources of income, with that from employment falling by at least 10–15 percentage points, to below a half of the total, while income from home production and the informal sector rose by a similar amount. (Although the direction of change is the same, the figures differ substantially between Mroz et al., 1997, and Commander et al., 1999.) The overall impact of these changes on income inequality seems to have been small.

appears that by OECD standards some substantial inequality in measured incomes was also present elsewhere.[50]

4.4. Interpreting the evidence

As with the socialist period, the qualification of "measured" incomes is important to note. What do the estimates of inequality of earnings and incomes from the transition period tell us about differences in economic welfare? We consider again price subsidies, nonwage benefits from work, and social benefits in kind from the state. We produce only limited evidence and inevitably we are in part just raising issues that need to be subjected to further measurement.

The story with subsidies seems as if it might be straightforward. If subsidies in the socialist period were equalising in their effect (even if they were not targeted on the lower part of the income distribution), their removal through price liberalisation will have had a regressive impact. The rise in inequality of economic welfare will have therefore been greater than that shown by data on cash incomes alone.

Newbery (1995), however, concludes from an analysis of household budget survey data that price changes in Hungary over 1988–1991 had relatively little redistributive impact, noting that this may be because the indirect tax system had already been re-formed in the early 1980s. As we noted earlier in commenting on the socialist period, it is the entire set of tools for manipulating the price system that should be the focus of attention and not just explicit consumption subsidies. For example, the distributional impact of the new Value Added Taxes needs to be analysed.

Some subsidies certainly remain. Schaffer (1995) reports that total subsidies (to producer and consumer) in 1993 in former Czechoslovakia, Hungary and Poland were about 3–5% of GDP (down from 15% or more in 1986), and around the level of those in the European Union, with the bulk of those that were left due to "remaining price controls (notably transport) and social/political factors (notably housing)" (p. 117). The distributional impact of those subsidies that are retained may differ from those that were removed.

The housing market has seen significant continuing price intervention, and there is also the distributive impact of privatisation of the state housing stock to be considered. Pudney (1995) estimates the subsidy to households renting public sector property in Hungary in 1991 and concludes that the effect was equalising (in contrast to Dániel's results for the 1970s reported earlier) although the absolute value of the subsidy rose with income level (a concentration curve below the 45° line). As Pudney points out, a key issue in considering the distributive effect of a market-orientated rent reform is what

---

[50] The surveys for the countries we mention by name are all new ones and the estimates from them should not be compared directly with those from the 1989 FBS in Table 2. In those countries for which there are also per capita expenditure data a switch to this alternative measure of household welfare would not greatly alter the picture. For example, the Gini for Russia in the RLMS is effectively unchanged (although that for Kyrgystan falls by a fifth). (The conceptual advantages of expenditure data are often stressed but the problems of measurement should not be underestimated.)

the state would do with the revenue from higher rents—one cannot simply focus on the removal of the subsidy alone.

The period considered by Pudney was already one when the public sector owned only a small part of the housing stock in Hungary and in the event a large part of the remaining public sector housing at the start of the 1990s was sold off in the following years, rather than the rents being raised. Dániel (1997) reports that this privatisation was on highly advantageous terms for the buyer, while existing owner-occupiers with state mortages were offered a huge write-down of their mortgage debt in return for a switch to market interest rates. She makes illustrative calculations of the annualized value of the ensuing privatisation using household budget survey data for 1989 (taking into account a range of costs, including those of renovation due to the backlog of maintenance). These indicate a regressive impact.

The housing sector underwent enormous change in Russia in the first half of the 1990s. Buckley and Gurenko (1997) argue that by mid-1992 the implicit housing subsidy to renters, already high by the end of the Soviet period, had risen hugely, since nominal rents were unchanged in the liberalization of prices beginning that year. Data from round one of RLMS, collected in Summer 1992, show average expenditure on rent and utilities as a percentage of total average expenditure to have been only 2.8% (Mroz et al., 1997: figure 3). Buckley and Gurenko's estimate of the value of the subsidy "income" to renters in 1992 reduces the Gini coefficient of per capita income in RLMS by 6 percentage points (a figure that of course depends on a whole series of assumptions), and they argue that housing policy at this time therefore provided an important cushion against the consequences of transition.

Subsequent events included a (literal) give-away privatization of massive proportions of the public sector housing stock. By late 1996, only a third of Russian households lived in housing owned by the state or by enterprises and well over half owned their own homes, compared to figures of two-thirds and a quarter respectively in 1992 (Mroz et al., 1997: Table 9). Buckley and Gurenko argue that its give-way nature, coupled with the prior distribution of housing, imply that this privatization was strongly progressive. This is supported by the results of Struyk and Daniell (1995) who analyse a random sample of several thousand dwellings from seven cities (including Moscow and St. Petersburg) collected at the end of 1993 (the year in which privatization appears to have peaked). They find no clear evidence linking income (or occupational status) of the household to the probability that the dwelling had been privatised.

The Russian privatisation, including the terms under which it took place, underline the importance of taking into account imputed rent from owner occupation in calculations of households' incomes, as recommended in UN guidelines (UN, 1977), although this is not in general the practice in Western countries either. If only the "subsidy income" for renters is taken into account, then the Russia privatisation would appear to have *worsened* the distribution of income, as households lose their rent subsidy and have no other income imputed in its place.

Large subsidies appear to have remained for those still renting in Russia in the mid-1990s. Commander and Schankerman report expenditures on housing subsidies to have been 4% of GDP in 1995, and "on a rising trend" (1997: p. 2). RLMS data show households' average expenditure on rent and utilities as a percentage of the total to have risen to only 5.8% by end 1996 (Mroz et al., 1997: Fig. 3), although the smaller proportion of renters at that time needs to be borne in mind.

We noted in Section 2 the importance of nonwage benefits from work during the socialist period. Part of this importance (or one of the reasons for their existence) should have declined during transition with price liberalisation and the increasing variety of goods available for purchase on the open market. But the general view is that fringe benefits from employers did not decline as quickly as expected (Commander and Schankerman, 1997: Rein et al., 1997). Nor did these benefits remain a feature of state enterprises alone. Evidence from various countries show both privatised firms and new firms supplying nonwage benefits as well, although not necessarily to the same extent.

The reasons for the continued importance of nonwage benefits seem mixed. They include inertia and weak alternative state social support (for example in Russia) on the one hand, and, on the other, both the desire to retain or attract staff and the managers' views of the role of the firm towards its employees. While the latter reasons may appear to be an inheritance from the past, neither are out of line with good management practice in Western market economies, although the scale on which the benefits are paid may differ. In some transition countries there have been tax incentives (intentional or otherwise) to managers to pay part of employees' remuneration other than through wages (a feature also familiar from the West). For example, Standing (1996) argues that this was the case in Russia with the excess wage tax, as do Filer et al. (1997) for the Czech Republic.

As one might expect, the situation from country to country in the mid 1990s displayed substantial variation. Earle (1997) using aggregate data on the Czech Republic and Romania for 1992–1993 argues that "every type of measured benefit falls within the Western range" (p. 69). On the other hand, Russia and (even more so) Ukraine still saw extensive provision, especially (but not only) that part of the subsidised housing referred to above that remained with enterprises. The desire to provide continued access to fringe benefits appears to have been an important reason for avoiding lay-offs. Nevertheless, enterprise survey data showed some declines for Russia over 1991–1994 (Commander and Schankerman, 1997). (See also OECD, 1996b.) A feature that seems to have been common to all transition countries is a very large withdrawal by enterprises from provision of pre-schools (kindergartens). A good number were divested to local authorities but many closed.[51]

---

[51] Across the CIS as a whole, there were 32,000 fewer pre-schools in 1995 than there had been in 1991. The example of Kazakhstan illustrates the decline of enterprise kindergartens, much the more important type at the end of the Soviet period. Their number fell by nearly 60% over 1991–1995 while the number of local authority facilities rose by only 10% (UNICEF, 1998: figure 2.5). (The enrolment rate of pre-school children fell by 30 percentage points.) Remaining enterprise kindergartens in Kazakhstan appear to have provided places that were still heavily subsidised (Klugman et al., 1997).

There is less direct evidence on the distributional impact of fringe benefits in transition (as opposed to indirect evidence from the link with firm size or type). Two studies for Russia in 1994 indicate that fringe benefits went to better paid workers. Commander and Schankerman (1997) report the number of benefits provided by industrial firms rising with the average firm wage. Kolev (1998) uses data from a random sample of employees and finds a clear positive relationship with the monthly wage for the probability of receipt for various benefits (but not for housing), even when controlling for other characteristics that could be correlated with wages. (Without these controls, the probability of receipt rises between the bottom and top quarters of the wage distribution by a factor of 1.5–4.0, depending on the benefit concerned, falling only for housing.) More evidence of this type is needed.

Kolev then goes on to try to estimate the value of fringe benefits using respondents' evaluation of their job satisfaction. He finds that all fringe benefits are positively associated with higher reported job satisfaction and that very large increases in the wage would be needed to compensate for the benefits' removal. While self-reported satisfaction may be a rather weak proxy for indirect utility, the analysis resonates with the comment of Rein et al. (1997) that the value of fringe benefits to workers may differ from their measured cost to firms. It is the former that we are most interested in while it is the latter on which the analysis of firm data—the standard approach—focuses.

Finally, we consider social benefits in kind in the form of education and health. This is another example of an issue where more work is needed. Although there has been a lot of interest in reforms to education and health systems in the transition countries, published work on the new distributional incidence of state expenditures, similar to that, for example, of Milanovic (1995) for the socialist period remains thin on the ground, although internal World Bank reports have considered the issue.

One might certainly expect there to have been some changes. In the case of education, there were some marked falls in total expenditure as a proportion of GDP in some countries in the first half of the 1990s—Georgia and Armenia were probably the worst cases, with a virtual collapse in state expenditures due to a precipitous decline in tax revenue (UNICEF, 1998: Fig. 2.10). Of course, the value of the educational benefit may not be well proxied by expenditure but it would indeed be surprising if the distributional incidence of these changes were neutral.[52] Enrolments also fell in a number of countries, with declines at all levels of schooling in parts of Central Asia and the Caucasus. Overall, the number of children of school-age rose in the transition countries as a whole in the first half of the 1990s but the number of children enrolled in school fell (Cusan and Motivans, 1999).

---

[52] One concrete benefit from schools that is relatively easy to value is free-school meals. There have been notable falls in provision in many countries, especially in the successor states of the former Soviet Union. For example, the proportion of children in primary schools receiving such meals fell by around 15–20 percentage points over 1989–1996 in Russia and Belarus and by 50 points in Kazakhstan and Kyrgyzstan (UNICEF, 1998: figure 2.15). Since there have been no compensatory increases in state transfers to families it seems safe to label these changes as regressive, given the typical position of children in the income distribution.

There is varied evidence suggesting a growth in inequalities in education systems in the 1990s, especially in the former Soviet republics and poorer parts of South-East Europe, implying that the incidence of state spending on education may have shifted in a regressive fashion (UNICEF, 1998; Micklewright, 1999). Enrolment and attendance may have fallen off in particular in lower income households due to a rising price of education and falling and more unequally distributed household incomes. On the price side there has been formal and informal charging for places or for teaching, both in schools and in tertiary level institutions (formal charges in compulsory level schooling still seems absent), and large increases in the real costs of textbooks, children's clothing and shoes, and local transport.

5. Conclusions

We saw in Section 2 that it was dangerous to generalise about income distribution in the socialist economies, especially in relation to market economies since these too display considerable heterogeneity. As far as earnings of full-time workers are concerned, dispersion towards the end of the socialist period in the countries that have been most studied in the literature matched that in several OECD economies—the decile ratio in Czechoslovakia was essentially the same as that in Germany, Poland the same as Australia, Russia the same as Britain. Dispersion in Britain and Russia (and in the rest of the Soviet Union) was much larger than in Germany or Czechoslovakia—and in the other Central European countries. In both parts of Europe, East and West, earnings were less dispersed than in North America.

But this was the picture at only one point in time and we emphasised the significant changes that had taken place in the distribution of earnings in several of the socialist economies. Nor was the situation stable in the OECD area. There is no fixed socialist versus market comparison to be made.

The picture for household incomes was clearer, at least for the 1980s—the socialist countries that we have covered in this chapter were apparently more equal than was typical of OECD countries, with a difference between the mean per capita Gini coefficient of 7 percentage points, although the Scandinavian and Benelux countries were at about the same level as the socialists.

Not only does this conclusion refer to just one period but it also refers to measured incomes only. We emphasised the importance of accounting for subsidies (and indirect taxes), fringe benefits and social income in kind. These change the picture in a way that defies easy summary. The same is true for market economies although the extent to which conclusions are affected may be less.

Although earnings inequality increased through the 1990s, the scale of the effect of the transition varied greatly. While the decile ratio rose by the order of 30–50% between 1980 and 1997 (mostly after 1989) in Central Europe, it doubled in the Ukraine and quadrupled, as least temporarily, in Russia although we noted reasons for doubting the veracity of everything one sees here.

The switch to the broader concept of household income dampens these changes, with an increase of around 25% recorded in the per capita Gini coefficient in Central Europe and 100% in Russia. The Central European countries by the late 1990s were well up into the OECD range for income inequality. Russia was well above it and there can be little doubt that this is now a very unequal country (even if the situation under socialism is still open to debate). This relatively simple message has to be qualified, however, by the fact that there is (or was as of 1997) perhaps more evidence that Russian inequality was stabilising than was true for the less dramatic rises in Central Europe—although the different Russian sources do not tell the same story. And again we emphasised the need to consider other forms of income that affect the distribution of economic welfare and the difficulties in doing so. The issue of housing illustrates the problems, including the failure of the data to capture the impact on the distribution of income of housing privatisation.

We have not found satisfactory analytical models encompassing enough features of the transition, such as combining the relative price effects of liberalisation with the distinctive wage setting processes of state and privately owned enterprises to generate an evolving pattern of inequality. This is a major deficiency that has not only deprived us of an effective analytical framework within which to consider the evidence but also limits the treatment of distributional considerations which may constrain government policy. Dewatripont and Roland (1992, 1995 and 1996) (and others) have considered how changes in ownership structure may modify attitudes to successive phases of reform.

The study of changes in the transition countries, or the comparison of socialist and market economies, involves datasets that are not strictly comparable. This underlines the data problems to which we have referred many times. Such problems are serious both at the conceptual and at the practical level and considerable care is needed with those data that are available.

The data problems would be even more serious if we were attempting to compare the *levels* of income before and after rather than relying, as we do, exclusively on indices of *relative* dispersion. We know, however, that indices of per capita GDP, though also presenting statistical problems, fell in all cases. Poland recovered and passed its previous peak first, and recovery was general in Central Europe in the mid 1990s—but not in the CIS.

We have not presented data such as mortality or morbidity, which would reinforce the welfare implications of falling GDP and rising inequality, especially for the countries of the CIS. These are relevant to the "capability approach" to human welfare described by Sen in the first chapter of this handbook. It might be that the distribution of capabilities has widened more than that of incomes and this would be an interesting hypothesis to investigate.

We started by saying that we were reporting on an episode of changing income distributions in a particular group of countries. An episode of a relatively concentrated period of change such as typified those occurring in the course of the long runs of data reported in other chapters of this handbook. We are not, however, tempted to make any claims for the representativeness of the (incomplete) episode we have studied as an example of those earlier in the historical record.

Appendix A

Suppose that each sector consists of numerous enterprises using equipment of different vintages earning different per capita quasi-rents at the unique competitive wage. Suppose also that workers in each enterprise appropriate a proportion α of their per capita quasi-rent in addition to the competitive wage.

In this case a wage subsidy adds less to profits and investment, and more to earnings and consumption, thus the condition for further employment subsidisation to raise output more than consumption becomes more demanding at $s < (1-\alpha)b$.

As before, output rises by $(\underline{w}-s)dn$, but now household income rises by $(\underline{w}-b)dn + \alpha(n.ds - dt)$, where the second term is α times the net addition to profits on which tax, t, is levied. Revenue neutrality implies that $dt + b.dn = n.ds$ so that household income rises by $(\underline{w} - b)dn + \alpha b.dn$ and net profits rise if $(\underline{w} - s)dn > (\underline{w} - (1-\alpha)b)dn$, that is if $s < (1-\alpha)b$.

If the minimum wage were driven by considerations of distribution of earnings amongst the employed, for example

$$\underline{w} = \beta e, \text{ where } \beta < 1 \text{ and } e = \text{average earnings,}$$

then, with $\alpha > 0$, $\underline{w}$ itself would rise with an employment subsidy: while as before output again rises by $(\underline{w} - s)dn$, household income rises by $(\underline{w} - b)dn + \alpha(n.ds - dt - n.dw) + n.d\underline{w}$, and $n.d\underline{w} = \beta n.de$, where $n.de = n.d\underline{w} + \alpha(n.ds - dt - n.d\underline{w})$. Revenue neutrality again implies that $dt + b.dn = n.ds$, so that $n.de = n.d\underline{w} + \alpha(b.dn - n.d\underline{w})$, and $n.d\underline{w} = \beta(1-\alpha)n.d\underline{w} + \alpha\beta b.dn$, and $n.d\underline{w} = \alpha\beta.b.dn/(1 - (1-\alpha)\beta)$. Household income rises by

$$(\underline{w} - b)dn + \alpha b.dn + (1 - \alpha)\alpha\beta b.dn/(1 - (1-\alpha)\beta)$$

so that net profits rise if $s < (1-\alpha)(1-\beta)b/(1 - (1-\alpha)\beta)$.

Thus there would seem to be scope for a profits-tax-financed employment subsidy even if quasi-rents are shared with labour and rising average earnings raise the *de facto* minimum wage as long as the relevant coefficients are not very close to unity. For instance $\alpha = \beta = 1/2$ makes the necessary condition that $s < b/3$, while $\alpha = \beta = 3/4$ makes it $s < b/13$.

Appendix B

This appendix gives data points for the transition period that are not otherwise reported in published sources given in the sources to the figures.

1. Distribution of earnings of employees (Figs. 7 and 8)

Q90/Q10	1989	1990	1991	1992	1993	1994	1995	1995	1997
Poland	2.43		2.85	2.91	3.01	3.40	3.35	3.48	3.53
Hungary		3.40		3.56	3.70	3.75			4.17
Czech Rep.	2.43		2.60	2.75	3.20	3.14	3.70	2.86	2.98
Russia	3.33	3.36	4.28	8.17	15.55	9.41	9.96	9.60	10.40
Ukraine				3.12	5.51			5.74	

Q90/Q50 (%)	1989	1990	1991	1992	1993	1994	1995	1995	1997
Poland	159.0		175.5	179.0	181.6	195.9	196.2	199.1	200.3
Hungary		196.4		201.5	204.9	205.6			214.4
Czech Rep.	148.7		163.3	167.5	182.4	181.2	179.2	173.1	173.7
Russia	182.2	178.3	207.5	228.6	270.6	272.8	286.6	282.4	290.0
Ukraine				177.9	219.4			234.4	

Q10/Q50 (%)	1989	1990	1991	1992	1993	1994	1995	1995	1997
Poland	65.4		61.5	61.5	60.3	57.6	58.6	57.2	56.7
Hungary		57.7		56.7	55.3	54.8			51.4
Czech Rep.	61.3		62.8	60.7	57.0	57.6	48.4	60.6	58.2
Russia	54.7	53.1	48.5	28.0	17.4	29.0	28.8	29.4	27.8
Ukraine	59.5		62.1	57.1	39.8	37.2	33.5	40.8	

2. Distribution of individuals by per capita income (Figures 9, 10 and 11)

Gini coefficient	1989	1990	1991	1992	1993	1994	1995	1995	1997
Poland	0.275	0.268	0.265	0.274	0.317	0.323	0.321	0.328	0.334
Hungary	0.225		0.209		0.231	0.234	0.242	0.246	0.254
Czech Rep. (MC)				0.228				0.258	
Czech Rep. (BS)					0.214	0.230	0.216	0.230	0.239
Russia (FBS)	0.265			0.289	0.398	0.409	0.381	0.375	0.375

Note: The two sets of figures for the Gini coefficient for per capita income in the Czech Republic are from the microcensus (MC) and the budget survey (BS). The former are calculations using the survey microdata reported in Večerník (1998). The Russian FBS figures are from Frolova (1998). All other results are from the files of the "MONEE project" at UNICEF International Child Development Centre, Florence. The project collaborates with statistical offices throughout the region and produces regular reports on social conditions and public policy in the transition in Central and Eastern Europe and the former Soviet Union (UNICEF, 1993, 1994, 1995, 1997, 1998). Inequality indices have been estimated from the grouped data collected by the project using the INEQ package written by F.A. Cowell, LSE, using the Pareto assumption both within ranges and for the top interval (see Atkinson and Micklewright, 1992: pp. 279–281).

References

Ackland, R. and J. Falkingham (1997), A profile of poverty in Kyrgyzstan, in J. Falkingham, J. Klugman, S. Marnie and J. Micklewright, eds., Household Welfare in Central Asia (Macmillan, Basingstoke).

Aghion, P. and O. Blanchard (1994), On the speed of transition in Central Europe, NBER Macroeconomic Annual, 283–300.

Alderman, H. (1998), Social assistance in Albania: Decentralization and targeted transfers, LSMS Working Paper 134 (The World Bank, Washington DC).

Alexeev, M. (1988), The effect of housing allocation on social inequality: A Soviet perspective, Journal of Comparative Economics 12: 228–234.

Alexeev, M. (1990), Distribution of housing subsidies in the USSR, with some Soviet-Hungarian comparisons, Comparative Economic Studies 32: 138–157.

Allison, C. and D. Ringold (1996), Labor markets in transition in Central and Eastern Europe, World Bank Technical Paper 352, Social Challenges of Transition Series (The World Bank, Washington DC).

Andorka, R., Z. Ferge and I. Toth (1996), Is Hungary really the least unequal? A discussion of data on income inequalities and poverty in Central and Eastern European countries (TARKI, Budapest).

Atkinson, A.B. and J. Micklewright (1983), On the reliability of income data in the family expenditure survey 1970–77, Journal of the Royal Statistical Society, series A 146: 33–61.

Atkinson, A.B. and J. Micklewright (1992), Economic Transformation in Eastern Europe and the Distribution of Income (Cambridge University Press, Cambridge).

Atkinson, A.B., L. Rainwater and T. Smeeding (1995), Income Distribution in OECD Countries, Social Policy Studies No. 18 (OECD, Paris).

Bergson, A. (1984), Income inequality under Soviet socialism, Journal of Economic Literature 22: 1052–1099.

Boeri, T. (1994), 'Transitional' unemployment, Economics of Transition 2: 1–26.

Boeri, T. (1995), Unemployment dynamics and labour market policies, in S. Commander and F. Coricelli, eds., Unemployment, Restructuring and The Labour Market in Eastern Europe and Russia (World Bank, Economic Development Institute Development Studies, Washington, DC).

Boeri, T. and S. Edwards (1998), Long-term unemployment and short-term unemployment benefits: The changing nature of non-employment subsidies in Central and Eastern Europe, Empirical Economics 23: 31–54.

Bourit, F., P. Hernu and M. Perrot (1983), Les salaires en 1982, Economie et Statistique 154 (April): 17–32.

Boyle Torrey, B., T. Smeeding, and D. Bailey (1996), Rowing between Scylla and Charybdis: Income transitions in Central European households, Luxembourg Income Study Working Paper 132.

Bruinooge, G., Ö. Éltetö, G. Fajth and G. Grubben (1990), Income distributions in an international perspective – the case of Hungary and the Netherlands, Statistical Journal of the United Nations 7: 39–53.

Buckley R.M. and E.N. Gurenko (1997), Housing and income distribution in Russia: Zhivago's legacy, World Bank Research Observer 12: 19–34.

Buckley R.M. and E.N. Gurenko (1998), Housing demand in Russia: Rationing and reform, Economics of Transition 6: 197 210.

Burda, M. (1993), Unemployment, labour markets and structural change in Eastern Europe, Economic Policy 16: 101-137.

Burda, M. (1995), Labour market institutions and the economic transformation of Central and Eastern Europe, in S. Commander and F. Coricelli, eds., Unemployment, Restructuring and The Labour Market in Eastern Europe and Russia (World Bank, Economic Development Institute Development Studies, Washington, DC).

Cardoso, A. (1997), Earnings Inequality in Portugal: The Relevance and the Dynamics of Employer Behaviour, PhD thesis (European University Institute, Florence).

Commander, S., J. McHale, and R. Yemtsov (1995), Russia, in S. Commander and F. Coricelli, eds., Unemployment, Restructuring, and the Labor Market in Eastern Europe and Russia, EDI Development Studies (The World Bank, Washington DC).

Commander, S., A. Tolstopiatenko, and R. Yemtsov (1999), Channels of redistribution: Inequality and poverty in the Russian transition, Economics of Transition 7: 411–448.

Commander, S. and U. Lee (1998), How does public policy affect the income distribution? Evidence from Russia 1992-1996, mimeo (European Bank for Reconstruction and Development, London).

Commander, S. and M. Schankerman (1997), Enterprise restructuring and social benefits, Economics of Transition 5: 1–24.

Cornes, R. (1995), Measuring the distributional impact of public goods, in D van de Walle and K. Nead, eds., Public Spending and the Poor (Johns Hopkins University Press, Baltimore).

Cusan, A. and A. Motivans (1999), Changing expenditures and enrolment, in J. Micklewright, ed., Education After Communism (Macmillan, Basingstoke) (forthcoming).

Dániel, Z. (1985), The effect of housing distribution on social inequality in Hungary, Journal of Comparative Economics 9: 391–409.

Dániel, Z. (1997), The paradox in the privatization of Hungary's public housing: A national gift or a bad bargain? Economics of Transition 5: 147–170.

Dewatripont, M. and G. Roland (1992), Economic reforms and dynamic political constraints, Review of Economic Studies, 59: 703–730.

Dewatripont, M. and G. Roland (1995), The design of reform packages under uncertainty, American Economic Review 85: 1207–1233.

Dewatripont, M. and G. Roland (1996), Transition as a process of large scale institutional change, Economics of Transition 4: 1–30.

Diamond, P.A. and J.A. Mirrlees (1971), Optimal taxation and public production I: Production efficiency and II: Tax rules, American Economic Review 61: 8–27 and 261–278.

Doyle, C. (1996), The distributional consequences during the early stages of Russia's transition, Review of Income and Wealth 42: 493–506.

Earle, J. (1997), Do East European enterprises provide social protection? Employee benefits and labour market behaviour in the East European transition, in M. Rein, B. Friedman and A. Wörgötter, eds., Enterprise and Social Benefits After Communism (Cambridge University Press, Cambridge).

Éltetö, Ö. (1997), Disparities in the economic well-being of Hungarian society from the late 1970s to the 1980s, in P. Gottschalk, B. Gustafsson and E. Palmer, Changing Patterns in the Distribution of Economic Welfare: An International Perspective (Cambridge University Press, Cambridge).

Éltetö, Ö. and E. Frigyes (1968), New income inequality measures as efficient tools for causal analysis and planning, Econometrica 36: 383–396.

EBRD (1997), Transition Report 1997 (European Bank for Reconstruction and Development, London).

EBRD (1998), Transition Report 1998 (European Bank for Reconstruction and Development, London).

Eurostat (1998), The distribution of earnings in the European Union, Statistics in Focus, Population and Social Conditions, number 8.

Falkingham, J. and J. Micklewright (1997), Surveying households in Central Asia: Problems and progress, in J. Falkingham, J. Klugman, S. Marnie and J. Micklewright, eds., Household Welfare in Central Asia (Macmillan, Basingstoke and St. Martin's Press, New York).

Falkingham, J. (1997), Public transfers and targeting in Kyrgyzstan, in J. Falkingham, J. Klugman, S. Marnie and J. Micklewright, eds., Household Welfare in Central Asia (Macmillan, Basingstoke and St. Martin's Press, New York).

Filer, R., O. Schneider, and J. Svejnar (1997), Wage and non-wage labour costs in the Czech Republic—The impact of fringe benefits, in M. Rein, B. Friedman and A. Wörgötter, eds., Enterprise and Social Benefits After Communism (Cambridge University Press, Cambridge).

Flakierski, H. (1991), Social policies in the 1980s in Poland: A discussion of new approaches, in J. Adam, ed., Economic Reforms and Welfare Systems in the USSR, Poland and Hungary (Macmillan, Basingstoke).

Flemming, J. (1993), Public finance, unemployment and economics in transition, in A.B. Atkinson, ed., Economics in a changing world, vol. 3. Public Policy and Economic Organisation. Proceedings of Tenth World Congress of the International Economic Association (Macmillan, Basingstoke and St. Martin's Press, New York).

Frolova, E. (1998), Problems on poverty and income inequality in the Russian Federation: Methodological issues and conclusions, Department for Living Condition Statistics and Population Surveys, State Committee of the Russian Federation on Statistics (Goskomstat, Moscow).

Galasi, P. (1998), Income Inequality and Mobility in Hungary, 1992-96, Innocenti Occasional Paper 64 (UNICEF International Child Development Centre, Florence).

Garner, T. (1998), Changing welfare in a changing world?: Income and expenditure inequalities in the Czech and Slovak Republics, in S. Jenkins, A. Kapteyn and B. van Praag, eds., The Distribution of Welfare and Household Production: International Perspectives (Cambridge University Press, Cambridge).

Garner, T. and K. Terrell (1998), A Gini decomposition analysis of inequality in the Czech and Slovak Republics during the transition, Economics of Transition 6: 23–46.

Gregg, P. and J. Wadsworth (1996), It takes two: Employment polarization in the OECD, Centre for Economic Performance Discussion Paper 304 (London School of Economics, London).

Grossman, G. (1987), Roots of Gorbachev's Problems: Private Income and Outlay in the Late 1970s, Gorbachev's Economic Plans (US Congress Joint Economic Committee, Washington DC).

Hughes, G. and P. Hare (1992), Trade policy and restructuring in Eastern Europe, in J. Flemming and J. Rollo, eds., Trade Payments and Adjustment in Central and Eastern Europe (Royal Institution of International Affairs and European Bank for Reconstruction and Development, London).

ILO (1984), World Labour Report (International Labour Organization, Geneva).

ILO (1987), World Labour Report (International Labour Organization, Geneva).

IMF, The World Bank, OECD and EBRD (1991), A Study of the Soviet Economy (OECD, Paris).

Jarvis, S. and J. Micklewright (1995), The targeting of family allowance in Hungary, in D. van de Walle and K. Nead, eds., Public Spending and the Poor (Johns Hopkins University Press, Baltimore).

Jarvis, S. and S. Pudney (1995), Redistributive policy in a transition economy: The case of Hungary, in D. Newbery, ed., Tax and Benefit Reform in Central and Eastern Europe (Centre for Economic Policy Research, London).

Klugman, J. (ed.) (1997), Poverty in Russia: Public Policy and Private Responses, EDI Development Studies (The World Bank, Washington DC).

Klugman, J., S. Marnie, J. Micklewright and P. O'Keefe (1997), The impact of kindergarten divestiture on household welfare in Central Asia, in J. Falkingham, J. Klugman, S. Marnie and J. Micklewright, eds., Household Welfare in Central Asia (Macmillan, Basingstoke and St. Martin's Press, New York).

Knight, J. and L. Song (1990), The determinants of urban income inequality in China, Institute of Economics and Statistics, Applied Economics Discussion Paper 91 (University of Oxford, Oxford).

Kolev, A. (1998), The determination of enterprise benefits in Russia and their impact on individual well-being, Working Paper ECO 98/5, Department of Economics (European University Institute, Florence).

Kordos, J. (1996), Forty years of the household budget surveys in Poland, Statistics in Transition (Journal of the Polish Statistical Association) 2: 1119–1138.

Lapins, J. and E. Vaskis (1996), The new household budget survey in Latvia, Statistics in Transition (Journal of the Polish Statistical Association) 2: 1085–1103.

Layard, P.R.G. and A. Richter, How much unemployment is needed for restructuring? Economics of Transition 3: 39–58.

Lydall, H.F. (1968), The Structure of Earnings (Oxford University Press, Oxford).

Lydall, H.F (1979), Some problems in making international comparisons of inequality, in J.R. Moroney, ed., Income Inequality: Trends and International Comparisons (D.C. Heath, Lexington, MA).

Marchal, J. and B. Ducros (eds.) (1968), The Distribution of National Income (Macmillan, Basingstoke).

Marnie, S. (1992), The Soviet Labour Market in Transition, EUI Monograph in Economics (European University Institute, Florence).

Marnie, S. and J. Micklewright (1994), Poverty in pre-reform Uzbekistan: What do official data really reveal? Review of Income and Wealth 40: 395–414.

Martini, A, A. Ivanova and S. Novosyolova (1996), The income and expenditure survey of Belarus: Design and implementation, Statistics in Transition (Journal of the Polish Statistical Association) 2: 1063–1084.

McAuley, A.N.D. (1979), Economic Welfare in the Soviet Union (University of Wisconsin Press, Madison).

McKinnon, R. (1991), The Order of Economic Liberalization (Johns Hopkins University Press, Baltimore).

Messerlin, P. (1992), The association agreements between the EC and Central Europe, in J. Flemming and J. Rollo, eds., Trade Payments and Adjustment in Central and Eastern Europe (Royal Institution of International Affairs and European Bank for Reconstruction and Development, London).

Micklewright, J. (1999), Education, inequality and transition, Economics of Transition 7: 343–376.

Mikhalev, V. and N. Bjorksten (1995), Wage formation during the period of economic restructuring in the Russian Federation, Centre for Co-operation with the Economies in Transition, Paper GD (95) 102 (OECD, Paris).

Milanovic, B. (1995), The distributional impact of cash and in-kind transfers in Eastern Europe and Russia, in D. van de Walle and K. Nead, eds., Public Spending and the Poor (Johns Hopkins University Press, Baltimore).

Milanovic, B. (1998), Income, Inequality, and Poverty during the Transition from Planned to Market Economy, World Bank Regional and Sectoral Studies (The World Bank, Washington DC).

Milanovic, B. (1999), Explaining the growth in inequality during the transition, Economics of Transition 7: (forthcoming).

Morrisson, C. (1984), Income distribution in East European and Western countries, Journal of Comparative Economics 8: 21–138.

Mroz, T. and B. Popkin (1995), Poverty and the economic transition in the Russian Federation, Economic Development and Cultural Change 44: 1–32.

Mroz, T., B. Popkin, D. Mancini, E. Glinskaya and M. Loshkin (1997), Monitoring economic conditions in the Russian Federation: The Russia Longitudinal Monitoring Survey 1992-96, Report submitted to USAID, Carolina Population Centre (University of North Carolina at Chapel Hill).

National Statistical Committee of the Kyrgyz Republic (1997), Kyrgyzstan Analysis Report 1996: Living Standards and Measurement Survey (National Statistical Committee of the Kyrgyz Republic, Bishkek).

Newbery, D. (1995), The distributional impact of price changes in Hungary and the United Kingdom, Economic Journal 101: 847–863.

Newell, A. and B. Reilly (1996), The gender wage gap in Russia: Some empirical evidence, Labour Economics 3: 337–356.

Newell, A. and M. Socha (1998), Wage distribution in Poland: The roles of privatisation and international trade, 1992–96, Economics of Transition 6: 47–66.

OECD (1993), Employment Outlook (OECD, Paris).

OECD (1996a), Employment Outlook (OECD, Paris).

OECD (1996b), The Changing Social Benefits in Russian Enterprises (OECD, Paris).

Ofer, G. and A. Vinokur (1992), The Soviet Household under the Old Regime (Cambridge University Press, Cambridge).

Oliver, R. (1997), Model Living Standards Measurement Study survey questionnaire for the countries of the former Soviet Union, Living Standards Measurement Study Working Paper No. 130 (The World Bank, Washington DC).

Phelps Brown, H. (1977), The Inequality of Pay (Oxford University Press, Oxford).

Pryor, F.L. (1973), Property and Industrial Organization in Communist and Capitalist Nations (Indiana University Press, Bloomington).

Pudney, S. (1994a), Earnings inequality in Hungary since 1988, Economics of Transition 2: 101–106.

Pudney, S. (1994b), Earnings inequality in Hungary: A comparative analysis of household and enterprise survey data, Economics of Planning 27: 251–276.

Pudney, S. (1995), Income distribution and the reform of public housing in Hungary, Economics of Transition 3: 75–106.

Redor, D. (1992), Wage Inequalities East and West (Cambridge University Press, Cambridge).

Rein, M., B. Friedman and A. Wörgötter (1997), Introduction, in M. Rein, B. Friedman and A. Wörgötter, eds., Enterprise and Social Benefits After Communism (Cambridge University Press, Cambridge).

Renaud, B. (1991), Housing reform in socialist economies, World Bank Discussion Paper 125 (The World Bank, Washington DC).

Rodrigues, C. (1993), Measurement and decomposition of inequality in Portugal 1980/81–1989/90, Discussion Paper MU9302 (The Microsimulation Unit, Department of Applied Economics, University of Cambridge, Cambridge).

Rosen, S. (1981), Economics of superstars, American Economic Review 71: 845–858.

Rutkowski, J. (1996a), Changes in the wage structure during economic transition in Central and Eastern Europe, World Bank Technical Paper 340, Social Challenges of Transition Series (The World Bank, Washington DC).

Rutkowski, J. (1996b), High skills pay off: The changing wage structure during economic transition in Poland, Economics of Transition 4: 89–112.

Rutkowski, J. (1998), Welfare and the labor market in Poland, World Bank Technical Paper 417, Social Challenges of Transition Series (The World Bank, Washington DC).

Schaffer, M., (1995), Government subsidies to enterprises in Central and Eastern Europe: Budgetary subsidies and tax arrears, in D. Newbery, ed., Tax and Benefit Reform in Central and Eastern Europe (Centre for Economic Policy Research, London).

Sefton, T. (1997), The Changing Distribution of the Social Wage, STICERD Occasional Paper 21 (London School of Economics, London).

Shenfield, S. (1984), The Mathematical-Statistical Methodology of the Contemporary Soviet Family Budget Survey, PhD thesis (Centre for Russian and East European Studies, Faculty of Commerce and Social Science, University of Birmingham).

Smeeding, T.M., P. Saunders, J. Coder, S. Jenkins, J. Fritzell, A.J.M Hagenaars, R. Hauser and M. Wolfson (1993), Poverty, inequality, and family living standards impacts across seven nations: The effect of noncash subsidies for health, education and housing, Review of Income and Wealth 39: 229–255.

Sniukstiene, G, G. Vanagaite and G. Binkauskiene (1996), Household budget survey in Lithuania, Statistics in Transition (Journal of the Polish Statistical Association) 2: 1085–1103.

Standing, G. (1996), Russian Unemployment and Enterprise Restructuring: Reviving Dead Souls (Macmillan, Basingstoke).

Standing, G. and D. Vaughan-Whitehead (1995), Minimum Wages in Central and Eastern Europe: From Protection to Destitution (Central European University Press, Budapest).

Steiner, V. and K. Wagner (1996), Has earnings inequality in Germany changed in the 1980s? ZEW Discussion Paper 96–32 (University of Mannheim).

Stewart, K. (1998), Decentralisation and Regional Equity in Russia: Three Essays on Intergovernmental Transfers and the Financing of Education, PhD thesis (Department of Economics, European University Institute, Florence).

Struyk, R. and J. Daniell (1995), Housing privatization in urban Russia, Economics of Transition 3: 197–214.

Szakolczai, G. (1979), Limits to redistribution: the Hungarian experience, in D. Collard, R. Lecomber and M. Slater, eds., Income Distribution: The Limits to Redistribution: Proceedings of the 31st Symposium of the Colston Research Society (Scientechnica, Bristol).

United Nations (1977), Provisional guidelines on statistics of the distribution of income, consumption and accumulation of households, Department of Economic and Social Affairs, Studies in Methods, Series M, no. 61 (United Nations, New York).

UNICEF (1993), Public policy and social conditions, Regional Monitoring Report 1 (UNICEF International Child Development Centre, Florence).

UNICEF (1994), Crisis in mortality, health and nutrition, Regional Monitoring Report 2 (UNICEF International Child Development Centre, Florence).

UNICEF (1995), Poverty, children and policy: Responses for a brighter future, Regional Monitoring Report 3 (UNICEF International Child Development Centre, Florence).

UNICEF (1997), Children at risk in Central and Eastern Europe: Risks and promises, Regional Monitoring Report 4 (UNICEF International Child Development Centre, Florence).

UNICEF (1998), Education for all? Regional Monitoring Report 5, (UNICEF International Child Development Centre, Florence).

Večerník, J. (1991), Earnings distribution in Czechoslovakia: Intertemporal changes and international comparison, European Sociological Review 7: 237–252.

Večerník, J. (1993), The labour market, poverty and social policy in the Czech and Slovak republics, 1990-92: Data and analysis, ACE Grant Report (Institute of Sociology, Academy of Sciences, Prague) Luxembourg Income Study Working Paper 198.

Večerník, J. (1995), Changing earnings distribution in the Czech Republic, Economics of Transition 3: 355–372.

Večerník, J. (1996), Markets and People: The Czech Reform Experience in a Comparative Perspective (Avebury, Aldershot) .

Večerník, J. (1997), The emergence of the labour market and earnings distribution: The case of the Czech Republic, in P. Gottschalk, B. Gustafsson and E. Palmer, eds., Changing Patterns in the Distribution of Economic Welfare: An International Perspective (Cambridge University Press, Cambridge).

Večerník, J. (1998), Household Income Distribution and Redistribution in the Czech Republic: Readjustment to the Market (Institute of Sociology, Academy of Sciences, Prague) Luxembourg Income Study Working Paper 198.

Wiles, P.J.D. (1974), Distribution of Income: East and West (North-Holland, Amsterdam).

Wiles, P.J.D. (1978), Our shaky data base, in W. Krelle and A.F. Shorrocks, eds., Personal Income Distribution (North-Holland, Amsterdam).

Wiles, P.J.D. and S. Markowski (1971), Income distribution under communism and capitalism, Soviet Studies, Part I, 22: 344–369 and Part II 22: 487–511.

Williamson, J. (1997), The Washington consensus revisited, in L. Emmerij, ed., Economic and Social Development into the XXI Century (Latin American Development Bank, Washington, DC).

World Bank (1996), World Development Report (Oxford University Press, New York).

AUTHOR INDEX

SUBJECT INDEX

ability
  family transmission of 446–53
    productive abilities 446–8
    redistribution, costs of 448–51
    taste-based inequality 451–3
  in selection theory 389–90
absolute income differences in OECD countries 280–4
absolute poverty 313
affirmative-action and discrimination 470
age/ageing and wealth distribution 607, 648, 649
agency theory
  in agricultural sector 568
  in distribution of earnings 412–13, 417–19
  in labor markets 25
aggregate accumulation and economic growth 483–98
  factor income distribution 490–8
    and long-run growth 493–8
    savings and classes 491–3
  and neoclassical allocation 483–90
    and optimal savings 487–90
    and saving propensities 484–7
aggregate utility and unenforceable contracts 544
agriculture
  employment in 856
  income inequality in 242–3
  insurance in 567
Albania 885
altruism
  intergenerational 440, 443–4
  in redistribution
    constraints 757
    motives for 684–7
anonymity in measurement of inequality 97
Argentina 816, 817
Armenia
  earnings, full-time 860–1
  economic transition, indicators 885
  household income, per capita 869
asset inequality and economic performance 587–95
Atkinson index in social welfare function (SWF) 115

augmented wealth 629
Australia
  earnings, full-time 862
  income distribution, per capita 870
  income inequality in
    data on 270
    decile ratios 279
    disposable, increases in 285–6, 301
    Gini coefficients on 279, 302
    Lorenz curve
      absolute income 284
      relative income 278
  poverty in
    in children 347–8, 367, 371
    data sources 364
    dominance
      first-order 339, 341, 343
      normalized gap 340, 342, 344
    in elderly 349–50, 368, 372
    estimated head counts 371–2
    in female-headed households 351–2, 369, 372
    rates and changes 335
    TIP curves 337
  wealth distribution in 634
    estate tax 640
    estimates 641
    and housing ownership 645
    investment income 642
    tax data on 637
Austria
  income inequality in 270
  poverty in
    in children 347–8, 367, 371
    data sources 364
    dominance
      first-order 339, 341, 343
      normalized gap 340, 342, 344
    in elderly 349–50, 372
  poverty in
    estimated head counts 371–2
  poverty in
    in female-headed households 351–2, 372

937

HANDBOOKS IN ECONOMICS

1. HANDBOOK OF MATHEMATICAL ECONOMICS (in 4 volumes)
    Volumes 1, 2 and 3 edited by Kenneth J. Arrow and Michael D. Intriligator
    Volume 4 edited by Werner Hildenbrand and Hugo Sonnenschein

2. HANDBOOK OF ECONOMETRICS (in 5 volumes)
    Volumes 1, 2 and 3 edited by Zvi Griliches and Michael D. Intriligator
    Volume 4 edited by Robert F. Engle and Daniel L. McFadden
    Volume 5 is in preparation (editors James J. Heckman and Ed E. Leamer)

3. HANDBOOK OF INTERNATIONAL ECONOMICS (in 3 volumes)
    Volumes 1 and 2 edited by Ronald W. Jones and Peter B. Kenen
    Volume 3 edited by Gene M. Grossman and Kenneth Rogoff

4. HANDBOOK OF PUBLIC ECONOMICS (in 4 volumes)
    Volumes 1 and 2 edited by Alan J. Auerbach and Martin Feldstein
    2 volumes in preparation (editors Alan J. Auerbach and Martin Feldstein)

5. HANDBOOK OF LABOR ECONOMICS (in 5 volumes)
    Volumes 1 and 2 edited by Orley C. Ashenfelter and Richard Layard
    Volumes 3A, 3B and 3C edited by Orley C. Ashenfelter and David Card

6. HANDBOOK OF NATURAL RESOURCE AND ENERGY ECONOMICS
    (in 3 volumes). Edited by Allen V. Kneese and James L. Sweeney

7. HANDBOOK OF REGIONAL AND URBAN ECONOMICS (in 3 volumes)
    Volume 1 edited by Peter Nijkamp
    Volume 2 edited by Edwin S. Mills
    Volume 3 edited by Paul C. Cheshire and Edwin S. Mills

8. HANDBOOK OF MONETARY ECONOMICS (in 2 volumes)
    Edited by Benjamin Friedman and Frank Hahn

9. HANDBOOK OF DEVELOPMENT ECONOMICS (in 4 volumes)
    Volumes 1 and 2 edited by Hollis B. Chenery and T.N. Srinivasan
    Volumes 3A and 3B edited by Jere Behrman and T.N. Srinivasan

10. HANDBOOK OF INDUSTRIAL ORGANIZATION (in 3 volumes)
    Volumes 1 and 2 edited by Richard Schmalensee and Robert R. Willig
    Volume 3 is in preparation (editors Mark Armstrong and Robert H. Porter)

11. HANDBOOK OF GAME THEORY with Economic Applications (in 3 volumes)
    Volumes 1 and 2 edited by Robert J. Aumann and Sergiu Hart
    Volume 3 is in preparation (editors Robert J. Aumann and Sergiu Hart)

12. HANDBOOK OF DEFENSE ECONOMICS (in 1 volume)
    Edited by Keith Hartley and Todd Sandler

13. HANDBOOK OF COMPUTATIONAL ECONOMICS (in 1 volume)
    Edited by Hans M. Amman, David A. Kendrick and John Rust

14. HANDBOOK OF POPULATION AND FAMILY ECONOMICS (in 2 volumes)
    Volumes 1A and 1B edited by Mark R. Rosenzweig and Oded Stark

15. HANDBOOK OF MACROECONOMICS (in 3 volumes)
    Edited by John B. Taylor and Michael Woodford

16. HANDBOOK OF INCOME DISTRIBUTION (in 1 volume)
    Edited by Anthony B. Atkinson and François Bourguignon

17. HANDBOOK OF HEALTH ECONOMICS (in 2 volumes)
    Edited by Anthony J. Culyer and Joseph P. Newhouse

FORTHCOMING TITLES

HANDBOOK OF AGRICULTURAL ECONOMICS
Editors Bruce l. Gardner and Gordon C. Rausser

HANDBOOK OF SOCIAL CHOICE AND WELFARE ECONOMICS
Editors Kenneth J. Arrow, Amartya K. Sen and Kotaro Suzumura

HANDBOOK OF RESULTS IN EXPERIMENTAL ECONOMICS
Editors Charles Plott and Vernon L. Smith

HANDBOOK OF ENVIRONMENTAL ECONOMICS
Editors Karl-Goran Mäler and Jeff Vincent

HANDBOOK OF FINANCE AND ECONOMICS
Editors George M. Constantinides, Milton Harris and René M. Stulz

All published volumes available